The Gun Digest Book Of
MODERN GUN VALUES

Seventh Edition

By Jack Lewis
Edited by Harold A. Murtz

DBI BOOKS, INC.

Publisher
Sheldon L. Factor

Art Director
Rueselle Gilbert

Technical Editor
Chuck Karwan

Production Coordinator
Sonya Kaiser

Copy Coordinator
Dorine Imbach

Produced by

GALLANT/CHARGER
PUBLICATIONS

ISBN 0-87349-034-7
Library of Congress Catalog Card Number 75-10067

THE AUTHOR

Jack Lewis has been the editor of *Gun World* Magazine, as well as its publisher, for nearly thirty years, capping a many-faceted career. Over the years he has been a ranch hand, farm worker, horse wrangler, structural steel worker, laborer, private detective, motion-picture stuntman, newspaper reporter, and screen and television writer. He is the author of a number of adventure and Western novels, as well as a humorous series dealing with Marine Corps combat corrspondents and photographers.

A veteran of World War II and Korean actions, he is a retired lieutenant-colonel of the Marine Corps Reserve and was called to active duty in 1970 to pursue a special study in Vietnam. In addition to firearms publications, he is publisher of *Horse and Horseman and Bow & Arrow Hunting* and *Fishing & Boating Illustrated magazines.*

THE EDITOR

Harold Murtz has been associated with firearms for more than three decades. His collecting career started in the late 1950s with a well-worn 7mm Remington Rolling Block rifle ordered through the mail. Since then, he has developed an enviable collection of U.S., British and Japanese military firearms.

Born and raised in the Midwest, Murtz joined the staff of *Guns* Magazine as associate editor in 1969. Shortly after joining DBI Books in 1972, Murtz became the editor of *Guns Illustrated.* Murtz' editorial accomplishments include *The Gun Digest Book Of Exploded Firearms Drawings,* Vols. I, II and III, all editions of *Modern Gun Values* and the six-part *Firearms Assembly/Disassembly* series. He has also had an active part in nearly all the rest of DBI's shooting/hunting books.

CONTENTS

RIFLES: The worth of a rifle has overtones of philosophy **138**

SHOTGUNS: The steel shot requirement may well have
an adverse effect on some shotgun prices **304**

INTRODUCTION

BEFORE WE get into reasons and philosophies, let's all turn to the inside front cover of this book.

Listed there are the standards and classifications for used firearms. This system was devised by the National Rifle Association and serves as the ultimate guide for evaluating used guns in this country.

While there are various classifications, *please understand that all of the values listed here are for NRA Excellent.* If the gun is better than that and seems to fit into a higher category, it probably is worth more than the price listed in these pages. If it qualifies as being in poor shape, the value will be downgraded accordingly. Just how much that value drops will depend largely upon your abilities as a gun trader.

But remember, please: NRA Excellent. That's our basis for judgement. If you're going to use this book, it will have to be yours, too.

Now on to other matters —

Some people will not like this book. They are the same people who have not liked the first six editions of *The Gun Digest Book Of Modern Gun Values* — and they probably won't like the eighth edition either.

"Your prices are too low," some of them say. I listen, then I begin to question. Invariably these are folks who paid more for a gun than it really was worth and don't like to feel they've been had. There also are gun traders who don't like MGV, as we call it, because they have found the prices contained herein are more realistic than the price tags they have on some of their for-sale firearms...and they have trouble selling to those who own an up-to-date copy.

But from the general gun-fancying public, I'm gratified that this continuing series has received more than its share of accolades. Admittedly, we don't have prices and photos on *every* gun made since the turn of the century. We continue to attempt, however, to update the volumes as errors or omissions are brought to our attention.

Colt, Remington and Smith & Wesson all have historians on their staffs and can be a big help in

tracking down lesser known models, but once in awhile even they are puzzled. Colt, for example, had a factory fire decades ago that wiped out an entire segment of records. Thus, there are some blanks in the official verification picture and, on occasion, Colt historians call upon collecting buffs who have made their own studies and discoveries.

Remington maintains a museum and staff in Ilion, New York, and is highly helpful in running down needed information and photos.

One problem lies in the fact that a specific model may have been advertised under some glamorous name dreamed up by local dealers or distributors, without any great mention of model and style numbers. This parochial approach to marketing creates a whole new set of problems, since it's highly likely that the originating factory knew nothing of the out-in-the-sticks marketing plan and how it was carried out.

Winchester maintained an excellent museum and research staff that was an aid in running down

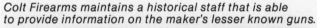
Colt Firearms maintains a historical staff that is able to provide information on the maker's lesser known guns.

wayward, disappeared models so long as Olin operated the factory in New Haven. But in recent years, the Winchester collection and most of the records that went with it have been transferred to the Buffalo Bill Museum in Cody, Wyoming. The staff there is helpful, but surely does not have the expertise of the gun experts who were on the payroll in New Haven and charged with keeping track of such knowledge decade after decade, generation after generation.

Smith & Wesson has continued to maintain its authorities on the many models turned out by the company over the years. Roy Jinks has been highly helpful since the first edition of this tome appeared more than ten years ago.

When I first told Jinks and others of the plan to produce that first edition, there were some doubtful looks, but offers of help and wishes of luck. Over years, the continuing effort has required a lot of both.

Everyone involved has my thanks for this effort and the preceeding volumes that seem to grow thicker with each new outing; adding new guns — and old ones on which we have accomplished additional research — always calls for more pages. This particular effort contains forty-eight pages and nearly three hundred guns more than the sixth edition.

One thing I have learned — and many of you probably have learned along with me — is the fact that the value of used firearms, whether rifle, shotgun or handgun, is closely tied to the economy of the moment.

All too often, I'm approached at a gun show by some worthy who states, "I bought such-and-such used gun in 1978. Everyone told me it would increase in value, but it hasn't. The price has gone down instead."

Without meaning to indulge in political finger-pointing, the fact is that a gent named Jimmy Carter was President of these United States in 1978. As I recall, we had double-digit inflation; interest, if you *had* to borrow money, was in the twenty percent bracket; more, if you couldn't offer proper security for the loan...like a mortagage on your children!

In such times, the values of what I call "hard currencies" tend to rise. Today, the price of gold is somewhere in the vicinity of $400 an ounce; the price of silver runs up and down on both sides of the $7 mark. But in the late 1970s, gold had leaped to something like $800 per ounce — more than twice its current world market value. The price of silver had risen to some $50, as the Hunt Brothers worked hard at getting a corner on the world supply of this precious metal. The value of used guns rose accordingly, since they were being gobbled

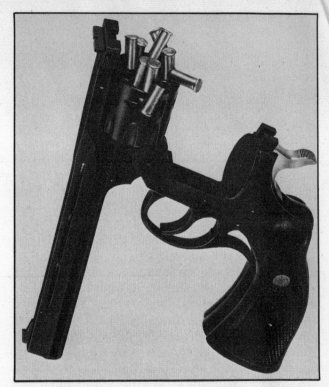

With the demise of Harrington & Richardson, guns made by that manufacturer have gained in collector interest. Prices probably will increase on some of the H&R models.

up as a hedge against inflation just as was the case with gold, silver, diamonds and other precious metals and gems.

I have been a longtime collector of Indian-made turquoise jewelry. During that period of the Seventies, I saw the value of such jewelry double and even triple. When silver hit the unlikely neighborhood of about $50 per ounce, the Navajos and Zunis were pulling the stones out of their silver jewelry and selling the remaining metal on the silver market!

Like everything else — well, almost everything — when times returned to what might be considered relatively "normal," the price of these commodities returned to a more realistic level. The only instance I can think of in which the price of silver did not decrease was with photographic film.

As most of us realize, photographic film utilizes silver in its manufacture. When one develops that film, the dark coating that remains on the transparent base is a type of silver. Based upon the increase in the cost of silver, Kodak quickly jumped the price of film to several times what it had been costing. They had the obvious answer: The increased cost of the silver used in the manufacture of photographic film forced them to increase the price.

Winchester expected great things for the commemorative dedicated to the late John Wayne. However, demand has not met the supply. The manufacturer turned out some 50,000 of the carbines, which have gained little in price.

In the meantime, the value of silver is about one-seventh of what it was ten or twelve years ago, but when it returned to a more ralistic value, this fact went ignored by the makers of photo goods. The price of film hasn't dropped a penny! Perhaps we all would have been much better off to sell our guns at the then high value and buy Kodak stock! Hindsight, as they say, is a wonderful, if hurtful thing!

Years ago, when he was first beginning to make money as a movie actor, Joel McCrea asked the late Will Rogers how he should invest his wages. Rogers replied in his whimsical Oklahoma drawl, "Buy land, son. It's the only thing they ain't makin' more of."

The actor invested in huge tracts. The city of Thousand Oaks, California, now stands on what once was his hay ranch...and Joel McCrea probably owns the bank!

Some of this same approach can be taken toward some firearms. With the consolidations, buy-outs and closing of factories, there are some guns that just aren't going to be made any more. Working with the theory of supply and demand, this seems to hold some promise. A case in point might involve the guns once made by Harrington & Richardson. Most of the handguns, for example, were cheaply made — and cheaply sold. None of them were any great wonders of engineering, but they filled a void in the handgun market.

But a few years ago, the H&R factory closed down. Its then owner now is an executive with another firearms company. In short, the H&R, regardless of model, is something they "ain't makin' more of."

Chances are the H&R guns never will become really valued collector items like some of the pre-World War II single-actions, Colt for example.

First, they weren't that expensively made and there were — and are — one hell of a lot of them around.

However, they have maintained their value, while some other guns have dropped considerably in resale return. Today, Harrington & Richardson revolvers are bringing about the same price as they did in 1978, when the first edition of this book was produced.

Where are we headed with all of this? Frankly, I don't have the slightest idea. I'm the one who once owned all rights to the first four chapters of "Jonathan Livingston Seagull" and returned those rights to the author. He made a fortune off the book and I have copies of some old aviation magazines in which I published those first four chapters.

Like I said before, hindsight is wonderful. It's also a totally worthless commodity.

Incidentally, this introduction would be incomplete if I did not offer my thanks to Harold Murtz, who has looked over my shoulder on all seven editions. He has questioned some of the compiled knowledge and, on some occasions, has shown it to be faulty. As a result, we have been able to compile a more complete and honest book than would be the case had I not had his input. He knows where to find the answers when I don't...and that's a valuable asset in any endeavor.

Guns, I figure, are sort of like Confederate money. Don't burn the loot or your guns. Genuine Confederate bills now enjoy a healthy price on the collector market. If any gun is maintained in good condition, it ultimately will be worth more than what you paid for it. History says so.

Jack Lewis,
Capistrano Beach, California

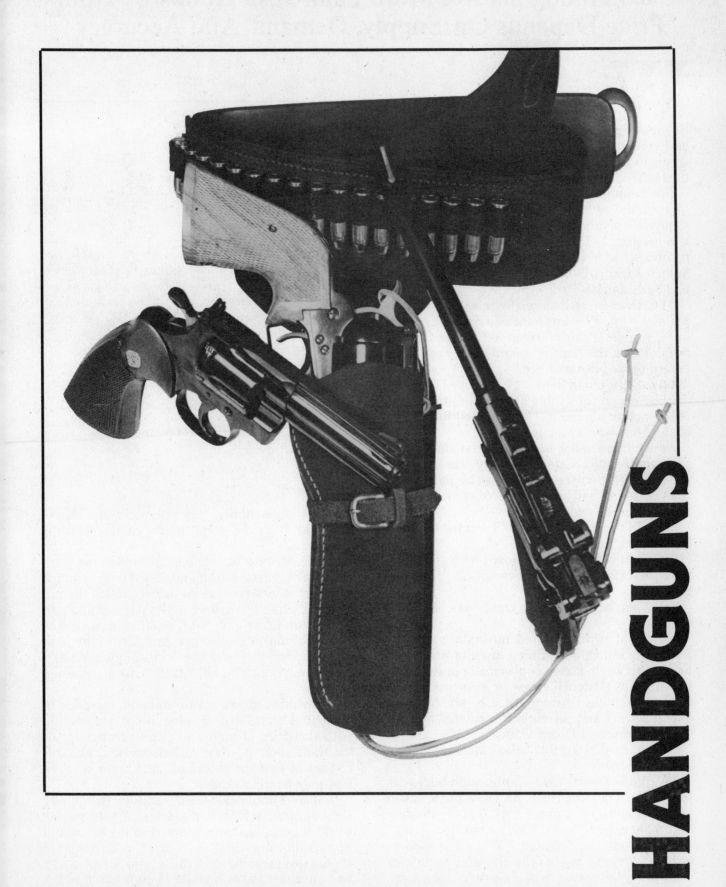

HANDGUNS

Used Handguns Are More Than Just Hunks Of Iron; Price Depends On Supply, Demand And Accuracy!

WHEN ONE looks at the Handgun Scene and considers the prices of used automatics and revolvers, the explanation regarding prices seems to come down to the old law of supply and demand.

For example, a few years ago, a retired Western film star called me and asked for help. It seems as though his saddle, twin silver-mounted holster rig and his matched pair of Colt Single Action Army revolvers had been on display in a museum in his hometown in Arizona to which all of his film tack had been donated.

"Those holsters look mighty empty," he complained. "I don't want to spend a batch of money, but if you see a pair of cheap old junker Colt .45 six-shooters, buy 'em for me and I'll pay you back. I want those holsters filled."

I wasn't of much help.

"There's no such thing as a cheap junker Colt single-action anymore," I had to tell him. "Any such gun is worth money."

As it turned out I hadn't understood the full problem. All of his movie cowboy gear had been stolen from the museum. All except his pair of Colt SAA revolvers had been recovered eventually and returned to the museum.

"How's the display set up?" I wanted to know, considering alternatives.

"It's in a case and all enclosed with glass."

"How close to it can a viewer get?" I wanted to know.

"Oh, maybe four or five feet," was his recollection.

Instead of paying a retired movie star's ransom, I suggested he think of filling those holsters with one of the single-action copies made in Italy and imported by Mitchell Arms or even the Uberti model which has been imported by several firms over the years and currently is marketed by Benson Firearms and Uberti USA.

"What do they go for?" the retiree wanted to know, frowning.

"Well, the Uberti 1873 Cattleman model goes for around $350 when new. And now the Mitchell guns in .45 go for just under $300. They both bring over $200 at gun shows. That's used."

"My, God!" he declared. "When I started in pictures, I could buy a fully engraved Colt with ivory grips for not much more'n that." The com-

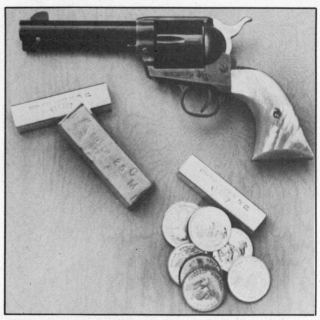

While gold and silver fluctuate a great deal, firearms have a tendency to hold their value to a greater degree.

parison, incidentally, may give you some idea of how far back he went in the movie heroing business.

Since no one was going to handle the guns except the museum staff and they'd be far enough away from viewers that no one could tell the difference, it finally was decided we'd round up a pair of the non-firing Colt SAA replicas marketed by Tom Nelson at Collectors Armoury. With new custom grips, they're sitting in those holsters today, bringing "ooohs" and "aaahs" from museum visitors.

As mentioned in our introduction, the price of used guns seems to bear some sort of relationship with the price of gold and other precious commodities such as silver and diamonds. The difference is that the prices of guns don't seem to fluctuate nearly as much.

Someone once made the observation that, under normal circumstances, the price of gold on the world market can be compared to the price of a new quality suit. Back in the days when the price of gold was established in the United States at $35 an ounce, a good suit could be purchased at between $30 and $40. We maintained the $35 price of gold in this country, but some years later, it was selling for $70 to $100 abroad. That was the price range for a top-line three-piecer during that same era. With the world price of gold hovering around the $380.00 mark, as of this writing, that's what you'll probably have to pay for a good suit at a shop you can trust.

In 1982, when Colt came out with the John Wayne Commemorative revolver, they announced that the .45 Single-Action Army model was being taken out of production. Some, however, have been made since from available parts. Several other commemoratives have been produced in limited numbers. But today, if you want a brand new, out-of-the box Colt Single-Action Army revolver, it is assembled in the Colt Custom Shop from that shrinking supply of available parts and the price is somewhere around $2500!

I've mentioned before that I have an old pre-WWII SAA with a relatively low serial number. I bought it years ago in a pawn shop for $45. A few years back, when we needed a photo of such a revolver, I handed it to Dean Grennell and asked that he snap the picture. When he returned, the handgun was cradled delicately in his arms.

"Have you checked the serial number on this?" he wanted to know.

"Not lately." I admitted, knowing I'd hardly looked at the Colt from the day I'd bought it.

"This thing's worth $2500!" That was during the era when gold on the world market was selling for around $800 per ounce. Today, gold sells for less than half that price, but my old Pawn Shop Special is still worth $2500 — and a bit more!

Again, we seem to be discussing supply and demand.

Not long ago, I was listening to a teenager complain that he was being paid $5 an hour to dig ditches and that wasn't enough! Rather grandly, I informed him that, a lot of years ago, I dug ditches for twenty-five cents an hour. He wasn't impressed.

"Money bought a lot more then," he declared.

"Not exactly. In those days, beer was twenty-five cents a bottle and I had to work an hour for a beer. I don't see anyone paying $5 for a beer!" I told him. I still don't think he was impressed.

During the Great Depression, one could buy new handguns for about $30 per copy. That, all too often, equated to a month's pay. Today, you can buy a respectable handgun for $300 to $500. That rarely *equates* to a month's pay. If it does, in your case, I suggest you find another line of work!

Which brings us back to the matter of gold. A lot of people bought gold a decade back as a hedge against inflation when it was selling for $800 an ounce. They've lost their shirts, based upon today's values. Some of the people we both know invested in guns in that same era, being told by the supposedly knowing that the guns would increase in value as inflation increased.

Such has not been the case. Inflation has been greatly reduced. Gold and silver certainly are not what they used to be pricewise; gold is less than half and silver is about one-seventh of its peak price. But I can't think of any handgun that has come anywhere close to decreasing that much in value. They may not have increased a great deal in value, but they haven't decreased all that much either.

There are those who feel the introduction of plastics in handguns will do much to disrupt the value of all-metal guns. The theory is that the guns with polymer frames can be produced more cheaply, therefore they eventually will glut the market at lower prices.

The only handgun marketed in this country that has a plastic frame at this point is the Glock, which is being made in three slightly differing versions. The Glock 17, with a 4.48-inch barrel, sells at retail for around $510. The same model, with a six-inch barrel, is roughly $740. A newer version, the Glock 19, introduced in 1988, five years after the original, retails new for the same price as the 17. The difference is that the later version has a four-inch barrel and the magazine holds fifteen rounds instead of seventeen. I think that pretty well sinks the theory that plastics will ruin the market for steel guns. It hasn't happened with handguns and the polymer-stocked rifles, either.

In the case of automatics, some of them have seen a drop in prices as used guns, but this again has to do, I think, with supply and demand. With the acceptance of the Beretta M9 as the sidearm for our Armed Forces, the whole world seems to have gone crazy for 9mm autos...and manufacturers around the world have been waiting to supply them. Over the past half dozen years, literally hundreds of new models — or updated variations of old ones — have found their way into the marketplace. The result is something of a glut. Yet, certain autos, including specific models turned out by Colt, Smith & Wesson and Springfield Armory, are in demand. This demand is based largely upon performance. Shooters have found these models will shoot where they are pointed...and that's what they want. They will pay a premium for a handgun with a track record for accuracy and reliability.

I guess what it all comes down to is a fact that we all recognize: Guns that perform will continue to maintain their values; those that don't probably will suffer in the marketplace.

ALLEN

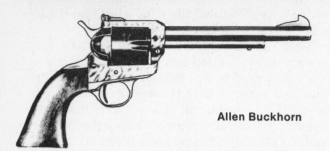

Allen Buckhorn

ALLEN Buckhorn: revolver; single-action; .44 magnum, .44-40; 6-rd. cylinder; 4¾", 6", 7½" barrel lengths; grooved rear sight, blade front; one-piece uncheckered walnut stocks; steel or brass backstrap, trigger guard; color case-hardened frame; blued cylinder, barrel. Made in Italy by Uberti. Formerly imported by Iver Johnson. Reintroduced, 1986; importation dropped by Allen Fire Arms, 1987. Used values: fixed sights, $200 to $225; with convertible cylinder, $225 to $250.

Buckhorn Target Model has same specs, except has flat-top frame, adjustable rear sight, ramp front. No longer imported by Allen. Used values: $225 to $250; with convertible cylinder, $250 to $275.

Buckhorn Buntline Model has 18" barrel. No longer imported by Allen. Used value, $250 to $275.

ALLEN Cattleman: revolver; single-action; .22 LR, .22 WMR, .38 Special, .357 magnum; .44-40, .45 Colt; 6-rd. cylinder; 4¾", 5½", 7½" barrels; fixed groove rear sight, blade front; one-piece uncheckered walnut stocks; steel or brass backstrap, trigger guard; blued barrel, cylinder; case-hardened frame. polished hammer flats. Made in Italy by Uberti. Formerly imported by Iver Johnson. Reintroduced, 1986; no longer imported by Allen Fire Arms. Used value, $200 to $220.

Target Cattleman has same specs, except for flat-top frame, fully adjustable rear sight. No longer imported by Allen. Used value, $200 to $220.

Buntline Cattleman has 18" barrel, .357, .44-40. .45 Colt only. No longer imported by Allen. Used value, $200 to $220.

Sheriff's Model Cattleman has 3" barrel, .44-40 only. No longer imported by Allen. Used value, $200 to $220.

ALLEN 1875 Army Outlaw: revolver; single-action; .357 magnum, .44-40, .45 Colt; 6-rd. cylinder; 7½" barrel; 13¾" overall length; weighs 44 oz.; notch rear sight, blade front; uncheckered walnut stocks; brass trigger guard; color case-hardened frame, rest is blued. Made in Italy by Uberti. Introduced, 1986; importation dropped, 1987. Used value, $190 to $200.

ALLEN Rolling Block: single-shot; .22 LR, .22 WMR, .357 magnum; 9⅞" half-round, half-octagon barrel; 14" overall length; weighs 44 oz.; fully adjustable rear sight, blade front; walnut stocks, forend; brass trigger guard; color case-hardened frame, blued barrel. Replica of 1871 target rolling block. Made in Italy by Uberti. Introduced, 1986; no longer imported by Allen Fire Arms; currently imported by Benson Firearms, Uberti U.S.A. Used value, $160 to $175.

AMERICAN DERRINGER

**American Derringer
Semmerling LM-4**

American Derringer Model 1

AMERICAN DERRINGER Semmerling LM-4: repeater; manually operated; 9mmP, with 8-rd. magazine; .45 ACP, 5 rds.; 3½" barrel; ramp front sight, fixed rear; blued or stainless steel; checkered black plastic stocks. Introduced, 1977; still in production. Used values: blued, $900 to $950; stainless, $1000 to $1100.

AMERICAN DERRINGER Model 1: over/under; 2-shot capability; break-action; .22 LR, .22 WRFM, .22 Hornet, .223 Rem, .30 Luger, .30-30, .32 ACP, .38 Super, .380 ACP, .38 Special, 9x18, 9mmP, .357 magnum, .41 magnum, .44-40, .44 Special, .44 magnum, .45 Colt, .410; 3" barrel; 4.82" overall length; weighs 15½ oz. in .38 Special; rosewood, zebra wood stocks; blade front sight; stainless steel; manual hammer block safety. Introduced, 1980;

still in production. Used value, depending on caliber, $165 to $285; engraved model, $285 to $325, depending on caliber.

AMERICAN DERRINGER Model 4 Alaskan Survival Model: has same specs as Model 4, except for upper barrel chambered for .45-70. Introduced, 1980; still in production. Used value: $270 to $290.

AMERICAN DERRINGER Model 3: single-shot; .38 Special; 2½" barrel; 4.9" overall length; weighs 8.5 oz.; rosewood stocks; blade front sight; manual hammer block safety; stainless steel. Introduced, 1985; still in production. Used value, $75 to $80.

AMERICAN DERRINGER Model 4: has same specs as Model 1, except has 4.1" barrel, overall length of 6"; chambered for 3" .410 shotshell or .45 Colt; also made with .45-70 upper barrel, .410 or

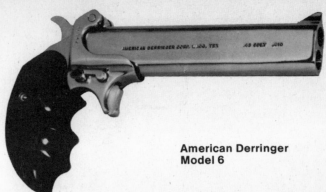

American Derringer Model 6

American Derringer Model 4

.45 Colt bottom barrel; stainless steel. Introduced, 1985; still in production. Used value, $260 to $280.

AMERICAN DERRINGER Model 6: has same general specs as Model 1, except has 6" barrels chambered for 3" .410 shotshell or .45 Colt. 8.2" overall length; weighs 21 oz.; rosewood stocks; manual hammer block safety. Introduced, 1986; still in production. Used value, $285 to $300.

AMERICAN FIREARMS

American 25

American .380

AMERICAN FIREARMS 25: .25 auto; 8-rd. magazine; 4.4" overall length; 2.1" barrel; fixed sights; walnut grips; blued ordnance steel or stainless steel; manufactured by American Firearms Co., Inc. Introduced in 1966; dropped, 1974. Used values: blued steel model, $100 to $110; stainless steel model, $110 to $120.

AMERICAN FIREARMS Derringer: over/under; 2-shot; .38 Special, .22 LR, .22 WRFM; 3" barrel; fixed open sights; checkered plastic grips; entirely of stainless steel; spur trigger, half-cock safety. Introduced in 1972; dropped, 1974. Used value, $125 to $145.

AMERICAN FIREARMS 380: automatic; .380 auto; stainless steel; 8-rd. magazine; 5½" overall; 3½" barrel; smooth walnut stocks. Limited manufacture, 1972. Used value, $250 to $300.

AMT

AMT Hardballer: automatic; .45 ACP; 5" barrel, 8½" overall; adjustable combat sights; checkered walnut grips; stainless steel construction; extended combat safety; serrated matted slide rib; long grip safety; beveled magazine well; grooved front, back straps; adjustable trigger; custom barrel bushing. Introduced, 1978; still in production. Used value, $300 to $325.

Hardballer Long Slide has same general specs as Hardballer, except for 7" barrel, 10½" overall length; fully adjustable micro rear sight. Introduced, 1977; still in production. Used value, $325 to $350.

AMT Skipper has same specs as Hardballer, but 1" shorter in overall length. Introduced, 1978; dropped, 1980. Used value, $325 to $350.

AMT Combat Government: automatic; .45 ACP; 5" barrel; 8½" overall length; fixed combat sights; checkered walnut grips; stainless steel construction; extended combat safety; adjustable target-type trigger; flat mainspring housing; custom-fitted barrel bushing. Introduced, 1978; dropped, 1980. Used value, $300 to $325.

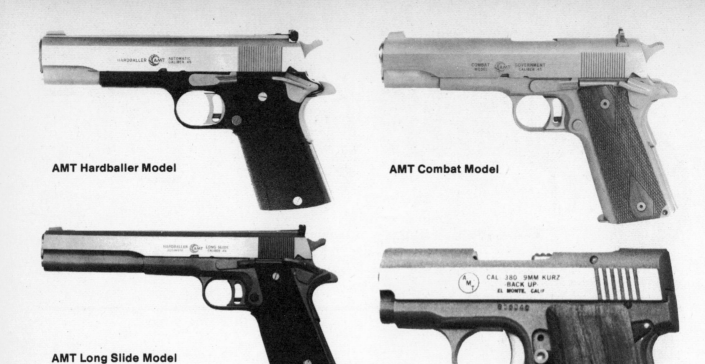

AMT Hardballer Model

AMT Combat Model

AMT Long Slide Model

AMT Backup

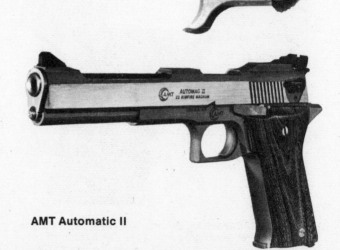

AMT Backup: automatic; .22 LR, 8-rd. magazine; .380 ACP, 5 rds.; 2½" barrel; weighs 17 oz.; 5" overall length; smooth wood stocks; fixed, open, recessed sights; concealed hammer; manual, grip safeties; blowback operated; stainless steel. .380 introduced, 1974; .22 introduced, 1982; still in production. Used value, $155 to $165.

AMT Lightning: automatic; .22 LR; 10-rd. magazine; tapered barrels, 6½", 8½", 10½", 12½"; bull barrels, 5", 6½", 8½", 10½", 12½"; weighs 45 oz. with 6½" barrel; overall length with 6½" barrel 10¾"; checkered wrap-around rubber stocks; blade front sight, fixed rear, adjustable rear at extra cost; stainless steel; Clark trigger with adjustable stops; receiver grooved for scope; interchangeable barrels. Introduced, 1984; still in production. Used value, $180 to $190, depending on barrel length.

AMT Automag II: automatic; .22 WMR; 10-rd. magazine; 6" barrel; 9¾" overall length; weighs 23 oz.; Millett adjustable rear sight, blade front; smooth black composition stocks; squared trigger guard; stainless steel construction; gas-assisted action; brushed finish on slide flats, rest sandblasted. Introduced, 1987; still in production. Used value, $200 to $225.

AMT Automatic II

ASTRA

ASTRA Model 900: automatic; 7.63mm; 5½" barrel; 11½" overall length; 10-rd. fixed magazine; adjustable rear sight, fixed front; small ring hammer on early models, larger hammer on later; grooved walnut grips; lanyard ring. Based upon design of "broomhandle" Mauser, but has barrel, barrel extension as two parts rather than one as in German Mauser, different lockwork, etc. Introduced in 1928; dropped, 1940. Originally priced at $37; has collector value. Used value, $550 to $600.

Astra Model 900

Astra Model 400

Astra M300/3000

ASTRA Model 400: automatic; 9mm Bergmann-Bayard; 6" barrel, 10" overall length; 9-rd. magazine; fixed sights; blowback action; some will also chamber and fire 9mm Luger and .38 ACP but it isn't recommended; blued finish; hard rubber or walnut grips. Introduced in 1921; dropped, 1946. Used value, $165 to $185.

ASTRA Model 300/3000: pocket automatic; .32 auto, .380 auto; 4" barrel; 5⅝" overall length, hard rubber grips. Introduced in 1922; dropped, 1958. Used value, $200 to $225.

ASTRA 4000: advertised as Falcon; automatic; .22 LR, .32 auto, .380 auto; 3⅔" barrel; 6½" overall length; 10-rd. magazine in .22, 8 rds. in .32, 7 rds. in .380; thumb safety; exposed hammer; fixed sights; checkered black plastic grips; blued. Introduced in 1956; U.S. importation dropped, 1968. Used value, $250 to $300; .22 model, $300 to $350; with conversion kit to another caliber add $150.

Astra Model 800

ASTRA Model 800: automatic; also called Condor; 9mm Luger; tubular-type design; 5-5/16" barrel; 8¼" overall length; 8-rd. magazine; fixed sights; blued finish; grooved plastic grips. Based on Model 400 design. Introduced in 1958; dropped, 1968. Few imported; produced primarily for European police, military use. Used value, $750 to $850.

ASTRA Model 200: vest pocket automatic; advertised as the Firecat; .25 ACP only; 2¼" barrel, 4⅜" overall length; 6-rd. magazine; fixed sights; blued finish; plastic grips. Introduced in 1920; still in production; U.S. importation dropped in 1968. Used value, $150 to $175.

Astra Cub

ASTRA Cub: pocket automatic; .22 short, .25 auto; 2¼" barrel; 4-7/16" overall length; 6-rd. magazine; fixed sights; blued or chrome finish; plastic grips. Introduced in 1957; still in production, but U.S. importation dropped, 1968. Used value, $125 to $145.

Astra Model 600

Astra Cadix

ASTRA Model 600: military, police automatic; 9mm Luger; 5¼" barrel, 8" overall length; 8 rds.; fixed sights; blued finish, hard rubber or walnut grips. Introduced in 1942; dropped, 1946. Used value, $175 to $185.

ASTRA Camper: same basic design as Cub, but has 4" barrel, overall length, 6¼"; chambered for .22 short only. Spanish-made. Manufactured 1953 to 1960. Used value, $125 to $145.

ASTRA Cadix: revolver, double-action; .22 caliber, 9-rd. cylinder; 5 rds. in .38 Special; 4" or 6" barrel; blued finish; adjustable rear sight, ramp front; checkered plastic stocks. Manufactured 1960 to 1968. Used value, $140 to $150.

Astra Constable

ASTRA Constable: automatic; .22 LR, .32 ACP; 3½" barrel; 10-rd. magazine in .22 LR, 8-rd. in .32 ACP, 7 rds. in .380 ACP; adjustable rear sight, fixed front; moulded plastic grips; double-action; non-glare rib on slide; quick, no-tool take-down feature; blued or chrome finish except .32, which is no longer available. Current importer is Interarms. Introduced in 1969; still in production. Used values, blued finish, $185 to $210; chrome, $200 to $225.

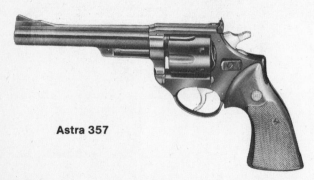

Astra 357

ASTRA 357: revolver; .357 magnum; 3", 4", 6", 8½" barrels; 6-rd. swing-out cylinder; integral rib, ejector rod; click-adjustable rear sight, ramp front; target hammer; checkered walnut grips; blued. Imported by Interarms. Introduced in 1972; still in production. Used value, $185 to $210.

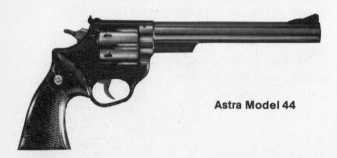

Astra Model 44

ASTRA Model 44: revolver, double-action; .44 magnum; similar in design to .357 magnum version; 8½" barrel length. Introduced, 1980; still in production. Used value, $215 to $240.

Astra Model A-80

ASTRA Model 41: same specs as Model 44, except chambered for .41 magnum rd.; 6" barrel length only. Introduced, 1980; still imported by Interarms. Used value, $210 to $255.

ASTRA Model 45: revolver, double-action; same specs as Model 41, except is chambered for .45 Colt cartridge. Manufactured in Spain. Introduced, 1980; still being imported by Interarms. Used value, $215 to $240.

ASTRA A-60: automatic; double-action; has the same general specs as Constable model, but in .380 only; 13-rd. magazine; slide-mounted ambidextrous safety; blued steel only. Made in Spain. Introduced, 1980; still imported by Interarms. Used value, $280 to $300.

ASTRA A-80: automatic, double-action; 9mm Parabellum, .38 Super, 15 rds.; .45 ACP, 9 rds.; 3¾" barrel; weighs 40 oz.; 7" overall length; checkered black plastic stocks; square blade front sight, drift-adjustable square notch rear; loaded-chamber indicator; combat-style trigger guard; optional right-side slide release; automatic internal safety; decocking lever; blued or chrome finish. Imported from Spain by Interarms. Introduced, 1982; dropped, 1985. Used values: blued, $275 to $300; chrome finish, $300 to $315.

ASTRA A-90: automatic; double-action; 9mm Parabellum, .45 ACP; 15-rd. magazine in 9mm, 9rds. for .45; 3¾" barrel; 7" overall length; weighs 40 oz.; checkered black plastic stocks; square blade front sight, square notch rear adjustable for windage; double or single action; loaded chamber indicator; optional right or left-side slide release; combat-type trigger guard; auto internal safety; decocking lever. Made in Spain. Introduced 1985; still imported by Interarms. Used value, $300 to $325.

BAYARD

BAYARD Model 1908: pocket automatic; .25 auto, .32 auto, .380 auto; 2¼" barrel; 4⅞" overall length; 6-rd. magazine; fixed sights, blued finish; hard rubber grips. Introduced in 1908; dropped, 1939. Used value, $165 to $185.

Bayard Model 1908

BAYARD Model 1923: small model pocket auto; .25 auto only; 2⅛" barrel; 4-5/16" overall length; fixed sights, blued finish; checkered grips of hard rubber. Scaled-down model of large Model 1923. Introduced in 1923; dropped, 1940. Used value, $165 to $175.

BAYARD Model 1923: larger model pocket auto; .32 auto, .380 auto; 3-5/16" barrel; 4-5/16" overall length; 6-rd. magazine; fixed sights; blued finish, checkered grips of hard rubber. Introduced in 1923; dropped, 1930. Used value, $150 to $175.

BAYARD Model 1930: pocket auto; .25 auto; has same general specifications as small Model 1923 auto pistol with improvements in finish, internal mechanism. Introduced in 1930; dropped, 1940. Used value, $175 to $185.

BERETTA

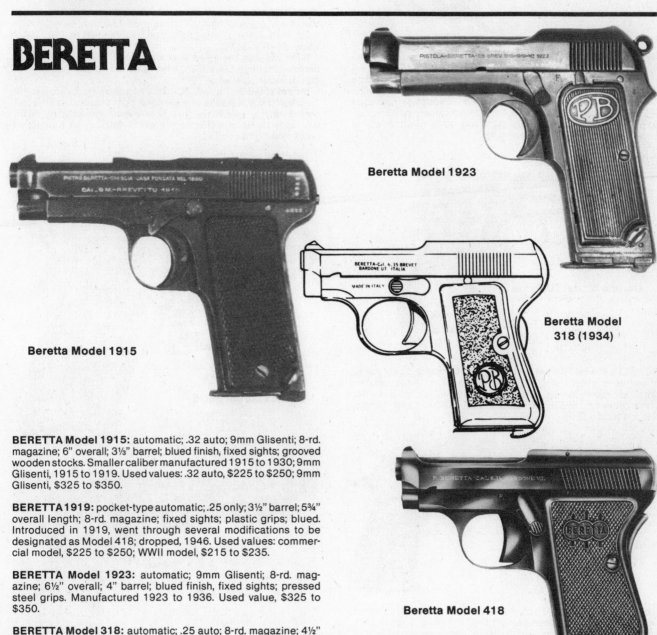

Beretta Model 1923

Beretta Model 1915

Beretta Model 318 (1934)

Beretta Model 418

BERETTA Model 1915: automatic; .32 auto; 9mm Glisenti; 8-rd. magazine; 6" overall; 3⅓" barrel; blued finish, fixed sights; grooved wooden stocks. Smaller caliber manufactured 1915 to 1930; 9mm Glisenti, 1915 to 1919. Used values: .32 auto, $225 to $250; 9mm Glisenti, $325 to $350.

BERETTA 1919: pocket-type automatic; .25 only; 3½" barrel; 5¾" overall length; 8-rd. magazine; fixed sights; plastic grips; blued. Introduced in 1919, went through several modifications to be designated as Model 418; dropped, 1946. Used values: commercial model, $225 to $250; WWII model, $215 to $235.

BERETTA Model 1923: automatic; 9mm Glisenti; 8-rd. magazine; 6½" overall; 4" barrel; blued finish, fixed sights; pressed steel grips. Manufactured 1923 to 1936. Used value, $325 to $350.

BERETTA Model 318: automatic; .25 auto; 8-rd. magazine; 4½" overall; 2½" barrel; weighs 14 oz.; blued finish, fixed sights; plastic stocks. Manufactured 1934 to 1939. Used value, $200 to $225.

BERETTA Model 418: pocket-type automatic; has same specs as Model 1919, except that grip safety was redesigned to match contour of backstrap. Also marketed as the Panther Model. Introduced, 1946; dropped, 1958. Used value, $200 to $225.

Beretta Model 950BS

Beretta Cougar

BERETTA Cougar, also Model 1934 or 934: pocket-type automatic; .380 auto, .32 auto; 3⅜" barrel. 5⅞" overall length; 7-rd. magazine; fixed sights; plastic grips; thumb safety; blued or chrome finish. Official Italian service sidearm in WWII; wartime version lacks quality of commercial model. Introduced in 1934; no longer legally importable; still in production. Used values: WWII model, $250 to $275; commercial model, blued, $275 to $300; nickel finish, add $15; for .32, subtract $30.

BERETTA Model 950B Minx M2: automatic; .22 short only; 2⅜" barrel; 4½" overall length; 6-rd. magazine; rear sight milled in slide; fixed front; black plastic grips; blued. Introduced in 1950. Used value, $140 to $150.

Minx M4 has the same specs as Model M2, except for 3¾" barrel. Introduced in 1956. Used value, $150 to $165. Neither model importable since 1968.

Model 950 BS .22 short, .25 ACP; 2½" barrel; 4½" overall length; checkered black plastic stocks; fixed sights; thumb safety, half-cock safety; hinged barrel for single loading, cleaning; blued finish. Made by Beretta USA. Introduced, 1982; still in production. Used value, $125 to $130.

Beretta Model 70 Puma

BERETTA Model 70 Puma: pocket-type automatic; .32 auto only; 4" barrel; 6" overall length; 8-rd. magazine; fixed sights; plastic grips; crossbolt safety; blued, chrome finish. Introduced after WWII; dropped, 1968. Used values: blued, $175 to $195; chrome finish, $180 to $200.

Beretta Model 95OB

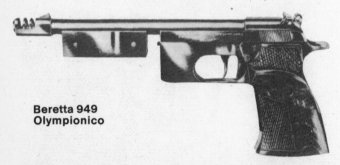

Beretta 949 Olympionico

Beretta Model 951

BERETTA Model 949 Olympionico: target automatic; .22 short only; 8¾" barrel; 12½" overall length; 5-rd. magazine; target sights; adjustable barrel weight; muzzle brake; hand-checkered walnut thumbrest grips; blued. Introduced in 1949; dropped, 1968. Used value, $500 to $525.

BERETTA Model 950B Jetfire: automatic; .25 auto; 2⅜" barrel; 4½" overall length; 7-rd. magazine; has the same general specs as Minx M2. Introduced in 1950; not importable since 1968. Now being made in U.S. Used value, $125 to $130.

BERETTA Model 951: automatic; 9mm Luger; 4½" barrel; 8" overall length; advertised originally as Brigadier model; 8-rd. magazine; external hammer; crossbolt safety; slide stays open after last shot; fixed sights; moulded grooved plastic grips; blued. Introduced in 1951; still in production. Used value, $275 to $300.

Beretta Model 90

Beretta Model 76

Beretta Model 81

Beretta Model 84

Beretta Model 71

BERETTA Model 71 and Model 72 Jaguar Plinker: automatic; .22 LR only; 3½" (Mod. 71) or 6" (Mod. 72) barrels; 8-rd. magazine; rear sight adjustable for windage only, fixed front; checkered plastic grips; blued. Introduced in 1956; dropped, 1968. Used value, $175 to $185.

Jaguar Model 101 has the same general specs as Jaguar Plinker, except for 6" barrel only; overall length, 8¾"; adjustable rear sight; wrap-around checkered plastic grips; lever thumb safety. Introduced in 1969; discontinued. Used value, $185 to $200.

Beretta Model 70T

BERETTA Model 70T: automatic; .32 auto; 6" barrel; 8½" overall length; 9-rd. magazine; adjustable rear sight, fixed front; external hammer; slide stays open after last shot; checkered plastic wrap-around grips. Introduced in 1969; dropped, 1975. Used value, $200 to $225.

BERETTA Model 90: double-action automatic; .32 auto; 3⅝" barrel; 6¾" overall length; 8-rd. magazine; fixed sights, matted rib on slide; chamber-loaded indicator; external hammer; stainless steel barrel; moulded plastic wrap-around grips; blued. Introduced in 1969; dropped, 1982. Used value, $175 to $185.

BERETTA Model 70S: automatic; .380 auto; 3⅝" barrel; 6½" overall length; 7-rd. magazine; external hammer; fixed sights; checkered plastic wrap-around grips; blued. Introduced in 1977; dropped, 1985. Used value, $175 to $200.

BERETTA Model 76: automatic; .22 LR only; 6" barrel; 9½" overall length; 10-rd. magazine; adjustable rear sight, interchangeable blade front; non-glare, ribbed slide; heavy barrel; external hammer; checkered plastic wrap-around grips; blued. Introduced in 1971; dropped, 1985. Used value, $250 to $275.

BERETTA Model 81: automatic, double-action; .32 auto; 12-rd. magazine; 6.8" overall; 3.8" barrel; blued finish, fixed sights; plastic stocks. Introduced in 1976; dropped, 1981. Used value, $210 to $225.

BERETTA Model 84: automatic; same as Model 81, except in .380 auto with 13-rd. magazine. Introduced in 1976; still in production. Used value, $300 to $320.

Beretta Model 92

Beretta Model 82W

BERETTA Model 82W: automatic; .32 ACP; has same specs as Model 81, except has wood grips, 9-rd. magazine. Introduced, 1977; dropped, 1984. Used value, $225 to $235.

BERETTA Model 85W: automatic; .380 ACP; has same specs as Model 84, except has wood grips, 9-rd. magazine. Introduced, 1977; dropped, 1984. Used value, $275 to $285.

BERETTA Model 92: automatic; double-action; 9mm Parabellum; 15-rd. magazine; 8½" overall; 5" barrel; blued finish; fixed sights; plastic stocks. Introduced, 1976; dropped, 1981. Used value, $325 to $350.

   Model 92 SB has same general specs as standard model, except chambered for 9mm Parabellum; 15-rd. magazine; 4.92" barrel; 8.54" overall length; blade front sight, windage-adjustable rear; black plastic stocks, wood optional. Introduced, 1977; dropped, 1985. Used value, $400 to $425.

   Model 92 SB Compact has same specs as 92 SB, except magazine holds 14 rds. Introduced, 1977; dropped, 1985. Used value, $400 to $425.

   Model 92 F has the same general specs as standard Model 92, except has matte finish, squared trigger guard, grooved front, back

straps, inertia firing pin; extractor acts as chamber loaded indicator; wood or plastic grips. Made in Italy. Introduced, 1977; still imported by Beretta USA. Used value, $425 to $450.

Beretta Model 20

BERETTA Model 20: automatic; double-action; .25 ACP; 8-rd. magazine; 2.5" barrel; 4.9" overall length; weighs 10.9 oz.; fixed sights; plastic or walnut stocks. Made in Italy. Introduced, 1984; dropped, 1986. Used value, $135 to $145.

BERETTA Model 21: automatic; .22 LR, .25 ACP; has the same general specs as Model 950 BS, except has 2.5" barrel, 4.9" overall length, 7-rd. magazine. Introduced, 1985; still produced. Made in U.S. Used value, $150 to $160.

BERNARDELLI

BERNARDELLI Standard: automatic; .22 LR only, 6", 8", 10" barrels; with 10" barrel, 13" overall length; 10-rd. magazine; target sights; adjustable sight ramp; walnut target grips; blued. Introduced in 1949; still in production. Used value, $185 to $200.

Bernardelli Vest Pocket Model

Bernardelli Model 80

BERNARDELLI Vest Pocket Model: automatic; .22 LR, .25 auto; 2⅛" barrel; 4⅛" overall length; 6-rd. magazine in .22, 5-rd. in .25; 8-rd. extension magazine also available in .25; no sights, but sighting groove milled in slide; plastic grips; blued. Introduced in 1948; U.S. importation dropped, 1968. Used value, $160 to $175.

Bernardelli Model 90

BERNARDELLI Match 22: automatic .22 LR only; 5¾" barrel; 9" overall length; 10-rd. magazine; manual, magazine safeties; external hammer; adjustable rear sight, post front; hand-checkered thumbrest walnut grips; blued. Introduced in 1971; replaced by Model 100. Used value, $200 to $210.

BERNARDELLI Model 60: automatic; .22 LR, 10 rds.; .32 ACP, 9 rds.; .380 ACP, 7 rds.; 3½" barrel; 6½" overall length; weighs 26½ oz.; checkered plastic grips, thumb rest; ramp front sight, adjustable white-outlined rear; hammer block slide safety; loaded chamber indicator; dual recoil buffer springs; serrated trigger; interia-type firing pin. Made in Italy. Introduced, 1978; still imported by Mandell Shooting Supplies. Used value, $200 to $225.

BERNARDELLI Model 80: automatic; .22 LR, .32 auto, .380 auto; .22 magazine holds 10 rds., .32 holds 8, .380 holds 8; 6½" overall, 3½" barrel; blued finish; adjustable rear sight, white dot front; plastic thumbrest stocks. Introduced 1968 as modification of Model 60 to meet U.S. import requirements. Used value, $150 to $160.

Model 90 has same specs, except for 9" overall length; 6" barrel; .22 or .32 cal. only. Introduced, 1968; still in production. Used value, $160 to $175.

Bernardelli Model 69

BERNARDELLI Model 69: target auto; .22 LR; 10-rd. magazine; 5.9" barrel; 9" overall length; weighs 38 oz.; interchangeable target sights; wrap-around hand-checkered walnut stocks; thumbrest; meets UIT requirements; manual thumb safety, magazine safety; grooved trigger. Made in Italy. Introduced, 1987; still imported by Mandall Shooting Supplies. Used value, $200 to $225.

Bernardelli Model 100

BERNARDELLI Model 100: automatic, target model; .22 LR only; 10-rd. magazine; 9" overall; 6" barrel; blued finish; adjustable rear sight, interchangeable front; checkered walnut thumbrest stocks. Introduced in 1969 as Model 68; dropped, 1983. Used value, $250 to $275.

Bernardelli PO18

BERNARDELLI PO18: automatic; double-action; 9mmP; 16-rd. magazine; 4.8" barrel; 6.2" overall length; weighs 36.3 oz.; low-profile combat sights; checkered, contoured plastic or optional walnut stocks; manual thumb safety, half-cock, magazine safeties; ambidextrous magazine release; auto-locking firing pin block safety. Made in Italy. Introduced, 1987; still imported by Mandall Shooting Supplies. Used values: plastic grips, $300 to $325; walnut, $325 to $350.

PO18 Combat Model has same specs as standard PO18, except has 4.1" barrel, 14-rd. magazine. Introduced, 1987; no longer imported. Used values: with plastic stocks, $300 to $325; walnut, $325 to $350.

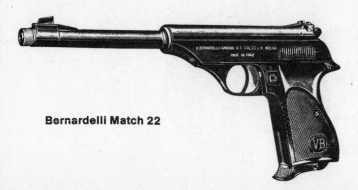

Bernardelli Match 22

BROWNING

Browning Hi-Power 9mm

Browning Renaissance Hi-Power

Browning Louis XVI

BROWNING Hi-Power 9mm: automatic; 9mm Parabellum only; 4⅝" barrel; 7¾" overall length; based on Browning-Colt .45 auto; adjustable or fixed rear sight; checkered walnut grips; thumb, magazine safeties; external hammer with half-cock safety feature; blued finish; 13-rd. magazine. Introduced in 1935, still in production. Used value, $350 to $375; with adjustable rear sight, $375 to $400.

Hi-Power Renaissance model has the same specs as standard model, except for chrome-plated finish, full engraving, polyester pearl grips. Introduced in 1954; dropped, 1982. Used value, $900 to $1000.

Browning Hi-Power 88 II

Louis XVI Hi-Power: same as standard Hi-Power 9mm, except for fully engraved silver-gray frame, slide, gold-plated trigger, hand-checkered walnut grips; issued in deluxe walnut case. Introduced in 1981; still in production. Used values: fixed sights, $1400 to $1450; adjustable sights, $1480 to $1525.

Hi-Power 88 II has same general specs as standard model, except has fixed rear sight, Parkerized military finish, black checkered polyamid grips; marketed with extra magazine. Imported from Belgium by Howco Distributors, Inc. Introduced, 1982; dropped, 1985. Used value, $350 to $375.

Browning Model 1906

BROWNING Model 1906 .25 Automatic: .25 ACP only; 2" barrel; 4½" overall length; 6-rd. magazine; fixed sights; blued or nickel finish; hard rubber grips. Almost identical to Colt Vest Pocket .25 auto. Introduced in 1906; dropped, 1940. Used value, $275 to $300.

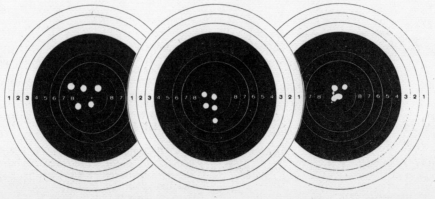

Browning 380

BROWNING Model 1910 380: automatic; .380, .32 ACP; 3-7/16" barrel; 6" overall length; 9-rd. magazine; pre-'68 models have fixed sights, later adjustable; hard rubber grips; blued finish. Introduced in 1910, and a longer-barreled version in 1922; redesigned in 1968; dropped, 1981. Used value, $275 to $285 except WWII manufacture, $245 to $250. Last models had 4½" barrel, are 7" overall.

The 380 Renaissance model has the same specs as the standard Browning 380, except for chrome-plated finish, full engraving, polyester pearl grips. Introduced in 1954; dropped, 1981. Used value, $900 to $1000.

Browning Baby Model 25

BROWNING 25 "Baby": automatic; .25 ACP only; 2⅛" barrel; 4" overall length; 6-rd. magazine; fixed sights, hard rubber grips; blued finish. Introduced in 1940; dropped, not importable, 1968. Used value, $250 to $300.

Browning 25 Lightweight has the same general specs as the standard model, except that it is chrome plated, has polyester pearl grips, alloy frame. Introduced in 1954; dropped, 1968. Used value, $300 to $350.

Browning 25 Renaissance Model has the same specs as the standard Browning 25, except for chrome-plated finish, polyester pearl grips, full engraving. Introduced in 1954; dropped, 1968. Used value, $650 to $750.

BROWNING Renaissance Set: includes Renaissance versions of Hi-Power 9mm, .380 Automatic, .25 Automatic in a specially fitted walnut case. Oddly, value depends to a degree upon condition of the case. Introduced in 1954; dropped, 1968. Used value, collectors, $3500 to $3750, unfired.

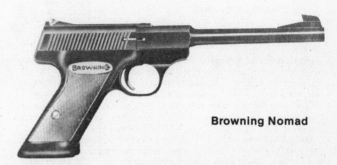

Browning Nomad

BROWNING Nomad: automatic; .22 LR only; 4½", 6¾" barrels; overall length, 8-15/16" with 4½" barrel; 10-rd. magazine; screw-adjustable rear sight, removable blade front; brown plastic grips; blued finish. Introduced in 1962; dropped, 1973. Used value, $200 to $225.

Browning Challenger Gold Model

BROWNING Challenger: automatic; .22 LR only; 4½", 6¾" barrels; overall length, 11-7/16" with 6¾" barrel; 10-rd. magazine; screw-adjustable rear sight, removable blade front; hand-checkered walnut grips; blued finish. Introduced in 1962; dropped, 1974. Used value, $275 to $300.

Challenger II has same specs as Challenger I, except for changed grip angle, impregnated hardwood stocks. Introduced, 1976; replaced by Challenger III, 1984. Used value, $160 to $180.

Challenger Gold Model has the same general specs as standard Browning Challenger, except for gold wire inlays in metal; figured, hand-carved, checkered walnut grips. Introduced in 1971; dropped, 1974. Used value, $850 to $900.

Challenger Renaissance Model has the same exact specs as standard Challenger, except for chrome-plated finish, full engraving, top-grade, hand-carved, figured walnut grips. Introduced in 1971; dropped, 1974. Used value, $750 to $850.

BROWNING Medalist: automatic; .22 LR only; 6¾" barrel; 11⅛" overall length; 10-rd. magazine; vent rib; full wrap-around grips of select walnut, checkered with thumb rest; matching walnut forend; left-hand model available; screw-adjustable rear sight, removable blade front; dry-firing mechanism; blued finish. Introduced in 1962; dropped, 1974. Used value, $525 to $550.

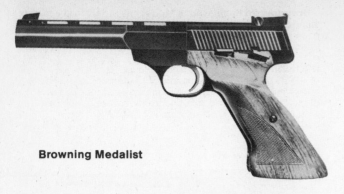

Browning Medalist

Browning BDA-380

International Medalist has same general specs as standard Medalist, but is sans forend; 5.9" barrel, overall length, 10-15/16"; meets qualifications for International Shooting Union regulations. Introduced in 1964; dropped, 1974. Used value, $550 to $600.

Medalist Gold Model has the same specs as standard Browning Medalist, except for gold wire inlays; better wood in grip. Introduced in 1963; dropped, 1974. Used value, $1200 to $1300.

Medalist Renaissance Model has the same specs as standard Medalist, except for finely figured, hand-carved grips, chrome plating, full engraving. Introduced in 1964; dropped, 1974. Used value, $1100 to $1200.

manufactured by Sauer, also known as SIG-Sauer P220. Imported 1977 to 1981. Used value, $400 to $450.

BDA 380: automatic; .380 auto; 12-rd. magazine; 3-13/16" barrel; 6¾" overall length; blade front sight, windage-adjustable rear; combination safety, de-cocking lever; inertia firing pin; unchechkered walnut grips. Manufactured in Italy. Introduced 1978; still in production. Used value, $275 to $300.

BROWNING Double Action 9mm: automatic; firing pin safety block; 15-rd. magazine; twin ambidextrous decocking levers; wrap-around moulded grips; squared trigger guard; drift-adjustable rear sight; Parkerized finish. Introduced, 1985; importation dropped, 1988. Used value, $350 to $375.

BROWNING Buck Mark: automatic; .22 LR; 10-rd. magazine; 5½" barrel; 9" overall length; weighs 32 oz.; adjustable rear sight, ramp front; skip-line checkered moulded black composition stocks; all-steel construction; gold-colored trigger; matte blue finish. Introduced, 1985; still in production. Used value, $120 to $130.

Buck Mark Plus has same specs as standard model, except has laminated wood stocks. Introduced, 1985; still in production. Used value, $150 to $160.

Buck Mark Silhouette has same basic specs as standard model, except has 9⅞" heavy barrel, hooded front sight, interchangeable posts. Millett Gold Cup 360 SIL rear; grip, forend are of black laminated wood. Introduced, 1987; still in production. Used value, $200 to $225.

Buck Mark Varmint has same specs as standard version, except has 9⅞" heavy barrel, full-length scope base, no sights, black laminated wood stocks, optional forend; weighs 48 oz. Introduced, 1987; still in production. Used value, $190 to $210.

Browning BDA

BROWNING BDA: automatic; 9mm Luger, .38 Super Auto, .45 ACP; 9-rd. magazine in 9mm, .38 Super Auto; 7 rds. in .45 ACP; 7-4/5" overall; 4-2/5" barrel; blued finish, fixed sights, plastic stocks;

CHARTER ARMS

CHARTER ARMS Undercover: double-action revolver; swing-out 5-rd. cylinder; .38 Special; 2", 3" barrels; with 2" barrel, 6¾" overall length; walnut standard or Bulldog grips; fixed rear sight, serrated ramp front; blued or nickel finish. Introduced in 1965; still in production. Used values, blued, with regular grips, $135 to $145; Bulldog grips, $140 to $150; nickel finish, $150 to $160.

Stainless Steel Undercover: has the same specs as the standard model, except is made of stainless steel; 2" barrel length only. Introduced, 1980; still in production. Used value, $180 to $195.

CHARTER ARMS Pathfinder: double-action revolver; has the same general specs as Undercover model, except in .22 LR only; 3" barrel only; adjustable rear sight, ramp front; blued finish only. Introduced in 1971; still in production. Used value, $125 to $135.

Dual Pathfinder has the same general specs as standard Pathfinder model, except an extra cylinder is chambered for .22 WRFM cartridge; hand-checkered walnut grips. Introduced in 1971; dropped, 1971. Used value, $155 to $165.

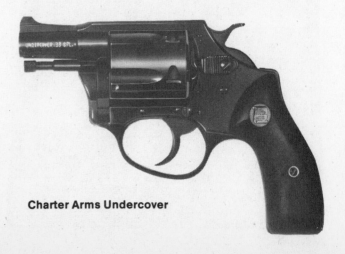

Charter Arms Undercover

Charter Arms Pathfinder

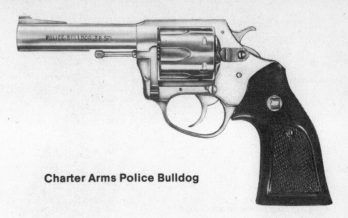

Charter Arms Police Bulldog

Charter Arms Undercoverette

Charter Arms Target Bulldog

CHARTER ARMS Undercoverette: double-action revolver; has same general specs as Undercover, but with 6-rd. .32 S&W Long chambering; 2" barrel only; designed for policewomen or ladies' purse; blued only. Introduced in 1969; dropped, 1981. Used value, $125 to $135.

Bulldog Pug has 2½" barrel; 7¼" overall length; weighs 19 oz.; notch rear sight, ramp front; Bulldog walnut or neoprene stocks; wide trigger, hammer spur; shrouded ejector rod. Introduced, 1986; still in production. Used value, $180 to $190.

Bulldog Tracker has same general specs as standard Bulldog, except is chambered for .357 magnum; has 2½", 4", or 6" bull barrel; adjustable rear sight, ramp front; square-butt checkered walnut or Bulldog-style neoprene stocks; blued finish. Introduced, 1986; still in production. Used value, $160 to $175.

Charter Arms .44 Special Bulldog

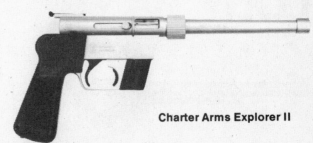

Charter Arms Explorer II

CHARTER ARMS Bulldog: revolver, double-action; .44 Special; 5-rd. swing-out cylinder; 3" barrel only; chrome-moly steel frame; wide trigger, hammer; square notch fixed rear sight, Patridge-type front; checkered walnut grips; blued only. Introduced in 1973. Used value, $150 to $165.

Police Bulldog is .38 Special, has 6-rd. cylinder; 4" barrel; adjustable rear sight, ramp front. Introduced in 1976; still in production. Used value, $140 to $150.

Target Bulldog is .357 magnum, .44 Special; adjustable rear sight, ramp front. Introduced in 1976; dropped, 1984. Used value, $165 to $175.

Bulldog 357 has same general specs as .44 Special model, except for .357 caliber, 6" barrel. Introduced in 1977; still in production. Used value, $150 to $165.

CHARTER ARMS Explorer II: automatic; .22 LR; 8-rd. magazine; 8" barrel; 15½" overall; blade front sight, open rear adjustable for elevation; satin finish; serrated simulated walnut stocks; action adapted from Explorer carbine. Introduced in 1980; still in production. Used values: $70 to $80; with extra magazine, 6" or 10" barrel, $90 to $95.

CHARTER ARMS Model 79K: automatic; double-action; .32 ACP, .380 ACP; 7-rd. magazine; 3.6" barrel; weighs 24.5 oz.; overall length, 6.5"; fixed sights; hammer block; firing pin, magazine safeties; stainless steel finish. Imported from West Germany. Introduced, 1984; no longer imported. Used value, $285 to $300.

Charter Arms Model 79K

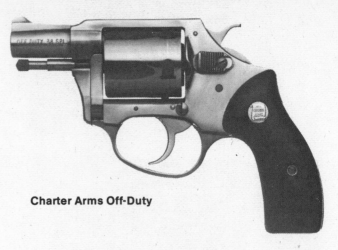

Charter Arms Off-Duty

Charter Arms Model 40

CHARTER ARMS Model 40: automatic; double-action; .22 LR; similar to Model 79K, except has 3.3" barrel; weighs 21.5 oz. Introduced, 1984; no longer imported. Used value, $230 to $240.

CHARTER ARMS Off-Duty: revolver; .38 Special only; 2" barrel; has same general specs as Undercover; Mat-Black finish; all steel; Red-Dot front sight; choice of smooth or checkered walnut, neoprene; also available in stainless steel. Introduced, 1984; still in production. Used values: Mat-Black finish, $120 to $130; stainless steel, $160 to $170.

CHARTER ARMS Police Undercover: revolver; .32 H&R magnum, .38 Special; 6 rds.; Patridge front sight, fixed square-notch rear; checkered walnut grips; blued finish or stainless steel; 2" barrel. Introduced, 1984; still in production. Used values: stainless steel, $190 to $200; blued, $160 to $170.

CHARTER ARMS Target Bulldog: revolver; double-action; .357 magnum, .44 Special; 5-rd. cylinder; 4" barrel; 9" overall length; weighs 21 oz.; adjustable rear sight, blade front; square-butt walnut stocks; all-steel frame; shrouded barrel, ejector rod. Introduced, 1986; still in production. Used values: .357 magnum, $175 to $185; .44 Special, $180 to $190.

COLT

Colt Model 1873

COLT Model 1873: also known as Frontier, Peacemaker, Single-Action Army; single-action revolver; originally made in black powder calibers; .22 LR, long, short; .22 WRFM, .32 Colt, .32-20, .32 S&W, .32 rimfire, .38 Colt, .38 S&W, .38 Special, .38-40, .357 magnum, .41 Colt, .44 rimfire, .44 Russian, .44-40, .44 Special, .45 Colt, .45 ACP, .450 Boxer, .450 Ely, .455 Ely, .476 Ely; recent production in .357 magnum, .45 Colt only; barrels, 3", 4" sans ejector, dropped;

4¾", 5½" 7½" with ejector; overall length, 10¼" with 4¾" barrel; one-piece uncheckered walnut grip or checkered black rubber; standard model has fixed sights; target model has target sights, flat top strap; blued finish, case-hardened frame or nickel plated. Those with serial numbers after 165,000 fire smokeless powder; black powder only should be used in lower-numbered guns. Change was made in 1896, when spring catch was substituted for cylinder pin screw. Introduced in 1873; dropped, 1942. New production began in 1955 with serial number 1001SA. Production dropped, 1982. Used values for pre-WWII models, .22 Target Model, $4000 to $5000; other calibers, $5000 to $6000; Storekeeper Model, sans ejector, $3500 to $4000; .45 Artillery Model with 5½" barrel, $1750 to $1800; .45 Cavalry Model, 7½" barrel, $1750 to $2000; .44-40 Frontier Model, $1250 to $1500; standard model, $1000 to $1200; post-1955 model, $500 to $600.

Colt .45 Buntline Special is same as post-1955 standard Model 1873, except for 12" barrel; .45 Colt only; designed after guns made as presentation pieces by author Ned Buntline. Introduced in 1957; dropped, 1975. Used value, $600 to $700.

New Frontier Single Action Army has the same specs as Model 1873, except for flat-top frame, smooth walnut grips, 5½", 7½" barrel; .357 magnum, .45 Colt; adjustable target-type rear sight, ramp front. Introduced in 1961; dropped, 1982. Used value, $475 to $525.

New Frontier Buntline Special has the same specs as New Frontier Single Action Army model, except for 12" barrel. Introduced in 1962; dropped, 1966. Used value, $750 to $1000.

COLT Bisley: revolver, single-action; same general specs and calibers as Single Action Army (1873) Model, with trigger, hammer and grips redesigned for target shooting. Target model features target sights, flat-top frame. Manufactured from 1894 to 1915; sought after by collectors. Used values: standard model, $850 to $1250; target model, $2000 to $3000.

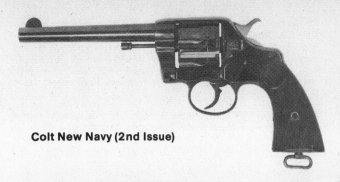

Colt New Navy (2nd Issue)

Colt Lightning Model

COLT Lightning: revolver, double-action; .38 and .41 (known as the "Thunderer") calibers; 6-rd. cylinder; with ejector, barrel lengths are 4½", 6"; sans ejector, 2½", 3½", 4½", 6"; fixed sights; blued or nickel finish; hard rubber grips. Manufactured 1877 to 1909. Used value, $350 to $400.

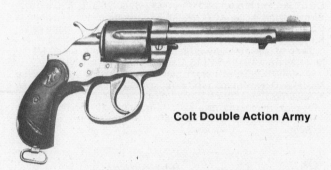

Colt Double Action Army

COLT Double Action Army: revolver, double-action; .38-40, .44-40, .45 Colt; similar to Lightning model, but with heavier frame; 6-rd. cylinder; barrel lengths, with ejector, 4¾", 5½", 7½"; sans ejector, 3½", 4"; lanyard ring in butt; hard rubber grips, fixed sights; blued or nickel finish. Manufactured 1878 to 1905. Used value, $750 to $800.

Colt New Navy (1st Issue)

COLT New Navy (First Issue): revolver, double-action; .38 Short Colt, .38 Long Colt, .41 Short, Long Colt; left-revolving 6-rd. cylinder; 3", 4½", 6" barrel lengths; fixed blade front sight, V-notched rear; Colt's first solid-frame, swing-out cylinder model; hard rubber or walnut grips; blued or nickel; also called the New Army, adopted by both Army and Navy. Manufactured 1889 to 1894. In demand by collectors. Used value, $325 to $350.

COLT New Navy (Second Issue): revolver; same general specs as First Issue, except for double cylinder notches, double locking

bolt; lanyard loop on butt; added calibers: .38 Special, .32-20; does not fire modern high-velocity loads safely. Manufactured 1892 to 1905. Used value, $300 to $325.

COLT New Pocket Model: revolver, double-action; .32 Short Colt, Long Colt; 6-rd. cylinder; 2½", 3½", 6" barrel lengths; hard rubber grips, fixed blade front sight, notched V rear. Manufactured 1895 to 1905. Used value, $225 to $275.

Colt New Police

COLT New Police: revolver, double-action; .32 caliber; built on New Pocket Model frame, with larger hard rubber grips; 2½", 4", 6" barrels; same sights as New Pocket Colt, blued or nickel finish. Manufactured 1896 to 1905. Used value, $225 to $250.
  New Police Target Model has same specs, except for target sights, 6" barrel only. Manufactured 1896 to 1905. Used value, $365 to $385.

Colt New Service

COLT New Service: double-action revolver; large frame, swing-out 6-rd. cylinder; .38 Special, .357 magnum, .38-40, .38-44, .44 Russian, .44 Special, .44-40, .45 Colt, .45 ACP, .450 Ely, .476 Ely; 4", 4½", 5", 5½", 6", 7½" barrels. Special run in .45 auto during WWI was designated as Model 1917 Revolver under government contract. Fixed open notch rear sight milled in top strap, fixed front; checkered hard rubber grips on commercial New Service; lanyard loop on most variations; blued, nickel finish. Introduced in 1897; dropped, 1943. Used values: 1917 military model, $300 to $325; .357 magnum, which was introduced in 1936, $550 to $650; other models, $450 to $550.

New Service Target Model has the same general specs as standard New Service model, except for rear sight adjustable for windage, front adjustable for elevation; top strap is flat; action is hand finished; 5", 6", 7½" barrels; .44 Special, .44 Russian, .45 Colt, .45 ACP, .450 Ely, .455 Ely, .476 Ely; blued finish, hand-checkered walnut grips. Introduced in 1900; dropped, 1940. Used value, $650 to $750.

COLT Model 1900: automatic; .38 ACP; 7-rd. magazine; 6" barrel; 9" length overall; fixed sights, plain walnut stocks, spur hammer; blued finish. Dangerous to fire modern high-velocity loads. Manufactured 1900 to 1903. Collector value. Used value, $550 to $650.

Colt Model 1902 Military

COLT Model 1902 Military: automatic; .38 ACP; 8-rd. magazine; 9" overall; 6" barrel; fixed sights; fixed blade front sight, notched V rear; checkered hard rubber grips; round back hammer (changed to spur type in 1908); sans safety; blued finish. Do not fire modern high-velocity loads. Manufactured from 1902 to 1929. Collector value. Used value, $500 to $525.

COLT Model 1902 Sporter: automatic; .38 ACP; 8-rd. magazine; 6" barrel, 9" overall; sans safety; checkered hard rubber grips, blade front sight, fixed notch V rear, round hammer. Not safe with modern loads. Manufactured 1902 to 1929. Collector value. Used value, $575 to $600.

COLT Model 1903: pocket automatic; .38 ACP; same general specs as Model 1902 Sporter, except for 4½" barrel; 7½" overall length; round back hammer changed to spur type in 1908. Not safe with modern ammo. Manufactured 1903 to 1929. Collector value. Used value, $425 to $450.

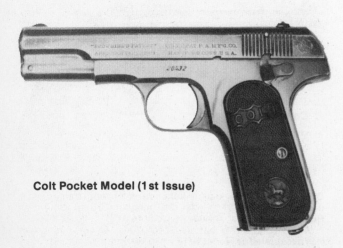

Colt Pocket Model (1st Issue)

COLT Pocket Model 32, First Issue: automatic; .32 auto; 8-rd. magazine; 3¾" barrel, 7" overall; fixed sights, hammerless, slide lock, grip safeties, hard rubber stocks, blued finish, barrel locking bushing. Manufactured from 1903 until 1911. Used value, $325 to $350.

Colt Pocket Model (2nd Issue)

Second Issue is same as original issue, except for redesign without barrel bushing. Made from 1911 until 1945. Used value, $275 to $300.

Model 32 (Third Issue) has same specs as second issue, except for 3¾" barrel; overall length, 6¾"; machine-checkered walnut grips. On all guns above serial No. 468097, safety disconnector prevents firing cartridge in chamber if magazine is removed. Introduced in 1926; dropped, 1945. Used values: $275 to $300; U.S. property marked $450 to $550.

COLT Pocket Model 380 (First Issue): automatic; .380 auto; 7-rd. magazine; 4" barrel, 7" overall. Same general design, specs as Pocket Model 32. Manufactured from 1908 to 1911. Used value, $375 to $400.

Second Issue is same as first issue, sans barrel bushing. Manufactured from 1911 to 1945. Used value, $325 to $350.

Model 380 (Third Issue) has same specs as second issue Model 380, except for 3¾" barrel; overall length, 6¾"; machine-checkered walnut grips. Safety disconnector installed on guns with serial numbers above 92,894. Introduced in 1926; dropped, 1945. Used values: $325 to $350; U.S. Property marked $550 to $650.

Colt Marine Corps Model

COLT Marine Corps Model: double-action revolver, same specs as Second Issue New Navy, except for round butt, 6" barrel only. Made in .38 Short, Long Colt, .38 Special. Manufactured 1905 to 1909. Used value, $775 to $825.

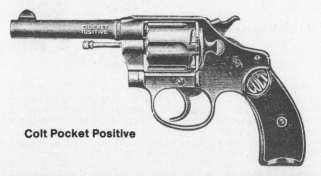

Colt Pocket Positive

COLT Pocket Positive: double-action revolver, based upon New Pocket model; dropped in 1905; .32 Short Colt, .32 Long Colt, .32

Colt New Police (interchangeable with .32 S&W Long, S&W Short cartridges); 2½", 3½", 6" barrels; overall length, 7½" with 3½" barrel; 6-rd. cylinder; rear sight groove milled in top strap, rounded front sight; positive lock feature; hard rubber grips; blued or nickel finish. Introduced in 1905; dropped, 1940. Used value, $225 to $250.

Colt Police Positive

COLT Police Positive: double-action revolver; 6-shot swing-out cylinder; replaced New Police model; dropped in 1905; .32 Short Colt, .32 Long Colt, .32 Colt New Police, .38 S&W; 2½", 4", 5", 6" barrel lengths; overall length, 8½" with 4" barrel; fixed sights; checkered walnut, plastic, hard rubber grips; top of frame matted to reduce glare. Introduced in 1905; dropped, 1947. Used value, $175 to $195.

Police Positive Target model has same general specs as standard Police Positive. Chambered for .32 Short Colt, .32 Long Colt, .32 New Police, .32 S&W Short, .32 S&W Long; .22 LR. Introduced in 1910; in 1932, cylinder was modified by countersinking chambers for safety with high-velocity .22 ammo; those with noncountersunk chambers should be fired only with standard-velocity .22 LR ammo. Has 6" barrel, overall length, 10½"; rear sight adjustable for windage, front for elevation; checkered walnut grips; blued; backstrap, hammer spur, trigger checkered. Introduced in 1905; dropped, 1940. Used value, $350 to $375.

Police Positive Special has generally the same specs as standard Police Positive, except that frame is lengthened to accommodate a longer cylinder, permitting chambering of .38 Special, .32-20; also made in .32 and .38 Colt New Police; 4", 5", 6" barrels; with 4" barrel, overall length, 8¾"; blued or nickel. Introduced in 1907; dropped, 1973. Used values: blued, $200 to $225; nickel finish, $225 to $250.

Police Positive (Second Issue) is same as Detective Special, except has 4" barrel, measures 9" overall, weighs 26½ oz. Introduced, 1977; dropped, 1980. Used value, $165 to $175.

Colt Officer's Model Target

Colt Officer's Model Match

COLT Officer's Model Target: double-action revolver; second issue replaced first issue, discontinued in 1908; .22 LR, .32 New Police, .38 Special; 6" barrel in .22 LR and .32 NP, 4", 4½", 5", 6", 7½", in .38 Special; overall length, 11¼" with 6" barrel; hand-finished action; 6-rd. cylinder; hand-checkered walnut grips; adjustable rear target sight, blade front; blued finish. The .38 Special was introduced in 1908, .22 LR in 1930, .32 NP in 1932; .32 NP dropped in 1942; model dropped, 1949. Used values: .22 LR, $375 to $385; .32NP, $350 to $400; .38 Special, $325 to $350.

Officers' Model Special is basically the same as second issue Officer's Model Target gun, but with heavier barrel, ramp front sight, Coltmaster adjustable rear sight, redesigned hammer; checkered plastic stocks; 6" barrel, .22 LR, .38 Special; blued finish. Introduced in 1949; dropped, 1955. Used value, $350 to $375.

Officers' Model Match has the same general specs as Officers' Model Special, which it replaced. Exceptions are target grips of checkered walnut, tapered heavy barrel, wide hammer spur. Introduced in 1953; dropped, 1970. Used value, $400 to $425.

Colt Army Special

COLT Army Special: double-action revolver, .41 caliber frame; .32-20, .38 Special, .41 Colt; 6-rd. cylinder; barrel lengths, 4", 4½", 5", 6"; overall length, 9¼" with 4" barrel; hard rubber grips; fixed sights; blued or nickel finish. Not safe for modern .38 Special high-velocity loads in guns chambered for that caliber. Introduced in 1908; dropped, 1928. Used value, $285 to $300.

Colt Pocket Model 25

COLT Pocket Model 25: advertised as vest pocket model; hammerless automatic; .25 ACP only; 2" barrel; 4½" overall length; 6-rd. magazine; hard rubber or checkered walnut grips; fixed sights, milled in top of slide; incorporates straight-line striker, rather than pivoting hammer, firing pin; slide-locking safety, grip safety; magazine disconnector added in 1917 at serial No. 141,000; blued, with case-hardened safety lever, grip safety, trigger, or nickel finished. Introduced in 1908; dropped, 1941. Used values: blued, $225 to $250; nickel finish, $275 to $295; U.S. Property marked, $650 to $750.

COLT Model 1911: automatic, also known as Government Model; .45 ACP only; 5" barrel; 8½" overall length; 7-rd. magazine; checkered walnut grips; fixed sights; military versions have Parkerized or nonglare blued finish; commercial versions have blued finish with letter "C" preceding serial number. Introduced in 1911; produced from 1923 on as Model 1911A1. Used value, $550 to $600.

Colt Model 1911

Colt 1911 Commercial Model

Colt Model 1911A1

Model 1911A1 has the same specs as Model 1911, except for a longer grip safety spur, checkered, arched mainspring housing; finger relief cuts in frame behind trigger; plastic grips. During WWI and WWII, other firms produced the Government Model under Colt license; included were Remington UMC, Remington-Rand, Ithaca Gun Co., North American Arms of Canada (rare), Singer Sewing Machine (rare), Union Switch & Signal Co. and Springfield Armory. These government models bear imprint of licensee on slide. Model was redesigned and redesignated as Government Model MKIV Series 70 in 1970; approximately 850 1911A1 guns were equipped with split-collet barrel bushing, BB prefix on serial number — this adds to their collector value. Introduced in 1923. Used values: .45 autos of WWI to WWII, U.S. Model of 1911: Colt, $500 to $550; North American Arms Co., approx. 100 manufactured, $5000-plus; Remington-UMC, 21,676 manufactured, $750 to $800; Springfield Armory, 25,767 manufactured, $700 to $750; Commercial

Model M1911 Type, $550 to $600. U.S. Model of 1911A1: Singer, only 500 manufactured, extremely well made, $6000 to $7000; Union Switch & Signal Co., 40,000 manufactured, $525 to $550; Colt, $425 to $450; Ithaca, $375 to $400; Remington Rand, $375 to $400; Commercial Model of 1911A1, $550 to $600; Colt .45-22 Conversion unit, $185 to $210; Colt .22-45 Conversion unit, quite rare, collector item, $600 to $700.

COLT Model 1917 Army: double-action, swing-out 6-rd. cylinder; based upon New Service revolver to fire .45 ACP cartridge with steel half-moon clips; later, shoulder permitted firing ammo sans clip; .45 Auto Rim cartridge can be fired in conventional manner; 5½" barrel, 10.8" overall length; smooth walnut grips; fixed sights; dull finish. Should be checked for damage by corrosive primers before purchase. Introduced in 1917; dropped, 1925. Used value, $300 to $325.

COLT Camp Perry Model (First Issue): target single-shot; built on frame of Colt Officers' Model; .22 LR only, with countersunk chamber for high-velocity ammo after 1930; 10" barrel; 13¾" overall length; checkered walnut grips; hand-finished action; adjustable target sights; trigger, backstrap, hammer spur checkered; blued finish, with top, back of frame stippled to reduce glare. Resembles Colt revolvers, but chamber, barrel are single unit, pivoting to side for loading and extraction when latch is released. Introduced in 1926; dropped, 1934. Used value, $850 to $875.
  Camp Perry Model (Second Issue) has the same general specs as first issue, except for 8" barrel, 12" overall length; shorter hammer fall. As only 440 were produced, it has collector value over original version. Introduced in 1934; dropped, 1941. Used value, $950 to $1000.

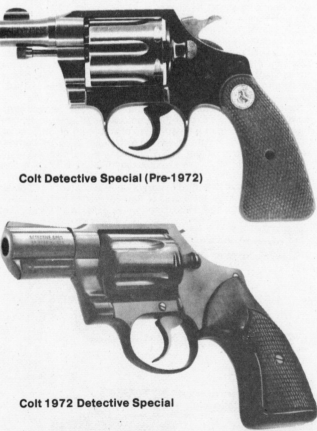

Colt Detective Special (Pre-1972)

Colt 1972 Detective Special

COLT Detective Special: swing-out cylinder; double-action revolver; 6-rd. capacity; .32 New Police, .38 New Police, .38 Special; 2" barrel, 6¾" overall length. Other specs are identical to those of Police Positive Special, with rounded butt introduced in 1933. Introduced in 1926; dropped, 1972. Used values, .32 variations, $235 to $245; .38 Special, $250 to $275.
  Detective Special (1972) is revamp of original with heavier barrel; integral protective shroud enclosing ejector rod; frame, side plate, cylinder, barrel, internal parts are of high-tensile alloy

steel; .38 Special only; walnut Bulldog-type grips; rear sight is fixed; notch milled in top strap, serrated ramp front; checkered hammer spur; blued, nickel finish. Introduced in 1972; dropped, 1987. Used values: blued, $250 to $275; nickel finish, $275 to $300.

Colt Bankers Special

COLT Bankers Special: double-action revolver; swing-out 6-rd. cylinder essentially the same as pre-1972 Detective Special, but with shorter cylinder of Police Positive rather than that of Police Positive Special; .22 LR, with countersunk chambers after 1932, .38 New Police, .38 S&W; 2" barrel, 6½" overall length; a few produced with Fitzgerald cutaway trigger guard; checkered hammer spur, trigger; blued or nickel finish. Low production run on .22 gives it collector value. Introduced in 1926; dropped, 1940. Used values: .22, blued, $725 to $750; nickel finish, $850 to $900; .38 blued, $400 to $425; nickel, $475 to $500.

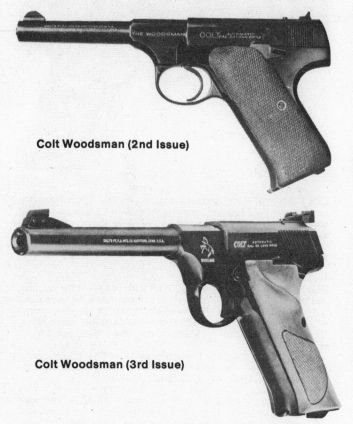

Colt Woodsman (2nd Issue)

Colt Woodsman (3rd Issue)

COLT Woodsman (First Issue): target automatic; .22 LR standard velocity; 6½" barrel; 10½" overall length; 10-rd. magazine; prior to 1927, designated as .22 Target Model. Designation, "The Woodsman," added after serial No. 34,000; adjustable sights, check-

ered walnut grips. Introduced in 1915; dropped, 1932. Collector value. Used value, $475 to $500.

Woodsman Second Issue has basically the same specs as first issue, except for substitution of heat-treated mainspring housing for use with high-velocity cartridges, heavier barrel. Introduced in 1932; dropped, 1948. Used value, $425 to $450.

Woodsman Third Issue has the same basic specs as earlier Woodsman issues, except for longer grip, larger thumb safety, slide stop, magazine disconnector, plastic or walnut grips, magazine catch on left side; click-adjustable rear sight, ramp front. Introduced in 1948; dropped, 1977. Used value, $375 to $400.

Colt Woodsman Sport Model

COLT Woodsman Sport Model (First Issue): has the same general specs as second issue Woodsman Target model, except for adjustable rear sight, adjustable or fixed front; 4½" barrel, 8½" overall length; fires standard- or high-velocity .22 LR ammo. Introduced in 1933; dropped, 1948. Used value, $500 to $525.

Woodsman Sport Model (Second Issue) has the same specs as the third-issue Woodsman Target model, except for 4½" barrel, overall length of 9"; plastic grips. Introduced in 1948; dropped, 1976. Used value, $275 to $300.

Woodsman Targetsman has generally the same specs as third-issue Woodsman Target model, except for no automatic slide stop, less expensive adjustable rear sight. Introduced 1969; dropped, 1976. Used value, $250 to $275.

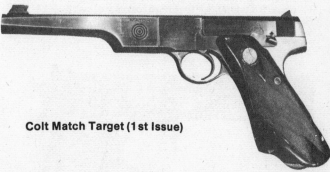

Colt Match Target (1st Issue)

COLT Match Target (First Issue): target automatic; .22 LR only; 6½" flat-sided barrel, 11" overall length; adjustable rear sight, blade front; checkered walnut one-piece extension grips; blued; same basic design as earlier Woodsman models. Introduced in 1938; dropped, 1942. Used value, $725 to $750.

Match Target (Second Issue) has the same general specs as third-issue Target Woodsman. Flat-sided 6" heavy barrel, 10½" overall length; .22 LR, standard- or high-velocity ammo; checkered walnut or plastic grips; click-adjustable rear sight, ramp front; blued. Introduced in 1948; dropped, 1976. Used value, $425 to $450.

Match Target 4½ has the same specs as second-issue Match Target, except for 4½" barrel; measures 9" overall. Introduced in 1950; dropped, 1976. Used value, $425 to $500.

Colt Official Police

COLT Official Police: double-action revolver; .22 LR, .32-20, .38 Special, .41 Long Colt; 2", 6" heavy barrels in .38 Special only; 4", 6", in .22 LR only; 4", 5", 6", in other calibers; checkered walnut grips, plastic grips on post-WWII models. Version made to military specs in WWII was called Commando model, had sand-blasted blue finish. Introduced in 1928 as a replacement for Army Special; dropped, 1969. Collector value. Used values, standard model, $215 to $235; military model, $225 to $250.

Colt Super 38

COLT Super 38: identical to Government Model or 1911A1 automatic, except for capacity of magazine, caliber; .38 Colt Super; 9-rd. magazine; fixed sights. Introduced in 1928; still in production as Government Model MKIV/Series 80. Used value, $350 to $375; for pre-WWII add 75%. From 1935 to 1941 a few "Super Match" Super .38s were made with adjustable target sights. Rare collector value. Used value, $1500 to $1750.

Colt Service Model Ace

COLT Ace: automatic; built on same frame as Government Model .45 automatic; .22 LR only, standard or high velocity; does not have floating chamber; 4¾" barrel, 8¼" overall length; adjustable rear sight, fixed front; target barrel, hand-honed action. Introduced in 1930; dropped, 1947. Collector value. Used value, $850 to $900.

Service Model Ace has specs identical to those of National Match Model 45 automatic, except for magazine capacity, caliber; .22 LR, standard or high velocity; 10-rd. magazine; specially designed chamber increases recoil four-fold to approximate that of .45 auto. Introduced in 1935; dropped, 1945; reintroduced, 1978; dropped, 1986. Collector interest affects value. Used values: old model, $850 to $900; new manufacture, $375 to $400.

Colt Shooting Master

COLT Shooting Master: double-action revolver; swing-out 6-rd. cylinder; deluxe target version of New Service; .38 Special, .357 magnum, .44 Special, .45 ACP/Auto Rim; .45 Colt; 6" barrel, 11¼" overall length; checkered walnut grips, rounded butt; rear sight adjustable for windage, front for elevation; blued. Introduced in 1932; dropped, 1941. Used value, $650 to $750; add $150 for .45 ACP; add $250 for .44 Special.

Colt National Match 45

COLT National Match: target automatic; .45 ACP; has same specs as Government Model .45 automatic, except for adjustable rear sight, ramp front; match-grade barrel, hand-honed action. Also available with fixed sights. Introduced in 1932, dropped 1940. Used values, fixed sights, rare, $1250 to $1300; target sights, $1250 to $1300.

COLT Challenger: automatic; .22 LR only; has same basic specs as third-issue Target Woodsman, with fewer features; slide does not stay open after last shot; fixed sights; 4½", 5" barrels; overall length, 9" with 4½" barrel; checkered plastic grips; blued finish. Challenger introduced in 1950; dropped, 1955. Used value, $225 to $250.

Huntsman has exactly the same specs as Challenger model, with name change for marketing purposes. Introduced in 1955; dropped, 1976. Used value, $225 to $250.

COLT Commander: lightweight automatic; .45 ACP; .38 Super auto; 9mm Luger; 4¼" barrel, 8" overall length; 7-rd. magazine for .45, 9 rds. for other calibers; weighs 26½ oz.; basic design of Government Model auto, but is of lightweight alloy, reducing weight; early versions had checkered plastic grips, present production have checkered walnut; fixed sights; rounded hammer spur; blued, nickel finish. Introduced in 1950; still in production. Used values: 70 Series, $400 to $425; 80 Series, $375 to $400.

Colt Huntsman

Cobra 1973 Model like original version, has frame, side plate of alloy, steel cylinder, barrel; integral protective shroud enclosing ejector rod; other specs are identical to 1972 Detective Special, with exception of lighter Cobra barrel, blued, nickel finish. Introduced in 1973; dropped, 1981. Used values, blued, $225 to $235; nickel finish, $235 to $250.

Colt Viper

COLT Viper: revolver; double-action; .38 Special; has same general specs as Colt Cobra, except for 4" barrel; 9" overall length. Introduced in 1977; dropped, 1978. Used value, $200 to $225.

Colt Commander

Colt Three-Fifty-Seven

COLT Three-Fifty-Seven: double-action revolver; 6-rd. swing-out cylinder; .357 magnum only; 4", 6" barrels; 9¼" overall length with 4" barrel; available as service revolver or in target version; latter has wide hammer spur, target grips; checkered walnut grips; Accro rear sight, ramp front; blued finish. Introduced in 1953; dropped, 1961. Used values: standard model, $275 to $295; target model, $325 to $350.

Colt Cobra

Colt Agent

COLT Cobra: double-action revolver; 6-rd. swing-out cylinder; .32 New Police, .38 New Police, .38 Special; based upon design of pre-1972 Detective Special, except that frame, side plate are of Colt-alloy, high-tensile aluminum alloy; 2", 3", 4", 5" barrels; Coltwood plastic grips on later guns, checkered wood on early issues; square butt was on early issue, replaced by round butt; optional hammer shroud; blue finish, matted on top, rear of frame. Old model shown. Introduced in 1951; dropped, 1972; 3", 4", 5" barrel styles were special order. Used value,. $225 to $250.

Colt Agent (1982)

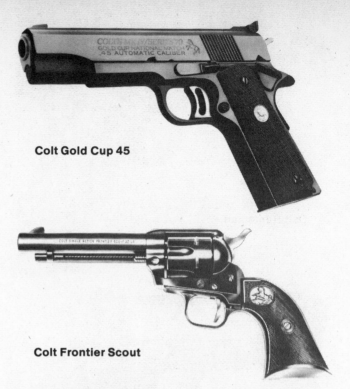

Colt Gold Cup 45

Colt Frontier Scout

COLT Agent: double-action revolver; 6-rd. swing-out cylinder; .38 Special only; 2" barrel, 6¾" overall length; minor variation of Cobra Model with shorter, stub grip for maximum concealment; Coltalloy frame, side plate; steel cylinder, barrel; no housing around ejector rod; square butt; blued finish. Old model shown. Introduced in 1955; dropped, 1972. Used value, $250 to $275.

    Agent 1973 Model closely resembles 1973 Cobra model, except for grip design, which extends just below bottom of frame; 2" barrel; overall length, 6⅝"; checkered walnut grips; .38 Special only; blued finish. Introduced in 1973; dropped, 1981. Used value, $190 to $210.

    Agent 1982 Model is lightweight version of Detective Special; .38 Special only; 6-rd. cylinder; 2" barrel; weighs 16¾ oz.; 6⅞" overall length; fixed sights; Parkerized-type finish. Reintroduced, 1982; no longer in production. Used value, $190 to $210.

Colt Python

COLT Python: double-action revolver; 6-rd. swing-out cylinder; .357 magnum only, but will handle .38 Special; made first appearance in 6" barrel, later with 2½", 4"; checkered walnut grips contoured for support for middle finger of shooting hand; vent-rib barrel; ramp front sight, rear adjustable for windage, elevation; full-length ejector rod shroud; wide-spur hammer, grooved trigger; blued, nickel finish; hand-finished action. Introduced in 1955; still in production. Used values: blued, $400 to $425; nickel finish, $425 to $450.

    Stainless Python has same specs as standard models, except is made of stainless steel; 4", 6" barrel lengths only. Used value, $475 to $500.

COLT Gold Cup 45: National Match grade automatic; .45 ACP only; same general specs as Government Model .45 auto; has match-grade barrel, bushing; long, wide trigger; adjustable trigger stop; flat mainspring housing; adjustable rear sight, target front; hand-fitted slide; wider ejection port; checkered walnut grips. Introduced in 1957; still in production. Used values: 70 Series, $500 to $550; 80 Series, $450 to $500.

    Gold Cup 38 Special has same general specs as Gold Cup 45 except it is chambered only for .38 Special mid-range ammo. Introduced in 1960; dropped, 1974. Collector value. Used value, $550 to $600.

COLT Frontier Scout: single-action revolver; scaled-down version of Model 1873 Army; .22 LR, long, short; interchangeable

cylinder for .22 WRFM; 4½" barrel, 9-15/16" overall length; originally introduced with alloy frame; steel frame, blue finish introduced in 1959; fixed sights; plastic or wooden grips. Introduced in 1958; dropped, 1971. Used values, alloy frame, $200 to $225; blue finish, plastic grips, $225 to $250; nickel finish, wood grips, $185 to $205; interchangeable magnum cylinder, add $25.

    Scout Buntline has same specs as Frontier Scout with steel frame, wood grips, except for 9½" barrel. Introduced in 1959; dropped, 1971. Used value, $275 to $300.

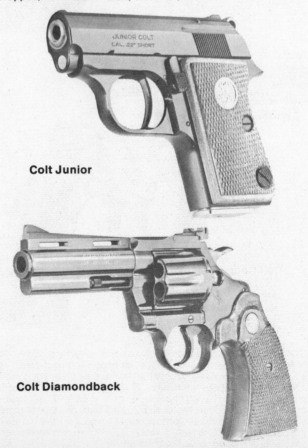

Colt Junior

Colt Diamondback

COLT Junior: pocket model automatic; .22 short, .25 ACP; 2¼" barrel; overall length, 4⅜"; 6-rd. magazine; exposed hammer with round spur; checkered walnut stocks; fixed sights; blued. Initially produced in Spain by Astra, with early versions having Spanish markings as well as Colt identity; parts were assembled in U.S., sans Spanish identification after GCA '68 import ban. Introduced in 1968; dropped, 1973. Used values: Spanish versions, collector value, $250 to $275; U.S.-made versions, $165 to $185.

COLT Diamondback: double-action revolver; swing-out 6-rd. cylinder; scaled down version of Python; .38 Special, .22 LR; 2½", 4", 6" barrel; available in nickel, .22 with 4" only; vent-rib barrel; target-type rear sight adjustable for windage, elevation; ramp front; full checkered walnut grips; integral rounded rib beneath barrel shrouds ejector rod; broad checkered hammer spur. Introduced in 1966; no longer in production. Used values: .38 nickel-plated with 4" barrel, $265 to $285; .22 LR, $265 to $285.

COLT Metropolitan MKIII: double-action revolver; swing-out 6-rd. cylinder; designed for urban law enforcement; 4" barrel; .38 Special only; fixed sights; choice of service, target grips of checkered walnut; blued finish, standard; nickel, optional. Introduced in 1969; dropped, 1972. Used values: blued, $175 to $195; nickel finish, $180 to $200.

Colt Official Police MKIII

COLT Official Police MKIII: double-action revolver; an old name, but a renewed design, incorporating coil mainsprings in place of leaf springs; .38 Special only; 4" barrel, 9⅜" overall length; square-butt, checkered walnut grips; fixed rear sight notch milled in top strap, fixed ramp front; grooved front surface on trigger, checkered hammer spur. Introduced in 1969; dropped, 1975. Used value, $185 to $195.

COLT Lawman MKIII: similar to Official Police MKIII, but beefed up to handle .357 magnum; will also chamber .38 Special; 2", 4" barrels; with 4" barrel, overall length, 9⅜"; choice of square, round-butt walnut grips; fixed sights; blued, nickel finish. Introduced in 1969; no longer in production. Used values: blued, $175 to $190; nickel, $180 to $200.
Lawman Mark V is modification of Mark III; redesigned lockwork reduces double-action trigger pull; faster lock time; redesigned grips; 2", 4" barrel lengths; fixed sights; solid rib. Introduced, 1984; dropped, 1987. Used value, $215 to $225.

Colt Trooper

COLT Trooper: double-action revolver; swing-out 6-rd. cylinder; has the same specs as Officer's Match model, except for 4" barrel; .38 Special, .357 magnum; ramp front sight; choice of standard hammer, service grips, wide hammer spur, target grips. Introduced in 1953; dropped, 1969. Used values: standard service model, $250 to $250; target model, $250 to $275.

Colt Trooper MKV

COLT Trooper MKIII: double-action revolver; .357 magnum only; chambers .38 Special as well; 4", 6" barrels; with 4" barrel, overall length, 9½"; rear sight adjustable for windage/elevation, ramp front; shrouded ejector rod; checkered walnut target grips; target hammer, wide target trigger; blued, nickel finish. Introduced in 1969; dropped, 1983. Used values: blued, $185 to $200; nickel, $190 to $210.
Trooper Mark V is modified version of Mark III; redesigned lockwork reduces double-action trigger pull; faster lock time; redesigned grips; adjustable rear sight, red insert front; 4", 6", 8" vent-rib barrel; blued or nickel finish. Introduced, 1984. Used value, $225 to $235.

Colt MKIV/Series '70 45 Govt Model

COLT MK IV/Series '70 45 Govt. Model: .45 ACP, 9mm Luger, .38 Super; is identical to .38 Super and previous .45 Government Model, except for improved collet-type barrel bushing and reverse taper barrel to improve accuracy. Introduced in 1970. Model most in demand for combat modification. Used values: 70 Series, $425 to $450; 80 Series, $400 to $425; 70 Series "Rarest of 70's", $650-700.
Combat Grade Government Model has same general specs as standard Government Model, except has higher undercut front sight, white outlined rear; flat mainspring housing; longer trigger; beveled magazine well; angled ejection port; Colt/Pachmayr wrap-around grips; internal firing pin safety. Introduced, 1983; no longer in production. Used value, $425 to $450.
MK IV/Series '80 has same general specs as Series '70; .45 version has blued, nickel or satin nickel finish; Pachmayr grips optional; 9mm, .38 Super are blued only; .45 only also available in stainless steel with high profile sights. Used value, $375 to $425, depending on caliber, finish.

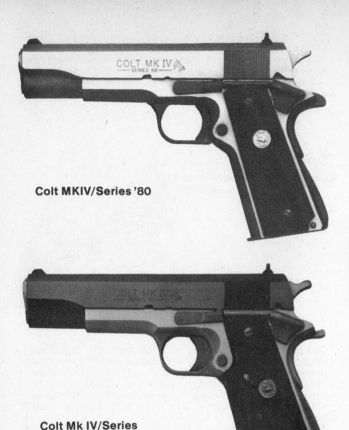

Colt MKIV/Series '80

Colt Mk IV/Series '80 Combat Elite

MK IV/Series '80 Combat Elite is similar to Government Model, but in .45 ACP only; has stainless steel frame, ordnance steel slide, internal parts; checkered rubber grips; beveled magazine well; high-profile sights with 3-dot system; extended grip safety. Introduced, 1986; still in production. Used value, $475 to $500.

Colt New Frontier 22

COLT New Frontier .22: single-action revolver; scaled-down version of New Frontier .45; 6-rd. capacity; furnished with dual cylinders for .22 LR, .22 WRFM ammo; 4⅜", 6", 7½" barrels; with 6" barrel, overall length, 11½"; target-type rear sight adjustable for windage, elevation, ramp front; checkered black plastic grips; flat top strap; color case-hardened frame, rest blued. Introduced in 1973; dropped, 1975; reintroduced, 1981; dropped, 1982. Used values: 7½" barrel, $225 to $250; others, $185 to $195.

COLT Peacemaker .22: single-action revolver; scaled-down version of century-old Model 1873; 6-rd. capacity; furnished with dual cylinders for .22 LR, .22 WRFM ammo; rear sight notch milled into rounded top strap, fixed blade front; color case-hardened frame, rest blued; black plastic grips; 4⅜", 6", 7½" barrels; overall length with 6" barrel, 11¼". Introduced in 1973; dropped, 1975. Used values: 7½" barrel, $215 to $225; others, $185 to $195.

Colt Peacemaker 22

Colt Combat Commander

COLT Combat Commander: automatic; .45 ACP, 7 rds; .38 Super Auto, 9mm Luger, 9 rds.; 4¼" barrel; overall length, 8"; fixed blade front sight; grooved trigger, hammer spur; arched housing, grip and thumb safeties. Introduced, 1979; called Commander until 1981; still in production. Blued finish, except for satin nickel (no longer offered) .45 version. Used values: 9mm, $375 to $400; .45, $400 to $425; .38 Super, $375 to $400; .45 satin finish, $410 to $435.

Lightweight Commander has same specs as Commander, except for wood panel grips, frame of aluminum alloy; .45 ACP only; blued finish. Introduced, 1949; still in production as Mk. IV Series 80 .45 ACP only. Used values: $375 to $400; Series 70, $400 to $425; add $50 for 9mm or .38 Super (discontinued).

Colt 380 Government

COLT 380 Govt. Model: automatic; .380 ACP; 7-rd. magazine; scaled-down version of 1911A1; 3" barrel; weighs 21¾ oz.; 6" overall length; checkered composition stocks; ramp front sight, fixed square-notch rear; thumb and internal firing pin safeties; blued, nickel or satin nickel finish. Introduced, 1983; still in production. Used value, $240 to $265, depending on finish.

Colt Commando Special

COLT Commando Special: revolver; has same specs as Detective Special, except has combat grade finish, rubber grips. Introduced, 1984; dropped, 1987. Used value, $190 to $200.

Colt Peacekeeper

COLT Peacekeeper: revolver; has same general specs as Trooper MK V; 4", 6" barrels; weighs 42 oz. with 6" barrel; red insert ramp front sight, white outline adjustable rear; rubber round-bottom combat grips; matte blue finish. Introduced, 1985; dropped, 1987. Used value, $200 to $225.

Colt King Cobra

COLT King Cobra: revolver; double-action; .357 magnum; 6-rd. cylinder; 2½", 4", 6" barrels; 9" overall length, with 4" barrel; weighs 42 oz.; adjustable white outline rear sight, red insert ramp front; full-length contoured ejector rod housing, barrel rib; matte finish; stainless steel construction. Introduced, 1986; still in production. Used value, $290 to $315.

Colt Delta Elite

COLT Delta Elite: automatic; 10mm auto; 5" barrel; 8½" overall length; same general design as Government Model; 3-dot high-profile combat sights; rubber combat stocks; internal firing pin safety; new recoil spring/buffer system; blued finish. Introduced, 1987; still in production. Used value, $450 to $475.

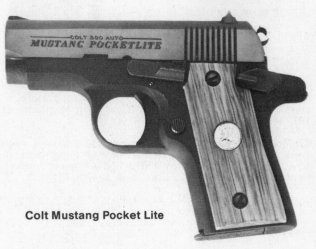

Colt Mustang 380

Colt Mustang Pocket Lite

COLT Mustang 380: automatic; .380; similar to standard .380 Government Model; 2¾" barrel; 8" overall length; weighs 18.5 oz.; steel frame; blued or nickel finish. Introduced, 1987; still in production. Used value, $240 to $275, depending on finish.

Mustang Pocket Lite model has same specs as Mustang 380, except has alloy frame; weighs 12.5 oz. Introduced, 1987; still in production. Used value, $250 to $265.

CZ

CZ Model 38

CZ Pocket Duo

CZ Pocket Duo: automatic; .25 auto; 6-rd. magazine; 2⅛" barrel; 4½" overall; manufactured in Czechoslovakia; plastic stocks; fixed sights; blued or nickel finish. Manufactured 1926 to 1960. Used value, $145 to $165.

CZ Model 1945

CZ Model 27

CZ New Model 006

CZ Model 27: automatic; .32 auto; 8-rd. magazine; 4" barrel, 6" overall; plastic stocks, fixed sights, blued finish. Manufactured 1927 to 1951. Used value, $175 to $185.

CZ Model 38: automatic, double-action; .380 auto; 9-rd. magazine; 3¾" barrel, 7" overall; plastic stocks, fixed sights, blued finish. Also listed as CZ Pistole 39(t) during German occupation. Manufactured 1939 to 1945. Used value, $250 to $275.

CZ Model 1945: automatic, double-action; .25 auto; 8-rd. magazine; 2" barrel, 5" overall; plastic stocks, fixed sights, blued finish. Manufactured 1945 to approximately 1960. Used value, $155 to $175.

CZ New Model .006: automatic, double-action; .32 auto; 8-rd. magazine; 3⅛" barrel, 6½" overall; plastic stocks, fixed sights, blued finish. Issued to Czech police as Model VZ50. Manufactured 1951 to approximately 1967. Used value, $250 to $275.

DAKOTA

DAKOTA Single-Action: revolver; .22 LR, .22 WRFM, .357 magnum, .30 Carbine, .44-40, .45 Colt; 6-rd. cylinder; 3½", 4⅝", 5½", 7½", 12", 16¼" barrel lengths; smooth European walnut stocks; blade front sight, fixed rear; Colt-type hammer, firing pin; color

Dakota Single-Action

case-hardened frame; brass grip frame, trigger guard; blued barrel, cylinder; also available in nickel finish. Made in Italy. Introduced, 1967; early sporadic production. Currently imported by EMF. Used value, $210 to $240, depending on caliber, barrel length.

Dakota Bisley Model

DAKOTA Bisley Model: revolver; single-action; .22 LR, .22 WRFM, .32-20, .32 H&R magnum, .357 magnum, .30 Carbine, .38-40, .44 Special, .44-40, .45 Colt, .45 ACP; 4⅝", 5½", 7½" barrel lengths; with 5½" barrel, overall length is 10½", weighs 37 oz.; fixed groove rear sight, blade front; uncheckered walnut stocks; color case-

hardened frame, blued barrel, cylinder; steel trigger guard, backstrap; Colt-type firing pin on hammer. Also available with nickel finish, factory engraving. Made in Italy. Introduced, 1985; still imported by EMF. Used values: blued, $300 to $325; nickel, $350 to $375; engraved, $475 to $500.

DAKOTA 1875 Outlaw Model: revolver; single-action; .357 magnum, .44-40, .45 Colt; 7½" barrel; 13½" overall length; weighs 46 oz.; fixed groove rear sight, blade front; unchecked walnut stocks; color case-hardened frame, blued cylinder, barrel; steel backstrap; brass trigger guard; also made with nickel finish, factory engraving. Authentic copy of 1875 Remington. Made in Italy. Introduced, 1986; still imported by EMF. Used values: blued, $275 to $300; nickel, $340 to $365; engraved, $450 to $475.

Dakota 1890 Police Model

DAKOTA 1890 Police Model: revolver; single-action; .357 magnum, .44-40, .45 Colt; has the same general specs as 1875 Outlaw model, except has 5½" barrel, overall length of 12" and weighs 40 oz.; has lanyard ring in the butt. Made in Italy. Introduced, 1986; still imported by EMF. Used values: blued, $300 to $325; nickel, $325 to $350; engraved, $475 to $500.

DETONICS

Detonics 45

DETONICS .45: automatic; .45 ACP; 6-rd. magazine; 9mm Parabellum, 8 rds.; 3¼" barrel; overall length, 6¾"; fixed sights, adjustable rear sight available; checkered walnut stocks; throated barrel, polished feed ramp, blued finish. Later in stainless steel. Introduced in 1977; still in production. Used values: blued, $360 to $385; stainless, $375 to $400.

DETONICS Scoremaster: target automatic; .45 ACP, .451 Detonics magnum; 7-rd. clip; 5" heavy match barrel, recessed muz-

zle; 6" barrel optional; weighs 41 oz.; 8¾" overall length; blade front sight, Bomar low-base rear; checkered Pachmayr stocks, matching mainspring housing; stainless steel; Detonics recoil system; extended grip safety; ambidextrous safety; extended magazine release. Marketed with 2 spare magazines, 3 interchangeable front sights, carrying case. Introduced, 1983; still in production. Used value, $750 to $775.

Detonics Super Compact

DETONICS Super Compact: automatic; double-action; 9mm Parabellum; 7-rd. clip; 3" barrel; weighs 22 oz.; 5.7" overall length; smooth composition stocks; fixed sights; stainless steel; ambidextrous firing pin safety; trigger guard hook. Introduced, 1983; no longer in production. Used value, $325 to $350.

Detonics Service Master

length; checkered walnut stocks; fixed or adjustable combat-type sights; throated barrel, polished feed ramp; self-adjusting cone barrel centering system; beveled magazine inlet; full-clip indicator; matte finish. Introduced, 1977; still in production. Used value, $450 to $475.

Combat Master Mark VI has same specs as Mark I, except has adjustable sights, is of polished stainless steel. Introduced, 1977; still in production. Used value: $480 to $500.

DETONICS Pocket Nine: automatic; double-action; 9mmP; 6-rd. clip; 3" barrel; 5.7" overall lenght; weighs 26 oz.; fixed sights; black micarta stocks; stainless steel construction; trigger guard hook hammer; captive recoil spring. Introduced, 1984; dropped, 1987. Used value, $300 to $325.

Pocket 9LS has same general specs as Pocket 9, except has 4" barrel, weighs 28 oz. Used value, $300 to $325.

Power 9 has the same specs as 9LS except has polished slide flats. Used value, $325 to $350.

DETONICS Servicemaster: automatic; .45 ACP; 7-rd. magazine; 4½" barrel; 7⅞" overall length; weighs 32 oz.; fixed combat sights; Pachmayr rubber stocks; stainless steel construction; extended grip safety; thumb and grip safeties; matte finish. Introduced, 1986; still in production. Used value, $500 to $525.

Service Master II has same specs as Servicemaster, except has polished slide flats. Used value, $550 to $575.

Detonics Combat Master Mark I

Detonics Pocket 380

DETONICS Combat Master Mark I: automatic; .45 ACP, 6-rd. clip; 9mmP, .38 Super, with 7-rd. clip; 3¼" barrel; 6¾" overall

DETONICS Pocket 380: automatic; double-action; .380 ACP; 6-rd. clip; 3" barrel; overall length, 5¾"; weighs 23 oz.; fixed sights; grooved black micarta stocks; stainless steel construction; trigger guard hook; snag-free hammer; captive recoil spring; ambidextrous firing pin safety. Introduced, 1986; dropped, 1987. Used value, $300 to $325.

ERMA

ERMA Automatic: .22 LR target pistol; 10-rd. magazine; interchangeable 8-3/16", 11¾" barrels; adjustable target sights; checkered plastic grips; blued finish. Used value, $125 to $135.

ERMA KGP 68: automatic; .32 auto (KGP32), 6-rd. magazine; .380 auto (KGP38), 5-rd. magazine; 3½" barrel; overall length, 6¾"; adjustable blade front sight, fixed rear, checkered walnut grips; side-lock manual safety. No longer imported by Excam. Used value, $125 to $145.

Erma KGP 68

Erma KGP 69

ERMA KGP69: automatic; .22 LR; 8-rd. magazine; 4" barrel; overall length, 7-5/16"; checkered plastic grips; adjustable blade front sight, fixed rear; slide stays open after last shot. Was imported from Germany by Excam as the KGP22. Used value, $125 to $135.

ERMA KGP38: automatic; .380 ACP; 5-rd. magazine; same basic design as KGP32. Imported by Excam. Introduced, 1978; no longer imported. Used value, $125 to $135.

ERMA-EXCAM RX 22: automatic; double-action; .22 LR; 8-rd. magazine; 3¼" barrel, 5.58" overall length; fixed sights; plastic wrap-around grips; polished blued finish, thumb safety; patented ignition safety system. Assembled in USA. Introduced, 1980; no longer in production. USed value, $110 to $120.

ERMA KGP22: automatic; .22 LR; 8-rd. magazine; 4" barrel; 7¾" overall length; fixed sights; checkered plastic stocks; blued finish; has toggle action similar to that of original Luger. Was imported from West Germany by Excam, now by Beeman. Introduced, 1978; still in production. Used value, $125 to $135.

ERMA KGP32: automatic; .32 ACP; 6-rd. magazine; 4" barrel; 7⅜" overall; rear sight adjustable for windage only; same basic design as KGP22; checkered plastic stocks, wood optional; blued finish; magazine and sear disconnect safety system. Was imported by Excam. Introduced, 1978; no current importer. Used value, $125 to $135.

F.I.E.

F.I.E. Hombre

F.I.E. Super Titan II

F.I.E. Hombre: revolver, single-action; .357 magnum, .44 magnum, .45 Colt; 5½", 7½" barrels; blade front sight, grooved backstrap rear; blued finish; color case-hardened frame; smooth walnut grips, medallion. Introduced, 1970; still imported. Used values: .44 magnum, $175 to $200; other calibers, $150 to $175.

F.I.E. E27 Titan: automatic; .25 ACP; 6-rd. magazine; 4", 6" barrel lengths; checkered walnut stocks, wide trigger; fixed sights; blued or chromed finish. Manufactured by Firearms Import & Export. Introduced, 1977; dropped, 1982. Used values: blued, $25 to $27.50; chromed, $30 to $32.50.

F.I.E. G27 Guardian: automatic; .25 ACP; 6-rd. magazine; 2-7/16" barrel; 4¾" overall length; contoured plastic stocks; fixed sights; blued, gold or chromed finish. Introduced, 1977; dropped, 1982. Used values: blued, $25 to $27.50; chromed, $30 to $32.50; gold, $35 to $37.50.

F.I.E. TITAN II: automatic; .32 ACP, .380 ACP, .22 LR; 6-rd. magazine in .32, .380; 10 rds. in .22 LR; 3⅞" barrel; 6¾" overall length; adjustable sights; checkered nylon thumbrest grips; checkered walnut optional; magazine disconnector; firing pin block; standard slide safety; blued or chromed finish. Introduced, 1978; still in production; .32 made in Italy, .380 in USA. Used values: .32 blued, $95 to $100; chromed, $105 to $110; .380 blued, $125 to $130; chromed, $135 to $140; .22 LR, blued only, $95 to $100.

Super Titan II has same specs as Titan II, except .32 ACP, .380 ACP only; blued finish only; 12-rd. magazine in .32 ACP; 11 rds. in .380. Imported from Italy. Introduced, 1981; still in production. Used values: .32 ACP, $135 to $145; .380 ACP, $155 to $165.

F.I.E. Titan II

F.I.E. A27B

F.I.E. A27 B: automatic; .25 ACP; 6-rd. magazine; 2½" barrel; 4⅜" overall; checkered walnut stocks; fixed sights; all-steel construction; thumb, magazine safeties; exposed hammer; blued finish. Introduced in 1978; still in production. Used value, $85 to $100.

F.I.E. Model F38

F.I.E. Model F38: marketed as Titan Tiger; revolver, double-action; .38 Special; 2", 4" barrel lengths; Bulldog-style checkered plastic grips; walnut optional at added cost; fixed sights; swing-out cylinder; one-stroke ejection. Manufactured in USA by F.I.E. Introduced, 1978; still in production as N38. Used values: blued finish, $65 to $85; chrome finish, $85 to $95.

F.I.E. E15 Buffalo Scout

F.I.E. E15 Buffalo Scout: revolver, single-action; .22 LR/.22 WRFM combo; 4¾" barrel; overall length, 10"; adjustable sights; sliding spring ejector; black checkered plastic or uncheckered red walnut grips; blued, chromed or blue/brass finish. Introduced, 1978; still imported. Used value, $45 to $60, depending upon finish.

F.I.E. Legend: revolver; single-action; .22 LR/.22 WRFM combo; 6 rds.; 4¾", 5½" barrel lengths; fixed sights; black checkered plastic grips, walnut available at added cost; brass backstrap, trigger guard; case-hardened steel frame. Introduced, 1978 by F.I.E.; dropped, 1983. Used values: rimfire combo, $70 to $75; .22 LR only, $65 to $70.

F.I.E. Model D-38

F.I.E. Model D-38: over/under derringer; copy of original Remington derringer, .38 Special, .38 S&W; 2" barrel; checkered plastic grips, fixed sights; chrome finish; spur trigger. Introduced, 1979; still in production. Used value, $60 to $65.

F.I.E. TZ-75

F.I.E. TZ-75: automatic; double-action; 9mm Parabellum; 15-rd. magazine; 4.72" barrel; weighs 33⅓ oz.; 8.25" overall length; smooth European walnut stocks; undercut blade front sight; windage-adjustable open rear; squared-off trigger guard; rotating slide-mounted safety. Imported from Italy. Introduced, 1983; still in production. Used value, $275 to $300.

F.I.E. Texas Ranger

F.I.E. Texas Ranger: revolver; single-action; .22 LR, .22 WRFM; 4¾", 6½", 9" barrel lengths; American hardwood stocks; blade front sight, notch rear; blue/black finish; available with extra cylinder. Introduced, 1983; still in production. Used value, $45 to $60, depending upon barrel length, combo.

F.I.E. Little Ranger

F.I.E. Little Ranger: revolver; single-action; has the same general specs as the Texas Ranger model, except has 3½" barrel, bird's head grips; .22 LR or .22 WRFM convertible. Introduced, 1986; still in production. Used values: standard model, $75 to $80; convertible, $90 to $95.

F.I.E. Yellow Rose: revolver; single-action; same as the Buffalo Scout model, but is plated overall in 24-karat gold. Introduced, 1987; still in production. Used value, $200 to $225.

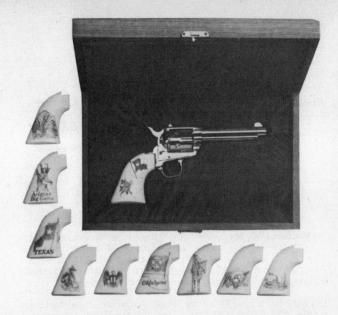

**F.I.E. Yellow Rose
Limited Edition**

Yellow Rose Limited Edition is the same as the standard edition, except has polymer grips scrimshawed with map of Texas, Texas state flag, yellow rose with green leaves; other scrimshawed depictions available. Marketed in French fitted American walnut presentation case. Introduced, 1987 in a limited edition. Used value, $300 to $325.

FN BROWNING

FN Browning Model 1900

**FN Browning Model 1910
Pocket Auto**

FN Browning Model 1910 Pocket Auto: automatic; .32 Auto, .380 Auto; 7-rd. magazine in .32, 6 rds., .380; 3½" barrel; 6" overall length; weighs 20½ oz.; hard rubber stocks; fixed sights; blued finished. Made in Belgium. Introduced, 1910; still produced, but not imported. Used value, $475 to $500.

FN BROWNING Model 1900: automatic; .32 auto; 7-rd. magazine; 4" barrel; 6¾" overall length; checkered hard rubber stocks; fixed sights; blued finish. Manufactured in Belgium, 1899 to 1910. Used value, $250 to $275.

FN Browning Model 1903

FN Browning Model 1922

FN BROWNING Model 1903: automatic; 9mm Browning; 7-rd. magazine; 5" barrel; 8" overall; hard rubber checkered stocks; fixed sights; blued finish. Designed primarily for military use; design, function similar to Browning FN 380. Manufactured 1903 to 1939. Used value, $300 to $350.

FN BROWNING Model 1922: automatic; .32 auto, with 9-rd. magazine; .380 auto, 8 rds.; 4½" barrel; 7" overall; checkered hard rubber stocks; fixed sights; blued finish. Introduced in 1922; still in production, but not imported. Used value, $225 to $250.

HAMMERLI

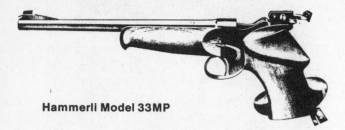

Hammerli Model 33MP

HAMMERLI Model 33MP: single-shot competition free pistol; .22 LR; Martini-type action, set trigger; 11½" octagonal barrel, 16½" overall length; micrometer rear sight, interchangeable front; European walnut stocks, forearm, blued finish. Manufactured in Switzerland, 1933 to 1949. Used value, $750 to $800.

HAMMERLI Model 100 Free Pistol: single-shot, slow-fire target model; .22 LR only; 11½" barrel; adjustable set trigger; micrometer rear sight, interchangeable post or bead front; European walnut grips, forearm; blued. Introduced in 1947; redesigned as Model 101 in 1960; dropped, 1962. Used value, $750 to $800.

Hammerli Model 200 Olympia

Hammerli Model 205

HAMMERLI WALTHER Model 200 Olympia: automatic; also advertised as Quickfire model; .22 LR, short; 7½" barrel; 8-rd. magazine; muzzle brake; adjustable barrel weights; walnut thumbrest grip; micrometer rear sight; ramp front; blued. Based on 1936 Olympia with some parts interchangeable. Introduced in 1950. In 1957 muzzle brake was redesigned. Dropped, 1963. Used value, $575 to $600.

Model 201 has the same specs as Model 200, except for standard adjustable sights and adjustable custom grip. Introduced in 1950; dropped, 1957. Used value, $600 to $650.

Model 202 has the same specs as Model 201, except for 9½" barrel. Introduced in 1957; dropped, 1959. Used value, $600 to $650.

Model 203 called the American Model, has the same general specs as Model 201, except for micrometer rear sight, slide stop. Introduced in 1957; dropped, 1959. Used value, $675 to $725.

Model 204 is the same as the Model 203, except is equipped with the standard thumbrest grips. Introduced in 1947; dropped, 1963. Used value, $675 to $700.

Model 205 has the same specs as Model 204, except for hand-checkered French walnut grip, detachable muzzle brake. Introduced in 1960; dropped, 1964. Used value, $725 to $750.

HAMMERLI Model 110 Free Pistol: single-shot, slow-fire target model. Has exactly the same specs as Model 100, except for highly polished, blued barrel. Introduced in 1957; redesignated as Model 102 in 1960; dropped, 1962. Used value, $550 to $575.

Hammerli Model 103 Free Pistol

HAMMERLI Model 103 Free Pistol: single-shot, slow-fire target model. Has the same specs as Model 103, except for deluxe carving of wood. Introduced in 1960; dropped, 1963. Used values: $600 to $650; with inlaid ivory carvings, $850 to $900.

Hammerli International Model 206

Hammerli Model 207

HAMMERLI International Model 206: automatic; rapid-fire target model; .22 LR and short; 7-1/16" barrel; 8-rd. magazine; muzzle brake; slide stop; checkered walnut thumbrest grips; adjustable trigger, blued. Cartridges not interchangeable. Introduced in 1964; dropped, 1967. Used value, $575 to $600.

International Model 207 has exactly the same specs as Model 206, except for uncheckered walnut grips, with adjustable grip plates. Introduced in 1964; dropped, 1969. Used value, $600 to $625.

Hammerli Model 208 has the same specs as Model 207, except that barrel is shortened to 6", no muzzle brake, adjustable trigger pull; .22 LR only. Introduced in 1958; still in production. Used value, $875 to $900.

Hammerli Model 104

Hammerli Model 120

Hammerli Model 106

HAMMERLI Match Pistol Model 104: single-shot free pistol; .22 LR only; 11½" barrel; micrometer rear sight, post front; uncheckered selected walnut grips with trigger-finger ramp, adjustable hand plate, custom finish; blued. Introduced in 1963; dropped, 1965. Used value, $625 to $675.

Match Pistol Model 105 has exactly the same specs as Model 104, except for octagonal barrel, highly polished metal, French walnut grip plates. Introduced in 1963; dropped, 1965. Used value, $675 to $700.

Model 106 has the same general specs as Model 104, but with matte blue finish on barrel to reduce glare; other minor changes. Replaced Model 104. Introduced in 1966; dropped, 1972. Used value, $700 to $725.

Model 107 has the same specs as Model 105, which it replaced. Has matte blue finish on barrel to reduce glare, other minor improvements. Introduced in 1966; dropped, 1972. Used value, $700 to $725.

HAMMERLI International Model 210: automatic; .22 short only; has the same general design as Model 207, but with lightweight bolt to reduce the recoil movement; six gas-escape ports in rear of barrel; barrel vents, adjustable muzzle brake to reduce muzzle jump, adjustable grip plates. Introduced in 1967; dropped, 1970. Used value, $675 to $700.

Model 209 has exactly the same specs as Model 210, except for nonadjustable grips. Introduced in 1967; dropped, 1970. Used value, $650 to $675.

Hammerli Model 230-1

HAMMERLI Model 230-1: automatic; .22 short; 5-rd. magazine; 6⅓" barrel; 11-3/5" overall length; micrometer rear sight, post front; uncheckered European walnut thumbrest grips; blued finish. Designed for rapid-fire International competition. Introduced in 1970; dropped. 1983. Used value, $650 to $700.

Model 230-2 has same specs as Model 230-1, except for partially checkered stocks, adjustable heel plate. Introduced in 1970; still in production. Used value, $700 to $725.

HAMMERLI Model 120: single-shot free pistol; .22 LR only; 10" barrel; 14¾" overall length; internally adjustable trigger for two-stage, single-stage pull; micrometer rear sight, post front; hand-

checkered walnut target grips; blued. Introduced in 1972; dropped, 1985. Redesignated as Model 120-1 in 1972. Used value, $350 to $400.

Model 120-2 has the same general specs as Model 120-1, except for special contoured walnut hand rest. Both sights can be moved forward or rearward; blued. Introduced in 1973; dropped, 1985. Used value, $425 to $450.

Model 120 Heavy Barrel Style was designed for sale in Great Britain to conform with existing laws governing sporting handgun specs. It has the same specs as Model 120-1, except for 5¾" barrel. Introduced in 1973; dropped, 1985. Used values: with standard grips, $425 to $450; with adjustable grips, $475 to $500.

Hammerli International
Model 211

HAMMERLI International Model 211: automatic; .22 LR only; 5-9/10" barrel; 10" overall length; micrometer bridged rear sight, post ramp front; externally adjustable trigger with backlash stop; hand-checkered European walnut thumbrest grips; blued. Introduced in 1973; still in production. Used value, $875 to $900.

Hammerli Model 150

HAMMERLI Model 150: single-shot free pistol; .22 LR only; 11⅜" barrel; 15⅜" overall length; movable front sight on collar, micrometer rear; Martini-type action; straight-line firing pin, no hammer; adjustable set trigger; uncheckered adjustable palm-shelf grip. Introduced in 1973; still in production. Used value, $1250 to $1350.

HAMMERLI Virginian: revolver, single-action; .357 magnum, .45 Colt; 6-rd. cylinder; 4⅝", 5½", 7½" barrels; same general design as Colt SAA, except for base pin safety feature. Has grooved rear

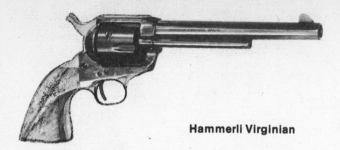

Hammerli Virginian

Hammerli 212 Hunter's Model

sight, blade front; barrel and cylinder are blued, frame case-hardened, with chromed grip frame, trigger guard, one-piece European walnut grip. Manufactured in Europe, 1973 to 1976, for exclusive Interarms importation. Used value, $250 to $300.

HAMMERLI 212 Hunter's Model: automatic; .22 LR; 4.9" barrel; overall length 8.5"; weighs 31 oz.; based on Model 208; fully adjustable target trigger system; checkered walnut stocks; white dot front sight, adjustable for elevation; rear adjustable for windage only. Made in Switzerland. Introduced, 1984; still imported by Osborne's Supplies. Used value, $725 to $750.

HAMMERLI Model 232: automatic; .22 short; 6-rd. magazine; 5" barrel with 6 exhaust ports; 10.4" overall length; weighs 44 oz.; stippled walnut wrap-around stocks; interchangeable front, rear blades, fully adjustable micrometer rear sight; recoil-operated; adjustable trigger. Made in Switzerland. Introduced, 1984; imported by Osborne's, Beeman. Used value, $750 to $800.

Hammerli Model 232

HARRINGTON & RICHARDSON

H&R American

H&R Young America

H&R Vest Pocket Model

HARRINGTON & RICHARDSON American: double-action solid-frame revolver; .32 S&W Long, .38 S&W; 2½", 4½", 6" barrels; 6-rd. cylinder in .32, 5-rd. in .38; fixed sights, hard rubber grips; blued, nickel finish. Introduced in 1883; dropped during WWII. Used value, $50 to $75.

HARRINGTON & RICHARDSON Young America: double-action solid-frame revolver; .22 LR, .32 S&W Short; 2", 4½", 6" barrels; 7-rd. cylinder in .22, 5-rd. in .32; fixed sights, hard rubber grips; blued, nickel finish. Introduced in 1885; dropped during WWII. Used value, $50 to $75.

HARRINGTON & RICHARDSON Vest Pocket Model: double-action solid-frame revolver; .22 long, .32 S&W Short; 1⅛" barrel; spurless hammer; 7-rd. cylinder in .22, 5-rd. in .32; no sights except for milled slot in top frame; hard rubber grips; blued, nickel finish. Introduced in 1891; dropped during WWII. Used value, $85 to $100.

HARRINGTON & RICHARDSON Automatic Ejecting Model: double-action hinged-frame revolver; .32 S&W Long, .32 S&W; 3¼", 4", 5", 6" barrels; 6-rd. cylinder in .32, 5-rd. in .38; fixed sights; hard rubber grips; blued, nickel finish. Introduced in 1891; dropped, 1941. Used value, $75 to $85.

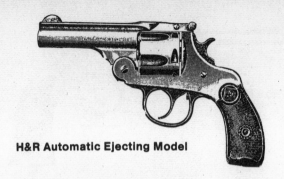

H&R Automatic Ejecting Model

H&R Model 4

H&R Premier Model

HARRINGTON & RICHARDSON Premier Model: double-action hinged-frame revolver; .22 LR, .32 S&W Short; 2", 3", 4", 5", 6" barrels; 7-rd. cylinder in .22, 5-rd. in .32; fixed sights; hard rubber grips; blued, nickel finish. Introduced in 1895; dropped, 1941. Used value, $75 to $85.

H&R Model 5

H&R Model 40 Hammerless

H&R Model 6

HARRINGTON & RICHARDSON Model 40 Hammerless: double-action small hinged-frame revolver; .22 LR, .32 S&W Short; 2", 3", 4", 5", 6" barrels; 7-rd. cylinder in .22, 5-rd. in .32; fixed sights; hard rubber stocks; blued, nickel finish. Also listed during late production as Model 45. Introduced in 1899; dropped, 1941. Used value, $80 to $90.

HARRINGTON & RICHARDSON Model 50 Hammerless: double-action large hinged-frame revolver; .32 S&W Long, .38 S&W; 3¼", 4", 5", 6" barrels; 6-rd. cylinder in .38; fixed sights; hard rubber grips; blued, nickel finish. Also listed in later production as Model 55. Introduced in 1899; dropped, 1941. Used value, $85 to $90.

HARRINGTON & RICHARDSON Model 4: double-action solid-frame revolver; .32 S&W Long, .38 S&W; 2½", 4½", 6" barrels; 6-rd. cylinder for .32, 5-rd. for .38; fixed sights, hard rubber grips; blued, nickel finish. Introduced in 1905; dropped, 1941. Used value, $55 to $65.

HARRINGTON & RICHARDSON Model 5: double-action solid-frame revolver; .32 S&W Short only; 2½", 4½", 6" barrels; 5-rd. cylinder; fixed sights; hard rubber grips; blued, nickel finish. Introduced in 1905; dropped, 1939. Used value, $55 to $65.

HARRINGTON & RICHARDSON Model 6: double-action solid-frame revolver; .22 LR only; 2½", 4½", 6" barrels; 7-rd. cylinder; fixed sights; hard rubber grips; blued, nickel finish. Introduced in 1906; dropped, 1941. Used value, $55 to $65.

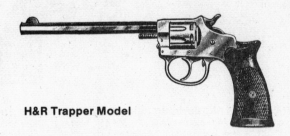

H&R Trapper Model

HARRINGTON & RICHARDSON Trapper Model: double-action solid-frame revolver; .22 LR only; 6" octagonal barrel; 7-rd. cylinder; fixed sights; checkered walnut stocks; blued. Introduced in 1924; dropped during WWII. Used value, $95 to $115.

H&R 22 Special

H&R Model 922

HARRINGTON & RICHARDSON .22 Special: double-action heavy hinged-frame revolver, .22 LR; 6" barrel; 9-rd. cylinder; fixed rear sight, gold-plated front; checkered walnut grips; blued. Originally introduced as Model 944; later version with recessed cylinder for high-speed ammo was listed as Model 945. Introduced in 1925; dropped, 1941. Used value, $90 to $100.

Introduced in 1919. Early production had 10" octagonal barrel, later dropped. Dropped, 1981. Used value, $75 to $85.

   Model 922 Bantamweight has the same specs as standard model, except for 2½" barrel; rounded butt. Introduced in 1951; no longer produced. Used value, $75 to $85.

H&R Model 766

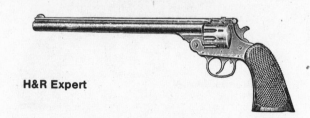

H&R Expert

HARRINGTON & RICHARDSON Model 766: double-action target revolver; hinged frame; .22 LR; 6" barrel; 7-rd. cylinder; fixed sights; checkered walnut grips; blued. Introduced in 1926; dropped, 1936. Used value, $100 to $115.

HARRINGTON & RICHARDSON Expert: has the same general specs as the .22 Special Model 945, except for being produced with 10" barrel. Listed as Model 955. Introduced in 1929; dropped, 1941. Used value, $125 to $135.

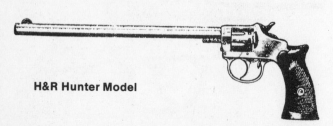

H&R Hunter Model

H&R Self-Loading 25

HARRINGTON & RICHARDSON Hunter Model: double-action solid-frame revolver; .22 LR only; 10" octagon barrel; 9-rd. cylinder; fixed sights; checkered walnut grips; blued. Introduced in 1926; dropped, 1941. Used value, $115 to $125.

HARRINGTON & RICHARDSON Self-Loading 25: automatic; .25 auto; 6-rd. magazine; 2" barrel, 4½" overall; checkered hard rubber stocks, fixed sights, blued finish. Variation of Webley & Scott design. Manufactured approximately 1929 to 1941. Used value, $250 to $300.

H&R USRA Model

HARRINGTON & RICHARDSON USRA Model: single-shot hinged-frame target pistol; .22 LR only; 7", 8", 10" barrels; adjustable target sights; checkered walnut grips; blued. Introduced in 1928; dropped, 1943. Used value $375 to $425.

HARRINGTON & RICHARDSON Model 922: double-action solid-frame revolver; .22 LR only; 4", 6", 10" barrels; 9-rd. cylinder; fixed sights; checkered walnut or Tenite grips; blued or chrome finish.

H&R Self-Loading 32

HARRINGTON & RICHARDSON Self-Loading 32: automatic; .32 auto; 8-rd. magazine; 3½" barrel, 6½" overall; checkered hard rubber stocks, fixed sights, blued finish. Variation of Webley & Scott design. Manufactured approximately 1929 to 1941. Used value, $275 to $300.

H&R No. 199

HARRINGTON & RICHARDSON No. 199: advertised as Sportsman Model; single-action hinged-frame revolver; .22 LR only; 6" barrel; 11" overall length; 9-rd. cylinder; adjustable target sights; checkered walnut grips; blued. Introduced in 1933; dropped, 1951. Used value, $115 to $125.

H&R New Defender

HARRINGTON & RICHARDSON New Defender: also listed as Model 299; double-action hinged-frame revolver; .22 LR only; 2" barrel; 6¼" overall length; has the same basic specs, except for barrel length, as Model 999; adjustable sights; checkered walnut grips, round butt; blued. Introduced in 1936; dropped, 1941. Used value, $125 to $140.

H&R Bobby Model

HARRINGTON & RICHARDSON Bobby Model: also listed as Model 15; double-action hinged-frame revolver; .32 S&W Long, .38 S&W; 4" barrel; 9" overall length; 6-rd. cylinder in .32, 5-rd. in .38; fixed sights; checkered walnut grips; blued. Designed for use by London police during WWII. Introduced in 1941; dropped, 1943. Collector value. Used value, $145 to $165.

HARRINGTON & RICHARDSON Guardsman: double-action solid-frame revolver; .32 S&W Long only; 2½", 4" barrels; 6-rd. cylinder; fixed sights; checkered Tenite grips; blued, chrome finish. Introduced in 1946; dropped, 1957. Used values: blued, $75 to $95; chrome finish, $80 to $100.

H&R Model 929

HARRINGTON & RICHARDSON Model 929: advertised as Sidekick Model; double-action revolver; solid-frame; swing-out cylinder; .22 LR, short; 2½", 4", 6" barrels; 9-rd. cylinder; fixed sights; checkered plastic grips; blued. Introduced in 1956; dropped, 1985. Used value, $65 to $70.

H&R Model 622

HARRINGTON & RICHARDSON Model 622: double-action revolver; solid frame; .22 LR, long, short; 2½", 4", 6" barrels; 6-rd. cylinder; fixed sights; checkered plastic grips; blued. Introduced in 1957; dropped, 1963. Used value, $55 to $70.

Model 623 has exactly the same specs as Model 622, except for chrome finish. Introduced in 1957; dropped, 1963. Used value, $75 to $85.

H&R Model 732

HARRINGTON & RICHARDSON Model 732: double-action revolver; solid-frame; 6-rd. swing-out cylinder; .32 S&W, .32 S&W Long; 2½", 4" barrels; rear sight adjustable for windage on 4" model, fixed on shorter barrel; ramp front; plastic checkered grips; blued. Introduced in 1958; dropped, 1985. Used value, $75 to $80.

Model 733 has the same specs as Model 732, except for nickel finish. Used value, $80 to $85.

HARRINGTON & RICHARDSON Model 939: advertised as Ultra Sidekick Model; double-action revolver; solid-frame; swing-out 9-rd. cylinder; 6" barrel, with vent rib; adjustable rear sight, ramp front; checkered walnut grips; blued. Introduced in 1958; dropped, 1981. Used value, $95 to $100.

H&R Model 939

HARRINGTON & RICHARDSON Model 949: advertised as Forty-Niner Model; double-action revolver; solid-frame; side-loading, ejection; 9-rd. cylinder; .22 LR, long, short; 5½" barrel; adjustable rear sight, blade front; one-piece plain walnut grip; blued, nickel finish. Introduced in 1960; dropped, 1985. Used value, $75 to $85.

Model 950 has same specs as Model 949, except has nickel finish. Used value, $90 to $95.

H&R Model 900

HARRINGTON & RICHARDSON Model 900: double-action revolver; solid-frame; swing-out, 9-rd. cylinder; .22 LR, long, short; 2½", 4", 6" barrels; fixed sights; high-impact plastic grips; blued. Introduced in 1962; dropped, 1973. Used value, $65 to $75.

Model 901 has the same specs as Model 900, except for chrome finish, white plastic grips. Introduced in 1962; dropped, 1963. Used value, $85 to $95.

H&R Model 925

HARRINGTON & RICHARDSON Model 925: advertised as the Defender Model; originally introduced as Model 25; double-action revolver; hinged-frame; .38 S&W only; 5-rd. cylinder; 2½" barrel; adjustable rear sight, fixed front; one-piece smooth plastic grip; blued. Introduced in 1964; dropped, 1981. Used value, $100 to $125.

HARRINGTON & RICHARDSON Model 976: revolver, double-action; hinged frame; .22 LR, with 9-rd. cylinder; .38 S&W, 5 rds.; 4" barrel; fixed front sight, adjustable rear; checkered walnut stocks, blued finish. Introduced in 1968; dropped, 1981. Used value, $75 to $85.

H&R Model 926

HARRINGTON & RICHARDSON Model 926: revolver, double-action; hinged frame; .22 LR, with 9-rd. cylinder; .38 S&W, 5 rds.; 4" barrel; fixed front sight, adjustable rear; checkered walnut stocks, blued finish. Introduced 1968; dropped 1980. Used value, $100 to $125.

HARRINGTON & RICHARDSON Model 666: revolver, double-action; solid frame; combo with two 6-rd. cylinders; .22 LR, .22 WRFM; 6" barrel; fixed sights; plastic stocks; blued finish. Introduced 1976; dropped 1980. Used value, $65 to $75.

H&R Model 649

HARRINGTON & RICHARDSON Model 649: revolver, double-action, solid frame; combo with two 6-rd. cylinders: .22 LR, .22 WRFM; 5½" barrel; blade front sight, adjustable rear; one-piece walnut grip, blued finish. Introduced in 1976; dropped 1980. Used value, $85 to $95.

H&R Model 650

HARRINGTON & RICHARDSON Model 650: revolver, double-action; solid frame. Has same specs as Model 649, except is nickel finished. Introduced 1976; dropped 1980. Used value, $85 to $95.

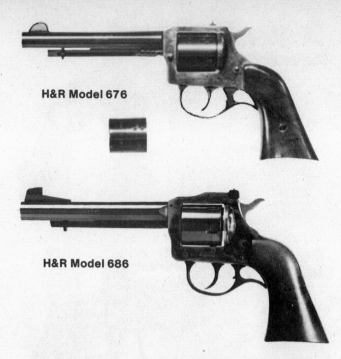

H&R Model 676

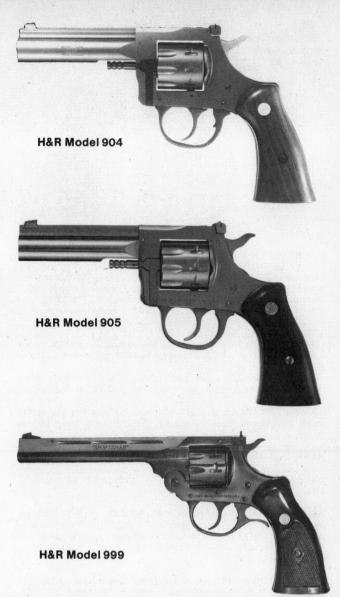

H&R Model 904

H&R Model 686

H&R Model 905

HARRINGTON & RICHARDSON Model 676: revolver, double-action; solid frame; combo with two 6-rd. cylinders: .22 LR, .22 WRFM; 4½", 5½", 7½", 12" barrel lengths; blade front sight, adjustable rear; one-piece walnut grip, color case-hardened frame, blued finish. Introduced 1976; dropped, 1985. Used value, $85 to $95.

Model 686 has same general specs as Model 676, except for ramp and blade front sight, fully adjustable rear; 4½", 5½", 7½", 10" barrel lengths. Introduced, 1981; dropped, 1985. Used value, $85 to $100, depending on barrel length.

H&R Model 999

H&R Model 940

HARRINGTON & RICHARDSON Model 999: revolver; double-action; marketed as Sportsman Model; .22 short, long, LR; 9-rd. cylinder; 4", 6" top-break barrel; weighs 34 oz.; checkered hardwood grips; front sight adjustable for elevation, rear for windage; automatic ejection; trigger guard extension; blued finish; optional engraving. Introduced, 1936; dropped, 1985. Used values: standard model, $125 to $150; engraved model, $250 to $300.

HARRINGTON & RICHARDSON Model 940: advertised as Ultra Sidekick; revolver, double-action; .22 short, long, LR; 9 rds.; 6" barrel; vent rib; ramp front sight; adjustable rear; checkered hardwood grips; thumbrest; swing-out cylinder, blued. Introduced, 1978; dropped, 1982. Used value, $80 to $85.

HARRINGTON & RICHARDSON Model 602: revolver, double-action; .22 WRFM; 6-rd. cylinder; 6" flat-sided barrel; blade front sight, fully adjustable rear; smooth walnut grips; swing-out cylinder; coil spring construction; blued finish. Introduced, 1981; dropped, 1983. Used value, $85 to $90.

Model 604 has same specs as Model 603, except for target-style bull barrel with raised solid rib. Introduced, 1981; dropped, 1985. Used value, $95 to $100.

HARRINGTON & RICHARDSON Model 903: has same specs as Model 603, except for .22 LR chambering; 9-rd. cylinder. Introduced, 1981; dropped, 1985. Used value, $80 to $85.

Model 904 has same specs as Model 604, except for .22 LR chambering; 9-rd. cylinder. Introduced, 1981; dropped, 1985. Used value, $90 to $95.

Model 905 has same specs as Model 904, except has 4" barrel, H&R Hard-Guard finish. Used value, $115 to $120.

H&R Model 826

H&R Model 830

H&R Model 504

H&R Model 532

H&R Model 586

HARRINGTON & RICHARDSON Model 829: revolver; double-action; .22 LR; 9-rd. cylinder; 3" bull barrel; weighs 27 oz.; uncheckered American walnut stocks; ramp/blade front sight, adjustable rear; blued finish; recessed muzzle; swing-out cylinder. Introduced, 1982; dropped, 1984. Used value, $95 to $105.

Model 826 has same specs as Model 829, except is chambered for .22 LR, .22 magnum; 6-rd. cylinder. Introduced, 1982; dropped, 1984. Used value, $100 to $110.

Model 830 has same specs as Model 826, except for nickel finish. Introduced, 1982; dropped, 1984. Used value, $100 to $110.

Model 832 has same specs as Model 826, except is chambered for .32 S&W Long. Introduced, 1982; dropped, 1984. Used value, $100 to $110.

Model 833 has same specs as Model 832, except has nickel finish. Introduced, 1982; dropped, 1984. Used value, $100 to $110.

HARRINGTON & RICHARDSON Model 504: revolver; .32 H&R magnum; 5-rd. cylinder; 3", 4", 6" barrel lengths; blued finish; other specs those of Model 904 swing-out. Introduced, 1984; dropped, 1985. Used value, $150 to $155.

HARRINGTON & RICHARDSON Model 532: revolver; .32 H&R magnum; has same general specs as Model 622; 5-rd. cylinder; solid frame; 2½", 4" barrel lengths; round butt; wood grips; blued finish. Introduced, 1984; dropped, 1985. Used value, $100 to $125.

HARRINGTON & RICHARDSON Model 586: revolver; .32 H&R magnum; 5-rd. cylinder; same general specs as Model 686; 4½", 5½", 7½", 10" barrel lengths. Introduced, 1984; dropped, 1985. Used value, $160 to $165.

HAWES

Hawes Montana Marshal

HAWES Western Marshal: revolver, single-action; 6-rd. cylinder; .357 magnum, .44 magnum, .45 Colt, .45 auto, .22 magnum, .22 LR; 6" barrels for centerfire calibers, 5" for rimfires; rosewood grips in centerfire models, plastic stag grips for rimfires; also available with interchangeable cylinder combos: .357 magnum/9mm Luger, .45 Colt/.45 auto, .44 magnum/.44-40, .22 LR/.22 WRFM. Introduced, 1968; manufactured in West Germany by Sauer & Sohn exclusively for Hawes; dropped, 1980. Used values: .357 magnum, $140 to $155; .45 Colt, $155 to $170; .44 magnum, $145 to $155; .45 auto, $155 to $165; .22 LR, $115 to $130. Combo values: .357 magnum/9mm Luger, $150 to $160; .45 Colt/.45 auto, $150 to $160; .44 magnum/.44-40, $155 to $165; .22 LR/.22 WRFM, $125 to $130.

HAWES Montana Marshal: revolver, single-action; has same specs, caliber combinations as Western Marshal, except for brass grip frame. Introduced, 1968; dropped, 1980. Used values: .357 magnum. $155 to $170; .45 Colt, $165 to $170; .44 magnum, $160 to $170; .45 auto, $155 to $170; .22 LR, $145 to $155; .357 magnum/9mm Luger, $185 to $190; .45 Colt/.45 auto, $185 to $190; .44 magnum/.44-40, $195 to $205.

Hawes Texas Marshal

HAWES Texas Marshal: revolver, single-action, same specs, caliber combos as Western Marshal, except for pearlite grips, nickel finish. Introduced, 1969; dropped, 1980. Used values, same as for Montana Marshal.

HAWES Deputy Marshal: revolver, single-action; .22 LR; also available as combo with .22 WRFM cylinder; 6-rd. cylinders; 5½" barrel, 11" overall length; blade front sight, adjustable rear; plastic or walnut grips; blued finish. Introduced, 1973; dropped, 1980. Used values: .22 LR with plastic grips, $70 to $80, with walnut grips $80 to $90. Combo values: .22 LR/.22 WRFM with plastic grips, $85 to $90, with walnut grips, $95 to $100.

HAWES Deputy Denver Marshal: revolver, single-action; same specs as Deputy Marshal, except for brass frame. Introduced, 1973; dropped, 1980. Used values: .22 LR with plastic grips, $75 to $80, with walnut grips $80 to $85. Combo values: .22 LR/.22 WRFM, with plastic grips $90 to $95, walnut grips, $100 to $105.

HAWES Deputy Montana Marshal: revolver, single-action; same specs as Deputy Marshal, except has walnut grips only; brass grip frame. Introduced, 1973; dropped, 1980. Used values: .22 LR, $75 to $80; combo value, .22 LR/.22 WRFM, $90 to $100.

Hawes Federal Marshal

Hawes Deputy Texas Marshal

HAWES Federal Marshal: revolver, single-action, same specs as Western Marshal, except never manufactured in .22 rimfire; has color case-hardened frame, one-piece European walnut grip, brass grip frame. Introduced, 1969; dropped, 1980. Used values: .357 magnum, $165 to $170; .45 Colt, $165 to $170; .44 magnum, $175 to $180; .357 magnum/9mm Luger, $200 to $205; .45 Colt/.45 ACP, $200 to $205; .44 magnum/.44-40, $205 to $230.

HAWES Deputy Texas Marshal: revolver, single-action; same specs as Deputy Marshal, except for chrome finish. Introduced, 1973; dropped, 1980. Used values: .22 LR with plastic grips $70 to $75, with walnut grips $80 to $85. Combo values: .22 LR/.22 WRFM with plastic grips, $85 to $90; with walnut grips, $95 to $100.

HAWES Deputy Silver City Marshal: revolver, single-action; same specs as Deputy Marshal, except for brass grip frame, chromed frame, blued barrel and cylinder. Introduced, 1973; dropped, 1980. Used values: .22 LR with plastic grips, $75 to $80, with walnut grips, $85 to $90. Combo values: .22 LR/.22 WRFM with plastic grips, $85 to $90; with walnut grips $95 to $105.

Hawes Silver City Marshal

Hawes Favorite

HAWES Silver City Marshal: revolver, single-action, same basic specs as Western Marshal. Differs with pearlite grips, brass frame. Not made in .22. Introduced, 1969; dropped, 1980. Used values: .357 magnum, $165 to $170; .45 Colt, $170 to $175; .44 magnum, $180 to $190; .357 magnum/9mm Luger, $200 to $205; .44 magnum/.44-40, $205 to $230; .45 Colt/.45 ACP, $200 to $205.

HAWES Chief Marshal: revolver, single-action; same specs as Western Marshal, except for target-type front sight, adjustable rear; oversize stocks. Not made in .22 RF. Introduced, 1969; dropped, 1980. Used values: .357 magnum, $175 to $200; .45 Colt, $175 to $200; .44 magnum, $185 to $210; .357 magnum/9mm Luger, $200 to $225; .44 magnum/.44-40, $205 to $230; .45 Colt/.45 ACP, $200 to $225.

HAWES Favorite: single-shot; tip-up action; .22 LR; 8" barrel, 12" overall length; target sights, plastic or rosewood stocks, blued barrel; chromed frame. Replica of Stevens No. 35 target model. Manufactured, 1968 to 1976. Used value, $85 to $90.

HAWES/SAUER Double Action: automatic; 9mm Luger, .38 Super, .45 ACP; 9-rd. magazine in 9mm, .38 Super; 7 rds. in .45; 4⅜" barrel, 7¾" overall length; checkered European walnut stocks or black plastic; windage-adjustable rear sight, blade front; square combat trigger guard. Manufactured in Germany. Introduced, 1977; still in production; dropped by Hawes in 1980; also known as Browning BDA, SIG/Sauer P-220. Used value, $425 to $450.

HECKLER & KOCH

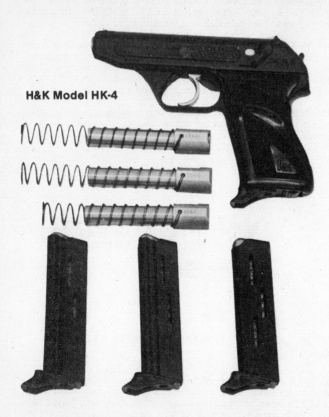

H&K Model HK-4

H&K Model P9S

H&K Model P9S 45

HECKLER & KOCH HK-4: automatic, double-action; .380 auto; 8-rd. magazine; 3½" barrel; 6" overall length; checkered black plastic grips; rear sight adjustable for windage, front fixed. Early version was available with interchangeable barrels, magazines for four calibers. Imported from Germany originally by Harrington & Richardson, then by Heckler & Koch; importation dropped, 1985. Used values: single caliber, $275 to $300; with four barrels as set, $425 to $450.

HECKLER & KOCH P9S: automatic; double-action; 9mm Parabellum, 9-rd. magazine; 4" barrel; 5.4" overall length; fixed sights; checkered plastic grips; loaded/cocked indicators; hammer cocking lever; originally imported from Germany by Gold Rush Gun Shop, then by Heckler & Koch, Inc.; importation dropped, 1986. Used value, $400 to $425.

P9S Target Model has same specs as Model P9S 9mm, except for adjustable trigger, trigger stop and adjustable rear sight. Used value, $650 to $700.

P9S 45 has same specs as Model P9S 9mm, except for being made for .45 auto cartridge; has 7-rd. magazine. Still in production. Used value, $450 to $475.

P9S Competition Kit is the same as P9S 9mm, but has interchangeable 5½" barrel; barrel weight; choice of standard plastic or walnut competition stocks. Used values: with plastic stocks, $775 to $800; with walnut competition stocks, $800 to $825.

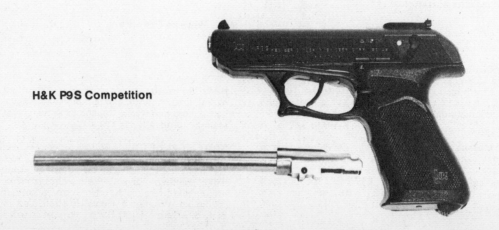

H&K P9S Competition

H&K Model VP'70Z

H&K Model P7

HECKLER & KOCH VP'70Z: automatic; double-action; 9mm Parabellum; 18-rd. magazine; 4½" barrel; 8" overall length; stippled black plastic stocks; ramp front sight, channeled rear on slide; recoil operated; only 4 moving parts; double column magazine. Manufactured in West Germany. Introduced, 1978; importation dropped, 1985. Used value, $350 to $375.

HECKLER & KOCH P7 (PSP): automatic; 9mm Parabellum; 8-rd. magazine; 4.13" barrel; weighs 29 oz.; 6.54" overall length; cock-

ed by pressure on front strap; squared combat trigger guard; blued finish. Imported from West Germany. Introduced, 1982; still in production. Used value, $600 to $650.

P7-M13 has same specs as P7, except has 13-rd. magazine, matte black finish, ambidextrous magazine release, forged steel frame. Introduced, 1986; still imported. Used value, $725 to $775.

HIGH STANDARD

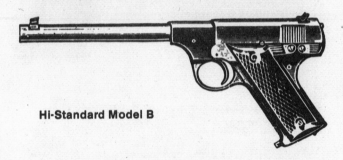

Hi-Standard Model B

Hi-Standard Model H-B

HI-STANDARD Model B: automatic; hammerless; .22 LR only; 4¾", 6¾" barrels; 10¾" overall length with 6¾" barrel; 10-rd. magazine; fixed sights; checkered hard rubber grips; blued. Introduced in 1932; dropped, 1942. Used value, $275 to $300.

Model S-B has the same specs as Model B, except with 5¾" barrel only; smoothbore for .22 shot cartridge. Introduced in 1939; dropped, 1940. Used value, $325 to $350.

Model H-B has the same general specs as the Model B, except there is no thumb safety; has visible hammer. Introduced in 1940; dropped, 1942. Used value, $285 to $310.

HI-STANDARD Model C: automatic; hammerless; .22 short only. Other specs are identical to those of Model B Hi-Standard auto. Introduced in 1936; dropped, 1942. Used value, $285 to $310.

Hi-Standard Model H-A

HI-STANDARD Model A: automatic; hammerless; .22 LR only; 4½", 6¾" barrel; 11½" overall length, with 6¾" barrel; adjustable target-type sights; checkered walnut grips; blued. Actually an updated version of Model B. Introduced in 1938; dropped, 1942. Used value, $275 to $300.

Model H-A has the same specs as Model A, but has visible hammer, sans thumb safety. Introduced in 1940; dropped, 1942. Used value, $325 to $350.

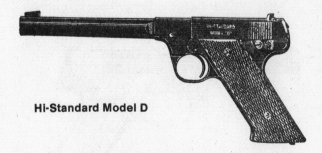

Hi-Standard Model D

HI-STANDARD Model D: automatic; hammerless; .22 LR only; has the same specs as Model A, except with heavy barrel. Introduced in 1938; dropped 1942. Used value, $285 to $310.

Model H-D has the same specs as Model D, except for visible hammer, sans thumb safety. Introduced in 1940; dropped, 1942. Used value, $250 to $275.

Model H-DM has the same general specs as Model H-D, but with thumb safety added. Introduced in 1946; dropped, 1951. Used value, $250 to $275.

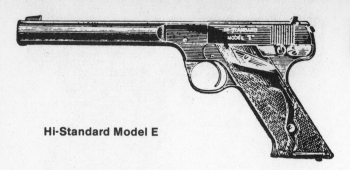

Hi-Standard Model E

**Hi-Standard Olympic
(2nd Model)**

HI-STANDARD Model E: automatic; hammerless; .22 LR only; has same general specs as Model A, except for thumbrest grips, heavy barrel. Introduced in 1937; dropped, 1942. Used value, $350 to $375.

Model H-E has the same specs as Model E, except for visible hammer, sans thumb safety. Introduced in 1941; dropped, 1942. Used value, $425 to $475.

HI-STANDARD Model G-380: automatic; take-down; .380 auto only; 5" barrel; visible hammer; thumb safety; fixed sights; checkered plastic grips; blued. Introduced in 1947; dropped, 1950. Used value, $275 to $300.

Olympic (Second Model) is hammerless, take-down automatic; .22 short only; interchangeable 4½", 6¾" barrels; with 6¾" barrel, 11½" overall length; 10-rd. magazine; target sights; adjustable barrel weights; alloy slide; checkered plastic thumbrest grips; blued. Introduced in 1951; dropped, 1958. Used values: with both barrels, $375 to $400; one barrel, $300 to $325.

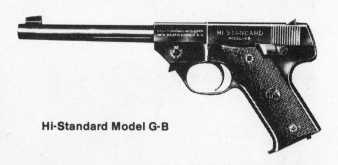

Hi-Standard Model G-B

Hi-Standard Supermatic

HI-STANDARD Model G-B: automatic; hammerless; take-down; .22 LR only; interchangeable barrels of 4½", 6¾"; with 6¾" barrel, overall length, 10¾"; fixed sights; checkered plastic grips; blued. Introduced in 1949; dropped, 1951. Used values: with two barrels, $250 to $275; one barrel, $175 to $200.

Model G-D has same general specs as Model G-B, including interchangeable barrels; except for target sights, checkered walnut grips. Introduced in 1949; dropped, 1951. Used values: with two barrels, $300 to $325; one barrel, $200 to $225.

Model G-E has same general specs as Model G-D, except for thumbrest walnut grips, heavy barrels. Introduced in 1949; dropped, 1951. Used values: with both barrels, $300 to $325; one barrel, $275 to $300.

**Hi-Standard Supermatic
Tournament**

Hi-Standard Model Olympic

Hi-Standard Supermatic Citation

HI-STANDARD Olympic (First Model): automatic; hammerless; .22 short only; light alloy slide; other specs are same as Model G-E, including interchangeable barrels. Introduced in 1950; dropped, 1951. Used values: with both barrels, $500 to $550; one barrel, $400 to $450.

HI-STANDARD Supermatic: automatic; hammerless; take-down; .22 LR only; 4½", 6¾" interchangeable barrels; 10-rd. magazine; late models have recoil stabilizer on longer barrel; 11½" overall length, with 6¾" barrel; 2-, 3-oz. adjustable barrel weights; target sights; checkered plastic thumbrest grips; blued. Introduced in 1951; dropped, 1958. Used values: with both barrels, $250 to $275; one barrel, $200 to $225.

Supermatic Tournament model is .22 LR only, with same specs of standard Supermatic, except for interchangeable 5½" bull barrel, and 6¾" barrel; barrels drilled, notched for stabilizer, weights; click-adjustable rear sight, undercut ramp front; checkered walnut grips; blued finish. Introduced in 1958; dropped, 1963. Used values: both barrels, $275 to $300; one barrel, $200 to $225.

Supermatic Citation has the same general specs as Tournament model, except for choice of 5½" bull barrel, 6¾", 8", 10" tapered barrels, with stabilizer, 2 removable weights; adjustable trigger pull; click-adjustable rear sight; ramp front; checkered laminated wood grips; bull-barrel model has checkered walnut grips with thumbrest. Introduced in 1958; dropped, 1966. Used values: tapered barrel, $275 to $300; bull barrel, $300 to $325.

Supermatic Standard Citation is a simplified version of original Citation, but with 5½" bull barrel only; 10" overall length; over-travel trigger adjustment; rebounding firing pin; click-adjustable square-notch rear sight, undercut ramp front; checkered walnut grips with or without thumbrest, right or left hand. Dropped, 1977 Used value, $225 to $250.

Supermatic Citation Survival Pack includes Citation auto, extra magazine; electroless nickel finish; padded canvas carrying case has interior pockets for magazine, knife, compass. Introduced, 1982; dropped, 1984. Used value, $300 to $325.

Supermatic Citation Military model has same specs as Standard Citation model, except for military-style grip, positive magazine latch, stippled front, backstraps; 5½" bull barrel or 7¾" fluted barrel. Dropped, 1984. Used value, $300 to $325.

Supermatic Trophy has the same specs as original Citation model, except for choice of 5½" bull barrel, 7¼" fluted style; extra magazine; high-luster blue finish. Introduced in 1963; dropped, 1966. Used value, $275 to $300.

Supermatic Trophy Military model has same general specs as standard Trophy model, except that grip duplicates feel of Government Model .45; trigger adjustable for pull, over-travel; stippled front, backstrap; checkered walnut grips with or without thumbrest; right or left hand; frame-mounted click-adjustable rear sight; undercut ramp front. Dropped, 1984. Used value, $325 to $350.

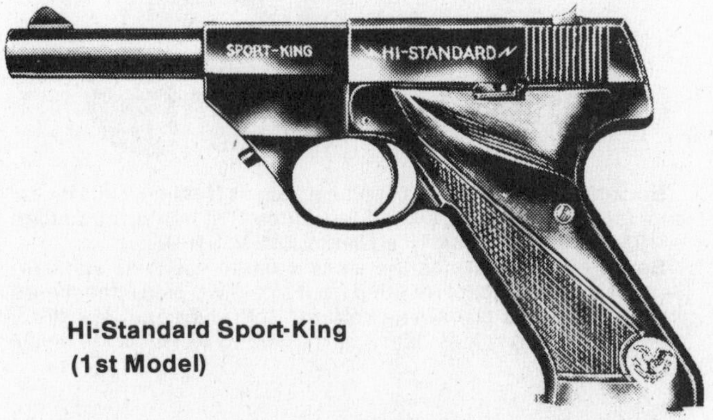

HI-STANDARD Flight-King (First Model): automatic; hammerless; .22 short only; other specs are identical to those of Sport-King model, except for aluminum alloy frame, slide. Introduced in 1953; dropped, 1958. Used values: with both barrels, $250 to $275; one barrel, $210 to $250.

Flight-King (Second Model) has the same general specs as first-model Flight-King, except for all-steel construction; .22 LR only. Introduced in 1958; dropped, 1966. Used values: with both barrels, $200 to $225; one barrel, $185 to $200.

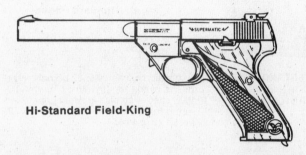

Hi-Standard Field-King

HI-STANDARD Field-King: automatic; hammerless .22 LR only; has the same general specs as Sport-King model, but with target sights, heavier 6¾" barrel; late model with recoil stabilizer. Introduced in 1951; dropped, 1958. Used value, $185 to $195.

Hi-Standard Dura-Matic

HI-STANDARD Dura-Matic: automatic; hammerless take-down; .22 LR only; 4½", 6½" interchangeable barrels; with 6½" barrel, overall length, 10⅞"; usually sold with one barrel only; fixed sights; checkered plastic grips; blued. Introduced in 1955; dropped, 1969. Used value, $125 to $135.

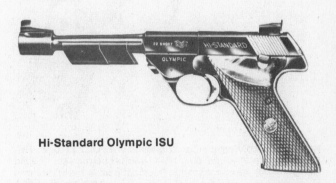

Hi-Standard Olympic ISU

HI-STANDARD Olympic ISU: target automatic; hammerless; .22 short only; 6¾" barrel; (5½" bull, 8" tapered, dropped 1964) 10-rd. magazine; detachable weights; integral stabilizer; trigger adjustable for pull, over-travel; click-adjustable square-notch rear sight; undercut ramp front; checkered walnut grips with or without thumbrest; left, right hand; blued finish. Meets International Shooting Union regulations. Introduced in 1958; dropped 1977. Used value, $325 to $350.

Hi-Standard Sport-King
(1st Model)

HI-STANDARD Sport-King (First Model): automatic; hammerless; .22 LR only; 4½", 6¾" intechangeable barrels; with 6¾" barrel, 11½" overall length; 10-rd. magazine; fixed sights; checkered thumbrest plastic grips; blued. Introduced in 1951; dropped, 1958. Used values: with both barrels, $210 to $230; one barrel, $185 to $200.

Lightweight Sport-King has the same specs as the standard Sport-King model, except frame is of forged aluminum alloy. Introduced in 1954; dropped, 1965. Used values: both barrels, $200 to $225; one barrel, $185 to $200.

Sport-King (Second Model) is all-steel, .22 LR; minor interior design changes from first model Sport-King, interchangeable barrel retained. Introduced in 1958; dropped, 1984. Used values: both barrels, $200 to $225; one barrel, $185 to $200.

Hi-Standard Plinker

HI-STANDARD Plinker: automatic; hammerless; .22 LR only; interchangeable 4½", 6½" barrels; 9" overall length with 4½" barrel; 10-rd. magazine; grooved trigger; checkered plastic target grips; fixed square-notch rear sight; ramp front; blued. Introduced in 1972; dropped, 1975. Used value, $125 to $145.

Hi-Standard Sharpshooter

HI-STANDARD Sharpshooter: automatic; hammerless; .22 LR only; 5½" barrel; 9-rd. magazine; push-button take-down feature; scored trigger; adjustable square-notch rear sight, ramp front; slide lock; checkered laminated plastic grips; blued. Introduced in 1972; dropped, 1982. Used value, $190 to $215.

Hi-Standard Victor

HI-STANDARD Victor: automatic; hammerless; .22 LR only; 4½", 5½" barrels; 8¾" overall length with shorter barrel; vent or solid aluminum rib; 10-rd. magazine; interchangeable barrel feature; rib-mounted click-adjustable rear sight, undercut ramp front; checkered walnut grips with thumbrest; blued. Introduced in 1973; dropped, 1984. Used values: solid rib, $275 to $300; vent rib, $325 to $350.

HI-STANDARD Sentinel: double-action revolver; solid aluminum alloy frame; 9-rd. swing-out cylinder; .22 LR only; 3", 4", 6" barrels; with 4" barrel, overall length, 9"; fixed sights; checkered plastic

grips; blued, nickel finish. Introduced in 1955; dropped, 1974. Used values: blued, $85 to $100; nickel, $95 to $110.

Sentinel Deluxe has the same specs as the standard Sentinel, except for movable rear sight, two-piece square-butt checkered walnut grips, wide triggers; 4", 6" barrels only. Introduced in 1957; dropped, 1974. Used value, $110 to $125.

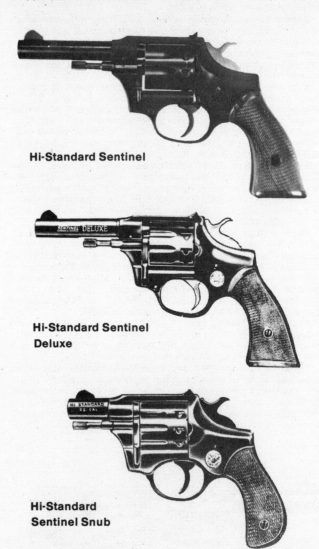

Hi-Standard Sentinel

Hi-Standard Sentinel Deluxe

Hi-Standard Sentinel Snub

Sentinel Snub model has same specs as Sentinel Deluxe, except for checkered bird's-head-type grips; 2⅜" barrel. Introduced in 1957; dropped, 1974. Used value, $85 to $100.

Sentinel Imperial has the same general specs as standard Sentinel model, except for ramp front sight, two-piece checkered walnut grips, onyx-black or nickel finish. Introduced in 1962; dropped, 1965. Used values: black finish, $95 to $110; nickel finish, $100 to $120.

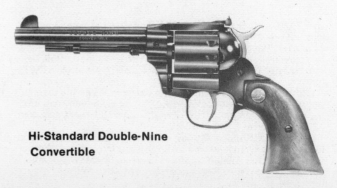

Hi-Standard Double-Nine Convertible

HI-STANDARD Double-Nine: double-action revolver; Western-styled version of Sentinel; .22 short or LR; 5½" barrel; 11" overall length; 9-rd. swing-out cylinder; dummy ejection rod housing; spring-loaded ejection; rebounding hammer; movable notch rear sight, blade front; plastic grips; blued, nickel finish. Introduced in 1959; dropped, 1971. Used values: blued, $100 to $125; nickel, $110 to $135.

Double-Nine Convertible model has the same general specs as original Double-Nine, except primary cylinder is chambered for .22 LR, long, short; extra cylinder fires .22 WRFM; smooth frontier-type walnut grips; movable notched rear sight, blade front; blued, nickel finish. Introduced in 1972; dropped, 1984. Used values: blued $115 to $125; nickel, $125 to $140.

Hi-Standard Derringer

HI-STANDARD Derringer: double-action; hammerless; over/under 2" barrels; 5" overall length; 2-shot; .22 LR, long, short, .22 WRFM; plastic grips; fixed sights; standard model has blue, nickel finish. Presentation model is gold plated, introduced in 1965; dropped, 1966. Presentation model has some collector value. Standard model, introduced in 1963, dropped, 1984. Used values: standard model, $100 to $115; presentation model, $175 to $200; matched pair, presentation model, consecutive serial numbers, $400 to $450; .22 magnum, $115 to $125.

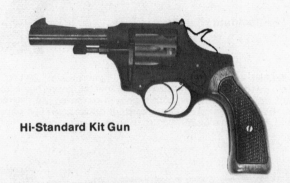

Hi-Standard Kit Gun

HI-STANDARD Kit Gun: double-action; .22 LR, long, short; 4" barrel; 9" overall length; 9-rd. swing-out cylinder; micro-adjustable rear sight, target ramp front; checkered walnut grips; blued. Introduced in 1970; dropped, 1973. Used value, $100 to $120.

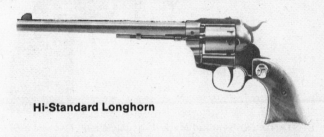

Hi-Standard Longhorn

HI-STANDARD Longhorn: double-action revolver; same general specs as Double-Nine; original version has 4½" barrel, pearl-like plastic grips; model with 5½" barrel has plastic staghorn grips; later model has walnut grips, 9½" barrel; aluminum alloy frame; blued finish. Long-barreled model introduced in 1970, dropped, 1971. Other models introduced in 1961; dropped, 1966. Used values: 9½" barrel, walnut grips, $100 to $125; other models, $90 to $100.

Longhorn Convertible has the same general specs as standard Longhorn, but with 9½" barrel only; smooth walnut grips; dual cylinder to fire .22 WRFM cartridge. Introduced in 1971; dropped, 1984. Used value, $115 to $125.

Hi-Standard Natchez

HI-STANDARD Natchez: double-action revolver; same general specs as Double-Nine, except for 4½" barrel; 10" overall length; ivory-like plastic bird's-head grips; blued. Introduced in 1961; dropped, 1966. Used value, $100 to $120.

Hi-Standard Durango

HI-STANDARD Durango: double-action revolver; has the same general specs as the Double-Nine model; .22 LR, long, short; 4½", 5½" barrels; 10" overall length with shorter barrel; brass-finished trigger guard, backstrap; uncheckered walnut grips; blued only in shorter barrel length; blued, nickel in 5½" barrel. Introduced in 1972; dropped, 1975. Used values: blued, $85 to $95; nickel, $95 to $105.

Hi-Standard Posse

HI-STANDARD Posse: double-action revolver; same general design as Double-Nine, except for 3½" barrel; 9" overall length; uncheckered walnut grips; brass grip frame, trigger guard; blued. Introduced in 1961; dropped, 1966. Used value, $85 to $95.

Hi-Standard Mark I

HI-STANDARD Sentinel Mark I: double-action revolver; .22 LR; 9-rd. cylinder; 2", 3", 4" barrel lengths; unchecked walnut stocks; ramp front sight, fixed or adjustable rear; blued or nickel finish. Introduced, 1974; dropped, 1984. Used value, $150 to $175.

Hi-Standard Mark II

HI-STANDARD Sentinel Mark II: double-action revolver; .357 magnum; 6-rd. cylinder; 2½", 4", 6" barrel lengths; walnut combat grips; fixed sights; blued finish. Manufactured 1973 to 1975 by Dan Wesson Arms. Used value, $165 to $185.

HI-STANDARD Sentinel Mark III: double-action revolver; has the same specs as Sentinel Mark II, except for ramp front sight, adjustable rear. Manufactured 1973 to 1975 by Dan Wesson Arms. Used value, $175 to $200.

HI-STANDARD Sentinel Mark IV: double-action revolver; .22 WRFM; except for caliber, has same specs as Sentinel Mark I. Introduced in 1974; dropped, 1979. Used value, $165 to $185.

HI-STANDARD Camp Model: double-action revolver; .22 LR, .22 WRFM; has same specs as Sentinel Mark IV, except for target-type checkered walnut grips; 6" barrel; adjustable rear sight. Introduced, 1976; dropped, 1979. Used value, $165 to $185.

Hi-Standard High Sierra

HI-STANDARD High Sierra: double-action revolver; .22 LR, .22 WRFM; 9 rds.; 7" octagonal barrel; 12½" overall length; blade front sight, adjustable rear; smooth walnut grips; swing-out cylinder; gold-plated backstrap, trigger guard. Introduced, 1978; dropped, 1984. Used value: $125 to $135.

Hi-Standard Custom 10-X

HIGH STANDARD Custom 10-X: automatic; .22 LR; 10-rd. magazine; 5½" bull barrel; weighs 44½ oz.; 9¾" overall length; checkered walnut stocks; undercut ramp front sight, frame-mounted adjustable rear; custom-made, fitted; fully adjustable target trigger; stippled front, backstraps; slide lock; marketed with two extra magazines; non-reflective blued finish; signed by maker. Introduced, 1983; dropped, 1984. Used value, $575 to $600.

IVER JOHNSON

Iver Johnson Safety Hammer Model

IVER JOHNSON Safety Hammer Model: double-action revolver; hinged frame; .22 LR, .32 S&W Long, .32 S&W; 2", 3", 3¼", 4", 5", 6" barrels; in .22 LR, 7-rd. cylinder; in .32 S&W Long, 6 rds., 5-rd.

capacity in others; fixed sights; hard rubber grips with round butt, square butt in rubber or walnut; heavier frame for .32 S&W Long, .38 S&W; blued, nickel finish. Introduced in 1892; dropped, 1950. Used value, $75 to $85.

Iver Johnson Safety Hammerless

IVER JOHNSON Safety Hammerless Model: double-action revolver; hinged frame; basic design comparable to Safety Hammer model; .22 LR, .32 S&W Long, .32 S&W, .38 S&W; 2", 3", 3¼", 4", 5",

6" barrels; in .22 LR, 7-rd. cylinder; in .32 S&W Long, 6 rds., 5-rd. capacity in others; fixed sights, hard rubber grips with round butt, square butt in rubber or walnut; heavier frame for .32 S&W Long, .38 S&W; blued, nickel finish. Introduced in 1895; dropped, 1950. Used value, $85 to $95.

Iver Johnson Model 1900

IVER JOHNSON Model 1900: double-action revolver; solid frame; .22 rimfire, .32 S&W Long, .32 S&W, .38 S&W; 2½", 4½", 6" barrels; 7-rd. cylinder in .22, 6 rds. in .32 S&W, 5 rds. in .32 S&W Long; fixed sights; hard rubber grips; blued, nickel finish. Introduced in 1900; dropped, 1947. Used value, $55 to $65.

Model 1900 Target utilizes same frame as standard model; .22 LR only; 6", 9" barrels; 7-rd. cylinder; fixed sights; checkered walnut grips; blued finish. Introduced in 1925; dropped, 1942. Used value, $100 to $125.

Iver Johnson Supershot

IVER JOHNSON 22 Supershot: double-action revolver; hinged frame; .22 LR only; 6" barrel; 7-rd. cylinder; fixed sights; checkered walnut grips; blued finish. Introduced in 1929; dropped, 1949. Used value, $75 to $85.

Supershot 9-shot has hinged frame, .22 LR only; 9-rd. cylinder; pre-WWII model has adjustable finger rest. Other specs are same as standard model. Introduced in 1929; dropped, 1949. Used value, $85 to $95.

IVER JOHNSON Target 9-Shot: double-action revolver; solid frame; .22 LR only; 6", 10" barrels; 10¾" overall length with 6" barrel; 9-rd. cylinder; fixed sights; checkered diamond panel walnut grips; blued finish. Introduced in 1929; dropped, 1946. Used value, $85 to $95; add $20 for 10" barrel.

Iver Johnson Sealed 8 Target

IVER JOHNSON Sealed Eight Supershot: double-action revolver; hinged frame; .22 LR only; 6" barrel; 8-rd. cylinder counterbored for high-velocity ammo; 10¾" overall length; pre-WWII ver-

sion has adjustable finger rest; adjustable target sights; checkered diamond panel walnut grips; blued finish. Introduced in 1931; dropped, 1957. Used value, $115 to $125.

Sealed Eight Target has solid frame; 6", 10" barrels; fixed sights; other specs are same as Sealed Eight Supershot. Introduced in 1931; dropped, 1957. Used value, $85 to $95.

Sealed Eight Protector has hinged frame; 2½" barrel; 7¼" overall length; fixed sights; checkered walnut grips; blued finish. Introduced in 1933; dropped, 1949. Used value, $85 to $95.

Iver Johnson Champion

IVER JOHNSON Champion: single-action target revolver; hinged frame; .22 LR only; 6" barrel; 10¾" overall length; 8-rd. cylinder; countersunk chambers for high-velocity ammo; adjustable finger rest; adjustable target-type sights; checkered walnut grips; blued finish. Introduced in 1938; dropped, 1948. Used value, $120 to $135.

Iver Johnson Trigger-Cocking Model

IVER JOHNSON Trigger-Cocking Model: single-action target revolver; hinged frame; .22 LR only; 6" barrel; 10¾" overall length; 8-rd. cylinder, with countersunk chambers; adjustable target sights, grips; blued finish; checkered walnut grips. First pull on the trigger cocks the hammer; second releases hammer. Introduced in 1940; dropped, 1947. Some collector value. Used value, $100 to $125.

Iver Johnson Supershot Model 844

IVER JOHNSON Supershot Model 844: double-action revolver; hinged frame; .22 LR only; 4½", 6" barrel; 9¼" overall length with 4½" barrel; 8-rd. cylinder; adjustable sights; one-piece checkered walnut grip; blued finish. Introduced in 1955; dropped, 1956. Used value, $75 to $85.

Iver Johnson Model 855

IVER JOHNSON Armsworth Model 855: single-action revolver; hinged frame; .22 LR only; 6" barrel; 10¾" overall length; adjustable finger rest; adjustable sights; one-piece checkered walnut grip; blued finish. Introduced in 1955; dropped, 1957. Used value, $85 to $95.

Iver Johnson Model 55

Iver Johnson Model 55A

IVER JOHNSON Model 55: double-action target revolver; solid frame; .22 LR, long, short; 4½", 6" barrels; 10¾" overall length, with 6" barrel; 8-rd. cylinder; fixed sights; checkered walnut grips; blued finish. Introduced in 1955; dropped, 1961. Used value, $60 to $75.

Model 55A has the same specs as Model 55, except for incorporation of a loading gate. Introduced in 1952; no longer in production. Used value, $80 to $85.

Iver Johnson Model 57

Iver Johnson Model 57A

IVER JOHNSON Model 57: double-action target revolver; solid frame; .22 LR, long, short; 4", 5" barrels; 8-rd. cylinder; 10¾" overall length with 6" barrel; adjustable sights; checkered plastic grip with thumb channel; blued finish. Introduced in 1956; dropped, 1961. Used value, $65 to $75.

Model 57A has the same specs as Model 57, except for addition of loading gate. Introduced in 1962; dropped, 1980. Used value, $80 to $90.

Iver Johnson Model 66 Trailsman

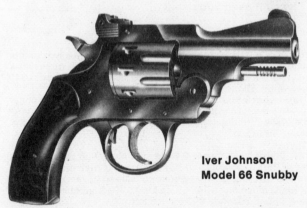

Iver Johnson Model 66 Snubby

IVER JOHNSON Model 66 Trailsman: double-action revolver; hinged frame; .22 LR, long, short; 6" barrel; 11" overall length; 8-rd. cylinder; rebounding hammer; adjustable sights; checkered plastic grips with thumb channel; blued finish. Introduced in 1958; dropped, 1980. Used value, $95 to $110.

Trailsman 66 Snubby model has same general specs as standard Model 66, except for 2¾" barrel; 7" overall length; smooth, rounded plastic grips; also available in .32 S&W, .38 S&W with 5-rd. cylinder. Introduced in 1961; dropped, 1972. Used value, $95 to $110.

IVER JOHNSON Model 50A Sidewinder: frontier-style double-action revolver; solid frame; .22 LR, long, short; 6" barrel; 11¼" overall length; 8-rd. cylinder; fixed sights; plastic staghorn grips; blued finish. Introduced in 1961; dropped, 1980; in varying configurations as Models 524, 624, 724, 824, some with adjustable sights. Used value, $75 to $85.

Iver Johnson Model 50A

Iver Johnson Model 55S Cadet

IVER JOHNSON Model 67 Viking: double-action revolver; hinged frame; .22 LR, long, short; 4½", 6" barrels; 11" overall length; with 6" barrel; 8-rd. cylinder; adjustable sights; plastic grips with thumb channel. Introduced in 1964; dropped, 1974. Used value, $85 to $95.

Iver Johnson Model 67S

Model 67S Viking Snubby has the same general specs as standard Model 67, except for 2¾" barrel, 7" overall length; small plastic grips; also available in .32 S&W, .38 S&W, with 5-rd. cylinder. Introduced in 1964; dropped, 1974. Used value, $85 to $95.

Iver Johnson Model 55S-A

IVER JOHNSON Model 55S Cadet: double-action revolver; solid frame; .22 LR, long, short, .32 S&W, .38 S&W; 2½" barrel; 7" overall length; .22 has 8-rd. cylinder, others, 5-rd. capacity; fixed sights; plastic grips; blued finish. Introduced in 1955; dropped, 1961. Used value, $60 to $65.

Model 55S-A has the same specs as Model 55S, except for addition of a loading gate. Introduced in 1962; dropped, 1980. Used value, $75 to $85.

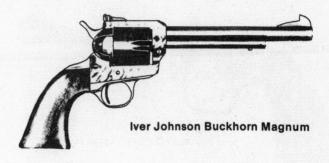

Iver Johnson Buckhorn Magnum

IVER JOHNSON Cattleman: single-action revolver; .357 magnum, .44 magnum, .45 Colt; 6-rd. cylinder; 4¾", 5½", 6" barrel lengths; one-piece uncheckered walnut grip, fixed sights, brass grip frame; color case-hardened frame; blued barrel and cylinder. Manufactured in Italy. Introduced, 1973; dropped, 1980. Used value, $165 to $185.

Cattleman Buckhorn has the same specs as Cattleman, except for ramp front sight, adjustable rear; additional barrel lengths of 5½" and 12". Introduced in 1973; dropped, 1980. Used value, $190 to $200, depending on caliber, barrel length.

Iver Johnson Model 67 Viking

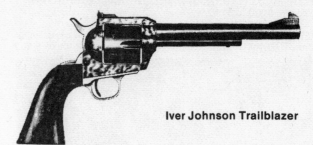

Iver Johnson Trailblazer

Cattleman Buntline has same specs as Cattleman Buckhorn, except for 18" barrel, shoulder stock with brass fittings. Introduced in 1973; dropped, 1980. Used values, $300 to $325.

Cattleman Trailblazer has same general specs as Cattleman Buckhorn, except .22 caliber; has combo .22 LR, .22 WRFM cylinders; 5½", 6½" barrel lengths. Introduced in 1973; dropped, 1980. Used value, $125 to $145.

IVER JOHNSON Sportsman: double-action revolver; solid frame; .22 LR; 6-rd. cylinder; 4¾", 6" barrel lengths; checkered plastic stocks; fixed sights; blued finish. Manufactured 1974 to 1976. Used value, $65 to $75.

IVER JOHNSON American Bulldog: double-action revolver; solid frame; .22 LR, .22 WRFM, .38 Special; in .22, 6-rd. cylinder, in .38 Special, 5 rds.; 2½", 4" barrel lengths; checkered plastic stocks; adjustable rear sight, fixed front; blued or nickel finish. Manufactured 1974 to 1976. Used value, $75 to $80.

Iver Johnson Rookie

IVER JOHNSON Rookie: double-action revolver; solid frame; .38 Special; 5-rd. cylinder; 4" barrel; 9" overall length; checkered plastic stocks; fixed sights; blued finish. Introduced, 1975; dropped, 1976. Used value, $85 to $95.

Iver Johnson Deluxe Target Model

IVER JOHNSON Deluxe Target Model: double-action revolver; solid frame; .22 LR; same specs as Sportsman model, except for substitution of adjustable sights. Manufactured 1975 to 1976. Used value, $85 to $95.

IVER JOHNSON Swing Out Model: double-action revolver; .22 LR, .22 WRFM, .32 S&W Long, .38 Special; in .22, 6-rd. cylinder; in centerfire calibers, 5 rds.; plain barrels are 2", 3", 4"; with vent rib, 4", 6", 8¾'" fixed sights with plain barrel, adjustable sights with vent-rib barrel; walnut stocks; blued or nickel finish. Introduced in 1977; dropped, 1979. Used values: plain barrel, $90 to $100; vent-rib barrel, $100 to $110.

IVER JOHNSON X300 Pony: automatic; .380 ACP; 6-rd. magazine; 3" barrel; 6" overall length; checkered walnut stocks; blade

Iver Johnson Pony

front sight, windage-adjustable rear; all-steel construction; inertia firing pin; loaded chamber indicator; lanyard ring; no magazine safety; matte, blued or nickel finish. Introduced in 1978; no longer in production. Used values: blued finish, $175 to $200; nickel, $185 to $210; matte finish, $175 to $200.

Iver Johnson TP25B

IVER JOHNSON TP25B: automatic; double-action; .25 ACP; 7-rd. magazine; 2.85" barrel; weighs 14½ oz.; 6.39" overall length; fixed sights; black checkered plastic stocks. Introduced, 1981; still in production. Used value, $125 to $135.

    TP22B has same specs as TP25B, except is chambered for .22 LR only. Introduced, 1981; still in production. Used value, $125 to $135.

Iver Johnson Trailsman

IVER JOHNSON Trailsman: automatic; .22 LR; 10-rd. magazine; 4½", 6" barrel lengths; with shorter barrel, measures 8¼" overall, weighs 46 oz.; checkered composition stocks; slide hold-open latch; push-button magazine release; positive sear-block safety; fixed target-type sights; blued only. Introduced, 1983; no longer in production. Used value, $120 to $130.

IVER JOHNSON ENforcer Model 3000: automatic; .30 M1 Carbine; 15 or 30-rd. magazine; 9½" barrel; 17" overall length; weighs 4 lbs.; American walnut stock, metal handguard; gold bead ramp front sight, peep rear. Originally made by Universal Firearms. Introduced, 1984; still produced. Used value, $200 to $225.

LLAMA

Llama Model IIIA

Llama Model VIII

Llama Model IXA

Llama Model XI

Llama Martial

LLAMA Model IIIA: automatic; .380 auto only; 3-11/16" barrel; 6½" overall length; 7-rd. magazine; checkered thumbrest plastic grips; adjustable target sights; vent rib; grip safety; blued. Early versions were sans vent rib, had lanyard ring, no thumbrest on grips. Imported by Stoeger. Introduced in 1951; still in production. Used value, $135 to $155.

LLAMA Model XA: automatic; .32 auto only; 3-11/16" barrel; 6½" overall length; 8-rd. magazine; checkered thumbrest plastic grips; adjustable target sights; grip safety; blued. Imported by Stoeger. Introduced in 1951; no longer in production. Used value, $125 to $145.

Llama Model XV

LLAMA Model XV: automatic; .22 LR only; 3-11/16" barrel; 6½" overall length; 8-rd. magazine; checkered thumbrest plastic grips; adjustable target sights; vent rib; grip safety; blued. Imported by Stoeger. Introduced in 1951; still in production. Used value, $150 to $165.

LLAMA Model VIII: automatic; .38 Super only; 5" barrel; 8½" overall length; 9-rd. magazine; hand-checkered walnut grips; rear sight adjustable for windage; vent rib; grip safety; blued. Imported by Stoeger. Introduced in 1952; still in production. Used value, $200 to $225.

LLAMA Model IXA: automatic; .45 auto only; 5" barrel; 8½" overall length; 7-rd. magazine; hand-checkered walnut grips; vent rib; fixed sights; grip safety; blued. Introduced in 1952; still in production. Used value, $225 to $250.

LLAMA Model XI: automatic; 9mm Parabellum; 5" barrel; 8½" overall length; 8-rd. magazine; checkered thumbrest plastic grips; adjustable rear sight, fixed front; vent rib; blued. Imported by Stoeger Arms. Introduced in 1954 by Stoeger; still in production. Used value, $200 to $225.

Llama Martial Deluxe

LLAMA Martial: double-action revolver; .22 LR, .22 WRFM, .38 Special; 4" barrel in .38 only, 6" in .22; 11¼" overall length with 6" barrel; hand-checkered walnut grips; target sights; blued. Imported by Stoeger. Introduced in 1969; still in production. Used value, $150 to $165.

Martial Deluxe has same specs as standard Martial model, except for choice of satin chrome, chrome engraved, blued engraved, gold damascened finishes; simulated pearl stocks. Used values: satin chrome, $225 to $250; chrome-engraved, $250 to $275; blued-engraved, $250 to $275; gold-damascened finish, $1200 to $1250.

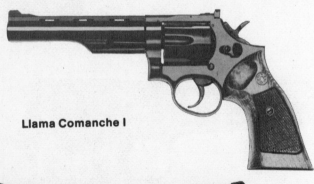

Llama Comanche I

Llama Super Commanche

LLAMA Comanche I: double-action revolver; .22 LR; 6-rd. cylinder; 6" barrel; 11¼" overall length; checkered walnut stocks; target-type sights; blued finish. Introduced in 1977, replacing Martial .22 model; no longer in production. Used value, $165 to $175.

Comanche II has same general specs as Comanche I, except chambered in .38 Special; 4" barrel. Introduced in 1977; no longer in production. Used value, $175 to $185.

Comanche III was introduced in 1975 as original Comanche; .357 magnum; 6-rd. cylinder; 4", 6" barrel; 9¼" overall; ramp front sight, adjustable rear; checkered walnut stocks, blued finish. Still in production. Used value, $200 to $225.

Super Comanche is similar to the Comanche except for .44

magnum chambering; 6" barrel only; 6-rd. cylinder; has smooth, extra-wide trigger; wide spur hammer; oversize target walnut grips; blued finish only. Introduced, 1979; still imported from Spain by Stoeger. Used value, $225 to $250.

Super Comanche IV is similar to the Commanche except has large frame; .357 magnum only; 4", 6', 8½" barrel lengths; wide spur hammer; extra-wide trigger; ovresize walnut target grips; blued finish. Still imported from Spain by Stoeger. Used value, $275 to $390.

Super Commanche V has the same space as Comanche V, except is .44 magnum only; no 4" barrel available. Still imported by Stoeger. Used value, $300 to $325.

Llama Omni

LLAMA Omni: automatic; double-action; 9mm, .45 ACP; 13-rd. magazine in 9mm, 7-rd. in .45; 4¼" barrel length; 7¾" overall length in .45, 8" in 9mm; weighs 40 oz.; ball-bearing action; double sear bars; articulated firing pin; low-friction rifling; checkered plastic stocks; ramped blade front sight, adjustable rear sight on .45; drift adjustable on 9mm. Made in Spain. Introduced, 1982; dropped, 1986. Was imported by Stoeger Industries. Used values: .45 ACP, $300 to $325; 9mm, $275 to $300.

Llama Medium Frame Model

LLAMA Medium Frame Model: 9mmP, .45 ACP; 9-rd. magazine in 9mm, 7 rds. in .45; 4-5/16" barrel; weighs 37 oz.; rear adjustable sight, blade-type front; scaled-down version of large frame model; locked breech mechanism; manual, grip safeties. Made in Spain. Introduced, 1985; still imported by Stoeger Industries. Currently called Compact Frame. Used value, $200 to $225.

MAB

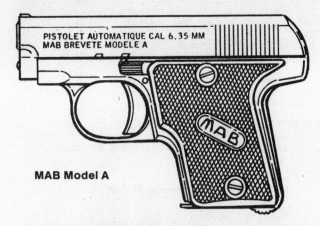

MAB Model A

MAB Model D: automatic; .32, .380 auto; 3½" barrel; 7" overall length; 9-rd. magazine in .32, 8 rds. in .380; push-button magazine release; fixed sights; black checkered hard rubber grips; blued. Introduced in 1933; made under German supervision in WWII. Imported to U.S. as WAC Model D or MAB Le Gendarme. Importation dropped, 1968. Used value, $145 to $155.

MAB Model E

MAB Model A: automatic; .25 auto; 2½" barrel; 4½" overall length; based on Browning design; 6-rd. magazine; no rear sight, fixed front; checkered plastic or hard rubber grips; blued. Introduced in 1921; production suspended in 1942; production resumed in 1945 for importation into U.S. as WAC Model A or Le Defendeur; importation dropped in 1968. Manufactured by Manufacture d'armes de Bayonne, France. Used value, $145 to $165.

MAB Model B: automatic; .25 auto; 2" barrel; 4½" overall length; 6-rd. magazine; no rear sight; fixed front; hard rubber grips; blued. Introduced in 1932; dropped in 1967. Never imported to U.S. Used value, $150 to $165.

MAB Model E: automatic; .25 auto; 3¼" barrel; 6.1" overall length; 10-rd. magazine; fixed sights; plastic grips; blued. Introduced in 1949; imported into U.S. as WAC Model E. Importation dropped, 1968. Used value, $135 to $145.

MAB Model R: automatic; .22 LR; 4½" or 7" barrel; external hammer; 10-rd. magazine. Introduced in 1950; never imported into U.S. Still in production. Used value, $150 to $160.

MAB Model C

MAB Model P-15

MAB Model C: automatic; .32, .380 auto; 3¾" barrel; 6" overall length; 7-rd. magazine in .32, 6 rds. in .380; push-button magazine release behind trigger; fixed sights; black checkered hard rubber grips; blued. Introduced in 1933; made under German supervision during WWII. Importation dropped, 1968. Used value, $150 to $160.

MAB Model P-15: 9mm Parabellum; 4½" barrel; 8" overall length; 15-rd. magazine; fixed sights; checkered plastic grips; blued; still in production; not currently imported. Used value, $275 to $300.

MAB Model F

MAB Model D

MAB Model F: automatic; .22 LR; 3¾", 6", 7¼" barrels; 10¾" overall length; 10-rd. magazine; windage-adjustable rear sight, ramp front; plastic thumbrest grips; blued. Introduced in 1950; variation imported into U.S. as Le Chasseur model. Importation dropped, 1968. Used value, $160 to $170.

MAUSER

Mauser Bolo Model 96

MAUSER Bolo Model 96: automatic; 7.63mm Mauser; locked-bolt design; 4" barrel; 10¾" overall length; 10-rd. box magazine; adjustable rear sight, fixed front; grooved walnut grips. Based upon original Model 96 design, but barrel reduced in length in accordance with Versailles Treaty. Introduced in 1922 for export; dropped, 1930. Used value, $750 to $800.

**Mauser Model 1910
Pocket Pistol**

MAUSER Model 1910 Pocket Pistol: automatic; .25 auto; 3-3/16" barrel; 5⅜" overall length; 9-rd. magazine; fixed sights; checkered hard rubber or walnut grips; blued. Introduced in 1910; dropped, 1939. Used value, $250 to $275.

MAUSER Model 1914 Pocket Pistol: .32 auto; 8-rd. magazine; 3-2/5" barrel; 6" overall length; checkered walnut, hard rubber stocks; fixed sights; blued finish. Similar in design to Model 1910. Manufactured 1914 to 1935. Used value, $225 to $250.

**Mauser WTP
(1st Model)**

**Mauser WTP
(2nd Model)**

MAUSER WTP (First Model): automatic; advertised as Westen-taschen-Pistole or vest-pocket pistol; .25 auto only; 2½" barrel; 4½" overall length; 6-rd. magazine; checkered hard rubber grips; blued. Introduced in 1922; dropped, 1938. Used value, $225 to $250.

Second Model WTP is smaller, lighter in weight. Introduced in 1938; dropped during WWII. Used value, $250 to $275.

MAUSER Model 1930: 7.63mm Mauser; 5¼" barrel; serrated walnut grips. Introduced in 1930; dropped, ca. 1939. Used value, $950 to $1000.

MAUSER Model 1934 Pocket Pistol: .32 auto; has the same general specs as Model 1914, except for substitution of one-piece walnut stock. Manufactured 1934 to 1939. Used value, $250 to $275.

Mauser Model HSc

MAUSER Model HSc: double-action automatic; .32 auto, .380 auto; 3⅜" barrel; 6.05" overall length; 7-rd. magazine; fixed sights; checkered walnut grips; blued, nickel finish. Introduced in 1939; dropped about 1976. Imported by Interarms. Used values: blued, $325 to $350; nickel, $350 to $375.

MAUSER HSc Super: automatic; .32, .380 ACP; 3.56" barrel; weighs 29 oz.; 6" overall length; blade front sight, drift-adjustable rear; double- or single-action; low-profile exposed hammer; combat trigger guard; blued finish. Made in Italy. Imported by Interarms. Introduced, 1983; still in production; no longer imported. Used value, $300 to $310.

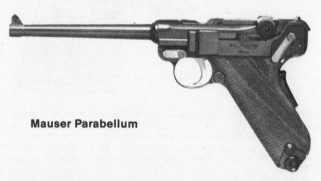

Mauser Parabellum

MAUSER Parabellum: automatic; .30 Luger, 9mm Parabellum; 4" barrel in 9mm, 4", 6" in .30; with 4" barrel, overall length, 8.7"; fixed sights; manual, grip safeties; checkered walnut grips; blued; American eagle over chamber; follows Swiss Luger style. Imported by Interarms. Introduced in 1966; dropped, 1978. Used value, $750 to $800.

Parabellum P-08 has the same general specs as 1906 model, except for redesigned take-down lever; curved front strap; improved safety, trigger; Mauser banner on toggle. Introduced in 1908; resurrected in 1975; dropped, 1978. Imported by Interarms. Used value, $750 to $800.

Pre-WWII MAUSER LUGERS: 9mm (rarely 7.65mm) marked "Mauser," "S/42," or "byf" on toggle. Prices often reflect collector interest. Used value, $450 up.

M-S SAFARI ARMS

M-S SAFARI ARMS Matchmaster: automatic; .45 ACP; 7-rd. magazine; 5" barrel; weighs 45 oz.; 8.7" overall length; rubber or checkered walnut combat grips; combat adjustable sights; blued, Armaloy, Parkerized or electroless nickel finish; beavertail grip safety; extended slide release; combat hammer; threaded barrel bushing; also available in 30-oz. lightweight and stainless steel models. Introduced, 1983; dropped, 1985. Used value, $460 to $475.

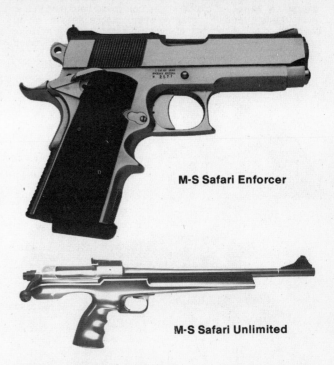

M-S Safari Enforcer

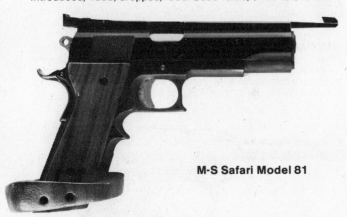

M-S Safari Model 81

M-S Safari Unlimited

M-S SAFARI ARMS Model 81: automatic; same general specs as Matchmaster, except is chambered for .45 ACP or .38 Special mid-range wadcutter; fixed or adjustable walnut target grips; optional Aristocrat rib with extended front sight optional; Model 81L has long slide. Introduced, 1983; dropped, 1985. Used values: Model 81, $500 to $525; Model 81L, $575 to $550.

Model 81 NM has same general specs as Matchmaster, except weighs 28 oz.; 8.2" overall length; Ron Power match sights; blued, Armaloy, Parkerized, stainless steel or electroless nickel. Introduced, 1983; dropped, 1985. Used value, $500 to $550.

Model 81 BP has same general design as Matchmaster; designed for bowling pin matches; extended slide; 6" sight radius; faster slide cycle time; adjustable combat sights; magazine chute. Introduced, 1983; dropped, 1985. Used value, $600 to $625.

Model 81 BP Super has same specs as Model 81 BP, except for shorter, lighter slide. Introduced, 1983; dropped, 1985. Used value, $550 to $600.

M-S SAFARI ARMS Enforcer: automatic; .45 ACP; shortened version of Matchmaster; 3.8" barrel; weighs 40 oz.; overall length, 7.7"; lightweight version weighs 28 oz. Introduced, 1983; dropped, 1985. Used value, $350 to $400.

M-S SAFARI ARMS Unlimited: silhouette pistol; single-shot bolt-action; electronic trigger; any caliber in .308 or smaller; 14-15/16" barrel; weighs 72 oz.; 21½" overall length; fiberglass stock; open iron sights. Introduced, 1983; dropped, 1985. Used value, $500 to $525.

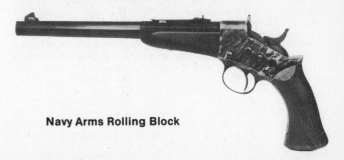

M-S Unlimited Silhouette

M-S SAFARI Unlimited Silhouette Model: bolt-action; single-shot; any caliber smaller than .308; 14-15/16" barrel; 21½" overall length; weighs 72 oz.; fiberglass stock; open iron sights; electronic trigger. Introduced, 1984; dropped, 1985. Used value, $700 to $725.

NAVY ARMS

NAVY ARMS Model 1875: single-action revolver; .357 magnum, .44-40, .45 Colt; 6-rd. cylinder; 7½" barrel; 13½" overall length; smooth European walnut grips; fixed sights, blued or nickel finish. Manufactured in Italy. Introduced, 1955; dropped, 1982. Replica of Remington Model 1875. Used value, $145 to $165.

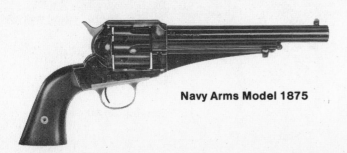

Navy Arms Model 1875

Navy Arms Rolling Block

NAVY ARMS Rolling Block: single-shot; .22 LR, .22 Hornet, .357 magnum; 8" barrel; 12" overall length; color case-hardened frame; brass trigger guard; uncheckered walnut stocks, forearm; blued barrel; adjustable sights. Manufactured in Italy. Introduced in 1965; Hornet chambering dropped, 1975. .22 LR dropped, 1979. Used value, $125 to $145.

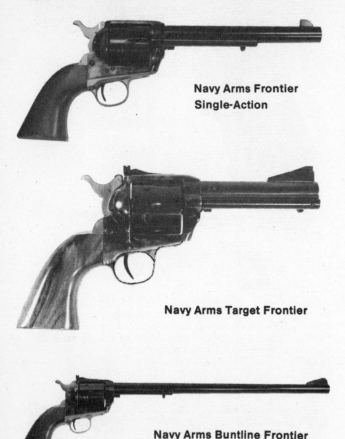

Navy Arms Frontier Single-Action

Navy Arms Target Frontier

Navy Arms Buntline Frontier

NAVY ARMS Frontier Model: .22 LR, .22 WRFM, .357 magnum, .45 Colt; 6-rd. cylinder; 4½", 5½", 7½" barrels; brass grip frame; color case-hardened frame; blued barrel and cylinder; fixed sights; one-piece uncheckered walnut grip. Manufactured in Italy. Introduced 1976; dropped, 1978. Used value, $120 to $130.

Frontier Target Model has the same specs as Frontier, except for ramp front sight, adjustable rear. Introduced, 1976; dropped, 1978. Used value, $175 to $195.

Frontier Buntline has same general specs as Frontier Target Model; made in .357 magnum and .45 Colt only; has 16½" barrel; detachable shoulder stock. Introduced 1976; dropped, 1978. Used value, $200 to $225.

Navy Arms Grand Prix

NAVY ARMS Grand Prix: silhouette pistol; single-shot rolling block; .44 magnum, .30-30, 7mm Special, .45-70; 13¾" barrel; weighs 4 lb.; walnut forend, thumbrest grip; adjustable target sights; adjustable aluminum barrel rib; matte blue finish. Introduced, 1983; dropped, 1985. Used value, $290 to $300.

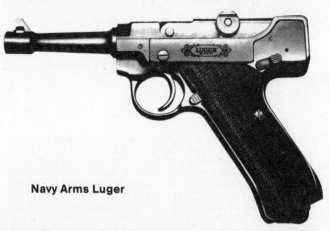

Navy Arms Luger

NAVY ARMS Luger: automatic; .22 LR; 10-rd. magazine; 4" barrel; 9" overall length; weighs 44 oz.; fixed sights; checkered walnut stocks; all-steel construction; blowback toggle action. Made in U.S. Introduced, 1986; dropped, 1987. Used value, $115 to $120. $120.

War Model Luger has same specs as standard version, except has matte finish. Used value, $115 to $120.

Naval Model Luger has same specs as standard model, except has 6" barrel, adjustable rear sight. Used value, $115 to $120.

Artillery Model Luger is same as standard model, except has 8" barrel, adjustable rear sight mounted on barrel. Used value, $115 to $120.

REMINGTON

REMINGTON Model 95: superposed double-barrel derringer; single-action; .41 short rimfire; 3" barrels; 4⅞" overall length. Introduced in 1866; dropped 1935. Prior to 1888 the model was stamped "E. Remington & Sons"; from 1888 to 1910 the derringers were marked "Remington Arms Co."; from 1910 to 1935 guns were marked "Remington Arms-U.M.C. Co." The early styles have a two-armed extractor, long hammer spur. In later models a few have no extractor; majority have sliding extractor, short hammer spur. Available with all-blued finish, full nickel plate, blued barrels, nickel-plated frame; factory engraving; choice of checkered hard rubber, walnut, mother-of-pearl, ivory grips; fixed rear groove sight, front blade integral with top barrel. Value of gun on modern market is primarily as collector item. Used values: plain model, $400 to $450; all nickel, $425 to $475; engraved model with mother-of-pearl or ivory grips, $1000-plus.

Remington Model 95

REMINGTON Model 1901: single-shot, rolling-block action; .22 short, .22 LR, .44 S&W Russian; 10" barrel; 14" overall length; checkered walnut grips, forearm; target sights; blued finish. Manufactured 1901 to 1909. Collector value. Used value, $1200 to $1400.

Remington Model XP-100

Remington Model 51

Remington Model XP-100 Silhouette

REMINGTON Model 51: automatic; .32 auto, .380 auto; 7-rd. magazine; 3½" barrel; 3⅝" overall length; fixed sights; blued finish; hard rubber grips. Introduced in 1918; dropped, 1934. Used value, $300 to $325.

REMINGTON Model XP-100: single-shot pistol; bolt-action; .221 Rem. Fireball only; 10½" barrel; 16¾" overall length; vent rib; blade front sight, adjustable rear; receiver drilled, tapped for scope mounts; one-piece brown nylon stock; blued finish. Introduced in 1963; dropped, 1985. Used value, $250 to $275.

    XP-100 Silhouette has same specs as standard version, except chambered in 7mm BR Rem.; no sights furnished but drilled, tapped for scope mounting; 14¾" barrel; 21¾" overall length. Introduced, 1981; still in production. Used value, $275 to $300.

    XP-100 Varmint Special has same specs as standard model, except is chambered for .223 Rem., cavity in forend allows insertion of weights to adjust balance; marketed in black vinyl case. Introduced, 1985; still in production. Used value, $290 to $315.

Remington Model XP-100 Custom Long Range Model

    XP-100 Custom Long Range Model has same specs as Varmint Special, except is chambered for 7mm-08 Rem., .35 Rem.; has adjustable Bo-Mar rear sight, interchangeable ramp blade front, custom 14½" barrel, custom English walnut stock. Introduced, 1986; still in production. Used value, $650 to $675.

ROSSI

Rossi Double-Action Model

Rossi Double-Action Model: revolver; .22 LR, .32 S&W Long, .38 Special; 5-rd. cylinder in .38 Special, 6 rds. in other calibers; 3", 6" barrels; wood or plastic stocks; ramp front sight, adjustable rear; blued, nickel finish. Manufactured in Brazil; currently imported by Interarms. Introduced in 1965; still in production. Used value, $95 to $105.

ROSSI Model 68: revolver; double-action; .38 Special; 3" barrel; weighs 22 oz.; checkered wood stocks; ramp front sight; low-profile adjustable rear; blued or nickel finish; all-steel frame;

swing-out cylinder. Made in Brazil. Introduced, 1978; still imported by Interarms. Used value, $100 to $110.

    Model 31 has same specs as Model 68, except has 4" barrel. Used value, $95 to $100.

Rossi Model 69

ROSSI Model 69: revolver; double-action; .32 S&W; has same specs as Model 68, except for chambering. Made in Brazil. Introduced, 1978; still imported by Interarms. Used value, $100 to $110.

ROSSI Model 70: revolver; double-action; .22 LR; has same specs as Model 68, except for chambering. Made in Brazil. Introduced, 1978; still imported by Interarms. Used value, $95 to $100.

    Model 51 has same specs as Model 70, except blued only, 6" barrel. Made in Brazil. Introduced, 1978; still imported by Interarms. Used value, $115 to $120.

ROSSI Model 88: revolver; double-action; .38 Special; 5-rd. cylinder; 3" barrel; weighs 32 oz.; 8¾" overall length; stainless steel construction; ramp front sight, drift-adjustable square-notch rear; small frame; matte finish; checkered wood stocks. Introduced, 1983; imported from Brazil by Interarms. Used value, $110 to $125.

Model 89 has same specs as Model 88, except is chambered for .32 S&W. Introduced, 1983; dropped, 1986. Used value, $150 to $160.

Rossi Model 941

Rossi Model 84

ROSSI Model 84: revolver; double-action; .38 Special; 6-rd. cylinder; 3" barrel; 8" overall length; weighs 27½ oz.; stainless steel. Made in Brazil. Introduced, 1984; importation dropped by Interarms, 1986. Used value, $110 to $120.

Model 85 has the same specs as the Model 84, except is equipped with a ventilated rib. Introduced, 1984; dropped, 1986. Used value, $115 to $126.

Rossi Model 851

Rossi Model 951

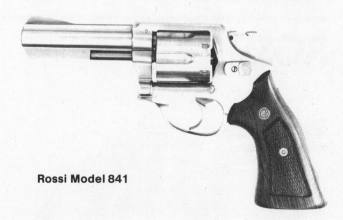

Rossi Model 841

ROSSI Model 951: revolver; .38 Special; 6 rds.; 4" vent-rib barrel; 9" overall length; weighs 30 oz.; checkered hardwood combat stocks; colored insert front sight, adjustable rear; shrouded ejector rod; blued finish. Made in Brazil. Introduced, 1985; still imported by Interarms. Used value, $140 to $150.

Model 941 has same specs as 951, except has solid rib. Used value, $120 to $125.

ROSSI Model 851: revolver; has same specs as Model 951, but is of stainless steel. Introduced, 1985; still imported by Interarms. Used value, $160 to $170.

Model 841 has same specs as 851, except has 3" barrel. Used value, $140 to $150.

ROSSI Model 511: revolver; .22 LR; 6-rd. cylinder; 4" barrel; 9" overall length; weighs 30 oz.; adjustable square-notch rear sight; orange-insert ramp front; checkered wood stocks; stainless steel construction; heavy barrel; integral sight rib; shrouded ejector rod. Made in Brazil. Introduced, 1986; still imported by Interarms. Used value, $150 to $160.

RUGER

RUGER Standard Model: automatic; .22 LR only; 4¾", 6" barrels; with 4¾" barrel, 8¾" overall length; 9-rd. magazine; checkered hard rubber grips, walnut optional; square-notch rear sight adjustable for windage only, fixed wide blade front; blued. Introduced in 1949; dropped, 1982 in favor of Mark II. Until 1951 featured red eagle insignia in grips; changed to black upon death of Alex Sturm. This type has considerable collector value. Used values: red eagle model, $525 to $550; current model, $125 to $150.

Ruger Standard Model (Black Eagle)

Ruger Mark I

RUGER Mark I: automatic, target model; .22 LR only; 5¼" bull barrel, 6⅞" tapered barrel; with 6⅞" barrel, 10⅛" overall length; 9-rd. magazine; adjustable micrometer rear sight, fixed ⅛" blade front; checkered hard rubber grips, walnut optional; blued. Basically the same design as Standard model. Introduced in 1951; dropped, 1982 in favor of Mark II. Early issue had red eagle in grips; changed to black late in 1951. Former has collector value. Used value current model, $150 to $175.

Ruger Mark II

Ruger Mark II Government Target

RUGER Mark II: automatic; .22 LR; 10-rd. magazine; 4¼" 6" barrel lengths; checkered hard rubber stocks; fixed blade front sight, square-notch windage-adjustable rear; new bolt hold-open device, magazine catch; new receiver contours; stainless steel or blued. Introduced, 1982; still in production. Used values: blued, $120 to $130; stainless steel, $160 to $185.

Mark II Target has same general specs as standard model, except has 6⅞" barrel length; .125" blade front sight, adjustable micro click rear; sight radius, 9⅜". Introduced, 1982; still in production. Used values: blued, $150 to $160; stainless steel, $200 to $215.

Mark II Bull Barrel has same specs as Target model, except has 5½" or 10" heavy barrel. Introduced, 1982; still in production. Used values: blued, $150 to $160; stainless, $200 to $215.

Mark II Government Target Model has same specs as Mark II Target Model, except has higher sights, roll-stamped "Government Target Model" on right side of receiver; blued finish. Introduced, 1987; still in production. Used value, $180 to $200.

Ruger Lightweight Single-Six

RUGER Single-Six: single-action revolver; .22 LR, .22 WRFM; 4⅝", 5½", 6½", 9½" barrels; with 4⅝" barrel, overall length, 10"; 6-rd. cylinder; checkered hard rubber grips on early production, uncheckered walnut on later versions; rear sight adjustable for windage only; blued. Introduced in 1953; dropped, 1972. Used value, $200 to $225.

Lightweight Single-Six has same specs as standard model, except cylinder, cylinder frame, grip frame are of alloy; 4⅝" barrel only. Aluminum cylinder has Moultin Hard Coat finish. Some guns have blued steel cylinder. Introduced in 1956; dropped, 1958. Used value, $250 to $275.

Single-Six Convertible has the same general specs as standard model, except for interchangeable cylinders, one handling .22 LR, long, short, the other .22 WRFM cartridges; 5½", 6½" barrels only. Introduced in 1962; dropped, 1972. Used value, $225 to $250.

Super Single-Six Convertible has same general specs as standard model, except for interchangeable .22 LR, .22 WRFM cylinders; ramp front sight, click-adjustable rear sight with protective ribs. Introduced in 1964; dropped, 1972. Used value, $225 to $250.

New Model Super Single-Six is improved version of original model, with new Ruger interlocked mechanism, independent firing pin, music wire springs throughout, hardened chrome-moly steel frame, other improvements; .22 LR, long, short; .22 WRFM in extra cylinder; fully adjustable rear sight, ramp Patridge front; 4⅝", 5½", 6½", 9½" barrels. Introduced in 1973; still in production. Used values: 9½" barrels, $150 to $175; other lengths, $145 to $165.

Ruger New Model Blackhawk

RUGER .357 Magnum Blackhawk: single-action revolver; .357 magnum; 4⅝", 6½", 10" barrels; with 6½" barrel, 12" overall length; 6-rd. cylinder; checkered hard rubber or uncheckered walnut grips; click-adjustable rear sight, ramp front; blued. Introduced in 1955; dropped, 1972. Used values: $225 to $250; 10" barrel, $700 to $800; "Flatty", $300 to $350.

Ruger New Model Blackhawk has same general outward specs as original .357 model, but is chambered for .357 magnum, .41 magnum; 6-rd. cylinder; new Ruger interlocked mechanism; transfer bar ignition; hardened chrome-moly steel frame; wide trigger; music wire springs; independent firing pin; blued. Introduced in 1973; still in production. Used value, $175 to $185.

Ruger .357/9mm has the same specs as .357 magnum, except furnished with interchangeable cylinders for 9mm Parabellum, .357 magnum cartridges. Introduced in 1967; dropped, 1985. Used value, $225 to $235.

RUGER 44 Magnum Blackhawk: single-action revolver; .44 magnum; 6½", 7½", 10" barrels; 12⅛" overall length; 6-rd. cylinder; adjustable rear sight, ramp front; uncheckered walnut grips; blued. Introduced in 1956; dropped, 1963. Used value, $400 to $450; $700 to $800 for 7½" and 10".

Ruger Super Bearcat

RUGER Bearcat: single-action revolver; .22 LR, long, short; 4" barrel; 8⅞" overall length; 6-rd. nonfluted cylinder; fixed sights; uncheckered walnut grips; blued. Introduced in 1958; dropped, 1971. Used value, $225 to $250.

Super Bearcat is improved version of original, but with same general specs. All-steel construction; music wire coil springs throughout; nonfluted engraved cylinder. Introduced in 1971; dropped, 1975. Used value, $250 to $275.

Ruger Super Blackhawk

RUGER Super Blackhawk: single-action revolver; .44 magnum; 7½" barrel; 13⅜" overall length; 6-rd. unfluted cylinder; steel, brass grip frame; uncheckered walnut grips; click adjustable rear sight, ramp front; square-back trigger guard; blued. Introduced in 1959; dropped, 1972. Used value, $300 to $325.

New Model Super Blackhawk has the same exterior specs as original, fires .44 Special as well as .44 magnum cartridge; has new interlocked mechanism; steel grip frame; wide trigger; wide hammer spur; nonfluted cylinder. Introduced in 1973; still in production. Used value, $200 to $225; add $25 for stainless.

Ruger Hawkeye

RUGER Hawkeye: single-shot, single-action pistol; standard frame with cylinder replaced with rotating breech block; 8½" barrel; 14½" overall length; chambered for short-lived .256 magnum cartridge; uncheckered walnut grips; click-adjustable rear sight, ramp front; barrel drilled, tapped for scope mounts; blued. Introduced in 1963; dropped, 1964. Used value, $850 to $900.

RUGER 41 Magnum Blackhawk: single-action revolver; .41 magnum; 4⅝", 6½" barrel; with 6½" barrel, 12" overall length. Has same general specs as Ruger Blackhawk .357 magnum, except for chambering, smaller frame. Introduced in 1965; dropped, 1972. Used value, $275 to $300; New Model, $175 to $200.

RUGER 30 Carbine Blackhawk: single-action revolver; has the same general specs as the pre- and post-1972 Blackhawk models, except for chambering for .30 military carbine cartridge; 7½" barrel only, has fluted cylinder; round-back trigger guard. Introduced in 1967; still in production. Used values: New Model, $165 to $175; Old Model, $250 to $275.

RUGER .45 Colt: single-action revolver; .45 Colt only; 4⅝", 7½" barrel; with 7½" barrel, 13⅛" overall; adjustable micro-click rear sight, ⅛" ramp front; uncheckered walnut grips; Ruger interlocked mechanism; similar in design to Super Blackhawk. Introduced in 1971; still in production. Used values: New Model, $175 to $200; Old Model, $250 to $270.

Ruger .45 Colt/.45 ACP convertible has the same specs as .45 Colt, but is furnished with interchangeable .45 ACP cylinder. Introduced in 1971; dropped, 1983. Used values: New Model, $200 to $220; Old Model, $275 to $300.

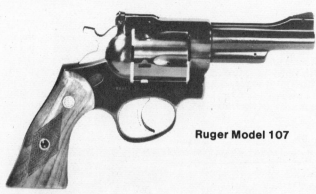

Ruger Model 107

RUGER Police Service-Six Model 107: double-action revolver; .357 magnum; 2¾", 4", 6" barrels; 6" barrel dropped in 1973; with 4" barrel, 9¼" overall length; 6-rd. cylinder; integral ejector rod shroud and sight rib; semi-target-type checkered walnut grips; early model had choice of fixed or adjustable rear sight; blued. Introduced in 1972; dropped, 1987. Used value, $165 to $185.

Ruger Model 108

RUGER Police Service-Six Model 108: double-action revolver; .38 Special. Has exactly the same specs as Model 107, except for chambering. Introduced in 1972; dropped, 1987. Used value, $150 to $160.

RUGER Police Service-Six Model 109: revolver; has same specs as Model 108, except is chambered for 9mm Parabellum. Introduced, 1976; dropped, 1984. Used value, $225 to $250.

RUGER Police Service-Six Model 707: has same specs as Model 107, except is constructed of stainless steel; 4" standard or heavy barrel. Introduced, 1973; dropped, 1987. Used value, $180 to $200.

**Ruger Police
Service-Six Model 708**

RUGER Police Service-Six Model 708: has same specs as Model 108, except for stainless steel construction; 4" standard or heavy barrel. Introduced, 1973; dropped, 1987. Used value, $165 to $175.

RUGER Security-Six Model 117: double-action revolver; .357 magnum; 2¾", 4", 6" barrels; with 4" barrel, 9¼" overall length; 6-rd. cylinder; externally has same general appearance as Model 107. Has hand-checkered semi-target walnut grips; adjustable rear sight, Patridge-type front on ramp; music wire coil springs throughout. Introduced in 1974; dropped, 1985. Used value, $200 to $215.

RUGER Security-Six Model 717: double-action revolver; .357 magnum. Has exactly the same specs as Model 117, except that all metal parts except sights are of stainless steel. Sights are black alloy for visibility. Introduced in 1974; dropped, 1985. Used value, $225 to $250.

RUGER Speed-Six Model 207: double-action revolver; .357 magnum; 2¾", 4" barrel; 9¼" overall length; square-notch fixed rear sight, Patridge-type front; all-steel construction; music wire coil springs throughout; round-butt, diamond-pattern checkered walnut grips; blued. Also available without hammer spur. Introduced in 1974; dropped, 1987. Used value, $175 to $185.

Ruger Speed-Six Model 208

RUGER Speed-Six Model 208: double-action revolver; .38 Special. Has exactly the same specs as Model 207, except for chambering. Introduced in 1974; dropped, 1987. Used value, $160 to $170.

    Speed-Six Model 737 has same specs as Model 207, except made of stainless steel. Introduced, 1975; dropped, 1987. Used value, $185 to $200.

    Speed-Six Model 738 has same specs as Model 208, except made of stainless steel. Introduced, 1975; dropped, 1987. Used value, $175 to $185.

Speed-Six Model 209 has same exact specs as Model 208, but is chambered for 9mm Parabellum cartridge. Introduced, 1981; dropped, 1984. Used value, $235 to $255.

RUGER Speed-Six Model 739: has same specs as Model 209, except is chambered for 9mm Parabellum; made of stainless steel. Introduced, 1981; dropped, 1984. Used value, $225 to $250.

Ruger Redhawk

Ruger Super Redhawk

RUGER Redhawk: revolver, double-action; .41 magnum, .44 magnum; stainless steel; brushed satin finish; 7½" barrel; 13" overall length; 5½" barrel added 1984; Patridge-type front sight, fully adjustable rear; square-butt American walnut grips. Introduced, 1979; still in production. Used value, $295 to $310.

    Super Redhawk has same general specs as standard Redhawk, except has heavy extended frame, Ruger integral scope mounting system; wide hammer spur has been lowered; incorporates mechanical design of GP-100 series; 7½", 9½" barrel lengths; live rubber stocks with goncalo alves inserts; constructed of satin-polished stainless steel. Introduced, 1987; still in production. Used value, $350 to $375.

RUGER New Model Super Blackhawk RMR: revolver; single-action; 6-rd. cylinder; .44 magnum only; same general specs as standard NM Super Blackhawk, except has 10½" untapered bull barrel; longer full length ejector rod, housing; target front, rear sights; weighs 54 oz. Introduced, 1983; dropped, 1984. Used value, $240 to $250.

RUGER New Model Blackhawk 357 Maximum: revolver; single-action; 6-rd. cylinder; .357 Maximum only; same general specs as standard NM Blackhawk; 7½", 10" bull barrel; overall length with 10½" barrel, 16⅞". Introduced, 1983; dropped, 1984. Used value, $275 to $300.

**Ruger New Model Super
Blackhawk Stainless**

RUGER New Model Super Blackhawk Stainless: revolver; single-action; 6-rd. cylinder; .44 magnum; 7½", 10" barrels; uncheckered American walnut stocks; ramp front sight, micro-click-adjustable rear; stainless steel construction; non-fluted cylinder; new interlocked mechanism; steel grip, cylinder frame; square-back, trigger guard; wide serrated trigger; wide hammer spur. Introduced, 1982; still in production. Used value, $240 to $255.

RUGER New Model Bisley Single-Six: revolver; single-action; .22 LR, .32 H&R magnum; 6½" barrel; similar to New Model Single-Six, except frame is styled after Bisley "flat-top"; oval trigger guard; drift-adjustable rear sight, interchangeable front; weighs 41 oz. Introduced, 1985; still in production. Used value, $190 to $200.

Ruger New Model Bisley Blackhawk

RUGER New Model Bisley Blackhawk: revolver; single-action; .357, .41 magnum, .44 magnum, .45 Colt; 7½" barrel; overall length 13"; has same specs as standard New Model Blackhawk, except hammer is lower with deeply checkered wide spur; wide, smooth trigger; longer grip frame; unfluted cylinder; roll engraved with Bisley marksman, trophy. Introduced, 1985; still in production. Used value, $220 to $240.

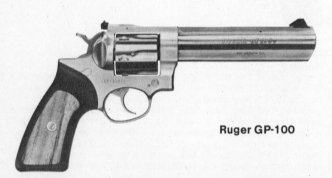

Ruger GP-100

RUGER GP-100: revolver; double-action; .357 magnum; 6-rd. cylinder; 4" heavy barrels, 6" standard; weighs 40 oz.; fully adjustable rear sight, interchangeable blade front; Ruger cushioned grip with goncalo alves inserts; new design action, frame; full-length ejector shroud; satin blue finish or stainless steel. Introduced, 1986; still in production. Used value, $280 to $300.

RUGER GP-141: revolver; .357 magnum; 6-rd. cylinder; 4" heavy barrel; 9.3" overall length; weighs 40 oz.; adjustable rear sight, interchangeable blade front; stocks of live rubber with goncalo alves inserts; all new action, frame; full-length ejector shroud/ Introduced, 1986; still in production. Used value, $240 to $255.

GP-160 has same specs as the GP-141, except has 6" barrel. Introduced, 1986; still in production. Used value, $240 to $260.

GP-161 has same specs as GP-141, except has 6" heavy barrel. Introduced, 1986; still in production. Used value, $240 to $260.

KGP-141 has same specs as GP-141, except is constructed of stainless steel. Introduced 1986; still produced. Used value, $260 to $280.

KGP-160 is the same as the GP-160, except is of stainless steel. Introduced, 1986; still produced. Used value, $260 to $280.

KGP-161 has same specs as GP-161, except is of stainless steel. Introduced, 1986; still produced. Used value, $260 to $280.

Ruger P-85

RUGER P-85: automatic; double-action; 9mmP; 15-rd. magazine; 4.5" barrel; 7.84" overall length; weighs 32 oz.; windage-adjustable square-notch rear sight, square post front; grooved composition stocks; ambidextrous magazine release. Introduced, 1986; still in production. Used value, $200 to $225.

RG

RG Model 57

RG 57: revolver, double-action; .357 magnum; 4" barrel, 9½" overall length; 6-rd. swing-out cylinder; checkered plastic stocks; fixed sights; steel frame. Manufactured in Germany, imported by RG Industries. Introduced, 1977; importation dropped, 1986. Used value, $75 to $85.

RG Model 38S

RG 38S: revolver, double-action; .38 Special; 6-rd. swing-out cylinder; 3", 4" barrel lengths; windage-adjustable rear sight, fixed front; checkered plastic stocks; blued or nickel finish. Introduced, 1977; importation dropped, 1986. Used values: blued, $55 to $60; nickel, $65 to $70.

RG Model 30

RG Model 26

RG 30: revolver, double-action; .22 LR, .32 S&W ; 6-rd. swing-out cylinder; 4" barrel; 9" overall length; windage-adjustable rear sight, fixed front; checkered plastic stocks; blued or nickel finish. Introduced, 1977; importation dropped, 1986. Used values: blued, $45 to $50; nickel, $50 to $52.50.

RG Model 63

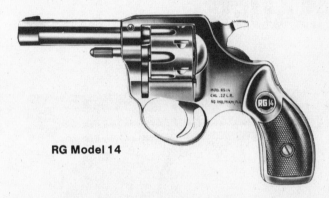

RG Model 14

RG 63: revolver, double-action; .22 LR, .38 Special; 8-rd. cylinder in .22, 6 rds. in .32; 5" barrel; 10¼" overall length; checkered plastic stocks; fixed sights; Western configuration with slide ejector rod; blued or nickel finish. Introduced, 1976; importation dropped, 1986. Used values: .22 LR, $35 to $40; .38 Special, blued, $45 to $50; .38 Special, nickel, $50 to $55.

RG 14: revolver; double-action; .22 LR; 6 rds.; 1¾", 3" barrel lengths; 5½" overall length with shorter barrel; fixed sights; checkered plastic grips; cylinder swings out when pin is removed. Introduced, 1978; importation dropped, 1986. Used value, $20 to $25.

RG Model 88

RG Model 23

RG Model 88: revolver, double-action; .38 Special, .357 magnum; 6-rd. swing-out cylinder; 4" barrel; 9" overall length; checkered walnut stocks; fixed sights; wide spur hammer, trigger; blued. Introduced, 1977; importation dropped, 1986. Used value, $65 to $70.

RG Super 66: revolver, single-action; .22 LR, .22 magnum; 6-rd. cylinder; 4¾" barrel; 10" overall length; checkered plastic stocks; adjustable rear sight, fixed front; slide ejector rod; blued or nickel finish. Introduced, 1977; importation dropped, 1986. Used values: blued, $40 to $45; nickel, $50 to $55.

RG 23: revolver, double-action; has same specs as RG 14, except for central ejector system, not requiring cylinder pin removal. Used value, $25 to $30.

RG 26: automatic; .25 ACP; 6-rd. magazine; 2½" barrel; 4¾" overall length; checkered plastic stocks; fixed sights; blued finish; thumb safety. Introduced in 1977; importation dropped, 1986. Used value, $35 to $40.

RG Model 74

RG 31: revolver; double-action; .32 S&W; 6 rds.; .38 Special, 5 rds.; 2" barrel; 6¾" overall length; fixed sights; checkered plastic grips; blued finish; cylinder swings out when pin is removed. Introduced, 1978; importation dropped, 1986. Used value, $35 to $45.

RG Model 74: revolver, double-action; .22 LR; 6 rds.; 3" barrel; 7¾" overall length; fixed sights; checkered plastic grips; swing-out cylinder with spring ejector; blued finish. Introduced, 1978; importation dropped, 1986. Used value, $50 to $55.

RG Model 39: revolver, double-action; .38 Special, .32 S&W; 6 rds.; 2" barrel; 7" overall length; fixed sights; checkered plastic grips; blued finish; swing-out cylinder; spring ejector. Introduced, 1980; importation dropped, 1986. Used value, $50 to $55.

RG Model 39

SAUER

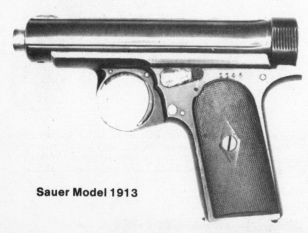

Sauer Model 1913

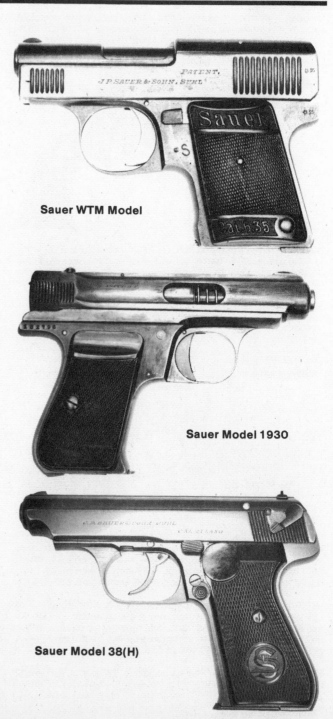

Sauer WTM Model

Sauer Model 1930

Sauer Model 38(H)

SAUER Model 1913: pocket automatic; .32 auto; 3" barrel; 5⅞" overall length; 7-rd. magazine; fixed sights; checkered hard rubber black grips; blued finish. Introduced in 1913; dropped, 1930. Used value, $175 to $200.

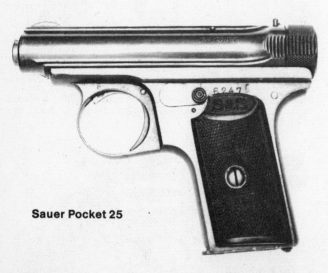

Sauer Pocket 25

SAUER Pocket 25: automatic; same general design as Model 1913, but smaller in size; .25 auto; 2½" barrel; 4¼" overall length; improved grip, safety features. Introduced about 1920; dropped, 1930. Used value, $175 to $200.

SAUER WTM: automatic; .25 auto; 4⅛" overall length; top ejection; 6-rd. magazine; fixed sights; checkered hard rubber grips; fluted slide; blued. Introduced about 1924; dropped about 1927. Used value, $175 to $200.

SAUER Model 28: automatic; .25 auto; 3-15/16" overall length; slanted serrations on slide; top ejection; same general design as WTM, but smaller in size; checkered black rubber grips with Sauer imprint; blued. Introduced about 1928; dropped about 1938. Used value, $175 to $200.

SAUER Model 1930 (Behorden Modell): improved version of the Model 1913; .32 auto; black plastic grips; blued finish. Introduced, 1930; dropped, 1938. Used value, $200 to $240.

SAUER Model 38(H): double-action automatic; .32 auto; 3¼" barrel; 6¼" overall length; 7 rds.; fixed sights; black plastic grips; blued. Introduced in 1938; dropped, 1944. Used value, $250 to $275. Note: .22 and .380 very rare, very valuable.

SIG

SIG Model P210-1

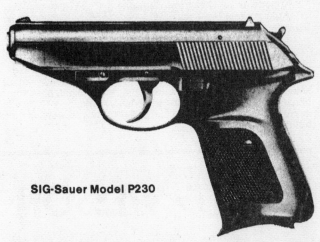

SIG-Sauer Model P230

SIG Model P210-1: automatic; .22 LR, 7.65 Luger, 9mm Luger; 6-rd. magazine; 4¾" barrel; 8½" overall length; checkered hardwood stocks; fixed sights; polished blue finish. Introduced in 1949; still in production. Manufactured in Switzerland. Used value, $1200 to $1300.

  Model P210-2 has the same general specs as Model P210-1, except it is not chambered for .22 LR cartridge; has plastic stocks and a sandblasted finish. Still in production. Used value, $1000 to $1250.

SIG Model 210-5 Target Model: automatic; .22 LR, 7.65 Luger, 9mm Luger; has same specs as Model P210-2, except for 6" barrel, adjustable rear sight, target front, adjustable trigger stop. Introduced, 1950; dropped, 1960. Used value, $1350 to $1400.

  Model P210-6 target model has the same specs as Model P210-2, except for micrometer rear sight, target front, adjustable trigger stop. Still in production. Used value, $1250 to $1350.

SIG-Sauer Model P230: automatic, double-action; .22 LR, .32 auto, .380 auto, 9mm Police; 10-rd. magazine in .22 LR, 8 rds. in .32 auto, 7 rds. in other calibers; 3-3/5" barrel; 6¾" overall length; checkered plastic stocks; fixed sights; blued finish. Introduced, 1977; still in production. Manufactured in West Germany. Currently imported by Sigarms. Used value, $300 to $325.

SIG-Hammerli Model P240

SIG-Sauer Model P220

Sig-Sauer Model P225

SIG-Sauer Model P220: automatic, double-action; .22 LR, 7.65mm Luger, 9mm Luger, .38 Super, .45 auto; 10-rd. magazine in .22 LR, 7 rds. in .45 auto, 9 rds. in other calibers; 4-2/5" barrel; 7-4/5" overall length; checkered plastic stocks; fixed sights; blued. Sold in U.S. as Browning BDA. Also sold by Hawes. Introduced, 1976; still in production. Manufactured in West Germany. Currently imported by Sigarms. Used values: bottom mag release, $375 to $395; side mag release, $450 to $475.

SIG-Sauer Model P225: automatic; double-action; 9mmP; 8-rd. magazine; 3.8" barrel length; weighs 26 oz.; checkered black plastic stocks; blade-type front sight, windage-adjustable rear; squared combat-type trigger guard; shorter, lighter version of P-220; Made in West Germany. Introduced, 1985; still imported by Sigarms. Used value, $450 to $475.

SIG-Sauer P-226: automatic; double-action; has same specs as P-220 model, except has 15-rd. magazine, 4.4" barrel; weighs 26½ oz. Made in West Germany. Introduced, 1986; still imported by Sigarms, Inc. Used value, $450 to $475.

SIG-Hammerli Model P240: automatic; .38 Special; 5-rd. magazine; 6" barrel; 10" overall length; uncheckered European walnut stocks with target thumbrest; micrometer rear sight, post front; blued finish. Manufactured in Switzerland. Introduced, 1975; still in production. Used values: $900 to $1000; .22 conversion unit, $400 to $425.

SIG-Sauer P-226

SMITH & WESSON

S&W New Model No. 3

S&W Target Model

SMITH & WESSON New Model No. 3: revolver, single action; hinged frame; .44 Russian; 4", 5", 6", 6½", 7", 7½", 8" barrel lengths; rounded hard rubber or walnut stocks; fixed or target sights; blued or nickel finish; manufactured 1878 to 1908; has broad collector value. Used value, $1000 to $1100.

No. 3 Frontier model has same general specs as New Model, but chambered for .44-40 Win. only; made in barrel lengths of 4", 5", 6¾". Manufactured 1885 to 1908. Great collector interest. Used value, $1100 to $1200.

No. 3 Target model has same specs as New Model, but is made with 6½" barrel only; available in .32-44 S&W, .38-44 S&W calibers only. Collector interest. Manufactured 1887 to 1910. Used value, $1100 to $1200.

S&W 38 Model

SMITH & WESSON 38: revolver, double-action; hinged frame; .32 S&W; 5-rd. cylinder; 4", 4½", 5", 6", 7", 10" lengths; hard rubber checkered stocks; fixed sights; blued or nickel. Several design variations. Manufactured 1880 to 1911. Some collector value. Used values: serial numbers through 4000, $300 to $350; guns with 8", 10" barrels, $425 to $450; other versions, $160 to $175.

S&W 32

SMITH & WESSON 32: revolver, double-action; hinged frame; .32 S&W; 5-rd. cylinder; 3", 3½", 6" barrel lengths; hard rubber stocks; fixed sights; blued or nickel. Manufactured 1880 to 1919. Early serial numbers have great collector significance, with numbers through 50 bringing as high as $2500. Used value, standard model, $150 to $175.

S&W 44

SMITH & WESSON 44: revolver, double-action; .44 Russian, .38-40; 6-rd. cylinder; 4", 5", 6", 6½" barrel lengths; hard rubber stocks; fixed sights; blued or nickel finish. Manufactured 1881 to 1913. Collector interest based upon number manufactured. Used values: .44 Russian, $750 to $800; .38-40, $1000 to $1200.

Frontier 44 model has same specs as standard .44, except being chambered for .44-40 cartridge only. Manufactured 1881 to 1910. Collector interest. Used value, $750 to $850.

Favorite 44 has same specs as standard model, except for lightweight frame. Manufactured 1881 to 1913. Collector interest. Used value, $1900 to $2000.

S&W Model 1891 Single-Shot

S&W 1891 Target Model

SMITH & WESSON Model 1891: revolver, single-action; hinged frame; .38 S&W; 3¾", 4", 5", 6" barrel lengths; hard rubber stocks; blued or nickel finish; fixed sights. Also available with .22 LR single-shot target barrel. Manufactured 1891 to 1911. Used values: $475 to $500; with single-shot barrel, $800 to $850.

Model 1891 Target Model, First Issue, was built on same frame as standard Model 1891; .22 LR, .32 S&W, .38 S&W; 6", 8", 10" barrel lengths; target sights; square butt hard rubber stocks; blued finish only. Also furnished with .38 S&W barrel, cylinder to convert to single-action revolver. Manufactured 1893 to 1905. Collector interest. Used values: .22 LR single-shot, $325 to $350; .32 S&W single-shot, $850 to $900; .38 S&W single-shot, $850 to $900; combo set with single-shot barrel, single-action conversion unit, $1000 to $1150.

Model 1891 Target Model, Second Issue, has basically the same specs as First Issue, except that it cannot be converted to revolver configuration; redesigned adjustable rear sight; 10" barrel only; .22 LR only. Collector interest. Manufactured 1905 to 1909. Used value, $425 to $450.

SMITH & WESSON Olympic Model: single-shot target model; .22 LR; hinged frame; same general specs as Model 1891 Target, Second Issue, except incorporates lockwork of S&W double-ac-

tion; 10" barrel; prior to 1920, was known as Perfected Target model, but was used by Olympic team that year, leading to name; target-type checkered walnut stocks. Produced 1909 to 1923. Collector interest. Used values: Perfected Target model, $450 to $500; Olympic model, $575 to $625.

S&W Model I

SMITH & WESSON Model I: revolver, double-action, hand-ejector; .32 S&W Long; 3¼", 4¼", 6" barrel lengths; fixed sights; blued or nickel finish; hard rubber stocks. First S&W solid-frame revolver with swing-out cylinder. Manufactured 1896 to 1903. Collector interest. Used value, $350 to $400.

S&W Safety Hammerles

SMITH & WESSON Safety Hammerless: produced for nearly 60 years; discontinued at the start of WWII; also called the New Departure; was the last of S&W's top-break designs. Having no exposed hammer, it was a true pocket gun and would not snag on the draw; could be fired without removing from the pocket. Capacity, 5 rds.; chambered for .32 S&W and .38 S&W; 17 oz., with overall length of 6¼"; anti-snag-type sights with fixed blade front and U-notch rear; checkered Circassian walnut or hard rubber grips with S&W monogram; blued or nickel finish; featured grip safety and the action provided a distinct pause prior to let-off, giving the effect of single-action pull. Used value, $300 to $325.

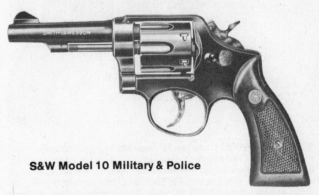

S&W Model 10 Military & Police

SMITH & WESSON Model 10 Military & Police: the backbone of S&W's line; basic frame is termed S&W's K-frame, the derivative source of the K-38, et al. It is, quite possibly, the most popular, widely accepted police duty revolver ever made. Introduced about 1902. Has been made with square-butt checkered walnut stocks and in round-butt pattern with choice of hard rubber or checkered walnut, in barrel lengths from 2" to 6½", as well as Airweight version.

Currently made in .38 Special; capacity, 6 rds.; with 6" barrel, overall length is 11⅛" in square butt, about ¼" less for round butt type; weight is 31 oz.; sights, 1/10" service-type front and square-notch rear, nonadjustable; finishes, blued or nickel. Currently available in standard or heavy-barrel version, nickel or blue finish. Used values: blue, $145 to $150; nickel, $155 to $160. A version of the Military & Police was offered in .32 WCF (also called .32-20), from the introduction of the design to beginning of WWII; current used value: $225 to $250.

SMITH & WESSON Military & Police Target Model: from the early 1920s to 1941 S&W introduced various versions of their M&P, refined for target work; modifications included rear sights adjustable for windage and elevation; with few, if any, exceptions, barrel lengths were 6". Calibers, .38 Special, .32 S&W Long, .22 LR; a few were made up on a custom basis in .32 WCF. All had 6-shot cylinders, with overall lengths of 11⅛"; weights spanned from 32 oz. for the .38 to 35 oz. for the .22 versions. Pre-WWII target models are identifiable by the absence of a rib on the barrel. Stocks, checkered walnut, but not of the later Magna pattern. Used value: $245 to $250 for the .32 S&W Long and .22 LR; $265 to $275 for the .38 Special; up to $600 for the .32 WCF from original factory production.

S&W Model 30 Hand Ejector

SMITH & WESSON Model 30 Hand Ejector: early swing-out cylinder design. Chambered for .32 S&W Long; will accept the .32 S&W and the .32 S&W Long wadcutter load; capacity, 6 rds.; made with 2", 3" and 4" barrels; 6" was available at one time; checkered walnut with medallion; formerly hard rubber; fixed sights, with 1/10" serrated ramp front and square notch rear; overall length, 8" with 4" barrel; weight, 18 oz.; finish, blue or nickel. Introduced in 1903; no longer produced. Used value, $250 to $275.

S&W Perfected Model 38

SMITH & WESSON Perfected Model 38: revolver, double-action; hinged frame; .38 S&W; 5-rd. cylinder; 3¼", 4", 5", 6" barrel lengths; hard rubber or simulated pearl stocks; fixed sights; blued or nickel. Same general specs as S&W 38, except has heavier frame; side latch. Manufactured 1909 to 1920. Some collector value. Used value, $350 to $375.

SMITH & WESSON .22/32 Target: a forerunner of the Model 35; made for the .22 LR, capacity 6 rds.; chambers were countersunk at the heads around 1935, for the high-velocity cartridges introduced at that time; furnished only in blued finish; 6" barrel, with overall length of 10½"; won the "Any Revolver" event at the USRA matches several times; sights, 1/10" or ⅛" Patridge front, square notch rear sight adjustable for windage and elevation; stocks, special, oversize, square-butt pattern in checkered Circassian walnut,

with S&W monogram. Introduced in 1911; superseded by the Model 35 in 1953. Retail price, new, just before WWII, $35. Used value, $400 to $425.

S&W 22/32 Target

S&W 35

SMITH & WESSON 35: automatic; .35 S&W auto; 7-rd. magazine; 3½" barrel, 6½" overall length; uncheckered walnut stocks; fixed sights; blued or nickel finish. Manufactured 1913 to 1921. Collector interest. Used values: $575 to $625; S&W .32 auto, $1250 to $1300.

S&W Military Model of 1917

SMITH & WESSON Military Model of 1917: entry of the U.S. into WWI found facilities unable to produce sufficient quantities of the recently adopted Government Model auto pistol, so approximately 175,000 Smith & Wesson revolvers were manufactured, being chambered to fire the .45 ACP cartridge by means of the two 3-rd. steel clips; also fires the .45 Auto Rim round, introduced after the war, without clips. The wartime units had a duller blued finish and smooth walnut grips, with 5½" barrel; overall length, 10¼"; weight, 36¼ oz. with lanyard ring in the butt. A commercial version remained in production after the end of WWI to the start of WWII, distinguished by a bright blue finish and checkered walnut stocks. Used value: $300 to $325 for military; $425 to $450 for commercial.

SMITH & WESSON Model 31 Regulation Police: similar to the Model 33, except for caliber; chambered for the .32 S&W Long, it

S&W Model 31 Regulation Police

will accept the .32 S&W, .32 Colt New Police; capacity, 6 rds.; barrel lengths, 2", 3", 3¼", 4", 4¼" and 6"; currently, 2", 3" and 4" only. With 4" barrel, 8½" in length, weight 18¾ oz.; fixed sights, with 1/10" serrated ramp front and square notch rear; stocks, checkered walnut, with medallion; finish, blue, nickel. Introduced, 1917; still in production. Used value, $225 to $235.

S&W Model 33 Regulation Police

SMITH & WESSON Model 33 Regulation Police: similar to Model 31, except for its caliber; chambered for the .38 S&W, it will accept the .38 Colt New Police; capacity, 5 rds.; 4" barrel; overall length, 8½"; weight, 18 oz.; fixed sights, with 1/10" serrated ramp front and square notch rear; stocks, checkered walnut, with medallion; blue, nickel finish. Introduced in 1917; dropped, 1974. Used value, $185 to $200.

S&W Police Target Model

SMITH & WESSON Regulation Police, Target Model: target version of the Model 31; 6" barrel and adjustable target sights; made only in .32 S&W Long (accepting .32 S&W and .32 Colt New Police); length, 10¼"; weight 20 oz.; checkered walnut stocks; blued finish; capacity, 6 rds. Introduced, 1917; dropped, 1941. Used value, $350 to $375.

S&W Straightline Single-Shot Target

SMITH & WESSON Straightline Single-Shot Target: chambered for the .22 LR cartridge, the S&W Straightline was made from 1925 through 1936; had a 10" barrel and was 11-5/16" overall; weighing 34¼ oz.; was made only in blued finish; with target sights; stocks were of walnut, usually not checkered. As with many long-discontinued pistols, the current market value is weighted by the interest of dedicated collectors, rather than shooters, most of whom would be disappointed by the accuracy potential of typical examples. Used values: $850 to $900, if complete with original metal case and accessories; $600 to $625 without.

S&W Model 1926 .44 Military

SMITH & WESSON Model 1926 .44 Military: modified version of S&W's earlier New Century hand-ejector, minus the triple-lock feature, but retaining the heavy shroud around the ejector rod; primarily produced in .44 Special, sometimes encountered in .45 Colt, .455 Webley or .455 Ely; barrel lengths, 4", 5" and 6½"; overall length, 11¾" with 6½" barrel; weight, 39½ oz. with 6½" barrel; capacity, 6 rds.; sights, 1/10" service-type front and fixed square-notch rear; stocks, checkered walnut, square or Magna-type, with S&W medallion; finish, blued or nickel. Discontinued at the start of WWII; replaced after the war by the 1950 model. Used values: $400 to $425 in blue; $450 to $475 in nickel; Post WWII, $550 to $650.

S&W Model 1926 Target

SMITH & WESSON Model 1926 Target: a target version of the 1926 Model; rear sight adjustable for windage and elevation; produced from 1926 to the beginning of WWII; replaced after the war by the 1950 Target Model 24. Used values: Pre-War, $650 to $750; Post-War, $550 to $600.

S&W Model 20 38/44 Heavy Duty

SMITH & WESSON Model 20 .38/44 Heavy Duty: six-shot, .38 Special revolver, built on the S&W .44 frame, often termed their N-frame, hence the .38/44 designation; designed to handle high-velocity .38 Special ammunition; barrel lengths, 4", 5" and 6½"; with 5" barrel, overall length, 10⅜" and weight, 40 oz.; fixed sights, with 1/10" service-type (semi-circle) front and square notch rear; stocks, checkered walnut, Magna-type with S&W medallion; finish, blued or nickel. Introduced in 1930; discontinued, 1967. Used values: Pre-War, $425 to $450; Post-War, $250 to $300.

S&W 22/32 Kit Gun

S&W 38/44 Outdoorsman Model 23

SMITH & WESSON .22/32 Kit Gun: a compact, outdoorsman's revolver, based on the .22/32 Target, modified by a round-butt stock pattern and 4" barrel; made with 1/10" Patridge or pocket revolver front sight, with rear sight adjustable for elevation and windage; checkered Circassian walnut or hard rubber stocks; blued or nickel finishes; barrel length, 4"; overall length, 8" with round butt (small or special oversized target square-butt stocks were offered on special order); weight, 21 oz.; capacity, 6 rds.; chambered only for the .22 LR. Introduced in 1935; replaced in 1953 by the Model 34. Used value, $225 to $250.

SMITH & WESSON .38/44 Outdoorsman Model 23: introduced in 1930 as a companion to the Model 20; reintroduced about 1950 with ribbed barrel and Magna-type stocks; was made only in blue, with 6½" barrel; plain Patridge ⅛" front sight, S&W micrometer-click rear adjustable for windage and elevation; capacity, 6 rds. of .38 Special; overall length, 11¾"; weight, 41¾ oz. Discontinued, 1967. Used values: Pre-War, $550 to $600; Post-War, $450 to $475.

S&W Model 27 .357 Magnum

S&W Model 32 Terrier

SMITH & WESSON Model 32 Terrier: essentially a 2" version of the Model 30 Hand Ejector; stocks, round-butt pattern in checkered walnut with medallion; blued finish standard, nickel at extra cost; length, 6¼"; weight, 17 oz.; capacity, 5 rds. of .38 S&W (or .38 Colt New Police); fixed sights, with 1/10" serrated ramp front and square notch rear. Introduced in 1936; discontinued, 1974. Used value, $225 to $250.

SMITH & WESSON Model 27 .357 Magnum: introduced with the .357 magnum cartridge in 1935; essentially the same as the .38 Special, except case is lengthened by 0.135", loaded to substantially higher pressures in order to obtain higher velocities. (The case was lengthened to prevent its use in guns chambered for the .38 Special round.) Pre-WWII Model 27s offered in barrel lengths of 3½", 5", 6", 6½", 8⅜" and 8¾"; could be custom-ordered with barrels of any length up to 8¾"; weights were 41 oz. for 3½", 42½ oz. for 5", 44 oz. for 6", 44½ oz. for 6½" and 47 oz. for 8⅜"; overall length, 11⅜" for 6" barrel; could be ordered with any of S&W's standard target sights; the 3½" version usually was furnished with a Baughman quick-draw sight on a plain King ramp; finely checkered top strap matched barrel rib, with vertically grooved front and rear grip straps and grooved trigger; capacity, 6 rds. of .357 magnum; also could fire .38 Special; S&W bright blue or nickel finishes; checkered Circassian walnut stocks, with S&W medallion in choice of square or Magna type. Retail price at beginning of WWII, $60. Post-WWII production was similar, with the hammer redesigned to incorporate a wider spur and inclusion of the present pattern of S&W click micrometer rear sight; blue or nickel finish. Still in production. Model 27 was the first centerfire revolver with recessed cylinder; the .357 required registration with registration no. stamped in yoke of frame; about 6000 made before registration stopped. The papers, themselves, have some collector value without the gun!

Used values: up to $850 to $1000 for pre-WWII model with registration papers furnished at that time (subtract $150 if no papers); $350 to $375 for post-war versions.

S&W Model 17 K-22 Masterpiece

SMITH & WESSON Model 17 K-22 Masterpeice: redesigned version of Model 16. Introduced around 1947; still in production. Postwar production added the refinement of a broad barrel rib, intended to compensate for weight variations between the three available calibers: .38 Special, .32 S&W Long and .22 LR. Likewise added were the redesigned hammer, with its broad spur and thumb-tip relief notch, an adjustable anti-backlash stop for the trigger and the Magna-type grips developed in the mid-Thirties to help cushion the recoil of the .357 magnum. 6" barrel is standard, with 8⅜" available. Capacity, 6 rds.; overall length, 11⅛" with 6" barrel; loaded weight, 38½ oz. for 6"; 42½ oz. for 8⅜". Blue finish only. Currently offered in .22 LR only. Used values: 6" barrel, $250 to $275; 8⅜" barrel, $275 to $295; add $100 for Pre-WWII.

SMITH & WESSON Victory Model: WWII version of the Model 10; usually in 4" barrel length, Parkerized with sandblasted or brushed finish, smooth (non-Magna) walnut stocks and lanyard ring in square butt; usually in .38 Special, though a version termed the .38-200 was made for the British forces. The Victory Model is inferior in external fit, finish to commercial production, though collectors may be willing to pay prices slightly higher than those listed for the standard Model 10 revolver. Used value, $155 to $175.

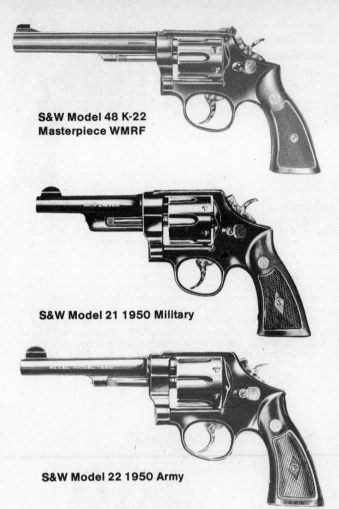

S&W Model 48 K-22 Masterpiece WMRF

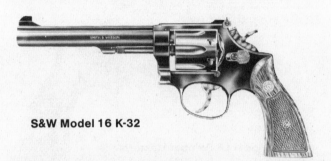

S&W Model 16 K-32

SMITH & WESSON Model 16 K-32 Masterpiece: Originating as a target version of the hand-ejector in .32 S&W Long about 1935, and dropped at the beginning of WWII, the Model 16 appeared in its present form in the late Forties, designated the K-32 as a companion to the K-22 and K-38. A double-action revolver, holding 6 rds. of .32 S&W Long, it was made only with 6" barrel and blued finish. Walnut, Magna-pattern stocks with medallions were standard, factory target stocks in exotic woods available as options. Other options included target hammer, target trigger, red-insert front sight, white-outline rear sight and choice of Patridge or Baughman front sights. Dropped in 1973. Used values: .32 hand-ejector model, $650 to $675; post-war version, $450 to $500.

S&W Model 21 1950 Military

S&W Model 22 1950 Army

SMITH & WESSON Model 22 1950 Army: post-WWII version of the Model '17, with minor design refinements; remained in production until 1967; has the usual semi-circular front sight and U-shaped notch rear sight milled in the top of the receiver strap, the same as the M'17. A target version was made, having adjustable rear sight. Used value, $550 to $600.

S&W Model 14 Single Action

SMITH & WESSON Model 14 K-38 Masterpiece: double-action revolver; .38 Special only; 6", 8⅜" barrels; with 6" barrel, 11⅛" overall length; 6-rd. swing-out cylinder; built on S&W K frame; micrometer rear sight; ⅛" Patridge-type front; hand-checkered service-type walnut grips; blued. Introduced in 1947; dropped, 1983. Used values: 6" barrel, $250 to $275; 8⅜" barrel, $265 to $285.

Model 14 Masterpiece Single Action has the same general specs as standard Model 14, except for being single-action only; has target hammer, target trigger. Used values: 6" barrel, $225 to $250; 8⅜" barrel, $245 to $265.

SMITH & WESSON Model 48 K-22 Masterpiece WMRF: a modification of the K-22 Model 17; chambered to accept the .22 WMRF cartridge; available with 4" barrel, without being distinctly designated as a Combat Masterpiece, and in the 6" and 8⅜" lengths, as well; weight, with the 6" barrel, 39 oz.; auxiliary cylinder was offered to permit the use of this model with the .22 LR cartridge. The quoted price of this accessory was $35.50, as of 1969. Used values: with 6" barrel, $250 to $275; $275 to $300 for 8⅜" barrel; add $100 if equipped with .22 LR as well as .22 WMRF cylinder.

SMITH & WESSON Model 21 1950 .44 Military: post-WWII version of the S&W Model 1926 with minor design refinements; made in 5" barrel; chambered for the .44 Special (also handles the .44 Russian); length, 10¾"; weight, 36¼ oz.; fixed sights; finish, blued or nickel; stocks, checkered walnut, Magna-type, with S&W medallion. Discontinued, 1967. Used value, $550 to $600.

S&W 1950/1955 Model 25 Target

SMITH & WESSON 1950/1955 Model 25 .45 Target: introduced in 1950 as a companion to the 1950 Model 24 .44 Target; identical except being chambered for .45 ACP/Auto Rim. The 1950 .45 Target was redesigned in 1955 to become the 1955 .45 Target, superseding the 1950 version. Modifications consisted of a heavier barrel with broad rib, similar to that of the K-38; S&W target stocks in place of the Magna-type; a target hammer and broad, target-type trigger. Standard barrel length, 6½"; no factory production of 4" has been reported, although some owners have had them cut down to 4" length; capacity, 6 rds.; overall length, 11⅞"; weight 45 oz.; sights, ⅛" plain Patridge front, S&W micrometer-click rear, adjustable for windage and elevation; finish, blue; stocks, checkered walnut, pattern as noted, with S&W medallion. Dropped, 1983. Used value, $300 to $325; M1950 version, $550 to $600. The .45 Colt made on special order only.

S&W Model 24

lengths, 2" and 4"; stocks, checkered walnut Magna-type, round or square butt; weight, 18 oz.; with 2" barrel and round butt; overall length, 6⅞" (2", round butt); sights, fixed ⅛" serrated ramp front, square-notch rear. Introduced about 1952; still produced. Used values: $200 to $225, blue; $235 to $245, nickel; subtract $25 for 4".

SMITH & WESSON Model 24 1950 .44 Target: introduced in 1950 as a refined version of the 1926 Target Model; customarily produced with 6½" barrel and Patridge-type front sight having vertical rear blade surface, with S&W micrometer-click rear sight adjustable for windage and elevation; limited quantity was produced in a 4"-barreled version, with Baughman quick-draw front sight on serrated ramp, with the same type of rear sight. As with most S&W target models, blued finish was standard, although a few specimens have been custom-ordered in nickel. Chambered for the .44 Special (also handles the shorter .44 Russian cartridge); capacity, 6 rds.; with 4" barrel, overall length is 9¼" and weight is 40 oz. Discontinued about 1966. Used values: $550 to $600 for the 6½" barrel; $600 to $650 for the 4" barrel.

Model 24 (1983) was limited to production of 7500 guns; .44 Special only, built to specs of original model; 4", 6½" barrels; grooved top strap; barrel rib. Made in 1983 only. Used values: 4" barrel, $270 to $290; 6½" barrel, $300 to $310.

S&W Model 18 Combat Masterpiece

S&W Model 34 1953

S&W Model 15 Combat Masterpiece

SMITH & WESSON Model 15 .38 Combat Masterpiece: it took some years after WWII to reestablish commercial production and begin catching up with civilian demands at S&W. By the early Fifties, the situation was bright enough to warrant introducing a 4" version of the K-38, which was designated the .38 Combat Masterpiece. Its only nominal companion was the .22 Combat Masterpiece and no attempt was made to match loaded weights, as in the K-series; the .38 weighing 34 oz. empty, compared to 36½ oz. for the .22 version. Barrel ribs were more narrow than the K-series and front sights were of the Baughman, quick-draw ramp pattern, replacing the vertical surface of the K-series Patridge-type; overall length, 9⅛"; finish, blue or nickel; capacity, 6 rds.; chambered for .38 Special. Used values: $200 to $225; $225 to $250, nickel.

SMITH & WESSON Model 18 .22 Combat Masterpiece: companion to the .38 Combat Masterpiece Model 15, with Baughman ⅛" quick-draw front sight on plain ramp and S&W micrometer-click rear sight adjustable for windage and elevation; chambered for .22 LR, handling .22 long and .22 short, as well; capacity, 6 rds.; length of barrel, 4"; overall length, 9⅛"; loaded weight, 36½ oz.; stocks, checkered walnut, Magna-type, with S&W medallion; finish, blue only; available options include broad-spur target hammer, wide target trigger; hand-filling target stocks; red front sight insert and white outlined rear sight notch. Dropped, 1985. Used value, $225 to $245.

SMITH & WESSON Model 12 Military & Police Airweight: similar to the Model 10, except for the incorporation of an aluminum alloy frame; made only in .38 Special, with capacity of 6 rds.; barrel

SMITH & WESSON Model 34 1953 .22/32 Kit Gun: updated version of the earlier .22/32 Kit Gun, the 1953 version — still in production — features a ribbed barrel, micrometer rear sight adjustable for elevation and windage; Magna-type stocks; flattened cylinder latch employed on many of S&W's later small pocket designs. Available barrel lengths, 2" and 4"; overall length, 8" with 4" barrel and round butt; weight, 22½ oz. in 4" barrel; stocks, checkered walnut, round or square butt; sights, 1/10" serrated ramp front, square-notch rear adjustable for windage and elevation. Used value, $225 to $250

S&W Model 36 Chiefs Special

SMITH & WESSON Model 36 Chiefs Special: double-action revolver; descended from Model 32 Terrier Model, with longer cylinder. Round-butt pattern of grips is most common, although square-butt design was available. Barrel lengths, 2", 3"; with 3" barrel, 7½" overall length; fixed square-notch rear sight, 1/10" serrated ramp front; 5-rd. cylinder; .38 Special only; blued or nickel. Introduced in 1952; still in production. Used values: blued, $200 to $225; nickel, $225 to $245.

S&W Model 60 Stainless
Chiefs Special

Chiefs Special Model 60 has same specs as Model 36, except has 2" barrel; round butt only; stainless steel construction. Used value, $225 to $250.

S&W Model 37 Chiefs
Special Airweight

SMITH & WESSON Model 37 Chiefs Special Airweight: lightweight version of the Model 36, incorporating aluminum alloy frame, reducing weight to 14 oz.; general specs are the same as for Model 36; finish, blue, nickel. Used values: blue, $200 to $225; nickel, $225 to $235.

S&W Model 43 Airweight

SMITH & WESSON Airweight Kit Gun Model 43: identical to Model 34, except for aluminum alloy frame; made only in 3½" barrel; weight, 14¼ oz.; square-butt stocks of checkered walnut; overall length, 8"; blue or nickel finish. Discontinued about 1974. Collector value. Used values: blue, $275 to $300; nickel, $300 to $325.

Model 63 has same specs as Model 34 1953, except is of stainless steel construction; 4" barrel only. Introduced, 1977; still in production. Used value, $220 to $230.

S&W Model 40 Centennial

SMITH & WESSON Model 40 Centennial: swing-out version of earlier, top-break Safety Hammerless; has hammerless design, with grip safety. In .38 Special only, with capacity of 5 rds.; barrel length 2", with overall length of 6½"; weight, 19 oz.; fixed sights with 1/10" serrated ramp front and square-notch rear. Introduced in 1953; dropped, 1974. Collector value. Used values: Airweight (Model 42), blue, $400 to $425; nickel, $500 to $525.

S&W Model 35 1953

SMITH & WESSON Model 35 1953 .22/32: a redesign of the .22/32 which had been developed on the .32 Hand Ejector. Departing from the .22/32 Target Model, it added the post-war Magna stocks; a rib atop the barrel; and modern S&W front sight and micrometer rear sight. Chambered for the .22 LR, capacity, 6 rds; barrel length, 6", with 10½" overall length; weight 25 oz.; finished only in blue. Introduced in 1953; dropped, 1974. Collector value. Used value, $375 to $400.

S&W Model 28 Highway Patrolman

SMITH & WESSON Model 28 Highway Patrolman: introduced in 1954 as a functional version of the Model 27 minus the cost-raising frills such as the checkered top strap; made only in 4" and 6" barrel lengths; overall length, 11¼" with 6" barrel; weight, 41¾ oz. with 4" barrel; 44 oz. with 6" barrel; sights, ⅛" Baughman quick-draw front on plain ramp, S&W micrometer-click rear, adjustable for elevation and windage; stocks, checkered walnut, Magna-type with S&W medallion; target stocks at extra cost; finish, blued with sandblast stippling on barrel rib and frame edging. Still in production. Used value, $215 to $225.

Model 38 Bodyguard Airweight

**S&W Model 19
Combat Magnum**

SMITH & WESSON Model 38 Bodyguard Airweight: features a shrouded hammer that can be cocked manually for single-action firing; .38 Special only; capacity, 5 rds.; length of barrel, 2"; overall length, 6⅜"; weight 14½ oz.; fixed sights, with 1/10" serrated ramp front and square-notch rear. Introduced in 1955; still in production. Used values: blue, $235 to $255; nickel, $275 to $285.

Bodyguard Model 49 has same specs as Model 38, except is of steel construction; weighs 20½ oz.; blued or nickel finish. Used values: blued finish, $200 to $215; nickel, $215 to $225.

SMITH & WESSON Model 19 Combat Magnum: introduced about 1956; built on the lighter S&W K-frame, as used on the K-38, et al., rather than on the heavier N-frame, used for the Model 27 and 28; its six-shot cylinder is chambered for the .357 magnum cartridge; capable of firing .38 Special ammo; finish, S&W bright blue or nickel; stocks, checkered goncalo alves with S&W medallion; sights, ⅛" Baughman quick-draw front plain ramp, S&W micrometer-click rear, adjustable for windage and elevation; available with 2½", 4" or 6" barrel; with 4" barrel, length is 9½" and weight is 35 oz. Used value, $215 to $235.

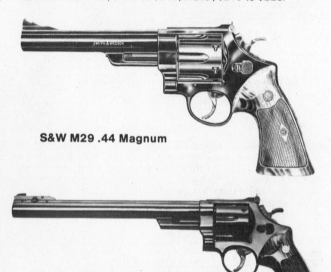

S&W M29 .44 Magnum

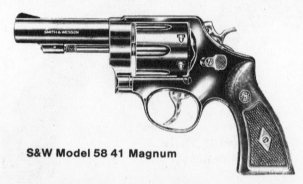

S&W Model 58 41 Magnum

SMITH & WESSON Model 58 .41 Magnum: also known as the .41 Military & Police, this is a fixed-sight version of the Model 57; available only in 4" barrel; in blue or nickel; capacity, 6 rds.; overall length, 9¼"; weight, 41 oz.; sights, ⅛" serrated ramp front, square-notch rear; stocks, checkered walnut, with S&W medallion, in Magna pattern. No longer produced. Used values: blue, $300 to $325; nickel, $325 to $350.

S&W Model 29 Silhouette

**S&W Model 53
.22 Magnum**

SMITH & WESSON Model 29 .44 Magnum: introduced in 1956. As with the Model 27, the Model 29 was developed to take a new cartridge developed by lengthening the .44 Special case by 0.125" — this being intended to prevent use of .44 magnum ammo in guns chambered for the .44 Special. The .44 magnum is loaded to pressures approximately twice that of the .44 Special. The 6-shot cylinder also will handle .44 Special or .44 Russian. Barrel lengths, 4", 5", 6½", 8⅜"; length, 11⅞" with 6½" barrel; weighs 43 oz. with 4", 47 oz. with 6½" and 51½ oz. with 8⅜" barrel; sights, ⅛" red ramp front, S&W micrometer-click rear, adjustable for elevation and windage; stocks, target type of goncalo alves, with S&W medallion. Broad, grooved target trigger, wide-spur target hammer. Finish, bright blue or nickel. Used values: $350 to $375; 6" to 4", $345 to $365; Model 629 stainless, $350 to $375; 5" rare, $750 to $800.

Model 29 Silhouette has same general specs as standard model, except has 10⅝" barrel; oversize target-type stocks of checkered goncalo alves; 4-position click-adjustable front sight; weighs 58 oz.; 16⅛" overall length. Introduced, 1983; still in production. Used values: with presentation case, $350 to $365; without case, $300 to $315.

SMITH & WESSON Model 53 .22 Magnum: starting in the late Fifties there was considerable interest in converting K-22s to centerfire wildcat (i.e., nonstandard cartridge) configurations, usually being chambered for a shortened version of the .22 Hornet, known as the .22 Harvey K-Chuck. With the intent of capitalizing on this interest, S&W introduced the .22 Rem. CFM or centerfire magnum cartridge — also termed the .22 Jet — and the Model 53, chambered for it. The .22 Jet was a necked-down .357 case, designed to use a bullet of .222 to .223" diameter. The Model 53 was supplied with 6 chamber bushings, adapting it for firing .22 rimfire ammo, by means of repositioning the striker on the hammer. Alternatively, a standard .22 LR cylinder was offered as a factory-fitted accessory, at about $35.30, for interchanging with the .22 Jet cylinder. Capacity, 6 rds.; barrel, 4", 6" and 8⅜"; with 6" barrel, length was 11¼" and weight, 40 oz.; finish, blued only; stocks, checkered walnut with S&W medallion; sights, ⅛" Baughman ramp front, S&W micrometer-click rear, adjustable for elevation and windage; Model 53 was dropped from production in 1974, having been introduced about 1960. Used values: $550 to $600 if complete with chamber inserts and/or fitted .22 LR cylinder; $50 higher with 8⅜" barrel.

S&W Model 57 41 Magnum

S&W Model 51 Kit Gun MRF

SMITH & WESSON Model 51 1960 .22/32 Kit Gun M.R.F.: identical to the Model 43, except that it is chambered for the .22 WRFM cartridge and weighs 24 oz.; has an all-steel frame, 3½" barrel. Introduced in 1960; dropped, 1974. Retail, new, was $105.50 in blue, $113.50 in nickel. Used value, $325 to $350, blue; $350 to $360, nickel.

S&W Model 41 Auto Target

SMITH & WESSON .22 Auto Target Model 41: introduced about 1957; still in production. Chambered for the .22 LR, the Model 41 was at one time also available in .22 short for international competition; capacity, either caliber, 10 rds. in magazine; barrel lengths, 5" or 7⅜". With 7⅜" barrel, overall length is 12"; weight is 43½ oz. Sights, ⅛" undercut Patridge-type in front, S&W micrometer-click rear, adjustable for windage and elevation; stocks, checkered walnut with modified thumbrest, usable by right- or left-handed shooters; finish, S&W bright blue, only; trigger, ⅜" wide, grooved, with adjustable stop; detachable muzzle brake was supplied with 7⅜" barrel only (muzzle brake recently dropped). Used value, $320 to $340.

The Model 41 was also made in a heavy-barrel variant, with or without an extendable front sight and in a less elaborate version, called the **Model 46,** with moulded nylon stocks. Values are approximately the same as quoted here even though the Model 46 is somewhat more collectible due to lower production figures. Used value, $350 to $400.

Model 41 .22 Match has 5½" heavy barrel, weighs 44½ oz.; 9" overall length; .22 LR; 10-rd. clip; checkered walnut stocks, modified thumbrest; ⅛" Patridge front sight on ramp base, S&W micro-click adjustable rear; grooved trigger; adjustable trigger stop; bright blued finish; matted top area. Extension front sight added, 1965. Introduced, 1963; still in production. Used value, $325 to $350.

SMITH & WESSON Model 57 .41 Magnum: introduced as a deluxe companion to the Model 58, both being chambered for a new cartridge developed especially for them at that time, carrying a bullet of .410" diameter. The old .41 Long Colt cartridge cannot

be fired in guns chambered for the .41 magnum, nor can any other standard cartridge. Capacity, 6 rds.; barrel lengths, 4", 6" and 8⅜"; finish, bright blue or nickel; with 6" barrel, length is 11⅜" and weight is 48 oz. Sights, ⅛" red ramp front, S&W micrometer-click rear, adjustable for elevation and windage, with white-outline notch; stocks, special oversize target-type of goncalo alves, with S&W medallion; wide, grooved target trigger and broad-spur target hammer; blued, nickel. Introduced in 1964; still in production. Used values: 4" and 6" barrels, $265 to $285; 8⅜" barrel, $300 to $325.

S&W Model 61 Escort

SMITH & WESSON Model 61 Escort: automatic; hammerless; .22 LR only; 2.175" barrel; 4-13/16" overall length; 5-rd. magazine; thumb safety on left side of grip; fixed sights; cocking indicator; checkered plastic grips; blued or nickel finish. Introduced in 1970; dropped, 1973. Collector value. Used values: blued, $185 to $210; nickel finish, $225 to $250.

S&W 32 Auto

SMITH & WESSON .32 Auto: successor to S&W's original auto pistol, which was chambered for the .35 S&W auto caliber cartridge, this gun was chambered for the common .32 auto or 7.65mm cartridge; it has a magazine capacity of 8 rds., barrel length of 4" and weight of about 28 oz., measuring 7" overall; walnut, stocks, not checkered; finish, blued or nickel. Features included an unusual grip-safety, just below the trigger guard. Introduced in 1924; discontinued, 1937. Collector value. Used value, $1000 to $1200.

S&W Model 39

SMITH & WESSON Model 39 9mm Auto: introduced in 1954; dropped, 1981. Furnished with two 8-rd. magazines; barrel length, 4"; length overall, 7-7/16"; weight, 26½ oz., without magazine; sights, ⅛" serrated ramp front, rear sight adjustable only for windage, with square notch; stocks, checkered walnut, with S&W medallion; finish, S&W bright blue or nickel. During the first dozen years of its production, a limited number of Model 39s were made with steel frames, rather than the standard aluminum alloy type, currently commanding premium prices, as noted here. Collector value. Used values: blued, $275 to $300; nickel, $285 to $310; steel-frame model, $950 to $1000.

S&W Model 52 Target

SMITH & WESSON Model 52 .38 Target Auto: introduced in 1961; still in production. Designed to fire a mid-range loading of the .38 Special cartridge, requiring a wadcutter bullet seated flush with the case mouth; action is straight blowback, thus not suited for firing of high-velocity .38 Special ammo; magazine holds 5 rds.; barrel, 5"; length overall, 8⅝"; weight, 41 oz.; sights, Patridge-type front on ramp, S&W micrometer-click rear, adjustable for elevation and windage; stocks, checkered walnut, with S&W medallion; available only in blue. Used value, $450 to $475.

S&W Model 59

SMITH & WESSON Model 59 9mm Auto: similar to the Model 39, except for incorporation of a staggered-column magazine holding 14 rds.; weight, 27½ oz. without magazine; stocks, checkered, high-impact moulded nylon. Like the Model 39, the 59 offers the option of carrying a round in the chamber, with hammer down, available for firing via a double-action pull of the trigger. Other specs are the same as for the Model 39; blue or nickel finish. Introduced in the early Seventies; dropped, 1983. Used values: $275 to $300 for blue finish; $285 to $310 for nickel.

S&W Model 66 Combat Magnum

SMITH & WESSON Model 66 Combat Magnum: revolver; double-action; stainless steel; .357 magnum; 6-rd. cylinder; 2½", 4", 6" barrel lengths; 9½" overall with 4" barrel; checkered goncalo alves target stocks; Baughman Quick Draw front sight on plain ramp, micro-click adjustable rear; grooved trigger, adjustable stop; satin finish. Introduced, 1971; still in production. Used value, $225 to $235.

S&W Model 67 K-38

SMITH & WESSON Model 67 K-38: revolver; double-action; .38 Special; 6-rd. cylinder; stainless steel; marketed as Combat Masterpiece; 4" barrel; 9½" overall length; service-style checkered American walnut stocks; Baughman Quick Draw front sight on ramp, micro-click adjustable rear; square butt with grooved tangs; grooved trigger, adjustable stop. Introduced, 1972; still in production. Used value, $215 to $220.

S&W Model 439

S&W Model 439

S&W Model 64

SMITH & WESSON Model 439: automatic; double-action; 9mm Parabellum; 8-rd. magazine; has same general specs as Model 39, except that rear sight has protective shields on both sides of sight blade, new trigger-actuated firing pin lock, magazine disconnector, new extractor design; blued or nickel finish. Introduced in 1980; still in production. Used values: blued, $290 to $310; nickel finish, $300 to $320.

    Model 639 has same specs as Model 439, except is manufactured of stainless steel. Introduced, 1981; still in production. Used value, $320 to $345.

SMITH & WESSON Model 64: revolver; double-action; .38 Special; 6-rd. cylinder; 4" barrel; weighs 30½ oz.; 9½" overall length; Military & Police design; stainless steel construction; service-style checkered American walnut stocks; fixed, serrated front ramp sight, square-notch rear; square butt; satin finish. Introduced, 1981; still in production. Used value, $180 to $190.

SMITH & WESSON Model 547: revolver; double-action; 9mm Parabellum; 3", 4" heavy barrel; 9⅛" overall length with 4" barrel; checkered square-butt Magna Service stocks with 4" barrel; checkered round-butt target stocks with 3"; serrated ramp front sight, fixed square-notch rear; half-spur hammer; K-frame design; special extractor system; blued finish. Introduced, 1981; no longer in production. Used value, $200 to $225.

S&W Model 459

S&W Model 659

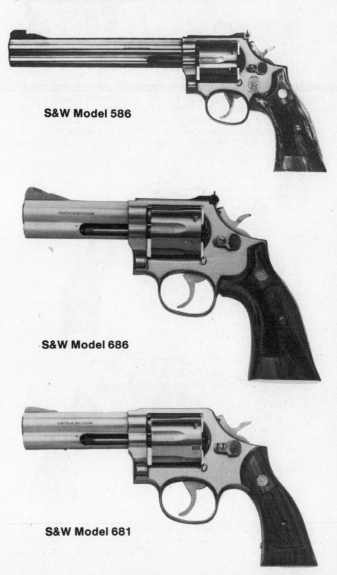

S&W Model 586

S&W Model 686

S&W Model 681

SMITH & WESSON Model 459: automatic, double-action; 9mm Parabellum; 14-rd. magazine; has same general specs as Model 439, except for increased magazine capacity, straighter, longer grip frame; blued or nickel finish. Introduced, 1980; still in production. Used values: blued, $300 to $320; nickel finish, $310 to $330.

    Model 659 has same specs as Model 459, except is of stainless steel. Introduced, 1981; still in production. Used value, $335 to $355.

SMITH & WESSON Model 586: revolver; double-action; marketed as Distinguished Combat Magnum; .357 magnum; 4" heavy, 6" heavy barrels; goncalo alves target stocks; Baughman red ramp front sight, micrometer-click rear; L-frame design; ejector rod shroud; combat-type trigger; semi-target hammer; blued, or nickel. Introduced, 1981; still in production. Used value, $245 to $265.

    Model 581 has same specs as Model 586, except has fixed sights, 4" barrel only. Introduced, 1981; still in production. Used value, $235 to $245.

    Model 686 has same specs as Model 586, except is of stainless steel construction. Introduced, 1981; still in production. Used value, $245 to $255.

    Model 681 has same specs as Model 686, but has fixed sights. Introduced, 1981; still in production. Used value, $215 to $225.

S&W Model 469

SMITH & WESSON Model 469: automatic; cut-down version of Model 459; 3½" barrel; weighs 26 oz.; 7⅞" overall length; 12-rd. magazine; accepts 14-rd. 459 magazine; cross-hatching on front of trigger guard, backstrap; plastic pebble-grain grips; curved finger-extension magazine; bobbed hammer; sandblasted blued finish. Introduced, 1983; still in production. Used value, $315 to $325.

S&W Model 6 50

S&W Model 651

SMITH & WESSON Model 650: revolver; double-action; .22 WRFM; 6-rd. cylinder; 3" barrel; similar to Model 34; rounded butt; fixed sights; stainless steel construction. Introduced, 1983; no longer in production. Used value, $215 to $225.

    Model 651 has same specs as Model 650, except has 4" barrel, square butt, adjustable rear sight. Introduced, 1983; no longer in production. Used value, $235 to $245.

S&W Model 624

SMITH & WESSON Model 624: revolver; .44 Special; 6-rd. cylinder; 4", 6" barrel lengths; with 4" barrel, overall length is 9½", weight is 41½ oz.; target-type checkered goncalo alves stocks; black ramp front sight, adjustable micrometer click rear; stainless steel version of Model 24. No longer in production. Used value, $325 to $350, depending on barrel length.

S&W Model 645

SMITH & WESSON Model 645: automatic; double-action; .45 ACP; 8-rd. magazine; 5" barrel' 8.7" overall length; weight, 37.6 oz.; red ramp front sight, drift-adjustable rear; checkered nylon stocks; stainless steel construction; cross-hatch knurling on recurved front trigger guard, backstrap; beveled magazine well. Introduced, 1985; still in production. Used value, $400 to $425.

S&W Model 422

SMITH & WESSON Model 422: automatic; .22 LR; 10-rd. magazine; 4½", 6" barrel lengths; 7½" overall length with shorter barrel; weighs 22 oz. with shorter barrel; fixed or adjustable sights; checkered plastic stocks on field model, checkered walnut on target version; aluminum frame, steel slide; brushed blued finish; internal hammer. Introduced, 1987; still in production. Used values: with fixed sights, $140 to $150; adjustable sights, $160 to $175.

SMITH & WESSON Model 745: automatic; .45 ACP; 8-rd. magazine; 5" barrel; 8⅝" overall length; weighs 38¾ oz.; windage adjustable square-notch rear sight, serrated ramp front; blued slide, trigger, hammer, sights. Marketed with two magazines. Introduced, 1987; still in production. Used value, $550 to $575.

S&W Model 745

STAR

Star Model A

STAR Model A: automatic; 7.63mm Mauser, 9mm Bergmann (9mm Largo); modified version of Colt Model 1911 .45 auto; appears almost identical to Browning patent; 5" barrel; 8½" overall length; 8-rd. magazine; checkered walnut grips; fixed sights; blued. The first locked-breech pistol manufactured commercially by Bonifacio Echeverria, S.A., in Eibar, Spain. Currently designated as Model AS, in .38 Super auto only. Not currently imported. Introduced in 1972; no longer in production. Used value, $200 to $225; add $80 for 7.63mm, $50 for .45.

STAR Model B: automatic; 9mm Parabellum; 9-rd. magazine; has the same design, other specs as Model A. Early versions had choice of barrel lengths: 4-3/16", 4⅛", or 6-5/16". Introduced in early Twenties; dropped during WWII. Used value, $200 to $225.

Star Model CO

STAR Model CO: automatic, pocket model; .25 auto only; 2¾" barrel; 4½" overall length; fixed sights; 6-rd. magazine; checkered plastic grips; blued. Introduced in 1934; dropped, 1957. Engraved models, pearl-like grips were available at added cost. Used value, $135 to $140 for standard model.

Star Model H

STAR Model H: pocket automatic; .32 auto; 7-rd. magazine. Identical in design to Model CO, except for caliber, magazine capacity. Introduced in 1934; dropped, 1941. Used value, $125 to $145.

Model HN has same general specs as Model H, except for .380 auto chambering, 6-rd. magazine. Manufactured 1934 to 1941. Used value, $125 to $150.

Star Model I

STAR Model I: automatic, police model; .32 auto; 4¾" barrel; 7½" overall length; 9-rd. magazine; fixed sights; checkered plastic grips; blued. Not imported into U.S. Introduced in 1943; dropped, 1945. Used value, $150 to $165

Model IN has the same general specs as Model I, except is chambered for .380 auto only; 8-rd. magazine. Introduced in 1934; still in production, but importation prohibited by Firearms Act of 1968. Used value, $150 to $175.

Star Super Star Model

Star Model M

STAR Model M: automatic; .38 ACP, 9mm Luger, 9mm Bergmann, .45 auto; 5" barrel, 8½" overall length; 7-rd. magazine for .45 auto, 8 rds. for all other calibers; modification of Model 1911 Colt automatic model; fixed sights; checkered walnut grips; blued. Not imported into U.S. Introduced in 1935; still in production and marketed abroad. Used value, $210 to $245.

Star Model F Target

Star Model S

STAR Model F: automatic; .22 LR only; 4½" barrel; 7¼" overall length; 10-rd. magazine; fixed sights; checkered thumbrest plastic grips; blued. Introduced in 1942; dropped, 1969. Used value, $135 to $145.

Model F Sport model has the same general specs as standard Model F, but with substitution of 6" barrel, adjustable target-type rear sight. Introduced in 1942; dropped, 1969. Used value, $145 to $155.

Model F Target model has the same general specs as standard Model F, except for substitution of adjustable target sights, 7" barrel, weights. Introduced in 1942; dropped, 1969. Used value, $165 to $185.

Model FRS is improved version of Model F, replacing the original version, but with same general specs; 6" barrel; alloy frame. Available in blued, chrome finish, with checkered walnut grips. Introduced in 1969; still in production. No longer imported. Used values: blued, $125 to $135; chrome, $145 to $155.

Model FM has the same general specs as the Model FRS, except for 4¼" barrel. Introduced in 1969; still in production. No longer imported. Used values: blued, $145 to $155; chrome, $150 to $160.

STAR Model S: automatic; .380 auto only; 4" barrel, 6½" overall length; 7-rd. magazine; fixed sights; checkered plastic grips; blued. Scaled-down modification of Colt 1911 automatic. Introduced in 1941; still in production, but importation into U.S. banned in 1968. Used value, $185 to $200.

Model SI has the same general specs as Model S, except for chambering in .32 auto only; 7-rd. magazine. Introduced in 1941; still in production, but importation banned in 1968. Used value, $165 to $185.

Super S has the same general specs as standard Model S, but with improved luminous sights for aiming in darkness, magazine safety, disarming bolt, indicator to show number of unfired cartridges. Introduced in 1942; dropped, 1954. Used value, $200 to $225.

Super SI has the same specs as Super S, except for being chambered in .32 auto only. Introduced in 1942; dropped, 1954. Used value, $175 to $195.

STAR Super Star Model: 9mm Parabellum, .38 Super auto; has the same general specs as the Model M, except for addition of disarming bolt, improved luminous sights, magazine safety, indicator for number of unfired cartridges. Introduced in 1942; dropped, 1954. Not imported. Used value, $225 to $250.

Super Star Target Model has the same general specs as Super Star model, except for substitution of adjustable target-type rear sight. Introduced in 1942; dropped, 1954. Used value, $300 to $325.

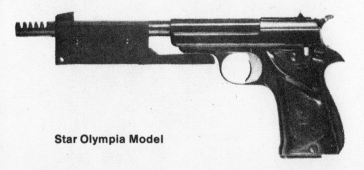

Star Olympia Model

STAR Olympia Model: automatic; designed for International rapid-fire target competition; .22 short only; 7" barrel; 11-1/16" overall length; 9-rd. magazine; alloy slide; muzzle brake; adjustable rear target sight; checkered plastic grips. Introduced in 1950; still in production. Not currently imported. Used value, $275 to $300.

Star Model HK

Star Super SM

Star Model PD

Star Model BKM

Star Model 28

STAR Model HK: automatic; .32 auto, .380 auto; 2¾" barrel; 5-9/16" overall length; 6-rd. magazine in .380, 7 rds. in .32; fixed sights; plastic grips; blued. Introduced in 1955; still in production. Never imported into U.S. Used value, $165 to $185.

STAR Model DK: automatic; .380 auto; overall length, 5-11/16" has aluminum alloy frame. Designation originally used for long discontinued .22 pistol. New .380 version introduced in 1958; never imported into U.S. Used value, $185 to $200.

STAR Model BKS: automatic; advertised as Star Starlight model; 9mm Parabellum only; 4½" barrel; 8-rd. magazine; fixed sights; magazine, manual safeties; checkered plastic grips; blued, chrome finish. Introduced in 1970; still in production as BKM with duraluminum frame. Model BM has steel frame. Imported by Interarms. Used values: blued, $185 to $200; chrome finish, $195 to $210.
  Model BKM has same specs as Model BKS, except for 4" barrel; hand-checkered walnut stocks; checkered backstrap. Introduced in 1976; still in production. Used value, $185 to $200.

STAR Super SM: automatic; .380 auto; 10-rd. magazine; 4" barrel; 6⅝" overall length; checkered plastic stocks, adjustable rear sight, blade front; blued or chromed finish; thumb safety, loaded chamber indicator. Manufactured in Spain. Introduced, 1977; still in production. Used values: blued, $195 to $210; chromed, $205 to $225.

STAR Model PD: automatic; .45 auto; 6-rd. magazine; 3¾" barrel; 7" overall length; checkered walnut stocks; adjustable rear sight, ramp front; blued finish. Introduced, 1975; still in production. Used value, $225 to $235.

STAR Model 28: automatic; double-action; 9mm Parabellum; 15-rd. magazine; 4¼" barrel; weighs 40 oz.; 8" overall length; square blade front sight, square-notch click-adjustable rear; grooved trigger guard face, front and backstraps; checkered black plastic stocks; ambidextrous safety. Imported from Spain by Interarms. Introduced, 1983; importation dropped, 1984; replaced by Model 30. Used value, $275 to $300.

Star Model 30 PK

STAR Model 30M: automatic; double-action; 9mm Parabellum; 15-rd. magazine; 4.33" barrel; overall length 8"; weighs 40 oz.; checkered black plastic stocks; square blade front sight, click-adjustable rear; grooved front, backstraps, trigger guard face; ambidextrous safety; steel frame. Imported from Spain by Interarms. Introduced, 1984; still imported. Used value, $350 to $375.

    Model 30 PK has same specs as Model 30M, except has alloy frame, 3.86" barrel, 7.6" overall length, weighs 30 oz. Introduced, 1984; still imported. Used value, $350 to $375.

STERLING

Sterling Model 283

Sterling Model 285

STERLING Model 283: also designated as the Target 300; automatic; .22 LR only; 4½", 6", 8" barrels; overall length, 9" with 4½" barrel; 10-rd. magazine; micrometer rear sight, blade front; checkered plastic grips; external hammer; adjustable trigger; all-steel construction; blued finish. Introduced in 1970; dropped, 1972. Used value, $100 to $125.

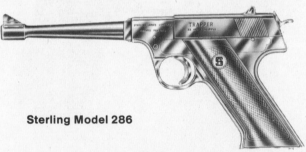

Sterling Model 286

Sterling Model 284

STERLING Model 284: also designated as Target 300L; automatic; .22 LR only; 4½", 6" tapered barrel; overall length, 9" with 4½" barrel; 10-rd. magazine; micrometer rear sight, blade front; checkered plastic grips; adjustable trigger; all-steel construction; blued finish. Introduced in 1970; dropped, 1972. Used value, $110 to $135.

STERLING Model 285: advertised as the Husky; automatic; .22 LR; has the same specs as the Model 283, but manufactured only with 4½" barrel, has fixed sights. Manufactured 1970 to 1971. Used value, $85 to $100.

STERLING Model 286: advertised as the Trapper Model; automatic; .22 LR only; 4½", 6" tapered barrel; overall length, 9" with 4½" barrel; 10-rd. magazine; fixed rear sight, serrated ramp front; checkered plastic grips; external hammer; target-type trigger; all-steel construction; blued finish. Introduced in 1970; dropped, 1972. Used value, $100 to $125.

STERLING MODEL 295: advertised as Husky Model; automatic; .22 LR only; 4½" heavy barrel; overall length, 9"; 10-rd. magazine; fixed rear sight, serrated ramp front; checkered plastic grips; external hammer; target-type trigger; all-steel construction; blued finish. Introduced in 1970; dropped, 1972. Used value, $100 to $125.

STERLING Model 300: automatic; blowback action; .25 auto; 2½" barrel; overall length, 4½"; 6-rd. magazine; no sights; black, white plastic grips; blue, satin nickel finish; all-steel construction. Introduced in 1971; dropped, 1984. Used values: blued, $65 to $70; nickel, $75 to $80.

Sterling Model 300

Sterling Model 400

Model 300S has same specs as Model 300, except is manufactured from stainless steel. Introduced, 1976; dropped, 1984. Used value, $85 to $95.

Sterling Model 302

Sterling Model 400S

STERLING Model 400: automatic; blowback double-action; .380 ACP; 3½" barrel; overall length, 6½"; micrometer rear sight, fixed ramp front; checkered rosewood grips; blue, satin nickel finish; thumb-roll safety; all-steel construction. Introduced in 1973; dropped, 1984. Used values: blued, $145 to $160; nickel, $150 to $165.

Model 400S has same specs as Model 400, except is manufactured of stainless steel. Introduced, 1977; dropped, 1984. Used value, $175 to $180.

STERLING Model 402: automatic; blowback double-action; .22 LR only; other specs are generally the same as those of the Model 400. Introduced in 1973; dropped, 1974. Used values: blued, $135 to $150; nickel, $140 to $155.

Sterling Model 302S

Sterling Model 450

STERLING Model 302: automatic; blowback action; .22 LR; other specs are generally the same as those of the Model 300, except that grips are available only in black plastic. Introduced in 1972; dropped, 1984. Used values: blued, $85 to $100; nickel, $95 to $105.

Model 302S has same specs as Model 302, except is manufactured from stainless steel. Introduced, 1976; dropped, 1984. Used value, $100 to $115.

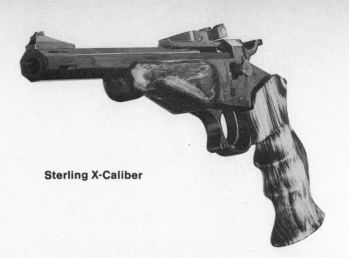

Sterling X-Caliber

STERLING Model 450: automatic; double-action; .45 auto; 8-rd. magazine; 4" barrel; 7½" overall length; uncheckered walnut stocks; blued finish; adjustable rear sight. Introduced, 1977; dropped, 1984. Used value, $375 to $400.

STERLING X-Caliber: single-shot; .22 LR, .22 WRFM, .357 magnum, .44 magnum; interchangeable 8", 10" barrels; 13" overall length with 8" barrel; goncalo alves stocks; Patridge front sight, fully adjustable rear; drilled/tapped for scope mounts; notched hammer for easy cocking; finger-grooved grip. Introduced, 1980; dropped, 1984. Used value, $180 to $190.

TAURUS

Taurus Model 74

TAURUS Model 74: revolver; double-action; .32 S&W Long; 6-rd. cylinder; 3" barrel; 8¼" overall length; hand-checkered walnut stocks; blued or nickel finish; adjustable rear sight, ramp front. Manufactured in Brazil. Imported by International Distributors. Introduced, 1971; dropped, 1978. Used value, $85 to $100.

Taurus Model 80

TAURUS Model 80: revolver; double-action; .38 Special; 6-rd. cylinder; 3", 4" barrel lengths; hand-checkered walnut stocks; blued or nickel finish; fixed sights. Imported by Taurus International. Introduced, 1971; still in production. Used value, $85 to $100.

Taurus Model 82

TAURUS Model 82: revolver, double-action; .38 Special; has the same specs as Model 80, except for heavy barrel. Introduced, 1971; still in production. Used value, $85 to $100.

Taurus Model 84

TAURUS Model 84: revolver, double-action; .38 Special; has same specs as Model 83, except for standard weight barrel. Introduced, 1971; dropped, 1978. Used value, $100 to $125.

TAURUS Model 86 Target Master: revolver, double-action; .38 Special; 6-rd. cylinder; 6" barrel; 11¼" overall length; hand-checkered walnut stocks; blued finish; adjustable rear sight, Patridge-design front. Introduced, 1971; still in production. Used value, $150 to $170.

TAURUS Model 94: revolver, double-action; .22 LR; other specs are the same as those of Model 74, except for 4" barrel, 9¼" overall length. Introduced, 1971; dropped, 1978. Used value, $90 to $100.

TAURUS Model 96 Scout Master: revolver; has same specs as Model 86 Master, except is chambered for .22 rimfire only. Introduced, 1971; still in production. Used value, $125 to $145.

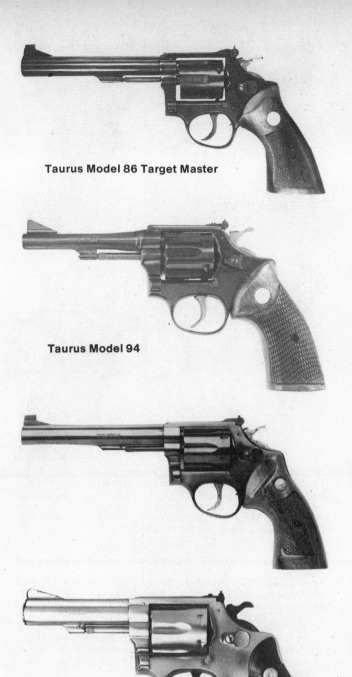

Taurus Model 86 Target Master

Taurus Model 94

Taurus Model 83

Taurus Model 66

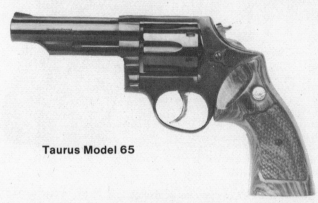

Taurus Model 65

Taurus Model 85

TAURUS Model 85: revolver, double-action; .38 Special; 5 rds.; 2", 3" barrels; ramp front sight, square-notch rear; checkered Brazilian hardwood grips; blued or satin blue finish. Introduced, 1980; still imported by Taurus International. Used value, $125 to $135.

TAURUS Model 83: revolver, double-action; .38 Special; 6-rd. cylinder; 4" heavy barrel, 9½" overall length; hand-checkered walnut grips; blued or nickel finish; adjustable rear sight, ramp front. Introduced, 1977; still in production. Used value, $110 to $125.

TAURUS Model 66: revolver; double-action; .357 magnum; 6-rd. cylinder; 3", 4", 6" barrels; standard stocks on 3", checkered European walnut target stocks on others; serrated ramp front sight, micro-click adjustable rear; wide target hammer spur; floating firing pin; heavy barrel; shrouded ejector rod; blued, satin blue finish. Manufactured in Brazil. Introduced, 1978; imported by Taurus International. Used value, $165 to $175.

    Model 65 has same specs as Model 66, except has ramp front sight, fixed rear. Used value, $145 to $155.

Taurus Model 73

TAURUS Model 73: revolver, double-action; .32 S&W Long; 6 rds.; 3" heavy barrel; listed as Sport model; 8¼" overall length; ramp front sight, notch rear; target-type Brazilian walnut grips; blued or satin blued finish. Manufactured in Brazil; imported by Taurus International. Introduced, 1979; still in production. Used values: blued finish, $140 to $145; satin blued, $150 to $160.

Taurus PT 92

Taurus PT-22

Taurus PT 99

TAURUS PT-22: automatic; double-action; .22 LR, .25 ACP; 2¾" barrel; weighs 18 oz.; serrated front sight, fixed square-notch rear; unchecked Brazilian walnut stocks; blued finish; pop-up barrel. Made in U.S. by Taurus International. Introduced, 1983; dropped, 1984. Used value, $125 to $150.

TAURUS PT-92AF: automatic; double-action; 9mm Parabellum; 15-rd. magazine; 4.92" barrel; weighs 34 oz.; 8.54" overall length; fixed sights; black plastic stocks; exposed hammer; chamber loaded indicator; inertia firing pin; blued finish. Imported from Brazil. Introduced, 1983; still imported. Used value, $245 to $260.

TAURUS PT-99AF: automatic; has same general specs as PT-92, except has fully adjustable rear sight, unchecked Brazilian walnut stocks; polished or satin blued finish. Imported from Brazil. Introduced, 1983; still in production. Used values: polished finish, $260 to $275; satin nickel, $270 to $285.

UBERTI

or with convertible .44 magnum/.44-40 cylinders. Made in Italy. Imported earlier by Iver Johnson, Allen Firearms. Now imported by Benson Firearms, Uberti U.S.A. Used values: standard model, $220 to $240; with convertible cylinders, $250 to $275.

   1987 Buntline Model has same specs as model imported earlier by Iver Johnson, Allen Firearms; 18" barrel, overall length, 23"; same sights, options as Cattleman, Buckhorn. Currently imported by Benson Firearms, Uberti U.S.A. Used value, $275 to $325, depending on options.

Uberti 1873 Cattlemen

Uberti 1873 Stallion

UBERTI 1873 Cattleman: revolver; single-action; .22 LR, .22 WRFM, .38 Special, .357 magnum, .44-40, .45 Colt; 3", 4¾", 5½", 7½" barrel lengths; with 5½" barrel, overall length is 10¾", weight is 38 oz.; same as the Cattleman model imported earlier by Iver Johnson and Allen Firearms; fixed or adjustable sights; also in stainless steel. Made in Italy, now imported by Benson Firearms and Uberti U.S.A. Used value, $240 to $275. depending on options.

   1873 Buckhorn Model is a slightly larger version of the Cattleman; specs are the same, except it is chambered for .44 magnum

UBERTI 1873 Stallion: revolver; single-action; .22 LR/.22 WRFM convertible; 5½" barrel; 10¾" overall length; weighs 36 oz.; grooved rear or adjustable rear sight, blade front; one-piece unchecked European walnut stocks; smaller version of Cattleman, has same options, including steel or brass trigger guard and backstrap; also made in stainless steel. Made in Italy. Introduced, 1986; still imported by Benson Firearms, Uberti U.S.A. Used value, $240 to $285, depending on options.

UBERTI Phantom SA Silhouette Model: single-shot; .357 magnum, .44 magnum; 10½" barrel; adjustable rear sight, blade on ramp front; target-style walnut stocks; hooked trigger guard. Made in Italy. Introduced, 1986; still imported by Benson Firearms and Uberti U.S.A. Used value, $300 to $325.

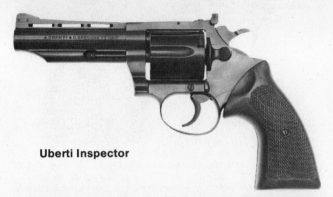

Uberti Inspector

UBERTI Inspector: revolver; double-action; .32 S&W Long, .38 Special; 6-rd. cylinder; 3", 4", 6" barrels; 8" overall length with 3" barrel; weighs 24 oz.; fixed or adjustable rear sight, blade on ramp front; checkered walnut stocks; blued or chrome finish. Made in Italy. Introduced, 1986; still imported by Benson Firearms and Uberti U.S.A. Used values: blued, fixed sights, $240 to $260; blued, adjustable sights, $275 to $300; chrome, fixed sights, $250 to $275; chrome, adjustable sights, $300 to $325.

UBERTI 1875 Army Outlaw: revolver; single-action; .357 magnum, .44-40, .45 Colt; 6-rd. cylinder; 7½" barrel; 13¾" overall length; weighs 44 oz.; notch rear sight, blade front; uncheckered European walnut stocks; brass trigger guard, color case-hardened frame; blued or nickel finish. Replica of 1875 Remington SA Army model. Made in Italy. Introduced, 1987; still imported by Benson Firearms, Uberti U.S.A. Used values: blued finish, $240 to $260; nickel finish, $275 to $300.

1890 Army Outlaw has same general specs as 1875 Army Outlaw, except has 5½" barrel, 12½" overall length, weighs 37 oz. Used values: blued finish, $240 to $260; nickel finish, $275 to $300.

Uberti 1875 SA Army

Uberti Rolling Block

UBERTI Rolling Block: single-shot; .22 LR, .22 WRFM, .22 Hornet, .357 magnum; 9½" barrel; 14" overall length; weighs 44 oz.; fully adjustable rear sight, blade front; walnut grip, forend; brass trigger guard; color case-hardened frame; blued barrel. Introduced, 1987; still imported by Benson Firearms and Uberti U.S.A. Used value, $200 to $225.

UNIQUE

Unique Kriegsmodell

Unique Model Rr

UNIQUE Kriegsmodell: automatic; .32 auto; 9-rd. magazine; 3-2/5" barrel, 5-4/5" overall length; grooved plastic stocks; blued finish; fixed sights. Manufactured in France 1940 to 1945 during WWII German occupation. Used value, $185 to $200.

Model Rr is the commercial version of Kriegsmodell, with the same specs, improved finish. Introduced, 1951; still in production, but not imported. Used value, $165 to $185.

Unique Model B/Cf

Unique Model Mikros

UNIQUE Model B/Cf: automatic; .32 auto, .380 auto; 9-rd. magazine in .32, 8 rds. in .380; 4" barrel; 6⅔" overall length; thumbrest plastic stocks; fixed sights; blued finish. Manufactured in France. Introduced, 1954; still in production, but not imported. Used value, $165 to $185.

UNIQUE Model Mikros: automatic, pocket type; .22 short, .22 LR; 6-rd. magazine; 2¼" barrel; 4-7/16" overall length; either alloy or steel frame; fixed sights; checkered plastic stocks; blued finish. Introduced, 1957; still in production, but not imported. Used value, $130 to $150.

Unique Model D6

Unique Model DES/69

UNIQUE Model D2: automatic; .22 LR; 10-rd. magazine; 4¼" barrel; 7½" overall length; thumbrest plastic stocks; adjustable sights; blued finish. Introduced, 1954; still in production, but not imported. Used value, $175 to $195.

   Model D6 has the same specs as Model D2, except for 6" barrel, 9¼" overall length. Introduced, 1954; still in production, but not imported. Used value, $175 to $195.

UNIQUE Model DES/69: automatic, match type; .22 LR; 5-rd. magazine; 5⅞" barrel; 10⅝" overall length; checkered walnut thumbrest stocks; adjustable handrest; click-adjustable rear sight, ramp front; blued finish. Introduced, 1969; still in production. Imported by Beeman. Used value, $650 to $700.

Unique Model DES/VO

Unique Model L

Unique Model 2000-U Match

UNIQUE Model L: automatic; .22 LR, .32 auto, .380 auto; 10-rd. magazine in .22 LR, 7 rds. in .32 auto, 6 rds. in .380 auto; 3⅓" barrel; 5-4/5" overall length; either steel or alloy frame; fixed sights; checkered plastic stocks; blued finish. Introduced, 1955; still in production, but not imported. Used value, $150 to $175; subtract $25 for .32.

UNIQUE Model DES/VO: automatic; rapid-fire match type; .22 short; 5-rd. magazine; 5⅞" barrel; 10-2/5" overall length; adjustable trigger; hand-checkered walnut thumbrest stocks; adjustable handrest; adjustable rear sight, blade front; blued finish. Introduced, 1974; importation dropped, 1983. Used value, $650 to $700.

UNIQUE Model 2000-U Match: automatic; .22 Short, 5-rd. magazine; 5.9" barrel; 11.3" overall length; weighs 43 oz.; adjustable stippled walnut stocks; blade front sight, fully adjustable rear; alloy frame, steel slide and shock absorber; 5 barrel vents; adjustable trigger; 340- or 160-gram weight housing; right- or left-hand style. Made in France. Introduced, 1984; still imported by Beeman. Used values: right-hand, $750; left-hand, $850 to $900.

WALTHER

Walther Model 3

Walther Model 1

Walther Model 4

WALTHER Model 1: automatic; .25 auto; 6-rd. magazine; 2" barrel; 4-2/5" overall length; checkered hard rubber stocks; fixed sights; blued finish. Manufactured in Germany, 1908 to 1918; collector value. Used value, $300 to $325.

WALTHER Model 4: automatic; .32 auto; 8-rd. magazine; 3½" barrel; 5⅞" overall length; checkered hard rubber stocks; fixed sights; blued finish. Manufactured 1910 to 1918; collector value. Used value, $265 to $285.

Walther Model 2

Walther Model 5

WALTHER Model 2: automatic; .25 auto; 6-rd. magazine; 2" barrel; 4-2/5" overall length; checkered hard rubber stocks; fixed sights; blued finish. Has same general internal design as Model 1. Manufactured, 1909 to 1918; collector value. Used value, $300 to $325.

WALTHER Model 3: automatic; .32 auto; 8-rd. magazine; 2⅔" barrel; 5" overall length; checkered hard rubber stocks; fixed sights; blued finish. Manufactured 1909 to 1918; collector value. Used value, $850 to $900 (rare).

WALTHER Model 5: automatic; .25 auto; has the same specs as Model 2, except with better workmanship; improved finish. Manufactured 1913 to 1918; collector value. Used value, $275 to $300.

Walther Model 6

WALTHER Model 6: automatic; 9mm Luger; 8-rd. magazine; 4¾" barrel; 8¼" overall length; checkered hard rubber stocks; fixed sights; blued finish. Manufactured 1915 to 1917. Used value, $2000-plus (extremely rare).

Walther Model 7

WALTHER Model 7: automatic; .25 auto; 8-rd. magazine; 3" barrel; 5⅓" overall length; checkered hard rubber stocks; fixed sights; blued finish. Manufactured 1917 to 1918. Used value, $375 to $400.

Walther Model 8

WALTHER Model 8: automatic; .25 auto only; 2⅞" barrel; 5⅛" overall length; 8-rd. magazine; fixed sights; checkered plastic grips; blued. Manufactured by Waffenfabrik Walther, Zella-Mehlis, Germany. Introduced in 1920; dropped, 1945. Used value, $325 to $350.

Model 8 Lightweight has exactly the same specs as the standard Model 8, except for use of aluminum alloy in slide, elements of frame. Introduced in 1927; dropped, 1945. Used value, $350 to $375.

Walther Model 9

WALTHER Model 9: automatic, vest pocket type; .25 auto only; 2" barrel; 3-15/16" overall length; 6-rd. magazine; checkered plastic grips; fixed sights; blued. Introduced in 1921; dropped, 1945. Used value, $350 to $375.

Walther Model PP

WALTHER Model PP: automatic; designed as law-enforcement model; .22 LR, .25 auto, .32 auto, .380 auto; 3⅞" barrel; 6-5/16" overall length; 8-rd. magazine; fixed sights; checkered plastic grips; blued. WWII production has less value because of poorer workmanship. Introduced in 1929; dropped, 1945. Used values: wartime models, $450 to $475; .32 caliber, $450 to $500; .380 caliber, $700 to $750; .22 caliber, $550 to $600; .25 caliber, $1500 to $2000.

Model PP Lightweight has the same specs as standard model, except for use of aluminum alloy in construction. Introduced in 1929; dropped, 1945. Used values: .32, .380 calibers, $525 to $550; .22 caliber, $600 to $650; .25 caliber, $1250 to $1500.

Post-WWII Model PP is being manufactured currently by Carl Walther Waffenfabrik, Ulm/Donau, West Germany. It has the same specs as the pre-war model except not made in .25. Still in production. Imported by Interarms. Used value, $375 to $400.

Model PP Mark II is being made in France by Manufacture De Machines Du Haut-Rhin and has the same specs as the pre-WWII model. Introduced in 1953; still in production, but not imported. Used value, $250 to $300.

WALTHER Model PPK: automatic; designated as the detective pistol; .22 LR, .25 auto, .32 auto, .380 auto; 3¼" barrel; 5⅞" overall length; 7-rd. magazine; checkered plastic grips; fixed sights; blued finish. WWII production has less value due to poorer workmanship. Introduced in 1931; still in production. Used values: wartime models, $400 to $425; .32, caliber, $400 to $425; .380 caliber, $850 to $1000; .22 caliber, $600 to $650; .25 caliber, $2000 and up.

Model PPK Lightweight has the same specs as standard model, except for incorporation of aluminum alloys. Introduced in 1933; dropped, 1945. Used values: .32, $500 to $525; .380, $950 to $1050; .22, .25, $2000 and up.

Post-WWII Walther PPK

Walther PPK/S American

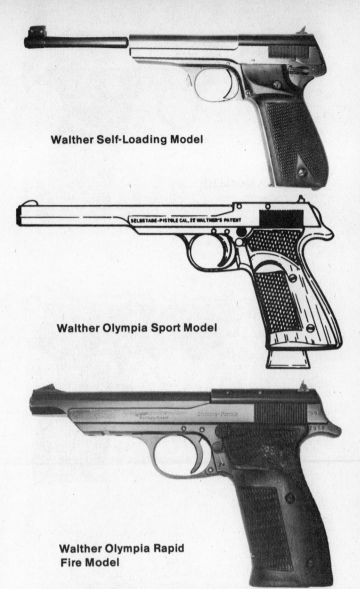

Walther Self-Loading Model

Walther Olympia Sport Model

Walther Olympia Rapid Fire Model

Post-WWII PPK model is being manufactured in West Germany by Carl Walther Waffenfabrik. It has the same general specs as the pre-war model, with construction either of steel or aluminum alloy. Still in production, although U.S. importation was dropped in 1968. Used value, $300 to $325.

Model PPK Mark II is produced in France by Manufacture De Machines Du Haut-Rhin. It has the same specs as pre-WWII model. Introduced in 1953; still in production, but not imported. Used value, $275 to $325.

Model PPK Mark II Lightweight has the same specs as the standard model, except that the receiver is of Dural and chambering is .22 LR, .32 auto only. Introduced in 1953; still in production, but not imported. Used value, $325 to $350.

PPK American has same general specs as PPK/S American, except has 6-rd. magazine, weighs 21 oz.; .380 ACP only; blued or stainless finish. Made in U.S. Introduced, 1986; still marketed by Interarms. Used value, $375 to $400.

PPK/S (German) has the same general specs as Walther PP, except has grip frame ½-inch longer and one shot larger magazine capacity to meet GCA'68 factoring system. Has 3.27" barrel; 6.1" overall length. Made in West Germany. Calibers .22 LR, .32, .380 ACP. Introduced 1968; dropped, 1982. Used values: .22 LR, $280 to $500; .32 ACP, .380 ACP, $225 to $400.

PPK/S/American has same specs as German-made PPK/S, except is made entirely in the USA by Interarms. Made only in .380 ACP, in blue ordnance steel or stainless. Introduced 1980; still in production. Used values: blued, $250 to $260; stainless, $295 to $315.

WALTHER Self-Loading Model: automatic; sport design; .22 LR only; 6", 9" barrels; with 6" barrel, 9⅞" overall length; checkered one-piece walnut or plastic grip; adjustable target sights; blued. Introduced in 1932; dropped during WWII. Used value, $500 to $525.

WALTHER Target Model: automatic; hammerless; .22 LR only; 6", 9" barrels; adjustable trigger; spring-driven firing pin; 10-rd. magazine capacity; safety on left rear side of frame; fixed front sight; rear adjustable for windage; hard rubber grips. Introduced in 1932; dropped during WWII. Collector value. Used value, $800 to $900.

WALTHER Olympia Sport Model: automatic; .22 LR only; 7⅜" barrel; 10-11/16" overall length; checkered plastic grips; adjustable target sights; blued. Available with set of four detachable weights. Introduced in 1936; dropped during WWII. Used value, $750 to $800.

Olympia Hunting Model has the same specs as Sport Model, except for 4" barrel. Introduced in 1936; dropped during WWII. Used value, $725 to $750.

Olympia Rapid Fire Model is automatic design; .22 short only; 7-7/16" barrel; 10-11/16" overall length; detachable muzzle weight; checkered plastic grips; adjustable target sights; blued finish. Introduced in 1936; dropped during WWII. Used value, $825 to $850.

Olympia Funkampf Model is automatic design; .22 LR only; 9⅝" barrel; 13" overall length; set of four detachable weights; checkered plastic grips; adjustable target sights; blued. Introduced in 1937; dropped during WWII. Used value, $1150 to $1200.

WALTHER Model HP: automatic; 9mm Parabellum; 5" barrel; 8⅜" overall length; 10-rd. magazine; checkered walnut or plastic grips; fixed sights; blued. Introduced as commercial handgun in 1939; dropped during WWII. Used value, $900 to $1000.

WALTHER P-38 Military Model: 9mm Parabellum; same specs as the Model HP, but adopted as official German military sidearm in 1938 and produced throughout World War II by Walther, Mauser and others. Quality, in most cases, is substandard to that of HP due to wartime production requirements. Introduced in 1938; dropped, 1945. Used value, $350 to $375.

Walther Model HP

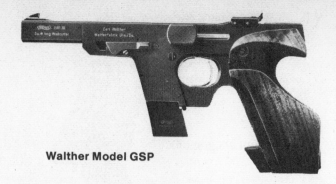

Walther Model GSP

WALTHER GSP Match Model: .22 LR; 5-rd. magazine; 5¾" barrel; 11-4/5" overall length; hand-fitting walnut stocks; adjustable rear sight, fixed front; marketed with spare magazine, barrel weight; blued finish. Imported by Interarms. Introduced, 1977; still in production. Used value, $750 to $800.

GSP-C Match Model has the same specs as GSP, but is chambered for .32 S&W wadcutter cartridge. Introduced, 1977; still in production. Used value, $800 to $850.

Walther P-38 (Post-WWII)

Walther P-5

WALTHER P-5: has same basic double-action mechanism as basic P-38 but differs externally; 9mm Parabellum only; 3½" barrel; overall length, 7"; Introduced, 1978; still imported from West Germany by Interarms. Used value, $650 to $700.

Walther P-38 K

Walther Model TPH

Post-war Model P-38 is manufactured currently by Carl Walther Waffenfabrik in West Germany. It has the same general specs as the WWII military model, except for improved workmanship and use of alloys in construction. Still in production. Imported by Interarms. Used value, $350 to $375.

P-38IV has same specs as standard post-WWII P-38 except for 4½" barrel, 8" overall length. Introduced in 1977; imported by Interarms. Used value, $475 to $500.

P-38K is streamlined version of original with 2¼" barrel; 6½" overall length; has strengthened slide, no dust cover, windage-adjustable rear sight; hammer decocking lever; non-reflective matte finish. Imported from West Germany by Interarms, 1976; dropped, 1980. Used value, $475 to $500.

WALTHER Model TPH: automatic; .22 LR; 6-rd. magazine; 2¼" barrel; 5⅜" overall length; weighs 14 oz.; drift-adjustable rear sight, blade front; constructed of stainless steel; scaled-down version of PP/PPK series. Made in U.S. by Interarms. Introduced, 1987; still in production. Used value, $200 to $225.

WEBLEY

Webley Mark III Police Model

WEBLEY Mark III Police Model: revolver; double-action; hinged frame; .38 S&W only; 6-rd. cylinder; 3", 4" barrels; with 4" barrel, overall length, 9½"; fixed sights; checkered Vulcanite or walnut grips; blued finish. Introduced in 1897; dropped, 1945. Used value, $185 to $210.

Webley-Fosbery Automatic Revolver

WEBLEY-Fosbery Automatic Revolver: .455 Webley, .38 Colt Auto; 6-rd. cylinder in .455, 8 rds. in .38 Colt Auto; hinged frame; 6" barrel; 12" overall length; hand-checkered walnut stocks; fixed sights; blued finish. Recoil revolves cylinder, cocking hammer, leading to automatic terminology. Manufactured 1901 to 1939. Both calibers have collector value. Used values: .455 Webley, $450 to $425; .38 Colt Auto, $800 to $850.

Webley Model 1906

WEBLEY Model 1906: automatic; .380 auto, .32 auto; 3½" barrel; 6¼" overall length; 7-rd. magazine in .380, 8 rds. in .32; exposed hammer; checkered hard rubber grips; checkered walnut grips on special order; blued; popular in Commonwealth for police use; law-enforcement version has rear sight; those for civilian consumption have sight groove full length of slide. Introduced in 1905; dropped, 1940. Used values: .32, $165 to $185; .380, $200 to $225.

Webley Model 1906 .25

WEBLEY Model 1906: automatic; .25 auto only; 2⅛" barrel; overall length, 4¼"; 6-rd. magazine; checkered hard rubber grips; resembles Model 1913 in appearance, but had no sights, no sight groove on slide, and is much smaller. Introduced in 1906; dropped, 1940. Used value, $185 to $210.

WEBLEY Police & Civilian Pocket Model: revolver; double-action; hinged frame; .32 S&W only; 3½" barrel; 6¼" overall length; 8-rd. cylinder; checkered plastic grips; fixed sights; blued finish. Introduced in 1906; dropped, 1940. Used value, $175 to $200.

Webley Model 1909 Auto

WEBLEY Model 1909: automatic; hammerless; .25 auto only; 2⅛" barrel; 4¼" overall length; 6-rd. magazine; front, rear sights mounted on slide; ejection port at top of slide; checkered black composition grips. Introduced in 1909; dropped, 1940. Used value, $185 to $210.

    Model 1909 Improved is in 9mm Browning Long only; limited production, some for the government of the Union of South Africa. It differs from the original in several features: grip frame is angled more than on other Webley autos; magazine release button is behind trigger guard; no grip safety; lanyard ring mounted at bottom of backstrap; safety lever on left side of slide; checkered black plastic grips. Introduced in 1909; dropped, 1930. Has considerable collector value. Used value, $500 to $550.

Webley Model 1909 Single-Shot

WEBLEY Model 1909: single-shot; tip-up action; .22, .32 S&W, .38 S&W; 9⅞" barrel; blade front sight; plastic thumbrest target grips; late versions had ballast chamber in butt to permit weight adjustment; rebounding hammer; matte-finish barrel; blued. Introduced in 1909; dropped, 1965. Used value, $225 to $250.

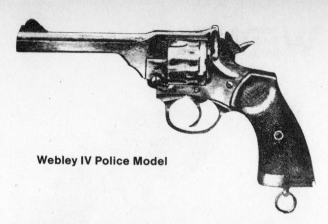

Webley IV Police Model

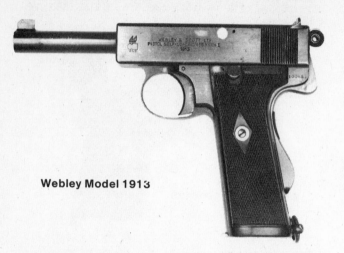

Webley Model 1913

WEBLEY Model 1913: automatic; .455 Webley only; commercial version of model adopted by Royal Navy in 1913; overall length, 8½"; 7-rd. magazine grip safety; movable rear sight; fixed blade front; checkered black composition grips; checkered walnut grips on special order. Introduced in 1911; dropped, 1931. Has some collector value. Used value, $350 to $375.

WEBLEY Mark IV Police Model: revolver; double-action; hinged frame; .38 S&W only; 6-rd. cylinder; 3", 4", 5", 6" barrels; with 5" barrel, overall length, 9⅛"; fixed or target sights; checkered plastic grips; lanyard ring; blued finish. Introduced in 1929; dropped, 1968. Used value, $160 to $185.

    Mark IV War Model has the same general specs as the Police Model. Built during WWII, it usually has poor-fitting, blued-over unpolished surfaces. To protect the corporate reputation, most were stamped, "War Finish." Used value, $145 to $155.

Webley Model 1911 (9" barrel)

Webley Mark IV Target Model

WEBLEY Model 1911: single-shot; .22 rimfire only; has appearance of automatic as it is built on Model 1906 frame; 4½" and 9" barrels; originally introduced as police training arm; some were available with removable wooden stock. Introduced in 1911; dropped, 1927. Only a few hundred produced, affording it collector interest. Used value, $500 to $525.

WEBLEY Mark IV Target Model: revolver; double-action; .22 LR only; built in small quantities on the Mark IV .38 frame; fitted with adjustable rear sight. Introduced in 1931; dropped, 1968. Virtually a custom-produced handgun. Used value, $300 to $325.

WEBLEY Mark IV .32 Police: revolver; double-action; .32 S&W; has the same specs as .38 S&W Mark IV Police version, except is chambered for smaller caliber. Introduced in 1929; dropped, 1968. Used value, $160 to $185.

DAN WESSON

DAN WESSON Model 11: double-action revolver; .357 magnum only; 2½", 4", 6" interchangeable barrels; with 4" barrel, 9¼" overall length; 6-rd. cylinder; interchangeable grips; adjustable dovetail rear sight, serrated ramp front. Marketed with tools for changing barrels, grips; non-recessed barrel nut, blued. Introduced in 1969; dropped, 1974. Used value, $145 to $165.

DAN WESSON Model 12: double-action revolver; .357 magnum only; 2¼", 3¾", 5¾" interchangeable barrels and grips; 6-rd. cylinder; adjustable target-type rear sight, serrated ramp front. Marketed with tools for changing barrels, grips; blued. Introduced in 1969; dropped, 1974. Used value, $165 to $175.

DAN WESSON Model 14: double-action revolver; .357 magnum only; 2¼", 3¾", 5¾" interchangeable barrels; with 3¾" barrel, 9" overall length; 6-rd. cylinder; interchangeable walnut grips; fixed dovetail rear sight, serrated ramp front; wide trigger with adjustable overtravel stop; wide spur hammer; recessed barrel nut; blued, nickel, matte nickel finish. Introduced in 1971; dropped, 1975. Replaced by Model 14-2. Used values: blued, $165 to $175; nickel, $165 to $175; matte nickel, $170 to $190.

Dan Wesson Model 11

Dan Wesson Model 12

Dan Wesson Model 14-2

Model 14-2 has same general specs as Model 14, except for 2", 4", 6" Quickshift interchangeable barrels; Quickshift grips interchangeable with 3 other styles. Introduced in 1976; still in production. Used value, $180 to $190.

Dan Wesson Model 15

Dan Wesson Model 15-2

DAN WESSON Model 15: double-action revolver; .357 magnum only; 2¼", 3¾", 5¾" interchangeable barrels; has same general specs as Model 14, except for rear sight adjustable for windage, elevation. Introduced in 1971; dropped, 1975. Replaced by Model 15-2. Used values: blued, $175 to $190; nickel, $175 to $190; matte nickel, $185 to $195.

Model 15-1 is the same as Model 15, except that size of the rear sight was reduced. Introduced, 1973, dropped 1975. Blued, nickel or matte nickel finish. Used values, blued, $175 to $190; nickel, $175 to $190; matte nickel, $190 to $200.

Model 15-2 is the same as Model 15-1, except shroud was discontinued. Introduced, 1973, still in production. Used value, $200 to $225.

Model 15-2H has same specs as the Model 15-2, except for

heavy barrel options. Introduced, 1975; still in production. Values depend upon barrel length, ranging from 2" through 15" barrel. Values: $170 to $175; extra barrels, $60 to $100, depending upon length.

Model 15-2HV has same specs as Model 15-2, except for heavy vent-rib barrel, ranging from 2" to 15". Introduced, 1975; still in production. Used values comparable to those of Model 15-2H.

DAN WESSON Model 8-2: revolver, double-action; .38 Special. Except for caliber, other specs are the same as the Model 14-2. Introduced, 1975; still in production. Used values, $135 to $140.

DAN WESSON Model 9-2H: revolver, double-action; .38 Special; has the same general specs as Model 15-2H, except for caliber. Introduced, 1975; still in production. Used value: $175 to $200, depending upon barrel length; extra barrels, $60 to $100, depending upon length.

Model 9-2V has same specs as Model 9-2H, except for standard vent-rib barrel, ranging from 2" to 15". Introduced, 1975; still in production. Values are comparable to those of Model 9-2H.

Model 9-2HV has same specs as Model 9-2, except for heavy vent-rib barrel; made in .38 Special only. Introduced, 1975; still in production. Used value comparable to that of Model 9-2H.

DAN WESSON Model 22: revolver; double-action; .22 LR, .22 WRFM; 6-rd. cylinder; 2½", 4", 6", 8", 10" interchangeable barrels; checkered, undercover, service or target stocks of American walnut; serrated, interchangeable front sight; adjustable white-outline rear; blued or stainless steel; wide trigger; over-travel trigger adjustment; wide hammer spur. Introduced, 1982; still in production. Used values: blued, $210 to $250, depending on barrel length; stainless, $230 to $275, depending on barrel length.

Dan Wesson Model 41V

DAN WESSON Model 41V: revolver; double-action; .41 magnum; 6-rd. cylinder; 4", 6", 8", 10" interchangeable barrels; smooth walnut stocks; serrated front sight, adjustable white-outline rear; wide trigger; adjustable trigger over-travel feature; wide hammer spur; blued or stainless steel. Introduced, 1982; still in production. Used values: blued, $280 to $325, depending on barrel length; stainless, $305 to $350, depending on barrel length.

DAN WESSON model 32M: revolver; has the same specs as the Model 14-2, except is chambered for the .32 Harrington & Richardson magnum; blued or stainless steel. Introduced, 1984. Used values: blued, $240 to $250; stainless, $270 to $280.

Dan Wesson Model 44V

DAN WESSON Model 44V: revolver; double-action; .44 magnum; has same specs as Model 41V, except for chambering. Introduced, 1982; still in production. Used values: blued finish, $300 to $340, depending on barrel length; stainless steel, $330 to $385, depending on barrel length.

DAN WESSON Model 9-2: revolver; has the same specifications as the Model 14-2, except has adjustable sights and is chambered for the .38 special; blued or stainless steel. Introduced, 1986. Used values: $240 to $250; stainless $270 to $280.

DAN WESSON Model 40 Silhouette: revolver; .357 Maximum; 6-rd. cylinder; 6", 8", 10" barrels; overall length with 8" barrel, 14.3"; weighs 64 oz.; adjustable rear sight, serrated front; blued or stainless steel; meets IHMSA competition criteria. Introduced,

**Dan Wesson
Model 40 Silhouette**

1986; still in production. Used values: blued finish, $350 to $400, depending on barrel length; stainless steel, $375 to $400, depending on barrel length.

MISCELLANEOUS HANDGUNS U.S.-MADE

Advantage Arms 442

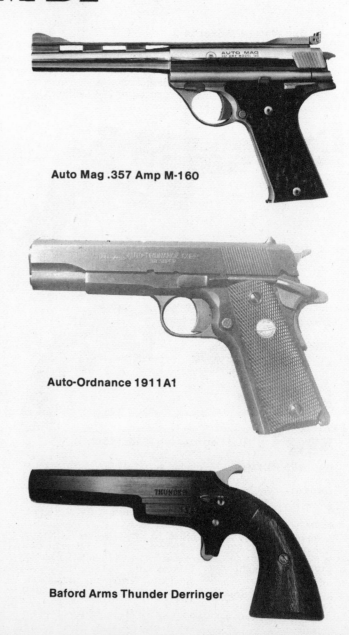

Auto Mag .357 Amp M-160

Auto-Ordnance 1911A1

Baford Arms Thunder Derringer

ADVANTAGE ARMS 442 Derringer: break-top action; .22 LR, .22 WRFM; 4 rds.; 2½" barrel; 4½" overall length; weighs 15 oz.; smooth walnut stocks; fixed sights; double-action trigger; rotating firing pin; spring-loaded extractors; nickel, blued or black finish. Introduced, 1983; dropped, 1985. Used value, $115 to $120.

AMERICAN ARMS TP-70: automatic, double-action; .22 LR, .25 ACP; 2.6" barrel, 4.72" overall; open fixed sights, checkered composition grips; stainless steel construction; exposed hammer; manual and magazine safeties. Distributed by M&N Distributors. Introduced, 1980; dropped 1983. Used value $200 to $225.

ARM TECH Derringer: 4 barrels, rotating firing pin; .22 LR, .22 WRFM; 2.6" barrel; 4.6" overall length; weighs 19 oz.; hard rubber or walnut stocks; fixed sights; stainless steel; double-action only; blued model available. Introduced, 1983; still in production. Used value, $140 to $150.

AUTO MAG: automatic; .357 Auto Mag, .44 Auto Mag; 6½" barrel; 11½" overall length; 7-rd. magazine; short recoil; rotary bolt system; stainless steel construction; checkered plastic grips; fully adjustable rear sight, ramp front. Manufactured 1970 to 1975. Used value, $1250 to $1500.

AUTO-ORDNANCE 1911A1: automatic; 9mm Parabellum, .38 Super, .41 Action Express, .45 ACP; .45 ACP has 7-rd. magazine, .41 A.E. 8 rds., others 9-rd.; 5" barrel; weighs 39 oz.; overall length, 8½"; blade front sight, windage-adjustable rear; same specs as military 1911A1, parts interchangeable; blued, non-glare finish. Made in U.S. by Auto-Ordnance Corp. Introduced, 1983; still in production. Used value, $230 to $240.

BAFORD ARMS Thunder Derringer: .410 2½" shotshell and .44 Special; insert sleeves available for .22 short, .22 LR, .25 ACP, .32 ACP, .32 H&R magnum, .30 Luger, .380 ACP, .38 Super, .38 Special, .38 S&W, 9mm; barrel lengths vary with caliber inserts; weighs 8½ oz., sans inserts; no sights; uncheckered walnut stocks; blued steel barrel, frame; polished stainless steel hammer, trigger. Sideswinging barrel; positive lock, half-cock safety; roll block safety. Introduced, 1986; dropped, 1988. Used values: basic model, $90 to $100; extra barrel inserts, $10 to $12 each.

Bren Ten Special Forces Model

Bauer .25 Auto

Special Forces Model is similar to Pocket Model, except has standard grip frame, 11-rd. magazine; weighs 33 oz.; 4" barrel; black or natural light finish. Introduced, 1984; no longer in production. Used values: black finish, $800 to $850; light finish, $775 to $800.

Budischowsky TP-70

BAUER 25: automatic; 25 auto; 2⅛" barrel; 4" overall length; 6-rd. magazine; stainless steel construction; fixed sights; plastic pearl or checkered walnut grips; manual, magazine safeties. Introduced in 1973; dropped, 1984. Used value, $75 to $95.

BAUER 22: automatic; .22 LR only; same design as Bauer .25 except has 5-rd. magazine; 2¼" barrel, measures 4⅛" overall. Manufacture began 1977; dropped, 1984. Used value, $125 to $150.

BUDISCHOWSKY TP-70: double-action automatic; .22 LR, .25 auto; 2-7/16" barrel; 4⅔" overall length; 6-rd. magazine; fixed sights; all stainless steel construction; manual, magazine safeties. Introduced in 1973; no longer in production. Used values: .25 ACP, $250 to $275; .22 LR, $350 to $375.

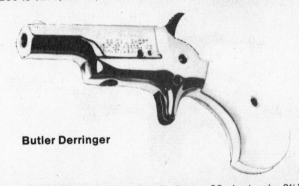

Butler Derringer

Bren Ten

BUTLER Derringer: single-shot derringer; .22 short only; 2½" barrel; blade front sight, no rear; smooth walnut or pearlite grips; spur trigger; blued, gold, chrome finish. Introduced, 1978; dropped, 1980. Used value, $40 to $50.

Century Model 100

BREN TEN: automatic; 10mm Auto; 11-rd. magazine; 5" barrel; weighs 38 oz.; 8¾" overall length; textured black nylon stocks; adjustable, replaceable combat sights; double- or single-action; stainless steel frame; blued slide; reversible thumb safety, firing pin block. Made by Dornaus & Dixon. Introduced, 1983; no longer in production. Used values: Standard model, $800 to $850; Military/Police, with overall black matte finish, $775 to $800; Dual Presentation 10mm & .45 ACP, $1250 to $1500.

Pocket Model similar to standard Bren Ten, but smaller; has 4" barrel, 7.37" overall length; weighs 28 oz.; fires 10mm Auto ammo; 9-rd. magazine; hard chrome slide, stainless frame. Introduced, 1984; no longer in production. Used value, $800 to $850.

CENTURY Model 100: revolver; single-action; .375 Winchester, .444 Marlin, .45-70; 6½", 8", 10", 12" barrels; weighs 6 lb.; Millett adjustable square-notch rear sight, ramp front; uncheckered walnut stocks; manganese bronze frame, blued cylinder, barrel; coil spring trigger mechanism. Introduced, 1975; still in production. Used values: 6½", 8" barrels, $450 to $475; 10", 12" barrels, $500 to $525.

Chipmunk Silhouette

CHIPMUNK Silhouette Model: bolt-action; single-shot; .22 LR; 14⅞" barrel; 20" overall length; weighs 32 oz.; American walnut stock; post ramp front sight, peep rear; meets IHMSA .22 unlimited competition rules. Introduced, 1985; still in production. Used value, $90 to $100.

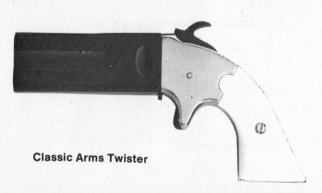

Classic Arms Twister

CLASSIC ARMS Twister: derringer, over/under; .22 LR, 9mm rimfire; 3¼" barrel; no sights; pearlite grips; barrels rotate on axis for two shots; spur trigger. Originally marketed by Navy Arms. Introduced, 1980; dropped, 1984. Used value, $45 to $50.

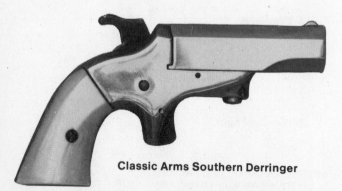

Classic Arms Southern Derringer

CLASSIC ARMS Southern Derringer: single-shot; .22 LR, .41 rimfire; 2½" barrel; weighs 12 oz.; 5" overall length; blade front sight; white plastic stocks; steel barrel; brass frame. Introduced, 1982; dropped, 1984. Used value, $45 to $55.

CLERKE First Model: double-action revolver; .32 S&W, .22 LR, long, short; 2¼" barrel; 6¼" overall length; fixed sights; 5-rd. swing-out cylinder in .32, 6 rds. in .22; checkered plastic grips; blued, nickel finish. Introduced in 1973; dropped, 1975. Used value, $20 to $25.

COMPETITION ARMS Competitor: single-shot; .22 LR, .223, 7mm TCU, 7mm International, .30 Herrett, .357 magnum, .41 magnum, .454 Casull, .375 Super Mag; other calibers on special order; 10", 14" barrel lengths; adjustable open rear sight, ramp front;

Clerke 1st Model

Competition Arms Competitor

interchangeable barrels of blued ordnance or stainless steel; vent barrel shroud; integral scope mount. Introduced, 1987; still in production. Used values: 10½" barrel, $350 to $375; 14" barrel, $360 to $385; extra barrels, standard calibers, $60 to $70 each; special calibers, $100 to $120.

COONAN .357 Magnum: automatic; .357 magnum; 7-rd. magazine; 5" barrel; weighs 42 oz.; 8.3" overall length; smooth walnut stocks; open adjustable sights; barrel hood; many parts interchangeable with Colt autos; grip, hammer, half-cock safeties. Introduced, 1983; limited production to date. Used value, $450 to $500.

COP

COP: 4-barrel double-action; stainless steel construction; .357 magnum; 3¼" barrels, 5½" overall length; open fixed sights; checkered composition grips. Introduced, 1981; still in production. Used value, $190 to $210.

DAVIS P-32: automatic; .32 ACP; 6-rd. magazine; 2.8" barrel; overall length, 5.4"; laminated wood stocks; fixed sights; chrome or black Teflon finish. Introduced, 1986; still in production. Used value, $150 to $175.

Davis P-32

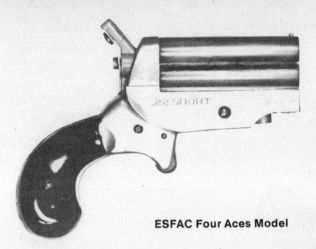

ESFAC Four Aces Model

DAVIS Derringer: over-under; .22 LR, .22 WRFM, .25 ACP, .32 ACP; 2.4" barrel; overall length; 4"; weighs 9.5 oz.; fixed notch rear sight, blade front; laminated wood stocks; black Teflon or chrome finish; spur trigger. Introduced, 1986; still in production. Used value, $40 to $45.

Four Aces Model 2 has same specs as Model 1, except has square-butt frame. Used value, $45 to $50.

Four Aces Model 3 has same specs as Model 2, except has 2" barrels, chambered for .22 LR cartridge. Used value, $50 to $55.

Four Aces Model 4 has same specs as Model 3, except overall length is slightly longer. Used value, $50 to $55.

ESFAC Pocket Pony

Falcon Portsider

ESFAC Pocket Pony: revolver; single-action; .22 LR; 6 rds.; 1⅜" barrel; fixed sights; black plastic grips; manganese bronze frame; blued barrel; color case-hardened trigger, hammer; non-fluted cylinder. Introduced, 1973; maker ceased business, 1974. Used value, $60 to $75.

FALCON Portsider: automatic; .45 ACP; 7-rd. magazine; 5" barrel; 8½" overall length; weighs 38 oz.; fixed combat sights; checkered walnut stocks; stainless steel construction; extended safety; wide grip safety; enlarged left-hand ejection port; extended ejector. Introduced, 1986; still in production. Used value, $425 to $450.

ESFAC Little Ace Derringer

Fraser Automatic

ESFAC Little Ace Derringer: single-shot; .22 short; 2" barrel; black plastic grips; no sights; manganese bronze frame; blued barrel; color case-hardened spur trigger, hammer; Introduced, 1973; maker ceased business, 1974. Used value, $30 to $35.

ESFAC Four Aces Model 1: derringer; .22 short; 4 rds.; 4 barrels 1-11/16" in length; black plastic grips; round butt; post front sight; manganese bronze frame; spur trigger; barrel selector on hammer; blued steel barrels. Introduced, 1973; maker ceased business, 1974. Used value, $45 to $50.

FRASER Automatic: automatic; .25 ACP; 6-rd. magazine; 2¼" barrel; 4" overall length; weighs 10 oz.; recessed fixed sights; checkered walnut or plastic pearl stocks; stainless steel construction; positive manual and magazine safeties; satin stainless, gold-plated or black QPQ finishes. Introduced, 1983; dropped, 1986. Used values: satin stainless, $75 to $85; gold-plated, $175 to $190; QPQ finish, $80 to $90.

FTL Auto Nine

Freedom Arms Mini Revolver

FREEDOM ARMS Mini Revolver: single-action; .22 short, .22 LR, .22 WRFM; 5 rds.; 4" barrel for magnum; 1", 1¾" barrel for LR, 4" overall length; blade front sight, notched rear; black ebonite grips; stainless steel construction; marketed in presentation case. Introduced, 1978; still in production. Used value, $85 to $90.

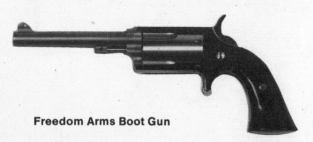

Freedom Arms Boot Gun

FREEDOM ARMS Boot Gun: revolver; single-action; has same specs as Freedom Arms Mini Revolver, except chambered for .22 LR, .22 WRFM only; has 3" barrel; weighs 5 oz.; 5⅞" overall length; oversize grips; floating firing pin; stainless steel construction. Introduced, 1982; still in production. Used values: .22 LR, $110 to $115; .22 WRFM, $120 to $125.

Freedom Arms .454 Casull

FREEDOM ARMS .454 Casull: revolver; single-action; .454 Casull; 5-rd. cylinder; 4¾", 7½", 10", 12" barrel lengths; weighs 50 oz. with 7½" barrel; impregnated hardwood stocks; blade front sight, notch or adjustable rear; stainless steel; sliding bar safety. Introduced, 1983; still in production. Used values: fixed sights, $675 to $725; adjustable sights, $775 to $825.

FTL Auto Nine: automatic; .22 LR; 6-rd. magazine; 2¼" barrel, 4⅜" overall length; checkered plastic grips; U-notch in slide as sight; alloy frame; barrel support sleeve bushing; hard chrome finish. Introduced in 1978; dropped, 1982. Used value, $145 to $150.

GUARDIAN-SS: automatic; double-action; .380 ACP; 6-rd. magazine; 3¼" barrel; weighs 20 oz.; 6" overall length; checkered walnut stocks; ramp front sight, windage-adjustable combat rear; narrow polished trigger; Pachmayr grips; blue slide; hand-fitted barrel; polished feed ramp; funneled magazine well; stainless steel. Introduced, 1982; dropped, 1985. Marketed by Michigan Armament, Inc. Used values: standard model, $200 to $225; custom model, $275 to $300.

Great Western Frontier

GREAT WESTERN Frontier: revolver, single-action; .22 LR, .22 Hornet, .38 Special, .357 magnum, .44 Special, .44 magnum, .45 Colt; 6-rd. cylinder; 4¾", 5½", 7½" barrel lengths; grooved rear sight, fixed blade front; imitation stag grips; blued finish. Sold primarily by mail order. Manufactured 1951 to 1962. Used values: .22, $150 to $165; centerfires, $225 to $275.

GREAT WESTERN Derringer: over/under, 2-shot; .38 S&W; 3" barrels; 5" overall length; checkered black plastic grips; fixed sights; blued finish. Replica of Remington Double Derringer. Manufactured 1953 to 1962. Used value, $95 to $100.

GUNWORKS Model 9 Derringer: over/under; .38/.357 magnum, 9mm/9mm magnum; bottom-hinged action; 3" barrel; weighs 15 oz.; smooth wood stocks; Millett orange bar front sight, fixed rear; all steel; half-cock, through-frame safety; dual extraction; electroless nickel finish; marketed with in-pant holster. Introduced, 1984, no longer in production. Used value, $85 to $90.

HARTFORD Target Automatic: in .22 LR only; 6¾" barrel; 10¾" overall length; 10-rd. magazine; checkered black rubber grips; target sights; blued finish. Bears close resemblance to early High Standard automatic models. Introduced in 1929; dropped, 1930. Has more collector than shooter value. Used value, $450 to $500.

HARTFORD Repeating Pistol: has the same general outward design characteristics as target auto; .22 LR only; hand-operated repeater, with slide being moved rearward by hand to eject cartridge case, forward to chamber new round. Introduced in 1929; dropped, 1930. Used value, $350 to $400.

HARTFORD Target Single-Shot: same general outward appearance as Hartford target auto, but with 5¾" barrel; 10¾" overall

Hartford Target Auto

length; .22 LR only; black rubber or walnut grips; target sights; color case-hardened frame; blued barrel. Introduced in 1929; dropped, 1930. Used value, $350 to $400.

Indian Arms DA

INDIAN ARMS Stainless: automatic, double-action; .380 auto; 6-rd. magazine; 3½" barrel; 6-1/16" overall length; checkered walnut stocks; adjustable rear sight, blade front; made of stainless steel, but with natural or blued finish; optional safety lock. Introduced, 1977; dropped, 1978. Used value, $250 to $275.

Interarms Virginian Dragoon

INTERARMS Virginian Dragoon: revolver, single-action; .357 magnum, .44 magnum, .45 Colt; 6-rds.; 6", 7½", 8⅜" barrel lengths; 12" Buntline on special order; ramp-type Patridge front sight, micro-adjustable target rear; smooth walnut grips; spring-loaded firing pin; color case-hardened frame; blued finish. Introduced, 1977;

dropped, 1986. Used values: standard barrel lengths, $210 to $230; Buntline barrel, $230 to $250.

Virginian Dragoon Silhouette has same general specs as standard model, except is of stainless steel; .357 magnum, .41 magnum, .44 magnum; 7½", 8⅜", 10½" barrels; smooth walnut and Pachmayr rubber grips; undercut blade front sight, adjustable square-notch rear; meets IHMSA standards. Made by Interarms. Introduced, 1982; dropped, 1986. Used values, $310 to $325.

Virginian Dragoon Engraved Models are same as standard Dragoon, except in .44 magnum; 6", 7" barrel; fluted or unfluted cylinders; stainless or blued; hand-engraved frame, cylinder, barrel; marketed in felt-lined walnut case. Introduced, 1983; dropped, 1986. Used value, $450 to $475.

Virginian Dragoon Deputy Model is similar to standard Dragoon, except has fixed sights; 5" barrel in .357, 6" in .44 magnum. Introduced, 1983; dropped, 1986. Used value, $200 to $220.

INTERDYNAMIC KG-99: automatic; 9mm Parabellum; 36-rd. magazine; 5" barrel; 12½" overall length; weighs 46 oz.; straight blowback action; fires from closed bolt; frame, stocks of high-impact nylon; blade front sight, fixed open rear. Introduced, 1982; still in production. Used value, $175 to $200.

KG-99K has same general specs as KG-99, except has 3" barrel; overall length 10"; weighs 44 oz.; 25-rd. standard magazine. Introduced, 1983; still in production. Used value, $180 to $200.

JANA Bison: revolver, single-action; .22 LR, .22 WRFM; 4¾" barrel; fixed front sight, adjustable rear; imitation stag grips; blued finish. Introduced, 1978; imported from West Germany; dropped, 1980. Used value, $65 to $75.

Jennings Model J-22

JENNINGS J-22: automatic; .22 LR; 6-rd. magazine; 2½" barrel; weighs 12 oz.; 4-15/16" overall length; fixed sights; walnut stocks. Introduced, 1981; still in production. Used value, $40 to $45.

Kimber Predator Supergrade

KIMBER Predator Hunter: single-shot; .221 Fireball, .223 Rem., 6mm TCU, 6x45, 7mm TCU; 15¾" barrel; weighs 88 oz.; no sights furnished; accepts Kimber scope mount system; AA claro walnut stock; uses Kimber Model 84 mini-Mauser action. Introduced, 1987; still in production. Used value, $700 to $800.

Predator Supergrade has same specs as Predator Hunter, except stock is of French walnut, has ebony forend tip, 22-line hand checkering. Introduced, 1987; still in production. Used value, $850 to $950.

LAR Grizzly Model

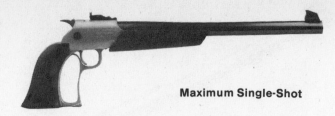

Maximum Single-Shot

LAR Grizzly: automatic; .45 Win. magnum; 7-rd. magazine; conversion units available for 9mm Win. magnum, .45 ACP, .357 magnum, .30 Mauser, .38 Super, .38 Special, 9mm Steyr, 9mm Browning Long, 9mm Luger; 5-7/16" barrel; weighs 51 oz.; 8⅞" overall length; no-slip rubber combat grips; ramped blade front sight, fully adjustable rear; beveled magazine well; flat, checkered rubber mainspring housing; polished feed ramp; throated barrel; solid barrel bushings. Introduced, 1983; limited production to date. Used value: $575 to $600; conversion units, $120 to $125.

LES P-18: automatic; 9mm Parabellum; 18-rd. magazine; 5½" barrel; checkered resin stocks; post front sight, V-notch rear, drift adjustable for windage; stainless steel; gas-assisted action; single- and double-action models in standard matte, deluxe polished finishes. Introduced in 1977; dropped 1981. Used values: standard finish, $225 to $235; deluxe finish, $285 to $295.

MAXIMUM Single-Shot: single-shot; falling-block action; .223, .22-250, 6mm BR, .243, .250 Savage, 7mm BR, 7mm TCU, 7mm-08, .30 Herrett, .308 Win.; 10½", 14" barrels; smooth walnut stocks, forend; ramp front sight, fully adjustable open rear; integral grip frame/receiver; drilled/tapped for scope mounts; adjustable trigger; Armaloy finish; interchangeable barrels. Made by MOA Corp. Introduced, 1983; still in production. Used value, $360 to $375.

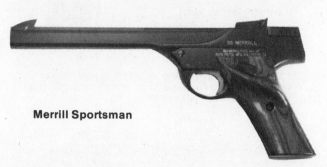

Merrill Sportsman

MERRILL Sportsman: single-shot; .22 short, .22 LR, .22 WRFM, .22 Rem Jet, .22 Hornet, .357 magnum, .38 Special, .256 Win. magnum, .45 Colt, .30-30, .44 magnum, and many others; 9", 12", 14" semi-octagon hinged barrel; uncheckered walnut grips with thumb, heel rest; adjustable rear sight, fixed front; hammerless; top rib grooved for scope mounts. Introduced, 1972; still in production as the RPM XL pistol. Used value, $325 to $350.

Liberty Mustang

Mitchell Single Action

LIBERTY Mustang: revolver, single-action; .22 LR, .22 WRFM or combo; 8 rds.; 5" barrel; 10½" overall length, blade front sight, adjustable rear; side ejector rod; smooth rosewood grips. Imported from Italy; introduced, 1976; dropped, 1980. Used value, $45 to $50.

LJUTIC LJ II: 2-shot derringer; double-action; .22 WRFM; 2¾" side-by-side barrels; checkered walnut stocks; fixed sights; vent rib; positive safety; stainless steel construction. Introduced, 1981; still in limited production. Used value, $400 to $425.

MITCHELL Single Action: revolver; .22 LR/.22 WRFM combo; .357 magnum, .44 magnum, .44 magnum/.44-40 combo, .45 Colt; 4¾", 5½", 6", 7½", 10", 12", 18" barrel lengths; ramp front sight, adjustable rear; one-piece walnut grips; brass grip frame; color case-hardened frame; hammer block safety; blued finish. Introduced, 1980; dropped, 1983. Used value, $125 to $150, depending on barrel length.

MITCHELL Derringer: over/under barrels; 2 rds.; .38 Special; 2¾" barrel; 5¼" overall length; polished blue finish; checkered walnut grips; has same basic design as original Remington, except for ramp front sight. Introduced, 1981; still in production. Used value, $90 to $100.

MOSSBERG Brownie: double-action, pocket pistol; four 2½" barrels; revolving firing pin; .22 LR, long, short; break-open action; steel extractor. Introduced in 1919; dropped, 1932. Has some collector interest. Used value, $250 to $275.

MOSSBERG Abilene: revolver; single-action; .357 magnum, .44 magnum, .45 Colt; 6 rds.; 4⅝", 6", 7½" barrel lengths; serrated ramp front sight, click-adjustable rear; smooth walnut grips; wide hammer spur; transfer bar ignition; blued or Magnaloy finish. Intro-

Ljutic Space Pistol

LJUTIC Space Pistol: single-shot; .22 WRFM, .357 magnum, .44 magnum, .308 Win.; 13½" barrel; American walnut grip, forend; twist-bolt action; button trigger; scope mounts furnished. Introduced, 1981; still in limited production. Used value, $625 to $650.

Mossberg Abilene

duced, 1978 by United States Arms, taken over by Mossberg; not currently in production. Used values: blued finish, $175 to $200; Magnaloy, $220 to $235.

Mitchell Derringer

Mossberg Brownie

NAM Mini Model

NAM Mini Model: revolver; single-action; .22 short, .22 LR, .22 WRFM; 1⅛", 1¼", 1⅝" barrels; weighs 4½ oz.; smooth plastic or walnut stocks; blade front sight only; stainless steel construction; spur trigger. Introduced, 1982; still in production. Used values, $85 to $95.

NORTH AMERICAN ARMS Model 22S: single-action revolver; .22 short; 5-rd. cylinder; 1⅛" barrel, 3½" overall length; made of stainless steel; plastic stocks; fixed sights. Introduced, 1981; still in production. Used value, $75 to $85.
   Model 22 LR has the same general specs as Model 22S, but chambered for .22 LR cartridge; 3⅞" overall length. Introduced, 1976; still in production. Used value, $85 to $95.

NORTH AMERICAN ARMS Model 454C: single-action revolver; .454 Casull; 5-rd. cylinder; 7½" barrel; 14" overall length; made of stainless steel; uncheckered hardwood stocks; fixed sights. Introduced in 1977; sporadic production since. Used value, $375 to $400.

NORTH AMERICAN 450 Magnum Express: revolver; single-action; .450 Magnum Express, .45 Win. magnum; 5-rd. cylinder; 7½", 10½" barrels; weighs 52 oz. with 7½" barrel; fully adjustable rear sight, blade front; uncheckered walnut stocks; patented hammer safety; stainless steel construction. Only 550 made. Introduced, 1984; dropped, 1985. Used value, $1400 to $1600.

ODI Viking: combat automatic; double-action; .45 ACP; 7-rd. magazine; 5" barrel; weighs 36 oz.; fixed sights; smooth teakwood stocks; stainless steel; brushed satin finish; spur-type hammer. Introduced, 1983; dropped, 1985. Used value, $400 to $415.

ODI Viking

ODI Viking Combat Model: automatic; 9mm, 9 rds.; .45 ACP, 7 rds.; 5" barrel; weighs 39 oz.; fixed notched rear sight, blade front; smooth teak stocks; made of stainless steel; brushed satin finish; Seecamp double-action system; spur-type hammer. Introduced, 1982, dropped, 1985. Used value, $375 to $395.
   Viking II has same general specs, except has 4½" barrel, weighs 37 oz.; slide-mounted thumb-activated firing pin safety. Used value, $375 to $395.

Phelps Heritage I

PHELPS Heritage I: revolver; single-action; .45-70; 6-rd. cylinder; 8", 12" barrels; weighs 5½ lb. with 12" barrel; adjustable rear sight, ramp front; safety bar; polished blued finish. Introduced, 1986; still in production. Used value, $450 to $475.
   Eagle I Model has same specs as Heritage, except is chambered for .444 Marlin. Introduced, 1986; still in production. Used value, $475 to $500.

Plainfield Model 71

Randall Service Model

PLAINFIELD Model 71: automatic; .22 LR, .25 auto; 10-rd. magazine in .22 LR; .25 auto, 8 rds.; 2½" barrel; 5⅛" overall length; stainless steel slide, frame; fixed sights; checkered walnut stocks. Also made with caliber conversion kit. Introduced, 1970; dropped, 1980 (approx.). Used values: .22 LR, .25 auto, $65 to $70; with conversion kit, $125 to $135.

Plainfield Model 72

Randall Raider Left-Hand Model

PLAINFIELD Model 72: automatic; has the same general specs as Model 71, except for 3½" barrel; 6" overall length; aluminum slide. Introduced, 1970; dropped about 1978. Used values: .22 LR, .25 auto, $70 to $75; with conversion kit, $125 to $135.

Randall Curtis E. LeMay Model

Pocket Partner

RANDALL Service Model: automatic; 9mm, .38 Super, .45 ACP; 5" barrel; weighs 38 oz.; 8½" overall length; blade front sight, fixed or adjustable rear; checkered walnut stocks; all stainless steel construction; round-top or ribbed slide. Introduced, 1983; dropped, 1984. Used values: with fixed sights, $275 to $285; adjustable sights, $295 to $315.

Compact Service Model has same specs as standard model, except has 4½" barrel; 7¾" overall length; weighs 36 oz. Introduced, 1983; dropped, 1984. Used values: fixed sights, $265 to $275; adjustable sights, $265 to $285.

Raider Model has same general specs as Service Model, except has 4½" barrel, measures 7¾" overall; 6-rd. magazine; weighs 35 oz.; also made in left-hand model; has squared trigger guard, extended magazine base plate. Introduced, 1984; dropped, 1985. Used value, $325 to $425, depending on sight options.

Curtis E. LeMay Four Star Model is almost identical to Raider Model, except for cosmetics. Introduced, 1984; dropped, 1985. Used value, depending on options, $450 to $480.

POCKET PARTNER: automatic; .22 LR; 6-rd. magazine; 2¼" barrel; overall length, 4¾"; weighs 10 oz.; fixed sights; checkered plastic stocks; all-steel construction; brushed blue finish. Introduced, 1985; still in production. Used value, $70 to $80.

Raven 25

Savage Model 1910

RAVEN: automatic; .25 auto; 3" barrel; 5½" overall length uncheckered walnut or pearlite stocks; fixed sights; blued, nickel or satin nickel finish. Manufactured in U.S., marketed by Early and Modern Firearms. Introduced, 1977; still in production and marketed by Raven Arms. Used value, $35 to $40.

SAVAGE Model 1910: automatic; .32 auto, .380 auto; .32 auto has 10-rd. magazine, 3¾" barrel, 6½" overall length; .380 auto has 9-rd. magazine, 4½" barrel, 7" overall length; grip safety; either hammerless or with exposed hammer; checkered hard rubber stocks; fixed sights; blued finish. Manufactured 1910 to 1917 Collector value. Used value, $225 to $250.

Reising Target Model

Savage Model 1917

REISING Target Model: automatic; hinged frame; .22 LR; 12-rd. magazine; 6½" barrel; external hammer; hard rubber checkered stocks; fixed sights; blued finish. Manufactured 1921 to 1924. Collector value. Used value, $350 to $400.

SAVAGE Model 1917: automatic pistol; .32 auto, 10-rd. magazine; .380 auto, 9-rd. magazine; 3¾" barrel in .32, 4½" barrel in .380; spurred hammer; blued finish; fixed sights; hard rubber grips. Instroduced in 1920; dropped, 1928. Used value, $225 to $250.

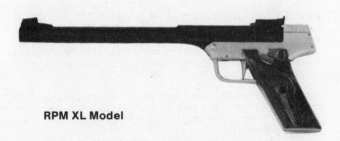

RPM XL Model

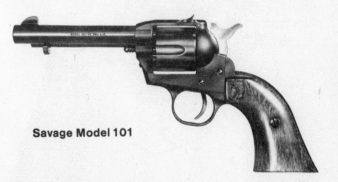

Savage Model 101

RPM XL Model: single-shot; .22 LR, .22 WRFM, .225 Win., .25 Rocket, 6.5mm Rocket, .32 H&R magnum, .357 Maximum, .357 magnum, .30-30, .30 Herrett, .357 Herrett, .41 magnum, .44 magnum, .454 Casull, .375 Win., 7mm UR, 7mm Merrill, .30 Merrill, 7mm Rocket, .270 Rocket, .270 Maximum, .45-70; 8", 10", 10¾", 12", 14" barrels; wide vent rib; adjustable Millett or ISGW rear sight, blade front; uncheckered walnut stocks; thumb and heel rests; barrel drilled, tapped for scope mounts; cocking indicator; spring-loaded barrel lock; positive hammer block thumb safety; adjustable trigger; blued or hard chrome finish; right- or left-hand models. Was made as the Merrill Sportsman until 1986. Introduced, 1986; still in production. Used value, depending on options, $425 to $475.

SAVAGE Model 101: single-action single-shot; .22 LR, long, short; 5½" barrel integral with chamber; overall length, 9"; fake cylinder swings out for loading, ejection; manual ejection with spring-rod ejector; compressed, plastic-impregnated wood grips; adjustable slotted rear sight, blade front; blued. Introduced in 1968; dropped, 1969. Used value, $100 to $125.

SECURITY INDUSTRIES Model PSS38: double-action revolver; .38 Special; 5-rd. cylinder; 2" barrel; 6½" overall length; made of stainless steel; checkered or smooth American walnut stocks; fixed sights. Introduced, 1973; dropped, 1977. Used value, $125 to $130.

SECURITY INDUSTRIES Model PM357: double-action revolver; .357 magnum; 5-rd. cylinder; 2½" barrel; 7½" overall length;

Security Industries Model PSS38

Security Industries Model PM357

made of stainless steel; uncheckered American walnut target stocks; fixed sights. Introduced in 1973; dropped, 1977. Used value, $125 to $135.

Security Industries Model PPM357

SECURITY INDUSTRIES Model PPM357: double-action revolver; .357 magnum; 5-rd. cylinder; 2" barrel; 6⅛" overall length; made of stainless steel; checkered American walnut target stocks; fixed sights. Introduced in 1976 with spurless hammer; converted to conventional hammer, 1977; dropped, 1977. Used value, $145 to $155.

SEDGLEY Baby Hammerless Model: double-action revolver; solid frame; .22 LR; 6-rd. cylinder; folding trigger; 4" overall length; hard rubber stocks; fixed sights; blued or nickel. Manufactured 1930 to 1939. Some collector interest. Used value, $175 to $200.

SEVILLE Single-Action: revolver; 6-rd. cylinder; .357 magnum, 9mm Win. magnum, .41 magnum, .45 ACP, .45 Colt, .45 Win. magnum; 4⅝", 5½", 6½", 7½" barrel lengths; smooth walnut, Pachmayr or thumbrest stocks; ramp front sight with red insert, fully adjustable rear; blued finish or stainless steel. Made in U.S. Introduced, 1981; no longer in production. Was made by United Sporting Arms, Inc. Used values: blued finish, $200 to $215; stainless steel, $225 to $250.

Seville Stainless Super Mag

SEVILLE Stainless Super Mag: revolver; single-action; 6-rd. cylinder; .357 Rem. Maximum, .454 magnum; 7½", 10" barrel lengths; mesquite or Pachmayr rubber stocks; stainless steel; other specs are same as standard Seville single-action. Made in U.S. Introduced, 1983; no longer in production. Used values: .357 Maximum, $300 to $350; .454 magnum, $400 to $450.

Seville Sheriff's Model

SEVILLE Sheriff's Model: revolver; single-action; 6-rd. cylinder; .44-40, .44 magnum, .45 ACP, .45 Colt; 3½" barrel; square-butt or bird's-head smooth walnut grips; ramp or blade front sight, adjustable or fixed rear; blued finish or stainless steel. Made in U.S. Introduced, 1983; dropped, 1983. Used values: blued finish, $215 to $225; stainless steel, $275 to $290.

SEVILLE Silhouette: revolver; single-action; .357, .41, .44, .45 Win. magnum; 6 rds.; 10½" barrel; weighs 55 oz.; smooth walnut thumbrest or Pachmayr stocks; undercut Patridge-style front sight, adjustable rear; stainless steel or blued finish. Marketed by United Sporting Arms. No longer in production. Used values: stainless steel, $300 to $325; blued, $225 to $250.

SHERIDAN Knockabout: single-shot pistol; tip-up action; .22 short, long; 5" barrel; 8¾" overall length; checkered plastic grips; blued finish; fixed sights. Introduced in 1953; dropped, 1960. Used value, $110 to $125.

SILE-SEECAMP II: automatic; double-action; .25 ACP, 8-rd. magazine; .32 ACP, 6-rd.; 2" barrel, 4⅛" overall length; smooth, non-snag contoured barrel sights on slide; cut-checkered walnut grips; stainless steel construction; inertia-operated firing pin; magazine disconnector; blued finish. Introduced in 1980; still in production as Seecamp LWS 32. Used value, $200 to $225.

SOKOLOVSKY 45 Automaster: automatic; .45 ACP; 6-rd. magazine; 6" barrel; 9½" overall length; weighs 3.6 lb.; smooth walnut stocks; ramp front sight, Millett adjustable rear; semi-custom built with precise tolerances for target shooting; special safety trigger; primarily stainless steel. Introduced, 1985; still in production. Used value, $2300 to $2400.

Sile-Seecamp II

Sokolovsky 45 Automaster

Springfield Armory 1911-A1

Steel City Double Duece

SPRINGFIELD ARMORY 1911-A1: automatic; 9mm, .45 ACP; 8-rd. magazine; reproduction of original Colt model; all new forged parts. Introduced, 1985; still in production. Used value, $225 to $250.

STEEL CITY Double Deuce: automatic; double-action; .22 LR, .25 ACP; 7-rd. magazine in .22, 6 rds. in .25; 2½" barrel; 5½" overall length; weighs 18 oz.; fixed groove sights; ambidextrous slide-mounted safety; stainless steel construction; matte finish. Introduced, 1985; still in production. Used value, $200 to $225.

Steel City War Eagle

STEEL CITY War Eagle: automatic; double-action; 9mmP; 13-rd. magazine; 4" barrel; fixed or adjustable sights; rosewood stocks; ambidextrous safety; matte-finished stainless steel construction. Introduced, 1986; still in production. Used value, $275 to $300.

Stevens No. 35

STEVENS No. 35: single-shot target pistol; .22 LR only; 6", 8", 12¼" barrels; tip-up action; walnut grips; target sights; blued. Also produced to handle .410 shotshell. Introduced in 1907; dropped, 1939. Has mostly collector value. Used value, $175 to $225.

Stevens No. 10

STEVENS No. 10: single-shot target model; tip-up action; .22 LR; 8" barrel; 11½" overall length; hard rubber stocks; blued finish; target sights. Manufactured 1919 to 1939. Some collector interest. Used value, $165 to $185.

Stoeger Target Luger

STOEGER Luger: automatic; .22 LR only; 11-rd. magazine; 4½", 5½" barrels; based upon original Luger design, but made in U.S. for Stoeger Arms; checkered or smooth wooden grips; blued. Introduced in 1970; dropped, 1978; all-steel model reintroduced, 1980; dropped, 1985. Made briefly by Navy Arms; dropped, 1987. Used value, $85 to $110.

Luger Target model has the same specs as standard Stoeger Luger, except for checkered hardwood stocks; target sights. Introduced, 1975; all-steel model reintroduced, 1980; dropped, 1985. Used value, $100 to $125.

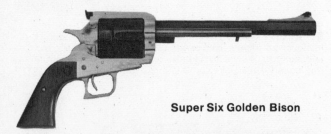

Super Six Golden Bison

SUPER SIX Golden Bison: revolver; single-action; .45-70; 6-rd. cylinder; 8", 10½" octagonal barrels; with 8" barrel, overall length is 15"; weighs 92 oz.; adjustable Millett rear sight, blaze orange blade on ramp front; manganese bronze used in cylinder frame, grip frame; coil springs; half-cock, crossbolt traveling safeties; antique brown or blued finish. Marketed in fitted walnut presentation case by Super Six Limited. Used values: with 8" barrel, $900 to $950; with 10½" barrel, $950 to $1000.

Tanarmi Over/Under Derringer

TANARMI Over/Under Derringer: single-shot; .38 Special; 3" barrel; 4¾" overall length; weighs 14 oz.; checkered white nylon stocks; fixed sights; tip-up barrel; blued finish. Assembled in U.S. by Excam; still in production. Used value, $55 to $60.

TDE Backup: automatic; .380 ACP; 5-rd. magazine; 2½" barrel; 5" overall length; uncheckered hardwood stocks; recessed fixed sights; concealed hammer; blowback operation; stainless steel. Introduced, 1977; still in production. Used value, $145 to $165.

Texas Longhorn Border Special

TEXAS LONGHORN Border Special: revolver; single-action; all centerfire pistol calibers; 3½" barrel; grooved top-strap rear sight, blade front; one-piece fancy walnut bird's-head style stocks; loading gate, ejector housing on left side; cylinder rotates to left; color case-hardened frame; high-polish blue finish; music wire coil springs. Marketed in glass-top display case. Introduced, 1984; still in production. Used value, $1200 to $1400.

**Texas Longhorn
West Texas Flat Top Target Model**

TEXAS LONGHORN West Texas Flat Top Target Model: revolver; single-action; has same features, specs as Border Special, except has standard stock rear sight, contoured ramp front; flat-top style frame. Marketed in display case. Introduced, 1984; still in production. Used value, $1200 to $1400.

Texas Longhorn Jezebel

TEXAS LONGHORN Jezebel: single-shot; .22 short, .22 LR; 6" barrel; 8" overall length; weighs 15 oz.; one-piece walnut grip, forend; fixed rear sight, bead front; top-break action; all stainless steel construction. Introduced, 1986; still in production. Used value, $130 to $140.

THOMAS 45: automatic; double-action; .45 ACP; 6-rd. magazine; 3½" barrel; 6½" overall length; checkered plastic stocks; windage-adjustable rear sight, blade front; blued finish; matte sighting surface; blowback action. Introduced, 1977; dropped, 1978. Only about 600 guns ever made. Collector value. Used value, $425 to $450.

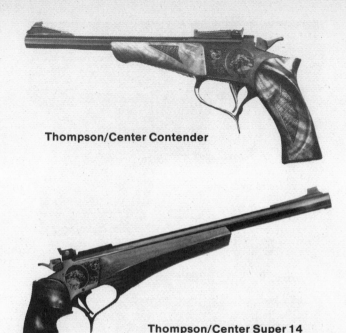

Thompson/Center Contender

Thompson/Center Super 14

THOMPSON/CENTER Contender: introduced in 1967; still in production. Single-shot, break-open pistol with exposed hammer, the action being opened by pressing rearward and upward on the tang of the trigger guard. Barrels are interchangeable, permitting the firing of different calibers from the same receiver. A circular insert in the face of the hammer is pivoted one-half turn to switch between the centerfire and rimfire firing pins. Barrels have been factory chambered and custom rechambered for a variety of different cartridges, many of them nonstandard, or "wildcat" numbers. A detachable choke tube was developed originally for a barrel chambered for the .45 Colt which, with choke installed, could fire 3" .410 shotshells effectively. Production of this barrel was discontinued at the suggestion of BATF; the .45 Colt/.410 barrels have changed hands at prices of $175 or more, due to their scarcity. Currently, an internal choke is furnished on the vent-rib barrel and bull barrel in .44 magnum and .45 Colt permitting the firing of solid-bullet loads when the choke is removed or T/C's "Hot-Shot" capsules with choke in place.

Rimfire calibers are .22 LR (also handling .22 BB caps, CB caps, short, long or shot loads), .22 WRFM, 5mm Rem.; centerfire calibers are .22 Hornet, .22 K-Hornet, .22 Rem. Jet, .218 Bee, .221 Rem. Fire Ball, .222 Rem., .256 Win. magnum, .25-35 WCF, .30 M-1 Carbine, .30-30 WCF, .38 Super Auto, .38 Special, .357 magnum, .357/44 Bain & Davis, 9mm Parabellum (Luger), .45 ACP, .45 Long Colt, .44 magnum. The .44 and .45 Colt can be had with choke or without; unfluted "bull barrels" are offered in .30 Herrett and .357 Herrett, these being two wildcat cartridges based upon the .30-30 case; standard barrel lengths, 8¾" and 10" although a few have been made in 6" length; standard forends snap on, but a special screw-held forend is supplied with the bull barrels; two designs of grips have been furnished, the early type having a decorative metal butt cap and the current one having a black plastic butt cap; decorative game scene etching is standard on both sides of all receivers; later models have adjustable trigger-stop in rear of trigger guard; standard sights consist of an undercut Patridge front sight on a ramp, with square-notch rear sight adjustable for windage or elevation; scope mounts available from T/C and other suppliers to fit the holes drilled and tapped for rear sight; weight, with 10" barrel, about 43 oz.; finish, blued; stocks, checkered walnut forend and handgrip, with thumbrest grips that must be ordered for right- or left-hand use, no extra charge for left-hand grips. Most early models embody a receiver design that makes it necessary to reset the action by pulling the trigger guard tang rearward before the hammer can be cocked. Used values: $175 to $200 for standard gun, complete with one barrel; $200 to $225 for gun with vent-rib/internal choke or full bull barrel less sights; $200 to $225 for gun with bull barrel and iron sights; $75 to $95 for standard barrel alone; $100 to $125 for vent-rib/internal choke or bull barrel less

sights; $75 to $95 for bull barrel alone, fitted with iron sights. Scarce, discontinued barrels in exotic chamberings may command higher figures.

Super 14 Contender has same general specs as standard Contender, except for 14" barrel; fully adjustable target sights; chambered for .30 Herrett, .357 Herrett, .30-30 Win., .35 Rem., .41 magnum, .44 magnum, .45 Win. magnum. Introduced, 1979; still in production. Used value, $225 to $235.

ULTRA LIGHT ARMS Model 20 Reb Hunter: bolt-action; .22-250 through .308 Win.; most silhouette calibers on request; 5-rd. magazine; 14" barrel; weighs 64 oz.; Kevlar/graphite reinforced stock in camouflage pattern; two-position safety; Timney adjustable trigger; matte or bright stock, metal finish; left- or right-hand action. Marketed in hard case. Introduced, 1987; still in production. Used value, $900 to $950.

U.S. ARMS Abilene Model: revolver, single-action; .357 magnum, .41 magnum, .44 magnum, .45 Colt; 4⅝", 5½", 6½", 7½", 8½" barrel lengths; adjustable rear sight, ramp front; uncheckered American walnut stocks; blued finish or stainless steel. Introduced in 1976; dropped, 1983. Used values: blued finish, $150 to $175; stainless steel, $175 to $200.

Abilene Convertible has same general specs as standard model, except for interchangeable .357 magnum, 9mm Luger cylinders; available only in blued finish. Used value, $175 to $200.

VEGA Stainless 45: automatic; .45 ACP; 7-rd. magazine; stainless steel construction; 5" barrel; 8⅜" overall length; almost exact copy of 1911A1 Colt; fixed sights or adjustable sights; slide, frame flats are polished, balance sandblasted. Introduced, 1980 by Pacific International Merchandising; dropped about 1984. Used values: fixed sights, $250 to $275; adjustable sights, $285 to $300.

Warner Infallible Model

WARNER Infallible Model: automatic, pocket configuration; .32 auto; 7-rd. magazine; 3" barrel; 6½" overall length; checkered hard rubber stocks; fixed sights; blued finish. Manufactured 1917 to 1919. Used value, $165 to $185.

Weatherby Mark V Silhouette

WEATHERBY Mark V Silhouette: bolt-action, single-shot; .22-250, .308; 15" barrel; globe front sight with inserts, target-type rear peep; thumbhole Claro walnut stock, rosewood forend tip, grip cap; featured modified Mark V Varmintmaster action; drilled and tapped for scope. Introduced, 1980; dropped, 1981. Used value, $1500 and up (rare).

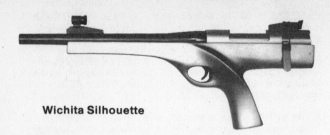

Wichita Silhouette

WICHITA Silhouette: bolt-action, single-shot; 7mm PPC, .308x1½, .308, also custom calibers; 14-15/16" barrel; 27⅜" overall length; Lyman globe front sight with inserts, Lyman or Williams peep rear; glass-bedded American walnut stock; right- or left-hand action;, fluted bolt; drilled, tapped for scope mounts; Remington-type trigger; non-glare blued satin finish. Introduced, 1979; still in production. Used value, $650 to $700.

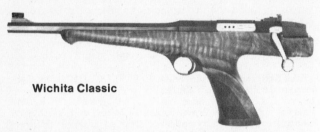

Wichita Classic

WICHITA Classic: bolt-action, single-shot; any caliber to .308; 11¼" octagonal barrel; micro open sights; receiver drilled, tapped for scope mounts on special order; checkered black walnut stock; non-glare blue finish. Introduced, 1980; still in production. Used value, $900 to $950.

WICHITA Hunter: single-shot; break-open action; 7mm INT-R, .30-30, .357 magnum, .357 Super magnum; 10½" barrel; weighs 3 lb. 14 oz.; walnut grip, forend; scope mount, no sights; stainless steel; safety; extra barrels available; grip dimensions same as .45 Colt Auto. Introduced, 1983; still in production. Used value, $425 to $450.

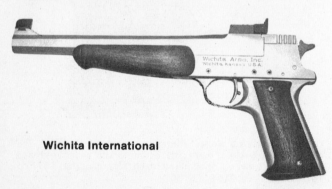

Wichita International

WICHITA International: has same specs as Hunter model, except weighs 3 lb. 13 oz.; no safety; target front sight, adjustable rear. Introduced, 1983; still in production. Used value, $425 to $450.

WILKINSON Diane: automatic; .22 LR, .25 ACP; 8-rd. magazine for .22 LR, 8-rd. for .25 ACP; 2⅛" barrel; 4½" overall length; checkered styrene stocks; fixed sights integral with slide, matte blued finish; internal hammer; separate ejector. Introduced, 1977; still in production. Used value, $95 to $110.

WILKINSON Linda: automatic; 9mm Parabellum; 31-rd. magazine; 8-5/16" barrel; weighs 4 lb. 13 oz.; 12¼" overall length; protected blade front sight, Williams adjustable rear; maple forend, checkered black plastic stocks; blowback action; crossbolt safety. Introduced, 1982; still in production. Used value, $340 to $360.

WILKINSON Sherry: automatic; .22 LR; 8-rd. magazine; 2⅛" barrel; 4¾" overall length; weighs 9¼ oz.; no sights; checkered

Wilkinson Diane

Wilkinson Linda

Whitney Wolverine

black plastic stocks; crossbolt safety; blued finish or gold-plated frame, blued slide, trigger. Introduced, 1985; still in production. Used value, $120 to $130.

WHITNEY Wolverine: automatic; .22 LR only; 4½" barrel; 9" overall length; aluminum alloy frame; rear sight movable for windage only; ⅛" Patridge-type front; top of slide serrated to reduce reflection; checkered plastic grips; blued or nickel finish. Introduced in 1956; dropped, 1963. Has some collector interest. Used values: blued finish, $350 to $375; nickel, $375 to $400.

FOREIGN

ACTION ARMS AT-84: automatic; double-action; 9mmP, .41 Action Express; 15-rd. magazine in 9mm, 10 rds. in .41 AE: 4.72" barrel; 8.1" overall length; weighs 35.5 oz.; drift-adjustable rear sight, blade front; polished blued finish. Made in Switzerland. Introduced, 1987; still imported by Action Arms. Used value, $350 to $375.

    AT-84P has same specs, except for 3.66" barrel, weighs 32.1 oz.; magazine carries 13 rds. of 9mm, 8 rds. of .41 AE. Used value, $350 to $375.

Anschutz Exemplar

ANSCHUTZ Exemplar: bolt-action; .22 LR, 5-rd. magazine; .22 WRFM, 5 rds.; 10" barrel; 17" overall length; weighs 56 oz.; open-notch adjustable rear sight, hooded front on ramp; European walnut stock, stippled grip, forend; built on Anschutz Match 64 rifle action with left-hand bolt; Anschutz #5091 two-stage trigger; receiver grooved for scope mount. Made in West Germany. Introduced, 1987; still imported by Precision Sales. Used values: .22 LR, $260 to $275; .22 WRFM, $275 to $290.

Agner Model 80

AGNER Model 80: automatic; .22 LR; 5-rd. magazine; 5.9" barrel; 9.5" overall length; weighs 36 oz.; adjustable French walnut stocks; fixed blade front sight, adjustable rear; safety key locks trigger, slide, magazine; dry fire button; right- or left-hand models. Made in Denmark. Introduced, 1984; dropped, 1987; was imported by Beeman. Used values: right-hand, $925 to $950; left-hand, $1000 to $1025.

AIR MATCH 500: single-shot target pistol; .22 LR; 10.4" barrel; weighs 28 oz.; match grip of stippled hardwood; left or right hand; match post front sight, adjustable match rear; adjustable sight radius; marketed in case with tools, spare sights. Made in Italy. Introduced, 1984; dropped, 1987; was imported by Kendall International Arms. Used value, $500 to $585.

Arminus Model

ARMINIUS Model: revolver; double-action; .357 magnum, .38 Special, .32 S&W, .22 WRFM, .22 LR; 6 rds. in centerfire, 8 rds. in rimfire; 4", 6", 8⅜" barrel lengths; checkered plastic grips; walnut at added cost; ramp front sight, fixed rear on standard versions, adjustable rear on target versions; vent rib, solid frame, swing-out cylinder; interchangeable cylinder for .22 WRFM available with standard .22 caliber. Imported from West Germany by F.I.E., 1978; still in production. Used values: rimfires, $75 to $85; centerfires, $145 to $165.

Alkartasuna Ruby

ALKARTASUNA Ruby: automatic; .32 auto; 9-rd. magazine; 6⅜" overall; 3⅜" barrel; checkered hard rubber or wooden stocks; blued finish; fixed sights. Manufactured in Spain, 1917 to 1922; distributed primarily in Europe; some used by French army in World Wars I, II. Used value, $100 to $125.

Arminex Trifire

ARMINEX Trifire: automatic; single-action; 9mm Parabellum. 9-rd.; .38 Super, 9-rd.; .45 ACP, 7-rd.; 5" barrel; weighs 38 oz.; 8" overall length; smooth contoured walnut stocks; interchangeable post front sight, adjustable rear; slide-mounted firing pin safety; contoured backstrap; blued or electroless nickel finish; convertible by changing barrel, magazine, recoil spring. Introduced, 1982; dropped, 1987. Used value, $300 to $320.

Armscor 38

Bersa Model 224

ARMSCOR 38: revolver; double-action; .38 Special; 4" barrel; 6-rd. cylinder; weighs 32 oz.; adjustable rear sight, ramp front; checkered Philippine mahogany stocks; vent rib; polished blue finish. Made in the Philippines. Introduced, 1986; still imported by Pacific International Merchandising Corp. Used value, $90 to $100.

Model 226 has same specs as Model 224, except has 6" barrel. Used value, $180 to $190.

Model 223 is same as Model 224, except is double-action, has wood stocks, 3½" barrel. Used value, $180 to $190.

Beeman SP Deluxe

BEEMAN SP Deluxe: single-shot; .22 LR; 8", 10", 11.2", 15" barrel lengths; European walnut stocks; adjustable palm rest; blade front sight, adjustable notch rear; detchable forend, barrel weight; standard version has no forend or weight. Imported by Beeman. Introduced, 1984; dropped, 1987. Used values: $230 to $250; standard model $180 to $200.

Bersa Model 383

BERSA Model 383: automatic; single-action; .380 ACP; 9-rd. magazine; 3½" barrel; weighs 25 oz.; square-notch windage-adjustable rear sight, blade front; target-type black nylon stocks; blowback action; combat-type trigger guard; magazine safety; blued finish. Made in Argentina. Introduced, 1984; now imported by Eagle Imports. Used value, $120 to $130.

Model 383DA has same specs as standard model, except is double-action; Used values: blued finish, $175 to $190; satin nickel finish, $200 to $220.

BRNO CZ 75: automatic; double-action; 9mmP; 15-rd. magazine; 4.7" barrel; 8" overall length; weighs 35 oz.; windage-adjustable rear sight, blade front; checkered wood stocks; blued finish. Made in Czechoslovakia. Introduced, 1986; still imported by Saki International. Used value, $450 to $475.

BRNO CZ-85: automatic; double-action; 9mmP, 7.65mm; has the same specs as CZ-75, except has ambidextrous slide release, safety lever, contoured composition stocks, matte finish on top of slide. Made in Czechoslovakia. Introduced, 1986; still imported by Saki International. Used value, $475 to $500.

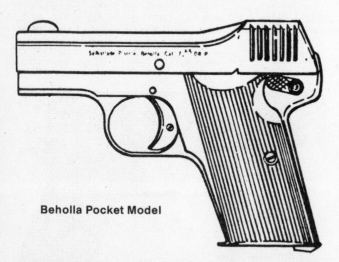

Beholla Pocket Model

BEHOLLA Pocket Auto: automatic; .32 auto; 7-rd. magazine; 5½" overall; 3" barrel; blued finish; fixed sights; grooved hard rubber or wooden stocks. German-made. Manufactured 1915 to 1925. Used value, $125 to $150.

BERSA Model 224: automatic; single-action; .22 LR; 11-rd. magazine; 5" barrel; weighs 26 oz.; checkered target-type nylon stocks; thumbrest; blade front sight, square-notch rear adjustable for windage; blowback action; conbat-type trigger guard; magazine safety; blued finish. Made in Argentina. Introduced, 1984; now imported by Eagle Imports. Used value, $180 to $190.

BRNO CZ 83: automatic; double-action; .32, .380; 15-rd. magazine in .32, 13 rds. in .380; 3.7" barrel; 6.7" overall length; weighs 26.5 oz.; windage-adjustable rear sight, blade front; checkered black plastic stocks; ambidextrous magazine release, safety; matte blue or polished. Made in Czechoslovakia. Introduced, 1987; still imported by Saki International. Used value, $300 to $325.

BRONCO Model 1918: automatic; .32 auto; 6-rd. magazine; 5" overall; 2½" barrel; blued finish; fixed sights; hard rubber stocks. Manufactured in Spain 1918 to 1925. Used value, $100 to $125.

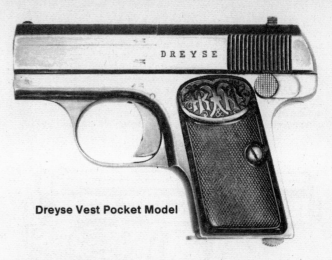

Bronco Model 1918

Dreyse Vest Pocket Model

Desert Eagle

DESERT EAGLE: automatic; .357 magnum, .41 magnum, .44 magnum; 9-rd. magazine in .357, 8 rds. in .41, .44; interchangeable 6", 8", 10", 14" barrels; with 6" barrel, weighs 52. oz., measures 10¼" overall; wrap-around soft rubber stocks; blade ramp front sight, combat-style rear; rotating 3-lug bolt; ambidextrous safety; combat trigger guard; optional adjustable trigger; military epoxy finish; alloy or stainless steel frame; Made in Israel. Introduced, 1982; still imported by Magnum Research. Used values: .357 magnum, $475 to $600, depending on barrel length; .41 magnum, $500 to $650, depending on barrel length; .44 magnum, $550 to $700, depending on barrel length.

DOMINO Model SP-601: automatic, match pistol design; .22 short; 5-rd. magazine; 5½" barrel length; 11¼" overall length; open notch adjustable rear sight, blade front; single-lever take-down, European walnut match stocks; adjustable palm rest; barrel ported to reduce recoil. Manufactured in Italy. Was imported by Mandall Shooting Supplies. Introduced, 1977; no longer imported. Used value, $600 to $650.
Model SP-602 has same general specs as Model SP-601, but is chambered for .22 LR; has adjustable one-piece walnut stock; no gas ports; different trigger, sear mechanism. Introduced, 1977; no longer imported. Used value, $575 to $625.

Dreyse Model 1907

DREYSE Model 1907: automatic; .32 auto; 8-rd. magazine; 3½" barrel; 6¼" overall; fixed sights; hard rubber checkered stocks; blued finish. Manufactured in Germany, 1907 to 1914. Used value, $145 to $150.

DREYSE Vest Pocket Model: automatic; .25 auto; 6-rd. magazine; 2" barrel; 4½" overall length; fixed sights; checkered hard rubber stocks; blued finish. Manufactured 1909 to 1914. Used value, $150 to $175.

DRULOV 75: target; single-shot; .22 LR; 9¾" ribbed barrel; 14½" overall length; weighs 44 oz.; micro-click rear sight, blade front; uncheckered walnut stocks; thumbrest; button-type set trigger. Made in Czechoslovakia. Introduced, 1987; still imported by Saki International. Used value, $250 to $275.

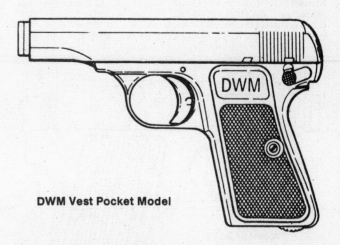

DWM Vest Pocket Model

DWM Vest Pocket Model: automatic; .32 auto; 3½" barrel; 6" overall; hard rubber checkered stocks; blued finish. Design resembles Browning FN Model 1910. Manufactured in Germany, 1920 to 1931. Used value, $250 to $300.

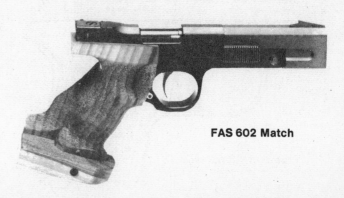

FAS 602 Match

FAS 602 Match: automatic; .22 LR; 5-rd. magazine; 5.6" barrel; 11" overall length; weighs 37 oz.; wrap-around adjustable walnut stocks; match blade front sight, fully adjustable open notch rear; magazine inserts from top; adjustable, removable trigger group; single-lever take-down. Made in Italy. Introduced, 1984; still imported by Beeman, Osborne's. Used value, $800 to $850.

    601 Match has same specs as 602, except has different stocks; .22 Short only for rapid-fire; weighs 40 oz.; barrel has gas ports to reduce recoil; different trigger/sear mechanism. Introduced, 1984; still imported by Beeman, Osborne's. Used value, $750 to $785.

Frommer Stop Pocket Model

FROMMER Stop Pocket Model: automatic; .32 auto, with 7-rd. magazine; .380 auto, with 6 rds.; 3⅞" barrel; 6½" overall length; grooved hard rubber stocks; fixed sights; blued finish. Manufactured in Hungary, 1912 to 1920. Used value, $165 to $175.

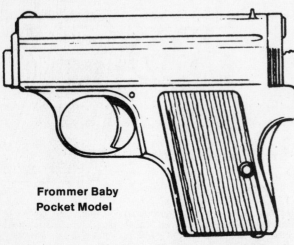

Frommer Baby Pocket Model

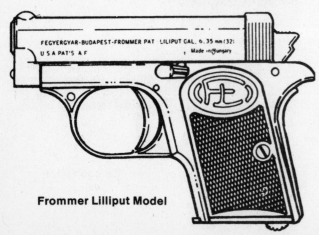

Frommer Lilliput Model

FROMMER Baby Pocket Model: automatic; .32 auto; 6-rd. magazine; smaller version of Stop Pocket model with 2" barrel; 4¾" overall. Manufactured from 1919 to approximately 1922. Used value, $175 to $195.

FROMMER Lilliput Pocket Model: automatic, blowback action; .25 auto; 6-rd. magazine; 2⅛" barrel; 4⅓" overall length; hard rubber stocks; fixed sights; blued finish. Manufactured 1921 to 1924. Used value, $185 to $195.

Galesi Model 6

GALISI Model 6: automatic; .25 auto; 6-rd. magazine; 2½" barrel; 4⅜" overall length; plastic stocks; fixed sights; blued finish. Manufactured in Italy. Introduced in 1930; still in production. Used value, $50 to $60.

Galesi Model 9

GALISI Model 9: automatic; .22 LR, .32 auto, .380 auto; 8-rd. magazine; 3¼" barrel; plastic stocks; fixed sights; blued finish. Introduced in 1930; still in production. Used value, $100 to $115.

GARCIA Regent: revolver; .22 LR only; 3", 4", 6" barrels; 8-rd. swing-out cylinder; fixed rear sight, ramp front; checkered plastic grips; blued. Introduced in 1972; dropped, 1977. Used value, $65 to $75.

GARCIA/FI Model D: automatic; .380 ACP; 6-rd. magazine; 3⅛" barrel; 6⅛" overall length; checkered American walnut stocks; windage-adjustable rear sight, blade front; blued; lanyard ring. Manufactured by Firearms International, 1977 to 1979. Used value, $185 to $200.

GLOCK 17: automatic; double-action; 9mmP; 17-rd. magazine; 4.48" barrel; 7.4" overall length; weighs 22 oz.; white outline rear

Garcia/FI Model D

Glock 17

adjustable sight, dot on front blade; polymer frame; steel slide; trigger safety; recoil-operated action; firing pin safety, drop safety. Made in Austria. Introduced, 1986; still imported by Glock, Inc. Used value, $300 to $325.

Helwan 9mm

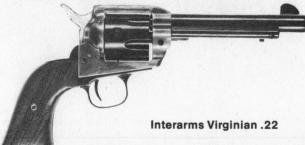

Interarms Virginian .22

HELWAN 9mm: automatic; 9mm Parabellum; 8-rd. magazine; 4½" barrel; weighs 33 oz.; 8¼" overall length; blade front sight, drift-adjustable rear; grooved black plastic stocks; updated version of Beretta Model 951. Imported from Egypt by Steyr Daimler Puch of America. Introduced, 1982; dropped, 1983. Used value, $165 to $185.

INTERARMS Virginian .22 Convertible is smaller version of standard Dragoon; .22 LR, .22 WRFM; 5½" barrel; 10¾" overall length; weighs 38 oz., comes with both cylinders; case-hardened frame, rest blued or stainless steel. Made in Italy. Introduced, 1983; dropped, 1987; was imported by Interarms. Used values: blued, $150 to $160; stainless, $165 to $180.

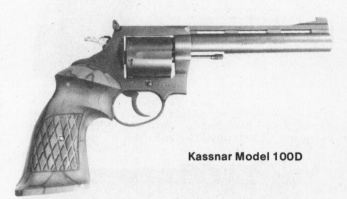

Kassnar Model 100D

KASSNAR M-100D: revolver; double-action; .22 LR, .22 WRFM, .38 Special; 6-rd. cylinder; 3", 4", 6" barrel lengths; target-style checkered hardwood stocks; elevation-adjustable rear sight, ramp front; vent-rib barrel. Manufactured in the Philippines by Squires Bingham; imported by Kassnar. Introduced, 1977; no longer imported. Used value, $70 to $75.

   Model 100TC is refined version of Model 100C; full ejector rod shroud has been added. Imported from Philippines by Kassnar. Used value, $90 to $95.

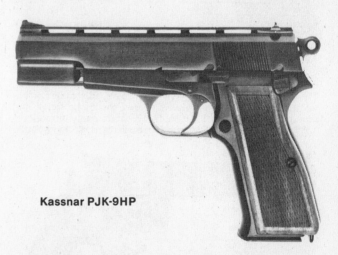

Kassnar PJK-9HP

KASSNAR PJK-9HP: automatic; single-action; 9mmP; 13-rd. magazine; 4¾" barrel; 8" overall length; weighs 32 oz.; adjustable rear sight, ramp front; checkered European walnut stocks; with or without full-length vent rib. Made in Hungary. Introduced, 1986; no longer imported. Used value, $200 to $225.

KLEINGUENTHER R-15: revolver, double-action; .22 LR, .22 WRFM, .32 S&W; 6-rd. cylinder; 6" barrel; 11" overall length; checkered thumbrest walnut stocks; adjustable rear sight, fixed front; full-length solid barrel rib; adjustable trigger; blued finish. Manufactured in Germany. Introduced in 1976; dropped, 1978. Used value, $145 to $150.

KORRIPHILA HSP 701: automatic; double-action; 9mmP, .38 WC, .38 Super, .45 ACP; 9-rd. magazine in 9mm, 7 rds. in .45; 4" or 5" barrels; weighs 35 oz.; adjustable rear sight, ramp or target front;

Korriphila HSP 701

Lahti Model 40

checkered walnut stocks; delayed roller lock action; limited production. Made in West Germany. Introduced, 1986; still imported by Osborne's. Used value, $1400 to $1450.

LAHTI Model 40: automatic; 9mm Luger; 8-rd. magazine; 4¾" barrel; checkered plastic stocks; fixed sights; blued finish. Manufactured in Sweden by Husqvarna. Manufactured 1940 to 1941. Collector value. Used value, $280 to $300.

Model L-35 is basically the same as Model 40, but was manufactured on limited basis in Finland from 1935 until World War II. Has better finish, quality and, because of limited number, has greater value to collectors. Used value, $650 to $700.

Korth Auto

LeFrancais Policeman Model

KORTH Auto: automatic; double-action; 9mmP; 13-rd. magazine; 4¼" barrel; 10½" overall length; weighs 35 oz.; adjustable combat sights; checkered walnut stocks; forged, machined frame and slide; matte or polished finish. Made in West Germany. Introduced, 1985; still imported by Osborne's. Used value, $1850 to $1900.

LE FRANCAIS Policeman Model: double-action automatic; .32 auto; 3½" hinged barrel; 6" overall length; 7-rd. magazine; checkered hard rubber stocks; fixed sights; blued finish. Manufactured in France. Introduced, 1914; still in production, but not imported. Used value, $250 to $300 (rare).

Korth Revolver

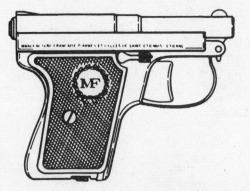

LeFrancais Staff Officer Model

KORTH Revolver: revolver; double-action; .22 LR, .22 WRFM, .357 magnum, 9mmP; 3", 4", 6" barrel lengths; 8" to 11" overall lengths; weighs 33 to 38 oz., depending on barrel length; adjustable rear sight, blade front; checkered walnut combat or sport stocks; four interchangeable cylinders available; hammer-forged steel construction; high-polish blued or matte finish; gold-trimmed presentation models available. Made in Germany. Introduced, 1986; still imported by Beeman, Osborne's. Used values: polished blue finish, $1250 to $1300; matte finish, $1000 to $1050; presentation models to $1600, depending upon amount of gold trim.

LE FRANCAIS Staff Officer Model: double-action automatic; .25 auto; has same general specs as Policeman Model, except for 2½" barrel; no cocking piece head. Introduced, 1914; still in production, but not imported. Used value, $200 to $225.

LE FRANCAIS Army Model: double-action automatic; 9mm Browning Long; has same general specs as Policeman Model, except for 8-rd. magazine; 5" barrel; 7¾" overall length; checkered European walnut stocks. Manufactured 1928 to 1938. Used value, $325 to $350.

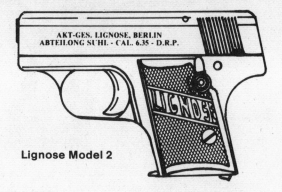

Lignose Model 2

Lignose Einhand Model 2A

Lignose Model 3A

LIGNOSE Model 2: pocket automatic; .25 auto; follows conventional Browning design; 2" barrel; 4½" overall length; 6-rd. magazine; checkered hard rubber stocks; blued finish. Manufactured in Germany. Used value, $175 to $200.

Lignose Model 2A Einhand has same general specs as Model 2, except trigger-type mechanism at front of trigger guard allows trigger finger to retract the slide. Used value, $200 to $225.

Lignose Model 3A Einhand has same specs as Model 2A, except for extended grip; 9-rd. magazine. Used value, $200 to $225.

Luna Model 300

LUNA Model 300: single-shot, free pistol; .22 short; 11" barrel; set trigger; checkered, carved walnut stock, forearm; adjustable palm rest; target sights; blued finish. Manufactured in Germany, approximately 1929 to 1939. Used value, $725 to $750.

Manurhin Model PPK/S

MANURHIN Walther PP: automatic; double-action; .22 LR, 10 rds.; .32 ACP, 8 rds.; .380 ACP, 7 rds.; 3.87" barrel; 7.7" overall length; weighs 23 oz.; white-outline front, rear sights; hammer drop safety; all-steel construction; blued; checkered composition stocks; supplied with two magazines. Made in France. Importation began, 1984, by Manurhin International; dropped, 1986. Used Value, $285 to $300.

PPK/S Model has same specs as Model PP, except has 3.25" barrel; overall length is 6.12". Used value, $285 to $300.

Manurhin MR 32 Match

MANURHIN MR 32 Match: revolver; .32 S&W Long; 6 rds.; 6" barrel; 11¾" overall length; weighs 42 oz.; anatomical target grips are shaped, but not finished; interchangeable blade front sight, adjustable micrometer rear; externally adjustable trigger; trigger shoe. Made in France. Introduced, 1984; dropped, 1986; was imported by Manurhin International. Used value, $500 to $525.

Model MR 38 has same specs, except is chambered for .38 Special; has 5¾" barrel. Used value: $500 to $525.

MANURHIN MR 73: revolver; .357 magnum; 6 rds.; 9" long-range barrel; 10¾" silhouette barrel; checkered walnut stocks; interchangeable blade front sight, adjustable micrometer rear; externally adjustable trigger; single-action only. Made in France. Introduced, 1984; dropped, 1986; was imported by Manurhin International. Used value, $575 to $600.

MR 73 Sport model has same general specs as standard model, except is chambered for .32 S&W Long, .357 magnum; has 5.25" barrel; overall length, 10.4"; double-action; blued finish; straw-colored hammer, trigger; marketed with adjusting tool. Made in France. Introduced, 1984; dropped, 1986; was imported by Manurhin International. Used value, $575 to $600.

MKE Model TPK

MKE Model TPK: double-action auto pistol; .32 auto; 8-rd. magazine, .380, 7-rd. magazine; 4" barrel; 6½" overall length; adjustable notch rear sight, fixed front; checkered plastic grips; exposed hammer; safety blocks firing pin, drops hammer; chamber-loaded indicator pin. Copy of Walther PP. Imported from Turkey by Firearms Center, Inc., then by Mandall Shooting Supplies; no longer imported. Used value, $185 to $210.

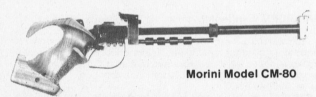

Morini Model CM-80

MORINI Model CM-80: single-shot; .22 LR; 10" free-floating barrel; 21.25" overall length; weighs 30 oz.; listed as Super Competition model; adjustable or wrap-around stocks; adjustable match sights; adjustable grip/frame angle; adjustable barrel alignment; adjustable trigger weight, sight radius. Made in Italy. Introduced, 1985; still imported by Osborne's. Used values: standard model, $580 to $600; deluxe, $725 to $750.

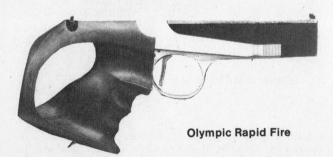

Olympic Rapid Fire

OLYMPIC Rapid Fire Pistol: automatic; .22 short; 5" barrel, exhaust ports; 10.4" overall length; weighs 43 oz.; wrap-around walnut stocks; fully adjustable micrometer rear sight; recoil-operated; adjustable trigger. Made in Spain. Introduced, 1985; no longer imported by Osborne's. Used value, $650 to $675.

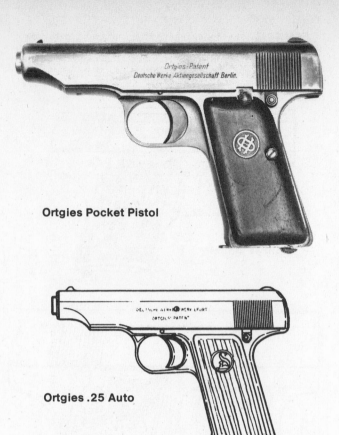

Ortgies Pocket Pistol

Ortgies .25 Auto

ORTGIES Pocket Pistol: automatic; blowback action; .32 auto; 3¼" barrel; 6½" overall length; 8-rd. magazine; constructed without screws, uses pins and spring-loaded catches; grip safety protrudes only when firing pin is cocked; fixed sights; uncheckered walnut grips; blued. Introduced about 1919; dropped, 1926. Used value, $125 to $145.

Ortgies .380 Auto has same specs as the .32, except for additional thumb-operated safety catch; 7-rd. magazine. Introduced in 1922; dropped, 1926. Used value, $135 to $165.

Ortgies .25 Auto is scaled-down version of .32 auto; 6-rd. magazine; 2¾" barrel; 5-3/16" overall length. Introduced in 1920; dropped, 1926. Used value, $125 to $135.

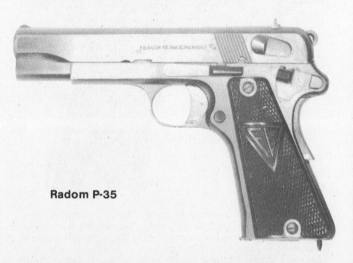

Radom P-35

RADOM P-35: automatic; 9mm Luger; 8-rd. magazine; 4¾" barrel; 7¾" overall length; checkered plastic stocks; fixed sights; blued finish. Design based on Colt Model 1911A1. Manufactured in Poland 1935 to 1945. Used value, $275 to $300; Pre-Nazi add 100%.

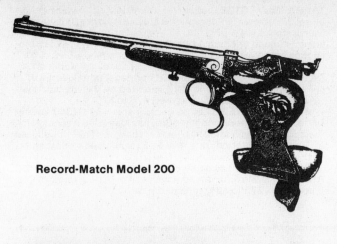

Record-Match Model 200

Record-Match Model 210

SILE-BENELLI B76: automatic; double-action; 9mm Parabellum; 8-rd. magazine; 4¼" chrome-lined barrel, 8-1/16" overall length; blade front sight, windage-adjustable rear; cut-checkered walnut stocks; fixed barrel, locked breech, exposed hammer, stainless steel inertia firing pin; loaded-chamber indicator; all-steel construction. Imported from Italy; introduced in 1979; no longer in production. Used value, $300 to $325.

S.P.A. GAMBA Mauser Hsc 80 G.15: automatic; .32 ACP, 9mm Ultra; 15-rd. magazine; 3.34" barrel; 5.9" overall length; weighs 24 oz.; windage-adjustable rear sight, blade front; checkered walnut stocks; also made in 9-rd. version. Made in Italy. Introduced, 1987; importation dropped by Armes de Chasse, 1988. Used values: standard model, $525 to $550; 9-shot version, $575 to $600.

S.P.A. GAMBA Trident Super 4: revolver; double-action; .32 S&W, .38 Special; 6-rd. cylinder; 4" barrel; 9.4" overall length; weighs 24 oz.; adjustable rear sight, blade front; checkered walnut stocks; vent rib; polished blue finish. Made in Italy. Introduced, 1987; importation dropped by Armes de Chasse, 1988. Used value, $400 to $425.

STEYR Model SP: automatic; double-action pocket pistol; .32 auto; 7-rd. detachable magazine; revolver-type trigger; movable rear sight, fixed front; checkered black plastic grips; blued finish. Introduced in 1957; still in production, but not imported since 1968 Gun Control Act. Used value, $225 to $250.

Steyr GB

RECORD-MATCH Model 200: single-shot free pistol; Martini action; .22 short; 11" barrel; micrometer rear sight, target-type front; carved, checkered European walnut stock, forearm, with adjustable hand base; blued finish; set trigger, spur trigger guard. Manufactured in Germany prior to WWII. Used value, $725 to $750.

Model 210 single-shot free pistol has same general design, specs as Model 210, except for more intricate carving, checkering; button release on set trigger. Manufactured prior to WWII. Used value, $1000 to $1100.

Model 210A is identical to Model 210, except for dual action. Manufactured prior to WWII. Used value, $1000 to $1100.

S.A.B. GAMBA Model SAB G 90: automatic; double-action; 9mm Ultra, .30 Luger; 15-rd. magazine; 4.7" barrel; weighs 33 oz.; uncheckered European walnut stocks; windage-adjustable rear sight, undercut blade front; squared trigger guard. Made in Italy. Introduced, 1986; importation dropped by Armes de Chasse, 1988. Used value, $475 to $500.

Model SAB G 91 has same specs as G 90, except has 3½" barrel, magazine holds 12 rds. Introduced, 1986; importation dropped, 1988. Used value, $475 to $500.

STEYR GB: automatic; double-action; 9mm Parabellum; 18-rd. magazine; 5.39" barrel; weighs 53 oz.; 8.4" overall length; post front sight, fixed rear; checkered European walnut stocks; delayed blowback action; gas-operated. Imported from Germany by Gun South, Inc. Introduced, 1981; no longer in production. Used value, $325 to $350.

TANARMI Model TA22S: revolver; single-action; .22 short, long, LR, .22 LR/.22 WRFM combo; 6 rds.; 4¾" barrel; 10" overall length; blade front sight, drift adjustable rear; checkered nylon grips, walnut optional; manual hammer block safety frame. Imported from Italy by Excam; introduced, 1978; still imported. Used values: .22 rimfire, $70 to $75; .22 WRFM, $80 to $85; .22 rimfire/.22 WRFM combo, $90 to $95.

Model TA76 has same basic design as TA22S, except has blued trigger guard, backstrap. Introduced, 1978; still imported. Used values: blued, $50 to $60; chromed, $55 to $65.

Sile-Bennelli B76

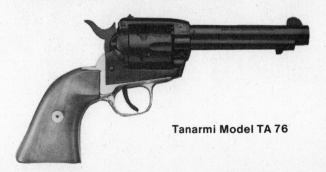

Tanarmi Model TA 76

TANARMI Model TA 76: revolver; single-action; .22 LR, .22 WRFM; 6-rd. cylinder; 4¾" barrel; 10" overall length; weighs 32 oz.; adjustable rear sight, blade front; uncheckered walnut stocks; color case-hardened frame; brass backstrap, trigger guard; manual hammer block safety; blued or chrome finish. Also available with combo cylinders. Made in Italy. Introduced, 1987; still imported by Excam. Used values: blued, .22 LR, $45 to $50; blued, combo, $55 to $60; chrome, .22 LR, $55 to $60; chrome, combo, $65 to $70.

TARGA Model GT27: automatic; .25 ACP; 6-rd. magazine; 2-7/16" barrel; 4⅝" overall length; checkered nylon stocks; fixed sights; external hammer with half-cock feature; safety lever take-down; blued, chromed finish. Assembled in U.S. by Excam. Introduced, 1977; still in production. Used values: blued, $30 to $35; chromed, $35 to $40.

TARGA Model GT32: automatic; .32 ACP; 7-rd. magazine; 4⅞" barrel; 7⅜" overall length; optional checkered nylon thumbrest or walnut stocks; windage-adjustable rear sight, blade front; external hammer; blued or chromed finish. Introduced, 1977; still in production. Used values: blued, $60 to $70; chromed, $65 to $70.

Model GT380 has the same general specs as Model GT32, except is chambered for .380 ACP cartridge; introduced, 1977; still in production. Made in Italy, imported by Excam, Inc. Used values: blued, $70 to $75; chromed, $70 to $75.

Model GT380XE has same general specs as GT380, except barrel is 3.88", overall length, 7.38"; has magazine disconnector, firing pin and thumb safeties; blued or satin nickel finish. Introduced in 1980; still imported from Italy by Excam. Used values: blued, $100 to $110; satin nickel, $110 to $120.

Model GT32XE has same specs as TA380XE, except for .32 ACP chambering. Introduced, 1980; still imported. Used values: blued finish, $75 to $85; satin nickel, $85 to $95.

HANDGUN NOTES

RIFLES

The Worth Of A Rifle Has Overtones Of Philosophy!

The pre-1964 Winchester Model 70 has a mystique among shooters that is a facet manufactured by gun traders. The present-day version of the rifle shoots just as well as this model.

WHAT IS a rifle of specific model and caliber worth?

That's a simple question that has endless ramifications when it comes to a complete answer. In fact, it may be that there is no *complete* answer. Special circumstances call for special needs. I guess what it all comes down to, regarding worth, is what do you want to do with the rifle — and what do you expect it to do for you? There probably are as many answers to that as there are riflemen!

An illustration, though, might be made out of an incident from my own experience. I was hunting in Zimbabwe a few years back and had shot a Cape buffalo. Something of a neophyte, I was settling for heart and lung shots, when I undoubtedly should have shot the beast through the shoulders to anchor it.

I had seven rounds in the animal when it decided to charge me. I had been firing a .375 H&H magnum for this hunt and, as the two tons of meat came down on me, I had exactly two thoughts: First, it's fifty yards to the nearest tree and I won't make it. The second thought was a bit more practical: I wish to hell I had a 105mm howitzer, but I'd have settled for a .458!

Frankly, I've never been a fancier of the .458. I always figured there was just too much recoil for the benefits derived therefrom, unless you wanted to level mountains with it. But as that black mountain of wild meat bore down on me in the African bush, I saw the error of my thinking. There are, indeed, special guns for special purposes.

My professional hunter on that outing, a gent named Mark Sparrow, always insists that I killed the buffalo with the last round in my rifle, when it was roughly a dozen feet from me. However, I am quick to tell him he got paid for saying I killed it. He fired in the same moment as I, using a .458 that had been a long time off the Winchester Model 70 assembly line, but was a veritable gem for dangerous game.

I still think those who take a .458 out for plinking have had their brains addled by too much recoil, but should I ever again face a charging Cape buffalo — or even one that's not headed in my direction with violence in mind — I'd want a .458...or the earlier mentioned 105mm!

Oddly, several months ago, I was in Zimbabwe again. With a young professional, Nigel Theissen, I had been following a herd of elephants through the bush. We finally came upon them and hunkered down, trying to determine the size and weight of the ivory. Finally, the pro lowered his binoculars, shaking his head.

"Nothing here worth taking," he muttered. Frankly, I was a little relieved. Again, I was armed with a .375 H&H and I was't all that certain I wanted to take on an elephant with that caliber. I've read all those books, too, about how the old ivory hunters used to down elephants with slingshots or something else of equal velocity. Well, I'm not an old ivory hunter. In fact, I don't even consider myself old; just well seasoned. And I got that way by trying to match caliber and rifle to the game I plan to hunt.

As an addendum to the above, we still were looking over the half-dozen elephants from about forty yards away, when the wind switched 180 degrees. A big female elephant suddenly turned toward us, trunk going up and her ears pivoting forward, seeking us out.

"I think this is a great time to haul out of here," I

In Africa, even the ants grow king-size. Dangerous big game calls for a choice of the proper caliber and rifle, but there are a number of reasonably priced models today.

ventured under my breath.

"Five minutes ago was a great time to haul arse," friend Nigel announced aloud in his British-tinged Zimbabwean accent. He was already moving. Right behind him, I wasn't all that certain about the Sako .375 H&H I was carrying. I kept glancing over my shoulder, wondering if the big cow elephant planned on following; the hunted becoming the hunter. On the other hand, Nigel Theissen seemed to have full confidence in the oldish model British-made .375 H&H Whitworth rifle that is his professional companion.

That takes care of the talk about what you want the gun to do and what you want to do with it. Now we get down to the nitty-gritty: price.

Early in my gun writing career, everyone I talked to about Africa kept insisting that one should have a double rifle of big bore. That, they insisted, was the only thing.

So I did some checking on the guns made by Holland & Holland in their London gunworks. When you start talking about these guns, there are two sets of prices: modern-day manufacture and pre-World War II guns. The world is convinced that the guns made in the years before the start of the Late Great Hate were better. Back in the Twenties you could buy a Holland & Holland No. 2 Model double rifle for about ninety-five English pounds. In those days, the pound was worth about five bucks U.S. That translates to $475; high-priced for that era, true. But if you want a pre-WWII No. 2 in this day and age, plan on rounding up $10,000 or more! The post-war version goes for a bit less: upward of $7000! For what it might be worth, calibers range from .240 to .577, so such a rifle will hurl a lot of lead in the direction of dangerous game, but at the price, most of us would put such a rifle in a safe and never take it out except to be sure it wasn't rusting!

Incidentally, the professional African hunters can't afford those prices, either. There may be a few such guns around, handed down from father to son through the generations, but I've never seen one in use in the parts of Africa I've visited.

Instead, the professional hunters go for bolt-actions such as the Winchester Model 70, Remington's Model 700, the aforementioned Whitworth and there are a batch of Sako rifles with black plastic stocks in .375 H&H in the hands of the pros. They are efficient, they offer more than two shots — and no one has to mortgage his wife and kids to own one.

Then comes the matter of mystique.

Mystique is what the pre-1964 Winchester Model 70 is supposed to have. This, no doubt, is going to upset a batch of Winchester collectors, but it is my own opinion that the Model 70 rifles being made today under Winchester license by U.S. Repeating Arms are every bit as good as those made prior to 1964.

Admittedly, Winchester went through a period extending from the mid-Sixties into the late Seventies, wherein the corporate thinking seemed to be that they could sell the sizzle instead of the steak. Admittedly, inflation was running as rampant as the famed Colt mustang and engineers and bean counters had to put their heads together in an effort to decrease the cost of production and not send the price of the rifle totally out of the prospective buyer's sight. Plastic was substituted for a lot of what had been steel. Impressed checkering replaced hand-cutting. There were other changes, too.

But through modern technology, USRA has, a lot of folks feel, including myself, that the Model 70 has regained most — if not all — of what it lost during that one period in history. Computer science has helped, with programmed checkering cut by machine rather than by hand. New steels have added to the strength of the rifles. And through actual test, I and others have found that the current crop of Model 70s are just as accurate as the praised and oft-heralded pre-64 variety.

The supposed mystique of the older version is largely the result of salesmanship on the part of collectors and dealers who have pumped up the advantages of the pre-64 Winchester...and a batch of money has been paid for said rifles in the years since that particular modification went out of production.

All of this, of course, gets us back to the question of what a rifle is worth.

Basically, it's worth what you can afford and still have a rifle that will do what you want it to do, when you want it done.

ANSCHUTZ

Anschutz Model 64S (Early Production)

Anschutz Model 64S (Late Production)

Anschutz Model 64MS

ANSCHUTZ Model 64: bolt-action, single-shot match rifle; .22 LR only; 26" barrel; walnut-finished hardwood stock; cheekpiece; hand-checkered pistol grip, beavertail forearm; adjustable butt plate; no sights; scope blocks, receiver grooved for Anschutz sights; adjustable single-stage trigger; sliding side safety; forward sling swivel for competition sling. Marketed in U.S. as Savage/Anschutz Model 64. Introduced in 1967; no longer in production. Used value, $300 to $325.

Model 64L has the same specs as Model 64, except for left-hand action. No longer in production. Used value, $325 to $350.

Model 64S has the same specs as standard Model 64, except for addition of Anschutz No. 6723 match sight set. No longer in production. Used value, $400 to $425.

Model 64SL has the same specs as Model 64S except for left-hand action. No longer in production. Used value, $425 to $450.

Model 64MS has same basic specs as standard Model 64 except for 21¾" barrel; silhouette-type stock; no sights; drilled, tapped for scope mounts; stock has stippled checkering, contoured thumb groove with Wundhammer swell; adjustable two-stage trigger. Introduced by Savage Arms, 1981; still imported from West Germany by Precision Sales International. Used value, $425 to $450.

Anschutz Model 1407

ANSCHUTZ Model 1407: bolt-action, single-shot match rifle; action based upon that of Savage/Anschutz Model 54; .22 LR only; 26" barrel; length, weight conform to ISU competition requirements, also suitable for NRA matches; French walnut prone-style stock; Monte Carlo, cast-off cheekpiece; hand-stippled pistol grip, forearm; swivel rail, adjustable swivel; adjustable rubber butt plate; no sights; receiver grooved for Anschutz sights; scope blocks; single-stage trigger; wing safety. Marketed in U.S. by Savage. Introduced in 1967; still in production; not currently imported. Used value: right-hand model, $325 to $350; left-hand stock, $335 to $365.

Anschutz Model 1411

ANSCHUTZ Model 1411: bolt-action, single-shot match rifle; built on same action as Savage/Anschutz Model 54; .22 LR only; has same basic specs as Model 1407, except for longer overall length of 46"; 27½" barrel. Introduced in 1967; still in production; not currently imported. Used values: $350 to $365; adjustable stock, $475 to $500.

Anschutz Model 1413

ANSCHUTZ Model 1413: bolt-action, single-shot match rifle; has the same specs as Model 1411, except for International-type French walnut stock; adjustable aluminum hook butt plate; adjustable cheekpiece. Introduced in 1967; still in production; not currently imported. Used value: $500 to $550; adjustable stock, $750 to $775.

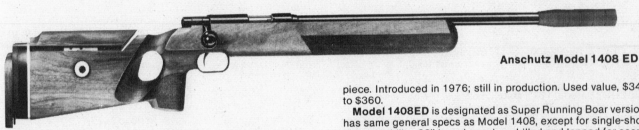

Anschutz Model 1408 ED

ANSCHUTZ Model 1408: bolt-action, sporter; .22 LR; 5- or 10-rd. magazine; 19¾" barrel; receiver grooved for scope mount; folding leaf rear sight, hooded ramp front; European walnut Mannlicher-type stock; hand-stippled pistol grip, forearm; adjustable cheek-piece. Introduced in 1976; still in production. Used value, $340 to $360.

Model 1408ED is designated as Super Running Boar version; has same general specs as Model 1408, except for single-shot-only capability, 23" barrel, receiver drilled and tapped for scope mount, no metallic sights; has oversize bolt knob, European walnut thumbhole stock, adjustable comb and butt plate, single-stage adjustable trigger. Introduced in 1976; still in production; not currently imported. Used value, $600 to $650.

Anschutz Model 1432

ANSCHUTZ Model 1432: bolt-action; .22 Hornet; 5-rd. box magazine; 24" barrel; receiver grooved for scope mount; folding leaf rear sight, hooded ramp front; European walnut Monte Carlo-type stock; hand-checkered pistol grip, forearm; cheekpiece. Introduced in 1976, no longer in production. Used value, $600 to $650.

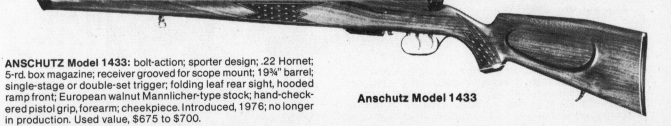

ANSCHUTZ Model 1433: bolt-action; sporter design; .22 Hornet; 5-rd. box magazine; receiver grooved for scope mount; 19¾" barrel; single-stage or double-set trigger; folding leaf rear sight, hooded ramp front; European walnut Mannlicher-type stock; hand-checkered pistol grip, forearm; cheekpiece. Introduced, 1976; no longer in production. Used value, $675 to $700.

Anschutz Model 1433

ANSCHUTZ Model 1533: bolt-action; .222 Rem.; has same general specs as Model 1433, except for chambering, 3-rd. box magazine. Introduced, 1976; no longer in production. Used value, $675 to $700.

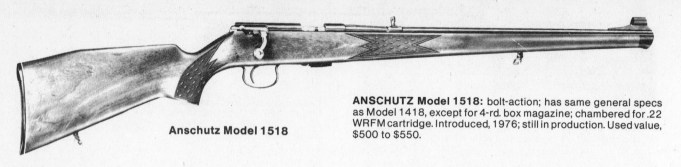

Anschutz Model 1518

ANSCHUTZ Model 1518: bolt-action; has same general specs as Model 1418, except for 4-rd. box magazine; chambered for .22 WRFM cartridge. Introduced, 1976; still in production. Used value, $500 to $550.

ANSCHUTZ Model 1432D: bolt-action; .22 Hornet; 5-rd. clip; 23½" barrel; 42½" overall length; no sights; drilled/tapped for scope mounts; checkered European walnut stock; adjustable single-stage trigger. Now called Classic 1700. Introduced, 1982; still imported from Germany by Precision Sales International. Used value, $600 to $650.

    Model 1532D has same specs as 1432D, except is chambered for .222 Remington; 2-rd. clip. Now called Classic 1700. Introduced, 1982; still imported. Used value, $600 to $650.

    Model 1432D Custom has same specs as standard model, except has roll-over Monte Carlo cheekpiece, slim forend, Schnabel tip; palm swell on pistol grip; rosewood grip cap; white diamond insert; skip-line checkering. Now called Custom 1700. Introduced, 1982; still imported. Used value, $625 to $675.

Anschutz Model 2000

ANSCHUTZ Mark 2000: .22 LR; bolt-action; single-shot; heavy 26" barrel; 43" overall length; globe insert front sight, micro-click peep rear; walnut-finished hardwood stock; designed as target rifle; thumb groove in stock; pistol grip swell. Made in West Germany. Introduced, 1980; still imported by Precision Sales International. Used value, $250 to $285.

ANSCHUTZ Model 1811 Match: bolt-action; single-shot; 27¼" heavy round barrel; 46" overall length; no sights, but grooved for Anschutz sights; scope blocks; French walnut stock; Monte Carlo cast-off cheekpiece; adjustable rubber butt plate; checkered pistol grip, beavertail forend; swivel rail, adjustable swivel; single-stage adjustable trigger. Now called Model 1911 Match. Made in West Germany. Introduced, 1979; still imported by Precision Sales International. Used value, $700 to $725.

    Model 1811L has same specs as standard model, except has left-hand action, stock. Now called 1911L Match. Used value, $725 to $750.

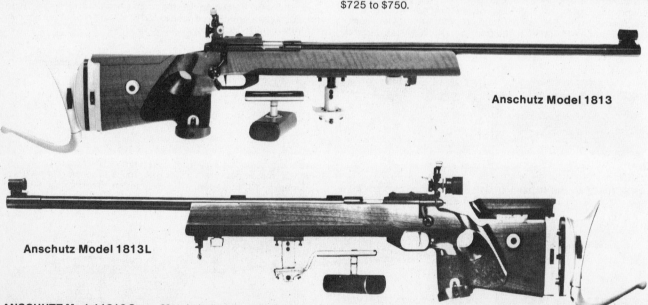

Anschutz Model 1813

Anschutz Model 1813L

ANSCHUTZ Model 1813 Super Match: bolt-action, single-shot; same specs as Model 1811, except has International-type stock, adjustable cheekpiece, adjustable aluminum hook-type butt plate. Now called Model 1913. Made in West Germany. Introduced, 1979; still imported by Precision Sales International. Used value, $1000 to $1100.

    Model 1813L has same specs as standard 1813, except has left-hand stock, action. Now called Model 1913L. Used value, $1050 to $1150.

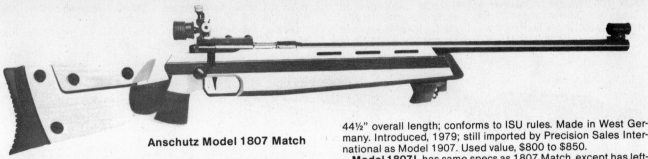

Anschutz Model 1807 Match

ANSCHUTZ Model 1807 Match: bolt-action; single-shot; .22 LR; has same specs as Model 1811, except has 26" heavy barrel, 44½" overall length; conforms to ISU rules. Made in West Germany. Introduced, 1979; still imported by Precision Sales International as Model 1907. Used value, $800 to $850.

Model 1807L has same specs as 1807 Match, except has left-hand action, stock. Now called Model 1907L. Used value, $825 to $875.

ANSCHUTZ Model 1810 Super Match II: bolt-action; single-shot; .22 LR; same general specs as Super Match 1813, except has hardwood stock, tapered forend; no hand or palm rest; adjust-able hook butt plate, cheekpiece. Made in West Germany. Introduced, 1980; still imported by Precision Sales International as Model 1910 Super Match II. Used value, $850 to $925.

Anschutz Model 54.18

ANSCHUTZ Model 54.18: bolt-action; single-shot; .22 LR; same general specs as 1813 Super Match, except has metallic silhou-ette stock, 2-stage trigger. Made in West Germany. Introduced, 1981; still imported by Precision Sales International. Used value, $725 to $775.

Model 54.18L has same specs as standard model, except is left-hand version. Used value, $750 to $800.

ANSCHUTZ 1827B Biathlon: bolt-action; .22 LR; 5-rd. maga-zine; 21½" barrel; 42½" overall length; special Biathlon globe front sight, micrometer rear has snow cap; adjustable trigger; adjust-able wooden butt plate; adjustable handstop rail; Biathlon butt hook. Special order only. Made in West Germany. Introduced, 1982; still imported by Precision Sales International. Used values: $900 to $975; left-hand version, $950 to $1050.

Anschutz 1808ED

ANSCHUTZ 1808ED: bolt-action; single-shot; .22 LR; 23½" heavy barrel; 42" overall length; designed as running target gun; no sights; receiver grooved for scope mount; hardwood stock; adjust-able cheekpiece; beavertail forend; stippled pistol grip, forend; removable barrel weights; adjustable trigger. Special order only. Made in West Germany. Introduced, 1982; still imported by Preci-sion Sales International. Used value, $750 to $800.

Model 1808EDL has same specs as 1808ED, except is de-signed for left-handed shooter. Used value, $800 to $850.

Anschutz Model 1403D

ANSCHUTZ Model 1403D Match: bolt-action; single-shot; .22 LR; no sights; walnut-finished hardwood stock; cheekpiece; checkered pistol grip, beavertail forend; adjustable butt plate; slide safety; adjustable single-stage trigger; receiver grooved for sights. Made in West Germany. Introduced, 1980; still imported by Precision Sales International. Used value, $400 to $425.

Model 1403DL has same specs as 1403D, except has left-hand stock and action. Used value, $425 to $450.

Anschutz 1416 Deluxe

ANSCHUTZ 1416 Deluxe: bolt-action; .22 LR; 5-rd. clip; 22½" barrel; 41" overall length; hooded ramp front sight, folding leaf rear; European walnut Monte Carlo stock; cheekpiece; checkered pistol grip. Schnabel forend; adjustable single-stage trigger; receiver grooved for scope mounts. Made in West Germany. Introduced, 1982; still imported by Precision Sales International. Used value, $300 to $325.

Model 1516 Deluxe: has same specs as 1416 Deluxe, except is chambered for .22 WRFM; 4-rd. clip. Introduced, 1982; still imported. Used value, $325 to $350.

Anschutz Model 1418D

ANSCHUTZ 1418D Deluxe: bolt-action; .22 LR; has same specs as 1416D, except has full-length Mannlicher-style stock, 19¾" barrel, buffalo horn Schnabel tip. Made in West Germany. Introduced, 1982; still imported by Precision Sales International. Used value, $450 to $500.

1518D Deluxe has same specs as 1418D Deluxe, except is chambered for .22 WRFM, has 4-rd. clip. Introduced, 1983; still imported. Used value, $475 to $525.

Anschutz 1422D Classic

ANSCHUTZ 1422D Classic: bolt-action; .22 LR; 5-rd. clip; 24" barrel; 43" overall length; hooded ramp front sight, folding leaf rear; select European walnut stock; checkered pistol grip, forend; adjustable single-stage trigger; drilled/tapped for scope mount. Made in West Germany. Introduced, 1982; still imported by Precision Sales International. Used value, $450 to $500.

Model 1422D Custom has same specs as Deluxe model, except has roll-over Monte Carlo cheekpiece, slim forend, Schnabel tip; palm swell on pistol grip; rosewood grip cap, diamond insert; skip-line checkering. Made in West Germany. Introduced, 1982; still imported by Precision Sales International. Used value, $550 to $600.

ANSCHUTZ 1522D Classic: bolt-action; .22 WRFM; 4-rd. clip; all other specs identical to 1422D. Made in West Germany. Introduced, 1982; still imported by Precision Sales International. Used value, $500 to $525.

Model 1522D Custom has same specs as 1422D Custom, except is chambered for .22 WRFM, has 4-rd. clip. Introduced, 1982; still imported. Used value, $575 to $625.

Anschutz Model 520

ANSCHUTZ Model 520: autoloader; .22 LR; overall length, 43"; weighs 6½ lb.; European Monte Carlo walnut stock, forend; hand checkering; rotary-style safety; 10-rd. clip magazine; single-stage trigger; folding adjustable rear sight, hooded ramp front; receiver grooved for scope mounts. Made in West Germany. Introduced, 1982; still imported by Precision Sales International as Model 525. Used value, $200 to $215.

ANSCHUTZ Model 1810 Super Match II: called Model 1910, as of 1988; single-shot; .22 LR; has same general specs as Super Match 1813, except has European hardwood stock, tapered forend, deep receiver area; no hand, palm rests; no sights; uses Match 54 action; adjustable hook butt plate, cheekpiece; right- or left-hand styles. Made in West Germany. Introduced, 1982; still imported by Precision Sales. Used values: right-hand model, $1150 to $1200; left-hand, $1225 to $1275.

Anschutz Achiever

ANSCHUTZ Achiever: bolt-action; .22 LR; 5-rd. clip; 19½" barrel; 35½" to 36⅔" overall length; weighs 5 lb.; fully adjustable open rear sight, hooded front; walnut-finished European hardwood stock; Mark 2000-type action; adjustable two-stage trigger; grooved for scope mounts. Made in West Germany. Introduced, 1987; still imported by Precision Sales. Used value, $220 to $230.

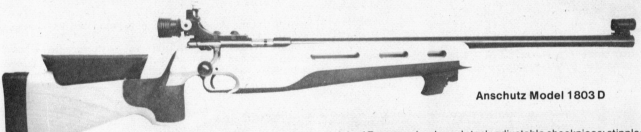

Anschutz Kadett

ANSCHUTZ Kadett: bolt-action; .22 LR; 5-rd. clip; 22" barrel; 40" overall length; weighs 5½ lb.; Lyman adjustable folding leaf rear sight, hooded bead on ramp front; checkered walnut-finished European hardwood stock; Mark 2000 target action; single-stage trigger; grooved for scope mount. Made in West Germany. Introduced, 1987; imported by Precision Sales; dropped, 1988. Used value, $190 to $200.

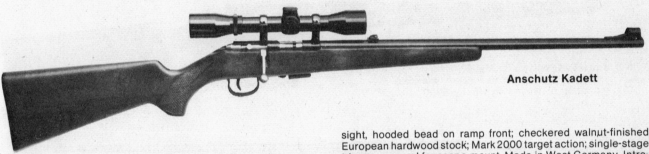

Anschutz Model 1803 D

ANSCHUTZ Model 1803D: single-shot; .22 LR; 25½" heavy barrel; 43¾" overall length; weighs 8.6 lb.; no sights; walnut-finished European hardwood stock; adjustable cheekpiece; stippled grip, forend; built on Anschutz Match 64 action; two-stage trigger; right- or left-hand models. Made in West Germany. Introduced, 1987; still impotred by Precision Sales. Used values: right-hand model, $490 to $515; left-hand, $415 to $525.

ARMSCOR

ARMSCOR Model 14P: bolt-action; .22 LR; 5-rd. magazine; 23" barrel; 41½" overall length; weighs 6 lb.; elevation-adjustable rear sight, bead front; grooved for scope mounts; blued finish. Made in the Philippines. Introduced, 1987; still imported by Armscor. Used value, $70 to $75.

ARMSCOR Model 1500: bolt-action; .22 LR; has the same general specs as the Model 14P, except is chambered for .22 WRFM; has 21½" barrel; double-lug bolt, checkered stock. Made in the Philippines. Introduced, 1987; still imported by Armscor. Used value, $120 to $125.

ARMSCOR Model 20P: autoloader; .22 LR; 15-rd. magazine; 20¾" barrel; 39¾" overall length; weighs 5½ lb.; elevation-adjustable rear sight, bead front; walnut-finished Philippine mahogany stock; receiver grooved for scope mounts; blued finish. Made in the Philippines. Introduced, 1987; still imported by Armscor. Used value, $70 to $75.

Model 2000 has the same specs as Model 20P, except has fully adjustable rear sight, checkered stock. Used value, $75 to $80.

ARMSCOR Model 1600: autoloader; .22 LR; 15-rd. magazine; 18" barrel; 38½" overall length; weighs 5¼ lb.; aperture rear sight, post front; black ebony wood stock; matte black finish; resembles Colt AR-15. Made in the Philippines. Introduced, 1987; still imported by Armscor. Used value, $85 to $90.

Model 1600 R has same specs as 1600, except has retractable butt stock, ventilated forend. Used value, $95 to $100.

BRNO

Brno Model 21 H

BRNO Model 21 H: bolt-action, Mauser-type; 6.5x55, 7x57, 8x57mm; 5-rd. box magazine; 20½" barrel; 2-leaf rear sight, ramp front; half-length sporting stock; hand-checkered pistol grip, forearm; sling swivels; double-set trigger. Manufactured prior to World War II. Used value, $625 to $650.

BRNO Hornet: bolt-action; .22 Hornet; 5-rd. box magazine; 23" barrel; 3-leaf rear sight, hooded ramp front; double-set trigger; sling swivels; hand-checkered pistol grip, forearm. Manufactured in Czechoslovakia prior to World War II. Used value, $650 to $675.

BRNO Model 22F: bolt-action, Mauser-type; has same general specs as Model 21, except for Mannlicher-type stock. Produced prior to World War II. Used value, $850 to $900.

Brno Model 22F

Brno Model II

BRNO Model I: bolt-action; .22 LR; 5-rd. magazine; 3-leaf rear sight, hooded ramp front; sling swivels; sporting stock, hand-check-ered pistol grip. Manufactured prior to World War II. Used value, $450 to $475.

Model II: has same specs as Model I, except for better grade of European walnut stock. Manufactured prior to World War II. Used value, $525 to $550.

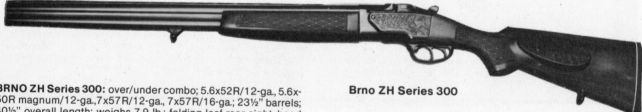

BRNO ZH Series 300: over/under combo; 5.6x52R/12-ga., 5.6x-50R magnum/12-ga.,7x57R/12-ga., 7x57R/16-ga.; 23½" barrels; 40½" overall length; weighs 7.9 lb.; folding leaf rear sight, bead front; walnut stock; box-lock action; eight-barrel set for combo calibers and o/u shotgun barrels. Made in Czechoslovakia. Intro-

Brno ZH Series 300

duced, 1986; still imported by Saki International. Used value, $2300 to $2500.

Brno XHB 680 Fox

BRNO ZKB 680 Fox: bolt-action; .22 Hornet, .222 Rem.; 5-rd. magazine; 23½" barrel; 42½" overall length; weighs 5¾ lb.; open adjustable rear sight, hooded front; Turkish walnut Monte Carlo stock; adjustable double-set triggers; detachable box magazine. Made in Czechoslovakia. Introduced, 1986; still imported by Saki International. Used value, $350 to $375.

Brno ZKK 600

Brno ZKK 602

BRNO ZKK 600: bolt-action; .30/06, .270, 7x57, 7x64; 5-rd. magazine; 23½" barrel; 43" overall length; open folding adjustable rear sight, hooded ramp front; uncheckered walnut stock; adjustable set trigger; easy-release sling swivels. Made in Czechoslovakia. Introduced, 1986; still imported by Saki International. Used value, $450 to $475.

BRNO Super Express: over/under double rifle; 7x65R, 9.3x74R, .375 H&H, .458 Win. magnum; 23½" barrel; 40" overall length; weighs about 8½ lb.; quarter-rib with open rear sight, bead on ramp front; checkered European walnut stock; side-lock action; en-

ZKK 601 has the same specs as ZKK 600, except is chambered for .223, .243. Introduced, 1986; still imported. Used value, $400 to $425.

ZKK 602 has same general specs as ZKK 600, except has 25" barrel, is chambered for 8x68S, .375 H&H, .458 Win. magnum. Introduced, 1986; still imported. Used value, $500 to $525.

NOTE: All models available with Monte Carlo stock at $60 premium.

graved side plates; double-set triggers; selective auto ejectors; rubber recoil pad. Made in Czechoslovakia. Introduced, 1986; still imported by Saki International. Used value, $2900 to $3100.

BROWNING

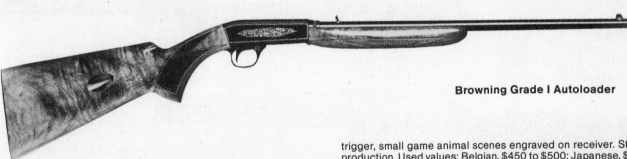

Browning Grade I Autoloader

BROWNING Grade I Autoloader .22: same action as discontinued Remington Model 241A; take-down; .22 LR, .22 short, not interchangeable; 19¼" barrel for LR, 22¼" for short cartridge; butt stock tube magazine holds 11 LR, 16 short cartridges; select European walnut stock; hand-checkered pistol grip, semi-beavertail forearm; open rear sight, bead front; engraved receiver, grooved for tip-off scope mount; cross-bolt safety. Introduced in 1958. Manufactured in Belgium until 1972; production transferred to Miroku in Japan; still in production. Used values: Belgian, $250 to $275; Japanese, $200 to $225.

Grade II has identical specs to Grade I, except for gold-plated

trigger, small game animal scenes engraved on receiver. Still in production. Used values: Belgian, $450 to $500; Japanese, $250 to $300.

Grade III has same specs as Grade I, except for gold-plated trigger, extra-fancy walnut stock, forearm; skip checkering on pistol grip, forearm; satin chrome-plated receiver; hand-carved, engraved scrolls, leaves, dog/game bird scenes; .22 LR only. No longer in production. Used values: Belgian, $950 to $1000; Japanese, $600 to $625.

Grade VI has the same general specs as Grade I, except has grayed or blued receiver; extensive engraving, gold-plated animals; stock, forend of high-grade walnut with double-border cut checkering. Made in Japan. Introduced, 1987; still in production. Used value, $500 to $525.

Browning Safari Grade Heavy Barrel

BROWNING High-Power Safari Grade: standard Mauser-type bolt-action; .270 Win., .30/06, 7mm Rem. magnum, .300 Win. mag-

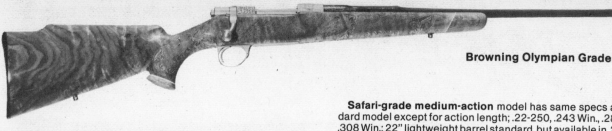

Browning Olympian Grade

num; .308 Norma magnum, .338 Win. magnum, .375 H&H magnum, .458 Win. magnum; 24" barrel in magnum calibers, 22" in others; 4-rd. magazine capacity for magnum cartridges, 6 rds. for others; European walnut stock; hand-checkered pistol grip, forearm; Monte Carlo cheekpiece; recoil pad on magnum models; folding leaf rear sight, hooded ramp front; quick-detachable sling swivels. Introduced in 1960; dropped, 1974. Used value, $625 to $650.

Safari-grade short-action has the same specs as standard-grade Safari except for short action; .222 Rem., .222 Rem. magnum; 22" lightweight, 24" heavy barrel. Dropped, 1974. Used value, $550 to $600.

Safari-grade medium-action model has same specs as standard model except for action length; .22-250, .243 Win., .284 Win., .308 Win.; 22" lightweight barrel standard, but available in .22-250, .243 with heavy barrel. Dropped, 1974. Used value, $575 to $625.

Medallion grade has the same specs as standard Safari grade with exception of scroll-engraved receiver, barrel; engraved ram's head on floor plate; select European walnut stock has rosewood grip cap, forearm tip. Dropped, 1974. Used value, $1200 to $1250.

Olympian-grade High-Power has the same specs as Safari, except for engraving on barrel; chrome-plated floor plate, trigger guard, receiver, all engraved with game scenes; figured European walnut stock; rosewood forearm tip, grip cap; grip cap is inlaid with 18-karat gold medallion. Discontinued, 1974. Used value, $1850 to $2250.

Browning Model T-2

BROWNING Model T-1 T-Bolt: straight-pull bolt-action; .22 LR only; 24" barrel; 5-rd. clip magazine; uncheckered walnut pistol-grip stock; peep rear sight, ramped blade front; in either left- or right-hand model. Introduced in 1965; not regularly imported. Used value, $225 to $250.

Model T-2 has the same specs as Model T-1, except for figured, hand-checkered walnut stock. Not regularly imported. Used values: $300 to $325; last run T-2 with plain stock and no peep sight, $185 to $210.

Browning BAR Grade II

Browning BAR Grade IV

BROWNING BAR: not to be confused with military Browning selective-fire rifle; semiautomatic; .243 Win., .308 Win., .270 Win., .280 Rem., .30/06, 7mm Rem. magnum, .300 Win. magnum, .338 Win. magnum; 22" barrel; 4-rd. detachable box magazine for standard calibers, 3-rd. for magnums; adjustable folding leaf rear sight, gold bead hooded ramp front; receiver tapped for scope mounts; checkered walnut pistol-grip stock, forearm. Grades I, II introduced in 1967; Grades II, III, V still in production. Grades vary according to amount of checkering, carving, engraving, inlay work. Used values, standard calibers: Grade I, $375 to $400; II, $550 to $600; III $800 to $850; IV, $1200 to $1300, V, $1900 to $2000; magnum calibers: Grade I, $400 to $450; II, $600 to $650; III, $800 to $850; IV, $1250 to $1350; V, $2000 to $2250.

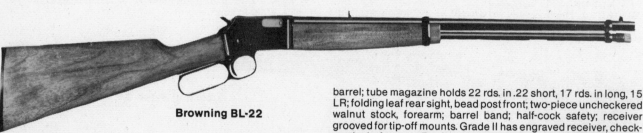

Browning BL-22

BROWNING BL-22 Grade I: lever-action; .22 LR, long, short; 20" barrel; tube magazine holds 22 rds. in .22 short, 17 rds. in long, 15 LR; folding leaf rear sight, bead post front; two-piece uncheckered walnut stock, forearm; barrel band; half-cock safety; receiver grooved for tip-off mounts. Grade II has engraved receiver, checkered grip, forearm. Produced by Miroku Firearms, Tokyo, Japan, to Browning specs. Introduced in 1970; still in production. Used values: $175 to $200 for Grade I; $235 to $250 for Grade II.

Browning BLR

BROWNING BLR: lever-action; .222, .223, .22-250, .257 Roberts, 7mm-08, .308 Win., .243 Win., .358 Win.; 20" barrel; 4-rd. detachable magazine; square-notch adjustable rear sight, gold bead hooded ramp front; receiver tapped for scope mount; recoil pad; checkered straight-grip stock, forearm, oil finished; wide, grooved trigger, Introduced, 1971; made to Browning specs by Miroku Firearms, Tokyo, Japan, since May '74; still in production. Used value, $300 to $325.

Browning BAR-22

BROWNING BAR-22: semiautomatic; .22 LR; 15-rd. tubular magazine; 20¼" barrel; receiver grooved for scope mount; folding leaf rear sight, gold bead ramp front; French walnut stock, hand-checkered pistol grip, forearm. Introduced, 1977; dropped, 1986. Manufactured in Japan. Used values: Grade I, $175 to $195; Grade II, $225 to $250.

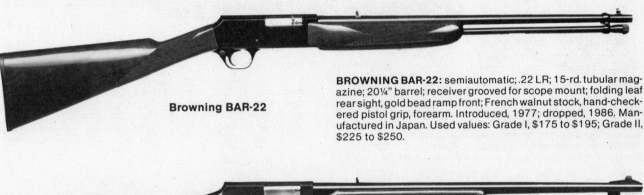

Browning BPR-22

BROWNING BPR-22: pump-action; .22 LR; .22 WRFM hammerless; other specs generally the same as those of BAR-22, except for magazine capacity of 11 rds. Made in Japan. Introduced in 1977; .22 LR dropped, 1981; .22 WRFM dropped, 1982. Used values: Grade I, $200 to $225; Grade II, $300 to $325.

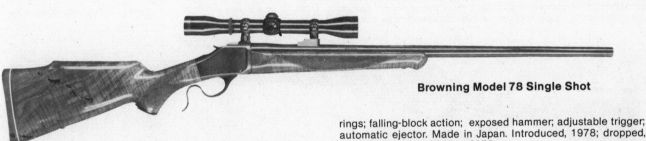

Browning Model 78 Single Shot

rings; falling-block action; exposed hammer; adjustable trigger; automatic ejector. Made in Japan. Introduced, 1978; dropped, 1983. Used value, $350 to $375.

Model B-78: has same general specs as standard model, except is .45-70 only; 24" heavy octagon barrel; blade front sight, step-adjustable rear; drilled, tapped for scope mounts; straight-grip hand-checkered walnut stock, semi-Schnabel forend; sling swivels; curved, blued steel butt plate. Introduced, 1978; dropped, 1981. Used value, $400 to $425.

BROWNING Model 78: single-shot; .30/06, .25/06, 6mm Rem., .243, .22-250, 7mm Rem. magnum; 26" tapered octagon or heavy round barrel; hand-rubbed, hand-checkered select walnut stock; rubber recoil pad; no sights; furnished with scope mounts and

Browning Model B-92

BROWNING B-92: lever-action, .357 magnum, .44 magnum; 11-rd. magazine; 20" round barrel; post front sight, classic cloverleaf rear with notched elevation ramp; straight-grip European walnut stock, high-gloss finish; steel butt plate; tubular magazine. Designed from original Model 92 lever-action. Manufactured in Japan. Introduced, 1979; dropped, 1988. Used value, $250 to $285.

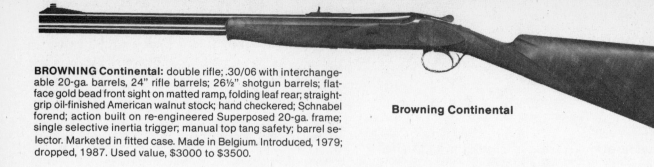

BROWNING Continental: double rifle; .30/06 with interchangeable 20-ga. barrels, 24" rifle barrels; 26½" shotgun barrels; flatface gold bead front sight on matted ramp, folding leaf rear; straight-grip oil-finished American walnut stock; hand checkered; Schnabel forend; action built on re-engineered Superposed 20-ga. frame; single selective inertia trigger; manual top tang safety; barrel selector. Marketed in fitted case. Made in Belgium. Introduced, 1979; dropped, 1987. Used value, $3000 to $3500.

Browning Continental

Browning BBR

BROWNING BBR: bolt-action; .25/06, .270, .30/06, 7mm Rem. magnum, .300 Win. magnum, .338 Win. magnum; 22" sporter barrel, recessed muzzle; American walnut Monte Carlo stock; high cheekpiece; full/checkered pistol grip, forend; recoil pad on magnums; grooved, gold-plated adjustable trigger; detachable box magazine; 4 rds. in standard calibers, 3 in magnums; tang slide safety; low profile swing swivels. Made in Japan. Introduced, 1978; dropped, 1984. Used value, $375 to $400.

BBR Short Action has same general design as standard model, except has short action; .22-250, .243, .257 Roberts, 7mm-08, .308; 22" light or 24" heavy barrel. Introduced, 1983; dropped, 1984. Used value, $375 to $400.

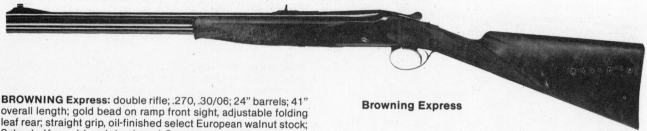

BROWNING Express: double rifle; .270, .30/06; 24" barrels; 41" overall length; gold bead on ramp front sight, adjustable folding leaf rear; straight grip, oil-finished select European walnut stock; Schnabel forend; hand checkered; Superposed action; reinforced breech face; single selective trigger; selective ejectors; manual safety; hand-engraved receiver; marketed in fitted case. Made in

Browning Express

Belgium. Introduced, 1981; dropped, 1987. Used value, $3200 to $3300.

Browning Model 1895

BROWNING Model 1895: lever-action; .30/06, .30-40 Krag; 4-rd. magazine; 24" round barrel; overall length, 42"; weighs 8 lb.; straight-grip walnut stock, forend; matte finish; buckhorn rear sight with elevator, gold bead front on ramp; replica of Browning's first box-magazine lever-action; top-loading magazine; half-cock hammer safety; High Grade Model has gold-plated moose, grizzly on gray engraved receiver. Made in Japan. Introduced, 1984; dropped, 1985. Used values: Grade I, $375 to $400; High Grade, $550 to $600.

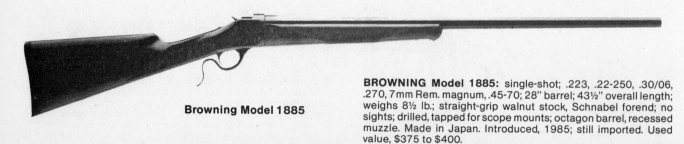

Browning Model 1885

BROWNING Model 1885: single-shot; .223, .22-250, .30/06, .270, 7mm Rem. magnum, .45-70; 28" barrel; 43½" overall length; weighs 8½ lb.; straight-grip walnut stock, Schnabel forend; no sights; drilled, tapped for scope mounts; octagon barrel, recessed muzzle. Made in Japan. Introduced, 1985; still imported. Used value, $375 to $400.

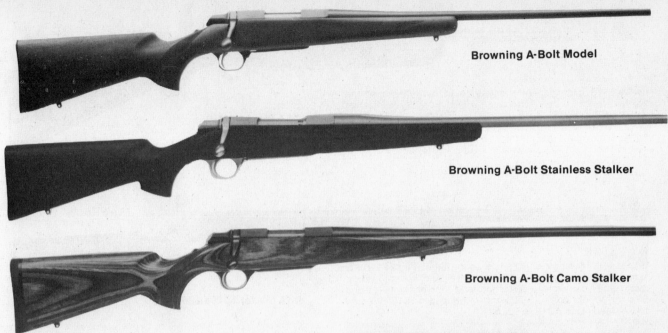

Browning A-Bolt Model

Browning A-Bolt Stainless Stalker

Browning A-Bolt Camo Stalker

BROWNING A-Bolt: bolt-action; .25/06, .270, .30/06, .280, 7mm Rem. magnum, .300 Win. magnum, .338 Win. magnum, .375 H&H; 22" barrel, recessed muzzle; magnum and standard action, overall length is 44¾"; short action's overall length, 41¾"; classic-style American walnut stock; recoil pad on magnum calibers; short-throw fluted bolt; 3 locking lugs; plunger-type ejector; adjustable, grooved gold-plated trigger; hinged floor plate; detachable box magazine; slide tang safety; rosewood grip, forend caps; Medallion and Hunter grades. Made in Japan. Introduced, 1985; still imported. Used values: Medallion, no sights, $300 to $325; Hunter, no sights, $275 to $300; Hunter, with sights, $300 to $325.

A-Bolt Short Action model has sames general specs as standard A-Bolt, except for shorter action; .22-250, .243, .257 Roberts, 7mm-08, .308. Made in Japan. Introduced, 1985; still imported.

Used values same as standard model.

A-Bolt Stainless Stalker has the same general specs as the standard A-Bolt, except the receiver is of stainless steel; other exposed metal is finished in matte silver-gray; stock is finished with black stipple paint. Made in .270, .30/06, 7mm Rem. magnum. Made in Japan. Introduced, 1987; still imported by Browning. Used value, $375 to $400.

A-Bolt Left-Hand is the same as the standard version, except has left-hand action; made in .270, .30/06, 7mm Rem. magnum. Made in Japan. Introduced, 1987; still imported. Used value, $350 to $375.

A-Bolt Camo Stalker has same specs as standard model, except stock is of camo-stained laminated wood; has cut checkering, non-glare finish on metal; made in .270, .30/06, 7mm Rem. magnum. Made in Japan. Introduced, 1987; still in production. Used value, $300 to $325.

Browning Model 71

BROWNING Model 71: lever-action; .348 Win.; 4-rd. magazine; 20", 24" barrels; 45" overall rifle length; rifle weighs 8 lb. 2 oz.; pistol-grip stock; classic-style forend; metal butt plate; reproduction of Winchester Model 71; has half-length magazine; High Grade has blued barrel and magazine, grayed lever and receiver with scroll engraving, gold-plated game scene. Production limited to 3000 rifles, 3000 carbines. Made in Japan. Introduced, 1987; still marketed. Used values: Grade I, $425 to $475; High Grade, $725 to $775.

BSA

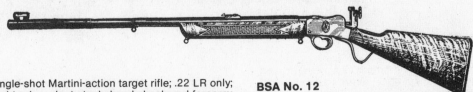

BSA No. 12: single-shot Martini-action target rifle; .22 LR only; 29" barrel; straight-grip walnut stock; hand-checkered forearm; Parker-Hale No. 7 rear sight, hooded front. Introduced in 1912; dropped, 1929. Used value, $225 to $250.

BSA No. 12

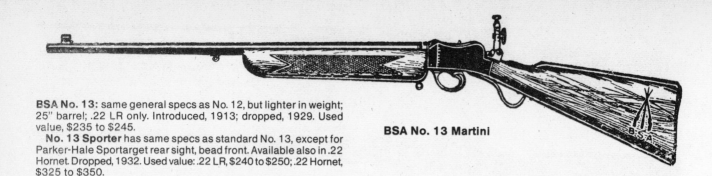

BSA No. 13 Martini

BSA No. 13: same general specs as No. 12, but lighter in weight; 25" barrel; .22 LR only. Introduced, 1913; dropped, 1929. Used value, $235 to $245.

No. 13 Sporter has same specs as standard No. 13, except for Parker-Hale Sportarget rear sight, bead front. Available also in .22 Hornet. Dropped, 1932. Used value: .22 LR, $240 to $250; .22 Hornet, $325 to $350.

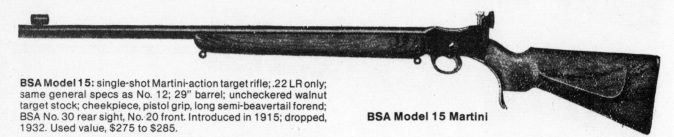

BSA Model 15 Martini

BSA Model 15: single-shot Martini-action target rifle; .22 LR only; same general specs as No. 12; 29" barrel; uncheckered walnut target stock; cheekpiece, pistol grip, long semi-beavertail forend; BSA No. 30 rear sight, No. 20 front. Introduced in 1915; dropped, 1932. Used value, $275 to $285.

BSA Centurion: has the same basic specs as Model 15, but was outfitted with Centurion match barrel; maker guaranteed 1.5" groups at 100 yards. Dropped, 1932. Used value, $375 to $400.

BSA-Parker Model 12/15

BSA-Parker Model 12/15: single-shot Martini-action target rifle: allegedly combined best features of No. 12 and Model 15; .22 LR only; 29" barrel; walnut target stock with high comb, cheekpiece, beavertail forend; forward sling swivel; Parker-Hale PH-7A rear sight, PH-22 front. Introduced in 1938; dropped at beginning of WWII. Used value, $300 to $325.

BSA Model 12/15: has the same specs as BSA-Parker Model 12/15, but this was designation given rifle when reintroduced following WWII. Dropped, 1950. Used value, $275 to $300.

BSA Heavy Model 12/15 has same specs as standard Model 12/15, except for extra-heavy competition barrel. Used value, $350 to $375.

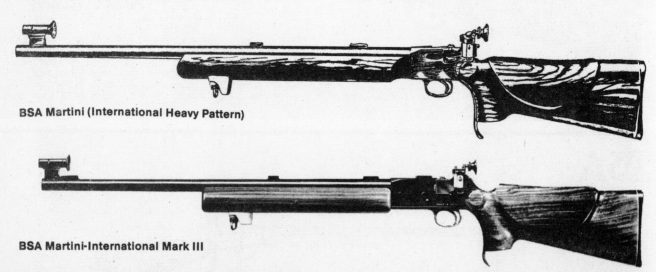

BSA Martini (International Heavy Pattern)

BSA Martini-International Mark III

BSA Martini-International Heavy Pattern: single-shot match rifle, Martini-type action; .22 LR only; 29" heavy barrel; uncheckered two-piece target stock; full cheekpiece, pistol grip, broad beavertail forend; hand stop; swivels; right- or left-hand styles. Introduced in 1950; dropped, 1953. Used value, $350 to $375.

Martini-International Light Pattern has same general specs, except for lightweight 26" barrel. Used value, $325 to $350.

Martini ISU Match model has same general specs except for 28" barrel; flat cheekpiece; available with standard or heavy barrel; adjustable trigger; modified PH-1 Parker-Hale tunnel front sight, PH-25 Aperture rear. Imported by Freelands; dropped, 1986. Used values: standard barrel, $450 to $475; heavy barrel, $475 to $485.

Martini-International Mark II has same specs as 1950 model, with choice of light, heavy barrel. Improvements to original include redesigned stock, forearm, trigger mechanism, ejection system. Introduced in 1953; dropped, 1959. Used value, $350 to $375.

Martini-International Mark III has same specs as Mark II heavy barrel model, plus redesigned stock, forend, free-floating barrel, longer frame with alloy strut to attach forend. Introduced in 1959; dropped, 1967. Used value, $400 to $425.

BSA Imperial

BSA Imperial: bolt-action; .270 Win., .308 Win., .30/06 in lightweight model; .22 Hornet, .222 Rem., .243 Win., .257 Roberts, 7x57mm, .300 Savage and .30/06 in standard weight; 22" barrel; recoil reducer cut into muzzle; fully adjustable trigger; European walnut cheekpiece stock; hand-checkered pistol grip, Schnabel forend; black butt plate, pistol grip cap with white spacers; drilled, tapped for scope mounts. Introduced in 1959; dropped, 1964. Used value, $250 to $275.

BSA Majestic Deluxe

BSA Majestic Deluxe: Mauser-type bolt-action; .22 Hornet, .222 Rem., .243 Win., .308 Win., .30/06, 7x57mm; 22" barrel; 4-rd. magazine; European walnut stock; checkered pistol grip, forend; cheekpiece, Schnabel forend; folding leaf rear sight, hooded ramp front; sling swivels. Introduced in 1959; dropped, 1965. Used value, $250 to $275.

Majestic Deluxe Featherweight has the same general specs as standard Majestic Deluxe, except for recoil pad, lightweight barrel, recoil reducer; .243 Win., .270 Win., .308 Win., .30/06, .458 Win. magnum. Used values: .458 Win. magnum, $350 to $400; other calibers, $350 to $375.

BSA Monarch Deluxe

BSA Monarch Deluxe: Mauser-type bolt-action; .22 Hornet, .222 Rem., .243 Win., .270 Win., 7mm Rem. magnum, .308 Win., .30/06; 22" barrel. Has same general specs as Majestic Deluxe standard model, except for redesigned stock, with hardwood forend tip, grip cap. Introduced in 1965; dropped, 1977. Used value, $250 to $300.

Monarch Deluxe Varmint model has same specs as standard Monarch Deluxe except for 24" heavy barrel; .222 Rem., .243 Win. Used value, $275 to $325.

BSA CF-2

BSA CF-2 Stutzen

BSA CF-2: bolt-action; .222 Rem., .22-250, .243, 6.5x55, 7mm Mauser, 7x64, .270, .308, .30/06, 7mm Rem. magnum, .300 Win. magnum; 24" barrel; open adjustable rear sight, hooded ramp front; roll-over Monte Carlo stock of European walnut; high-gloss finish; pistol grip, skip-line checkering; adjustable single trigger or optional double-set trigger. Manufactured in England. Introduced by Precision Sports, 1980; dropped, 1985. Used values: standard calibers, $275 to $300; magnum calibers, $300 to $325.

CF-2 Stutzen has same specs as standard model, except has full-length Stutzen-style stock, contrasting Schnabel forend tip, grip cap; improved bolt guide; 20½" barrel; available with double-set triggers; .222, 6.5x55, .308 Win., .30/06, .270, 7x64. Introduced by Precision Sports in 1982; dropped, 1985. Used values: standard trigger, $375 to $400; double-set triggers, $400 to $450.

CABANAS

Canabas Master Model

Canabas Varmint Model

CABANAS Master Model: bolt-action, single-shot; .177; 19½" barrel; 45½" overall length; weighs 8 lb.; Monte Carlo target-type walnut stock; adjustable rear sight, blade front; fires round ball or pellet with .22 blank cartridge. Made in Mexico. Introduced, 1984; still imported by Mandall Shooting Supplies. Used value, $85 to $90.

Varmint Model has same specs as Master model. except has 21½" barrel, weighs 4½ lb.; has varmint-type stock. Used value, $70 to $75.

Canabas Leyre Model

Canabas Model R83

Canabas 82 Mini Youth

CABANAS Leyre Model is similar to Master model, except is 44" overall, has sport/target stock. Used value, $90 to $95.

Model R83 has same specs as Leyre model, except has 17" barrel, hardwood stock, measures 44" overall. Used value, $55 to $60.

Model 82 Mini Youth has 16½" barrel, overall length of 33". Used value, $50 to $55.

CABANAS Espronceda: single-shot; has same specs as the Leyre model, except has full sporter stock, 18¾" barrel; 40" overall length; weighs 5½ lb. Made in Mexico. Introduced, 1986; still imported by Mandall. Used value, $75 to $80.

Cabanas Laser Model

CABANAS Laser Model: single-shot; .177; fires round ball or pellet with .22-caliber blank cartridge; 19" barrel; 42" overall length; weighs 6¾ lb.; open fully adjustable rear sight, blade front; target-type thumbhole stock. Made in Mexico. Introduced, 1987; still imported by Mandall. Used value, $110 to $120.

CENTURY

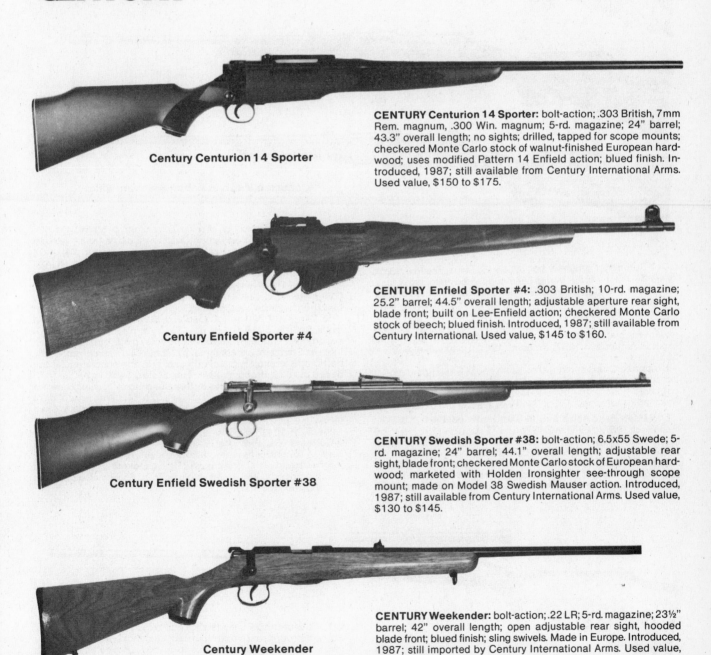

Century Centurion 14 Sporter

CENTURY Centurion 14 Sporter: bolt-action; .303 British, 7mm Rem. magnum, .300 Win. magnum; 5-rd. magazine; 24" barrel; 43.3" overall length; no sights; drilled, tapped for scope mounts; checkered Monte Carlo stock of walnut-finished European hardwood; uses modified Pattern 14 Enfield action; blued finish. Introduced, 1987; still available from Century International Arms. Used value, $150 to $175.

Century Enfield Sporter #4

CENTURY Enfield Sporter #4: .303 British; 10-rd. magazine; 25.2" barrel; 44.5" overall length; adjustable aperture rear sight, blade front; built on Lee-Enfield action; checkered Monte Carlo stock of beech; blued finish. Introduced, 1987; still available from Century International. Used value, $145 to $160.

Century Enfield Swedish Sporter #38

CENTURY Swedish Sporter #38: bolt-action; 6.5x55 Swede; 5-rd. magazine; 24" barrel; 44.1" overall length; adjustable rear sight, blade front; checkered Monte Carlo stock of European hardwood; marketed with Holden Ironsighter see-through scope mount; made on Model 38 Swedish Mauser action. Introduced, 1987; still available from Century International Arms. Used value, $130 to $145.

Century Weekender

CENTURY Weekender: bolt-action; .22 LR; 5-rd. magazine; 23½" barrel; 42" overall length; open adjustable rear sight, hooded blade front; blued finish; sling swivels. Made in Europe. Introduced, 1987; still imported by Century International Arms. Used value, $60 to $65.

COLT

COLT Lightning: slide-action; .32-20, .38-40, .44-40; 26" round or octagonal barrel; 15-rd. tubular magazine; open rear sight, blade front; American walnut stock, forend. Manufactured 1884 to 1902. Collector value. $500 to $1250.

Lightning Carbine has same specs except for 20" barrel, adjustable military-type sights, 12-rd. magazine. Collector value. Manufactured 1884 to 1902. Used value, $650 to $1500.

Lightning Baby Carbine has same specs as Lightning Carbine, except lighter in weight; 22" round barrel; weighs 8 lb. Collector value. Manufactured 1885 to 1900. Used value, $1500 to $3500.

Lightning Small Frame model .22 short, .22 long; 24" round or octagonal barrel; tubular magazine holds 16 shorts, 15 longs; open rear sight, bead front; American walnut stock, forearm. Collector value. Manufactured 1887 to 1904. Used value, $400 to $800.

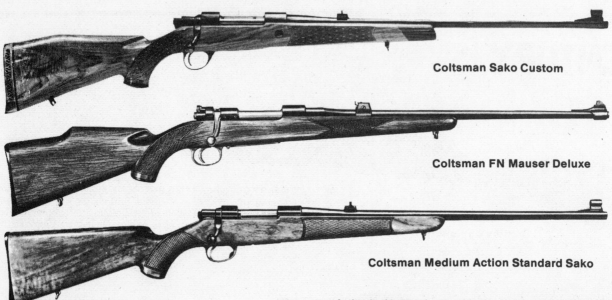

Coltsman Sako Custom

Coltsman FN Mauser Deluxe

Coltsman Medium Action Standard Sako

COLT Standard Coltsman: bolt-action; FN Mauser action; .30/06, .300 H&H magnum; 22" barrel; hand-checkered pistol-grip walnut stock; 5-rd. box magazine; no rear sight, ramp front; quick-detachable sling swivels. Introduced in 1957; replaced in 1962 by Sako action model; dropped, 1965. Used value, $450 to $475.

Coltsman Deluxe model has the same specs as standard model, except for better checkering, wood. Adjustable rear sight, ramp front. Introduced in 1957; dropped, 1962. Used value, $525 to $550.

Coltsman Custom model has same specs as standard model, except for fancy walnut stock, Monte Carlo comb, cheekpiece, engraved floor plate. Introduced in 1957; replaced in 1962 by Sako action; dropped, 1965. Used value, $600 to $625.

Coltsman Sako short-action Standard model is bolt-action; made from 1957 to 1961 in .243 Win., .308 Win.; from 1962 to 1966 in .222, .222 magnum only; other specs are virtually the same as those of the FN Mauser model. Used value, $450 to $475.

Coltsman Sako short-action Deluxe model has same general specs as FN Mauser version except made in .243, .308 Win. calibers only from 1957 to 1961. Dropped in this grade in 1961.

Action had integral scope blocks. Used value, $450 to $475.

Coltsman Sako short-action Custom model has same general specs as FN Mauser version except for action; made in .243, .308 Win. calibers only from 1957 to 1961; in .222, .222 magnum from 1962 to 1966; dropped, 1966. Used value, $600 to $625.

Coltsman medium-action Sako Standard model has hinged floor plate, hand-checkered walnut stock, standard sling swivels; bead front sight on hooded ramp, folding leaf rear; sliding safety; in .243 Win., .308 Win. Introduced in 1962; dropped, 1966. Used value, $400 to $450.

Coltsman Custom medium-action Sako has same specs, calibers as Standard, except for fancy Monte Carlo stock, recoil pad, dark wood forend tip, pistol-grip cap, skip-line checkering. Introduced in 1962; dropped, 1966. Used value, $475 to $500.

Coltsman Standard long-action Sako model is chambered for .264 Win., .270 Win., .30/06, .300 H&H, .375 H&H. With exception of action, calibers, other specs are same as those of Standard Sako medium-action version. Introduced in 1962; dropped, 1966. Used value, $450 to $475; $100 premium for .300 and .375 H&H.

Coltsman Custom long-action Sako is the same as Standard version, except for fancy Monte Carlo stock, recoil pad, dark wood forend tip and pistol-grip cap, skip-line checkering. Introduced in 1962; dropped, 1966. Used value, $525 to $550; $100 premium for .300 and .375 H&H.

Colteer 1-22 Model

COLT Colteer 1-22: single-shot bolt-action; .22 LR, long, short; 20" barrel; open rear sight, ramp front; uncheckered walnut pistol-grip Monte Carlo stock. Introduced in 1957; dropped, 1967. Used value, $175 to $200.

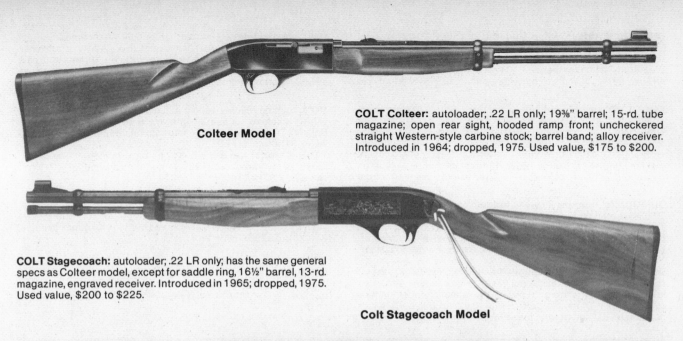

Colteer Model

COLT Colteer: autoloader; .22 LR only; 19⅜" barrel; 15-rd. tube magazine; open rear sight, hooded ramp front; uncheckered straight Western-style carbine stock; barrel band; alloy receiver. Introduced in 1964; dropped, 1975. Used value, $175 to $200.

COLT Stagecoach: autoloader; .22 LR only; has the same general specs as Colteer model, except for saddle ring, 16½" barrel, 13-rd. magazine, engraved receiver. Introduced in 1965; dropped, 1975. Used value, $200 to $225.

Colt Stagecoach Model

Colt-Sauer Standard Sporter

num; 24" barrel; 3-rd. detachable box magazine; no sights; hand-checkered American walnut pistol-grip stock; rosewood pistol grip, forend caps; recoil pad; quick-detachable sling swivels. Introduced in 1971; dropped, 1986. Used value, $700 to $725.

Colt-Sauer short action has the same general specs as standard long-action model, except has shorter action, chambering for .22-250, .243 Win., .308 Win. Introduced in 1974; dropped, 1986. Used value, $700 to $725.

COLT-Sauer Sporter: bolt-action; standard model uses long action made in Germany by Sauer and Sohn; .25/06, .270 Win., .30/06, 7mm Rem. magnum, .300 Weatherby magnum, .300 Win. mag-

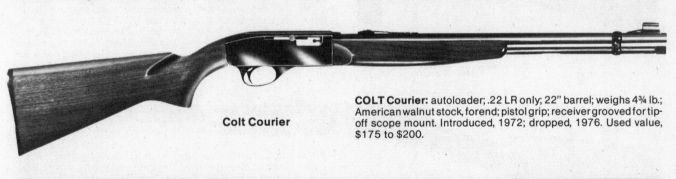

Colt Courier

COLT Courier: autoloader; .22 LR only; 22" barrel; weighs 4¾ lb.; American walnut stock, forend; pistol grip; receiver grooved for tip-off scope mount. Introduced, 1972; dropped, 1976. Used value, $175 to $200.

DUMOULIN

Dumoulin Sporter

DUMOULIN Sporter: bolt-action; all commercial calibers; 25" barrel; no sights; checkered pistol-grip French walnut stock, rosewood pistol-grip cap, forend tip, recoil pad; built on Sako or FN actions. Manufactured in Belgium; imported by Firearms Center; no longer imported. Used value, $850 to $900.

DUMOULIN African Safari Model: bolt-action; .264 Win., 7mm Rem. magnum, .300 Win., .338 Win., 6.5x58, 8x68S, .300 H&H, 9.3x64, .458 Win., .404 Jeffery, .416 Rigby, .416 Hoffman, 7mm Weatherby, .300 Weatherby, .340 Weatherby; 24" to 26" barrels; 44" overall length with 24" barrel; weighs 8½ to 9 lb.; two-leaf rear

DUMOULIN Bavaria Model: bolt-action; .222, .222 Rem. magnum, .223, .270, .280 Rem., .30/06, 6.5x57, 7x57, 7x64, .243, .264 Win., 7mm Rem. magnum, .300 Win., .338 Win., 6.5x68, 8x68S, .25/06, .22-250, 6mm, .300 Weatherby, .308 Norma, .240 Weatherby, .375 H&H, 9.3x64, .458 Win.; 21", 24", 25" octagonal barrels; weighs about 7 lb.; classic two-leaf rear sight, hooded blade on ramp front; hand-checkered, oil-finished select European walnut

DUMOULIN Pionnier Express Model: double rifle; .338 Win., .375 H&H, .458 Win., .470 NE, .416 Rigby, .416 Hoffman, .500 NE; also standard calibers; 24", 26" barrels; 45" overall length with 24" barrel; weighs 9½ lb.; two-leaf rear sight on quarter-rib, bead on ramp front; box-lock triple-lock system; Greener crossbolt; H&H-

DUMOULIN Sidelock Prestige: double rifle; has same general specs as Pionnier model, except has side-lock action, reinforced table; internal parts are gold-plated; traditional chopper lump or classic Ernest Dumoulin barrel system; 22" to 24" barrels, depending on caliber; grande luxe European walnut stock; Purdey

sight, hooded front on banded ramp; built on modified Sako or Mauser Oberndorf actions; classic English-style deluxe European walnut stock; oil finish; buffalo horn grip cap; rubber butt pad; Model 70-type or side safety. Custom built in Belgium. Introduced, 1986; importation dropped, 1987. Used value, $2000 to $2200.

stock; built on Mauser action; adjustable trigger; Model 70-type safety; quick-detachable sling swivels; solid butt pad. Made in Belgium. Introduced, 1986; importation dropped, 1987. Used value, $1500 to $1700.
 Diane Model has same specs as Bavaria model, except has round barrel. Introduced, 1986; importation dropped, 1987. Used value, $1250 to $1400.

type ejectors; articulated front trigger. Made in Belgium. Introduced, 1987; no longer imported by Midwest Gun Sport. Used values: standard calibers, $4000 to $4250; magnum calibers, $6000 to $6250.

lock system; 10 grades, built to customer specs; differing engraving styles. Made in Belgium. Introduced, 1987; no longer imported by Midwest Gun Sport. Used value, $9500 to $15,000, depending on grade.

ERMA

Erma Model EM1 22

ERMA Model EM1: semiautomatic; .22 LR; 10- or 15-rd. magazine; 18" barrel; patterned after U.S. Cal. .30 M1 carbine; M1-type sights; receiver grooved for scope mounts; sling swivel in barrel band, oiler slot in stock; European walnut M1-Carbine-type stock. Introduced, 1966; no longer imported. Used value, $145 to $150.
 Model EGM1 has same specs as Model EM1, but no oiler slot in stock; has ramp front sight, 5-rd. magazine. Introduced, 1970, no longer imported. Used value, $135 to $140.

Erma Model EG72

ERMA EG72: pump-action; .22 LR; 15-rd. magazine; 18½" barrel; visible hammer; open rear sight, hooded ramp front; grooved slide handle, straight hardwood stock; receiver grooved for scope mounts. Manufactured 1970 to 1976 in Germany; now made in U.S. by Iver Johnson as Targetmaster. Used value, $100 to $125.

Erma Model EG712

ERMA Model EG712: lever-action; .22 short, long, LR.; tubular magazine holds 21 shorts, 17 longs, 15 LR; 18½" barrel; near replica of Model 94 Winchester; open rear sight, hooded ramp front; carbine-style stock, forearm of European hardwood, barrel band; receiver grooved for scope mount. Introduced in 1976, still in production by Iver Johnson as the Wagonmaster. Used value, $145 to $165.
 Model EG712 L has same specs as EG712, except has European walnut stock, heavy octagon barrel, engraved, nickel silver-finished receiver. Introduced, 1978; no longer imported by Excam. Used value, $210 to $225.

ERMA Model EG73: lever-action; has same gene l specs as Model EG712, except for .22 WRFM chambering, 19.3" barrel; magazine holds 12 rds. Originally made in Germany. Introduced in 1973, still in production by Iver Johnson. Used value, $165 to $175.

ERMA ESG22 Carbine: autoloader; .22 WRFM, .22 LR; 12-rd. magazine for magnum, 15 rds. for LR; military post front sight, adjustable peep rear; 18" barrel; 35½" overall length; walnut-stained beech stock; gas-operated or blowback action; styled after M-1 carbine; receiver grooved for scope mounts. Made in Italy. Introduced, 1978; no longer imported by Excam. Used values: magnum, $215 to $220; LR blowback, $120 to $130.

FEINWERKBAU

Beeman/Feinwerkbau 2000

Beeman/Feinwerkbau 2000 Metallic Silhouette

FEINWERKBAU 2000 Target Model: single-shot; .22 LR; 26¼" barrel; 43¾" overall length; weighs 8¾ lb.; standard walnut match stock; stippled pistol grip, forend; micrometer match aperture rear sight, globe front with interchangeable inserts; electronic or mechanical trigger. Made in West Germany. Introduced, 1979; still imported by Beeman. Used value, $850 to $900.

    2000 Mini-Match Model has same specs as 2000 Target, except has walnut-stained birch stock, 22" barrel. Introduced, 1979; still imported by Beeman. Used value, $800 to $850.

    2000 Metallic Silhouette Model has same action as target model; single-shot; .22 LR; 21.8" barrel; overall length 39"; weighs 6.8 lb.; anatomical grip; no sights; grooved for standard mounts; fully adjustable match trigger; heavy bull barrel. Made in West Germany. Introduced, 1985; no longer imported by Beeman. Used value, $700 to $750.

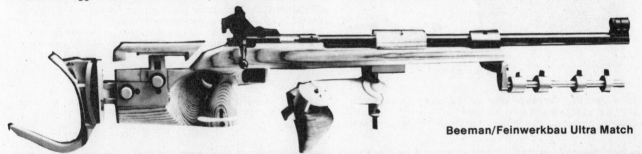

Beeman/Feinwerkbau Ultra Match

FEINWERKBAU Ultra Match 22 Free Model: single-shot; .22 LR; 26.4" barrel; weighs 17 lb. with accessories; micrometer match aperture rear sight, globe front with interchangeable inserts; laminated wood thumbhole stock; electronic or mechanical trigger; accessory rails for movable weights; adjustable cheekpiece, hooked butt plate; right- or left-hand styles. Made in West Germany. Introduced, 1983; importation dropped by Beeman, 1988. Used values: right-hand, mechanical trigger, $1400 to $1450; electronic trigger, $1650 to $1700; left-hand model, mechanical trigger, $1500 to $1550; electronic trigger, $1850 to $1900.

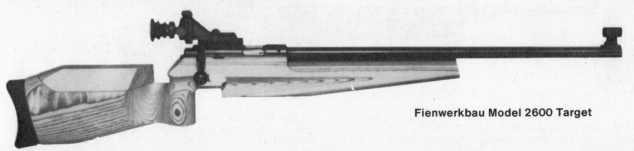

Fienwerkbau Model 2600 Target

FEINWERKBAU Model 2600 Target: single-shot; .22 LR; 26.3" barrel; 43.7" overall length; weighs 10.6 lb.; micrometer match aperture rear sight, globe front with interchangeable inserts; lam- inated European hardwood stock; free-floating barrel; adjustable match trigger. Made in West Germany. Introduced, 1986; still im- ported by Beeman. Used value, $1400 to $1500.

FEINWERKBAU Ultra Match Free Rifle: single-shot; .22 LR; 26.4" barrel; 40.4" overall length; weighs 14.06 lb.; match-type stock; adjustable butt plate. Made in West Germany. Introduced, 1987; importation dropped by Beeman, 1988. Used value, $1300 to $1400.

FINNISH LION

Finnish Lion Match Model

FINNISH Lion Match Model: bolt-action, single-shot; .22 LR; 28¾" barrel; extension-type rear peep sight, aperture front; Euro- pean walnut free rifle-type stock; full pistol-grip, beavertail forearm, thumbhole, palm rest, hand stop, hooked butt plate, swivel. Manu- factured 1937 to 1972. used value, $550 to $650.

FINNISH Lion Standard Target Model: bolt-action; single-shot; .22 LR; 27⅝" barrel; 46" overall length; no sights; French walnut target stock; adjustable trigger; many accessories available. Made in Finland. Introduced, 1978; still imported by Mandall Shooting Sup- plies. Used value, $475 to $550.

Finnish Lion Champion Model

FINNISH Lion Champion: bolt-action, single-shot; free rifle de- sign; .22 LR; 28¾" barrel; extension-type rear peep sight, aperture front; European walnut free-rifle stock; full pistol-grip, beavertail forearm, thumbhole, palm rest, hand stop, hooked butt plate swivel. Manufactured 1965 to 1972. Used value, $600 to $650.

FINNISH Lion ISU Target Model: bolt-action, single-shot; .22 LR; 27½" barrel; extension-type rear peep sight, aperture front; European walnut target-design stock; hand-checkered beavertail forearm, full pistol grip, adjustable butt plate, swivel. Manufac- tured 1966 to 1977. Used value, $300 to $325.

HAMMERLI

Hammerli Model Olympia

HAMMERLI Model Olympia: bolt-action, single-shot designed for 300-meter event; chambered in Europe for 7.5mm, marketed in U.S. in .30/06, .300 H&H magnum; other calibers on special order; 29½" heavy barrel, double-pull or double-set trigger; micrometer peep rear sight, hooded front; free-type rifle stock with full pistol grip, thumbhole; cheekpiece, palm rest, beavertail forearm; swivels, Swiss-type butt plate. Introduced in 1949; dropped, 1959. Used value, $750 to $775.

Hammerli Model 45

HAMMERLI Model 45: bolt-action, single-shot; match rifle; .22 LR; 27½" barrel; free-rifle stock with full pistol grip, thumbhole, cheekpiece; palm rest, beavertail forearm; Swiss-type butt plate, sling swivels: micrometer peep rear sight, blade front; thumbhole pistol-grip hardwood stock. Used value, $550 to $600.

HAMMERLI Model 54: bolt-action, single-shot; match rifle; .22 LR, 21½" barrel; micrometer peep rear sight, globe front; European walnut free-rifle stock; cheekpiece, adjustable hook butt plate, palm rest, thumbhole, swivel. Manufactured 1954 to 1957. Used value, $600 to $650.

Hammerli Model 503

HAMMERLI Model 503: bolt-action, single-shot; free rifle; .22 LR; 27½" barrel; micrometer rear sight, globe front; European walnut free-rifle stock; cheekpiece, adjustable hook butt plate, palm rest, thumbhole, swivel. Manufactured 1957 to 1962. Used value, $550 to $575.

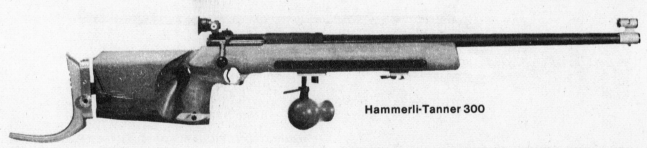

Hammerli-Tanner 300

HAMMERLI-Tanner 300 Meter: bolt-action, single-shot; free rifle design; 7.5mm Swiss; 29½" barrel; micrometer peep rear sight, globe front; uncheckered European walnut free-rifle stock; cheekpiece, adjustable hook butt plate, thumbhole, palm rest, swivel. Manufactured in Switzerland. Introduced, 1962; still in production. Used value, $800 to $850.

Hammerli Model 506

HAMMERLI Model 506: bolt-action, single-shot; match rifle; .22 LR; 26¾" barrel; micrometer peep rear sight, globe front; European walnut free-rifle stock; cheekpiece, adjustable hook butt plate, palm rest, thumbhole, swivel. Manufactured 1963 to 1966. Used value, $575 to $600.

HARRINGTON & RICHARDSON

H&R Model 60

HARRINGTON & RICHARDSON Reising Model 60: semiautomatic; .45 ACP; 12-, 20-rd. detachable box magazines; 18¼" barrel; open rear sight, blade front; uncheckered hardwood pistol-grip stock. Manufactured 1944 to 1946. Some collector value. Used value, $350 to $400.

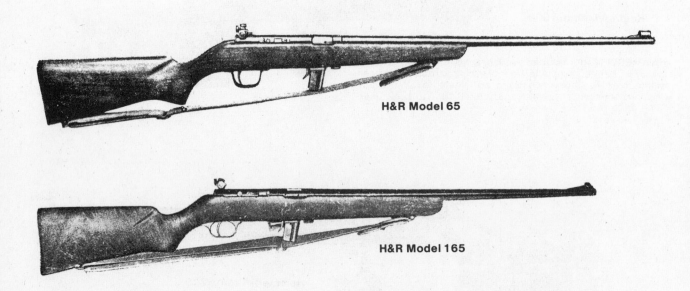

H&R Model 65

H&R Model 165

HARRINGTON & RICHARDSON Model 65: semiautomatic; .22 LR; 10-rd. detachable box magazine; 23" barrel; rear peep sight, blade front; uncheckered hardwood pistol-grip stock; used as training rifle by the Marine Corps in WWII, has same general dimensions as M-1 Garand. Manufactured 1944 to 1946. Used value, $250 to $275.

HARRINGTON & RICHARDSON Model 165: called the Leatherneck Model, it was a variation of Model 65 military autoloader used to train Marines in basic marksmanship during WWII. Blowback autoloader; .22 LR only; 23" barrel; 10-rd. detachable box magazine; uncheckered hardwood pistol-grip stock; Redfield No. 70 rear peep sight, blade front on ramp; sling swivels, web sling. Introduced in 1945; dropped, 1961. Used value, $150 to $175.

H&R Model 265

HARRINGTON & RICHARDSON Model 265: called the Reg'lar Model in advertising; bolt-action repeater; .22 LR only; 22" barrel; 10-shot detachable box magazine; uncheckered hardwood pistol-grip stock; Lyman No. 55 rear peep sight, blade front on ramp. Introduced in 1946; dropped, 1949. Used value, $90 to $100.

HARRINGTON & RICHARDSON Model 365: called the Ace in advertising; bolt-action single-shot; .22 LR only; 22" barrel; uncheckered hardwood pistol-grip stock; Lyman No. 55 rear peep sight, blade front on ramp. Introduced in 1946; dropped, 1947. Used value, $65 to $75.

H&R Model 465

HARRINGTON & RICHARDSON Model 465: advertised as Targeteer Special; bolt-action repeater; .22 LR only; 25" barrel; 10-shot detachable box magazine; uncheckered walnut pistol-grip stock; Lyman No. 57 rear peep sight, blade front on ramp; sling swivels, web sling. Introduced in 1946; dropped, 1947. Used value, $125 to $135.

HARRINGTON & RICHARDSON Model 450: bolt-action repeater; .22 LR only; 26" barrel; 5-shot detachable box magazine; uncheckered walnut target stock with full pistol grip, thick forend;

Targeteer Jr. has the same basic specs as Model 465, except for 22" barrel; shorter youth stock; 5-rd. detachable box magazine; Redfield No. 70 rear peep sight, Lyman No. 17A front. Introduced in 1948; dropped, 1951. Used value, $135 to $145.

scope bases; no sights; sling swivels, sling. Introduced in 1948; dropped, 1961. Used value, $125 to $135.

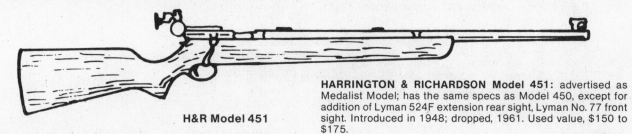

H&R Model 451

HARRINGTON & RICHARDSON Model 451: advertised as Medalist Model; has the same specs as Model 450, except for addition of Lyman 524F extension rear sight, Lyman No. 77 front sight. Introduced in 1948; dropped, 1961. Used value, $150 to $175.

HARRINGTON & RICHARDSON Model 250: advertised as the Sportster Model; bolt-action repeater; .22 LR only; 22" barrel; 5-rd. detachable box magazine; uncheckered hardwood pistol-grip stock; open rear sight, blade front on ramp. Introduced in 1948; dropped, 1961. Used value, $85 to $95.

HARRINGTON & RICHARDSON Model 251: has the same specs as Model 250, except for addition of Lyman No. 55H rear sight. Introduced in 1948; dropped, 1961. Used value, $100 to $110.

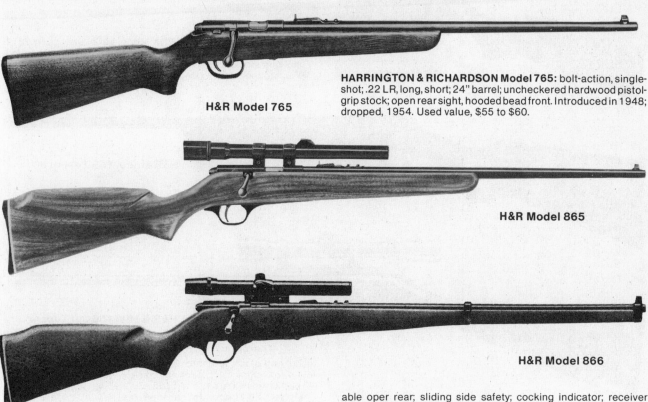

H&R Model 765

H&R Model 865

H&R Model 866

HARRINGTON & RICHARDSON Model 765: bolt-action, single-shot; .22 LR, long, short; 24" barrel; uncheckered hardwood pistol-grip stock; open rear sight, hooded bead front. Introduced in 1948; dropped, 1954. Used value, $55 to $60.

HARRINGTON & RICHARDSON Model 865: bolt-action; .22 short, long, LR; 5-rd. clip magazine; 22" round tapered barrel; 39" overall length; weighs 5 lb.; walnut-finished American hardwood stock with Monte Carlo, pistol grip; blade front sight, step-adjust-able oper rear; sliding side safety; cocking indicator; receiver grooved for tip-off scope mounts. Introduced, 1949; dropped, 1985. Used value, $75 to $85.

Model 866 has the same specs as Model 865, except has a Mannlicher stock. Manufactured only in 1971. Used value, $100 to $125.

HARRINGTON & RICHARDSON Model 150: autoloader; .22 LR only; 22" barrel; 5-rd. detachable box magazine; unchecked pistol-grip stock; open rear sight, blade front on ramp. Introduced in 1949; dropped, 1953. Used value, $115 to $125.

HARRINGTON & RICHARDSON Model 151: has the same specs as Model 150, except for substitution of Redfield No. 70 peep rear sight. Introduced in 1949; dropped, 1953. Used value, $125 to $140.

H&R Model 422

HARRINGTON & RICHARDSON Model 422: slide-action repeater; .22 LR, long, short; 24" barrel; tube magazine, capacity of 15 LR, 17 long, 21 short cartridges; unchecked walnut pistol-grip stock, grooved slide handle; open rear sight, ramp front. Introduced in 1952; dropped, 1958. Used value, $85 to $90.

HARRINGTON & RICHARDSON Model 852: bolt-action repeater; .22 LR, long, short; 24" barrel; tube magazine with capacity of 15 LR, 17 long, 21 short cartridges; unchecked pistol-grip hard-wood stock; open rear sight, bead front. Introduced in 1952; dropped, 1953. Used value, $85 to $90.

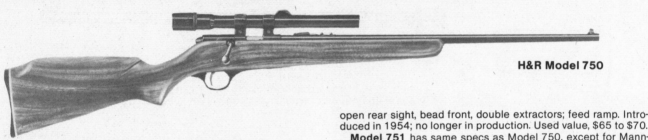

H&R Model 750

HARRINGTON & RICHARDSON Model 750: bolt-action single-shot; .22 LR, long, short; 24" barrel; unchecked hardwood stock;

open rear sight, bead front, double extractors; feed ramp. Introduced in 1954; no longer in production. Used value, $65 to $70.

Model 751 has same specs as Model 750, except for Mannlicher stock. Manufactured only in 1971. Used value, $100 to $125.

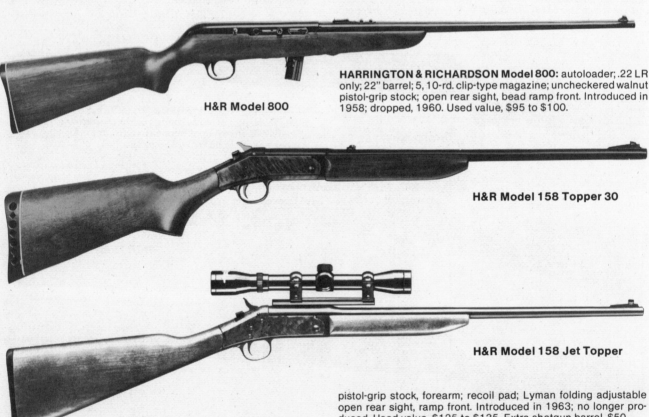

H&R Model 800

HARRINGTON & RICHARDSON Model 800: autoloader; .22 LR only; 22" barrel; 5, 10-rd. clip-type magazine; unchecked walnut pistol-grip stock; open rear sight, bead ramp front. Introduced in 1958; dropped, 1960. Used value, $95 to $100.

H&R Model 158 Topper 30

H&R Model 158 Jet Topper

HARRINGTON & RICHARDSON Model 158 Topper 30: single-shot combo rifle; shotgun-type action; visible hammer; side lever; automatic ejector; 22" interchangeable barrels, available in .22 Hornet, .30-30, .357 magnum, .44 magnum; unchecked walnut

pistol-grip stock, forearm; recoil pad; Lyman folding adjustable open rear sight, ramp front. Introduced in 1963; no longer produced. Used value, $125 to $135. Extra shotgun barrel, $50.

Model 158 Topper Jet has the same general specs as Model 158 Topper 30, except standard caliber is .22 Rem. Jet, interchangeable with 20-ga., .410-bore, .30-30 barrels. Introduced in 1963; dropped, 1967. Used values: standard .22 Rem. Jet, $125 to $135; additional .30-30 barrel, $65 to $75; 20-ga. barrel, $50 to $60; .410 barrel, $40 to $45.

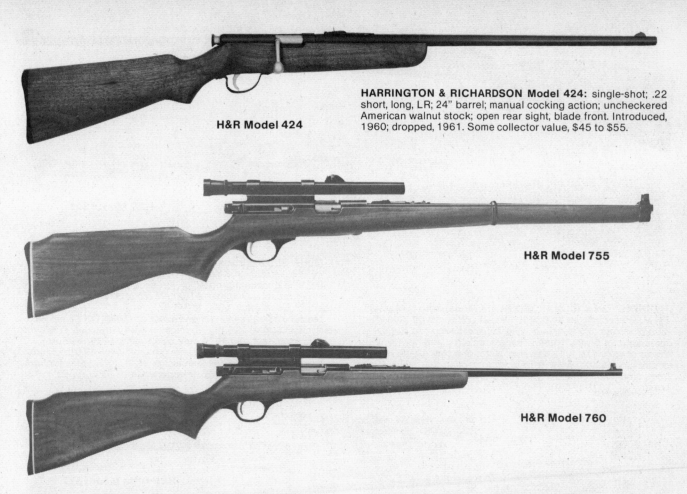

H&R Model 424

HARRINGTON & RICHARDSON Model 424: single-shot; .22 short, long, LR; 24" barrel; manual cocking action; uncheckered American walnut stock; open rear sight, blade front. Introduced, 1960; dropped, 1961. Some collector value, $45 to $55.

H&R Model 755

H&R Model 760

HARRINGTON & RICHARDSON Model 755: advertised as the Sahara Model; single-shot .22 LR, long, short; 22" barrel; blowback action; automatic ejection; hardwood Mannlicher-type stock; open rear sight, military front. Introduced in 1963; dropped, 1971.

Some collector interest. Used value, $125 to $135.
Model 760 has the same specs as Model 755, except for substitution of conventional hardwood sporter stock. Introduced in 1965; dropped, 1970. Used value, $85 to $90.

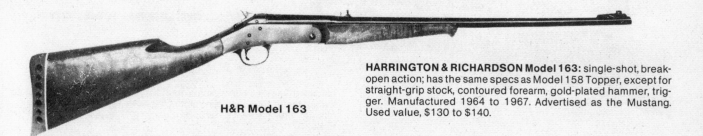

H&R Model 163

HARRINGTON & RICHARDSON Model 163: single-shot, break-open action; has the same specs as Model 158 Topper, except for straight-grip stock, contoured forearm, gold-plated hammer, trigger. Manufactured 1964 to 1967. Advertised as the Mustang. Used value, $130 to $140.

HARRINGTON & RICHARDSON Model 164: single-shot; has same specs as Model 158, except for straight-grip uncheckered

walnut stock, contoured forearm; gold-plated hammer, trigger. Introduced in 1964; dropped, 1967. Used value, $125 to $135.

H&R Model 300

H&R Model 330

H&R Model 301

HARRINGTON & RICHARDSON Ultra Model 300: bolt-action, FN Mauser action; .22-250, .243 Win., .270 Win., .30/06, .308 Win., .300 Win. magnum, 7mm Rem. magnum; 22" barrel; 3-rd. magazine for magnums, 5-rd. for others; hand-checkered American walnut stock; cheekpiece, full pistol grip; pistol-grip cap, forearm tip of contrasting exotic wood; with or without open rear sight, ramp front; rubber butt plate, sling swivels. Manufactured 1965 to 1978. Used value, $375 to $400.

Model 330 has same general specs as Model 300; .243 Win., .270 Win., .30/06, .308 Win., 7mm Rem. magnum, .300 Win. magnum; less checkering on stock, no sling swivels, forend tip, or pistol-grip cap. Advertised as Hunters Model. Manufactured 1967 to 1972. Used value, $350 to $400.

Model 333 has same general specs as Model 300; 7mm Rem. magnum, .30/06; 22" barrel; uncheckered hardwood stock, no sights. Manufactured 1974 only. Used value, $275 to $300.

Ultra Model 301 has the same general specs as Ultra Model 300, except for 18" barrel, Mannlicher-style stock; metal forearm tip. Not available in .22-250. Introduced in 1978; dropped, 1978. Used value, $375 to $400.

H&R Ultra Model 317

H&R Model 317P

loads; 20" tapered barrel; same general specs as Ultra Model 300, except for 6-rd. magazine, no sights; receiver dovetailed for scope mounts. Introduced in 1966; dropped, 1976. Used value, $400 to $425.

Ultra Model 317P has same specs as Model 317, except for better grade of walnut, basketweave checkering. Dropped, 1976. Used value, $500 to $525.

HARRINGTON & RICHARDSON Ultra Model 317: advertised as the Ultra Wildcat; .17 Rem., .222 Rem., .223 Rem., .17/223 hand-

H&R Ultra Model 370

HARRINGTON & RICHARDSON Ultra Model 370: advertised as Ultra Medalist; built on Sako action; .22-250, .243 Win., 6mm

Rem.; 24" heavy target/varmint barrel; uncheckered, oil-finished walnut stock; roll-over comb; no sights; tapped for open sights and/or scope mounts; adjustable trigger; recoil pad, sling swivels. Introduced in 1967; dropped, 1974. Used value, $375 to $400.

H&R Ultra Model 360

HARRINGTON & RICHARDSON Model 360: autoloader, gas operated; .243 Win., .308 Win.; 22" barrel; 3-rd. detachable box magazine; hand-checkered walnut stock; roll-over cheekpiece, full pistol grip, exotic wood pistol-grip cap, forearm tip; sling swivels; open adjustable rear sight, gold bead front. Introduced in 1967; dropped, 1973. Used value, $300 to $325.

Model 361 has same general specs as Model 360, except for full roll-over cheekpiece. Manufactured 1970 to 1973. Used value, $315 to $335.

HARRINGTON & RICHARDSON Model 058: single-shot; .22 Hornet, .30-30 Win., .357 magnum, .44 magnum, plus 20-ga.; has same specs as Model 158 except is fitted with 28" 20-ga. barrel as accessory. Introduced, 1968; dropped, 1985. Used value, $130 to $150.

H&R Model 749

HARRINGTON & RICHARDSON Model 749: pump-action; .22 short, long, LR; tube magazine holds 18 shorts, 15 longs, 13 LR; 19" barrel; overall length, 35½"; weighs 14 lb. 13 oz.; dovetail blade front sight, adjustable rear; positive ejection; walnut-finished American hardwood stock, contoured forend. Made only in 1971. Used value, $85 to $95.

H&R Model 155

HARRINGTON & RICHARDSON Model 155 "Shikari": single-shot; .44 Rem. magnum or .45-70; 24" or 28" barrel; folding-leaf rear-sight, blade front; unchecked straight-grip hardwood stock, forearm, barrel band; built on Model 158 action, has brass cleaning rod. Introduced, 1972; dropped, 1982. Used value, $125 to $145.

H&R Model 171 Deluxe

H&R Model 172

HARRINGTON & RICHARDSON Model 171: single-shot, trap-door action; .45-70; 22" barrel; leaf rear sight, blade front; unchecked walnut stock. Replica of Model 1873 Springfield cavalry carbine. Introduced, 1972; dropped, 1985. Used value, $245 to $265.

Model 171 Deluxe has same specs, except for an engraved action. Introduced, 1972; dropped, 1985. Used value, $335 to $355.

Model 172 has same specs as Model 171 Deluxe, except for fancy checkered walnut stock, tang-mounted aperture sight, silver-plated hardware. Introduced, 1972; dropped, 1977. Used value, $500 to $550.

H&R Model 173

HARRINGTON & RICHARDSON Model 173: single-shot, trap-door action; .45-70; 26" barrel; replica of Model 1873 Springfield Officer's Model; engraved breech block, receiver, hammer, barrel band, lock, butt plate; checkered walnut stock; ramrod; peep rear sight, blade front. Introduced, 1972; dropped, 1977. Used value, $300 to $350.

HARRINGTON & RICHARDSON Model 178: single-shot, trap-door action; .45-70; 32" barrel; replica of Model 1873 Springfield infantry rifle; uncheckered full-length walnut stock; leaf rear sight, blade front; barrel bands, sling swivels, ramrod. Manufactured 1973 to 1975. Used value, $325 to $350.

H&R Model 157

HARRINGTON & RICHARDSON Model 157: single-shot; .22 WRFM, .22 Hornet, .30-30; 22" barrel; folding leaf rear sight, blade front; uncheckered hardwood pistol-grip butt stock, full-length forearm; swing swivels; built on Model 158 action. Introduced, 1976; dropped, 1985. Used value, $140 to $160.

H&R Model 700 Deluxe

HARRINGTON & RICHARDSON Model 700: autoloader; .22 WRFM; 5- or l0-rd. magazine; 22" barrel; folding leaf rear sight, blade front on ramp; American walnut Monte Carlo stock. Introduced, 1977; dropped, 1985. Used value, $155 to $165.

Model 700 Deluxe has same specs as Model 700, except has walnut stock with cheekpiece; checkered grip, forend; rubber recoil pad; no sights; marketed with H&R Model 432 4X scope, base and rings. Introduced, 1979; dropped, 1985. Used value, $225 to $235.

H&R Model 5200

HARRINGTON & RICHARDSON Model 5200: single-shot; .22 LR; target rifle; 28" barrel; no sights; drilled, tapped for sights, scope; target-style American walnut stock; full-length accessory rail, rubber butt pad, palm stop; fully adjustable trigger; dual extractors; polished blue-black metal finish. Introduced, 1981; dropped, 1985. Used value, $350 to $375.

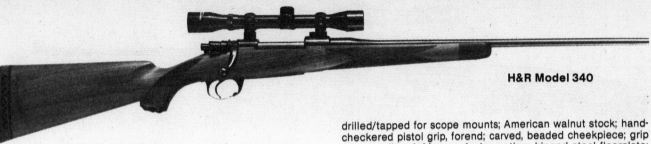

H&R Model 340

HARRINGTON & RICHARDSON Model 340: bolt-action; .243, 7x57, .308, .270, .30/06; 22" barrel; 43" overall length; no sights; drilled/tapped for scope mounts; American walnut stock; hand-checkered pistol grip, forend; carved, beaded cheekpiece; grip cap; recoil pad; Mauser-design action; hinged steel floorplate; adjustable trigger; high-luster blued finish. Introduced, 1983; dropped, 1984. Used value, $290 to $300.

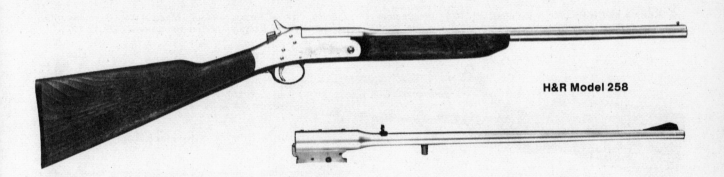

H&R Model 258

HARRINGTON & RICHARDSON 258 Handy Gun II: single-shot; interchangeable rifle/shotgun barrels; .22 Hornet, .30-30, .357 magnum, .357 Maximum, .44 magnum, 20-ga. 3"; 22" barrel; 37" overall length; ramp blade front sight, adjustable folding leaf rear; bead front sight on shotgun barrel; walnut-finished American hardwood stock; electroless matte nickel finish. Introduced, 1982; dropped, 1985. Used value, $150 to $160.

HECKLER & KOCH

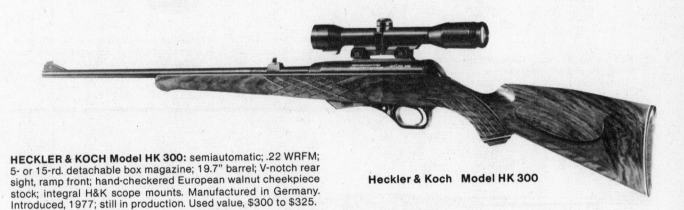

Heckler & Koch   Model HK 300

HECKLER & KOCH Model HK 300: semiautomatic; .22 WRFM; 5- or 15-rd. detachable box magazine; 19.7" barrel; V-notch rear sight, ramp front; hand-checkered European walnut stock; integral H&K scope mounts. Manufactured in Germany. Introduced, 1977; still in production. Used value, $300 to $325.

HECKLER & KOCH Model HK91-A-2: semiautomatic; .308 Win.; 5- or 20-rd. detachable box magazine; 19" barrel; V and aperture rear sight, post front; plastic butt stock, forearm; delayed roller-lock blowback action. Introduced, 1978; still in production. Used value, $550 to $600.
   Model HK-91-A-3 has same specs as A-2, except for collapsible metal butt stock. Introduced, 1978; still in production. Used value, $650 to $700.

HECKLER & KOCH Model HK-93-A-2: semiautomatic; .223 Rem., has the same general specs as Model HK-91-A-2, except for 16.13" barrel. Introduced, 1978; still in production. Used value, $550 to $600.
   Model HK-93-A-3 has same specs as A-2, except for collapsible metal butt stock. Introduced, 1978; still in production. Used value, $650 to $700.

Heckler & Koch HK 770

HECKLER & KOCH HK770: semiautomatic; .308 Win.; 3-rd. magazine; 19.6" barrel; vertically adjustable blade front sight, open

HECKLER & KOCH HK270: autoloader; .22 LR; 5-rd. magazine; 19¾" barrel; 38.2" overall length; elevation-adjustable post front sight, windage-adjustable diopter rear; straight blowback action;

fold-down windage-adjustable rear; checkered European walnut pistol-grip stock; polygonal rifling, delayed roller-locked bolt system; receiver top dovetailed for clamp-type scope mount. Imported from West Germany. Introduced, 1979; still imported. Used value, $500 to $525.

receiver grooved for scope mount. Made in West Germany. Introduced, 1978; no longer imported. Used value, $200 to $225.

Heckler & Koch SL7

HECKLER & KOCH SL7: autoloader; .308 Win.; 3-rd. magazine; 17" barrel; overall length, 39¾"; weighs 8 lb.; oil-finished European walnut stock; adjustable aperture rear sight, hooded post

front; polygon rifling; delayed roller-locked action; dovetailed for H&K quick-detachable scope mount. Made in West Germany. Introduced, 1983; still imported by H&K. Used value, $525 to $575.
   Model SL6 has same specs as SL7, except is chambered for .223 Rem. Introduced, 1983; still imported. Used value, $525 to $575.

Heckler & Koch
PSG-1 Marksman

HECKLER & KOCH PSG-1 Marksman: autoloader; .308 Win.; 5-. 20-rd. magazines; 25.6" heavy barrel; 47.5" overall length; weighs 17.8 lb.; marketed with 6x42 Hendsoldt scope; no iron sights;

matte black high-impact plastic stock adjustable for length; pivoting butt cap, adjustable cheekpiece; target-type pistol grip, palm shelf; built on H&K 91 action; T-way rail for tripod, sling swivel. Made in West Germany. Introduced, 1986; still imported. Used value, $6250 to $6350.

HEYM

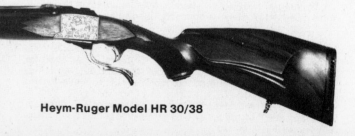

HEYM-RUGER Model HR 30: single-shot; .243, 6.5x57R, 7x64, 7x65R, .270, .308, .30/06; 24" round barrel; bead ramp front sight, leaf rear; hand-checkered European walnut Mannlicher or sporter stock; oil finish; recoil pad; Ruger No. 1 action. New custom-made gun, many options available. Introduced, 1978; still in production; importation dropped, 1987. Used values: sporter stock, $1700 to $1900; full stock, $1800 to $2000.

Heym-Ruger Model HR 30/38

Model HR 30G has same specs as HR 30, except is chambered for 6.5x68R, .300 Win. magnum, 8x68S, 9.3x74R. Used value, $1800 to $2000.

HR-38N has same specs as HR 30G, except for octagon barrel, sporter stock only. Used value, $1900 to $2100.

HR-38G has same specs as HR-38N, except is chambered for same magnum calibers as HR 30G. Used value, $2000 to $2200.

Model HR 30/38: single-shot; .243, 6.5x57R, 7x64, 7x65R, .308, .30/06, 6.5x68R, .300 Win. magnum, 8x68S, 9.3x74R; 24", 26" barrels; Ruger No. 1 action, safety; bead/ramp front sight, leaf rear; European walnut stock; hand-checkered pistol grip, forend; recoil pad; Mannlicher or sporter design; Schnabel forend, Bavarian cheekpiece; Canjar single-set trigger; hand-engraved animal scene; optional deluxe engraving, stock carving. Made in West Germany. Introduced, 1981; no longer imported by Paul Jaeger, Inc. Used values: standard calibers, with round barrel, sporter stock, $1600 to $1800; round barrel, Mannlicher stock, $1700 to $1900; magnum calibers, with round barrel, sporter stock, $1600 to $1800; with octagon barrel, add $200; with side plates, large engraved hunting scenes, add $750 to $1000.

Heym Model SR-20

Heym Model SR-20 Classic

HEYM Model SR-20: bolt-action; 5.6x57, .243, 6.5x57, .270, 7x57, 7x64, .308, .30/06, 9.3x62, 6.5x68, 7mm Rem. magnum, .300 Win. magnum, 8x68S, .375 H&H; 20½", 24", 26" barrel lengths; silver bead ramp front sight, adjustable folding leaf rear; hand-checkered pistol-grip stock or full Mannlicher-style of dark European walnut; recoil pad, rosewood grip cap, oil finish; hinged floor plate, 3-position safety. Made in West Germany. Introduced, 1978 ; was imported by Paul Jaeger, Inc.; importation dropped, 1986. Used values: 20½" barrel, $875 to $900; 24" barrel, $800 to $850; 26" barrel (magnum calibers), $800 to $850.

Model SR-20G: bolt-action; 6.5x68, 7mm Rem. magnum; .300 Win. magnum, 8x68S, .375 H&H; 26" barrel; silver bead on ramp front sight, adjustable folding leaf rear; oil-finished European walnut Monte Carlo stock; rosewood grip cap; Schnabel tip; 3-position safety; hinged floorplate; drilled/tapped for scope mounts; adjustable trigger; numerous options. Introduced, 1981; importation dropped, 1988. Used value, $750 to $800.

Model SR-20N has same general specs as SR-20G, except is chambered for 5.6x57, .243, 6.5x55, 6.5x57, .270, 7x57, 7x64, .308, .30/06, 9.3x62. Used value, $700 to $800.

Model SR-20L has same specs as Model SR-20N, except has full Mannlicher-style stock; same chamberings, sans 9.3x62. Used value, $900 to $950.

Model SR-20 Classic is similar to SR-20N, except is chambered for 5.6x57, 6.5x57, 6.5x55SM, 7x57, 7x64, 9.3x62, .243, .270, .308, .30/06 in standard calibers, 6.5x68, 8x68S, 7mm Rem. magnum, .300 Win. magnum, .375 H&H in magnums; 24" barrel, standard calibers, 25" for magnums; classic-style French walnut stock; hand checkering; Pachmayr Old English pad; quick-detachable sling swivels; steel grip cap; right- or left-hand action. Made in West Germany. Introduced, 1985; importation dropped, 1988. Used values: right-hand, $800 to $850; left-hand, $900 to $950; magnum calibers, add $30.

Model SR-40: bolt-action; same as SR-20, except has short action; .222, .223, 5.6x50 magnum; 24" barrel; overall length, 44"; weighs 6¼ lb.; carbine-length Mannlicher-style stock. Introduced, 1984; importation dropped, 1988. Used value, $800 to $850; left-hand model, $900 to $950.

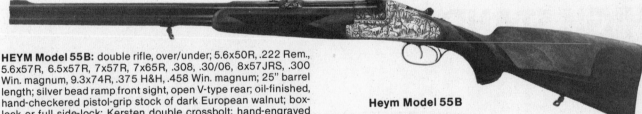

Heym Model 55B

HEYM Model 55B: double rifle; over/under; 5.6x50R, .222 Rem., 5.6x57R, 6.5x57R, 7x57R, 7x65R, .308, .30/06, 8x57JRS, .300 Win. magnum, 9.3x74R, .375 H&H, .458 Win. magnum; 25" barrel length; silver bead ramp front sight, open V-type rear; oil-finished, hand-checkered pistol-grip stock of dark European walnut; box-lock or full side-lock; Kersten double crossbolt; hand-engraved hunting scenes. Made in West Germany. Introduced, 1980; was imported by Paul Jaeger, Inc.; importation dropped, 1986. Used values: box-lock, $4000 to $4500; side-lock, $5000 to $6000.

Model 55BF has same specs as 55B/77B except chambered for 12-, 16-, 20-ga. over rifle barrel. Used values: box-lock, $3000 to $3500; side-lock, $5000 to $6000.

Model 55BFSS has same specs as Model BFSS, except has side-lock action. Importation dropped, 1986. Used value, $5000 to $6000.

Model 55BSS has same specs as Model 55B, except has side-lock action. Made in West Germany; importation dropped, 1986. Used value, $5000 to $6000.

HEYM Model 77B: double rifle; over/under; has same specs as Model 55B, except is chambered for 9.3x74R, .375 H&H, .458 Win. magnum. Introduced, 1980; importation dropped, 1986. Used value, $4000 to $5000.

Model 77BSS has same specs as 55BSS, but with same chamberings as Model 77B. Introduced, 1980; importation dropped, 1986. Used value, $5500 to $6500.

Model 77BF: combo gun; box-lock; over/under; has same specs as Model 55BF, except rifle barrel is chambered for magnum cartridges. Made in West Germany. Was imported by Paul Jaeger, Inc.; importation dropped, 1986. Used value, $4500 to $5500.

Model 77BFSS has same specs as Model 77BF, except has side-lock action. Made in West Germany. Importation dropped, 1986. Used value, $6000 to $7000.

Heym Model 22s

HEYM Model 22s: combo; 16- or 20-ga. over .22 Hornet, .22 WRFM, .222 Rem., .222 Rem. magnum, .223, .22-250, .243 Win., 5.6x50R, 6.5x57R, 7x57R; 25" barrels; solid rib; silver bead front sight, folding leaf rear; oil-finished, hand-checkered pistol-grip stock of dark European walnut; tang-mounted cocking slide, single-set trigger. Made in West Germany. Introduced, 1980; not currently imported. Used value, $1200 to $1500.

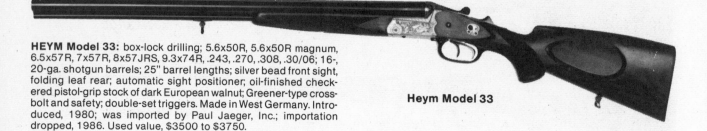

Heym Model 33

HEYM Model 33: box-lock drilling; 5.6x50R, 5.6x50R magnum, 6.5x57R, 7x57R, 8x57JRS, 9.3x74R, .243, .270, .308, .30/06; 16-, 20-ga. shotgun barrels; 25" barrel lengths; silver bead front sight, folding leaf rear; automatic sight positioner; oil-finished checkered pistol-grip stock of dark European walnut; Greener-type crossbolt and safety; double-set triggers. Made in West Germany. Introduced, 1980; was imported by Paul Jaeger, Inc.; importation dropped, 1986. Used value, $3500 to $3750.

HEYM Model 37: double rifle drilling; 7x65R, .30/06, 8x57JRS, 9.3x74R; 20-ga. shotgun barrels; 25" barrel lengths; silver bead front sight, folding leaf rear; oil-finished, hand-checkered pistol-grip stock of dark European walnut; full side-lock construction; Greener-type crossbolt, cocking indicators; deluxe model has engraved scene. Made in West Germany. Introduced, 1980; was im-

ported by Paul Jaeger, Inc.; importation dropped, 1986. Used values: standard model, $5500 to $6000; deluxe, $6200 to $6750.

Model 37 side-lock drilling is similar to standard model, except has choice of 12-, 16-, 20-ga. shotgun barrels; rifle barrel is manually cocked, uncocked. Used values: $4000 to $4200; with engraved hunting scenes, $4750 to $5000.

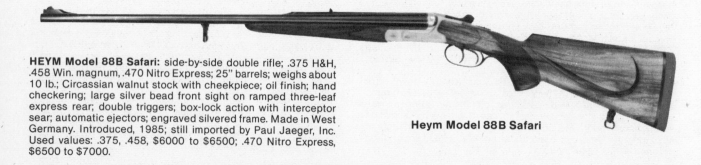

Heym Model 88B Safari

HEYM Model 88B Safari: side-by-side double rifle; .375 H&H, .458 Win. magnum, .470 Nitro Express; 25" barrels; weighs about 10 lb.; Circassian walnut stock with cheekpiece; oil finish; hand checkering; large silver bead front sight on ramped three-leaf express rear; double triggers; box-lock action with interceptor sear; automatic ejectors; engraved silvered frame. Made in West Germany. Introduced, 1985; still imported by Paul Jaeger, Inc. Used values: .375, .458, $6000 to $6500; .470 Nitro Express, $6500 to $7000.

HIGH STANDARD

Hi-Standard Sport King

HIGH STANDARD Sport King: autoloader; standard version was advertised as Field Model; .22 LR, long, short; 22¼" barrel; tube magazine has capacity of 15 LR, 17 long, 21 short cartridges; uncheckered pistol-grip stock; open rear sight, bead post front. Introduced in 1960; dropped, 1976. Used value, $75 to $85.

Sport King Special has the same specs as the standard or Field Model, except for Monte Carlo stock, semi-beavertail forearm. Introduced in 1960; dropped, 1966. Used value, $95 to $110.

Sport King Deluxe has the same specs as Special Model, except for impressed checkering on stock. Introduced in 1966; dropped, 1975. Used value, $120 to $140.

Sport King Carbine has the same action as Sport King Special; 18¼" barrel; open rear sight, bead post front; straight-grip stock; brass butt plate; sling swivels. Tube magazine holds 12 LR, 14 long, 17 short cartridges; receiver grooved for scope mounts; golden trigger guard, trigger, safety. Introduced in 1962; dropped, 1972. Used value, $100 to $110.

Hi-Standard Hi-Power Field

Hi-Standard Hi-Power Deluxe

HIGH STANDARD Hi-Power: bolt-action; standard model was advertised as Field Model; built on Mauser-type action; .270, .30/06; 22" barrel; 4-rd. magazine; uncheckered walnut field-style pistol-grip stock; sliding safety; quick-detachable sling swivels; folding leaf open rear sight, ramp front. Introduced in 1962; dropped, 1966. Used value, $275 to $300.

    Hi-Power Deluxe model has the same specs as the standard version, except for impressed checkering on Monte Carlo stock, sling swivels. Introduced in 1962; dropped, 1966. Used value, $300 to $325.

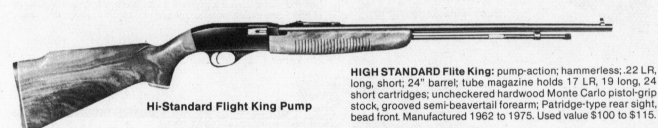

Hi-Standard Flight King Pump

HIGH STANDARD Flite King: pump-action; hammerless; .22 LR, long, short; 24" barrel; tube magazine holds 17 LR, 19 long, 24 short cartridges; uncheckered hardwood Monte Carlo pistol-grip stock, grooved semi-beavertail forearm; Patridge-type rear sight, bead front. Manufactured 1962 to 1975. Used value $100 to $115.

HUSQVARNA

Husqvarna Hi-Power

HUSQVARNA Hi-Power: Mauser-type bolt-action; .220 Swift, .270 Win., .30/06, 6.5x55, 8x57, 9.3x57; 23¾" barrel; 5-rd. box magazine; hand-checkered pistol-grip beech stock; open rear sight, hooded ramp front; sling swivels. Introduced in 1946; dropped, 1959. Used value, $300 to $325.

HUSQVARNA Model 1950: Mauser-type bolt-action; has the same specs as Hi-Power model, except chambered only in .220 Swift, .270 Win., .30/06. Introduced in 1950; dropped, 1952. Used value, $300 to $325.

HUSQVARNA Model 1951 Hi-Power: has the same specs as the Model 1950, except for a high-comb stock, low safety. Produced under model designation only in 1951. Used value, $300 to $325.

Husqvarna Series 1100

HUSQVARNA Series 1100: Mauser-type bolt-action sporter; .220 Swift, .30/06, 6.5x55, 8x57, 9.3x57; 23½" barrel; other specs generally the same as Model 1951 except for European walnut stock, jeweled bolt. Introduced in 1952; dropped, 1956. Used value, $350 to $375.

HUSQVARNA Series 1000: Mauser-type bolt-action; has the same general specs as Model 1951, except for substitution of European walnut stock, with cheekpiece, Monte Carlo comb. Introduced in 1952; dropped, 1956. Used value, $350 to $375.

Husqvarna Series 3100

HUSQVARNA Series 3100: advertised as Crown Grade; Husqvarna improved Mauser action; .243 Win., .270 Win., 7mm Rem., .30/06, .308 Win.; 23¾" barrel; 5-rd. box magazine; hand-checkered European walnut pistol-grip stock; cheekpiece; black forearm tip, pistol-grip cap; open rear sight, hooded ramp front; sling swivels. Introduced in 1954; dropped, 1976. Used value, $375 to $400.

Husqvarna Series 3000

HUSQVARNA Series 3000: Husqvarna improved Mauser action; has the same specs as Series 3100, except for substitution of Monte Carlo-style stock. Introduced in 1954; dropped, 1976. Used value, $375 to $400.

Husqvarna Series 4000

HUSQVARNA Series 4000: Husqvarna improved Mauser action; .243 Win., .270 Win., .30/06, .308 Win., 7mm Rem. magnum; 20½" barrel; 5-rd. box magazine; no rear sight, hooded ramp front; drilled, tapped for scope mounts; European walnut Monte Carlo stock; hand-checkered pistol grip, forearm; sling swivels. Introduced in 1954; dropped, 1976. Used value, $375 to $400.

Husqvarna Series 4100

HUSQVARNA Series 4100: bolt-action; Husqvarna improved action; specs identical to those of Series 4000, except for substitution of lightweight European walnut stock with cheekpiece and has adjustable open rear sight. Introduced in 1954; dropped, 1976. Used value, $375 to $400.

Husqvarna Model 456

HUSQVARNA Model 456: full-stock bolt-action sporter; has the same general specs as Series 4000, except for full-length sporter stock, open adjustable rear sight, metal forearm cap, slope-away cheekpiece. Introduced in 1959; dropped, 1970. Used value, $450 to $475.

HUSQVARNA Series 6000: advertised as Imperial Custom Grade; .243 Win., .270 Win., .30/06, .308 Win., 7mm Rem. magnum; other specs the same as Series 3100, except for fancy walnut stock, adjustable trigger, three-leaf folding rear sight. Introduced in 1968; dropped, 1970. Used value, $475 to $500.

HUSQVARNA Series 7000: advertised as Imperial Monte Carlo Lightweight Model; .243 Win., .270 Win., .30/06, .308 Win.; other specs are identical to those of Series 4000, except for fancy walnut stock, adjustable trigger, three-leaf folding rear sight. Introduced in 1968; dropped, 1970. Used value, $425 to $450.

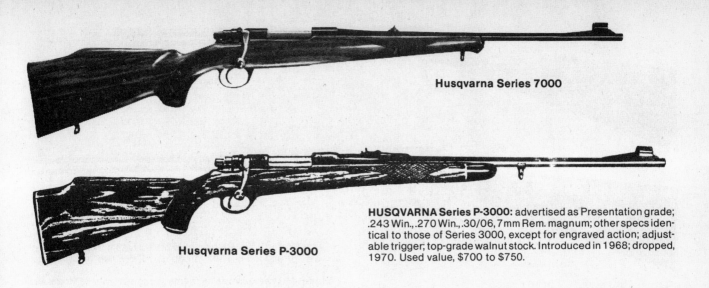

Husqvarna Series 7000

Husqvarna Series P-3000

HUSQVARNA Series P-3000: advertised as Presentation grade; .243 Win., .270 Win., .30/06, 7mm Rem. magnum; other specs identical to those of Series 3000, except for engraved action; adjustable trigger; top-grade walnut stock. Introduced in 1968; dropped, 1970. Used value, $700 to $750.

HUSQVARNA Model 8000: advertised as Imperial grade; improved Husqvarna bolt-action; .270 Win., .30/06, .300 Win. magnum, 7mm Rem. magnum; 23¾" barrel; jeweled bolt; hand-checkered deluxe French walnut stock; Monte Carlo cheekpiece; rosewood forearm tip; pistol-grip cap; adjustable trigger; 5-rd. box magazine; hinged engraved floor plate; no sights. Introduced in 1971; dropped, 1972. Used value, $525 to $550.

HUSQVARNA Model 9000: advertised as Crown grade; has the same specs as Model 8000, except for folding leaf rear sight, hooded ramp front; Monte Carlo cheekpiece stock; no jeweling on bolt; no engraving on floor plate. Introduced in 1971; dropped, 1972. Used value, $400 to $425.

ITHACA

Ithaca Model X5-T

Ithaca Model X-15

ITHACA Model X5-C: take-down autoloader; .22 LR only; 22" barrel; 7-rd. clip-type magazine; uncheckered hardwood pistol-grip stock, grooved forearm; open rear sight, Raybar front. Intro-

duced in 1958; dropped, 1964. Used value, $95 to $100.

Model X5-T has the same specs as the Model X5-C, except for 16-rd. tube magazine; smooth forearm. Introduced in 1959; dropped, 1963. Used value, $100 to $115.

Model X-15 has same specs as Model X5-C, except that forearm is not grooved. Manufactured 1964 to 1967. Used value, $70 to $75.

Ithaca Model 49 Standard

ITHACA Model 49: advertised as Saddlegun; lever-action single-shot; .22 short, long, LR; 18" barrel; blank tube magazine for appearance only; straight uncheckered Western-style carbine stock; barrel band on forearm; open adjustable rear sight, bead post front. Introduced in 1961; dropped, 1976. Used value, $55 to $60.

Ithaca Model 49 Presentation

Ithaca Model 49R

cept for figured walnut stock, gold-plated hammer, trigger, sling swivels. Introduced in 1962; dropped, 1975. Used value, $65 to $70.

Model 49 Presentation has same specs as standard Model 49, except for fancy figured walnut stock, gold nameplate inlay, gold trigger and hammer, engraved receiver; in .22 LR, .22 WRFM. Introduced in 1962; dropped, 1974. Used value, $175 to $185.

Model 49R has same general specs as Model 49 single-shot; but is repeater; .22 short, long, LR; tubular magazine; 20" barrel; open rear sight, bead front; checkered grip. Manufactured 1968 to 1971. Used value, $120 to $130.

Model 49 Youth Saddlegun has same specs as the standard model, except for shorter stock. Introduced in 1961; dropped, 1976. Used value, $55 to $60.

Model 49 Magnum has same specs as standard Model 49 except is chambered for .22 WRFM cartridge. Introduced in 1962; dropped, 1976. Used value, $60 to $65.

Model 49 Deluxe has the same specs as standard model, ex-

Ithaca Model 72

for scope mounts. Introduced in 1972; dropped, 1977. Used values: .22 LR, $115 to $125; .22 WRFM, $125 to $135.

Model 72 Deluxe has same specs as Model 72, but receiver is engraved, silver-finished; has octagonal barrel, higher grade American walnut stock, forearm. Manufactured 1974 to 1976. Used value, $175 to $200.

Model 72 Magnum has same specs as Model 72, except for .22 WRFM chambering; 11-rd. tubular magazine; 18½" barrel. Manufactured 1975 to 1977. Used value, $155 to $165.

ITHACA Model 72: lever-action repeater; .22 LR; 18½" barrel; uncheckered Western-style straight American walnut stock, barrel band on forearm; 15-rd. tube magazine; half-cock safety; step-adjustable open rear sight, hooded ramp front; receiver grooved

Ithaca Model LSA-55 Standard

duced in 1972; dropped about 1976. Used values: $350 to $375; with heavy barrel .222, .22-250 only, $365 to $385.

LSA Deluxe has same specs as standard model, except pre-'74 version had hand-checkered stock; also, roll-over cheekpiece; rosewood forearm tip, grip cap; white spacers; sling swivel; no heavy barrel. Used value, $375 to $400.

LSA-55 Heavy Barrel has same specs as standard model, except for 23" heavy barrel; no sights; redesigned stock; beavertail forearm; made in .22-250, .222 Rem. Manufactured 1974 to 1976. Used value, $385 to $395.

ITHACA LSA-55: bolt-action repeater; .243 Win., .308 Win., .22-250, .222 Rem., 6mm Rem., .25/06, .270 Win., .30/06; 23" free-floating barrel; European walnut pistol-grip Monte Carlo stock. Early versions had impressed checkering on pistol grip, forearm; as of 1974, stocks are hand checkered. Removable adjustable rear sight, hooded ramp front; 3-rd. detachable box magazine; adjustable trigger; receiver drilled, tapped for scope mounts. Intro-

ITHACA Model LSA-65: bolt-action repeater; has same specs as standard-grade Model LSA-55, except for 4-rd. magazine; made in .25/06, .270 Win., .30/06. Manufactured 1969 to 1976. Used value, $350 to $375.

Model LSA-65 Deluxe has same specs as standard model, except for roll-over cheekpiece, skip-line checkering, rosewood grip cap, forend tip, no sights; scope mount included. Manufactured 1969 to 1976. Used value, $375 to $400.

ITHACA BSA CF-2: bolt-action; .222 Rem., .22-250, .243, 6.5x55, 7mm Mauser, 7x64, .270, .308, .30/06, 7mm Rem. magnum, .300 Win. magnum; 24" barrel; open adjustable rear sight, hooded ramp front; European walnut stock; roll-over Monte Carlo; palm swell on pistol grip; skip-line checkering; adjustable single or optional double-set triggers; side safety; visible cocking indicator; vented rubber recoil pad; high gloss or oil finish on stock. Manufactured in England. Introduced, 1980; dropped by Precision Sports, 1985.

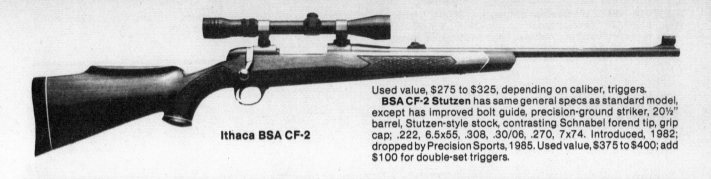

Ithaca BSA CF-2

Used value, $275 to $325, depending on caliber, triggers.

BSA CF-2 Stutzen has same general specs as standard model, except has improved bolt guide, precision-ground striker, 20½" barrel, Stutzen-style stock, contrasting Schnabel forend tip, grip cap; .222, 6.5x55, .308, .30/06, .270, 7x74. Introduced, 1982; dropped by Precision Sports, 1985. Used value, $375 to $400; add $100 for double-set triggers.

IVER JOHNSON

IVER JOHNSON Model X: bolt-action, single-shot; take-down; .22 LR., .22 long, .22 short; 22" barrel; open rear sight, blade front; hardwood pistol-grip stock; knob forearm tip; uncheckered. Introduced in 1928; dropped, 1932. Used value, $50 to $60.

Iver Johnson Model 2X

IVER JOHNSON Model 2X: same general specs as Model X, but has larger stock, without forearm knob; heavier 24" barrel. Introduced in 1932; dropped, 1955. Used value, $85 to $90.

IVER JOHNSON PM30HB Carbine: autoloader; .30 U.S. Carbine, 5.7mm MMJ; 18" barrel; overall length, 35½"; weighs 6½ lb.; hardwood or walnut stock; click-adjustable peep rear sight, post front with protective wings; copy of WWII military carbine; gas-operated; 15-rd. detachable magazine; blued finish or stainless steel. Introduced, 1983; still produced. Used values: blued, $150 to $160; stainless steel, $180 to $190.

Iver Johnson PM30HB

Iver Johnson Survival Carbine

IVER JOHNSON Survival Carbine: has same general specs as PM30HB Carbine, except has black Zytel stock; vertical pistol grip; folding stock optional. Introduced, 1983; dropped, 1986. Used values: stainless steel, $180 to $190; blued, $160 to $170; with folding stock, add $25 to $30.

Iver Johnson Model EW .22HBA

IVER JOHNSON Model EW .22HBA: autoloader; .22 LR; 15-rd. magazine; 18½" barrel; overall length 38"; weighs 5.8 lb.; walnut-finished hardwood stock; adjustable rear peep sight, blade front; resembles M-1 .30 Carbine. Introduced, 1985; no longer imported. Used value, $125 to $135.

IVER JOHNSON Li'l Champ: single-shot; .22 short, long, LR; 16¼" barrel; 32½" overall length; weighs 3⅛ lb.; adjustable rear sight, blade on ramp front; moulded composition stock; designed for young shooters; nickel-plated bolt. Introduced, 1986; still in production. Used value, $65 to $70.

KIMBER

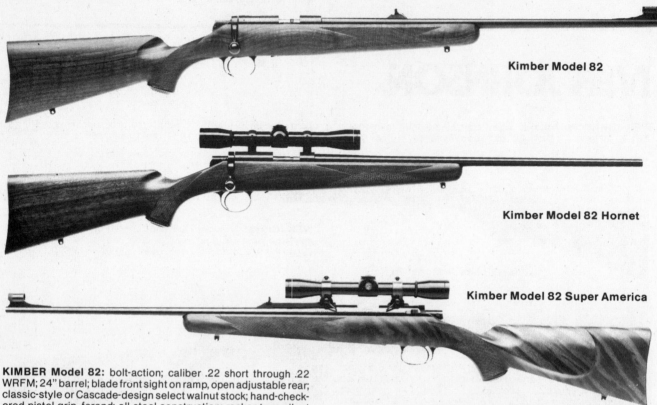

Kimber Model 82

Kimber Model 82 Hornet

Kimber Model 82 Super America

KIMBER Model 82: bolt-action; caliber .22 short through .22 WRFM; 24" barrel; blade front sight on ramp, open adjustable rear; classic-style or Cascade-design select walnut stock; hand-checkered pistol grip, forend; all-steel construction; rocker-type silent safety; blued finish; receiver grooved for special Kimber scope mounts; checkered steel butt plate; steel grip cap; available with or without sights. Introduced, 1980 by Kimber of Oregon. Used value, $375 to $400.

Model 82 Hornet: bolt-action; .22 Hornet; 3-rd. magazine; 22½" barrel; 41" overall length; blade on ramp front sight, open adjustable rear; available without sights; classic or Cascade-design claro walnut stock, hand-checkered pistol grip, forend; all-steel construction; rocker-type silent safety; twin locking lugs; double extractors; receiver grooved for special Kimber scope mounts; checkered steel butt plate; steel grip cap. Introduced, 1982; still in production. Used values: Classic stock, with sights, $480 to $500; without sights, $450 to $465; Cascade stock, with sights, $550 to $575; without sights, $520 to $540.

Model 82 Super America has same general specs as standard 82, except available in .22 LR, .22 WRFM, .22 Hornet; classic stock only; Continental cheekpiece; borderless, wrap-around checkering; folding leaf rear sight on quarter-rib; quick-detachable, double-lever scope mounts. Introduced, 1982; still in production. Used values: .22 LR, $700 to $725; .22 WRFM, $740 to $760; .22 Hornet, $775 to $800.

Kimber Model 84 Classic

KIMBER Model 84 Sporter: bolt-action; .223; 5-rd. magazine; 22½" barrel; 42" overall length; weighs 6¼ lb.; made in Classic, Cascade, Custom Classic grades; all have hand-cut borderless checkering, steel grip cap, checkered steel butt plate; hooded ramp front sight with bead, folding leaf rear are optional; new Mauser-type head locking action; steel trigger guard; hinged floor plate; Mauser-type extractor; fully adjustable trigger; grooved for scope mounts. Introduced, 1984; still in production. Used values, without optional sights: Classic, $500 to $550; Cascade, $550 to $600; Custom Classic, $650 to $700.

Model 84 Super America has the same specs as the 82 Super America, except it is dovetailed to accept Kimber scope mounts; chambered for .223. Introduced, 1985; still in production. Used value, $800 to $850.

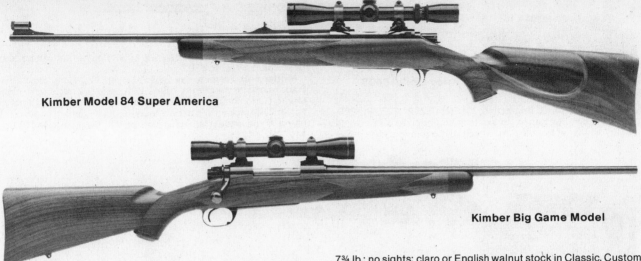

Kimber Model 84 Super America

Kimber Big Game Model

KIMBER Big Game Model: bolt-action; .270, .280, 7mm Rem. magnum, .30/06, .300 Win. magnum, .338 Win. magnum, .375 H&H; 22", 24" barrel lengths; 42" overall length with 22" barrel; weighs 7¾ lb.; no sights; claro or English walnut stock in Classic, Custom Classic, Super America design; Model 70-type trigger, ejector design; Mauser-type extractor; three-position safety. Introduced, 1987; still in production. Used values: Classic, $700 to $750; Custom Classic, $900 to $950; Super America, $1050 to $1100.

KRICO

KRICO Sporter: bolt-action; .22 Hornet, .222 Rem.; 4-rd. clip magazine; 22", 24", 26" barrel lengths; miniature Mauser-type action, single- or double-set trigger; open rear sight, hooded ramp front; hand-checkered European walnut stock, cheekpiece, pistol grip, forend tip; sling swivels. Manufactured in Germany, 1956 to 1962. Used value, $500 to $550.

KRICO Model 311: bolt-action; .22 LR; 5- or 10-rd. clip magazine; 22" barrel; open rear sight, hooded ramp front; single- or double-set trigger; hand-checkered European walnut stock, pistol grip,

Krico Carbine has same specs as Sporter model except for Mannlicher-type stock, 22" barrel. Manufactured 1956 to 1962. Used value, $475 to $500.

Krico Varmint Model has same specs as Sporter, except for heavy barrel, no sights, .222 Rem. only. Manufactured 1956 to 1962. Used value, $500 to $525.

cheekpiece; sling swivels. Also available with 2½X scope. Manufactured 1958 to 1962. Used values: iron sights, $250 to $275; with scope, $300 to $325.

Krico Model 330S Match

KRICO Model 330S Match: single-shot; .22 LR; 25.6" heavy barrel; hooded front sight with interchangeable inserts; diopter match rear, rubber eye-cup; walnut-finished beechwood match stock; built-in hand stop; adjustable recoil pad; factory-set match trigger; stippled pistol grip. Introduced, 1981; not currently imported. Used value, $425 to $450.

Krico Model 430S Match

KRICO Model 430S Match: bolt-action; single-shot or repeater; .22 Hornet; 24" barrel; no sights, drilled and tapped for scope mounts; target-style walnut stock, stippled pistol-grip, forend; dovetail rail for scope mounting; double-set or match trigger. Introduced, 1981; not currently imported. Used values: single-shot, $350 to $375; repeater, $425 to $450.

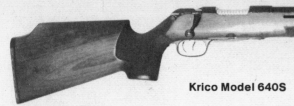

Krico Model 640S

KRICO Model 640S: bolt-action; .17 Rem., .222, .223, .22-250, .308; 20" semi-bull barrel; no sights; pistol-grip stock of French walnut; ventilated forend; 5-rd. detachable box magazine; single-

or double-set triggers. Introduced, 1981; not currently imported. Used value, $750 to $800.

Model 640 Varmint has 23.75" barrel; .222 Rem. only; 4-rd. magazine; cut-checkered select European walnut stock; high Monte Carlo comb; Wundhammer palm swell; rosewood forend tip; drilled, tapped for scope mounts; free-floating heavy bull barrel. Made in West Germany. Imported by Beeman. Used value, $1200 to $1250.

Krico Model 650S

Krico Model 650 S/2

KRICO Model 650S: bolt-action; detachable 3-shot box magazine; .222, .223, .243, .308; 26" bull barrel, muzzle brake/flash hider; no sights; drilled, tapped for scope mounts; oil-finished select European walnut stock; adjustable cheekpiece, recoil pad; match trigger, single- or double-set trigger available; all metal has matte blue finish; marketed as Sniper Rifle. Currently available only in .308 as Model 640 Super Sniper. Introduced, 1981; still imported. Used value, $950 to $1000.

Model 650 S/2 single-shot has same general specs as Model 650S but marketed as Benchrester model; .223, .243, 6mm, .308; 23.6" bull barrel; special benchrest stock of French walnut; adjustable recoil pad. Introduced, 1981; dropped, 1983. Used value, $900 to $950.

Model 650 Super Sniper has same specs as standard model, except is chambered only for .223, .308; 26" bull barrel; matte blue finish; muzzle brake/flash hider; adjustable cheekpiece, recoil pad. Made in West Germany. No longer imported. Used value, $900 to $950.

Krico Model 302

KRICO Model 302: bolt-action; .22 LR; 5- or 10-rd. magazine; single- or double-set trigger; 24" barrel; hooded post front sight, windage-adjustable rear; European walnut stock; checkered pistol grip, forend. Made in West Germany. Introduced, 1982; dropped, 1984. Used values: single-set trigger, $375 to $400; double-set trigger, $425 to $450.

Model 352 has same specs as Model 302, except has single-set trigger only; chambered for .22 WRFM. Introduced, 1982; was

imported briefly as Model 354; no longer imported. Used value, $400 to $425.

Model 302E has same specs as Model 302, except has straight forend, stock is walnut-finished hardwood. Introduced, 1982; importation dropped, 1983. Used value, $375 to $400.

Model 352E has same specs as 302E, except is chambered for .22 WRFM. Introduced, 1982; importation dropped, 1983. Used value, $350 to $375.

Model 302 DR C is chambered for .22 LR, .22 WRFM; 24" barrel; 43" overall length; classic-style European walnut stock; other specs the same as standard Model 302. Introduced, 1983; dropped, 1984. Used values: .22 LR, $350 to $375; .22 WRFM, $375 to $400.

Krico Model 304

KRICO Model 304: bolt-action; same specs as Model 302, except has 20" barrel, full-length Mannlicher-type stock. Made in West Germany. Introduced, 1982; dropped, 1984. Used values: .22 LR, $365 to $375; .22 WRFM, $450 to $475.

Krico Model 340S

Krico 340 Mini-Sniper

KRICO Model 340S: bolt-action; .22 LR; 5-rd. clip; 21" match barrel; 39½" overall length; designed as silhouette rifle; no sights; receiver grooved for tip-off mounts; European walnut match-style stock; stippled grip, forend; free-floating barrel; adjustable two-stage match trigger or double-set trigger; meets NRA MS rules. Made in West Germany. Introduced, 1983; still imported. Used value, $500 to $525.

Model 340 Mini-Sniper Rifle has same general specs as 340S, but weighs 8 lb., measures 40" overall; high comb; palm swell, stippled ventilated forend; receiver grooved for scope mounts; free-floating bull barrel; muzzle brake; large bolt knob; match quality single trigger; sandblasted barrel, receiver. Made in West Germany. Introduced, 1984; imported by Beeman; dropped, 1986. Used value, $700 to $750.

Kricotronic 340 has same basic specs as 340S, except has electronic ignition system, replacing firing pin; fast lock time. Made in West Germany. Introduced, 1985; imported by Beeman; dropped, 1988. Used value, $750 to $800.

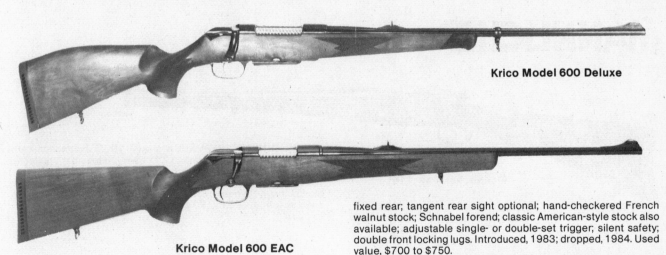

Krico Model 400D

KRICO Model 400D: bolt-action; .22 Hornet; detachable 5-rd. magazine; 23.5" barrel; hooded post front sight, windage-adjustable open rear; deluxe European walnut stock; Schnabel forend; solid rubber recoil pad; detachable box magazine; rear locking lugs; twin extractors; sling swivels; hand-checkered pistol grip, forend; single- or double-set triggers. Introduced, 1983; still im-

ported from West Germany. Used values: $500 to $550; with Mannlicher stock, $600 to $650.

Model 400E has same general specs as 400E, except has straight forend, walnut-finished beech stock; no forend tip; hard rubber butt plate; single- or double-set trigger. Introduced, 1982; importation dropped, 1983. Used values: single trigger, $325 to $350; double trigger, $350 to $375.

Model 400L has same specs as Model 400D, except has select French walnut stock, no Schnabel. Introduced, 1982; importation dropped, 1983. Used value, $550 to $650.

Model 420L has same specs as Model 400L, except has full Mannlicher-type stock, 20" barrel, solid rubber butt pad. Introduced, 1982; importation dropped, 1983. Used value, $850 to $950.

Krico Model 600 Deluxe

Krico Model 600 EAC

KRICO Model 600: bolt-action; .17 Rem., .222, .222 Rem. magnum, .223, .243; 24" barrel; overall length, 44"; hooded ramp front sight,

fixed rear; tangent rear sight optional; hand-checkered French walnut stock; Schnabel forend; classic American-style stock also available; adjustable single- or double-set trigger; silent safety; double front locking lugs. Introduced, 1983; dropped, 1984. Used value, $700 to $750.

Model 600L Deluxe has same specs as standard model, except has gold-plated single-set trigger; traditional European-style select fancy walnut stock; rosewood Schnabel forend tip; Bavarian cheekpiece; fine checkering; front sling swivel attaches to barrel; butterknife bolt handle. Introduced, 1983; dropped, 1984. Used value, $700 to $750.

Model 600 EAC has same specs as basic model, except has

KRICO Model 700E: bolt-action; .308, 7x57, 7x64, .270, .30/06; has same specs as Model 600, except for chamberings. Introduced, 1983; dropped, 1984. Used value, $750 to $800.

Model 700EM has same specs as Model 700E, except is chambered for 7mm Rem. magnum, .300 Win. magnum; 26" barrel. Introduced, 1983; dropped, 1984. Used value, $800 to $850.

Model 700EC has same specs as 700E, except is chambered for .308, 7x57, 7x64, .270, .30/06, 9.3x62. Introduced, 1983;

American-style classic stock, sling swivels. Introduced, 1983; importation dropped, 1984. Used value, $700 to $750.

dropped, 1984. Used value, $750 to $800.

Model 700L Deluxe has same specs as Model 600L, except is chambered for .17 Rem., .222, .223, .22-250, .243, .308, 7x57, 7x64, .270, .30/06, 9.3x62, 8x68S, 7mm Rem. magnum, .300 Win. magnum, 9.3x64. Introduced, 1983; still imported by Beeman. Used values: standard calibers, $850 to $875; magnum calibers $900 to $950.

Krico Model 620L

KRICO Model 620L: has same general specs as Model 600,

except has full Mannlicher-style stock, 20.75" barrel; chambered for .243 Win. only; optional match trigger; drilled, tapped for scope mounts. Introduced, 1983; still imported. Used value, $800 to $850.

KRICO Model 720L: has same specs as Model 620L, except is chambered for .270 Win., .30/06. Introduced, 1983; still in production. Used value, $850 to $900.

Krico Model 120M

KRICO Model 120M: bolt-action; .22 LR; 5-rd. magazine; 19½" barrel; overall length 46"; weighs 6 lb.; European hardwood stock; tangent rear sight adjustable for elevation, hooded blade front; blued finish; adjustable trigger; receiver grooved for scope mounts. Made in West Germany. No longer imported. Used value, $175 to $200.

Krico Model 320

KRICO Model 320: bolt-action; .22 LR; 5-rd. magazine; 19½" barrel; 38½" overall length; weighs 6 lb.; windage-adjustable open rear sight, blade front on ramp; Mannlicher-style select European walnut stock; cut-checkered grip, forend; blued steel forend cap; detachable box magazine; single- or double-set triggers. Made in West Germany. Introduced, 1986; still imported by Beeman. Used value, $520 to $535.

MANNLICHER

Mannlicher Model 1903

MANNLICHER-SCHOENAUER Model 1903: bolt-action carbine sporter; 6.5x53mm only; 17.7" barrel; full-length uncheckered European walnut Mannlicher-style stock; metal forearm cap; pistol grip; cartridge trap in butt plate; 5-rd. rotary magazine; double-set trigger; two-leaf rear sight, ramp front; flat bolt handle; sling swivels. Introduced in 1903; dropped, 1937. Used value, $700 to $750.

MANNLICHER-SCHOENAUER Model 1905: bolt-action carbine sporter; 9x56mm only; 19.7" barrel; other specs identical to those of Model 1903. Introduced in 1905; dropped, 1937. Used value, $750 to $850.

MANNLICHER-SCHOENAUER Model 1908: bolt-action carbine; 7x57mm and 8x56mm; all other specs identical to those of Model 1905. Introduced in 1908; dropped, 1947. Used values: 8x50mm, $650 to $700; 7x57mm, $750 to $850.

MANNLICHER-SCHOENAUER Model 1910: bolt-action sporting carbine; 9.5x57mm only; other specs identical to those of

MANNLICHER-SCHOENAUER High Velocity: bolt-action sporting rifle; .30/06, 7x64 Brenneke, 8x60 magnum, 9.3x62, 10.75x-57mm; 23.6" barrel; hand-checkered traditional sporting stock of

MANNLICHER-SCHOENAUER Model 1924: bolt-action carbine; .30/06 only; aimed at American market; other specs identical

MANNLICHER-SCHOENAUER Model 1950: bolt-action sporter; designed primarily for the U.S. market; .257 Roberts, .270 Win., .30/06; 24" barrel; standard hand-checkered European walnut sporting stock; pistol grip, cheekpiece; ebony forend tip; 5-rd. rotary magazine; single- or double-set trigger; flat bolt handle; folding leaf open rear sight, hooded ramp front; shotgun-type safety; sling swivels. Introduced in 1950; dropped, 1952. Used value, $725 to $750.

Model 1908. Introduced in 1910; dropped, 1937. Used value, $750 to $800.

European walnut; cheekpiece, pistol grip; 5-rd. rotary magazine; British-type three-leaf open rear sight, ramp front; sling swivels. Introduced in 1922; dropped, 1937. Used value, $750 to $1000.

to those of Model 1908. Introduced in 1924; dropped, 1937. Used value, $800 to $1000.

   Model 1950 Carbine has the same specs as standard Model 1950 rifle, except for full-length Mannlicher-type stock, metal forend cap; 20" barrel. Introduced in 1950; dropped, 1952. Used value, $750 to $800.
   Model 1950 6.5 Carbine has same specs as Model 1950 carbine, except for 18¼" barrel chambered for 6.5x53mm only. Introduced in 1950; dropped, 1952. Used value, $750 to $800.

Mannlicher Model 1952 Carbine

MANNLICHER-SCHOENAUER Model 1952: bolt-action sporting rifle; .257 Roberts, .270 Win., .30/06, 9.3x62mm; improved version of Model 1950; has same specs except for swept-back bolt handle, improved stock design. Introduced in 1952; dropped, 1956. Used value, $650 to $750.
   Model 1952 Carbine has the same specs as the Model 1950 Carbine, except for full-length Mannlicher stock design, swept-back bolt handle; .257 Roberts, .270 Win., .30/06. Introduced in 1952; dropped, 1956. Used value, $750 to $850.
   Model 1952 6.5 Carbine has the same specs as Model 1950 6.5 Carbine, except for swept-back bolt handle, improved stock

design. Chambered for 6.5x53mm only. Introduced in 1952; dropped, 1956. Used value, $750 to $850.

Mannlicher-Schoenauer Model 1956

Mannlicher-Schoenauer Model 1956 Carbine

MANNLICHER-SCHOENAUER Model 1956: bolt-action sporting rifle; .243 Win., .30/06; has the same general specs as Model 1952 rifle, except for high-comb improved walnut stock, 22" barrel. Introduced in 1956; dropped, 1960. Used value, $650 to $700.
   Model 1956 Carbine has the same general specs as Model 1952 Carbine, except for redesigned high-comb walnut stock;

.243 Win., .257 Roberts, .270 Win., .30/06. Introduced, 1956; dropped, 1960. Used value, $700 to $800.

Mannlicher-Schoenauer Model 1961-MCA Carbine

MANNLICHER-SCHOENAUER Model 1961-MCA: bolt-action rifle; .243 Win., .270 Win., .30/06; has the same specs as Model 1956 rifle, except for substitution of Monte Carlo-style walnut stock. Introduced in 1961; dropped, 1971. Used value, $600 to $625.

1961-MCA Carbine has the same general specs as Model 1956 Carbine, except for substitution of walnut Monte Carlo stock; .243 Win., .270 Win., .30/06, .308 Win., 6.5x53mm. Introduced in 1961; dropped, 1971. Used value, $650 to $750.

MANNLICHER Model SL: bolt-action; .222 Rem., .222 Rem. magnum, .223 Rem.; 5-rd. detachable rotary magazine; 23" barrel; interchangeable single- or double-set trigger; open rear sight, hooded ramp front; Steyr-Mannlicher SL action; European walnut half-stock; Monte Carlo comb, cheekpiece; skip-checkered pistol grip, forearm; detachable sling swivels; butt pad. Introduced, 1967; still in production. Used value, $650 to $750.

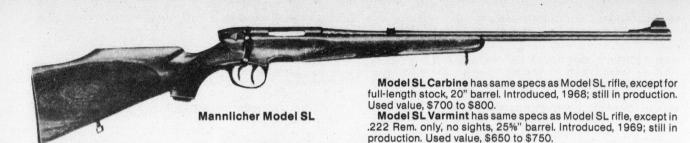

Mannlicher Model SL

Model SL Carbine has same specs as Model SL rifle, except for full-length stock, 20" barrel. Introduced, 1968; still in production. Used value, $700 to $800.

Model SL Varmint has same specs as Model SL rifle, except in .222 Rem. only, no sights, 25⅝" barrel. Introduced, 1969; still in production. Used value, $650 to $750.

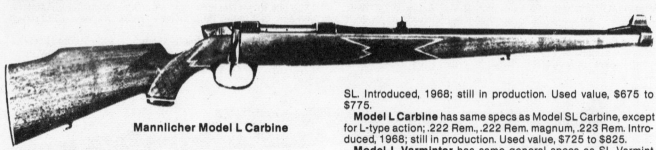

Mannlicher Model L Carbine

MANNLICHER Model L: bolt-action; .22-250, 5.6x57mm, .243 Win., 6mm Rem., .308 Win.; other specs are the same as the Model

SL. Introduced, 1968; still in production. Used value, $675 to $775.

Model L Carbine has same specs as Model SL Carbine, except for L-type action; .222 Rem., .222 Rem. magnum, .223 Rem. Introduced, 1968; still in production. Used value, $725 to $825.

Model L Varminter has same general specs as SL Varmint model except for L-type action; chambered for .22-250, .243 Win., .308 Win. Introduced, 1969; still in production. Used value, $675 to $770.

Mannlicher Model SSG Match

MANNLICHER Model SSG Match Target: bolt-action; .308 Win.; 5- or 10-rd. magazine; L-type action; 25½" heavy barrel; single-shot plug; single trigger; micrometer peep rear sight, globe front; European walnut target stock; full pistol grip; wide forearm, swivel

rail, adjustable butt plate; also made with high-impact plastic stock. Introduced, 1969; still in production; not imported. Used values: walnut stock, $1100 to $1250; plastic stock, $850 to $950.

Mannlicher Model M

Mannlicher Model M Professional

MANNLICHER Model M: bolt-action; 6.5x57mm, 7x57mm, 7x64mm, .25/06, .270 Win., .30/06, 8x57JS, 9.3x62; M-type action; other specs are the same as Model SL rifle, except for forend tip, recoil pad. Also made in left-hand model, with bolt on left and 6.5x55, 7.5mm Swiss as additional calibers. Standard version in-

troduced, 1969; left-hand version, 1977; still in production. Used values: standard model, $750 to $800; left-hand model, $800 to $825.

Model M Carbine has the same general specs as the Model SL carbine, except is built on M-type action, has recoil pad. Also made in left-hand action, with added 6.5x55mm, 7.5mm Swiss chamberings. Introduced, 1977; still in production. Used values: standard carbine, $775 to $800; left-hand model, $800 to $825.

Model M Professional has the same specs as standard model, except for Cycolac stock; Parkerized finish; right-hand action only. Introduced, 1977; still in production. Used value, $750 to $800.

Mannlicher Model S

MANNLICHER Model S: bolt-action; 6.5x68mm, .257 Weatherby magnum, .264 Win. magnum, 7mm Rem. magnum, .300 Win. magnum, .300 H&H magnum, .308 Norma magnum, 8x68S, .338 Win. magnum, 9.3x64mm, .375 H&H magnum; has the same specs as SL model, except is built on S-type action, forend tip, recoil pad, 25⅝" barrel. Introduced, 1970; still in production. Used value, $750 to $800.

Model S/T has the same specs as Model S, except chambered for 9.3x64mm, .375 H&H magnum, .458 Win.; heavy barrel. Introduced, 1975; still in production. Used value, $900 to $950.

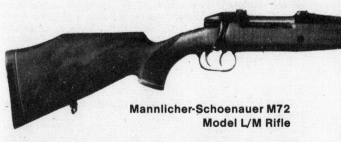

Mannlicher-Schoenauer M72 Model L/M Rifle

MANNLICHER-SCHOENAUER M72 Model L/M: bolt-action; .22-250, 5.6x57mm, 6mm Rem., .243 Win., 6.5x57mm, .270 Win., 7x57mm, 7x64mm, .308 Win., .30/06; 23⅝" barrel; L/M receiver, 5-rd. rotary magazine; front-locking bolt; open rear sight, hooded ramp front; interchangeable single- or double-set trigger; European walnut half-stock, hand-checkered pistol-grip forearm, rosewood forend tip; recoil pad, detachable sling swivels. Introduced, 1972; no longer in production. Used value, $650 to $700.

M72 Model L/M Carbine has same general specs as standard M72 Model L/M, except for full-length stock, 20" barrel. Introduced, 1972; no longer in production. Used values, $675 to $775.

M72 Model S has same general specs as standard M72 Model L/M, except for magnum action; 4-rd. magazine; 25⅝" barrel; chambered for 6.5x68, 7mm Rem. magnum, 8x68S, 9.3x64mm, .375 H&H magnum. Introduced, 1972; no longer in production. Used value, $700 to $800.

M72 Model S/T has same specs as standard M72 Model S, except for optional 25⅝" barrel; chambered for .300 Win. magnum, 9.3x64mm, .375 H&H magnum, 9.3x64mm, .375 H&H magnum, .458 Win. magnum. Introduced, 1975; no longer in production. Used value, $750 to $850.

MARLIN

MARLIN Model 92: lever-action; .22 short, long, LR, .32 short, long rimfire or centerfire with interchangeable firing pin; barrel lengths, 16", 24", 26", 28"; tubular magazine; open rear sight, blade front; uncheckered straight-grip stock, forearm. Originally marketed as Model 1892. Manufactured 1892 to 1916. Collector value. Used values: .22, $425 to $450; .32, $525 to $550.

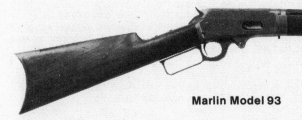

Marlin Model 93

MARLIN Model 93: lever-action; .25-36 Marlin, .30-30, .32 Special, .32-40, .38-55; solid frame or take-down; 10-rd. tubular magazine; 26", 28", 30", 32" round or octagonal barrel; open rear sight, bead front; uncheckered straight-grip stock, forearm. Originally marketed as Model 1893. Manufactured 1893 to 1936. Collector value. Used value, $425 to $475.

Model 93 Carbine has same specs as standard model except for 20" barrel, 7-rd. magazine; chambered for .30-30, .32 Special; carbine sights. Collector value. Used value, $525 to $575.

Model 93SC, designated as the Sporter Carbine, has same specs as standard carbine, except for shorter 5-rd. magazine. Collector value. Used value, $575 to $600.

Marlin Model 94

MARLIN Model 94: lever-action; .25-20, .32-20, .38-40, .44-40; 10-rd. magazine; 24" round or octagonal barrel; solid frame or take-down; open rear sight, bead front; uncheckered pistol grip or straight stock, forearm. Originally marketed as Model 1894. Manufactured 1894 to 1934. Collector value. Used value, $550 to $575.

Marlin Model 95

MARLIN Model 95: lever-action; .32 WCF, .38-56, .40-65, .40-70, .40-82, .45-70; 9-rd. tubular magazine; 24" round or octagonal barrel, other lengths on special order; open rear sight, bead front; uncheckered straight or pistol-grip stock, forearm. Manufactured 1895 to 1915. Collector value. Used value, $700 to $750.

Marlin Model 97

MARLIN Model 97: lever-action; .22 short, long, LR; tubular magazine; 16", 24", 26", 28" barrel lengths; open rear sight, bead front; uncheckered straight or pistol grip stock, forearm. Originally marketed as Model 1897. Manufactured 1897 to 1922. Collector value. Used value, $500 to $550.

MARLIN Model 18: slide-action; .22 short, long, LR; tube magazine; round or octagonal 20" barrel; solid frame; exposed hammer; open rear sight, bead front; uncheckered straight stock, slide han- dle. Manufactured 1906 to 1909. Some collector value. Used value, $200 to $225.

Marlin Model 20

MARLIN Model 20: slide-action; .22 short, long, LR; full-length tubular magazine holds 18 LR, half-length holds 10 LR; 24" octagonal barrel; open rear sight, bead front; uncheckered straight-grip stock. Later versions designated as 20S. Manufactured 1907 to 1922. Some collector value. Used value, $200 to $225.

MARLIN Model 25: slide-action; .22 short; 15-rd. tubular magazine; 23" barrel; open rear sight, bead front; uncheckered straight- grip stock, slide handle. Manufactured 1909 to 1910. Some collector value. Used value, $225 to $250.

Marlin Model 27

MARLIN Model 27: slide-action; .25-20, .32-20; 7-rd. tubular magazine; 24" octagonal barrel; open rear sight, bead front; unchecked- ered straight-grip stock, grooved slide handle. Manufactured 1910 to 1916. Some collector value. Used value, $200 to $225.

Model 27S has the same specs as standard model, except for round barrel; chambered also for .25 Stevens RF. Manufactured 1920 to 1932. Used value, $160 to $175.

MARLIN Model 32: slide-action; .22 short, long, LR; short tubular magazine holds 10 LR; full-length magazine holds 18 LR; 24" octagonal barrel; open rear sight, bead front; uncheckered pistol- grip stock, grooved slide handle. Some collector value. Manufac- tured 1914 to 1915. Used value, $250 to $275.

Marlin Model 38

MARLIN Model 38: slide-action repeater; hammerless take-down; .22 short, long, LR; tube magazine holds 10 LR, 12 long, 15 short cartridges; 24" octagon barrel; open rear sight, bead front; un- checkered pistol-grip walnut stock, grooved slide handle. Intro- duced in 1920; dropped, 1930. Used value, $200 to $225.

MARLIN Model 50: autoloader; take-down; .22 LR only; 6-rd. detachable box magazine; 22" barrel; open rear sight adjustable for elevation, bead front; uncheckered pistol-grip walnut stock, grooved forearm. Introduced in 1931; dropped, 1934. Used value, $115 to $125.

Model 50E has same specs as Model 50, except for hooded front sight, peep rear. Used value, $125 to $135.

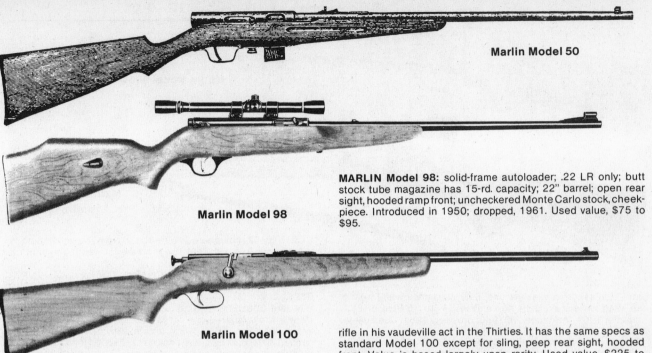

Marlin Model 50

MARLIN Model 98: solid-frame autoloader; .22 LR only; butt stock tube magazine has 15-rd. capacity; 22" barrel; open rear sight, hooded ramp front; uncheckered Monte Carlo stock, cheek-piece. Introduced in 1950; dropped, 1961. Used value, $75 to $95.

Marlin Model 98

Marlin Model 100

MARLIN Model 100: bolt-action, take-down single-shot; .22 short, long, LR; 24" barrel; open rear sight adjustable for elevation, bead front; uncheckered walnut pistol-grip stock. Introduced in 1936; dropped, 1960. Used value, $65 to $75.

Model 100S was introduced in 1936; dropped, 1946. It is known as the Tom Mix Special, allegedly because Tom Mix used such a rifle in his vaudeville act in the Thirties. It has the same specs as standard Model 100 except for sling, peep rear sight, hooded front. Value is based largely upon rarity. Used value, $225 to $250.

Model 100SB is the same as Model 100, except it is smooth-bore for use with .22 shot cartridge; has shotgun sight. Actually, this probably is the version used by Tom Mix in his act, as he used shot cartridges for breaking glass balls and other on-stage targets. Introduced in 1936; dropped, 1941. Used value, $225 to $250.

Marlin Model 101

MARLIN Model 101: improved version of Model 100; this version has improved bolt, redesigned stock, 22" barrel; semi-buckhorn sight adjustable for windage, elevation, hooded Wide-Scan front; black plastic trigger guard; T-shaped cocking piece; uncheckered walnut stock has beavertail forearm; receiver grooved for tip-off scope mount. Introduced in 1951; dropped, 1976. Used value, $65 to $75.

Model 101DL has same specs as Model 101, except for peep rear sight, hooded front; sling swivels. Manufactured 1952 to 1964. Used value, $85 to $90.

Marlin-Glenfield Model 101G has same specs as Model 101, with hardwood stock. Manufactured 1960 to 1965. Used value, $50 to $55.

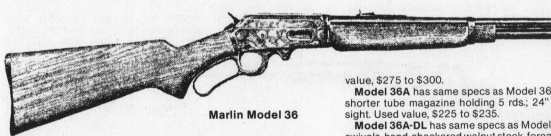

Marlin Model 36

value, $275 to $300.

Model 36A has same specs as Model 36 standard, except for shorter tube magazine holding 5 rds.; 24" barrel; hooded front sight. Used value, $225 to $235.

Model 36A-DL has same specs as Model 36A, except for sling swivels, hand-checkered walnut stock, forearm. Used value, $325 to $350.

Model 36 Sporting carbine has same general specs as Model 30A, except for a 20" barrel. Used value, $245 to $265.

Model 1936 only produced one year, add $100 to $150.

MARLIN Model 36: lever-action, carbine repeater; .32 Special, .30-30; 6-rd. tube magazine; 20" barrel; uncheckered walnut pistol-grip stock; semi-beavertail forearm; carbine barrel band; open rear sight, bead front. Introduced in 1936; dropped, 1948. Used

MARLIN Model 336C: lever-action repeating carbine; updated version of Model 36 carbine; specs are virtually the same, except for round breech bolt; gold-plated trigger; offset hammer spur; semi-buckhorn adjustable folding rear sight; ramp front with Wide-Scan hood; receiver tapped for scope mounts; top of receiver sandblasted to reduce glare. Introduced in 1948; still in production in .30-30, .35 Rem.; latter was introduced in 1953; .32 Win. Special discontinued, 1963. Used values: .32 Win. Special, $195 to $215; other calibers, $190 to $210.

Model 336A is the same as 336C, except it has 24" round

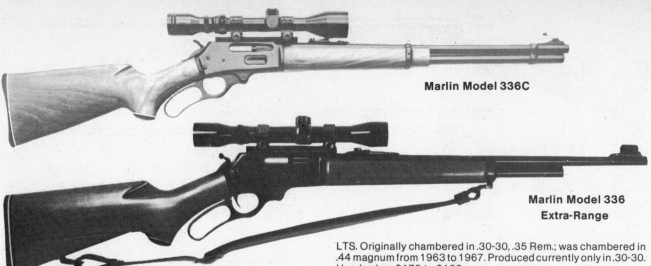

Marlin Model 336C

Marlin Model 336
Extra-Range

barrel; half-length magazine tube; 5-rd. capacity; blued forearm cap, sling swivels; available now only in .30-30; .35 Rem. discontinued in 1963. Introduced in 1950; dropped, 1981. Used value, $225 to $250.

Model 336A-DL has the same specs as Model 336A, except for sling, swivels, hand-checkered stock, forearm. Dropped, 1962. Used value, $250 to $275.

Model 336 Sporting carbine has same specs as Model 336A, except for 20" barrel. Dropped, 1963. Used value, $225 to $250.

Model 336 Zipper is same as Model 336 sporting carbine, but was chambered only in .219 Zipper. Introduced in 1955; dropped, 1961. Used value, $350 to $375.

Model 336T, called the Texan Model, has same specs as Model 336 carbine, except for straight-grip uncheckered walnut stock, squared lever. Introduced in 1953; still in production as Model

LTS. Originally chambered in .30-30, .35 Rem.; was chambered in .44 magnum from 1963 to 1967. Produced currently only in .30-30. Used value, $175 to $185.

Model 336 Marauder is same as Model 336T, except with 16¾" barrel. Introduced in 1963; dropped, 1964. Used value, $300 to $325.

Model 336CS has same general specs as standard model, except is chambered only for .30-30, .35 Rem.; 6-rd. tube magazine; 20" barrel; 38½" overall length; select black walnut stock; capped pistol grip; hammer-block safety; tapped for scope mounts; offset hammer spur; top of receiver sand-blasted. Still in production. Used value, $225 to $250.

Model 30AS has same specs as 336CS, except has walnut-finished hardwood stock; .30-30 only. Still in production. Used value, $225 to $250.

Model 336 Extra-Range Carbine has same specs as 336CS. except is chambered for .356 Win. and .307 Win.; has new hammer-block safety; 4-rd. magazine; rubber butt pad; marketed with detachable sling swivels, branded leather sling. Introduced, 1983; dropped, 1987. Used value, $225 to $250.

Marlin Model 81-DC

hooded front sight, peep rear. Used value, $80 to $85.

Model 81C is an improved version of standard Model 81; specs differ only in that the stock has semi-beavertail forearm. Introduced in 1940; dropped, 1970. Used value, $80 to $85.

Model 81-DC has same specs as Model 81-C, except for hooded front sight, peep rear, sling swivels. Introduced in 1940; dropped, 1965. Used value, $90 to $95.

Marlin-Glenfield Model 81G has same specs as Model 81C, except the stock is of less expensive wood; has bead front sight. Introduced in 1960; dropped, 1965. Used value, $65 to $70.

MARLIN Model 81: bolt-action, take-down repeater; .22 short, long, LR; tube magazine holds 18 LR, 20 long, 24 short cartridges; 24" barrel; open rear sight, bead front; uncheckered pistol-grip stock. Introduced in 1937; dropped, 1965. Used value, $70 to $75.

Model 81E differs from standard Model 81 only in that it has

Marlin Model 39

Marlin Model 39A

MARLIN Model 39: lever-action take-down repeater; .22 short, long, LR; tube magazine holds 18 LR, 20 long, 25 short cartridges; 24" octagon barrel; open rear sight, bead front; uncheckered pistol-grip walnut stock, forearm. Introduced in 1938; dropped, 1958. Used value, $300 to $325.

Marlin Model 39A Mountie

Model 39A has the same general specs as Model 39 but with heavier stock, semi-beavertail forearm, round barrel. Introduced in 1939; still in production. Used value, $165 to $185.

Golden Model 39A has gold-plated trigger, other refinements. Used value, $185 to $195.

Model 39A Mountie is virtually the same as the Model 39A but with straight-grip stock, slim forearm; 20" barrel; tube magazine holds 15 LR, 16 long, 21 short cartridges. Introduced in 1953; dropped, 1960. Used value, $165 to $185.

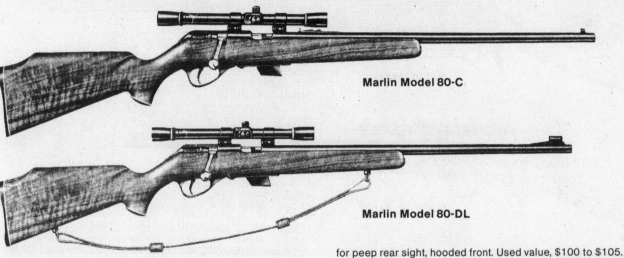

Marlin Model 80-C

Marlin Model 80-DL

MARLIN Model 80: bolt-action, take-down; .22 short, long, LR; 8-rd. detachable box magazine; 24" barrel; open rear sight, bead front; uncheckered walnut pistol-grip stock; black butt plate. Introduced in 1934; dropped, 1939. Used value, $85 to $95.

Model 80E has the same specs as standard Model 80, except for peep rear sight, hooded front. Used value, $100 to $105.

Model 80-C replaced standard Model 80 in 1940; dropped in 1970. Has same general specs as Model 80, except that stock has semi-beavertail forearm. Used value, $65 to $75.

Model 80-DL introduced in 1940; dropped, 1965; has same specs as the Model 80-C, except for peep rear sight, hooded front; sling swivels. Used value, $75 to $85.

Marlin Model A-1

MARLIN Model A-1: autoloader, take-down; .22 LR only; 6-rd. detachable box magazine; 24" barrel; open rear sight, bead front; uncheckered walnut pistol-grip stock. Introduced in 1935; dropped, 1946. Used value, $95 to $100.

MARLIN Model 332: bolt-action, varmint rifle; .222 Rem. only; short Sako Mauser-type action; 24" barrel; 3-rd. clip-type magazine; checkered walnut stock; two-position peep sight in rear,

Model A-1E has the same specs as standard Model A-1, except for a hooded front sight, peep rear. Used value, $105 to $110.

Model A-1C was introduced in 1940; dropped, 1946; has same specs as Model A-1, except that stock has semi-beavertail forearm. Used value, $105 to $110.

Model A-1DL has same specs as Model A-1C, except for sling swivels, hooded front sight, peep rear. Used value, $110 to $115.

hooded ramp front. Introduced in 1954; dropped, 1957. Used value, $350 to $375.

Marlin Model 455

MARLIN Model 455: bolt-action; FN Mauser action; Sako trigger; .308, .30/06, .270 Win.; 5-rd. box magazine; 24" stainless steel barrel; checkered walnut Monte Carlo stock with cheekpiece; Lyman No. 48 receiver sight, hooded ramp front. Introduced in 1957; dropped, 1959. Used value, $400 to $425.

Marlin-Glenfield Model 30A

MARLIN-Glenfield Model 30: lever-action; .30-30; has the same general specs as the Model 336C, except for 4-rd. magazine;

lower-quality stock of American hardwood. Manufactured 1966 to 1968. Used value, $135 to $150.

Model 30A has same specs as Model 30, except for impressed checkering on stock, forearm. Introduced in 1969; still in production as Model 30AS. Used value, $145 to $160.

Marlin Model 57

MARLIN Model 57: lever-action; .22 short, long, LR; tube magazine holds 27 short, 21 long, 19 LR cartridges; 22" barrel; unchecked Monte Carlo-type pistol-grip stock; open rear sight, hooded ramp front. Introduced in 1959; dropped, 1965. Used value, $100 to $125.

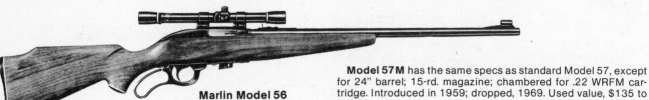

Marlin Model 56

Model 57M has the same specs as standard Model 57, except for 24" barrel; 15-rd. magazine; chambered for .22 WRFM cartridge. Introduced in 1959; dropped, 1969. Used value, $135 to $150.

Model 56 is same as Model 57, except equipped with clip-loading magazine; 8-rd. capacity. Introduced in 1955; dropped, 1964. Used value, $95 to $115.

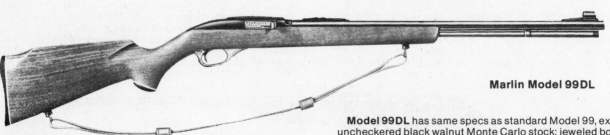

Marlin Model 99DL

Model 99DL has same specs as standard Model 99, except for unchecked black walnut Monte Carlo stock; jeweled bolt; gold-plated trigger, sling, sling swivels. Introduced in 1960; dropped, 1965. Used value, $75 to $80.

Model 99M1 carbine, designed after U.S. 30M1 carbine, but otherwise using same action as Model 99C; 18" barrel; 9-rd. tube magazine; unchecked pistol grip carbine stock; hand guard with barrel band; open rear sight, military-type ramp front; sling swivels. Introduced in 1966; dropped, 1978. Used value, $115 to $125.

MARLIN Model 99: autoloader; .22 LR only; 22" barrel; 18-rd. tube magazine; unchecked walnut pistol-grip stock; open rear sight, hooded ramp front. Introduced in 1959; dropped, 1961. Used value, $75 to $95.

Model 99C has same specs as standard Model 99, except for unchecked Monte Carlo stock; grooved receiver for tip-off scope mounts; gold-plated trigger. Later production features checkering on pistol-grip, forearm. Introduced in 1962; dropped, 1978. Used value, $75 to $85.

Model 99G has same specs as 99C, except for plainer stock, bead front sight. Manufactured 1960 to 1965. Used value, $75 to $80.

MARLIN Model 65: bolt-action single-shot; .22 short, long, LR; 24" barrel; open rear sight, bead front; unchecked walnut pistol-grip stock, grooved forearm. Introduced in 1932; dropped, 1938.

Used value, $100 to $115.

Model 65E is the same as Model 65, but is equipped with hooded front sight, peep rear. Used value, $115 to $120.

Marlin Model 88-C

MARLIN Model 88-C: take-down autoloader; .22 LR only; tube magazine in butt stock; 14-rd. capacity; open rear sight, hooded

front; unchecked pistol-grip stock. Introduced in 1947; dropped, 1956. Used value, $65 to $80.

Model 88-DL was introduced in 1953; dropped, 1956; same specs as Model 88-C, except for hand-checkered stock, sling swivels, receiver peep sight in rear. Used value, $125 to $145.

Marlin Model 89C

MARLIN Model 89C: same general specs as Model 88-C, except with clip magazine. Early version had 7-rd. clip; 12-rd. clip in later versions. Introduced in 1950; dropped, 1961. Used value, $65 to $75.

Marlin Model 89DL has same specs as Model 89-C, except for addition of sling swivels, receiver peep sight. Used value, $85 to $95.

Marlin Model 122

MARLIN Model 122: single-shot; bolt-action, junior target model with shortened uncheckered stock; .22 short, long, LR; 22" barrel; open rear sight, hooded ramp front; walnut Monte Carlo pistol-grip stock. Introduced in 1961; dropped, 1965. Used value, $75 to $85.

Marlin Model 980

MARLIN Model 980: bolt-action repeater; .22 WRFM only; 8-rd. clip-type magazine; 24" barrel; open rear sight adjustable for elevation, hooded ramp front; uncheckered walnut Monte Carlo style stock with white spacers at pistol grip and butt plate; sling, sling swivels. Introduced in 1962; dropped, 1970. Used value, $90 to $100.

Marlin Model 989M2

Model 989M2 carbine is the same as Model 99M1, except for 7-rd. clip-type detachable magazine. Introduced in 1966; dropped, 1979. Used value, $75 to $85.

Model 989G Marlin-Glenfield is the same as the Model 989, except for plain stock, bead front sight. Introduced in 1962; discontinued, 1964. Used value, $60 to $65.

Model 989MC Carbine has same specs as Model 99M1, except for 7-rd. clip-loading magazine. Introduced, 1966; no longer in production. Used value, $75 to $85.

MARLIN 989: autoloader; .22 LR only; 7-rd. clip magazine; 22" barrel; open adjustable rear sight; hooded ramp front; uncheckered Monte Carlo-type pistol-grip stock of black walnut; black butt plate. Introduced in 1962; dropped, 1966. Used value, $85 to $95.

Marlin Model 62

MARLIN Model 62: lever-action repeater; .256 magnum, .30 carbine; 23" barrel; 4-rd. clip magazine; open rear sight, adjustable for elevation, hooded ramp front; swivels, sling; uncheckered Monte Carlo-type pistol-grip stock. The .256 magnum was introduced in 1963; dropped, 1969. Used values: .256 magnum, $225 to $250; .30 carbine, $250 to $275.

Marlin 444 Sporter

hooded ramp front; straight-grip Monte Carlo stock of uncheckered walnut; recoil pad; carbine forearm, barrel band; sling, sling swivels. Introduced in 1965; dropped, 1972. Used value, $225 to $250.

Model 444 Sporter has same specs as 444 rifle, except for 22" barrel, Model 336A-type pistol-grip stock, forearm; recoil pad; detachable swivels; sling. Introduced, 1972; still in production as 444 SS. Used value, $245 to $265.

MARLIN Model 444: lever-action repeater; action is strengthened version of Model 336; .444 Marlin cartridge only; 4-rd. tube magazine; 24" barrel; open rear sight adjustable for elevation,

Marlin-Glenfield Model 60

Marlin Model 49

MARLIN-Glenfield Model 60: semiautomatic; .22 LR; same general specs as Model 99C, except for checkered or uncheckered walnut-finished hardwood stock. Introduced, 1966; still in production as Marlin Model 60. Used value, $70 to $80.

MARLIN Model 49: semiautomatic; .22 LR; has same specs as Model 99C, except for two-piece checkered or uncheckered hard-wood stock. Manufactured 1968 to 1971. Used value, $70 to $80.

Model 49DL: autoloader; .22 LR only; same specs as Model 99 standard model, except for two-piece stock/forend, capped pistol grip, checkered forearm and pistol grip, gold trigger; scroll-engraved receiver; grooved for tip-off scope mounts. Introduced in 1970; no longer in production. Used value, $115 to $125.

Marlin-Glenfield Model 70

MARLIN-Glenfield Model 70: semiautomatic; .22 LR; has same specs as Model 989 M2 carbine, except for walnut-finished hardwood stock. Manufactured 1966 to 1969. Used value, $60 to $65.

Model 70P Papoose has same general specs as Model 70, except is take-down; has 16¼" barrel, walnut-finished hardwood stock, no forend, open adjustable rear sight, ramp front; crossbolt safety; weighs 3¾ lb.; receiver grooved for scope mounts; marketed with 4X scope, mounts, zippered carrying case. Introduced, 1986; still in production. Used value, $90 to $100.

Marlin Model 780

Marlin Model 781

Marlin Model 782

MARLIN Model 780: bolt-action; .22 short, long, LR; 7-rd. clip magazine; 22" barrel; open rear sight, hooded ramp front; Monte Carlo stock, checkered pistol grip, forearm; receiver grooved for scope mounts. Introduced, 1971; still in production. Used value, $75 to $85.

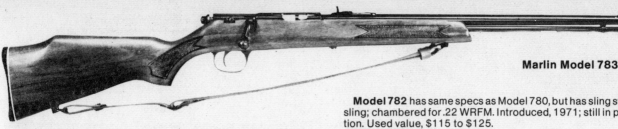

Marlin Model 783

Model 781 has same specs as Model 780, except for tubular magazine holding 17 LR. Introduced, 1971; still in production. Used value, $75 to $85.

Model 782 has same specs as Model 780, but has sling swivels; sling; chambered for .22 WRFM. Introduced, 1971; still in production. Used value, $115 to $125.

Model 783 has same specs as Model 782, except for tubular magazine. Introduced, 1971; still in production. Used value, $115 to $125.

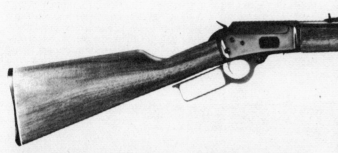

Marlin Model 1894C

MARLIN Model 1894: lever-action; .44 magnum only; 10-rd. tube magazine; 20" carbine barrel; uncheckered straight grip black walnut stock, forearm; gold-plated trigger; receiver tapped for scope mount; offset hammer spur; solid top receiver is sandblasted to reduce glare; hooded ramp front sight, semi-buckhorn adjustable rear. Supposedly a re-creation of the Model 94 of the last century, actually it is built on the Model 336 action. Introduced, 1971; still in production as Model 1894S. Used value, $185 to $200.

Model 1894 Sporter has same specs as Model 1894 carbine, except for 22" barrel, 6-rd. magazine. Manufactured 1973. Used value, $250 to $275.

Model 1894 Octagon has same specs as 1894 carbine, except for octagonal barrel, bead front sight. Manufactured 1973. Used value, $250 to $300.

Model 1894C has same specs as standard 1894, except is chambered for .357 magnum; 9-rd. tube magazine; 18½" barrel. Introduced, 1980; no longer in production. Used value, $195 to $210.

Model 1894CS Carbine has same specs as standard 1894 Sporter, except is chambered for .38 Special, .357 magnum; 9-rd. magazine; brass bead front sight; 18½" barrel; hammer block safety. Introduced 1983; still in production. Used value, $190 to $205.

Model 1894M has same specs as standard model, except chambered for .22 WRFM, has 11-rd. magazine; no gold-plated trigger; receiver tapped for scope mount or receiver sight. Introduced, 1983; still in production. Used value, $200 to $225.

Marlin Model 1895

MARLIN Model 1895: lever-action; .45-70 only; 22" round barrel; 4-rd. tube magazine; uncheckered straight grip stock, forearm of black walnut; solid receiver tapped for scope mounts, receiver sights; offset hammer spur; adjustable semi-buckhorn folding rear sight, bead front. Meant to be a re-creation of the original Model 1895, discontinued in 1915. Actually built on action of Marlin Model 444. Introduced in 1972; still in production as 1895 SS. Used value, $200 to $225.

Marlin Model 375

MARLIN 375: has same specs as Model 444, except is chambered for .375 Win.; has 5-rd. tube magazine; 20" barrel; quick-detachable swivels. Introduced, 1979; dropped, 1984. Used value, $240 to $250.

MARLIN-Glenfield Model 15: bolt-action; single-shot; .22 short, long, LR; 22" barrel; 41" overall length; ramp front sight, adjustable open rear; Monte Carlo walnut-finished hardwood stock, checkered full pistol grip; red cocking indicator; thumb safety; receiver grooved for tip-off scope mount. Introduced, 1979; dropped, 1983. Used value, $55 to $60.

MARLIN-GLENFIELD 30GT: lever-action; .30-30; 6-rd. tube magazine; 18½" barrel; brass bead front sight, adjustable rear; straight-grip walnut-finished hardwood stock; receiver sandblasted. Introduced, 1979; dropped, 1981. Used value, $145 to $165.

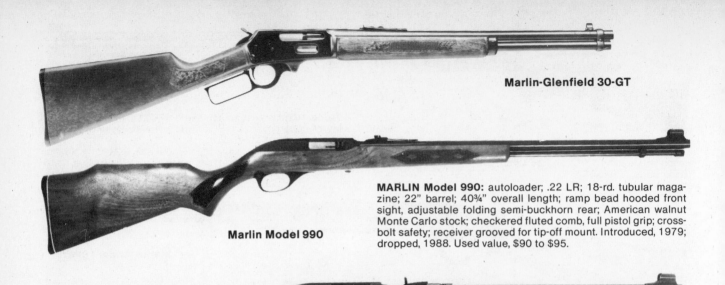

Marlin-Glenfield 30-GT

Marlin Model 990

MARLIN Model 990: autoloader; .22 LR; 18-rd. tubular magazine; 22" barrel; 40¾" overall length; ramp bead hooded front sight, adjustable folding semi-buckhorn rear; American walnut Monte Carlo stock; checkered fluted comb, full pistol grip; cross-bolt safety; receiver grooved for tip-off mount. Introduced, 1979; dropped, 1988. Used value, $90 to $95.

Marlin Model 995

MARLIN Model 995: autoloader; .22 LR; 7-rd. clip magazine; 18" barrel; 36¾" overall length; hooded ramp bead front sight, adjustable folding semi-buckhorn rear; American walnut Monte Carlo stock; full pistol grip; checkered pistol grip, forend; crossbolt safety; receiver grooved for tip-off scope. Introduced, 1979; still produced. Used value, $85 to $95.

Marlin Model 25M

Marlin Midget Magnum

is chambered for .22 WRFM; has 22" barrel, walnut-finished hardwood stock; 7-rd. clip magazine. Introduced, 1983; still in production. Used value, $75 to $85.

    Model 25MB Midget Magnum has same general specs as Model 25M, except has 16¼" barrel, 35¼" overall length, weighs 4¾ lb.; take-down; walnut-finished hardwood stock; grooved for tip-off scope; marketed with iron sights, 4X scope, zippered nylon case. Introduced, 1987; still in production. Used value, $120 to $125.

MARLIN Model 25: bolt-action; .22 short, long, LR; has same basic specs as Model 780, except has walnut-finished hardwood pistol-grip stock, ramp front sight, open rear. Introduced, 1982; still in production. Used value, $65 to $75.

    Model 25M has same general specs as standard model, except

Marlin Model 15Y

MARLIN Model 15Y "Little Buckaroo": bolt-action single-shot; .22 short, long, LR; 16¼" barrel; overall length 33¼"; weighs 4¼ lb.; walnut-finished hardwood stock; adjustable open rear sight, ramp front; marketed with 4x15 scope, mount. Introduced, 1984; dropped, 1986. Used value, $70 to $75.

Marlin Model 9

MARLIN Model 9: autoloader; 9mm Parabellum; 12-rd. magazine; 16½" barrel; wood stock; rubber butt pad; adjustable open rear sight, ramp front with bead, hood; manual hold-open; Garand-type safety; magazine safety; loaded chamber indicator; drilled, tapped for scope mount. Introduced, 1985; still in production. Used value, $180 to $190.

Marlin Model 45 Carbine

MARLIN Model 45 Carbine: has same general specs as the Model 9 Camp Carbine, except is chambered for .45 ACP, has 7-rd. magazine. Introduced, 1986; still in production. Used value, $260 to $280.

MAUSER

Mauser Model 98

MAUSER Standard Model 98: introduced after World War I; commercial version of the German military 98k model; bolt-action repeater; 7mm Mauser, 7.9mm Mauser; 23½" barrel, 5-rd. box magazine; military-style uncheckered European walnut stock; straight military-type bolt handle; adjustable rear sight, blade front; sling swivels; Mauser trademark on receiver ring. Dropped, 1938. Used value, $275 to $325.

Mauser Special British Model

MAUSER Special British Model: bolt-action Type A standard Mauser Model 98 action; 7x57, 8x60, 9x57, 9.3x62mm, .30/06; 23½" barrel; 5-rd. box magazine; hand-checkered pistol-grip Circassian walnut sporting stock; buffalo horn grip cap, forearm tip; Express rear sight, hooded ramp front; military-type trigger; detachable sling swivels. Introduced before WWI; dropped, 1938. Used value, $1250 to $1500.

Mauser Type A Magnum Model

8x51mm, .250-3000. Introduced before WWI; dropped, 1938. Used value, $1500 to $2000.

Type A Magnum Model has the same general specs as standard Type A model, except for heavier magnum action; 10.75x-68mm, .280 Ross, .318 Westley Richards Express, .404 Nitro Express. Introduced before WWI; dropped, 1939. Used value, $1500 to $2000.

MAUSER Type A Short Model: has the same general specs as standard Type A, except for short action, 21½" barrel; 6.5x54,

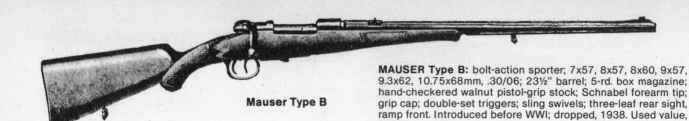

Mauser Type B

MAUSER Type B: bolt-action sporter; 7x57, 8x57, 8x60, 9x57, 9.3x62, 10.75x68mm, .30/06; 23½" barrel; 5-rd. box magazine; hand-checkered walnut pistol-grip stock; Schnabel forearm tip; grip cap; double-set triggers; sling swivels; three-leaf rear sight, ramp front. Introduced before WWI; dropped, 1938. Used value, $1000 to $1250.

Mauser Sporter

Short Model Sporter has the same specs as the standard rifle, except for 19¾" barrel; chambered only for 6.5x54, 8x51 cartridges. Manufactured prior to WWI. Used value, $2000 to $2500.

Sporter Carbine has same specs as standard rifle, except for 19¾" barrel; chambered only for 6.5x54, 6.5x58, 7x57, 8x57, 9x57. Manufactured prior to WWI. Used value, $1250 to $1500.

Military Sporter has the same specs as standard rifle, except for Model 98-type barrel, double-pull trigger, military front sight; chambered for 7x57, 8x57, 9x57. Manufactured prior to WWI. Used value, $700 to $750.

MAUSER Sporter: bolt-action; 6.5x55, 6.5x58, 7x57, 9x57, 9.3x62, 10.75x68; 5-rd. box magazine; 23½" barrel; double-set trigger; tangent-curve rear sight, ramp front; uncheckered European walnut stock, pistol grip, Schnabel-tipped forearm; sling swivels. Manufactured in Germany prior to World War I. Used value, $1000 to $1250.

MAUSER Model EN310: bolt-action, single-shot; .22 LR only; 19¾" barrel; fixed open rear sight, blade front; uncheckered European walnut pistol-grip stock. Manufactured from post World War I era to 1935. Used value, $275 to $350.

Mauser Model ES350

MAUSER Model ES350: bolt-action repeater; .22 LR only; 27½" barrel; target-style walnut stock; hand-checkered pistol grip, forend; grip cap; open micrometer rear sight, ramp front. Introduced in 1925; dropped, 1935. Used value, $400 to $425.

MAUSER Model EL320: bolt-action, single-shot; .22 LR only; 23½" barrel; sporting-style European walnut stock; hand-checkered pistol grip, forearm; grip cap; adjustable open rear sight, bead front; sling swivels. Introduced in 1927; dropped, 1935. Used value, $275 to $300.

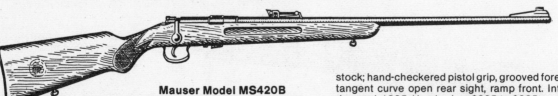

Mauser Model MS420B

MAUSER Model MS420: bolt-action repeater; .22 LR only; 25½" barrel; 5-rd. detachable box magazine; European walnut sporting stock; hand-checkered pistol grip, grooved forearm, sling swivels; tangent curve open rear sight, ramp front. Introduced in 1925; dropped, 1935. Used value, $265 to $285.

Model MS420B has the same general specs as MS420, except for better wood, 25¾" barrel. Introduced in 1935; dropped, 1939. Used value, $350 to $375.

Mauser Model MM410

MAUSER Model MM410: bolt-action repeater; .22 LR only; 23½" barrel; 5-rd. detachable box magazine; European walnut sporting stock; hand-checkered pistol grip; tangent curve open rear sight, ramp front; sling swivels. Introduced in 1926; dropped, 1935. Used value, $325 to $350.

Model MM410B has the same general specs as MM410, except for lightweight sporting stock. Introduced in 1935; dropped, 1939. Used value, $350 to $375.

MAUSER Model DSM34: bolt-action single-shot; .22 LR only; 26" barrel; Model 98 Mauser military-type stock; no checkering; tangent curve open rear sight, barleycorn front; sling swivels. Introduced in 1934; dropped, 1939. Used value, $250 to $300.

MAUSER Model ES340: bolt-action single-shot target rifle; .22 LR only; 25½" barrel; European walnut sporting stock; hand-checkered pistol grip, grooved forearm; tangent curve rear sight, ramp front; sling swivels. Introduced in 1923; dropped, 1935. Used value, $275 to $300.

MAUSER Model KKW: bolt-action single-shot target rifle; .22 LR; 26" barrel; Model 98 Mauser military-type walnut stock; no checkering; tangent curve open rear sight, barleycorn front; sling swivels; improved model was used in training German troops in WWII. Target model introduced in 1935; dropped, 1939. Used value, $325 to $385.

MAUSER Model EX340B: bolt-action single-shot target rifle; replaced ES340; has same general specs, except for 26¾" barrel, uncheckered pistol-grip stock. Introduced in 1935; dropped, 1939. Used value, $335 to $350.

Mauser Model MS350B

MAUSER Model MS350B: bolt-action repeater, replacing Model ES350; same general specs; .22 LR only; 26¾" barrel; 5-rd. detachable box magazine; target stock of European walnut; hand-checkered pistol grip, forearm; barrel grooved for detachable rear sight/scope; micrometer open rear sight, ramp front; sling swivels. Introduced in 1935; dropped, 1939. Used value, $375 to $400.

MAUSER Model ES350B: bolt-action single-shot target rifle; has the same general specs as Model MS350B, except is single-shot. Introduced in 1935; dropped, 1938. Used value, $300 to $325.

Mauser Model 660

Mauser Model 660 Safari

MAUSER Model 660: bolt-action; .243 Win., .25/06, .270 Win., .308 Win., .30/06, 7x57, 7mm Rem. magnum; 24" barrel; short action; adjustable single-stage trigger; push-button safety; no sights; drilled, tapped for scope mounts; checkered European Monte Carlo walnut stock; white line pistol-grip cap, recoil pad. Introduced in 1973; importation discontinued, 1975; still in production. Used value, $750 to $850.

Model 660 Safari has the same basic specs as standard 660, except chambered in .458 Win. magnum, .375 H&H magnum, .338 Win. magnum, 7mm Rem. magnum; 28" barrel; Express rear sight, fixed ramp front. Importation discontinued, 1975; still in production. Used value, $850 to $950.

Model 660 Ultra has same specs as standard model, except for 20.9" barrel. Introduced, 1965; still in production; importation discontinued. Used value, $750 to $850.

MAUSER Model 2000: bolt-action; .270 Win., .308 Win., .30/06; 5-rd. magazine; modified Mauser action; folding leaf rear sight, hooded ramp front; hand-checkered European walnut stock, Monte

Model 660T Carbine has same specs as standard rifle, except for 20.9" barrel, full-length stock. Introduced, 1965; still in production; importation discontinued. Used value, $850 to $950.

Model 660SH has same specs as standard rifle, except for 23-3/5" barrel; chambered for 6.5x68, 7mm Rem. magnum, 7mm SE V Hoff, .300 Win. magnum, 8x68S, 9.3x64. Introduced, 1965; still in production; importation discontinued. Used value, $800 to $900.

Model 660S Deluxe has the same specs as standard rifle, except available in carbine version also, with engraving, gold/silver inlay work, heavy carving on select walnut stock. Special order only; no longer imported. Used value, $2500-plus.

Model 660P Target manufactured in .308 Win., other calibers on special order; short action; adjustable single-stage trigger; 26-3/5" heavy barrel, muzzle brake; 3-rd magazine; dovetail rib for scope mounting; European walnut target stock, with full pistol grip, thumbhole, adjustable cheekpiece, adjustable rubber butt plate. Not imported. Used value, $1000 to $1100.

Carlo comb, cheekpiece; forend tip; sling swivels. Manufactured 1969 to 1971; replaced by Model 3000. Used value, $325 to $350.

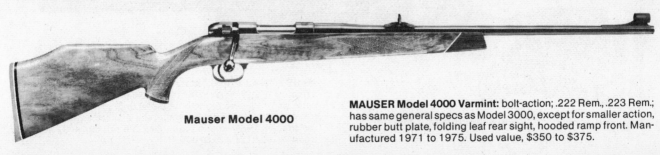

Mauser Model 4000

MAUSER Model 4000 Varmint: bolt-action; .222 Rem., .223 Rem.; has same general specs as Model 3000, except for smaller action, rubber butt plate, folding leaf rear sight, hooded ramp front. Manufactured 1971 to 1975. Used value, $350 to $375.

MAUSER Model 10 Varminter: bolt-action; .22-250 only; 24" heavy barrel; no sights; drilled, tapped for scope mounts; externally adjustable trigger; hammer-forged barrel; hand-checkered European walnut Monte Carlo pistol-grip stock; 5-rd. box magazine. Introduced in 1973; importation discontinued, 1975; still in production. Used value, $375 to $400.

Mauser Model 3000

MAUSER Model 3000: bolt-action; .243 Win., .270 Win., .308 Win., .30/06, .375 H&H magnum, 7mm Rem. magnum; 22" barrel in standard calibers, 26" in magnum; no sights; drilled, tapped for scope mounts; sliding safety; fully adjustable trigger; hand-checkered, European walnut, Monte Carlo stock; white line spacer on pistol-grip cap, recoil pad. Left-hand action at added cost. Introduced in 1973; dropped, 1975. Used values: standard calibers, $400 to $425; left-hand action, $425 to $450; magnums, $475 to $500; left-hand magnums, $500 to $525.

MAUSER Model 77: bolt-action; .243, 6.5x57, 7x64, .308, .30/06; 24" barrel; ramp front sight, open adjustable rear; oil-finished European walnut stock; palm-swell pistol grip, Bavarian cheekpiece, recoil pad; detachable 3-rd. magazine; same trigger system as Model 66. Introduced, 1981; no longer imported. Used values: half stock, $900 to $950; full-length stock, $1000 to $1050.

Model 77 Magnum has same specs as standard Model 77 except has 26" barrel; chambered for 7mm Rem. magnum, 6.5x68, .300 Win. magnum, 9.3x62, 9.3x64, 8x68S. Used value, $1000 to $1050.

Model 77 Big Game version has same specs as magnum model, except is chambered for .375 H&H, .458 Win. magnum. Used value, $1100 to $1200.

Mauser Model 66

Mauser Model 66S Magnum

MAUSER Model 66: bolt-action; 5.6x61, .243, 6.5x57, .270, 7x64, .308 Win., .30/06, 9.3x62; 24" barrel; hooded ramp front sight, Williams open adjustable rear; oil-finished European walnut stock; rosewood pistol-grip cap, forend sling swivels, Pachmayr recoil pad; interchangeable barrels within caliber groups; double-set or single trigger interchangeable. Manufactured in West Germany by Mauser. Introduced, 1981; no longer imported. Used values: standard calibers, $900 to $950; Model 66S with 21" barrel, $950 to $975; Model 66SM, with single-set trigger, special wood, finish, $1250 to $1300.

Model 66S Magnum has same general specs as standard model, except for 26" barrel, chambered for 7mm Rem. magnum, 6.5x68, .300 Win. magnum, 7mm SE v. H, .300 Weatherby magnum, 9.3x64, 8x68S. Used value, $1100 to $1150.

Model 66S Big Game version has same specs as standard Model 66 except for 26" barrel, chambering for .375 H&H magnum, .458 Win. magnum. Used value, $1400 to $1450.

Mauser Model 66 SP Match

MAUSER Model 66 SP Match: bolt-action; .308 Win.; 3-rd. magazine; 27½" barrel, muzzle brake; no sights; match design European walnut stock; thumbhole pistol grip, spring-loaded cheekpiece, Morgan adjustable recoil pad; adjustable match trigger. Introduced, 1981; still in production but not currently imported. Used value, $1250 to $1300.

MOSSBERG

Mossberg Model K

MOSSBERG Model K: take-down slide-action repeater; hammerless; .22 short, long, LR; tube magazine holds 14 LR, 16 long, 20 short cartridges; 22" barrel; unchecked straight-grip walnut stock, grooved slide handle; open rear sight, bead front. Introduced in 1922; dropped, 1931. Used value, $125 to $135.

Mossberg Model L

MOSSBERG Model L: take-down, single-shot; .22 short, long, LR; Martini-design falling-block lever-action; 24" barrel; unchecked walnut pistol-grip stock; forearm; open rear sight, bead front. Introduced in 1929; dropped, 1932. Used value, $200 to $225.

MOSSBERG Model M: has same specs as Mossberg Model K, except for 24" octagonal barrel, pistol-grip stock. Introduced in 1928; dropped, 1931. Used value, $135 to $150.

MOSSBERG Model B: single-shot, take-down; .22 short, long, LR; 22" barrel; unchecked pistol-grip walnut stock. Introduced in 1930; dropped, 1932. Used value, $75 to $85.

MOSSBERG Model R: bolt-action repeater; take-down; .22 short, long, LR; 24" barrel; tube magazine; unchecked pistol-grip stock; open rear sight, bead front. Introduced in 1930; dropped, 1932. Used value, $85 to $95.

MOSSBERG Model 10: bolt-action, take-down, single-shot; .22 short, long, LR; 22" barrel, unchecked walnut pistol-grip stock, swivels, sling; open rear sight, bead front. Introduced in 1933; dropped, 1935. Used value, $60 to $65.

MOSSBERG Model 20: bolt-action, take-down, single-shot; .22 short, long, LR; 24" barrel; unchecked pistol-grip stock, forearm with finger grooves; open rear sight, bead front. Introduced in 1933; dropped, 1935. Used value, $70 to $75.

MOSSBERG Model 30: bolt-action, take-down, single-shot; .22 short, long, LR; 24" barrel; unchecked pistol-grip stock, grooved forearm; rear peep sight, hooded ramp bead front. Introduced in 1933; dropped, 1935. Used value, $65 to $75.

MOSSBERG Model 40: bolt-action, take-down repeater; has same general specs as Model 30, except for tube magazine with capacity of 16 LR, 18 long, 22 short cartridges. Introduced in 1933; dropped, 1935. Used value, $75 to $85.

MOSSBERG Model 14: bolt-action, take-down, single-shot; .22 short, long, LR; 24" barrel; unchecked pistol-grip stock, semi-beavertail forearm; rear peep sight, hooded ramp front; sling swivels. Introduced in 1934; dropped, 1935. Used value, $65 to $70.

MOSSBERG Model 34: bolt-action, take-down, single-shot; .22 short, long, LR; 24" barrel; unchecked pistol-grip stock with semi-beavertail forearm; rear peep sight, hooded ramp front. Introduced in 1934; dropped, 1935. Used value, $60 to $65.

MOSSBERG Model 44: bolt-action, take-down, repeater; .22 short, long, LR; 24" barrel; tube magazine holding 16 LR, 18 long, 22 short cartridges; unchecked walnut pistol-grip stock, semi-beavertail forearm; rear peep sight, hooded ramp front; sling swivels. Introduced in 1934; dropped, 1935. Used value, $100 to $125.

MOSSBERG Model 25: bolt-action, take-down, single-shot; .22 short, long, LR; 24" barrel; unchecked pistol-grip stock, semi-beavertail forearm; rear peep sight, hooded ramp front; sling swivels. Introduced in 1935; dropped, 1936. Used value, $75 to $85.

Model 26A is the same as Model 25, except for minor improvements, including better wood and finish. Introduced in 1936; dropped, 1938. Used value, $85 to $95.

Mossberg Model L42A

Mossberg Model 42C

MOSSBERG Model 42: bolt-action, take-down, repeater; .22 short, long, LR; 7-rd. detachable box magazine; 24" barrel; unchecked walnut pistol-grip stock; receiver peep sight, open rear sight, hooded ramp front; sling swivels. Introduced in 1935; dropped, 1937. Used value, $75 to $85.

Model 42A has same general specs as Model 42, with only minor upgrading. Introduced in 1937 to replace dropped Model 42; dropped, 1938. Used value, $85 to $95.

Model L42A is the same as Model 42A, but with left-handed action. Introduced in 1938; dropped, 1941. Used value, $95 to $100.

Model 42B has same general specs as Model 42A with minor design improvements and replaced the latter; had micrometer peep sight, with open rear; 5-rd. detachable box magazine. Introduced in 1938; dropped, 1941. Used value, $75 to $80.

Model 42C has same specs as Model 42B, except it is sans rear peep sight. Used value, $65 to $70.

Model 42M is updated version of Model 42, replacing discontinued models. Has 23" barrel; .22 short, long, LR; 7-rd. detachable box magazine; two-piece Mannlicher-type stock with pistol-grip, cheekpiece; micrometer receiver peep sight, open rear sight, hooded ramp front; sling swivels. Introduced in 1940; dropped, 1950. Used value, $70 to $75.

Model 42MB has the same specs as Model 42M, except no cheekpiece; made specifically for Great Britain, British proofmarks. Produced only during World War II. Some collector value. Used value, $125 to $145.

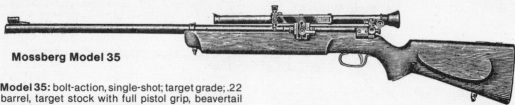

Mossberg Model 35

MOSSBERG Model 35: bolt-action, single-shot; target grade; .22 LR only; 26" barrel, target stock with full pistol grip, beavertail forearm; micrometer rear peep sight; hooded ramp front; sling swivels. Introduced in 1935; dropped, 1937. Used value, $125 to $145.

Model 35A: bolt-action, single-shot; .22 LR only; 26" heavy barrel; unchecked target stock with cheekpiece, full pistol grip; micrometer rear peep sight, hood front; sling swivels. Introduced in 1937; dropped, 1938. Used value, $125 to $145.

Model 35A-LS is the same as standard Model 35A, except for substitution of Lyman 17A front sight, Lyman No. 57 rear. Used value, $130 to $150.

Model 35B is not a variation of Model 35, as might plausibly be expected. Instead, it has the same specs as the Model 44B, but is single-shot. Introduced in 1938; dropped, 1940. Used value, $90 to $95.

Mossberg Model 45

MOSSBERG Model 45: bolt-action, take-down, repeater; .22 short, long, LR; tube magazine holds 15 LR, 18 long, 22 short cartridges; unchecked pistol-grip stock; receiver peep sight, open rear, hooded ramp front; sling swivels. Introduced in 1935; dropped, 1937. Used value, $75 to $85.

Model 45C has same specs as standard Model 45, except that it has no sights; designed for use only with scope sight. Used value, $65 to $75.

Model 45A is improved version of discontinued Model 45, with minor design variations. Introduced in 1937; dropped, 1938. Used value, $75 to $85.

Model 45AC is the same as the Model 45A, but without receiver peep sight. Used value, $65 to $75.

Model L45A is the same as the Model 45A, except for having a left-hand action. Introduced in 1937; dropped, 1938. Used value, $85 to $95.

Model 45B has same general specs as Model 45A, but with open rear sight. Introduced in 1938; dropped, 1940. Used value, $65 to $75.

Mossberg Model 46

Mossberg Model 46B

MOSSBERG Model 46: bolt-action, take-down repeater; .22 short, long, LR; 26" barrel; tube magazine holds 15 LR, 18 long, 22 short cartridges; unchecked walnut pistol-grip stock with cheekpiece, beavertail forearm; micrometer rear peep sight; hooded ramp front; sling swivels. Introduced in 1935; dropped, 1937. Used value, $75 to $85.

Model 46C has same specs as standard Model 45, except for heavier barrel. Used value, $85 to $90.

Model 46A has virtually the same specs as discontinued Model 46, but with minor design improvements, detachable sling swivels.

Introduced in 1937; dropped, 1938. Used value, $85 to $95.

Model 46AC differs from Model 46A only in that it has open rear sight instead of micrometer peep sight. Used value, $65 to $70.

Model 46A-LS is the same as the Model 46A, except it is equipped with factory-supplied Lyman No. 57 receiver sight. Used value, $90 to $110.

Model L-46A-LS differs from model 46A-LS only in fact that it has left-hand action. Used value, $90 to $110.

Model 46B is updated version of Model 46A, but with receiver peep and open rear sights. Introduced in 1938; dropped, 1940. Used value, $75 to $85.

Model 46BT differs from Model 46B only in the fact that it has a heavier barrel, target-styled stock. Introduced in 1938; dropped, 1939. Used value, $85 to $90.

Model 46M dates back to design of original Model 46, incorporating many of changes in discontinued models. Has 23" barrel; .22 short, long, LR; tube magazine holds 15 LR, 18 long, 22 short cartridges; two-piece Mannlicher-type stock with pistol grip, cheek-piece; micrometer receiver peep sight, open rear, hooded ramp front; sling swivels. Introduced in 1940; dropped, 1952. Used value, $85 to $90.

Mossberg Model 43B

MOSSBERG Model 43: bolt-action repeater; .22 LR only; adjustable trigger, speed lock; 26" barrel; 7-rd. detachable box magazine; target stock with cheekpiece, full pistol grip; beavertail forend; Lyman No. 57 rear sight, selective aperture front; adjustable front swivel. Introduced in 1937; dropped, 1938. Used value, $125 to $135.

Model L43 is the same as standard Model 43, except it was made with left-hand action. Used value, $135 to $145.

Model 43B is not styled after standard Model 43, but has same specs as Model 44B, except for substitution of Lyman No. 57 receiver sight, Lyman No. 17A front sight. Introduced in 1938; dropped, 1939. Used value, $115 to $125.

Mossberg Model 44B

MOSSBERG Model 44B: bolt-action repeater; target configuration; bears little resemblance to standard Model 44; .22 LR only; 26" heavy barrel; 7-rd. detachable box magazine; walnut target stock with cheekpiece, full pistol grip; beavertail forearm; adjustable sling swivels; micrometer receiver peep sight, hooded front. Introduced in 1938; dropped, 1943. Used value, $85 to $95.

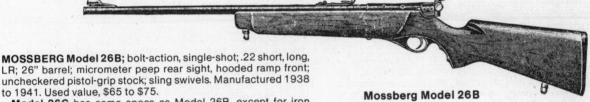

MOSSBERG Model 26B; bolt-action, single-shot; .22 short, long, LR; 26" barrel; micrometer peep rear sight, hooded ramp front; uncheckered pistol-grip stock; sling swivels. Manufactured 1938 to 1941. Used value, $65 to $75.

Model 26C has same specs as Model 26B, except for iron sights, no sling swivels. Used value, $55 to $60.

Mossberg Model 26B

Mossberg Model 50

MOSSBERG Model 50: take-down autoloader; .22 LR only; 24" barrel; 15-rd. tube magazine in butt stock; uncheckered walnut pistol-grip stock; finger grooves in grip; open rear sight, hooded ramp front. Introduced in 1939; dropped, 1942. Used value, $75 to $85.

Mossberg Model 51

MOSSBERG Model 51: has the same general specs as Model 50, except for addition of receiver peep sight, sling swivels, cheekpiece stock, beavertail forearm. Made only in 1939. Used value, $85 to $95.

Model 51M has the same specs as Model 51, except for substitution of two-piece Mannlicher-style stock, 20" barrel. Introduced in 1946; dropped, 1949. Used value, $100 to $115.

Mossberg Model 51M

Mossberg Model 44US

MOSSBERG Model 44US: bolt-action repeater; redesign of Model 44B, designed primarily for teaching marksmanship to Armed Forces during World War II; .22 LR only; 26" heavy barrel; 7-rd. detachable box magazine; unchecked walnut target stock; sling swivels; micrometer receiver peep sight, hooded front. Introduced in 1943; dropped, 1948. Collector value. Used value, $125 to $145; $25 premium for U.S. Property markings.

Mossberg Model 151M

MOSSBERG Model 151M: take-down autoloader; has same general specs of Model 51M with minor mechanical improvements. The action is removable without tools. Introduced in 1946; drop-

ped, 1958. Used value, $75 to $85.

Model 151K has same general specs as Model 151M, except for 24" barrel; is without peep sight, sling swivels. Unchecked stock has Monte Carlo comb, cheekpiece. Introduced in 1950; dropped, 1951. Used value, $70 to $80.

Mossberg Model 152

MOSSBERG Model 152: autoloading carbine; .22 LR only; 18" barrel; 7-rd. detachable box magazine; Monte Carlo pistol-grip stock; hinged forearm swings down to act as forward handgrip;

MOSSBERG Model 142: bolt-action carbine; .22 short, long, LR; 18" barrel; 7-rd. detachable box magazine; as with Model 152, sling swivels mount on left side of stock, forearm hinges down to act as handgrip; rear peep sight, military-style ramp front. Introduced in 1949; dropped,

sling swivels are mounted on left side; rear peep sight, military-type ramp front. Introduced in 1948; dropped, 1957. Used value, $75 to $85.

Model 152K has same specs as Model 152, except peep sight is replaced by open sight. Introduced in 1950; dropped, 1957. Used value, $70 to $75.

1957. Used value, $75 to $80.

Model 142K has same specs as Model 142, except peep sight is replaced by open sight. Introduced in 1953; dropped, 1957. Used value, $70 to $75.

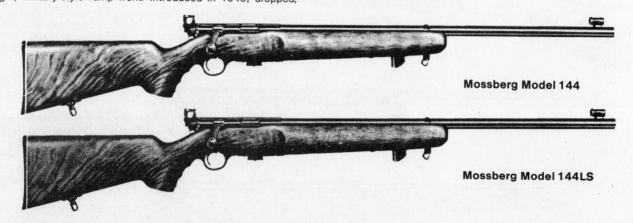

Mossberg Model 144

Mossberg Model 144LS

MOSSBERG Model 144: bolt-action target model; .22 LR only; 26" heavy barrel; 7-rd. detachable box magazine; pistol-grip target stock; adjustable hand stop; beavertail forearm; sling swivels; micrometer receiver peep sight, hooded front. Introduced in 1949; dropped, 1954. Used value, $90 to $110.

Model 144LS has the same specs as Model 144, except for substitution of Lyman No. 57MS receiver peep sight, Lyman No.

17A front. Introduced in 1954; no longer in production. Used value, $110 to $125.

Model 144 Target has same general specs as Standard Model 144, except for 27" round barrel, Lyman 17A hooded front sight with inserts, Mossberg S331 receiver peep sight; target-style American walnut stock; adjustable forend hand stop. Introduced, 1978; dropped, 1985. Used value, $140 to $150.

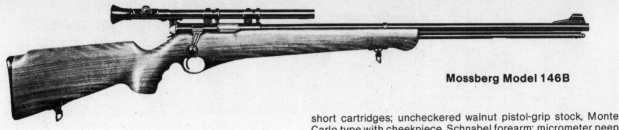

Mossberg Model 146B

MOSSBERG Model 146B: bolt-action, take-down repeater; .22 short, long, LR; 26" barrel; tube magazine holds 20 LR, 23 long, 30 short cartridges; uncheckered walnut pistol-grip stock, Monte Carlo type with cheekpiece, Schnabel forearm; micrometer peep sight, hooded front sight; sling swivels. Introduced in 1949; dropped, 1954. Used value, $75 to $80.

Mossberg Model 140B

MOSSBERG Model 140K: bolt-action repeater; .22 short, long, LR; 7-rd. clip magazine; 24½" barrel; uncheckered walnut pistol-grip stock, Monte Carlo with cheekpiece; open rear sight, bead front; sling swivels. Introduced in 1955; dropped, 1958. Used value, $75 to $85.

Model 140B is target/sporter version of Model 140K; only difference in specs is substitution of peep rear sight, ramp front. Introduced in 1957; dropped, 1958. Used value, $80 to $90.

Mossberg Model 346B

MOSSBERG Model 346K: hammerless bolt-action repeater; .22 short, long, LR; 24" barrel; tube magazine with capacity of 18 LR, 20 long, 25 short cartridges; uncheckered walnut stock with pistol grip, Monte Carlo comb, cheekpiece; open rear sight, bead front; quick-detachable sling swivels. Introduced in 1958; dropped, 1971. Used value, $65 to $70.

Model 346B has same specs as Model 346K, except for hooded ramp front sight, receiver peep with open rear. Introduced in 1958; dropped, 1967. Used value, $70 to $75.

Mossberg Model 320K

MOSSBERG Model 320K: single-shot, hammerless bolt-action; same specs as Model 346K, except single-shot with drop-in loading platform; automatic safety. Introduced in 1958; dropped, 1960. Used value, $50 to $55.

Model 320B, designated by manufacturer as a Boy Scout target model, has the same specs as the Model 340K, except it is single-shot with automatic safety. Introduced in 1960; dropped, 1971. Used value, $75 to $85.

Mossberg Model 340B

MOSSBERG Model 340B: hammerless, bolt-action repeater; target/sporter model is the same as Model 346K, except for clip-type 7-rd. magazine; rear peep sight, hooded ramp front. Introduced in 1958; no longer in production. Used value, $65 to $75.

Model 340K is the same as Model 340B, except for open rear sight, bead front. Introduced in 1958; dropped, 1971. Used value, $65 to $75.

Model 340TR has same general specs as Model 340K, except for smooth bore; rifled and choke adapters screw on muzzle for shooting bullets or shot. Smooth bore was designed for trap shooting with hand trap. Special device fitted barrel to allow shooter to spring trap. Introduced in 1960; dropped, 1962. Used values: $100 to $115; with Model 1A trap installed, $150 to $160.

Model 340M is the same as Model 340K, except for 18½" barrel, Mannlicher-style stock, sling, sling swivels. Introduced in 1970; dropped, 1971. Used value, $75 to $85.

Mossberg Model 342

MOSSBERG Model 342: hammerless bolt-action carbine; .22 short, long, LR; 18" tapered barrel; 7-rd. clip magazine; unchecked walnut Monte Carlo pistol-grip stock; two-position forearm that folds down for rest or handgrip; peep rear sight, bead front; receiver grooved for scope mounts; thumb safety; sling swivels; web sling. Introduced in 1958; no longer in production. Used value, $75 to $85.

Model 342K is the same as Model 342, except with open rear sight. Used value, $65 to $75.

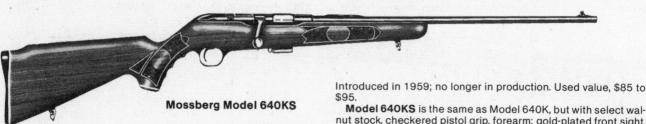

Mossberg Model 350K

MOSSBERG Model 350K: autoloader; .22 high-speed short, long, LR; 23½" barrel; 7-rd. clip magazine; walnut Monte Carlo pistol-grip stock; open rear sight, bead front. Introduced in 1958; dropped, 1971. Used value, $65 to $75.

Mossberg Model 352K

MOSSBERG Model 352: autoloading carbine; .22 short, long, LR; 18" barrel; uncheckered walnut Monte Carlo pistol-grip stock; two-position Tenite forearm extension folds down for rest or handgrip; peep rear sight, bead front; sling swivels, web sling. Introduced in 1958; dropped, 1971. Used value, $65 to $75.

Model 352K is the same as Model 352, except with open rear sight. Used value, $65 to $70.

Mossberg Model 640KS

MOSSBERG Model 640K: hammerless bolt-action; .22 WRFM only; 24" barrel, 5-rd. detachable clip magazine; walnut Monte Carlo pistol-grip stock, with cheekpiece; open rear sight, bead front; sling swivels; impressed checkering on pistol grip, forearm. Introduced in 1959; no longer in production. Used value, $85 to $95.

Model 640KS is the same as Model 640K, but with select walnut stock, checkered pistol grip, forearm; gold-plated front sight, rear sight elevator and trigger. Dropped, 1974. Used value, $95 to $115.

MOSSBERG Model 620K: same as Model 640K, except is single-shot. Introduced in 1958; dropped, 1974. Used value, $65 to $75.

Mossberg Model 351K

Mossberg Model 351C

MOSSBERG Model 351K: autoloading sporter; .22 LR only; 24" barrel; 15-rd. tube magazine in butt stock; walnut Monte Carlo pistol-grip stock; open rear sight, bead front. Introduced in 1960; dropped, 1971. Used value, $65 to $75.

Model 351C carbine is the same as Model 351K, except for 18½" barrel, straight Western-type carbine stock, with barrel band; sling swivels. Introduced in 1965; dropped, 1971. Used value, $70 to $80.

Mossberg Model 400

MOSSBERG Model 400 Palomino: lever-action repeater; .22 short, long, LR; 24" barrel; tube magazine has capacity of 15 LR, 17 long, 20 short cartridges; open notch rear sight adjustable for windage, elevation; bead front; blued finish receiver grooved for scope. Introduced in 1959, dropped, 1963. Used value, $85 to $105.

Model 402 Palomino has same specs as Model 400 except for 18½" or 20" barrel; barrel band on forearm; magazine holds two less rounds in specified .22 rimfire lengths. Manufactured 1961 to 1971. Used value, $90 to $110.

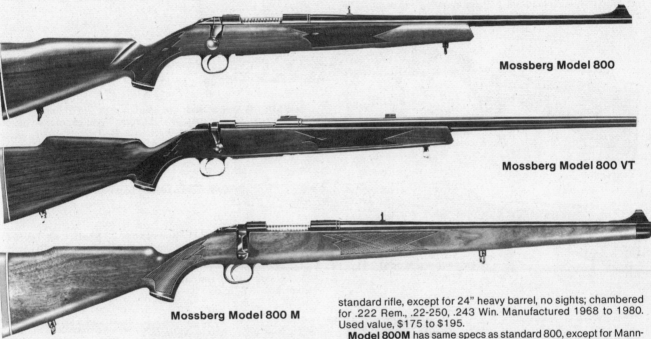

Mossberg Model 800

Mossberg Model 800 VT

Mossberg Model 800 M

MOSSBERG Model 800: bolt-action; .222 Rem., .22-250, .243 Win., .308 Win.; 4-rd. magazine in all but .222; 3 rds. for that caliber; 22" barrel; folding leaf rear sight, ramp front; checkered pistol-grip Monte Carlo stock, forearm; cheekpiece; sling swivels. Manufactured 1967 to 1980. Used value, $175 to 195.

Model 800VT for varmint/target shooting, has same specs as standard rifle, except for 24" heavy barrel, no sights; chambered for .222 Rem., .22-250, .243 Win. Manufactured 1968 to 1980. Used value, $175 to $195.

Model 800M has same specs as standard 800, except for Mannlicher-type stock, flat bolt handle, 20" barrel; chambered for .22-250, .243 Win., .308 Win. Manufactured 1969 to 1972. Used value, $250 to $265.

Model 800D Super Grade has same general specs as standard model, except for roll-over comb, cheekpiece; rosewood forend tip, pistol-grip cap; chambered for .22-250, .243 Win., .308 Win. Manufactured 1970 to 1973. Used value, $275 to $300.

Mossberg Model 810

MOSSBERG Model 810: bolt-action; .270 Win., .30/06, 7mm Rem. magnum, .338 Win. magnum; 22" barrel in standard calibers, 24" in magnum chamberings; detachable box magazine or internal magazine, hinged floorplate; 4-rd. magazine in standard calibers, 3 rds. for magnums; leaf rear sight, ramp front; checkered pistol-grip stock, forearm; Monte Carlo comb, cheekpiece; pistol grip cap, sling swivels. Manufactured 1970 to 1980. Used values: standard calibers, $200 to $225; magnum calibers, $225 to $250.

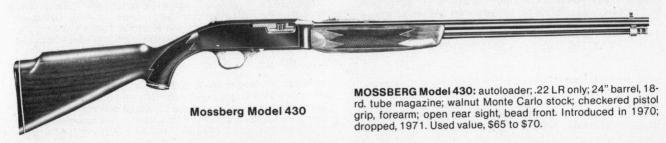

Mossberg Model 430

MOSSBERG Model 430: autoloader; .22 LR only; 24" barrel, 18-rd. tube magazine; walnut Monte Carlo stock; checkered pistol grip, forearm; open rear sight, bead front. Introduced in 1970; dropped, 1971. Used value, $65 to $70.

Mossberg Model 432

MOSSBERG Model 432: autoloading carbine; same as Model 430, except for uncheckered straight-grip carbine stock, forearm; barrel band; sling swivels. 15-rd. tube magazine. Introduced in 1970; dropped, 1971. Used value, $70 to $75.

MOSSBERG Model 321K: bolt-action, single-shot; .22 short, long, LR; 24" barrel; hardwood stock with walnut finish; cheekpiece; checkered pistol grip, forearm; hammerless bolt-action with drop-in loading platform; automatic safety; adjustable open rear sight, ramp front. Introduced in 1972; no longer in production.

Used value $50 to $55.
   Model 321B is the same as Model 321K, except with S330 peep sight with ¼-minute click adjustments. Dropped, 1976. Used value, $55 to $65.

Mossberg Model 333

MOSSBERG Model 333: autoloader; .22 LR; 20" barrel; 15-rd. tubular magazine; open rear sight, ramp front; checkered pistol-grip Monte Carlo stock, forearm; barrel band; sling swivels. Manufactured 1972 to 1973. Used value, $65 to $75.

Mossberg Model 341

MOSSBERG Model 341: bolt-action; .22 short, long, LR; 24" barrel; 7-rd. clip magazine; walnut Monte Carlo stock with checkered pistol grip, forearm; plastic butt plate with white line spacer; open rear sight adjustable for windage, elevation; bead post front; sliding side safety. Introduced in 1972; dropped, 1976. Used value, $65 to $75.

Mossberg Model 353

MOSSBERG Model 353: autoloader; updated version of Model 352K; specs are primarily the same; pistol grip, forearm are checkered; receiver is grooved for scope mount. Introduced in 1972; no longer in production. Used value, $75 to $85.

Mossberg Model 472 Carbine

   Model 472 Rifle has same specs as carbine except for 24" barrel, 5-rd. magazine; pistol-grip stock only. Manufactured 1974 to 1976. Used value, $150 to $165.
   Model 472 Brush Gun has same specs as 472 Carbine, except for 18" barrel; .30-30 only, 5-rd. magazine; straight stock. Manufactured 1974 to 1976. Used value $160 to $165.
   Model 472 "1 of 5000" has same specs as 472 Brush Gun, except for etched frontier scenes on receiver; gold-plated trigger; brass saddle ring, butt plate, barrel bands; select walnut stock, forearm; limited edition, numbered 1 through 5000. Manufactured 1974. Used value, $300 to $350.

MOSSBERG Model 472 Carbine: lever-action; .30-30, .35 Rem.; 6-rd. tubular magazine; 20" barrel; open rear sight, ramp front; pistol grip or straight stock; barrel band on forearm; sling swivels on pistol-grip style, saddle ring on straight-stock model. Manufactured 1972 to 1980. Used value, $145 to $165.

MOSSBERG Model 377: autoloader; .22 LR; 15-rd. tubular magazine; advertised as the Plinkster; 20" barrel; moulded polystyrene thumbhole stock, roll-over cheekpiece; Monte Carlo comb; no open sights, comes with 4X scope mounted. Introduced, 1977; dropped, 1985. Used value, $70 to $75.

MOSSBERG Model RM-7: bolt-action; .30/06, 7mm Rem. magnum; 22", 24" barrels; gold bead front sight on ramp, adjustable folding leaf rear; drilled, tapped for scope mounts; classic-style checkered pistol-grip stock of American walnut; rotary magazine; 3-position bolt safety; sling swivel studs. Introduced in 1978; drop-

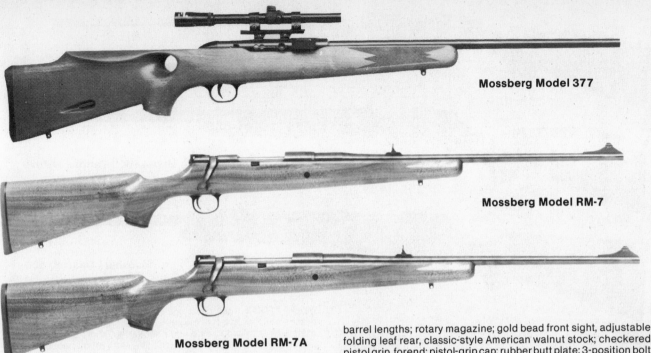

Mossberg Model 377

Mossberg Model RM-7

Mossberg Model RM-7A

ped, 1981. Used value, $350 to $400, quite rare.
Model RM-7 A: bolt-action; .30/06, 7mm Rem. magnum; 22", 24"

barrel lengths; rotary magazine; gold bead front sight, adjustable folding leaf rear, classic-style American walnut stock; checkered pistol grip, forend; pistol-grip cap; rubber butt plate; 3-position bolt safety, sling swivel studs; drilled, tapped for scope mounts. Introduced, 1978; dropped, 1981. Used values, $350 to $400, quite rare.

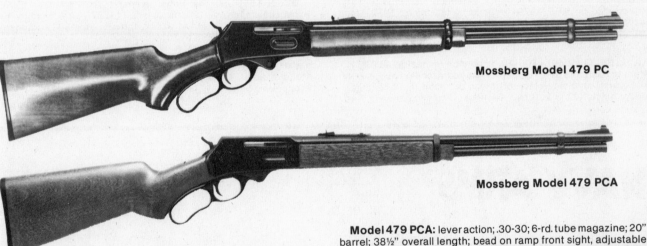

Mossberg Model 479 PC

Mossberg Model 479 PCA

MOSSBERG Model 479 PC: lever-action; .30-30, .35 Rem.; 6-rd. tube magazine; 20" barrel; ramp front sight, elevation-adjustable rear, American walnut stock, fluted comb; composition butt plate; pistol-grip cap, hammer-block safety; side ejection. Introduced, 1978; dropped, 1981. Used value, $150 to $160.
Model 479 SC has same specs as 479 PC, except has straight-grip stock. Introduced, 1978; dropped, 1981. Used value, $150 to $160.

Model 479 PCA: lever action; .30-30; 6-rd. tube magazine; 20" barrel; 38½" overall length; bead on ramp front sight, adjustable open rear; walnut-finished hardwood stock; hammer-block safety; rebounding hammer, trigger built into cocking lever, blued finish; right-side ejection port. Reintroduced, 1983; no longer in production. Used value, $145 to $155.
Model 479RR Roy Rogers has same specs as 479 PCA, except has 5-rd. magazine; 18" barrel; 36½" overall length; gold bead on ramp front sight, adjustable semi-buckhorn rear; American walnut stock; gold-finished trigger, barrel bands; Rogers' signature, American eagle, stars and stripes etched in receiver. 5000 guns produced only in 1983. Used value, $300 to $325.

Mossberg Model 380

MOSSBERG Model 380: autoloader; .22 LR; 15-rd. tubular magazine in stock; 20" tapered barrel; bead front sight, open rear; walnut-finished hardwood stock; black plastic butt plate; receiver grooved for scope mounting. Introduced, 1981; no longer produced. Used value, $65 to $75.

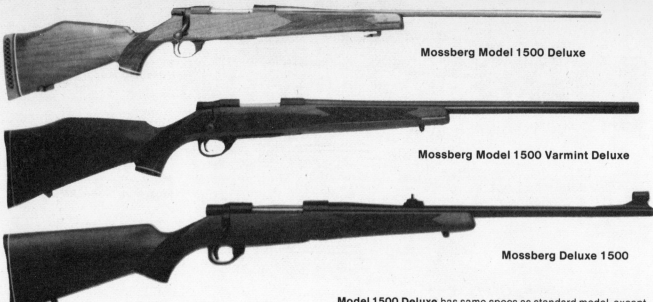

Mossberg Model 1500 Deluxe

Mossberg Model 1500 Varmint Deluxe

Mossberg Deluxe 1500

MOSSBERG Model 1500 Mountaineer: bolt-action; .222, .223, .22-250, .243, .25/06, .270, .30/06, .308, 7mm Rem. magnum, .300 Win. magnum, .338 Win. magnum; 22", 24" barrel lengths; weighs 7½ lb.; American walnut stock; Monte Carlo comb, cheekpiece; cut checkering; open round-notch adjustable rear sight, hooded ramp gold bead front; single-unit trigger guard/magazine box; hinged floor plate; swivel studs; composition butt plate; magnums have rubber recoil pad. Made in Japan. Originally marketed by S&W. Introduced by S&W, 1979; dropped by Mossberg, 1987. Used values: standard calibers, $240 to $250; magnums, $250 to $260.

MOSSBERG Model 1700LS: bolt-action; marketed as Classic Hunter; has same general specs as standard model 1500, except has classic-style stock; tapered forend, Schnabel tip; hand-checkering; black rubber butt pad; flush-mounted sling swivels; 4-rd.

Model 1500 Deluxe has same specs as standard model, except comes sans sights; has engine-turned bolt; floor plate is decorated with scrollwork; skip-line checkering; sling, swivels, swivel posts included; magnum models have vent, recoil pad. Used values: standard calibers, $260 to $275; magnums, $265 to $280.
Model 1500 Varmint Deluxe has same specs as standard model, except has heavy 22" barrel, fully adjustable trigger; chambered for .222, .22-250, .223; skip-line checkering; quick-detachable swivels. Originally marketed by S&W. Introduced, 1982; dropped by Mossberg, 1987. Used value, $300 to $325.
Model 1550 has the same general specs as Model 1500, except has removable box magazine; .243, .270, .30/06 only; with or without sights. Made in Japan. Introduced, 1986; dropped, 1987. Used value, $285 to $315.

magazine; jeweled bolt body; chambered for .243, .270, .30/06. Made in Japan. Originally marketed by S&W. Introduced, 1983; dropped by Mossberg, 1987. Used value, $325 to $350.

NAVY ARMS

Navy Arms Model 66

NAVY ARMS Model 66: lever-action; reproduction of Winchester Model 1866; .38 Special and .44-40; polished brass frame, butt

plate, other parts blued; full-length tube magazine; walnut straight-grip stock, forearm; barrel band; open leaf rear sight, blade front. Introduced in 1966; no longer imported. Used value, $200 to $235.
  Model 66 Carbine has same specs as Model 66 rifle, except for 19" barrel, 10-rd. magazine; carbine forearm, barrel band. Introduced, 1967; no longer in production. Used value, $185 to $195.
  Model 66 Trapper has same specs as carbine version, except for 16½" barrel, magazine holds two rounds less. Used value, $185 to $195.

NAVY ARMS Model 1873: lever-action; .357 magnum, .44-40; barrels 24" octagon, 20" round carbine, 16½" trapper style; walnut stock, forearm; step adjustable rear sight, blade front; designed after the Winchester '73 model; finish is blue, case hardened or

nickel, last in .44-40 only; sliding dust cover, lever latch. Manufactured in Italy; imported by Navy Arms. Introduced in 1973; no longer imported. Used value, $200 to $225.
  Model 1873 Carbine has same specs as rifle, except for 19"

Navy Arms Model 1873 Carbine

Navy Arms Revolving Carbine

Navy Arms Rolling Block Baby Carbine

**Navy Arms Rolling Block
Buffalo Rifle**

round barrel, 10-rd. magazine, carbine forearm, barrel band. Introduced, 1973; no longer imported. Used value, $200 to $225.

Model 1873 Trapper has same specs as carbine, except for 16½" barrel, 8-rd. magazine. Used value, $215 to $235.

NAVY ARMS Revolving Carbine: .357 magnum, .44-40, .45 Colt; 6-rd. cylinder; 20" barrel; action based on Remington Model 1874 revolver; open rear sight, blade front; straight-grip stock, brass butt plate, trigger guard. Manufactured in Italy. Introduced, 1968; no longer imported. Used value, $185 to $200.

NAVY ARMS Baby Carbine: single-shot; .22 LR, .22 Hornet, .357 magnum, .44-40; 20" octagonal barrel, 22" round barrel; case-hardened frame; brass trigger guard; based on Remington rolling-block action; open rear sight; blade front; unchecked straight-grip stock, forearm; brass butt plate. Introduced, 1968; no longer imported by Navy. Used value, $160 to $170.

Rolling Block Buffalo Rifle has same general design as Baby Carbine except is larger; .444 Marlin, .45-70, .50-70; 26", 30" half or full octagonal barrel; open rear sight, blade front; brass barrel band. Introduced, 1971; still in production only in .45-70. Used value, $275 to $300.

Rolling Block Creedmore Model has same specs as Buffalo

Rifle, except for 26", 28", 30" heavy half or full octagon barrel; .45-70, .45-90; currently available only in .45-70; Creedmore tang peep sight. Used value, $425 to $450.

Rolling Block Buffalo Carbine has same specs as Buffalo Rifle, except for 18" barrel. Used value, $250 to $275.

NAVY ARMS Martini: single-shot; .444 Marlin, .45-70; 26", 30" half or full octagon barrel; Creedmore tang peep sight, open middle sight, blade front; checkered pistol-grip stock, Schnabel for-

end, cheekpiece. Introduced, 1972; importation dropped, 1978. Used value, $350 to $400.

Navy Arms .45-70 Rifle

open rear sight, ramp front; hand-checkered Monte Carlo stock. Introduced, 1973; no longer in production. Used value, $300 to $325.

.45-70 Mauser Carbine has same specs as rifle, except for 18" barrel, straight stock. Used value, $300 to $325.

NAVY ARMS .45-70 Mauser: bolt-action; .45-70 Government; 3-rd. magazine; 24", 26" barrel; built on Siamese Mauser action;

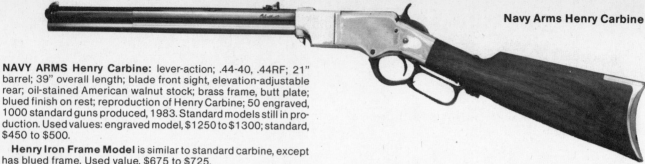

Navy Arms Henry Carbine

NAVY ARMS Henry Carbine: lever-action; .44-40, .44RF; 21" barrel; 39" overall length; blade front sight, elevation-adjustable rear; oil-stained American walnut stock; brass frame, butt plate; blued finish on rest; reproduction of Henry Carbine; 50 engraved, 1000 standard guns produced, 1983. Standard models still in production. Used values: engraved model, $1250 to $1300; standard, $450 to $500.

Henry Iron Frame Model is similar to standard carbine, except has blued frame. Used value, $675 to $725.

Henry Military Model is similar to Henry Carbine, except has different type rear sight, sling swivels. Used value, $475 to $525.

Henry Trapper Model is same as standard carbine, except has 16½" barrel, measures 34½" overall. Used value, $475 to $525.

NOBLE

NOBLE Model 33: slide-action hammerless repeater; .22 LR, long, short; 24" barrel; tube magazine holds 15 LR, 17 long, 21 short cartridges; Tenite stock, grooved wood slide handle; open rear sight, bead front. Introduced in 1949; dropped, 1953. Used value, $65 to $75.

Model 33A has the same general specs as the Model 33, except that the stock and slide handle are of hardwood. Introduced in 1953, as replacement for Model 33. Dropped, 1955. Used value, $75 to $80.

Noble Model 236

NOBLE Model 236: slide-action hammerless repeater; .22 LR, long, short, 24" barrel; tube magazine holds 15 LR, 17 long, 21 short cartridges; hardwood pistol-grip stock, grooved wood slide handle; open rear sight, ramp front. Introduced in 1951; dropped, 1973. Used value, $75 to $80.

Noble Model 10

NOBLE Model 10: bolt-action, single-shot; .22 LR, long, short; 24" barrel; unchecked hardwood pistol-grip stock; open rear sight, bead front. Introduced in 1955; dropped, 1958. Used value, $40 to $50.

Noble Model 20

NOBLE Model 20: bolt-action, single-shot; same general specs as Model 10, except for 22" barrel, walnut pistol-grip stock. Introduced in 1958; dropped, 1963. Used value, $40 to $50.

Noble Model 222

NOBLE MODEL 222: bolt-action, single-shot; .22 LR, long, short. Barrel, receiver milled as integral unit; unchecked hardwood pistol-grip stock; interchangeable peep and V-notch rear sight, ramp front; scope mounting base. Introduced in 1958; dropped, 1971. Used value, $40 to $55.

Noble Model 275

NOBLE Model 275: lever-action, hammerless; .22 LR, long, short; 24" barrel; tube magazine holds 15 LR, 17 long, 21 short cartridges; unchecked hardwood full pistol-grip stock; open rear sight, ramp front. Introduced in 1958; dropped, 1971. Used value, $75 to $85.

PARKER-HALE

Parker-Hale 1200 Super

PARKER-HALE 1200 Super: bolt-action; .22-250, .243 Win., 6mm Rem., .25/06, .270 Win., 6.5x55mm, 7x57, 7x64, .30/06, .308 Win., 8mm, 7mm Rem. magnum, .300 Win. magnum; 4-rd. magazine; 24" barrel; Mauser-design action; folding open rear sight, hooded ramp front; checkered European walnut pistol-grip stock; Monte Carlo cheekpiece; recoil pad; sling swivels. Introduced, 1968; still imported. Manufactured in England. Used value, $275 to $295.

1200 Super Magnum has same specs as 1200 Super except for 3-rd. magazine; chambered for 7mm Rem. magnum, .300 Win. magnum. Introduced, 1969; dropped, 1983. Used value, $300 to $325.

1200P Presentation has same general specs as 1200 Super, sans sights; has engraved action, floor plate, trigger guard; detachable sling swivels; chambered for .243 Win., .30/06. Manufactured, 1969 to 1975. Used value, $350 to $400.

1200V Varminter has same general specs as 1200 Super, sans sights; 24" heavy barrel; chambered for .22-250, 6mm Rem., .25/06, .243 Win. Introduced, 1969; dropped, 1983. Used value, $295 to $315.

Model 1200 Super Clip has the same specs as Model 1200 Super, except has detachable steel box magazine, steel trigger guard; optional set trigger. Made in England. Introduced, 1984; still imported by Precision Sports, Inc. Used value, $500 to $550; with set trigger, $525 to $575.

PARKER-HALE Model 1000: Has same general specs as Model 1200 Super, except has standard satin-finished Monte Carlo walnut stock; no rosewood grip or forend caps; sling swivels; checkered butt plate; optional set trigger. Made in England. Introduced, 1984; still imported by Precision Sports, Inc. Used value, $325 to $375; with set trigger, $350 to $400.

Parker-Hale Model 2100

PARKER-HALE Model 2100: bolt-action; marketed as Midland Rifle; .22-250, .243, 6mm, .270, 6.5x55, 7x57, 7x64, .308, .30/06; 22" barrel; overall length 43"; weighs 7 lb.; flip-up open rear sight, hooded post front; European walnut stock; cut-checkered pistol grip, forend; sling swivels; Mauser-type action; twin front locking lugs; rear safety lug; claw extractor; hinged floor plate; adjustable single-stage trigger; slide-type safety. Made in England. Introduced, 1984; still imported by Precision Sports. Used value, $250 to $275.

Parker-Hale Model 81 Classic

PARKER-HALE Model 81 Classic: bolt-action; .22-250, .243, 6mm Rem., .270, 6.5x55, 7x57, 7x64, .308, .30/06, .300 Win. magnum, 7mm Rem. magnum; 4-rd. magazine; 24" barrel; overall length 44½"; weighs 7¾ lb.; classic-style European walnut stock; oil-finish; hand-cut checkering; rosewood grip cap; no sights; drilled, tapped for sights, scope mounts; Mauser-style action; Oberndorf-style trigger guard; hinged floor plate; rubber butt pad; quick-detachable sling swivels; optional set trigger. Made in England. Introduced, 1984; still imported by Precision Sports. Used value, $450 to $475.

Model 81 African has same specs as Classic Model 81, except is chambered for .300 H&H, .308 Norma magnum, .375 H&H, 9.3x62; adjustable trigger; barrel band front swivel; African Express rear sight; engraved receiver; checkered pistol grip, forend; solid butt pad. Made in England. Introduced, 1986; still imported. Used value, $725 to $775.

Parker-Hale Model 1100 Lightweight

PARKER-HALE Model 1100 Lightweight: bolt-action; similar to Model 81 Classic, except has slim barrel, hollow bolt handle; alloy trigger guard, floor plate; Monte Carlo stock has Schnabel forend, hand-cut checkering; adjustable Williams rear sight, hooded ramp front; same calibers as Model 81; 22" barrel. Made in England. Introduced, 1984; still imported by Precision Sports. Used value, $375 to $400.

Parker-Hale Model 1100M African Magnum

Model 1100M African Magnum has same general specs as Model 1100 standard, except has 24" barrel; .375 H&H magnum, .404 Jeffery, .458 Win. magnum; stock is heavily reinforced, glass bedded, weighted; rubber recoil pad. Made in England. Introduced, 1984; still imported by Precision Sports. Used value, $550 to $575.

Parker-Hale M87 Target

PARKER-HALE M87 Target: bolt-action; .243, 6.5x55, .30/06, .300 Win. magnum; other calibers on request; 5-rd. detachable box magazine; 26" heavy barrel; 45" overall length; weighs 10 lb.; no sights; receiver dovetailed for Parker-Hale mounts; target-type walnut stock adjustable for length of pull; stippled grip, forend; solid butt pad; accessory rail with hand-stop; Mauser-type action; large bolt knob; Parkerized finish. Made in England. Introduced, 1987; still imported by Precision Sports. Used value, $725 to $775.

PERUGINI-VISINI

PERUGINI-VISINI Double Rifle: over/under; 7mm Rem. magnum, 7x65R, 9.3x74R, .270 Win., .338 Win. magnum, .375 H&H, .458 Win. magnum; 24" barrels; 40½" overall length; oil-finished European walnut stock; cheekpiece; hand-checkered pistol grip, forend; box-lock action; ejectors; bead on ramp front sight, Express rear on rib; silvered receiver; other metal parts blued; marketed in trunk-type case. Made in Italy. Introduced, 1983; no longer imported by Wm. Larkin Moore. Used value, $3500 to $4000.

PERUGINI-VISINI Side-By-Side Double: same calibers as over/under double rifle, plus .470 Nitro; 22", 26" barrels; oil-finished walnut stock; hand-checkered grip, forend; cheekpiece; side-lock action; ejectors; bead on ramp front sight, express rear on rib; hand-detachable side plates; marketed in trunk-type case. Made in Italy. Introduced, 1983; no longer imported by Wm. Larkin Moore. Used value, $7500 to $7750.

Perugini-Visini Side-By-Side

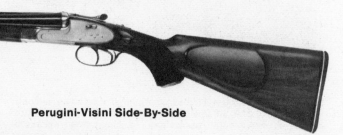

PERUGINI-VISINI Boxlock Double: side-by-side; 9.3x74R, .444 Marlin; 25" barrel; 41½" overall length; bead on ramp front sight, express rear on rib; oil-finished European walnut stock; hand-checkered pistol grip, forend; cheekpiece; non-ejector action; double triggers; color case-hardened receiver; rubber recoil pad; marketed in trunk-type case. Made in Italy. Introduced, 1983; no longer imported by Wm. Larkin Moore. Used value, $1800 to $2200.

Perugini-Visini Boxlock Double

PERUGINI-VISINI Eagle: single-shot; .17 Rem., .222, .22-250, .243, .270, .30/06, 7mm Rem. magnum, .300 Win. magnum, 5.6x-50R, 5.6x57R, 6.5x68R, 7x57R, 9.3x74R, 10.3x60R; various barrel lengths; no sights; claw-type scope mounts; oil-finished European walnut stock; box-lock action; adjustable set trigger; ejector; engraved, case-hardened receiver. Made in Italy. Introduced, 1986; no longer imported by Armes de Chasse. Used value, $3700 to $3800.

PERUGINI-VISINI Professional: bolt-action; calibers from .222 Rem. through .458 Win. magnum; various barrel lengths; no sights; oil-finished European walnut stock; modified Mauser 98K action; single- or double-set triggers. Made in Italy. Introduced, 1986; importation dropped, 1988. Used value, $3000 to $3100.

PERUGINI-VISINI Selous: double-rifle; 9.3x74R, .375 H&H magnum, .458 Win. magnum; other calibers on request; barrels to customer specs; folding leaf rear sight, gold bead on matted rib front; hand-detachable H&H-type side-locks; internal parts gold plated; auto ejectors; double triggers; fine engraving. Made in Italy. Introduced, 1987; still imported by Wm. Larkin Moore. Used value, $16,000 to $17,000, depending on options.

PERUGINI-VISINI Victoria: double-rifle; box-lock action; has same general features as Selous model; 7x65R, .30/06, 9.3x74R, .375 H&H magnum, .458 Win. magnum; auto ejectors; double triggers; optional 20-ga. barrels, other options. Made in Italy. Introduced, 1987; still imported by Wm. Larkin Moore. Used value, $4200 to $4500, depending on options.

REMINGTON

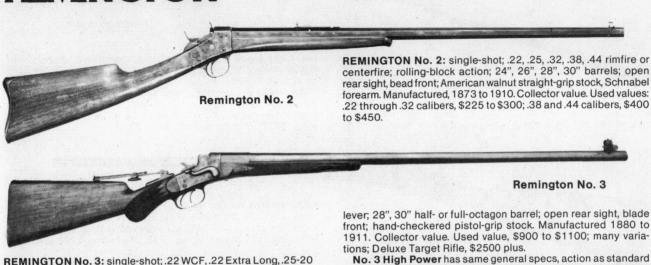

Remington No. 2

REMINGTON No. 2: single-shot; .22, .25, .32, .38, .44 rimfire or centerfire; rolling-block action; 24", 26", 28", 30" barrels; open rear sight, bead front; American walnut straight-grip stock, Schnabel forearm. Manufactured, 1873 to 1910. Collector value. Used values: .22 through .32 calibers, $225 to $300; .38 and .44 calibers, $400 to $450.

Remington No. 3

REMINGTON No. 3: single-shot; .22 WCF, .22 Extra Long, .25-20 Stevens, .25-21 Stevens, .25-25 Stevens, .32 WCF, .32 Ballard & Marlin, .32-40 Rem., .38 WCF, .38-40 Rem., .38-50 Rem., .38-55 Ballard & Marlin, .40-60 Ballard & Marlin, .40-60 WCF, .45-60 Rem., .40-82 WCF, .45-70 Govt., .45-90 WCF; falling-block action, side lever; 28", 30" half- or full-octagon barrel; open rear sight, blade front; hand-checkered pistol-grip stock. Manufactured 1880 to 1911. Collector value. Used value, $900 to $1100; many variations; Deluxe Target Rifle, $2500 plus.

No. 3 High Power has same general specs, action as standard No. 3; .30-30, .30-40, .32 Special, .32-40, .38-55, .38-72 high-power cartridges; 28", 30" barrels; open rear sight, bead front; hand-checkered pistol-grip stock, forearm. Manufactured 1893 to 1907. Collector value. Used value, $1000 to $1200.

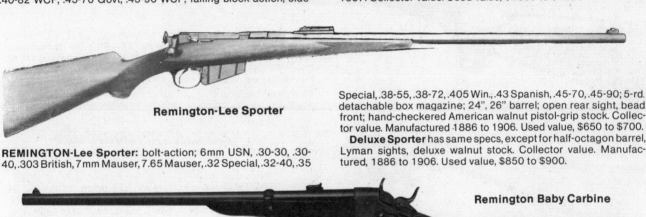

Remington-Lee Sporter

REMINGTON-Lee Sporter: bolt-action; 6mm USN, .30-30, .30-40, .303 British, 7mm Mauser, 7.65 Mauser, .32 Special, .32-40, .35 Special, .38-55, .38-72, .405 Win., .43 Spanish, .45-70, .45-90; 5-rd. detachable box magazine; 24", 26" barrel; open rear sight, bead front; hand-checkered American walnut pistol-grip stock. Collector value. Manufactured 1886 to 1906. Used value, $650 to $700.

Deluxe Sporter has same specs, except for half-octagon barrel, Lyman sights, deluxe walnut stock. Collector value. Manufactured, 1886 to 1906. Used value, $850 to $900.

Remington Baby Carbine

REMINGTON Baby Carbine: single-shot; .44 Win.; 20" barrel; rolling-block action; open rear sight, blade front; uncheckered American walnut carbine-style straight stock, forearm; barrel band. Manufactured, 1883 to 1910. Collector value. Used value, $475 to $550.

Remington No. 4

REMINGTON No. 4: single-shot, rolling-block action; solid frame or take-down; .22 short, long, LR; .25 Stevens rimfire; .32 short, long rimfire; has 22½" octagonal barrel; 24" barrel available for .32 rimfire only; blade front sight, open rear; plain walnut stock, forearm. Introduced in 1890; dropped, 1933. (1890 to 1901, solid frame; 1901 to 1926 first take-down with lever on right side; 1926 to 1933, second take-down with large screw head.) Used value, $195 to $250.

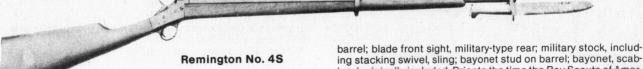

Remington No. 4S

REMINGTON No. 4S: Also known as Model 22 military single-shot rifle; rolling-block action; in .22 short or .22 LR only; 26" barrel; blade front sight, military-type rear; military stock, including stacking swivel; sling; bayonet stud on barrel; bayonet, scabbard originally included. Prior to the time the Boy Scouts of America downgraded militarism for fear of being compared with the Hitler Youth Movement, this was called the Boy Scout rifle and was the official rifle of the BSA. Introduced in 1913; dropped, 1933. Collector value. Used value, $475 to $650.

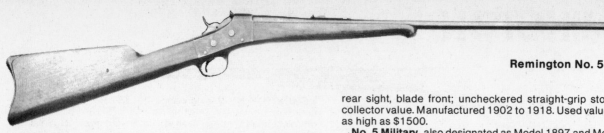

Remington No. 5

REMINGTON No. 5: single-shot; 7mm Mauser, .30-30, .30-40 Krag, .303 British, .32-40, .32 Special, .38-55 high-power cartridges; 24", 26", 28" barrels; rolling-block action; open sporting rear sight, blade front; uncheckered straight-grip stock. Some collector value. Manufactured 1902 to 1918. Used value, $650 to as high as $1500.

No. 5 Military, also designated as Model 1897 and Model 1902, has same specs as standard No. 5 except for 30" barrel, chambering for 8mm Lebel, 7mm Mauser, 7.62 Russian, .30 U.S. Used value, $350 to $375; deduct $50 for 7mm.

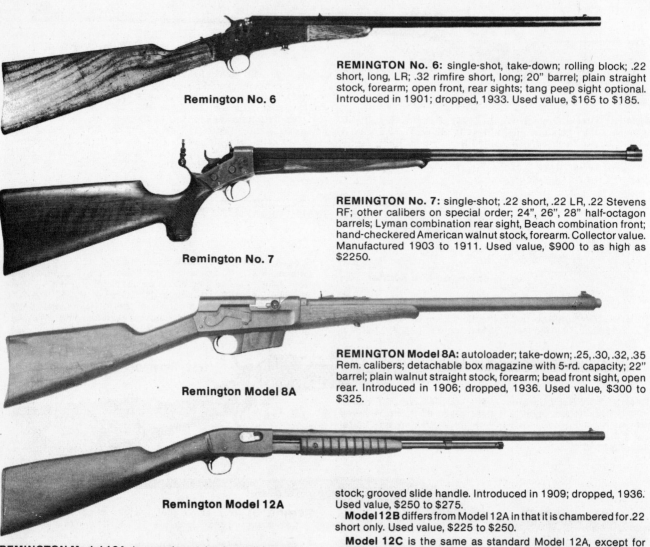

Remington No. 6

REMINGTON No. 6: single-shot, take-down; rolling block; .22 short, long, LR; .32 rimfire short, long; 20" barrel; plain straight stock, forearm; open front, rear sights; tang peep sight optional. Introduced in 1901; dropped, 1933. Used value, $165 to $185.

Remington No. 7

REMINGTON No. 7: single-shot; .22 short, .22 LR, .22 Stevens RF; other calibers on special order; 24", 26", 28" half-octagon barrels; Lyman combination rear sight, Beach combination front; hand-checkered American walnut stock, forearm. Collector value. Manufactured 1903 to 1911. Used value, $900 to as high as $2250.

Remington Model 8A

REMINGTON Model 8A: autoloader; take-down; .25, .30, .32, .35 Rem. calibers; detachable box magazine with 5-rd. capacity; 22" barrel; plain walnut straight stock, forearm; bead front sight, open rear. Introduced in 1906; dropped, 1936. Used value, $300 to $325.

Remington Model 12A

REMINGTON Model 12A: hammerless, take-down slide action; .22 short, long, LR; tube magazine holds 15 shorts, 12 longs, 10 LR; 22" barrel, bead front sight, open rear; uncheckered straight stock; grooved slide handle. Introduced in 1909; dropped, 1936. Used value, $250 to $275.

Model 12B differs from Model 12A in that it is chambered for .22 short only. Used value, $225 to $250.

Model 12C is the same as standard Model 12A, except for pistol-grip stock, octagonal barrel. Used value, $275 to $300.

Model 12CS is the same as Model 12C, except it is chambered for .22 WRF; magazine holds 12 rds. Used value, $275 to $300.

Remington Model 14½

REMINGTON Model 14A: centerfire slide-action repeater; hammerless, take-down: .25, .30, .32 Rem. calibers; 5-rd. tube magazine; 22" barrel, bead front sight, open rear; uncheckered walnut straight stock, grooved slide handle. Introduced in 1912; dropped, 1935. Used value, $250 to $275.

Model 14R carbine; same as standard Model 14A, except for 18" barrel. Used value, $300 to $325.

Model 14½ rifle is same as Model 14A, except in .38/40, .44/40 calibers; 11-shot full-length tube magazine; 22½" barrel. Introduced in 1912; dropped, 1925. Used value, $325 to $350.

Model 14½ carbine is same as 14½ rifle, except for 9-rd. magazine, 18½" barrel. Used value, $350 to $400.

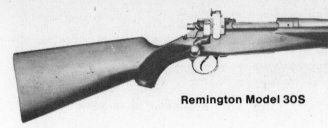

Remington Model 30S

REMINGTON Model 30A: bolt-action centerfire; modified commercial version of 1917 Enfield action; early models had 24" barrel; military-type double-stage trigger, Schnabel forearm tip; later versions have 22" barrel. In .25, .30, .32, .35 Rem., 7mm Mauser, .30/06; 5-rd. box magazine; checkered walnut stock, forearm on later versions, uncheckered on earlier with finger groove in forearm; pistol grip; bead front sight, open rear. Introduced in 1921; dropped, 1940. Used value, $425 to $450.

Model 30R carbine is same as Model 30A, except for 20" barrel, plain stock. Used value, $450 to $475.

Model 30S sporting model has same action as 30A; .257 Roberts, 7mm Mauser, .30/06; 5-shot box magazine, 24" barrel; bead front sight, No. 48 Lyman receiver sight; has long full forearm, high-comb checkered stock. Introduced in 1930; dropped, 1940. Used value, $500 to $550.

REMINGTON Model 33: take-down bolt-action single-shot; .22 short, long, LR; 24" barrel; bead front sight, open rear; uncheckered pistol-grip stock, grooved forearm. Introduced in 1931; dropped, 1936. Used value, $115 to $125.

Model 33 NRA Junior target model is same as standard Model 33, except for 7/8" sling, swivels; Patridge front sight, Lyman peep-style rear. Used value, $125 to $135.

REMINGTON Model 24A: take-down autoloader; .22 short only or .22 LR only; tube magazine in butt stock carries 10 LR or 15 short cartridges; 21" barrel; bead front sight, open rear; uncheckered walnut stock, forearm. Introduced, 1922; dropped, 1935. Used value, $165 to $185.

Remington Model 241A Speedmaster replaces standard Model 24A; introduced in 1935; dropped, 1951. Has same general configuration as original model, but with 24" barrel. Used value, $200 to $250.

Remington Model 25A

REMINGTON Model 25A: slide-action repeater; hammerless, take-down; .25-20, .32-20; 10-rd. tube magazine; 24" barrel; blade front sight, open rear; uncheckered walnut pistol-grip stock, grooved slide handle. Introduced in 1923; dropped, 1936. Used value, $275 to $285.

Model 25R carbine is same as standard Model 25A, except for 18" barrel, 6-rd. magazine; straight stock. Used value, $285 to $315.

Remington Model 34

REMINGTON Model 34: bolt-action, take-down repeater; .22 short, long, LR; tube magazine holds 15 LR, 17 long or 22 short cartridges; 24" barrel; bead front sight, open rear; uncheckered hardwood pistol-grip stock, grooved forearm. Introduced in 1932; dropped, 1936. used value, $135 to $145.

Model 34 NRA target model is the same as standard Model 34, except for Patridge front sight, Lyman peep in rear; swivels, 7/8" sling. Used value, $145 to $165.

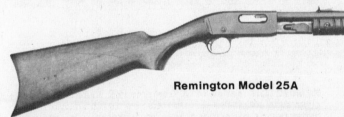

Remington Model 341A

REMINGTON Model 341A: take-down bolt-action repeater; .22 short, long, LR; tube magazine holds 15 LR, 17 long, 22 short; 27" barrel; bead front sight, open rear; uncheckered hardwood pistol-grip stock. Introduced in 1936; dropped, 1940. Used value, $115 to $125.

Model 341P for target shooting, is same as standard Model 341A, except for hooded front sight, peep rear. Used value, $135 to $145.

Model 341SB is same as Model 341A, except it is smoothbore for use with .22 shot cartridges. Used value, $140 to $150.

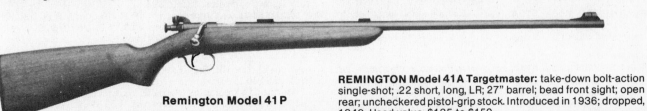

Remington Model 41P

REMINGTON Model 41A Targetmaster: take-down bolt-action single-shot; .22 short, long, LR; 27" barrel; bead front sight; open rear; uncheckered pistol-grip stock. Introduced in 1936; dropped, 1940. Used value, $135 to $150.

Model 41AS differs from 41A Targetmaster only in that it is chambered only for .22 WRF cartridge. Used value, $115 to $125.

Model 41P is same as standard Model 41A, except that it has hooded front sight, peep-type rear. Used value, $125 to $135.

Model 41SB is same as standard 41A Targetmaster, except it is smoothbore only for .22 shot cartridges. Used value, $125 to $140.

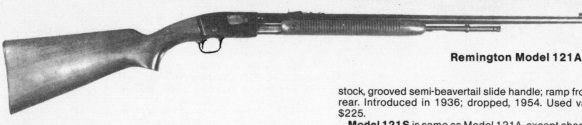

Remington Model 121A

REMINGTON Model 121A Fieldmaster: slide-action take-down, hammerless repeater; .22 short, long, LR; tube magazine holds 20 short, 15 long, 14 LR; 24" round barrel; unchecked pistol-grip stock, grooved semi-beavertail slide handle; ramp front sight, open rear. Introduced in 1936; dropped, 1954. Used value, $200 to $225.

Model 121S is same as Model 121A, except chambered for .22 WRF; magazine holds 12 rds. Used value, $250 to $300.

Model 121SB; same as Model 121A, except smoothbore for use of .22 shot cartridge. Used value, $300 to $350.

Remington Model 81A

REMINGTON Model 81A Woodsmaster: autoloader; .30, .32, .35 Rem., .300 Savage; 5-shot nondetachable box magazine; 22" barrel; bead front sight, open rear; unchecked walnut pistol-grip stock, forearm. Introduced in 1936; dropped, 1950. Used value, $275 to $285; $50 to $100 premium for .35 Rem. and .300 Savage.

Remington Model 141A

REMINGTON Model 141A Gamemaster: hammerless, take-down slide-action; .30, .32, .35 Rem.; 5-shot tube magazine; 24" barrel; bead front sight, open rear; unchecked walnut pistol-grip stock, grooved slide handle. Introduced in 1936; dropped, 1950. Used value, $250 to $275; slight premium for .35 Rem.

Remington Model 37 Rangemaster

REMINGTON Model 37 Rangemaster: produced in two variations; the first was produced from 1937 to 1940; the second from 1940 to 1954; 1937 model is .22 LR only; 5-shot box magazine; single-shot adapter supplied as standard; 22" heavy barrel; Remington peep rear sight, hooded front; scope bases; unchecked target stock, with sling, swivels. When introduced, barrel band held forward section of stock to barrel; with modification of forearm, barrel band was eliminated in 1938. Used values: without sights, $375 to $400; with factory sights, $450 to $500.

Model 37 of 1940 has same basic configuration as original; changes include Miracle trigger mechanism; high-comb stock, beavertail forearm. Used values: without sights, $400 to $425; with factory sights, $475 to $525.

Remington Model 510A

REMINGTON Model 510A: take-down bolt-action single-shot; .22 short, long, LR; 25" barrel; bead front sight; open rear; unchecked walnut pistol-grip stock. Introduced in 1939; dropped, 1962. Used value, $75 to $85.

Model 510P is same as standard Model 510, except for Patridge-design front sight on ramp, peep rear. Used value, $85 to $95.

Model 510SB is same as standard model, except for being smoothbore for .22 shot cartridge; shotgun bead front sight, no rear sight. Used value, $85 to $95.

Model 510X was introduced in 1964; dropped, 1966. Had aspirations to be a target rifle; differed from original model only in improved sights. Used value, $90 to $110.

REMINGTON Model 511A: take-down bolt-action repeater; .22 short, long, LR; 6-rd. detachable box magazine; 25" barrel; bead front sight; open rear; unchecked pistol-grip stock. Introduced in 1939; dropped, 1962. Used value, $80 to $95.

Model 511P is same as standard model, except for peep sight on rear of receiver; Patridge-type ramp blade front. Used value, $80 to $100.

Model 511X same as Model 511A, except for clip-type magazine; improved sight. Introduced in 1953; dropped, 1966. Used value, $110 to $125.

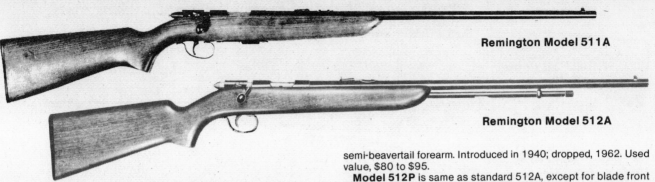

Remington Model 511A

Remington Model 512A

semi-beavertail forearm. Introduced in 1940; dropped, 1962. Used value, $80 to $95.

Model 512P is same as standard 512A, except for blade front sight on ramp, peep rear. Used value, $80 to $95.

Model 512X is same as standard Model 512A, except for improved sight. Introduced in 1964; dropped, 1966. Used value, $100 to $125.

REMINGTON Model 512A: take-down bolt-action repeater; .22 short, long, LR; tube magazine holds 22 short, 17 long, 15 LR; 25" barrel; bead front sight, open rear; uncheckered pistol-grip stock;

Remington Model 513TR

Remington Model 513S

uncheckered target stock; sling, swivels; globe front sight, Redfield No. 70 peep-type rear. Introduced in 1941; dropped, 1969. Used value, $225 to $250.

Model 513S differs from 513TR Matchmaster in that it has checkered sporter-style stock; Patridge-type front sight, Marble open rear. Introduced in 1941; dropped, 1956. Used value, $300 to $350.

REMINGTON Model 513TR Matchmaster: bolt-action target rifle; .22 LR only; 6-shot detachable box magazine; 27" barrel;

Remington Model 550A

hardwood pistol-grip stock; bead front sight, open rear. Introduced in 1941; dropped, 1971. Used value, $100 to $115.

Model 550P is same as standard 550A, except for blade front sight on ramp, peep-type rear. Used value, $115 to $125.

Model 550-2G was originally listed as Gallery Special; same as standard model, except for fired shell deflector; screw eye for counter chain; 22" barrel. Used value, $100 to $120.

REMINGTON Model 550A: autoloader; features floating chamber for interchangeable use of .22 short, long, LR ammo; tube magazine holds 22 short, 17 long, 15 LR; 24" barrel; unchecked

Remington Model 720A

Model 1917 Enfield; checkered pistol-grip stock; bead front sight on ramp, open rear; made only in 1941, as factory facilities were converted to wartime production. Used value, $750 to $1000.

Model 720R is the same as standard 720A, except for 20" barrel. Used value, $750 to $1000.

Model 720S is same as Model 720A, except for 24" barrel. Used value, $750 to $1000.

REMINGTON Model 720A: bolt-action; .30/06, .270 Win., .257 Roberts; 5-rd. box magazine; 22" barrel; action is modification of

REMINGTON Model 521TL: called the Junior Target Model, this is a take-down bolt-action repeater; .22 LR only; 6-rd. detachable box magazine; 25" barrel; unchecked target stock; came with sling, swivels; blade front sight, Lyman 57RS rear peep type. Introduced in 1947; dropped, 1969. Used value, $145 to $155.

REMINGTON Model 514: bolt-action single-shot; .22 short, long, LR; 24" barrel; unchecked pistol-grip stock; black plastic butt plate; bead front sight, open rear. Introduced in 1948; dropped, 1971. Used value, $75 to $85.

Model 514P is the same as standard 514, except for ramp front sight, peep type in rear. Used value, $75 to $95.

Remington Model 514

Remington Model 521TL

Remington Model 721
H&H Magnum

REMINGTON Model 721A: standard grade bolt-action; .30/06, .270 Win.; 24" barrel, 4-rd. box magazine; bead front sight on ramp, open rear; uncheckered walnut sporter stock. Introduced in 1948; dropped, 1962. Used value, $250 to $275.

Model 721ADL differs from standard-grade 721A in that the wood has deluxe checkering on stock and forearm. Used value, $325 to $345.

REMINGTON Model 722A: same as Model 721 series, except for shorter action; .257 Roberts, .300 Savage, .308 Win. Introduced in 1948; dropped, 1962. Used value, $275 to $300.

Model 722ADL, so-called deluxe grade, is same as standard

Model 721 BDL is the same as the Model 721ADL, except that the checkered stock is from more select wood. Used value, $350 to $365.

Model 721 Remington was also offered in .300 H&H, in all variations. In the case of the 721A Magnum, the changes were a heavy 26" barrel, 3-shot magazine and addition of a recoil pad. Used value, $350 to $375.

Model 721 ADL H&H Magnum boasted checkering on walnut stock. Used value, $400 to $425.

.300 H&H Model 721 BDL, with select walnut, has a used value of $450 to $475.

model, except for checkered stock. Used value, $325 to $350.

Model 722 BDL, termed the deluxe special grade, has same checkering as ADL, but has better wood. Used value, $400 to $425.

Remington Model 722A 222

REMINGTON Model 722A 222: this series of rifles differs from standard 722A primarily in the fact that it is in .222 Rem.; has 5-

REMINGTON Model 722A 244: has same specs as Model 722A 222, except it is .244 Rem. only and magazine capacity is 4 rds. Introduced in 1955; dropped, 1962. Used value, $275 to $300.

Model 722 ADL 244 differs from standard model only in check-

shot magazine and 26" barrel. Introduced in 1950; dropped, 1962. Used value, $275 to $300.

Model 722 ADL 222 is the same as 722A 222, except for deluxe checkering on walnut stock. Used value, $325 to $350.

Model 722 BDL 222 differs from ADL configuration only in that walnut stock is of better grade. Used value, $375 to $400.

ering on pistol grip, forearm. Used value, $325 to $345.

Model 722 BDL 244 is the same as the ADL configuration except for better-grade walnut. Used value, $375 to $400.

Remington Model 760 BDL

REMINGTON Model 760: hammerless slide-action repeater; made originally in .223 Rem., 6mm Rem., .243 Win., .257 Roberts, .270 Win., .30/06, .300 Savage, .308 Win., .35 Rem. Models from mid-'60s to early '70s had impressed checkering; others are hand checkered on pistol grip, slide handle; early versions had no check-

ering on stock, had grooved slide handle; 4-shot magazine; 22" barrel; bead front sight on ramp, open rear. Introduced in 1952; dropped, 1980. Used value, $230 to $250; .222, .223, and .257 bring 200% to 300% premiums.

Model 760 carbine: same as standard Model 760, except in .308 Win., .30/06 only; 18½" barrel. Used value, $250 to $265.

Model 760 ADL is same as standard Model 760, except for deluxe checkered stock, grip cap, sling swivels, choice of standard or high comb. Used value, $250 to $275.

Model 760 BDL is same as standard model, except for basket-weave checkering on pistol grip, forearm; black forearm tip; early versions available in right- or left-hand styles; .308 Win., .30/06, .270 Win.; Monte Carlo cheekpiece. Used value: $275 to $300;

760 BDL(D), with fine checkering, engraving, $750 to $800; **760 BDL(F),** with fine checkering, top-grade wood, engraving, $1350 to $1500; 760 BDL(F) with gold inlays, $2500 to $2750.

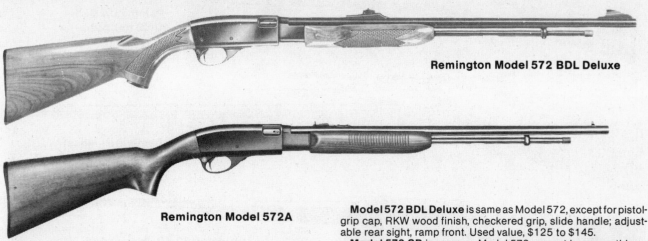

Remington Model 572 BDL Deluxe

Remington Model 572A

REMINGTON Model 572: slide-action; .22 rimfire; tube magazine holding 20 short, 17 long, 14 LR cartridges; 24" round tapered barrel; walnut pistol-grip stock, grooved slide handle; step-adjustable rear sight, bead post front; crossbolt safety; receiver grooved for tip-off scope mount. Introduced in 1955; still in production. Used value, $115 to $125.

Model 572 BDL Deluxe is same as Model 572, except for pistol-grip cap, RKW wood finish, checkered grip, slide handle; adjustable rear sight, ramp front. Used value, $125 to $145.

Model 572 SB is same as Model 572, except has smoothbore barrel for .22 LR shot cartridge. Used value, $120 to $130.

Model 572A Fieldmaster: hammerless slide-action repeater; .22 short, long, LR; tube magazine holds 20 short, 17 long, 15 LR; 25" barrel; ramp front sight; open rear; unchecked hardwood pistol-grip stock, grooved forearm. Introduced in 1955; still in production. Used values: standard, $100 to $115; BDL, $125 to $145.

Remington Model 740A

REMINGTON Model 740A: gas-operated autoloader; .308 Win., .30/06; 4-rd. detachable box magazine; 22" barrel, unchecked

pistol-grip stock; grooved semi-beavertail forearm; ramp front sight, open rear. Introduced in 1955; dropped, 1960. Used value, $225 to $245.

Model 740 ADL is same as standard model, except for deluxe checkered stock, grip cap, sling swivels, standard or high comb. Used value, $250 to $260.

Model 740 BDL is same as ADL model, except for selected walnut stock. Used value, $275 to $300.

Remington Model 40X

Remington Model 40X Centerfire

REMINGTON Model 40X: .22 LR single-shot bolt-action target rifle; action is similar to Model 722; adjustable trigger; 28" heavy barrel; Redfield Olympic sights optional; scope bases; target stock; bedding device; adjustable swivel; rubber butt plate. Introduced in 1955; dropped, 1964. Used values: with sights, $450 to $460; sans sights, $350 to $375.

Model 40X standard, with lighter barrel, is otherwise same as heavyweight model listed above. Used values: with sights, $400 to $425; sans sights, $325 to $350.

Model 40X Centerfire has same basic specs as the 40X rimfire heavy-barrel target rifle; standard calibers, .30/06, 7.62 NATO, .222 Rem. magnum, .222 Rem., with other calibers on special request at additional cost. Introduced, 1961; dropped, 1964. Used values: sans sights, $450 to $500; with sights, $550 to $600.

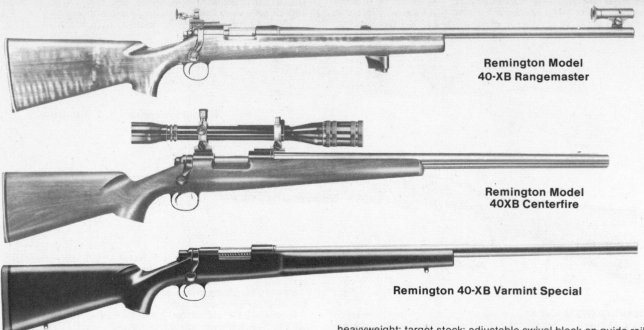

Remington Model
40-XB Rangemaster

Remington Model
40XB Centerfire

Remington 40-XB Varmint Special

REMINGTON Model 40-XB Rangemaster: rimfire bolt-action single-shot, replacing rimfire Model 40X; .22 LR; 28" barrel, standard or heavyweight; target stock, adjustable swivel block on guide rail; rubber butt plate; furnished without sights. Introduced in 1964; dropped, 1974. Used value, $400 to $425.

Model 40-XB Centerfire: bolt-action single-shot designed to replace Model 40X Centerfire; .308 Win., .30/06, .223 Rem., .222 Rem. magnum, .222 Rem.; stainless steel 27¼" barrel, standard or heavyweight; target stock; adjustable swivel block on guide rail; rubber butt plate; furnished without sights. Introduced in 1964; still in production. Used value, $650 to $750.

40-XB KS Varmint Special has same general specs as 40-XB Centerfire model, except has Kevlar aramid fiber stock; straight comb; cheekpiece; palm-swell grip; black recoil pad; removable swivel studs; single-shot or repeater; chamberings include .220 Swift and others for the Model 40-XB Rangemaster Target; custom-built to order. Introduced, 1987; still in production. Used values: single-shot, $725 to $775; repeater, $800 to $850.

Remington Model 725ADL

Remington Model 725

REMINGTON Model 725 ADL: bolt-action; in .243, .244, .270, .280, .30/06; rifle has 22" barrel, 4-rd. box magazine; in .222, has 24" barrel, 5-rd. magazine; Monte Carlo comb, walnut stock; hand-checkered pistol grip, forearm; swivels; hooded ramp front sight,

open rear. Introduced in 1958; dropped, 1961. Used value, $325 to $350.

Model 725 Kodiak Magnum: rifle is built on the same basic action as 725 ADL; .375 H&H magnum; .458 Win. magnum; 26" barrel; 3-rd. box magazine; reinforced deluxe Monte Carlo stock; recoil pad; special recoil reduction device built into barrel; black forearm tip; sling, swivels; made only in 1962. Used value, $700 to $750.

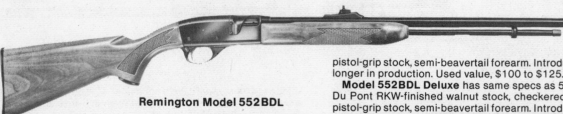

Remington Model 552BDL

REMINGTON Model 552A Speedmaster: standard model auto-loader handles .22 short, long, LR cartridges interchangeably; tube magazine holds 20 short, 17 long, 15 LR; 25" barrel, bead front sight, open rear; uncheckered walnut-finished hardwood

pistol-grip stock, semi-beavertail forearm. Introduced in 1958; no longer in production. Used value, $100 to $125.

Model 552BDL Deluxe has same specs as 552A, except has Du Pont RKW-finished walnut stock, checkered forend, capped pistol-grip stock, semi-beavertail forearm. Introduced in 1958; no longer in production. Used value, $100 to $125.

Model 552C carbine is the same as standard Model 552A, except for 21" barrel. Used value, $100 to $135.

Model 552GS Gallery Special has same specs as standard model, except for being chambered in .22 short only. Used value, $100 to $125.

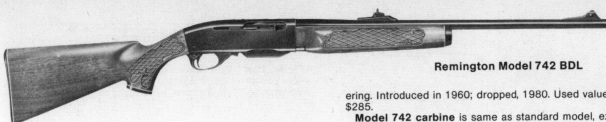

Remington Model 742 BDL

REMINGTON Model 742: gas-operated semi-auto; 6mm Rem., .243 Win., .280 Rem., .308 Win., .30/06; 4-rd. box magazine; 22" barrel; bead front sight on ramp, open rear; versions of 1960s had impressed checkering on stock, forearm; later versions, cut check-ering. Introduced in 1960; dropped, 1980. Used value, $275 to $285.

Model 742 carbine is same as standard model, except has 18½" barrel; .308 Win., .30/06 only. Used value, $285 to $295.

Model 742 BDL is same as standard 742, except in .308 Win., .30/06 only; available in right-, left-hand models; Monte Carlo cheekpiece; black tip on forearm; basketweave checkering. Used value, $275 to $300.

Remington International Match Free Rifle

REMINGTON International Match Free Rifle: bolt-action single-shot; special-order calibers were available, but standard chamberings are .22 LR, .222 Rem., .222 Rem. magnum, .30/06, 7.62mm NATO; used same action as earlier Model 40X; 28" barrel, 2-oz. adjustable trigger; freestyle hand-finished stock, with thumbhole; interchangeable, adjustable rubber butt plate and hook-type butt plate; adjustable palm rest; adjustable sling swivel; furnished without sights. Introduced in 1961; dropped, 1964. Used value, $700 to $750.

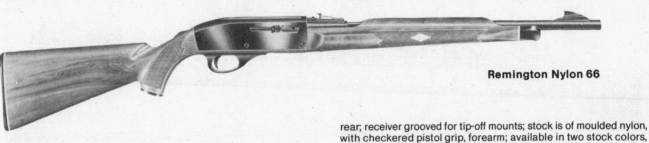

Remington Nylon 66

REMINGTON Nylon 66: autoloader; .22 LR only; tube magazine in butt stock holds 14 rds.; 19½" barrel; blade front sight, open rear; receiver grooved for tip-off mounts; stock is of moulded nylon, with checkered pistol grip, forearm; available in two stock colors, Mohawk brown and Apache black; latter has chrome-plated receiver cover. Introduced in 1959; dropped, 1988. Used value either color/style, $80 to $90.

Remington Nylon 76

REMINGTON Nylon 76: .22 LR only; same as standard Mohawk brown 66, except has short-throw lever-action. Introduced in 1962; dropped, 1964. Used value, $125 to $150.

Remington Nylon 11

REMINGTON Nylon 11: bolt-action repeater; .22 short, long, LR; 6-, 10-rd. clip-type magazines; 19⅝" barrel; blade front sight, open rear; Mohawk brown nylon stock; checkered pistol grip, forearm. Introduced in 1962; dropped, 1964. Used value, $125 to $135.

Remington Nylon 10

REMINGTON Nylon 10: bolt-action single-shot; same as Nylon 11, except single-shot. Introduced in 1962; dropped, 1964. Used value, $85 to $100.

Remington Nylon 12

REMINGTON Nylon 12: bolt-action repeater; same as Nylon 11 model, except for tube magazine holding 22 short, 17 long, 15 LR. Introduced in 1962; dropped, 1964. Used value, $125 to $135.

Remington Model 700 Varmint

Remington Model 700 BDL Left-hand

Remington Model 700 Classic

Remington Model 700 Custom KS Mountain Rifle

Remington Model 700 FS

Remington Model 700 RS

REMINGTON Model 700: this is another of those guns that verges on being an empire. Introduced in 1962, the Model 700 has been Remington's most recent continuing success and is still a top seller, in spite of price increases each year.

Model 700 ADL is bolt-action, .222, .22/250, .243, 6mm Rem., .270, 7mm Rem. magnum, .308, .30/06; 22" and 24" round tapered barrel; walnut Monte Carlo stock, with pistol grip; originally introduced with hand-checkered pistol grip, forearm, was made for several years with RKW finish, impressed checkering; more recent models have computerized cut checkering; removable, adjustable rear sight with windage screw; gold bead ramp front; tapped for scope mounts. Used value, $275 to $300; except for 7mm Rem. magnum, $300 to $325.

Model 700 BDL is same as 700 ADL, except for black forearm tip, pistol grip cap, skip-line checkering; matted receiver top; quick-release floor plate; quick-detachable swivels, sling; hooded ramp front sight; additional calibers, .17 Rem., 6.5mm Rem. magnum, .350 Rem. magnum, .264 Win. magnum, .300 Win. magnum. Used value: $350 to $375; **Peerless grade,** with better wood, checkering, custom work, $950 to $1000; **Premier grade,** with inlays, engraving, $2250 to $2500.

Model 700 BDL left-hand is the same as 700 BDL, except for left-hand action, stock; available only in .243, .308, .270 Win., .30/06 in current production. Used value. $350 to $375.

Model 700 Safari is same as Model 700 BDL, except in .458 Win. magnum, 375 H&H; recoil pad, oil-finished, hand-checkered stock. Used value, $650 to $700.

Model 700 C custom rifle is same as Model 700 BDL, except for choice of 20", 22", 24" barrel; with or without sights, hinged floor plate; select walnut, hand-checkered stock; rosewood forearm tip, grip cap; hand-lapped barrel. Dropped, 1984. Used value: in standard calibers, $700 to $750; magnum calibers, $650 to $700; with optional recoil pad, add $20.

Model 700 Classic is a classic version of Model 700 ADL with straight-comb stock; sling swivel studs installed. Introduced, 1979; still in production. Used value, $325 to $375.

Model 700 Varmint has same specs as 700 BDL except for 24" heavy barrel, no sights. Made in .222, .223, .22-250, 6mm Rem., .243, 7mm-08 Rem., .308 in current production. Used value, $350 to $375.

Model 700 Mountain Rifle has same specs as 700 BDL, except has 22" tapered barrel, weighs 6¾ lb.; has redesigned pistol grip, straight comb, contoured cheekpiece, satin stock finish, fine checkering, hinged floor plate, magazine follower; two-position thumb safety; 4-rd. magazine; chambered for .270 Win., .280 Rem., .30/06; added in 1988: .243, 7mm-08, .308. Introduced, 1986; still

in production. Used value, $325 to $350.

Model 700 Custom KS Mountain Rifle has same specs as Mountain model, except has 24" barrel, Kevlar reinforced resin stock; left- and right-hand versions; .270 Win., .280 Rem., .30/06, 7mm Rem. magnum, .300 Win. magnum, .338 Win. magnum, 8mm Rem. magnum, .375 H&H; weighs 6 lb. 6 oz. Introduced, 1986; still in production. Used value, $600 to $625.

Model 700 FS has same specs as 700 BDL, except has classic-style fiberglass stock reinforced with Kevlar, black Old English-type rubber recoil pad; blind magazine; stock in gray or camouflage pattern; right- or left-hand actions; .243, .308, 7mm Rem. magnum, .270, .30/06; weighs 6⅝ lb. Introduced, 1987; still in production. Used value, $400 to $425.

Model 700 RS has same general specs as Mountain Rifle, except has glass-reinforced thermoplastic resin stock; textured gray or camouflage finish; solid butt pad; hinged floor plate; 22" barrel; weighs 6¾ lb.; .270, .280 Rem., .30/06. Introduced, 1987; still in production. Used value, $325 to $350.

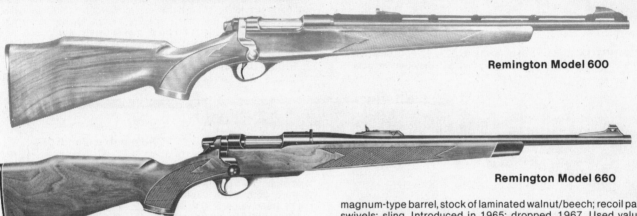

Remington Model 600

Remington Model 660

REMINGTON Model 600: bolt-action carbine; 5-rd. box magazine for 6mm Rem., .243 Win., .308 Win.; 6-rd. magazine for .222 Rem.; 18½" round barrel, with vent. nylon rib; checkered walnut Monte Carlo pistol-grip stock; blade ramp front sight, open rear; drilled, tapped for scope mounts. Introduced in 1964; dropped, 1967. Used value, $250 to $400.

Model 600 magnum is the same as Model 600, but with 4-rd. box magazine for 6.5mm Rem. magnum, .350 Rem. magnum; heavy

magnum-type barrel, stock of laminated walnut/beech; recoil pad; swivels; sling. Introduced in 1965; dropped, 1967. Used value, $450 to $550.

Model 660: bolt-action carbine, replacing Model 600; 5-rd. box magazine for 6mm Rem., .243 Win., .308 Win.; 6-rd. magazine for .222 Rem.; 20" barrel; bead front sight on ramp, open rear; checkered Monte Carlo stock; black pistol-grip cap, forearm tip. Introduced in 1968; dropped, 1971. Used value, $300 to $350.

Model 660 magnum is same as 660 standard, except in 6.5mm Rem. magnum, .350 Rem. magnum; 4-rd. magazine; recoil pad; laminated walnut/beech stock for added strength; quick-detachable sling swivels, sling. Introduced in 1968; dropped, 1971. Used value, $400 to $500.

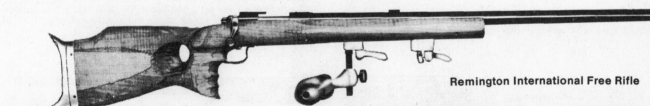

Remington International Free Rifle

REMINGTON International Free Rifle: in both rimfire, centerfire; has same action as Model 40-XB; .22 LR; .222 Rem., .222 Rem.

magnum, .223 Rem., 7.62 NATO, .30/06; 2-oz. adjustable trigger; no sights; hand-finished stock; adjustable butt plate and hook; movable front sling swivel; adjustable palm rest. Introduced in 1964; dropped, 1974. Used value, $750 to $850.

Remington Model 581

REMINGTON Model 581: bolt-action, .22 short, long, LR: 5-rd. magazine; 24" round barrel; hardwood Monte Carlo pistol-grip

stock; screw-adjustable open rear sight, bead on post front; side safety; wide trigger; receiver grooved for tip-off mounts. Introduced, 1967; dropped, 1984. Used value: $90 to $100; left-hand action, $95 to $105.

Model 581-S Sportsman has same specs as 581; comes with single-shot adapter. Reintroduced, 1986; still in production. Used value, $130 to $140.

Remington Model 582

REMINGTON Model 582: same as Model 581, except for tubular magazine holding 20 short, 15 long, 14 LR cartridges. Dropped, 1984. Used value, $100 to $110.

Remington Model 788

REMINGTON Model 788: bolt-action; .222, .22-250, 6mm Rem., .243, 7mm-08, .308, .30-30, .44 magnum; .222 has 5-rd. magazine, others 4-rd.; 24" tapered barrel for .222, .22-250, 22" for other calibers; walnut-finished hardwood pistol-grip stock, unchecked-ered with Monte Carlo comb; open rear sight adjustable for win-dage, elevation, blade ramp front; thumb safety; detachable box magazine; receiver tapped for scope mounts. Introduced in 1967, dropped, 1983. Used value, $175 to $200; left-hand model, $180 to $205; $50 to $75 premium for .30-30 and .44 magnum.

Remington Model 580

REMINGTON Model 580: single-shot, bolt-action; .22 short, long, LR; 24" tapered barrel; hardwood stock with Monte Carlo comb, pistol grip; black composition butt plate; screw-lock adjustable rear sight, bead post front; side safety; integral loading platform; receiver grooved for tip-off mounts. Introduced in 1957; dropped, 1976. Used value, $70 to $75.

Model 580 SB is same as standard Model 580, except for smooth-bore barrel for shot cartridges. Used value, $65 to $70.

Remington Model 591

REMINGTON Model 591: bolt-action; 5mm Rem. rimfire; 4-rd. clip magazine; 24" barrel; uncheckered hardwood stock, with Monte Carlo comb; black composition pistol-grip cap, butt plate; screw-adjustable open rear sight, bead post front; side safety, wide trigger; receiver grooved for tip-off scope mounts. Introduced in 1970; dropped, 1975. Used value, $100 to $125.

Remington Model 592

REMINGTON Model 592: same as Model 591, except for tube magazine; holds 10 5mm Rem. rimfire rds. Introduced in 1970; dropped, 1974. Used value, $110 to $135.

Remington Model 541-S

REMINGTON Model 541-S: bolt-action; .22 short, long, LR; 24" barrel; walnut stock; checkered pistol grip, forearm; no sights; drilled, tapped for scope mounts, receiver sights; 5-rd. clip; thumb safety; engraved receiver, trigger guard. Introduced, 1972; drop-ped, 1983. Used value, $350 to $375.

Model 541-T has same general specs as 541-S, except no engraving; has satin finish; drilled, tapped for scope mounts only; .22 short, long, LR; 5-rd. clip. Reintroduced, 1986. Used value, $240 to $255.

**Remington Model
40-XC National Match**

REMINGTON 40-XC National Match: bolt-action; 7.62 NATO; 5-rd. top-loading clip-slot magazine; 23¼" stainless steel barrel; no sights; position-style American walnut stock; palm swell; adjust-able butt plate; adjustable trigger; meets all ISU Army Rifle specs. Introduced, 1978; still in production. Used value, $725 to $750.

Remington Model 40XB-BR

REMINGTON Model 40XB-BR: bolt-action, single-shot; .22 BR Rem., .222, .223, 6mmx47, 6mm BR Rem., 7.62 NATO; 20" light var-mint barrel, 26" heavy varmint; no sights; supplied with scope blocks; select walnut stock; stainless steel barrel, adjustable trigger. Introduced, 1978; still in production. Used value, $700 to $750.

Remington Model 40-XR

REMINGTON 40-XR: bolt-action single-shot; .22 LR; 24" heavy target barrel; no sights, drilled, tapped, furnished with scope blocks; American walnut position-style stock, with front swivel block, forend guide rail; adjustable butt plate, adjustable trigger. Meets ISU specs. Introduced, 1978; still in production. Used value, $700 to $750.

Remington Model 540-XR

REMINGTON 540-XR: bolt-action, single-shot; .22 LR; 26" barrel; no sights; drilled, tapped for scope blocks; fitted with front sight base; Monte Carlo position-style stock; thumb groove, cheek-piece; adjustable butt plate; full length guide rail; adjustable match trigger. Introduced, 1978; dropped, 1983. Used value, $300 to $325.

540-XRJR has same specs as 540-XR, except has 1¾" shorter stock to fit junior shooter; adjustable length of pull. Introduced, 1978; dropped, 1983. Used value, $300 to $325.

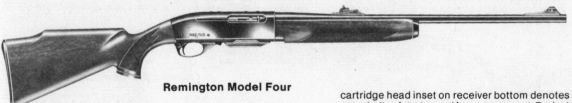

Remington Model Four

REMINGTON Model Four: semiautomatic; .243 Win., 6mm Rem., .280 Rem., .308 Win., .30/06; 4-rd. clip magazine round tapered barrel; gold bead ramp front sight, windage-adjustable step rear; checkered American walnut pistol-grip stock with Monte Carlo; cartridge head inset on receiver bottom denotes caliber; positive crossbolt safety; tapped for scope mount. Redesign of Model 742. Introduced, 1981; dropped, 1988. Used value, $300 to $350.

Model Four Collectors Edition: has same specs as standard Model Four, except has etched receiver, 24K gold inlays, all metal parts have high-luster finish. Made in .30/06 only. Only 1500 made in 1982. Used value, $1600 to $2000.

REMINGTON Model Six: slide-action; 6mm Rem., .243, .270, .308 Win., .30/06; 22" round tapered barrel; gold bead front sight on matted ramp, open step adjustable rear; cut-checkered Monte Carlo walnut stock with full cheekpiece; detachable 4-rd. clip mag-azine; crossbolt safety, tapped for scope mount; cartridge head medallion on receiver bottom to denote caliber. Improved version of Model 760. Introduced, 1981; dropped, 1988. Used value, $300 to $350.

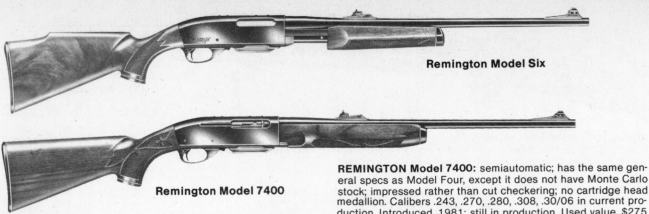

Remington Model Six

Remington Model 7400

REMINGTON Model 7400: semiautomatic; has the same general specs as Model Four, except it does not have Monte Carlo stock; impressed rather than cut checkering; no cartridge head medallion. Calibers .243, .270, .280, .308, .30/06 in current production. Introduced, 1981; still in production. Used value, $275 to $295.

REMINGTON Model 7600: slide-action; has same specs as Model Six, except does not have Monte Carlo stock, cheekpiece, no cartridge head medallion; impressed checkering. Calibers .243, .270, .280, .30/06 in current production. Introduced, 1981; still in production. Used value, $265 to $285.

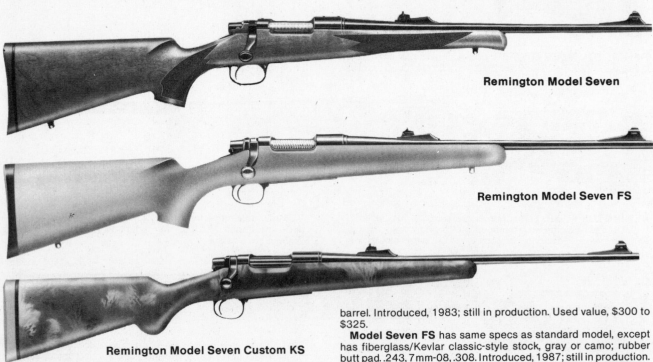

Remington Model Seven

Remington Model Seven FS

Remington Model Seven Custom KS

REMINGTON Model Seven: bolt-action; .223 Rem., .243, 7mm-08, 6mm, .308; 5-rd. magazine in .223 Rem., 4 rds. in other calibers; 18½" barrel; 48½" overall length; ramp front sight, adjustable open rear; American walnut stock; modified Schnabel forend; machine-cut checkering; short action; silent side safety; free-floated barrel. Introduced, 1983; still in production. Used value, $300 to $325.

Model Seven FS has same specs as standard model, except has fiberglass/Kevlar classic-style stock, gray or camo; rubber butt pad. .243, 7mm-08, .308. Introduced, 1987; still in production. Used value, $400 to $425.

Model Seven Custom KS has same specs as standard model, except stock is of Kevlar aramid fiber; has 20" barrel; .35 Rem., .350 Rem. magnum; weighs 5¾ lb.; iron sights; drilled, tapped for scope mounts. Special order through Remington Custom Shop. Introduced, 1987; still in production. Used value, $600 to $650.

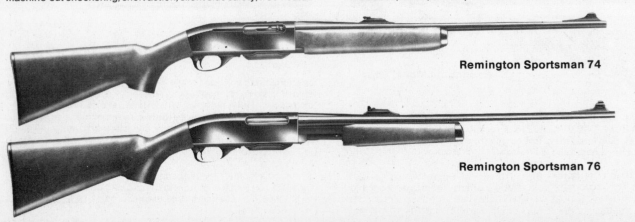

Remington Sportsman 74

Remington Sportsman 76

REMINGTON Sportsman 74: autoloader; .30/06; 4-rd. magazine; 22" barrel; walnut-finished hardwood stock, forend; open

REMINGTON Sportsman 76: slide-action; .30/06; 4-rd. magazine; 22" barrel; walnut-finished hardwood stock, forend; open

adjustable sights; other specs similar to those of Model Four. Introduced, 1984; dropped, 1987. Used value, $270 to $290.

adjustable sights. Other specs similar to those of Model Six. Introduced, 1984; dropped, 1987. Used value, $220 to $240.

Remington Sportsman 78

REMINGTON Sportsman 78: bolt-action; .223, .243, .308, .270, .30/06; 4-rd. magazine; 22" barrel; straight-comb walnut-finished hardwood stock; open adjustable sights; other specs similar to Model 700. Introduced, 1984; still in production. Used value, $240 to $260.

RIGBY

Rigby Best Quality

Rigby Second Quality

RIGBY Best Quality: hammerless ejector double rifle; .275 magnum, .350 magnum, .470 Nitro Express; side-lock action; 24" to 28" barrels; hand-checkered walnut stock; pistol grip, forearm; folding leaf rear sight, bead front; engraved receiver. Discontinued prior to World War II. Used value, $15,000 to $20,000.

Rigby Second Quality has the same general specs as the Best

Quality model, but features box-lock action. Used value, $9500 to $12,000.

Rigby Third Quality has the same specs as the Best Quality rifle, except for lower-grade wood, not as well finished. Used value, $7500 to $10,000.

Rigby 350 Magnum

RIGBY 350 Magnum: Mauser-type action; .350 magnum only; 24" barrel; 5-rd. box magazine; high-quality walnut stock with checkered full pistol grip, forearm; folding leaf rear sight, bead front. No longer in production. Used value, $2500 to $3500.

RIGBY 416 Magnum: Mauser-type action; .416 Big Game only; 24" barrel; 4-rd. box magazine; walnut sporting stock with check-

ered pistol grip, forearm; folding leaf rear sight, bead front. Still in production. Used value, $3500 to $4500.

Rigby 275

RIGBY 275: Mauser-type action; .275 High Velocity, 7x57mm; 25" barrel; 5-rd. box magazine; walnut sporting stock with hand-checkered full pistol grip, forearm; folding leaf rear sight, bead front. Still in production. Used value, $2000 to $2250.

Rigby 275 Lightweight has same specs as the standard model, except for 21" barrel. Still in production. Used value, $2000 to $2250.

RUGER

NOTE: In 1976, Ruger marked virtually all then-current models with the words: "Made in the 200th yr. of American Liberty." Guns carrying this line command prices twenty-five percent above the standard versions. This applies to new, unfired guns w/boxes.

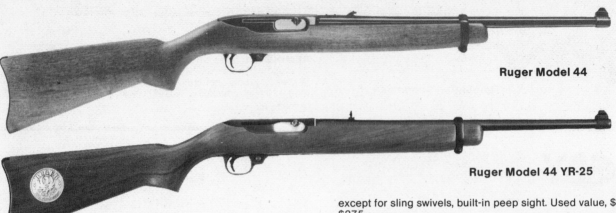

Ruger Model 44

Ruger Model 44 YR-25

RUGER Model 44: autoloading carbine; .44 magnum only; 18½" barrel; 4-rd. tube magazine; magazine release button incorporated in 1967; uncheckered walnut pistol-grip carbine stock; barrel band; receiver tapped for scope mount; folding leaf rear sight, gold bead front. Introduced in 1961; dropped, 1985. Used value, $250 to $275.

Model 44RS carbine is the same as the standard Model 44, except for sling swivels, built-in peep sight. Used value, $250 to $275.

Model 44 Sporter is the same as the standard Model 44, except for sling swivels, Monte Carlo sporter stock, grooved forearm, grip cap, flat butt plate. Dropped, 1971. Used value, $350 to $400.

Model 44 International is the same as standard Model 44, except for full-length Mannlicher-type walnut stock, sling swivels. Dropped, 1971. Used value, $500 to $550.

Model 44 YR-25 Carbine has same specs as earlier versions, but this is the 25th Anniversary model, the last year of manufacture. Made only in 1985. Used value, $375 to $400.

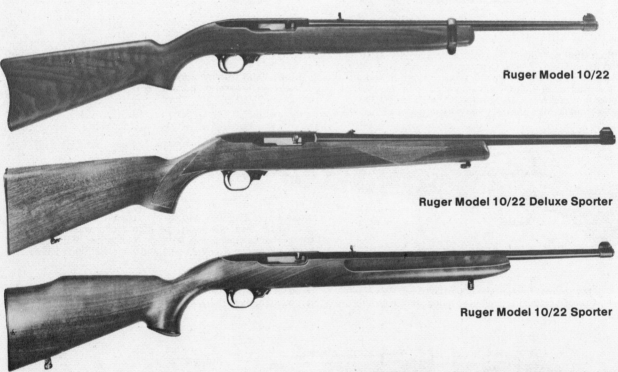

Ruger Model 10/22

Ruger Model 10/22 Deluxe Sporter

Ruger Model 10/22 Sporter

RUGER Model 10/22: autoloading carbine; .22 LR only; 18½" barrel; detachable 10-rd. rotary magazine; uncheckered walnut carbine stock on early versions; as of 1980, standard models have birch stocks; barrel band; receiver tapped for scope blocks or tip-off mount; adjustable folding leaf rear sight, gold bead front. Introduced in 1964; still in production. Used value, $95 to $100.

Model 10/22 Sporter is the same as standard Model 10/22, except for Monte Carlo stock with grooved semi-beavertail forearm, black plastic grip cap with white eagle, sling swivels. Introduced 1966; dropped, 1971. Used value, $125 to $135.

Model 10/22 Deluxe Sporter has the same general specs as the standard model, except has checkered walnut stock, flat butt plate, sling swivels; no barrel band. Introduced, 1971; still in production. Used value, $140 to $150.

Model 10/22 International has the same specs as standard model, except has full-length Mannlicher-type walnut stock, sling swivels. Early production was uncheckered; later production had two different types of checkering. Introduced, 1966; dropped, 1971. Used value, $350 to $400.

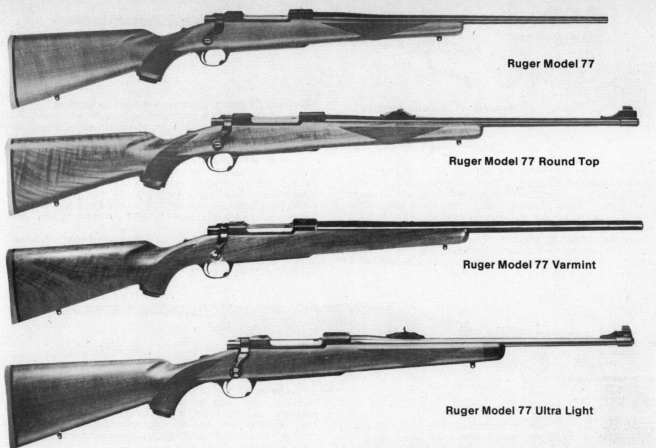

Ruger Model 77

Ruger Model 77 Round Top

Ruger Model 77 Varmint

Ruger Model 77 Ultra Light

RUGER Model 77 R: bolt-action; .22-250, .220 Swift, .243 Win., .25/06, .257 Roberts, .250-3000, 6mm, .270 Win., 7x57mm, 7mm Rem. magnum, .30/06; 22" tapered barrel, 3- or 5-rd. capacity, depending upon caliber; hinged floor plate; adjustable trigger; hand-checkered American walnut stock; pistol-grip cap; sling swivel studs; recoil pad; integral scope mount base; optional folding leaf adjustable rear sight, gold bead ramp front. Introduced in 1968; still in production. Used values: $250 to $265; with sights, $265 to $285.

Model 77RS magnum-size action, made in .257 Roberts, .25/06, .270 Win., .30/06, 7mm Rem. magnum, .300 Win. magnum, .338 Win. magnum; magazine capacity, 3 or 5 rds., depending upon caliber; .270, .30/06, 7x57, .280 Rem. have 22" barrels, all others, 24". Used value, $285 to $295, depending upon caliber.

Model 77 Round Top Magnum (77ST) has round top action; drilled, tapped for standard scope mounts, open sights; .25/06, .270 Win., 7mm Rem. magnum, .30/06, .300 Win. magnum, .338 Win. magnum; other specs generally the same as Model 77 Standard. Introduced in 1971; dropped, 1985. Used value, $285 to $295.

Model 77 Varmint (77V) is made in .22-250, .220 Swift, .243 Win., .25/06 and .308; 24" heavy straight tapered barrel, 26" in .220 Swift; drilled, tapped for target scope mounts or integral scope mount bases on receiver; checkered American walnut stock. Introduced, 1970; still in production. Used value, $275 to $300.

Model 77 Ultra Light (77RL) has same specs as standard model, except .243, .308, .270, .30/06, .257, .22-250, .250-3000; 20" light barrel; Ruger 1" scope rings supplied. Introduced, 1983; still in production. Used value, $330 to $355.

Model 77 International (77RSI) has the same specs as standard model, except has 18½" barrel, full-length Mannlicher-style stock, steel forend cap, loop-type sling swivels, open sights, Ruger steel scope rings, improved front sight; .22-250, .250-3000, .243, .308, .270, .30/06; weighs 7 lb; 38⅜" overall length. Introduced, 1986; still in production. Used value, $375 to $400.

Model 77 Ultra Light Carbine (77RLS) has same specs as Model 77 Ultra Light rifle, except has 18½" barrel, Ruger scope mounting system, iron sights, hinged floor plate; .270, .30/06, .243, .308; overall length is 38⅞"; weighs 6 lb. Introduced, 1987; still in production. Used value, $375 to $400.

Ruger No. 1 Light Sporter

Ruger No. 1 Medium Sporter

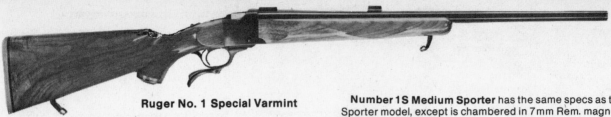

Ruger No. 1 Special Varmint

RUGER No. 1 B: under-lever single-shot; .22-250, .220 Swift, .243 Win., .223, .257 Roberts, .280, 6mm Rem., .25/06, .270 Win., .30/06, 7mm Rem. magnum, .300 Win. magnum, .338 magnum, .270 Weatherby, .300 Weatherby; 26" barrel, with quarter rib; American walnut, two-piece stock; hand-checkered pistol grip, forearm; open sights or integral scope mounts; hammerless falling-block design; automatic ejector; top tang safety. Introduced in 1967; still in production. Used value, $325 to $350.

Number 1 A Light Sporter has the same general specs as standard model, except for 22" barrel, Alex Henry-style forearm, iron sights; .243 Win., .270 Win., .30/06, 7x57mm. Introduced in 1968; still in production. Used value, $325 to $350.

Number 1S Medium Sporter has the same specs as the Light Sporter model, except is chambered in 7mm Rem. magnum, .300 Win. magnum, .338 Win. magnum, .45-70; 26" barrel, except .45-70, with 22" barrel. Introduced in 1968; still in production. Used value, $325 to $350.

Number 1H Tropical Model is chambered for .375 H&H magnum, .458 Win. magnum; has 24" heavy barrel; open sights. Introduced in 1968; still in production. Used value, $350 to $375.

Number 1V Special Varminter has 24" heavy barrel, chambered for .22-250, .220 Swift, .223, .25/06, 6mm; supplied with target scope bases. Introduced in 1970; still in production. Used value, $300 to $325.

Number 1 RSI International has same features as No. 1B, except has full-length Mannlicher-style stock of American walnut. Calibers .243, .30/06, 7x57, .270. Introduced, 1983; still in production. Used value, $325 to $350.

Ruger No. 3

RUGER No. 3: under-lever single-shot carbine; .22 Hornet, .223, .30-40 Krag, .375 Win., .44 magnum, .45-70; 22" barrel; same action as Ruger No. 1, except for different lever; unchecked American walnut, two-piece carbine-type stock; folding leaf rear sight, gold bead front; adjustable trigger; barrel band on forearm; automatic ejector. Introduced in 1969; .30-40 chambering dropped 1978; model discontinued, 1986. Used value, $225 to $250.

Ruger Min-14

Ruger Mini-14 Ranch Rifle

RUGER Mini-14: gas-operated, fixed-piston carbine; .223 Rem. only; 18½" barrel; 5-rd. detachable box magazine; unchecked, reinforced American hardwood carbine-type stock (early versions had walnut); positive primary extraction; fully adjustable rear sight, gold bead front. Introduced in 1973; still in production. Used value, $225 to $235.

Mini-14 Stainless has same general specs as standard model, except that barrel, action are built of stainless steel. Introduced in 1978; still in production. Used value, $275 to $285.

Mini-14 Ranch Rifle has same general specs as standard rifle, except is chambered for .222 (1984 only), .223; has steel-reinforced hardwood stock; ramp-type front sight; marketed with Ruger S100R scope rings; 20-rd. magazine available; blued or stainless steel. Used values: blued, $270 to $285; stainless, $285 to $295.

Ruger Model 77/22

RUGER Model 77/22: bolt-action; .22 LR; 10-rd. magazine; 20" barrel; 39¾" overall length; straight-grain American walnut stock; folding leaf rear sight, gold bead front; rotary magazine; three-position safety; patented bolt locking system; integral scope-mounting system. Introduced, 1983; still in production. Used value, $240 to $260.

S.A.B. GAMBA

S.A.B. GAMBA Bayern 88: over/under combo; 2¾" 12 ga. over 5.6x50R, 6.5x57R, 7x57R, 7x65R, .222 Rem. magnum, .30/06; 24½" barrels; modified choke; weighs 7½ lb.; folding leaf rear sight, bead front on ramp; checkered European walnut stock; box-lock action; double-set trigger; case-hardened receiver; game, floral scene engraving; extractors; solid barrel rib. Made in Italy. Introduced, 1987; no longer imported. Used value, $1100 to $1250.

S.A.B. GAMBA Mustang: single-shot; .222 Rem. magnum, 5.6x50, 6.5x57R, 7x65R, .270 Win., .30/06; 25½" barrel; weighs 6¼ lb.; leaf rear sight, bead on ramp front; hand-checkered. oil-finished figured European walnut stock; H&H-type single-shot side-lock action; double-set trigger; silvered receiver; Renaissance engraving signed by engraver; claw-type scope mounts. Made in Italy. Introduced, 1987; no longer imported. Used value, $9400 to $9600.

S.A.B. GAMBA Safari Express: over/under; 7x65R, 9.3x74R, .375 H&H; 25" barrel; weighs about 9 lb.; leaf rear sight, bead on ramp front; checkered select European walnut stock; cheekpiece; rubber recoil pad; box-lock action; triple Greener locking system; auto ejectors; double-set triggers; engraved floral, game scenes. Made in Italy. Introduced, 1987; no longer imported. Used value, $4800 to $5000.

S.A.B. GAMBA RGZ 1000 Game: bolt-action; .270, 7x64, 7mm Rem. magnum, .300 Win. magnum; 23¾" barrel; weighs 7¾ lb.; open adjustable rear sight, hooded blade front; Monte Carlo-style European walnut stock; modified 98K Mauser action; double-set trigger. Made in Italy. Introduced, 1987; dropped, 1988; was imported by Armes de Chasse. Used value, $950 to $1000.

RGZ 1000 Battue has same specs as Game model, except has 20½" barrel; special open notch ramp rear sight, bead front; single trigger. Introduced, 1987; dropped, 1988. Used value, $1000 to $1050.

SAKO

Sako Vixen Sporter

Sako Vixen Carbine

Sako Vixen Heavy Barrel

SAKO Vixen Sporter: bolt-action; .218 Bee, .22 Hornet, .222 Rem., .222 Rem. magnum, .223; built on L461 short Mauser-type action; 23½" barrel; checkered European walnut, Monte Carlo, pistol-grip stock; cheekpiece; no rear sight; drilled, tapped for scope mounts; hooded ramp front; sling swivels. Introduced in 1946; dropped, 1976. Used value, $500 to $525.

Vixen Carbine has same specs as the Vixen Sporter, except for Mannlicher-type stock, 20" barrel. Used value, $550 to $575.

Vixen Heavy Barrel model has same specs as sporter, except in .222 Rem., .222 Rem. magnum, .223 only; target-style stock; beavertail forearm; heavy barrel. Used value, $475 to $500.

Sako Mauser

SAKO Mauser: bolt-action sporter; .270, .30/06; 24" barrel; built on FN Mauser action; 5-rd. magazine; hand-checkered European walnut, Monte Carlo cheekpiece stock; open leaf rear sight, Patridge front; sling swivel studs. Introduced in 1946; dropped, 1961. Used value, $450 to $500.

Magnum Mauser has same general specs as standard Sako Mauser; .300 H&H magnum, .375 H&H magnum only; recoil pad. Dropped, 1961. Used value, $550 to $600.

Sako Forester Sporter

SAKO Forester Sporter: bolt-action; .22-250, .243 Win., .308 Win.; 23" barrel; built on L579 medium Mauser-type action; 5-rd. magazine; hand-checkered walnut Monte Carlo pistol-grip stock; no rear sight, hooded ramp front; drilled, tapped for scope mounts; sling swivel studs. Introduced in 1957; dropped, 1971. Used value, $425 to $450.

Forester Carbine has same specs as Forester Sporter, except for Mannlicher-type stock, 20" barrel. Used value, $450 to $475.

Forester Heavy Barrel model has same specs as standard model, except for 24" heavy barrel. Used value, $425 to $450.

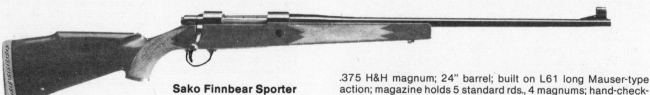

Sako Finnbear Sporter

SAKO Finnbear Sporter: bolt-action; .25/06, .264 Win. magnum, .270, .30/06, .300 Win. magnum, .338 magnum, 7mm Rem. magnum, .375 H&H magnum; 24" barrel; built on L61 long Mauser-type action; magazine holds 5 standard rds., 4 magnums; hand-checkered European walnut, Monte Carlo, pistol-grip stock; recoil pad; sling swivels; no rear sight, hooded ramp front; drilled, tapped for scope mounts. Introduced in 1961; dropped, 1971. Used value, $450 to $475; $550 to $575 for .375.

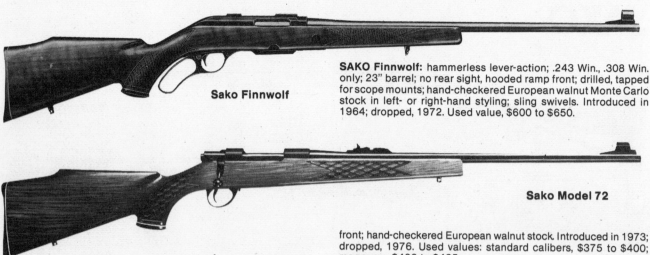

Sako Finnwolf

SAKO Finnwolf: hammerless lever-action; .243 Win., .308 Win. only; 23" barrel; no rear sight, hooded ramp front; drilled, tapped for scope mounts; hand-checkered European walnut Monte Carlo stock in left- or right-hand styling; sling swivels. Introduced in 1964; dropped, 1972. Used value, $600 to $650.

Sako Model 72

SAKO Model 72: bolt-action; .222 Rem., .223 Rem., .22-250, .243 Win., .25/06, .270 Win., .30/06, 7mm Rem. magnum, .300 Win. magnum, .338 Win. magnum, .375 H&H magnum; 23" or 24" barrel; adjustable trigger; hinged floor plate; short action in .222, .223, long action on all other calibers; adjustable rear sight, hooded front; hand-checkered European walnut stock. Introduced in 1973; dropped, 1976. Used values: standard calibers, $375 to $400; magnums, $400 to $425.

SAKO Model 73: lever-action; .243 Win., .308 Win.; has same specs as Finnwolf model, except for flush floorplate, 3-rd. clip magazine, no cheekpiece. Manufactured 1973 to 1975. Used value, $375 to $400.

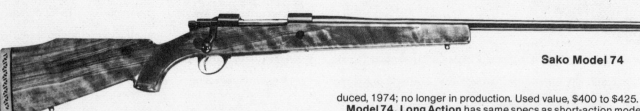

Sako Model 74

SAKO Model 74, Short Action: bolt-action; .222 Rem., .223 Rem.; 5-rd. magazine; 23½" standard or heavy barrel; no sights; hand-checkered European walnut Monte Carlo stock; Mauser-type action; detachable sling swivels. Introduced, 1974; no longer in production. Used value, $425 to $450.

Model 74, Medium Action has same specs as short-action model, except chambering for .220 Swift, .22-250, .243 Win. Intro-

SAKO Model 78: bolt-action; .22 LR, .22 Hornet; 5-rd. magazine for rimfire, 4 rds. for Hornet; 22½" barrel; no sights; hand-checkered European walnut Monte Carlo stock. Introduced, 1977; no longer

duced, 1974; no longer in production. Used value, $400 to $425.

Model 74, Long Action has same specs as short-action model, except for 24" barrel; 4-rd. magazine for magnum cartridges; chambered for .25/06, .270 Win., 7mm Rem. magnum, .30/06, .300 Win. magnum, .338 Win. magnum, .375 H&H. Heavy-barrel version chambered only for .25/06, 7mm Rem. magnum. Introduced, 1974; no longer in production. Used value, $400 to $425.

Model 74 Carbine has same specs as long-action Model 74, except for 20" barrel; Mannlicher-design full-length stock; 5-rd. magazine, chambered only for .30/06. Introduced, 1974; no longer in production. Used value, $450 to $475.

in production. Used values: .22 RF, $325 to $350; .22 Hornet, $350 to $375.

Sako Model 78

Sako Standard Sporter

Sako Classic Sporter

Sako Deluxe Sporter

Sako Super Deluxe Sporter

Sako Safari Grade

SAKO Standard Sporter: bolt-action; .17 Rem., .222, .223 (short action); .22-250, .220 Swift, .243, .308 (medium action); .25/06, .270, .30/06, 7mm Rem. magnum, .300 Win. magnum, .338 Win. magnum, .375 magnum, .375 H&H magnum (long action); 23", 24" barrels; no sights; hand-checkered European walnut pistol-grip stock; hinged floor plate, adjustable trigger. Imported from Finland by Stoeger; introduced, 1978; no longer imported. Used values: short action, $450 to $475; medium action, $450 to $475; long action, $475 to $500; magnum calibers, $500 to $525.

Classic Sporter has same specs as Standard Sporter, except has straight-comb stock with oil finish, solid rubber recoil pad, recoil lug; receiver drilled, tapped for scope mounts; in .243, .270, .30/06, 7mm Rem. magnum only. Introduced, 1980; no longer imported. Used value, $700 to $725.

Deluxe Sporter has same specs as Standard Sporter except has select wood, rosewood pistol-grip cap, forend tip; metal checkering on dovetail bases, bolt sleeve, bolt handle; ventilated recoil pad; skip-line checkering. Used value, $700 to $750.

Super Deluxe Sporter has same specs as Deluxe Sporter except has select European walnut stock with deep-cut oak leaf carving, high-gloss finish; metal has super-high polish. Used value, $1600 to $1750.

Heavy Barrel Sporter has same basic specs as Standard Sporter except for beavertail forend. Made with short, medium actions only. Used value, $575 to $600.

Carbine model has same specs as Standard Sporter, except has full Mannlicher-type stock, 20" barrel; made in .222, .243, .270, .30/06 only. Introduced, 1977; still imported by Stoeger. Used value, $625 to $650.

Safari Grade has same general specs as Standard Sporter, except is made in long action only; 7mm Rem. magnum, .300 Win. magnum, .338 Win. magnum, .375 H&H magnum only; hand-checkered European walnut stock, solid rubber recoil pad; pistol-grip cap, forend tip; quarter-rib express rear sight, hooded ramp front, front sling swivel mounted on barrel. Used value, $1250 to $1300.

Sako Finnsport 2700

SAKO Finnsport 2700: bolt-action; short, long, medium actions; same general specs as standard Sako Sporter model; same calibers; Monte Carlo stock design; comes with scope mounts; different checkering pattern. Introduced, 1983; no longer imported by Stoeger. Used value, $640 to $660.

Sako Fiberclass Sporter

SAKO Fiberclass Sporter: bolt-action; .25/06, .270, .30/06, 7mm Rem. magnum, .300, .338 Win. magnum, .375 H&H; has same general specs as Standard Sporter, except has black fiberglass stock; wrinkle finish; rubber butt pad; 23" barrel; marketed with scope mounts. Made in Finland. Introduced, 1985; still imported by Stoeger. Used values: standard calibers, $775 to $800; magnums, $790 to $815.

Sako Hunter

Sako Hunter LS

Sako Hunter Carbine

SAKO Hunter has same specs as the Sako Sporter, but with redesigned stock; scope mounts are marketed with the rifle. Made in Finland. Introduced under new name, 1986; still imported by Stoeger. Used value, $625 to $650.

Hunter LS has same specs as Hunter model, except has laminated stock with dull finish; chambered for the same calibers. Introduced, 1987; still imported by Stoeger. Used value, $700 to $750.

Hunter Carbine has same specs as Sako Hunter, but with 18½" barrel; oil-finished stock; .22-250, .243, 7mm-08, .308, .300 Win., .25/06, 6.5x55, .270, 7x64, .30/06, 7mm Rem. magnum, .375 H&H. Introduced, 1986; still imported by Stoeger. Used value, $650 to $675.

SAVAGE

SAVAGE Model 99A: lever-action repeater. Every gun company of major proportions seems to have one or two models that have become legend and upon which much of the company's reputation has been built. This is true of the Model 99 — and it's many variations — for the Savage Arms Corporation. The original Model 99 was introduced in 1899 and replaced in 1922 by the Model 99A. The Model 99A is in .30-30, .300 Savage, .303 Savage; hammerless, solid frame; 24" barrel; 5-rd. rotary magazine; uncheckered straight-grip American walnut stock, tapered forearm; open rear sight, bead front on ramp. Introduced in 1922; dropped, 1983. Used value, $300 to $325; $100 premium for pre-WWII.

Model 99B is the same as Model 99A, except has take-down design. Dropped, 1937. Used value, $500 to $550.

Model 99E, pre-World War II model had solid frame and was chambered for .22 Hi-Power, .250-3000, .30-30, .300 Savage, .303 Savage; 24" barrel for .300 Savage, 22" for all others; other specs are the same as Model 99A. Model was dropped in 1940; reintroduced in 1961; dropped, 1984. The current model is chambered in .243 Win., .300 Savage, .308 Win.; 20" barrel; checkered pistol-grip stock. Used values: pre-WWII, $550 to $650; current model, $235 to $250.

Model 99H is solid-frame model, with same general specs as Model 99A, except for carbine stock with barrel band; .250-3000, .30-30, .303 Savage. Used value, $425 to $450.

Model 99F Featherweight model was discontinued in 1940; reintroduced in 1955; dropped, 1973. Pre-WWII model was takedown style, with same specs as pre-war Model 99E, except for lighter weight. The 1955 version has solid frame, 22" barrel; .243 Win., .300 Savage, .308 Win.; checkered walnut pistol-grip stock. Used values: pre-WWII model, $425 to $450; 1955 model, $275 to $300.

Model 99G has the same specs as pre-WWII Model 99E, except for take-down feature; hand-checkered pistol grip, forearm. Dropped, 1940. Used value, $400 to $450.

Model 99K is a deluxe version of Model 99G. Has engraved receiver, barrel, Lyman peep rear sight, folding middle sight; fancy-grade walnut stock; other specs identical. Dropped, 1940. Used value, $1500 to $2000.

Model 99EG has same specs as Model G except for uncheckered stock in pre-WWII styling. Dropped in 1940; reintroduced in 1955; dropped, 1961. The 1955 version is in .250 Savage, .243 Win., .300 Savage, .308 Win., .358 Win. Used values: pre-WWII,

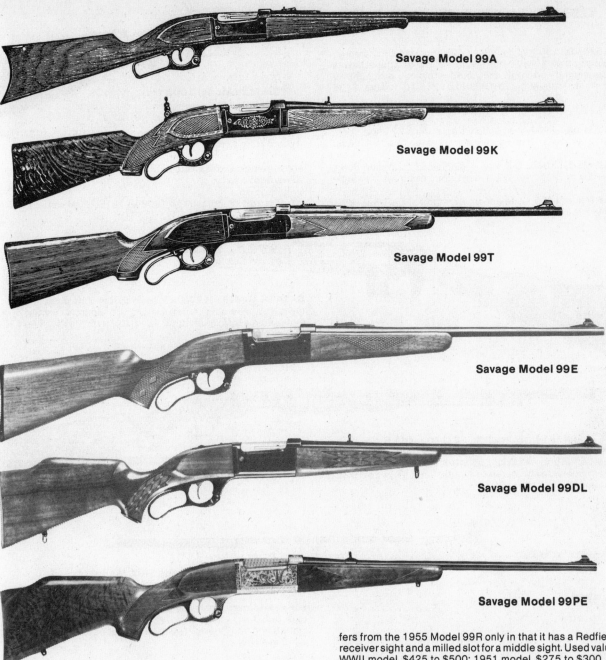

Savage Model 99A

Savage Model 99K

Savage Model 99T

Savage Model 99E

Savage Model 99DL

Savage Model 99PE

$400 to $425; 1955 model, $275 to $300.

Model 99T Featherweight has same general specs as standard Model 99s; solid-frame design; .22 High-Power, .30-30, .303 Savage, .300 Savage; 22" barrel on .300 Savage, 20" for other calibers; hand-checkered walnut pistol-grip stock; beavertail forend; weighs approximately 1½ lb. less than standard. Dropped, 1940. Used value, $350 to $375.

Model 99R pre-WWII was solid-frame design; .250-3000, .300 Savage; 22" barrel for .250-3000, 24" for .300 Savage; oversize pistol-grip stock, forearm; hand-checkered American walnut. Dropped, 1940; reintroduced, 1951; dropped, 1961. The 1951 version has the same specs as pre-WWII version, except for 24" barrel; sling swivel studs; .243 Win., .250 Savage, .300 Savage, .308 Win., .358 Win. Used values: pre-WWII model, $400 to $425; 1951 model, $250 to $300.

Model 99RS was made prior to WWII, dropped in 1940, then reintroduced in 1955, finally being discontinued in 1961. The pre-war model is the same as the pre-war Model 99R, except that it is equipped with quick-detachable sling swivels and sling, a Lyman rear peep sight and a folding middle sight. The pre-war version dif-

fers from the 1955 Model 99R only in that it has a Redfield 70LH receiver sight and a milled slot for a middle sight. Used values: pre-WWII model, $425 to $500; 1951 model, $275 to $300.

Model 99DL Deluxe has same general specs as discontinued Model 99F, except for sling swivels, high-comb Monte Carlo stock; .243 Win., .308 Win. Introduced, 1960; dropped, 1974. Used value, $300 to $325.

Model 99C has same specs as Model 99F, except clip magazine replaces rotary type; .243 Win., .284 Win., .308 Win. (.284 dropped in 1974); 4-rd. detachable magazine; 3-rd for .284. Introduced in 1965; still in production. Used value, $275 to $300.

Model 99CD is same as Model 99C, except for removable bead ramp front sight, removable adjustable rear sight, white line recoil pad, pistol-grip cap, hand-checkered pistol grip, grooved forearm, quick-detachable swivels, sling; .250-3000, .308 Win. Used value, $285 to $300.

Model 99PE Presentation Grade has same specs as Model 99DL, plus game scene engraved on receiver sides, engraved tang, lever; fancy American walnut Monte Carlo stock, forearm; hand checkering; quick-detachable swivels; .243 Win., .284 Win., .308 Win. Introduced in 1968; dropped, 1970. Used value, $750 to $900.

Model 99DE Citation Grade is same as Model 99PE, but engraving is less elaborate. Introduced in 1968; dropped, 1970. Used value, $500 to $650.

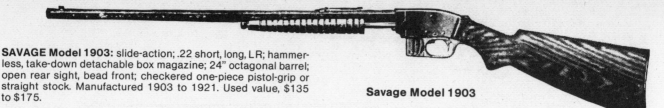

SAVAGE Model 1903: slide-action; .22 short, long, LR; hammerless, take-down detachable box magazine; 24" octagonal barrel; open rear sight, bead front; checkered one-piece pistol-grip or straight stock. Manufactured 1903 to 1921. Used value, $135 to $175.

Savage Model 1903

SAVAGE Model 1904: bolt-action, single-shot; .22 short, long, LR; take-down; 18" barrel; open rear sight, bead front; uncheck-

ered one-piece straight stock. Manufactured 1904 to 1917. Used value, $75 to $85.

SAVAGE Model 1905: bolt-action, single-shot; .22 short, long, LR; take-down; 22" barrel; open rear sight, bead front; uncheck-

ered one-piece straight stock. Manufactured 1905 to 1918. Used value, $85 to $95.

SAVAGE Model 1909: slide-action; .22 short, long, LR; has same general specs as Model 1903, except for uncheckered stock, 20"

round barrel. Manufactured 1909 to 1915. Used value, $110 to $135.

Savage Model 1912

SAVAGE Model 1912: autoloader; .22 LR; 7-rd. detachable box magazine; take-down; open rear sight, bead front; uncheckered straight stock. Manufactured 1912 to 1916. Used value, $200 to $250.

SAVAGE Model 1914: slide-action; .22 short, long, LR; hammerless, take-down; tubular magazine holds 17 LR cartridges; 24" octagonal barrel; open rear sight, bead front; uncheckered pistol-grip stock, grooved slide handle. Manufactured 1914 to 1924. Used value, $150 to $195.

Savage Model 1914

Savage NRA Model 19

SAVAGE NRA Model 19: bolt-action match rifle; .22 LR only; 25"

barrel; 5-rd. detachable box magazine; American walnut military-type full stock, pistol grip, uncheckered; adjustable rear peep sight, blade front. Introduced in 1919; dropped, 1933. Used value, $145 to $155.

SAVAGE Model 19: bolt-action target rifle, replacing NRA Model 19; .22 LR only; 25" barrel; 5-rd. detachable box magazine; target-type uncheckered walnut stock, full pistol grip, beavertail forearm. Early versions have adjustable rear peep sight, blade front; later models have hooded front sight, extension rear. Introduced in 1933; dropped, 1946. Used value, $145 to $155.

Model 19H is same as 1933 Model 19, except chambered for .22 Hornet only. Used value, $350 to $400.
Model 19L has same specs as 1933 Model 19, except for Lyman 48Y receiver sight, No. 17A front. Used value, $200 to $250.
Model 19M has same specs as 1933 Model 19, except for heavy 28" barrel, with scope bases. Used value, $200 to $250.

SAVAGE Model 1920: bolt-action, short Mauser action; .250-3000, .300 Savage; 22" barrel in .250-3000, 24" in .300 Savage; 5-rd. box magazine; hand-checkered American walnut pistol-grip

stock, slender Schnabel forearm; open rear sight, bead front. Introduced in 1920; dropped, 1926. Used value, $325 to $350.

Savage Model 20-1926

SAVAGE Model 20-1926: bolt-action; has same specs as Model 1920, except for redesigned stock, 24" barrel, Lyman No. 54 rear peep sight. Introduced in 1926; dropped, 1929. Used value, $325 to $350.

Savage Model 23AA

Savage Model 23B

Model 23AA has the same general specs as Model 23A, with exception of checkered stock, swivel studs, speed lock. Introduced in 1933; dropped, 1942. Used value, $175 to $185.

Model 23B has same specs as Model 23A, but is chambered for .25-20 cartridge; no Schnabel; 25" barrel; swivel studs. Dropped, 1942. Used value, $150 to $175.

Model 23C has the same specs as the Model 23B, except it is chambered for .32-20. Dropped, 1942. Used value, $150 to $185.

Model 23D has the same specs as the Model 23B, except it is chambered for .22 Hornet. Dropped, 1947. Used value, $250 to $275.

SAVAGE Model 23A: bolt-action; .22 LR only; 23" barrel; 5-rd. detachable box magazine; uncheckered American walnut pistol-grip stock, thin forearm, Schnabel tip; open rear sight, blade or bead front. Introduced in 1923; dropped, 1933. Used value, $145 to $155.

SAVAGE Model 25: side-action hammerless take-down repeater; .22 short, long, LR; 24" octagon barrel; tube magazine holds 15 LR, 17 long, 20 short cartridges; uncheckered American walnut pistol-grip stock; grooved slide handle; open rear sight, blade front. Introduced in 1925; dropped, 1929. Used value, $200 to $225.

Savage Model 40

SAVAGE Model 40: bolt-action sporter; .250-3000, .30-30, .300 Savage, .30/06; 24" barrel in .300 Savage, .30/06; 22" in other calibers; uncheckered American walnut pistol-grip stock, tapered forearm, Schnabel tip; open rear sight, bead front on ramp; detachable box magazine; release button on right side of stock. Introduced in 1928; dropped, 1940. Used value, $200 to $250.

Savage Model 45

SAVAGE Model 45: termed Super Sporter, it has same specs as Model 40, except for chamberings, hand-checkered pistol grip, forearm. Introduced in 1928; dropped, 1940. Used value, $300 to $325.

Savage Model 29

SAVAGE Model 29: slide-action hammerless take-down repeater; .22 short, long, LR; 24" barrel; tube magazine holds 15 LR, 17 long, 20 short cartridges; open rear sight, bead front. Pre-WWII version had octagon barrel, hand-checkered walnut pistol-grip stock, slide-handle; post-war model had round barrel, uncheckered wood. Introduced in 1929; dropped, 1967. Used values: pre-WWII, $225 to $250; post-war, $175 to $185.

Savage Model 3

SAVAGE Model 3: bolt-action take-down single-shot; .22 short, long, LR; pre-WWII version has 26" barrel, later models, 24"; uncheckered American walnut pistol-grip stock; checkered hard rubber butt plate; open rear sight, bead front. Introduced in 1933; dropped, 1952. Used value, $65 to $75.

Model 3S has same specs as Model 3, except for substitution of rear peep sight, hooded front sight. Used value, $85 to $95.

Model 3ST has the same specs as the Model 3S, but was sold with swivels, sling. Dropped, 1941. Used value, $95 to $100.

Savage Model 4

SAVAGE Model 4: bolt-action take-down repeater; .22 short, long, LR; 24" barrel; 5-rd. detachable box magazine; pre-WWII version has checkered pistol-grip American walnut stock, grooved forearm; post-war model has uncheckered stock; open rear sight, bead front. Introduced in 1933; dropped, 1965. Used values: pre-WWII, $95 to $100; post-war, $75 to $85.

Model 4S has the same specs as Model 4, except for substitution of rear peep sight, hooded front. Used values: pre-WWII, $115 to $125; post-war, $85 to $95.

Model 4M has same specs as post-war Model 4, except is chambered for .22 WRFM cartridge. Introduced in 1961; dropped, 1965. Used value, $100 to $115.

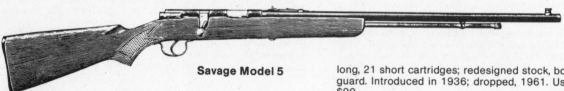

Savage Model 5

SAVAGE Model 5: bolt-action take-down repeater; has the specs of Model 4, except for tube magazine with capacity of 15 LR, 17 long, 21 short cartridges; redesigned stock, bolt handle, trigger guard. Introduced in 1936; dropped, 1961. Used value, $80 to $90.

Model 5S has the same specs as the Model 5, except for substitution of peep rear sight, hooded front. Used value, $100 to $110.

Savage Model 219

Savage Model 219L

SAVAGE Model 219: hammerless, take-down single-shot; 25" barrel; .22 Hornet, .25-20, .30-30, .32-20; shotgun-type action with top lever; uncheckered walnut pistol-grip stock, forearm; open rear sight, bead front on ramp. Introduced in 1938; dropped,1965. Used value, $125 to $135.

Savage Model 219L has same specs as Model 219 except action is opened with side lever. Introduced in 1965; dropped, 1967. Used value, $110 to $125.

SAVAGE Model 221: termed a utility gun, it has the same specs as the Model 219, except for chambering in .30-30 only, with interchangeable 30" 12-ga. shotgun barrel. Introduced in 1939; discontinued, 1960. Used value, $145 to $155.

SAVAGE Model 222: has the same specs as Model 221, except shotgun barrel is 16-ga., 28" Used values: $120 to $130; both barrels, $150 to $165.

SAVAGE Model 223: has same specs as the Model 221, except shotgun barrel is 20-ga., 28". Used values: $120 to $130; both barrels, $160 to $170.

SAVAGE Model 227: has same specs as the Model 221, except that shotgun barrel is 12-ga., 30"; rifle barrel chambered for .22 Hornet. Used value, $145 to $165.

SAVAGE Model 228: has same specs as Model 221, except shotgun barrel is 16-ga., 28"; rifle barrel is chambered for .22 Hornet. Used value, $145 to $150.

SAVAGE Model 229: has same specs as Model 221, except shotgun barrel is 20-ga., 28"; rifle barrel is chambered for .22 Hornet. Used value, $145 to $150.

Savage Model 6

SAVAGE Model 6: take-down autoloader; .22 short, long, LR; 24" barrel; tube magazine has capacity of 15 LR, 17 long, 21 short cartridges; pre-WWII version had checkered pistol-grip stock; post-war style has uncheckered walnut stock; open rear sight, bead front. Introduced in 1938; dropped, 1968. Used value, $75 to $85.

Model 6S has identical specs to Model 6, except for substitution of peep rear sight. Used value, $85 to $95.

SAVAGE Model 7: take-down autoloader; same specs as Model 6, except for 5-rd. detachable box magazine. Introduced in 1939; dropped, 1951. Used value, $85 to $90.

Model 7S has same specs as Model 7, except for substitution of peep rear sight, hooded front. Used value, $95 to $100.

Savage Model 340C

.222 Rem. was introduced in 1964; .22 Hornet dropped, 1964. Used values: .30-30, $135 to $145; .222 Rem., $135 to $145; .22 Hornet, $165 to $190.

Model 340C carbine has identical specs as standard Model 340, except for 18½" barrel, in .30-30 only. Introduced in 1962; dropped, 1965. Used value, $145 to $150.

Model 340S Deluxe has same specs as Model 340, except for peep rear sight, hooded front; hand-checkered stock, swivel studs. Dropped, 1958. Used value, $200 to $225.

SAVAGE Model 340: bolt-action repeater; .22 Hornet, .222 Rem., .30-30; 24" barrel in .22 Hornet, .222 Rem., 22" in .22 Hornet, .30-30, 20" in .30-30; uncheckered American walnut pistol-grip stock; open rear sight, ramp front. Introduced in 1950; dropped, 1986;

SAVAGE Model 342: bolt-action repeater; .22 Hornet only; has same specs as Model 340 and after 1953 was incorporated in manufacturer's line as Model 340. Introduced in 1950; dropped, 1953 as model. Used value, $175 to $200.

Model 342S has same specs as Model 340S, but is in .22 Hornet only. Incorporated into Model 340 line in 1953. Used value, $175 to $200.

Savage Model 110C

Savage Model 110 B

Savage Model 110CL

Savage Model 110 V

Savage Model 110E

Savage Model 110D

Savage Model 110DL

Savage Model 110DL Magnum

Savage Model 110S

Savage Model 110EL

SAVAGE Model 110: bolt-action repeater; .243 Win., .270 Win., .308 Win., .30/06; 22" barrel; 4-rd. box magazine; hand-checkered American walnut pistol-grip stock; open rear sight, ramp front. Introduced in 1958; dropped, 1963. This is another of those corporate successes that goes on and on in one variation or another. Used value, $145 to $150.

Model 110MC has same specs as Model 110, except for 24" barrel; Monte Carlo stock; in .22-250, .243 Win., .270 Win., .308 Win., .30/06. Introduced in 1959; dropped, 1969. Used value, $155 to $165.

Model 110MCL has same specs as Model 110MC, except it is built on left-hand action. Introduced in 1959; dropped, 1969. Used value, $175 to $200.

Model 110M magnum has specs of Model 110MC, except has recoil pad; in .264, .300, .308, .338 Win., 7mm Rem. magnum. Introduced in 1963; dropped, 1969. Used value, $175 to $200.

Model 110ML magnum has same specs as Model 110M, except for being built on a left-hand action. Used value, $175 to $200.

Model 110E has the same general specs as earlier versions of Model 110; .223, .243 Win., .30/06, .270, 7mm Rem. magnum; 24" stainless steel barrel for magnum, 20" ordnance steel for other calibers; 3-rd. box magazine for magnum, 4-rd. for others; uncheckered Monte Carlo stock on early versions; current models have checkered pistol grip, forearm; 7mm magnum has recoil pad; open rear sight, ramp front. Introduced in 1963; still in production. Used values: 7mm Rem. magnum, $200 to $225; other calibers, $165 to $185.

Model 110EL has the same specs as Model 110E, except in 7mm Rem. magnum, .30/06 only; left-hand action. Used values:

7mm magnum, $185 to $195; .30/06, $170 to $180.

Model 110P Premier Grade comes in .243 Win., .30/06, 7mm Rem. magnum; 24" barrel of stainless steel for 7mm magnum, 22" for other calibers; 3-shot box magazine for magnum, 4-shot for others; skip-checkered Monte Carlo French walnut stock, rosewood pistol-grip cap, forearm tip; magnum version has recoil pad; open rear sight, ramp front. Introduced in 1964; dropped, 1970. Used values: 7mm magnum, $400 to $425; other calibers, $375 to $400.

Model 110PL Premier Grade has the same specs as Model 110P, except for left-hand action. Used values: 7mm magnum, $400 to $425; other calibers, $375 to $400.

Model 110PE Presentation Grade has same specs as Model 110P, except for engraved receiver, trigger guard, floor plate; stock is of choice French walnut. Introduced in 1958; dropped, 1970. Used values: 7mm magnum, $550 to $575; other calibers, $500 to $525.

Model 110EL Presentation Grade has same specs as Model 110PE, except it is built on a left-hand action. Used values: 7mm magnum, $550 to $575; other calibers, $500 to $525.

Model 110C was introduced in 1966; no longer in production; .22-250, .243 Win., .25/06, .270 Win., .30/06, .308 Win., 7mm Rem. magnum, .300 Win. magnum. Magnum calibers have 3-shot detachable box magazine; other calibers, 4-rd. magazine; magnum calibers, .22-250 have 24" barrel, others, 22"; hand-checkered Monte Carlo American walnut pistol-grip stock; magnum has recoil pad; open folding leaf rear sight, ramp front Used values: magnum calibers, $275 to $300; standard calibers, $250 to $275.

Model 110B (right-hand bolt) and **110BL** (left-hand bolt) were introduced in 1977 and are same as Model 110E except chambered for .30/06, .270 Win., and .243 Win. and have internal magazines. Reintroduced, 1988 with laminated stock. Used values: Model 110B, $185 to $200; Model 110BL, $185 to $200.

Model 110S Silhouette has the same general specs as standard Model 110, except for heavy tapered 22" barrel, 5-rd. maga-

zine; chambered for .308 Win., 7mm-08 Rem. only; special silhouette stock, stippled pistol grip, forend; rubber recoil pad; no sights; drilled, tapped for scope mounts. Introduced, 1978; no longer in production. Used value, $275 to $325.

Model 110-V Varmint has same specs as 110-C, except is chambered for .22-250 only; 26" heavy barrel; varmint stock. Introduced, 1983; dropped, 1987. Used value, $300 to $325.

Model 110K has same specs as standard 110, except has laminated camouflage stock; .243, .270, .30/06, 7mm Rem. magnum, .338 Win. magnum. Introduced, 1986; dropped, 1988. Used value, $300 to $325.

SAVAGE/ANSCHUTZ Model 153: bolt-action; .222 Rem. only; 24" barrel; manufactured to Savage specs by J.G. Anschutz, West Germany; skip-checkered French walnut stock; cheekpiece; rose-

wood grip cap, forearm tip; sling swivels; folding leaf open rear sight, hooded ramp front. Introduced in 1964; dropped, 1967. Used value, $350 to $375.

Savage Model 65

SAVAGE Model 65: bolt-action; .22 short, long, LR; 20" free-floating barrel; 5-rd. detachable box magazine; sliding safety; dou-

ble extractors; American walnut Monte Carlo stock; checkered pistol grip, forearm; step-adjustable open rear sight, gold bead ramp front. Introduced in 1965; dropped, 1974. Used value, $75 to $85.

Model 65M has same specs as Model 65, but is chambered for .22 WRFM cartridge. Introduced in 1966; dropped, 1981. Used value, $100 to $115.

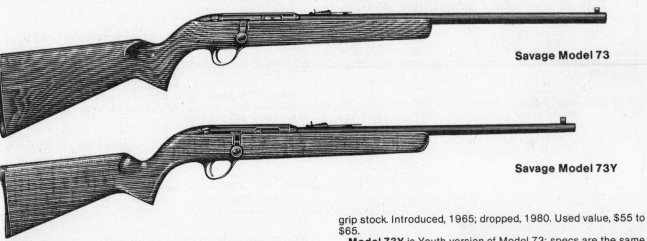

Savage Model 73

Savage Model 73Y

SAVAGE-Stevens Model 73: bolt-action, single-shot; .22 short, long, LR; open rear sight, bead front; uncheckered hardwood pistol-

grip stock. Introduced, 1965; dropped, 1980. Used value, $55 to $65.

Model 73Y is Youth version of Model 73; specs are the same except for shorter butt stock, 18" barrel. Introduced, 1965; dropped, 1980. Used value, $50 to $60.

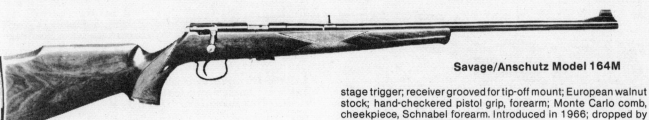

Savage/Anschutz Model 164M

SAVAGE/ANSCHUTZ Model 164: bolt-action; .22 LR only; 24" barrel; 5-rd. detachable clip magazine; fully adjustable single-

stage trigger; receiver grooved for tip-off mount; European walnut stock; hand-checkered pistol grip, forearm; Monte Carlo comb, cheekpiece, Schnabel forearm. Introduced in 1966; dropped by Savage in 1981. Used value, $250 to $275.

Model 164M has same specs as Model 164, except magazine holds 4 rds.; chambered for .22 WRFM cartridge. Used value, $275 to $300.

SAVAGE/ANSCHUTZ Model 54: bolt-action; .22 LR only; 23" barrel; 5-rd. clip magazine; adjustable single-stage trigger; wing safety; receiver grooved for tip-off mount, tapped for scope blocks; French walnut stock, with Monte Carlo roll-over comb, Schnabel forearm tip; hand-checkered pistol grip, forearm; folding leaf sight,

hooded ramp gold bead front. Introduced in 1966; dropped by Savage in 1981. Used value, $425 to $450.

Model 54M has same specs as Model 54, except chambered for .22 WRFM. Introduced in 1973; dropped by Savage, 1981. Used value, $450 to $475.

Savage/Anschutz Model 54

Savage/Anschutz Model 184

SAVAGE/ANSCHUTZ Model 184: bolt-action; .22 LR only; 21½" barrel; 5-rd. detachable clip magazine; factory-set trigger; receiver grooved for scope mounts; European walnut stock with Monte Carlo comb, Schnabel forearm; hand-checkered pistol grip, forearm; folding leaf rear sight, hooded ramp front. Introduced in 1966; dropped, 1974. Used value, $250 to $300.

Savage/Anschutz Model 10D

SAVAGE-Anschutz Mark 10: bolt-action, single-shot; .22 LR; 26" barrel; micrometer rear sight, globe front; European walnut pistol-grip target stock; cheekpiece; adjustable hand stop; sling swivels. Imported 1967 to 1972. Used value, $175 to $200.

    Mark 10D has same general specs as standard Mark 10, except for Monte Carlo stock, different rear sight. Imported 1972 only. Used value, $200 to $225.

SAVAGE-Stevens Model 46: bolt-action; .22 short, long, LR; tubular magazine holds 15 LR; 20" barrel; uncheckered hardwood pistol-grip stock, or checkered Monte Carlo stock. Manufactured 1969 to 1973. Used value, $60 to $65.

Savage Model 60

SAVAGE Model 60: autoloader; .22 LR; 15-rd. tubular magazine; 20" barrel; open rear sight, ramp front; American walnut Monte Carlo stock; checkered pistol grip, forearm. Manufactured 1969 to 1972. Used value, $65 to $75.

Savage Model 88

SAVAGE Model 88: autoloader; .22 LR; has same general specs as Model 60, except for blade front sight, uncheckered hardwood stock. Manufactured 1969 to 1972. Used value, $65 to $75.

Savage Model 90

SAVAGE Model 90 Carbine: autoloader; .22 LR; same general specs as Model 60, except for 10-rd. tubular magazine, 16½" barrel; folding leaf rear sight, bead front; uncheckered walnut carbine stock; barrel band; sling swivels. Manufactured 1969 to 1972. Used value, $75 to $85.

Savage Model 63K

SAVAGE Model 63K: bolt-action, single-shot; .22 short, long, LR; 18" barrel; furnished with key to lock trigger; open rear sight, hooded ramp front; full-length hardwood pistol-grip stock; sling swivels. Manufactured 1970 to 1972. Used value, $75 to $85.

Model 63M has same specs as Model 63K, except chambered for .22 WRFM. Manufactured 1970 to 1972. Used value, $95 to $100.

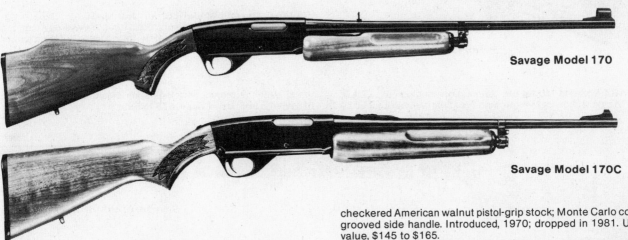

Savage Model 170

Savage Model 170C

SAVAGE Model 170: pump-action; .30-30, .35 Rem.; 3-rd. tubular magazine; 22" barrel; folding leaf rear sight, ramp front; select checkered American walnut pistol-grip stock; Monte Carlo comb, grooved side handle. Introduced, 1970; dropped in 1981. Used value, $145 to $165.

Model 170C Carbine has same specs as Model 170 rifle, except for straight-comb stock, 18½" barrel; chambered for .30-30 only. Introduced, 1974; dropped in 1981. Used value, $145 to $165.

Savage Model 72

SAVAGE-Stevens Model 72: lever-action, single-shot; .22 short, long, LR; 22" octagonal barrel; falling-block action; case-hardened frame; open rear sight, bead front; uncheckered American walnut straight-grip stock, forearm. Advertised as Crackshot, but differs from original made by Stevens. Introduced, 1972; dropped, 1987. Used value, $85 to $95.

SAVAGE-Stevens Model 74: lever-action; single-shot; same specs as Model 72, except for 22" round barrel; black-finished frame; hardwood stock. Manufactured 1972 to 1974. Used value, $85 to $95.

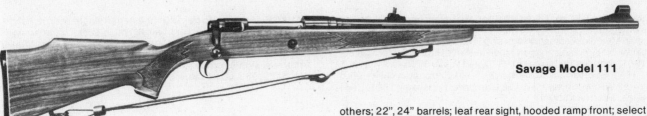

Savage Model 111

SAVAGE Model 111: bolt-action; .243 Win., .270 Win., 7x57, 7mm Rem. magnum, .30/06; 3-rd. clip in 7mm Rem. magnum, 4 rds. in others; 22", 24" barrels; leaf rear sight, hooded ramp front; select checkered American walnut pistol-grip stock; Monte Carlo comb, cheekpiece; pistol-grip cap; detachable swivels, sling. Advertised as Chieftain. Introduced, 1974; dropped in 1978. Used value, $250 to $275.

SAVAGE Model 112V: bolt-action, single-shot; .220 Swift, .222 Rem., .223 Rem., .22-250, .243 Win., .25/06; 26" heavy varmint barrel, scope bases; no sights; select American walnut varminter stock; high comb; checkered pistol grip; detachable sling swivels. Introduced, 1975; dropped, 1979. Used value, $250 to $275.

Model 112R has same general design specs as standard model, except for 5-rd. magazine; .22-250, .25/06; 26" tapered free-floating barrel; American walnut stock; fluted comb, Wundhammer swell at pistol grip; drilled, tapped for scope mounts; top tang safety. No longer in production. Used value, $275 to $300.

Savage Model 112V

Savage-Stevens Model 80

SAVAGE-Stevens Model 80: autoloader; 15-rd. tubular magazine; 20" barrel open rear sight, bead front; checkered American walnut pistol-grip stock; side safety. Introduced, 1976; no longer in production. Used value, $65 to $75.

SAVAGE-Stevens Model 89: lever-action; single-shot; .22 LR; 18½" barrel; 35" overall length; Martini action; hammer cocked by hand; automatic ejection; black satin finish. Introduced, 1977; dropped, 1985. Used value, $75 to $85.

Savage/Anschutz Mark 12

SAVAGE/ANSCHUTZ Mark 12: bolt-action, single-shot; .22 LR; globe front sight, micro-click peep rear; 26" heavy barrel; walnut-finished hardwood stock; thumb groove, Wundhammer pistol-grip swell, adjustable hand stop; sling swivels. Imported from West Germany. Introduced, 1978; dropped, 1981. Used value, $200 to $250.

Savage/Anschutz Model 64

SAVAGE/ANSCHUTZ Model 64: bolt-action, single-shot; .22 LR; 26" round barrel; no sights, scope blocks furnished; walnut-finished hardwood stock; cheekpiece, checkered pistol grip, beavertail forend; adjustable butt plate; sliding side safety; adjustable single-stage trigger; receiver grooved for Anschutz sights; left-hand model available. Introduced, 1978; importation dropped by Savage, 1981. Used value, $325 to $350.

SAVAGE/ANSCHUTZ 1418 Sporter: bolt-action; .22 LR; has same general specs as Savage/Anschutz 164, except has European Mannlicher stock, inlays, skip-line hand-checkering, double-set or single-stage trigger. Made in West Germany. Introduced, 1981; dropped by Savage, 1981. Used value, $425 to $450.
    1518 Sporter has same specs as 1418, except is chambered for .22 WRFM. Introduced, 1981; dropped by Savage, 1981. Used value, $450 to $500.

SAVAGE-Stevens Model 120: bolt-action, single-shot; .22 short, long, LR; 20" round, tapered barrel; action cocks on opening of bolt; thumb safety; double extractors; recessed bolt face; tubular magazine; walnut-finished hardwood stock; pistol grip; sporting front/rear sights; grooved for scope mounts. Introduced 1979; dropped, 1983. Used value, $60 to $70.

Savage-Stevens Model 125

SAVAGE-Stevens Model 125: bolt-action, single-shot; 22" barrel; 39" overall length; walnut-finished stock; manual cocking; sporting front sight, open rear with elevator; blued finish. Introduced, 1981; no longer made. Used value, $60 to $70.

SMITH & WESSON

Smith & Wesson Model A

Smith & Wesson Model B

Smith & Wesson Model C

Smith & Wesson Model D

Smith & Wesson Model E

Model B has same specs as Model A, except for 20¾" light barrel, Schnabel forend tip; chambered for .243 Win., .270 Win., .30/06. Imported, 1969 to 1972. Used value, $300 to $350.

Model C has same specs as Model B, except for straight-comb stock. Imported 1969 to 1972. Used value, $300 to $350.

Model D has same specs as Model C, except for full-length Mannlicher-type stock. Imported 1969 to 1972. Used value, $400 to $425.

Model E has same specs as Model B, except for full-length Mannlicher-type stock. Imported 1969 to 1972. Used value, $400 to $425.

SMITH & WESSON Model A: bolt-action; .22-250, .243 Win., .270 Win., .308 Win., .30/06, 7mm Rem. magnum, .300 Win. magnum; 5-rd. magazine in standard calibers, 3 rds. for magnums; 23¾" barrel; folding leaf rear sight, hooded ramp front; hand-checkered European walnut stock; Monte Carlo, rosewood pistol grip cap, forend tip; sling swivels. Manufactured in Sweden by Husqvarna. Imported, 1969 to 1972. Used value, $275 to $325.

Smith & Wesson Model 125

SMITH & WESSON Model 125: bolt-action; .270 Win., .30/06; 5-rd. magazine; 24" barrel; step-adjustable rear sight, hooded ramp front; action drilled, tapped for scope mounts; thumb safety. Standard grade has hand-checkered stock of European walnut; deluxe grade adds rosewood forearm tip, pistol-grip cap. Introduced in 1973; dropped, 1973. Used value: standard grade, $275 to $300; deluxe grade, $350 to $400.

Smith & Wesson Model 1500

Smith & Wesson Model 1500 Deluxe

Smith & Wesson Model 1500 Mountaineer

SMITH & WESSON Model 1500: bolt-action; .243, .270, .30/06, .308, 7mm Rem. magnum, 22" barrel; 24" in 7mm Rem. magnum; hooded gold bead front sight, open round-notch rear, adjustable for windage, elevation; Monte Carlo checkered American walnut stock with Monte Carlo cheekpiece; single-set trigger; one-piece trigger guard, magazine box; hinged floor plate; quick-detachable swivel studs; composition non-slip butt plate; magnum model has rubber recoil pad. Introduced, 1979; importation from Japan dropped by S&W, 1984. Used values: $240 to $250 in standard calibers; $250 to $250 in magnum.

Model 1500 Deluxe has same specs as standard Model 1500, except has no sights, engine-turned bolt; decorative scrollwork on

floor plate; skip-line checkering; pistol-grip cap with S&W seal; sling, swivels included; magnum has ventilated recoil pad. Introduced, 1980; importation from Japan dropped by S&W, 1984. Used values: standard calibers, $260 to $275; magnum, $265 to $280.

Model 1500 Varmint Deluxe has same specs as standard 1500, except has satin-finished stock; checkering; no sights; drilled, checkering, quick-detachable swivels; .222, .22-250, .223; blued or Parkerized finish; oil-finished stock. Introduced, 1982; importation from Japan dropped by S&W, 1984. Used value, $275 to $300.

Model 1500 Mountaineer has same specs as standard model, except has satin-finished stock; checkering; no sights; drilled/tapped for scope mounts; 22" or 24" barrel; .223, .243, .270, .30/06, 7mm Rem. magnum; magnum model has recoil pad. Introduced, 1979; importation from Japan dropped by S&W, 1984. Used value, $240 to $260.

Smith & Wesson Model 1700LS

SMITH & WESSON Model 1700LS: bolt-action; .243, .270, .30/06; marketed as Classic Hunter; similar to Model 1500, except has

classic stock, tapered forend, Schnabel tip; ribbon checkering pattern; black rubber butt pad; flush-mounted sling swivels; jeweled bolt body, knurled bolt knob; removable 5-rd. magazine. Introduced, 1983; importation from Japan dropped by S&W, 1984. Used value, $340 to $360.

SPRINGFIELD ARMORY

Springfield Armory M1A

SPRINGFIELD ARMORY M1A: semi-automatic gas-operated; .308 Win. (7.62 NATO), .243 Win.; 5-, 10-, 20-rd. box magazine; 25-1/16" barrel, flash suppressor; adjustable aperture rear sight, blade front; walnut, birch or fiberglass stock; fiberglass hand guard; sling

Springfield Armory Supermatch

swivels, sling. Same general specs as military M14 sans full-auto capability. Maker is private Illinois firm, not a U.S. Government facility. Introduced, 1974; still in production. Used values: fiber-glass stock, $525 to $550; birch stock, $550 to $575; walnut $575 to $600.

Match M1A has same general specs as standard model, except for National Match grade barrel, sights; better trigger pull; modified gas system, mainspring guide; glass-bedded American walnut stock. Used value, $750 to $775.

Super Match M1A has same specs as Match model, except for heavier, premium-grade barrel. Used value, $800 to $850.

Springfield Armoury M6

SPRINGFIELD ARMORY M6: over/under; .22 LR, .22 WRFM, .22 Hornet over .410 shotgun; designed as survival arm; 18" barrels; 31½" overall length; blade front sight, military aperture for .22, V-notch for .410; folds for compact storage; quick disassembly features; all-metal construction. Introduced, 1982; still in production. Used value, $90 to $100.

SPRINGFIELD ARMORY Model 700 BASR: bolt-action; .308 Win.; 5-rd. magazine; 26" heavy Douglas Premium barrel; 46¼" overall length; weighs 13.5 lb. complete; no sights; synthetic fiber stock; rubber recoil pad; marketed with military leather sling; adjustable, folding Parker-Hale bipod. Introduced, 1987; still in production. Used value, $1600 to $1650.

Springfield Armory M-21 Sniper

SPRINGFIELD ARMORY M-21 Sniper: autoloader, .308 Win.; 20-rd. box magazine; 22" heavy barrel; 44¼" overall length; weighs 15¼ lb. with bipod, scope mount; National Match sights; heavy American walnut stock with adjustable comb, ventilated recoil pad; based on M1-A rifle; folding, removable bipod; leather military sling. Introduced, 1987; still in production. Used value, $1700 to $1750.

STEVENS

STEVENS Ideal No. 44: single-shot, lever-action, rolling-block; take-down; .22 LR, .25 rimfire, .32 rimfire, .25-20, .32-20, .32-40, .38-40, .38-55, .44-40; 24" or 26" barrel, round, full octagon, half octagon; uncheckered straight-grip walnut stock, forearm; open rear sight, Rocky Mountain front. Introduced in 1894; dropped, 1932. Primarily of collector interest. Used value, $350 to $375.

Ideal No. 44½ has the same general specs as No. 44, except for falling-block lever-action replacing rolling-block of earlier model. Manufactured 1903 to 1916. Collector interest. Used value, $375 to $450; premium for centerfires.

Other Ideal versions, through No. 56, are virtually identical in basic specs, differing only in type of updated improvements. Prices vary from standard and No. 44½ depending upon improvements. Used values, $500-plus.

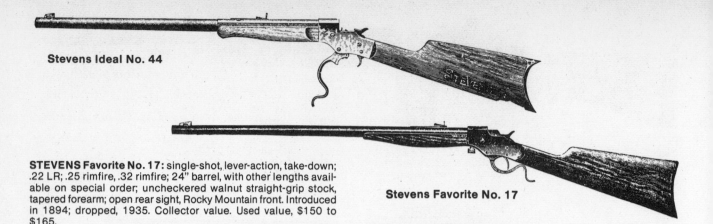

Stevens Ideal No. 44

Stevens Favorite No. 17

STEVENS Favorite No. 17: single-shot, lever-action, take-down; .22 LR; .25 rimfire, .32 rimfire; 24" barrel, with other lengths available on special order; uncheckered walnut straight-grip stock, tapered forearm; open rear sight, Rocky Mountain front. Introduced in 1894; dropped, 1935. Collector value. Used value, $150 to $165.

STEVENS Favorite No. 18: has the same specs as the No. 17, except for substitution of vernier peep rear sight, Beach combination front, addition of leaf middle sight. Introduced in 1894; dropped, 1935. Collector value. Used value, $175 to $200.

STEVENS Favorite No. 19: has same specs as No. 17, except for substitution of Lyman combination rear sight, Lyman front, addition of leaf middle sight. Introduced in 1895; dropped, 1935. Collector value. Used value, $175 to $210.

STEVENS Favorite No. 20: has same specs as No. 17, except for smoothbore barrel for .22 rimfire, .32 rimfire shot cartridges only. Introduced in 1895; dropped, 1935. Collector value. Used value, $135 to $145.

STEVENS Favorite No. 27: has the same specs as No. 17, except for substitution of octagon barrel. Introduced in 1896; dropped, 1935. Collector value. Used value, $175 to $185.

STEVENS Favorite No. 28: has same specs as No. 18, except for substitution of octagon barrel. Introduced in 1896; dropped, 1935. Collector value. Used value, $175 to $200.

STEVENS Favorite No. 29: has same specs as No. 19, except for substitution of octagon barrel. Introduced in 1896; dropped, 1935. Collector value. Used value, $175 to $200.

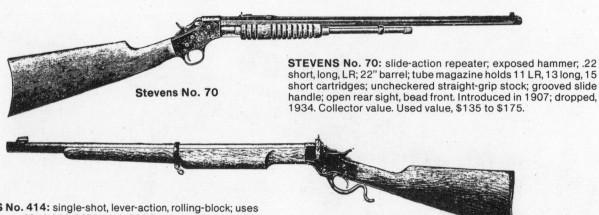

Stevens No. 70

Stevens No. 414

STEVENS No. 70: slide-action repeater; exposed hammer; .22 short, long, LR; 22" barrel; tube magazine holds 11 LR, 13 long, 15 short cartridges; uncheckered straight-grip stock; grooved slide handle; open rear sight, bead front. Introduced in 1907; dropped, 1934. Collector value. Used value, $135 to $175.

STEVENS No. 414: single-shot, lever-action, rolling-block; uses same action as Model 44; 26" barrel; .22 LR only or .22 short only; uncheckered straight-grip walnut stock, military-style forearm, sling swivels; Lyman receiver peep sight, blade front. Introduced in 1912; dropped, 1932. Known as Armory Model, has some collector value affecting price. Used value, $350 to $375.

STEVENS Crack Shot No. 26: single-shot, take-down, lever-action; .22 LR, .32 rimfire; 18", 22" barrel; uncheckered straight-grip walnut stock, tapered forearm; open rear sight, blade front.

STEVENS No. 26½: has the same specs as No. 26 except for smoothbore barrel for .22, .32 rimfire shot cartridges. Introduced

Introduced in 1913; dropped, 1939. Collector value. Used value, $125 to $135.

in 1914; dropped, 1939. Collector value. Used value, $115 to $125.

Stevens No. 66

STEVENS No. 66: bolt-action take-down repeater; .22 short, long, LR; 24" barrel; tube magazine holds 13 LR, 15 long, 19 short cartridges; uncheckered walnut pistol-grip stock, grooved forearm; open rear sight, bead front. Introduced in 1931; dropped, 1935. Used value, $75 to $80.

Stevens No. 419

STEVENS No. 419: bolt-action, take-down single-shot; termed the Junior Target Model; .22 LR only; 26" barrel; uncheckered walnut junior target stock; pistol grip; sling, swivels; Lyman No. 55 peep rear sight, blade front. Introduced in 1932; dropped, 1936. Used value, $95 to $120.

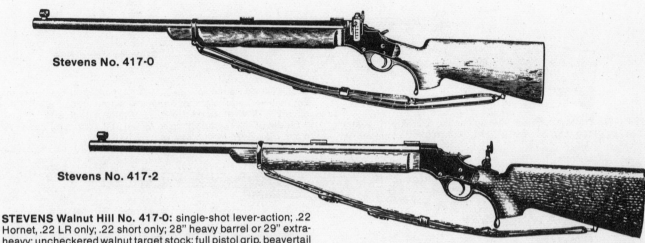

Stevens No. 417-0

Stevens No. 417-2

STEVENS Walnut Hill No. 417-0: single-shot lever-action; .22 Hornet, .22 LR only; .22 short only; 28" heavy barrel or 29" extra-heavy; uncheckered walnut target stock; full pistol grip, beavertail forearm; sling swivels, barrel band, sling; Lyman No. 52L extension rear sight, No. 17A front. Introduced in 1932; dropped, 1947. Value largely based upon collector appeal. Used value, $450 to $500.

No. 417-1 Walnut Hill has same specs as the No. 417-0, except for substitution of Lyman No. 48L receiver sight. Dropped, 1947. Used value, $475 to $525.

No. 417-2 Walnut Hill model has same specs as No. 417-0, except for substitution of Lyman No. 1441 tang sight. Dropped, 1947. Used value, $495 to $525.

No. 417-3 Walnut Hill has the same specs as No. 417-0, except that it was sold without sights. Dropped, 1947. Used value, $400 to $425.

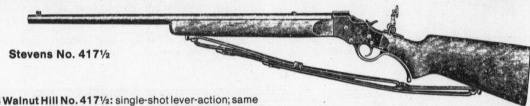

Stevens No. 417½

STEVENS Walnut Hill No. 417½: single-shot lever-action; same general specs as 417-0; .22 Hornet, .25 rimfire, .22 WRF, .22 LR; 28" barrel; uncheckered walnut sporting-style stock; pistol-grip, semi-beavertail forearm; swivels; sling; Lyman No. 144 tang peep sight, folding middle sight, bead front. Introduced in 1932; dropped, 1940. Used value, $475 to $500.

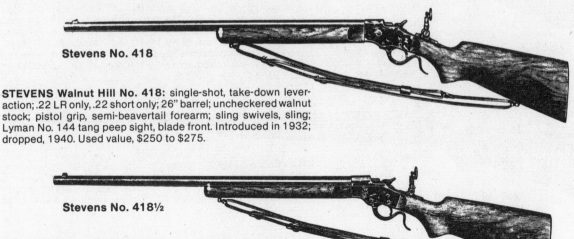

Stevens No. 418

STEVENS Walnut Hill No. 418: single-shot, take-down lever-action; .22 LR only, .22 short only; 26" barrel; uncheckered walnut stock; pistol grip, semi-beavertail forearm; sling swivels, sling; Lyman No. 144 tang peep sight, blade front. Introduced in 1932; dropped, 1940. Used value, $250 to $275.

Stevens No. 418½

STEVENS Walnut Hill No. 418½: has the same general specs as No. 418, except for availability in .25 Stevens rimfire, .22 WRF also; substitution of Lyman No. 2A tang peep sight, bead front. Introduced in 1932; dropped, 1940. Used value, $250 to $275.

Stevens Model 053

STEVENS Buckhorn Model 053: bolt-action, take-down single-shot; .25 Stevens rimfire, .22 WRF, .22 short, long, LR; 24" barrel; uncheckered walnut stock; pistol grip, black forearm tip; receiver peep sight, open middle sight, hooded front. Introduced in 1935; dropped, 1948. Used value, $75 to $85.

Model 53 has the same specs as Model 053, except for open rear sight, plain bead front. Used value, $60 to $65.

Stevens Model 056

STEVENS Buckhorn Model 056: bolt-action, take-down repeater; .22 short, long, LR; 24" barrel; 5-rd detachable box magazine; uncheckered walnut sporter-type stock; pistol grip, black forearm tip; receiver peep sight, open middle sight, hooded front. Introduced in 1935; dropped, 1948. Used value, $85 to $95.

Model 56 has same specs as Model 056, except for open rear sight, plain bead front. Used value, $70 to $75.

Stevens Model 066

Stevens No. 66

STEVENS Buckhorn Model 066: bolt-action, take-down repeater; .22 short, long, LR; 24" barrel; tube magazine holds 15 LR, 17 long, 21 short cartridges; uncheckered walnut sporting stock; pistol grip, black forearm tip; receiver peep sight, open middle sight, hooded front. Introduced in 1935; dropped, 1948. Used value, $85 to $95.

Model 66 has the same specs as Model 066, except for open rear sight, plain bead front. Used value, $70 to $75.

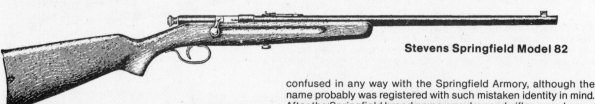

Stevens Springfield Model 82

STEVENS Springfield Model 82: bolt-action, take-down single-shot. Springfield was used as a brand name from 1935 until 1948, with the designation being dropped at that time. It should not be confused in any way with the Springfield Armory, although the name probably was registered with such mistaken identity in mind. After the Springfield brand name was dropped, rifles were known strictly by the Stevens name. In .22 short, long, LR; 22" barrel; uncheckered walnut pistol-grip stock, grooved forearm; open rear sight, bead front. Introduced in 1935; dropped, 1939. Used value, $45 to $55.

Stevens Springfield Model 83

STEVENS Springfield Model 83: bolt-action, take-down single-shot; same basic action as Model 82, but chambered for .25 Stevens, .22 WRF, .22 short, long, LR; 24" barrel; other specs are identical to those of Model 82. Introduced in 1935; dropped, 1939. Used value, $75 to $85.

STEVENS-Springfield Model 86: bolt-action, take-down repeater; .22 short, long, LR; 24" barrel; plated bolt, trigger; tube magazine holds 15 LR, 17 long, 21 short cartridges; uncheckered walnut stock; pistol grip, black forearm tip. Introduced in 1935; produced until 1948 under Springfield brand name; produced from 1948 to 1965 under Stevens name when dropped. Used value, $75 to $85.

Model 086 has the same specs as Model 86, except for sub-

Stevens Model 86

Stevens Springfield Model 86S

stitution of peep rear sight, hooded front. Marketed under Springfield brand name from 1935 to 1948. Used value, $85 to $95.

Model 86-S is exactly the same as Model 086, but designation was changed when Springfield name was dropped in 1948; marketed as Stevens thereafter, until dropped, 1952. Used value, $85 to $95.

Stevens Model 416

STEVENS Model 416: bolt-action, target model; .22 LR only 26" heavy barrel; 5-rd. detachable box magazine; uncheckered walnut target-type stock; sling swivels, sling; receiver peep sight, hooded front. Introduced in 1937; dropped, 1949. Used value, $155 to $165; $175 to $225 with U.S. Property markings.

Stevens Model 15Y

STEVENS-Springfield Model 15: bolt-action, take-down single-shot; .22 short, long, LR; 22" barrel; uncheckered pistol-grip stock; open rear sight, bead front. Introduced in 1937; dropped, 1948. Used value, $50 to $55.

Stevens Model 15 has identical specs to Stevens-Springfield Model 15, except for substitution of 24" barrel, redesigned stock, including black forearm tip. Introduced in 1948; dropped, 1965. Used value, $55 to $60.

Model 15Y, the so-called Youth Model, has same specs as standard Stevens Model 15, except for 21" barrel, shorter butt stock. Introduced in 1958; dropped, 1965. Used value, $55 to $60.

Stevens No. 076

STEVENS Buckhorn No. 76: take-down autoloader; .22 LR only; 24" barrel; 15-rd. tube magazine; uncheckered sporter-style stock, black forearm tip; open rear sight, plain bead front. Introduced in 1938; dropped, 1948. Used value, $85 to $90.

No. 076 has same specs as No. 76, except for peep receiver sight, open middle sight, hooded front. Introduced in 1938; dropped, 1948. Used value, $100 to $110.

STEVENS Model 87: take-down autoloader; .22 LR only; 24" barrel until late '60s, then with 20" barrel; uncheckered pistol-grip stock, black forearm tip; open rear sight; bead front. Marketed as Springfield Model 87 from 1938 to 1948, when trade name dropped. Dropped, 1976. Used value, $70 to $75.

Model 087, Springfield designation, has same specs as Model 87, except for peep rear sight, hooded front. Introduced in 1938; redesignated, 1948. Used value, $75 to $85.

Model 87-S is Stevens designation for 087, as of 1948. Dropped, 1953. Used value, $75 to $85.

STEVENS Buckhorn No. 57: take-down autoloader; has the same specs as No. 76, except for 5-rd. detachable box magazine. Introduced in 1939; dropped, 1948. Used value, $75 to $85.

No. 057 has the same specs as the No. 57. Also introduced in 1939; dropped, 1948. Used value, $75 to $85.

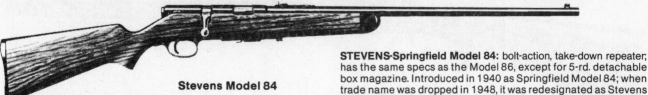

Stevens Model 84

STEVENS-Springfield Model 84: bolt-action, take-down repeater; has the same specs as the Model 86, except for 5-rd. detachable box magazine. Introduced in 1940 as Springfield Model 84; when trade name was dropped in 1948, it was redesignated as Stevens Model 84 and continued until dropped, 1965. Used value, $65 to $70.

Stevens Model 84S

Model 084 has the same specs as Springfield Model 84, except for substitution of rear peep sight, hooded front. Introduced in 1940; when trade name was dropped in 1948, it was redesignated.

STEVENS-Springfield Model 85: has the same specs as Model 87, except for 5-rd. detachable box magazine. From introduction in 1939 until 1948, was designated as Springfield Model 85. Has been Stevens Model 85 since 1948; dropped, 1976. Used value, $75 to $85.

STEVENS Model 322: bolt-action carbine; .22 Hornet only; 21" barrel; 4-rd. detachable box magazine; unchecked walnut pistol-grip stock; open rear sight, ramp front. Introduced in 1947; dropped, 1950. Used value, $165 to $175.

STEVENS Model 325: bolt-action carbine; .30-30 only; 21" barrel; 3-rd. detachable box magazine; unchecked pistol-grip stock; open rear sight, bead front. Introduced in 1947; dropped, 1950. Used value, $165 to $175.

Used value, $65 to $75.

Model 84-S is exactly the same as Model 084, but designation was changed when Springfield name was dropped. Marketed as Stevens Model 84-S from 1948 until dropped, 1952. Used value, $65 to $70.

Model 085 is same as Model 85, except for peep rear sight, hooded front. This designation was used on Springfield brand rifles from 1939 until 1948. Used value, $85 to $95.

Model 85-S is exactly the same as Model 085, but carries Stevens name since 1948; dropped, 1976. Used value, $80 to $90.

Model 322-S has the same specs as the Model 322, except for substitution of a peep rear sight. Introduced in 1947; dropped, 1950. Used value, $185 to $195.

Model 325-S has same specs as Model 325, except for substitution of peep rear sight. Introduced in 1947; dropped, 1950. Used value, $185 to $195.

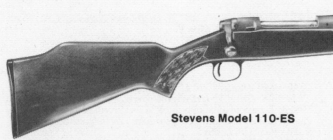

Stevens Model 110-ES

STEVENS Model 110E: bolt-action; .308, .30/06, .243; 4-rd. magazine; 22" round tapered barrel; removable bead ramp front sight, step-adjustable rear; walnut-finished hardwood Monte Carlo stock;

checkered pistol grip, forend; hard rubber butt plate; top tang safety; drilled, tapped for peep sight or scope mounts. Bears direct resemblance to Savage standard Model 110. Introduced, 1978; dropped, 1984. Used value, $170 to $180.

Model 110-ES has same general specs as 110E except for 5-rd. magazine; free-floating barrel; marketed with 4X scope, mounts. Introduced, 1981; dropped, 1985. Used value, with scope, $185 to $195.

Stevens Model 35

STEVENS Model 35: bolt-action; .22 LR; detachable 5-rd. clip; 11" barrel; 41" overall length; ramp front sight, step-adjustable open rear; walnut-finished hardwood stock; checkered pistol grip,

forend; receiver grooved for scope mount. Introduced, 1982; no longer in production. Marketed by Savage. Used value, $60 to $65.

Model 35M has same specs as standard model, except is chambered for .22 WRFM cartridge. Used value, $75 to $85.

Model 36 has same basic specs as standard model, but is single-shot. Used value, $50 to $55.

STEYR-MANNLICHER

Steyr .22 Carbine

STEYR Carbine: bolt-action; .22 LR; 5-rd. detachable box magazine; 19" barrel; leaf rear sight, hooded bead front; hand-checkered European walnut Mannlicher-type stock; sling swivels. Manufactured in Austria, 1953 to 1967. Used value, $450 to $475.

STEYR-MANNLICHER Model M: bolt-action; 7x64, 7x57, .25/06, .270, .30/06; optional calibers: 6.5x57, 8x57JS, 9.3x62, 6.5x55, 7.5x55; available in left-hand action in standard calibers; 20" barrel with full Mannlicher stock, 23.6" with half-stock; full Mannlicher or half-stock with Monte Carlo, pistol-grip of hand-checkered European walnut; rubber recoil pad; ramp front sight, open U-notch rear; interchangeable double- or single-set triggers; detachable 5-rd. rotary magazine; drilled, tapped for scope mounts. Introduced, 1981; still imported. Used values: Mannlicher stock, $750 to $800; half stock, $800 to $825.

Model M Professional has same specs as standard model, except has Parkerized finish, synthetic stock, right-hand only. Used value, $750 to $800.

Steyr-Mannlicher ML 79 Luxus

STEYR-MANNLICHER ML 79 Luxus: has same general specs as Models L and M, except has single-set trigger, detachable 3-rd. steel magazine, 6-rd. magazine optional; same calibers as Models L and M; oil finish or high-gloss lacquered stock. Introduced, 1981; no longer imported. Used values: Mannlicher stock, $800 to $850; half stock, $950 to $950.

Steyr-Mannlicher Model S

STEYR-MANNLICHER Model S: bolt-action; .300 Win. magnum, .338 Win. magnum, 7mm Rem. magnum, .300 H&H magnum, .375 H&H magnum, 6.5x68, 8x68S, 9.3x64; 25.6" barrel; ramp front sight, U-notch rear; half stock with pistol grip, Monte Carlo of hand-checkered European walnut; rubber recoil pad; available with optional spare magazine inletted in butt; detachable 4-rd. magazine; interchangeable single- or double-set triggers; drilled, tapped for scope mounts. Introduced, 1981; still imported. Used value, $750 to $800.

Model S/T has same specs as Model S except is chambered for .375 H&H magnum, .458 Win. magnum, 9.3x64. Introduced, 1981; still imported. Used value, $900 to $950.

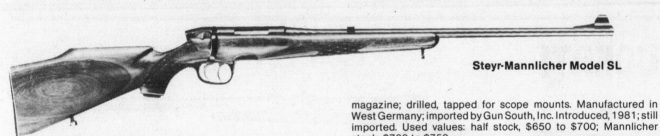

Steyr-Mannlicher Model SL

STEYR-MANNLICHER Model SL: bolt-action; .222, .222 Rem. magnum, .223; 20" barrel with full stock; 23.6" with half stock; ramp front sight, open U-notch rear; hand-checkered full Mannlicher or half stock with Monte Carlo in European walnut; interchangeable single- or double-set triggers; 5-rd. detachable rotary magazine; drilled, tapped for scope mounts. Manufactured in West Germany; imported by Gun South, Inc. Introduced, 1981; still imported. Used values: half stock, $650 to $700; Mannlicher stock, $700 to $750.

Model SL Varmint has same specs as standard model except is chambered only for .222 Rem., .22-250, .243, .308, 26" heavy barrel; 5-rd. detachable magazine; no sights; drilled, tapped for scope mounts; choice of single- or double-set trigger. Used value, $700 to $750.

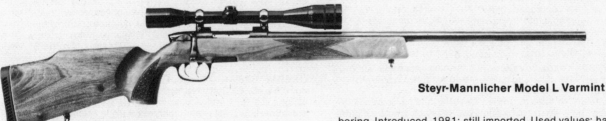

Steyr-Mannlicher Model L Varmint

STEYR-MANNLICHER Model L: bolt-action; .22-250, 6mm, .243, .308 Win.; has same specs as Model SL, except for caliber chambering. Introduced, 1981; still imported. Used values: half stock, $700 to $750; Mannlicher stock, $750 to $800.

Model L Varmint has same specs as Model SL Varmint except is chambered for .22-250, .243, .308. Used value, $700 to $750.

STEYR-MANNLICHER SSG Marksman: .308 Win.; 25.6" barrel; hooded blade front sight, folding leaf rear; ABS Cycolac synthetic or walnut half stock; 5-rd. rotary magazine; Parkerized finish; interchangeable single- or double-set triggers; drilled, tapped for scope mounts. Manufactured in West Germany. Introduced, 1981 by Steyr Daimler Puch of America; still imported by Gun South, Inc. Used values: synthetic stock, $750 to $850; walnut stock, $675 to $725.

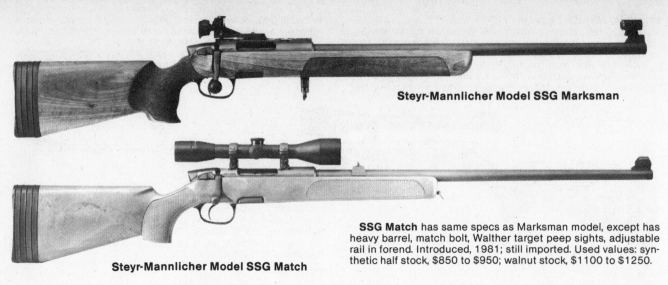

Steyr-Mannlicher Model SSG Marksman

Steyr-Mannlicher Model SSG Match

SSG Match has same specs as Marksman model, except has heavy barrel, match bolt, Walther target peep sights, adjustable rail in forend. Introduced, 1981; still imported. Used values: synthetic half stock, $850 to $950; walnut stock, $1100 to $1250.

Sterr-Mannlicher Match UTI

STEYR-MANNLICHER Match UIT: bolt-action; .243, .308; 10-rd. magazine; 25.5" barrel; 44.48" overall length; weighs 10.9 lb.; UIT

Match walnut stock; stippled grip, forend; Walther rear peep sight, globe front; adjustable double-pull trigger; adjustable butt plate. Made in Austria. Introduced, 1984; still imported by Gun South. Used value, $1500 to $1550.

UBERTI

Uberti Rolling Block Baby Carbine

UBERTI Model 1866: lever-action; .22 LR, .22 WRFM, .38 Special, .44-40; 24½" octagonal barrel; 43¼" overall length; weighs 8.1 lb.; elevation-adjustable rear sight, windage-adjustable blade front; polished brass frame, butt plate, forend cap, balance charcoal blued. Made in Italy. Introduced, 1987; still imported by Benson Firearms, Uberti USA. Used value, $350 to $375.

Model 1866 Yellowboy Carbine has same specs as standard model, except has 19" round barrel. Introduced, 1987; still imported. Used value, $325 to $350.

Model 1866 Yellowboy Indian Carbine has same specs as 1866 Yellowboy, except has engraved receiver, brass nails in stock. Introduced, 1987; still imported. Used value, $360 to $385.

Model 1866 Trapper's Model has same specs as standard model, except has 16" barrel. Introduced, 1987; still imported. Used value, $325 to $350.

UBERTI 1873 Sporting Model: lever-action; .22 LR, .22 WRFM, .38 Special, .357 magnum, .44-40, .45 Colt; 24¼" octagonal barrel; 43¼" overall length; weighs 8.1 lb.; elevation-adjustable rear

UBERTI Rolling Block Baby Carbine: single-shot; .22 LR, .22 WRFM, .22 Hornet, .357 magnum; 22" barrel; 35½" overall length; weighs 4.8 lb.; copy of Remington New Model No. 4 carbine; brass butt plate, trigger guard; blued barrel; color case-hardened frame. Introduced, 1986; still imported by Benson Firearms, Uberti USA. Used value, $200 to $225.

UBERTI Henry Model: lever-action; .44-40; 24½" half-octagon barrel; 43¾" overall length; weighs 9.2 lb.; elevation-adjustable rear sight, blade front; uncheckered walnut stock; butt plate, frame, elevator, magazine follower of brass; balance charcoal blued or of polished steel; 22¼" barrel also available. Made in Italy. Introduced, 1987; still imported by Benson Firearms, Uberti USA. Used value, $475 to $500.

UBERTI 1875 Army Target Model: revolving carbine; .357 magnum, .44-40, .45 Colt; 6-rd. cylinder; 18" barrel; 37" overall length; weighs 4.9 lb.; carbine version of 1875 single-action revolver; elevation-adjustable rear sight, ramp front; uncheckered walnut stock; polished brass butt plate, trigger guard; case-hardened frame; blued or nickel-plated cylinder, barrel. Made in Italy. Introduced, 1987; still imported by Benson Firearms, Uberti USA. Used values: blued, $350 to $375; nickel, $425 to $450.

sight, windage-adjustable blade front; uncheckered walnut stock; brass elevator; color case-hardened frame; blued barrel, hammer, lever, butt plate. Made in Italy. Introduced, 1987; still imported by

Benson Firarms, Uberti USA. Used value, $460 to $480.

1873 Sporting Carbine has same specs as standard model, except has 18" round barrel; available with nickel plating. Used values: blued finish, $475 to $500; nickel finish, $500 to $525.

1873 Trapper's Model has same specs as standard model, except has 16" barrel. Used value, $425 to $440.

UBERTI 1873 Cattleman: revolving carbine; .22 LR/.22 WRFM, .38 Special, .357 magnum, .44-40, .45 Colt; 6-rd. cylinder; 18" barrel; 34" overall length; weighs 4.4 lb.; grooved or target rear sight, blade front; carbine version of single-action revolver; case-hardened frame; blued cylinder, barrel; brass butt plate. Made in Italy. Introduced, 1987; still imported by Benson Firearms, Uberti USA. Used values: fixed sights, $250 to $275; target sights, $300

Uberti 1873 Sporting Model

to $325; .22 convertible model, fixed sights, $300 to $325; convertible, target sights, $310 to $325.

1873 Buckhorn Model revolving carbine has same specs as 1873 Cattleman, except slightly larger; made in .44 magnum, or convertible .44 magnum/.44-40. Introduced, 1987; still imported. Used values: fixed sights, $280 to $300; target sights, $300 to $325; convertible, fixed sights, $300 to $325; convertible, target sights, $325 to $350.

VOERE

Voere Model 1007

VOERE Model 1007: bolt-action; Biathlon model; .22 LR; 18" barrel; weighs 5½ lb.; military-type oil-finished beech stock; open

adjustable rear sight, hooded front; single-stage trigger; sling swivels; convertible to single-shot. Made in Austria. Introduced, 1984; still imported. Used value, $165 to $175.

Model 1013 has same general specs as Model 1007, except is chambered for .22 WRFM and has double-set trigger. Used value, $200 to $225.

Voere Model 2155

VOERE Model 2155: bolt-action; .22-250, .270, .308, .243, .30/06, 7x64, 5.6x57, 6.5x55, 8x57 JRS, 7mm Rem. magnum, .300 Win.

magnum, 8x68S, 9.3x62, 9.3x64, 6.5x68; 5-rd. detachable box magazine; Mauser-type action; European walnut stock; checkered pistol grip, forend; open adjustable rear sight, ramp front; single- or double-set trigger; drilled, tapped for scope mount. Made in Austria. Introduced, 1984; still imported by L. Joseph Rahn. Used value, $375 to $400, depending on options.

VOERE Model 2115: autoloader; .22 LR; 8-, 15-rd. clip magazines; 18.1" barrel; 37.7" overall length; weighs 5.75 lb.; leaf rear sight, hooded ramp front; walnut-finished beechwood stock; checkered pistol grip, forend; cheekpiece; single-stage trigger; wing-

type safety. Made in Austria. Introduced, 1984; still imported by L. Joseph Rahn. Used value, $180 to $190.

Model 2114S has same specs as Model 2115, except has no cheekpiece, no checkering. Used value, $160 to $170.

Voere Model 2107

VOERE Model 2107: bolt-action; .22 LR; 5-, 8-shot magazine; 19½" barrel; 41" overall length; weighs 6 lb.; fully adjustable open

rear sight, hooded front; European hardwood Monte Carlo stock; swivel studs; butt pad. Made in West Germany. Introduced, 1986; importation by KDF, Inc., dropped, 1988. Used value, $140 to $150.

Model 2107 Deluxe has same basic specs as Model 2107, except has checkered stock, raised cheekpiece. Introduced, 1986; importation dropped, 1988. Used value, $155 to $165.

Voere Titan

VOERE Titan: bolt-action; .243, .25/06, .270, .7x57, .308, .30/06, .257 Weatherby, 7mm Rem. magnum, .,300 Win. magnum, .300 Weatherby, .308 Norma magnum, .375 H&H; 3- or 4-rd. magazine, depending on caliber; 24", 26" barrels; 44½" overall length with

24" barrel; weighs 8 lb.; no sights; drilled, tapped for scope mounts; hand-checkered, oil-finished European walnut Monte Carlo stock; recoil pad; swivel studs; three-lug, front-locking ac-

VOERE Titan Menor: bolt-action; .222 Rem., .223 Rem.; 3-rd. magazine; 23½" barrel; 42" overall length; weighs 6 lb.; no sights; drilled, tapped for scope mounts; hand-checkered, oil-finished European walnut Monte Carlo stock; rosewood grip cap, forend

tion. Made in Austria. Introduced, 1986; importation by KDF, Inc., dropped, 1988. Used values: standard calibers, $750 to $800; magnums, $850 to $900. Now imported as the Mauser 225.

tip. Made in Austria. Introduced, 1986; dropped, 1988. Used values: standard model, $550 to $600; competition model, $600 to $650.

WALTHER

Walther Olympic

WALTHER Olympic Model: bolt-action, single-shot; .22 LR; 26" heavy barrel; extension micrometer rear sight, interchangeable front; hand-checkered pistol-grip target stock of European walnut; full rubber-covered beavertail forend; thumbhole, palm rest, adjustable butt plate; sling swivels. Manufactured in Germany prior to WWII. Used value, $750 to $800.

Walther Model 2

WALTHER Model 1: autoloader; .22 LR, 5-, 9-rd. detachable box magazine; 20" barrel; tangent curve rear sight, ramp front; hand-

WALTHER Model V: bolt-action, single-shot; .22 LR; 26" barrel; open rear sight, ramp front; uncheckered European walnut pistol-grip sporting stock, grooved forend; sling swivels. Manufactured prior to World War II. Used value, $300 to $325.

checkered European walnut sporting stock; pistol grip; grooved forend; sling swivels. Has bolt-action feature, making it possible to fire as autoloader, single-shot or as bolt-operated repeater. Manufactured prior to WWII. Used value, $300 to $325.

Model 2 has same basic specs as Model 1, except for 24½" barrel, heavier stock. Used value, $325 to $350.

Model V Meisterbusche has same general specs as standard model, except for checkered pistol grip, micrometer open rear sight. Used value, $375 to $400.

Walther Model KKJ

WALTHER Model KKJ: bolt-action; .22 LR, .22 WRFM, .22 Hornet; 24" medium-heavy target barrel; 5-rd. clip; checkered European walnut pistol-grip stock, forearm; high tapered comb; sling swivels. Imported originally by Interarms; no longer imported. Introduced in 1957; .22 Hornet still in production. Used values: rimfires, $450 to $500; .22 Hornet, $600 to $650.

Walther Model KKM Match

WALTHER Model KKM Match Model: bolt-action, single-shot; .22 LR only; 28" barrel; fully adjustable match trigger; micrometer rear sight, Olympic front with post, aperture inserts; European walnut stock with adjustable hook butt plate, hand shelf, ball-type

offset yoke palm rest. Imported from Germany by Interarms. Introduced in 1957; still in production; no longer imported. Used value, $700 to $750.

Model KKM-S has same specs as Model KKM, except for adjustable cheekpiece. Used value, $775 to $800.

Model KKJ-Ho has same specs as KKJ, except chambered for .22 Hornet cartridge. Used value, $600 to $650.

Model KKJ-Ma has same specs as KKJ, except chambered for .22 WRFM. Used value, $450 to $500.

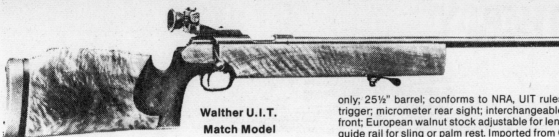

**Walther U.I.T.
Match Model**

WALTHER U.I.T. Match Model: bolt-action; single-shot; .22 LR

only; 25½" barrel; conforms to NRA, UIT rules; fully adjustable trigger; micrometer rear sight; interchangeable post or aperture front; European walnut stock adjustable for length, drop; forearm guide rail for sling or palm rest. Imported from Germany by Interarms. Introduced in 1966; still in production. Used value, $750 to $800.

Walther Moving Target Model

WALTHER Moving Target Model: bolt-action; single-shot; .22 LR only; 23.6" barrel; micrometer rear sight, globe front; especially

designed for running boar competition; receiver grooved for dovetail scope mounts; European walnut thumbhole stock; stippled forearm, pistol grip; adjustable cheekpiece, butt plate. Imported from Germany by Interarms. Introduced in 1972; still in production. Used value, $750 to $800.

**Walther Prone
400 Model**

WALTHER Prone 400 Model: bolt-action; single-shot; .22 LR only; has the same general specs as U.I.T. Match Model except for scope blocks, split stock for cheekpiece adjustment; especially designed for prone shooting. Introduced in 1972; still in production; no longer imported. Used value, $750 to $800.

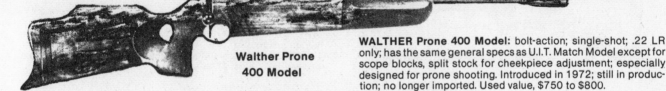

WALTHER Model SSV: bolt-action, single-shot; .22 LR, .22 Hornet; 25½" barrel; no sights; European walnut Monte Carlo stock; high cheekpiece; full pistol grip, forend. Used value, $500 to $525.

**Walther
Model SSV**

WALTHER Model GX-1: bolt-action, single-shot; .22 LR; 25½" heavy barrel; free rifle design; micrometer aperture rear sight, globe front; European walnut thumbhole stock; adjustable cheekpiece, butt plate; removable butt hook; accessory rail; hand stop, palm rest, counterweight; sling swivels. Used value, $900 to $1000.

Model GX-1 Match: bolt-action, single-shot; .22 LR; has same specs as U.I.T. Special except has stock designed for total adjustments; weighs 15½ lb. Introduced, 1978; still imported by Interarms. Used value, $1000 to $1200.

Walther U.I.T. Special

walnut stock, adjustable for length, drop; forend rail for sling or palm rest; left-hand stock available; fully adjustable trigger; conforms to NRA, UIT requirements. Imported from West Germany by Interarms. Introduced, 1978; still imported. Used value, $850 to $1000.

WALTHER U.I.T. Special: bolt-action; single-shot; .22 LR; 25½" barrel; globe-type front sight, adjustable aperture rear; European

Walther Running Boar Match Model

LR; 23.6" barrel; globe-type front sight, fully adjustable aperture rear; European walnut thumbhole stock, stippled pistol grip, forend; receiver grooved for dovetail scope mounts; adjustable cheekpiece, butt plate; left-hand stock available. Introduced, 1978; still imported by Interarms. Used value, $750 to $800.

WALTHER Running Boar Match: bolt-action, single-shot; .22

WEATHERBY

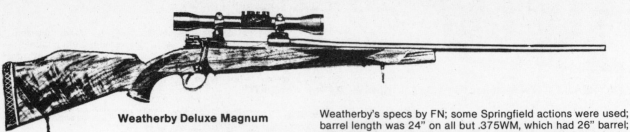

Weatherby Deluxe Magnum

WEATHERBY Deluxe Magnum: Roy Weatherby's first rifle; bolt-action in .220 Rocket, .257 Weatherby magnum, .270 Weatherby magnum, 7mm Weatherby magnum, .300 Weatherby magnum and .375 Weatherby magnum. Mauser actions were built to Weatherby's specs by FN; some Springfield actions were used; barrel length was 24" on all but .375WM, which had 26" barrel; Monte Carlo stock with cheekpiece; hand-checkered pistol grip, forearm; black grip cap, forearm tip; quick-detachable sling swivels. Introduced in 1948; dropped, 1955. Used value, $650 to $700.

   Deluxe Model has same specs as Deluxe Magnum, except chambered for .270 Win., .30/06. Dropped, 1955. Used value, $600 to $650.

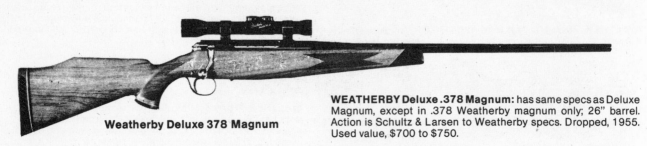

Weatherby Deluxe 378 Magnum

WEATHERBY Deluxe .378 Magnum: has same specs as Deluxe Magnum, except in .378 Weatherby magnum only; 26" barrel. Action is Schultz & Larsen to Weatherby specs. Dropped, 1955. Used value, $700 to $750.

Weatherby Mark V Deluxe

Weatherby Lazer Mark V

WEATHERBY Mark V Deluxe: bolt-action in .22-250, .30/06, .224 Weatherby Varmintmaster and Weatherby magnum chamberings of .240, .257, .270, 7mm, .300, .340, .378 and .460. Mark V action available in right- or left-hand model; some actions made by Sauer in Germany to Weatherby specs; depending on caliber, box magazine holds 2 to 5 rds.; 24" barrels; no sights; drilled, tapped for scope mounts; Monte Carlo stock, cheekpiece; skip checkering on pistol grip, forearm; forearm tip, pistol grip cap, recoil pad; quick-detachable sling swivels. Introduced in 1958; made in U.S. from 1958 to 1960, then production transferred to Germany; still in production, except made in Japan. Left-hand action worth $50 more than right-hand. Used values: for right-hand models, .460 Weatherby magnum, $1000 to $1100; .378 Weatherby magnum, $750 to $800; other calibers, $500 to $525; German rifle: .460, $1250 to $1500; .378, $950 to $1000; others, $650 to $675; Japan models: .460, $950 to $1000; .378, $750 to $800; others, $475 to $525.

   Lazer Mark V has same specs as standard Mark V, except has laser carving on butt, pistol grip, forend; 24", 26" barrel lengths; .22-250 and Weatherby calibers from .224 through .460 WM. Introduced, 1981; still produced. Used value, $640 to $800, depending on caliber, barrel length.

Weatherby Mark XXII Deluxe

WEATHERBY Mark XXII Deluxe: .22 LR; semi-automatic; 24" barrel; 5-, 10-shot clip magazines; Monte Carlo stock, cheekpiece; skip checkering on pistol grip, forearm; forearm tip, grip cap, quick-

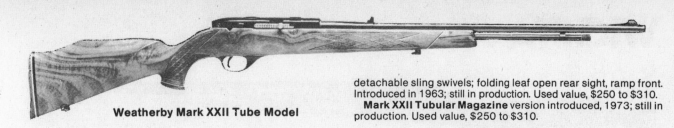

Weatherby Mark XXII Tube Model

detachable sling swivels; folding leaf open rear sight, ramp front. Introduced in 1963; still in production. Used value, $250 to $310.

Mark XXII Tubular Magazine version introduced, 1973; still in production. Used value, $250 to $310.

Weatherby Vanguard

Weatherby Vanguard VGL

Weatherby Vanguard Fiberguard

WEATHERBY Vanguard: bolt-action; .25/06, .243, .270, .30/06, .308, .264, 7mm Rem. magnum, .300 Win. magnum; 3- or 5-rd. magazines, depending on caliber; 24" barrel, adjustable trigger; no sights; receiver drilled, tapped for scope mounts; hinged floor plate; American walnut stock; pistol-grip cap; forearm tip; hand-checkered forearm, pistol-grip. Introduced in 1970; dropped, 1983. Used value, $325 to $350.

Vanguard VGL is similar to standard Vanguard, but has short action; 20" barrel; .223, .243, .270, .30/06, 7mm Rem. magnum; non-glare blued finish; satin-finished stock; hand-checkering; black butt pad, spacer. Made in Japan. Introduced, 1984; still imported. Used value, $275 to $300.

Vanguard VGS has same general specs as standard model; chambered for .22-250, .25/06, .243, .270, .30/06, 7mm Rem., .300 Win. magnum; 3- or 5-rd. magazines; American walnut stock; pistol-grip cap, forend tip; hand-inletted, checkered; sights optional; drilled, tapped for scope mounts; side safety; adjustable trigger; hinged floor plate. Made in Japan. Introduced, 1984; still imported. Used value, $290 to $300.

Vanguard VGX has same specs as VGS model, except has deluxe wood, different checkering style, ventilated recoil pad. Made in Japan. Introduced, 1984; still imported. Used value, $350 to $375.

Vanguard Fiberguard uses Vanguard barreled action, forest green wrinkle-finished fiberglass stock; matte blued metal; 20" barrel; weighs 6½ lb.; .223, .243, .308, .270, 7mm Rem. magnum, .30/06. Made in Japan. Introduced, 1985; still imported. Used value, $385 to $425.

Weatherby Fibermark

Weatherby Euromark

WEATHERBY Fibermark: bolt-action; .240 WM through .340 WM calibers; has same specs as standard Mark V, except has fiberglass stock with black wrinkle, non-glare finish; black recoil pad; receiver, floor plate sandblasted, blued; fluted bolt; 24", 26" barrel lengths. Introduced, 1983; still produced. Used value, $650 to $700.

WEATHERBY Euromark: bolt-action; all Weatherby calibers, except .224, .22-250; 24", 26" round tapered barrels; 44½" overall length with 24" barrel; optional sights; hand-checkered, oil-finished Monte Carlo walnut stock; ebony forend tip, grip cap; solid butt pad; adjustable trigger; cocking indicator; hinged floor plate; thumb safety; quick-detachable sling swivels; right- or left-hand action. Made in Japan. Introduced, 1986; still in production. Used value, $775 to $975, depending on caliber.

WICHITA

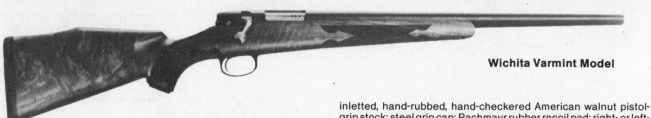

Wichita Varmint Model

WICHITA Varmint Model: bolt-action; calibers .17 Rem. through .308 Win., including .22 and 6mm PPC; 21⅛" Atkinson chrome-moly barrel; no sights, drilled and tapped for scope mounts; hand-inletted, hand-rubbed, hand-checkered American walnut pistol-grip stock; steel grip cap; Pachmayr rubber recoil pad; right- or left-hand action; 3 locking lugs; single-shot or 3-rd. magazine; checkered bolt handle; hand-fitted, lapped and jeweled bolt; non-glare blued finish. Introduced, 1978; still in production. Used value, $1200 to $1400.

Wichita Classic Model

WICHITA Classic Model: bolt-action; calibers .17 through .308 Win., including .22 and 6mm PPC; 21⅛" barrel; has same general specs as Varmint model, except has octagonal barrel. Introduced, 1978; still in production. Used value, $1800 to $2000.

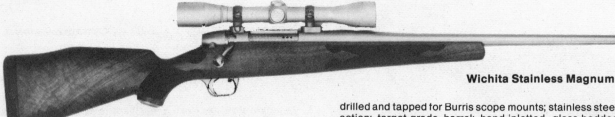

Wichita Stainless Magnum

WICHITA Stainless Magnum: bolt-action; calibers .270 Win. through .458 Win. magnum; 22", 24" barrel lengths; no sights, drilled and tapped for Burris scope mounts; stainless steel barrel, action; target-grade barrel; hand-inletted, glass-bedded fancy American walnut stock; hand-checkered; steel pistol-grip cap; Pachmayr rubber recoil pad; single-shot or with blind magazine; fully adjustable trigger. Introduced, 1980; no longer in production. Used value, $1200 to $1400.

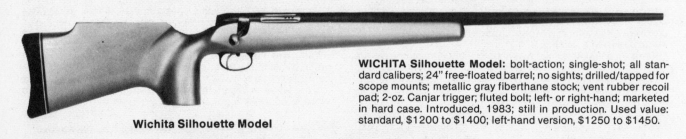

Wichita Silhouette Model

WICHITA Silhouette Model: bolt-action; single-shot; all standard calibers; 24" free-floated barrel; no sights; drilled/tapped for scope mounts; metallic gray fiberthane stock; vent rubber recoil pad; 2-oz. Canjar trigger; fluted bolt; left- or right-hand; marketed in hard case. Introduced, 1983; still in production. Used value: standard, $1200 to $1400; left-hand version, $1250 to $1450.

WINCHESTER

Winchester Model 73

WINCHESTER Model 73: lever-action; .22 RF, .32-20, .38-40, .44-40; 6-, 12-, 15- or 17-rd. tubular magazine; 24" barrel; open rear sight, bead or blade front; uncheckered American walnut straight-grip stock, forend. Manufactured 1873 to 1924. Collector value. Used values: $850 to $1700; Win. 1 of 1000, $25,000 to $100,000, Win. 1 of 100, $20,000 to $75,000.

Winchester Model 73 Carbine

Model 73 Carbine has same general specs as rifle, except for 20" barrel; 12-rd. magazine. Collector value. Used value, $1250

WINCHESTER Low-Wall Sporter: lever-action, single-shot; .22 RF; 28" round, octagonal barrel; solid frame; open rear sight, blade

WINCHESTER High-Wall Sporter: lever-action, single-shot; .22 RF through .50; solid frame or take-down; light 30" barrel; open rear sight, blade front; uncheckered American walnut straight-grip stock, forend. Manufactured 1885 to 1920. Collector value. Used value, $750 to $1250.

High-Wall Special Grade has same specs as standard high-wall, except for better wood; hand-checkered stock, forend. Collector value. Used value, $1500 to $2000.

High-Wall Schuetzen has same basic action as standard high-wall; solid frame or take-down; spur finger lever; double-set trig-

to $2000.

Model 73 Special Sporter has same specs as standard rifle, except for octagon barrel only, color case-hardened receiver, select American walnut pistol-grip stock. Collector value. Used value, $1500 to $2500.

front; uncheckered American walnut straight stock, forend. Manufactured 1885 to 1920. Collector value. Used value, $700 to $1200.

ger; 30" octagonal barrel; Vernier rear tang peep sight, wind-gauge front; European walnut Schuetzen-type stock; hand-checkered forend, pistol grip; Schuetzen butt plate, adjustable palm rest. Collector value. Used value, $2000 to $3000.

High-Wall Winder Musket has same basic specs of other high-wall models; chambered for .22 short, .22 LR; 28" round barrel; solid frame or take-down; musket-type rear sight, blade front; straight-grip military-type stock, forend. Collector value. Used value, $400 to $450.

Winchester Model 1886

WINCHESTER Model 1886: lever-action repeating rifle; it is more a collector's item than practical rifle; .45-70, .45-90, .40-82, .40-65, .38-56, .40-70, .38-70, .50-100-450, .50-110 Express, .33

WCF; 8-shot tube magazine or 4-shot half magazine; 26" barrel, round, half-octagonal, octagonal; open rear sight; bead or blade front; plain straight stock, forearm. Introduced in 1886; discontinued, 1935. Price when discontinued, $53.75. Used value, $1500 to $2500.

Model 1886 Carbine is same as rifle but with 22" barrel. Used value, $3000 to $5000, rare.

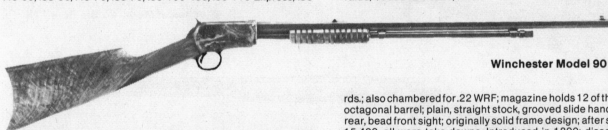

Winchester Model 90

WINCHESTER Model 90: slide-action repeater, with visible hammer; tubular magazine holds 15 .22 rimfire short, 12 long, 11 LR

rds.; also chambered for .22 WRF; magazine holds 12 of these; 24" octagonal barrel; plain, straight stock, grooved slide handle; open rear, bead front sight; originally solid frame design; after serial No. 15,499, all were take-downs. Introduced in 1890; discontinued, 1932. Retail when discontinued, $22.85. Used values: take-down, $450 to $550; solid frame, $1500 to $2000.

Winchester Model 92

WINCHESTER Model 92: lever-action repeater; 24" barrel, round, half-octagonal, octagonal; 13-shot tube magazine, 7-shot half-magazine, 10-shot two-thirds magazine; available in .25-20, .32-20, .38-40, .44-40; plain, straight stock, forearm; open rear, bead front sight. Introduced in 1892; dropped, 1941. Price when discontinued, $22.80. Used value, $650 to $1500.

Model 92 Carbine had 20" barrel, 11- or 5-shot magazine. Used value, $750 to $1600.

Model 92 was redesignated as **Model 53** in 1924, with mod-

ifications, including 6-shot tube half-magazine in solid frame; 7-shot in take-down. Barrel was 22", nickel steel; open rear sight, bead front; straight stock; pistol-grip stock optional; forearm was redesigned. Introduced in 1924; dropped, 1932. Collector value. Used value, $700 to $1200.

WINCHESTER Model 94: carbine, center-fire lever-action; originally available in .30-30, .32 Special, .25-35 Win., .32-40, .38-55, .44 magnum added in 1967. Originally introduced in rifle length, but discontinued in 1936. Currently made only in .30-30. Rifles had 22", 26" barrels; carbine, 20" barrel; carbine has full-length tube magazine with 6-rd. capacity, half-length magazine with 4-rd. capacity; plain, uncheckered American walnut stock; open rear sight; blade front on early versions; ramp front sight introduced in 1931. Production of receiver mechanism revised from 1964 to 1971. Post-'71 version has redesigned steel carrier with sturdier block design, redesigned lever camming slot, improved loading

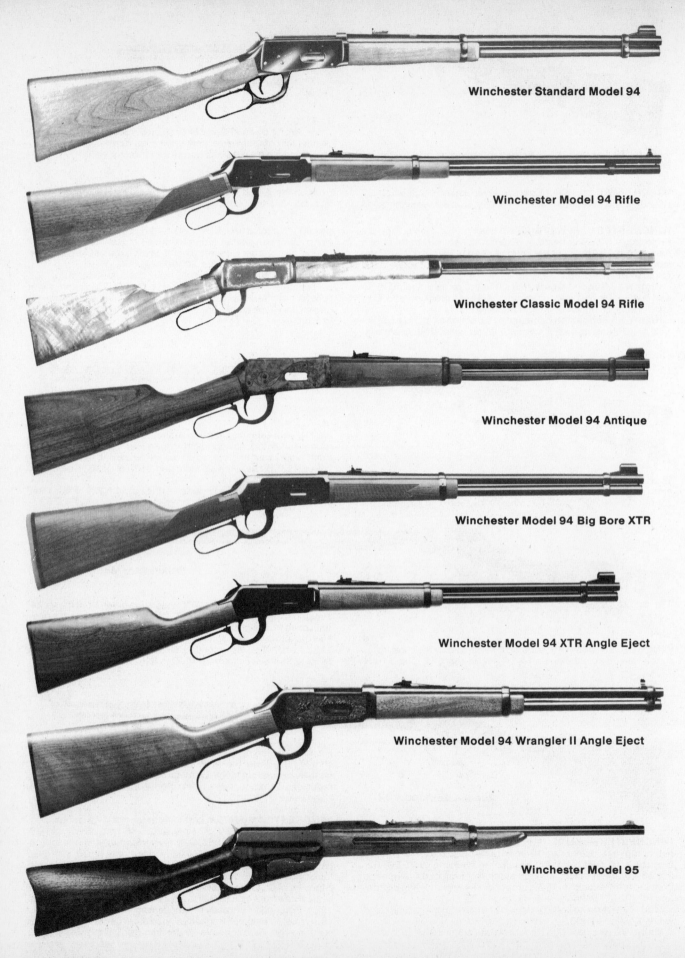

Winchester Standard Model 94

Winchester Model 94 Rifle

Winchester Classic Model 94 Rifle

Winchester Model 94 Antique

Winchester Model 94 Big Bore XTR

Winchester Model 94 XTR Angle Eject

Winchester Model 94 Wrangler II Angle Eject

Winchester Model 95

Winchester XTR 7x30 Waters

port; barrel band on forearm; saddle ring. Introduced in 1894; still in production by U.S. Repeating Arms. Used values: pre-1964 version, $450 to $750; pre-1971 version, $125 to $175; post-1971 version, $175 to $200.

Model 94 Magnum carbine has same general specs as the standard Model 94, except that magazine holds 10 .44 magnum cartridges. Introduced in 1968; dropped, 1972. Used value, $200 to $250.

Model 94 Classic has same general specs as standard Model 94, except for octagonal barrel in 20", 26" lengths; steel butt plate, semi-fancy American walnut stock, forearm; scrollwork on receiver; .30-30 only. Introduced in 1957; dropped, 1970. Used values: carbine, $275 to $300; rifle length, $265 to $285.

Model 94 Antique has same general specs as standard Model 94, except for case-hardened receiver with scrollwork. Introduced in 1968; dropped, 1974. Used value, $195 to $250.

Model 94 Big Bore XTR has same general specs as basic model; chambered for .375 Win.; 6-rd. tube magazine; 20" barrel; cut-checkered satin-finish American walnut stock; rubber recoil pad. Introduced, 1978; now manufactured under license by U.S. Repeating Arms. Used value, $250 to $275.

Model 94 XTR Angle Eject has same specs as Model 94 XTR Big Bore, except is chambered for .307 Win., .356 Win., .375 Win.; 6-rd. tube magazine; 20" barrel; 38⅝" overall length; ejects cartridge cases at forward angle. Made under license by U.S. Repeating Arms. Introduced, 1983; still in production. Used value, $250 to $275.

Model 94 Wrangler has same general specs as standard Model 94, except has 16" barrel; roll-engraved Western scene on receiver; hoop finger lever; .32 Win. Special only. Introduced, 1983; no longer in production. Used value, $185 to $200.

Model 94 Wrangler II Angle Eject is similar to standard Model 94. except has 16" barrel; hoop-type finger lever; roll-engraved Western scenes on receiver; .38-55 only. Introduced, 1983 by U.S. Repeating Arms; dropped, 1986. Used value, $195 to $215.

Model 94XTR Angle Eject, 7x30 Waters has same specs as standard Angle Eject model, except has 24" barrel; chambered for 7x30 Waters caliber; 7-rd. tubular magazine; overall length 41¾"; weighs 7 lb.; rubber butt pad. Introduced, 1984; still marketed by U.S. Repeating Arms. Used value, $200 to $250.

Model 94 Side Eject has same general specs as basic Model 94, except for side ejection feature; 16", 20", 24" barrels; straight-grip stock; .30-30, .44 magnum, .44 Special, .45 Colt. Introduced, 1984; no longer in production. Used value, $200 to $225.

Ranger Side Eject Carbine has same specs as the Model 94 Side Eject Model, except has 5-rd. magazine, no front sight hood, has American hardwood stock. Introduced, 1985; still in production by U.S. Repeating Arms. Used value, $150 to $165.

WINCHESTER Model 95: lever-action; .30-40 Krag, .30 Govt. (03), .30 Govt. (06), .303 British, 7.62mm Russian, .35 Win., .38-72, .405 Win., .40-72; .30-40, .303 have 5-rd. box magazine, 4 rds. for other calibers; 24", 26", 28" barrel; open rear sight, bead or blade front; unchecked straight-grip stock, forend; solid frame, or take-down. Manufactured 1895 to 1931. Collector value. Used value, $800 to $1200.

Model 95 Carbine has same specs as Model 95 rifle, except for carbine stock, solid frame only, 27" barrel; chambered for .30-40, .30-30, .30/06 (see above), .303 British. Collector value. Used value, $750 to $1000.

Winchester-Lee Sporter

front; military semi-pistol-grip stock. Commercial version of Lee Navy Model 1895 rifle. Manufactured 1897 to about 1902. Collector value. Used value, $650 to $700.

Lee Sporter has same specs as musket, except for sporter stock, 24" barrel; open rear sight, bead front. Manufactured 1897 to about 1902. Collector value. Used value, $750 to $800.

WINCHESTER-Lee Musket: bolt-action; 6mm (.236 USN); 5-rd. clip-loaded box magazine; 28" barrel; folding leaf rear sight, post

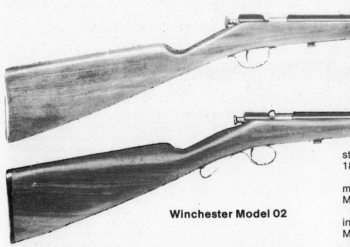

Winchester Model 1900

Winchester Model 02

WINCHESTER Model 1900: bolt-action, single-shot; .22 short, long; 18" round barrel; take-down; open rear sight, blade front;

straight-grip one-piece American walnut stock. Manufactured 1899 to 1902. Some collector interest. Used value, $200 to $225.

Model 02 has same basic specs as Model 1900, with minor cosmetic improvements; .22 short, long, extra long, LR; take-down. Manufactured 1902 to 1931. Used value, $125 to $135.

Model 04 has same basic specs as Model 02, with slight changes in stock design; .22 short, long, extra long, LR; 21" round barrel. Manufactured 1904 to 1931. Used value, $135 to $150.

Thumb Trigger Model 99 has same specs as Model 02, except button at rear of cocking piece serves as trigger. Manufactured 1904 to 1923. Some collector interest. Used value, $275 to $300.

Winchester Model 04

Winchester Model 03

Winchester Model 05

Winchester Model 07

Winchester Model 10

WINCHESTER Model 03: self-loader; .22 Win. Auto RF; 10-rd. tubular magazine in butt; 20" barrel; take-down; open rear sight, bead front; unchecked straight-grip stock, forend. Manufactured 1903 to 1932. Collector value. Used value, $300 to $350.

grip stock, forend. Manufactured 1905 to 1920. Collector value. Used value, $375 to $400.

Model 07 has same general design specs as Model 05, except chambered for .351 Win. Self-Loading only; 20" barrel. Manufactured 1907 to 1957. Collector value. Used value, $350 to $375.

Model 10 has same general design specs as Model 07, except chambered for .401 Win. Self-Loading. Manufactured 1910 to 1936. Collector value. Used value, $375 to $450.

WINCHESTER Model 05: self-loader; .32 Win. Self-Loading, .35 Win. Self-Loading; 5-, 10-rd. box magazine; 22" barrel; take-down; open rear sight, bead front; unchecked American walnut pistol-

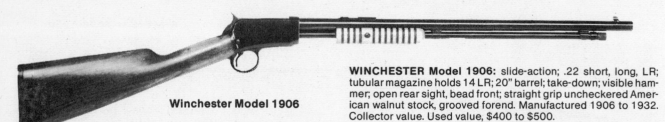

Winchester Model 1906

WINCHESTER Model 1906: slide-action; .22 short, long, LR; tubular magazine holds 14 LR; 20" barrel; take-down; visible hammer; open rear sight, bead front; straight grip unchecked American walnut stock, grooved forend. Manufactured 1906 to 1932. Collector value. Used value, $400 to $500.

WINCHESTER Model 52: bolt-action rifle. Like taxes, this rifle just goes on, some models being dropped to be replaced by updates; there have been no less than 14 variations. Model 52 target rifle was introduced in 1919; dropped in 1937. Had standard barrel, 28"; .22 LR; 5-shot box magazine; folding leaf peep rear sight, blade front sight, with options available; scope bases; originally

had semi-military stock; pistol grip; grooves on forearm; later versions had higher comb, semi-beavertail forearm; slow lock model was replaced in 1929 by speed lock; last arms of model bore serial number followed by letter "A." Used values: slow lock style, $425 to $450; speed lock, $475 to $500.

Model 52 heavy barrel model had speed lock; same general

Winchester Model 52 Sporter

Winchester Model 52D Heavy Barrel

Winchester Model 52B Sporter

Winchester Model 52-D

Winchester Model 52 International Match

specs as standard model, except for heavy barrel; a Lyman 17G front sight. Dropped, 1939. Used value, $500 to $525.

Model 52 sporting rifle same as standard model, except for 24" lightweight barrel; deluxe sporting stock, checkered, with black forend tip; cheekpiece; has Lyman No. 48 receiver sight, gold bead on hooded ramp at front. Dropped, 1958. Used value, $1500 to $1800.

Model 52-B target rifle, introduced in 1935; dropped, 1947; has 28" barrel, redesigned action; choice of target stock or Marksman stock, with high comb, full pistol grip, beavertail forearm; wide variety of sights was available at added cost. Used value, sans sights, $475 to $500.

Model 52-B heavy barrel has same specs as standard 52-B, except for heavier barrel. Used value, $525 to $550.

Model 52-B bull gun has extra-heavy barrel, Marksman stock; other specs are same as standard Model 52-B. Used value, $550 to $575.

Model 52-B sporting rifle is same as first type Model 52 sporting rifle, except that it utilizes Model 52-B action. Dropped, 1961. Used value, $1400 to $1700.

Model 52-C target rifle — and others in "C" series — introduced in 1947; dropped, 1961. Target rifle has improved action, trigger mechanism, with new Marksman stock, heavy barrel; vari-

ous sight combinations available at added cost; other specs are same as original model. Used value, sans sights, $525 to $550.

Model 52-C standard model has same specs as the original Model 52 heavy barrel, but with the standard barrel. Used value, $475 to $500.

Model 52-C bull gun has same general specs as Model 52 heavy barrel model, but has extra-heavy bull barrel, giving gun weight of 12 lb. Used value, $575 to $625.

Model 52-D target rifle was introduced in 1961. Action has been redesigned as single-shot only for .22 LR; has 28" free-floating standard or heavy barrel; blocks for standard target scopes; redesigned Marksman stock; rubber butt plate; accessory channel in stock with forend stop. Used value, sans sights, $450 to $500.

Model 52 International Match Rifle, introduced in 1976, features laminated international-style stock with aluminum forend assembly, adjustable palm rest. Used values, sans sights: with ISU trigger, $550 to $575; with Kenyon trigger, $600 to $625.

Model 52 International Prone Rifle, introduced in 1976, has same features as International Match model, except for oil-finished stock with removable roll-over cheekpiece for easy bore cleaning. Used value, sans sights, $600 to $625.

Winchester Model 55 Centerfire

WINCHESTER Model 55 Centerfire: lever-action; .25-35, .30-30, .32 Win. Special; 3-rd. tubular magazine; 24" round barrel; open rear sight, bead front; uncheckered American walnut straight-grip stock, forend. Based on Model 94 design. Collector value. Manufactured 1924 to 1932. Used value, $500 to $750.

Winchester Model 54 Improved Sporter

Winchester Model 54 National Match

Winchester Model 54 Target

WINCHESTER Model 54: bolt-action centerfire. This is another of those models that verged on being an empire. There were numerous models and styles, in spite of the fact that it had a relatively short life. What the manufacturer calls the "first type" was made from 1925 to 1930; the improved type, from 1930 to 1936.

The early type sporting rifle had a 24" barrel; 5-shot box magazine and was in .270 Win., 7x57mm, .30-30, .30/06, 7.65x53mm, 9x57mm; two-piece firing pin; open rear sight, bead front; stock was checkered, pistol-grip design; scored steel butt plate, checkered from 1930 on; tapered forearm. Retail, when dropped, 1936, $59.75. Used value, $375 to $425; high premium for metric calibers.

Model 54 carbine — first type — was added in 1927; it had plain stock, grasping grooves on forearm, 20" barrel. Used value, $475 to $500.

Model 54 super grade was same as the early sporter, except for deluxe stock with pistol grip cap, cheekpiece, black forend tip. Came with quick-detachable sling swivels, 1" leather sling. Used value, $550 to $600.

Model 54 sniper's rifle has heavy 26" barrel, Lyman No. 48 rear peep sight, blade front sight; semi-military type stock only in .30/

06. Used value, $600 to $625.

Model 54 sniper's match rifle sort of gilds the lily; it is the same as the early sniper model, but with Marksman target stock, scope bases and the same variety of calibers as standard model. Used value, $700 to $725.

Model 54 National Match rifle differs from standard model only in that it has Lyman sights, Marksman target stock, scope bases. Used value, $650 to $700.

Model 54 target rifle is same as standard model, but has 24" medium-weight barrel, 26" in .220 Swift; has Marksman target stock, Lyman sights, scope bases. Used value, $625 to $650.

Model 54 improved sporter has speed lock, one-piece firing pin; NRA-type stock; checkered pistol grip, forearm; 5-shot box magazine; in .22 Hornet, .220 Swift, .250-3000, .257 Roberts, .270 Win., 7x57mm, .30/06; has 24" barrel, except for 26" for .220 Swift. Used value, $500 to $525.

Model 54 improved carbine is same as improved sporter, but has 20" barrel; stock may be NRA type or lightweight stock used on original version. Used value, $550 to $575.

Winchester Model 56

WINCHESTER Model 56: bolt-action .22 rimfire, choice of .22 short or LR; 5-, 10-shot magazines; 22" barrel; uncheckered pistol-grip stock, Schnabel-type forearm; open rear sight, bead front. Introduced in 1926 dropped, 1929. Retail when discontinued, $21. Used value, $325 to $350.

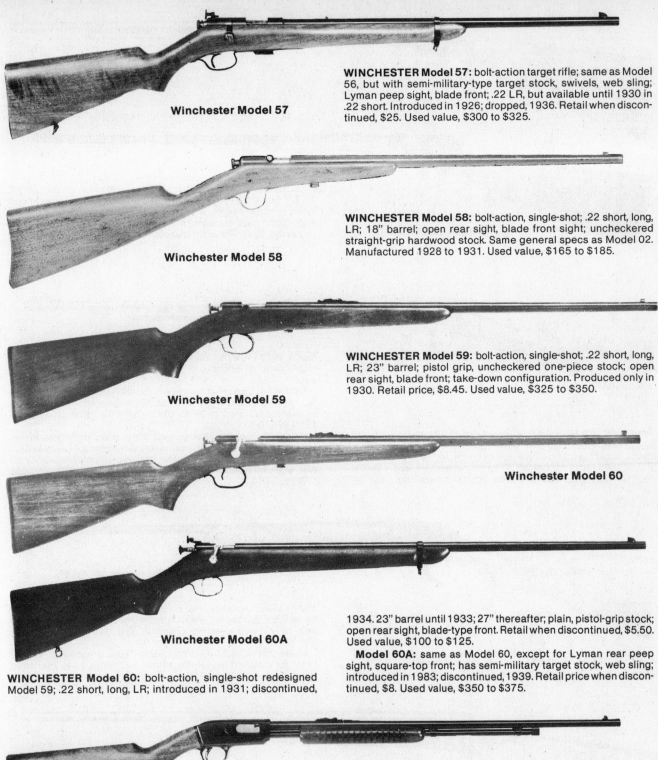

Winchester Model 57

WINCHESTER Model 57: bolt-action target rifle; same as Model 56, but with semi-military-type target stock, swivels, web sling; Lyman peep sight, blade front; .22 LR, but available until 1930 in .22 short. Introduced in 1926; dropped, 1936. Retail when discontinued, $25. Used value, $300 to $325.

Winchester Model 58

WINCHESTER Model 58: bolt-action, single-shot; .22 short, long, LR; 18" barrel; open rear sight, blade front sight; uncheckered straight-grip hardwood stock. Same general specs as Model 02. Manufactured 1928 to 1931. Used value, $165 to $185.

Winchester Model 59

WINCHESTER Model 59: bolt-action, single-shot; .22 short, long, LR; 23" barrel; pistol grip, uncheckered one-piece stock; open rear sight, blade front; take-down configuration. Produced only in 1930. Retail price, $8.45. Used value, $325 to $350.

Winchester Model 60

Winchester Model 60A

1934. 23" barrel until 1933; 27" thereafter; plain, pistol-grip stock; open rear sight, blade-type front. Retail when discontinued, $5.50. Used value, $100 to $125.

Model 60A: same as Model 60, except for Lyman rear peep sight, square-top front; has semi-military target stock, web sling; introduced in 1983; discontinued, 1939. Retail price when discontinued, $8. Used value, $350 to $375.

WINCHESTER Model 60: bolt-action, single-shot redesigned Model 59; .22 short, long, LR; introduced in 1931; discontinued,

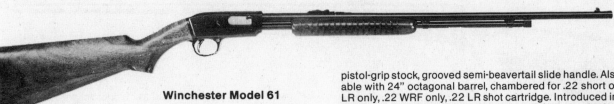

Winchester Model 61

WINCHESTER Model 61: hammerless slide-action, take-down repeater; .22 short, long, LR; tubular magazine holds 20 short, 16 long, 14 LR; 24" barrel, open rear sight, bead front; uncheckered

pistol-grip stock, grooved semi-beavertail slide handle. Also available with 24" octagonal barrel, chambered for .22 short only, .22 LR only, .22 WRF only, .22 LR shot cartridge. Introduced in 1932; dropped, 1963. Retail when discontinued, $70. Used value, $350 to $400.

The Model 61 Magnum introduced in 1960; dropped, 1963; differs from the standard model only in that it is chambered for .22 WRFM; magazine holds 12 rds. Used value, $450 to $500.

WINCHESTER Model 62: slide-action, visible hammer repeater; chambered for .22 short, long, LR; tube magazine holds 20 short, 16 long, 14 LR; 23" barrel; plain, straight-grip stock; grooved semi-

beavertail slide handle; also available in gallery model in .22 short only. Introduced in 1932; dropped, 1959. Retail when discontinued, $53. Used value, $325 to $345.

Winchester Model 62

Winchester Model 63

WINCHESTER Model 63: take-down, self-loading rifle; .22 LR, .22 LR Super Speed; 23" barrel; 10-shot tube magazine in butt stock; open rear sight, bead front; plain pistol-grip stock, forearm; available in early series with 20" barrel. Introduced in 1933; discontinued, 1958. Retail when discontinued, $85. Used value, $350 to $400.

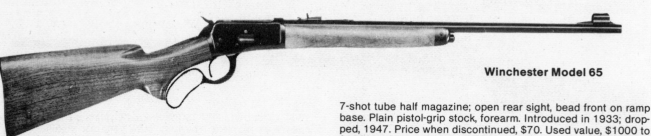

Winchester Model 64

WINCHESTER Model 64: lever-action; .219 Zipper, .25-35, .30-30, .32 Win. Special; 20", 24" barrel; open rear sight, ramped bead front; unchecked American walnut pistol-grip stock, forend. Improved version of Model 55. Originally manufactured 1933 to 1957; additional production with .30-30 chambering only, 24"

barrel, 1972 to 1973. Collector value on original production. Used value: early production, $550 to $600; later production model, $300 to $325.

Model 64 Zipper has same general specs as original Model 64, but with peep rear sight, 26" barrel, chambered for .219 Zipper only. Manufactured 1938 to 1941. Collector value. Used value, $950 to $1000.

Model 64 Deer Rifle has same specs as standard original model, except for hand-checkered pistol-grip stock, forend, 1" sling swivels, sling; checkered steel butt plate; chambered only for .30-30, .32 Win. Manufactured, 1933 to 1956. Collector value. Used value, $700 to $750.

Winchester Model 65

WINCHESTER Model 65: improvement on the Model 53, it's a lever-action solid-frame repeater, in .25-20, .32-20; has 22" barrel,

7-shot tube half magazine; open rear sight, bead front on ramp base. Plain pistol-grip stock, forearm. Introduced in 1933; dropped, 1947. Price when discontinued, $70. Used value, $1000 to $1500.

Model 65 .218 Bee introduced in 1939; dropped, 1947. It is same as standard model, except for 24" barrel, peep rear sight. Used value, $1000 to $1500.

Winchester Model 67

WINCHESTER Model 67: bolt-action, take-down, single-shot; in .22 short, long, LR, .22 WRF; also made with smoothbore for shot;

WINCHESTER Model 677: similar to standard Model 67, except for no sights; scope mounts were mounted on barrel; fired .22 short, long, LR interchangeably. Enjoyed little success due to poor

27" barrel; open rear sight, bead front; unchecked pistol-grip stock; early models had grooved forearm. Introduced in 1934; dropped, 1963. Retail price when discontinued, $22. Used value, $100 to $115.

Model 67 Boy's Rifle is the same as standard model, but has shorter stock, 20" barrel. Used value, $110 to $115.

scope-mounting system. Introduced, 1937; dropped, 1939. Enjoys some value as a collector item, as only 2239 were produced. Retail price, when dropped, $5.95. Used value, $250 to $275.

Winchester Model 68

WINCHESTER Model 68: bolt-action, single-shot take-down; the same as the Model 67, except for being equipped with rear peep sight. Introduced in 1934; discontinued, 1946. Retail price when discontinued, $6.95. Used value, $100 to $125.

Winchester Model 69

WINCHESTER Model 69: bolt-action, take-down repeater; .22 short, long, LR, detachable 5-, 10-rd. box magazine; 25" barrel. Peep or open rear sight; bead ramp front; uncheckered pistol-grip

WINCHESTER Model 697: similar to standard Model 69, except that there were no sight cuts in barrel; scope bases were attached to barrel; no sights; rifle fired .22 short, long, LR cartridges inter-

stock, Introduced in 1935; discontinued, 1963. Retail price when discontinued, $36. Used value, $175 to $195.

Model 69 Target Rifle is same as standard Model 69, except for rear peep sight, blade front sight, sling swivels. Used value, $200 to $215.

Model 69 Match Rifle differs from the target model only in that it has Lyman No. 57EW receiver sight. Used value, $215 to $225.

changeably; came equipped with choice of 2¾ or 5X scope; 25" round barrel. Introduced, 1937; dropped, 1941. Retail when dropped, $12.50. Collector interest. Used value, $200 to $215.

Winchester Model 70 Super Grade (pre-1964)

Winchester Model 70 National Match

Winchester Model 70 African

Winchester Model 70 Alaskan

Winchester Model 70 Lightweight Carbine

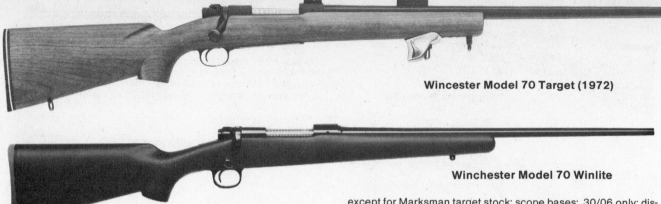

Wincester Model 70 Target (1972)

Winchester Model 70 Winlite

WINCHESTER Model 70: this bolt-action centerfire repeating rifle is a versatile longarm, having been produced in more variations and configurations than any other of the manufacturer's firearms. The rifle is divided into roughly three historical categories, the original variations having been made from 1936 to 1963; at that time the rifle was redesigned to a degree, actually downgraded in an effort to meet rising costs, but to hold the retail price. This series of variations was produced from 1964 until 1972, at which time the rifle was upgraded and the retail price increased. Additional changes have been made in years since.

Model 70 Standard Grade (1936-1963): available in .375 H&H magnum, 8x57mm, .300 H&H magnum, .308 Win., .30/06, 7x57mm .270 Win., .257 Roberts, .250-3000, .243 Win., .220 Swift, .22 Hornet (other rare calibers exist, including 9x57mm, .35 Rem., and .300 Savage). 4-shot box magazine in magnum calibers, 5-shot for others; for a short period, a 20" barrel was available; standard was 24", with 26" for .300 magnum, .220 Swift; 25" for .375 H&H magnum; hooded ramp front sight, open rear; hand-checkered walnut stock; later production had Monte Carlo comb as standard. Retail price when introduced, $62. Used value: $550 to $600 in standard calibers; $2500 to $3500 in rare calibers.

Model 70 Standard Grade (1964-1971); available in .30/06, .308 Win., .270, .243, .225, .22-250, .222 Rem.; 24" barrel, 5-shot box magazine; hooded ramp front sight, open rear, Monte Carlo cheekpiece, impressed checkering; sling swivels. Used value, $300 to $325.

Model 70 Standard Grade (1971 to present); available in .30/06, .308, .270, .243, .25/06, .222, .22-250; 22" swaged, floating barrel; walnut Monte Carlo stock; cut checkering on pistol grip, forearm; has removable hooded ramp bead front sight, open rear; receiver tapped for scope mounts; steel grip cap; sling swivels. Used value, $325 to $350.

Model 70 Target Model (1937-1963); same as standard model of period, except for scope bases, 24" medium-weight barrel, Marksman stock; when introduced, it was available in same calibers as standard model; when discontinued, only in .30/06, .243 Win. Used value, $750 to $850, depending upon caliber.

Model 70 Target Model (1964-1971); .30/06, .308 Win.; 24" barrel, 5-shot box magazine; target scope blocks, no sights; high-comb Marksman stock; aluminum hand stop; swivels. Used value, $550 to $650.

Model 70 Target Model (1972 to discont.); same as current standard model, except has 24" heavy barrel; contoured aluminum hand stop for either left- or right-handed shooter; high-comb target stock; clip slot in receiver; tapped for micrometer sights. Used value, $600 to $750.

Model 70 Super Grade (1937-1960); same as standard model of early production period, except for deluxe stock, cheekpiece, black forearm tip, sling, quick-detachable sling swivels; grip cap. Used value: $900 to $1000 in standard calibers; rare calibers, $4000 to $4500.

Model 70 Super Grade (recent production); .300 Win. magnum; .30/06, .270, .243; .300 magnum has recoil pad; same as standard model, except for semi-fancy, presentation-checkered walnut stock; ebony forearm tip with white spacer; pistol grip; non-slip rubber butt plate; knurled bolt handle. Used value, $400 to $425.

Model 70 National Match; same as early standard model,

except for Marksman target stock; scope bases; .30/06 only; discontinued, 1960. Used value, $650 to $850.

Model 70 Featherweight Sporter: introduced in 1952; dropped, 1963; same as standard model of period, but has redesigned stock, aluminum trigger guard, butt plate, floor plate; 22" barrel; .358 Win., .30/06, .308 Win., .270 Win., .264 Win. magnum, .243 Win. Used value, $550 to $600; $1000 for .358.

Model 70 Featherweight Super Grade; same as Featherweight Sporter, but with deluxe stock, cheekpiece, sling, quick-detachable swivels, black pistol-grip cap, forearm tip; discontinued, 1960. Used value, $850 to $1000.

Model 70 Varmint (1956-1963); same as early standard model, except with 26" heavy barrel; varminter stock; scope bases; .243 Win., .220 Swift. Used value, $600 to $700.

Model 70 Varmint (1974 to present); same as earlier version, but in .243, .22-250, .222 only. Used value, $300 to $325.

Model 70 Bull Gun; same as early model, except for 28" extra-heavy barrel, scope bases; Marksman stock; .30/06, .300 H&H magnum; discontinued, 1963. Used value, $675 to $750.

Model 70 African (1956-1963); same as super grade of the era, but with 24" barrel, 3-shot magazine; recoil pad, Monte Carlo stock; .458 Win. magnum only. Used value, $1750 to $2250.

Model 70 African (1964-1971); same as original version, except for special sights, 22" barrel; hand-checkered stock; twin stock-reinforcing bolts, Monte Carlo stock, ebony forearm tip; recoil pad; quick-detachable swivels. Used value, $600 to $650.

Model 70 African (1971 to present); same as earlier version, except for floating heavy barrel. Used value, $425 to $450.

Model 70 Alaskan (1960-1963); same as early standard model, except for 25" barrel, recoil pad; 3-shot magazine in .338 Win., 4-shot in .375 H&H magnum. Used value, $900 to $1100.

Model 70 Westerner (1960-1963); same as standard model of era, except for 26" barrel in .264 Win. magnum. 24" barrel in .300 Win. magnum. Used value, $675 to $725.

Model 70 Westerner (1981); has same general specs as basic Model 70; standard iron sights; .223, .243, .270, .30/06, 7mm Rem. magnum, .300 Win. magnum; 22", 24" barrel lengths. Introduced, 1981; dropped, 1984. Used value, $325 to $335.

Model 70 Deluxe (1964-1971); in .243, .270 Win., .30/06, .300 Win. magnum; 3-shot magazine, 24" barrel in magnum caliber, 5-shot magazine, 22" barrel in others; hooded ramp front sight, open rear; recoil pad on magnum, hand-checkered forearm, pistol grip, Monte Carlo walnut stock, ebony forearm tip. Used value, $400 to $450.

Model 70 Magnum (1964-1971); in .375 H&H magnum, .338, .300, .264 Win. magnum, 7mm Rem. magnum; 24" pad, swivels, checkered Monte Carlo stock; hooded ramp front sight, open rear. Used value: .375 H&H magnum, $450 to $475; other calibers, $400 to $425.

Model 70 Mannlicher (1969-1971); Mannlicher-type stock with Monte Carlo comb, cheekpiece, quick-detachable swivels, checkered wood, steel forearm cap, hooded ramp front sight, open rear; in .30/06, .308 Win., .270, .243; 19" barrel; 5-shot box magazine. Used value, $650 to $675.

Model 70 International Army Match; produced in 1971 only; .308 Win.; 5-shot box magazine, 24" heavy barrel; externally adjustable trigger; International Shooting Union stock; forearm rail for accessories; adjustable butt plate; optional sights. Used value, sans sights, $675 to $700.

Model 70 Lightweight Carbine; bolt-action; .270, .30/06 in standard action; .22-250, .223, .243, .308 in short action; 20" barrel; 5-rd. magazine, 6-rd. in .223; satin-finished American walnut stock; cut checkering; no sights; drilled, tapped for scope mounts;

plate; sling swivel studs. Introduced, 1984; no longer in production. Used value, $230 to $250.

Model 70 Winlite has same specs as Model 70 XTR Sporter, except has brown fiberglass stock; no sights; drilled, tapped for scope mounts; 22", 24" barrel lengths; .270, .30/06, 7mm Rem. magnum, .338 Win. magnum; .280, .300 Weatherby, .300 Win. magnum added, 1988; 3- or 4-rd. magazine, depending on caliber. Introduced, 1986; still in production. Used value, $425 to $450.

Winchester Model 70 XTR

Winchester Model 70 XTR Magnum

Winchester Model 70 XTR Featherweight

Winchester Model 70 XTR Varmint

Winchester Model 70XTR Sporter Magnum

WINCHESTER Model 70 XTR: bolt-action; .222, .22-250, .25/06, .243, .270, .308, .30/06; 5 rds.; 22" swaged floating barrel; removable hooded bead ramp front sight, adjustable open rear, flips down for scope mount; cut-checkered pistol-grip Monte Carlo walnut stock; steel pistol-grip cap, hinged floor plate; sling swivels; blued finish. Introduced, 1978; currently produced by U.S. Repeating Arms in fewer calibers. Used values, $375 to $400.

Model 70 XTR Magnum has same specs as standard sporter except for 24" barrel; chambered for .264 Win. magnum, 7mm Rem. magnum, .300 Win. magnum, .338 Win. magnum; 3-rd. magazine; satin-finished stock. Introduced, 1978; no longer in production. Used value, $400 to $425.

Model 70 XTR Featherweight has same general specs as Model 70 XTR Magnum, except for chambering in .22-250, .243, .257 Roberts, .270, .280, 7x57, .30/06, .308; 22" tapered barrel; Classic American walnut stock, Schnabel forend, wrap-around cut checkering, red rubber butt pad; detachable sling swivels; satin-finished stock, high-polished blued finish on metal; optional blade front sight, adjustable folding rear. Introduced, 1981; manufactured under license by U.S. Repeating Arms. Used value, $360 to $375.

Model 70 XTR Varmint version has same specs as XTR Magnum except is chambered for .22-250, .243 only; 24" heavy barrel, no sights; black serrated butt plate; black forend tip; high-luster finish. Introduced, 1980; no longer in production. Used value, $360 to $375.

Model 70 XTR Sporter Magnum has same general specs as standard XTR model; .264 Win. magnum, 7mm Rem. magnum, .300 Win. magnum, .338 Win. magnum; 3-rd. magazine; 24" barrel; 44½" overall length; Monte Carlo cheekpiece; satin finish; adjustable folding leaf rear sight, hooded ramp front; 3-position safety; detachable sling swivels; stainless steel magazine follower; rubber butt pad; epoxy-bedded recoil lug. Made under license by U.S. Repeating Arms. Introduced, 1981; no longer produced. Used value, $340 to $360.

Model 70 XTR Super Express Magnum; bolt-action; has 3-rd. magazine; .375 H&H magnum, .458 Win. magnum; 22", 24" barrels; Monte Carlo cheekpiece; wrap-around checkering; open rear sight, hooded ramp front; 2 steel crossbolts strengthen stock; front sling swivel mounted on barrel; contoured rubber butt pad. Made under license by U.S. Repeating Arms. Introduced, 1981; still produced. Used value, $475 to $575.

Model 70 Lightweight Rifle: .22-250, .223 Remington, .243 Winchester, .270 Winchester, .308 Winchester, .30/06; 5-rd. magazine for all calibers, except .223; it has 6-rd. capacity; 22" barrel; no sights; drilled, tapped for scope mounts; satin-finished American walnut stock; machine-cut checkering; three-position safety; stainless steel magazine follower; hinged floor plate; sling swivel studs; also available with Win-Tuff laminated stock, Win-Cam green-shaded laminated stock in .270, 30/06. Introduced, 1984; still in production. Used values: standard model, $300 to $325; with Win-Tuff stock, $310 to $330; with Win-Cam stock, $350 to $375.

WINCHESTER Model 71: solid-frame lever-action repeating rifle; 20", 24" barrel; .348 Win.; 4-rd. tubular magazine; open rear sight, bead front on ramp with hood; plain walnut stock, forearm. Intro-

Winchester Model 71 Special

duced in 1936; dropped, 1957. Retail when discontinued, $138. Used value, $700 to $750.

Model 71 Special is same as standard grade, but has peep rear sight, checkered stock, forearm; grip cap, quick-detachable sling swivels, leather sling. Used value, $800 to $900; 71 Carbine with 20" barrel, $1400 to $1500.

Winchester Model 77

WINCHESTER Model 77: semi-automatic, solid-frame, clip type;

.22 LR only; 8-shot clip magazine; 22" barrel; bead front sight, open rear; plain, one-piece hardwood stock, pistol grip. Introduced, 1955; dropped, 1963. Retail when dropped, $40; used value, $125 to $135.

Model 77, tubular magazine type; same as clip-type Model 77, except for 15-rd. tube magazine. Retail when dropped, $40. Used value, $125 to $135.

Winchester Model 75

WINCHESTER Model 75 Sporter: bolt-action solid-frame sporting model fires .22 LR ammo; 5-rd. box magazine; 24" barrel; bolt-action repeater, cocked with opening movement of bolt; check-

ered select walnut stock, pistol grip; hard rubber grip cap; swivels; checkered steel butt plate. Introduced in 1939; dropped, 1958. Retail, when dropped, $70.95; used value, $550 to $600.

Model 75 Target Model is same as standard model, but equipped with target scope or variety of sights; predated sporting model. Introduced in 1938; dropped, 1958; unchecked walnut stock, semi-beavertail forearm; pistol grip, checkered steel butt plate; came with 1" army-type leather sling. Retail price, when dropped, $80.55. Used value, $350 to $375.

Winchester Model 72

WINCHESTER Model 72: bolt-action take-down repeater; tubular magazine holds 22 short, 16 long, 15 LR; 25" barrel; peep or open rear sight, bead front; unchecked pistol-grip stock. Introduced in 1938; dropped, 1959. Price when discontinued, $38.45. Used value, $150 to $175.

Winchester Model 74

WINCHESTER Model 74: semi-automatic, take-down; chambered for .22 short only or .22 LR only; tube magazine in butt stock holds 20 short, 14 LR rds. 24" barrel; open rear sight, bead front; unchecked one-piece pistol-grip stock. Introduced in 1939; discontinued, 1955. Price when dropped, $39.20. Used value, $135 to $150.

Winchester Model 43

WINCHESTER Model 43: bolt-action sporting rifle; .218 Bee, .22 Hornet; .25-20; last two dropped, 1950. 24" barrel; 3-shot detach-

able box magazine; open rear sight, bead front on hooded ramp; unchecked pistol-grip stock with swivels. Introduced in 1949; dropped, 1957. Retail when dropped, $75. Used value, $450 to $475.

Model 43 Special Grade; same as standard Model 43, except for grip cap, checkered pistol grip, forearm; open rear sight or Lyman 59A micrometer. Used value, $550 to $600.

Winchester Model 47

WINCHESTER Model 47: bolt-action single-shot; .22 short, long, LR; 25" barrel; uncheckered pistol grip stock; peep or open rear sight; bead front. Introduced in 1949; dropped, 1954. Price when discontinued, $24.25. Used value, $125 to $135.

Winchester Model 88

WINCHESTER Model 88: lever-action rifle; available in .243 Win., .284 Win., .308 Win., .358 Win.; barrel length, 22"; weighs 6½ lb.; measures 39½" overall; fitted with hooded bead front sight, fold-

ing leaf rear sight. Stock is one-piece walnut with steel-capped pistol grip, fluted comb, carbine barrel band, sling swivels. Has four-shot detachable magazine of staggered, box-type, held with double latches. Hammerless action, with three-lug bolt, crossbolt safety; side ejection. Introduced in 1955; dropped, 1974. Last retail price, $169.95. Used value, $300 to $325; slightly higher for .284; $550 to $650 for .358; $350 to $375 for carbine.

Winchester Model 55

WINCHESTER Model 55: semi-automatic single-shot; .22 short, long, LR; 22" barrel; open rear sight, bead front; one-piece uncheckered walnut stock. Introduced in 1957; dropped, 1961. Retail price when discontinued, $20.45. Used value, $135 to $150.

Winchester Model 100

WINCHESTER Model 100: semi-automatic, gas-operated carbine; available in .243 Win., .284 Win., .308 Win. Barrel is 22"; weight, 7½

lb.; measures 42½" overall. In 1967 barrel length was reduced to 19". Stock is one-piece walnut with checkered pistol grip and forearm, sling swivels. Magazine holds 4 rds., except .284, which holds 3 rds.; tapped for receiver sights or scope mounts; equipped with hooded bead front sight, folding leaf rear. Introduced in 1960; dropped in 1974. Last retail price, $179.95. Used values: pre-'64, $350 to $375; post-'64, $250 to $275.

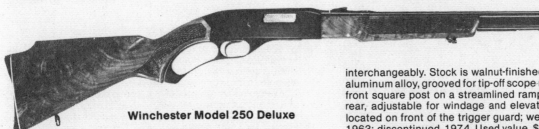

Winchester Model 250 Deluxe

WINCHESTER Model 250: .22 rimfire lever-action rifle; standard and deluxe models; 20½" barrel; tubular magazine, with capacity of 21 short 17 long, 15 LR cartridges, chambered to handle these

interchangeably. Stock is walnut-finished hardwood; receiver of aluminum alloy, grooved for tip-off scope mounts; sights include a front square post on a streamlined ramp; square notch sight in rear, adjustable for windage and elevation; crossbolt safety is located on front of the trigger guard; weight, 5 lb. Introduced in 1963; discontinued, 1974. Used value, $85 to $90.

  The Model 250 Deluxe model included select walnut stock, fluted comb, cheekpiece, basketweave checkering, white spacers between butt plate and stock, sling swivels. Manufactured from 1965 to 1971. Used value, $100 to $125.

Winchester Model 255

WINCHESTER Model 255: lever-action rifle; same as Model

250, except chambered for .22 WRFM cartridge. Introduced in 1963, discontinued in 1974. Retail price on standard model $74.95. Used value, $135 to $155.

  Model 255 Deluxe has same general specs as standard 255, except has high-gloss Monte Carlo select walnut stock, fluted comb, cheekpiece, basketweave checkering, white spacer between butt plate and stock, sling swivels. Introduced, 1965; dropped, 1974. Used value, $175 to $195.

Winchester Model 270

WINCHESTER Model 270: slide-action rifle; .22 rimfire; available in standard and deluxe models; 20½" barrel; tubular magazine with capacity of 21 short, 17 long, 15 LR; chambered to handle all three interchangeably; stock is walnut-finished hardwood; one version, discontinued in 1965, offered forearm of cycolac;

had square post front sight on streamlined ramp; rear sight was square notch type, adjustable for windage, elevation; receiver was of aluminum alloy, grooved for tip-off scope mounts; crossbolt safety; weight about 5 lb. Deluxe style featured high-gloss Monte Carlo stock of walnut with fluted comb, basketweave checkering, cheekpiece. Introduced in 1963, dropped in 1974. Last retail price for standard version, $72.95. Used value for standard, $85 to $100.

Model 270 Deluxe has same specs as standard model, except has high-gloss Monte Carlo select walnut stock, fluted comb, cheekpiece, basketweave checkering, white butt spacer. Introduced, 1965; dropped, 1974. Used value, $115 to $125.

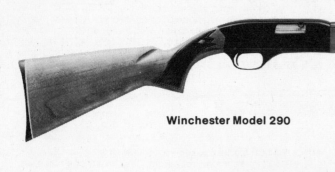

Winchester Model 290

WINCHESTER Model 290: semi-automatic; .22 short, long, LR; tubular magazine holds 15 LR rds.; 20½" barrel; open rear sight, ramp front; uncheckered or impress-checkered hardwood pistol-grip stock, forend. Introduced, 1963; dropped, 1977. Used value, $80 to $85.

Model 290 Deluxe has same specs as standard version, except for fancy American walnut Monte Carlo stock, forend. Manufactured 1965 to 1977. Used value, $90 to $100.

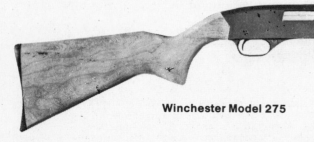

Winchester Model 275

WINCHESTER Model 275: slide-action rifle; same as Model 270, but chambered for .22 WRFM cartridge. Introduced in 1964, dropped in 1971. Last retail price for standard model, $77.95. Used value for standard $90 to $95.

Model 275 Deluxe has same specs as standard model, except has select American walnut stock, Monte Carlo, fluted comb, cheekpiece, basketweave checkering, white butt spacer. Introduced, 1965; dropped, 1971. Used value, $115 to $120.

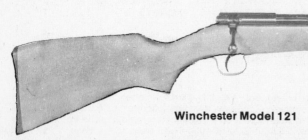

Winchester Model 121

WINCHESTER Model 121: bolt-action, single-shot; .22 rimfire; fires short, long, LR cartridges; barrel length is 20½"; weighs 5 lb.;

one-piece stock is of American hardwood with modified Monte Carlo profile; sights are standard post bead, adjustable V at rear. Receiver is steel, with front locking bolt; grooved to accommodate tip-off mounts for scope sight. Introduced in 1967; discontinued, 1973. Available in three versions: a **Youth Model** with short butt stock and **Standard Model,** both at $23.95; a **Deluxe Version** with Monte Carlo, fluted comb and sling swivels at $27.95. Used value for Youth model, $65 to $75; Standard model, $65 to $70; Deluxe, $90 to $100.

Winchester Model 131

WINCHESTER Model 131: bolt-action, clip-loading .22 rimfire; 20" barrel, overall weight about 5 lb.; stock is one-piece American

hardwood with fluted comb, modified Monte Carlo profile; ramped bead post front, adjustable rear sight; clip-type magazine holds 7 rds., short, long, LR; steel receiver is grooved for telescopic sight mounts; barrel has 1:16" twist ratio; front locking bolt; red safety and red cocking indicator. Introduced in 1967; dropped, 1973; last retail price $38.45. Used value, $85 to $90.

Winchester Model 141

WINCHESTER Model 141: bolt-action; .22 rimfire; tubular magazine in butt holds 19 short, 15 long, 13 LR cartridges interchangeably; barrel is 20½"; weight, 5 lb.; stock is American hardwood with fluted comb, modified Monte Carlo; front locking bolt, ramped bead post front and adjustable rear sight; red cocking indicator and red-marked safety. Introduced in 1967; dropped in 1973. Last retail price, $41.95. Used value, $85 to $90.

Winchester Model 150

WINCHESTER Model 150: lever-action carbine; .22 rimfire; has 20½" barrel, weighs 5 lb.; stock is walnut-finished American hardwood; forearm has frontier-style barrel band; straight grip; no checkering; tube magazine holds 21 short, 17 long, 15 LR cartridges; receiver is aluminum alloy, grooved for scope sight. Introduced in 1967; dropped, 1974. Retail price, $53.95. Used value, $100 to $120.

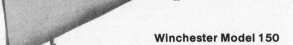

Winchester Model 770

WINCHESTER Model 770: bolt-action; available in .222 Rem., .22-250, .243 Win., .270 Win., .308 Win., .30/06; also in .264 Win. magnum, 7mm Rem. magnum, .300 Win. magnum. Available with 22" barrel for standard calibers, 24" for magnums; weighs 7½ lb. Stock is walnut with high-comb Monte Carlo, undercut cheekpiece; has front sight ramp and hood with adjustable rear sight. Magazine capacities vary, depending upon caliber. Standard models have composition butt plates; magnums, rubber recoil pads. There is a red cocking indicator, serrated trigger. Pistol grip is capped, and grip and forearm checkered. This rifle was designed as a lower-echelon Model 70, but failed to meet acceptance, thus was dropped after only four years in the line, being replaced by Model 70A. Introduced, 1969; dropped, 1973; retailed at $139.95 for standard models, $154.95 for magnums. Used value for standards, $225 to $250; magnums, $250 to $275.

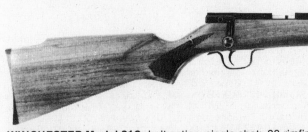

Winchester Model 310

WINCHESTER Model 310: bolt-action; single-shot; .22 rimfire, 22" barrel; weighs 5⅝ lb.; 39" overall in length; 13½" length of pull; stock is American walnut with Monte Carlo, fluted comb; checkered pistol grip, forearm. Has ramped bead post front sight, adjustable rear sight; receiver is grooved for scope sight; also drilled, tapped for micrometer rear sight. Is equipped with serrated trigger, positive safety lever. Introduced in March 1971; dropped, 1974. Last retail price, $44.95. Used value, $125 to $135.

Winchester Model 320

WINCHESTER Model 320: bolt-action; .22 rimfire; 22" barrel; weighs 5⅝ lb.; measures 39½" overall; stock is American walnut, with Monte Carlo, fluted comb; checkered pistol grip and forearm; ramped bead post front sight, adjustable rear; grooved for scope mounts; drilled, tapped for micrometer rear sight; magazine holds 5 rds. of .22 short, long, LR. Is equipped with sling swivels, serrated trigger, positive safety. Introduced in March 1971; dropped, 1974. Last retail price, $57.50. Used value, $275 to $300.

WINCHESTER Model 70A: bolt-action rifle; available in .222 Rem.; .22-250; .243 Win.; .270 Win., .30/06, .308 Win. with 22" barrels, 24" barrels in .264 Win. magnum, 7mm Rem. magnum and .300 Win. magnum. Incorporates features of Model 70 rifle; action is of chrome molybdenum steel; three-position safety; serrated trigger; engine-turned bolt; rear sight is adjustable leaf with white

Winchester Model 70A

diamond for quick sighting; front sight is hooded ramp type; stock is dark American walnut with high-comb Monte Carlo, undercut cheekpiece. Introduced in 1972 as replacement for Model 770, more closely following style of Model 70. Used value, $275 to $300; magnum used value, $300 to $325.

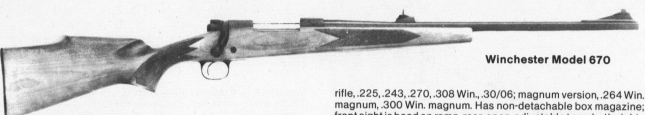

Winchester Model 670

WINCHESTER Model 670: bolt-action; available in carbine style with 19" barrel, sporting rifle with 22", magnum version with 24" barrel; sporting rifle, carbine held 4 rds. in magazine; magnum, 3 rds.; carbine chambered for .243 Win., .270 Win., .30/06; sporting rifle, .225, .243, .270, .308 Win., .30/06; magnum version, .264 Win. magnum, .300 Win. magnum. Has non-detachable box magazine; front sight is bead on ramp, rear, open, adjustable type; both sights easily detached for scope mounting; stock is hardwood with walnut finish, high-comb Monte Carlo style; redesigned in 1972, with only 22" version being produced in .243 and .30/06. Dropped in 1974. Last retail price, $134.95. Used values: $200 to $225; magnum, $250 to $275; carbine, $250 to $275.

Winchester Model 9422

Winchester 9422 XTR Classic

WINCHESTER Model 9422: lever-action; duplicates appearance of Model 94; in .22 short, long, LR and WRFM. Has 20½" barrel; weighs 6½ lb.; stock, forearm are of American walnut, with steel barrel band around latter; front sight is ramp, dovetail bead and hood, with adjustable semi-buckhorn at rear. Standard model holds 21 short, 17 long, 15 LR, interchangeable. Magnum model holds 11 .22 WRFM cartridges. Receiver is of forged steel, with all-steel action. Both styles are grooved for scope mounts. Both styles were introduced in 1972. Used value: $185 to $225 for standard; $225 to $250 for WRFM.

Model 9422 XTR has same specs as basic model, except no magnum chambering; has XTR wood, metal finish. Made under license by U.S. Repeating Arms. Used value, $200 to $235.

Model 9422M XTR has same specs as 9422 XTR, except is chambered for .22 WRFM, has 11-rd. magazine. Made under license by U.S. Repeating Arms. Used value, $200 to $250.

Model 9422 XTR Classic has same specs as standard model, except has satin-finished walnut stock, fluted comb; no checkering; crescent steel butt plate; curved finger lever; capped pistol grip; 22½" barrel; 39⅛" overall length; .22 short, long, LR, .22 WRFM. Introduced, 1985; still produced under license by U.S. Repeating Arms. Used value, $200 to $250.

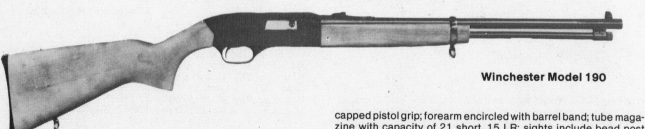

Winchester Model 190

WINCHESTER Model 190: semi-auto carbine; .22 rimfire; 20½" barrel with 1:16" twist. American hardwood stock, with plain, un- capped pistol grip; forearm encircled with barrel band; tube magazine with capacity of 21 short, 15 LR; sights include bead post front, adjustable V at rear; aluminum alloy receiver is grooved for scope mounts. Weight is approximately 5 lb., overall length, 39"; sling swivels included. Introduced in 1974; dropped, 1980. Last retail price, $78.75. Used value, $85 to $90.

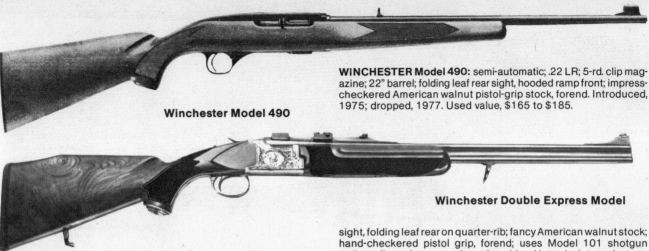

Winchester Model 490

WINCHESTER Model 490: semi-automatic; .22 LR; 5-rd. clip magazine; 22" barrel; folding leaf rear sight, hooded ramp front; impress-checkered American walnut pistol-grip stock, forend. Introduced, 1975; dropped, 1977. Used value, $165 to $185.

Winchester Double Express Model

WINCHESTER Double Express: over/under; .30/06-.30/06, 9.3x74R-9.3x74R, .270-.270, 7.65R-7.65R, .257 Roberts-.257 Roberts; 23½" barrel; 39⅝" overall length; bead on ramp front sight, folding leaf rear on quarter-rib; fancy American walnut stock; hand-checkered pistol grip, forend; uses Model 101 shotgun action; silvered, engraved receiver; blued barrels; integral scope bases; quick-detachable sling swivels; marketed in hard case. Made in Japan. Introduced, 1982; dropped, 1985. Was imported by Winchester Group, Olin Corp. Used value, $2250 to $2500.

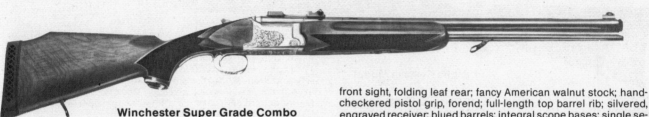

Winchester Super Grade Combo

WINCHESTER Super Grade Combo: over/under; .30/06, 12-ga.; 25" barrel; Winchoke shot barrel; 41¼" overall length; bead front sight, folding leaf rear; fancy American walnut stock; hand-checkered pistol grip, forend; full-length top barrel rib; silvered, engraved receiver; blued barrels; integral scope bases; single selective mechanical trigger. Made in Japan. Introduced, 1982; dropped, 1985. Was imported by Winchester Group, Olin Corp. Used value, $2500-plus.

Winchester Ranger

Winchester Ranger Youth Model

WINCHESTER Ranger: bolt-action; .243, .270, .30/06, 7mm Rem. magnum; 22", 24" barrel lengths; similar to Model 70 XTR Sporter; American hardwood stock; no checkering; composition butt plate; matte blue finish. Introduced, 1985; still produced under license by U.S. Repeating Arms. Used value, $220 to $245.

Ranger Youth Model has same general specs, except has scaled-down stock; .223, .243 only. Used value, $220 to $245.

MISCELLANEOUS RIFLES U.S.-MADE

ACKLEY Standard Model: bolt-action; .22-250, .25/06, .257 Roberts, .270, 7x57, .30/06, 7mm Rem. magnum, .300 Win. magnum; 4-rd. magazine for standard calibers, 4 rd. for magnums; 24" barrel; no sights; drilled, tapped for scope mounts; hand-checkered American walnut stock, rubber recoil pad, swivel studs; Ackley barrel; hinged floor plate; fully adjustable trigger; Mark X Mauser action. Introduced, 1971; dropped, 1975. Used value, $350 to $375.

Olympus Grade has same specs as standard model, except for better wood. Used value, $400 to $425.

Olympus Grade II has same specs as Olympus Grade, except for finer finishing, better blued surfaces. Used value, $450 to $475.

Varmint Special has same specs as standard model, except has 26" barrel, varmint stock, available also in .220 Swift. Used value, $350 to $375.

Ackley Standard Model

ALPHA 1: bolt-action; .243, 7mm-08, .308; 4-rd. magazine; 20" round tapered barrel; 39½" overall length; no sights; drilled, tapped for scope mounts; satin-finish American walnut Monte Carlo stock; rubber butt pad; swivel studs; medium-length action; side safety; cocking indicator; aluminum bedding block; Teflon-coated trigger guard, floor plate assembly. Introduced, 1982; dropped, 1984, when new model introduced. Used value, $550 to $650.

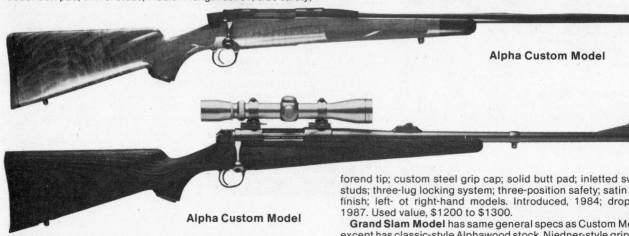

Alpha Custom Model

Alpha Custom Model

ALPHA Custom Model: bolt-action; .17 Rem., .222, .223, .22-250, .338-284, .25/06, .35 Whelan, .257 Weatherby, .338 Win. magnum; other calibers available in short, medium, long actions; 20" to 23" barrel lengths; 40" to 43" overall length; weighs 6 to 7 lb.; no sights; drilled, tapped for scope mounts; hand-checkered classic-style California claro walnut stock; hand-rubbed oil finish; ebony forend tip; custom steel grip cap; solid butt pad; inletted swivel studs; three-lug locking system; three-position safety; satin blue finish; left- ot right-hand models. Introduced, 1984; dropped, 1987. Used value, $1200 to $1300.

Grand Slam Model has same general specs as Custom Model, except has classic-style Alphawood stock, Niedner-style grip cap. Marketed with hard case, sling. Introduced, 1984; dropped, 1987. Used value, $900 to $1000.

Alaskan Model has same specs as Custom Model, except has stainless steel barrel, receiver; other parts coated with Nitex; has Alphawood stock, Neidner-style grip cap, barrel band swivel stud. Introduced, 1984; dropped, 1987. Used value, $1100 to $1200.

American Firearms Stainless

AMERICAN FIREARMS Stainless Model: bolt-action .22-250, .243, 6mm Rem., 6mm Win. magnum, .25/06, .257 Win. magnum, .264 Win. magnum, 6.5mm Rem. magnum, 6.5x55, .270 Win. magnum, .284 Win., 7x57, 7mm Rem. magnum, 7.62x39, .308 Win., .30/06, .300 Win. magnum, .338 Win. magnum, .458 magnum; 16½", 18", 20", 22", 24", 26", 28" barrel lengths; no sights; drilled, tapped for scope mounts; hand-checkered walnut/maple laminated stock; side safety; hinged floor plate; adjustable trigger; made of blued or satin stainless steel. Manufactured in four grades. Introduced, 1972; dropped 1974. Used values: Grade I Presentation, $650 to $675; Grade II Deluxe, $450 to $475; Grade III Standard, $300 to $325; Grade IV Standard .338, .458 magnum, $425 to $450.

AMT Lightning

AMT Lightning 25/22: autoloader; .22 LR; 25-rd. magazine; 18" tapered or bull barrel; weighs 6 lb.; windage-adjustable rear sight, ramp front; folding stainless steel stock; made of stainless steel; matte finish; receiver dovetailed for scope mounts; extended magazine release. Introduced, 1984; still in production. Used value, $180 to $190.

Lightning Small-Game Hunting Model has same specs as Lightning 25/22, except has black fiberglass-filled nylon stock, checkered pistol grip, forend; fitted with swivel studs; removable recoil pad for storage in stock; no sights; marketed with 1" scope,

mounts; 22" target-weight barrel; overall length 40½"; weighs 6¾ lb. Introduced, 1987; still in production. Used value, $185 to $195.

ARMALITE AR-7 Explorer: survival rifle originally designed for use by U.S. Air Force; .22 LR, semi-automatic; take-down; 8-rd. box

BIG HORN Custom: take-down bolt-action; chambered to customer's specs; furnished with 2 barrels to customer specs; classic-style claro walnut stock; no sights; drilled, tapped for scope mounts;

Armalite AR-7

magazine; 16" cast aluminum barrel, with steel liner; moulded plastic stock, hollow for storing action, barrel, magazine; designed to float; peep rear sight; blade front. Introduced in 1959; still in production, but manufactured since 1973 by Charter Arms Corporation. Used value, $75 to $80.

    Custom AR-7: same specs as AR-7 Explorer, except with walnut stock; pistol grip, cheekpiece; not designed to float. Introduced in 1964; dropped, 1970. Used value, $135 to $145.

    Charter AR-7 Explorer: is the same as the Armalite AR-7, except is available with black, silvertone or camouflage finish. Still in production by Charter Arms. Used value, $75 to $80.

Mauser action; Pachmayr flush swivel sockets; recoil pad. Introduced, 1983; no longer in production. Used value, $1500 to $1550.

Bortmess Big Horn

BORTMESS Big Horn: bolt-action; all calibers from .22-250 through .458 Win.; 24", 25" barrel lengths; no sights; drilled tapped for

scope mounts; recoil pad; built on Ranger Arms action; Monte Carlo stock of American walnut; roll-over cheekpiece; half-curl pistol grip; rosewood cap; tapering forend; rosewood forend cap; high-gloss finish. Introduced, 1974; dropped, 1977. Used value, $450 to $475.

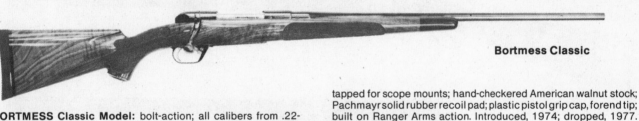

Bortmess Classic

BORTMESS Classic Model: bolt-action; all calibers from .22-250 through .458 Win.; 24", 25" barrel lengths; no sights; drilled,

tapped for scope mounts; hand-checkered American walnut stock; Pachmayr solid rubber recoil pad; plastic pistol grip cap, forend tip; built on Ranger Arms action. Introduced, 1974; dropped, 1977. Used value, $500 to $550.

Bortmess Omega

BORTMESS Omega: bolt-action; all calibers from .22-250 through .358 Norma; 24", 25" barrel lengths; no sights; drilled, tapped for scope mounts; American walnut stock; high-gloss finish. Introduced, 1974; dropped, 1977. Used value, $450 to $475.

CHIPMUNK Single Shot: bolt-action single-shot; .22 short, long, LR, WRFM; 16⅛" barrel; 30" overall length; post on ramp front sight, adjustable peep rear; American walnut stock; drilled/tapped for scope mounting. Introduced, 1982; still produced by Chipmunk Mfg. Used value, $85 to $95.

    Chipmunk Presentation Model has same specs as basic model, except is fully engraved, with hand-checkered fancy walnut stock. Introduced, 1982; limited production. Used value, $350 to $400.

CLERKE Hi-wall: single-shot; .223, .22-250, .243, 6mm Rem., .250 Savage, .257 Roberts, .25/06, .264 Win., .270, 7mm Rem. magnum, .30-30, .30/06, .300 Win., .375 H&H, .458 Win., .45-70; barrel, 26" medium-weight; walnut pistol-grip stock, forearm; no checkering; black butt plate; no sights; drilled, tapped for scope mounts; exposed hammer; Schnabel forearm, curved finger lever. Introduced in 1970; dropped, 1975. Used value, $250 to $275.

Deluxe Hi-Wall: same specs as standard model, except for half-octagon barrel, adjustable trigger, checkered pistol grip, forearm,

COMMANDO Mark III: semi-automatic; .45 auto; 16½" barrel; 15- or 30-rd. magazine; muzzle brake, cooling sleeve; peep-type rear sight, blade front; walnut stock and forearm; available with choice of vertical or horizontal foregrip. Manufactured 1969 to 1976. Used value, $225 to $250.

Mark 9 has the same specs as Mark III, except chambered for

cheekpiece; plain or double-set trigger. Used values: single trigger, $275 to $300; double-set trigger, $300 to $325.

9mm Luger, redesigned trigger housing. Introduced, 1976; no longer in production. Used value, $225 to $250.

Mark 45 has same specs as Mark 9, but chambered for .45 auto; choice of 5-, 15-, 30-, 90-rd. magazines. Introduced, 1976; no longer in production. Used value, $225 to $250.

C. Sharps Model 1874 Sporting Rifle

C. Sharps Model 1874 Sporting Rifle #3

C. Sharps Model 1874 Long Range Express Rifle

C. Sharps Model 1874 Military Rifle

C. Sharps Model 1874 Business Rifle

C. SHARPS ARMS 1874 Sporting Model: single-shot; .40, .45, .50; 30" octagon barrel; weighs 9½ lb.; Lawrence-type open rear sight, blade front; American walnut stock; color case-hardened receiver, butt plate, barrel bands; blued barrel; re-creation of original Sharps models in six variations. Introduced, 1985; no longer in production. Used values: Sporting Rifle No. 1, $550 to $600; Sporting Rifle No. 3, $450 to $500; Long Range Express Rifle, $575 to $625; Military Rifle, $575 to $625; Carbine, $450 to $500; Business Rifle, $425 to $475.

C. SHARPS ARMS New Model 1875: single-shot; .22 LR Stevens, .32-40 Ballard, .38-55 Ballard, .40-90-2⅝", .40-70X-2 1/10", .40-70-2¼", .40-70-2½", .40-50-1 11/16", .40-50-1⅞", .45-90-2 4/10", .45-70-2 1/10"; 30" tapered octagonal barrel; improved Lawrence-type buckhorn rear sight, blade front; straight-grip walnut stock; case-colored receiver; reproduction of 1875 Sharps rifle. Introduced, 1986; still in production. Used value, $450 to $500.

C. Sharps New Model 1875

C. Sharps 1875 Saddle Ring Carbine

1875 Carbine has same specs as standard sporting model, except has 24" round tapered barrel. Introduced, 1986; still in production. Used value, $425 to $500.

1875 Saddle Ring Model has same specs as standard version, except has saddle ring, 26" tapered octagonal barrel. Introduced, 1986; still in production. Used value, $450 to $500.

C. Sharps 1875 Classic Sharps

C. SHARPS ARMS 1875 Classic Sharps: single-shot; has same general specs as New Model 1875 sporting model, except has 30" full octagon barrel, Rocky Mountain buckhorn rear sight, crescent butt plate with toe plate, Hartford-style forend with German silver nose cap; weighs 10 lb. Introduced, 1987, still in production. Used value, $700 to $750.

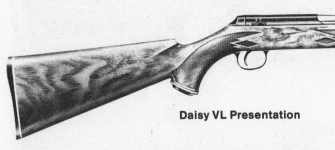

Daisy VL Presentation

DAISY V/L: single-shot; under-lever action; .22 V/L caseless cartridge; 18" barrel; adjustable open rear sight, ramp blade front; stock of wood-grained Lustran plastic. Manufactured 1968 to 1969; only 19,000 produced. Used value, $100 to $125.

V/L Presentation Grade has same specs as standard model, except for American walnut stock. Manufactured, 1968 to 1969; only 4000 produced. Used value, $125 to $150.

V/L Collector Kit includes Presentation Grade rifle, gold plate engraved with owner's name, gun's serial number; included gun case, brass wall hangers for gun, 300 rounds of V/L ammo. Manufactured 1968 to 1969; only 1000 produced. Some collector value. Used value, $250 to $300.

DuBiel Custom

DuBIEL Custom: bolt-action; .22-250 through .458 Win. magnum, selected wildcats; barrel weights, lengths dependent upon caliber; Douglas Premium barrel; stocks in 5 styles, walnut, maple or laminates; hand-checkered; no sights; has integral milled scope mount bases; left- or right-hand models; 5-lug locking mechanism; 36° bolt rotation; adjustable Canjar trigger; oil or epoxy stock finish; slide-type safety; floor plate release; jeweled, chromed bolt; sling swivel studs; recoil pad. Introduced, 1978; still in production. Used value, $1900 to $2000.

Fajen Acra Model S-24

FAJEN Acra S-24: bolt-action; .270, .30/06, .243, .308, .284, .22-250, 6mm, .25/06, 7x57, .257 Roberts, 7mm Rem. magnum, .308 Norma magnum, .300 Win. magnum, .264 Win. magnum; 24" barrel; no sights; Santa Barbara Mauser action; checkered Monte Carlo stock of American walnut, recoil pad; glass-bedded stock; blued finish, rosewood pistol-grip cap, forend tip. Introduced, 1969; dropped, 1973. Used value, $275 to $300.

Acra M-18 has same specs as S-24 except has 18" barrel, full-length Mannlicher-type stock; not made in magnum calibers. Used value, $325 to $350.

FAJEN Acra Model RA: bolt-action; standard calibers; has same specs as Model S-24, except has less extensive checkering. Tenite butt plate, pistol-grip cap, forend tip. Used values, $275 to $300.

Acra Varmint Model: bolt-action; 26" heavy barrel; has same specs as S-24 otherwise. Used value, $275 to $300.

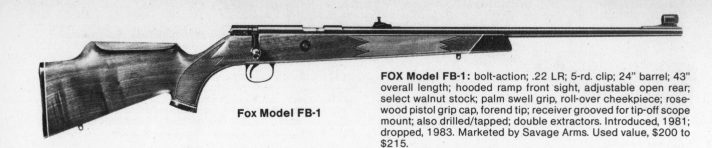

Fox Model FB-1

FOX Model FB-1: bolt-action; .22 LR; 5-rd. clip; 24" barrel; 43" overall length; hooded ramp front sight, adjustable open rear; select walnut stock; palm swell grip, roll-over cheekpiece; rosewood pistol grip cap, forend tip; receiver grooved for tip-off scope mount; also drilled/tapped; double extractors. Introduced, 1981; dropped, 1983. Marketed by Savage Arms. Used value, $200 to $215.

LJUTIC Space Gun: single-shot; .22-250, .30-30, .30/06, .308; 24" barrel; 44" overall length; iron sights or scope mounts; American walnut stock, grip, forend; anti-recoil mechanism; twist-bolt action. Introduced, 1981; still in limited production. Used value, $2400 to $2500.

M-S Safari Arms Varmint

M-S SAFARI ARMS Varmint Model: bolt-action; single-shot; any standard centerfire chambering; 24" stainless steel barrel; no sights; drilled/tapped for scope mounts; custom painted thumbhole or pistol-grip fiberglass stock; stainless steel action; electronic trigger; custom built to customer specs. Introduced, 1983; dropped, 1985. Used value, $950 to $1000, depending on options.

M-S Safari Arms Silhouette

M-S SAFARI ARMS Silhouette Model: bolt-action; single-shot; .22 LR, all standard centerfires; 23" barrel for .22 LR, 24" for centerfires; no sights; drilled/tapped for scope mounts; custom-painted fiberglass silhouette stock; stainless steel action; electronic trigger; custom built to customer's specs. Introduced, 1982; dropped, 1985. Used value, $900 to $950.

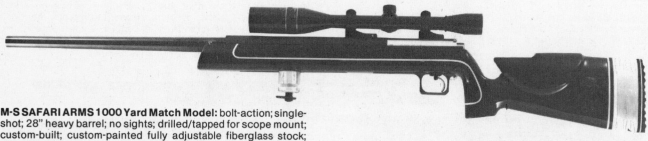

M-S Safari Arms 1000 Yard Match

M-S SAFARI ARMS 1000 Yard Match Model: bolt-action; single-shot; 28" heavy barrel; no sights; drilled/tapped for scope mount; custom-built; custom-painted fully adjustable fiberglass stock; sleeved stainless steel action; electronic trigger. Introduced, 1982; dropped, 1985. Used value, $1450 to $1500.

NEWTON-Mauser Sporter: bolt-action; .256 Newton; 5-rd. box magazine; double-set triggers; 24" barrel; Mauser action; hinged floor plate; open rear sight, ramp front; American walnut pistol-grip stock. Manufactured 1914 to 1915. Used value, $600 to $650.

NEWTON Standard Sporter (Type I): bolt-action; .22, .256, .280, .30, .33, .35 Newton; .30/06; 24" barrel; open rear sight, ramp front; hand-checkered pistol-grip stock; Newton action. Manufactured, 1916 to 1918. Collector value. Used value, $750 to $800.

Standard Sporter (Type II) has same general specs as Type I, except improved design; .256, .30, .35 Newton, .30/06; 5-rd. box magazine; reversed set-trigger, Enfield-design bolt handle. Collector value. Manufactured 1921 to 1922. Used value, $650 to $700.

Buffalo Newton Sporter has same specs as Type II, but manufactured by Buffalo Newton Rifle Co. Collector value. Manufactured 1922 to 1924. Used value, $600 to $650.

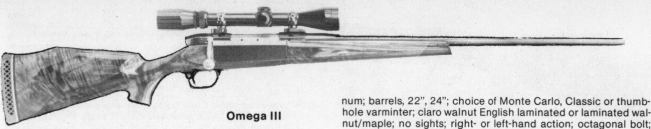

Omega III

OMEGA III: bolt-action; .25/06, .270, .30/06, 7mm Rem. magnum, .300 Win. magnum, .338 Win. magnum, .358 Norma magnum; barrels, 22", 24"; choice of Monte Carlo, Classic or thumbhole varminter; claro walnut English laminated or laminated walnut/maple; no sights; right- or left-hand action; octagonal bolt; square locking system, enclosed bolt face; rotary magazine holds 5 standard or 4 belted cartridges; fully adjustable trigger. Introduced in 1973; dropped, 1976. Used value, $525 to $550.

Pederson 3000

PEDERSEN 3000: bolt-action, Mossberg Model 800 action; .270, .30/06, 7mm Rem. magnum, .338 Win. magnum; 3-rd. magazine; barrels 22" in .270, .30/06; 24", all other calibers; American walnut stock, roll-over cheekpiece; hand-checkered pistol grip, forearm; no sights; drilled, tapped for scope mount; adjustable trigger; sling swivels. Grades differ in amount of engraving and quality of stock wood. Introduced in 1972; dropped, 1975. Used values: Grade I, $750 to $775; Grade II, $575 to $600; Grade III, $500 to $525.

PEDERSEN 3500: bolt-action; .270 Win., .30/06, 7mm Rem. magnum; 22" barrel in standard calibers, 24" for 7mm mag.; 3-rd. magazine; drilled, tapped for scope mounts; hinged steel floor plate; damascened bolt; adjustable trigger; hand-checkered black walnut stock, forearm; rosewood pistol-grip cap, forearm tip. Introduced in 1973; dropped, 1975. Used value, $400 to $425.

PEDERSEN Model 4700: lever-action; .30-30, .35 Rem.; 5-rd. tubular magazine; 24" barrel; Mossberg Model 472 action; open rear sight, hooded ramp front; black walnut stock, beavertail forearm; barrel band swivels. Manufactured, 1975. Used value, $175 to $200.

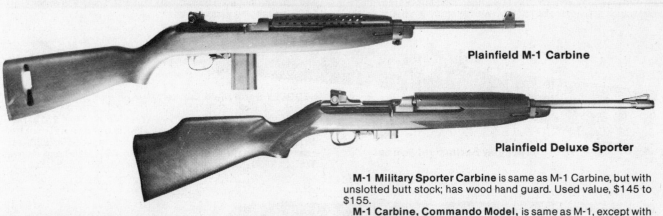

Plainfield M-1 Carbine

Plainfield Deluxe Sporter

PLAINFIELD M-1 Carbine: same as U.S. military carbine, except available in 5.7mm, as well as standard .30 M-1; early models had standard military fittings, some from surplus parts; later model had ventilated metal hand guard, no bayonet lug. Introduced in 1960; dropped, 1976. Used value, $150 to $155.

M-1 Military Sporter Carbine is same as M-1 Carbine, but with unslotted butt stock; has wood hand guard. Used value, $145 to $155.

M-1 Carbine, Commando Model, is same as M-1, except with telescoping wire stock, pistol grips front and rear. Used value, $165 to $175.

Deluxe Sporter is same as M-1, except for Monte Carlo sporting stock. Introduced in 1960; dropped, 1973. Used value, $165 to $175.

Rahn Deer Series

RAHN Deer Series: bolt-action; .25/06, .308, .270; 24" barrel; open adjustable rear sight, bead front; drilled, tapped for scope mounts; Circassian walnut stock with rosewood forend, grip caps or Monte Carlo style with semi-Schnabel forend; hand-checkered; one-piece trigger guard; hinged, engraved floor plate; rubber recoil pad; .22 rimfire conversion insert available. Introduced, 1986; still produced by Rahn Gun Works, Inc. Used value, $550 to $600.

Elk Series has same general specs as Deer Series, except is chambered for .30/06, 7mm Rem. magnum; has elk head engraved on floor plate. Introduced, 1986; still produced. Used value, $575 to $625.

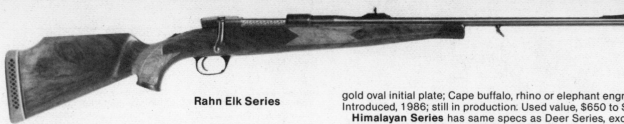

Rahn Elk Series

Safari Series has same specs as Deer Series, except is chambered for .308 Norma magnum, .300 Win. magnum, 8x68S, 9x64;

gold oval initial plate; Cape buffalo, rhino or elephant engraving. Introduced, 1986; still in production. Used value, $650 to $700.

Himalayan Series has same specs as Deer Series, except is chambered for 5.6x57, 6.5x68S; has short walnut or fiberglass stock; floor plate engraved with yak with scroll border. Introduced, 1986; still in production. Used value, $600 to $650.

Ranger Arms Texas Maverick

RANGER ARMS Texas Maverick: bolt-action; .22-250, .243, 6mm Rem., .308 Win., 6.5mm, .350 Rem. magnum; 22", 24" round tapered barrels; no sights; drilled, tapped for scope mounts; Monte Carlo

RANGER ARMS Standard Model: bolt-action; all major calibers from .22-250 through .458 Win. magnum; barrel lengths, contour to order; choice of hand-checkered roll-over cheekpiece, thumbhole, Mannlicher stock in variety of woods; rosewood pistol-grip

RANGER ARMS Texas Magnum: bolt-action; .270 Win., .30/06, 7mm Rem. magnum, .300 Win. magnum, .338 Win. magnum, .358 Norma magnum; 24", 25" barrel lengths; hand-checkered American walnut or Claro stock; hand rubbed to high polish, epoxy finish;

stock of English or Claro walnut; skip-line checkering; cheekpiece; rosewood pistol-grip cap; forend tip; recoil pad; adjustable trigger; push-button safety; made in right- and left-hand models. Introduced, 1969; dropped, 1974. Used values: Governor Grade, $350 to $375; thumbhole model, $375 to $400; Mannlicher model, $375 to $400.

cap, forend tip; recoil pad; no sights, drilled, tapped for scope mounts; push-button safety; adjustable trigger; choice of left-, right-hand models. Introduced, 1969; dropped, 1974. Used value, $325 to $350; more with added options.

no sights; drilled, tapped for scope mounts; recoil pad; swivel studs; jeweled, chromed bolt body; rosewood pistol-grip cap; forend tip. Introduced, 1969; dropped, 1974. Used value, $350 to $400, depending upon options.

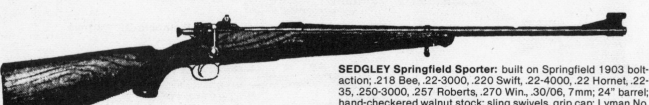

Sedgely Springfield Sporter

SEDGLEY Springfield Sporter: built on Springfield 1903 bolt-action; .218 Bee, .22-3000, .220 Swift, .22-4000, .22 Hornet, .22-35, .250-3000, .257 Roberts, .270 Win., .30/06, 7mm; 24" barrel; hand-checkered walnut stock; sling swivels, grip cap; Lyman No. 48 rear sight, bead front on matted ramp. Introduced in 1928; discontinued, 1941. Used values: $550 to $600; left-hand model, $750 to $800; Mannlicher stock, 20" barrel, $700 to $750.

SERRIFLE Schuetzen Model: single-shot; .32, .22, .38, .41, .44, .45; octagon, half-octagon or round barrels to 32" at customer's preference; fancy Helm-pattern walnut stock; no sights; furnished with scope blocks; Niedner-type firing pin; coil spring striker; based on Winchester Hi-Wall action. Introduced, 1984; dropped, 1986. Made by Serrifle, Inc. Used value, $1200 to $1250.

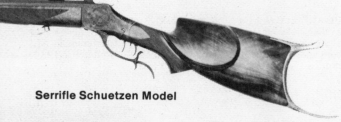

Serrifle Schuetzen Model

Shilen DGA Sporter

SHILEN DGA Model: bolt-action; .17 Rem., .222, .223, .22-250, .220 Swift, 6mm Rem., .243 Win., .250 Savage, .257 Roberts, .284

Win., .308 Win., .358 Win., 3-rd. magazine; 24" barrel; no sights; uncheckered Claro walnut stock; cheekpiece; pistol-grip; sling swivels. Introduced, 1976; still in production. Used value, $500 to $525.

DGA Varminter has same specs as standard model, except for 25" heavy barrel. Introduced, 1976; still in production. Used value, $525 to $550.

Shilen DGA Varminter

SHILOH SHARPS 1874 Long Range Express: single-shot; .40-50 BN, .40-90 BN, .45-70 ST, .45-110 ST, .40-70 ST, .50-90 ST, .50-110 ST, .32-40, .38-55, .40-70 ST, .40-90 ST; 34" tapered octagon barrel; 52" overall length; weighs 10½ lb.; sporting tang rear sight, globe front; semi-fancy, oil-finished pistol-grip walnut stock; shotgun-type butt plate; Schnabel forend; re-creation of Model 1874 Sharps; double-set triggers. Introduced, 1985, still in production. Used value, $675 to $725.

Sharps 1874 Sporting Rifle No. 1 has same specs as Long Range Express, except has 30" barrel, blade front, buckhorn rear sight. Introduced, 1985; still produced. Used value, $650 to $675.

Sharps 1874 Sporting Rifle No. 3 has same general specs as No. 1, except has straight-grip stock, standard wood. Introduced, 1985; still produced. Used value, $500 to $525.

Sharps 1874 Montana Roughrider has same general specs as Sporting Rifle No. 1, except has half-octagon or full-octagon barrel in 24", 26", 28", 30", 34" barrels; .30-40, .30-30, .40-50x1-11/16 BN, .40-70x2-1/10, .45-70x2-1/10 ST; globe front and tang sight optional; standard supreme or semi-fancy wood; shotgun, pistol-grip or military-style butt. Introduced, 1985; still produced. Used

DGA Benchrest Model is single-shot bolt-action, but built on same basic specs as standard model; has 26" medium or heavy barrel; classic or thumbhole walnut or fiberglass stock. Introduced, 1977; still in production. Used value, $600 to $625.

values: standard supreme wood, $550 to $575; semi-fancy, $575 to $600.

Sharps 1874 Military Model has same general specs as Long Range Express, except has 30" round barrel; Lawrence-style rear ladder sight, iron block front; military butt; patchbox; three barrel bands; single trigger; .40-50x1-11/16" BN, .40-70x2-1/10" BN, .40-90 BN, .45-70x2-1/10" ST, .50-70 ST. Introduced, 1985; still produced. Used value, $600 to $650.

Sharps 1874 Business Rifle is similar to Sporting Rifle No. 3, except has 28" heavy round barrel, military-type butt stock, steel butt plate; .40-50 BN, .40-70 BN, .40-90 BN, .45-70 ST, .45-90 ST, .50-70 ST, .50-100 ST, .32-40, .38-55, .40-70 ST .40-90 ST. Introduced, 1986, still produced. Used value, $450 to $475.

Sharps 1874 Carbine has same specs as Business model, except has 24" round barrel, single trigger. Introduced, 1986; still produced. Used value, $450 to $475.

Sharps 1874 Saddle ring Model has same specs as 1874 Carbine, except has 26" octagon barrel, semi-fancy shotgun-type butt. Introduced, 1986; still in production. Used value, $550 to $575.

Shiloh Sharps Jaeger

SHILOH Sharps Jaeger: single-shot; .30-40, .30-30, .307 Win., .45-70; has same general specs as 1874 Montana Roughrider model, except has 26" half-octagon lightweight barrel, standard supreme black walnut stock. Introduced, 1986; still in production. Used value, $550 to $575.

STANDARD Model G: semiautomatic, gas-operated; .23-35, .30-30, .25 Rem., .30 Rem., .35 Rem.; magazine holds 4 rds. in .35, 5 rds. in other calibers; hammerless; take-down; 22⅜" barrel; open rear sight, ivory bead front; gas port, when closed required manual slide action; American walnut butt stock, slide handle-type fore-

arm. Manufactured, 1910. Some collector value. Used value, $325 to $350.

Model M has same general specs as Model G, sans gas-operating feature; operates as slide-action. Manufactured, 1910. Used value, $325 to $350.

Thompson/Center Single-Shot

THOMPSON/CENTER Single-Shot: single-shot; .223, .22-250, .243 Win., 7mm Rem. magnum, .30/06; 23" barrel; 39½" overall length; blade on ramp front sight, windage-adjustable open rear; American black walnut stock; cut-checkering on pistol grip, forend; break-open design; interchangeable barrels; crossbolt safety; single-stage or double-set trigger. Introduced, 1983; still produced. Used value, $275 to $300.

Thompson/Center Contender Carbine

THOMPSON/CENTER Contender Carbine: single-shot; .22 LR, .22 Hornet, .222 Rem., .223 Rem., 7mm TCU, 7x30 Waters, .30-30, .357 Rem. Maximum, .35 Rem., .44 magnum, .410; 21" barrel; overall length 35"; weighs 5⅛ lb.; open adjustable rear sight, blade front; checkered American walnut stock; rubber butt pad; built on T/C Contender action; interchangeable barrels; drilled, tapped for scope mounts. Introduced, 1985; still in production. Used value, $275 to $300.

THOMPSON/CENTER TCR '87: single-shot; .22 Hornet, .222 Rem., .223 Rem., .22-250, .243 Win., .270, .308, 7mm-08, .30/06, .32-40 Win., 12-gauge slug; 23" standard, 25⅞" heavy barrels; no sights; checkered American black walnut stock; break-open de- sign; interchangeable barrel feature; single-stage trigger; cross-bolt safety. Used value, $275 to $300; add $120 to $125 for extra 12-ga. slug barrel.

Ultra Light Model 20

ULTRA LIGHT ARMS Model 20: bolt-action; .22-250, .243, 6mm Rem., .257 Roberts, 7x57, 7mm-08, .284, .308; other calibers on request; 22" barrel; 41½" overall length; weighs 4½ lb.; no sights; marketed with scope mount; Kevlar/graphite stock in green, black, brown or camo; two-position, three-function safety; Timney trigger; bright or matte finish; marketed in hard case; left- or right-hand action. Introduced, 1986; still in production. Used values: standard model, $950 to $1000; left-hand action, $1100 to $1200.

Model 20S has same specs as standard model, except uses short action; 41" overall length; .17 Rem., .222 Rem., .223 Rem., .22 Hornet. Introduced, 1986; still in production. Used values: right-hand action, $975 to $1025; left-hand action, $1100 to $1200.

ULTRA LIGHT Model 24: bolt-action; has same specs as Model 20, except is chambered for .25/06, .270, .280, .30/06; has longer magazine length. Introduced, 1986; still in production. Used values: right-hand action, $975 to $1025; left-hand, $1150 to $1200.

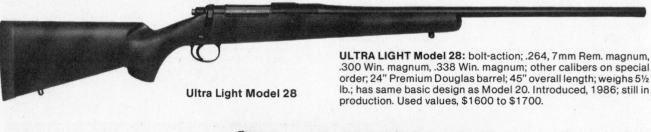

Ultra Light Model 28

ULTRA LIGHT Model 28: bolt-action; .264, 7mm Rem. magnum, .300 Win. magnum, .338 Win. magnum; other calibers on special order; 24" Premium Douglas barrel; 45" overall length; weighs 5½ lb.; has same basic design as Model 20. Introduced, 1986; still in production. Used values, $1600 to $1700.

Universal .30 Carbine

Universal Deluxe Carbine

Universal 1000

UNIVERSAL .30 Carbine: same as .30 M-1 military carbine, but sans bayonet lug; 5-rd. clip magazine; made for short period in mid-1960s with Teflon-coated barrel, action; matte finish on metal. Introduced in 1964; dropped, 1984. Used value, $145 to $155. $155.

    Deluxe .30 Carbine is same as standard model, except for choice of gold-finished, nickel or blued metal parts; Monte Carlo stock; dropped, 1973. Used values: gold-finish, $175 to $185; nickel, $145 to $155; blue, $130 to $140.

    Ferret Semiauto rifle is the same as Universal deluxe .30 Carbine, except for blued finish only, .256 caliber only, no iron sights, equipped with 4X Universal scope. Dropped, 1973. Used value, $165 to $175.

    In 1974 models were revised and redesignated by model numbers.

    Universal 1000 is same as military issue, except for better walnut stock, receiver tapped for scope mounts; dropped, 1977. Used value, $150 to $160.

    Model 1002 is the same as Model 1000, except it has blued metal miliary-type perforated hand guard; dropped, 1977. Used value, $140 to $150.

WICKLIFFE Model '76: single-shot, .22 Hornet, .223 Rem., .22-250, .243 Win., .25/06, .308 Win., .30./06, .45-70; 22" lightweight, 26" heavy sporter barrel; no sights; American walnut Monte Carlo stock; cheekpiece, pistol-grip, semi-beavertail forend; falling-block action. Introduced, 1976; dropped, 1979. Used value, $300 to $325.

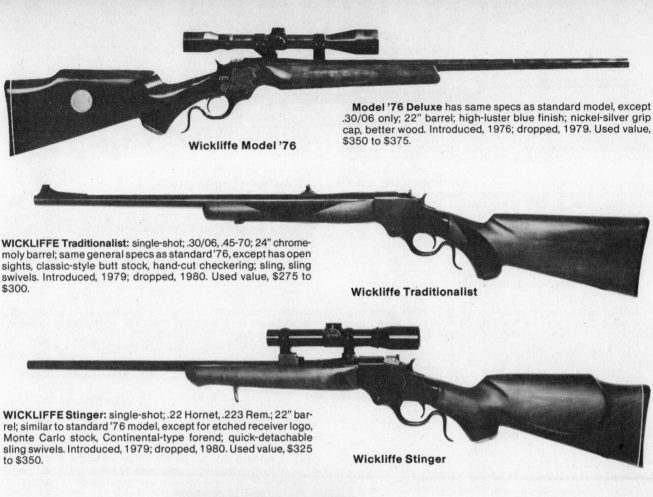

Wickliffe Model '76

Model '76 Deluxe has same specs as standard model, except .30/06 only; 22" barrel; high-luster blue finish; nickel-silver grip cap, better wood. Introduced, 1976; dropped, 1979. Used value, $350 to $375.

WICKLIFFE Traditionalist: single-shot; .30/06, .45-70; 24" chrome-moly barrel; same general specs as standard '76, except has open sights, classic-style butt stock, hand-cut checkering; sling, sling swivels. Introduced, 1979; dropped, 1980. Used value, $275 to $300.

Wickliffe Traditionalist

WICKLIFFE Stinger: single-shot; .22 Hornet, .223 Rem.; 22" barrel; similar to standard '76 model, except for etched receiver logo, Monte Carlo stock, Continental-type forend; quick-detachable sling swivels. Introduced, 1979; dropped, 1980. Used value, $325 to $350.

Wickliffe Stinger

Winslow Standard Model

WINSLOW Bolt-Action: chambered in all standard and magnum centerfire calibers; 24" barrel, 26" for magnums; choice of 3 stock styles; hand-rubbed black walnut, hand-checkered pistol grip, forearm; 4-rd. blind magazine; no sights, receiver tapped for scope mounts; recoil pad; quick-detachable swivel studs; ebony forearm tip, pistol-grip cap. Introduced, 1963; dropped, 1978. Used value: $400 to $425; varmint model in .17/222, .17/223, $415 to $450; left-hand models, add $60.

FOREIGN-MADE

Alpine Sporter

ALPINE Sporter: bolt-action; .22-250, .243 Win., .264 Win., .270, .30/06, .308, .308 Norma magnum, 7mm Rem. magnum, 8mm, .300 Win. magnum; 5-rd. magazine, 3 rds. for magnums; 23" barrel in standard calibers, 24" for magnums; ramp front sight, open adjustable rear; checkered pistol-grip Monte Carlo stock of European walnut; recoil pad, sling swivels. Imported from England by Mandall Shooting Supplies. Introduced, 1978; dropped, 1987. Used value, $375 to $400.

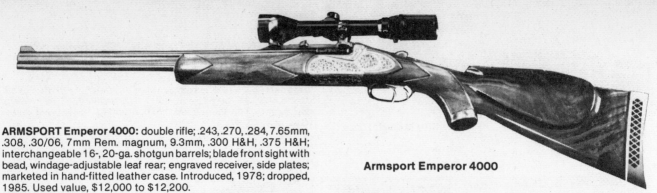

Armsport Emperor 4000

ARMSPORT Emperor 4000: double rifle; .243, .270, .284, 7.65mm, .308, .30/06, 7mm Rem. magnum, 9.3mm, .300 H&H, .375 H&H; interchangeable 16-, 20-ga. shotgun barrels; blade front sight with bead, windage-adjustable leaf rear; engraved receiver, side plates; marketed in hand-fitted leather case. Introduced, 1978; dropped, 1985. Used value, $12,000 to $12,200.

    Emperor 4010 is side-by-side version of Model 4000; chambered for .243, .270, .284, 7.65mm, .308, .30/06, 7mm Rem. mag-num, 9.3mm, .300 H&H, .338 Win., .375 H&H; choice of length and choke for shotgun barrels. Used value, $9200 to $9300.

ARMSPORT 2801: bolt-action; .243, .308, .30/06, 7mm Rem. magnum, .300 Win. magnum; 24" barrel; weighs 8 lb.; open adjustable rear sight, ramp front; European walnut Monte Carlo stock; blued finish. Made in Italy. Introduced, 1986; still imported by Armsport. Used value, $400 to $425.

BERETTA Sporting Carbine: .22 LR, 4-, 8- or 20-rd. magazine; 20½" barrel; 3-leaf folding rear sight, Patridge-type front; European walnut stock, sling swivels, hand-checkered pistol-grip. When bolt handle is dropped, acts as conventional bolt-action; with bolt handle raised fires semiauto. Produced in Italy following World War II. Used value, $325 to $350.

Beretta Model 500

BERETTA Model 500: bolt-action; .222, .223; barrel length 23.62" to 24.41"; European walnut stock; oil-finished, hand-checkered; no sights; drilled, tapped for scope mounts; short action; rubber butt pad. Made in Italy. Introduced 1984; still imported by Beretta USA. Used value, $500 to $550, depending on extras.

    Model 501 has same general specs as Model 500, except is built on medium action; chambered for .243, .308. Introduced, 1984, still imported. Used value, $500 to $550.

    Model 502 has same general specs as Model 500, except is built on long action; chambered for 6.5x55, .270, 7x64, 7mm Rem. magnum, .30/06, .330 Win. magnum, .375 H&H. Introduced, 1984; still imported. Used value, depending on extras, $550 to $600.

BERETTA Express S689: double rifle; .30/06, 9.3x74R; 23" barrel; weighs 7.7 lb.; European walnut stock; checkered grip, forend; open V-notch rear sight, blade front on ramp; box-lock action; silvered, engraved receiver; double triggers; ejectors; solid butt plate. Made in Italy. Introduced, 1984; still imported by Beretta USA. Used value, $1800 to $2000.

    Express SSO has same general specs as S689, except is chambered for .375 H&H, .458 Win. magnum. Used value, $4500 to $5000.

Bernardelli Carbine

BERNARDELLI Carbine: autoloader; .22 LR; 5-rd. magazine; 21" barrel; 40" overall length; weighs 5 lb. 3 oz.; open adjustable rear sight, hooded post front; European hardwood stock; blued barrel; painted receiver. Made in Italy. Introduced, 1986; still imported by Mandall Shooting Supplies. Used value, $215 to $225.

CHAPUIS Express Model: double rifle, over/under; 7x57R, 7x65R, .30/06, 9.3x74R, .444 Marlin, .45-70, .375 H&H; 20-ga. barrels optional; 23.6", 21.5" rifle barrels; express sights; optional rear with folding leaves; checkered oil-finish French or American walnut stock; auto ejectors; game motif, scroll engraving on receiver; side plates. Comes in 3 grades: RG Box lock; R Deluxe with false side plates; President with blued side plates, gold inlays. Introduced, 1978; dropped, 1983. Used values: RG Box lock, $2100 to $2200; R Deluxe, $2450 to $2600; President, $2900 to $3100.

CHURCHILL Regent Combo: over/under combo; 3" 12-ga. over .222, .223, .243, .270, .308, .30/06; 25" barrels; 42" overall length; weighs 8 lb.; open rear sight, blade on ramp front; hand-checkered, oil-finished European walnut Monte Carlo stock; dovetail scope mount; double triggers; silvered engraved receiver. Made in Europe. Introduced, 1985; still imported by Kassnar Imports. Used value, $575 to $625.

CHURCHILL Highlander: bolt-action; .243, .25/06, .300 Win. magnum, .270, .308, .30/06, 7mm Rem. magnum; 3- or 4-rd. magazine, depending on caliber; 22", 24" barrel lengths; 42½" overall length with 22" barrel; weighs 7½ to 8 lb.; no sights or with fully adjustable rear sight, gold bead on ramp front; checkered classic-style European walnut stock; oil-finished wood; swivel posts; recoil pad; positive safety. Made in Europe. Introduced, 1986; still

Churchill Regent Combo

Churchill Highlander

imported by Kassnar Imports. Used values: without sights, $200 to $225; with sights, $225 to $250.

Regent Grade has the same specs as Highlander, except has Monte Carlo-style stock. Introduced, 1986; still imported. Used values: without sights, $400 to $425; with sights, $425 to $450.

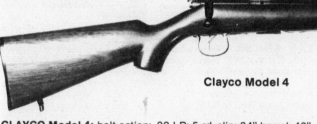

Clayco Model 4

CLAYCO Model 4: bolt-action; .22 LR; 5-rd. clip; 24" barrel; 42"

overall length; weighs 5¾ lb.; walnut-finished hardwood stock; adjustable open rear sight, ramp front with bead; wing-type safety; black composition butt plate, pistol-grip cap; receiver grooved for tip-off scope. Made in China. Introduced, 1983 by Clayco Sports; dropped, 1985. Used value, $100 to $110.

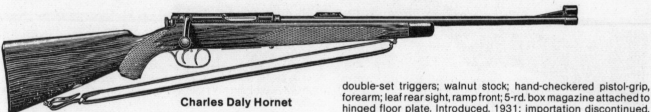

Charles Daly Hornet

CHARLES DALY Hornet: originally made by Franz Jaeger Co. of Germany; miniaturized Mauser action; .22 Hornet only; 24" barrel,

double-set triggers; walnut stock; hand-checkered pistol-grip, forearm; leaf rear sight, ramp front; 5-rd. box magazine attached to hinged floor plate. Introduced, 1931; importation discontinued, 1939. Imported by Charles Daly. (Note: Same model was imported by A.F. Stoeger and sold as Herold rifle.) Collector interest. Used value, $350 to $400.

Dixie Model 1873 Rifle

Dixie Model 1873 Carbine

forearm, receiver engraved with scrolls, elk, buffalo; color case-hardened. Replica of Winchester '73. Introduced, 1975; still imported. Used value, $250 to $275.

Model 1873 Carbine has same general specs as rifle version, except no engraving or color case-hardening; 20" barrel. Used value, $250 to $275.

DIXIE Model 1873: lever-action; .44-40; 11-rd. tubular magazine; 23½" octagonal barrel; leaf rear sight, blade front; walnut stock,

EMF Henry Carbine: lever-action; .44-40, .44 RF; 21" barrel; 39" overall length; weighs 9 lb.; elevation-adjustable rear sight, blade front; oil-stained American walnut stock; reproduction of original Henry model; brass frame, butt plate, balance blued; engraving

optional. Made in Italy. Introduced, 1986; still imported by EMF. Used values: standard model, $425 to $450; engraved, $725 to $775.

EMF Sharps Old Reliable: single-shot; .45-70, .45-120-3¼" Sharps; 28" full octagon barrel; 45" overall length; weighs 9½ lb.; folding leaf rear sight, sporting blade front; deluxe checkered walnut stock; falling block, lever action; color case-hardened butt plate, hammer, action; available also in sporter, military carbine, sporter carbine configurations. Made in Italy. Introduced, 1986; no longer imported by EMF. Used value, $250 to $275; engraved models, $400 to $450.

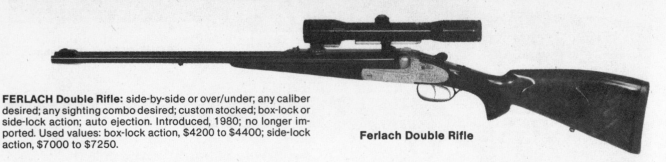

Ferlach Double Rifle

FERLACH Double Rifle: side-by-side or over/under; any caliber desired; any sighting combo desired; custom stocked; box-lock or side-lock action; auto ejection. Introduced, 1980; no longer imported. Used values: box-lock action, $4200 to $4400; side-lock action, $7000 to $7250.

FERLACH Custom Drilling: any combo of gauge/caliber desired; custom-built as to barrel length, stock dimensions, wood, sights; Blitz action; Greener crossbolt. Manufactured in Austria. Introduced, 1976; no longer imported by Ferlach (Austria) of North America. Used value, $3500 to $4000, depending upon options.

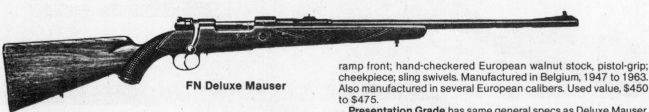

F.I.E. GR-8 Black Beauty

F.I.E. GR-8 Black Beauty: autoloader; .22 LR; 14-rd. magazine; 19⅜" barrel; 39½" overall length; weighs 4 lb.; adjustable open rear sight, band on ramp front; moulded black nylon stock; checkered pistol grip, forend; top tang safety; receiver grooved for tip-off scope mounts. Made in Brazil. Introduced, 1984; still imported. Used value, $60 to $75.

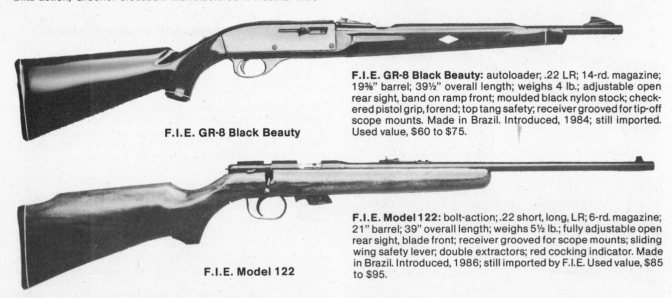

F.I.E. Model 122

F.I.E. Model 122: bolt-action; .22 short, long, LR; 6-rd. magazine; 21" barrel; 39" overall length; weighs 5½ lb.; fully adjustable open rear sight, blade front; receiver grooved for scope mounts; sliding wing safety lever; double extractors; red cocking indicator. Made in Brazil. Introduced, 1986; still imported by F.I.E. Used value, $85 to $95.

F.I.E./FRANCHI Para Carbine: autoloader; .22 LR; 11-rd. magazine; 19" barrel; 39¼" overall length; weighs 4¾ lb.; open adjustable rear sight, hooded front; take-down; receiver grooved for scope mounts; magazine feeds through butt plate. Marketed in fitted carrying case. Made in Italy. Introduced, 1986; still imported by F.I.E. Used value, $220 to $230.

FN Deluxe Mauser

F.N. Deluxe Mauser: bolt-action; .220 Swift, .243 Win., .244 Rem., .257 Roberts, .250/3000, .270 Win., 7mm, .300 Savage, .308 Win., .30/06; 5-rd. box magazine; 24" barrel; Tri-range rear sight, hooded ramp front; hand-checkered European walnut stock, pistol-grip; cheekpiece; sling swivels. Manufactured in Belgium, 1947 to 1963. Also manufactured in several European calibers. Used value, $450 to $475.

Presentation Grade has same general specs as Deluxe Mauser, except for engraved receiver, trigger guard, barrel breech, floor plate; selected walnut stock. Manufactured, 1947 to 1963. Used value, $850 to $900.

FN Supreme Mauser

F.N. Supreme Mauser: bolt-action; .243 Win., .270 Win., 7mm, .308 Win., .30/06; 22" barrel; 4-rd. magazine in .243, .308; 5 rds. in other calibers; Tri-range rear sight, hooded ramp front; hand-checkered European walnut stock; pistol grip, Monte Carlo cheekpiece, sling swivels. Manufactured, 1957 to 1975. Used value, $475 to $525.

Supreme Magnum has same general specs as Supreme Mauser, except chambered for .264 Win. magnum, 7mm Rem. magnum, .300 Win. magnum; 3-rd. magazine. Manufactured 1957 to 1973. Used value, $525 to $600.

Garcia Musketeer

GARCIA Musketeer: bolt-action; .243, .264, .30/06, .308 Win., .308 Norma magnum, 7mm Rem. magnum, .300 Win. magnum;

GARRET ARMS Rolling Block: single-shot; .45-70; 30" octagon barrel; 48" overall length; weighs 9 lb.; ladder-type tang sight, open folding rear on barrel, hooded globe front; European walnut

44½" overall length; 24" barrel; FN Mauser Supreme action; checkered walnut Monte Carlo stock, pistol grip; Williams Guide open rear sight, hooded ramp front; adjustable trigger; sliding thumb safety; hinged floor plate; 5-rd. capacity in standard calibers, 3 rds. in magnums. Imported. Introduced, 1970; dropped, 1972. Used value, $350 to $400.

stock; reproduction of Remington rolling block long-range sporter. Made in Italy. Introduced, 1987; no longer imported by Garrett Arms & Imports. Used value, $250 to $275.

Gevarm Model A2

GEVARM Model A2: autoloader; blowback action; take-down; .22 LR only; 21½" barrel; 8-rd. clip magazine; no firing pin (as such) or extractor; fires from open bolt; ridge on bolt face offers twin ignition; tangent rear sight, hooded globe front; uncheckered walnut stock, Schnabel forearm. Imported by Tradewinds, Inc., beginning in 1958; dropped, 1963. Used value, $150 to $165.

Golden Eagle Model 7000 Grade 1

GOLDEN EAGLE Model 7000 Grade I: bolt-action; .22-250, .243 Win., .25/06, .270 Win., .270 Weatherby magnum, 7mm Rem. magnum, .30/06, .300 Weatherby magnum, .300 Win. magnum .338

GREIFELT Sport Model: bolt-action; .22 Hornet; 5-rd. box magazine; 22" barrel; 2-leaf rear sight, ramp front; hand-checkered European walnut stock; pistol grip; made in Germany prior to World War II. Used value, $700 to $750.

CARL GUSTAF Standard Model: bolt-action; 6.5x55, 7x54, 9.3x-62mm, .270 Win., .308 Win., .30/06; 4-rd. magazine for the 9.3x-62mm, 5 rds. for other calibers; folding leaf rear sight, hooded ramp front; sling swivels; Classic-style French walnut stock; hand-checkered pistol grip, forearm. Available in left-hand model also. Manufactured in Sweden, 1970 to 1977. Used value, $350 to

Monte Carlo Model has same general specs as Standard model, except for addition of 7mm Rem. magnum chambering, Monte Carlo-style stock with cheekpiece. Manufactured 1970 to 1977. Used value, $375 to $400.

Model II has same specs as Monte Carlo model, except for chambering, select walnut stock, rosewood forend tip. Chambered for .22-250, .243 Win., .25/06, .270 Win., 6.5x55mm, 7mm Rem. magnum, .308 Win., .30/06, .300 Win. magnum; 3-rd. magazine in magnum calibers. Manufactured, 1970 to 1977. Used value, $500 to $525.

Model III has same specs as Monte Carlo model, except for higher-grade wood, high-gloss finish, rosewood forend tip, no sights. Chambered for .22-250, .26/06, .270 Win., 6.5x55mm, 7mm Rem. magnum, .308 Win., .30/06, .300 Win. magnum; 3-rd. magazine in magnum calibers. Manufactured 1970 to 1977. Used value, $600 to $625.

Deluxe Model has same general specs as Monte Carlo; chambered for 6.5x55mm, .308 Win., .30/06, 9.3x62mm; engraved trigger guard, floor plate; top-grade French walnut stock, rosewood forend tip. Manufactured 1970 to 1977. Used value, $700 to $725.

Win. magnum; 4-rd. magazine for .22-250, 3 rds. in other calibers; 24" or 26" barrels; no sights; checkered American walnut stock, contrasting grip cap, forend tip, golden eagle head inset in grip cap; recoil pad. Made in Japan. Introduced in 1976; dropped, 1979. Used value, $400 to $425.

Grade I African Model has same general specs, but is chambered for .375 H&H magnum, .458 Win. magnum; furnished with sights. Introduced in 1976; dropped, 1979. Used value, $475 to $500.

CARL GUSTAF Varmint-Target Model: bolt-action; .222 Rem., .22-250, .243 Win., 6.5x55mm; adjustable trigger; 26¾" barrel; no sights; target-style stock, French walnut. Introduced, 1970; no longer imported. Used value, $475 to $500.

CARL GUSTAF Grand Prix: single-shot target model; .22 LR; single-stage adjustable trigger; 26¾" barrel, adjustable weight; adjustable cork butt plate; no sights; uncheckered French walnut target-style stock. Introduced, 1970; no longer in production. Used value, $425 to $450.

HAENEL Mauser-Mannlicher: bolt-action; 7x57, 8x57, 9x57mm; 5-rd. Mannlicher-type box magazine; 22" or 24" barrel, half or full octagon; raised matted rib; action based on Model 88 Mauser; double-set trigger; leaf open rear sight, ramp front; hand-checkered European walnut sporting stock cheekpiece, Schnabel tip, pistol grip, sling swivels. Manufactured in Germany prior to WWII. Used value, $400 to $450.

'88 Mauser Sporter has the same general specs, except for 5-rd. Mauser box magazine. Manufactured in Germany prior to WWII. Used value, $400 to $450.

HOLLAND & HOLLAND Royal: hammerless side-lock double rifle; actually a special-order rifle in the realm of semi-production, with original buyer's options available; .240 Apex, 7mm H&H magnum, .300 H&H magnum. .375 H&H magnum, .458 Win. magnum, .465 H&H; 24", 26", 28" barrels; two-piece choice European stock; hand-checkered pistol grip, forearm; folding leaf rear sight, ramp front; swivels; custom-engraved receiver. Still in production. Used values: pre-WWII model, $12,500 to $15,000; post-war, $9000 to $10,000.

No. 2 Model has the same specs as H&H Royal except for less

ornate engraving, less figure in stock. Still in production. Used value: pre-WWII, $10,000 to $11,000; post-war, $7000 to $7250.

Model Deluxe has the same specs as Royal Model, except for more ornate engraving, better grade European walnut in stock; better fitting. Still in production. Used value: pre-WWII, $17,500 to $20,000; post-war, $12,500 to $15,000.

Holland & Holland Royal Model

HOLLAND & HOLLAND Best Quality: bolt-action; built on Mauser or Enfield action; .240 Apex, .300 H&H magnum, .375 H&H magnum; 24" barrel; 4-rd. box magazine; cheekpiece stock of European walnut; hand-checkered pistol grip, forearm; folding leaf rear sight, hooded ramp front; sling swivels, recoil pad. Still in production. Used value: pre-WWII, $4500 to $5000; post-war, $3500 to $4000.

Holland & Holland Best Quality Model

HOLLAND & HOLLAND Deluxe Magazine Model: bolt-action; has the same specs as Best Quality model, except for higher quality engraving, exhibition-grade European walnut stock. Introduced following World War II; still in production. Used value, $5000 to $7000.

Interarms Standard Mark X

Interarms Mark X Cavalier

Interarms Mark X Viscount

Interarms Mini-Mark X

INTERARMS Mark X: bolt-action; .22-250, .243 Win., .270 Win., .308 Win., .25/06, .30/06, 7mm Rem. magnum, .300 Win. magnum; 24" barrel; sliding safety; hinged floor plate; adjustable trigger at added cost; adjustable folding leaf rear sight, ramp front with removable hood; hand-checkered European walnut Monte Carlo stock, forearm; white spacer on grip cap, butt plate, forearm tip. Imported from Yugoslavia. Introduced in 1972; still in production. Four additonal variations have appeared since 1974. Used values: standard model, $225 to $250; with adjustable trigger, $250 to $275.

Mark X Cavalier has same specs as Mark X, but with roll-over cheekpiece, rosewood grip cap and forend tip, recoil pad. Intro-

duced in 1974; dropped, 1983. Used value, $275 to $300.

Mark X Viscount has same specs as Mark X, except for hand-checkered stock of European hardwood. Introduced, 1974; importation dropped, 1983; reintroduced, 1987; still imported. Used value, $300 to $325.

Mini-Mark X is a scaled-down version of standard rifle; uses miniature M98 Mauser action; 20" barrel; open adjustable sights; .223 Rem. only; 39¾" overall length; drilled, tapped for scope mounts; adjustable trigger. Made in Yugoslavia. Introduced, 1987; still imported by Interarms. Used value, $350 to $375.

Mark X Mannlicher Carbine has same specs as Mark X, except for Mannlicher-type stock, 20" barrel; made only in .270 Win., .308 Win., .30/06, 7x57mm. Introduced, 1976; dropped, 1983. Used value, $325 to $350.

Mark X Alaskan has same specs as Mark X, except for stock crossbolt, heavy-duty recoil pad; made in .375 H&H magnum, .458 Win. magnum. Introduced, 1976; dropped, 1985. Used value, $375 to $400.

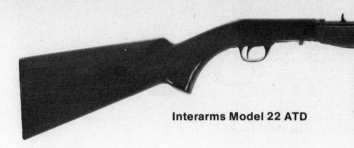

Interarms Model 22 ATD

INTERARMS Model 22 ATD: autoloader; .22 LR; 11-rd. magazine; 19.4" barrel; 36.8" overall length; weighs 4.6 lb.; open adjustable rear sight, blade front; checkered European walnut stock; Browning-type take-down action; crossbolt safety; tube magazine loads through butt plate; engraved receiver; blued finish. Made in China. Introduced, 1987; still imported by Interarms. Used value, $120 to $130.

KDF K-22

KDF K-22: bolt-action; .22 LR, .22 WRFM; 5- or 6-rd. magazine; 21½" barrel; 40" overall length; weighs 6½ lb.; no sights; receiver grooved for scope mounts; hand-checkered, oil-finished European walnut Monte Carlo stock; front-locking lugs on bolt; pillar bedding system. Made in West Germany. Introduced, 1984; importation dropped, 1988. Used values: .22 LR, $250 to $260; .22 WRFM, $280 to $300.

K-22 Deluxe has same specs as K-22, except has quick-detachable swivels, rosewood forend tip, rubber recoil pad; .22 LR only. Introduced, 1984; dropped, 1988. Used value, $350 to $375.

KDF K-15 Improved

KDF K-15 Improved: bolt-action; .243, .25/06, .270, 7x57, .308, .30/06, .257 Weatherby, .270 Weatherby, 7mm Rem. magnum, .300 Win. magnum, .300 Weatherby, .308 Norma magnum, .375 H&H; 3- or 4-rd. magazine. depending on caliber; 24", 26" barrel lengths; no sights furnished; drilled, tapped for scope mounts; hand-checkered, oil-finished European walnut stock in Featherweight Classic design with Schnabel or European Monte Carlo with rosewood grip cap, forend tip; fast lock time. Made in West Germany. Introduced, 1987; dropped, 1988. Used values: standard calibers, $900 to $950; magnum calibers, $975 to $1050.

K-15 Fiberstock Pro-Hunter has same specs as the K-15 Improved, except has Brown Precision fiberglass stock in choice of black, green, gray, brown, or camo with wrinkle finish; recoil arrestor; Parkerized, matte blue or electroless nickel finish; standard or magnum calibers. Introduced, 1987; dropped, 1988. Used values: standard calibers, $1200 to $1250; magnum calibers, $1225 to $1275.

K-15 Dangerous Game Model has same specs as K-15 Improved, except is chambered for .411 KDF magnum cartridge; choice of iron sights or scope mounts; hinged floor plate; gloss blue, matte blue, Parkerized or electroless nickel finish. Introduced, 1987; dropped, 1988. Used value, $1300 to $1350.

Kleinguenther K-15

KLEINGUENTHER K-15: bolt-action; .243, .25/06, .270, .30/06, .308 Win., 7x57, .308 Norma magnum, .300 Weatherby magnum, 7mm Rem. magnum, .375 H&H, .257 Weatherby, .270 Weatherby magnum, .300 Weatherby magnum; 24" barrel, standard calibers; 26" for magnums; no sights; drilled, tapped for scope mounts; hand-checkered Monte Carlo stock of European walnut; rosewood grip cap, high-luster or satin finish; recoil pad; many optional features available on special order. Manufactured in Germany. Imported and assembled by Kleinguenther; dropped, 1985. Used value, $775 to $800.

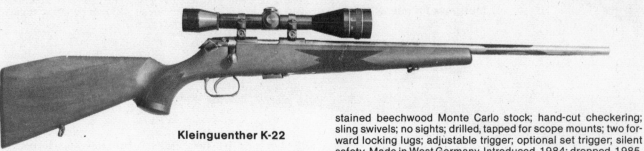

Kleinguenther K-22

KLEINGUENTHER K-22: bolt-action; .22 LR, .22 WRFM; 5-rd. magazine; 21½" barrel; overall length 40"; weighs 6½ lb.; walnut-stained beechwood Monte Carlo stock; hand-cut checkering; sling swivels; no sights; drilled, tapped for scope mounts; two forward locking lugs; adjustable trigger; optional set trigger; silent safety. Made in West Germany. Introduced, 1984; dropped, 1985. Used values: standard model, $275 to $300; with double-set trigger, $350 to $375; .22 WRFM, $350 to $375; with double-set trigger, $425 to $450.

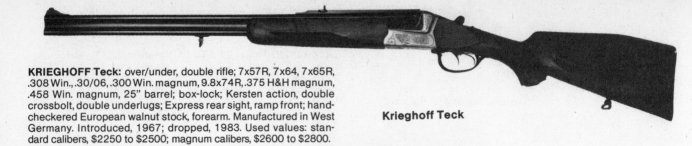

KRIEGHOFF Teck: over/under, double rifle; 7x57R, 7x64, 7x65R, .308 Win., .30/06, .300 Win. magnum, 9.8x74R, .375 H&H magnum, .458 Win. magnum, 25" barrel; box-lock; Kersten action, double crossbolt, double underlugs; Express rear sight, ramp front; hand-checkered European walnut stock, forearm. Manufactured in West Germany. Introduced, 1967; dropped, 1983. Used values: standard calibers, $2250 to $2500; magnum calibers, $2600 to $2800.

Krieghoff Teck

KRIEGHOFF Ulm: over/under, double rifle; has same general specs, caliber range as Teck model, except for side-lock, leaf arabesque engraving. Introduced, 1963; dropped, 1983. Used value, $6000 to $7000.

Krieghoff Ulm

KRIEGHOFF Ulm-Primus: over/under, double rifle; has same general specs as Ulm model, except for deluxe modifications including higher grade of engraving, wood, detachable side-locks. Introduced, 1963; dropped, 1983. Used value, $7500 to $8000.

Lebeau-Courally Sidelock

LEBEAU-COURALLY Sidelock: double rifle; 8x57 JRS, 9.3x74R, .375 H&H, .458 Win.; 23½" to 26" barrels; made to customer specs; express rear sight on quarter-rib, bead on ramp front; French walnut stock; pistol grip with cheekpiece, splinter or beavertail forend; steel grip cap; Holland & Holland-type side-lock; ejectors; reinforced action; chopper lump barrels; several engraving patterns. Made in Belgium. Introduced, 1987; still imported by Wm. Larkin Moore. Used value, $16,500 to $17,500.

MARATHON Super Shot 22: bolt-action, single-shot; .22 LR; 24" barrel; 41½" overall length; weighs 4.9 lb.; select hardwood stock; step-adjustable open rear sight, bead front; receiver grooved for scope mounts; blued finish. Made in Spain. Introduced, 1984; dropped by Marathon Products, 1986. Used value, $55 to $60.

MARATHON Sportsman: bolt-action; .243, .308, 7x57, .30/06, .270, 7mm Rem. magnum, .300 Win. magnum; 24" barrel; 45" overall length; weighs 7.9 lb.; selected walnut Monte Carlo stock; rubber recoil pad; open adjustable rear sight, bead front on ramp; uses Santa Barbara Mauser action; triple thumb locking safety; blued finish. Made in Spain. Introduced, 1984; dropped by Marathon Products, 1986. Used value, $250 to $275.

Musgrave Premier NR5

MUSGRAVE Premier NR5: bolt-action; .243 Win., .270 Win., .30/06, .308 Win., 7mm Rem. magnum; 5-rd. magazine; 25½" barrel; no sights; European walnut stock, Monte Carlo, cheekpiece; hand-checkered pistol grip, forearm; pistol-grip cap, forend tip; recoil pad; sling swivel studs. Introduced, 1972; importation stopped 1973. Used value, $450 to $475.

Musgrave Valiant NR6

MUSGRAVE Valiant NR6: bolt-action; .243 Win., .270 Win., .30/06, .308 Win., 7mm Rem. magnum; has same general specs as NR5, except for 24" barrel, straight-comb stock, skip checkering, sans grip cap, forend tip; leaf rear sight, hooded ramp front. Introduced, 1972; importation stopped 1973. Used value, $400 to $425.

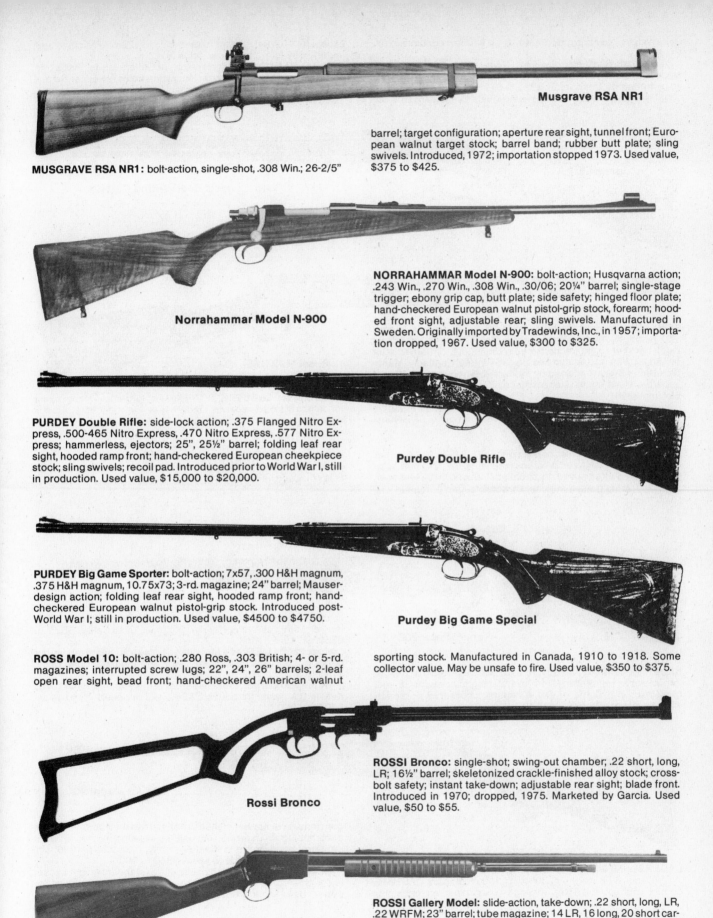

Musgrave RSA NR1

MUSGRAVE RSA NR1: bolt-action, single-shot, .308 Win.; 26-2/5"

barrel; target configuration; aperture rear sight, tunnel front; European walnut target stock; barrel band; rubber butt plate; sling swivels. Introduced, 1972; importation stopped 1973. Used value, $375 to $425.

Norrahammar Model N-900

NORRAHAMMAR Model N-900: bolt-action; Husqvarna action; .243 Win., .270 Win., .308 Win., .30/06; 20¼" barrel; single-stage trigger; ebony grip cap, butt plate; side safety; hinged floor plate; hand-checkered European walnut pistol-grip stock, forearm; hooded front sight, adjustable rear; sling swivels. Manufactured in Sweden. Originally imported by Tradewinds, Inc., in 1957; importation dropped, 1967. Used value, $300 to $325.

PURDEY Double Rifle: side-lock action; .375 Flanged Nitro Express, .500-465 Nitro Express, .470 Nitro Express, .577 Nitro Express; hammerless, ejectors; 25", 25½" barrel; folding leaf rear sight, hooded ramp front; hand-checkered European cheekpiece stock; sling swivels; recoil pad. Introduced prior to World War I, still in production. Used value, $15,000 to $20,000.

Purdey Double Rifle

PURDEY Big Game Sporter: bolt-action; 7x57, .300 H&H magnum, .375 H&H magnum, 10.75x73; 3-rd. magazine; 24" barrel; Mauser-design action; folding leaf rear sight, hooded ramp front; hand-checkered European walnut pistol-grip stock. Introduced post-World War I; still in production. Used value, $4500 to $4750.

Purdey Big Game Special

ROSS Model 10: bolt-action; .280 Ross, .303 British; 4- or 5-rd. magazines; interrupted screw lugs; 22", 24", 26" barrels; 2-leaf open rear sight, bead front; hand-checkered American walnut

sporting stock. Manufactured in Canada, 1910 to 1918. Some collector value. May be unsafe to fire. Used value, $350 to $375.

Rossi Bronco

ROSSI Bronco: single-shot; swing-out chamber; .22 short, long, LR; 16½" barrel; skeletonized crackle-finished alloy stock; cross-bolt safety; instant take-down; adjustable rear sight; blade front. Introduced in 1970; dropped, 1975. Marketed by Garcia. Used value, $50 to $55.

Rossi Gallery Model

ROSSI Gallery Model: slide-action, take-down; .22 short, long, LR, .22 WRFM; 23" barrel; tube magazine; 14 LR, 16 long, 20 short cartridge capacity; adjustable rear sight, fixed front; uncheckered straight-grip walnut stock, grooved slide handle. Imported from Brazil by Garcia. Introduced in 1973; still imported by Interarms.

Used values, standard model, $115 to $125; magnum model, $125 to $135.

Gallery Model Carbine has same specs as standard Gallery model except for 16¼" barrel. Introduced, 1975; no longer imported by Interarms. Used value, $115 to $125.

Gallery Model Magnum has same specs as standard version, except for 10-rd. magazine, chambering for .22 WRFM. No longer imported by Interarms. Used value, $125 to $135.

Model 62 SAC is carbine version of Gallery Model; has same specs, except has 16¼" barrel; magazine holds fewer cartridges; blued or nickel finish. Made in Brazil. Still imported by Interarms. Used value, $135 to $145.

Rossi Saddle-Ring Carbine

Rossi M92 SRS

ROSSI Saddle-Ring Carbine: lever-action; .38 Special, 9 rds.; .357 magnum, .44-40, .44 magnum, 8 rds.; 20" barrel; blade front sight, buckhorn rear; uncheckered walnut stock; patterned after Model 92 Winchester; handles .38, .357 interchangeably. Manufactured in Brazil; imported by Interarms. Introduced, 1978; still imported. Used values: standard model, $175 to $185; engraved, $240 to $250.

Puma M92 SRS has same general specs as standard Saddle Ring Carbine, except has 16" barrel; overall length of 33"; chambered only for .38 Special, .357 magnum; larger lever loop; puma medallion in side of receiver. Made in Brazil. Introduced, 1986; still imported by Interarms. Used value, $200 to $225.

SAUER Mauser Sporter: bolt-action; 7x57, 8x57, .30/06; other calibers on special order; 5-rd. box magazine; 22", 24" half-octagon barrels, matted raised rib; double-set trigger; three-leaf open rear sight, ramp front; hand-checkered pistol-grip European walnut stock, raised side panels, Schnabel tip; sling swivels; also manufactured with full-length stock, 20" barrel. Manufactured prior to WWII. Used value, $550 to $650.

Sauer Model 200

SAUER Model 200: bolt-action; .243, .308, .25/06, .270, .30/06; 24" interchangeable barrel; 44" overall length; no sights; drilled, tapped for iron sights or scope mounts; checkered European walnut pistol-grip stock; removable box magazine; left-hand model available; steel or alloy versions. Made in West Germany. Introduced, 1986; still imported by Sigarms. Used value, $625 to $650.

Model 200 LUX Grade has same specs as standard model, but better wood, finish. Introduced, 1986; still imported. Used value, $725 to $775.

Model 200 Carbon Fiber has stock of this material; other specs remain the same. Introduced, 1986; still imported. Used value, $900 to $950.

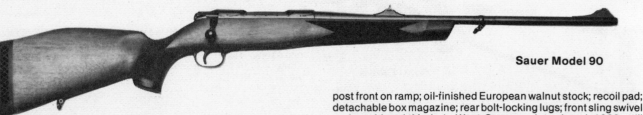

Sauer Model 90

SAUER Model 90: bolt-action; .22-250, .243, .308, .25/06, .270, .30/06, 7mm Rem. magnum, .300 Win., .300 Weatherby, .375 H&H; 20", 24", 26" barrel lengths; windage-adjustable open rear sight, post front on ramp; oil-finished European walnut stock; recoil pad; detachable box magazine; rear bolt-locking lugs; front sling swivel on barrel band. Made in West Germany. Introduced, 1986; still imported by Sigarms. Used value, $850 to $900.

Model 90 Safari has the same specs as standard model, except is chambered for .458 Win. magnum. Introduced, 1986; still imported. Used value, $1200 to $1250.

SCHULTZ & LARSEN Model 47: bolt-action, single shot; .22 LR; 28½" barrel; set trigger; micrometer receiver sight, globe front; free-rifle style European walnut stock; cheekpiece, thumbhole, butt plate, palm rest, sling swivels. Manufactured in Germany. Used value, $550 to $575.

SCHULTZ & LARSEN Model 54: bolt-action, single-shot; 6.5x-55mm, American calibers were availabe on special order; 27½" barrel; micrometer receiver sight, globe front; free-rifle style Euro- pean walnut stock; adjustable butt plate; cheekpiece; palm rest, sling swivels. Used value, $650 to $700.

SCHULTZ & LARSEN Model 54J: bolt-action, .270 Win., .30/06, 7x61 Sharpe & Hart; 3-rd. magazine; 24", 26" barrels; hand-check- ered European walnut sporter stock; Monte Carlo comb, cheek- piece. Used value, $550 to $600.

SIG-SAUER SSG 2000: bolt-action; .223, .308, 7.5 Swiss, .300 Weatherby magnum; 4-rd. detachable box magazine; 24", 25.9" barrel lengths; weighs 13.2 lb.; thumbhole walnut stock; adjust- able comb, butt plate, forend rail; stippled grip, forend; no sights; comes with scope mounts; right- or left-hand models; flash hider/ muzzle brake; double-set triggers; sliding safety. Made in West Germany. Introduced, 1985; no longer imported by Sigarms, Inc. Used value, $2000 to $2100.

SOVEREIGN TD .22: autoloader; .22 LR; 10-rd. clip; 21" barrel; 41" overall length; weighs 6½ lb.; fully adjustable open rear sight, hooded ramp front; walnut-finished hardwood stock; take-down; blued finish. Introduced, 1986; no longer imported. Used value, $60 to $70.

Squires Bingham Model 14D

SQUIRES BINGHAM Model 14D: bolt-action; .22 LR; 5-rd. box magazine; 24" barrel; V-notch rear sight, hooded ramp front; grooved receiver for scope mounts; exotic hand-checkered wood stock, contrasting forend tip, pistol-grip cap. Manufactured in the Philip- pines. Not currently imported. Used value, $65 to $75.
   Model 15 has same specs as Model 14D, except chambered for .22 WRFM. Used value, $70 to $75.

SQUIRES BINGHAM Model M16: semi-automatic; .22 LR; 19½" barrel, muzzle brake/flash hider; has general appearance of mili- tary M-16; integral rear sight, ramped post front; black painted mahogany butt stock, forearm. Not currently imported. Used value, $100 to $125.

SQUIRES BINGHAM Model M20D: semi-automatic; .22 LR; 15- rd. detachable box magazine; 19½" barrel, muzzle brake/flash hider; V-notch rear sight, blade front; grooved receiver for scope mount; hand-checkered exotic wood stock; contrasting pistol-grip cap, forend tip. Not currently imported. Used value, $75 to $85.

Star Rolling Block Carbine

STAR Rolling Block Carbine: single-shot; .30-30, .357 magnum, .44 magnum; 20" barrel; rolling-block action; folding leaf rear sight; ramp front; straight-grip European walnut stock, forearm; metal butt plate, barrel band. Manufactured in Spain, 1973 to 1975. Not imported. Used value, $150 to $185.

Swiss K-31 Target Model

SWISS K-31 Target Model: straight-pull bolt-action; .308; 6-rd. magazine; 26" barrel; 44" overall length; protected blade front sight, ladder-type adjustable rear; European walnut stock; based on straight-pull Schmidt-Rubin design; marketed with sling, muz- zle cap. Made in Switzerland. Introduced, 1982; no longer im- ported by Mandall Shooting Supplies. Used value, $700 to $750.

Tanner Standard UIT Model

TANNER Standard UIT Model: bolt-action; .308, 7.5mm Swiss; 10-rd. magazine; 25.8" barrel; overall length 40.6"; weighs 10.5 lb.; nutwood match-style stock; accessory rail; stippled pistol grip; ventilated forend; micrometer-diopter rear sight, globe front with interchangeable inserts; adjustable trigger. Made in Switzerland. Introduced, 1984; still imported by Osborne's. Used value, $2000 to $2200.

TANNER 50-Meter Free Rifle: single-shot, bolt-action; .22 LR; 27.7" barrel; 43.4" overall length; weighs 13.9 lb.; nutwood stock with palm rest; accessory rail; adjustable hook butt plate; same sights as UIT Model; adjustable set trigger. Made in Switzerland. Introduced, 1984; still imported by Osborne's. Used value, $1600 to $1800.

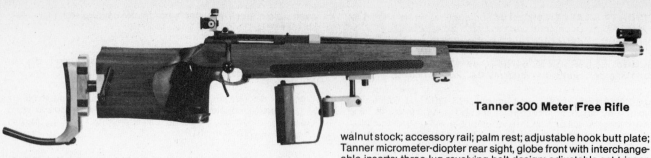

Tanner 300 Meter Free Rifle

TANNER 300 Meter Free Rifle: bolt-action, single-shot; .308, 7.5 Swiss; 28.7" barrel; 45.3" overall length; weighs 15 lb.; thumbhole walnut stock; accessory rail; palm rest; adjustable hook butt plate; Tanner micrometer-diopter rear sight, globe front with interchangeable inserts; three-lug revolving bolt design; adjustable set trigger. Made in Switzerland. Introduced, 1984; still imported by Osborne's. Used value, $1900 to $2000.

Tikka Model 55

Tikka Model 55 Sporter

Tikka Model 55 Deluxe

TIKKA Model 55: bolt-action; .17 Rem., .222, .22-250, 6mm Rem., .243, .308; 23" barrel; detachable 3-rd. magazine; bead ramped front sight, rear adjustable for windage, elevation; hand-checkered Monte Carlo stock of European walnut; palm swell on pistol grip; drilled, tapped for scope mounts. Imported by Ruko Sporting Goods. Introduced, 1979; importation dropped, 1981. Used value, $325 to $335.

Model 55 Sporter has same general specs as standard model, except has 23" heavy barrel, chambered for .222, .22-250, .243, .308; varmint-type stock; no sights; oil-finish on stock; detachable 5- or 10-rd magazine. Introduced, 1979; importation dropped, 1981. Used value, $325 to $350.

Model 55 Deluxe has same specs as standard Model 55, except has roll-over cheekpiece, forend tip, grip cap of rosewood. Used value, $375 to $400.

Model 55 Deluxe American has same specs as Deluxe model, except has gloss lacquer finish on stock, no sights. Used value, $375 to $400.

Tikka Model 65

TIKKA Model 65: bolt-action; has same general specs as Model 55, except is chambered for .25/06, 6.5x55, 7x57, 7x64, .270, .308, .30/06, 7mm Rem. magnum, .300 Win. magnum; 22" barrel; 5-rd. magazine; adjustable trigger. Introduced, 1979; importation dropped, 1981. Used value, $450 to $475.

Model 65 Target has same general specs as standard 65; chambered for .25/06, 6.5x55, .270, .308, .30/06; 22" heavy barrel; target-type walnut stock; no sights; stock designed to meet ISU requirements, with stippled forend, palm swell. Introduced, 1969; importation dropped, 1981. Used value, $550 to $650.

TIKKA Model 07: combo; .222, 5.6x52R, 5.6x50R magnum beneath 12-ga. barrel; barrel length, 22¾"; bead front sight, open windage-adjustable rear; Monte Carlo stock of European walnut; palm swell with pistol grip; exposed hammer, sling swivels; vent rib, rosewood pistol-grip cap. Introduced, 1979 by Ruko Sporting Goods; importation dropped, 1982. Used value, $425 to $450.

Model 77K has same specs as Model 07, except has hammerless shotgun-type action, double triggers. Used value, $550 to $575.

TRADEWINDS Husky Model 5000: bolt-action; .270, .30/06, .308, .243, .22-250; 23¾" barrel; fixed hooded front sight, adjustable rear; hand-checkered Monte Carlo stock of European walnut; white-line spacers on pistol-grip cap, forend tip, butt plate; removable magazine; recessed bolt head, adjustable trigger. Imported from Europe. Introduced, 1973; dropped, 1983. Used value, $350 to $375.

Tradewinds Husky Model 5000

Tradewinds Model 260-A

TRADEWINDS Model 260-A: autoloader; .22 LR; 5-rd. magazine; 22½" barrel; 41½" overall length; hooded ramp front sight, 3-leaf folding rear; walnut stock; hand-checkered pistol grip, forend; double extractors; sliding safety; sling swivels; receiver grooved for scope mount. Made in Japan. Introduced, 1975; still imported by Tradewinds. Used value, $165 to $170.

TRADEWINDS Model 311-A: bolt-action; .22 LR; 5-rd. magazine; 22½" barrel; 41¼" overall length; Monte Carlo walnut stock; hand-checkered pistol grip, forend; hooded ramp front sight, folding leaf rear; sliding safety; receiver grooved for scope mount. Made in Europe. Introduced, 1976; no longer imported. Used value, $125 to $135.

Tyrol Custom Crafted Model

TYROL Custom Crafted Model: bolt-action; .243, .25/06, .308, 7mm, .300 Win.; 23¾" barrel; hooded ramp front sight, adjustable rear; hand-checkered Monte Carlo stock of European walnut; drilled, tapped for scope mounts; adjustable trigger; shotgun-type tang safety. Manufactured in Austria. Introduced, 1973 by Firearms Center; dropped, 1975. Used value, $325 to $350.

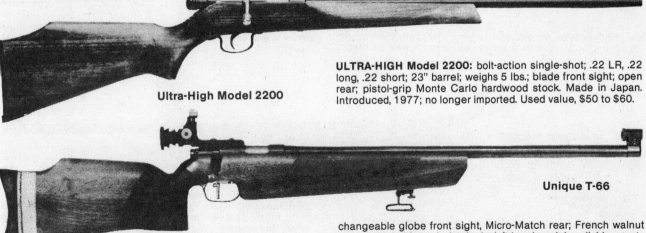

Ultra-High Model 2200

ULTRA-HIGH Model 2200: bolt-action single-shot; .22 LR, .22 long, .22 short; 23" barrel; weighs 5 lbs.; blade front sight; open rear; pistol-grip Monte Carlo hardwood stock. Made in Japan. Introduced, 1977; no longer imported. Used value, $50 to $60.

Unique T-66

UNIQUE T-66: bolt-action, single-shot; .22 LR; 25.6" barrel; interchangeable globe front sight, Micro-Match rear; French walnut stock; stippled forend, pistol grip; left-hand model available; meets NRA, UIT standards. Imported from France. Introduced, 1980, by Solersport; no longer imported. Used value, $450 to $475.

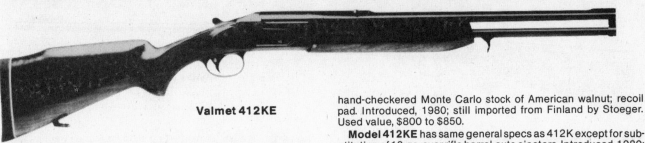

Valmet 412KE

VALMET 412K: double rifle; .308, .30/06; 24" barrels; ramp front sight, adjustable open rear; barrel selector mounted on trigger; hand-checkered Monte Carlo stock of American walnut; recoil pad. Introduced, 1980; still imported from Finland by Stoeger. Used value, $800 to $850.

Model 412KE has same general specs as 412K except for substitution of 12-ga. over rifle barrel, auto ejectors. Introduced, 1980; still imported by Stoeger. Redesignated as 412S. Used value, $700 to $750.

Valmet Hunter Model

VALMET Hunter Model: autoloader; .223, .243, .308; magazines hold from 5 to 30 rds., depending upon options, calibers; 20½"

barrel; 42" overall length; weighs 8 lb.; open rear sight, blade front; American walnut butt, forend; checkered palm-swell pistol grip, forend; Kalashnikov-type action. Made in Finland. Introduced, 1986; still imported by Stoeger. Used value, $500 to $550.

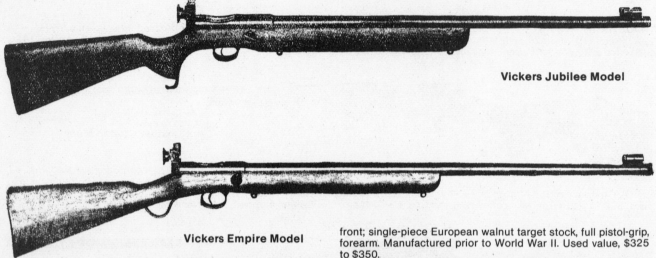

Vickers Jubilee Model

Vickers Empire Model

VICKERS Jubilee Model: Martini-type action; single-shot; .22 LR; 28" heavy barrel; Perfection rear peep sight, Parker-Hale No. 2

front; single-piece European walnut target stock, full pistol-grip, forearm. Manufactured prior to World War II. Used value, $325 to $350.

Empire Model has same general specs as Jubilee, except for straight-grip stock, 27", 30" barrels. Manufactured prior to WWII. Used value, $300 to $325.

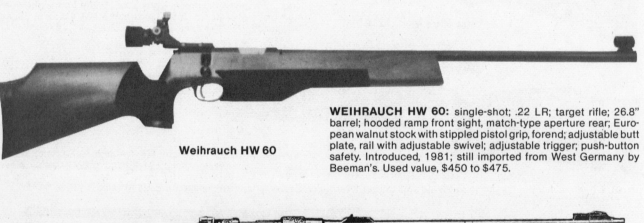

Weihrauch HW 60

WEIHRAUCH HW 60: single-shot; .22 LR; target rifle; 26.8" barrel; hooded ramp front sight, match-type aperture rear; European walnut stock with stippled pistol grip, forend; adjustable butt plate, rail with adjustable swivel; adjustable trigger; push-button safety. Introduced, 1981; still imported from West Germany by Beeman's. Used value, $450 to $475.

Westley Richards Magazine Model

WESTLEY RICHARDS Magazine Model: built on Mauser or magnum Mauser action; .30/06, 7mm High Velocity, .318 Accelerated Express, .375 magnum, .404 Nitro Express, .425 magnum; barrels, 22" for 7mm, 25" for .425, 24" for all other calibers; leaf

rear sight, hooded front; sporting stock of French walnut; hand-checkered pistol-grip, forearm; cheekpiece; horn forearm tip; sling swivels. Used value, $3000 to $5000, depending on chambering and features.

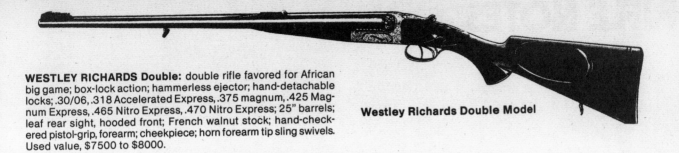

WESTLEY RICHARDS Double: double rifle favored for African big game; box-lock action; hammerless ejector; hand-detachable locks; .30/06, .318 Accelerated Express, .375 magnum, .425 Magnum Express, .465 Nitro Express, .470 Nitro Express; 25" barrels; leaf rear sight, hooded front; French walnut stock; hand-checkered pistol-grip, forearm; cheekpiece; horn forearm tip sling swivels. Used value, $7500 to $8000.

Westley Richards Double Model

Whitworth Express

WHITWORTH Express: bolt-action; ..22-250, .243, .25/06, .270, 7x57, .308, .30/06, .300 Win. magnum, 7mm Rem. magnum, .375 H&H, .458 Win. magnum; 24" barrel; 44" overall length; classic European walnut English Express stock; hand checkering; 3-leaf open sight on magnums; standard open sights on others; adjustable trigger; hinged floor plate; steel recoil crossbolt; solid recoil pad; barrel-mounted sling swivel. Made originally in England; barreled actions now produced in Yugoslavia. Introduced, 1974; still imported by Interarms. Used values: standard model, $360 to $385; with Express sights, $440 to $465.

Express Carbine has same specs as rifle version, except has Mannlicher-style stock, 20" barrel; .243, .270, .308, 7x57, .30/06. Introduced, 1986; dropped, 1988. Used value, $450 to $500.

A. ZOLI O/U Combo: .308, .222, .30/06; 12-ga. shotgun barrels; 24" barrel length; blade front sight, flip-up rear; European walnut stock; comes with set of 12-ga. barrels. Introduced, 1980; still imported from Italy by Mandall Shooting Supplies. Used value, $900 to $1000.

RIFLE NOTES

RIFLE NOTES

The Steel Shot Syndrome Doesn't Speak Well For Values Of Older Shotguns

Remington's SP 10 magnum shotgun is based upon the design of the old 10-gauge Ithaca auto. Redesigned, it is meant to furnish the waterfowler with more lead and power to down ducks and geese at extended ranges with steel.

THERE IS a quiet dread going on among serious shotgunners. As a group, they are beyond those progressive stages of anger and panic and finally have come to realize they face a situation over which they have little control.

All of this, of course, has to do with steel shot. The ecological studies of the past two decades more or less determined that lead shot ingested by waterfowl causes lead poisoning and death. The result was the series of laws relating to where lead shot can be used in waterfowl hunting; the lead-approved areas seem to be shrinking year by year. More recently, at least one state has decreed that *no* lead shot will be allowed in shotgun hunting, whether the game is waterfowl, upland game birds — or rabbits. Other states are expected to follow this lead.

So what does one do with the old Parker side-by-side that has been handed down through three or four generations of serious scattergunners? It's a bird slayer from way back and still knocks down geese with its thirty-two-inch barrels just as proficiently as it did in Granddad's day. At least, it did until the anti-lead decrees.

Are you going to chance running steel-loaded shot through the barrels of this old heirloom? You've had a gunsmith look it over and he says the gun certainly is strong enough to handle modern steel shot — up to a point. Said gunsmith also looked at you as though you were a little mad for even considering such desecrations of this classic.

Not everyone has a collector-grade Parker in his gun rack, but a batch of us have guns of one breed or another that were built years or decades back, when no one even had thought about steel shot or

reasoned it would become a necessity for waterfowl — and now, other types of hunting.

We've heard the talk about how steel shot can damage the barrels of such guns over a period of time. Of course, we've also heard a few arguments that dispute that claim — but not many.

With today's plastic shot collars that encase the shot as it travels down the barrel, there is a high degree of protection and it is pretty well established that it is in the choke area of the gun, as shot and collar start to part, that the damage is greatest.

New, harder steels have been introduced to shotgun barrel manufacture with the idea that they will stand up under wear and tear by steel pellets. Those who manufacture guns with interchangeable screw-in chokes are designing them to withstand the possible damage caused by steel pellets. As one maker pointed out, with interchangeable chokes, if one is damaged, at least you can replace it with a new one.

But it gets worse. The Friendship Gun Club, which operated in Connecticut for years, has been shut down as a result of the cries from the ecology-inspired. The shooting club is situated at the edge of a body of water and shot from guns used to powder millions of clay targets over the decades has landed in the sand and silt beneath the water.

Then some folks found other species of birds, including several bald eagles, that seemingly had died of lead poisoning. The theory was that the eagles may have died from feasting on ducks that had lead poisoning. Others, though, are claming that crows, ravens and even song birds are ingesting lead pellets that are thick in the soil of the impact area at gun clubs across the land.

A number of years ago, I had an opportunity to observe a clean-up at a gun club in Southern California. Some strange-looking equipment was brought into the impact area to strip the topsoil; sort it out, I think, by means of centrifugal force; and salvaged the lead that had rested on or in the ground for countless years. When it was all over, the salvage operators had gleaned some twenty tons of lead! Needless to say, this was a highly popular gun club.

I've never attempted to shoot trap or skeet with steel shot. I doubt I'd be much good at it, because my heart wouldn't be in it. I have a hunch a lot of other shooters feel the same. When it reaches the point that the problems outweigh the fun, sports tend to die.

For the hunting fields, numerous new steps are being taken to make it possible and plausible to bag your limit with steel shot. A year or so back, Federal and Mossberg jointly introduced the 3½-inch 12-gauge magnum shotshell, which throws a lot more steel pellets out there than the shorter types.

Some years ago, the Ithaca Gun Company came up with a 10-gauge autoloader that enjoyed a degree of success. When the company lasped into financial difficulties, the rights to the 10-gauge were purchased by Remington and the design underwent a couple of years of redevelopment and redesign work.

In 1989, this particular design was introduced, along with a new type of shotshell that combines shot in different sizes. The combination, I found, will put ducks down to stay at forty-five to fifty yards, although steel shot has not been recommended for shots beyond thirty-five yards.

This type of gun — and you can look for more 10-gauges from other makers in the future — is fine for the waterfowl hunter who'll be sitting in a blind or hunting from a camouflaged boat. But in the states that are advocating steel shot for other

Federal Cartridge has been a leader in developing new loads for steel shot. The 3-inch magnum steel round was introduced in 1987; a year later, a 3½-incher was made.

types of game, the type of hunting that requires hours and hours of walking through cornfields, et al, the Remington gun is going to get mighty heavy. Unloaded, it weighs roughly eleven pounds. I'd not choose it for a pheasant hunt, unless someone furnished a sturdy gun carriage of the type built for artillery pieces — and something to pull it!

In spite of the above, it would appear manufacturers are working hard at solving the steel shot problem on a continuing basis. After all, they should be able to sell a batch of new steel-proof guns. But it does nothing to solve the dilemma of the thousands upon thousands of gunowners who have those old lead throwers in their gun racks and are not quite certain what to do with them.

All of this, I seriously fear, is going to have an ultimate effect on the market for used shotguns. There are plenty of them, of course — including that old Parker mentioned earlier — that will maintain or even increase in value simply by virtue of being in short supply and, as a result, become sought-after collector items.

But a lot of other guns possibly are going to come to be thought of as obsolete; outmoded through modern technology and the demands of ecology. If the claybirding games also come to suffer due to the steel shot ultimatums, I foresee only increasing gloom...coupled with decreasing prices for used smokepoles of the common garden variety.

I have some shotguns I like. We've spent a lot of time afield together. I don't want to chance them being damaged by steel shot, so I'll probably put them in a gun rack behind some protective glass.

On long winter evenings, I can sit beside the fire and remember the good times we had together. For serious goose-getting, I'll probably have to buy one of those new-fangled 10-gauge howitzers.

Most manufacturers of shotguns now are furnishing screw-in interchangeable chokes that will handle steel shot. Even if a choke should be damaged, it can be replaced.

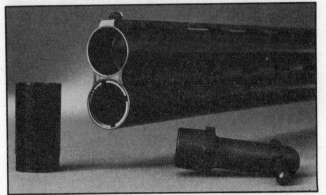

ARMSPORT

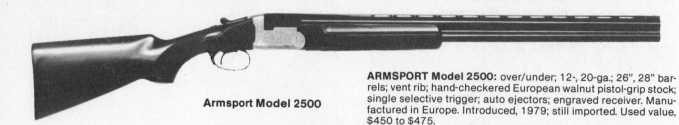

Armsport Model 2500

ARMSPORT Model 2500: over/under; 12-, 20-ga.; 26", 28" barrels; vent rib; hand-checkered European walnut pistol-grip stock; single selective trigger; auto ejectors; engraved receiver. Manufactured in Europe. Introduced, 1979; still imported. Used value, $450 to $475.

Armsport Goosegun

ARMSPORT Goosegun: side-by-side; 10-ga.; 3½" chambers only; 32" barrels; solid matted rib; checkered pistol-grip European walnut stock; double triggers; vent rubber recoil pad. Made in Spain. Introduced, 1979; imported by Armsport. Used value, $425 to $450.

Armsport Western Model

ARMSPORT Western: side-by-side; 12-ga. 3" chambers only; 20" barrels; checkered pistol-grip stock of European walnut, beavertail forend; metal front bead on matted solid rib; exposed hammers. Made in Spain. Introduced, 1979; still imported by Armsport. Used value, $300 to $325.

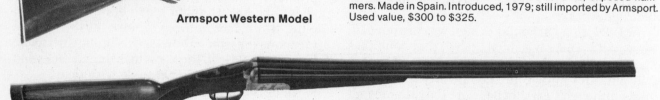

Armsport 1050

ARMSPORT 1050: side-by-side; 12-, 20-ga., .410; 3" chambers; 26", 28" barrel lengths; weighs 6 lb.; European walnut stock; boxlock action; double triggers; silvered, engraved receiver; extractors. Made in Italy. Introduced, 1986; still imported. Used values: 12-, 20-ga., $350 to $375; .410, $375 to $400.

ARMSPORT 2751: autoloader; gas-operated; 12-ga.; 3" chamber; 28" modified, 30" full choke barrels; weighs 7 lb.; European walnut stock; choke tube version available; blued or silvered receiver with engraving. Made in Italy. Introduced, 1986; still imported by Armsport. Used values: standard version, $400 to $425; with choke tubes, $450 to $475; silvered receiver, $475 to $500.

ARMSPORT 2755: pump-action; 12-ga.; 3" chamber; 28" modified, 30" full barrel; weighs 7 lb.; vent rib; European walnut stock; rubber recoil pad; blued finish; choke tubes available. Made in Italy. Introduced, 1986; still imported by Armsport. Used values: fixed chokes, $275 to $300; with choke tubes, $325 to $350.

ARMSPORT 2900 Tri-Barrel: over/under; 12-ga.; 3" chambers; 28" barrel; standard choke combos; weighs 7¾ lb.; European walnut stock; double triggers; top-tang barrel selector; silvered, engraved frame. Made in Italy. Introduced, 1986; still imported by Armsport. Used value, $1000 to $1050.

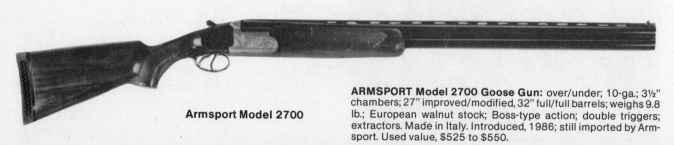

Armsport Model 2700

ARMSPORT Model 2700 Goose Gun: over/under; 10-ga.; 3½" chambers; 27" improved/modified, 32" full/full barrels; weighs 9.8 lb.; European walnut stock; Boss-type action; double triggers; extractors. Made in Italy. Introduced, 1986; still imported by Armsport. Used value, $525 to $550.

AYA

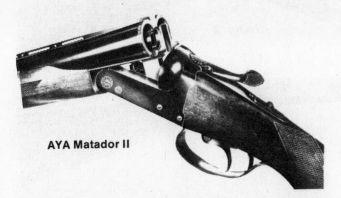

AYA Matador II

AYA Matador: side-by-side, hammerless double-barrel; 10-, 12-, 16-, 20-ga. magnum; barrels, 26", 28", 30", 32"; any standard choke combo; European walnut stock, forearm; checkered pistol grip, beavertail forearm; Anson & Deeley box-lock; single-selective trigger; selective automatic ejectors. Imported as Model 400E by Firearms International. Introduced in 1955; dropped, 1963. Used value, $375 to $400; $50 premium for 10-ga.

Matador II has same general specs as Matador I, except for better wood, vent-rib barrel. Manufactured 1964 to 1969. Used value, $450 to $500; $50 premium for 10-ga.

AYA Bolero: side-by-side, hammerless double-barrel; has the same general specs as standard Matador, except for non-selective ejectors, trigger; 12-, 16-, 20-, 28-ga., .410. Imported as Model 400 by Firearms International. Introduced in 1955; dropped, 1963. Used value, $325 to $335.

AYA Model 37 Super: side-lock over/under; 12-, 16-, 20-ga.; 26", 28", 30" barrels; any standard choke combo; vent rib; single selective trigger; automatic ejectors; hand-checkered stock, forearm; choice of pistol-grip or straight stock; heavily engraved. Introduced in 1963; no longer in production. Used value, $2000 to $2250.

AYA Model 56: side-lock, triple-bolting side-by-side; 12-, 20-ga.; barrel length, chokes to customer's specs; European walnut stock to customer's specs; semi-custom manufacture. Matted rib; automatic safety, ejectors; cocking indicators; gas escape valves; folding front trigger; engraved receiver. Introduced in 1972; no longer in production. Used value, $3000 to $3250.

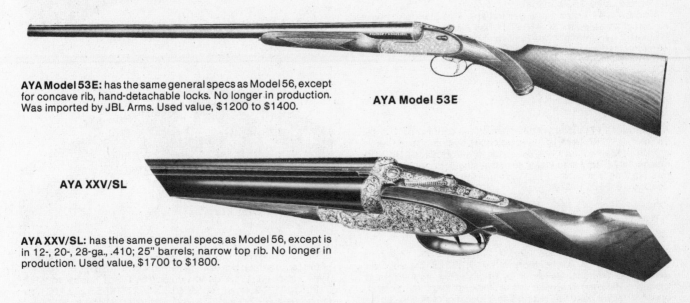

AYA Model 53E: has the same general specs as Model 56, except for concave rib, hand-detachable locks. No longer in production. Was imported by JBL Arms. Used value, $1200 to $1400.

AYA Model 53E

AYA XXV/SL

AYA XXV/SL: has the same general specs as Model 56, except is in 12-, 20-, 28-ga., .410; 25" barrels; narrow top rib. No longer in production. Used value, $1700 to $1800.

AYA Model XXV/BL: side-by-side; 12-, 16-, 20-ga.; 25" barrels; standard chokes; straight-grip European walnut stock; classic pistol grip; checkered butt; box-lock action; auto ejectors; single or double triggers; Churchill rib; color case-hardened or coin-finished receiver. Made in Spain. Introduced, 1981; no longer in production. Used value, $1100 to $1200.

AYA No. 1

AYA No. 1: has the same general specs as Model 56, except for concave rib, double bolting, lightweight frame. No longer in production. Was imported by JBL Arms. Used value, $2000 to $2100.

AYA No. 2

AYA No. 2: has the same general specs as AYA No. 1, except does not have folding trigger, cocking indicators. No longer in production. Used value, $950 to $1000.

AYA No. 4 Deluxe

AYA No. 4 Deluxe: side-by-side; 12-, 16-, 20-, 28-ga., .410; 26", 27", 28" barrels; improved/modified, modified/full chokes; straight-grip European walnut stock; checkered butt; classic forend; box-lock action; automatic ejectors; double or single triggers; color case-hardened receiver. Made in Spain. Introduced, 1981; no longer in production. Used values: 12- and 16-ga., $1550 to $1600; 20-ga., $1550 to $1600; 28-ga., .410, $1600 to $1650.

AYA Model 76

AYA Model 76: side-by-side; hammerless double; 12-, 20-ga.; 26", 28", 30" barrels; standard choke combos; hand-checkered European walnut stock, beavertail forend; Anson & Deeley box-lock; selective single trigger; auto ejectors. No longer in production. Used value, $500 to $525.

  Model 76 410: has same general specs as standard model, except chambered for 3" .410 shell; has extractors; 26" barrels; double triggers; straight-grip English-style stock. No longer in production. Used value, $550 to $600.

AYA Model 117

AYA Model 117: side-by-side; hammerless double; 10-, 12-ga.; 26", 27", 28", 30" barrels; standard choke combos; hand-checkered European walnut stock, beavertail forend; Holland & Holland-design detachable side-locks; selective single trigger; auto ejectors. No longer in production. Was imported by Precision Sports. Used value, $800 to $850.

AYA Model 2: side-by-side; 12-, 20-, 28-ga., .410; 2¾" chambers with 12-, 20-, 28-ga.; 3" chambers with .410; 26", 28" barrels; standard choke combos; weighs 7 lb.; English-style straight hand-rubbed, oil-finished European walnut stock; splinter forend; checkered butt; silver bead front sight; side-lock action; single selective or double triggers; selective auto ejectors; hand-engraved side plates; auto safety; gas escape valves. Made in Spain. Introduced, 1987; dropped, 1988. Used values: 12-, 20-ga. double triggers, $1200 to $1250; single trigger, $1350 to $1400; 28-ga., .410, double triggers, $1300 to $1350; single trigger, $1450 to $1500.

BAIKAL

BAIKAL MC-7: over/under; 12-, 20-ga.; 26", 28" barrels; hand-checkered fancy walnut stock, beavertail forend; fully chiseled, engraved receiver; chromed barrels, chambers, internal parts; double triggers; selective ejectors; solid raised rib; single selective trigger available. Marketed with case. Made in USSR. Introduced, 1975; importation dropped, 1982. Used value, $1400 to $1500.

BAIKAL MC-8-0: 12-ga.; 26", 28" barrels; available in two-barrel set; hand-checkered fancy walnut Monte Carlo stock; beavertail forend permanently attached to barrels; hand-engraved, blued receiver; single trigger, extractors; chromed barrels, chambers, internal parts; hand-fitted vent rib. Marketed with case. Made in USSR. Introduced, 1975; importation dropped, 1982. Used values: skeet version, $1100 to $1200; trap, $1100 to $1200; two-barrel set, $1400 to $1500.

BAIKAL MC-5-105: over/under; 20-ga.; 26" barrels; hand-fitted solid rib; fancy hand-checkered walnut stock; pistol-grip or straight stock; forend permanently attached to barrels; double triggers, extractors; fully engraved receiver; chromed barrels, chambers, internal parts; marketed with case. Manufactured in USSR. Introduced, 1975; importation dropped, 1982. Used value, $600 to $700.

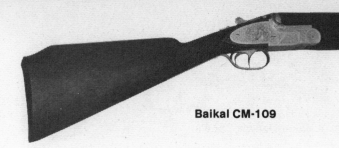

Baikal CM-109

BAIKAL MC-109: over/under; 12-ga.; 28" barrels; raised rib; hand-checkered fancy walnut stock, beavertail forend; hand-made side-locks; removable side plates; single selective trigger; chromed chambers, internal parts; selective ejectors; hand-chiseled scenes on receiver to customer specs. Marketed with case. Made in USSR. Introduced, 1975; importation dropped, 1982. Used value, $2000 to $2100.

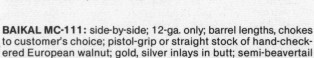

BAIKAL MC-110: side-by-side; 12-, 20-ga.; 26", 28" barrels; hand-checkered pistol grip or straight fancy walnut stock; semi-beavertail forend; fully engraved receiver, trigger guard, tang; double triggers; chromed barrels, chambers, internal parts; raised solid rib; hammer interceptors; extractors; auto safety; marketed in case. Made in Russia. Introduced, 1975; importation dropped, 1982. Used value, $1200 to $1300.

Baikal MC-110

BAIKAL MC-111: side-by-side; 12-ga. only; barrel lengths, chokes to customer's choice; pistol-grip or straight stock of hand-checkered European walnut; gold, silver inlays in butt; semi-beavertail forend; hand-chiseled bird, animal scenes on receiver; hand-made side-locks; removable side plates; chromed barrels, cham-

bers, internal parts; selective ejectors; single selective trigger; hammer interceptors; cocking indicators. Marketed with case. Made in Russia. Introduced, 1975; importation dropped, 1982. Special order only. Used value, $2100 to $2200.

Baikal IJ-27EIC

BAIKAL IJ-27EIC: over/under; 12-, 20-ga.; latter with 3" chambers; 26", 28" barrels; hand-checkered European walnut stock;

vent forend; rubber recoil pad; single selective trigger; hand-fitted ventilated rib; hand-engraved receiver; chromed barrels, chambers, internal parts; selective extractors, ejectors. Manufactured in USSR. Introduced, 1975; importation dropped, 1982. Used values: standard, skeet or trap, $300 to $350; with silver receiver inlays, $350 to $400.

BAIKAL IJ-58MAE: side-by-side; 12-, 20-ga.; 26", 28" barrels; hand-checkered European walnut stock, beavertail forend; hinged front double trigger; chromed barrels, chambers; hammer interceptors; hand-engraved receiver; selective ejection or extraction. Made in Russia. Introduced, 1975; importation dropped, 1982. Used value, $250 to $275.

Baikal IJ-58MAE

BAKER

Baker Batavia Leader

BAKER Batavia Leader: hammerless double; 12-, 16-, 20-ga.; 26" to 32" barrels; any standard choke combo; side-lock; automatic ejectors or plain extractors; hand-checkered pistol grip, forearm; American walnut stock. Introduced in 1921; discontinued, 1930. Manufactured by Baker Gun Co., Batavia, New York. Used values: with automatic ejectors, $425 to $450; plain extractors, $300 to $325.

Batavia Special has same specs as Batavia Leader, except for plain extractors, less expensive finish; 12-ga. only. Used value, $275 to $295.

Batavia Ejector has same specs as Leader, except for (in finer finish) Damascus or forged steel barrels; standard auto ejectors; 12-, 16-ga. only. Used value, $650 to $700.

BAKER Black Beauty Special: same specs as Batavia Leader, but with higher quality finish; dropped, 1930. Used values: with auto ejectors, $675 to $700; plain extractors, $575 to $600.

BAKER Grade S: side-by-side; hammerless double; 12-, 16-ga.; 26", 28", 30", 32" barrels; same general specs as Batavia Leader, but with finer finish, Fluid-tempered steel barrels; scroll, line engraving; hand-checkered European walnut pistol-grip stock, forend. Collector interest. Manufactured 1915 to 1933. Used values: with ejectors, $900 to $950; with plain extractors, $700 to $750.

Baker Batavia Special

Baker Grade R

BAKER Grade R: side-by-side; hammerless double; 12-, 16-ga.; 26", 28", 30", 32" barrels; same general specs as Batavia Leader except for Damascus or Krupp steel barrels, more extensive engraving, with game scene; hand-checkered European walnut stock, forend. Manufactured 1915 to 1933. Collector interest. Used values: auto ejectors, $1000 to $1150; plain extractors, $900 to $950; Paragon Grade: custom-made plain ext., $1250 to $1350; auto ejector, $1450 to $1650; Expert Grade, $2000 to $2250; Deluxe Grade, best quality, $3000 to $3250.

BERETTA

Beretta Model 409PB

BERETTA Model 409PB: hammerless box-lock double; 12-, 16-, 20-, 28-ga.; 27½", 28½", 30" barrels; engraved action; double triggers; plain extractors; improved/modified, modified/full chokes; hand-checkered European walnut straight or pistol-grip stock, beavertail forearm. Introduced in 1934; dropped, 1964. Used value, $550 to $600.

BERETTA Model 410: hammerless box-lock double; 10-ga. magnum only; 27½", 28½", 30" barrels; improved/modified, modified/full chokes; hand-checkered European walnut straight stock; recoil pad; plain extractors; double triggers. Introduced in 1934; dropped, 1963. Used value, $825 to $850.

   Model 410E is a hammerless box-lock double; has the same specs as Model 409PB except for better wood, finer engraving, automatic ejectors. Introduced in 1934; dropped, 1964. Used value, $1050 to $1100.

Beretta Model 410E

BERETTA Model 411E: hammerless box-lock double; 12-, 16-, 20-, 28-ga.; has the same general specs as Model 409PB, except for automatic ejectors, side plates and better wood, finer engraving. Introduced in 1934; dropped, 1964. Used value, $1000 to $1100.

BERETTA Model Asel: over/under box-lock; 12-, 20-ga.; 25", 28", 30" barrels; single nonselective trigger; selective automatic ejectors; improved/modified, modified/full chokes; hand-checkered pistol-grip stock, forearm. Introduced in 1947; dropped, 1964. Used value, $1000 to $1100.

Beretta Silver Hawk Featherweight

BERETTA Silver Hawk Featherweight: hammerless box-lock double; 12-, 16-, 20-, 28-ga.; 26" to 32" barrels; plain extractors, double or nonselective single trigger; all standard choke combos; matted rib; hand-checkered European walnut stock, beavertail forearm. Introduced in 1954; dropped, 1967. Used values: single trigger, $450 to $475; double triggers, $350 to $375.

Silver Hawk Magnum has the same general specs as Silver Hawk Featherweight, except for recoil pad, 10-ga. only; 3" and 3½" chambers; chrome-plated bores; raised rib; has 30", 32" barrels.

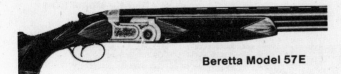

Beretta Model 57E

Introduced in 1954; dropped, 1967. Used values: single trigger, $600 to $625; double triggers, $500 to $525.

BERETTA Model 57E: over/under double; 12-, 20-ga., 12-magnum, 20-magnum; has the same general specs as Golden Snipe model, but overall quality is higher. Manufactured 1955 to 1967. Used value, $750 to $800.

BERETTA Silver Snipe: over/under box-lock; 12-, 20-ga., standard or magnum; 26", 28", 30" barrels; nickel steel receiver; plain or vent rib; improved/modified, modified/full, full/full chokes; selective, nonselective trigger; hand-checkered European walnut pistol-grip stock, forearm. Introduced in 1955; dropped, 1967. Used values: nonselective trigger, $550 to $575; selective trigger, $600 to $625.

Beretta Silver Snipe

BERETTA Golden Snipe: over/under box-lock; 12-, 20-ga., standard or magnum; has same general specs as the Silver Snipe model, except for ventilated rib as standard feature; automatic ejectors. Introduced in 1955; dropped, 1975. Used values: selective trigger, $650 to $675; nonselective trigger, $550 to $575.
Golden Snipe Deluxe has the same specs as standard Golden Snipe, except for finer engraving, better walnut; available in skeet, trap models. Introduced in 1955; dropped, 1975. Used value, $750 to $800.

BERETTA Grade 100: over/under double; 12-ga.; 26", 28", 30" barrels, standard choke combinations side-lock; double triggers; automatic ejectors; hand-checkered straight or pistol-grip European walnut stock, forend. Introduced, post-World War II; dropped, 1960s. Used value, $1500 to $1600.
Grade 200 has same general specs as Grade 100, except for chrome-plated action, bores; improved wood. Used value, $2000 to $2100.

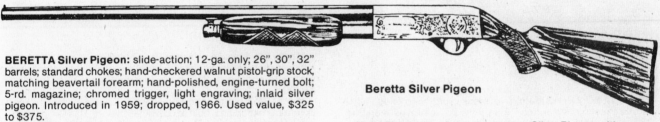

BERETTA Silver Pigeon: slide-action; 12-ga. only; 26", 30", 32" barrels; standard chokes; hand-checkered walnut pistol-grip stock, matching beavertail forearm; hand-polished, engine-turned bolt; 5-rd. magazine; chromed trigger, light engraving; inlaid silver pigeon. Introduced in 1959; dropped, 1966. Used value, $325 to $375.
Gold Pigeon has the same general specs as Silver Pigeon with vent rib, gold trigger, deluxe engraving, inlaid gold pigeon. Used value, $400 to $450.

Beretta Silver Pigeon

Ruby Pigeon has the same specs as Silver Pigeon, with exception of vent rib, extra-deluxe engraving, inlaid gold pigeon with ruby eye. Used value, $550 to $600.

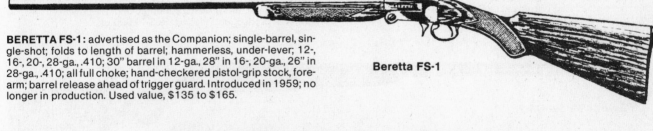

BERETTA FS-1: advertised as the Companion; single-barrel, single-shot; folds to length of barrel; hammerless, under-lever; 12-, 16-, 20-, 28-ga., .410; 30" barrel in 12-ga., 28" in 16-, 20-, 26" in 28-ga., .410; all full choke; hand-checkered pistol-grip stock, forearm; barrel release ahead of trigger guard. Introduced in 1959; no longer in production. Used value, $135 to $165.

Beretta FS-1

Beretta Silver Lark

BERETTA Silver Lark: autoloader; gas-operated, take-down; 12-ga. only; 26", 28", 30", 32" barrels; improved cylinder, modified, full choke; hand-checkered European walnut pistol-grip stock, beaver-

tail forearm; push-button safety in trigger guard; all parts hand-polished. Introduced in 1960; dropped, 1967. Used value, $300 to $325.
Gold Lark has the same specs as Silver Lark, except for fine engraving on receiver, ventilated rib. Used value, $375 to $400.
Ruby Lark has same specs as Silver Lark with the exception of a floating rib, stainless steel barrel, profuse engraving. Used value, $475 to $500.

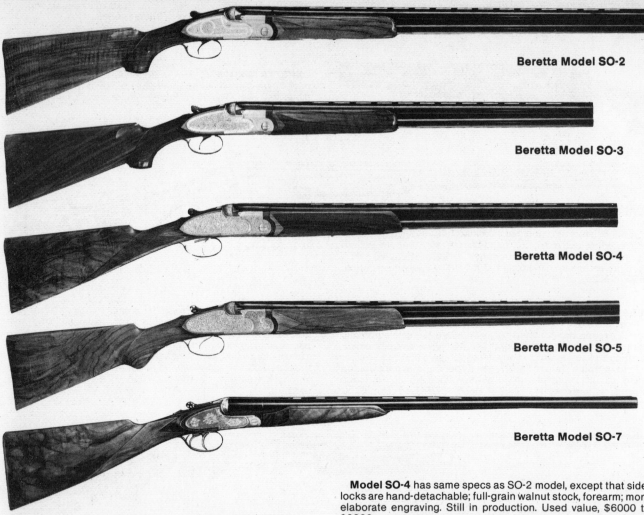

Beretta Model SO-2

Beretta Model SO-3

Beretta Model SO-4

Beretta Model SO-5

Beretta Model SO-7

Model SO-4 has same specs as SO-2 model, except that sidelocks are hand-detachable; full-grain walnut stock, forearm; more elaborate engraving. Still in production. Used value, $6000 to $6200.

Model SO-5 has the same basic specs as other SO models, but is virtually handmade, built to customer's specs. Has Crown grade symbol inlaid in gold in top lever. Still in production on special order basis. Used value, $7500 to $8000.

Model SO-6 is a side-by-side; hammerless double; 12-ga.; 2¾" or 3" chambers; other than barrel placement, has same general specs as over/under SO series guns. Introduced, 1948; no longer in production. Used value, $8000 to $8500.

Model SO-7 has same specs as Model SO-6, except for better grade of wood, more elaborate engraving. Introduced, 1948; no longer in production. Used value, $10,000 up.

BERETTA SO-2 Presentation: side-lock over/under; listed earlier as 502 Presentation series; 12-ga. only; 26" improved/modified, 28" modified/full barrels standard; skeet, trap models also made; vent rib; straight or pistol-grip stock of hand-checkered European walnut; chrome-nickel receiver; Boehler anti-rust barrels; all interior parts chromed; trigger, safety, top lever checkered; scroll engraving; silver pigeon inlaid in top lever. Introduced in 1965; no longer in production. Used value, $3200 to $3400.

Model SO-3 has same specs as Model SO-2, except for fancy selected walnut stock, profuse scroll and relief engraving. Still in production. Used value, $5400 to $5600.

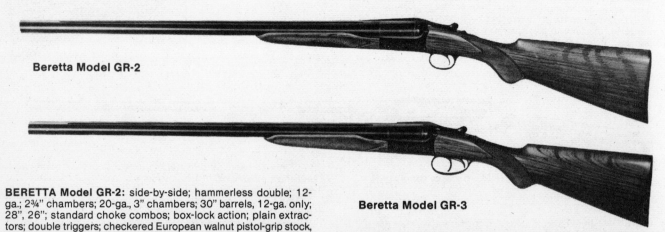

Beretta Model GR-2

Beretta Model GR-3

BERETTA Model GR-2: side-by-side; hammerless double; 12-ga.; 2¾" chambers; 20-ga., 3" chambers; 30" barrels, 12-ga. only; 28", 26"; standard choke combos; box-lock action; plain extractors; double triggers; checkered European walnut pistol-grip stock, forend. Manufactured 1968 to 1976. Used value, $500 to $550.

Model GR-3 has same general specs as Model GR-2, except for single selective trigger, chambering for 3" 12-ga. shells, recoil pad. Manufactured 1968 to 1976. Used value, $650 to $700.

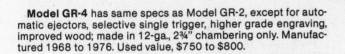

Beretta Model GR-4

Model GR-4 has same specs as Model GR-2, except for automatic ejectors, selective single trigger, higher grade engraving, improved wood; made in 12-ga., 2¾" chambering only. Manufactured 1968 to 1976. Used value, $750 to $800.

Beretta Model SL-2

BERETTA Model SL-2: pump-action; 12-ga. only; 3-rd. magazine; 26" improved, 28" full or modified, 30" full chokes; vent rib; hammerless; checkered European walnut stock, forend. Manufactured 1968 to 1971. Used value, $265 to $285.

BERETTA Model TR-1: single-shot trap model; 12-ga. only; 32" barrel, vent rib; hammerless; engraved frame; under-lever action; checkered European walnut Monte Carlo pistol-grip stock, beavertail forend; recoil pad. Manufactured 1968 to 1971. Used value, $225 to $250.

Model TR-2 has same specs as TR-1, except for extended vent rib. Manufactured 1968 to 1971. Used value, $275 to $300.

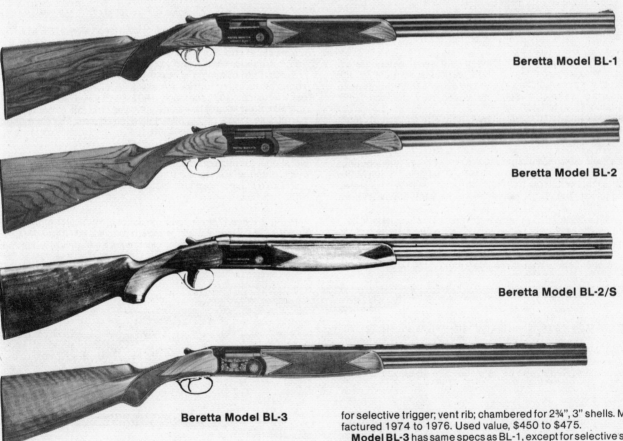

Beretta Model BL-1

Beretta Model BL-2

Beretta Model BL-2/S

Beretta Model BL-3

BERETTA Model BL-1: box-lock over/under; 12-ga. only; 26", 28", 30" barrels; improved/modified, modified/full chokes; Monoblock design; chrome-moly steel barrels; double triggers; no ejectors; ramp front sight with fluorescent inserts; 2¾" chambers; automatic safety; hand-checkered European walnut pistol-grip stock, forearm. Introduced in 1969; dropped, 1972. Used value, $400 to $425.

Model BL-2 has the same basic specs as BL-1, except for single selective trigger. Dropped in 1972. Used value, $450 to $475.

Model BL-2/S has same general specs as Model BL-2, except for selective trigger; vent rib; chambered for 2¾", 3" shells. Manufactured 1974 to 1976. Used value, $450 to $475.

Model BL-3 has same specs as BL-1, except for selective single trigger, vent rib, heavily engraved receiver; 12-ga. chambered for 2¾", 3" shells, 20-ga. for 3". Manufactured 1968 to 1976. Used value, $550 to $575.

Model BL-4 has same specs as Model BL-3, except for more engraving; improved wood; selective automatic ejectors. Manufactured 1968 to 1976. Used value, $650 to $700.

Model BL-5 has same specs as Model BL-4, except for additional engraving, fancier European walnut stock, forend. Manufactured 1968 to 1976. Used value, $800 to $900.

Model BL-6 has same specs as Model BL-5, except for side plates, more engraving, better wood. Manufactured 1973 to 1976. Used value, $1150 to $1250.

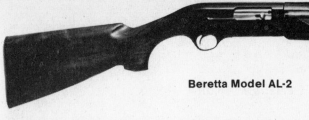

Beretta Model AL-2

BERETTA Model AL-2: autoloader; gas-operated; 12-ga. (2¾" or 3"), 20-ga.; 26", 28", 30" barrels; full, modified, improved cylinder, skeet chokes; interchangeable barrels; vent rib; medium front bead sight; 3-rd. magazine; European walnut stock, forearm; diamond-point hand checkering on pistol grip, forearm. Introduced in 1969; no longer in production. Used values: standard, $300 to $350; trap/skeet, $350 to $400; magnum, $400 to $425.

Model AL-3 has the same general specs as AL-2, but with improved wood, hand-engraved receiver; Monte Carlo pistol-grip stock on trap models. No longer in production. Used values: standard barrels, $350 to $375; skeet/trap, $400 to $425; 3" magnum, $400 to $425.

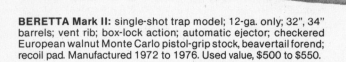

BERETTA Mark II: single-shot trap model; 12-ga. only; 32", 34" barrels; vent rib; box-lock action; automatic ejector; checkered European walnut Monte Carlo pistol-grip stock, beavertail forend; recoil pad. Manufactured 1972 to 1976. Used value, $500 to $550.

Beretta Mark II

Beretta Model A-301 Trap

BERETTA Model A-301: autoloader; field model; gas-operated; 12-ga., 2¾" chamber, 20-ga. 3"; 3-rd. magazine; vent rib; 26" improved, 28" full or modified choke barrels; checkered European walnut pistol-grip stock, forearm. Introduced, 1977; dropped, 1982. Used value, $350 to $400.

A-301 Magnum has same specs as field version, except chambered for 12-ga. 3" magnum shells; recoil pad, 30" full choke barrel only. Introduced, 1977; dropped, 1982. Used value, $375 to $400.

A-301 Skeet has same specs as field version, except for 26" barrel, skeet choke, skeet stock, gold-plated trigger. Introduced, 1977; dropped, 1982. Used value, $350 to $375.

A-301 Trap has same specs as field version, except for 30" full choke barrel only, Monte Carlo stock, recoil pad, gold-plated trigger. Introduced, 1977; dropped, 1982. Used value, $350 to $375.

A-301 Slug Model has same specs as field gun except for 22" barrel, slug choke, no rib, rifle sights. Introduced, 1977; dropped, 1982. Used value, $325 to $350.

BERETTA A-302: autoloader; 12-, 20-ga.; 2¾", 3" chambering; 22" slug barrel, 26" improved or skeet, 28" modified or full Multi-choke; 30" full or full trap barrels in 12-ga.; 26" improved or skeet, 28" modified or full, 20-ga.; European walnut stock; cut-checkered pistol grip, forend; scroll-engraved alloy receiver; gas-operated; push-button safety. Made in Italy. Introduced, 1983; still in production. Used values: standard, $350 to $375; Multi-choke 12-ga., $375 to $400.

BERETTA A-303: autoloader; 12-, 20-ga.; 2¾", 3" chambers; 22", 24", 26", 28", 30", 32" barrel lengths; 20-ga. weighs 6½ lb.; 12-ga., 7½ lb.; hand-checkered American walnut stock; gas-operated action; alloy receiver; magazine cut-off; push-button safety; Mobil-choke model comes with three interchangeable flush-mounted screw-in chokes. Made in Italy. Introduced, 1983; still imported by Beretta, USA. Used values: standard chokes, $375 to $450, depending on variations; Mobilchoke model, $425 to $500, depending on design variations.

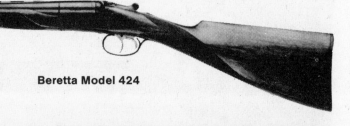

BERETTA Model 424: side-by-side; hammerless double; 12-, 20-ga.; box-lock action; 28" barrel, modified/full; 26", improved/modified; plain extractors; border engraving on action; straight-grip checkered European walnut stock, forend. Introduced, 1977; dropped, 1984. Redesignated as Model 625. Used value, $625 to $650.

Beretta Model 424

Beretta Model 426E

BERETTA Model S-55B: over/under double barrel; 12-ga., 2¾", 3" chambers; 20-ga., 3" chambers; 26", 28", 30" barrels, standard choke combos; selective single trigger; plain extractors; box-lock action; vent rib; checkered European walnut pistol-grip stock,

BERETTA Model 426E: side-by-side; hammerless double barrel; has same general specs as Model 424, except for selective single trigger, selective auto ejectors, finely engraved action, silver pigeon inlaid in top lever; higher grade wood. Introduced, 1977; dropped, 1984. Redesignated as Model 626. Used value, $850 to $900.

forend. Introduced, 1977; no longer in production. Used value, $450 to $500.

Model S-56E has same specs as Model S-55B, except for scroll engraving on receiver, selective auto ejectors. Introduced, 1977;

Beretta Model S-58 Trap

no longer in production. Used value, $500 to $550.

S-58 Skeet Model has same specs as Model S-56E, except for 26" barrels; skeet stock, forend; wide vent rib; skeet chokes. Introduced, 1977; no longer in production. Used value, $650 to $700.

S-58 Trap Model has same specs as skeet version, except for 30" barrels, improved modified/full trap choking; Monte Carlo European walnut stock; recoil pad. Introduced, 1977; no longer in production. Used value, $650 to $700.

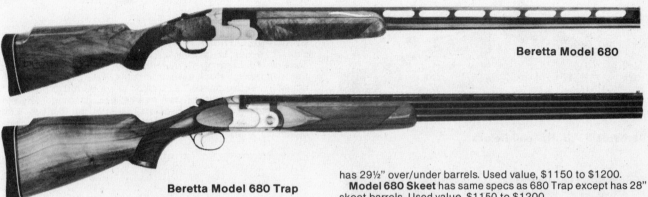

Beretta Model 680

Beretta Model 680 Trap

BERETTA 680: single-shot; 12-ga.; 32", 34" barrel; Monte Carlo stock of hand-checkered European walnut; luminous front sight, center bead; deluxe trap recoil pad. Introduced, 1979; no longer imported by Beretta USA Corp. Used values: $950 to $1000; Model 680 Combo Trap, with single barrel, $1600 to $1650.

Model 680 Trap has same specs as 680 single-barrel, except has 29½" over/under barrels. Used value, $1150 to $1200.

Model 680 Skeet has same specs as 680 Trap except has 28" skeet barrels. Used value, $1150 to $1200.

Model 685 has same specs as Model 680 over/under except is less ornate, less decorative wood. Used value, $600 to $650.

Model 686 has same specs as 685, except has better wood. Used value, $650 to $700.

Model 687 has same field gun specs as Model 686, except has more ornamentation, better finish on wood, metal. Used value, $800 to $2000-plus, depending on variation.

Beretta Model 626

BERETTA Model 626: side-by-side; 12-ga., 2¾" chambers; 20-ga., 3" chambers; 26", 28" barrels; standard choke combos; Beretta box-lock action; double underlugs, bolts; hand-checkered European walnut stock; coil springs; double triggers; auto safety; extractors; concave matted barrel rib. Made in Italy. Introduced, 1985; still imported by Beretta USA. USed value, $725 to $775.

Model 627 EL has same specs as 626, but has better wood, extensive engraving. Introduced, 1985; still imported. Used value, $1475 to $1550.

BERNARDELLI

Bernardelli Roma 6

BERNARDELLI Roma: side-by-side; hammerless; Anson & Deeley action; side plates; 12-ga. only in Roma 3 Model; 12-, 16-, 20-ga. in others; nonejector standard model; double triggers; 27½", 29½" barrels; modified/full chokes; hand-checkered European walnut stock, forearm; straight or pistol-grip style. Differences in grades are type of engraving, quality of wood, checkering, overall finish. Introduced in 1946; still in production. Used values: Roma 3, nonejector, $800 to $825; with ejectors, $850 to $900; Roma 4, nonejector, $900 to $950; with ejectors, $950 to $1000; Roma 6, nonejector, $1050 to $1100; with ejectors, $1125 to $1175.

Bernardelli Holland

Bernardelli V.B. Holland Deluxe

BERNARDELLI Holland: side-by-side; Holland & Holland-design side-lock action; 12-ga. only; 26" to 32" barrels; all standard choke combos; double triggers; automatic ejectors; hand-checkered European walnut stock, forearm; straight or pistol-grip style. Introduced in 1946; dropped, 1971. Used value, $3000 to $3250.

Deluxe Holland model has the same specs as standard Bernardelli Holland, except has beavertail forearm, hunting scene engraved on action. Introduced in 1946; still in production on special order only. Was imported by Sloans. Used value, $5000 to $5250.

BERNARDELLI St. Uberto No. 1: side-by-side; 12-, 16-, 20-, 28-ga.; 2¾", 3" chambers; 25⅝", 26¾", 28", 29⅛" barrels; modified/full; hand-checkered select European walnut stock; Anson & Deeley-style box-lock action; Purdey locks; choice of extractors or ejectors. Made in Italy. Originally introduced in 1946; importation renewed, 1987; still imported by Mandall Shooting Supplies, Armes de Chasse. Used values: with extractors, $750 to $800; with ejectors, $825 to $875.

St. Uberto No. 2 has same specs as No. 1, except has silvered receiver, more and better engraving. Introduced, 1946; dropped, 1972; importation renewed, 1987; still imported by Mandall and Armes de Chasse. Used values: with extractors, $775 to $850; with ejectors, $875 to $950.

St. Uberto F.S. Model has the same specs as No. 2, except has more, better engraving; carefully selected wood. Introduced, 1987; still imported by Mandall, Armes de Chasse. Used values: with extractors, $925 to $1000; with ejectors, $1050 to $1125.

Bernardelli S. Uberto 2

Bernardelli Brescia

Bernerdelli Italia

BERNARDELLI Brescia: side-by-side double barrel; 12-, 20-ga.; 25½" improved/modified barrels in 20-ga.; 27½" 29½" modified/full in 12-ga.; side-lock action; exposed hammers; engraved frame; double triggers; plain extractors; checkered European walnut English-style straight stock. Introduced circa 1960; still in produc-

tion. Used value, $900 to $950.

Italia Model has the same specs as Brescia, except for improved wood, higher grade of engraving. Still in production. Used value, $950 to $1000.

BERNARDELLI Elio: side-by-side double-barrel; 12-ga. only; lightweight game model; has same general specs as Game Cock model, except for automatic ejectors, English-style scroll engraving. Introduced circa 1970; still in production. Used value, $900 to $950.

Bernardelli Elio

Bernardelli Game Cock

Bernardelli Premier Game Cock

BERNARDELLI Game Cock: side-by-side; hammerless; box-lock action; 12-, 20-ga.; 25" improved/modified or 28" modified/full barrels; straight hand-checkered European walnut stock; double triggers on Standard model. Introduced in 1970; still in production. Was imported by Sloans. Used value, $600 to $650.

BERNARDELLI XXVSL: side-by-side; 12-ga.; 25" demi-block barrels; standard chokes; Holland & Holland-type side-lock action; double sears; custom-fitted European walnut stock; manual or

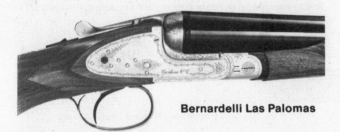

Bernardelli Las Palomas

BERNARDELLI System Holland H: 12 ga.; has same general specs as Las Palomas model, except has true side-lock action; reinforced breech, three Purdey locks; auto ejectors; folding right trigger; made in 3 grades; Model VB Liscio has color case-hardened receiver, side plates with light engraving; VB and VB Tipo

Deluxe Game Cock model has same specs as standard, except for light scroll engraving. Used value, $750 to $800.

Premier Game Cock has same specs as Roma 3 and is same gun by another designation. Value is the same.

auto safety; classic or beavertail forend; selective auto ejectors. Marketed in fitted luggage case. Made in Italy. Introduced, 1982, by Knight & Knight; dropped, 1984. Used value, $1300 to $1350.

BERNARDELLI Las Palomas: side-by-side; 12 ga.; 2¾" chambers; 28" barrels bored for pigeon shooting; select European walnut stock; reinforced Anson & Deeley action; single trigger; special trigger guard; manual safety; auto safety optional; Australian pistol grip with shaped heel, palm swell; vent recoil pad; optional features. Made in Italy. Introduced, 1984; still imported by Armes De Chasse and Quality Arms. Used value, $2000 to $2200.

Lusso models are silvered, engraved. Made in Italy. Introduced, 1984; still imported by Armes De Chasse, Quality Arms. Used values: VB Liscio, $3000 to $3100; VB, $4200 to $4300; VB Tipo Lusso, $4800 to $4900.

BRNO

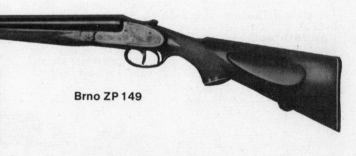

Brno ZP 149

BRNO ZP 149: side-by-side; 12-ga.; 2¾" chambers; 28½" full/modified barrels; weighs 7 lb. 3 oz.; Turkish or Yugoslavian walnut stock; raised cheekpiece; side-lock action; auto ejectors; barrel indicators; double triggers; auto safety; engraving available. Made in Czechoslovakia. Introduced, 1986; still imported by Saki International. Used values: standard model, $400 to $425; engraved, $425 to $450.

ZP 349 has same specs as ZP 149, except has extractors. Made in Czechoslovakia. Introduced, 1986; still imported. Used values: standard version, $440 to $470; engraved, $460 to $490.

Brno Super

BRNO Super: over/under; 12-ga.; 2¾" chambers; 27½" full/modified barrels; weighs 7¼ lb.; raised cheekpiece European walnut stock; side-lock action; double safety interceptor sears; double or

single triggers; selective auto ejectors; engraved side plates. Made in Czechoslovakia. Introduced, 1987; still imported by Saki International. Used value, $625 to $650.

BRNO 500: over/under; 2¾" chambers; 27" barrels, full/modified; weighs 7 lb.; European walnut stock; raised cheekpiece; box-lock action; double triggers; ejectors; acid-etched engraving. Made in Czechoslovakia. Introduced, 1987; still imported by Saki International. Used value, $650 to 675.

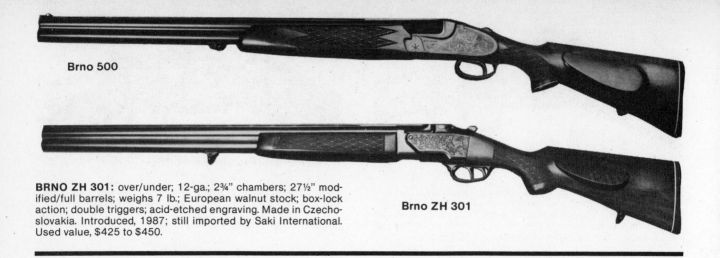

Brno 500

Brno ZH 301

BRNO ZH 301: over/under; 12-ga.; 2¾" chambers; 27½" modified/full barrels; weighs 7 lb.; European walnut stock; box-lock action; double triggers; acid-etched engraving. Made in Czechoslovakia. Introduced, 1987; still imported by Saki International. Used value, $425 to $450.

BROWNING

NOTE: Some models are made in Japan, some in Belgium and some in both countries. Collector interest has increased in Belgian-made models and prices are approximately 25% higher than for Japanese production.

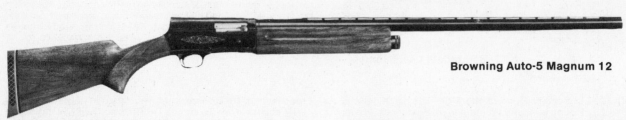

Browning Auto-5 Magnum 12

BROWNING Auto-5: autoloader; take-down, recoil-operated; has been made in a wide variety of configurations, grades and gauges. Browning Special or Standard model was introduced in 1900; redesignated as Grade I in 1940. Available in 12-, 16-ga.; 26" to 32" barrels; 4-rd. magazine; pre-WWII guns were available with 3-rd. magazine also; hand-checkered pistol-grip stock; forearm of European walnut; plain barrel, vent or raised matted rib. Variations still are being manufactured. Used values: with plain barrel, $375 to $400; with raised matted rib, $400 to $450; with vent rib, $450 to $500.

Auto-5 Grade III has the same general specs as the Grade I or Standard model, except for better wood, checkering and more engraving. Discontinued, 1940. Used values: plain barrel, $700 to $750; with raised matted rib, $775 to $825; with vent rib, $850 to $900.

Auto-5 Grade IV — sometimes called Midas Grade — has the same general specs as Grade III, except for profuse inlays of green, yellow gold. Discontinued, 1940. Used values: plain barrel, $1150 to $1250; with raised matted rib, $1350 to $1500; with vent rib, $1800 to $2000.

Auto-5 Trap model, in 12-ga. only, has the same specs as the Grade I, except for 30" vent-rib barrel, full choke only, trap stock. Used value, $550 to $575.

Auto-5 Magnum 12 has same general specs as Grade I, but is chambered for 3" magnum shell; has recoil pad, plain or vent-rib barrel; 28" barrel is modified or full, 30" and 32" are full choke. Introduced in 1958; still in production. Used values: plain barrel, $450 to $500; vent rib, $550 to $600.

Auto-5 Magnum 20 has the same general specs as the Magnum 12, except is chambered for 20-ga. magnum shell; 26" barrel is full, modified or improved, 28" is full or modified; vent rib. Used value, $450 to $500.

Browning Auto-5 Light Buck Special

Browning Auto-5 Light Standard

BROWNING Auto-5 Light: autoloader; take-down; recoil operated; 12-, 16-, 20-ga.; same general specs as Standard Auto-5;

5-rd. magazine with 3-rd. plug furnished; 2¾" chamber; 26", 28", 30" barrels, with standard choke choices; receiver is hand engraved; gold-plated trigger; double extractors; barrels are interchangeable; made with vent rib only on current models. Introduced in 1948; still in production. Used value, $425 to $450.

Browning Auto-5 Gold Classic

Browning Auto-5 Classic

Auto-5 Light Skeet model has the same specs as the Light Standard model except for skeet boring; available only in 12-, 20-ga.; 28" barrel with full or modified choke; 26" with full, modified or improved cylinder; plain barrel or vent rib; vent rib only on current model. Used value, $475 to $500.

Auto-5 Light Buck Special has the same specs as Standard model, except for 24" barrel; choked for slugs; adjustable rear sight, gold bead front on contoured ramp; detachable swivels, sling optional on current model. Dropped, 1985. Used value, $450 to $475; with sling, swivels, $475 to $500.

Auto-5 Classic has same specs as standard Auto-5 Light 12 ga. with 28" modified barrel, except has hunting, wildlife scenes engraved in satin gray receiver; engraved portrait of John M. Browning; also engraved is legend, "Browning Classic. One of Five Thousand"; select figured walnut stock; special checkering. Only 5000 manufactured. Introduced, 1984. Used value, $750 to $800.

Auto-5 Gold Classic has same specs as Classic, except engraved scenes are inlaid with gold animals, portrait; engraved with "Browning Gold Classic. One of Five Hundred." Only 500 made. Introduced, 1984. Used value, $4000 to $4500.

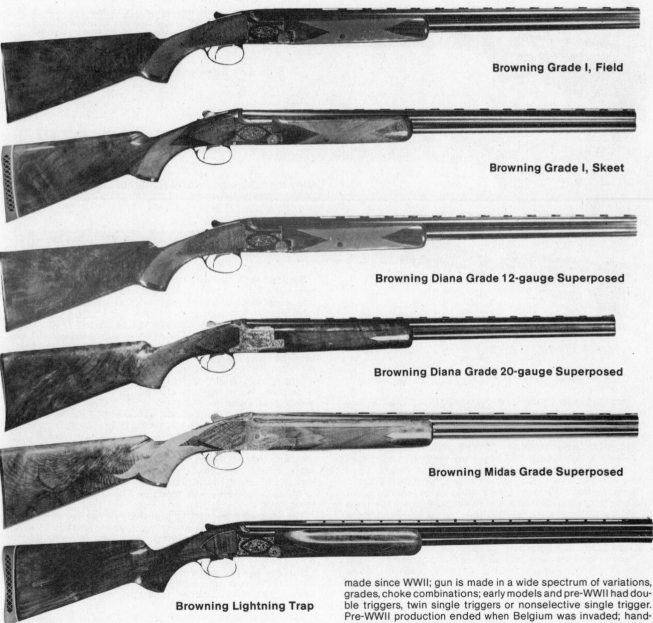

Browning Grade I, Field

Browning Grade I, Skeet

Browning Diana Grade 12-gauge Superposed

Browning Diana Grade 20-gauge Superposed

Browning Midas Grade Superposed

Browning Lightning Trap

BROWNING Superposed: over/under; Browning-designed action; 12-, 20-, 28-ga., .410; 26½", 28", 30" or 32" barrels; 32" not

made since WWII; gun is made in a wide spectrum of variations, grades, choke combinations; early models and pre-WWII had double triggers, twin single triggers or nonselective single trigger. Pre-WWII production ended when Belgium was invaded; hand-checkered stocks, forearms of French walnut; choice of pistol-grip or straight stock. Standard Grade is listed as Grade I, has raised matted rib or vent rib. Introduced in 1928; variations still in produc-

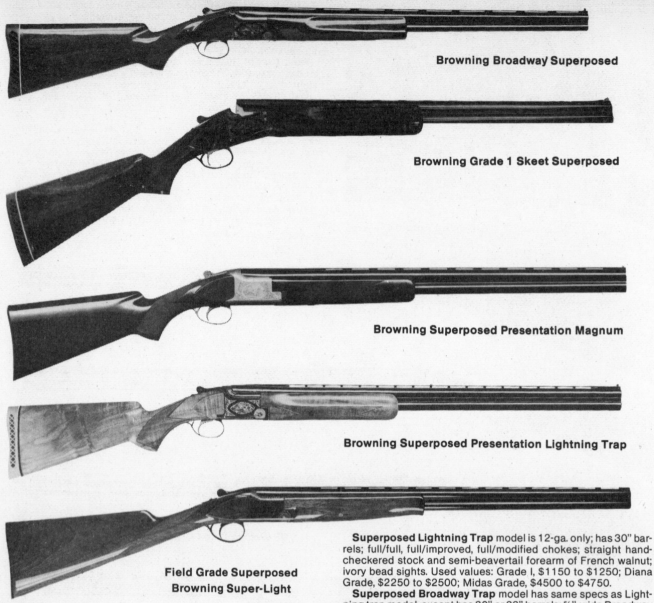

Browning Broadway Superposed

Browning Grade 1 Skeet Superposed

Browning Superposed Presentation Magnum

Browning Superposed Presentation Lightning Trap

**Field Grade Superposed
Browning Super-Light**

tion. Used values: with raised matted rib, $950 to $1000; vent rib, $1250 to $1500.

Lightning Model Grade I had only matted barrel, no rib before WWII; post-war models have vent rib. Other specs generally the same as Standard Superposed model. Used values: with matted barrel, $1000 to $1250; vent rib, $1250 to $1500.

Pigeon Grade Superposed was redesignated as Grade II after WWII. Had better wood, finer checkering, more engraving than Standard Superposed model; raised matted rib or vent rib. Used values: with matted rib, $1650 to $1750; vent rib, $1850 to $2000.

Diana Grade had either raised matted rib or vent rib before WWII; current models have only vent rib. Has same specs as Pigeon Grade, but with more engraving, better wood, improved general quality. Used values: with matted rib, $2250 to $2500; vent rib, $2500 to $2750.

Midas Grade in pre-war versions had raised matted rib or vent rib; current versions have only wide vent rib. Has same general specs as standard Superposed, but is heavily engraved, gold inlaid. Used values: raised matted rib, $4500 to $4750; vent rib, $5250 to $5500.

Superposed Magnum model has the same specs as Grade I, except is chambered for 12-ga. 3" shells; 30" vent-rib barrel, choked full/full or full/modified; recoil pad. Used values: Grade I, $1200 to $1250; Diana Grade, $2250 to $2500; Midas Grade, $4500 to $4750.

Superposed Lightning Trap model is 12-ga. only; has 30" barrels; full/full, full/improved, full/modified chokes; straight hand-checkered stock and semi-beavertail forearm of French walnut; ivory bead sights. Used values: Grade I, $1150 to $1250; Diana Grade, $2250 to $2500; Midas Grade, $4500 to $4750.

Superposed Broadway Trap model has same specs as Lightning trap model, except has 30" or 32" barrels; ⅝"-wide Broadway vent rib. Used values: Grade I, $1250 to $1500; Diana Grade, $2750 to $3000; Midas Grade, $4500 to $4750.

Superposed Skeet model has the same specs as Standard Superposed model, except for choice of 26½" or 28" barrels, choked skeet/skeet; made in 12-, 20-, 28-ga., .410. Used values: Grade I, $1250 to $1500; Pigeon Grade, $1650 to $1750; Diana Grade, $2250 to $2500; Midas Grade, $4500 to $4750.

Superposed Super-Light Presentation over/under is available in 4 grades; 12-, 20-ga.; box-lock action; top lever; single selective trigger; barrel selector combined with manual tang safety; 26½" barrels; hand-checkered straight-grip stock of select walnut. Options too numerous to mention. Introduced, 1977; still in production. Used value starts at $3000 to $3100; options bring more.

Superposed Presentation Lightning Skeet has same specs as standard Presentation, except has special skeet stock, forend; center and front ivory bead sights; all gauges. Introduced, 1977; dropped, 1982. Used value starts at $2250 to $2500; options bring more.

Superposed Presentation Magnum 12 has same specs as standard Presentation, except has 3" chambers, 30" barrels; factory-fitted recoil pad. Dropped, 1984. Used value, $2250 to $2500; options bring more.

Superposed Presentation Lightning Trap 12 has same specs as Lightning Skeet version, except has trap stock, 30" barrels, semi-beavertail forend. Dropped, 1984. Used value, $2000 to $2250.

Superposed Presentation Broadway Trap 12 has same specs as Lightning Trap 12, except has wide vent rib, different stock measurements, 30", 32" barrels. Dropped, 1984. Used value, $2000 to $2250; options bring more.

Superposed Super-Light: over/under; box-lock action; top lever; 12-, 20-ga.; 2¾" chambers; 26½" barrels only; choked mod- ified/full or improved/modified; barrel selector combined with manual tang safety; single selective trigger; straight-grip stock of select walnut; hand-checkered grip, forearm; vent rib; engraved receiver. Introduced in 1967; discontinued, 1976. Used values: Grade I, 12-ga., $1250 to $1350; 20-ga., $1500 to $1600.

BROWNING American Grade I: autoloader; 12-, 16-, 20-ga.; 2-, 4-rd. tube magazine; recoil-operated; 26", 28", 30", 32" barrel lengths, standard chokes; hand-checkered American walnut pistol-grip stock, forend. Identical to the Remington Model 11A, was manufactured by Remington for Browning, 1940 to 1949. Used value, $400 to $450.

American Special has same specs as Grade I, except for either vent rib or matted raised rib. Manufactured 1940 to 1949. Used values: vent rib, $475 to $500; raised rib, $425 to $450.

American Special Skeet version has same specs as Grade I, except for 26" barrel, vent rib, Cutts Compensator. Manufactured 1940 to 1949. Used value, $400 to $425.

American Field Model has same specs as Grade I, except for 28" barrel, Poly Choke. Manufactured 1940 to 1949. Used value, $375 to $400.

Browning Twelvette Double Auto

Browning Twentyweight Double Auto

BROWNING Double Auto: autoloader; take-down; short recoil system; 2-shot; 12-ga. only; 26", 28", 30" barrels; any standard choke; hand-checkered pistol-grip stock, forearm of European walnut; steel receiver; plain or recessed rib barrel; conservative engraving; weight, about 7¾ lb. Introduced in 1955; dropped, 1961. Used values: with plain barrel, $400 to $425; recessed rib, $450 to $475.

Twelvette Double Auto model is same as the standard Double Auto, except for aluminum receiver, barrel with plain matted top or vent rib; receiver is black anodized with gold-wiped engraving; some receivers are anodized in brown, gray or green with silver-wiped engraving; weighs about a pound less than standard model. Introduced in 1955; dropped, 1971. Used values: matted barrel, $375 to $400; vent rib, $425 to $450.

Twentyweight Double Auto model has the same specs as Twelvette model, but weighs 12 oz. less, largely due to thinner stock; 26½" barrel only. Introduced in 1956; dropped, 1971. Used values: matted barrel, $400 to $425; vent rib, $475 to $500.

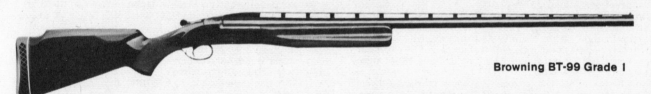

Browning BT-99 Grade I

BROWNING BT-99 Grade I: single-shot trap; 12-ga.; 32", 34" barrel; box-lock action; automatic ejector; vent rib; improved, full choke; checkered walnut pistol-grip stock, beavertail forend. Manufactured in Japan. Introduced, 1969; still in production. Used value, $500 to $550.

BT-99 Grade I Competition has same specs, except for high, wide rib, Monte Carlo-style stock. Introduced, 1976; Competition name dropped, 1978; still in production. Used value, $600 to $650.

BT-99 Competition Trap Special has same specs as Competition model, except has trap stock. Made in Japan. Still imported. Used value, $550 to $600.

Browning BSS Sporter

BROWNING BSS: side-by-side double; 12-, 20-ga.; 3" chambers; 26", 28", 30" barrels; standard choke combos; box-lock action; hammerless; non-selective single trigger; checkered walnut pistol-grip stock, beavertail forend. Manufactured in Japan. Introduced, 1972; dropped, 1987. Used value, $500 to $550.

Browning BSS Sidelock

BSS Sporter has same specs as BSS 20-ga., except for straight stock, selective trigger. Introduced, 1977; dropped, 1987. Used value, $500 to $550.

BSS Sidelock model is similar to BSS Sporter, except is true side lock; receiver, forend iron, trigger guard, top lever, tang are satin gray with rosettes, scrollwork; straight-grip French walnut stock; checkered butt; double triggers; auto safety; cocking indicator. Made in Japan. Introduced, 1984; dropped, 1987. Used value, $1100 to $1200.

Browning Liege

BROWNING Liege: over/under; double barrel; 12-ga.; 26½", 28" barrels, chambered for 2¾" shells; 30" for 3"; box-lock action; automatic ejectors; non-selective single trigger; standard choke combos; vent rib; checkered walnut pistol-grip stock, forearm. Manufactured 1973 to 1975. Used value, $650 to $700.

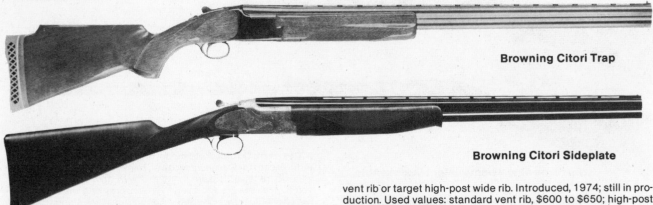

Browning Citori Trap

Browning Citori Sideplate

BROWNING Citori: over/under; double barrel; 12-, 20-ga.; 3" chambers; 26", 28", 30" barrels; improved/modified, modified/full, full/full chokes; automatic ejectors; box-lock action; selective single trigger; checkered pistol-grip stock, semi-beavertail forearm; recoil pad. Manufactured in Japan. Introduced, 1973; still in production. Used value, $525 to $550.

Citori Trap model has same general specs as standard Citori, except made in 12-ga. only, checkered walnut Monte Carlo stock, beavertail forearm; 30", 32" barrels; standard trap choke combos; vent rib or high-post target wide vent rib. Introduced, 1974; still in production. Used values: standard vent rib, $600 to $650; high-post vent rib, $650 to $700.

Citori Skeet model has same general specs as standard version, except for skeet stock, forearm; skeet-choked 26", 28" barrels; vent rib or target high-post wide rib. Introduced, 1974; still in production. Used values: standard vent rib, $600 to $650; high-post vent rib, $650 to $700.

Citori Sporter has same general specs as standard model, except made with 26" barrel only; straight-grip stock, Schnabel forend, satin oil finish. Introduced, 1978; still in production. Used value, $600 to $650.

Citori Superlight has same specs as standard Citori, except is made in 12-, 20-ga., 3" chambers; 26", 28" barrels; straight-grip stock; Schnabel forend tip. Made in Japan. Introduced, 1982; still imported. Used values: Grade I, $600 to $650; Grade VI, $1200 to $1300.

Citori Sideplate 20 Gauge has same specs as Citori Sporter, except is 20-ga. only; 26" barrels; improved/modified or modified/full; Grade V wood; hand-checkering; satin steel side plates; receiver, trigger guard tang etched with upland game scenes. Dropped, 1984. Used values: $1250 to $1300; four barrel skeet set, $2100 to $2200.

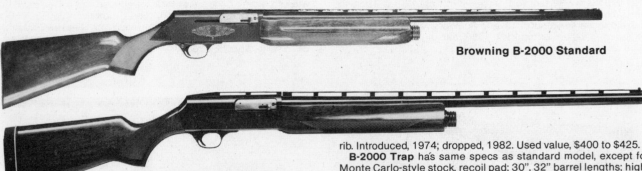

Browning B-2000 Standard

Browning B-2000 Skeet

BROWNING B-2000: autoloader; gas-operated; 12-, 20-ga.; 4-rd. magazine; chambered for 2¾" shells; 26", 28", 30" barrels; choice of standard chokes; vent rib or plain matted barrel; checkered pistol-grip stock of European walnut. Manufactured in Belgium, assembled in Portugal. Introduced, 1974; dropped, 1982. Used value, $375 to $400.

B-2000 Magnum has same specs as standard model, except 3" chambering, 3-rd. magazine; 26", 28", 30", 32" barrel lengths; vent rib. Introduced, 1974; dropped, 1982. Used value, $400 to $425.

B-2000 Trap has same specs as standard model, except for Monte Carlo-style stock, recoil pad; 30", 32" barrel lengths; high-post vent rib; modified, improved, full chokes; 12-ga. only; 2¾" chambering. Introduced, 1974; dropped, 1982. Used value, $400 to $425.

B-2000 Skeet has same specs as standard version, except for skeet stock, 26" skeet-choke barrel; 12-, 20-ga.; 2¾" chambering; recoil pad. Introduced, 1974; dropped, 1982. Used value, $400 to $425.

B-2000 Buck Special has same specs as standard model, except for 24" slug barrel, no rib, open rear sight, front ramp; 12-ga. chambered for 2¾" shell, 20-ga., 3". Introduced, 1974; dropped, 1982. Used value, $400 to $425.

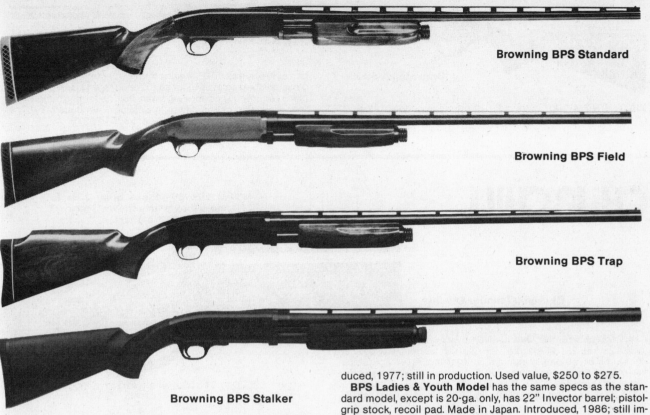

Browning BPS Standard

Browning BPS Field

Browning BPS Trap

Browning BPS Stalker

BROWNING BPS: pump-action; 12-ga.; 3" chamber; loads five 2¾" shells; four 3"; 26", 28", 30" barrels; standard choke choices; take-down; vent rib; checkered walnut pistol-grip stock, semi-beavertail slide handle; recoil pad. Manufactured in Japan. Intro-

duced, 1977; still in production. Used value, $250 to $275.

BPS Ladies & Youth Model has the same specs as the standard model, except is 20-ga. only, has 22" Invector barrel; pistol-grip stock, recoil pad. Made in Japan. Introduced, 1986; still imported. Used value, $300 to $325.

BPS Stalker is same as standard model, except has matte blued finish on metal, black-finished stock, black recoil pad; 12-ga. only; 3" chamber; 22", 28", 30" barrel lengths; Invector choke system. Introduced, 1987; still imported. Used value, $300 to $325.

Browning ST-100

BROWNING ST-100: over/under; 12-ga.; 30" barrels; five-position impact adjustment; floating under-barrel; floating rib designed for trap; hand-checkered select walnut stock, with high-gloss finish, semi-beavertail forend; floating Broadway rib; selective auto ejectors; single selective mechanical trigger; manual top tang manual safety. Introduced, 1979; dropped, 1982. Used value, $1900 to $2000.

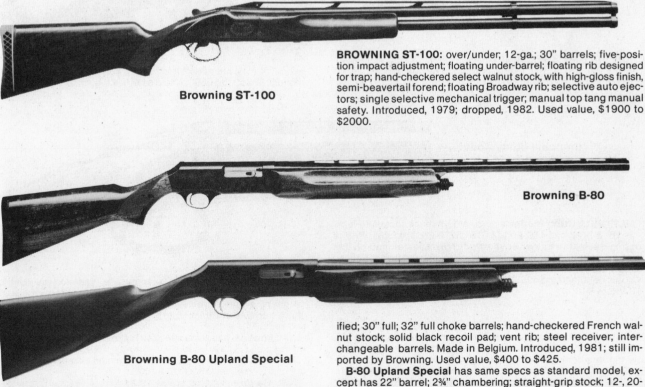

Browning B-80

Browning B-80 Upland Special

BROWNING B-80: autoloader; 12-, 20-ga.; 5 rds.; 22" slug barrel, 26" improved cylinder, cylinder, skeet, full, modified, 28" full, mod-

ified; 30" full; 32" full choke barrels; hand-checkered French walnut stock; solid black recoil pad; vent rib; steel receiver; interchangeable barrels. Made in Belgium. Introduced, 1981; still imported by Browning. Used value, $400 to $425.

B-80 Upland Special has same specs as standard model, except has 22" barrel; 2¾" chambering; straight-grip stock; 12-, 20-ga. Made in Belgium. Introduced, 1986; still imported by Browning. Used value, $375 to $400.

Browning A-500

BROWNING A-500: autoloader; short-recoil action; 12-ga.; 3" shells only; 26", 28", 30" barrels; Invector choke tubes; with 30" barrel, measures 49½", weighs 7 lb. 7 oz.; metal bead front sight; gloss-finished select walnut stock; checkered pistol grip, forend; black vent. recoil pad; four-lug rotary bolt; coil spring buffering system; magazine cut-off. Made in Belgium. Introduced, 1987; still imported by Browning. Used value, $350 to $375.

CHURCHILL

NOTE: 20-, 28-gauges bring 25% to 35% more than prices shown. The .410 is as much as 50% higher.

Churchill Premier Quality

CHURCHILL Premier Quality: side-by-side; hammerless; side-lock; 12-, 16-, 20-, 28-ga.; 25", 28", 30" 32" barrels; any desired choke combo; automatic ejectors; double triggers or single selective trigger; English engraving; hand-checkered European walnut stock, forearm; pistol-grip or straight English style. Introduced in 1900; firm went out of business in 1982. Used values: double triggers, $9000 to $10,000; single selective trigger, $10,000 to $12,500.

Churchill Field Model

CHURCHILL Field Model: side-by-side; hammerless; side-lock; 12-, 16-, 20-, 28-ga.; has the same general design specs as Premier Model but has lower grade of wood, less engraving, lower overall quality. Manufactured 1900 to 1982. Used values: double triggers, $6250 to $6500; single selective trigger, $7000 to $7250.

Churchill Utility Model

CHURCHILL Utility Model: side-by-side; hammerless; side-lock; 12-, 16-, 20-, 28-ga., .410; 25", 28", 30", 32" barrels; double triggers or single selective trigger; any desired choke combo; hand-checkered European walnut stock, forearm; pistol-grip or straight English style. Introduced in 1900; firm went out of business in 1982. Used values: double triggers, $3250 to $3500; single selective trigger, $3750 to $4000.

CHURCHILL Premier Over/Under: hammerless; side-lock; 12-, 16-, 20-, 28-ga.; 25", 28", 30", 32" barrels; automatic ejectors; double triggers or single selective trigger; English engraving; hand-checkered European walnut stock, forearm; pistol-grip or straight English style. Introduced in 1925; dropped, 1955. Used values: double triggers, $10,500 to $11,500; single selective trigger, $12,500 to $14,500.

CHURCHILL XXV Premier: side-by-side; hammerless double; 12-, 20-ga.; 25" barrels; standard choke combos; side-lock; assisted opening feature; auto ejectors; double triggers; narrow rib; checkered walnut straight-grip stock, forearm. Used value, $12,000 to $14,000.

XXV Imperial has same specs as Premier model, sans the assisted opening feature. Used value, $9000 to $10,000.

XXV Hercules has same specs as Premier, except has box-lock action. Used value, $6000 to $7000.

XXV Regal has same specs as XXV Hercules, sans assisted opening feature; made in 12-, 20-, 28-ga., .410. Used value, $3000 to $4000.

CHURCHILL/KASSNAR

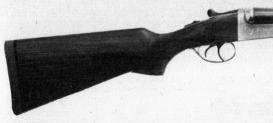

Churchill Windsor S/S

CHURCHILL WINDSOR S/S: side-by-side; 10-, 12-, 16-, 20-, 28-ga., .410; 2¾" chambers for 16-ga., 3" for all others; 24", 26", 28", 30", 32" barrel lengths; hand-checkered European walnut stock; rubber butt pad; Anson & Deeley box-lock action; silvered, engraved finish; auto top tang safety; double triggers; beavertail forend; Windsor I has extractors, Windsor II has selective auto ejectors. Made in Spain. Introduced, 1984; still imported by Kassnar. Used values: Windsor I, 10-ga., $350 to $375; Windsor I, other gauges, $275 to $300; Windsor II, $350 to $375.

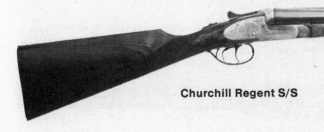

Churchill Regent S/S

CHURCHILL Regent S/S: side-by-side; has specs similar to Windsor Grade, except has fancier walnut, better checkering and engraving; tapered Churchill rib; 12-, 20-ga.; 25", 28" barrels; 2¾" chambers only; straight stock; double triggers; auto selective ejectors. Regent IV is box-lock, Regent VI is full side-lock. Made in Spain. Introduced, 1984; Regent VI still imported by Kassnar, others dropped, 1986. Used values: Regent IV, $400 to $425; Regent IV, left-handed, $475 to $500; Regent VI, $650 to $675.

Churchill Windsor O/U

CHURCHILL Windsor O/U: over/under; 12-, 20-ga., .410; 3" chambers; 26", 28", 30" barrels with standard choke combos or interchangeable choke tubes in 27", 30" barrel lengths; checkered European walnut stock, forend; pistol grip; box-lock action; silvered, engraved finish; single selective trigger; Windsor IV has auto ejectors; Windsor III has extractors only. Made in Italy. Introduced, 1984; still imported by Kassnar. Used values: Windsor III, fixed chokes, $450 to $475; ICT choke tubes, $490 to $525; Windsor IV, fixed chokes, $525 to $550; ICT choke tubes, $550 to $575.

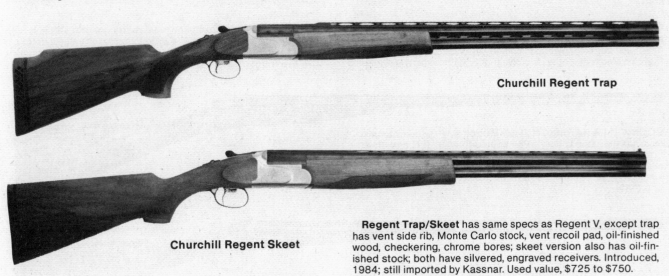

Churchill Regent Trap

Churchill Regent Skeet

CHURCHILL Regent O/U: over/under; same specs as Windsor, except has better wood, oil finish, better engraving; 12-, 20-ga. only; 27" barrels; interchangeable choke tubes only. Regent V has standard box-lock action; Regent VII has dummy side plates. Made in Italy. Introduced, 1984; Regent VII still imported by Kassnar, others dropped, 1986. Used values: Regent V, $700 to $725; Regent VII, $725 to $750.

Regent Trap/Skeet has same specs as Regent V, except trap has vent side rib, Monte Carlo stock, vent recoil pad, oil-finished wood, checkering, chrome bores; skeet version also has oil-finished stock; both have silvered, engraved receivers. Introduced, 1984; still imported by Kassnar. Used value, $725 to $750.

CHURCHILL Windsor Auto: autoloader; 12-ga.; 2¾" or 3" chambers; 26" to 30" barrel lengths; standard chokes or ICT choke tubes; weighs 7½ lb.; select Claro walnut stock; high gloss or matte finish wood; checkered pistol grip, forend; rosewood grip cap; stainless steel gas piston; crossbolt safety; anodized alloy

Churchill Windsor Auto

receiver. Made in Japan. Introduced, 1984; dropped, 1986. Used values: fixed chokes, $360 to $375; choke tubes, $380 to $395.

Windsor Flyweight has same specs as standard model, except has ICT choke tubes, 23" barrel, straight-grip stock. Used value, $380 to $395.

Churchill Regent Auto

Regent Flyweight has same specs as standard Regent, except has choke tubes, 23" barrel. Made in Japan. Introduced, 1984; dropped, 1986. Used value, $400 to $420.

CHURCHILL Regent Auto: autoloader; has same specs as Windsor model, except has etched, polished receiver. Made in Japan. Introduced, 1984; dropped, 1986. Used values: fixed chokes, $400 to $420; ICT choke tubes, $390 to $410.

CHURCHILL Deerfield: autoloader; has same specs as Windsor model, except has 20" slug barrel. Made in Japan. Introduced, 1984; dropped, 1986. Used value, $375 to $390.

Churchill Monarch

CHURCHILL Monarch: over/under; 12-, 20-ga.; 3" chambers; 26", 28" chrome-lined barrels; standard choke combos; 12-ga. weighs 7½ lb., 20-ga., 6½ lb.; checkered European walnut pistol-grip stock; box-lock action; engraved receiver; vent rib; single selective trigger or double triggers; blued finish. Introduced, 1987; still imported by Kassnar. Used values: double triggers, $275 to $300; single trigger, $300 to $325.

COGSWELL & HARRISON

COGSWELL & HARRISON Primac Model: side-by-side; hammerless; hand-detachable side locks; 12-, 16-, 20-ga.; 25", 26", 27½", 30" barrels; any choke combo; automatic ejectors; double triggers, single or single selective triggers; English-style engraving; hand-checkered European walnut straight-grip stock, forearm. Introduced in 1920s; still in production. Used values: double triggers, $4750 to $5000; single trigger, $5000 to $5250; single selective trigger, $5250 to $5500.

COGSWELL & HARRISON Victor Model: side-by-side; hammerless; has the same specs as Primac model except for better finish, finer wood, checkering, engraving patterns. Introduced in 1920s; still in production. Used values: double triggers, $7000 to $7250; single trigger, $7250 to $7500; single selective trigger, $7500 to $8000.

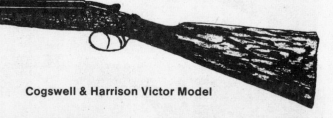

Cogswell & Harrison Victor Model

COGSWELL & HARRISON Konor Avant Tout: side-by-side; hammerless; box-lock action; 12-, 16-, 20-ga.; 25", 27½", 30" barrels; any desired choke combo; side plates; double, single or single selective triggers; hand-checkered European walnut straight-grip stock, forearm; pistol-grip stock available on special order; fine checkering, engraving. Introduced in 1920s; still in production. Used values: double triggers, $2500 to $2750; single trigger, $2750 to $3000; single selective trigger, $3000 to $3250.

Cogswell & Harrison Konor Avant Tout

Avant Tout Sandhurst model has the same specs as Konor model except for less-intricate engraving, checkering, lower grade of wood, overall workmanship. Still in production. Used values: double triggers, $2500 to $2700; single trigger, $2750 to $2850; single selective trigger, $2850 to $3000.

Avant Tout Rex model has the same specs as Sandhurst model except has no side plates, lower grade wood, checkering, engraving, overall finish. Still in production. Used values: double triggers, $1500 to $1600; single trigger, $1700 to $1800; single selective trigger, $1800 to $2000.

COGSWELL & HARRISON Huntic Model: side-by-side; hammerless; side-lock action; 12-, 16-, 20-ga.; 25", 27½", 30" barrels; any desired choke combo; automatic ejectors; double, single or single selective triggers; hand-checkered European walnut straight-grip stock, forearm; pistol-grip stock on special order. Introduced in late 1920s; still in production. Used values: double triggers, $2750 to $3000; single trigger, $3000 to $3250; single selective trigger, $3250 to $3500.

COGSWELL & HARRISON Markor Model: side-by-side; hammerless; box-lock action; 12-, 16-, 20-ga.; 27½", 30" barrels; any standard choke combo; double triggers; ejector or nonejector; hand-checkered European walnut straight-grip stock, forearm. Introduced in late 1920s; still in production. Used values: ejector model, $1500 to $1750; nonejector, $1250 to $1500.

COGSWELL & HARRISON Ambassador: side-by-side; hammerless double; 12-, 16-, 20-ga.; 26", 28", 30" barrels; any choke combo; box-lock action; side plates feature game engraving or rose scrollwork; auto ejectors; double triggers; hand-checkered European walnut straight-grip stock, forearm. Introduced, 1970; still in production. Used value, $3250 to $3500.

COLT

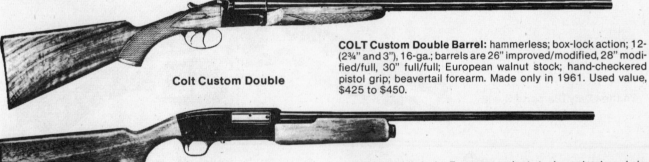

Colt Custom Double

COLT Custom Double Barrel: hammerless; box-lock action; 12-(2¾" and 3"), 16-ga.; barrels are 26" improved/modified, 28" modified/full, 30" full/full; European walnut stock; hand-checkered pistol grip; beavertail forearm. Made only in 1961. Used value, $425 to $450.

Colt Standard Pump

COLT Coltsman Pump Model: slide-action; take-down; 12-, 16-, 20-ga.; barrels are 26" improved, 28" modified or 30" full choke; magazine holds 4 rds.; European walnut stock; uncheckered pistol grip, forearm. Manufactured for Colt by Manufrance. Introduced in 1961; dropped, 1965. Used value, $225 to $250.

Coltsman Custom pump has the same specs as standard model, same manufacturer, except has hand-checkered pistol grip, forearm, vent rib. Introduced in 1961; dropped, 1963. Used value, $300 to $325.

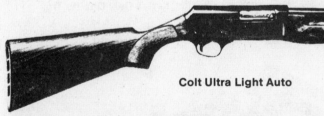

Colt Ultra Light Auto

COLT Ultra Light Auto: autoloader; take-down; alloy receiver; 12-, 20-ga.; chrome-lined barrels are 26" improved or modified, 28" modified or full, 30" full only, 32" full only; 4-rd. magazine; plain barrel, solid or vent rib; European walnut stock; hand-checkered pistol grip, forearm. Manufactured for Colt by Franchi. Introduced in 1964; dropped, 1966. Used values: plain barrel, $275 to $300; solid rib, $275 to $300; vent rib, $325 to $350.

Ultra Light Custom Auto is the same as the standard model, except for select walnut stock, forearm; engraved receiver; vent rib only. Introduced in 1964; dropped, 1966. Used values: solid rib, $350 to $375; vent rib, $400 to $425.

COLT Magnum Auto: autoloader; take-down; 12-, 20-ga.; chambered for 3" magnum shell; other specs generally the same as those for Ultra Light standard auto. In 12 magnum, barrels are 30" or 32"; 28" in 20 magnum. Produced for Colt by Franchi. Introduced in 1964; dropped, 1966. Used values: plain barrel, $325 to $350; solid rib, $350 to $375; vent rib, $400 to $425.

Custom Magnum Auto has same specs as standard Magnum Auto, except for select walnut stock, forearm; engraved receiver; vent rib only. Introduced in 1964; dropped, 1966. Used values: solid rib, $400 to $450; vent rib, $450 to $475.

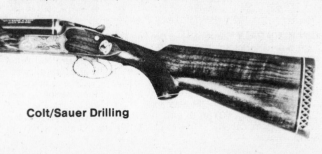

COLT Sauer Drilling: box-lock action; top lever; crossbolt; .30/06 or .243 Win. under side-by-side 12-ga. barrels; 25" barrels; set rifle trigger; side safety; shotgun barrels choked modified/full; folding leaf rear sight, blade front with brass bead; cocking indicators; tang barrel selector; automatic sight positioner; oil-finished American walnut stock; hand-checkered pistol grip, forearm; black pistol grip cap; recoil pad. Made for Colt by Sauer in West Germany. no longer imported by Colt. Used value, $2250 to $2500.

Colt/Sauer Drilling

CHARLES DALY

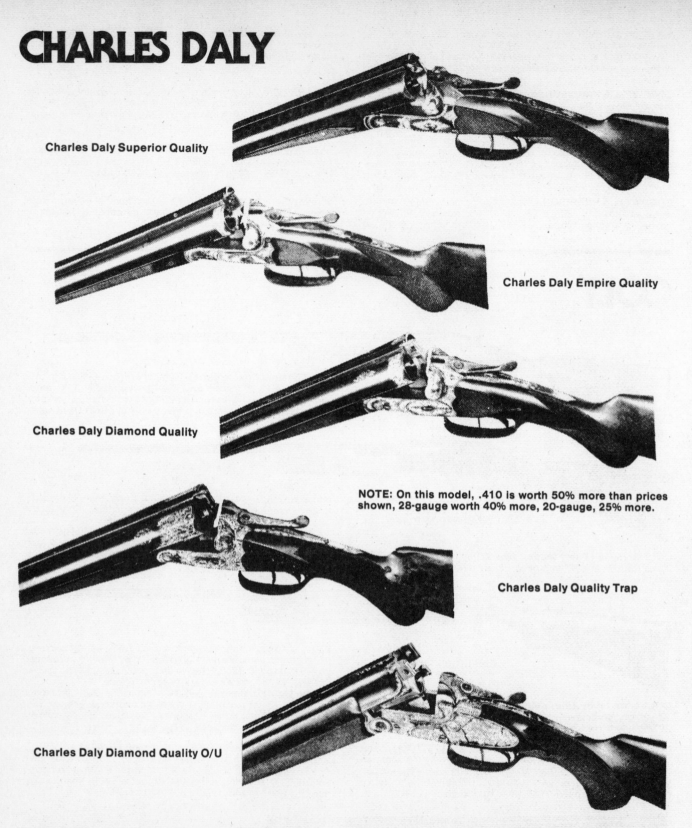

Charles Daly Superior Quality

Charles Daly Empire Quality

Charles Daly Diamond Quality

NOTE: On this model, .410 is worth 50% more than prices shown, 28-gauge worth 40% more, 20-gauge, 25% more.

Charles Daly Quality Trap

Charles Daly Diamond Quality O/U

CHARLES DALY Hammerless Double Barrel: Anson & Deeley-type box-lock action; 10-, 12-, 16-, 20-, 28-ga., .410; 26" to 28" barrels with any choke combo; walnut stock; checkered pistol grip, forearm; made in four grades; all have automatic ejectors, except Superior Quality; grades differ in grade of wood, checkering, amount of engraving, general overall quality. Made in Suhl, Germany, for Daly. Introduced about 1920; dropped, 1933. Used values: Regent Diamond Quality, $3750 to $4000; Diamond Quality, $2750 to $3250; Empire Quality, $1450 to $1650; Superior Quality, $700 to $800.

CHARLES DALY Empire Quality Over/Under: Anson & Deeley-type box-lock action; 12-, 16-, 20-ga.; 26" to 30" barrels; any standard choke combo; European walnut stock; hand-checkered pistol grip, forearm; double triggers; automatic ejectors. Made in Suhl, Germany, for Daly. Introduced about 1920; dropped, 1933. Used value, $2250 to $2500.

   Diamond Quality Over/Under has the same specs as Empire Quality, except has more extensive engraving, better wood and improved general overall quality. Used value, $3750 to $4000.

Charles Daly Empire Quality Trap

CHARLES DALY Empire Quality Trap: single-barrel; Anson & Deeley-type box-lock action; 12-ga. only; 30", 32", 34" vent-rib barrel; automatic ejector; European walnut stock; hand-checkered pistol grip, forearm. Made in Suhl, Germany, for Daly in one model only. Introduced about 1920; dropped, 1933. Used value, $1750 to $2000.

Charles Daly Sextuple Trap

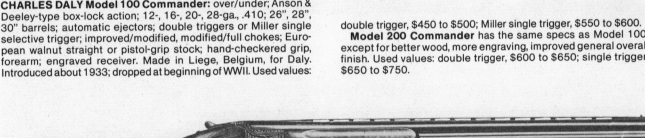

CHARLES DALY Sextuple Trap: single-barrel; Anson & Deeley-type box-lock action; 12-ga. only; 30", 32", 34" vent-rib barrel; six locking bolts; automatic ejector; European walnut stock; hand-checkered pistol grip, forearm. Made in two grades in Suhl, Germany, for Daly; grades differ only in checkering, amount of engraving, grade of wood, improved overall quality. Introduced about 1920; dropped, 1933. Used values: Empire Quality, $2000 to $2500; Regent Diamond Quality, $2500 to $3000.

CHARLES DALY Hammerless Drilling: Anson & Deeley-type box-lock action; 12-, 16-, 20-ga.; rifle barrel chambered for .25-20, .25-35, .30-30 cartridges; plain extractors; automatic rear sight operated by selector for rifle barrel; European walnut stock; hand-checkered pistol grip, forearm. Made in three grades in Suhl, Germany, for Daly; grades differ only in checkering, amount of engraving, wood, overall quality. Introduced about 1921; dropped, 1933. Used values: Superior Quality, $2250 to $2500; Diamond Quality, $3000 to $3250; Regent Diamond Quality, $3575 to $4000.

CHARLES DALY Model 100 Commander: over/under; Anson & Deeley-type box-lock action; 12-, 16-, 20-, 28-ga., .410; 26", 28", 30" barrels; automatic ejectors; double triggers or Miller single selective trigger; improved/modified, modified/full chokes; European walnut straight or pistol-grip stock; hand-checkered grip, forearm; engraved receiver. Made in Liege, Belgium, for Daly. Introduced about 1933; dropped at beginning of WWII. Used values:

double trigger, $450 to $500; Miller single trigger, $550 to $600.

Model 200 Commander has the same specs as Model 100, except for better wood, more engraving, improved general overall finish. Used values: double trigger, $600 to $650; single trigger, $650 to $750.

Charles Daly Superior Model

CHARLES DALY Field Grade: over/under; box-lock action; 12- (2¾", 3"), 20- (2¾", 3"), 28-ga., .410; 26", 28", 30" barrels; choked skeet/skeet, improved/modified, modified/full, full/full; vent rib; engraved receiver; selective single trigger; automatic selective ejectors; safety/barrel selector; walnut stock; hand-checkered pistol-grip, fluted forearm; recoil pad on 12-ga. magnum version.

This, like other Daly shotguns made following WWII, was manufactured in Japan. The 12- and 20-ga. standard and magnum guns were introduced in 1963; 28-ga., .410 in 1965. Used value, $450 to $500.

Superior Grade over/under has the same general specs as Field Grade, but is not chambered for magnum shells; other differences include beavertail forearm; selector device to select auto ejector or extraction only. Imported from Japan. Used values: $550 to $650; Superior skeet, $600 to $650; Superior trap, $625 to $650.

CHARLES DALY Diamond Grade: over/under; has the same general specs as the Superior Grade, but is stocked with French walnut, more extensively checkered, engraved receiver, trigger guard. Introduced in 1967; dropped, 1973. Imported from Japan. Used value, $750 to $800.

Diamond-Regent Grade over/under has same specs as Diamond Grade, except for highly figured French walnut stock, profuse engraving, hunting scenes inlaid in gold, silver; firing pins removable through breech face. Introduced in 1967; dropped, 1973. Imported from Japan. Used value, $1250 to $1500.

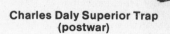

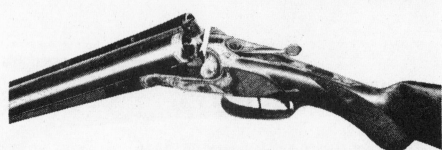

CHARLES DALY Superior Trap: single-shot, hammerless; 12-ga. only; 32", 34" barrels; full choke; vent rib; box-lock action; auto ejector; checkered walnut Monte Carlo pistol-grip stock, forearm; recoil pad. Manufactured in Japan, 1968 to 1976. Used value, $475 to $500.

Charles Daly Superior Trap (postwar)

Charles Daly Empire Double

CHARLES DALY Empire Double: side-by-side; hammerless; 12-, 16-, 20-ga.; 3" chambering for 12-, 20-ga.; 2¾" for 16; 26", 28", 30" barrel lengths; standard choke combos; box-lock action; plain extractors; non-selective single trigger; checkered walnut pistol-grip stock, beavertail forearm. Manufactured 1968 to 1971. Used value, $500 to $525.

CHARLES DALY Novamatic Lightweight: autoloader; 12-ga.; 3¾" chambering; 4-rd. tubular magazine; 26" barrel, improved cylinder or three-tube Quick-Choke system; plain or vent-rib barrel; checkered walnut pistol-grip stock, forearm. Manufactured in Italy by Breda, 1968. Used values: plain barrel, $225 to $275; vent rib, $275 to $300.

Novamatic Super Lightweight has same general specs as Lightweight, except standard vent rib, less weight, skeet choke available; 28" barrel in 12-ga.; plain barrel, Quick-Choke available in 20-ga. Manufactured 1968. Used value, $275 to $295.

Novamatic Super Lightweight 20 Magnum has same specs as Super Lightweight except for 3" chambering; 3-rd. magazine; 28" vent-rib barrel, full choke. Manufactured, 1968. Used value, $275 to $295.

Novamatic Trap Model has same specs as Lightweight, except for 30" vent-rib barrel; full choke; Monte Carlo trap stock; recoil pad. Manufactured, 1968. Used value, $300 to $325.

Novamatic 12 Magnum has same specs as Lightweight model except for 3" chambering, 3-rd. magazine capacity, 30" vent-rib barrel, full choke, recoil pad. Manufactured, 1968. Used value, $300 to $325.

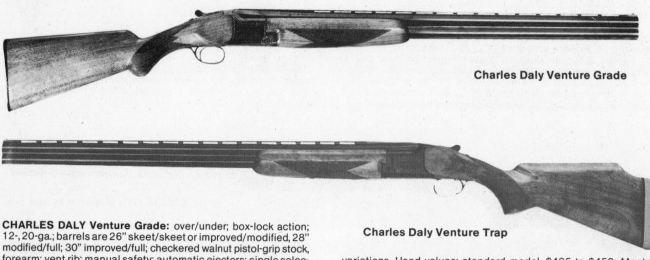

Charles Daly Venture Grade

Charles Daly Venture Trap

CHARLES DALY Venture Grade: over/under; box-lock action; 12-, 20-ga.; barrels are 26" skeet/skeet or improved/modified, 28" modified/full; 30" improved/full; checkered walnut pistol-grip stock, forearm; vent rib; manual safety; automatic ejectors; single selective trigger. Imported from Japan. Introduced in 1973. Made in 3 variations. Used values: standard model, $425 to $450; Monte Carlo trap, $475 to $500; skeet, $475 to $500.

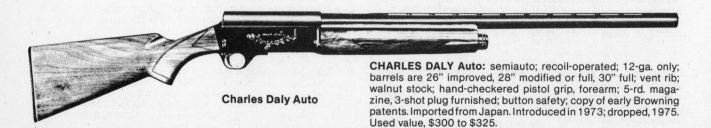

Charles Daly Auto

CHARLES DALY Auto: semiauto; recoil-operated; 12-ga. only; barrels are 26" improved, 28" modified or full, 30" full; vent rib; walnut stock; hand-checkered pistol grip, forearm; 5-rd. magazine, 3-shot plug furnished; button safety; copy of early Browning patents. Imported from Japan. Introduced in 1973; dropped, 1975. Used value, $300 to $325.

CHARLES DALY Field Auto: autoloader; 12-ga.; chambered for 2¾" or 3" shells; 27", 30" barrel lengths; standard chokes or Invector choke tubes; weighs 7¼ lb.; walnut stock; checkered pistol grip, forend; alloy receiver; chromed bolt; crossbolt safety; stainless steel gas piston. Made in Japan. Introduced, 1984; dropped, 1987. Was imported by Outdoor Sports Headquarters. Used value, $280 to $295.

Charles Daly Diamond Grade (1984)

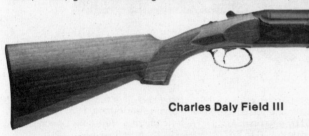

Charles Daly Diamond Trap (1984)

CHARLES DALY Diamond Grade: over/under; 12-, 20-ga.; 27" barrels; three choke tubes included; box-lock action; hand-checkered oil-finished European walnut stock; single selective competi-

CHARLES DALY Presentation Grade: over/under; has same specs as Diamond Grade, except has dummy side plates, better wood, finish; game scene engraved on silvered receiver, side

Made in Italy. Introduced, 1984; dropped, 1987. Was imported by Outdoor Sports Headquarters. Used value, $650 to $675.

    Diamond Trap is similar to Diamond Grade, except has competition vent top and middle ribs, target trigger, Monte Carlo stock; 12 ga. only; 30" barrels. Still imported by Outdoor Sports. Used value, $750 to $800.

    Diamond Skeet has same specs as Diamond Grade, except has skeet stock, competition vent rib, target trigger; 12 ga. only; 26" skeet barrels. Used value, $750 to $800.

plates. Introduced, 1984; dropped, 1986. Was imported by Outdoor Sports Headquarters. Used value, $800 to $850.

Charles Daly Field III

CHARLES DALY Field III: over/under; 12, 20 ga.; 26", 28", 30" barrels; vent rib; checkered European walnut stock, forend; single selective trigger; extractors; blued, engraved frame; chrome-lined bores. Made in Italy. Introduced, 1984; still imported by Outdoor Sports Headquarters. Used value, $325 to $350.

CHARLES DALY Superior II: over/under; 12-, 20-ga.; has same general specs as Field III model, except has single selective trigger, automatic ejectors, better wood, silvered receiver, more and better engraving. Introduced, 1984; still imported by Outdoor Sports Headquarters. Used values: standard model, $475 to $490; skeet model, $475 to $490; with 30" barrels, 3" chambers, $525 to $550.

CHARLES DALY Multi-XII: autoloader; has same general specs as the field auto, except has Multi-Action gas system, 3" chambers; shoots all loads without adjustment; Invector choke system; 27" barrel; scroll engraved receiver; rosewood grip cap; brown vent recoil pad. Made in Japan. Introduced, 1986; importation by Outdoor Sports Headquarters dropped, 1987. Used value, $325 to $350.

DAVIDSON

Davidson Model 63B

DAVIDSON Model 63B: double-barrel; 12-, 16-, 20-, 28-ga., .410; Anson & Deeley box-lock action; plain extractors, automatic safety; engraved, nickel-plated frame; barrel lengths: 25" in .410; 26", 28" and also 30" in 12-ga. only; chokes are improved cylinder/modified, modified/full, full/full; hand-checkered walnut stock; pistol grip. Manufactured in Spain; imported by Davidson Firearms Co., Greensboro, North Carolina. Introduced in 1963; still in production; no longer imported. Used value, $200 to $220.

DAVIDSON Model 63B Magnum: same specs as standard 63B, except chambered for 3" 12-ga. magnum shells and 3½" for 10-ga.; 10-ga. has 32" full/full barrels; still in production; no longer imported. Used values: 10-ga. magnum, $275 to $300; 12-, 20-ga. magnums, $300 to $325.

DAVIDSON Model 69SL: double; side-lock action, detachable side plates; 20-, 12-ga.; 26" barrels, modified/improved; 28" barrels, modified/full; nickel-plated, engraved action; hand-checkered European walnut stock. Introduced in 1963; still in production; no longer imported. Used value, $350 to $375.

DAVIDSON Model 73: side-by-side, hammer double; 12-, 20-ga.; 3" chambers; 20" barrels; side-lock action, detachable side plates; plain extractors; double triggers; checkered European walnut pistol-grip stock, forearm. Manufactured in Spain. Introduced, 1976; still in production; no longer imported. Used value, $225 to $250.

DIARM

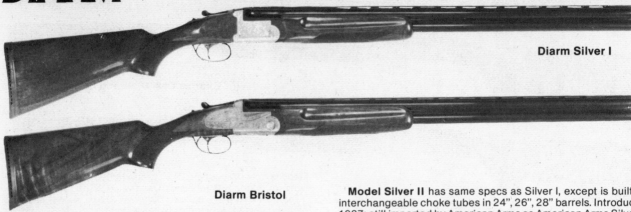

Diarm Silver I

Diarm Bristol

DIARM Model Silver I: over/under; 12-, 20-ga.; 3" chambers; 26", 28" barrels; standard choke combos; ¼" vent rib; hand-checkered walnut stock, forend; box-lock action; locking crossbolt; manual safety; auto selective ejectors; single selective trigger; brushed silver finish. Made in Spain. Introduced, 1987; still imported by American Arms as American Arms Silver I. Used value, $350 to $375.

Model Silver II has same specs as Silver I, except is built for interchangeable choke tubes in 24", 26", 28" barrels. Introduced, 1987; still imported by American Arms as American Arms Silver II. Used value, $450 to $475.

Bristol has same general specs as Silver II model, except has engraved dummy side plates, old silver-finished frame, gold trigger, front bead sight, glossy stock finish. Made in Spain. Introduced, 1987; still imported by American Arms as American Arms Bristol. Used values: fixed chokes, $550 to $575; with choke tubes, $575 to $600.

Diarm Waterfowl Special

DIARM Waterfowl Special: over/under; has same specs as Silver II, except has Parkerized finish, dull wood finish, sling swivels; 28" barrels, choke tubes; single selective trigger. Marketed with camouflaged sling. Made in Spain. Introduced, 1987; still imported by American Arms as American Arms Waterfowl Special. Used value, $450 to $475.

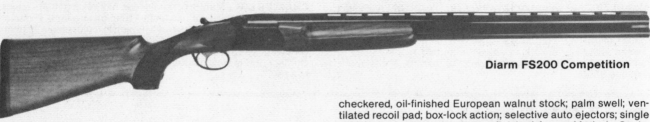

Diarm FS200 Competition

DIARM FS200 Competition: over/under; 12-ga.; 2¾" chambers; 32" barrels, skeet/skeet, improved/full; weighs 7 lb. 11 oz.; hand-checkered, oil-finished European walnut stock; palm swell; ventilated recoil pad; box-lock action; selective auto ejectors; single selective trigger; satin chrome-finished frame. Made in Spain. Introduced, 1987; dropped, 1987. Was imported by American Arms. Used value, $600 to $625.

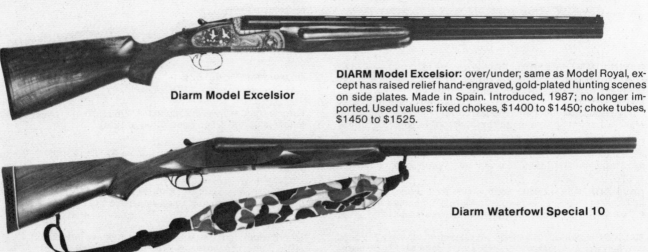

Diarm Model Excelsior

DIARM Model Excelsior: over/under; same as Model Royal, except has raised relief hand-engraved, gold-plated hunting scenes on side plates. Made in Spain. Introduced, 1987; no longer imported. Used values: fixed chokes, $1400 to $1450; choke tubes, $1450 to $1525.

Diarm Waterfowl Special 10

DIARM Waterfowl Special 10: side-by-side; 10-ga.; 3½" chambers; 32" full/full barrels; flat rib; weighs 10 lb. 13 oz.; dull-finished, hand-checkered European walnut stock, beavertail forend; full pistol grip; rubber recoil pad; box-lock action; double triggers; English scroll engraving; Parkerized metal finish; sling swivels. Marketed with camouflage sling. Made in Spain. Introduced, 1987; still imported by American Arms as American Arms Waterfowl Special. Used value, $400 to $435.

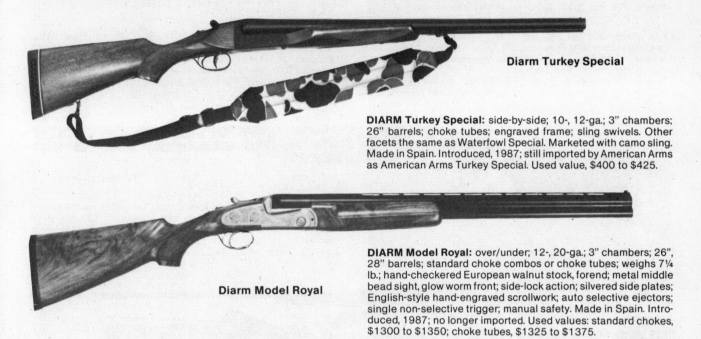

Diarm Turkey Special

DIARM Turkey Special: side-by-side; 10-, 12-ga.; 3" chambers; 26" barrels; choke tubes; engraved frame; sling swivels. Other facets the same as Waterfowl Special. Marketed with camo sling. Made in Spain. Introduced, 1987; still imported by American Arms as American Arms Turkey Special. Used value, $400 to $425.

Diarm Model Royal

DIARM Model Royal: over/under; 12-, 20-ga.; 3" chambers; 26", 28" barrels; standard choke combos or choke tubes; weighs 7¼ lb.; hand-checkered European walnut stock, forend; metal middle bead sight, glow worm front; side-lock action; silvered side plates; English-style hand-engraved scrollwork; auto selective ejectors; single non-selective trigger; manual safety. Made in Spain. Introduced, 1987; no longer imported. Used values: standard chokes, $1300 to $1350; choke tubes, $1325 to $1375.

Diarm York Model

DIARM York Model: side-by-side; 12-, 20-, 28-ga., .410; 3" chambers; 25", 28" barrels; standard choke combos; weighs 7¼ lb.; gloss-finished, hand-checkered European walnut stock; beavertail forend; pistol grip; box-lock action; gold bead front sight; double triggers; extractors; manual safety; independent floating firing pins. Made in Spain. Introduced, 1987; still imported by American Arms as American Arms York. Used value, $335 to $360, depending on gauge.

Diarm Derby Model

DIARM Derby Model: side-by-side; has same general specs as York model, except has single or double triggers; side-lock action; silvered side plates; English-type engraving; straight-grip, oil-finished walnut stock, splinter forend; selective auto ejectors; gas escape valve. Made in Spain. Introduced, 1987; still imported by American Arms as American Arms Derby. Used values: double triggers, $550 to $585, depending on gauge; single trigger, $585 to $640, depending on gauge.

EXEL

Exel Model 201

EXEL Model 201: side-by-side; 12-ga.; 2¾" chambers; 28" barrels; hand-checkered European walnut stock; straight or full pistol grip; metal bead front sight; box-lock action; color case-hardened finish; double triggers; extractors; high matted rib. Made in Spain. Introduced, 1984; dropped, 1987. Was imported by Exel Arms of America. Used value, $290 to $300.

    Model 202 has same specs as Model 201, except has 26" barrels. Introduced, 1984; dropped, 1987. Used value, $290 to $300.

    Model 203 has same specs as Model 201, except has 27" barrels, 3" chambers. Introduced, 1984; dropped, 1987. Used value, $290 to $300.

EXEL Model 204: side-by-side; 12-ga.; has same general specs as Model 201, except has silvered, engraved receiver, automatic selective ejectors, single or double triggers. Made in Spain. Introduced, 1984; dropped, 1987. Was imported by Exel Arms of America. Used value, $450 to $475.

Model 205 has same specs as Model 204, except has 26"

EXEL Model 207: side-by-side; 12-ga.; similar to Model 201, except has full side-lock action, 28" barrels. Made in Spain. Introduced, 1984; dropped, 1987. Was imported by Exel Arms of America. Used value, $550 to $600.

Model 208 has same specs as Model 207, except has better wood, finish. Introduced, 1984; dropped, 1987. Used value, $600 to $650.

barrels. Introduced, 1984; dropped, 1987. Used value, $450 to $475.

Model 206 has same specs as Model 204, except has 27" barrels. Introduced, 1984; dropped, 1987. Used value, $450 to $475.

Model 209 has same specs as Model 207, except has better wood, finish, 26" barrels, 20-ga., 3" chambers. Introduced, 1984; dropped, 1987. Used value, $475 to $500.

Model 210 has same specs as Model 209, except has 27" barrels. Introduced, 1984; dropped, 1987. Used value, $475 to $500.

Exel Series 300

EXEL Series 300: over/under; 12-ga.; 2¾" chambers; 28", 29" barrel lengths; European walnut stock; field or Monte Carlo con-

figuration; checkered grip, forend; box-lock action; silvered, engraved finish; vent rib; auto selective ejectors. Offered in 10 variations with differing degrees of ornamentation. Made in Spain. Introduced, 1984; dropped, 1987. Was imported by Exel Arms of America. Used value, $425 to $550, depending on ornamentation.

Exel Model 51

EXEL Model 51: folding single-shot; .410 only; 3" chamber; folding stock; splinter forend; non-ejector; case-hardened frame; exposed hammer. Made in Spain. Introduced, 1985; dropped, 1987. Was imported by Exel Arms. Used value, $150 to $160.

F.I.E.

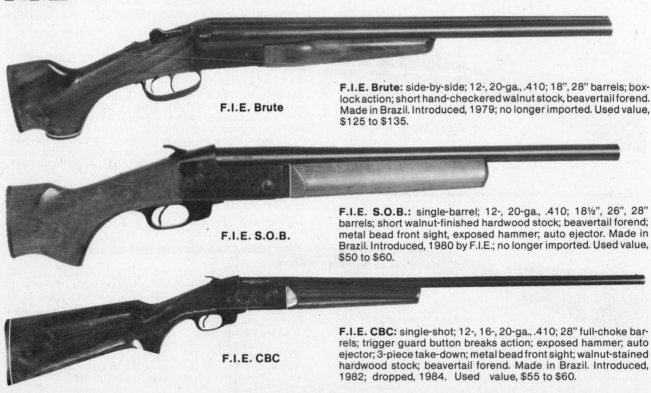

F.I.E. Brute

F.I.E. S.O.B.

F.I.E. CBC

F.I.E. Brute: side-by-side; 12-, 20-ga., .410; 18", 28" barrels; box-lock action; short hand-checkered walnut stock, beavertail forend. Made in Brazil. Introduced, 1979; no longer imported. Used value, $125 to $135.

F.I.E. S.O.B.: single-barrel; 12-, 20-ga., .410; 18½", 26", 28" barrels; short walnut-finished hardwood stock; beavertail forend; metal bead front sight, exposed hammer; auto ejector. Made in Brazil. Introduced, 1980 by F.I.E.; no longer imported. Used value, $50 to $60.

F.I.E. CBC: single-shot; 12-, 16-, 20-ga., .410; 28" full-choke barrels; trigger guard button breaks action; exposed hammer; auto ejector; 3-piece take-down; metal bead front sight; walnut-stained hardwood stock; beavertail forend. Made in Brazil. Introduced, 1982; dropped, 1984, Used value, $55 to $60.

F.I.E. Hamilton & Hunter

F.I.E. Hamilton & Hunter: single-shot; 12-, 20-ga., .410; 3" chambers; 28" barrel; weighs 6½ lb.; metal bead front sight; walnut-stained hardwood stock, beavertail forend; break-button on trigger guard; auto ejector; exposed hammer; three-piece take-down. Made in Brazil. Introduced, 1986; still imported. Used value, $75 to $80.

F.I.E. S.S.S. Model: single-barrel; 12-, 20-ga., .410; 3" chambers; 18½" cylinder barrel; break-button on trigger guard; weighs 6½ lb.; walnut-finished hardwood stock; full beavertail forend; exposed hammer; auto ejectors. Made in Brazil. Introduced, 1986; still imported. Used value, $90 to $95.

FOX

NOTE: 20-gauge versions worth 25% more than prices listed.

Fox Model AE

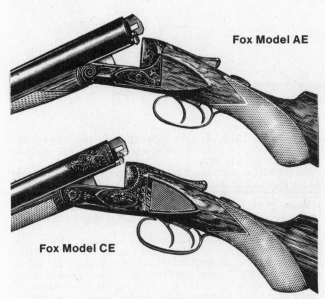

Fox Model CE

Fox Model XE

ing, quality of wood; 12-ga. introduced in 1906; dropped, 1942. With exception of Grade A, all have automatic ejectors. Fox-Kautzky single selective trigger, vent rib were optional at extra cost. Used values: Grade A, $850 to $900; Grade AE, $1100 to $1200; Grade BE, $1250 to $1500; Grade CE, $1850 to $2000; Grade XE, $3500 to $3750; Grade DE, $5750 to $6200; Grade FE, $12,500 to $13,000; add for single selective trigger, $200; add for vent rib, $250; add for beavertail forend, $200.

A.H. Fox 16-ga. has the same specs as 12-ga., except for chambering. Introduced in 1912; dropped, 1941. Used values are generally the same as for 12-ga., depending upon grade, extras, condition; $750 to $12,500.

A.H. Fox 20-ga. is a slightly scaled-down version of the 12-ga., but with same general design. Introduced in 1912; dropped, 1946. Used values generally 30% to 50% higher than for other gauges, dependent upon grade, extras, condition; $900 to $15,000.

FOX A.H. Fox Model: hammerless side-by-side; box-lock action; originally made in 12-ga. only with Damascus barrels with 2⅝" chambers; steel later changed to Chromex fluid steel and chambers extended to 2¾" for smokeless powder loads. Guns were made by Fox until firm was absorbed by Savage about 1930. Difference in grades depends upon workmanship, amount of engrav-

FOX Sterlingworth: side-by-side; hammerless; box-lock action; 12-, 16-, 20-ga.; 26", 28", 30" barrels; any standard choke combo; double triggers, plain extractors standard; automatic ejectors, single selective trigger extra; has the same general specs as earlier A.H. Fox doubles, but these were production-line guns without much handwork; American walnut stock; hand-checkered pistol grip, forearm. Introduced in 1910; dropped, 1947. Used values: $500 to $600; with automatic ejectors, $650 to $700; single selective trigger, $600 to $750; with ejectors and selective trigger, $750 to $800.

Sterlingworth Deluxe model has the same general specs as standard model, except it was also available with 32" barrel; single selective trigger is standard; has Lyman ivory bead sights, recoil pad. Introduced in 1930; dropped, 1946. Used values: $675 to $750; with automatic ejectors, $850 to $900.

Sterlingworth Skeet model has the same general specs as standard model, except for skeet bore only, straight grip stock; 26" or 28" barrels; 12-ga only. Introduced in 1935; dropped, 1946. Used values: $650 to $675; with automatic ejectors, $750 to $800.

Sterlingworth Trap model has the same general specs as standard Sterlingworth, except for trap stock, 32" barrels only; 12-ga.

Fox Sterlingworth Standard

only. Introduced in 1917; dropped, 1946. Used values: $700 to $750; with automatic ejectors, $850 to $950.

Sterlingworth Waterfowl Grade has the same general specs as the standard model, except for heavier frame, automatic ejectors; 12-ga. only. Introduced in 1934; dropped, 1939. Used value, $1250 to $1300.

FOX Single-Barrel Trap Model: box-lock action; 12-ga. only; 30", 32" barrel; automatic ejector; vent rib; American walnut stock and forearm, except Grade M, which had Circassian walnut; hand-checkered pistol grip, forearm; recoil pad optional. Originally made by A.H. Fox, but taken over by Savage about 1930. In 1932 the gun was redesigned, with full pistol-grip stock, Monte Carlo stock. Of Grade M, only 9 were made, giving it collector value. Difference in grades is based upon quality of wood and amount and quality of engraving on receiver. Introduced in 1919; dropped, 1935. Used values: Grade JE, $1250 to $1500; Grade KE, $1750 to $2000; Grade LE, $2750 to $3000; Grade ME, $7000 to $7500.

FOX Super Fox: side-by-side; box-lock action; 12-ga. only; chambered for 3" shells on special order; 30", 32" barrels; full choke only; double triggers; engraved action; American walnut stock; hand-checkered pistol grip, forearm; automatic ejectors. Introduced in 1925; dropped, 1942. Used value, $1200 to $1300.

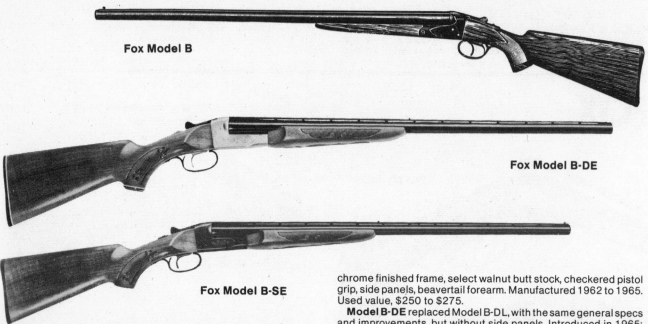

Fox Model B

Fox Model B-DE

Fox Model B-SE

FOX Model B: side-by-side; hammerless; box-lock action; 12-, 16-, 20-ga., .410; 26", 28", 30" barrels; double triggers; plain extractors; modified/full, improved/modified, full/full chokes; double triggers; American walnut stock, forearm; hand-checkered pistol grip, forearm; case-hardened frame. Introduced in 1940; no longer in production. Used value, $225 to $250.

Model B-ST has same specs as Fox Model B, except for nonselective single trigger. Manufactured 1955 to 1966. Used value, $250 to $275.

Model B-DL has same specs as Model B-ST, except for satin-chrome finished frame, select walnut butt stock, checkered pistol grip, side panels, beavertail forearm. Manufactured 1962 to 1965. Used value, $250 to $275.

Model B-DE replaced Model B-DL, with the same general specs and improvements, but without side panels. Introduced in 1965; dropped, 1966. Used value, $245 to $285.

Model B-SE has same specs as Model B, except for single trigger, selective ejectors. Introduced, 1966; dropped, 1987. Used value, $275 to $295.

Model B Lightweight is chambered for 12-, 20-ga., .410; barrels are 24" (12-, 20-ga.) improved/modified, 26" improved/modified, 28" modified/full, 30" modified/full in 12-ga. only; 26" full/full in .410 only; double triggers; select walnut stock; checkered pistol grip, beavertail forearm; vent rib; color case-hardened frame. Introduced in 1973; no longer in production. Used value, $225 to $275.

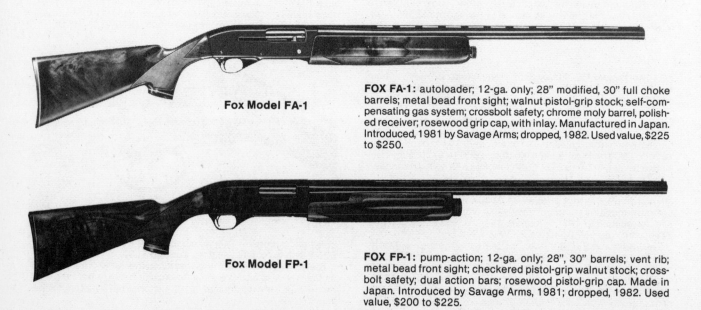

Fox Model FA-1

FOX FA-1: autoloader; 12-ga. only; 28" modified, 30" full choke barrels; metal bead front sight; walnut pistol-grip stock; self-compensating gas system; crossbolt safety; chrome moly barrel, polished receiver; rosewood grip cap, with inlay. Manufactured in Japan. Introduced, 1981 by Savage Arms; dropped, 1982. Used value, $225 to $250.

Fox Model FP-1

FOX FP-1: pump-action; 12-ga. only; 28", 30" barrels; vent rib; metal bead front sight; checkered pistol-grip walnut stock; crossbolt safety; dual action bars; rosewood pistol-grip cap. Made in Japan. Introduced by Savage Arms, 1981; dropped, 1982. Used value, $200 to $225.

FRANCHI

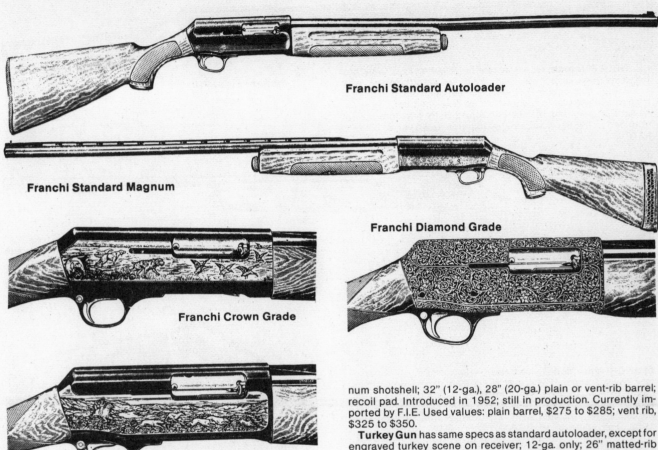

Franchi Standard Autoloader

Franchi Standard Magnum

Franchi Crown Grade

Franchi Diamond Grade

Franchi Imperial Grade

FRANCHI Standard Autoloader: recoil-operated autoloader; 12-, 20-ga.; 26", 28", 30" interchangeable barrels; 5-rd. magazine; plain barrel, solid or vent rib; improved, modified, full chokes; alloy receiver; chrome-lined barrels; simplified take-down; European walnut stock, forearm; pistol grip, forearm hand checkered. Introduced in 1950; still in production. Currently imported by F.I.E. Used values: plain barrel, $250 to $260; solid rib, $275 to $285; vent rib, $300 to $325.

Standard Magnum Autoloader has the same general specs as Standard model, except it is chambered for 12- or 20-ga., 3" magnum shotshell; 32" (12-ga.), 28" (20-ga.) plain or vent-rib barrel; recoil pad. Introduced in 1952; still in production. Currently imported by F.I.E. Used values: plain barrel, $275 to $285; vent rib, $325 to $350.

Turkey Gun has same specs as standard autoloader, except for engraved turkey scene on receiver; 12-ga. only; 26" matted-rib barrel; extra full choke. Manufactured 1963 to 1965. Used value, $350 to $400.

Skeet Model has same specs as standard autoloader except has skeet choke, 26" vent-rib barrel; fancier walnut stock, forearm. Manufactured 1972 to 1974. Used value, $350 to $400.

Crown Grade autoloader has same general specs as standard autoloader, except for hunting scene engraving on the frame. Manufactured 1954 to 1975. Used value, $1250 to $1300.

Diamond Grade autoloader has same specs as standard model, except that scroll engraving is silver inlaid. Manufactured 1954 to 1975. Used value, $1450 to $1600.

Imperial Grade features elaborate engraving, gold-inlaid hunting scene. Manufactured 1954 to 1975. Used value, $1750 to $2000.

Franchi Hunter Model

Franchi Hunter Magnum

FRANCHI Hunter Model Autoloader: recoil-operated autoloader; 12-, 20-ga.; has the same general specs as Standard model autoloader, except for better wood, engraved receiver; ribbed barrel only. Introduced in 1950; still in production. Used values: with hollow matted rib, $300 to $325; vent rib, $350 to $375.

Hunter Magnum has same specs as Hunter model, except is chambered for 12- or 20-ga.; 3" magnum shotshell; has 32" (12-ga.), 28" (20-ga.) vent rib, full choke barrel; recoil pad. Introduced in 1955; still in production. Used value, $350 to $375.

FRANCHI Eldorado: recoil-operated autoloader; 12-, 20-ga.; has the same general specs as Standard model autoloader, but with scroll engraving covering 75% of receiver surfaces; gold-plated trigger; chrome-plated breech bolt; chrome-lined bore; vent rib; select European stock; hand-checkered pistol grip, forearm. Introduced in 1955; no longer in production. Used value, $350 to $375.

Franchi Eldorado

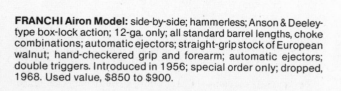

Franchi Slug Gun

FRANCHI Slug Gun: recoil-operated autoloader; 12-, 20-ga.; 22" barrel; alloy receiver; same general specs as Standard autoloader, except for short cylinder-bore barrel; raised gold bead front sight, Lyman folding leaf open rear; 5-rd. magazine; sling swivels. Introduced in 1955; no longer in production. Used value, $300 to $325.

FRANCHI Airon Model: side-by-side; hammerless; Anson & Deeley-type box-lock action; 12-ga. only; all standard barrel lengths, choke combinations; automatic ejectors; straight-grip stock of European walnut; hand-checkered grip and forearm; automatic ejectors; double triggers. Introduced in 1956; special order only; dropped, 1968. Used value, $850 to $900.

Franchi Airon

Franchi Astore S Model

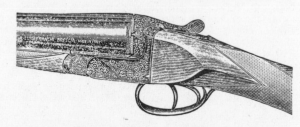

FRANCHI Astore Model: side-by-side; hammerless; Anson & Deeley-type box-lock action; 12-ga. only; all standard barrel lengths, choke combinations; plain extractors; double triggers; straight-grip European walnut stock; hand-checkered stock, forearm. Introduced in 1956; special order only; dropped, 1968. Used value, $700 to $750.

Astore S model has the same specs as standard Astore except for fine engraving on frame. Used value, $1500 to $1750.

Astore II has the same general specs as the Astore S, but is less elaborate; has double triggers, European walnut pistol-grip stock, plain extractors or auto ejectors; 27", 28" barrels, standard chokes. Currently in production. Used value, $925 to $950.

Franchi Condor Grade

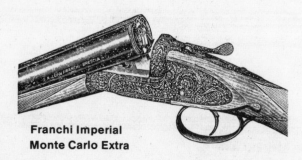

Franchi Imperial Monte Carlo Extra

FRANCHI Custom Sidelock Model: side-by-side; hammerless; 12-, 16-, 20-, 28-ga.; barrel lengths, chokes are to individual customer's requirements; automatic ejectors; hand-detachable locks; straight or pistol-grip stock of European walnut; hand-checkered grip section, forearm; self-opening action, single trigger optional.

Made in six grades; variations depending upon quality of wood, amount of engraving, checkering, overall workmanship. For self-opening action, add $75; for single trigger, add $200. Introduced in 1956, special order only; dropped, 1968. Used values: Condor Grade, $5900 to $6000; Imperial Grade, $8250 to $8500; Imperial S Grade, $8500 to $9000; Imperial Monte Carlo Grade No. 5, $9500 to $10,000; Imperial Monte Carlo Grade No. 11, $11,200 to $11,350; Imperial Monte Carlo Extra, $13,250 to $14,000.

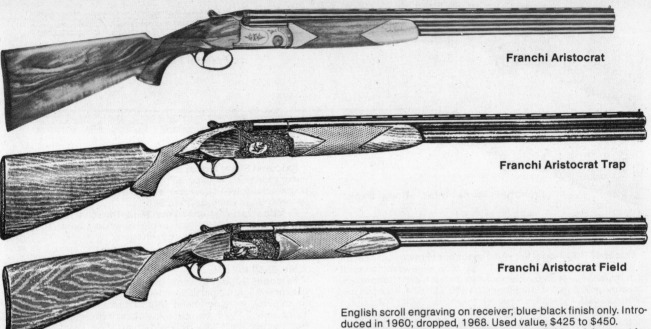

Franchi Aristocrat

Franchi Aristocrat Trap

Franchi Aristocrat Field

FRANCHI Aristocrat Trap Model: over/under; 12-ga. only; 30" barrels; 10mm wide rib; single selective trigger; automatic ejectors; non-auto safety; selected deluxe grade European walnut stock, beavertail forend; hand-checkered pistol grip; chrome-lined barrels are improved modified/full; Monte Carlo comb; color case-hardened receiver. Introduced in 1962; dropped, 1968. Used value, $500 to $550.

Aristocrat Skeet Model has the same specs as trap version, except for 26" barrels choked skeet/skeet, grooved beavertail forearm. Introduced in 1962; dropped, 1968. Used value, $475 to $500.

Aristocrat Field Model has same general design specs as other Aristocrat models, including vent rib; 12-ga. only; barrels are 24", cylinder/improved cylinder, 26" improved/modified, 28" modified/full, 30" modified/full; selective automatic ejectors; automatic safety; hand-checkered Italian walnut pistol-grip stock, forearm.

English scroll engraving on receiver; blue-black finish only. Introduced in 1960; dropped, 1968. Used value, $425 to $450.

Aristocrat Magnum has same specs as field model, except for 3" chambering; full-choke 32" barrels; recoil pad. Manufactured 1962 to 1965. Used value, $400 to $450.

Aristocrat Deluxe Grade has same specs as standard field, skeet or trap models, but with select walnut stock, forearm; heavy relief engraving on receiver, tang and trigger guard. Manufactured 1960 to 1965. Used value, $800 to $850.

Aristocrat Supreme Grade has same specs as Deluxe Grade, except for gold-inlaid game bird figures on receiver. Manufactured 1960 to 1965. Used value, $1100 to $1200.

Aristocrat Imperial Grade was made in field, skeet, trap configurations on a custom basis. Basic specs are the same as for standard models, but wood is top-quality European walnut, with exquisite engraving. Manufactured on individual order 1967 to 1969. Used value, $2000 to $2250.

Aristocrat Monte Carlo Grade has same general specs as Imperial Grade, except that engraving is more elaborate. Manufactured on individual order 1967 to 1969. Used value, $2750 to $3000.

Franchi Silver-King Aristocrat

FRANCHI Silver-King Aristocrat: over/under; 12-ga. only; deluxe version of Aristocrat design; has engraved, bright-finish receiver, selected ultra-deluxe walnut stock, forearm, cut from the same blank for match of grain, color, finish; hand-checkered pistol grip, forearm; vent rib; barrels are 24" cylinder/improved cylinder, 26" improved/modified, 28" modified/full, 30" modified/full; blue-black finish; chrome-lined barrels. Introduced in 1965; dropped, 1968. Used value, $525 to $550.

FRANCHI Dynamic 12: recoil-operated autoloader; 12-ga. only; has the same general specs and options as Franchi Standard model, except for heavy steel receiver, chrome-plated breech bolt and lifter; European walnut stock, forearm; chrome-lined barrel; 5-rd. magazine; trigger-safety-guard-lifter mechanism detachable as single unit; 3-shot plug furnished; plain or vent-rib barrel; also skeet, slug-gun configurations; slug gun has 22" barrel, sights. Introduced in 1965; dropped, 1970. Used values: with plain barrel, $250 to $275; with vent rib, $300 to $325; slug gun, $300 to $315; skeet model, $325 to $350.

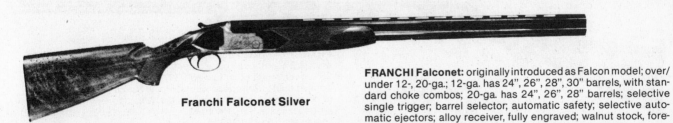

Franchi Falconet Silver

FRANCHI Falconet: originally introduced as Falcon model; over/under 12-, 20-ga.; 12-ga. has 24", 26", 28", 30" barrels, with standard choke combos; 20-ga. has 24", 26", 28" barrels; selective single trigger; barrel selector; automatic safety; selective automatic ejectors; alloy receiver, fully engraved; walnut stock, fore-

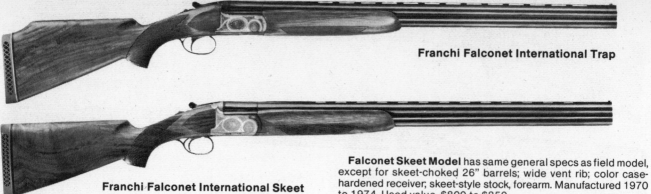

Franchi Falconet International Trap

Franchi Falconet International Skeet

Falconet Skeet Model has same general specs as field model, except for skeet-choked 26" barrels; wide vent rib; color case-hardened receiver; skeet-style stock, forearm. Manufactured 1970 to 1974. Used value, $800 to $850.
Falconet International Skeet Model has same specs as skeet model except for better finish, improved wood. Manufactured 1970 to 1974. Used value, $850 to $900.

arm; checkered pistol grip, forearm; epoxy finish. Introduced in 1969; no longer in production. Used value, $450 to $500.

Falconet Trap Model has same specs as field model, except for modified/full choke 30" barrel; 12-ga. only; wide vent rib; color case-hardened receiver; checkered trap-style Monte Carlo stock, forearm; recoil pad. Manufactured 1970 to 1974. Used value, $800 to $850.
Falconet International Trap Model has same specs as trap model except for better finish, improved wood; choice of straight stock or Monte Carlo style. Manufactured 1970 to 1974. Used

value, $850 to $875.
Falconet Super has same general specs as Diamond Grade, except has lightweight alloy receiver; single selective trigger; barrel selector on trigger; hand-engraved receiver; rubber butt pad; 12-ga. only; 27", 28" barrels; translucent front sight. Made in Italy. Reintroduced by F.I.E., 1982; dropped, 1986. Used value, $750 to $775.

FRANCHI Peregrin Model 400: over/under double; 12-ga.; 26½", 28" barrels; standard choke combos; steel receiver; auto ejectors; selective single trigger; checkered European walnut pistol-grip stock, forearm. Introduced 1975; still in production, no longer

imported. Used value, $550 to $600.
Peregrin Model 451 has same general specs as Model 400, except for alloy receiver. Introduced, 1975; still in production, no longer imported. Used value, $500 to $550.

FRANCHI Model 2003 Trap: over/under double; 12-ga.; 30", 32" barrels, bored modified/full, full/full; high vent rib; box-lock action; single selective trigger; auto ejectors; checkered European walnut straight or Monte Carlo stock, beavertail forearm; recoil pad; marketed with carrying case. Introduced, 1976; dropped, 1982. Used value, $900 to $950.

Model 2004 single-barrel trap has same specs as Model 2003, except for 32", 34" full-choke single barrel. Introduced, 1976; dropped, 1982. Used value, $900 to $1000.
Model 2005 Trap Set incorporates over/under barrels of Model 2004, single barrel of Model 2004 as interchangeable set. Introduced, 1976; dropped, 1982. Used value, $1400 to $1500.

Franchi Model 530

luxe, except for quality of wood, better engraving, gold inlays in receiver. Introduced, 1977; still in production, no longer imported. Used value, $700 to $750.
Model 530: autoloader; 12-, 20-, 28-ga.; 5-rd. magazine; 2¾" or 3" chamber; 30" barrel; interchangeable choke tubes; vent rib; oil-finished, hand-checkered straight or Monte Carlo French walnut stock with comb; interchangeable stock drilled, tapped for recoil reducer; specially tuned gas system; target-grade trigger; chrome-lined bore, chamber; matte blue finish. Introduced 1978; dropped, 1982. Used value, $450 to $475.

FRANCHI Model 500: autoloader; 12-ga.; 4-rd. magazine; gas operated; 26", 28" barrels, vent rib, any standard choke; checkered European walnut pistol-grip stock. Introduced, 1976; still in production, no longer imported. Used value, $275 to $295.
Model 520 Deluxe has same specs as Model 500, but with engraved receiver, better finish, wood. Introduced, 1976; still in production, no longer imported. Used value, $325 to $345.
Model 520 Eldorado Gold has same specs as Model 520 De-

FRANCHI Imperiale Monte Carlo Extra: side-by-side; 12-ga. only; Holland & Holland-type action; barrel length, choking to customer specs; walnut root custom stock; single or double triggers;

auto hammer ejectors; chrome-lined barrels. Custom-built gun made in Italy. Introduced, 1977 by Stoeger; no longer offered. Used value, $13,500 to $14,500.

FRANCHI 3000/2: over/under; has same specs as Model 2005, except has 30", 32" over and 32" or 34" under barrel, 3 inter-

changeable choke tubes. Marketed with fitted case. No longer imported. Used value, $2000 to $2250.

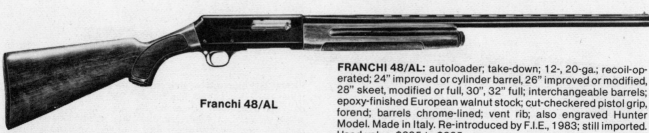

Franchi 48/AL

FRANCHI 48/AL: autoloader; take-down; 12-, 20-ga.; recoil-operated; 24" improved or cylinder barrel, 26" improved or modified, 28" skeet, modified or full, 30", 32" full; interchangeable barrels; epoxy-finished European walnut stock; cut-checkered pistol grip, forend; barrels chrome-lined; vent rib; also engraved Hunter Model. Made in Italy. Re-introduced by F.I.E., 1983; still imported. Used value, $295 to $325.

FRANCHI Alcione Super Deluxe: over/under; 12-ga.; 27" improved/modified, 28" modified/full barrels; similar to Falconet Super, except has better engraving, silvered receiver, gold-plated trigger; ivory bead front sight; gold-inlaid receiver; marketed in fitted case. Made in Italy. Re-introduced by F.I.E., 1982; still imported. Used value, $1200 to $1300.

FRANCHI Diamond Grade: over/under; 12-ga.; 2¾" chamber; 28" modified/full barrel; French walnut stock; cut-checkered pistol grip, forend; top tang safety; single selective trigger; auto ejectors; chrome-plated bores; silvered receiver; decorative scroll engraving. Made in Italy. Re-introduced by F.I.E., 1982; still imported. Used value, $600 to $625.

Franchi PG-80 Prestige

FRANCHI PG-80 Prestige: autoloader; gas-operated; 12-ga.; 2¾", 3" chamber; 24", 26", 28", 30", 32" barrel lengths; all standard

chokes; weighs 7 lb. 6 oz.; oil-finished, checkered European walnut stock; blued receiver; 7mm vent rib; stainless steel gas piston. Made in Italy. Introduced, 1985; still imported by F.I.E. Used value, $350 to $375.

PG-80 Elite has same specs as Prestige, except has engraved receiver. Introduced, 1985; still imported. Used value, $375 to $400.

FRANCOTTE

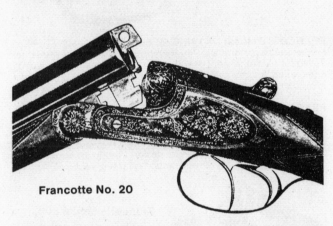

Francotte No. 20

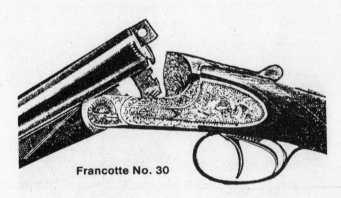

Francotte No. 30

FRANCOTTE A&F Series: side-by-side; Anson & Deeley-type box-lock action; 12-, 16-, 20-, 28-ga., .410; in 12-ga., 26" to 32" barrels; 26" to 28" in other gauges; any desired choke combo; crossbolt; side plates on all models except Knockabout; double triggers; automatic ejectors; series was made in seven grades for distribution exclusively in this country by Abercrombie & Fitch; grades varied only in overall quality, grade of wood, checkering and engraving. Introduced prior to WWII, dropped in 1960s. Used values: Knockabout Model, $1250 to $1300; Jubilee Model, $1450 to $1500; No. 14, $1800 to $1900; No. 18, $2000 to $2200; No. 20, $2250 to $2500; No. 25, $2500 to $2750; No. 30, $4000 to $4500; No. 45 Eagle Grade, $2750 to $3000.

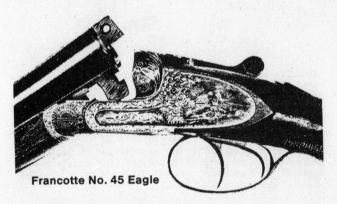

Francotte No. 45 Eagle

Francotte Model 6886

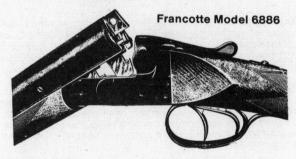

Francotte Model 8446

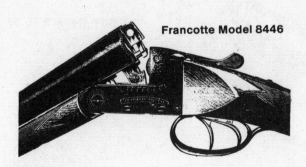

FRANCOTTE Model 6886: side-by-side; Anson & Deeley box-lock action; 12-, 16-, 20-, 28-ga., .410; all standard barrel lengths, choke combinations available; automatic ejectors; double triggers; hand-checkered European walnut stock, forearm; straight or pistol-grip design. Manufactured before World War II. Used value, $2250 to $2500.

FRANCOTTE Model 8446: side-by-side; Greener crossbolt; side clips; general specs are the same as Model 6886 except for finish, better construction. Manufactured before World War II. Used value, $2750 to $3000.

FRANCOTTE Model 6930: side-by-side; square crossbolt; Anson & Deeley box-lock action; 12-, 16-, 20-, 28-ga., .410; all standard barrel lengths, choke combos; automatic ejectors; double trig- gers; hand-checkered European walnut stock, forearm; straight or pistol-grip design. Manufactured before World War II. Used value, $2350 to $2500.

FRANCOTTE Model 4996: side-by-side; Anson & Deeley box-lock action; side clips; has the same general specs as Model 8446, except for minor variations in finish, checkering. Manufactured before World War II. Used value, $2750 to $3000.

FRANCOTTE Model 8457; side-by-side; Anson & Deeley box-lock action; 12-, 16-, 20-, 28-ga., .410; all standard barrel lengths, choke combos; Greener-Scott crossbolt; other specs are the same as those of Model 4996 except for better finish, checkering. Manufactured before World War II. Used value, $3000 to $3250.

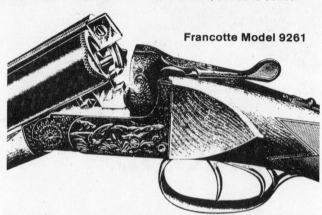

Francotte Model 9261

FRANCOTTE Model 9261: side-by-side; Anson & Deeley box-lock action; Greener crossbolt; other specs are the same as Model 8457. Manufactured before World War II. Used value, $2350 to $2500.

FRANCOTTE Model 11/18E: side-by-side; Anson & Deeley box-lock action; side clips; Purdey-type bolt; other specs are the same as those of Model 9261. Manufactured before World War II. Used value, $3000 to $3250.

FRANCOTTE Model 10/18E/628: side-by-side; Anson & Deeley box-lock action; side clips; Purdey-type bolt; other specs are same as Model 11/18E except overall quality is better, including wood, checkering, engraving, finish. Introduced before World War II; still in production. No current importer. Used value, $3000 to $3250.

FRANCOTTE Model 10594: side-by-side; Anson & Deeley box-lock action; side plates; 12-, 16-, 20-, 28-ga., .410; all standard barrel lengths, choke combos; reinforced frame, side clips; Purdey-type bolt; automatic ejectors; hand-checkered European walnut stock; straight or pistol-grip design. Introduced about 1950; still in production; no current importer. Used value, $2750 to $3000.

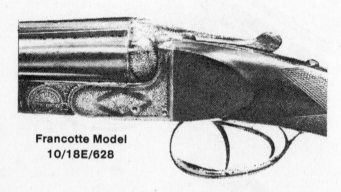

Francotte Model
10/18E/628

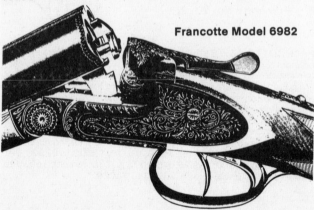

Francotte Model 6982

FRANCOTTE Model 8455: side-by-side; Anson & Deeley box-lock action; has the same specs as 10594 except for style of engraving. Greener crossbolt. Introduced about 1950; still in pro- duction; no current importer. Used value, $3125 to $3175.

FRANCOTTE Model 6982: side-by-side; Anson & Deeley box-lock action; has the same specs as Model 10594, except for style of engraving. Introduced about 1950; still in production; no current importer. Used value, $3125 to $3175.

FRANCOTTE Model 9/40E/38321: side-by-side; Anson & Deeley box-lock action; has the same general specs as Model 6982, ex- cept for better quality, fine English engraving. Introduced about 1950; still in production; no current importer. Used value, $4050 to $4150.

FRANCOTTE Model 120.HE/328: side-by-side; side-lock; auto- matic ejectors; double triggers; made in all standard gauges; chokes, barrel lengths to customer's order; hand-checkered European walnut stock, forearm; straight or pistol-grip design. Introduced about 1950; still in production; no current importer. Used value, $8100 to $8250.

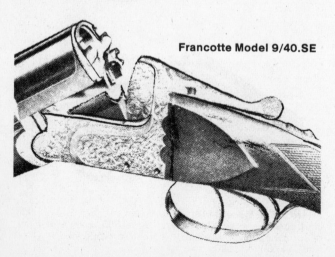

Francotte Model 9/40.SE

FRANCOTTE Model 9/40.SE: over/under, Anson & Deeley box-lock action; 12-, 16-, 20-, 28-ga., .410; all standard barrel lengths, choke combos; automatic ejectors; double triggers; hand-check- ered European walnut stock, forearm; straight or pistol-grip design; elaborate engraving. Introduced about 1950; still in production; no current importer. Used value, $8700 to $8850.

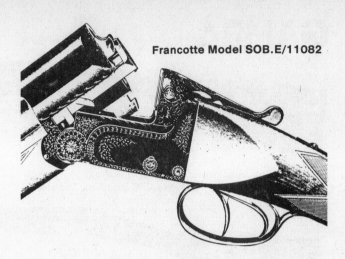

Francotte Model SOB.E/11082

FRANCOTTE Model SOB.E/11082: over/under; Anson & Deeley box-lock action; same general specs as Model 9/40SE, but not as profusely engraved. Introduced about 1950; no current importer. Used value, $6350 to $6500.

GALEF

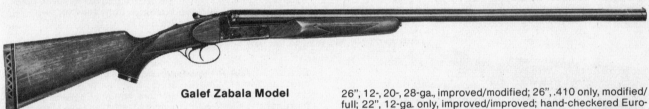

Galef Zabala Model

GALEF/ZABALA: double; 10-, 12-, 16-, 20-, 28-ga., .410; Anson & Deeley-type box-lock action; barrels, 32", 10-, 12-ga. only, full/full; 30". 12-ga. only, modified/full; 28", all except .410, modified/full; 26", 12-, 20-, 28-ga., improved/modified; 26", .410 only, modified/full; 22", 12-ga. only, improved/improved; hand-checkered European walnut stock; beavertail forearm; recoil pad; automatic safety, plain extractors. Imported from Spain; still in production; no current importer. Used values: 10-ga., $250 to $275; other gauges, $175 to $200.

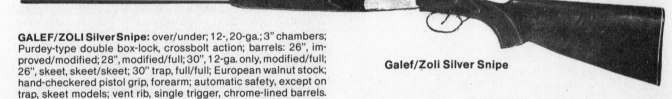

Galef/Zoli Silver Snipe

GALEF/ZOLI Silver Snipe: over/under; 12-, 20-ga.; 3" chambers; Purdey-type double box-lock, crossbolt action; barrels: 26", improved/modified; 28", modified/full; 30", 12-ga. only, modified/full; 26", skeet, skeet/skeet; 30" trap, full/full; European walnut stock; hand-checkered pistol grip, forearm; automatic safety, except on trap, skeet models; vent rib, single trigger, chrome-lined barrels. Manufactured in Italy. No longer imported. Used values: field model, $300 to $325; trap, skeet models, $350 to $400.

    Golden Snipe over/under has the same specs as Silver Snipe, except for automatic selective ejectors. No longer imported. Used values: field model, $425 to $450; trap, skeet, $450 to $475.

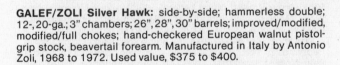

Galef/Zoli Silver Hawk

GALEF/ZOLI Silver Hawk: side-by-side; hammerless double; 12-, 20-ga.; 3" chambers; 26", 28", 30" barrels; improved/modified, modified/full chokes; hand-checkered European walnut pistol-grip stock, beavertail forearm. Manufactured in Italy by Antonio Zoli, 1968 to 1972. Used value, $375 to $400.

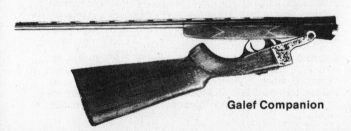

Galef Companion

GALEF Companion: single-shot; 12-magnum, 16-, 20-magnum, 28-ga., .410; 26", 28", 30" barrel lengths; has special folding feature; hammerless design; European walnut pistol-grip stock, forearm; plain or vent rib. Manufactured in Italy. Introduced, 1968; no longer imported. Used value, $100 to $110.

GALEF Monte Carlo Trap: single-shot; 12-ga. only; 32" barrel; full choke; vent rib; hammerless underlever design; plain extractor; checkered European walnut pistol-grip stock, beavertail forearm; recoil pad. Manufactured in Italy. Introduced, 1968; no longer imported. Used value, $200 to $225.

GAMBA

Gamba Edinburgh

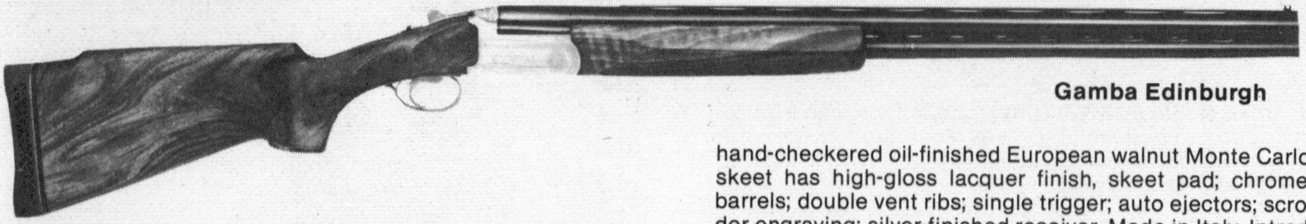

GAMBA Edinburgh: over/under; 26½" skeet barrels, 30", 32" trap, 32", 34" mono trap; 12-ga. only, 2¾" chambers; trap stock is

hand-checkered oil-finished European walnut Monte Carlo type, skeet has high-gloss lacquer finish, skeet pad; chrome-lined barrels; double vent ribs; single trigger; auto ejectors; scroll border engraving; silver-finished receiver. Made in Italy. Introduced, 1980 by Steyr Daimler Puch; no longer imported. Used value, $1200 to $1300.

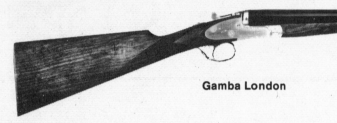
Gamba London

S.A.B. GAMBA London Model: side-by-side; 12-, 20-ga; 2¾" chambers; 26¾", 27½" barrels; weighs 6¾ lb.; straight English-style root walnut stock; checkered butt; Holland & Holland-type silvered receiver, side plates; fine English-type scroll, rosette engraving. Made in Italy. Originally marketed by Renato Gamba. Introduced, 1981; importation dropped. Reintroduced, 1987; importation by Armes de Chasse dropped, 1987. Used value, $4300 to $4450.

S.A.B. GAMBA Hunter Super: side-by-side; 12-ga. only; 2¾" chambers; 26¾" modified/full, 28" improved/modified barrels; weighs 6¾ lb.; checkered European walnut stock; box-lock action;

double triggers; extractors; silvered, engraved receiver. Made in Italy. Introduced, 1987, importation by Armes de Chasse dropped, 1987. Used value, $850 to $925.

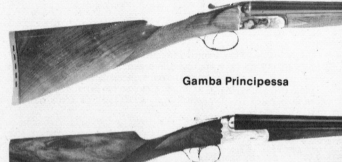
Gamba Principessa

S.A.B. GAMBA Principessa: side-by-side; has same general specs as Hunter Super, except is 12-, 20-ga. only; 2¾" chambers; double, single trigger; auto ejectors; straight English-style stock; fine English-style scroll engraving; silvered receiver. Made in Italy. Originally marketed by Renato Gamba. Introduced, 1981; importation dropped. Reintroduced, 1987; importation by Armes de Chasse dropped, 1987. Used value, $1100 to $1200.

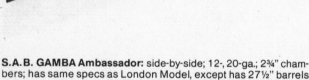
Gamba Oxford

S.A.B. GAMBA Oxford 90: side-by-side; has same general specs as the Hunter Super model, except has dummy side plates; choice of straight English or pistol-grip stock of root walnut; better grade of engraving; double or single trigger; auto ejectors; 26¾", 27½" barrels. Made in Italy. Originally marketed by Renato Gamba. Introduced, 1981; importation dropped. Reintroduced, 1987; importation by Armes de Chasse dropped, 1987. Used value, $1450 to $1550.

S.A.B. GAMBA LS 2000: over/under; folding design; 12-, 20-, 28-ga.; .410; 27½" modified/full barrels; weighs 6¼ lb.; European walnut stock; chromed box-lock action; single trigger; extractors; game scene engraving. Made in Italy. Introduced, 1987; importation by Armes de Chasse dropped, 1987. Used value, $450 to $475.

S.A.B. GAMBA Ambassador: side-by-side; 12-, 20-ga.; 2¾" chambers; has same specs as London Model, except has 27½" barrels choked to customer's specs; double or single trigger; Holland & Holland-type side locks; inlaid gold shield in forend; blued barrels, action. Made in Italy. Introduced, 1987; importation by Armes de Chasse dropped, 1987. Used value, $11,000 to $11,800.

Ambassador Executive has same specs as Ambassador model, except is custom built to customer's specs; has better wood, extensive signed engraving. Made in Italy. Introduced, 1987; importation by Armes de Chasse dropped, 1987. Used value, $17,200 to $18,200.

S.A.B. GAMBA Grifone: over/under; 12-ga.; 2¾" chambers; 26¾" improved cylinder/modified, modified/full barrels; weighs 7 lb.; checkered European walnut stock; box-lock action; double or single triggers; auto ejectors; silvered receiver; engraved game, floral scenes. Made in Italy. Introduced, 1987; importation by Armes de Chasse dropped, 1987. Used values: double triggers, $675 to $725; single trigger, $725 to $775.

S.A.B. GAMBA Europe 2000: over/under; has the same general specs as the Grifone model, except has dummy side plates; floral, English engraving patterns; anti-recoil butt plate; oil-finished, select walnut stock. Made in Italy. Introduced, 1987; importation by Armes de Chasse dropped, 1987. Used value, $1100 to $1200.

S.A.B. GAMBA Victory Trap: over/under; 12-ga.; 2¾" chambers; 29" modified/full barrels; weighs 7¾ lb.; removable rubber recoil pad; stippled European walnut stock; box-lock action; auto ejectors; single trigger; blued receiver; light engraving; gold name plate. Made in Italy. Introduced, 1987; importation by Armes de Chasse dropped, 1987. Used value, $1375 to $1475.

Victory Skeet Model has same specs as Victory Trap, except has 27" skeet/skeet barrels, recessed chokes, skeet-dimension stock. Introduced, 1987; no longer imported. Used value, $1375 to $1475.

Model Grinta Trap/Skeet has the same specs as Victory models, except has no engraving. Introduced, 1987; no longer imported. Used value, $1250 to $1325.

S.A.B. GAMBA Milano 3: single-shot; 12-, 16-, 20-, 28-, 32-ga., .410; 27½" full choke barrel; weighs 5¾ lb.; checkered European hardwood stock; chromed, photo-engraved receiver; folds for storage, transport; vent rib. Made in Italy. Introduced, 1987; importation by Armes de Chasse dropped, 1987. Used value, $260 to $280.

GARBI

GARBI Model 71: side-by-side; 12-, 16-, 20-ga.; 26", 28" barrels; straight-grip European walnut stock; checkered butt; classic forend; side-lock action; auto ejectors; double triggers; color case-hardened action. Made in Spain. Introduced, 1980; still imported by Wm. Larkin Moore. Used value, $1250 to $1500.

Garbi Model 71

GARBI Model 51A: side-by-side, 12-ga.; 2¾" chambers; 28" modified/full barrels; European walnut stock; box-lock action; hand-checkered pistol grip, forend; double triggers; extractors; hand-engraved receiver. Made in Spain. Introduced, 1980; no longer imported by L. Joseph Rahn. Used value, $350 to $375.

Model 51B has same specs as Model 51A, except has automatic ejectors; 12-, 16-, 20-ga. Introduced, 1980; still imported. Used value, $550 to $600.

GARBI Model 60A: side-by-side; 12-ga.; 2¾" chambers; 26", 28", 30" barrels; custom chokes; select European walnut custom stock; side-lock action; hand-checkered pistol grip, forend; double triggers; extractors; scroll-engraved receiver. Made in Spain. Introduced, 1981; still imported by L. Joseph Rahn. Used value, $550 to $575.

Model 60B has same specs as 60A, except has demi-block

barrels, ejectors; 12-, 16-, 20-ga. Introduced, 1981; still imported. Used value, $750 to $800.

GARBI Model 62A: side-by-side; same general design as Model 60A, except has plain receiver with engraved border; modified/full chokes; demi-block barrels; gas exhaust valves; extractors; jointed triggers. Made in Spain. Introduced, 1981; still imported by L. Joseph Rahn. Used value, $525 to $550.

Model 62B has same design as 62A, except has ejectors; 12-, 16-, 20-ga. Introduced, 1982; still imported. Used value, $750 to $800.

GARBI Model 110: side-by-side; 12-, 20-, 28-ga.; side-lock action; barrel lengths, chokes, stocks to custom order. Made in Spain. Introduced, 1982 by Toledo Armas; dropped, 1984. Used value, $1800 to $1900.

Garbi Model 100

GARBI Model 100: side-by-side; 12-, 16-, 20-, 28-ga.; 26", 28" custom-choked barrels; straight-grip European walnut stock, classic forend; checkered butt; side-lock action; double triggers; auto ejectors; color case-hardened action; numerous options. Made in Spain. Introduced, 1986; still imported by Wm. Larkin Moore, L. Joseph Rahn. Used value, $1800 to $2000, depending on options.

GARBI Model 101: side-by-side; 12-, 16-, 20-, 28-ga.; has same specs as Model 70, except has optional file-cut Churchill or vent top rib; Continental-style floral, scroll engraving; select European walnut stock; 12-ga. pigeon or wildfowl designs available; better quality than Model 71. Made in Spain. Introduced, 1982; still imported by Wm. Larkin Moore, L. Joseph Rahn. Used value, $2250 to $2500.

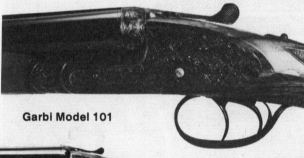

Garbi Model 101

GARBI Model 102: side-by-side; 12-, 16-, 20-ga.; 25" to 30" barrels; standard chokes as specified; select European walnut stock; Holland side-lock ejector; chopper lump barrels; scroll engraving;

hinged double triggers; non-selective single trigger optional; other options. Made in Spain. Introduced, 1982; still imported by Wm. Larkin Moore, L. Joseph Rahn. Used value, $2000 to $2150.

Garbi Model 102

GARBI Model 103A: side-by-side; 12-, 16-, 20-ga.; same general design as Model 71, except has Purdey-type scroll, rosette engraving; better overall quality. Made in Spain. Introduced, 1982; still imported by Wm. Larkin Moore, L. Joseph Rahn. Used value, $2500 to $2750.

Model 103B has same specs as 103A, except has nickel-chrome steel barrels, Holland & Holland-type opening mechanism. Introduced, 1982; still imported. Used values, $3500 to $3750.

GARBI Model 200: side-by-side; 12-, 16-, 20-, 28-ga.; has same design as Model 71, except barrels are nickel-chrome steel; heavy-duty locks; Continental-style floral, scroll engraving; finely figured European walnut stock. Made in Spain. Introduced, 1982; still imported by Wm. Larkin Moore, L. Joseph Rahn. Used value, $3500 to $3800.

GARBI Special Model: side-by-side; 12-, 16-, 20-, 28-ga.; same general specs as Model 71; has better metal work, wood; game

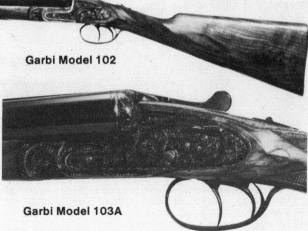

Garbi Model 103A

scene engraved in receiver; some with gold inlays; fancy European walnut stock. Made in Spain. Introduced, 1982; still imported by Wm. Larkin Moore. Used value, $3500 to $3800.

GREENER

GREENER Jubilee Model: Grade DH35; side-by-side; box-lock action; hammerless; 12-, 16-, 20-ga.; 26", 28", 30" barrels; any choke combo; double triggers; nonselective or selective single trigger at added cost; automatic ejectors; hand-checkered European walnut straight or pistol-grip stock, forearm; engraved action. Introduced in 1875; dropped, 1965. Used value, $2000 to $2250.

Sovereign Model, Grade DH40, has the same specs as Jubilee model except for better overall quality, better wood, checkering, engraving. Used value, $2250 to $2500.

Crown Model, Grade DH75 is top of the line for Greener hammerless ejector double style, with same general specs as others, but with top-quality workmanship, including checkering, engraving and figured walnut in stock, forearm. Used value, $3000 to $3250.

Note: on all variations, add $175 for nonselective single trigger; $350 for selective trigger.

GREENER Far-Killer Model: side-by-side; hammerless; box-lock action; 12-, 10-, 8-ga.; 28", 30", 32" barrels; any desired choke combination; nonejectors; automatic ejectors at added cost; hand-checkered European walnut straight or half-pistol-grip stock. Introduced about 1895; dropped, 1962. Used values: 12-ga. nonejector model, $1750 to $2000; with ejectors, $2500 to $2750; 8-, 10-ga., nonejector, $2000 to $2250; with ejectors, $2750 to $3000.

Greener Far-Killer Model

Greener Empire Model

GREENER Empire Model: side-by-side; hammerless; box-lock action; 12-ga. only; 28", 30", 32" barrels; any choke combo; hand-checkered European walnut straight or half-pistol-grip stock, forearm; nonejector; ejectors at additional cost. Introduced about 1893; dropped, 1962. Used values: nonejector model, $1000 to $1250; ejector model, $1300 to $1500.

Empire Deluxe Grade has same general specs as standard Empire model except has deluxe finish and better craftsmanship. Used values: nonejector model, $1350 to $1450; ejector model, $1550 to $1650.

GREENER General Purpose: single-shot; Martini-type action; take-down; 12-ga. only; 26", 30", 32" barrel; modified, full choke; ejector; hand-checkered European walnut straight-grip stock, forearm. Introduced in 1910; dropped, 1964. Used value, $275 to $300.

GREIFELT

GREIFELT Grade No. 1: over/under; Anson & Deeley box-lock action; 12-, 16-, 20-, 28-ga., .410; 26", 28", 30", 32" barrels; automatic ejectors; any desired choke combo; solid matted rib standard; vent rib at added cost; hand-checkered European walnut straight or pistol-grip stock, Purdey-type forearm; double triggers standard; single trigger at added cost; elaborate engraving. Manufactured in Germany prior to World War II. Used values: solid matted rib, $2750 to $3000; with vent rib, $3450 to $3650. Add $350 for single trigger.

Over/Under Combo Model has same design as Greifelt over/under shotguns; 12-, 16-, 20-, 28-ga., .410, any standard rifle caliber; 24", 26" barrels; folding rear sight; matted rib; auto or non-auto ejectors. Manufactured prior to World War II. Used values: auto ejectors, $4800 to $5000; non-auto ejectors, $4100 to $4250; obsolete rifle chamberings and 16-ga. worth less.

GREIFELT Grade No. 3: over/under; Anson & Deeley box-lock action; 12-, 16-, 20-, 28-ga., .410; same general specs as Grade No. 1 but engraving is less elaborate, wood has less figure. Manufactured prior to World War II. Used values: solid matted rib, $2250 to $2500; vent rib, $2800 to $2900; add $350 for single trigger.

GREIFELT Model 22: side-by-side; Anson & Deeley box-lock action; side plates; 12-, 16-ga.; 28", 30" barrels; modified/full choke only; plain extractors; double triggers; hand-checkered stock, forearm; pistol-grip, cheekpiece or straight English style. Introduced about 1950; still in production; no current importer. Used value, $1250 to $1500.

Model 22E has the same specs as standard Model 22 except for addition of automatic ejectors. Introduced about 1950; still in production; no current importer. Used value, $1750 to $2000.

GREIFELT Model 103: side-by-side; hammerless; Anson & Deeley box-lock action; 12-, 16-ga.; 28", 30" barrels, modified/full chokes;

Greifelt Grade No. 1

plain extractors; double triggers; hand-checkered European walnut stock, forearm; pistol-grip, cheekpiece or straight English style. Introduced about 1950; still in production; no current importer. Used value, $1250 to $1500.

Model 103E has same specs as Model 103 except for addition of automatic ejectors. Introduced about 1950; still in production; no current importer. Used value, $1400 to $1600.

GREIFELT Model 143E: over/under; Anson & Deeley box-lock action; 12-, 16-, 20-ga.; 26", 28", 30" barrels; has the same general design specs as the Pre-WWII Grade No. 1, but workmanship is of lower quality. Introduced about 1950; still in production; no current importer. Used values: with raised matted rib, double triggers, $1500 to $1600; vent rib, single selective trigger, $1750 to $1800.

HARRINGTON & RICHARDSON

H&R No. 3

HARRINGTON & RICHARDSON No. 3: single-barrel, hammerless; take-down; 12-, 16-, 20-ga., .410; 26", 28", 30", 32" barrels; automatic ejector; bead front sight; uncheckered American walnut pistol-grip stock, forearm; full choke only; top-lever break-open action. Introduced in 1908; dropped, 1942. Used value, $65 to $75.

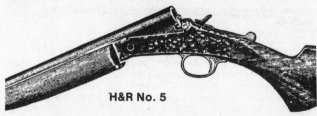

H&R No. 5

HARRINGTON & RICHARDSON No. 5: single-barrel, hammer model; take-down; lightweight configuration; 20-, 28-ga., .410; 26", 28" barrels; full choke only; automatic ejector; uncheckered American walnut pistol-grip stock, forearm; top-lever, break-open action; bead front sight. Introduced in 1908; dropped, 1942. Used value, $65 to $75.

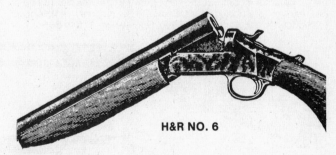

H&R NO. 6

HARRINGTON & RICHARDSON No. 6: single-barrel, hammer model; take-down; heavy breech; 10-, 12-, 16-, 20-ga.; 28", 30", 32", 34", 36" barrels; automatic ejector; uncheckered American walnut pistol-grip stock, forearm; bead front sight; top-lever, break-open action. Same basic design as No. 5 model except for heavier breech, gauges, barrel lengths. Introduced in 1908; dropped, 1942. Used value, $75 to $85.

HARRINGTON & RICHARDSON No. 8: single-barrel, hammer model; take-down; 12-, 16-, 20-, 28-ga., .410; 26", 28", 30", 32" barrels; full choke only; automatic ejector; uncheckered American walnut pistol-grip stock, forearm; bead front sight; same general design as Model 6 except for different forearm design, gauges, et al. Introduced in 1908; dropped, 1942. Used value, $75 to $85.

H&R NO. 8

H&R Bay State No. 7

HARRINGTON & RICHARDSON Bay State No. 7: also known as Model No. 9; single-barrel, hammer model; take-down; 12-, 16-, 20-ga., .410; 26", 28", 30", 32" barrels; full choke only; bead front sight; uncheckered American walnut pistol-grip stock, forearm; same specs as No. 8, except for fuller pistol grip, slimmer forearm. Introduced in 1908; dropped, 1942. Used value, $75 to $85.

H&R Folding Model

HARRINGTON & RICHARDSON Folding Model: single-barrel, hammer model; gun is hinged at front of frame so barrel folds against stock for storage, transport; full choke only; Light Frame version is 22" barrel only, 28-ga., .410; Heavy Frame is in 12-, 16-, 20-, 28-ga., .410; 26" barrel; bead front sight, checkered pistol-grip stock, forearm. Introduced about 1910; dropped, 1942. Used value, $100 to $125.

HARRINGTON & RICHARDSON No. 48 Topper: single-barrel, hammer model; take-down; 12-, 16-, 20-ga., .410; 26", 28", 30", 32" barrels; modified or full choke; automatic ejector; top-lever, break-open action; specs similar to those of Model 8. Introduced in 1946; dropped, 1957. Used value, $75 to $85.

   Model 488 Topper Deluxe has same specs as No. 48 Topper, except for black lacquered stock, forearm, recoil pad, chrome-plated frame. Introduced in 1946; dropped, 1957. Used value, $75 to $85.

H&R No. 48 Topper

HARRINGTON & RICHARDSON Model 148 Topper: single-barrel, hammer model; take-down; improved version of No. 48; 12-, 16-, 20-ga., .410; in 12-ga. barrels are 30", 32" or 36"; in 16-ga, barrels are 28" or 30"; in 20'ga., .410, barrels are 28"; full choke only; side lever; uncheckered American walnut pistol-grip stock, forearm; recoil pad. Introduced in 1958; dropped, 1961. Used

value, $75 to $85.

   Model 188 Deluxe Topper has the same specs as Model 148, except is .410 only; chrome-plated frame; stock, forearm finished with black, red, yellow, blue, green, pink or purple lacquer. Introduced in 1958; dropped, 1961. Used value, $75 to $80.

HARRINGTON & RICHARDSON Model 480 Jr. Topper: single-barrel, hammer model; has the same general specs as No. 48 Topper, except for shorter youth stock; 26" barrel only; .410 only. Introduced in 1958; dropped, 1960. Used value, $75 to $85.

   Model 580 Jr. Topper has the same specs as Model 480, except for variety of colored stock as with Model 188 Deluxe Topper. Introduced in 1958; dropped, 1961. Used value, $90 to $100.

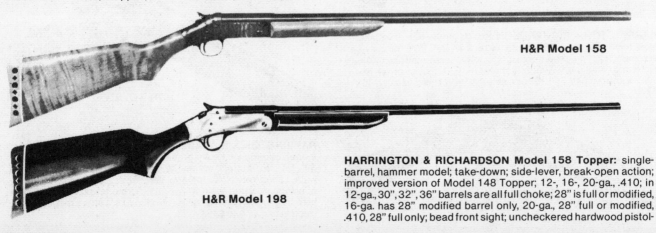

H&R Model 158

H&R Model 198

HARRINGTON & RICHARDSON Model 158 Topper: single-barrel, hammer model; take-down; side-lever, break-open action; improved version of Model 148 Topper; 12-, 16-, 20-ga., .410; in 12-ga., 30", 32", 36" barrels are all full choke; 28" is full or modified, 16-ga. has 28" modified barrel only, 20-ga., 28" full or modified, .410, 28" full only; bead front sight; uncheckered hardwood pistol-

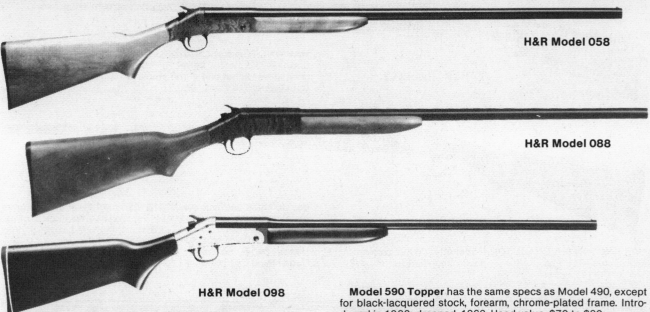

H&R Model 058

H&R Model 088

H&R Model 098

grip stock, forearm; recoil pad. Introduced in 1962; dropped, 1985. Used value, $75 to $85.

Model 198 Topper Deluxe has the same specs as Model 158, except for black-lacquered stock, forearm; chrome-plated frame; in 20-ga., .410 only. Introduced in 1962; dropped, 1985. Used value, $85 to $100.

Model 490 Topper has the same specs as Model 158, except for 26" barrel only, shorter youth stock; in 20-ga., modified; .410, full choke only. Introduced in 1962; dropped, 1985. Used value, $65 to $75.

HARRINGTON & RICHARDSON Model 159: advertised as the Golden Squire model; single-barrel; exposed hammer; 12-, 20-ga.; in 12-ga., 30" barrel, 20-ga., 28" barrel; full choke only; uncheckered hardwood straight-grip stock, forearm with Schnabel; bead front sight. Introduced in 1964; dropped, 1966. Used value, $75

HARRINGTON & Richardson Model 348: advertised as Gamester model; bolt-action; take-down; 12-, 16-ga.; 28" barrel; full choke only; 2-rd. tube magazine; uncheckered hardwood pistol-grip stock, forearm. Introduced in 1949; dropped, 1954. Used

HARRINGTON & RICHARDSON Model 351: advertised as the Huntsman model; bolt-action; take-down; 12-, 16-ga.; 26" barrel; Harrington & Richardson variable choke; push-button safety; 2-rd.

Model 590 Topper has the same specs as Model 490, except for black-lacquered stock, forearm, chrome-plated frame. Introduced in 1962; dropped, 1963. Used value, $70 to $80.

Topper Model 058 is 12-, 16-, 20-, 28-ga., .410; 26", 28", 30" barrels; take-down; side-lever opener, external hammer; auto ejector; case-hardened frame; walnut-finished hardwood pistol-grip stock. Introduced, 1978; dropped, 1981. Used value, $80 to $90.

Model 088 has same features as Model 058, except has semi-pistol-grip stock. No longer in production. Used value, $75 to $85.

Model 098 has same specs as 058, except has ebony-finished stock, nickel-plated frame; 26" barrel; 20-, 28-ga., .410. No longer produced. Used value, $75 to $85.

to $80.

Model 459 Golden Squire Jr. has same specs as Model 159, except for shorter youth stock, 26" full-choke barrel; 20-ga., .410 only. Made only in 1964. Used value, $70 to $75.

value, $75 to $85.

Model 349 Gamester Deluxe has the same specs as Model 348, except for adjustable choke device, 26" barrel; recoil pad. Introduced in 1953; dropped, 1955. Used value, $85 to $90.

tube magazine; uncheckered American hardwood Monte Carlo stock; recoil pad. Introduced in 1956; dropped, 1958. Used value, $75 to $85.

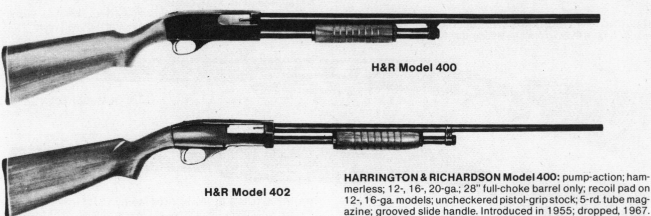

H&R Model 400

H&R Model 402

Model 402 has same general design as Model 400, but is only in .410 bore. Introduced in 1959; dropped, 1963. Used value, $145 to $155.

HARRINGTON & RICHARDSON Model 400: pump-action; hammerless; 12-, 16-, 20-ga.; 28" full-choke barrel only; recoil pad on 12-, 16-ga. models; uncheckered pistol-grip stock; 5-rd. tube magazine; grooved slide handle. Introduced in 1955; dropped, 1967. Used value, $115 to $125.

Model 401 has the same specs as Model 400, except for addition of Harrington & Richardson variable choke. Introduced in 1956; dropped, 1963. Used value, $135 to $145.

H&R Model 403

HARRINGTON & RICHARDSON Model 403: autoloader; take-down; .410 only; 26" barrel; full choke; 4-rd. tube magazine; uncheckered walnut pistol-grip stock, forearm. Made only in 1964. Used value, $175 to $195.

H&R Model 404C

ga., 26" modified/improved; .410, 25" full/full; double triggers; plain extractors; checkered hardwood pistol-grip stock, forearm. Made to H&R specifications in Brazil. Introduced in 1968; dropped, 1972. Used value, $165 to $175.

Model 404C has same specs as Model 404, except for Monte Carlo stock. Used value, $170 to $180.

HARRINGTON & RICHARDSON Model 404: double-barrel; box-lock action; 12-, 20-ga., .410; in 12-ga., 28" modified/full barrel; 20-

H&R Model 162

HARRINGTON & RICHARDSON Model 162: single-barrel, slug gun; has same specs as Model 158, except for cylinder bore, rifle sights, 24" barrel. Introduced, 1968; dropped, 1985. Used value, $60 to $65.

HARRINGTON & RICHARDSON Harrich No. 1: single-shot trap model; 12-ga. only; 32", 34" barrel; full choke; high vent rib; Anson & Deeley-type locking, Kersten top locks, double under lugs; hand-checkered European walnut Monte Carlo pistol-grip stock, beaver-tail forearm; recoil pad. Manufactured in Austria, 1971 to 1974. Used value, $1350 to $1500.

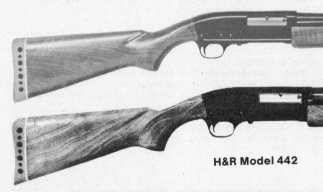

H&R Model 440

H&R Model 442

dard chokes; uncheckered American walnut pistol-grip stock, fore-arm; 4-rd. clip magazine; recoil pad. Introduced in 1972; dropped, 1975. Used value, $115 to $125.

Model 442 has same specs as Model 440 except for checkered pistol grip, forearm and full-length vent rib. Used value, $160 to $165.

HARRINGTON & RICHARDSON Model 440: pump-action, hammerless; 12-, 16-, 20-ga.; side ejection; 24", 26", 28" barrels; stan-

H&R Model 1212

H&R Model 1212 Waterfowler

HARRINGTON & RICHARDSON Model 1212: over/under; 12-ga., 2¾" chambers; 28" barrels; improved cylinder/improved modified chokes; box-lock; selective single trigger; plain extractors; vent rib; checkered European walnut pistol-grip stock, fluted forearm. Manufactured in Spain. Introduced in 1976; dropped, 1981. Used value, $275 to $300.

Manufactured in Spain. Introduced in 1976; dropped, 1981. Used value, $275 to $300.

Model 1212 Waterfowler has same specs as the standard field model, except for 30" barrels, modified/full choking; chambering for 3" magnum shells; recoil pad. Introduced, 1976; dropped, 1981. Used value, $325 to $350.

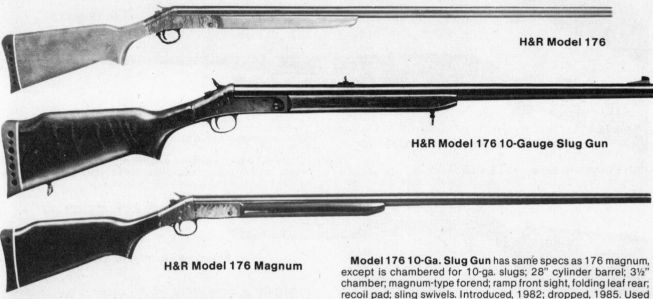

H&R Model 176

H&R Model 176 10-Gauge Slug Gun

H&R Model 176 Magnum

Model 176 10-Ga. Slug Gun has same specs as 176 magnum, except is chambered for 10-ga. slugs; 28" cylinder barrel; 3½" chamber; magnum-type forend; ramp front sight, folding leaf rear; recoil pad; sling swivels. Introduced, 1982; dropped, 1985. Used value, $100 to $110.

Model 176 Magnum: single-barrel; 10-, 12-ga.; 32" barrel; special long forend; recoil pad. Introduced, 1978; dropped, 1985. Used values: 12-ga., $80 to $85; 10-ga., $85 to $100.

HARRINGTON & RICHARDSON Model 176: single-shot; hammer-type; 10-ga. magnum only; has same general specs as Model 158, except for 36" heavy barrel; walnut stock, full forearm; recoil pad. Introduced, 1977; dropped, 1985. Used value, $85 to $100.

H&R Model 099 Deluxe

HARRINGTON & RICHARDSON Model 099 Deluxe: single-shot; 12-, 16-, 20-ga., .410; 2¾", 3" chambers; 25", 26", 28" barrels; semi-pistol grip walnut-finished hardwood stock; semi-beavertail forend; electroless matte nickel finish; bead front sight. Introduced, 1982; dropped, 1985. Used value, $75 to $85.

H&R Model 490

HARRINGTON & RICHARDSON Model 490: single-shot; has the same specs as Model 099, except stock is designed for smaller shooter; 26" barrel; 20-ga. modified or .410 full. Introduced, 1982; dropped, 1984. Used value, $70 to $80.

Model 490 Greenwing has same specs as Model 490, except has gold-finished trigger, inscription on frame; polished blued finish. Dropped, 1984. Used value, $80 to $85.

H&R Model 490 Greenwing

HIGH STANDARD

HIGH STANDARD Supermatic Field Model: autoloader; 12-ga. gas-operated; 26" improved, 28" modified or full, 30" full barrels; 4-rd. magazine; unchecked American walnut pistol-grip stock, forearm. Introduced in 1960; dropped, 1966. Used value, $175 to $185.

Field Model 20-ga. has same general design as 12-ga., but chambered for 3" magnum shell; 3-rd. magazine; 26" improved, 28" modified or full barrels; unchecked pistol-grip stock, forearm. Introduced in 1963; dropped, 1966. Used value, $180 to $190.

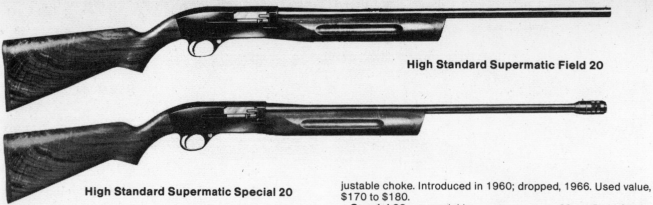

High Standard Supermatic Field 20

High Standard Supermatic Special 20

HIGH STANDARD Supermatic Special: autoloader; 12-ga.; has the same specs as 12-ga. Field model, except for 27" barrel, ad-

justable choke. Introduced in 1960; dropped, 1966. Used value, $170 to $180.

Special 20-ga. model has same specs as 20-ga. Field Grade, except for 27" barrel, adjustable choke. Introduced in 1963; dropped, 1966. Used value, $180 to $190.

High Standard Supermatic Trophy 20

HIGH STANDARD Supermatic Trophy Model: autoloader; 12-ga.; has same specs as Deluxe Rib 12-ga. model, except for 27"

vent-rib barrel, adjustable choke. Introduced in 1961; dropped, 1966. Used value, $185 to $195.

Trophy 20-ga. has the same specs as the Deluxe Rib 20, except for 27" vent-rib barrel, adjustable choke. Introduced in 1963; dropped, 1966. Used value, $185 to $195.

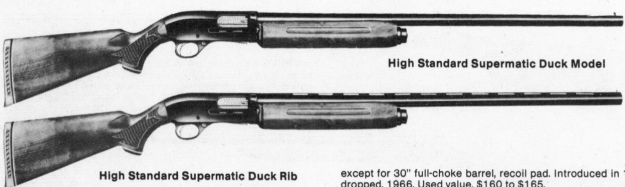

High Standard Supermatic Duck Model

High Standard Supermatic Duck Rib

HIGH STANDARD Supermatic Duck Model: autoloader; 12-ga. magnum only; has same general specs as 12-ga. field model,

except for 30" full-choke barrel, recoil pad. Introduced in 1961; dropped, 1966. Used value, $160 to $165.

Duck Rib 12 magnum has the same specs as the Duck 12 magnum, except for vent rib, checkered stock and forearm. Introduced in 1961; dropped, 1966. Used value, $200 to $210.

HIGH STANDARD Supermatic Skeet: autoloader; 12-ga.; 26" vent-rib barrel; skeet choke; other specs are the same as Deluxe Rib 12 model. Introduced in 1962; dropped, 1966. Used value, $175 to $185.

Skeet 20-ga. has same specs as Deluxe Rib 20 model, except for skeet choke, 26" vent-rib barrel. Introduced in 1964; dropped, 1966. Used value, $185 to $195.

HIGH STANDARD Supermatic Trap: autoloader; 12-ga.; 30" vent rib; full choke only; trap stock; recoil pad. Other specs the

same as Deluxe Rib 12 model. Introduced in 1962; dropped, 1966. Used value, $185 to $195.

HIGH STANDARD Supermatic Deer Model: 12-ga.; cylinder bore; same specs as Supermatic field model, except for 22" barrel;

rifle sights; checkered stock, forearm; recoil pad. Manufactured 1965. Used value, $175 to $185.

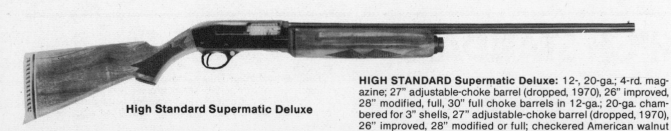

High Standard Supermatic Deluxe

HIGH STANDARD Supermatic Deluxe: 12-, 20-ga.; 4-rd. magazine; 27" adjustable-choke barrel (dropped, 1970), 26" improved, 28" modified, full, 30" full choke barrels in 12-ga.; 20-ga. chambered for 3" shells, 27" adjustable-choke barrel (dropped, 1970), 26" improved, 28" modified or full; checkered American walnut

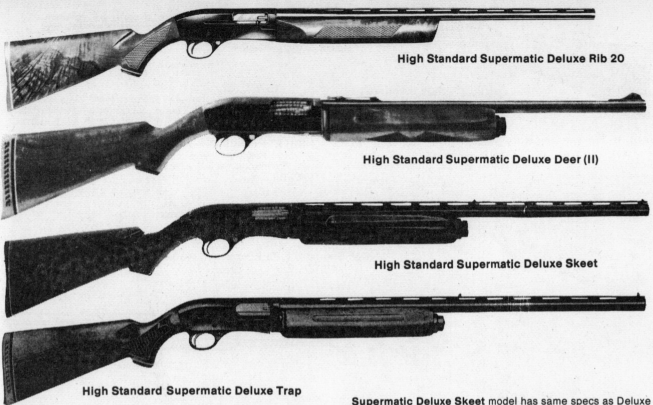

High Standard Supermatic Deluxe Rib 20

High Standard Supermatic Deluxe Deer (II)

High Standard Supermatic Deluxe Skeet

High Standard Supermatic Deluxe Trap

pistol-grip stock, forearm; recoil pad. Differs from original Super-matic; has new checkering, damascened bolt. Manufactured 1966 to 1975. Used values: with adjustable choke, $175 to $180; sans choke, $165 to $175.

Supermatic Deluxe Rib has same specs as Supermatic Deluxe, 12-, 20-ga, except for vent rib, no 26" barrel length. Manufactured 1966 to 1975. Used values: with adjustable choke, $160 to $165; sans choke, $200 to $225.

Supermatic Deluxe Duck Rib has same specs as Supermatic Deluxe, 12-ga. only, except for 3" magnum chambering; 3-rd. magazine; 30" full-choke vent-rib barrel. Manufactured 1966 to 1975. Used value, $210 to $235.

Supermatic Deluxe Duck model has same specs as Duck Rib model, sans vent rib. Manufactured 1966 to 1975. Used value, $190 to $200.

Supermatic Deluxe Skeet model has same specs as Deluxe Rib version, except was made only with 26" vent-rib barrel, skeet choke; 12-, 20-ga. Manufactured 1966 to 1975. Used value, $220 to $240.

Supermatic Deluxe Trap model has same specs as Deluxe Rib 12-ga. except has 30" vent-rib barrel, full choke, trap stock. Manufactured 1966 to 1975. Used value, $210 to $220.

HIGH STANDARD Flite-King Field Model: slide-action; 12-ga.; hammerless; 26" improved cylinder, 28" modified or full, 30" full barrel; 5-rd. magazine; unchecked walnut pistol-grip stock, grooved slide handle. Introduced in 1960; dropped, 1966. Used value, $130 to $140.

Field Model 20-ga. is chambered for 3" magnum shell; 4-rd. magazine; other specs, including barrel lengths, chokes are the same as 12-ga. version. Introduced in 1961; dropped, 1966. Used value, $140 to $150.

High Standard Flite-King Field 20

HIGH STANDARD Flite-King Special: slide-action; 12-ga.; has the same specs as Field version, except for 27" barrel, adjustable choke. Introduced in 1960; dropped, 1966. Used value, $135 to $140.

Special 20-ga. has same specs as Field 20, except for 27" barrel, adjustable choke. Introduced in 1961; dropped, 1966. Used value, $140 to $145.

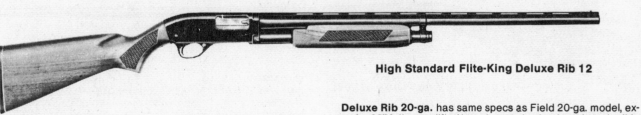

High Standard Flite-King Deluxe Rib 12

HIGH STANDARD Flite-King Deluxe Rib: slide-action; 12-ga.; has the same specs as Field 12 Flite-King, except for 28" full or modified, 30" full-choke barrel; vent rib; checkered walnut stock, slide handle. Introduced in 1961; dropped, 1966. Used value, $150 to $160.

Deluxe Rib 20-ga. has same specs as Field 20-ga. model, except for 28" full or modified barrel; vent rib; checkered stock, slide handle. Introduced in 1962; dropped, 1966. Used value, $165 to $170.

Flight-King Trap has the same specs as Deluxe Rib 12-ga., except for 30" barrel; full choke; vent rib; trap stock; recoil pad. Introduced, 1962; dropped, 1966. Used value, $175 to $185.

High Standard
Flite-King Trophy

HIGH STANDARD Flite-King Trophy: slide-action; 12-ga.; has the same specs as Deluxe Rib 12-ga., except for 27" vent-rib barrel, adjustable choke. Introduced in 1960; dropped, 1966. Used value, $165 to $170.

Trophy 20-ga. has the same specs as Field 20-ga., except for vent rib; 28" modified or full barrel, checkered stock, slide handle. Introduced in 1962; dropped, 1966. Used value, $175 to $180.

HIGH STANDARD Flite-King Skeet: slide-action; 12-ga.; same specs as 12-ga. Deluxe Rib, except for 26" skeet-choked barrel, vent rib. Introduced in 1962; dropped, 1966. Used value, $160 to $170.

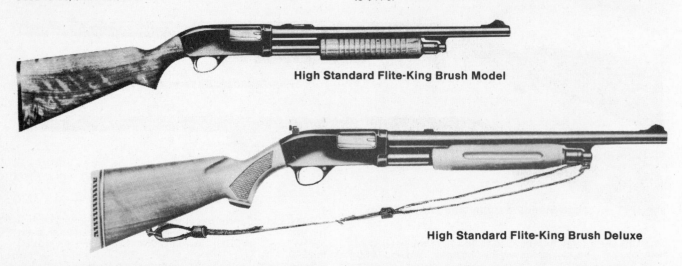

High Standard Flite-King Brush Model

High Standard Flite-King Brush Deluxe

HIGH STANDARD Flite-King Brush Gun: slide-action; 12-ga.; has same specs as Field model, except for 18" or 20" cylinder bore barrel; rifle sights. Introduced in 1962; dropped, 1964. Used value, $145 to $150.

Brush Deluxe model has same specs as Flite-King Brush Gun, except for recoil pad, adjustable peep rear sight; has checkered pistol grip, fluted slide handle, sling swivels, sling; made with 20" barrel only. Manufactured 1964 to 1966. Used value, $160 to $170.

HIGH STANDARD Flite-King 16 Series: slide-action; 16-ga.; has same general specs as various configurations of Flite-King 12-ga., but not available in Brush, Skeet or Trap models, nor in 30" barrel lengths. Introduced in 1961; dropped, 1965. Used values: Field, $110 to $120; Special, $125 to $130; Deluxe Rib, $145 to $150; Trophy, $150 to $155.

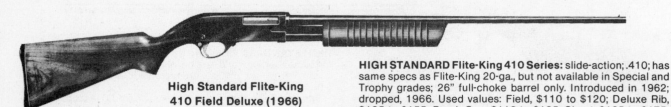

High Standard Flite-King
410 Field Deluxe (1966)

HIGH STANDARD Flite-King 410 Series: slide-action; .410; has same specs as Flite-King 20-ga., but not available in Special and Trophy grades; 26" full-choke barrel only. Introduced in 1962; dropped, 1966. Used values: Field, $110 to $120; Deluxe Rib, $135 to $155; Brush Gun, $110 to $125; Skeet, $165 to $175; Trap, $155 to $165.

High Standard Flite King Deluxe (1966)

HIGH STANDARD Flite-King Deluxe (1966): slide-action; 12-ga.; 5-rd. magazine, 26" improved cylinder barrel, 27" with adjustable choke; 28" modified or full; 30" full choke; checkered American walnut pistol-grip stock, forearm; recoil pad. General specs follow Flite-King series dropped in 1966, except for damascened bolt, new checkering design. Manufactured 1966 to 1975. Used values: with adjustable choke, $125 to $130; sans adjustable choke, $100 to $110.

Deluxe 20 (1966) has same specs as Deluxe 12-ga., except it is chambered for 3", 20-ga. shells; improved, modified, or full choking. Manufactured 1966 to 1975. Used value, $125 to $135.

Deluxe 28 (1966) has same specs as Deluxe 12-ga., except is chambered only for 28-ga., modified and full. Manufactured 1966 to 1975. Used value, $135 to $145.

Deluxe 410 (1966) has same specs as Deluxe 28, except is chambered for 3", .410 shell; full choke only. Manufactured 1966 to 1975. Used value, $120 to $130.

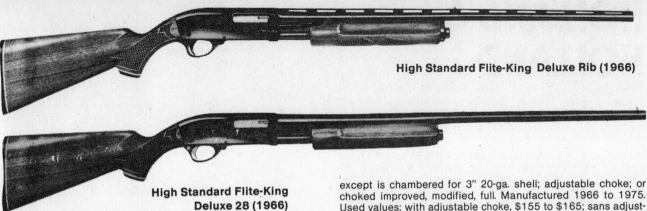

High Standard Flite-King Deluxe Rib (1966)

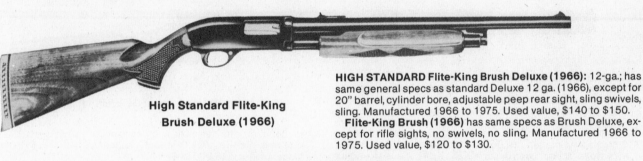

High Standard Flite-King
Deluxe 28 (1966)

HIGH STANDARD Flite-King Deluxe Rib (1966): 12-ga., has same specs as Flite-King Deluxe 12-ga., except for vent-rib barrel; made in 27" barrel length with adjustable choke, 28" modified or full, 30" full choke. Manufactured 1966 to 1975. Used values: with adjustable choke, $140 to $150; sans adjustable choke, $130 to $140.

Deluxe Rib 20 (1966) has same specs as 12-ga. 1966 version, except is chambered for 3" 20-ga. shell; adjustable choke; or choked improved, modified, full. Manufactured 1966 to 1975. Used values: with adjustable choke, $155 to $165; sans adjustable choke, $150 to $160.

Deluxe Rib 28 (1966) has same specs as 20-ga. version, except chambered for 28-ga. shell; no adjustable choke; made with modified, full chokes. Manufactured 1966 to 1975. Used value, $145 to $155.

Deluxe Rib .410 (1966) has same specs as 28-ga. version, except chambered for 3" .410 shell, full choke only. Manufactured 1966 to 1975. Used value, $150 to $160.

HIGH STANDARD Flite-King Deluxe Skeet (1966): slide-action; 12-ga.; has same specs as standard Deluxe (1966) model except for 26" vent-rib barrel, skeet choke; optional recoil pad. Manufactured 1966 to 1975. Used value, $165 to $175.

Deluxe Skeet 20 (1966) has same specs as 12-ga. except for 20-ga. chambering. Manufactured 1966 to 1975. Used value, $175 to $185.

Deluxe Skeet 28 (1966) has same specs as Deluxe Skeet 20, except for 28-ga. chambering. Manufactured 1966 to 1975. Used value, $180 to $190.

Deluxe Skeet .410 (1966) has same specs as Deluxe Skeet 20, except for .410 chambering,. Manufactured 1966 to 1975. Used value, $180 to $190.

Deluxe Trap (1966) has same general specs as standard Deluxe Rib 12 (1966), except was made only with 30" vent-rib barrel, full choke, trap stock. Manufactured 1966 to 1975. Used value, $165 to $175.

High Standard Flite-King
Brush Deluxe (1966)

HIGH STANDARD Flite-King Brush Deluxe (1966): 12-ga.; has same general specs as standard Deluxe 12 ga. (1966), except for 20" barrel, cylinder bore, adjustable peep rear sight, sling swivels, sling. Manufactured 1966 to 1975. Used value, $140 to $150.

Flite-King Brush (1966) has same specs as Brush Deluxe, except for rifle sights, no swivels, no sling. Manufactured 1966 to 1975. Used value, $120 to $130.

High Standard Shadow Indy

High Standard Shadow Seven

HIGH STANDARD Shadow Indy: over/under; 12-ga., 2¾" chambering; 27½" skeet-choked barrels; 29¾" improved modified/full, full/full; selective auto ejectors; selective single trigger; Airflow vent rib; box-lock action; engraved receiver; skip-checkered walnut pistol-grip stock, ventilated forearm; recoil pad. Manufactured in Japan 1974 to 1975. Used value, $600 to $625.

Shadow Seven has same general specs as Shadow Indy, except for less engraving, standard vent rib, forearm; no recoil pad; 27½" barrels made in improved cylinder/modified, modified/full. Manufactured in Japan 1974 to 1975. Used value, $500 to $525.

HIGH STANDARD Shadow Auto: gas-operated; 12-, 20-ga.; 2¾", 3" chambering in 12-ga., 3" in 20; magazine holds four 2¾" rounds, three 3"; 26" improved cylinder or skeet barrel, 28" modified, improved modified or full, 30" trap or full; magnum available only with 30" barrel; checkered walnut pistol-grip stock, forearm. Manufactured in Japan 1974 to 1975. Used value, $215 to $235.

HOLLAND & HOLLAND

NOTE: 20-gauge versions are valued at 20% more than indicated prices; 28-gauges, 40% additional; .410 at 60% higher.

Holland & Holland Royal Model

HOLLAND & HOLLAND Royal Model: side-by-side; hammerless; 12-, 16-, 20-, 28-ga.; barrel lengths, chokes to customer's specs; self-opening action; hand-detachable side-locks; automatic ejectors; double triggers or single nonselective trigger; made in Game, Pigeon, Wildfowl configurations; hand-checkered straight-grip stock, forearm; English engraving. Introduced in 1885; still in production. Used values: double triggers, $9000 to $11,000; single trigger, $10,000 to $12,000.

HOLLAND & HOLLAND Model Deluxe: side-by-side; hammerless; 12-, 16-, 20-, 28-ga.; barrel lengths and chokes to customer's specs; self-opening action; hand-detachable side-locks; has the same general specs as Royal Model, but with much more ornate engraving. Introduced in 1900; still in production. Used values: double triggers, $11,000 to $13,000; single trigger, $12,000 to $14,000.

Holland & Holland Badminton Model

HOLLAND & HOLLAND Badminton Model: side-by-side; hammerless; 12-, 16-, 20-, 28-ga.; has the same specs as Royal Model side-by-side except action is not self-opening. Introduced in 1902; still in production. Used values: double triggers, $9000 to $11,000; single trigger, $10,000 to $12,000.

Holland & Holland Royal Over/Under

HOLLAND & HOLLAND Royal Over/Under: hammerless; hand-detachable side-locks; 12-ga. only; barrel lengths, chokes to customer's specs; automatic ejectors; double triggers or single trigger; made in Game, Pigeon, Wildfowl configurations; hand-checkered European walnut straight-grip stock, forearm. Introduced in 1925; dropped, 1950. Used values: double triggers, $15,000 to $16,000; single trigger, $16,000 to $17,000.
   New Royal Model over/under has the same specs as original model, except for narrower, improved action. Introduced in 1951; dropped, 1965. Used values: double triggers, $18,000 to $19,000; single trigger, $19,000 to $20,000.

Holland & Holland Dominion Model

HOLLAND & HOLLAND Dominion Model: side-by-side; hammerless; side-lock; 12-, 16-, 20-ga.; 25", 28", 30" barrels; choked to customer's specs; double triggers; automatic ejectors; hand-checkered European walnut straight-grip stock, forearm. Introduced in 1935; dropped, 1965. Used value, $3250 to $3500.

HOLLAND & HOLLAND Northwood Game Model: side-by-side; 12-, 16-, 20-, 28-ga.; 28" barrels; any standard choke combo; Anson & Deeley box-lock action; double triggers, automatic ejectors; hand-checkered European walnut straight-grip or pistol-grip stock, forearm. Manufactured prior to World War II until late Sixties. Used value, $3500 to $4000.
   Northwood Wildfowl Model has same specs as Game Model, except made in 12-ga., 3" chambering only, 30" barrels. Used value, $4000 to $4500.
   Northwood Pigeon Model has same specs as Game Model, except has more engraving; not offered in 28-ga. Used value, $7000 to $7250.

HOLLAND & HOLLAND Super Trap: single-barrel; 12-ga.; 30", 32" barrel; extra-full choke; Anson & Deeley box-lock action; automatic ejector; no safety; Monte Carlo stock of European walnut, full beavertail forearm; recoil pad. Introduced prior to World War II; dropped in late Sixties. Used value, $4500 to $5000.
   Super Trap Deluxe Grade has same specs as standard model, except for upgraded wood, quality of engraving. Used value, $6000 to $7000.
   Super Trap Exhibition Grade has same specs as Deluxe Grade, except for better wood, additional engraving. Used value, $7000 to $8000.

HOLLAND & HOLLAND Riviera Model: side-by-side; hammerless; designed as pigeon gun; has the same specs as Badminton Model, except for double triggers, two sets of interchangeable barrels. Introduced in 1945; still in production. Used value, $10,000 to $12,000.

ITHACA

Ithaca Hammerless
Double Field Grade

Double No. 1 Grade
Ithaca Hammerless

Ithaca Hammerless
Double No. 2 Grade

Ithaca Hammerless
Double No. 3 Grade

Ithaca Hammerless
Double No. 4E

Ithaca Hammerless
Double No. 5E

ITHACA Hammerless Double Field Grade: side-by-side double-barrel; box-lock action; 12-, 16-, 20-, 28-ga., .410; 26", 28", 30", 32" barrels; any standard choke combination; top-lever breaking; hand-checkered American walnut pistol-grip stock, forearm; pistol-grip cap; various options at additional cost. Introduced with rotary bolt in 1926; dropped, 1948. Used values: standard model, $500 to $600; with automatic ejectors, add $175; with beavertail forearm, add $150; with vent rib, add $250; for 10-ga. magnum, 12-ga. magnum (only 900 made), add $350 to $400.

Hammerless Double No. 2 Grade has same general specs as Field Grade, with addition of black walnut stock, forearm, engrav-ing. Various options at added cost. Introduced in 1926; dropped, 1948. Used values: standard version, $700 to $750; with auto ejectors, add $175; with beavertail forearm, add $150; with vent rib, add $275; for 10-ga. magnum, 12-ga. magnum, add $400 to $450.

Hammerless Double No. 4 Grade has same basic design as Field Grade, but with many custom facets; double triggers are standard; hand engraved with scroll, line engraving; game scenes on frame, top lever, forearm iron, trigger guard; various options at added cost. Introduced in 1926; dropped, 1948. Used values: standard version, $1750 to $2000; with single selective trigger,

Ithaca Hammerless Double No. 7 Ejector

Ithaca Hammerless Double $2000 Grade

add $200; beavertail forearm, add $185; vent rib, add $300; 10-, 12-ga. magnums, add $500 and $300, respectively.

Hammerless Double No. 5 Grade has gold nameplate inset in stock; English pheasant inlaid in gold on left side, woodcock on right; American eagle is engraved on bottom; engraved leaf, flower background; has selective single trigger, beavertail forearm; vent rib extra. Introduced in 1926; dropped, 1948. Used values: $3500 to $4000; with vent rib, add $350; add $750 for 10-ga. magnums;

$400 for 12-ga. magnums.

Hammerless Double No. 7 Grade has select walnut stock, hand-fitted action, elaborately checkered wood; beavertail forearm with ebony tip; matted vent rib; profusely engraved receiver with oak leaf, acorn design; inlaid designs in green and yellow gold, silver; gold nameplate inset in stock; single selective trigger is triple gold-plated, hand checkered; automatic ejectors. Introduced in 1926; dropped, 1948. Used value, $7500 to $8000.

Hammerless Double $2000 Grade has same specs as other grades, but is inlaid with gold in elaborate designs; selective single trigger, vent rib, beavertail forearm. Prior to World War II, was listed as $1000 Grade. Introduced in 1926; dropped, 1948. Used value, $9000 to $10,000.

Ithaca One Barrel Trap 4E Grade

ITHACA One Barrel Trap Gun: single-shot, hammerless; box-lock action; 12-ga. only; 30", 32", 34" barrels; vent rib; hand-

checkered American walnut pistol-grip stock, forearm; recoil pad; made in four grades, differing only in quality of workmanship, grade of wood, amount of engraving, checkering. $5000 Grade was designated as $1000 model prior to World War II. Introduced in 1922; not currently produced. Used values: No. 4-E, $1200 to $1500; No. 5-E, $3000 to $3500; No. 7-E, $3500 to $3700; $5000 Grade, $7500 to $8000; Sousa Grade Single Barrel, $15,000 to $17,500.

ITHACA Single-Barrel Victory Model: single-shot, hammerless; box-lock action; 12-ga. only; 34" barrel; has same general specs as the other One Barrel models, but less extensive engraving, checkering, lower grade of wood. Introduced in 1922; dropped about 1938. Used value, $700 to $750.

Ithaca Model 37 Standard

Ithaca Model 37R Solid Rib

Ithaca Model 37R Deluxe Solid Rib

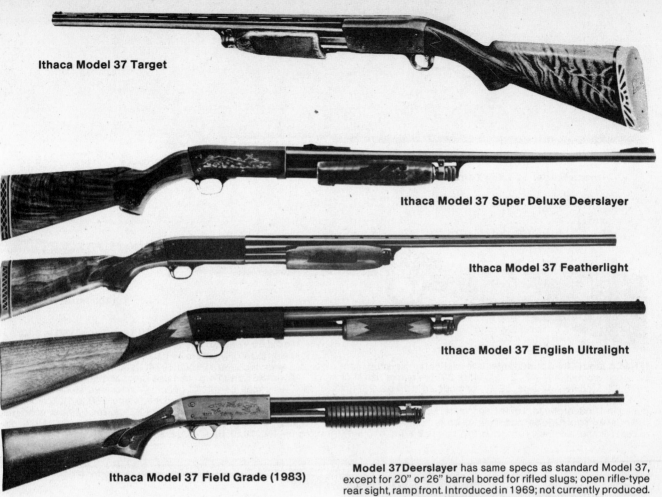

Ithaca Model 37 Target

Ithaca Model 37 Super Deluxe Deerslayer

Ithaca Model 37 Featherlight

Ithaca Model 37 English Ultralight

Ithaca Model 37 Field Grade (1983)

ITHACA Model 37: slide-action repeater; hammerless; take-down, 12-, 16-, 20-ga.; 26", 28", 30" barrels; 4-rd. tube magazine; hand-checkered American walnut pistol-grip stock, slide handle, or un-checkered stock, grooved slide handle. Introduced in 1937; dropped, 1986. Used values: with checkered pistol grip, slide handle, $175 to $195; with plain stock, grooved slide handle, $150 to $160.

Model 37R has the same general specs as standard Model 37 except for raised solid rib. Introduced in 1937; dropped, 1967. Used values: with checkered pistol grip, slide handle, $200 to $215; uncheckered stock, grooved slide handle, $170 to $180.

Model 37S Skeet Grade has same general specs as standard model, except for vent rib, extension slide handle. Introduced in 1937; dropped, 1955. Used value, $300 to $325.

Model 37T Trap Grade has same general specs as Model 37S except for straight trap stock of selected walnut, recoil pad. Introduced in 1937; dropped, 1955. Used value, $325 to $350.

Model 37T Target Grade replaced Model 37S Skeet Grade and Model 37T Trap Grade. Has same general specs as standard Model 37 except for hand-checkered stock, slide handle of fancy walnut; choice of skeet or trap stock; vent rib. Introduced in 1955; dropped, 1961. Used value, $375 to $400.

Model 37 Supreme Grade has same general specs as Model 37T, but available in skeet or trap configuration. Manufactured 1967 to 1979. Used value, $400 to $450.

Model 37 $3000 Grade was listed as $1000 Grade prior to World War II. Has same basic design as standard Model 37, but is custom-built, with gold-inlaid engraving; hand-finished parts; hand-checkered pistol-grip stock, slide handle of select figured walnut; recoil pad. Introduced in 1937; dropped, 1967. Used value, $4500 to $5000.

Model 37R Deluxe has same general specs as standard Model 37R, except for hand-checkered fancy walnut stock, slide handle. Introduced in 1955; dropped, 1961. Used value, $300 to $325.

Model 37 Deerslayer has same specs as standard Model 37, except for 20" or 26" barrel bored for rifled slugs; open rifle-type rear sight, ramp front. Introduced in 1969; not currently produced. Used value, $225 to $250.

Model 37 Super Deerslayer has same specs as standard Deerslayer, except for improved wood in stock, slide handle. Manufactured 1962 until 1979. Used value, $275 to $300.

Model 37 Basic Featherlight slide-action; 12-ga.; 26", 28", 30" barrels; tung-oil-finished walnut stock; traditional ringtail forend; matte finish on all metal; plain or vent rib. Introduced, 1980; dropped, 1983. Used values: plain barrel, $240 to $250; vent rib, $270 to $280; 3" magnum, full choke, $300 to $310.

Model 37 Featherlight has same general specs as Basic Featherlight; 12-, 20-ga.; 5 rds.; take-down.; bottom ejection; 26", 28", 30" barrels in 12-ga.; 26", 28" in 20; checkered American walnut pistol-grip stock; Ithaca Raybar front sight; decorated receiver; crossbolt safety. Manufactured in several grades. Introduced, 1980; not currently produced. Used values: standard model, $225 to $250; with vent rib, $260 to $270; 2500 Series, $600 to $625; Presentation Series, $1000 to $1050.

Model 37 Ultra-Featherlight has same specs as standard model, except is made in 20-ga. only; has 25" vent rib, recoil pad, gold-plated trigger, Sid Bell-designed grip cap. Used value, $310 to $325.

Model 37 Deluxe Featherlight has same specs as standard version except has vent rib, straight-grip stock, better wood, cut-checkered pump handle, grip; oil-finished wood. Introduced, 1981; not currently produced. Used value, $360 to $375.

Model 37 Magnum has same specs as standard model, except is chambered for 3" shells; longer receiver; grip cap has flying mallard; recoil pad, vent rib; 12-, 20-ga.; 28", 30" barrel. Introduced, 1978; not currently produced. Used value, $275 to $300.

Model 37 English Ultralight has same specs as standard Model 37 Ultralight, except has vent-rib barrel, oil-finished straight-grip stock; cut checkering on pump handle, grip and butt. Introduced, 1981; dropped, 1986. Used value: $375 to $400.

Model 37 Field Grade has same specs as standard Model 37 Featherlight, except has American hardwood stock, 12-, 20-ga.; 2¾" chamber only; ring-tail forend; standard or vent-rib barrel; Raybar front sight. Introduced, 1983; dropped, 1986. Used values: standard, $220 to $230; with vent rib, $240 to $250.

Ithaca Model 66

Ithaca Model 66 Long Tom

Ithaca Model 66RS

ITHACA Model 66 Supersingle: lever-action, single-shot; manually cocked hammer; 12-, 20-ga., .410; 30" full-choke barrel or 28" full or modified in 12-ga., 28" full or modified in 20-ga., 26" full in .410. Checkered straight stock, uncheckered forearm. Introduced in 1963; dropped, 1979. Used value, $85 to $95.

Model 66 Youth Model has same specs as standard Model 66, except for shorter stock, recoil pad, 25" barrel; 20-ga., .410 only.

Introduced in 1965; dropped, 1979. Used value, $80 to $90.

Model 66 Vent Rib has same specs as standard model, except for vent-rib barrel; made in 20-ga. only with checkered stock, recoil pad. Manufactured 1969 to 1974. Used value, $100 to $115.

Model 66 Long Tom has same specs as standard 66, except for 36" full-choke barrel; 12-ga. only; checkered stock; recoil pad. Manufactured 1969 to 1974. Used value, $80 to $90.

Model 66RS Buck Buster has 22" barrel, cylinder bore; rifle sights; 12-, 20-ga. Introduced in 1967; 12-ga. dropped, 1970; discontinued, 1979. Used value, $85 to $95.

Ithaca-SKB Model 100

ITHACA-SKB Model 100: side-by-side, double-barrel; box-lock action; 12-, 20-ga.; in 12-ga., 30" full/full barrels, 28" full/modified, 26" improved/modified; in 20-ga., 25" improved/modified only;

single selective trigger; plain extractors; automatic safety; hand-checkered pistol-grip stock, forearm. Made in Japan. Introduced in 1967; dropped, 1976. Used value, $375 to $400.

Ithaca-SKB Model 150 has same specs as Model 100, except for more ornate scroll engraving, beavertail forearm. Manufactured 1972 to 1974. Used value, $385 to $410.

Ithaca-SKB Model 200E Standard

ITHACA-SKB Model 200E: side-by-side, double barrel; box-lock action; has the same general specs as Model 100 except for automatic selective ejectors, engraved, silver-plated frame, gold-plated nameplate, trigger; beavertail forearm. Introduced in 1967;

dropped, 1977. Used value, $450 to $475.

Model 200E Skeet Grade has the same specs as standard model, except for 25" barrel in 12-ga., 25" in 20-ga.; skeet/skeet; non-automatic safety; recoil pad. Introduced in 1967; dropped, 1976. Used value, $450 to $475.

Ithaca-SKB Model 280 has same specs as Model 200E, except for English-type straight stock, game scene engraved on frame; not made with 30" barrels; quail gun has 25" barrels in improved cylinder. Imported 1971 to 1979. Used value, $450 to $475.

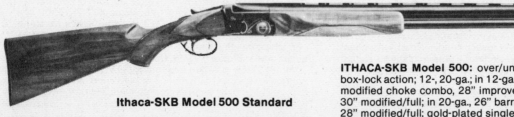

Ithaca-SKB Model 500 Standard

ITHACA-SKB Model 500: over/under; hammerless; top lever, box-lock action; 12-, 20-ga.; in 12-ga., 25" barrels have improved/modified choke combo, 28" improved/modified or modified/full, 30" modified/full; in 20-ga., 26" barrels have improved/modified, 28" modified/full; gold-plated single selective trigger; automatic ejectors, non-automatic safety; chrome-lined barrels, action; Ray-bar front sight; scroll-engraved border on receiver; hand-checkered walnut pistol-grip stock, forearm; pistol-grip cap; fluted comb.

Introduced in 1967; dropped, 1976. Used value, $450 to $475.

Model 500 Magnum has same specs as standard Model 600, except for magnum chambering. Used value, $475 to $500.

Ithaca-SKB Model 600 Skeet

ITHACA-SKB Model 600 Trap Grade: over/under; hammerless; box-lock action; 12-ga. only; 30", 32" barrels full/full or full/im-

proved; straight or Monte Carlo stock; recoil pad; other specs are the same as those of Model 500. Introduced in 1967; dropped, 1976. Used value, $525 to $550.

Model 600 Skeet Grade has the same specs as Model 500, except for 26", 28" skeet/skeet barrels, recoil pad. Introduced in 1967; dropped, 1976. Used value, $525 to $550.

Ithaca-SKB Model 700

ITHACA-SKB Model 700: over/under; hammerless; box-lock action; in both skeet, trap styles; has the same specs as Model 600, except for select oil-finished walnut stock, heavily engraved receiver. Introduced in 1967; dropped, 1976. Used value, $650 to $700.

ITHACA MX-8: over/under trap model; box-lock action; 12-ga.; 30", 32" barrels bored for international claybird competition; single nonselective trigger; interchangeable hammer/trigger groups;

hand-checkered European walnut pistol-grip stock, forearm; oil or lacquer wood finish; vent rib. Introduced in 1968; no longer in production. Used value, $4000 to $4500.

ITHACA Mirage: over/under; box-lock action; 12-ga.; 32", 30", 28" barrels; extra-full/modified, skeet/skeet boring; interchangeable hammer/trigger groups; single selective trigger; hand-checkered walnut pistol-grip stock, Schnabel forearm; recoil pad. Introduced in 1968; still in production; no longer imported. Used value, $2000 to $2250.

Ithaca Mirage

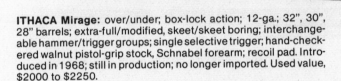

Ithaca Competition I

ITHACA Competition I: over/under trap gun; box-lock action; 12-ga.; 30", 32" barrels; interchangeable hammer/trigger groups; single nonselective triggers; improved/modified choke combo;

vent rib; standard or Monte Carlo stock design; hand-checkered American walnut pistol-grip stock, forearm. Introduced in 1968; dropped, 1974. Used value, $1150 to $1250.

Competition I Skeet model has same general specs as trap gun except for skeet stock, 26¾" skeet/skeet barrels; leather-faced recoil pad. Introduced in 1968; dropped, 1974. Used value, $1250 to $1500.

Ithaca Model 300

ITHACA Model 300: autoloader; recoil-operated; take-down; 12-ga. only; 30" full-choke barrel; 28" full or modified; 26" improved

cylinder; checkered American walnut pistol-grip stock, fluted forearm; crossbolt safety; automatic magazine cutoff allows changing loads without unloading magazine; vent rib at additional cost. Introduced in 1969; dropped, 1973. Used values: plain barrel, $150 to $175; vent rib, $200 to $225.

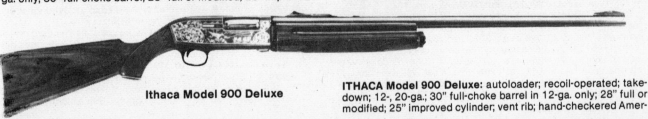

Ithaca Model 900 Deluxe

ITHACA Model 900 Deluxe: autoloader; recoil-operated; take-down; 12-, 20-ga.; 30" full-choke barrel in 12-ga. only; 28" full or modified; 25" improved cylinder; vent rib; hand-checkered American walnut pistol-grip stock, forearm; white spacers on grip cap, butt plate; interchangeable barrels, crossbolt safety; gold-filled engraving on receiver, gold-plated trigger, nameplate inlaid in stock. Introduced in 1969; dropped, 1973. Used value, $275 to $300.

Model 900 Deluxe Slug has same specs as standard model, except for 24" barrel, rifle sights. Introduced in 1969; dropped, 1973. Used value, $275 to $300.

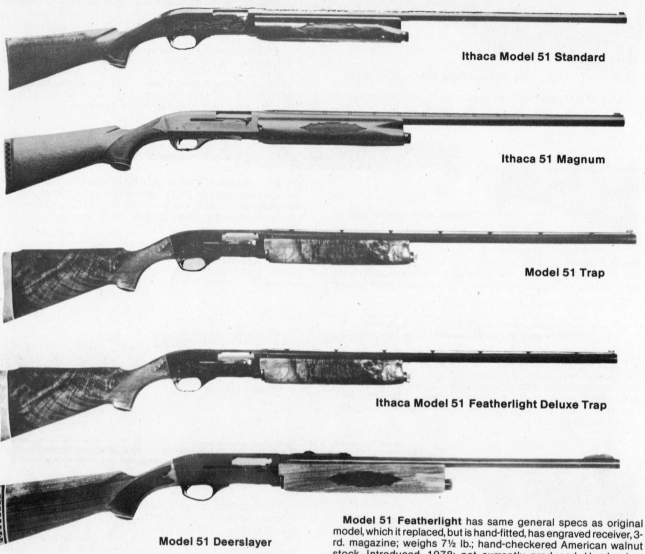

Ithaca Model 51 Standard

Ithaca 51 Magnum

Model 51 Trap

Ithaca Model 51 Featherlight Deluxe Trap

Model 51 Deerslayer

ITHACA Model 51: autoloader; gas-operated; take-down; 12-ga.; 30" full-choke barrel; 28" full, modified or skeet; 26" improved or skeet; Raybar front sight; hand-checkered American walnut pistol-grip stock; white spacer on pistol grip; 3-rd. tube magazine; reversible safety; engraved receiver; vent rib at added cost. Introduced in 1970; not currently produced. Used values: plain barrel, $210 to $225; vent rib, $300 to $325.

Model 51 Magnum has same specs as standard model, except for 3" chambers. Used value, $300 to $325.

Model 51 Trap has same specs as standard model, except for 30", 32" barrel, trap stock, trap recoil pad, vent rib. Used value, $300 to $325.

Model 51 Skeet has same specs as standard model, except for skeet stock, skeet recoil pad, vent rib. Used value, $325 to $350.

Model 51 Deerslayer is in 12-, 20-ga.; 24" special bore barrel for slugs; has Raybar front sight, open adjustable rear; sight base grooved for scope. Used value, $270 to $280.

Model 51 20-ga. has same general design as standard Model 51; 26" improved cylinder or skeet barrel; 28" full or modified; vent rib; magnum chambering at extra cost. Used values: standard model, $215 to $225; with vent rib, $300 to $325; standard magnum, $235 to $240; magnum with vent rib, $300 to $325; skeet version, $300 to $325.

Model 51 Featherlight has same general specs as original model, which it replaced, but is hand-fitted, has engraved receiver, 3-rd. magazine; weighs 7½ lb.; hand-checkered American walnut stock. Introduced, 1978; not currently produced. Used value, $350 to $365.

Model 51 Featherlight Deluxe Trap has same specs as 51 Featherlight, except has fancy walnut trap stock, 30" full or improved cylinder choke, 28" with full or improved modified. Used value, $400 to $425.

Model 51A has same general specs as basic Model 51, with cosmetic improvements. Introduced, 1982; dropped, 1986. Used value, $340 to $360; Presentation series, $1225 to $1250.

Model 51A Magnum has same basic specs as standard Model 51A, except is chambered for 3" shotshell. Used value, $375 to $400.

Model 51A Supreme Skeet has same specs as standard version, except has fancy American walnut skeet stock, 26" skeet barrel, Used value, $350 to $400.

Model 51A Deerslayer has same specs as standard 51A, except has 24" barrel, special bore; sight base grooved for scope mounts. Dropped 1984. Used value, $250 to $300.

Model 51A Supreme Trap has same specs as standard model, except has fancy American walnut trap stock, 30" full-choke barrel; Monte Carlo stock optional. Used value, $450 to $475; with Monte Carlo stock, $470 to $495.

Model 51 Waterfowler has basic model specs, except is 12-ga. only, 3" chamber; matte-finished metal; comes with sling, swivels and vent rib. Introduced, 1985; dropped, 1986. Used value, $375 to $400.

Ithaca LSA-55 Turkey Gun

ITHACA LSA-55 Turkey Gun: over/under combo; 12-ga./.222 Rem; 24½" ribbed barrels; plain extractor; single trigger; exposed hammer; folding leaf rear sight, bead front; checkered walnut Monte Carlo stock, forearm. Imported by Ithaca from Finland 1970 to 1979. Used value, $475 to $500.

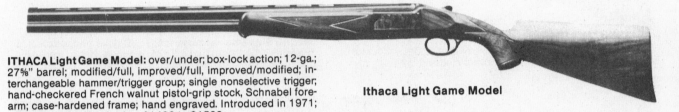

ITHACA Light Game Model: over/under; box-lock action; 12-ga.; 27⅝" barrel; modified/full, improved/full, improved/modified; interchangeable hammer/trigger group; single nonselective trigger; hand-checkered French walnut pistol-grip stock, Schnabel forearm; case-hardened frame; hand engraved. Introduced in 1971; dropped, 1974. Used value, $1400 to $1500.

Ithaca Light Game Model

ITHACA-SKB Century: single-barrel trap; 12-ga.; 30", 32" barrels, vent rib, full choke, auto ejector; box-lock action; checkered pistol-grip walnut stock, beavertail forearm; straight or Monte Carlo comb; recoil pad. Manufactured 1973 to 1974. Used value, $400 to $425.

Century II has same specs as Century, except for redesigned locking iron, reverse-taper forearm, higher stock. Manufactured 1975 to 1979. Used value, $465 to $485.

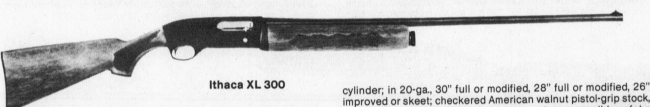

Ithaca XL 300

ITHACA Model XL 300: autoloader; gas-operated; 12-, 20-ga.; in 12-ga., 30" full-choke barrel, 28" full or modified, 26" improved cylinder; in 20-ga., 30" full or modified, 28" full or modified, 26" improved or skeet; checkered American walnut pistol-grip stock, fluted forearm; self-compensating gas system; reversible safety; vent rib at additional cost. Introduced in 1973; dropped, 1976. Used values: plain barrel, $195 to $205; vent rib, $225 to $250.

Ithaca-SKB Model 680 English

ITHACA-SKB Model 680 English: over/under; hammerless; box-lock action; 12-, 20-ga.; 26", 28" barrels, full/modified or modified/improved; single selective trigger; chrome-lined barrels, black chromed exterior surfaces; automatic selective ejectors; Bradley sights; vent rib; straight-grip stock; wraparound checkering. Introduced in 1973; dropped, 1976. Used value, $600 to $625.

Ithaca Model XL 900 Standard

ITHACA Model XL 900: autoloader; gas-operated; 12-, 20-ga.; 5-rd. tube magazine; in 12-ga., barrels are 30" full choke, 28" full or modified, 26" improved cylinder; in 20-ga., 28" full or modified, 26" improved; trap version has 30" full or improved choke; skeet version, 26" skeet; Bradley-type front sight on target-grade guns, Raybar front sight on vent-rib field guns; checkered walnut-finished stock; self-compensating gas system; reversible safety; action release button. Introduced in 1973; dropped, 1978. Used values: vent rib, $250 to $260; skeet grade, $265 to $285; trap grade (12-ga. only), $275 to $300.

Model XL 900 Slug Gun has same specs as standard Model XL 900, except for 24" slug barrel, rifle sights. Introduced in 1973; dropped, 1978. Used value, $250 to $265.

Ithaca Mag 10 Standard

ITHACA Mag 10: autoloader; gas-operated; 10-ga.; 3 rds.; 3½" magnum shells; full choke; plain or vent-rib barrel; walnut stock, forearm; recoil pad. Introduced, 1977; dropped, 1986. Used value, $450 to $475.

Ithaca Mag 10 Standard Vent Rib

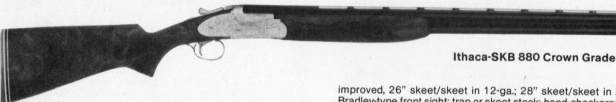

Ithaca Mag 10 Supreme

Mag 10 Deluxe has same specs as standard model, except for checkered semi-fancy wood, sling swivels; made with vent rib only.

Introduced, 1977; dropped, 1986. Used value, $550 to $600.

Mag 10 Supreme has same specs as Deluxe model, except for more fancy wood. Introduced, 1974; dropped, 1986. Used value, $600 to $625. Roadblocker Disc, $400 to $450.

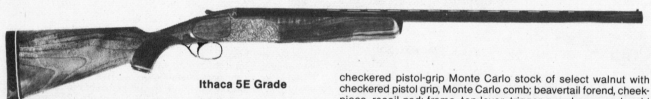

Ithaca-SKB 880 Crown Grade

ITHACA-SKB Model 880 Crown Grade: over/under; box-lock action; side plates; 12-, 20-ga.; 32" full/improved barrel, 30" full/

improved, 26" skeet/skeet in 12-ga.; 28" skeet/skeet in 20-ga.; Bradley-type front sight; trap or skeet stock; hand-checkered fancy French walnut pistol-grip stock, forearm; hand-honed action; engraved receiver; gold-inlaid crown on bottom of frame. Introduced in 1973; dropped, 1976. Used value, $1200 to $1300.

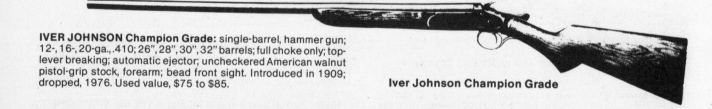

Ithaca 5E Grade

ITHACA 5E Grade: single-barrel; 12-ga. only; 30", 32" barrels; rampless vent rib; top lever break; dual locking lugs; hammerless;

checkered pistol-grip Monte Carlo stock of select walnut with checkered pistol grip, Monte Carlo comb; beavertail forend, cheekpiece, recoil pad; frame, top lever, trigger guard engraved, gold inlaid; gold nameplate in stock. Introduced, 1979; dropped, 1986. Used values: custom grade, $4250 to $5000; Dollar grade, $7000 to $7200.

IVER JOHNSON

IVER JOHNSON Champion Grade: single-barrel, hammer gun; 12-, 16-, 20-ga.,.410; 26", 28", 30", 32" barrels; full choke only; top-lever breaking; automatic ejector; uncheckered American walnut pistol-grip stock, forearm; bead front sight. Introduced in 1909; dropped, 1976. Used value, $75 to $85.

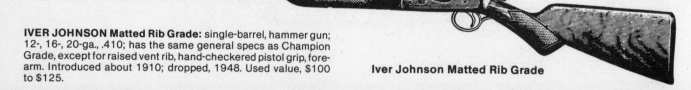

Iver Johnson Champion Grade

IVER JOHNSON Matted Rib Grade: single-barrel, hammer gun; 12-, 16-, 20-ga., .410; has the same general specs as Champion Grade, except for raised vent rib, hand-checkered pistol grip, forearm. Introduced about 1910; dropped, 1948. Used value, $100 to $125.

Iver Johnson Matted Rib Grade

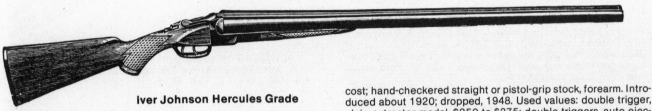

**Iver Johnson Special
Trap Model**

IVER JOHNSON Special Trap Model: single-barrel, hammer gun; 12-ga. only; 32" barrel only; other specs are the same as those of Matted Rib Grade. Introduced about 1912; dropped, 1949. Used value, $150 to $165.

Iver Johnson Hercules Grade

IVER JOHNSON Hercules Grade: double-barrel; box-lock action; hammerless; 12-, 16-, 20-ga., .410; 26", 28", 30", 32" barrels; full/full, modified/full chokes; double triggers; single nonselective or selective trigger at extra cost; automatic ejectors at additional cost; hand-checkered straight or pistol-grip stock, forearm. Introduced about 1920; dropped, 1948. Used values: double trigger, plain extractor model, $250 to $275; double triggers, auto ejectors, $275 to $300; plain extractors, nonselective trigger, $275 to $300; nonselective trigger, auto ejectors, $325 to $350; selective single trigger, plain extractors, $335 to $365; selective single trigger, auto ejectors, $375 to $400; add $100 for 20-ga., $150 for .410.

NOTE: 20-gauge is worth 25% more than prices listed; .410, 50% higher.

IVER JOHNSON Skeeter Model: double-barrel; box-lock action; hammerless; 12-, 16-, 20-, 28-ga., .410; 26" or 28" barrels; beavertail forearm. Other specs are same as Hercules grade, with the same options. Introduced about 1920; dropped, 1949. Used values: double triggers, plain extractors, $450 to $500; double triggers, auto ejectors, $500 to $525; nonselective trigger, auto ejectors, $500 to $525; selective single trigger, plain extractors, $525 to $550; selective trigger, auto ejectors, $575 to $625; add $100 for 20-ga., $200 for 28-ga., $200 for .410.

Iver Johnson Skeeter Model

Iver Johnson Super Trap Model

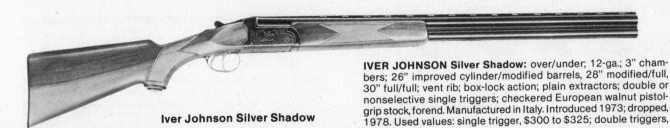

IVER JOHNSON Super Trap Model: side-by-side; hammerless; box-lock action; 12-ga. only; 32" barrel, full choke only; vent rib; hand-checkered pistol-grip stock, beavertail forearm; recoil pad. Introduced about 1924; dropped, 1949. Used values: double triggers, $525 to $550; nonselective single trigger, $575 to $600; single selective trigger, $650 to $700.

IVER JOHNSON Silver Shadow: over/under; 12-ga.; 3" chambers; 26" improved cylinder/modified barrels, 28" modified/full, 30" full/full; vent rib; box-lock action; plain extractors; double or nonselective single triggers; checkered European walnut pistol-grip stock, forend. Manufactured in Italy. Introduced 1973; dropped, 1978. Used values: single trigger, $300 to $325; double triggers, $265 to $275.

Iver Johnson Silver Shadow

KASSNAR

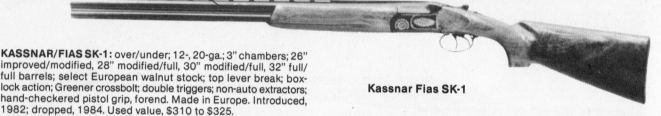

KASSNAR/FIAS SK-1: over/under; 12-, 20-ga.; 3" chambers; 26" improved/modified, 28" modified/full, 30" modified/full, 32" full/full barrels; select European walnut stock; top lever break; box-lock action; Greener crossbolt; double triggers; non-auto extractors; hand-checkered pistol grip, forend. Made in Europe. Introduced, 1982; dropped, 1984. Used value, $310 to $325.

   Model SK-3 has same specs as SK-1, except has single selective trigger. Made in Europe. Introduced, 1982; dropped, 1984. Used value, $325 to $335.

KASSNAR Fox: autoloader: 12-ga. only; 26", 28", 30" barrel lengths; standard choke combos; vent rib metal bead front sight, American walnut stock; crossbolt safety; interchangeable barrel. Imported

Kassnar Fias SK-1

   Model SK-4D has same specs as SK-3, except has side plates, better grade wood, deluxe engraving. Introduced, 1982; dropped, 1984. Used value, $350 to $375.

by Kassnar. Introduced, 1979; no longer imported. Used value, $175 to $200.

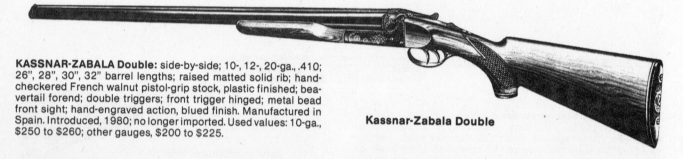

KASSNAR-ZABALA Double: side-by-side; 10-, 12-, 20-ga., .410; 26", 28", 30", 32" barrel lengths; raised matted solid rib; hand-checkered French walnut pistol-grip stock, plastic finished; bea-vertail forend; double triggers; front trigger hinged; metal bead front sight; hand-engraved action, blued finish. Manufactured in Spain. Introduced, 1980; no longer imported. Used values: 10-ga., $250 to $260; other gauges, $200 to $225.

Kassnar-Zabala Double

KASSNAR-SQUIRES BINGHAM Model 30D: slide-action; 12-ga.; 2¾" chamber; 20" improved or slug barrel, 24" slug, 26" improved, 28" modified, 30" full; Philippine mahogany stock; hand-

checkered pistol grip, forend; ramp front, open rear sight on slug models. Made in Philippines. Introduced, 1983; dropped, 1986. Was imported by Kassnar as Kassnar Omega. Used value, $90 to $100.

KASSNAR/Omega: pump-action; 12-ga.; 2¾" chambers; 20", 26", 28", 30" barrel lengths; stained hardwood or Philippine mahogany stock; bead front sight; rifle-type on slug gun; .damas-

cened bolt; crossbolt safety. Made in the Philippines. Introduced, 1984; dropped, 1986. Used values: Field model, $140 to $150; slug model, $145 to $155.

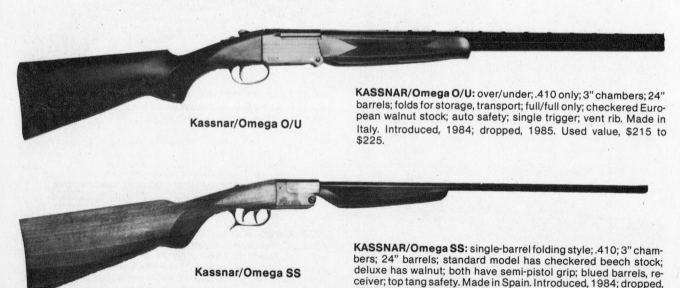

Kassnar/Omega O/U

KASSNAR/Omega O/U: over/under; .410 only; 3" chambers; 24" barrels; folds for storage, transport; full/full only; checkered European walnut stock; auto safety; single trigger; vent rib. Made in Italy. Introduced, 1984; dropped, 1985. Used value, $215 to $225.

Kassnar/Omega SS

KASSNAR/Omega SS: single-barrel folding style; .410; 3" chambers; 24" barrels; standard model has checkered beech stock; deluxe has walnut; both have semi-pistol grip; blued barrels, receiver; top tang safety. Made in Spain. Introduced, 1984; dropped, 1985. Used values: standard, $130 to $135; deluxe, $140 to $150.

KRIEGHOFF

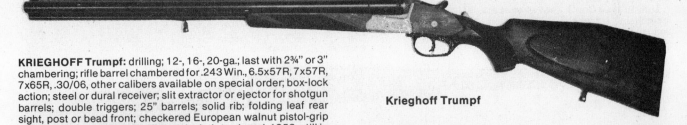

Krieghoff Trumpf

KRIEGHOFF Trumpf: drilling; 12-, 16-, 20-ga.; last with 2¾" or 3" chambering; rifle barrel chambered for .243 Win., 6.5x57R, 7x57R, 7x65R, .30/06, other calibers available on special order; box-lock action; steel or dural receiver; slit extractor or ejector for shotgun barrels; double triggers; 25" barrels; solid rib; folding leaf rear sight, post or bead front; checkered European walnut pistol-grip stock, forend; cheekpiece; sling swivels. Introduced, 1953; still in production. Used value, $3500 to $4000.

Neptun drilling; has the same specs as Trumpf model, except for side-locks, engraved hunting scene. Introduced, 1960; still in production. Used value, $6000 to $6500.

Neptun-Primus drilling; has same specs as Neptun model, except for detachable side-locks, fancier figured walnut, higher grade of engraving. Introduced, 1962; still in production. Used value, $7000 to $7500.

Krieghoff Model 32 Standard

Krieghoff Model 32 Skeet Set

KRIEGHOFF Model 32: over/under; 12-, 20-. 28-ga., .410; 26½", 28", 30", 32" barrels; any choke combo; box-lock action; single trigger; auto ejectors; checkered European walnut pistol-grip stock, forend; manufactured in field, skeet, trap configurations; patterned after Remington Model 32. Introduced, 1958; no longer in production. Used values: standard model, $1450 to $1650; low-rib two-barrel trap, $2250 to $2500; high-rib Vandalia two-barrel trap, $3000 to $3250.

Model 32 Single-Barrel Trap model has same specs as over/under, except 12-ga. only; 32", 34" barrels; modified, improved modified, full chokes; high vent rib; checkered Monte Carlo stock,

beavertail forend; recoil pad. Introduced, 1959; no longer in production. Used value, $1500 to $1600.

Model 32 Skeet Set has four sets of matched barrels (12-, 20-, 28-ga., .410); skeet chokes, stock design; marketed in fitted case in six grades, price depending upon quality of wood, amount and quality of engraving. Used values: Standard Grade, $3900 to $4000; Munchen Grade, $5750 to $6000; San Remo Grade, $7000 to $7500; Monte Carlo Grade, $11,000 to $12,250; Crown Grade, $13,000 to $14,500; Super Crown Grade, $15,000 to $17,500; Exhibition Grade, $24,500 to $25,000.

KRIEGHOFF Ulm: over/under; 12-, 16-, 20-ga.; has same specs as Teck Model over/under, except has side-locks, Arabesque engraving. Introduced, 1958; still in production. Used value, $6000 to $6500.

Ulm Combo has same specs, gauges, calibers as Teck combo, except for side-locks, Arabesque engraving. Introduced, 1963; still in production. Used value, $6500 to $7000.

Ulm-Primus over/under has same specs as Ulm over/under,

except for detachable side-locks, fancier figured walnut, higher grade engraving. Introduced, 1958; still in production. Used value, $7000 to $7500.

Ulm-Primus Combo has same specs as Ulm combo, except for detachable side-locks, fancier walnut, higher grade engraving. Introduced, 1963; still in production. Used value, $8000 to $10,000.

Krieghoff Ulm

KRIEGHOFF Teck: over/under; 12-, 16-, 20-ga., last chambered for 2¾", 3" shells; 28" vent-rib barrel; modified/full choke; box-lock action; Kersten double crossbolt; auto ejectors; double or single triggers; checkered European walnut pistol-grip stock, forend. Manufactured in West Germany. Introduced, 1967; still in production. Used value, $3250 to $3750.

Teck Combo has same general specs as Teck over/under, except receiver is steel or dural; slit extractor or ejector for shotgun barrel; rifle barrel in .22 Hornet, .222 Rem., .222 Rem. magnum, 7x57R, 7x64, 7x65R, .30-30, .300 Win. magnum, .30/06, .308, 9.3x-

Krieghoff Teck

74R; 25" barrels; solid rib; folding leaf rear sight, post or bead front; checkered European walnut pistol-grip stock, cheekpiece, semi-beavertail forend; sling swivels. Introduced, 1967; still in production. Used value, $4000 to $4500.

Krieghoff Single Barrel Trap Model

KRIEGHOFF Single Barrel Trap: single-shot; box-lock action; 12-ga. only; 32" or 34" full-choke barrel; thumb safety; vent rib;

hand-checkered Monte Carlo pistol-grip stock of European walnut, grooved beavertail forearm. Available in five grades, price depending upon grade of wood, decoration. Manufactured in West Germany. Introduced in 1970; still in production. Used values: standard grade, $1250 to $1300; San Remo Grade, $2250 to $2500; Monte Carlo Grade, $4500 to $4750; Crown Grade, $4750 to $5000; Super Crown Grade, $6000 to $6250.

Krieghoff Vandalia Trap

KRIEGHOFF Vandalia Trap: single-barrel or over/under; box-lock action; 12-ga. only; 30", 32", 34" barrels; three-way safety; selective single trigger; ejectors; vent rib; hand-checkered European walnut pistol-grip stock, beavertail forearm; available at additional cost with silver, gold inlays, relief engraving, fancier wood. Manufactured in West Germany. Introduced in 1973; dropped, 1976. Used value for standard model, $2750 to $3000.

LEFEVER

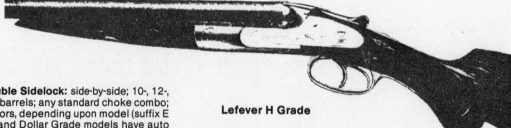

Lefever H Grade

LEFEVER Hammerless Double Sidelock: side-by-side; 10-, 12-, 16-, 20-ga.; 26", 28", 30" 32" barrels; any standard choke combo; plain extractors or auto ejectors, depending upon model (suffix E guns, A, AA, Optimus, Thousand Dollar Grade models have auto ejectors); double or single selective triggers; DS, DSE Grade models are sans cocking indicators; hand-checkered American walnut straight-grip or pistol-grip stocks, forends. Grades — 20 of them — differ in workmanship, quality of engraving, checkering, figure of wood, et al. Manufactured 1885 to 1919. Collector value. Used

values: Grade DS, $700 to $750; Grade DSE, $950 to $1000; Grade H, $800 to $850; Grade HE, $1100 to $1200; Grade G, $800 to $1000; Grade GE, $1250 to $1350; Grade F, $1000 to

$1100; Grade FE, $1400 to $1500; Grade E, $1250 to $1350; Grade EE, $1500 to $1600; Grade D, $1575 to $1625; Grade DE, $1800 to $1900; Grade C, $1900 to $2000; Grade CE, $2500 to $2600; Grade B, $3000 to $3600; Grade BE, $4000 to $4200; Grade A $6000 to $6500; Grade AA, $7500 to $8000; Optimus, $7000-plus; $1000 Grade, $10,000-plus.

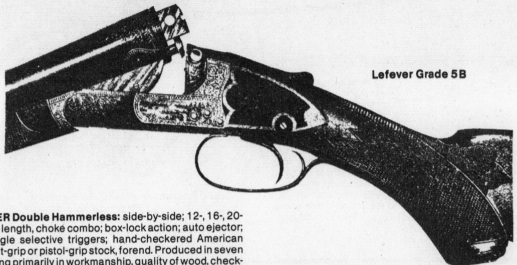

Lefever Grade 5 B

D.M. LEFEVER Double Hammerless: side-by-side; 12-, 16-, 20-ga.; any barrel length, choke combo; box-lock action; auto ejector; double or single selective triggers; hand-checkered American walnut straight-grip or pistol-grip stock, forend. Produced in seven grades, differing primarily in workmanship, quality of wood, checkering, engraving, et al. Marketed as New Lefever. Collector value, extremely rare, total production only 1000 to 1500 guns. Manufactured 1904 to 1906. Used values: O Grade, $1500 to $2000; O Grade with ejectors, $1600 to $2100; 9F Grade, $1800 to

$2400; 8E Grade, $3000 to $3500; 6C Grade, $3750 to $4000; 5B Grade, $4500 to $5000; 4AA Grade, $6000 to $6500; Uncle Dan, $10,000-plus.

D.M. LEFEVER Single-Barrel Trap: single-shot; 12-ga.; 26", 28", 30", 32" barrels; full choke only; box-lock action; auto ejector; hand-checkered American walnut pistol-grip stock, forend. Collector value. Manufactured 1904 to 1906. Used value, $600 to $650; extremely rare.

NOTE: 20-gauge 25% higher than prices shown; .410, 50% higher.

Lefever Nitro Express Model

LEFEVER Nitro Special: side-by-side double barrel; box-lock action; 12-, 16-, 20-ga., .410; 26", 28", 30", 32" barrels; standard choke combos; double triggers; single nonselective trigger at added cost; plain extractors; hand-checkered American walnut pistol-grip stock, forearm. Introduced in 1921; dropped, 1948. Used values: double triggers, $325 to $350; single trigger, $400 to $450.

Lefever Single Barrel Trap Model

LEFEVER Single Barrel Trap: single-shot; box-lock action; hammerless; 12-ga. only; 30", 32" barrels; ejector; full choke only; vent rib; bead front sight; hand-checkered American walnut pistol-grip stock, forearm; recoil pad. Introduced about 1923; dropped, 1942. Used value, $375 to $425.

Lefever Long Range Model

LEFEVER Long Range: single-shot; box-lock action; hammerless; 12-, 16-, 20-ga.; 26", 28", 30", 32" barrels; standard chokes; bead front sight; no recoil pad; field stock; other specs similar to those of single-barrel trap model. Introduced about 1923; dropped, 1942. Used value, $250 to $275.

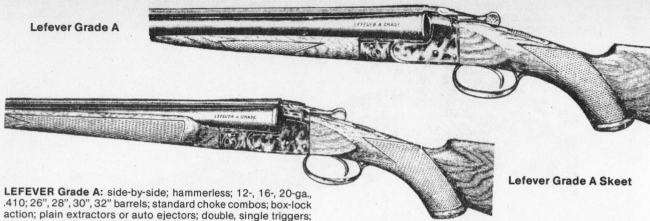

Lefever Grade A

Lefever Grade A Skeet

LEFEVER Grade A: side-by-side; hammerless; 12-, 16-, 20-ga., .410; 26", 28", 30", 32" barrels; standard choke combos; box-lock action; plain extractors or auto ejectors; double, single triggers; hand-checkered American walnut pistol-grip stock, forend. Manufactured in Ithaca plant, 1934 to 1942. Used values: plain extractors, double triggers, $550 to $600; auto ejector, double triggers, $650 to $700; plain extractors, single trigger, $700 to $750; auto ejectors, single triggers, $800 to $825.

Grade A Skeet model has same specs as standard Grade A, except for integral auto ejector, single trigger. 26" barrels, skeet chokes, beavertail forend. Manufactured 1934 to 1942. Used value, $900 to $950.

LJUTIC

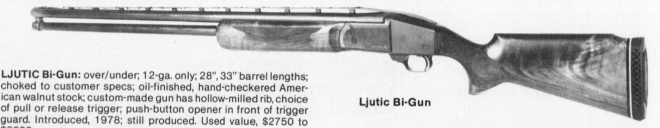

LJUTIC Bi-Gun: over/under; 12-ga. only; 28", 33" barrel lengths; choked to customer specs; oil-finished, hand-checkered American walnut stock; custom-made gun has hollow-milled rib, choice of pull or release trigger; push-button opener in front of trigger guard. Introduced, 1978; still produced. Used value, $2750 to $3000.

Bi-Gun Combo has same specs as standard design, except has

Ljutic Bi-Gun

two trigger assemblies, one for single trigger, one for double; interchangeable single barrel. Used value, $4000 to $4250.

LJUTIC Four Barrel Skeet has same general specs as Bi-Gun, except comes with matched 28" barrels in 12-, 20-, 28-ga., .410; custom American or French walnut stock, fancy checkering; Ljutic

Paternator chokes integral to barrels. Used value, $8500 to $9000.

Ljutic Mono Gun

Ljutic LTX Mono Gun

Adjustable Barrel Mono Gun has same specs, except has adjustable choke to adjust pattern; choice of Olympic, step-style or standard rib; custom stock, fancy wood. Introduced, 1978; dropped, 1983. Used value, $2500 to $2750.

LTX Mono Gun is similar to standard Mono Gun, except has exhibition quality wood, extra-fancy checkering, double recessed choking; extra-light 33" barrel; Olympic rib. Introduced, 1985; still produced. Used values: $3750 to $3800; with four screw-in choke tubes, $4200 to $4300.

LJUTIC Mono Gun: single-barrel; 12-ga. only; 34" barrel; hollow-milled rib; hand-checkered, oil-finished fancy walnut stock; pull or release trigger; removable trigger guard; push-button opener on trigger guard. Introduced, 1962; still produced. Used value, $2250 to $2500.

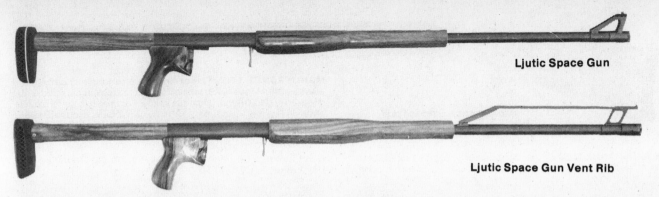

Ljutic Space Gun

Ljutic Space Gun Vent Rib

LJUTIC Space Gun: single-barrel; 12-ga. only; 30" barrel; fancy American walnut stock with medium or large pistol grip, universal comb; front sight or vent rib; pull or release button trigger; anti-

recoil device. Introduced, 1981; still produced. Used value, $2200 to $2300.

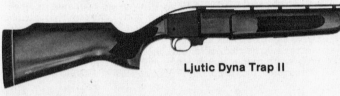

Ljutic Dyna Trap II

LJUTIC Dyna Trap II: single shot; has same specs as Mono Gun, except has 33" single barrel; straight or Monte Carlo stock. Introduced, 1981; dropped, 1984. Used value: $1100 to $1200.

LJUTIC Bi-Matic: autoloader; 12-ga.; 2¾" chamber; 2-rd. magazine; 26", 28", 30", 32" barrel, choked to customer's specs; custom-made; oil-finished, hand-checkered American walnut stock; de-

signed for trap, skeet; left- or right-hand ejection; many options. Introduced, 1983; dropped, 1984. Used value: $2000 to $2100.

MANUFRANCE

Manufrance Auto Model

MANUFRANCE Auto: autoloader; 12-ga. only; 3 rds.; gas-operated; 26" improved cylinder, 28" modified, 30" full choke barrels; vent rib; hand-checkered French walnut pistol-grip stock; black matte finish; quick take-down; interchangeable barrels. Manufactured in France. Imported by Interarms, 1978; no longer imported. Used value, $250 to $275.

Manufrance 254 Robust Deluxe

MANUFRANCE 254 Robust Deluxe: side-by side; 12-ga.; 2¾" chambers; 27½" chrome-lined barrels; hand-checkered French walnut stock, beavertail forend; box-lock action; double triggers;

auto ejectors; top tang safety; silver-gray finish; scroll engraving on receiver, top lever, trigger guard; optional retractable sling in butt. Made in France. Introduced, 1984 by Armsource, Inc.; dropped, 1985. Used value, $575 to $600.

222 Robust Field Model has same specs as Deluxe model, except has plain color case-hardened receiver; 27½" or 20½" barrels; extractors only. Introduced, 1984; dropped, 1985. Used value, $400 to $425.

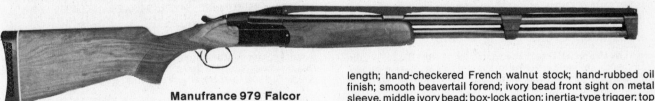

Manufrance 979 Falcor

MANUFRANCE 979 Falcor: over/under; competition trap model; 12-ga.; 2¾" chambers; 30" chrome-lined barrels; 48" overall

length; hand-checkered French walnut stock; hand-rubbed oil finish; smooth beavertail forend; ivory bead front sight on metal sleeve, middle ivory bead; box-lock action; inertia-type trigger; top tang safety/barrel selector; auto ejectors; alloy high-post rib. Made in France. Introduced, 1984 by Armsource; dropped, 1985. Used value, $1300 to $1500.

Manufrance Falcor Trap

MANUFRANCE 1985 Falcor Trap: over/under; has same general specs as Model 979, except has standard vent rib, middle rib, checkered grip, forend; luminous yellow front bead in metal sleeve. Made in France. Introduced, 1984 by Armsource; dropped, 1985. Used value, $700 to $750.

MANUFRANCE 1987 Falcor Skeet: over/under; has same specs as Model 1985 Falcor, except has 27½" skeet barrels, smooth skeet butt pad. Introduced, 1984 by Armsource; dropped, 1985. Used value, $700 to $750.

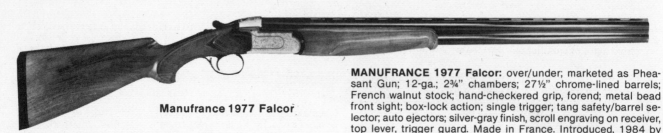

Manufrance 1977 Falcor

MANUFRANCE 1977 Falcor: over/under; marketed as Pheasant Gun; 12-ga.; 2¾" chambers; 27½" chrome-lined barrels; French walnut stock; hand-checkered grip, forend; metal bead front sight; box-lock action; single trigger; tang safety/barrel selector; auto ejectors; silver-gray finish, scroll engraving on receiver, top lever, trigger guard. Made in France. Introduced, 1984 by Armsource, Inc.; dropped, 1985. Used value, $675 to $725.

MARLIN

MARLIN Model 1898: slide-action; 12-ga.; 5-rd. tubular magazine; 26", 28", 30", 32" barrels; standard chokes; take-down; visible hammer; American walnut pistol-grip stock, grooved slide handle; checkering on higher grades. Grades differ in quality of woods, amount of engraving. Marlin's first shotgun, was manufactured 1898 to 1905. Collector value. Used values: Grade A, $450 to $475; Grade B, $500 to $525; Grade C, $600 to $650; Grade D, $1250 to $1350.

MARLIN Model 16: slide-action; 16-ga.; 5-rd. tubular magazine; 26", 28" barrels, standard chokes; take-down; American walnut pistol-grip stock, grooved slide handle. Manufactured in four grades, differing in quality of wood; engraving and checkering on Grades C, D; visible hammer. Manufactured 1904 to 1910. Used values: Grade A, $250 to $275; Grade B, $375 to $400; Grade C, $500 to $550; Grade D, $1000 to $1150.

Marlin Model 17 Standard

MARLIN Model 17: slide-action; 12-ga.; 5-rd. tubular magazine; 30", 32" barrels; full choke only; solid frame; uncheckered American walnut straight-grip stock, grooved slide handle, visible hammer. Collector value. Used value, $275 to $300.

    Model 17 Riot Gun has same specs as standard model, except for 20" barrel, cylinder bore. Manufactured 1906 to 1908. Some collector interest. Used value, $300 to $325.

    Model 17 Brush model has same specs as standard version, except for 26" barrel, cylinder bore. Manufactured 1906 to 1908. Some collector value. Used value, $300 to $325.

MARLIN Model 19: slide-action; 12-ga.; 5-rd. tubular magazine; has same general specs as Model 1898, except is lighter in weight, has two extractors, matted sighting groove on top of receiver; visible hammer. Made in four grades, differing in quality of workmanship and wood, amount of engraving. Manufactured 1906 to 1907. Collector value. Used values: Grade A, $250 to $265; Grade B, $325 to $350; Grade C, $425 to $450; Grade D, $925 to $950.

MARLIN Model 21 Trap: slide-action; 12-ga.; has the same general specs as Model 19, except for straight-grip stock; visible hammer. Made in four grades, differing in workmanship, quality of wood, engraving. Manufactured 1907 to 1909. Collector interest. Used values: Grade A, $275 to $300; Grade B, $400 to $425; Grade C, $500 to $550; Grade D, $1000 to $1100.

MARLIN Model 24: slide-action; 12-ga.; has same general specs as Model 19, but features solid matted rib attached to frame, automatic recoil safety lock, improved take-down. Made in four grades. Manufactured 1908 to 1915. Used values: Grade A, $275 to $300; Grade B, $425 to $450; Grade C, $500 to $550; Grade D, $1100 to $1200.

MARLIN Model 26: slide-action; 12-ga.; has same general specs as Model 24, Grade A, except for straight-grip stock, solid frame, 30", 32" full-choke barrel; visible hammer. Manufactured 1909 to 1915. Used value, $200 to $225.

Model 26 Riot model has same specs as standard Model 26, except for 20" barrel, cylinder bore. Manufactured 1909 to 1915. Used value, $250 to $275.

Model 26 Brush model has same specs as standard version except for 26" cylinder-bore barrel. Manufactured 1909 to 1915. Used value, $250 to $275.

Marlin Model 30 Grade D

MARLIN Model 30: slide-action; has same general specs as Model 16, except for improved take-down, auto recoil safety lock, solid matted rib on frame; visible hammer. Manufactured in four grades, depending upon quality of wood, amount and quality of engraving. Manufactured 1910 to 1915. Used values: Grade A, $250 to $275; Grade B, $325 to $350; Grade C, $440 to $460; Grade D, $1000 to $1100.

Model 30 Field has same specs as Grade B, except for 25" barrel, modified choke, straight-grip stock. Manufactured 1913 to 1914. Used value, $200 to $225.

Marlin Model 28B

MARLIN Model 28: slide-action; 12-ga.; 5-rd. tubular magazine; 26", 28", 30", 32" barrels, standard chokes; take-down; hammerless; made in four grades; all have matted barrel top, except for 28D, which has solid matted rib. Differences in grades are quality of wood, amount of engraving on 28C, 28D. Three grades manufactured 1913 to 1915; Model 28A manufactured 1913 to 1922. Used values: Model 28A, $225 to $250; 28B, $375 to $400; 28C, $450 to $500; 28D, $1000 to $1100.

Model 28T Trap has same specs as Model 28A, except for 30" barrel, matted rib; full choke; hand-checkered straight-grip walnut stock; high fluted comb; fancier wood. Manufactured 1915. Used value, $400 to $425.

Model 28TS has same specs as Model 28T, except for stock of plainer walnut, matted-top barrel instead of rib. Manufactured, 1915. Used value, $300 to $325.

MARLIN Model 31A: slide-action; 16-, 20-ga.; 25", 26", 28" barrel; hammerless; scaled-down version of Model 28; matted-top barrel; standard chokes; unchecked American walnut pistol-grip stock, grooved slide handle. Manufactured 1915 to 1922. Used value, $265 to $275.

Model 31B has same general specs as 31A, except for hand-checkered stock. Manufactured 1915 to 1917. Used value, $325 to $350.

Model 31C has same specs as Model 31B, except for improved wood, better checkering quality. Manufactured 1915 to 1917. Used value, $450 to $500.

Model 31D has same specs as Model 31C, except for improved wood, straight-grip stock optional. Manufactured 1915 to 1917. Used value, $875 to $950.

Model 31F has same specs as Model 31B, except for 25" barrel, modified choke, optional straight or pistol-grip stock. Manufactured 1915 to 1917. Used value, $325 to $350.

Marlin Model 42A

MARLIN Model 42A: slide-action repeater; take-down; 12-ga. only; 26" cylinder bore, 28" modified, 30" or 32" full choke; visible hammer; 5-rd. magazine; unchecked American walnut pistol-grip stock, grooved slide handle; bead front sight. Introduced in 1922; dropped, 1934. Used value, $165 to $175.

Marlin Model 43A

MARLIN Model 43A: slide-action; 12-ga.; has same general specs as Model 28, but lower in overall quality. Manufactured 1923 to 1930. Used value, $200 to $225.

Marlin Model 43T

Model 43T has same general specs as Model 28T, but is of lower quality. Manufactured 1923 to 1930. Used value, $325 to $350.

Model 43TS has same specs as Model 28TS, but is of lower quality. Manufactured 1923 to 1930. Used value, $350 to $375.

MARLIN Model 60: single-shot; 12-ga.; 30", 32" barrel; full choke; visible hammer; box-lock action; take-down; automatic ejector; pistol-grip walnut stock, beavertail forend. Only about 600 made; some collector interest. Manufactured, 1923. Used value, $175 to $200.

MARLIN Model 44A: slide-action; 20-ga.; hammerless; has same general specs as Model 31A, except is of slightly lower quality. Manufactured 1923 to 1935. Used value, $225 to $250.

Model 44S has same specs as Model 44A, except for hand-checkered American walnut stock; stock and slide handle of better quality wood. Manufactured 1932 to 1935. Used value, $325 to $350.

MARLIN Model 49: slide-action repeater; has same general specs as Model 42A, except not as well or expensively made. Used by Marlin as a premium, with purchase of four shares of corporate stock; less than 3000 made. Some collector value. Manufactured 1925 to 1928. Used value, $275 to $300.

Marlin Model 410

MARLIN Model 410: lever-action; .410, 2½" shell; 4-rd. tubular magazine; 22", 26" barrels; full choke; solid frame; visible hammer; uncheckered American walnut pistol-grip stock, grooved beavertail forend. Manufactured 1929 to 1932. Collector interest. Used value, $450 to $500.

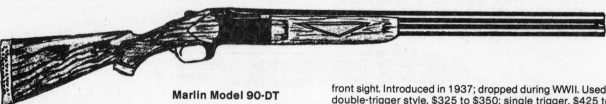

Marlin Model 53

MARLIN Model 53: slide-action; 12-ga.; has same general specs as Model 43A, except for redesigned tubular magazine, slide handle. Manufactured 1929 to 1930. Used value, $220 to $240.

MARLIN Model 63A: slide-action; 12-ga.; has same general specs as Model 43A, replacing it in line. Manufactured 1931 to 1935. Used value, $190 to $200.

Model 63T has same specs as Model 43T. Manufactured 1931 to 1935. Used value, $250 to $275.

Model 63TS Trap Special has same specs as Model 63T, except that stock dimensions were to special order. Manufactured 1931 to 1935. Used value, $320 to $335.

Marlin Model 90-DT

MARLIN Model 90: standard over/under; hammerless; box-lock action; 12-, 16- 20-ga., .410; 28", 30" barrels; improved/modified, modified/full choke combos; full-length rib between barrels; double triggers; single nonselective trigger at extra cost; hand-checkered American walnut pistol-grip stock, forearm; recoil pad; bead front sight. Introduced in 1937; dropped during WWII. Used values: double-trigger style, $325 to $350; single trigger, $425 to $450. .410 brings 50% higher.

Model 90-DT is post-WWII version of Model 90 with double triggers, no rib between barrels, no recoil pad. Introduced in 1949; dropped, 1958. Used value, $350 to $375.

Model 90-ST is post-war single nonselective trigger version; no rib between barrels, no recoil pad. Introduced in 1949; dropped, 1958. Used value, $450 to $475.

Marlin Model 55 Hunter

Marlin Model 55 Hunter Adjustable Choke

MARLIN Model 55 Hunter: bolt-action; take-down; 12-, 16-, 20-ga.; 28" barrel in 12-, 16-ga.; 26" in 20-ga.; full choke or with adjustable choke; uncheckered American walnut one-piece pistol-grip stock; 12-ga. has recoil pad. Introduced in 1950; dropped, 1965.

Marlin Model 55 Swamp Gun

Marlin Model 55 Goose Gun

Marlin Model 5510

Used values: plain barrel, $65 to $75; adjustable choke, $75 to $85.

Model 55-G was marketed as Marlin-Glenfield model. Has same specs as Model 55, except for walnut-finished hardwood stock. Used values: plain barrel, $55 to $60; with adjustable choke, $65 to $70.

Model 55 Swamp Gun has same specs as Model 55 Hunter except for 20½" barrel, chambered for 3" 12-ga. magnum shell; adjustable choke; sling swivels. Introduced in 1963; dropped, 1965. Used value, $75 to $85.

Model 55S Slug version has same specs as Model 55 Goose Gun except for 24" barrel, cylinder bore, rifle sights. Introduced, 1974; dropped, 1980. Used value, $95 to $110.

Model 55 Goose Gun bolt-action repeater; take-down; 12-ga. only; 36" barrel; full choke only; 2-rd. detachable clip magazine; thumb safety; uncheckered one-piece walnut pistol-grip stock; recoil pad; sling swivels; leather carrying strap; double-extractors; tapped for receiver sights. Introduced in 1964; still in production. Used value, $100 to $110.

Model 5510 has same general specs as Model 55, except chambered for 10-ga. 3½" magnum shell; 34" heavy barrel; full choke. Introduced, 1976; dropped, 1986. Used value, $150 to $165.

Marlin Model 59 Olympic

MARLIN Model 59 Olympic: single-shot, bolt-action; take-down; .410 only; 2½" or 3" shells; 24" barrel, full choke only; bead front sight; self-cocking bolt; automatic thumb safety; uncheckered one-piece walnut pistol-grip stock; also available with Junior stock with 12" length of pull. Introduced in 1960; dropped, 1962. Used value, $75 to $85.

MARLIN-Glenfield Model 60G: single-shot, bolt-action; take-down; .410 only; has exactly the same specs as Model 59, except

for walnut-finished hardwood stock. Introduced in 1961; dropped, 1962. Used value, $75 to $85.

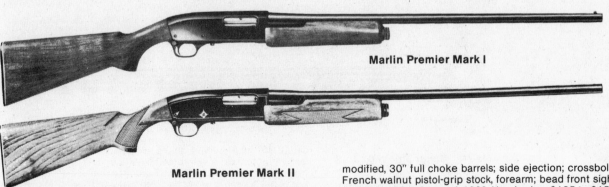

Marlin Premier Mark I

Marlin Premier Mark II

MARLIN Premier Mark I: slide-action repeater; take-down; hammerless; 12-ga. only; 3-rd. magazine; 26" improved or skeet, 28"

modified, 30" full choke barrels; side ejection; crossbolt safety; French walnut pistol-grip stock, forearm; bead front sight. Introduced in 1961; dropped, 1963. Used value, $135 to $150.

Premier Mark II has the same specs as Premier Mark I, except for scroll-engraved receiver, checkered pistol grip, forearm. Intro-

Marlin Premier Mark IV

duced in 1961; dropped, 1963. Used value, $145 to $165.

Premier Mark IV has the same specs as Premier Mark II, except for full-coverage engraved receiver, engraved trigger guard, fine checkering, better wood, pistol-grip cap, vent rib at added cost. Introduced in 1961; dropped, 1963. Used values: plain barrel, $200 to $225; vent rib, $245 to $265.

Marlin Model 50

MARLIN Model 50: bolt-action repeater; take-down; 12-, 20-ga.; 28" barrel in 12-ga., 26" in 20-ga.; 12-ga. has recoil pad; other specs are the same as Goose Gun, except 12-ga. was available with adjustable choke. Introduced in 1967; dropped, 1975. Used values: plain barrel, $75 to $85; with adjustable choke, $85 to $95.

Marlin Model 120 Magnum

vertail forearm; slide release button; crossbolt safety; interchangeable barrels; side ejection. Introduced in 1974; dropped, 1986. Used value, $200 to $225.

Model 120 Trap has same basic specs as 120 Magnum, except for hand-checkered Monte Carlo stock, full forearm; 30" full or modified trap choke. Introduced in 1974; dropped, 1986. Used value, $225 to $250.

MARLIN Model 120 Magnum: slide-action; hammerless; 12-ga.; 2¾" or 3" chamber, 26" improved cylinder barrel, 28" modified, 30" full choke; vent rib; checkered walnut pistol-grip stock, semi-bea-

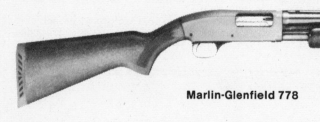

Marlin-Glenfield 778

MARLIN-Glenfield 778: slide action; 12-ga.; 2¾", 3" chambers; 5-rd. magazine; 20" slug barrel with sights, 26" improved, 28" modified, 30" full; plain or vent-rib barrel; walnut-finished hardwood stock; semi-beavertail forend; steel receiver; engine-turned bolt; double action bars; vent recoil pad. Introduced, 1978; dropped, 1984. Used values: plain barrel, $180 to $190; vent rib, $200 to $210.

MAUSER-BAUER

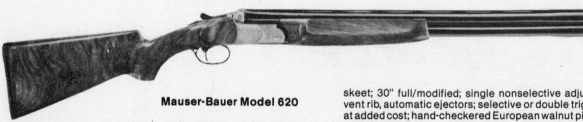

Mauser-Bauer Model 620

skeet; 30" full/modified; single nonselective adjustable trigger; vent rib, automatic ejectors; selective or double triggers available at added cost; hand-checkered European walnut pistol-grip stock, beavertail forearm; recoil pad. Produced in Italy for Mauser. Introduced in 1972; dropped, 1974. Used values: standard model, $650 to $675; single-selective trigger, $700 to $750; double triggers, $675 to $700.

MAUSER-BAUER Model 620: over/under; Greener crossbolt action; 12-ga.; 28" barrels, modified/full, improved/modified, skeet/

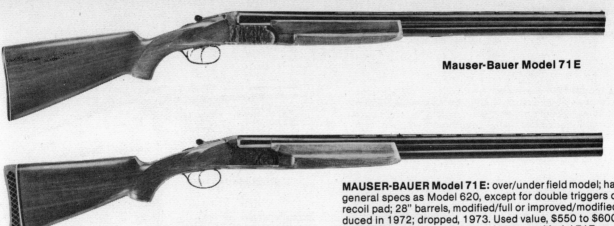

Mauser-Bauer Model 71E

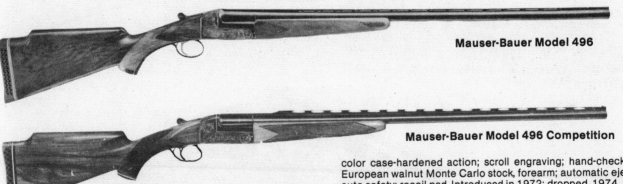

Mauser-Bauer Model 72E

MAUSER-BAUER Model 71E: over/under field model; has same general specs as Model 620, except for double triggers only; no recoil pad; 28" barrels, modified/full or improved/modified. Introduced in 1972; dropped, 1973. Used value, $550 to $600.

Model 72E has same general specs as Model 71E, except for wider rib, engraved receiver. Trap version has 30" trap/trap bored barrel; skeet has 28" full/modified. Introduced in 1972; dropped, 1973. Used value, $650 to $700.

Mauser-Bauer Model 496

Mauser-Bauer Model 496 Competition

color case-hardened action; scroll engraving; hand-checkered European walnut Monte Carlo stock, forearm; automatic ejector; auto safety; recoil pad. Introduced in 1972; dropped, 1974. Used value, $450 to $500.

Model 496 Competition Grade has same general specs as standard model, except for high ramp rib; front, middle sight bead; hand finishing on wood and metal parts. Introduced in 1973; dropped, 1974. Used value, $575 to $600.

MAUSER-BAUER Model 496: single-barrel trap model; single-shot; Greener crossbolt box-lock action; 12-ga.; 32" modified, 34" full-choke barrel; double underlocking blocks; matted vent rib;

Mauser-Bauer Model 610 Phantom

MAUSER-BAUER Model 610 Phantom: over/under; 12-ga.; 30", 32" barrels; standard choke combos; raised rib; vent rib between barrels for heat reduction; color case-hardened action; coil springs

throughout working parts; hand-checkered European walnut stock, forearm; recoil pad. Introduced in 1973; dropped, 1974. Used value, $650 to $700.

Model 610 Skeet version has same general specs as standard Model 610, except has set of Purbaugh tubes to convert gun for all-gauge competition. Tubes convert to 20-, 28-ga., .410. Introduced in 1973; dropped, 1974. Used value, $950 to $1000.

Mauser-Bauer Model 580

MAUSER-BAUER Model 580: advertised as St. Vincent model; side-by-side; side-lock Holland & Holland action; 12-ga.; 28", 30", 32" barrels; standard choke combos; split sear levers; coil hammer springs; single or double triggers; scroll-engraved receiver; hand-checkered European walnut straight stock, forearm. Introduced in 1973; dropped, 1974. Used value, $700 to $725.

MERKEL

MERKEL Model 100: over/under; hammerless; box-lock action; 12-, 16-, 20-ga.; standard barrel lengths, choke combos; Greener crossbolt safety; double triggers; plain extractors; plain barrel; ribbed barrel at added cost; hand-checkered European walnut stock, forearm; pistol-grip and cheekpiece or straight English type. Manufactured in Germany prior to World War II. Used values: plain barrel, $800 to $1000; ribbed barrel, $1000 to $1250.

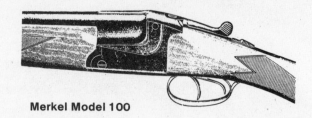

Merkel Model 100

Merkel Model 101

MERKEL Model 101: over/under; hammerless; box-lock action; has the same general specs as Model 100, except for English engraving motif, standard ribbed barrel, separate extractors. Manufactured in Germany prior to World War II. Used value, $900 to $1000.

   Model 101E has the same specs as Model 101, except for ejectors. Used value, $1100 to $1200.

Merkel Model 400

MERKEL Model 400: over/under; hammerless; box-lock action; has the same general specs as Model 101, except for Arabesque engraving on receiver, Kersten double crossbolt, separate extractors. Manufactured in Germany prior to World War II. Used value,

$850 to $950.

   Model 400E has same specs as Model 400, except for Merkel ejectors. Used value, $1000 to $1150.

MERKEL Model 200: over/under; hammerless; box-lock action; 12-, 16-, 20-, 24-, 28-, 32-ga.; Kersten double crossbolt; scalloped frame; Arabesque engraving; separate extractors; double triggers; standard barrel lengths, choke combos; ribbed barrels; hand-checkered European walnut stock, forearm; pistol-grip and cheekpiece or straight English style. Manufactured in Germany prior to WWII. Used value, $1000 to $1250.

   Model 200E has same general specs as Model 200, except for ejectors; double, single or single selective trigger. Introduced prior to WWII; still in production; 24-, 28-, 32-ga. dropped during WWII. Importation dropped by Champlin, 1979. No current importer. Used values: double triggers, $1150 to $1250; single trigger, $1250 to $1350; single selective trigger, $1350 to $1500.

Merkel Model 201

MERKEL Model 201: over/under; hammerless; box-lock action; has the same general specs as Model 200, except for better engraving, wood, checkering, overall quality. Manufactured in Germany prior to WWII. Used value, $1250 to $1400.

   Model 201E has the same specs as Model 201, except for ejectors; double, single or single selective trigger. Still in production.

No current importer. Used values: double triggers, $1400 to $1500; single trigger, $1450 to $1550; single selective trigger, $1550 to $1650.

MERKEL Model 202: over/under; hammerless; box-lock action; has same general specs as Model 201, except for better engraving, dummy side plates, finer wood, checkering. Manufactured in Germany prior to WWII. Used value, $1750 to $2000.
Model 202E has same specs as Model 202, except for ejectors. Manufactured prior to WWII. Used value, $2200 to $2400.

Merkel Model 202

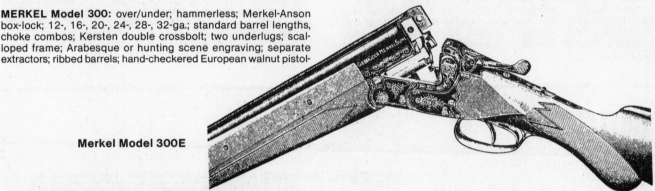

Merkel Model 203

MERKEL Model 203: over/under; hammerless; hand-detachable side-locks; 12-, 16-, 20-ga.; ribbed barrels in standard lengths, choke combos; Kersten double crossbolt; automatic ejectors; Arabesque or hunting scene engraving; hand-checkered European walnut stock, forearm; pistol-grip, cheekpiece or straight English style. Introduced in Germany prior to WWII. No current importer. Used values: double triggers, $3500 to $3750; single trigger, $3750 to $4000; single selective trigger, $4000 to $4250.

MERKEL Model 204E: over/under; hammerless; 12-, 16-, 20-ga.; has same general specs as Model 203, except for fine English-

style engraving, double triggers only. Merkel side-locks. Manufactured in Germany prior to WWII. Used value, $3750 to $4000.

MERKEL Model 300: over/under; hammerless; Merkel-Anson box-lock; 12-, 16-, 20-, 24-, 28-, 32-ga.; standard barrel lengths, choke combos; Kersten double crossbolt; two underlugs; scalloped frame; Arabesque or hunting scene engraving; separate extractors; ribbed barrels; hand-checkered European walnut pistol-

Merkel Model 300E

grip, cheekpiece or straight English-style stock. Manufactured in Germany prior to WWII. Used value, $1650 to $1850.
Model 300E has same general specs as Model 300, except for automatic ejectors. Used value, $1950 to $2050.

MERKEL Model 301: over/under; hammerless; Merkel-Anson box-lock action; has same general specs as Model 300, except for better engraving, wood, checkering. Manufactured in Germany prior to WWII. Used value, $1850 to $2000.
Model 301E has same specs as Model 301, except for automatic ejectors. Used value, $2150 to $2250.

MERKEL Model 302: over/under; hammerless; has the same general specs as Model 301E, except for dummy side plates. Manufactured in Germany prior to WWII. Used value, $2750 to $3000.

MERKEL Model 303E: over/under; hammerless; Holland & Holland-type hand-detachable side-locks; Kersten crossbolt, double underlugs, automatic ejectors. Has same general design specs as Model 203E, but is of better quality throughout. Introduced prior to WWII; still in production; no current importer. Used value, $5000 to $5250.

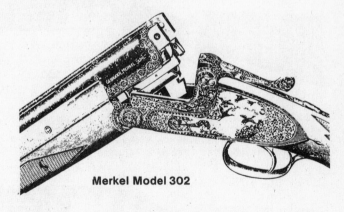

Merkel Model 302

Merkel Model 304E

MERKEL Model 304E: over/under; hammerless; Holland & Holland-type hand-detachable side-locks; has virtually the same specs as 303E, except for better workmanship and quality. Introduced in Germany prior to WWII; still in production, but not imported at this time. Used value, $6500 to $7000.

MERKEL Model 130: side-by-side; hammerless; box-lock action; 12-, 16-, 20-, 28-ga., .410; standard barrel lengths, choke combos; Anson & Deeley-type action; side plates; double triggers; automatic ejectors; elaborate Arabesque or hunting-scene engraving; hand-checkered European walnut stock, forearm; pistol-grip, cheekpiece or straight English style. Manufactured in Germany prior to WWII. Used value, $4500 to $5000.

MERKEL Model 127: side-by-side; hammerless; Holland & Holland-type action; hand-detachable side-locks; 12-, 16-, 20-, 28-ga., .410; standard barrel lengths, choke combos; elaborately engraved with Arabesque or hunting scene; hand-checkered European walnut stock, forearm; pistol-grip, cheekpiece or straight English style. Manufactured in Germany prior to WWII. Used value, $11,000 to $14,000.

MERKEL Model 47S: side-by-side; hammerless; side-locks; 12-, 16-, 20-ga.; 3" chamber available; all standard barrel lengths, choke combos; double hook bolting; Greener-type breech; double, single or single selective trigger; cocking indicators; English Arabesque engraving; hand-checkered European walnut stock, forearm; pistol-grip, cheekpiece or straight English style. Introduced prior to WWII; still in production; no current importer. Used values: double triggers, $2000 to $2250; single trigger, $2250 to $2500; single selective trigger, $2500 to $3000.

Merkel Model 47S

MERKEL Model 147E: side-by-side; 12-, 16-, 20-ga.; 26" barrels, other lengths on special order; any standard choke combo; Anson & Deeley lock system; auto ejectors; double triggers; hand-checkered straight-grip or pistol-grip stock, forend. Manufactured in Germany since WWII; no current importer. Used value, $1000 to $1200.

Model 147S has same specs as Model 147E, except for side-lock action, engraved hunting scene on action. Manufactured since WWII. Used value, $3000 to $3250.

Model 47S has same specs as Model 147S, except for less elaborate engraving pattern. Manufactured since WWII. Used value, $1500 to $1600.

MIIDA

Miida Model 612

MIIDA Model 612: over/under; 12-ga.; 26" improved cylinder/modified; 28" modified/full barrels; box-lock action; auto ejectors; single selective trigger; engraving; checkered walnut pistol-grip stock, forearm. Manufactured in Japan; imported by Marubeni America Corp., 1972 to 1974. Used value, $600 to $650.

Miida Model 2100

MIIDA Model 2100 Skeet: over/under; 12-ga.; 27" vent-rib barrels; skeet choke; selective single trigger; box-lock action; auto ejectors; skeet stock, forearm of select walnut; 50% of frame engraved. Imported 1972 to 1974. Used value, $750 to $800.

MIIDA Model 2200T Trap: over/under; 12-ga.; 29¾" improved modified/full choke barrels; vent rib; checkered fancy walnut trap stock, semi-beavertail forearm; recoil pad; 60% engraving coverage on frame. Imported 1972 to 1974. Used value, $800 to $850.

Model 2200S Skeet has same general specs as 2200T, except for 27" skeet-choked barrel; skeet stock; no recoil pad. Imported 1972 to 1974. Used value, $800 to $850.

Miida Model 2300

MIIDA Model 2300T Trap: has same general specs as Model 2200T, except for 70% coverage of frame with engraving. Imported 1972 to 1974. Used value, $850 to $900.

Model 2300S Skeet has same specs as Model 2200S, except for 70% engraving coverage of frame. Imported 1972 to 1974. Used value, $850 to $900.

Miida Grandee GRT

MIIDA Grandee GRT Trap: over/under; 12-ga.; 29" full choke-barrels; box-lock action, side plates; gold inlaid; fully engraved frame, breech ends of barrels, locking lever, trigger guard; single selective trigger; auto ejectors; wide vent rib; extra fancy walnut trap stock; semi-beavertail forearm; recoil pad. Imported 1972 to 1974. Used value, $1650 to $1750.

Model GRS Skeet has same general specs as GRT, except for 27" skeet-choked barrels, skeet stock, no recoil pad. Imported 1972 to 1974. Used value, $1650 to $1750.

MOSSBERG

Mossberg Model 83D

MOSSBERG Model 83D: bolt-action; take-down; .410 only; 23" barrel; interchangeable modified, full choke tubes; 2-rd. fixed top-loading magazine; unchecked one-piece finger-grooved pistol-grip stock. Introduced in 1940; replaced in 1947 by Model 183D. Used value, $60 to $65.

Mossberg Model 85D

MOSSBERG Model 85D: bolt-action; take-down; 20-ga. only; 25" barrel with interchangeable choke tubes for full, modified, improved cylinder; 2-rd. detachable box magazine; unchecked one-piece finger-grooved pistol-grip stock, black plastic butt plate. Introduced in 1940; replaced in 1947 by Model 185D. Used value, $60 to $65.

Mossberg Model 183D

MOSSBERG Model 183D: bolt-action; take-down; .410 only; 24" barrel; all other specs are the same as Model 83D. Introduced in 1947; dropped, 1971. Used value, $60 to $65.

Model 183K has the same specs as Model 183D, except for C-Lect-Choke instead of interchangeable tubes. Introduced in 1953; dropped, 1985. Used value, $65 to $70.

Mossberg Model 185K

MOSSBERG Model 185D: bolt-action; take-down; 20-ga. only; has same specs as Model 85D, except for 26" barrel, full, improved cylinder choke tubes. Introduced in 1947; dropped, 1971. Used value, $60 to $65.

Model 185K has the same specs as Model 185D, except for variable C-Lect-Choke replacing interchangeable tubes. Introduced in 1951 dropped, 1963. Used value, $70 to $75.

Mossberg Model 190D

MOSSBERG Model 190D: bolt-action; take-down; 16-ga. only; 26" barrel; other specs are identical to those of Model 185D, including full, improved cylinder choke tubes. Introduced in 1955; dropped, 1971. Used value, $60 to $65.

Model 190K has the same general specs as Model 185K, except for 16-ga. chambering. Introduced in 1956; dropped, 1963. Used value, $70 to $75.

Mossberg Model 195D

those of Model 185D. Introduced in 1955; dropped, 1971. Used value, $65 to $75.

Model 195K has same general specs as the Model 185K, except is in 12-ga. only; C-Lect-Choke. Introduced in 1956; dropped, 1963. Used value, $75 to $80.

MOSSBERG Model 195D: bolt-action; take-down; 12-ga. only; 26" barrel; interchangeable chokes; other specs are same as

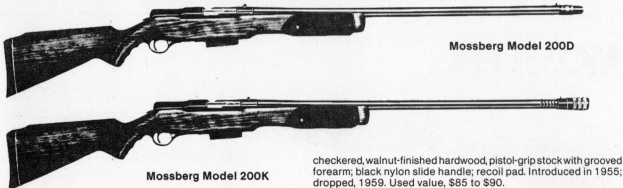

Mossberg Model 200D

Mossberg Model 200K

MOSSBERG Model 200D: slide-action; 12-ga. only; 28" barrel; interchangeable choke tubes; 3-rd. detachable box magazine; un-

checkered, walnut-finished hardwood, pistol-grip stock with grooved forearm; black nylon slide handle; recoil pad. Introduced in 1955; dropped, 1959. Used value, $85 to $90.

Model 200K has same specs as Model 200D, except for substitution of C-Lect-Choke. Introduced in 1955; dropped, 1959. Used value, $95 to $105.

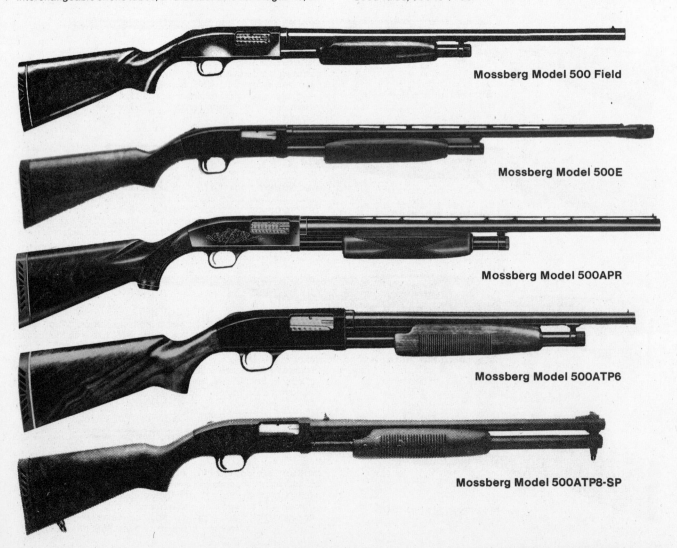

Mossberg Model 500 Field

Mossberg Model 500E

Mossberg Model 500APR

Mossberg Model 500ATP6

Mossberg Model 500ATP8-SP

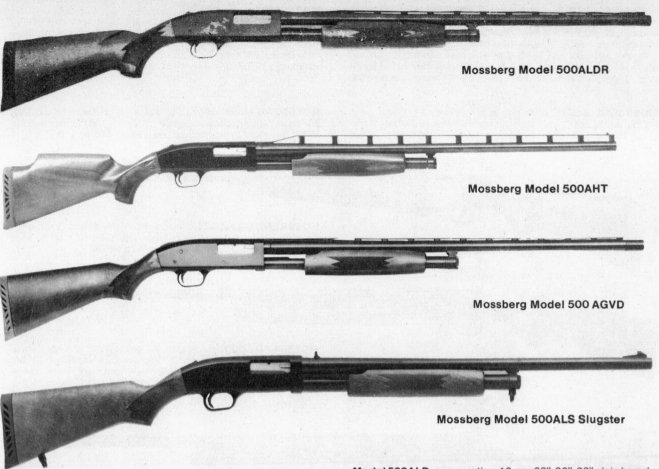

Mossberg Model 500ALDR

Mossberg Model 500AHT

Mossberg Model 500 AGVD

Mossberg Model 500ALS Slugster

MOSSBERG Model 500 Field Grade: slide-action; hammerless; take-down; 12-, 16-, 20-ga; 24" Slugster barrel with rifle sights in 12-ga. only, 26" improved or with adjustable C-Lect-Choke; 28" modified/full; 30" full choke in 12-ga. only; 6-rd. tube magazine; 3-shot plug furnished; uncheckered American walnut pistol-grip stock; grooved slide handle; recoil pad. Introduced in 1961; still in production. Used values: standard barrel, $150 to $165; Slugster barrel, $155 to $170; C-Lect-Choke barrel, $160 to $175; heavy magnum barrel, $175 to $190.

Model 500 Super Grade has the same basic specs as standard Model 500, except for checkered pistol grip, slide handle; vent-rib barrel. Introduced in 1961; no longer in production. Used values: standard barrel, $175 to $195; C-Lect-Choke, $180 to $200; heavy magnum barrel, $180 to $200.

Model 500E has the same general specs as standard Model 500, but is chambered for .410 only; 26" barrel; full, modified, improved chokes; tube magazine holds 6 standard rds., 5 magnum rds.; uncheckered walnut pistol-grip stock, grooved forearm, fluted comb; recoil pad. Used values: standard barrel, $150 to $165; skeet barrel with vent rib, checkering, $200 to $225.

Model 500APR Pigeon Grade trap gun has same specs as standard Model 500, except for vent-rib 30" barrel; full choke only; checkered walnut Monte Carlo stock, beavertail slide handle; recoil pad. Introduced in 1968; no longer in production. Used value, $350 to $375.

Model 500ATP6 has same general specs as pre-1977 Model 500 field grade, except 12-ga. only; 18½", 20" barrel; cylinder bore; 6-rd. magazine; uncheckered pistol-grip stock, grooved slide handle; shotgun or rifle sights. Designed specifically for law enforcement. Marketed as Persuader. Introduced, 1977; still in production. Used value, $175 to $185.

Model 500ATP8 has same specs as 500ATP6, except for 8-rd. magazine. Introduced, 1977; still in production. Used value, $185 to $195.

Model 500TP8-SP has same specs as 500ATP8, except for bayonet lug, Parkerized finish. Introduced, 1977; still in production. Used value, $195 to $205.

Model 500ALD: pump-action; 12-ga.; 28", 30", 32" plain barrel; has same general specs as pre-1977 Model 500 field version, except for game scene etched in receiver; also available with Accu-Choke, three interchangeable choke tubes; restyled stock, slide handle. Introduced, 1977; no longer in production. Used value, $185 to $200.

Model 500ALDR has same specs as 500ALD, except for vent rib. Introduced, 1977; no longer in production. Used value, $200 to $210.

Model 500ALMR has same specs as 500ALDR, except designated as Heavy Duck Model, chambered for 12-ga. magnum shells. Introduced, 1977; no longer in production. Used value, $210 to $220.

Model 500ALS Slugster has same specs as Model 500ALD, except for 24" cylinder-bore barrel, rifle sights. Introduced, 1977; no longer in production. Used value, $175 to $185.

Model 500CLD has same specs as Model 500ALD, except in 20-ga. Introduced, 1977; no longer in production. Used value, $185 to $200.

Model 500CLDR has same specs as 500CLD, except for vent rib. Introduced, 1977; no longer in production. Used value, $200 to $210.

Model 500CLS Slugster has same specs as 500ALS Slugster, except is 20-ga. Introduced, 1977; no longer in production. Used value, $175 to $185.

Model 500EL has same general specs as 500ALD, except made as .410. Introduced, 1977; no longer in production. Used value, $185 to $200.

Model 500ELR has same specs as Model 500EL, except for vent rib. Introduced, 1977; no longer in production. Used value, $210 to $220.

Model 500AHT has same specs as standard model, except 12-ga. only; Simmons Olympic-style free-floating rib, built-up Monte Carlo trap stock; 28", 30" barrels. Introduced, 1978; still in production. Used value, $360 to $370.

Model 500AHTD has same specs as 500AHT, except includes 3 interchangeable choke tubes. Used value, $370 to $400.

Model 500AGVD has same specs as standard 500, except has 3" chamber only; 12-, 20-ga.; 28" Accu-Choke system for improved, modified, full; vent rib only. Used value: $145 to $155.

Model 500ASG Slugster has the same specs as standard model, except has slug barrel; ramp front sight, open adjustable folding leaf rear; running deer etched on receiver; 12-ga. has 18½" barrel, 20-ga. has 24". Used value: $190 to $210.

Model 500EGV has same specs as standard model, except chambered for .410 only; 26" full choke barrel; checkered pistol grip, forend; fluted comb; recoil pad; vent rib barrel. Used value:

$190 to $200.

Model 500 Medallion has same specs as standard model, except has game bird medallion inset in receiver: pheasant, quail, grouse or duck; pheasant, duck guns are 12-ga.; others are 20-ga.; Accu-Choke; 28" vent-rib barrel; only 5000 made in each category. Introduced, 1983; dropped, 1984. Used value: $225 to $240.

MOSSBERG Model 385K: bolt-action; take-down; 20-ga. only; 26" barrel; C-Lect-Choke; walnut-finished hardwood Monte Carlo stock; two-rd. detachable clip magazine; recoil pad. Introduced in 1963; no longer in production. Used value, $75 to $85.

MOSSBERG Model 390K: bolt-action; take-down; 16-ga. only; 28" barrel; other specs are same as Model 385K. Introduced in 1963; no longer in production. Used value, $65 to $70.

Mossberg Model 395K

MOSSBERG Model 395K: bolt-action; take-down; 12-ga. only; 28" barrel; other specs same as Model 385K. Introduced in 1963; no longer in production. Used value, $75 to $85.

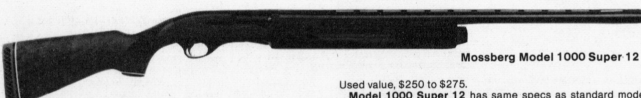

Mossberg Model 5500

MOSSBERG 5500: autoloader; 12-ga.; 2¾", 3" chamber; 18½" cylinder barrel, 24" slugster, 26" improved, 28" modified, 30" full; walnut-finished hardwood stock; bead front sight; interchangeable barrels; Accu-Choke tubes. Introduced, 1983; no longer produced. Used values: slug model, $210 to $220; all others, $230 to $240.

Mossberg Model 1000 Super 12

Used value, $250 to $275.

Model 1000 Super 12 has same specs as standard model, except has gas metering system for 2¾" and 3" shells; 26", 28", 30" Multi-Choke barrel; Parkerized Waterfowler has 28" Multi-Choke barrel. Used values: Super 12, $375 to $400; Super 12 Waterfowler, $425 to $450.

Model 1000S Super Skeet has same specs as standard 1000, except has recessed-type skeet choke; recoil-reduction compensator system; stock has palm swell; contoured trigger; forend cap weights for changing balance; oil-finished, select-grade walnut stock; 25" barrel; made in 12-, 20-ga. Used value, $475 to $500.

MOSSBERG Model 1000: autoloader; gas-operated; 12-ga.; 2¾" chambers; four-rd. tube magazine; 26", 28" barrel lengths; standard chokes; also available with screw-in choke tubes; American walnut stock; front, middle bead sights; vent rib; interchangeable crossbolt safety; engraved alloy receiver; pressure compensator, floating piston for recoil control. Made in Japan. Formerly marketed by Smith & Wesson and Mossberg; no longer imported.

NAVY ARMS

NAVY ARMS Model 83 Bird Hunter: over/under; 12-, 20-ga.; 3" chambers; 28" barrels; standard choke combos; weighs 7½ lb.; checkered European walnut stock; metal bead front sight; box-lock action; double triggers; extractors only; silvered, engraved receiver; vent top and middle rib. Made in Italy. Introduced, 1984; still imported by Navy Arms. Used value, $275 to $300.

Model 93 has same specs as Model 83, except has ejectors. Introduced, 1985; still imported. Used value, $335 to $360.

Navy Arms Model 84 Bird Hunter

NAVY ARMS Model 84 Bird Hunter: over/under; 12-, 20-ga.; 3" chambers; 28" barrels; checkered European walnut stock, forend; metal bead front sight; box-lock action; double triggers; extractors; silvered, engraved receiver; vented top, middle ribs. Made in Italy. Introduced, 1984; still imported by Navy Arms as Model 83/93. Used value: $225 to $250.

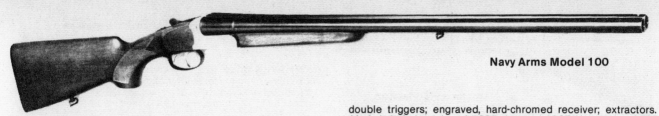

Navy Arms Model 100

NAVY ARMS Model 100: side-by-side; 12-, 20-ga.; 3" chambers; 28" improved cylinder/modified, modified/full chrome-lined barrels; weighs 7 lb.; checkered European walnut stock; gold-plated double triggers; engraved, hard-chromed receiver; extractors. Made in Italy. Introduced, 1985; dropped, 1987. Used value, $300 to $325.

Model 150 has same specs as Model 100, except has ejectors. Introduced, 1985; dropped, 1987. Used value, $375 to $400.

NAVY ARMS Model 600: single-shot; 12-, 20-ga., .410; 26", 28" barrels; checkered beech stock; chrome-lined barrel; engraved hard-chromed receiver; folds for storage, transport. Made in Italy. Introduced, 1986; dropped, 1987. Used value, $130 to $140.

NAVY ARMS Model 95: over/under; has same specs as Model 83 Bird Hunter, except is marketed with five interchangeable choke tubes. Made in Italy. Introduced, 1986; still imported by Navy Arms. Used value, $350 to $375.

Model 96 has same specs as Model 95, except has gold-plated single trigger, ejectors. Introduced, 1986; still imported. Used value, $450 to $475.

NAVY ARMS Model 410: over/under; .410; 3" chambers; 26" skeet/skeet, full/full barrels; weighs 6¼ lb.; checkered European walnut stock; box-lock action; engraved, hard-chrome finished receiver; chrome-lined barrels; vent rib; single trigger. Made in Italy. Introduced, 1986; still imported by Navy Arms. Used value, $200 to $225.

NAVY ARMS Model 105: 12-, 20-ga., .410; 3" chamber; 26", 28" barrel lengths; metal bead front sight; checkered walnut-stained hardwood stock; folds for storage, transport; hammerless; top-lever action; cross-bar action; chrome receiver. Made in Italy. Introduced, 1987; still imported. Used value, $90 to $95.

NEW HAVEN

New Haven Model 290

NEW HAVEN Model 290: bolt-action; take-down; 16-ga.; 28" barrel; detachable full-choke tube; other choke tubes available at added cost; two-rd. detachable clip; thumb safety; oil-finished American walnut Monte Carlo-style pistol-grip stock. Manufactured by Mossberg. Introduced in 1960; dropped, 1965. Used value, $50 to $55.

NEW HAVEN Model 295: bolt-action; take-down; 12-ga.; other specs are same as Model 290. Introduced in 1960; dropped, 1965. Used value, $65 to $75.

NEW HAVEN Model 283: bolt-action; take-down; .410; 25" barrel; 3" chamber; other specs as same as Model 290. Introduced in 1960; dropped, 1965. Used value, $65 to $75.

New Haven Model 285

New Haven Model 273

NEW HAVEN Model 285: bolt-action; take-down; 20-ga.; has same specs as Model 283, except for chambering. Introduced in 1960; dropped, 1965. Used value, $65 to $75.

NEW HAVEN Model 273: bolt-action; single-shot; top-loading; 24" tapered barrel; full choke only; thumb safety; oil-finished American walnut Monte Carlo-style pistol-grip stock. Introduced in 1960; dropped, 1965. Used value, $55 to $60.

NEW HAVEN Model 600: slide-action; take-down; 12-ga.; 26" improved-cylinder barrel, 28" full or modified, 30" full choke; 6-rd. magazine; choice of standard or 3" magnum barrel; safety on top of receiver; uncheckered walnut pistol-grip stock, extension slide handle. Same general design as Mossberg Model 500. Introduced in 1962; dropped, 1965. Used value, $120 to $130.

Model 600K has the same specs as Model 600, except for C-Lect-Choke feature. Used value, $130 to $140.

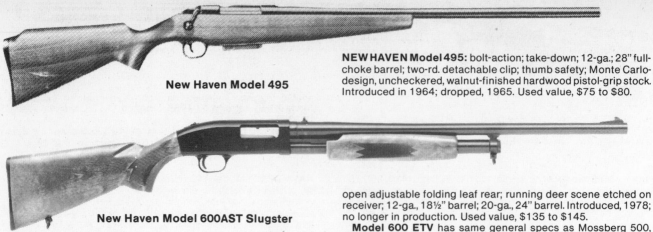

New Haven Model 495

New Haven Model 600AST Slugster

NEW HAVEN Model 495: bolt-action; take-down; 12-ga.; 28" full-choke barrel; two-rd. detachable clip; thumb safety; Monte Carlo design, uncheckered, walnut-finished hardwood pistol-grip stock. Introduced in 1964; dropped, 1965. Used value, $75 to $80.

NEW HAVEN 600AST Slugster: slide-action; has same specs as Mossberg Model 500, except has Slugster barrel; ramp front sight, open adjustable folding leaf rear; running deer scene etched on receiver; 12-ga., 18½" barrel; 20-ga., 24" barrel. Introduced, 1978; no longer in production. Used value, $135 to $145.

Model 600 ETV has same general specs as Mossberg 500, except .410 only; 26" barrels; walnut-finished stock; checkered pistol grip, forend, fluted comb, recoil pad, vent rib. Used value $165 to $175.

NOBLE

NOBLE Model 40: slide-action; 12-ga. only; 28" barrel; solid frame; 6-rd. magazine; Multi-Choke; recoil pad; uncheckered American walnut pistol-grip stock, grooved forearm; push-button safety. Introduced in 1952; dropped, 1956. Used value, $75 to $85.

NOBLE Model 50: slide-action; 12-ga. only; 28" barrel; solid frame; has same specs as Model 40, except without recoil pad and Multi-Choke. Introduced in 1954; dropped, 1956. Used value, $85 to $95.

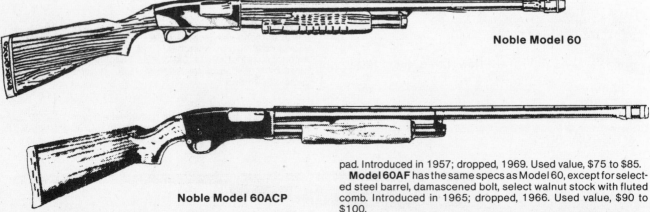

Noble Model 60

Noble Model 60ACP

NOBLE Model 60: slide-action; 12-, 16-ga.; 28" barrel; solid frame; crossbolt safety; 5-rd. magazine; uncheckered American walnut pistol-grip stock; grooved slide handle, VARY Choke choke; recoil pad. Introduced in 1957; dropped, 1969. Used value, $75 to $85.

Model 60AF has the same specs as Model 60, except for selected steel barrel, damascened bolt, select walnut stock with fluted comb. Introduced in 1965; dropped, 1966. Used value, $90 to $100.

Model 60ACP replaced Model 60, Model 60AF; has same general specs, except receiver is machined from single block of steel, all lock surfaces are hardened. Introduced in 1967; dropped, 1971. Used value, $90 to $100.

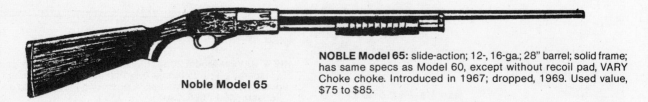

Noble Model 65

NOBLE Model 65: slide-action; 12-, 16-ga.; 28" barrel; solid frame; has same specs as Model 60, except without recoil pad, VARY Choke choke. Introduced in 1967; dropped, 1969. Used value, $75 to $85.

NOBLE Model 602: slide-action; 20-ga. only; solid frame; 28" barrel; adjustable choke; 5-rd. magazine; top safety; side ejection; uncheckered American walnut pistol-grip stock; grooved slide handle; recoil pad. Introduced in 1963; dropped, 1971. Used value, $85 to $90.

Model 602RCLP has same general specs as Model 602, except

Noble Model 602

for key lock safety mechanism, vent rib, checkered pistol-grip stock, slide handle. Manufactured 1967 to 1970. Used value, $100 to $110.

Model 602RLP has same specs as 602RCLP except is sans

adjustable choke; full or modified choke. Manufactured 1967 to 1970. Used value, $110 to $115.

Model 602CLP has same specs as 602RCLP, except for plain barrel. Manufactured 1958 to 1970. Used value, $95 to $100.

Mode 602XL has same specs as Model 602RCLP except for plain barrel, no recoil pad, only slide handle is checkered, full or modified choke. Manufactured 1958 to 1970. Used value, $85 to $95.

NOBLE Model 70: slide-action; .410 only; 26" barrel; full choke; solid frame; top safety; unchecked walnut pistol-grip stock; grooved forearm. Introduced in 1959; dropped, 1967. Used value, $85 to $95.

Model 70X replaced Model 70; specs are the same, except has side ejection, damascened bolt. Introduced in 1967; dropped, 1971. Used value, $95 to $100.

Model 70CLP has same general specs as Model 70, except for adjustable choke. Manufactured 1958 to 1970. Used value, $100

to $105.

Model 70XL has same specs as Model 70CLP, sans adjustable choke; checkered butt stock. Manufactured 1958 to 1970. Used value, $105 to $120.

Model 70RCLP has same specs as Model 70CLP, except for vent rib. Manufactured 1967 to 1970. Used value, $115 to $125.

Model 70RLP has same specs as Model 70CLP, but sans adjustable choke. Manufactured 1967 to 1970. Used value, $115 to $125.

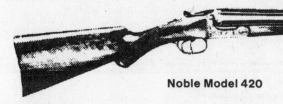

Noble Model 420

NOBLE Model 420: double-barrel; hammerless; 12-, 16-, 20-ga.; 28" barrels; full/modified only; top lever; double triggers; auto-

matic safety; matted rib; checkered pistol-grip stock, forearm. Introduced in 1959; dropped, 1971. Used value, $150 to $170.

Model 420EK has same general specs as Model 420, except for demi-block with triple lock; automatic selective ejectors, hand-checkered Circassian walnut pistol-grip stock; beavertail forearm; recoil pad; hand-engraved action; front and middle bead sights; gold inlay on top lever. Made only in 1968 under this designation. Used value, $250 to $275.

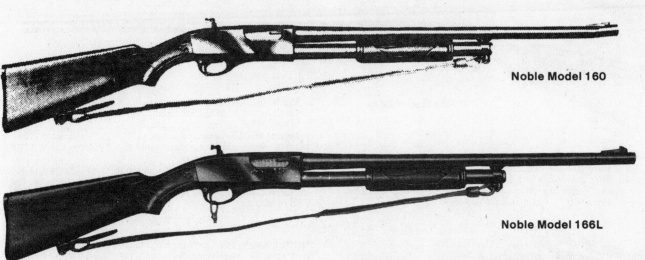

Noble Model 160

Noble Model 166L

NOBLE Model 160 Deergun: slide-action; 12-, 16-ga.; specs same as Model 60, except for 24" barrel; hard rubber butt plate; sling swivels; detachable carrying strap; Lyman adjustable peep

rear sight, ramp post front; tapped for scope. Introduced in 1965; dropped, 1966. Used value, $115 to $125.

Model 166L Deergun replaced Model 160; general specs are the same, except for improved workmanship. Introduced in 1967; dropped, 1971. Used value, $125 to $135.

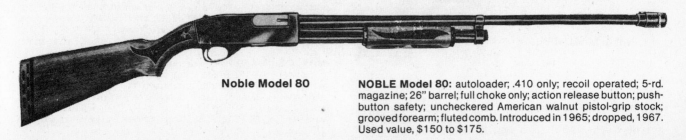

Noble Model 80

NOBLE Model 80: autoloader; .410 only; recoil operated; 5-rd. magazine; 26" barrel; full choke only; action release button; push-button safety; unchecked American walnut pistol-grip stock; grooved forearm; fluted comb. Introduced in 1965; dropped, 1967. Used value, $150 to $175.

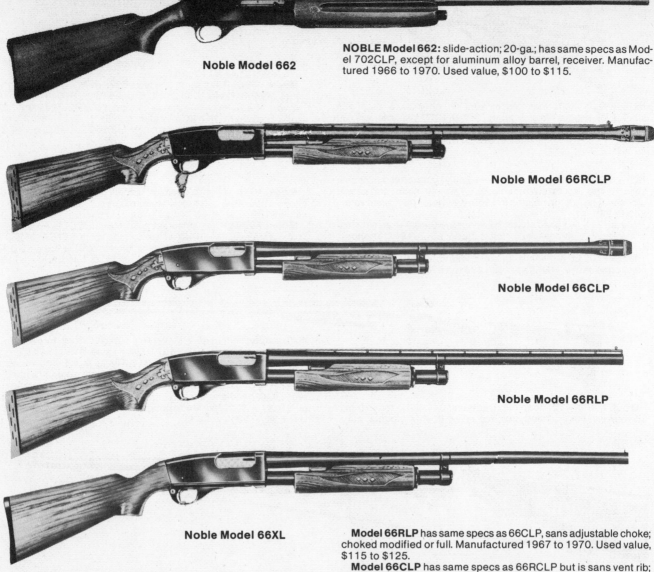

Noble Model 662

NOBLE Model 662: slide-action; 20-ga.; has same specs as Model 702CLP, except for aluminum alloy barrel, receiver. Manufactured 1966 to 1970. Used value, $100 to $115.

Noble Model 66RCLP

Noble Model 66CLP

Noble Model 66RLP

Noble Model 66XL

NOBLE Model 66RCLP: slide-action; 12-, 16-ga.; 3" chamber in 12-ga.; 5-rd. tubular magazine; 28" vent-rib barrel; adjustable choke; solid frame; key lock safety mechanism; checkered American walnut pistol-grip stock, slide handle; recoil pad. Manufactured 1967 to 1970. Used value, $125 to $150.

Model 66RLP has same specs as 66CLP, sans adjustable choke; choked modified or full. Manufactured 1967 to 1970. Used value, $115 to $125.

Model 66CLP has same specs as 66RCLP but is sans vent rib; plain barrel only. Manufactured 1967 to 1979. Used value, $105 to $115.

Model 66XL has same specs as Model 66RCLP, sans vent rib; no adjustable choke; bored modified or full; only slide handle is checkered; no recoil pad. Manufactured 1967 to 1970. Used value, $85 to $90.

Noble Model 450E

NOBLE Model 450E: double-barrel; 12-, 16-, 20-ga.; 28" barrel; modified/full chokes; demi-block with triple lock; double triggers; all specs the same as Model 420EK, which it replaced. Introduced in 1969; dropped, 1971. Used value, $165 to $195.

NOBLE Series 200: slide-action; 20-ga. only; 28" barrel; modified or full choke; solid frame; 5-rd. magazine; tang safety; side ejection; impressed checkering on slide handle; American walnut stock, slide handle; recoil pad. Made in 1972 only. Used values: standard model, $80 to $90; with VARY Choke choke, $90 to $100; with vent rib, $110 to $120; VARY Choke and vent rib, $120 to $150.

NOBLE Series 300: slide-action; 12-ga. only; 28" barrel; modified or full choke; solid frame; tang safety; side ejection; American walnut stock, slide handle; impressed checkering; 6-rd. magazine, 3-shot plug furnished. Made only in 1972. Used values: standard model, $80 to $90; with VARY Choke, $90 to $100; with vent rib, $110 to $120; VARY Choke and vent rib, $120 to $130.

NOBLE Series 400: slide-action; .410 only; 25" barrel; modified or full choke; solid frame, tang safety; side ejection; American walnut stock, slide handle; impressed checkering on pistol grip, slide handle; damascened bolt. Made only in 1972. Used values: standard model, $90 to $100; with VARY Choke, $100 to $110; with vent rib, $120 to $130; VARY Choke and vent rib, $130 to $140.

NOBLE Model 390 Deergun: slide-action; 12-ga. only; 24" rifled slug barrel; sling swivels; detachable carrying strap; Lyman adjustable peep rear sight, ramp post front; solid frame; tang safety; American walnut stock, slide handle; impressed checkering. Made only in 1972. Used value, $115 to $125.

NOBLE Model 520: side-by-side; hammerless; 12-, 20-, 16-, 28-ga. .410; 26", 28" barrel lengths; matted top rib; hand-checkered Circassian walnut stock, forend; hand-engraved frame; double triggers; Holland-design extractors. Has specs similar to Model 420. Introduced, 1970; dropped, 1972. Used value, $150 to $175.

NOBLE Model 550: side-by-side; hammerless; 12-, 20-ga.; 28" barrels; front, middle bead sights; double triggers; double auto selective ejectors; hand-checkered Circassian walnut pistol-grip stock, beavertail forend; grip cap; custom hand-engraved frame; rubber recoil pad; knight's head medallion inlaid on top snap; tang safety. Introduced, 1970; dropped, 1972. Used value, $250 to $275.

NOBLE Model 757: slide-action; 20-ga. only; 5-rd. magazine; solid frame; 28" barrel of aircraft alloy; adjustable choke; barrel, receiver black anodized; decorated receiver; tang safety; American walnut stock; impressed checkering on slide handle, pistol grip. Made only in 1972. Used value, $110 to $120.

PARKER

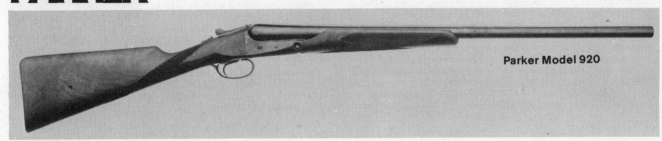

Parker Model 920

Parker A-1 Special Grade

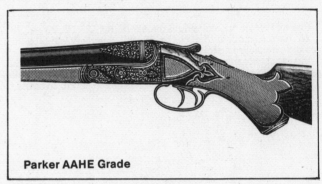

Parker AAHE Grade

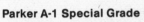

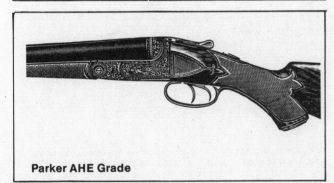

Parker AHE Grade

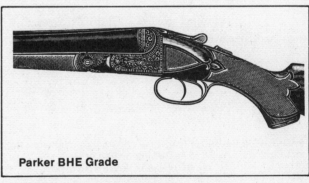

Parker BHE Grade

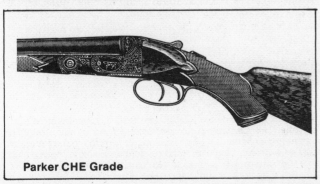

Parker CHE Grade

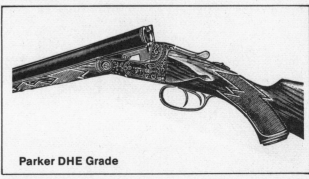

Parker DHE Grade

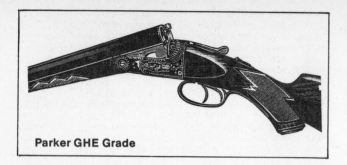
Parker GHE Grade

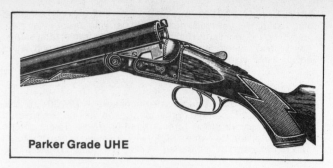
Parker Grade UHE

PARKER Model 920 Hammerless: after Parker Brothers was absorbed by Remington Arms in 1934, shotgun was designated as Remington Parker Model 920; prior to that, it was known simply as Parker Hammerless Double; side-by-side double; 10-, 12-, 16-, 20-, 28-ga., .410; 26" to 32" barrels; any standard choke combo; box-lock action; automatic ejectors; choice of straight, half or pistol-grip stock; hand-checkered pistol grip, forearm of select walnut; double or selective single trigger. Because of the wide variations in styles and extras, as well as the number of grades — differing in engraving, checkering and general workmanship — there is a wide range of values. The selective trigger was introduced in 1922, with the raised vent rib; the beavertail forend was introduced in 1923; all add to used value. Some guns were put together from available parts, stocks by Remington until 1942. Grades are in descending values, with the A-designated model being worth several times

that of the V model. Nonejector models — pre-1934 — are worth about 30% less than value shown for ejector models; if gun has interchangeable barrels, it is worth 30 to 35% more than shown. Those in 20-ga. are 35% higher, 28-ga. are 75% higher and .410 are 100% higher than values shown. Prices shown are for 12-, 16-ga. configurations. Used values: A-1 Special, $30,000 to $40,000; AAHE, $19,000 to $21,000; AHE, $12,500 to $15,000; BHE, $8500 to $9500; CHE, $7500 to $8000; DHE, $4000 to $4250; GHE, $2500 to $2750; VHE, $1250 to $1500; single trigger, add $250; vent rib, add $300; beavertail forearm, add $300.

With single selective trigger, add $200 to $300 to base price shown. For raised vent rib, add $325 to $350 For beavertail forearm addition in grades VHE, GHE, DHE, CHE, add $200 to $250 to base price; for grades BHE, AHE, AAHE, add $450 to $500 to base; for A-1 Special, add $500 to $750.

PARKER Trojan: hammerless double-barrel; 12-, 16-, 20-ga.; 26", 28" barrels, modified/full choke, 30" full; American walnut stock; hand-checkered pistol grip, forearm; box-lock action; plain extractors; double or single triggers. Introduced in 1915; dropped, 1939. Used values: double trigger, 12-, 16-ga., $1200 to $1400; 20-ga, $1600 to $1800; single trigger, 12-, 16-ga., $1300 to $1500; 20-ga., $1700 to $1900.

Parker Trojan Model

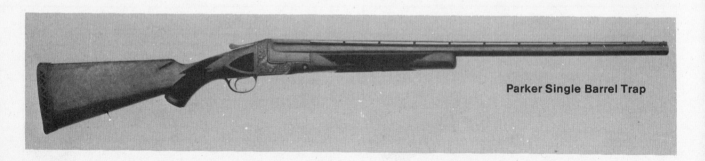
Parker Single Barrel Trap

PARKER Single-Barrel Trap: after absorption of Parker by Remington, model was listed as Remington Parker Model 930. In 12-ga. only; 30", 32", 34" barrels; any designated choke; vent rib; ejector; hammerless box-lock action; straight, half or pistol-grip stock of select American walnut; hand-checkered pistol grip, fore-

arm. Various grades differ with amount of workmanship, checkering, engraving, et al. General specs are the same for all variations. Introduced in 1917; dropped, 1942. Used values: SA-1 Special, $15,000 to $17,500; SAA, $7500 to $9500; SA, $4000 to $4250; SB, $2500 to $2750; SC, $1750 to $2000.

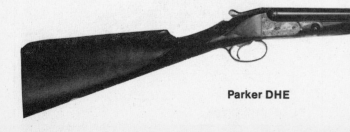
Parker DHE

PARKER DHE: side-by-side; 20 ga.; 2¾", 3" chambers; 26", 28" barrels; American walnut stock; checkered grip, forend; straight or pistol-grip style; metal bead front sight; reproduction of original; all parts interchange with original; double or single trigger; skeleton or hard rubber butt plate. Made in Japan. Introduced, 1984; imported by Parker Gun. Used value, $2100 to $2200.

PEDERSEN

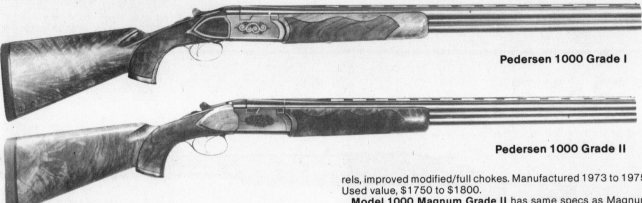

Pedersen 1000 Grade I

Pedersen 1000 Grade II

PEDERSEN 1000 Series Grade I: over/under; box-lock action; 12-, 20-ga.; barrel lengths, stock dimensions to customer specs; hand-checkered American walnut pistol-grip stock, forearm; rubber recoil pad; vent rib; automatic ejectors; single selective trigger; hand-engraved, gold-filled receiver. Introduced in 1973; dropped, 1975. Used value, $1750 to $1800.

Series 1000 Grade II has the same specs as Grade I, except for standard stock dimensions, no gold filling, less extensive engraving on receiver, less fancy wood in stock, forearm. Introduced in 1973; dropped, 1975. Used value, $1250 to $1300.

Series 1000 Grade III has the same specs as Grade II except for no receiver engraving; has gold-plated trigger, forearm release. Introduced in 1973; dropped, 1975. Used value, $750 to $800.

Model 1000 Magnum Grade I has same specs as Model 1000 Grade I, except for 12-ga. magnum 3" shell chambering, 30" bar-

rels, improved modified/full chokes. Manufactured 1973 to 1975. Used value, $1750 to $1800.

Model 1000 Magnum Grade II has same specs as Magnum Grade I, except for lower grade wood, less engraving, fewer silver inlays. Manufactured 1973 to 1975. Used value, $1250 to $1300.

Model 1000 Trap Grade I has same specs as Model 1000 Grade I, except made in 12-ga. only; 30", 32" barrels; modified/full or improved modified/full chokes; Monte Carlo trap stock. Manufactured 1973 to 1975. Used value, $1500 to $1750.

Model 1000 Trap Grade II has same specs as Grade I, except for lower grade wood, less engraving, fewer silver inlays. Manufactured 1973 to 1975. Used value, $1250 to $1300.

Model 1000 Skeet Grade 1 has same specs as basic Model 1000 Grade I, except 12-ga. only; 26", 28" barrels; skeet stock, skeet chokes. Manufactured 1973 to 1975. Used value, $1500 to $1750.

Model 1000 Skeet Grade II has same specs as Grade I, except has lower grade wood, less engraving, fewer silver inlays. Manufactured 1973 to 1975. Used value, $1250 to $1300.

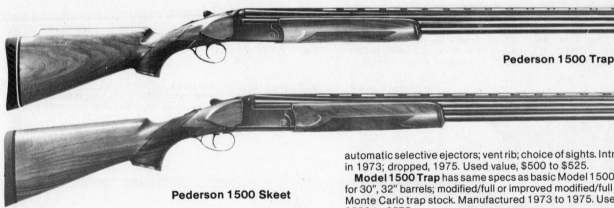

Pederson 1500 Trap

Pederson 1500 Skeet

PEDERSEN 1500: over/under; box-lock action; 12-ga. only; 26", 28", 30", 32" barrels; hand-checkered European walnut pistol-grip stock, forearm; rubber recoil pad; field version of Series 1000;

automatic selective ejectors; vent rib; choice of sights. Introduced in 1973; dropped, 1975. Used value, $500 to $525.

Model 1500 Trap has same specs as basic Model 1500, except for 30", 32" barrels; modified/full or improved modified/full chokes; Monte Carlo trap stock. Manufactured 1973 to 1975. Used value, $550 to $575.

Model 1500 Skeet has same specs as standard Model 1500, except for 27" barrels, skeet choke, skeet stock. Manufactured 1973 to 1975. Used value, $525 to $550.

PEDERSEN Series 2000 Grade I: side-by-side double-barrel; box-lock action; 12-, 20-ga.; barrel length, stock dimensions to customer's specs; hand-checkered American walnut pistol-grip stock, forearm; automatic selective ejectors; barrel selector/safety; single selective trigger; automatic safety; gold-filled, hand-engraved receiver Introduced in 1973; dropped, 1975. Used value, $1900 to

$2000.

Series 2000 Grade II has same specs as Grade I, except for standard stock dimensions, less extensive engraving, less fancy wood. Introduced in 1973; dropped, 1975. Used value, $1200 to $1300.

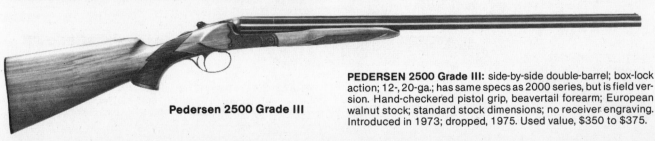

Pedersen 2500 Grade III

PEDERSEN 2500 Grade III: side-by-side double-barrel; box-lock action; 12-, 20-ga.; has same specs as 2000 series, but is field version. Hand-checkered pistol grip, beavertail forearm; European walnut stock; standard stock dimensions; no receiver engraving. Introduced in 1973; dropped, 1975. Used value, $350 to $375.

PEDERSEN Model 4000: slide-action; 12-, 20-ga., .410; 3" chambers; 26", 28", 30" barrels, standard chokes; based upon Mossberg Model 500; full-coverage engraving on receiver; checkered select American walnut stock, slide handle. Manufactured 1973. Used value, $325 to $350.

Model 4000 Trap has same specs, except made in 12-ga. only; 30" full-choke barrel, recoil pad, Monte Carlo trap stock. Manufac-

tured in 1975. Used value, $350 to $375.

PEDERSEN Model 4500: slide-action; has same general specs as standard Model 4000, except less engraving on receiver. Manufactured in 1975. Used value, $250 to $300.

Model 4500 Trap has same specs as Model 4000 Trap, except less engraving. Manufactured in 1975. Used value, $300 to $325.

PERAZZI

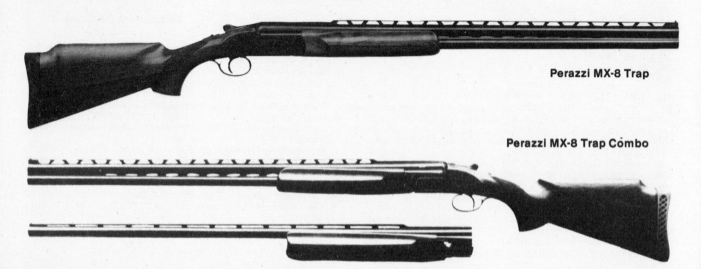

Perazzi MX-8 Trap

Perazzi MX-8 Trap Combo

PERAZZI MX-8 Trap: over/under; 12-ga.; 30", 32" barrels; high vent rib; box-lock action, auto selective ejectors; nonselective single trigger; improved modified/full chokes; checkered European walnut Monte Carlo stock, forend; recoil pad. Made in Italy. Imported by Ithaca 1969 to 1978. Used value, $3000 to $3200.

MX-8 Combo Trap model has same specs as MX-8 trap gun, except for extra single 32", 34" barrel; full choke; vent rib; forend; two trigger groups. Imported 1973 to 1978 by Ithaca. Used value, $4000 to $4300.

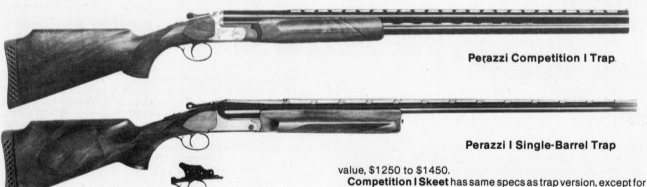

Perazzi Competition I Trap

Perazzi I Single-Barrel Trap

PERAZZI Competition I Trap: over/under; 12-ga.; 30", 32" barrels; vent rib; improved modified/full chokes; box-lock action, auto ejectors; single trigger; checkered European walnut pistol-grip stock, forend, recoil pad. Imported by Ithaca 1969 to 1974. Used

value, $1250 to $1450.

Competition I Skeet has same specs as trap version, except for 26¾" barrels; integral muzzle brakes; skeet chokes; skeet stock; forend. Imported by Ithaca 1969 to 1974. Used value, $1250 to $1450.

Competition I Single-Barrel Trap model has same general specs as over/under trap model, except for single 32", 34" barrel; full choke; checkered Monte Carlo stock, beavertail forend. Imported by Ithaca 1973 to 1978. Used value, $1100 to $1300.

Perazzi Single-Barrel Trap

PERAZZI Single-Barrel Trap: single-shot; 12-ga.; 34" barrel; full choke; vent rib; box-lock action; auto ejector; checkered European walnut pistol-grip stock, forend; recoil pad. Imported by Ithaca 1971 to 1972. Used value, $1000 to $1200.

PERAZZI Light Game Model: over/under; 12-ga.; 27½" barrels; modified/full, improved cylinder/modified chokes; single trigger; box-lock action; auto ejectors; checkered European walnut field stock, forend. Imported by Ithaca 1972 to 1974. Used value, $1100 to $1200.

Perazzi Light Game Model

PERAZZI Mirage Trap: over/under; 12-ga.; has same general specs as MX-8 trap model, except for tapered vent rib. Imported by Ithaca 1973 to 1978. Used value, $2000 to $2250.

Mirage Live Bird model has same specs as Mirage Trap, except for modified/extra-full 28" barrels; redesigned stock, forend for live bird competition. Imported by Ithaca 1973 to 1978. Used value, $2250 to $2500.

Mirage Skeet version has same specs as Mirage Trap, except

Perazzi Mirage Trap

for 28" barrels, integral muzzle brakes, skeet chokes; skeet stock, forend. Imported by Ithaca 1973 to 1978. Used value, $2000 to $2250.

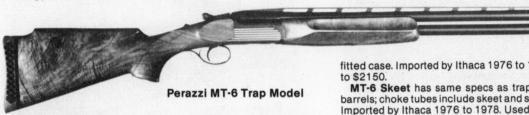

Perazzi MT-6 Trap Model

PERAZZI MT-6 Trap: over/under; 12-ga.; 30", 32" separated barrels; wide vent rib; five interchangeable choke tubes; non-selective single trigger; box-lock action; auto selective ejectors; checkered European walnut pistol-grip stock, forend; recoil pad; marketed in

fitted case. Imported by Ithaca 1976 to 1978. Used value, $2000 to $2150.

MT-6 Skeet has same specs as trap version, except for 28" barrels; choke tubes include skeet and skeet; skeet stock, forend. Imported by Ithaca 1976 to 1978. Used value, $2000 to $2150.

MT-6 Trap Combo is same as MT-6 trap model, except has extra single under-barrel, high aluminum vent rib; 32", 34" barrels; seven interchangeable choke tubes. Marketed in fitted case. Imported by Ithaca 1977 to 1978. Used value, $3250 to $3400.

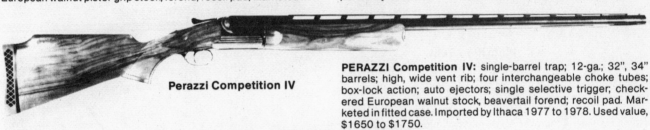

Perazzi Competition IV

PERAZZI Competition IV: single-barrel trap; 12-ga.; 32", 34" barrels; high, wide vent rib; four interchangeable choke tubes; box-lock action; auto ejectors; single selective trigger; checkered European walnut stock, beavertail forend; recoil pad. Marketed in fitted case. Imported by Ithaca 1977 to 1978. Used value, $1650 to $1750.

PERAZZI MX-20: over/under; 20-ga.; 3" chambers; standard fixed chokes or choke tubes; 26" barrels; weighs 6½ lb.; nickel silver front bead; select checkered European walnut stock; checkered butt; box-lock action; carved Schnabel forend; selective auto ejectors; manual safety; single selective trigger. Marketed in fitted case. Made in Italy. Introduced, 1986; still imported by Pachmayr, Ltd. Used value, $2450 to $2600.

Perazzi MX-20

PIOTTI

PIOTTI Piuma: side-by-side; 12-, 16-, 20-, 28-ga., .410; 25" to 30" barrels in 12-ga., 25" to 28" in other gauges; oil-finished, straight-grip European walnut stock; satin luster finish optional; splinter-type or beavertail forend; Anson & Deeley box-lock; ejectors; chopper lump barrels; file-cut rib; scroll, rosette, scallop engraving; double triggers, hinged front; optional single non-selective trigger; coin finish or color case hardening. Made in Italy. Introduced, 1983; still imported by Wm. Larkin Moore. Used value, $3250 to $3500.

PIOTTI King No. 1: side-by-side; 12-, 16-, 20-, 28-ga., .410; 25" to 30" barrels in 12-ga., 25" to 28" in other gauges; fine-figured straight-grip European walnut stock; split or beavertail forend; oil or satin luster finish; pistol grip; Holland & Holland-type side-lock action; double triggers, front hinged; single non-selective trigger optional; coin finish or color case hardening; file-cut or concave vent rib; full-coverage engraving; gold crown on top lever; name in gold; gold crest on forend. Made in Italy to customer's requirements. Introduced, 1983; still imported by Wm. Larkin Moore. Used value, $7500 to $8000.

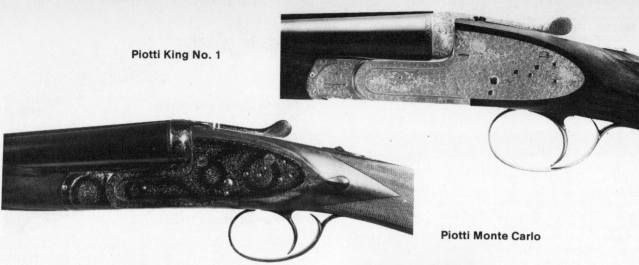

Piotti King No. 1

Piotti Monte Carlo

PIOTTI Monte Carlo: side-by-side; has same specs as King No. 1, except has Purdey-type engraving, no gold inlays; less detailed workmanship. Made in Italy. Introduced, 1983; still imported by Wm. Larkin Moore. Used value, $6750 to $7250.

PIOTTI Lunik: side-by-side; has same specs as King No. 1, except better quality; Rennaissance-style scroll engraving, gold crown on top lever, gold name and gold crest in forend; demi-block barrels. Made in Italy. Introduced, 1983; still imported by Wm. Larkin Moore. Used value, $8750 to $9250.

Piotti Lunik

Piotti King EELL

PIOTTI King EELL: side-by-side; same specs as King No. 1, but has highest quality wood, metal work; engraved scenes, gold inlays; signed by master engraver. Made in Italy. Introduced, 1983; no longer imported by Wm. Larkin Moore. Used value, $11,500 to $12,000.

PREMIER

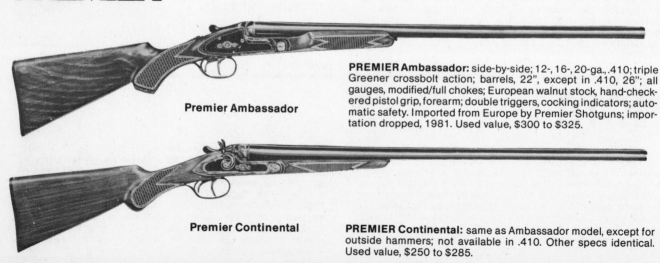

Premier Ambassador

PREMIER Ambassador: side-by-side; 12-, 16-, 20-ga., .410; triple Greener crossbolt action; barrels, 22", except in .410, 26"; all gauges, modified/full chokes; European walnut stock, hand-checkered pistol grip, forearm; double triggers, cocking indicators; automatic safety. Imported from Europe by Premier Shotguns; importation dropped, 1981. Used value, $300 to $325.

Premier Continental

PREMIER Continental: same as Ambassador model, except for outside hammers; not available in .410. Other specs identical. Used value, $250 to $285.

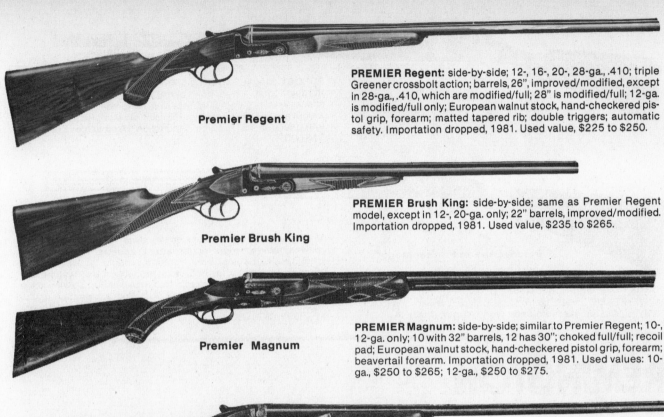

Premier Regent

PREMIER Regent: side-by-side; 12-, 16-, 20-, 28-ga., .410; triple Greener crossbolt action; barrels, 26", improved/modified, except in 28-ga., .410, which are modified/full; 28" is modified/full; 12-ga. is modified/full only; European walnut stock, hand-checkered pistol grip, forearm; matted tapered rib; double triggers; automatic safety. Importation dropped, 1981. Used value, $225 to $250.

Premier Brush King

PREMIER Brush King: side-by-side; same as Premier Regent model, except in 12-, 20-ga. only; 22" barrels, improved/modified. Importation dropped, 1981. Used value, $235 to $265.

Premier Magnum

PREMIER Magnum: side-by-side; similar to Premier Regent; 10-, 12-ga. only; 10 with 32" barrels, 12 has 30"; choked full/full; recoil pad; European walnut stock, hand-checkered pistol grip, forearm; beavertail forearm. Importation dropped, 1981. Used values: 10-ga., $250 to $265; 12-ga., $250 to $275.

Premier Monarch Supreme

PREMIER Monarch Supreme: side-by-side; 12-, 20-ga.; 2¾" chambers in 12-ga., 3" in 20; box-lock action; double triggers; auto ejectors; 26" improved cylinder/modified, 28" modified/full barrels; checkered European fancy walnut pistol-grip stock beavertail forearm. Introduced in 1959; importation dropped, 1981. Used value, $325 to $350.

PREMIER Presentation Custom Grade: has the same general specs as Monarch Supreme, but is made only to customer's order; has higher grade wood, engraved hunting scene, gold and silver inlays. Introduced, 1959; importation dropped, 1981. Used value, $750 to $800.

PURDEY

Purdey Hammerless Double Model

PURDEY Hammerless Double Model: side-by-side; side-lock; 12-, 16-, 20-ga.; 26", 27", 28", 30" barrels, last in 12-ga. only; double triggers or single trigger; any choke combo desired; choice of rib style; automatic ejectors; hand-checkered European walnut straight-grip stock, forearm standard; pistol-grip stock on special order; made in several variations including Game Model, Featherweight Game, Pigeon Gun, with side clips; Two-Inch Model for 2" shells. Prices are identical for all. Introduced in 1880; still in production. Used values: double triggers, $15,000 to $17,500; single trigger, $18,500 to $20,000.

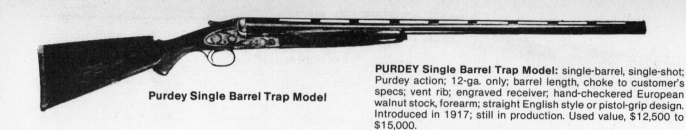

Purdey Single Barrel Trap Model

PURDEY Single Barrel Trap Model: single-barrel, single-shot; Purdey action; 12-ga. only; barrel length, choke to customer's specs; vent rib; engraved receiver; hand-checkered European walnut stock, forearm; straight English style or pistol-grip design. Introduced in 1917; still in production. Used value, $12,500 to $15,000.

Purdey Over-and-Under Model

PURDEY Over-and-Under Model: side-lock action; 12-, 16-, 20-ga.; 26", 27", 28" barrels, last in 12-ga. only; any choke combo; any rib style to customer's preference; pre-WWII guns are built on Purdey action, post-war versions on Woodward action; engraved receiver; double or single trigger, latter at added cost; hand-checkered European walnut stock, forearm; straight English or pistol-grip style. Introduced in 1925; still in production. Used values: with Purdey action, double triggers, $15,000 to $17,500; Purdey action with single trigger, $16,000 to $18,500; Woodward action, double triggers, $17,500 to $18,000; Woodward action, single trigger, $19,000 to $20,000.

REMINGTON

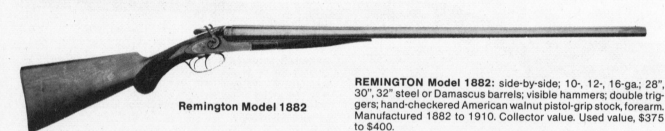

Remington Model 1882

REMINGTON Model 1882: side-by-side; 10-, 12-, 16-ga.; 28", 30", 32" steel or Damascus barrels; visible hammers; double triggers; hand-checkered American walnut pistol-grip stock, forearm. Manufactured 1882 to 1910. Collector value. Used value, $375 to $400.

REMINGTON Model 1889: side-by-side; 10-, 12-, 16-ga.; 28", 30", 32" steel or Damascus barrels; visible hammers; double triggers; hand-checkered American walnut stock, slim forend. Manufactured 1889 to 1908. Collector value. Used value, $500 to $550; steel barrels add $100.

Remington Model 1889

Remington Rider No. 3

REMINGTON Rider No. 3: single-shot; 10-, 12-, 16-, 20-, 24-, 28-ga.; 30", 32" barrel; hammerless; uncheckered American walnut pistol-grip stock, forearm. Manufactured 1893 to 1903. Collector value. Used value, $150 to $175.

Remington Model 1894

REMINGTON Model 1894: side-by-side; 10-, 12-, 16-ga.; 28", 30", 32" barrels; double triggers; box-lock action; auto ejectors; hammerless; hand-checkered American walnut straight-grip stock, forearm. Manufactured 1894 to 1910. Collector value. Used value, $450 to $500.

Model 1894 Trap has same specs as standard model, except for trap stock, 32" full-choke barrel. Manufactured 1894 to 1910. Collector value. Used value, $750 to $850.

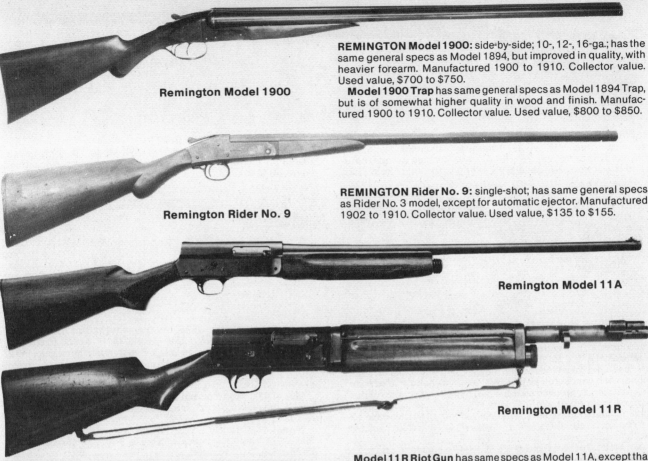

REMINGTON Model 1900: side-by-side; 10-, 12-, 16-ga.; has the same general specs as Model 1894, but improved in quality, with heavier forearm. Manufactured 1900 to 1910. Collector value. Used value, $700 to $750.

Model 1900 Trap has same general specs as Model 1894 Trap, but is of somewhat higher quality in wood and finish. Manufactured 1900 to 1910. Collector value. Used value, $800 to $850.

Remington Model 1900

Remington Rider No. 9

REMINGTON Rider No. 9: single-shot; has same general specs as Rider No. 3 model, except for automatic ejector. Manufactured 1902 to 1910. Collector value. Used value, $135 to $155.

Remington Model 11A

Remington Model 11R

REMINGTON Model 11A: hammerless, take-down, Browning-type autoloader; 5-rd. capacity; tube magazine; 12-, 16-, 20-ga.; barrel lengths, 26", 28", 30", 32"; full, modified, improved cylinder bore, skeet chokes; checkered pistol grip, forearm. Introduced in 1905; dropped, 1949. Was replaced by Model 11-48. Used values: with plain barrel, $200 to $225; solid rib, $245 to $265; vent rib, $275 to $300.

Model 11R Riot Gun has same specs as Model 11A, except that it is 12-ga. only; has sling swivels, special 20" barrel. Introduced in 1921; dropped, 1948. Used value, $300 to $350.

Model 11 custom grades, Expert, Special, Tournament and Premier styles, differ from Model 11A only in grade of walnut used in stock, forearm, engraving, checkering. Used values: Special grade (11B), $375 to $400; Tournament (11D), $700 to $800; Expert (11E), $900 to $1100; Premier, $1500 to $1800.

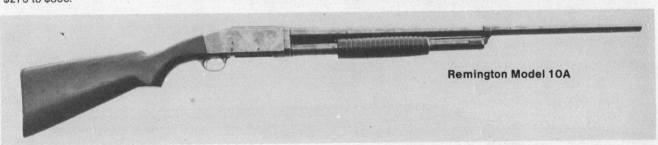

Remington Model 10A

REMINGTON Model 10A: slide-action repeater; hammerless, take-down; barrel lengths, 26", 28", 30", 32"; full, modified, cylinder bore; grooved slide handle; uncheckered pistol-grip stock; 12-ga. only; 6-rd. capacity; tube magazine. Introduced, 1907; dropped, 1929. Used value, $275 to $300.

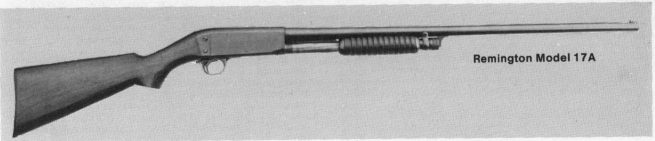

Remington Model 17A

REMINGTON Model 17A: slide-action repeater; hammerless, take-down; 5-rd. capacity; 20-ga. only; tube magazine; barrel lengths, 26", 28", 30", 32"; modified, full, cylinder-bore choke choice; grooved slide handle; uncheckered stock with pistol grip; Browning design. Introduced in 1921; dropped, 1933. Used value, $245 to $265.

Remington Model 29

REMINGTON Model 29: hammerless, take-down slide-action repeater; 12-ga. only; tubular magazine; 5-shot capacity; Model 29A has plain barrel, 26", 28", 30", 32"; full, modified, cylinder bore; hand-checkered slide handle, pistol-grip stock; made from 1929 to 1933. Used value, $200 to $225.

Model 29T Target Gun differs from Model 29A only in ventilated rib, longer slide handle, straight grip on trap stock. Used value, $375 to $400.

Remington Model 31A

REMINGTON Model 31: this model is one of those successes that leads to numerous versions. In all, there are ten variations, all introduced in 1931; dropped in 1949.

Model 31A, the standard grade slide-action repeater, is a hammerless, take-down model, with either 3- or 5-shot capacity; early models had checkered pistol-grip stock, slide handle; later styles had plain stock, grooved slide handle. Barrels, with choice of plain surface, solid rib or vent rib; were in 26", 28", 30", 32" lengths, choked full, modified, improved cylinder bore, skeet. Made in 12-, 16-, 20-ga. Used values: with plain barrel, $275 to $300; solid rib, $300 to $350; vent rib, $375 to $400.

Model 31 Custom Grades are Special Tournament, Expert and Premier, differing from Model 31A only in the grade of wood, amount and fineness of checkering and the amount and quality of engraving. Other specs remain the same. Used values: Special grade (31B), $450 to $475; Tournament (31D), $750 to $800; Expert (31E), $1000 to $1250; Premier (31F), $1750 to $1850.

Model 31TC Trap Grade is same as standard model, but in 12-ga. only, with 30", 32" vent-rib barrel, full choke, trap stock, pistol grip, recoil pad; extension beavertail forend; stock, forend are checkered. Used value, $475 to $525.

Model 31S Trap Special has same specs as Model 31TC, except half-pistol-grip stock, forend of standard walnut, solid-rib barrel. Used value, $450 to $475.

Model 31H Hunter's Special differs from Model 31S only in that it has a sporting stock with more drop and shorter length. Used value, $375 to $400.

Model 31R Riot Gun is same as Model 31A, but in 12-ga. only, with 20" barrel. Used value, $225 to $250.

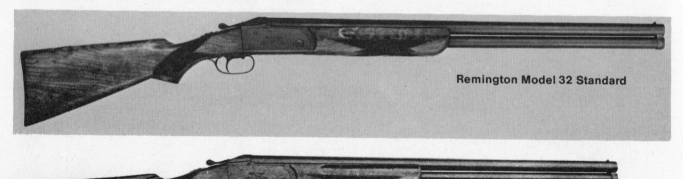

Remington Model 32 Standard

Remington Model 32 Custom

REMINGTON Model 32: this hammerless, take-down over/under is another of those on which the manufacturer built a lengthy reputation, making the model in its various configurations for a decade. Introduced in 1932; dropped, 1942. However, the nostalgia and demand resulted in the basic model which, with modern manufacturing techniques, was reintroduced in 1972 as the Model 3200.

Model 32A Standard Grade has automatic ejectors and the earlier model had double triggers; later, it was available only with a single selective trigger; in 12-ga. only, barrels are 26", 28", 30", 32"; standard chokes are full, modified, but options were offered for full, modified, improved, cylinder bore, skeet; choice of plain barrel, raised matted solid rib, vent rib; stock was walnut with checkered pistol grip, forend. Used values: with double triggers, $1000 to $1100; single trigger, $1200 to $1400; with vent rib, add $175 to $200; with raised solid rib, $75 to $100.

Model 32 Skeet Grade has same specs as Model 32A, except for choice of 26", 28" barrel, skeet boring; selective trigger only, beavertail forend. Used values: with plain barrels, $1200 to $1450; vent rib, $1500 to $1750; raised solid rib, $1400 to $1550.

Model 32 Custom stylings included Tournament, Expert and Premier grades, differing from standard 32A model only in engraving, fineness of checkering, grade of walnut used. Other specs are the same. Used values: Tournament grade (32D), $1750 to $2000; Expert (32E), $2750 to $3000; Premier (32F), $3500 to $4000.

Model 32TC Trap Grade has same specs as Model 32A, except for 30", 32" vent-rib barrel, trap stock with checkered beavertail forend, pistol grip; either double or single selective triggers; full choke only. Used values: with double triggers, $1350 to $1450; single trigger, $1600 to $1800.

Remington Model 11-48A Standard

Remington Model 11-48A .410

REMINGTON Model 11-48A: autoloader; half-pistol grip; hand-checkered stock, forend; 5-shot capacity in 12-, 16-, 20-ga.; 4-shot in 28-ga., .410; redesigned version of Model 11; introduced in 1949; dropped, 1969; hammerless, take-down; tube magazine; 26" barrel choked improved cylinder; 28" modified or full, 30" full in 12-ga. only; plain barrel; matted top surface, ventilated rib choices. Used values: $185 to $200; Special grade (11-48B),

Tournament grade (11-48D) and Premier grade (11-48F) had higher grades of wood, more and finer-line checkering, engraving. Used values: Special, $275 to $300; Tournament, $700 to $750; Premier, $1150 to $1250.

Model 11-48A .410 was introduced in 1954, 28-ga., 1952; both discontinued in 1969. Used values: with plain barrel, $225 to $250; with matted top surface, $250 to $275; vent rib, $300 to $325.

Model 11-48SA Skeet model is same as 28-ga. standard model, except for vent rib, skeet choke, 25" barrel; 28-ga. introduced, 1952; .410, 1954. Used value, $325 to $350.

Model 11-48A Riot Gun is same as standard model, but in 12-ga. only with 20" plain barrel. Used value, $200 to $225.

Remington Sportsman 48A

REMINGTON Sportsman 48A: autoloader; 12-, 16-, 20-ga.; 26" improved cylinder, 28" modified or full, 30" full-choke barrel; vent rib, matted barrel; plain barrel available; hammerless; take-down; 2-rd. tubular magazine; streamlined receiver; hand-checkered American walnut pistol-grip stock, grooved forend. Manufactured 1949 to 1959. Used values: vent rib, $250 to $275; matted barrel, $225 to $235; plain barrel, $160 to $170.

Sportsman 48B Special Grade has same general specs as standard 48A, except for higher quality wood, checkering; engraved receiver. Manufactured 1949 to 1959. Used value, $300 to $325.

Sportsman 48D Tournament Grade has same specs as 48B, except for improved wood, finer checkering, more engraving. Manufactured 1949 to 1959. Used value, $650 to $700.

Sportsman 48F Premier Grade has same specs as 48D, but features top-quality wood, fully engraved receiver. Manufactured 1949 to 1959. Used value, $1250 to $1400.

Sportsman 48SA Skeet has same specs as 48A, except for 26" barrel with matted surface or vent rib, skeet choke, ivory bead front sight, metal bead rear. Manufactured 1949 to 1960. Used values: vent rib, $275 to $300; matted barrel, $225 to $250.

Remington Model 870SA

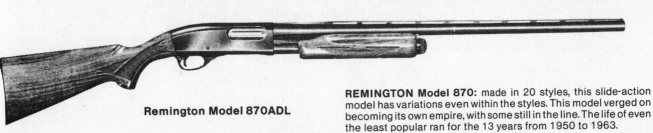

Remington Model 870ADL

REMINGTON Model 870: made in 20 styles, this slide-action model has variations even within the styles. This model verged on becoming its own empire, with some still in the line. The life of even the least popular ran for the 13 years from 1950 to 1963.

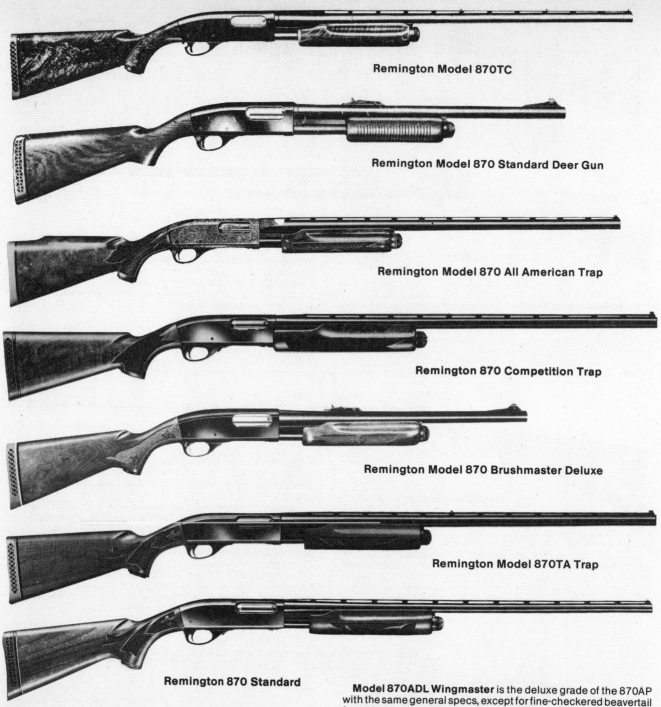

Remington Model 870TC

Remington Model 870 Standard Deer Gun

Remington Model 870 All American Trap

Remington 870 Competition Trap

Remington Model 870 Brushmaster Deluxe

Remington Model 870TA Trap

Remington 870 Standard

Model 870AP Wingmaster was the standard grade. A hammerless take-down, it had tube magazine, total capacity of 5 rds.; plug furnished with gun; barrels were 25" improved cylinder, 28" modified or full, 30" full, the last in 12-ga. only; choice of plain, matted top surface vent rib; walnut stock, no checkering, grooved slide handle. Introduced in 1950; dropped, 1963. Used values: plain barrel, $150 to $175; matted surface, $175 to $200; vent rib, $225 to $250.

Model 870 Wingmaster Field Gun still in production, was introduced, 1964. Specs are same as 870AP, except for checkered stock, slide handle. Used value: plain barrel, $165 to $185; vent rib, $185 to $200.

Model 870 Wingmaster Custom Grades include Tournament, Premier stylings. Only difference from Model 870AP is grade of walnut, amount of engraving, checkering; other specs are same. Introduced in 1960; still in production. Used values: Tournament (870D), $1400 to $1500; Premier, $2600 to $2800; Premier gold inlaid, $4200 to $4500.

Model 870ADL Wingmaster is the deluxe grade of the 870AP with the same general specs, except for fine-checkered beavertail forend, pistol-grip stock; choice of matted top surface barrel, vent rib. Introduced in 1950; dropped, 1963. Used values: matted surface, $200 to $225; vent rib, $235 to $265.

Model 870BDL Wingmaster varies from 870ADL only in selected American walnut for stock, forend. Introduced in 1950; dropped, 1963. Used values: with matted top surface barrel, $235 to $255; vent rib, $275 to $285.

Model 870SA Wingmaster Skeet gun is same as 870AP, except for 26" barrel, vent rib, skeet boring, ivory bead front sight, metal bead in rear; has extension beavertail slide handle, pistol-grip stock, both finely checkered. Introduced in 1950; dropped, 1982. Used values: Skeet grade (870SA) $225 to $250; Skeet Target (870SC), $275 to $300; Skeet Tournament (870SD), $950 to $1000; Skeet Premier grade (870SF), $1750 to $2000.

Model 870TB Wingmaster Trap Special has same specs as standard model, except for 28", 30" vent-rib barrel, full choke, no rear sight, metal bead front; checkered trap stock, slide handle. Introduced in 1950; no longer in production. Used value, $275 to $285.

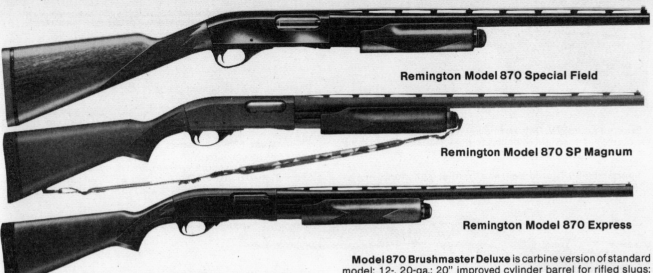

Remington Model 870 Special Field

Remington Model 870 SP Magnum

Remington Model 870 Express

Model 870TC Wingmaster Trap grade is same as 870TB, except for both front, rear sights, higher grade of walnut. Introduced in 1950; no longer in production. Used values: Trap grade (870TC), $300 to $325; Trap Tournament (870TD), $700 to $750; Trap Premier, $1750 to $2000.

Model 870 Wingmaster Magnum is same as 870AP, except in 12-ga.; 3" magnum only; 30" full-choke barrel; recoil pad. Introduced in 1955; discontinued, 1963. Used value, $250 to $300.

Model 870 Magnum Deluxe is same as standard 870 Magnum, including lifetime, except for checkered extension beavertail slide handle, stock, matted top surface barrel. Used value, $275 to $325.

Model 870 Magnum Duck Gun has same specs as 870 field gun, except chambered for 3", 12-, 20-ga. magnum shells only; 28", 30" barrel, plain vent rib, modified, full choke, recoil pad. Introduced in 1964; no longer in production. Used values: with plain barrel, $225 to $250; vent rib, $300 to $325.

Model 870 Wingmaster Field Gun has specs of 870AP standard model, except for checkered stock, slide handle. Introduced in 1965; no longer in production. Used values: with plain barrel, $185 to $210; vent rib, $225 to $235.

Model 870 Deer Gun standard configuration is same as 870 riot model, except for Winchester rifle-type sights. Used value, $225 to $235.

Model 870 All American Trap has same specs as Model 870TB, except for custom-grade engraved receiver, trigger guard, barrel; straight comb or Monte Carlo stock, forend of fancy American walnut; manufactured only with 30" full-choke barrel. Introduced, 1972; no longer in production. Used value, $650 to $700.

Model 870 Competition Trap has same specs as standard model, except is single shot, has 30" full-choke vent-rib barrel, gas reduction system, select walnut trap stock. Used value, $450 to $475.

Model 870 Brushmaster Deluxe is carbine version of standard model; 12-, 20-ga.; 20" improved cylinder barrel for rifled slugs; recoil pad; adjustable rear sight, ramp front; right- or left-hand models. Used values: $265 to $280; left-hand, $290 to $300.

Model 870D Tournament is same as standard 870, except has better wood, hand-checkered pistol grip, forend; vent rib; engraved barrel, receiver. Used value, $900 to $1000.

Model 870 20 Gauge Lightweight is the same as standard model, except weighs only 6 lb.; 28" improved barrel, 28" full or modified, 30" full; plain or vent-rib barrel. Used values: plain barrel, $250 to $260; vent rib, $270 to $280.

Model 870 TA Trap is same as standard model, except is chambered for 12-ga. only; 30" modified, full barrel; ivory front bead, white metal middle; hand-fitted action, parts; trap stock, recoil pad; special hammer, sear, trigger assembly. Used value, $300 to $320.

Model 870 Special Field has same specs as standard 870, except has 21" barrel only; 3" chamber; 12-, 20-ga.; straight-grip stock, shorter forend; cut checkering; vent rib. Introduced, 1984; still in production. Used value, $310 to $320.

Model 870 Special Purpose Magnum has same specs as standard model, except is chambered only for 12-ga. 3" shells; has vent rib, 26" or 28" Rem-Choke barrel; black metal finish; oil-finished wood; quick-detachable sling swivels; chrome-lined bores. Marketed with padded sling. Introduced, 1985; still in production. Used value, $290 to $315.

Model 870 Special Purpose Deer Gun has same specs as Special Purpose Magnum, except has 20" improved cylinder barrel; rifle sights; Parkerized barrel, receiver; black-finished bolt, carrier; oil-finished wood; recoil pad. Marketed with padded nylon sling. Introduced, 1986; still in production. Used value, $300 to $325.

Model 870 Express has same specs as 870 Wingmaster, except has walnut-finished hardwood stock, solid black recoil pad, pressed checkering; metal surfaces finished with black oxide; 28" vent-rib barrel; modified Rem-Choke tube. Introduced, 1987; still in production. Used value, $160 to $185.

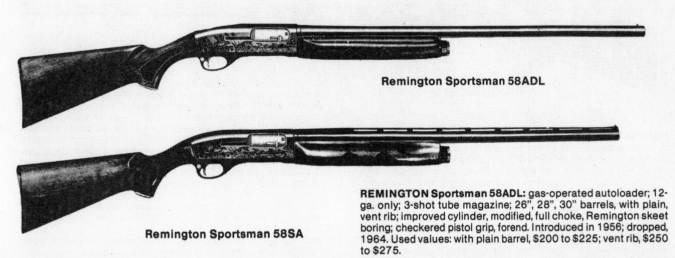

Remington Sportsman 58ADL

Remington Sportsman 58SA

REMINGTON Sportsman 58ADL: gas-operated autoloader; 12-ga. only; 3-shot tube magazine; 26", 28", 30" barrels, with plain, vent rib; improved cylinder, modified, full choke, Remington skeet boring; checkered pistol grip, forend. Introduced in 1956; dropped, 1964. Used values: with plain barrel, $200 to $225; vent rib, $250 to $275.

Remington Sportsman 58SC

Sportsman-58BDL Deluxe Special grade is same as 58ADL, except walnut wood is of select grade; manufactured during same period. Used values: with plain barrel, $250 to $275; vent rib, $325 to $350.

Sportsman-58 Tournament and Premier grades are same as 58ADL, except for vent rib, improved wood, checkering, engraving.

Used values: Tournament grade (58D), $725 to $775; Premier, $1250 to $1350.

Sportsman-58SA Skeet gun has same specs as 58ADL, except for vent rib, special skeet stock, forend. Used value, $300 to $325.

Sportsman-58 Skeet Target, Tournament and Premier grades verge on custom guns; with same general specs as Model 58SA, they have better wood, engraving, finer checkering. Used values: Skeet Target grade (58SC), $350 to $375; Skeet Tournament (58D), $725 to $775; Premier grade (58SF), $1250 to $1350.

Remington Model 878A

REMINGTON Model 878A Automaster: gas-operated autoloader; 12-ga. only; 3-shot tube magazine; plain or vent rib; uncheckedered pistol-grip stock, forend; barrels, 26" improved cylinder; 28" modified, 30" full choke. Introduced in 1959; dropped, 1962. Used values: $175 to $200; vent rib, $200 to $225.

Remington Model 1100 Field

Remington Model 1100 Magnum Duck Gun

Remington Model 1100SA

Remington Model 1100TB

REMINGTON Model 1100: a gas-operated, hammerless, take-down, autoloader, this model was introduced in 1963 in several configurations, most of them still in production. In its early days the stocks had impressed checkering, but this was replaced in 1972 by computerized cut checkering; crossbolt safety; steel receiver.

Model 1100 Field Gun has plain barrel or vent rib, in 12-, 16-, 20-ga.; barrels, 30" full, 28" modified or full, 26" improved cylinder; black plastic butt plate, white spacer. Used values: with plain barrel, $200 to $225; vent rib, $275 to $300.

Model 1100 Magnum Duck Gun is same as field model, except for chambering for 3" 12-, 20-ga. magnum shells only; 20-ga. has

28" full or modified barrel; 12-ga., 30" full, modified; recoil pad. Used values: plain barrel, $225 to $250; vent rib, $275 to $300.

Model 1100SA Skeet model; 12-, 20-ga.; same as 1100 field gun, except for 26" barrel, vent rib, skeet choke or Cutts Compensator. Used values: with skeet choke, $275 to $295; Cutts Compensator, $265 to $285.

Model 1100SB Skeet gun is the same as 1100SA, except for selected wood and in skeet choke only. No longer made. Used value, $285 to $320.

Model 1100TB Trap model; same as 1100 field style, except for trap stock, Monte Carlo or straight comb choice; 30" barrel, full, modified trap choke; vent rib; 12-ga. only; recoil pad. No longer made. Used values: straight stock, $300 to $325; Monte Carlo stock, $325 to $350.

Model 1100 Tournament, Premier Grades are same as standard models, except for grade of walnut, amount, fineness of check-

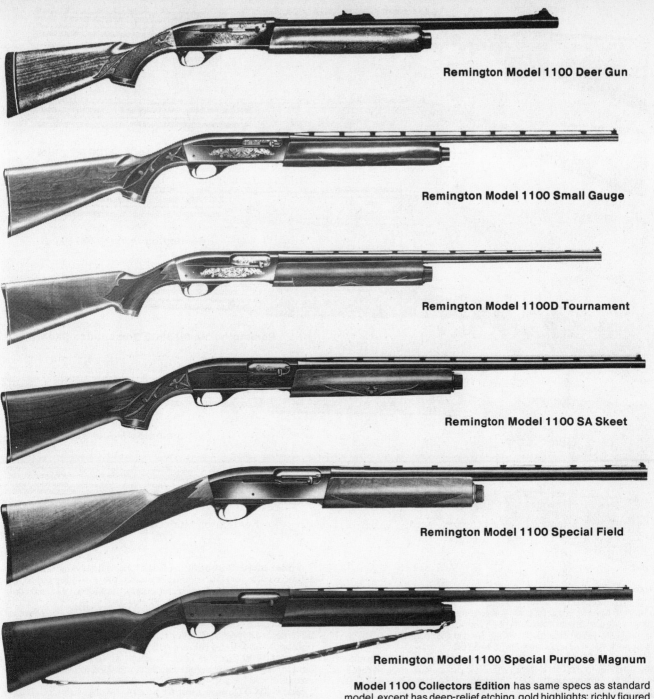

Remington Model 1100 Deer Gun

Remington Model 1100 Small Gauge

Remington Model 1100D Tournament

Remington Model 1100 SA Skeet

Remington Model 1100 Special Field

Remington Model 1100 Special Purpose Magnum

ering; engraving, gold inlays. Used values: Tournament (1100D), $1150 to $1400; Premier (1100F), $2750 to $3200; Premier, gold inlaid, $4500 to $4800.

Model 1100 Deer Gun; same as field gun, but with 22" barrel; 12-, 20-ga.; improved cylinder; rifle sights; recoil pad. Used value, $250 to $295.

Model 1100 Small Gauge has same specs as standard model, except is 20-ga. with 5-rd. magazine; .410 3". 4 rds.; available with 25" barrel, full, modified, improved cylinder; plain or vent rib. Introduced, 1978. Used values, $330 to $340.

Model 1100D Tournament has same specs as Model 1100 standard model, except has vent rib, better wood, more extensive engraving. Used value, $1400 to $1425.

Model 1100F Premier has same specs as 1100D except has better engraving, gold inlay work, select wood. Used values: sans gold inlay, $2700 to $3000; with gold inlay, $3000 to $3500.

Model 1100 LT-20 has same basic specs as standard model, except with weight-saving features; 26", 28" barrels. Used value, $300 to $325.

Model 1100 Collectors Edition has same specs as standard model, except has deep-relief etching, gold highlights; richly figured walnut stock, positive cut checkering; marketed with certificate showing serial number. Only 3000 made in 1981. Used value, $850 to $900.

Model 1100 Special Field has same general specs as standard model, except has 21" barrel; improved, modified, full; straight stock; shortened forend; cut checkering; vent rib; matte-finished receiver; no engraving. Introduced, 1983; still in production. Used value: $350 to $375.

Model 1100 SA Skeet has same specs as standard model, except has skeet boring, vent rib; ivory bead front sight, metal bead middle; cut checkering; new receiver scroll pattern. Used values: $320 to $350; Tournament models, $350 to $375.

Model 1100 Special Purpose Magnum has same specs as standard model, except is chambered for 12-ga. 3" shells; has vent rib; 26", 30" full-choke barrels; all exposed metal finished in non-reflective black; oil-finished wood; dark recoil pad; quick-detachable swivels; chrome-lined bore. Marketed with padded sling. Introduced, 1985; no longer in production. Used value, $320 to $350.

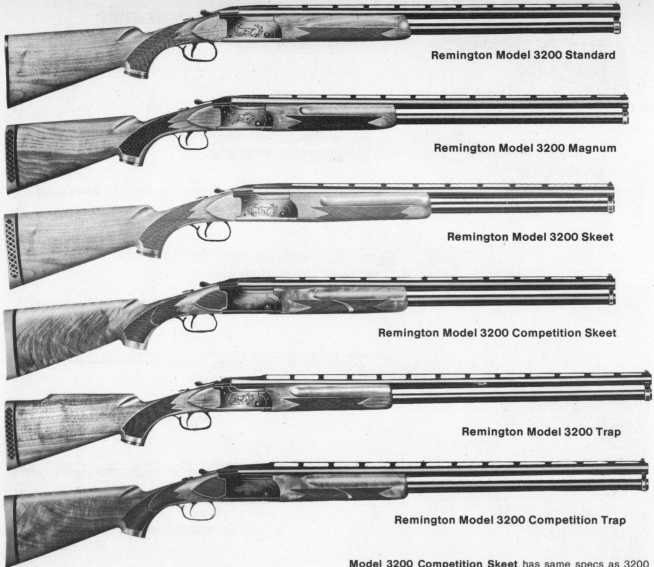

Remington Model 3200 Standard

Remington Model 3200 Magnum

Remington Model 3200 Skeet

Remington Model 3200 Competition Skeet

Remington Model 3200 Trap

Remington Model 3200 Competition Trap

REMINGTON Model 3200: over/under; 12-ga.; 2¾" chambering; 26" improved cylinder/modified, 28" modified/full, 30" modified/full barrels; vent rib; box-lock action; auto ejectors; selective single trigger; checkered American walnut pistol-grip stock, forearm. Bears resemblance to earlier Model 32. Introduced, 1973; dropped, 1984. Used value, $650 to $700.

Model 3200 Magnum has same specs as standard model, except chambered for 3" magnum shell; 30" barrels, modified/full or full/full. Introduced, 1973; dropped, 1984. Used value, $750 to $800.

Model 3200 Skeet has same specs as standard 3200, except for skeet-choked 26", 28" barrels, skeet stock, full beavertail forearm. Introduced, 1973; dropped, 1984. Used value, $750 to $800.

Model 3200 Competition Skeet has same specs as 3200 Skeet, except for engraved forend latch plate, trigger guard; gilt scrollwork on frame; select walnut wood. Introduced, 1973; dropped, 1984. Used value, $950 to $1000.

Model 3200 Trap has same specs as standard 3200, except for straight comb or Monte Carlo trap stock, beavertail forearm; 30", 32" improved modified/full or full/full chokes. Introduced, 1973; dropped, 1984. Used value, $750 to $800.

Model 3200 Special Trap has same specs as 3200 Trap, except for higher grade select walnut woodwork. Introduced, 1973; dropped, 1984. Used value, $775 to $825.

Model 3200 Competition Trap has same specs as Model 3200 Trap, except for engraved forend latch plate, trigger guard; gilt scrollwork on frame; select fancy walnut wood. Introduced, 1973; dropped, 1984. Used value, $900 to $950.

Remington Sportsman Pump

REMINGTON Sportsman Pump: pump-action; 12-ga.; 3" chamber; 28", 30" barrel lengths; checkered walnut-stained hardwood stock, forend; other specs similar to Model 870. Introduced, 1984; dropped, 1986. Used value, $175 to $185.

REMINGTON Sportsman Auto: autoloader; 12-ga. only; 2¾" chambering; 28", 30" barrel lengths; stock, forend of walnut-stained hardwood; weighs 7¾ lb.; other specs similar to Model 1100. Introduced, 1985; dropped, 1986. Used value, $290 to $300.

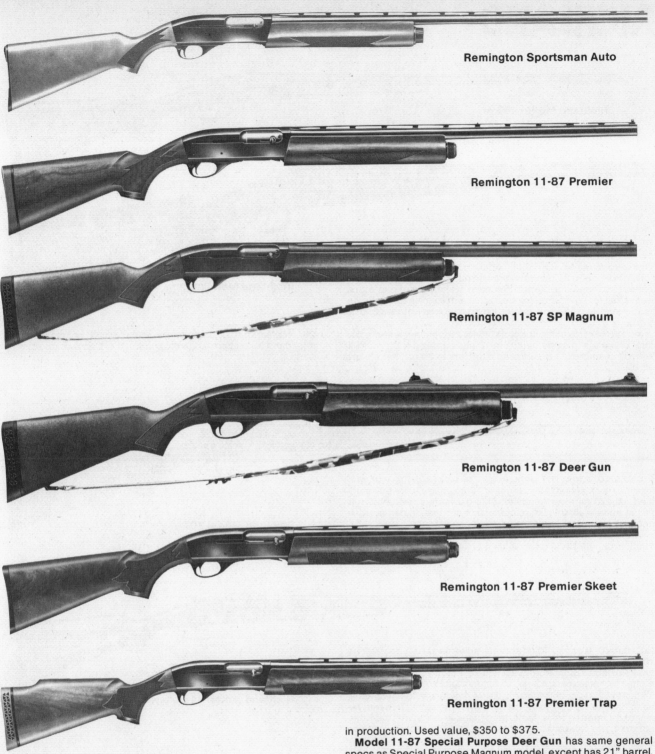

Remington Sportsman Auto

Remington 11-87 Premier

Remington 11-87 SP Magnum

Remington 11-87 Deer Gun

Remington 11-87 Premier Skeet

Remington 11-87 Premier Trap

REMINGTON 11-87 Premier: autoloader; gas-operated; 12-ga.; 3" chamber; 26", 28", 30" barrel lengths; Rem-Choke tubes; weighs 8¼ lb.; metal bead middle sight, Bradley-type white-faced front; satin-finished, cut-checkered walnut stock; brown butt pad; pressure compensating system handles 2¾" or 3" shells; stainless steel magazine tube; barrel support ring on operating bars; pinned forend; left- or right-hand versions. Introduced, 1987; still in production. Used values: standard, $350 to $375; left-hand. $385 to $410.

Model 11-87 Special Purpose Magnum has same specs as standard model, except has dull stock finish, Parkerized finish, blackened bolt, carrier; 20", 30" barrels; quick-detachable sling swivels. Marketed with padded nylon sling. Introduced, 1987; still

in production. Used value, $350 to $375.

Model 11-87 Special Purpose Deer Gun has same general specs as Special Purpose Magnum model, except has 21" barrel, rifle sights, fixed slug choke; gas system is set to handle all 2¾", 3" slug, buckshot, field and magnum loads; doesn't function with light field loads. Introduced, 1987; still in production. Used value, $300 to $325.

Model 11-87 Premier Skeet has same specs as standard model, except has skeet stock with cut checkering, satin finish, two-piece butt plate, 26" barrel with Rem-Chokes. Gas system is set for 2¾" shells only. Introduced, 1987; still produced. Used value, $400 to $425.

Model 11-87 Premier Trap has trap stock with straight or Monte Carlo comb; satin-finished, cut-checkered tournament-grade walnut stock; Rem-Choke 30" barrel. Gas system set for 2¾" shells only. Introduced, 1987; still in production. Used value, $385 to $415.

RICHLAND

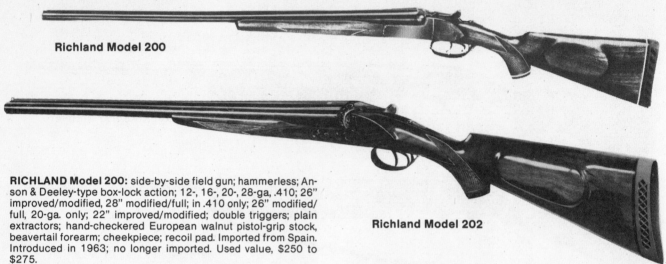

Richland Model 200

Richland Model 202

RICHLAND Model 200: side-by-side field gun; hammerless; Anson & Deeley-type box-lock action; 12-, 16-, 20-, 28-ga., .410; 26" improved/modified, 28" modified/full; in .410 only; 26" modified/full, 20-ga. only; 22" improved/modified; double triggers; plain extractors; hand-checkered European walnut pistol-grip stock, beavertail forearm; cheekpiece; recoil pad. Imported from Spain. Introduced in 1963; no longer imported. Used value, $250 to $275.

Model 202 has same specs as Model 200, but comes with two sets of barrels in same gauge. In 12-ga., barrels are 30" full/full with 3" chambers, 26" improved/modified; in 20-ga., barrels are 26" modified/full, 22" improved/modified with 3" chambers. Introduced in 1963; importation dropped, 1971. Used value, $225 to $250.

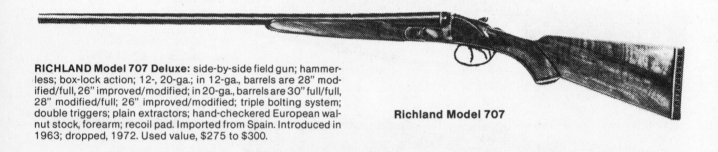

Richland Model 707

RICHLAND Model 707 Deluxe: side-by-side field gun; hammerless; box-lock action; 12-, 20-ga.; in 12-ga., barrels are 28" modified/full, 26" improved/modified; in 20-ga., barrels are 30" full/full, 28" modified/full; 26" improved/modified; triple bolting system; double triggers; plain extractors; hand-checkered European walnut stock, forearm; recoil pad. Imported from Spain. Introduced in 1963; dropped, 1972. Used value, $275 to $300.

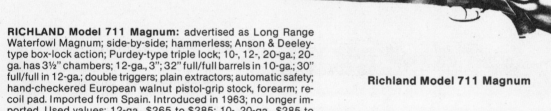

Richland Model 711 Magnum

RICHLAND Model 711 Magnum: advertised as Long Range Waterfowl Magnum; side-by-side; hammerless; Anson & Deeley-type box-lock action; Purdey-type triple lock; 10-, 12-, 20-ga.; 20-ga. has 3½" chambers; 12-ga., 3"; 32" full/full barrels in 10-ga.; 30" full/full in 12-ga.; double triggers; plain extractors; automatic safety; hand-checkered European walnut pistol-grip stock, forearm; recoil pad. Imported from Spain. Introduced in 1963; no longer imported. Used values: 12-ga., $265 to $285; 10-, 20-ga., $285 to $335.

Richland Model 808

RICHLAND Model 808: over/under; box-lock action; 12-ga. only; 30" full/full, 28" modified/full, 26" improved/modified barrels; plain extractors; nonselective single trigger; hand-checkered European walnut stock, forearm; vent rib. Imported from Italy. Introduced in 1963; importation dropped, 1968. Used value, $325 to $350.

RICHLAND Model 828: over/under; box-lock action; color case-hardened receiver; 28-ga. only; 26" improved/modified, 28" full/modified barrels; sliding crossbolt lock; non-automatic safety; plain extractors; vent rib; rosette engraving; hand-checkered European walnut stock, quick-detachable forearm. Imported from Italy. Introduced in 1971; no longer imported. Available on special order only. Used value, $575 to $625.

Richland Model 828

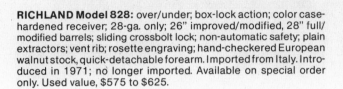

RICHLAND Model 844: over/under; nickel-chrome steel box-lock action; 12-ga., 12-ga. magnum; 26" improved/modified, 28" modified/full, 30" full/full barrels; plain extractors; non-selective single trigger; hand-checkered European walnut pistol-grip stock, forearm. Imported from Italy. Introduced in 1971; no longer imported. Used value, $300 to $325.

Richland Model 844

ROTTWEIL

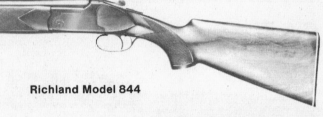

ROTTWEIL Field Supreme: over/under; 12-ga. only; 28" barrels, vent rib; box-lock action; metal bead front sight; hand-checkered, rubbed French walnut stock; checkered pistol grip, forend; plastic butt plate; removable interchangeable single trigger assembly; engraved action. Imported from West Germany. Introduced, 1976; dropped, 1986. Was imported by Dynamit Nobel. Used value, $2400 to $2500.

Rottweil Field Supreme

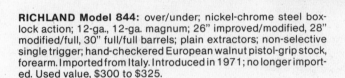

ROTTWEIL Olympia 72 Skeet: over/under; 12-ga. only; 27" barrels, vent rib; box-lock; metal bead front sight; hand-checkered, oil-finished French walnut stock, modified beavertail forend; chrome-lined barrels; flared chokes; inertia-type trigger; retracting spring-mounted firing pins; selective single trigger; engraved action. Introduced, 1976; dropped, 1986. Was imported by Dynamit Nobel. Used value, $1500 to $1800.

Rottweil Olympia 72 Skeet

Olympia 72 Trap has same specs as skeet version, except has 30" barrels. Used value, $1500 to $1800.

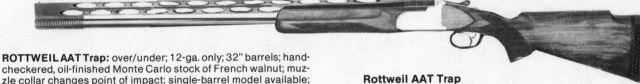

ROTTWEIL AAT Trap: over/under; 12-ga. only; 32" barrels; hand-checkered, oil-finished Monte Carlo stock of French walnut; muzzle collar changes point of impact; single-barrel model available; release/release or release/pull trigger group. Introduced, 1979; dropped, 1986. Was imported by Dynamit Nobel. Used values: single lower barrel model, $1700 to $1900; combo, with single and over/under barrels, $2400 to $2500.

Rottweil AAT Trap

ROTTWEIL American Trap Combo: 12-ga. only; box-lock action; separated 32" over/under barrels, single-barrel, 34"; high vent rib; center bead sight, plastic front in metal sleeve; hand-checkered, rubbed Monte Carlo stock of European walnut; double vent recoil pad; single selective or double triggers; hand-honed chokes; engraved action. Introduced, 1977; no longer imported. Used values: single-barrel, $2500 to $2600; over/under, $3250 to $3500.

American Skeet version has same general specs, except for 26" barrels. Used value, $1700 to $1900.

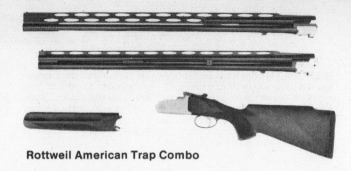

Rottweil American Trap Combo

SAE

SAE Model 70

SAE Model 66C: over/under; 12-ga. only; 26" skeet/skeet, 28" modified/full barrels; has same general specs as Model 70, except has oil-finished Monte Carlo stock, dummy side plates, gold inlays, extensive engraving. Made in Spain. Introduced, 1987; still imported by Spain America Enterprises. Used value, $900 to $950.

SAE Model 340X: side-by-side; 12-, 20-ga.; 2¾" chambers; 26" modified/full, 28" modified/improved cylinder barrels; true sidelock model; weighs 6.9 lb.; double triggers; selective ejectors; color case-hardened receiver; engraving. Made in Spain. Introduced, 1987; still imported by Spain America Enterprises. Used value, $950 to $1000.

SAE Model 70: over/under; 12-, 20-ga.; 3" chambers; 26" modified/full, 28" improved/modified cylinder barrels; weighs 6 lb. 10 oz.; European walnut stock; box-lock action; selective auto ejectors; auto safety; single mechanical trigger; engraved receiver; blued finish. Made in Spain. Introduced, 1987; still imported by Spain America Enterprises. Used value, $700 to $750.

Model 70 Multichoke has same specs as standard model, except has choke tubes, silvered receiver, 27" barrels; 12-ga. only. Made in Spain. Introduced, 1987; still imported. Used value, $750 to $800.

SAE Model 209E: side-by-side; has the same specs as Model 340X, except has engraved, coin-finished receiver, fancy oil-finished walnut stock, forend; made in 12-, 20-ga., .410; 2¾" chambers. Made in Spain. Introduced, 1987; still imported by Spain America Enterprises. Used value, $1100 to $1150.

SAE Model 210S

SAE Model 210S: side-by-side; 12-, 20-ga., .410; 3" chambers; 25" modified/full, 28" modified improved barrels; weighs 7 lb.; pistol-grip European walnut stock, splinter forend; box-lock action; auto safety; extractors; double triggers. Made in Spain. Introduced, 1987; still imported by Spain America Enterprises. Used value, $850 to $900.

SARASQUETA

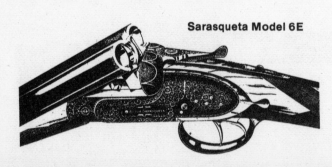

Sarasqueta Model 6E

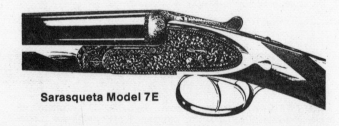

Sarasqueta Model 7E

SARASQUETA Sidelock Double: side-by-side; hammerless; 12-, 16-, 20-, 28-ga.; barrel lengths, choke combinations to customer's order; double triggers; hand-checkered European walnut straight-

Sarasqueta Model 4

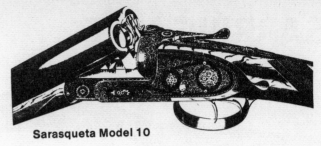

Sarasqueta Model 10

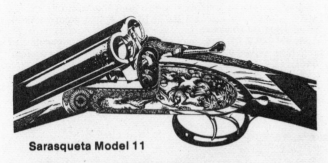

Sarasqueta Model 11

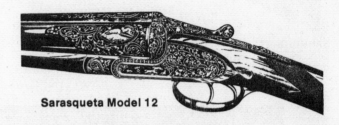

Sarasqueta Model 12

grip stock, forearm; gun is made in 18 grades; except for No. 6 and 7, all have automatic ejectors. Grades differ in quality of wood, checkering and amount and quality of engraving. Spanish manufacture. Used values: No. 4, $450 to $500; No. 4E, $550 to $600; No. 5, $550 to $600; No. 5E, $600 to $650; No. 6, $600 to $650;

No. 6E, $650 to $700; No. 7, $700 to $750; No. 7E, $750 to $800; No. 8, $800 to $850; No. 8E, $850 to $900, No. 9, $900 to $950; No. 9E, $950 to $1000, No. 10, $1400 to $1500; No. 10E, $1500 to $1600, No. 11, $1600 to $1700; No. 11E, $1700 to $1800, No. 12, $1800 to $1900, No. 12E, $2000 to $2100.

SARASQUETA No. 2: side-by-side; hammerless; box-lock action; 12-, 16-, 20-, 28-ga.; manufactured in all standard barrel lengths, choke combinations; plain extractors; double triggers; hand-checkered European walnut straight-grip stock, forearm; Greener crossbolt; engraved. Introduced in mid-1930s; still in production; no current importer. Used value, $400 to $425.

No. 3 has same specs as No. 2, but no Greener crossbolt; engraving style is different. Still in production. Used value, $420 to $450.

Sarasqueta No. 3

Sarasqueta Super Deluxe

SARASQUETA Super Deluxe: side-by-side; side-lock action; hammerless; 12-ga. only; barrel lengths, choke combos to customer's order; automatic ejectors; double triggers; hand-checkered European walnut pistol-grip stock, forearm; engraved action. Introduced in 1930s; still in production; no current importer. Used value, $1250 to $1300.

Sarasqueta Model 119E

SARASQUETA Model 119E: side-by-side; 12-ga.; 2¾" chambers; 28" barrels, modified/full, improved/modified; straight-grip European walnut stock; medium bead front sight; auto ejectors; double triggers; hand-engraved locks. Made in Spain. Introduced, 1982 by Toledo Armas; dropped, 1984. Used value, $475 to $500.

SARRIUGARTE

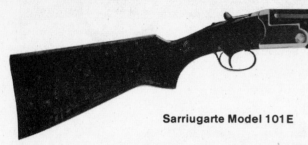

Sarriugarte Model 101E

SARRIUGARTE Model 101E: over/under; 12-ga.; 2¾" chambers; 26" improved/modified barrels, 28" modified/full; medium bead front sight; European walnut stock; hand-checkered full pistol grip; auto ejectors; single trigger; border engraving on receiver. Made in Spain. Introduced, 1982 by Toledo Armas; dropped, 1984. Used value: $425 to $450.

Model 101E DS has same specs as Model 101E, except has selective trigger. Introduced, 1982; dropped, 1984. Used value: $450 to $475.

Model 101DS has same specs as Model 101E, except has selective trigger, extractors; no auto ejectors. Introduced, 1982; dropped, 1984. Used value: $325 to $350.

SARRIUGARTE Model 200 Trap: over/under; 12-ga.; 2¾" chambers; has same specs as Model 101E, except has 30" full/full barrels; Monte Carlo-style stock; single trigger; auto ejectors; vent middle rib. Made in Spain. Introduced, 1982 by Toledo Armas; dropped, 1984. Used value: $650 to $675.

Sarriugarte Model 200 Trap

Sarriugarte Model 501E Special

SARRIUGARTE Model 501E Special: over/under; 12-ga.; 2¾" chambers; has same specs as Model 200 Trap, except has better wood, heavier engraving of customer's choice. Introduced, 1982; dropped, 1984. Used value: $1200 to $1250.

Model 501E Special Niger is same as 501E Special, but has higher grade wood, better engraving. Introduced, 1982; dropped, 1984. Used value: $1500 to $1600.

Model 501E Special Excelsior has same specs as 501E Special Niger, but is top of the line with best wood available; better grade of engraving. Introduced, 1982; dropped, 1984. Used value: $1600 to $1700.

SAUER

Sauer Royal Model

SAUER Royal Model: side-by-side; Anson & Deeley-type boxlock action; 12-, 20-ga.; 30" full/full barrels in 12-ga. only; 28" modified/full, 26" improved/modified in 20-ga. only; Greener crossbolt; single selective trigger; automatic ejectors; automatic safety; double underlugs; scalloped frame; Arabesque engraving; hand-checkered European walnut pistol-grip stock, beavertail forearm; recoil pad. Introduced in 1950s; still in production; no current importer. Used value, $1250 to $1300.

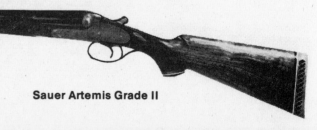

Sauer Artemis Grade II

SAUER Artemis Model: side-by-side; Holland & Holland-type sidelock action; 12-ga. only; 28" modified/full barrels; Greener-type crossbolt; double underlugs; double sear safeties; automatic ejectors; single selective trigger; hand-checkered European walnut pistol-grip stock, beavertail forearm; recoil pad. Grade I has fineline engraving; Grade II has English Arabesque motif. Introduced in 1950s; still in production; no current importer. Used values: Grade I, $3500 to $3750; Grade II, $4500 to $4750.

Sauer Model 66 Field Gun

**Sauer Model 66
Field Grade III**

SAUER Model 66 Field Gun: over/under; Purdey-type action; Holland & Holland side plates; 12-ga. only; 28" modified/full barrels; automatic safety; selective automatic ejectors; single selective trigger; hand-checkered European walnut stock, forearm; recoil pad; three grades of engraving. Introduced in 1950s; still in production; no current importer. Used values: Grade I, $1250 to $1500; Grade II, $1500 to $1750; Grade III, $2250 to $2500.

    Model 66 Trap has same general specs as field model except for 30" full/full or modified/full barrels; trap stock; wide vent rib; non-automatic safety; ventilated beavertail forearm. Introduced in 1960s; dropped, 1975. Used values: Grade I, $1300 to $1550; Grade II, $1550 to $1800; Grade III, $2300 to $2550.

    Model 66 Skeet has same specs as trap model. Used values: Grade I, $1300 to $1550; Grade II, $1550 to $1800; Grade III, $2300 to $2550.

Sauer Model BBF

SAUER Model BBF: over/under combo; blitz-action; Kersten lock; 16-ga. top barrel; choice of .30-30, .30/06, 7x65R rifle barrel; front set trigger activates rifle barrel; 25" barrels; shotgun barrel full choke only; sliding sear safety; folding leaf rear sight; hand-checkered European walnut pistol-grip stock, forearm; modified Monte Carlo comb, cheekpiece; sling swivels; Arabesque engraving pattern. Introduced in 1950s; still in production; no current importer. Used values: standard model, $1700 to $1900; Deluxe, $3250 to $3500.

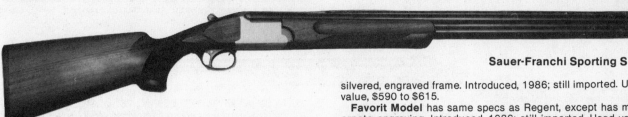

Sauer-Franchi Sporting S

SAUER-FRANCHI Standard Model: over/under; 12-ga.; 28", 29" barrels; standard choke combos; weighs 7 lb.; European walnut stock; blued finish; single selective trigger; selective auto ejectors; vent rib. Introduced, 1986; still imported from West Germany by Sigarms. Used value, $575 to $600.

    Regent Model has same specs as standard version, except has

silvered, engraved frame. Introduced, 1986; still imported. Used value, $590 to $615.

    Favorit Model has same specs as Regent, except has more ornate engraving. Introduced, 1986; still imported. Used value, $650 to $675.

    Diplomat Model has same specs as Favorite, except has more engraving, better wood. Introduced, 1986; still imported. Used value, $1100 to $1200.

    Sporting S has same specs as Favorit, except has trap and skeet configurations. Introduced, 1986; still imported. Used value, $925 to $975.

SAVAGE

SAVAGE Model 28A: slide-action; take-down; hammerless; 12-ga. only; 26", 28", 30", 32" plain barrel; 5-rd. tube magazine; modified, cylinder, full choke; uncheckered American walnut pistol-grip stock, grooved slide handle; black plastic butt plate. Introduced in 1920s; dropped, about 1940. Used value, $125 to $150.

    Model 28B has the same general specs as Model 28A, except has raised matted rib. Used value, $150 to $175.

    Model 28D trap gun has same specs as Model 28A, except for full-choke barrel, matted rib; hand-checkered pistol-grip, trap stock, checkered slide handle. Used value, $250 to $275.

SAVAGE Model 420: over/under; box-lock action; take-down; hammerless; 12-, 16-, 20-ga.; 26", 28", 30" barrels, last in 12-ga. only; double triggers; single non-selective trigger at extra cost; automatic safety; choked modified/full or cylinder/improved; checkered American walnut pistol-grip stock, forearm. Introduced in early 1930s; dropped, 1942. Used values: double triggers, $325 to $350; single trigger, $400 to $425.

SAVAGE Model 430: over/under; box-lock action; take-down; hammerless; has the same specs as Model 420, except for hand-checkered American walnut stock, forearm; recoil pad; matted top barrel. Introduced in early 1930s; dropped, 1942. Used values: double triggers, $350 to $375; single trigger, $425 to $450.

Savage Model 420

Savage Model 430

Savage Model 720

SAVAGE Model 720: autoloader; Browning design; take-down; 12-, 16-ga.; 26", 28", 30", 32" barrels, last in 12-ga. only; 4-rd. tube magazine; cylinder, modified, full chokes; hand-checkered American walnut pistol-grip stock, forearm; black plastic butt plate. Introduced in 1930; dropped, 1949. Used value, $175 to $195. Military riot version, rare, $300 to $350.

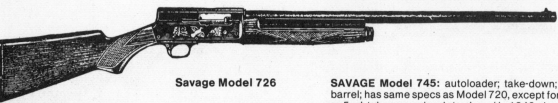

Savage Model 726

SAVAGE Model 740C: autoloader; skeet gun; take-down; 12-, 16-ga.; has the same specs as Model 726, except for skeet stock, beavertail forearm, Cutts Compensator; 24½" barrel. Introduced in late 1930s; dropped, 1949. Used value, $185 to $210.

SAVAGE Model 745: autoloader; take-down; 12-ga. only; 28" barrel; has same specs as Model 720, except for alloy receiver; 3- or 5-rd. tube magazine. Introduced in 1946; dropped, 1949. Used value, $150 to $175.

SAVAGE Model 726: autoloader; take-down; 12-, 16-ga.; has the same specs as Model 720, except tube magazine has 2-rd. capacity, engraved receiver. Introduced in 1930; dropped, 1949. Used value, $175 to $195.

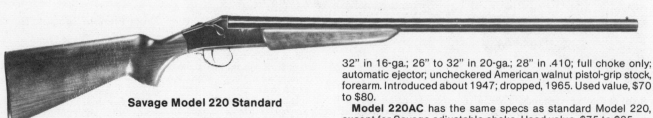

Savage Model 220 Standard

SAVAGE Model 220: single-barrel; single-shot; take-down; hammerless; 12-, 16-, 20-ga., .410; 28" to 36" barrels in 12-ga.; 28" to 32" in 16-ga.; 26" to 32" in 20-ga.; 28" in .410; full choke only; automatic ejector; uncheckered American walnut pistol-grip stock, forearm. Introduced about 1947; dropped, 1965. Used value, $70 to $80.

Model 220AC has the same specs as standard Model 220, except for Savage adjustable choke. Used value, $75 to $85.

Model 220P has the same specs as standard Model 220, except for Poly Choke; 12-ga. has 30" barrel only; 16-, 20-ga. have 28" barrel; not made in .410; recoil pad. Used value, $75 to $85.

Savage Model 755

Savage Model 755-SC

SAVAGE Model 755: autoloader; take-down; 12-, 16-ga.; 26" improved cylinder barrel; 28" full or modified, 30" full in 12-ga. only; hand-checkered American walnut pistol-grip stock, forearm; 2- or 4-rd. tube magazine. Introduced in 1949; dropped, 1958. Used value, $150 to $175.

Model 755-SC has same general specs as standard Model 755, except for 25" barrel, adjustable Savage Super Choke. Used value, $160 to $185.

Savage Model 24 Standard

SAVAGE Model 24: over/under combo; top barrel; .22 LR, long, short; lower barrel, .410 3" shotshell; full-choke bottom barrel; 24" barrels; open rear sight, ramp front rifle sight; uncheckered walnut pistol-grip stock; sliding button selector; single trigger. Introduced in 1950; dropped, 1965. Used value, $100 to $125.

Model 24-M has the same specs as Model 24, except top barrel is chambered for .22 WRFM cartridge. Used value, $120 to $140.

Model 24-DL has same specs as standard Model 24, except checkered stock has Monte Carlo comb, beavertail forearm; in 20-ga., .410 lower barrel; satin chrome-finished receiver, trigger guard. Used value, $110 to $135; add $20 for 20-ga.

Model 24-MDL has same specs as Model 24-DL, except upper barrel is chambered for .22 WRFM cartridge. Used value, $110 to $135; add $20 for 20-ga.

Savage Model 775 Lightweight

Savage Model 775-SC

SAVAGE Model 775 Lightweight: autoloader; take-down; 12-, 16-ga.; has same general specs as standard Model 755, except for alloy receiver. Introduced in 1953; dropped, 1960. Used value, $175 to $195.

Model 775-SC has same specs as Model 775 Lightweight, except for 26" barrel, Savage Super Choke. Used value, $180 to $200.

Savage Model 30

Savage Model 30-AC

Savage Model 30-T

Savage Model 30 Slug Gun

SAVAGE Model 30: slide-action; hammerless; solid frame; 12-, 20-ga., .410; 26", 28", 30" barrels; improved modified, full chokes; 5-rd. magazine in 12-, 20-ga., 4-rd. in .410; uncheckered American walnut stock, grooved slide handle; hard rubber butt plate. Introduced in 1958; dropped, 1979. Used value, $150 to $175.

Model 30-AC has the same specs as standard Model 30, except for 26" barrel, adjustable choke; 12-ga. only. Introduced in 1959; dropped, 1975. Used value, $160 to $185.

Model 30-ACL has same specs as Model 30-AC, but ejection port, safety are on left side. Introduced in 1960; dropped, 1964. Used value, $140 to $165.

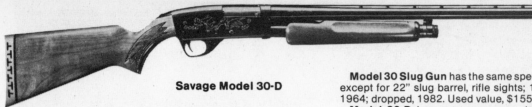

Savage Model 30-D

Model 30-T has same specs as standard model, except for 30" full-choke barrel only; 12-ga. only; Monte Carlo trap stock, recoil pad. Introduced in 1964; dropped, 1975. Used value, $155 to $175.

Model 30 Slug Gun has the same specs as standard Model 30, except for 22" slug barrel, rifle sights; 12-, 20-ga. Introduced in 1964; dropped, 1982. Used value, $155 to $175.

Model 30-D has same specs as standard model, except is chambered for 12-, 20-ga., .410 3" magnum shells; checkered pistol grip, fluted extension slide handle; alloy receiver; etched pattern on receiver; recoil pad. Introduced in 1972; dropped, 1979. Used value, $165 to $185.

Savage Model 750 Standard

SAVAGE Model 750: autoloader; Browning design; take-down; 12-ga. only; 26" improved, 28" full or modified barrel; 4-rd. tube magazine; checkered American walnut pistol-grip stock, grooved

forearm. Introduced in 1960; dropped, 1963. Used value, $165 to $175.

Model 750-SC has same specs as standard Model 750, except for 26" barrel only, Savage Super Choke. Introduced in 1962; dropped, 1963. Used value, $185 to $200.

Model 750-AC has same specs as Model 750, except for 26" barrel only, adjustable choke. Introduced in 1964; dropped, 1967. Used value, $185 to $200.

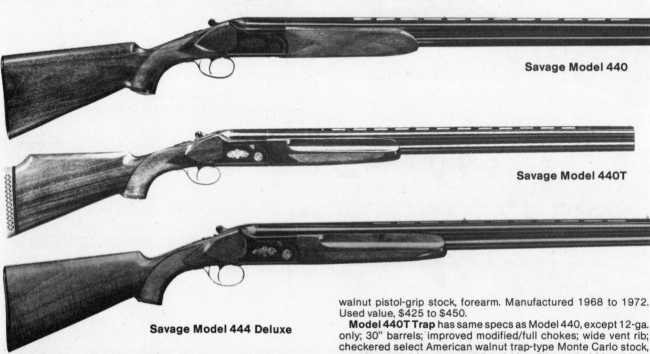

Savage Model 440

Savage Model 440T

Savage Model 444 Deluxe

SAVAGE Model 440: over/under; 12-, 20-ga.; 2¾" chambers in 12-ga., 3" in 20; 26" barrel with improved cylinder/modified or skeet chokes; 28" modified/full, 30" modified/full; box-lock action; single selective trigger; plain extractors; checkered American

walnut pistol-grip stock, forearm. Manufactured 1968 to 1972. Used value, $425 to $450.

Model 440T Trap has same specs as Model 440, except 12-ga. only; 30" barrels; improved modified/full chokes; wide vent rib; checkered select American walnut trap-type Monte Carlo stock, semi-beavertail forearm; recoil pad. Manufactured 1969 to 1972. Used value, $450 to $475.

Model 444 Deluxe has same general specs as Model 440, except for auto ejectors, select walnut stock, semi-beavertail forearm. Manufactured 1969 to 1972. Used value, $465 to $485.

Savage Model 330

SAVAGE Model 330: over/under; 12-, 20-ga.; 2¾" chambers for 12-ga., 3" for 20; 26" improved cylinder/modified barrel, 28" mod-

ified/full, 30" modified/full; box-lock action; selective single trigger; plain extractors; checkered European walnut pistol-grip stock, forearm. Manufactured in Finland by Valmet. Introduced, 1969; dropped, 1979. Used value, $375 to $400.

Model 333 has same general specs as Model 330, except for automatic ejectors; vent rib; 26" skeet choke, improved cylinder/modified barrels; 28" modified/full; 30" modified/full, fuller forearm. Introduced, 1973; dropped, 1979. Used value, $425 to $450.

Savage Model 333 12 Gauge

Savage Model 333 20 Gauge

Savage Model 333T

Model 333T Trap has same specs as Model 330, except 12-ga. only; 30" vent-rib barrel; improved modified/full chokes; Monte Carlo trap stock; recoil pad. Introduced. 1972; dropped, 1979. Used value, $450 to $475.

Savage Model 550

SAVAGE Model 550: side-by-side; 12-, 20-ga.; 2¾" chambers in 12-ga., 3" in 20; 26" improved cylinder/modified barrels, 28" modified/full, 30" modified/full; hammerless; box-lock action; non-selective single trigger; auto ejectors; checkered American walnut pistol-grip stock, semi-beavertail forearm. Manufactured 1971 to 1973. Used value, $245 to $275.

Savage Model 2400 Combo

SAVAGE Model 2400 Combo: over/under; 12-ga. full-choke top barrel, .308 Win. or .222 Rem. lower barrel; box-lock action based on Model 330; 23½" barrel; solid matted rib; blade front sight, folding leaf rear; dovetail for scope mounting; checkered European walnut Monte Carlo pistol-grip stock, semi-beavertail forearm; recoil pad. Introduced, 1975; dropped, 1979. Used value, $500 to $525.

Savage Model 242

SAVAGE Model 242: over/under; .410; 24" barrels; full choke; based upon design of Model 24D combo gun. Introduced, 1977; dropped, 1979. Used value, $125 to $150.

Savage-Fox Model B-SE

SAVAGE-Fox Model B-SE: side-by-side; 12-, 20-ga., .410; 26", 28" barrels; vent rib; hammerless take-down; non-selective single or double triggers; auto safety; ejectors; checkered pistol-grip American walnut stock; beavertail forend; white bead front, middle sights; case-hardened, decorated frame. Introduced, 1978; no longer in production. Used values: single trigger, $270 to $280; double triggers, $225 to $235.

Savage Model 311

SAVAGE-Stevens Model 311: side-by-side; 12-, 16-, 20-ga., .410; 26", 28", 30" barrels; hammerless; double triggers, auto top tang safety; walnut-finished hardwood pistol-grip stock, fluted comb; case-hardened finish on frame. Originally introduced in 1931 as Model 311, but was stamped *Model 5000.* In 1941 stamp was changed to *Model 5100,* but still listed in catalog as Model 311A. In 1950 gun was marked as *Model 311.* Still in production. Used value, $220 to $230.

SKB

SKB Model 680 English

SKB Model 680 English: over/under; 12-, 20-ga.; box-lock action; 26", 28" barrels; straight-grip walnut stock, wrap-around checkering; auto selective ejectors; Bradley-type sights; single selective trigger. Made in Japan. Introduced, 1977 by SKB Sports; dropped, 1980. Used value, $600 to $625.

SKB 100 Field

SKB 100 Field: side-by-side; 12-, 20-ga.; 2¾", 3" chambers; 26", 28½", 30" barrel lengths; European walnut hand-checkered pistol-grip stock, forend; pistol-grip cap; fluted comb; automatic safety; blued barrels, receiver. Made in Japan. Introduced, 1978 by SKB Sports; dropped, 1980. Used values: standard model, $375 to $400; magnum model, $385 to $410.

SKB 200 Field

scroll engraving; silver-plated receiver; beavertail forend, gold-plated trigger, name plate. Made in Japan. Introduced, 1978 by SKB Sports; dropped, 1980. Used values: standard model, $430 to $450; magnum model, $440 to $460.

Model 200E Skeet has same specs as standard 200E, except has recoil pad, non-auto safety; 25" barrels in 12-ga., 25" in 20-ga.; choked skeet/skeet. Introduced, 1978; dropped, 1980. Used value, $450 to $465.

SKB 200E Field: side-by-side; has same specs as Model 100 Field, except has automatic selective ejectors, bead middle sight,

SKB 280 English: side-by-side; 12-, 20-ga.; 25", 26", 28" barrel lengths; English-style straight-grip European walnut stock; wrap-around checkering; semi-beavertail forend; receiver hand engraved with quail, English scrollwork; simulated oil finish. Made in Japan. Introduced, 1978 by SKB Sports; dropped, 1980. Used

value, $475 to $500.

Model 280 Quail has same general specs as 280 English, except is 20-ga. only; 3" chambers; 25" barrels; single trigger; selective ejectors. Introduced, 1978; dropped, 1980. Used value, $485 to $510.

SKB 280 English

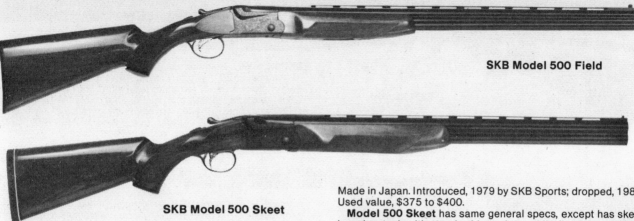

SKB Model 500 Field

SKB Model 500 Skeet

Made in Japan. Introduced, 1979 by SKB Sports; dropped, 1980. Used value, $375 to $400.

Model 500 Skeet has same general specs, except has skeet barrels, stock with standard butt plate, white line spacer. Used value, $425 to $450.

Model 500 Trap has same general specs, except has trap stock. Used value, $470 to $490.

Model 500 28 or .410 has same specs as standard field grade, except for gauges. Used value, $470 to $490.

SKB 500 Field Grade: over/under; 12-, 20-ga.; 26", 28", 30" barrels; checkered pistol-grip walnut stock, fluted comb; Ray-type front sight; box-lock action; gold-plated single selective trigger; auto ejectors, non-auto safety; border scroll-engraved receiver.

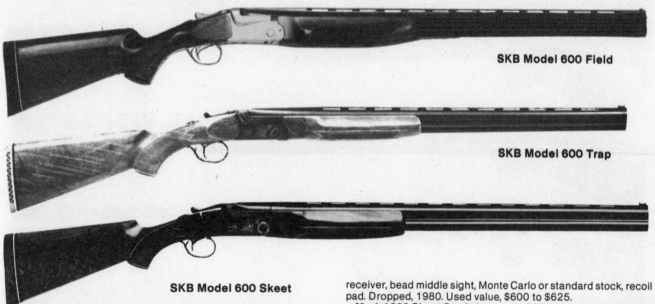

SKB Model 600 Field

SKB Model 600 Trap

SKB Model 600 Skeet

receiver, bead middle sight, Monte Carlo or standard stock, recoil pad. Dropped, 1980. Used value, $600 to $625.

Model 600 Skeet Grade is same as 600 trap, except is 12-, 20-, 28-ga., .410; has 26" or 28" barrels, skeet chokes; skeet pad. Dropped, 1980. Used value, $575 to $600.

Model 600 Small Bore is same as standard skeet grade, except features 3-barrel set for 20-, 28-ga., .410; all barrels are 28". Dropped, 1980. Used value, $1700 to $1800.

SKB 600 Field Grade: over/under; same specs as Model 500 field gun, except has better wood, fine scroll engraving on receiver. Introduced, 1979; dropped, 1980. Used value, $475 to $500.

Model 600 Trap Grade has 30" barrels, fine scroll engraved

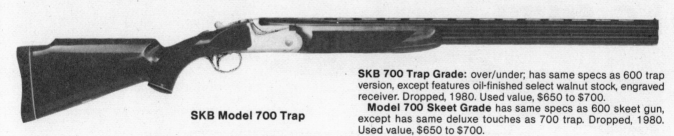

SKB Model 700 Trap

SKB 700 Trap Grade: over/under; has same specs as 600 trap version, except features oil-finished select walnut stock, engraved receiver. Dropped, 1980. Used value, $650 to $700.

Model 700 Skeet Grade has same specs as 600 skeet gun, except has same deluxe touches as 700 trap. Dropped, 1980. Used value, $650 to $700.

SKB Model 5600: over/under; 12-ga. only; 26", 28", 30" barrels; checkered pistol-grip walnut stock; hand-polished, blued frame, barrels; trap version has 16mm top rib; skeet rib is 13mm or 16mm; auto selective ejectors; mechanical single trigger. Made in Japan. Introduced, 1979 by SKB Sports; dropped, 1980. Used value, $475 to $500.

Model 5700 has same specs as 5600, except has better wood, checkering and grayed engraved receiver. Dropped, 1980. Used value, $550 to $600.

Model 5800 is same as Model 5700, except has fully engraved receiver. Dropped, 1980. Used value, $800 to $850.

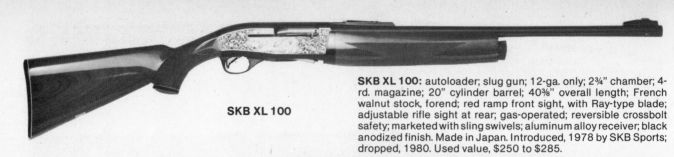

SKB XL 100

SKB XL 100: autoloader; slug gun; 12-ga. only; 2¾" chamber; 4-rd. magazine; 20" cylinder barrel; 40⅝" overall length; French walnut stock, forend; red ramp front sight, with Ray-type blade; adjustable rifle sight at rear; gas-operated; reversible crossbolt safety; marketed with sling swivels; aluminum alloy receiver; black anodized finish. Made in Japan. Introduced, 1978 by SKB Sports; dropped, 1980. Used value, $250 to $285.

SKB XL 900

SKB XL 900: autoloader; 12-, 20-ga.; 5-rd. magazine; 26", 28", 30" barrel lengths; 24" slug barrel; hand-checkered French walnut stock, forend; vent rib; Ray-type front sight on field grades, Bradley-type on target grades; self-compensating gas system; reversible

safety; action release button; gold trigger; inlaid name plate; silver game scene on receiver. Made in Japan. Introduced, 1979 by SKB Sports; dropped, 1980. Used values: vent rib, $250 to $275; skeet grade, $260 to $285; trap grade, $300 to $325; slug gun, $250 to $285.

XL 900MR has same general specs as standard XL 900, except is 12-ga. only; has magnum receiver to allow conversion to 3" shells by changing barrels. Introduced, 1979; dropped, 1980. Used values: vent rib, $260 to $275; skeet grade, $265 to $280; trap grade, $300 to $325; slug gun, $250 to $285.

SKB 7300

SKB 7900 Skeet

SKB 7900 Trap

SKB 7300: slide-action; 12-, 20-ga.; 2¾". 3" chambers; 24", 26", 28", 30" barrel lengths; hand-checkered French walnut stock, beavertail forend; recoil pad; white line spacer; Ray-type front sight; vent rib; double action bars. Made in Japan. Introduced,

1979 by SKB Sports; dropped, 1980. Used values: field grade, $225 to $250; slug gun, $225 to $250.

7900 Target Grade has same specs as Model 7300, except has 30" trap or 26" skeet barrels; target-type stocks; trap model has deluxe trap recoil pad; skeet has composition butt plate; blued, scroll-etched receiver; white front sight, middle bead. Introduced, 1979; dropped, 1980. Used values: trap model, $275 to $300; skeet, $275 to $300.

L.C. SMITH

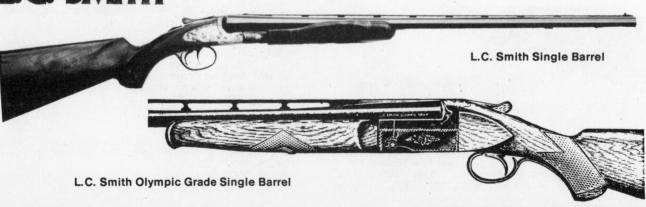

L.C. Smith Single Barrel

L.C. Smith Olympic Grade Single Barrel

L.C. SMITH Single-Barrel: single-shot; box-lock; hammerless; 12-ga. only; automatic ejector; 32", 34" barrels; vent rib; walnut stock; hand-checkered pistol grip, forearm; recoil pad. Made in 7 grades; original retail depending upon the quality of workmanship, engraving, quality of wood. Specialty Grade, introduced in 1917; dropped, 1948. Used value, $1200 to $1300. Eagle Grade, introduced in 1919; dropped, 1931. Used value, $2750 to $3000. Crown Grade, introduced in 1919; dropped, 1946. Used value, $3500 to $3750. Monogram Grade, introduced in 1919; dropped, 1946. Used value, $4500 to $5000. Olympic Grade, introduced in 1928; dropped, 1951. Used value, $1250 to $1500. Premier Grade, introduced in 1931; dropped, 1946. Used value, $7500 to $8000. Deluxe Grade, introduced in 1931; dropped, 1946. Used value, $12,500 to $15,000.

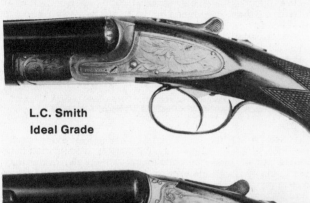

L.C. Smith
Ideal Grade

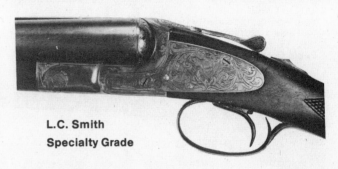

L.C. Smith
Specialty Grade

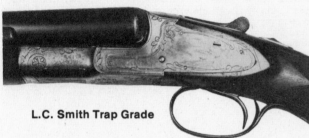

L.C. Smith Trap Grade

L.C. Smith Eagle Grade

L.C. Smith Skeet Special

L.C. Smith Premier Skeet

L.C. Smith Crown Grade

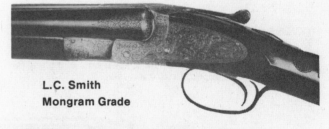

L.C. Smith
Mongram Grade

L.C. SMITH Hammerless: double-barrel; side-lock; 12-, 16-, 20-ga., .410; 26" to 32" barrels; standard choke combos; hand-checkered walnut stock, forearm; choice of straight stock, half or full pistol grip; beavertail or standard forearm; general specs are the same on all grades, but grades depend upon quality of workmanship, checkering, engraving and wood. Guns were made by Hunter Arms from 1913 until 1945; by L.C. Smith from 1945 to 1951. Values shown are for 12-ga. guns; 16-ga. are worth 10% less than 12s; 20-ga. guns are worth about 20% more than 12s; .410 guns are worth 50 to 75% more than 12-ga. guns; models made by L.C. Smith Gun Company are worth 5% less than Hunter Arms Company guns:

Field Grade, introduced in 1913; dropped, 1951; double triggers, plain extractors. Used values: $700 to $900; with automatic

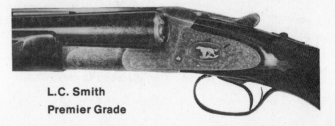

L.C. Smith
Premier Grade

ejectors, $800 to $1000; with non-selective single-trigger, plain extractors, $750 to $850; single trigger, automatic ejectors, $900 to $1100.

Ideal Grade, introduced in 1913; dropped, 1951; double triggers, plain extractors, $900 to $1100; double triggers, automatic ejectors, $1000 to $1200; single non-selective trigger, plain extractors, $950 to $1000; single selective trigger, automatic ejectors, $1200 to $1400.

Specialty Grade, introduced in 1913; dropped, 1951; double triggers, plain extractors, $1400 to $1600; double triggers, automatic ejectors, $1600 to $1800; single selective trigger, plain extractors, $1600 to $1800; single selective trigger, auto ejectors, $1900 to $2200.

Trap Grade, introduced in 1913; dropped, 1939; made only with single selective trigger, automatic ejectors. Used value, $1250 to $1500.

Eagle Grade, introduced in 1913; dropped, 1939; double trig-

gers, plain extractors, $3000 to $3200; double triggers, automatic ejectors, $3100 to $3300; single selective trigger, plain extractors, $3200 to $3400; single trigger, auto ejectors, $4000 to $4200.

Crown Grade, introduced in 1913; dropped, 1945; double triggers, automatic ejectors, $3500 to $3700; single selective trigger, auto ejectors, $4000 to $4200.

Monogram Grade, introduced in 1913; dropped, 1945; selective trigger, automatic ejectors, $7000 to $8000.

Premier Grade, introduced in 1913; dropped, 1941; single selective trigger; automatic ejectors, $15,000 to $16,000.

Deluxe Grade, introduced in 1913; dropped, 1945; $20,000 to $22,500.

Skeet Special, introduced in 1913; dropped, 1942; selective or nonselective single trigger, automatic ejectors, $1600 to $2000.

Premier Skeet Grade, introduced in 1949; dropped, 1951; single selective trigger, automatic ejectors, $1800 to $2200.

L.C. Smith Marlin Deluxe Grade

L.C. SMITH Marlin: double-barrel; hammerless; side-lock action; Field Grade is 12-ga. only; 28" barrels; modified/full only; double triggers; case-hardened frame; vent rib; standard extractors; automatic tang safety; checkered pistol-grip stock of select walnut; pistol-grip cap. Deluxe Grade has same specs as Field Grade, except for better wood, full beavertail forearm, Simmons floating vent rib. Introduced in 1968; dropped, 1972. Used values: Field Grade, $550 to $600; Deluxe Grade, $750 to $800.

STEVENS

Stevens Model 520

STEVENS Model 520: slide-action; 12-, 16-, 20-ga.; 30" barrel; weighs 7½ lb.; 5-rd. magazine; checkered American walnut stock, forend; safety inside trigger guard; made exclusively for Sears-Roebuck, marketed as Sears Ranger. Introduced, 1915; dropped, about 1930. Some collector value. Used value, $125 to $150.

Stevens Model 620

STEVENS Model 620: slide-action; hammerless; 12-, 16-, 20-ga.; 26", 28", 30", 32" barrels; take-down; 5-rd. tube magazine; cylinder, improved, modified, full chokes; hand-checkered American walnut pistol-grip stock, slide handle; black plastic butt plate. Introduced in 1927; dropped, 1953. Used value, $155 to $210.

STEVENS Model 621: slide-action; hammerless; 12-, 16-, 20-ga.; has the same specs as the Model 620, except for raised solid matted rib. Introduced in 1927; dropped, 1953. Used value, $200 to $220.

Stevens Model 311

STEVENS-Springfield Model 311: side-by-side; hammerless; box-lock action; 12-, 16-, 20-ga., .410; 26", 28", 30", 32" barrels; modified/full, cylinder/modified, full/full chokes; early guns had uncheckered American walnut pistol-grip stock, forearm; current production has walnut-finished hardwood stock, fluted comb; double triggers; plastic butt plate. Introduced in 1931; still in production as Savage-Stevens Model 311. Used value, $185 to $200.

Stevens Model 59

STEVENS Model 59: bolt-action repeater; take-down; .410 only; 24" barrel, full choke only; 5-rd. tube magazine; uncheckered one-piece walnut-finished hardwood pistol-grip stock; plastic butt plate. Introduced in 1934; dropped, 1973. Used value, $65 to $85.

Stevens Model 530ST

STEVENS Model 530: side-by-side; hammerless; box-lock action; 12-, 16-, 20-ga., .410; 26", 28", 30", 32" barrels; modified/full, cylinder/modified, full choke combos; double triggers; early models have recoil pads; hand-checkered American walnut pistol-grip stock, forearm. Introduced in 1936; dropped, 1954. Used value, $200 to $225.

Model 530M has the same specs as Model 530, except stock, forearm are of Tenite plastic. Introduced before WWII; dropped, 1947. Used value, $135 to $155.

Model 530ST has same specs as Model 530, except for single selective trigger. Introduced in 1947; dropped, 1954. Used value, $225 to $250.

Stevens Model 58

STEVENS Model 58: bolt-action repeater; take-down; .410 only; 24" barrel; full choke only; 3-rd. detachable box magazine; uncheckered, one-piece, walnut-finished hardwood pistol-grip stock; plastic butt plate; late model has machine-checkering on grip, forearm. Introduced in 1937; no longer in production as Savage-Stevens Model 58. Used value, $65 to $75.

Stevens Model 258

STEVENS Model 258: bolt-action repeater; take-down; 20-ga. only; 25" barrel, full choke only; uncheckered hardwood, one-piece, pistol-grip stock; black plastic forearm cap, butt plate. Introduced in 1937; dropped, 1965. Used value, $75 to $85.

Stevens Model 107

STEVENS Model 107: single-barrel; single-shot; hammer gun; take-down; 12-, 16-, 20-ga., .410; 28", 30" barrels in 12-, 16-ga., 28" in 20-ga., 26" in .410; full choke only; automatic ejector; uncheckered walnut-finished hardwood pistol-grip stock, forearm. Introduced in 1937; dropped, 1953. Used value, $70 to $80.

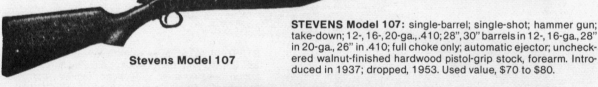

Stevens Model 22-410

STEVENS Model 22-410: over/under combo gun; .22 LR, long, short barrel over .410 shotgun barrel; visible hammer; take-down; 24" barrels; full choke shotgun barrel; single trigger; open rear sight, rifle-type ramp front; original models had uncheckered American walnut pistol-grip stock, forearm; later production had Tenite plastic stock, forearm. Introduced in 1938; dropped in 1950. Still in production by Savage Arms as Model 24, with variations. Used values: walnut stock, $100 to $125; plastic stock, $100 to $115.

Stevens Model 240

STEVENS Model 240: over/under; take-down; .410 only; 26" barrels, full choke only; double triggers; early models had uncheckered American walnut pistol-grip stock, forearm; later versions had stock, forearm of Tenite plastic. Introduced in 1939; dropped, 1942. Used values: walnut stock, $275 to $300; plastic stock, $250 to $275.

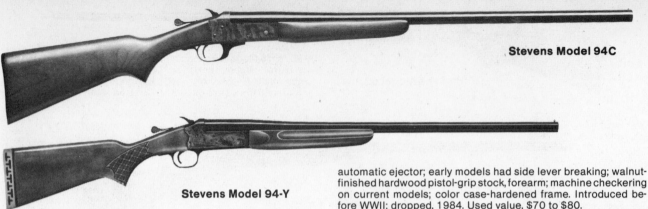

Stevens Model 94C

Stevens Model 94-Y

STEVENS Model 94C: single-barrel, single-shot; hammer gun; 12-, 16-, 20-ga., .410; full choke only; 28", 30", 32", 36" barrels;

automatic ejector; early models had side lever breaking; walnut-finished hardwood pistol-grip stock, forearm; machine checkering on current models; color case-hardened frame. Introduced before WWII; dropped, 1984. Used value, $70 to $80.

Model 94Y has same specs as Model 94C, except has 26" barrel, 20-ga. or .410, short stock with recoil pad for youth; top lever breaking. Dropped, 1984. Used value, $75 to $85.

STEVENS-Springfield Model 5151: side-by-side; hammerless; box-lock action; 12-, 16-, 20-ga., .410; has the same general specs as Stevens Model 311, except for hand-checkered pistol grip, forearm; recoil pad; two Ivoroid sights. Manufactured prior to WWII.

Used value, $250 to $275.

Model 5151-ST has the same specs as Model 5151, except for non-selective single trigger. Used value, $235 to $255.

Stevens Model 124

STEVENS Model 124: autoloader; solid frame, hammerless; 12-ga. only; 28" barrel; improved, modified, full chokes; 2-rd. tube magazine; checkered Tenite plastic stock, forearm. Introduced in 1947; dropped, 1952. Used value, $75 to $85.

Stevens Model 77 Standard

STEVENS Model 77: slide-action repeater; solid frame; hammerless; 12, 16-ga.; 26" improved; 28" modified or full choke; 5-rd. tube magazine; uncheckered walnut-finished hardwood stock, grooved slide handle. Introduced in 1954; dropped, 1971. Used value, $125 to $135.

Model 77SC has the same specs as standard Model 77, except for Savage Super Choke. Used value, $135 to $145.

Stevens 9478 Super Value

STEVENS 9478 Super Value: single-barrel; 10-, 12-, 20-ga., .410; 26", 28", 30", 36" barrel; walnut-finished hardwood stock; bottom action opening button; exposed hammer; auto ejection; color case-hardened frame. Introduced, 1979; dropped, 1986. Used value, $70 to $80.

Stevens Model 67

STEVENS Model 67: slide-action; 12-, 20-ga.; 26", 28", 30" barrel lengths; metal bead front sight; walnut-finished hardwood stock; checkered pistol grip, slide handle; tapered slide handle, top tang safety; steel receiver. Introduced, 1981 by Savage; still produced. Used values: standard model, $120 to $140; vent rib, $130 to $150.

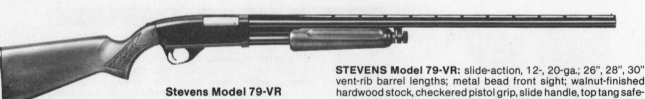

Stevens Model 79-VR

STEVENS Model 79-VR: slide-action, 12-, 20-ga.; 26", 28", 30" vent-rib barrel lengths; metal bead front sight; walnut-finished hardwood stock, checkered pistol grip, slide handle, top tang safety; tapered slide handle, interchangeable barrels. Introduced, 1981 by Savage; dropped, 1983. Used value, $115 to $120.

UNIVERSAL FIREARMS

UNIVERSAL Model 101: single-shot, external hammer; takedown; 12-ga. only; 28", 30" full-choke barrel; 3" chamber; top-breaking action; uncheckered pistol-grip stock, beavertail forearm.

UNIVERSAL Model 202: side-by-side; box-lock action; 12-, 20-ga.; 26" improved/modified barrels, 28" modified/full; 3" chambers; top breaking; double triggers; hand-checkered European walnut pistol-grip stock, European-style forearm. Introduced in 1967; dropped, 1969. Replaced by Double Wing model. Used

Introduced in 1967; dropped, 1969. Replaced by Single Wing model. Used value, $75 to $85.

value, $150 to $175.

   Model 203 has the same specs as Model 202, except is chambered for 3½" 10-ga. shells; has 32" full/full barrels. Introduced in 1967; dropped, 1969. Used value, $250 to $275.

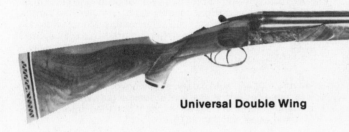

Universal Double Wing

UNIVERSAL Double Wing: side-by-side; box-lock; top-breaking action; 12-, 20-ga.; 26" improved/modified barrels, 28" and 30" modified/full; double triggers; recoil pad; checkered European walnut pistol-grip stock, beavertail forearm. Introduced in 1970; dropped, 1974. Used value, $175 to $200.

UNIVERSAL Model 2030: side-by-side; top-breaking box-lock action; has same general specs as Double Wing Model, except

chambered for 3½" 10-ga. shells; 32" full/full barrels only. Introduced in 1970; dropped, 1974. Used value, $275 to $295.

UNIVERSAL Auto Wing: autoloader; recoil operated; take-down; 12-ga. only; 5-shot magazine, 3-shot plug furnished; 2¾" chamber; 25", 28", 30" barrel; improved, modified, full chokes; vent rib; ivory bead front, middle sights; crossbolt safety; interchangeable

barrels; checkered European walnut pistol-grip stock, grooved forearm. Introduced in 1970; dropped, 1974. Used value, $165 to $175.

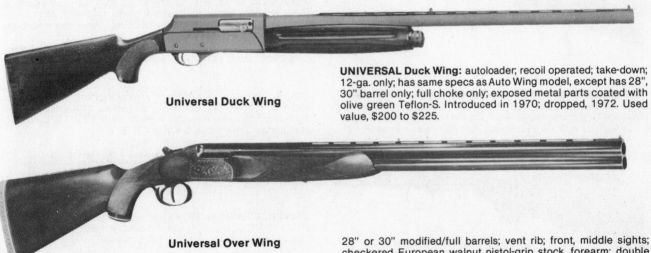

Universal Duck Wing

Universal Over Wing

UNIVERSAL Duck Wing: autoloader; recoil operated; take-down; 12-ga. only; has same specs as Auto Wing model, except has 28", 30" barrel only; full choke only; exposed metal parts coated with olive green Teflon-S. Introduced in 1970; dropped, 1972. Used value, $200 to $225.

UNIVERSAL Over Wing: over/under; hammerless; box-lock; top-breaking action; 12-, 20-ga.; 3" chambers; 26" improved/modified,

28" or 30" modified/full barrels; vent rib; front, middle sights; checkered European walnut pistol-grip stock, forearm; double triggers; single-trigger model with engraved receiver at added cost. Introduced in 1970; dropped, 1974. Used values: double-trigger model, $225 to $250; single-trigger, $275 to $300.

UNIVERSAL Single Wing: single-shot; external hammer; top-breaking action; 12-ga. only; 3" chamber; take-down; 28" full or modified barrel; uncheckered European walnut pistol-grip stock,

beavertail forearm; automatic ejector. Introduced in 1970; dropped, 1974. Used value, $75 to $85.

UNIVERSAL BAIKAL MC-21: autoloader; take-down; 12-ga. only; 5-rd. magazine; 26" improved, 28" modified, 30" full choke barrels; vent rib; hand-checkered European walnut cheekpiece stock; white spacers at pistol grip, butt plate; hand-rubbed finish; grooved

forearm; chrome-lined barrel, chamber; reversible safety; target-grade trigger. Manufactured in Russia. Introduced in 1973; no longer imported. Used value, $275 to $295.

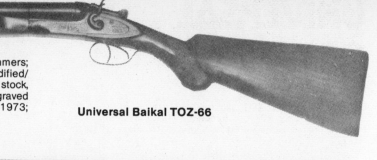

Universal Baikal TOZ-66

UNIVERSAL BAIKAL TOZ-66: side-by-side; exposed hammers; 12-ga. only; 2¾" chambers; 20" improved/modified, 28" modified/full barrels; hand-checkered European hardwood pistol-grip stock, beavertail forearm; chrome-lined barrels, chambers; hand-engraved receiver; extractors. Manufactured in Russia. Introduced in 1973; no longer imported. Used value, $250 to $275.

Universal Baikal IJ-58M

UNIVERSAL BAIKAL IJ-58M: side-by-side; hammerless; 12-ga. only; 2¾" chambers; 26" improved/modified, 28" modified/full barrels; hand-checkered European walnut pistol-grip stock, beavertail forearm; hinged front double trigger; chrome-lined barrels, chambers; hand-engraved receiver; extractors. Manufactured in Russia. Introduced in 1973; no longer imported. Used value, $250 to $275.

UNIVERSAL BAIKAL MC-10: side-by-side; hammerless; 12-, 20-ga.; 2¾" chambers; 12-ga. has 28" modified/full barrels; 20-ga., 26" improved/modified; hand-checkered fancy European walnut stock, semi-beavertail forearm; choice of pistol-grip or straight stock; chrome-lined barrels, chambers, internal parts; raised solid rib; double triggers; auto safety; extractors or selective ejectors; receiver engraved with animal, bird scenes; engraved trigger guard, tang. Manufactured in Russia; no longer imported. Introduced in 1973. Used value, $350 to $375.

UNIVERSAL BAIKAL IJ-25: over/under; 12-ga. only; 2¾" chambers; 26" skeet/skeet barrels, 28" modified/full, 30" improved/full; hand-checkered European walnut pistol-grip stock, ventilated forearm; white spacers at pistol-grip cap, recoil pad; single non-selective trigger chrome-lined barrels, chambers, internal parts; vent rib; hand-engraved, silver inlaid receiver, forearm latch, trigger guard. Manufactured in Russia. Introduced in 1973; no longer imported. Used value, $300 to $350.

Universal Baikal IJ-27

UNIVERSAL IJ-27: over/under; 12-ga. only; has same general specs as IJ-25, except for double triggers, automatic safety, non-selective ejectors. Introduced in 1973; no longer imported. Used value, $275 to $285.

 Universal Baikal IJ-27E has same specs as the IJ-27, except for substitution of selective ejectors. Used value, $300 to $325.

UNIVERSAL BAIKAL MC-5: over/under; 12-ga. only; 2¾" chambers; 26" improved/modified, skeet/skeet barrels; fancy hand-checkered European walnut stock; choice of straight or pistol-grip stock, with or without cheekpiece; non-removable forearm; engraved receiver; double triggers; extractors; hand-fitted solid rib; hammer interceptors; chrome-lined barrels, chambers, internal parts. Manufactured in Russia. Introduced in U.S. in 1973; no longer imported. Used value, $300 to $350.

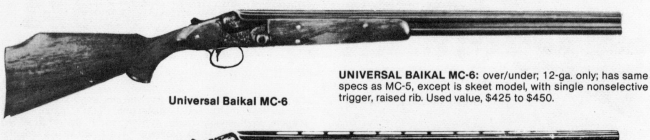

Universal Baikal MC-6

UNIVERSAL BAIKAL MC-6: over/under; 12-ga. only; has same specs as MC-5, except is skeet model, with single nonselective trigger, raised rib. Used value, $425 to $450.

Universal Baikal MC-8

UNIVERSAL BAIKAL MC-8: over/under; 12-ga. only; 2¾" chambers; 26" special skeet barrels; 28" modified/full; 2-barrel set; fancy hand-checkered European walnut Monte Carlo pistol-grip stock, non-removable forearm; double triggers; extractors; hand-fitted vent rib; blued, engraved receiver; chrome-lined barrels, chambers, internal parts; single selective trigger, selective ejectors available at extra cost. Manufactured in Russia. Introduced in U.S. in 1973; no longer imported. Used value, $750 to $800.

UNIVERSAL BAIKAL MC-7: over/under; 12-, 20-ga.; 2¾" chambers; 12-ga., 28" modified/full; 20-ga., 26" improved/modified barrels; hand-checkered European walnut straight or pistol-grip stock, beavertail forearm; double triggers; selective ejectors; solid raised rib; chrome-lined barrels, chambers, internal parts; hand-chiseled, engraved receiver. Manufactured in Russia. Introduced in U.S. in 1973; no longer imported. Used value, $700 to $750.

UNIVERSAL BAIKAL IJ-18: single-barrel, single-shot; 12-, 20-ga.; 2¾" chamber; in 12-ga., 28" modified, 30" full choke barrel; 20-ga., 26" modified; hand-checkered European walnut pistol-grip stock, forearm; white spacers at pistol grip, plastic butt plate; crossbolt safety in trigger guard; cocking indicator; chrome-lined barrel, chamber. Manufactured in Russia. Introduced in U.S. in 1973; no longer imported. Used value, $65 to $75.

VENTURA

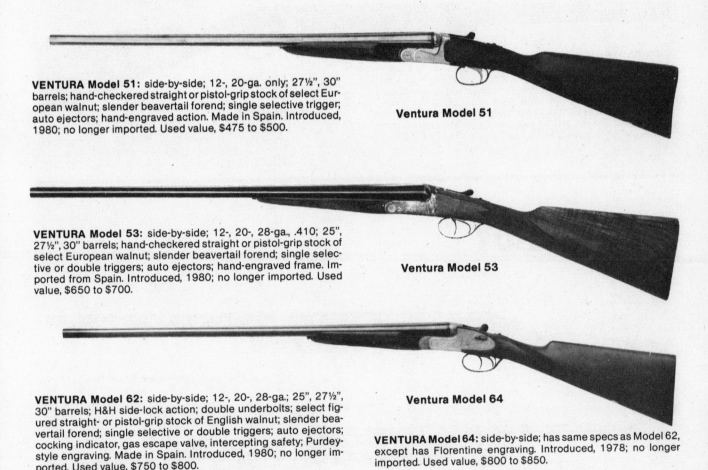

VENTURA Model 51: side-by-side; 12-, 20-ga. only; 27½", 30" barrels; hand-checkered straight or pistol-grip stock of select European walnut; slender beavertail forend; single selective trigger; auto ejectors; hand-engraved action. Made in Spain. Introduced, 1980; no longer imported. Used value, $475 to $500.

Ventura Model 51

VENTURA Model 53: side-by-side; 12-, 20-, 28-ga., .410; 25", 27½", 30" barrels; hand-checkered straight or pistol-grip stock of select European walnut; slender beavertail forend; single selective or double triggers; auto ejectors; hand-engraved frame. Imported from Spain. Introduced, 1980; no longer imported. Used value, $650 to $700.

Ventura Model 53

VENTURA Model 62: side-by-side; 12-, 20-, 28-ga.; 25", 27½", 30" barrels; H&H side-lock action; double underbolts; select figured straight- or pistol-grip stock of English walnut; slender beavertail forend; single selective or double triggers; auto ejectors; cocking indicator, gas escape valve, intercepting safety; Purdey-style engraving. Made in Spain. Introduced, 1980; no longer imported. Used value, $750 to $800.

Ventura Model 64

VENTURA Model 64: side-by-side; has same specs as Model 62, except has Florentine engraving. Introduced, 1978; no longer imported. Used value, $800 to $850.

VENTURA Model 66: side-by-side; has same specs as Model 64, except has treble bolting, side clips. Introduced, 1980; no longer imported. Used value, $900 to $1000.

VENTURA Model XXV: side-by-side; has same specs as Model 53, except has 25" barrels only, Churchill rib. Introduced, 1980; no longer imported. Used value, $575 to $600.

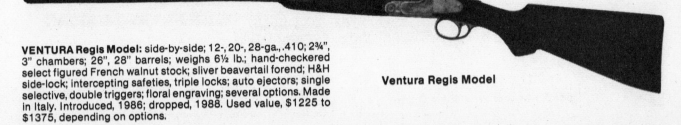

VENTURA Regis Model: side-by-side; 12-, 20-, 28-ga., .410; 2¾", 3" chambers; 26", 28" barrels; weighs 6½ lb.; hand-checkered select figured French walnut stock; sliver beavertail forend; H&H side-lock; intercepting safeties, triple locks; auto ejectors; single selective, double triggers; floral engraving; several options. Made in Italy. Introduced, 1986; dropped, 1988. Used value, $1225 to $1375, depending on options.

Ventura Regis Model

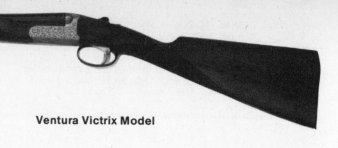

VENTURA Victrix Model: side-by-side; 12-, 20-, 28-ga., .410; 2¾", 3" chambers; 26", 28" barrel lengths; weighs 6½ lb.; hand-checkered French walnut stock, beavertail forend; Anson & Deeley boxlock; triple locks; auto ejectors; double or single selective trigger; optional screw-in chokes; marketed in leather trunk-type case. Made in Italy. Introduced, 1986; dropped, 1988. Used values: standard chokes, $600 to $625; screw-in chokes, $725 to $750.

Victrix Extra Lusso has the same specs as standard model, except has better quality wood, full floral engraving. Made in Italy. Introduced, 1986; dropped, 1988. Used values: standard chokes, $850 to $875; screw-in chokes, $875 to $925.

Ventura Victrix Model

VENTURA Avanti Small Gauge Model: over/under; 28-ga., 2¾"; .410, 3" chambers; 26" barrels; weighs 5¾ lb.; straight English-type French walnut stock; box-lock action; single selective trigger; auto ejectors; vent top, side ribs; fully engraved. Made in Italy. Introduced, 1987; dropped, 1988. Used value, $650 to $675.

Avanti Extra Lusso has same specs as Avanti, except has highly figured French walnut stock, more ornate engraving. Introduced, 1987; dropped, 1988. Used value, $850 to $900.

Ventura Avanti

WEATHERBY

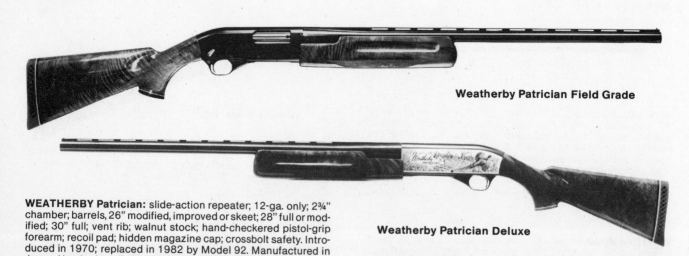

Weatherby Patrician Field Grade

Weatherby Patrician Deluxe

WEATHERBY Patrician: slide-action repeater; 12-ga. only; 2¾" chamber; barrels, 26" modified, improved or skeet; 28" full or modified; 30" full; vent rib; walnut stock; hand-checkered pistol-grip forearm; recoil pad; hidden magazine cap; crossbolt safety. Introduced in 1970; replaced in 1982 by Model 92. Manufactured in Japan. Used values: field or skeet grade, $275 to $300; trap grade, $325 to $350.

Patrician Trap has same specs as standard Patrician, except for trap stock, 30" full-choke barrel. Imported 1972 to 1982. Used value, $325 to $350.

Patrician Deluxe has same specs as standard grade, except for fancy-grade wood, etched receiver. Imported 1972 to 1982. Used value, $375 to $395.

Weatherby Centurion Field Grade

WEATHERBY Centurion: autoloader; 12-ga. only; 2¾" chamber; barrels, 26" skeet or improved cylinder; 28" improved, modified, full; 30" full; American walnut stock; hand-checkered pistol grip, forearm; vent rib with front, middle bead sights; engraved

Weatherby Centurion Deluxe

alloy receiver; pressure compensator. Introduced in 1970; replaced in 1982 by Model 82. Manufactured in Japan. Used value, $275 to $300.

Centurion Trap has same specs as standard Centurion, except for trap stock, 30" full choke barrel. Imported 1972 to 1982. Used value, $300 to $325.

Centurion Deluxe has same specs as standard version, except for fancy-grade wood, etched receiver. Imported 1972 to 1982. Used value, $315 to $335.

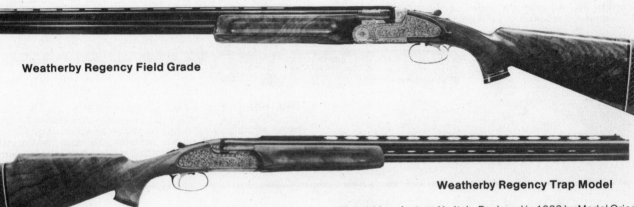

Weatherby Regency Field Grade

Weatherby Regency Trap Model

WEATHERBY Regency: over/under; 12-, 20-ga.; box-lock action with simulated side-locks; selective automatic ejectors; single selective trigger; barrels, 28" only, full/modified, modified/improved, skeet/skeet; vent rib; bead front sight; American walnut stock, hand-checkered pistol grip, forearm; fully engraved receiver; re-

coil pad. Manufactured in Italy. Replaced in 1982 by Model Orion. Used values: 12-, 20-ga., field, skeet, $650 to $700; trap, $700 to $750.

Regency Trap model has same specs as standard model, except has trap stock, straight or Monte Carlo comb; 30", 32" barrels, modified/full, improved modified/full, full/full chokes; vent side ribs; vent top rib. Imported 1965 to 1982. Used value, $700 to $750.

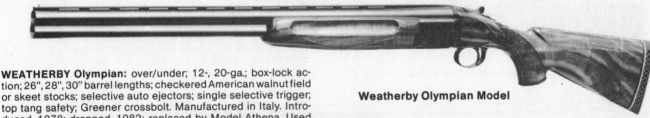

Weatherby Olympian Model

WEATHERBY Olympian: over/under; 12-, 20-ga.; box-lock action; 26", 28", 30" barrel lengths; checkered American walnut field or skeet stocks; selective auto ejectors; single selective trigger; top tang safety; Greener crossbolt. Manufactured in Italy. Introduced, 1978; dropped, 1982; replaced by Model Athena. Used values: trap or field, $675 to $700; skeet version, $700 to $725.

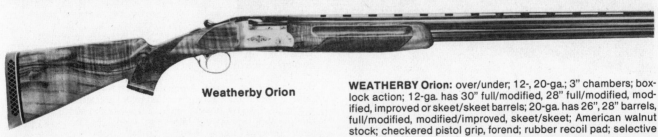

Weatherby Ninety-Two

WEATHERBY Ninety-Two: slide-action; 12-ga.; 3" chamber; 26" modified, improved or skeet barrels; 28" full or modified; 30" full,

full trap or 3" magnum; Multi-choke available; vent rib; American walnut stock; hand-checkered pistol grip, forend; grip cap; recoil pad; crossbolt safety; short-stroke action. Made in Japan. Introduced, 1982; dropped, 1988. Used values: field or skeet, fixed chokes, $290 to $310; trap grade, $310 to $325; with Multi-choke, $325 to $350.

Weatherby Orion

WEATHERBY Orion: over/under; 12-, 20-ga.; 3" chambers; box-lock action; 12-ga. has 30" full/modified, 28" full/modified, modified, improved or skeet/skeet barrels; 20-ga. has 26", 28" barrels, full/modified, modified/improved, skeet/skeet; American walnut stock; checkered pistol grip, forend; rubber recoil pad; selective auto ejectors; single selective trigger; top tang safety; Greener-type crossbolt; trap style has 2¾" chambers. Made in Japan. Introduced, 1982; still imported. Used values: standard, $575 to $625; skeet, $600 to $625; trap, $650 to $700.

Weatherby Athena

WEATHERBY Athena: over/under; 12-, 20-ga.; box-lock action; 28" barrels, full/modified, modified/improved, skeet/skeet; American walnut stock; checkered pistol grip, forend; mechanical selective trigger; top tang safety; selective auto ejectors; Greener-type crossbolt; recoil pad; engraved receiver; trap model has 2¾" chambers. Made in Japan. Introduced, 1982; still imported. Used values: standard model, $900 to $1000; skeet, $875 to $925; trap, $950 to $1150.

Weatherby Eighty-Two

WEATHERBY Eighty-Two: autoloader; 12-ga.; 2¾", 3" chambers; 26", 28", 30" barrels; interchangeable choke tubes; 22" slug barrel with sights available; hand-checkered pistol-grip stock, forend; rubber recoil pad; gas-operated with floating piston; gold-plated trigger; fluted bolt; crossbolt safety; Made in Japan. Introduced, 1982; still imported. Used value, $325 to $350.

WESTLEY RICHARDS

WESTLEY RICHARDS Best Quality: side-by-side; double barrel; hammerless; side-lock action; 12-, 16-, 20-ga.; barrel lengths, chokes to order; hand-detachable locks; hinged lock plate; selective ejectors; hand-checkered walnut stock, forearm; choice of straight, half-pistol grip; double or single selective trigger. Introduced in 1890; dropped, 1965. Used values: double-trigger model,

Westley Richards Best Quality

$6000 to $6500; single selective trigger, $7000 to $7500.

    Best Quality Pigeon or Wildfowl Model has same specs as standard model, except for stronger action; triple bolting; 12-ga. only; chambered for 2¾", 3" shells; 28", 30" full-choke barrels. Introduced in 1900; still in production. Used values: double-trigger model, $7000 to $7250; single selective trigger, $8000 to $8250.

WESTLEY RICHARDS Model DeLuxe Quality: side-by-side double-barrel; hammerless; box-lock action; hand-detachable locks; triple-bite lever work; other specs are same as Best Quality model, except for better workmanship throughout. Available in Pigeon or Wildfowl Model at same price. Introduced in 1890; still in production. Used values: double-trigger model, $10,000 to $11,000; single selective trigger, $11,000 to $12,000.

Westley Richards DeLuxe Box Lock

Westley Richards DeLuxe Sidelock

WESTLEY RICHARDS Sidelock Model DeLuxe Quality: side-by-side double-barrel; hammerless; hand-detachable side-locks; 12-, 16-, 20-ga.; barrel lengths, chokes to order; selective ejectors; double triggers, single selective trigger; hand-checkered European stock, forearm; straight or half-pistol grip available in Pigeon or Wildfowl Model at same price. Introduced in 1910; still in production. Used values: double-trigger model, $14,500 to $15,500; single selective trigger, $16,500 to $17,500.

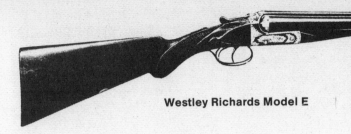

Westley Richards Model E

WESTLEY RICHARDS Model E: side-by-side double-barrel; hammerless; Anson & Deeley box-lock action; 12-, 16-, 20-ga.; barrel lengths, choking to order; selective or non-ejector; double triggers; hand-checkered European walnut stock, forearm; straight or half-pistol grip; Pigeon or Wildfowl Model available at same price. Introduced in late 1920s; still in production. Used values: ejector model, $3000 to $3500; non-ejector, $4000 to $4500.

WESTLEY RICHARDS Ovundo: over/under; hammerless; box-lock action; 12-ga. only; barrel lengths, chokes to order; hand-detachable locks, dummy side plates; single selective trigger; hand-checkered European walnut stock, forearm; straight or half-pistol grip. Introduced in 1920; dropped, 1945. Used value, $17,500 to $20,000.

WINCHESTER

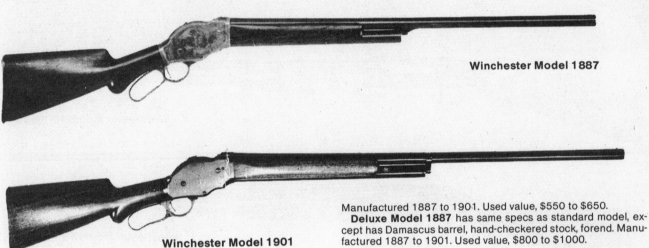

Winchester Model 1887

Winchester Model 1901

WINCHESTER Model 1887: lever-action; 10-, 12-ga.; 4-rd. tubular magazine; 30", 32" barrel, full choke; solid frame; uncheckered American walnut pistol-grip stock, forend. Collector value.

Manufactured 1887 to 1901. Used value, $550 to $650.
Deluxe Model 1887 has same specs as standard model, except has Damascus barrel, hand-checkered stock, forend. Manufactured 1887 to 1901. Used value, $800 to $1000.

WINCHESTER Model 1901: lever-action; 10-ga.; has same general specs as Model 1887, except for internal redesign features. Replaced Model 1887 in line. Collector interest. Manufactured 1901 to 1920. Used value, $750 to $850.

Winchester Model 97

WINCHESTER Model 97: slide-action; visible hammer; takedown or solid frame; 12-, 16-ga.; 5-shot tube magazine; barrel lengths are 26", 28", 30", 32", last in 12-ga. only; choked full, modified, cylinder bore, with intermediate chokes introduced in 1931. Gun introduced in 1897 was revamp of Model 1893. Numerous variations were introduced, discontinued over the years, with model discontinued, 1957. Standard grade has plain stock, grooved slide handle, side ejection port. Retail price when discontinued, $89.95. Used value, $325 to $375.

Model 97 also was available in higher grade trap, tournament, pigeon grades. Stocks on higher grades were of better walnut,

checkered. On these, slide handles also were of better wood, checkered in standard or semi-beavertail configuration, without the deep wood grooves of standard model. Higher grades were discontinued in 1939. Used values: trap grade, $600 to $650; tournament grade, $650 to $700; pigeon grade, $1000 to $1100.

Model 97 also was offered as riot gun with same specs as standard model; take-down or solid frame. In 12-ga. only, it had 20" cylinder bore barrel. Trench gun, the same as riot model, was issued with bayonet and ventilated steel handguard by U.S. government in 1917-18. Used values: riot model, $350 to $375; trench model, $425 to $450.

Winchester Model 1911

WINCHESTER Model 1911: autoloading shotgun; hammerless; take-down; 12-ga. only; barrels were plain in 26", 28", 30", 32"; standard chokes; 4-shot tubular magazine; stock and forearm plain or checkered. Introduced in 1911; discontinued, 1925. Collector value. Original retail price, $61.50. Used value, $275 to $300.

Winchester Model 12 Standard

Winchester Model 12 Trap

Winchester Model 12 Pigeon

Winchester Model 12 Super Pigeon Skeet

Winchester Model 12 Super Pigeon Trap

WINCHESTER Model 12: slide-action; 12-, 16-, 20-, 28-ga.; 3 standard versions; has blued receiver of chrome-moly steel; pigeon grade only has engine-turned bolt and carrier; optional ventilated rib; deluxe grade only has butt stock and slide handle of high-grade walnut with fine-line hand checkering; magazine capacity, 5 rds. Field gun has 26", 28", 30" barrels with choice of improved cylinder, modified or full chokes, respectively. Model 12 trap gun is full choke only with 30" barrel, choice of standard or Monte Carlo stock, recoil pad; skeet gun is skeet choked, with 26" barrel, fitted stock, recoil pad. Introduced originally in 1912; dropped from line in 1965; reintroduced in 1972; no longer produced. Price when dropped was $237.50 for skeet model. Used values: 1972 model, $375 to $425, depending on style; pre-1965 models, $450 to $500. Nostalgia has resulted in older Model 12s often selling for considerably more than original retail price. As an example of sup-

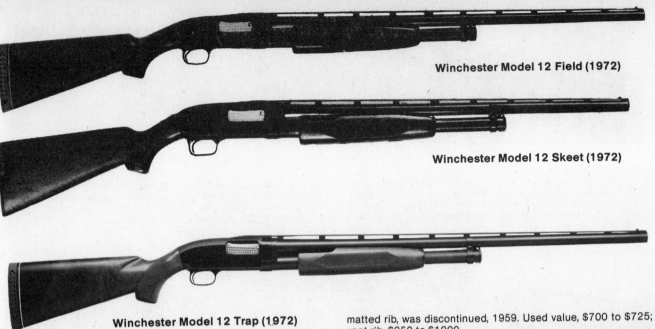

Winchester Model 12 Field (1972)

Winchester Model 12 Skeet (1972)

Winchester Model 12 Trap (1972)

ply and demand, in 1965, price for pigeon grade was $372.50. One year later — with Model 12 discontinued and considered a custom gun, price leaped to $825.

Prior to discontinuation in 1965, there were many variations of Model 12 and an even wider variation of used values. Model 12 Featherweight, made from 1959 to 1962, had plain barrel, modified take-down, alloy guard, in 12-ga. only; available in 26" improved cylinder, 28" modified or full, 30" full. Used value, $400 to $425. Standard version with matted rib, discontinued after WWII, has used value of $525 to $550. Standard grade, with vent rib, also discontinued after WWII, was 12-ga. only with 26¾", 30" barrel. Used value, $650 to $700. Manufactured from 1918 to 1963 was Model 12 riot model, in 12-ga., with 20" cylinder-bore barrel. Used value, $350 to $375.

The Model 12 has appeared in several skeet configurations. The standard skeet model, discontinued after WWII, was in 12-, 16-, 20-, 28-ga., with 5-shot tube magazine, 26" barrel, skeet choke. Featured red or ivory bead front sight, 94B mid-sight. Pistol grip was checkered as was extension slide handle. Used value, $650 to $700. Skeet model with plain barrel, sans sights, was manufactured from 1937 to 1947. Used value, $575 to $600. Style featuring Cutts Compensator, with plain barrel, was discontinued, 1954. Used value, $475 to $500. Discontinued in 1965, skeet style with ventilated rib was 12-, 20-ga. Used values: $850 to $950 for 12-ga.; $1150 to $1250 for 20-ga., $4000 to $4250 for 28-ga.

Of trap configurations, original was discontinued after WWII. It had specs of standard Model 12, plus extension slide handle, recoil pad, straighter stock, checkered pistol grip, recoil pad, 30" matted-rib barrel; 12-ga., full choke only. Used value, $700 to $750. Trap model with ventilated rib was same as standard trap otherwise. Used value, $750 to $800. Model 12 trap with Monte Carlo stock and vent rib has used value of $775 to $825.

Model 12 also was produced in 2 styles for duck hunters. The heavy duck gun, in 12-ga. only, handled 3" shells, had 3-shot magazine, recoil pad, 30" and 32" barrel lengths, full choke only. Discontinued, 1964. Used value, $550 to $600. Same style, with

matted rib, was discontinued, 1959. Used value, $700 to $725; vent rib, $950 to $1000.

Model 12 pigeon grade guns virtually constitute an empire unto themselves. These were deluxe versions of the standard, field, duck, skeet or trap guns made on special order only. Pigeon grade guns made on special order only. Pigeon grade guns had finer finishes, hand-worked actions, engine-turned bolts, carriers. Stock dimensions were to specs of individual, with top-grade walnut, fancy hand-checkering. At added cost from $50 to $250 or more, engraving and carving could be added. This particular grade was discontinued, 1965; prices are based upon variations, sans added engraving and carving. Range of used values is: field gun, plain barrel, $950 to $1000; with vent rib, $1250 to $1450; skeet gun, matted rib, $1250 to $1350; vent rib, $1500 to $1750; skeet, Cutts Compensator, $750 to $800; trap gun matted rib, $1450 to $1550; with vent rib, $1850 to $2200.

Used values for Winchester Model 12 Super Pigeon grade can be no more than an approximation, since these are rare and are worth what the buyer wants to pay. Super Pigeon grade, introduced 1965 in conjunction with the Model 12, was reintroduced to the trade in 1972; no longer produced. Custom Model 12 has same general specs as standard models; available in 12-ga. only, with any standard choke and barrel length choice of 26", 28", 30", with vent rib. Receiver is engraved; hand-honed and fitted action. Stocks, forearm are fancy walnut and made to individual order. Used value starts at $2500. After that, you're on your own.

Model 12 (1972) has same general specs as standard Model 12, except for engine-turned bolt, carrier; 12-ga. only; 26", 28", 30" standard-choke barrels; vent rib; hand-checkered American walnut stock, slide handle. Manufactured 1972 to 1975. Used value, $500 to $550.

Model 12 Skeet (1972) has same specs as standard Model 12 (1972), except for 26" skeet-choked barrel; hand-checkered skeet stock, slide handle; recoil pad. Manufactured 1972 to 1975. Used value, $525 to $575.

Model 12 Trap (1972) has same specs as standard Model 12 (1972); 30" full choke vent-rib barrel only; straight or Monte Carlo trap stock; recoil pad. Manufactured 1972 to 1975. Used value, $575 to $600.

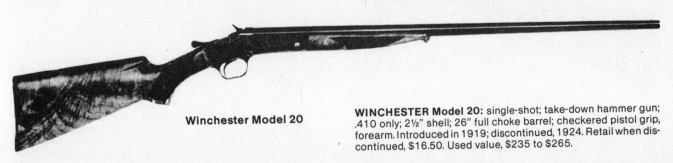

Winchester Model 20

WINCHESTER Model 20: single-shot; take-down hammer gun; .410 only; 2½" shell; 26" full choke barrel; checkered pistol grip, forearm. Introduced in 1919; discontinued, 1924. Retail when discontinued, $16.50. Used value, $235 to $265.

Winchester Model 36

WINCHESTER Model 36: single-shot bolt-action take-down; cocks by pulling rearward on knurled firing-pin head, the same mechanism used in some Winchester single-shot rifles; 9mm short or long, shot or ball cartridges interchangeably; one-piece plain wood stock, forearm; special trigger guard forms the pistol grip; composition butt plate; 18" round barrel. No guns were serialized. Introduced in 1920; discontinued, 1927. Price at time of discontinuation, $7.05. Used value, $200 to $225.

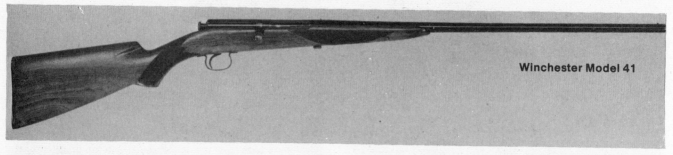

Winchester Model 41

WINCHESTER Model 41: single-shot bolt-action shotgun; standard take-down style only with 24" full-choke barrel; fires .410 2½" ammo; chambering changed in 1933 to 3" shell; stock is plain one-piece walnut; pistol grip; hard-rubber butt plate; straight grip optional at no increase in price; checkered stock on special order. Model 41s were not numbered serially. Increase in value reflects interest as a collector item. Introduced in 1920; discontinued, 1934. Original retail, $9.95. Used value, $250 to $275.

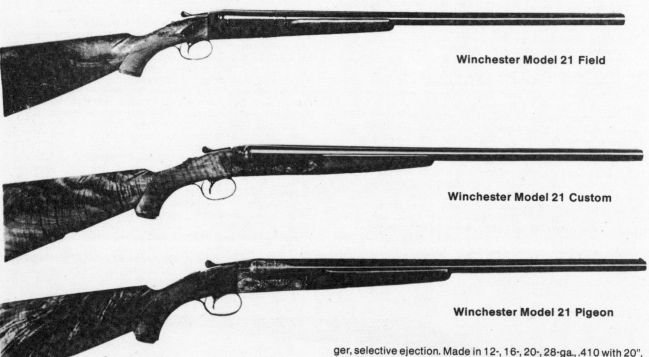

Winchester Model 21 Field

Winchester Model 21 Custom

Winchester Model 21 Pigeon

WINCHESTER Model 21: side-by-side, hammerless field gun; box-lock; automatic safety; early models have double triggers, non-selective ejection; post-WWII guns have selective single trigger, selective ejection. Made in 12-, 16-, 20-, 28-ga., .410 with 20", 28", 30", 32" barrels, last only in 12-ga.; raised matted or ventilated rib; chokes are full, improved modified, modified, improved cylinder, skeet; choice of straight or pistol-grip stock; regular, beavertail forearm; checkered walnut. Introduced in 1931; discontinued, 1959. Retail when discontinued, $425. Used values: double triggers, non-selective ejection, $1500 to $1800; double triggers, selective ejection, $1750 to $2000; selective single trigger, non-selective ejection, $2250 to $2500; selective single trigger, selec-

Winchester Model 21 Grand American

tive ejection, $2500 to $2750; with ventilated rib, add $250 to $300; .410 (only 57 made), $25,000 to $35,000; 28-ga., 50% higher than listed price.

Model 21 Skeet Gun is same general design as standard model, but has 26", 28" barrels only; skeet chokes; red bead front sight; selective single trigger, selective ejection; non-auto safety; checkered French walnut stock, beavertail forearm; wooden butt is checkered without pad or butt plate. Discontinued, 1958. Used values: with matted rib, $2250 to $2500; with ventilated rib, $2500 to $2750.

Model 21 Trap Gun differs from standard with 30" or 32" barrels; full choke; selective trigger; non-auto safety; selective ejection; pistol-grip or straight stock, beavertail forearm of checkered walnut. Discontinued, 1958. Used values: with matted rib, $2250

to $2500; with vent rib, $2500 to $2750.

Model 21 Duck Gun has same general specs as field gun, but is chambered for 3" 12-ga. shells; has 30", 32" barrels; full choke; selective ejection; selective single trigger; recoil pad; checkered beavertail forearm, pistol-grip stock. Discontinued, 1958. Used values: with matted rib, $2250 to $2500; with vent rib, $2750 to $3000.

As with the Model 12, the Winchester Model 21 became a special-order gun. After 1960, it was offered only in Custom, Pigeon and Grand American grades. General specs are same as standard Model 21, but have full fancy American walnut stocks, forearms, with fancy checkering, hand-honed working parts. Carved woodwork, gold inlays and engraving are available at added cost. Dropped in late 1970s. Used values: Custom grade, $4500 to $5000; Pigeon grade, $6500 to $7500; Grand American, $15,000-plus.

Winchester Model 42

WINCHESTER Model 42: hammerless, slide-action; .410 only; 26", 28" barrel; full or modified choke; chambered for 3" shells; available with plain walnut stock, no checkering; slide handle grooved; capacity of 6 shells in 2½" length; 5 shells in 3" length; weight, 5⅞ to 6 lb. Trap grade had full fancy wood and checkering,

until dropped in 1940. Introduced in May 1933; dropped, 1963. Last retail price, $101.95. Used values: $600 to $650; skeet with matted rib, $1200 to $1300; standard with matted rib, $850 to $900; Deluxe grade, $1500 to $1750; vent rib (Simmons), $2500 to $2750.

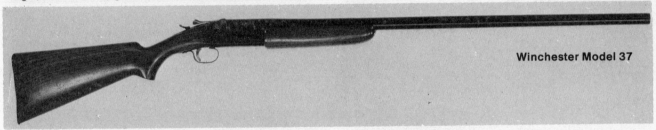

Winchester Model 37

WINCHESTER Model 37: single-shot shotgun; top-lever, breakdown construction with automatic ejector; semi-hammerless action; plain barrel only in 12-, 16-, 20-, 28-ga., .410; choice of 26", 28" barrel, full choke; stock is plain walnut with composition butt

plate, pistol grip, semi-beavertail forearm. On special order, at no extra charge, barrels could be modified or cylinder choke. Introduced in 1936; discontinued, 1963. Last retail price was $35. Used values: $85 to $140; 28-ga. (rare), $600 to $750.

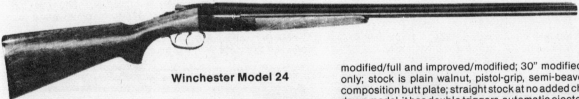

Winchester Model 24

WINCHESTER Model 24: hammerless double-barrel shotgun; 12-, 16-, 20-ga.; 26" barrels; chokes were improved/modified; 28"

modified/full and improved/modified; 30" modified/full in 12-ga. only; stock is plain walnut, pistol-grip, semi-beavertail forearm; composition butt plate; straight stock at no added charge; a breakdown model, it has double triggers, automatic ejectors. Introduced in 1940; discontinued, 1957. Price when discontinued, $96.20. Used values: $300 to $350; 20-ga., $400 to $450.

Winchester Model 40 Skeet

WINCHESTER Model 40: autoloading shotgun; 12-ga. only; streamlined receiver; hammerless action; 4-rd. tube magazine; 28", 30" barrels; choked modified or full; plain pistol-grip stock, semi-beavertail forend; ramp bead front sight. Introduced, 1940; discontinued, 1941. Retail when discontinued, $68.15. Used value, $350 to $400.

Model 40 Skeet had 24"barrel; Cutts Compensator; checkering on pistol grip, forearm; grip cap. Collector interest. Original price, $73.50. Used value, $450 to $500.

Winchester Model 50

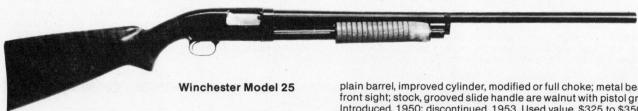

Winchester Model 50 Trap

WINCHESTER Model 50: autoloading shotgun; field grades available in 12-, 20-ga.; skeet, 12-ga.; trap, 12-ga.; 12-ga. barrels were 30" full choke, 28" full or modified, 28" improved or skeet. There were numerous options including a ventilated rib and gun could fire field or high-velocity loads without adjustment; stock was of American walnut, hand-checkered with fluted comb, composition butt plate; magazine tube was below barrel with 2-shell capacity; side ejection. Featherweight model was adopted in 1958. Weight for standard was 7¼ lb. for 12-ga., 7 lb. for Featherweight,

5¾ lb. for 20-ga. Pigeon grade was available with any combination of barrel lengths and chokes. Barrels interchangeable, with bead front sight. Gun worked on short recoil principle. When fired, floating chamber moved rearward to start the action moving to the rear. Bolt continued to rear, extracting and ejecting spent shell, lifting new one into position. Introduced in late 1954; discontinued in 1961. Retailed at $144.95 for standard grade. Used value, $300 to $325.

Model 50 Field gun is same as the standard, except for ventilated rib. Used value, $400 to $425. Skeet version has 26" vent-rib barrel, skeet stock in selected walnut, skeet choke. Used value, $425 to $450. Model 50 trap, 12-ga. only; full choke, 30" vent-rib barrel; Monte Carlo stock of select walnut. Used value, $450 to $475.

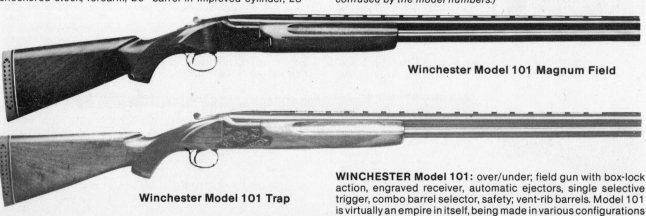

Winchester Model 25

WINCHESTER Model 25: slide-action repeating shotgun; solid frame; hammerless; 12-ga. only, with 4-rd. tubular magazine; 28"

plain barrel, improved cylinder, modified or full choke; metal bead front sight; stock, grooved slide handle are walnut with pistol grip. Introduced, 1950; discontinued, 1953. Used value, $325 to $350.

Model 25 was made in riot model from 1949 to 1955; only change from standard was a 20" cylinder-choke barrel. Used value, $350 to $375.

Winchester Model 59

WINCHESTER Model 59: autoloading shotgun; 12-ga. only; has checkered stock, forearm; 26" barrel in improved cylinder, 28"

modified or full, 30" full choke; special order 26" barrel has Versalite choke system of cylinder tubes (introduced in 1961) to allow any choke variation; barrel was fiberglass-wrapped steel tube. Introduced in 1959; discontinued, 1965. Retail price when discontinued, $160. Used value, $375 to $400.
(Winchester also made a Model 59 rimfire rifle in 1930 — don't be confused by the model numbers.)

Winchester Model 101 Magnum Field

Winchester Model 101 Trap

WINCHESTER Model 101: over/under; field gun with box-lock action, engraved receiver, automatic ejectors, single selective trigger, combo barrel selector, safety; vent-rib barrels. Model 101 is virtually an empire in itself, being made in various configurations

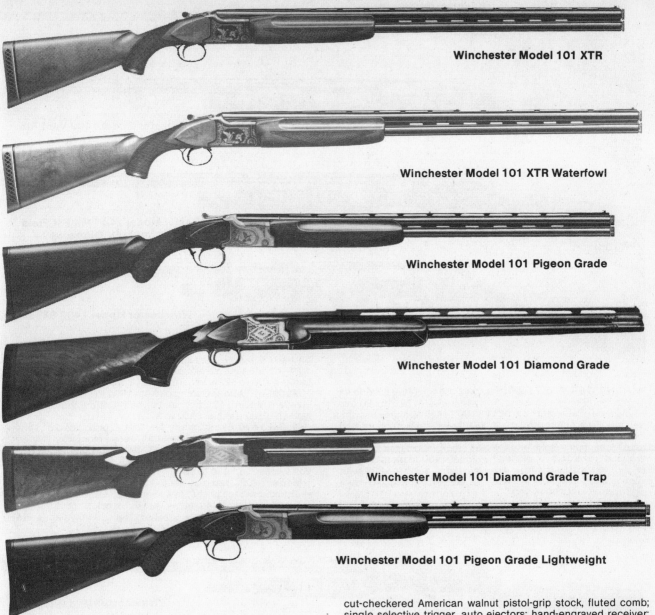

Winchester Model 101 XTR

Winchester Model 101 XTR Waterfowl

Winchester Model 101 Pigeon Grade

Winchester Model 101 Diamond Grade

Winchester Model 101 Diamond Grade Trap

Winchester Model 101 Pigeon Grade Lightweight

and styles. Handles 2¾" shells in 12-, 28-ga.; 3" in 20-ga., .410; 30" barrels on 12-ga. only, choked modified/full; 28" modified/full; ; 26½" choked improved/modified. Stock, forearm are checkered French walnut. Made in Japan by Olin Kodensha. The 12-ga. was introduced in 1963; other gauges, 1966; no longer in production. Model 101s now marketed by Winchester Group, Olin Corp. Used values: 12-, 20-ga., $550 to $600; 28-ga., .410, $650 to $700.

Model 101 Magnum Field gun is same as standard field gun, but chambered for 12- and 20-ga., 3" magnum shells; 30" barrels are choked full/full, modified/full; has recoil pad. Introduced, 1966; still in production. Used value, $650 to $700; Pigeon grade, $950 to $900.

Model 101 Skeet gun is same as field model, except for skeet stock, forearm; barrels for 12-ga. are 26", 20-ga. 26½"; 28-ga., .410, 28"; all gauges skeet choked. Introduced in 1966; no longer in production. Used values: 12-, 20-ga., $700 to $750; 28-ga., .410, $750 to $800.

Model 101 Trap gun has trap stock, Monte Carlo or straight; recoil pad; 12-ga. only; barrels are 30", 32" improved modified/full, full/full. Introduced in 1966; no longer in production. Used values: straight stock, $650 to $700; Monte Carlo, $700 to $750; single-barrel trap, $500 to $550; Pigeon grade, $950 to $1000.

Model 101 XTR replaces original field model; 12-, 20-ga.; 26", 28", 30" barrel lengths; top lever break; manual safety, barrel selector; metal bead front sight, chrome-plated chambers, bores;

cut-checkered American walnut pistol-grip stock, fluted comb; single selective trigger, auto ejectors; hand-engraved receiver; Winchokes. Introduced, 1978; still in production. Used value, $850 to $900.

Model 101 XTR Waterfowl has same basic specs as 101 XTR field version except has 32" barrels, 12-ga., 3" chambering only. Marketed with Winchoke tubes. Introduced, 1981; still produced. Used value, $850 to $900.

Model 101 Pigeon Grade has same general specs as 101 XTR field model, except has new vent rib; bead front and middle sights; hand-engraved satin-finished receiver; knurled non-slip trigger; hand-checkered French walnut stock; 12-, 20-ga.; 25½" to 32" barrels; full range of chokes; numerous options. Introduced, 1980. Used value, $950 to $1050.

Model 101 Diamond Grade has same general specs as standard model, except is designed for trap or skeet competition; trap is 12-ga. only, skeet in 12-, 20-, 28-ga., .410; tapered, elevated rib; contoured trigger; deep diamond-pattern engraving; available in several configurations, barrel lengths with Winchoke. Made in Japan. Introduced, 1982; still imported. Used values: trap o/u, $1250 to $1350; single-barrel trap, $1200 to $1250; trap combo set, $2000 to $2100; skeet, $1200 to $1300.

Model 101 Pigeon Grade Lightweight has same specs as standard model, except is made in Lightweight, Lightweight-Winchoke, Featherweight styles; 3" chambers; vent-rib barrel with middle bead; fancy American walnut stock. Marketed in hard case. Made in Japan. Introduced, 1983; still imported. Used value, $1100 to $1200.

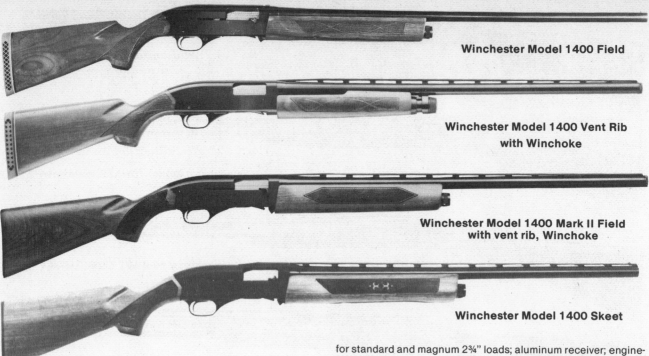

Winchester Model 1400 Field

Winchester Model 1400 Vent Rib
with Winchoke

Winchester Model 1400 Mark II Field
with vent rib, Winchoke

Winchester Model 1400 Skeet

WINCHESTER Model 1400: field gun; gas-operated take-down autoloader; 2-shot magazine; 2¾" chambered for 12-, 16-, 20-ga.; plain barrel or with vent rib in 26", 28", 30" lengths; improved cylinder, modified, full choke or with Winchoke; stock, forearm had impressed checkering on walnut; recoil pad was available with recoil reduction system and Cycolac stock. Introduced in 1964; dropped, 1968 to be replaced by Model 1400 Mark II. Original price, $149.95. Used values: with plain barrel, $200 to $225; with vent rib, $225 to $250; with Winchoke, add $45; with recoil reduction system, add $50 to $60.

Model 1400 Mark II, introduced in 1968, has restyled stock, forearm; push-button carrier release; has front-locking, rotating bolt locking into barrel extension; self-compensating gas system

for standard and magnum 2¾" loads; aluminum receiver; engine-turned bolt; push-button action release; crossbolt safety. Made in right- or left-hand versions. Dropped 1980. Used values: plain barrel, $200 to $225; vent rib, $225 to $250.

Model 1400 Deer Gun made from 1965 to 1968, was same as standard Model 1400, but had 22" barrel, rifle sights for slugs or buckshot. Used value, $200 to $225.

Model 1400 Skeet gun is 12-, 20-ga. only; has 26" vent-rib barrel; skeet choke; stock, forearm are semi-fancy walnut; stock is Cycolac when recoil reduction system is used. Introduced in 1965; discontinued, 1968. Used values: $275 to $300; with recoil reduction system, add $50 to $60.

Model 1400 Trap gun, made from 1965 to 1968, 12-ga.; 30" vent-rib barrel; full choke; has semi-fancy walnut stock or recoil reduction system. Used values: with trap stock, $275 to $300; with Monte Carlo, $300 to $325; with recoil reduction system, add $50 to $60.

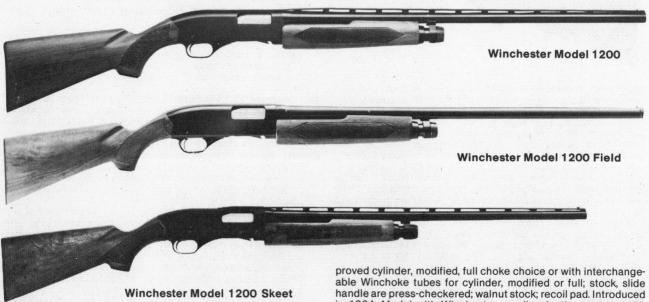

Winchester Model 1200

Winchester Model 1200 Field

Winchester Model 1200 Skeet

WINCHESTER Model 1200: slide-action take-down shotgun, with front-lock rotary bolt; 4-rd. magazine; 12-, 16-, 20-ga.; with 2¾" chambers; plain or vent-rib barrels, 26", 28", 30" length; im-

proved cylinder, modified, full choke choice or with interchangeable Winchoke tubes for cylinder, modified or full; stock, slide handle are press-checkered; walnut stock; recoil pad. Introduced in 1964. Model with Winchester recoil reduction system, with Cycolac stock, introduced in 1966; discontinued, 1970. Original plain model was priced at $185. Used values: with plain barrel, $150 to $175; with vent-rib barrel, $175 to $200; with Winchoke, add $45; with recoil reduction system, add $50 to $60.

Model 1200 Magnum Field gun introduced in 1966; same as

Winchester Model 1200 Trap

standard Model 1200 field gun, but chambered for 3" magnum shells in 12-, 20-ga.; choice of plain or vent rib; 28", 30" full-choke barrels. Used values: with plain barrel, $175 to $195; with vent-rib barrel, $200 to $215; recoil reduction system, add $50 to $60.

Model 1200 Deer gun appeared from 1965 to 1974; same as standard model; has rifle-type sights on 22" barrel; meant for rifled slugs or buckshot; 12-ga. only; with sling swivels. Used value,

$175 to $185.

Model 1200 Skeet gun, made from 1965 to 1973, was 12-, 20-ga. only; 2-shot magazine; tuned trigger; 26" vent-rib barrel; semi-fancy walnut stock, forend; skeet choke. Used values: $225 to $250; with Winchester recoil system, add $50 to $60.

Model 1200 Trap gun was in 12-ga. only; 2-shot magazine; 30" full choke vent-rib barrel; 28" with Winchoke; regular or Monte Carlo trap stock of semi-fancy walnut; made from 1965 to 1973. Used values: with regular trap stock, $235 to $250; Monte Carlo stock, $240 to $275; with Winchester recoil reduction system, add $50 to $60; with Winchoke, add $45.

Winchester Model 370

WINCHESTER Model 370: single-barrel shotgun; available in 12-ga. in 36", 32", 30" barrel lengths; 16-ga., 32", 30"; 20-and 28-ga., 28" barrel; .410 with 26" barrel; all chambered for 3" shells except 16-, 28-ga. using 2¾" shells; weight varies with gauges and barrel lengths, ranges from 5½ to 6¼ lb.; break-open type, auto-

matic ejection; plain American hardwood stock; uncapped pistol grip and hard-rubber butt plate; full choke only; bead front sight. Introduced in 1968; discontinued, to be replaced by Model 37A. Last retail price, $35.95. Used value, $80 to $90.

Winchester Model 37A

Winchester 37A Youth Model

WINCHESTER Model 37A: single-shot shotgun; available in all gauges from 12 through .410; choice of barrel lengths, 25", 28", 30", 32"; with exception of 16- and 28-ga., all chambered for 3"

shells; full chokes. Also available in Youth model with 26" barrel in 20-ga. and .410, improved modified and full chokes, respectively; stock is of walnut-stained hardwood with checkering on bottom of forearm and sides of capped pistol grip; features top lever opening to right or left, concave hammer spur; white spacer between grip cap and butt plate. Introduced in 1973; dropped, 1980. Retail price, $68.75 for 12-ga. with 36" barrel and Youth model; all others, $62.95. Used value, $85 to $95.

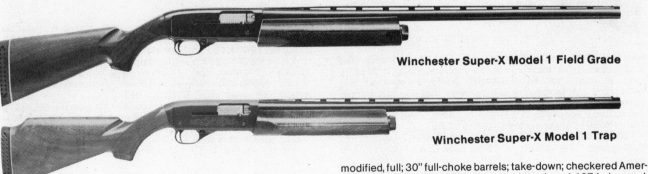

Winchester Super-X Model 1 Field Grade

Winchester Super-X Model 1 Trap

modified, full; 30" full-choke barrels; take-down; checkered American walnut pistol-grip stock, forearm. Introduced, 1974; dropped, 1981. Used value, $325 to $350.

Super-X Model 1 Trap has same specs as standard model, except 30" barrel only, improved modified or full choke; straight or Monte Carlo trap stock, forearm of select American walnut; recoil

WINCHESTER Super-X Model 1: autoloader; gas-operated; 12-ga.; 2¾" chamber; 4-rd. magazine; 26" improved cylinder, 28"

Winchester Super-X Model 1 Skeet

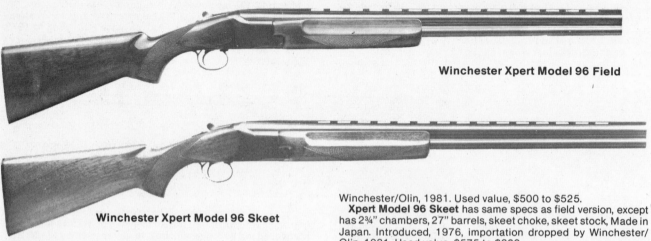

Winchester Xpert Model 96 Field

Winchester Xpert Model 96 Skeet

WINCHESTER Xpert Model 96 Field: over/under; box-lock action; 12-, 20-ga; 3" chambers; 26", 28", 30" barrels; vent rib; similar to the Model 101; depending on gauge, barrel length, weights 6¼ to 8¼ pounds; checkered walnut pistol grip stock, forend. Made in Japan. Introduced, 1976; importation dropped by

pad. Introduced, 1974; dropped, 1981. Used value, $375 to $400.

Super-X Model 1 Skeet has same specs as standard model, except for skeet stock, 26" skeet-choke barrels. Introduced, 1974; dropped, 1981. Used value, $400 to $425.

Winchester/Olin, 1981. Used value, $500 to $525.

Xpert Model 96 Skeet has same specs as field version, except has 2¾" chambers, 27" barrels, skeet choke, skeet stock, Made in Japan. Introduced, 1976, importation dropped by Winchester/Olin, 1981. Used value, $575 to $600.

Xpert Model 96 Trap has the same specs as field version, except has 2¾" chambers, 12-ga., only, 30" trap barrels, straight or Monte Carlo trap stock, recoil pad. Made in Japan. Introduced, 1976; importation dropped by Winchester/Olin, 1981. Used value, $575 to $600.

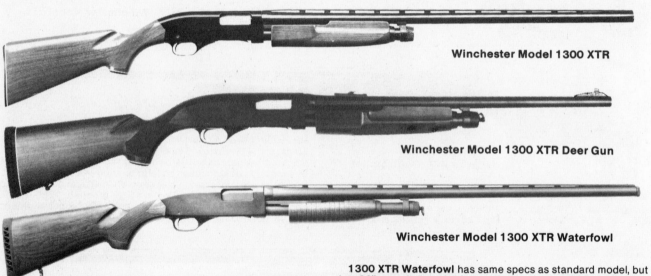

Winchester Model 1300 XTR

Winchester Model 1300 XTR Deer Gun

Winchester Model 1300 XTR Waterfowl

WINCHESTER 1300 XTR: slide-action; 12-, 20-ga; 3" chamber; 4-rd. magazine; 28" plain or vent-rib barrel; metal bead front sight; cut-checkered American walnut stock; XTR finish on wood; twin action bars; crossbolt safety; alloy receiver, trigger guard; engine-turned bolt. Introduced, 1978; no longer in production. Was produced under license by U.S. Repeating Arms. Used values: plain barrel, $250 to $260; vent rib, $260 to $270.

1300 XTR Deer Gun has same specs as 1300 XTR except has 24⅛" barrel; rifle-type sights; 12-ga. only. Used value, $235 to $245.

WINCHESTER Model 23 Pigeon Grade: side-by-side; 12-, 20-ga.; 26", 28", 30" barrels; cut-checkered high-luster stock of high-grade American walnut; beavertail forend; mechanical trigger;

1300 XTR Waterfowl has same specs as standard model, but has 30" vent-rib barrel; 12-ga. only. Used value, $260 to $270.

Model 1300 XTR Featherweight has same specs as standard model, except has 22" vent-rib barrel; marketed with three Winchoke tubes; roll-engraved receiver; crossbolt safety with red indicator. Made under license by USRA. Introduced, 1984; still in production. Used value, $240 to $260.

Model 1300 Turkey has same specs as standard model, except is 12-ga. only; 30" barrel, with modified, full, extra-full Winchoke tubes; matte finish on wood, metal; recoil pad; sling swivels; marketed with Cordura sling; also made with green-shaded laminated stock. Introduced, 1986; still in production. Used value, $230 to $250.

tapered vent rib; selective ejectors; silver-gray satin finish on receiver, top lever, trigger guard; fine-line scroll engraving. Made in Japan. Introduced, 1978; Pigeon Grade designation dropped,

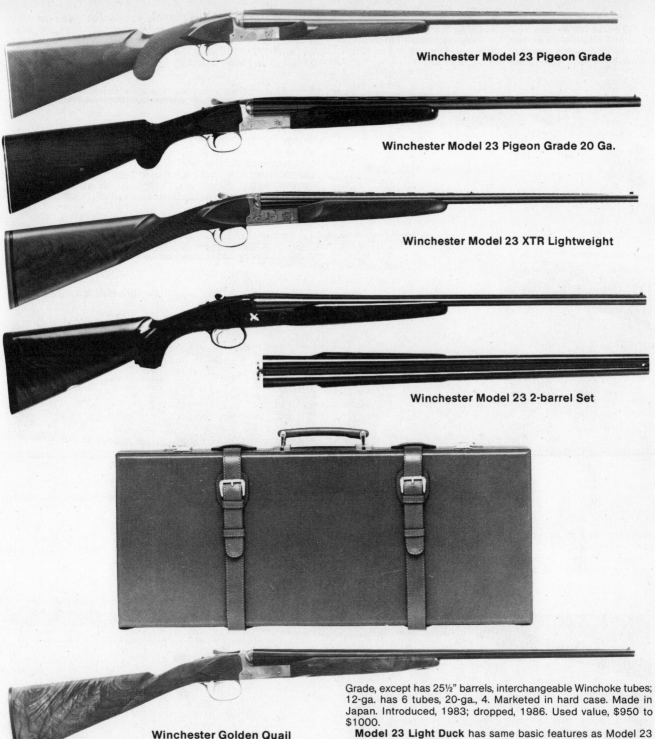

Winchester Model 23 Pigeon Grade

Winchester Model 23 Pigeon Grade 20 Ga.

Winchester Model 23 XTR Lightweight

Winchester Model 23 2-barrel Set

Winchester Golden Quail

1986. Marketed by Winchester Group, Olin Corp. Used value, $800 to $850.

Model 23 XTR Lightweight has same general specs as Pigeon Grade, except has 25½" barrels, English-style straight-grip stock; thin semi-beavertail forend; improved/modified choking; silver-gray frame; engraved bird scene. Marketed in hard case. Made in Japan. Introduced, 1982; no longer imported by Winchester/Olin. Used value, $900 to $950.

Model 23 Heavy Duck has same specs as Pigeon Grade, except has blued, plain receiver; 30" full/extra-full barrels; 3" chambers. Marketed in hard case. Made in Japan. Introduced, 1983; dropped, 1984. Used value, $1100 to $1200.

Model 23 Pigeon Grade (Winchoke) has same specs as Pigeon Grade, except has 25½" barrels, interchangeable Winchoke tubes; 12-ga. has 6 tubes, 20-ga., 4. Marketed in hard case. Made in Japan. Introduced, 1983; dropped, 1986. Used value, $950 to $1000.

Model 23 Light Duck has same basic features as Model 23 Pigeon Grade, except has plain blued frame, 28" full/full barrels; 20-ga.; 3" chambers; marketed in hard case. Made in Japan. Introduced, 1984; still imported by Winchester/Olin. Used value, $1200 to $1250.

Model 23 Classic has blued receiver, scroll engraving; 12-, 20-ga. have gold pheasant inlaid on bottom of receiver, 28-ga., .410 have gold quail inlaid; gold initial plate in stock; ebony inlay in forend; auto safety; auto ejectors; single selective trigger. Made in Japan. Introduced, 1986; still imported by Winchester/Olin. Used values: 12-, 20-ga., $1450 to $1500; 28-ga., .410, $1500 to $1550.

Model 23 Custom has same specs as Model 23 Classic, except has plain blued receiver, no engraving; internal Winchoke system with six tubes; chrome-lined bores, chambers for steel shot. Marketed in luggage-style case. Made in Japan. Introduced, 1986; still imported by Winchester/Olin. Used value, $1250 to $1300.

Model 23 Two-Barrel Set: built on basic Model 23 action, but comes with interchangeable 20, 28-ga. 25½" barrels, each fitted with its own full fancy American walnut semi-beavertail forend. Marketed in handmade leather luggage-style carrying case. Only 500 made in 1986. Used value, $3250 to $3300.

Model 23 Golden Quail limited edition was made over four years. In 1983, 28-ga. was made, 20-ga. in 1984, 12-ga. in 1985 and, in 1986, the .410-ga. Only 500 made each year. Used value, 28-ga. $1450 to $1500; 20-ga. $1450 to $1500; 12-ga., $1400 to $1450; .410, $1500 to $1550.

Winchester 1500 XTR

WINCHESTER 1500 XTR: autoloader; 12-, 20-ga.; 26", 28", 30" barrels plain or vent rib; with or without Winchoke tubes; cut-checkered pistol-grip stock of American walnut; metal bead front sight; gas-operated; front locking, rotating bolt; nickel-plated carrier, crossbolt safety. Introduced, 1978; dropped, 1983. Was made under license by U.S. Repeating Arms. Used value, $250 to $275.

Winchester Model 501

Winchester Model 501 Skeet

Winchester Model 501 Trap

WINCHESTER Model 501: over/under; 12-ga. only; marketed as Grand European; 27", 30", 32" barrel lengths; hand-rubbed oil-finish American walnut stock; engraved silvered receiver; engine-turned breech interior; selective auto ejectors; chromed bores; tapered vent rib. Trap model has Monte Carlo or regular stock, skeet version has rosewood butt plate. Made in Japan. Introduced, 1981; dropped, 1986. Marketed by Winchester Group, Olin Corp. Used value, $1400 to $1500.

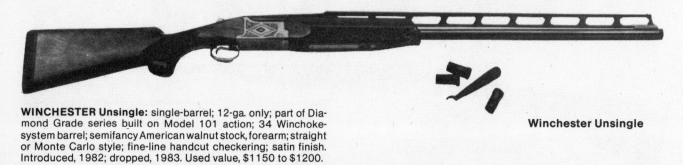

WINCHESTER Unsingle: single-barrel; 12-ga. only; part of Diamond Grade series built on Model 101 action; 34 Winchoke-system barrel; semifancy American walnut stock, forearm; straight or Monte Carlo style; fine-line handcut checkering; satin finish. Introduced, 1982; dropped, 1983. Used value, $1150 to $1200.

Winchester Unsingle

Winchester Ranger Standard

WINCHESTER Ranger: slide-action; 12-, 20-ga.; 3" chamber, 4-rd. magazine; 28", 30" plain or vent-rib barrel; metal bead front sight; walnut-finished hardwood stock, ribbed forend; crossbolt safety; twin-action bars; rotating bolt; black rubber butt pad. Introduced, 1981; still produced under license by U.S. Repeating Arms. Used values: plain barrel, $145 to $165; vent rib, $190 to $195.

Ranger Youth Model has same general specs as standard Ranger, except has 22" plain barrel, modified or Winchoke; 3" 20-ga. only; 13" pull length. Introduced, 1983; no longer produced. Used value, $140 to $150.

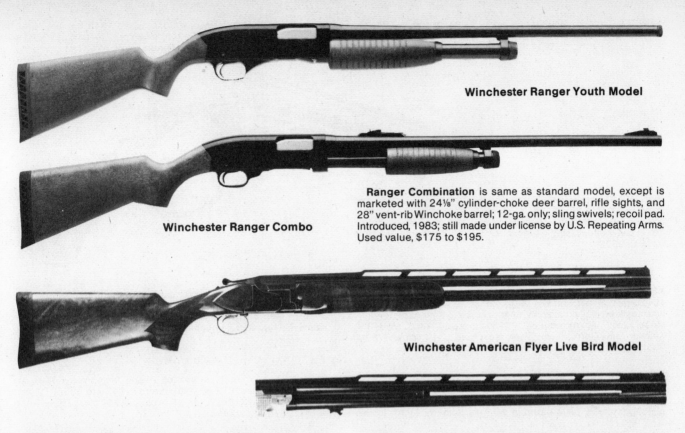

Winchester Ranger Youth Model

Winchester Ranger Combo

Ranger Combination is same as standard model, except is marketed with 24⅛" cylinder-choke deer barrel, rifle sights, and 28" vent-rib Winchoke barrel; 12-ga. only; sling swivels; recoil pad. Introduced, 1983; still made under license by U.S. Repeating Arms. Used value, $175 to $195.

Winchester American Flyer Live Bird Model

WINCHESTER American Flyer Live Bird Model: has the same specs as Model 101, except is 12-ga. only, has 2¾" chambers, 28" barrels; under barrel is fitted for internal Winchokes, marketed with four choke tubes; over barrel has extra-full choke; blued receiver, gold wire border inlays; competition vent rib; full fancy American walnut stock; matte finish on top of receiver. Marketed in luggage-type case. Made in Japan. Introduced, 1987; still imported by Winchester/Olin. Used value, $2100 to $2250.

American Flyer Combo Set has same specs as Live Bird Model, except has additional set of 29½" barrels, with same choke specs. Made in Japan. Introduced, 1987; still imported by Winchester/Olin. Used value, $2650 to $2800.

WINCHESTER Quail Special: over/under; has same general specs as Model 101, except is built with small frame for 28-ga., .410; 3" chambers; 28-ga. has internal Winchoke system, marketed with four choke tubes; .410 is choked full/modified; silvered, engraved receiver; 25½" barrels. Made in Japan. Introduced, 1987; still imported by Winchester/Olin. Used value, $1500 to $1650.

MISCELLANEOUS SHOTGUNS U.S.-MADE

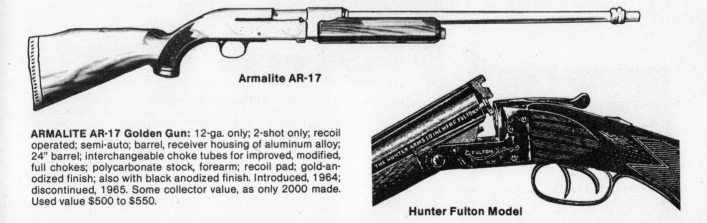

Armalite AR-17

ARMALITE AR-17 Golden Gun: 12-ga. only; 2-shot only; recoil operated; semi-auto; barrel, receiver housing of aluminum alloy; 24" barrel; interchangeable choke tubes for improved, modified, full chokes; polycarbonate stock, forearm; recoil pad; gold-anodized finish; also with black anodized finish. Introduced, 1964; discontinued, 1965. Some collector value, as only 2000 made. Used value $500 to $550.

Hunter Fulton Model

HUNTER Fulton: hammerless; side-by-side; box-lock; 12-, 16-, 20-ga.; 26" to 32" barrels; standard choke combos; double triggers or non-selective single trigger; walnut stock; hand-checkered pis- tol grip, forearm. Introduced, 1920; dropped, 1948. Manufactured by Hunter Arms Company, Fulton, New York. Used values: single trigger, $435 to $450; double triggers, $350 to $375.

Hunter Special Model

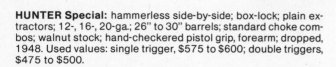

HUNTER Special: hammerless side-by-side; box-lock; plain ex- tractors; 12-, 16-, 20-ga.; 26" to 30" barrels; standard choke com- bos; walnut stock; hand-checkered pistol grip, forearm; dropped, 1948. Used values: single trigger, $575 to $600; double triggers, $475 to $500.

KESSLER Three-Shot Repeater: bolt-action, take-down; 12-, 16-, 20-ga.; 28" barrel in 12-, 16-ga.; 26" in 20-ga.; 2-rd. detachable box magazine; full choke only; uncheckered one-piece pistol-grip stock; recoil pad. Introduced in 1951; dropped, 1953. Made by Kessler Arms Corp., Silver Creek, New York. Used value, $75 to $85.

KESSLER Lever-Matic: lever-action repeater; take-down; 12-, 16-, 20-ga.; 26", 28", 30" barrels; full choke only; 3-rd. magazine; uncheckered pistol-grip stock; recoil pad; dropped, 1953. Used value, $125 to $150; uncommon and unusual.

MORONNE Model 46: over/under; 12-, 20-ga.; 26" improved cylinder/modified, 28" modified/full barrels; box-lock action; non- selective single trigger; plain extractors; checkered straight or pistol-grip stock; plain barrel or vent rib. Some collector value; fewer than 500 manufactured by Rhode Island Arms 1949 to 1953. Used values: 12-ga., plain barrels, $525 to $550; 12-ga., vent rib, $675 to $700; 20-ga. plain barrels, $675 to $700; 20-ga. vent rib, $750 to $800.

RUGER Red Label: over/under; 12-ga., 3" chambers; 20-ga., 3" chambers; 26", 28" vent-rib barrels; full/modified, improved cyl- inder/modified, skeet chokes; box-lock action; single selective trigger; auto ejectors; checkered American walnut pistol-grip stock, forearm; 20-ga. introduced, 1977; still in production. 12-ga. introduced, 1982; still in production. Used values: field, $550 to $600; skeet, $575 to $625.

Ruger Red Label

Smith & Wesson Model 916

slide handle; satin-finished steel receiver, no-glare top. Introduced in 1973; dropped, 1980. American made. Used values: plain barrels, sans recoil pad, $100 to $125; plain barrel with adjustable choke, $115 to $135; plain barrel, recoil pad, $105 to $130; vent rib, recoil pad, $140 to $165.

   Model 916T has same general specs as Model 916, except 12- ga. only; take-down; not made with 20" barrel; plain or vent rib. Introduced, 1976; dropped, 1980. Used values: vent rib, $140 to $160; plain barrel, $100 to $125.

SMITH & WESSON Model 916: slide-action; 12-, 16-, 20-ga.; 6- shot; barrel lengths, 20" cylinder choke, 26" improved cylinder, 28" modified, full or adjustable choke; 30" full; vent rib on 26", 28" barrels available; uncheckered walnut stock; fluted comb, grooved

Snake Charmer

SNAKE CHARMER: single-barrel; .410 3" only; 18⅛" barrel; no sights; plastic thumbhole stock; all stainless steel construction; storage compartment in butt stock for spare ammo. Introduced, 1978; no longer produced by Sporting Arms, Inc. Used value, $75 to $85.

WESTERN ARMS Long Range Hammerless: side-by-side, box- lock; double or single trigger; plain extractors; in 12-, 16-, 20-ga., .410; barrels, 26" to 32", modified/full chokes; uncheckered wal- nut stock, forearm. Introduced in 1924; discontinued, 1942. Made by Western Arms Corp., later absorbed by Ithaca Gun Co. Used values: single trigger, $275 to $300; double triggers, $225 to $250.

FOREIGN-MADE

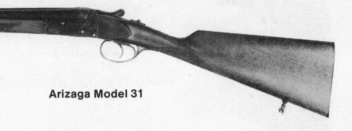

Arizaga Model 31

ARIZAGA Model 31: side-by-side; 12-, 16-. 20-ga., .410; 26", 28" barrels; standard choke combos; 45" overall length; weighs 6 lb. 9 oz.; European walnut English-style straight or pistol-grip stock; box-lock action; double triggers; engraved receiver; blued finish. Made in Spain. Introduced, 1986; still imported by Mandall Shooting Supplies. Used value, $295 to $300.

ARMSCOR Model 30: slide-action; 12-ga.; 5-rd. magazine; 28" modified, 30" full barrel lengths; weighs 7.3 lb.; metal bead front sight; Philippine mahogany stock; double action bars; grooved forend; blued finish. Made in the Philippines. Introduced, 1987; still imported by Armscor. Used value, $140 to $150.

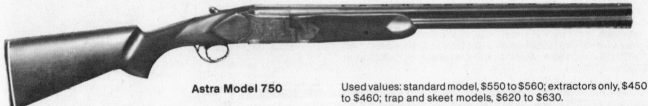

Astra Model 750

ASTRA Model 750: over/under; 12-ga.; 28", 30" barrels; vent rib; hand-checkered European walnut stock; single selective trigger; selective auto ejectors; scroll-engraved receiver. Introduced, 1980; no longer imported. Was imported from Spain by L. Jos. Rahn, Inc.

Used values: standard model, $550 to $560; extractors only, $450 to $460; trap and skeet models, $620 to $630.

ASTRA Model 650: over/under; has same specs as Model 750, except has double triggers. Introduced, 1980; no longer imported. Was imported from Spain by L. Jos. Rahn, Inc. Used values: with extractors, $370 to $380; with ejectors, $460 to $470.

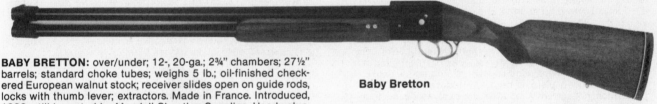

Baby Bretton

BABY BRETTON: over/under; 12-, 20-ga.; 2¾" chambers; 27½" barrels; standard choke tubes; weighs 5 lb.; oil-finished checkered European walnut stock; receiver slides open on guide rods, locks with thumb lever; extractors. Made in France. Introduced, 1986; still imported by Mandall Shooting Supplies. Used value, $475 to $500.
Baby Bretton Deluxe has same specs, except has silvered, engraved receiver; double triggers; 12-, 16-, 20-ga. Imported by Quality Arms. Used value, $700 to $725.

Beeman/Fabarm O/U

BEEMAN/Fabarm: over/under; 12-ga.; 2¾" chambers; 26½" skeet, 29" barrels; select walnut stock, forend; cut checkering; Schnabel forend; red bead front sight, white bead middle; box-lock action; single selective trigger; auto ejectors; chrome-lined bores, chambers; silvered, engraved receiver; skeet/trap combo has interchangeable barrels. Made in Italy. Introduced, 1984; no longer imported by Beeman. Used values: Field, $450 to $475; trap or skeet, $525 to $550; combo, $850 to $900.

Benelli Autoloader

BENELLI Autoloader: 12-ga.; 5-rd. magazine; 26", 28" barrels; vent rib; metal bead front sight; hand-checkered European walnut pistol-grip stock; crossbolt safety; hand-engraved receiver on higher grades; quick-interchangeable barrels. Manufactured in Italy. Introduced by Heckler & Koch, 1977; no longer imported. Used values: standard model, $300 to $325; engraved model, $360 to $385; slug model, $325 to $345.

Benelli 123-SL-80

BENELLI 123-SL-80: autoloader; gas-operated; 12-ga.; 2¾" chamber; 24⅛" rifled barrel; 45½" overall length; weighs 9 lb.; no sights; drilled, tapped for scope mounts; checkered European walnut stock; quick interchangeable barrel system; recoil pad; crossbolt safety; quick-detachable swivel mounts. Made in Italy. Introduced, 1986; still imported by Ballistic Research Industries. Used value, $650 to $675.

BENELLI Super 90: autoloader; gas-operated; 12-ga.; 3" chamber; 26" improved, 28" full choke barrel; weighs 7¼ lb.; metal bead front sight; high-impact polymer stock; sporting version of military/ police gun; vent rib; Montefeltro bolt system; blued finish. Made in Italy. Introduced, 1986; still imported by Heckler & Koch. Used value, $475 to $500.

BGJ 10 Gauge Magnum: side-by-side; 10-ga.; 3½" chambers; 32" full choke barrels; weighs 11 lb.; box-lock action; checkered European walnut stock; color hardened action; double triggers; matted rib; front, center metal bead sights; Purdey-type forend release; ventilated rubber recoil pad. Made in Spain. Introduced, 1986; still imported by Mandall Shooting Supplies. Used value, $350 to $375.

BGJ 10 Gauge Magnum

Boss Over/Under Model

BOSS Over/Under: side-lock action; 12-, 16-, 20-, 28-ga., .410; 26", 28", 30", 34" barrels; any desired choke combo; automatic ejectors; double or non-selective single trigger; selective single trigger extra; hand-checkered European walnut stock, forearm; recoil pad; matted or vent rib. Introduced about 1952; still in production; not currently imported. English made. Used values: dou-

ble triggers, $12,500 to $15,000; non-selective single trigger, $17,500 to $20,000; selective single trigger, $22,500 to $25,000.

BOSS Double Barrel: side-by-side; side-lock; 12-, 16-, 20-, 28-ga., .410; 26", 28", 30", 32" barrels; any desired choke combo; automatic ejectors; double or non-selective single trigger; selective single trigger extra; hand-checkered European walnut stock, forearm; straight or pistol-grip stock. Introduced after WWI; still in production; not currently imported. Used values: double triggers,

$10,000 to $12,500; non-selective single trigger, $15,000 to $17,500; selective single trigger, $20,000 to $22,500.

Breda Standard Autoloader

BREDA Autoloader: take-down autoloader; 12-ga. only; 4-rd. tube magazine; 25½", 27½" barrels; chrome bore; plain or with matted rib; hand-checkered European walnut stock, forearm; straight or pistol-grip style; available in 3 grades with chromed receivers,

Boss Double Barrel Model

engraving. Grade, value depends upon amount of engraving, quality of wood. Introduced in 1946; still in production. Made in Italy. Used values: Standard, with plain barrel, $225 to $250; with matted rib, $250 to $275; Grade I, $305 to $320; Grade II, $400 to $450; Grade III, $550 to $600.

Magnum 12 Autoloader model has same specs as Standard Breda Autoloader, except is chambered for 12-ga. 3" magnum shell. Introduced in 1950; still in production. Used values: with plain barrel, $275 to $300; with matted rib, $300 to $325.

CAPRINUS Sweden: over/under; 12-ga.; 2¾" chambers; 28", 30" barrels; interchangeable choke tubes; high-grade European walnut stock, optional Monte Carlo; oil finish; checkered butt; stainless steel construction; single selective trigger; ejectors; double safety system. Made in Sweden. Introduced, 1982; no longer imported by Caprinus USA. Used values: Skeet Special. $4700 to

Caprinus Sweden

$4800; Skeet Game, $4900 to $5000; Game Model, $4900 to $5000; Trap Model, $4950 to $5050.

Chapuis Progress RG

CHAPUIS Progress RBV: side-by-side; 12-, 20-ga.; 26½", 27½" barrels; chromed bores; fine-checkered oil-finished straight or pistol-grip stock of French or American walnut; single barrel joining rib; auto ejectors; double triggers; scroll engraving. Made in France. Introduced, 1979; no longer imported. Used value, $900 to $950.

Progress RG has box-lock action, but other specs are basically the same as RBV. Used value, $600 to $625.

Progress Slug has same specs as Progress RG, except right barrel is rifled for slugs. Used value, $750 to $800.

CLAYCO Model 6: over/under; 12-ga.; 2¾" chambers; 26", 28", barrels; walnut-finished hardwood stock; checkered pistol grip, forend; mechanical single trigger; auto safety; vent rubber recoil pad; blued scroll-engraved receiver; vent top rib. Made in China. Introduced, 1983; no longer imported. Used value, $175 to $200.

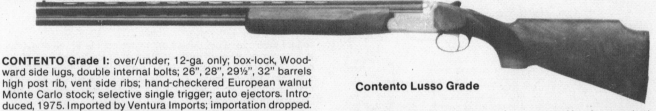

Contento Lusso Grade

CONTENTO Grade I: over/under; 12-ga. only; box-lock, Woodward side lugs, double internal bolts; 26", 28", 29½", 32" barrels high post rib, vent side ribs; hand-checkered European walnut Monte Carlo stock; selective single trigger; auto ejectors. Introduced, 1975. Imported by Ventura Imports; importation dropped. Used value, $800 to $850.

Lusso Grade has same specs as Grade I, except for better wood, engraved action. Used value, $1200 to $1300.

Extra Lusso has same specs as Lusso, except has fancy walnut stock, extensive Florentine engraving. Used value, $2000 to $2100.

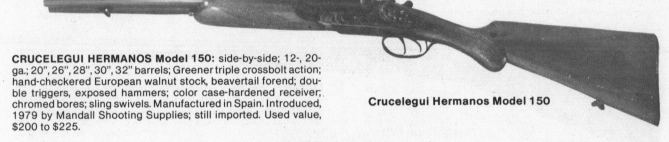

Crucelegui Hermanos Model 150

CRUCELEGUI HERMANOS Model 150: side-by-side; 12-, 20-ga.; 20", 26", 28", 30", 32" barrels; Greener triple crossbolt action; hand-checkered European walnut stock, beavertail forend; double triggers, exposed hammers; color case-hardened receiver; chromed bores; sling swivels. Manufactured in Spain. Introduced, 1979 by Mandall Shooting Supplies; still imported. Used value, $200 to $225.

Darne Bird-Hunter

DARNE Bird-Hunter: side-by-side; 20-, 12-ga.; sliding breech action; double triggers; automatic selective ejection; 25½" barrels; improved cylinder, modified; raised rib; deluxe walnut stock, hand-checkered forearm; case-hardened receiver. Manufactured in France; was imported by Firearms Center, Victoria, Texas, but manufacture now discontinued. Used value, $650 to $700.

Darne Pheasant Hunter is same as Bird-Hunter, except for highly engraved receiver, fancy walnut stock, forearm; 12-ga. only, 27½" barrels, modified and full chokes. Used value, $1300 to $1400.

Darne Quail-Hunter Supreme is same as Bird-Hunter model, except for premium-grade engraving, extra-fancy wood; 20-, 28-ga. only; 25½" barrels, improved/modified chokes. Used value, $1800 to $2000.

DUMOULIN Liege Model: side-by-side; 12-, 16-, 20-, 28-ga.; 2¾", 3" chambers; 26" to 32" barrels, choked to customer's specs; weighs 6.4 lb.; Anson & Deeley box-lock or side-lock action. Custom-built in Belgium. Introduced, 1986; dropped, 1988. Used value, $4200 to $4500.

ERA Bird Hunter

ERA Bird Hunter: side-by-side; 12-, 16-, 20-ga., .410; box-lock action; 26", 28", 30" barrel lengths; hand-checkered walnut stock, beavertail forend; raised matted rib; double triggers; engraved receiver; extractors; auto disconnector. Made in Brazil. Introduced, 1979 by F.I.E.; no longer imported. Used value, $85 to $95.

ERA Full Limit

ERA Full Limit: over/under; 12-, 20-ga.; 28" barrels; vent, top and middle ribs; hand-checkered walnut-finished hardwood stock; Monte Carlo or straight styles interchangeable; auto safety, extractors; double triggers; engraved receiver. Made in Brazil. Introduced by F.I.E., 1980; no longer imported. Used value, $175 to $200.

ERA Winner: single-barrel; 12-, 16-, 20-ga., .410; 28" barrel; walnut-stained hardwood stock; beavertail forend; metal bead front sight; trigger guard button opens action; exposed hammer; auto ejectors. Made in Brazil. Introduced, 1980 by F.I.E.; no longer imported. Used value, $45 to $50.

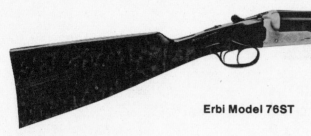

Erbi Model 76ST

ERBI Model 76ST: side-by-side; 10-, 12-, 20-, 28-ga.; 26", 28" modified/full barrels; hand-checkered straight-grip European walnut stock; medium bead front sight; double triggers; extractors; engraved, silvered receiver. Made in Spain. Introduced, 1982, by Toledo Armas; dropped, 1984. Used value, $350 to $375.

Model 76AJ has same specs as Model 76ST, except has automatic ejectors. Introduced, 1982, by Toledo Armas; dropped, 1984. Used value, $400 to $425.

Model 80 has same specs as standard model 76, except has side-lock action. Introduced, 1982, by Toledo Armas; dropped, 1984. Used value, $500 to $550.

FERLACH Constant Companion: side-by-side; Anson & Deeley-type action; 12-, 16-, 20-ga.; 28", 30" barrels; tapered boring; quadruple Greener bolt; auto safety; ejectors; engraved receiver; double triggers; hand-checkered black walnut pistol-grip stock; cheek-piece. Manufactured in Austria. Originally imported by Flaig's. Introduced in 1956; dropped, 1958. Used value, $550 to $600.

Ferlib Model FVII

FERLIB Model F VII: side-by-side; 12-, 20-, 28-ga., .410; 25", 26", 27", 28" barrels; standard chokes; oil-finished European walnut stock; checkered straight grip, forend; box-lock action; single or double triggers; beavertail forend optional; silvered, scroll-engraved receiver. Made in Italy. Introduced, 1983; still imported by Wm. Larkin Moore. Used values: 12-, 20-ga., $2200 to $2300; 28-ga., .410, $2400 to $2500.

Garcia Bronco

GARCIA Bronco: single-shot; .410; swing-out action; one-piece metal frame stock, receiver; crackle finish; 18½" barrel. Italian made. Manufactured 1968 to 1978. Used value, $45 to $50.

Garcia Bronco 22/410

GARCIA Bronco 22/410: over/under combo; swing-out action; take-down; .22 LR top barrel, .410 lower; 18½" barrel; one-piece metal frame stock, receiver; crackle finish. Manufactured 1976 to 1978. Italian made. Used value, $65 to $75.

GIB Magnum

GIB Magnum: side-by-side; 10-ga. only; 3½" chambers; box-lock action; 32" barrels; checkered pistol-grip stock of European walnut; double triggers, color case-hardened action; front, center metal bead sights; matted rib; vent rubber recoil pad. Made in Spain. Introduced, 1978; still imported by Mandall Shooting Supplies as BGJ model as of 1984. Used value, $250 to $275.

Golden Eagle 5000 Grade I Field

Golden Eagle 5000 Grade II

Golden Eagle Grade III Trap

GOLDEN EAGLE Model 5000 Grade I Field: over/under; 12-, 20-ga.; 2¾", 3" chambers in 12-ga.; 3" in 20; 26", 28", 30" barrels; box-lock action; selective single trigger; auto ejectors; improved/modified, modified/full choking; vent rib; engraved receiver; gold eagle head inlaid in frame; checkered walnut pistol-grip stock, semi-beavertail forearm. Manufactured in Japan; imported 1975 to 1980. Used value, $500 to $520.

Model 5000 Grade I Trap has same specs as Field model, except 30", 32" barrels; modified/full, improved modified/full, full/full choking; wide vent rib, trap-style stock; recoil pad. Imported 1975 to 1980. Used value, $600 to $625.

Model 5000 Grade I Skeet has same specs as Field model, except for 26", 28" skeet-choked barrels; vent rib. Imported 1975 to 1980. Used value, $540 to $560.

Model 5000 Grade II Field has same specs as Grade I Field model, except for more elaborate engraving, spread-wing eagle inlaid in gold; fancier wood. Imported 1975 to 1980. Used value, $560 to $575.

Model 5000 Grade II Trap has same specs as Grade I Trap model, except for more elaborate engraving; spread-wing eagle gold inlay; vent side ribs; inertia trigger; fancier wood. Imported 1975 to 1980. Used value, $680 to $700.

Model 5000 Grade II Skeet has same specs as Grade I Skeet model, except for more elaborate engraving, spread-wing eagle gold inlay, inertia trigger, vent side ribs, fancier wood. Imported 1975 to 1980. Used value, $620 to $640.

Model 5000 Grade III is available in field, trap, skeet versions; same specs as lower grades, except has game scene engraving, scroll-engraved frame, barrels, side plates, fancy wood; Trap model has Monte Carlo comb; full pistol grip; recoil pad. Imported 1976 to 1980. Used value, $1850 to $2000.

GOROSABEL Model Blackpoint: side-by-side; 12-, 20-ga.; 2¾", 3" chambers; 26", 27", 28" barrels; standard choke combos; select hand-checkered European walnut stock; splinter or beavertail forend; Holland & Holland-type side-lock action; Purdey-style scroll, rose engraving; numerous options. Made in Italy. Introduced, 1986, dropped, 1988. Used value, $1150 to $1200.

Model Silverpoint has same specs as Blackpoint, except has less fancy wood, Holland-type scroll engraving. Introduced, 1986; dropped, 1988. Used value, $775 to $825.

Gorosabel Model Blackpoint

GOROSABEL Model 503: side-by-side; 12-, 16-, 20-, 28-ga., .410; 26", 27", 28" barrels; standard choke combos; English or pistol-grip select hand-checkered walnut stock; splinter or beavertail forend; Anson & Deeley-type box-lock action; scalloped frame, scroll engraving; auto ejectors. Introduced, 1986; dropped, 1988. Used value, $825 to $875.

Gorosabel Model 503

Model 502 has the same basic specs as Model 503, except has less fancy wood, engraving. Introduced, 1986; dropped, 1988. Used value, $650 to $700.

Model 501 has same specs as Model 502, except is standard-grade model; no engraving. Introduced, 1986; dropped, 1988. Used value, $525 to $550.

HEYM Model 55/77: over/under; 12-, 16-, 20-ga.; 28" barrel standard; box-lock action; hand-checkered European walnut stock; Kersten double crossbolt; double under lugs; Arabesque or hunting engraving; numerous options at added cost. Introduced, 1979; no longer imported. Used value, $1800 to $2000.

Model 55SS/77FSS has same specs as standard model, except has side-lock action. No longer imported. Used value, $3500 to $3800.

Heym Model 55/77

IGA Model

IGA Model: side-by-side; 12-, 20-, 28-ga., 2¾" chambers; .410, 3"; 26", 28" barrels; standard chokes; oil-finished hardwood stock;

hand-checkered pistol grip, forend; extractors; solid matted rib; auto safety; double triggers. Made in Brazil. Introduced, 1983; still imported by Stoeger. Used value: $175 to $200.

IGA Coach Model has same specs as standard model, except has 20" barrels; 12-, 20-ga. Made in Brazil. Introduced, 1983; still imported by Stoeger. Used value: $175 to $200.

INDUSTRIAS DANOK Red Prince: side-by-side; 12-ga.; 2¾" chambers; modified/full barrels; straight-grip European walnut stock; checkered grip, forend; medium bead front sight; double

triggers; auto ejectors; hand-engraved action. Made in Spain. Introduced, 1982, by Toledo Armas; dropped, 1984. Used value: $500 to $525.

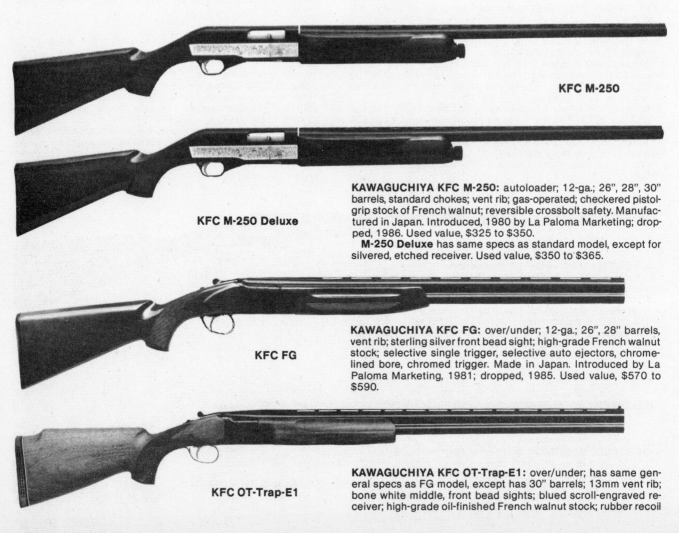

KFC M-250

KFC M-250 Deluxe

KAWAGUCHIYA KFC M-250: autoloader; 12-ga.; 26", 28", 30" barrels, standard chokes; vent rib; gas-operated; checkered pistol-grip stock of French walnut; reversible crossbolt safety. Manufactured in Japan. Introduced, 1980 by La Paloma Marketing; dropped, 1986. Used value, $325 to $350.

M-250 Deluxe has same specs as standard model, except for silvered, etched receiver. Used value, $350 to $365.

KFC FG

KAWAGUCHIYA KFC FG: over/under; 12-ga.; 26", 28" barrels, vent rib; sterling silver front bead sight; high-grade French walnut stock; selective single trigger, selective auto ejectors, chrome-lined bore, chromed trigger. Made in Japan. Introduced by La Paloma Marketing, 1981; dropped, 1985. Used value, $570 to $590.

KFC OT-Trap-E1

KAWAGUCHIYA KFC OT-Trap-E1: over/under; has same general specs as FG model, except has 30" barrels; 13mm vent rib; bone white middle, front bead sights; blued scroll-engraved receiver; high-grade oil-finished French walnut stock; rubber recoil

KFC OT-Trap-E2

pad. Introduced, 1981; dropped, 1985. Used value, $750 to $775.

OT-Trap-E2 has same specs as E1, except receiver is chromed, better scroll engraving, super-deluxe French walnut stock, forend. Used value, $1200 to $1250.

OT-Skeet-E1 version of FG model has 26" or 28" skeet barrels; 13mm vent rib, middle and front bead sights; gold-colored wide trigger; plastic butt plate; push-button forend release. Used value, $750 to $800.

OT-Skeet-E2 is skeet version of OT-Trap-E1. Used value, $1200 to $1250.

Kleinguenther Condor

KLEINGUENTHER Condor: over/under; 12-, 20-ga.; Purdey-type double-lock action; barrels, 26" improved/modified or skeet/skeet; 28" full/modified or modified/modified; 30" 12-ga. only, full/mod-ified, full/full; European walnut stock; hand-checkered pistol grip, forearm; single selective trigger; automatic ejectors, vent rib; skeet model has extra-wide rib. Imported from Italy; no longer imported. Used values: field grade, $350 to $375; skeet, $375 to $400.

Condor Trap: has same specs as field grade, except for wide vent rib, Monte Carlo stock; 12-ga. only; barrels, 28" full/modified; 30", 32" modified/full or full/full. No longer imported. Used value, $400 to $425.

Kleinguenther/Brescia

KLEINGUENTHER/BRESCIA: side-by-side; 12-, 20-ga.; Anson & Deeley-type action; barrels, 28" full/modified or improved/mod-ified, chrome lined; European walnut stock; hand-checkered pis-tol grip, forearm; recoil pad; double triggers; engraved action. Imported from Italy; no longer imported. Used value, $300 to $325.

Lanber Model 844

LANBER Model 844: over/under; 12-ga.; 2¾", 3" chambers; 28" improved cylinder/improved modified, 30" modified/full barrels; European walnut stock; checkered pistol grip, forend; single trig-ger, selective or non-selective; double triggers on magnum ver-sion; with or without ejectors. Made in Spain. Introduced, 1981; dropped, 1986. Used values: with selective triggers, extractors, $325 to $350; 3" magnum, $350 to $375; with ejectors, $400 to $425.

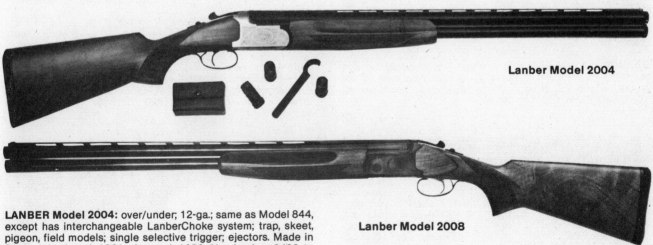

Lanber Model 2004

Lanber Model 2008

LANBER Model 2004: over/under; 12-ga.; same as Model 844, except has interchangeable LanberChoke system; trap, skeet, pigeon, field models; single selective trigger; ejectors. Made in Spain. Introduced, 1981; dropped, 1986. Used value, $400 to $425.

Model 2008 has same specs as Model 2004, but has no middle rib. Introduced, 1981; still imported. Used value, $400 to $425.

LAURONA Super Model: over/under; 12-, 20-ga.; 2¾", 3" cham-bers; 26", 28", 29" barrel lengths; standard choke combos or Multi-chokes; made in six different configurations; European walnut stock; box-lock action; silvered, engraved frame; auto selective

Model 208 has same specs as Model 2008, except has 30" barrels. Introduced, 1981; still imported. Used value, $400 to 425.

ejectors; single selective or twin single triggers; black chrome barrels. Made in Spain. Introduced, 1986; dropped, 1988. Used value, $425 to $525, depending upon configuration.

Miguel Larranaga Traditional

MIGUEL LARRANAGA Traditional: side-by-side; 12-, 20-ga.; 2¾" chambers; 28" modified/full barrels; straight-grip European walnut stock; hand checkering; medium bead front sight; exposed hammers; checkered butt; hand-engraved locks. Made in Spain. Introduced, 1982 by Toledo Armas; dropped, 1984. Used value, $360 to $375.

LEBEAU-COURALLY Boxlock Model: side-by-side; 12-, 16-, 20-, 28-ga.; 26" to 30" barrels; choked to custom specs; custom-built; hand-rubbed, oil-finished French walnut stock, forend; Anson & Deeley-type box-lock action; ejectors; with or without side plates;

Purdey-type fastener; choice of rib style, engraving. Made in Belgium to order. Introduced, 1987; still imported by Wm. Larkin Moore. You ain't gonna find many of these at the swap meet! Used value, $7500 to $8200, depending on options.

LEBEAU-COURALLY Sidelock: side-by-side; 12-, 16-, 20-, 28-ga.; 26" to 30" custom-choked barrels; dimensions to customer's specs; best quality French walnut custom stock; checkered butt, grip, splinter forend; Holland & Holland-type side-lock action; ejectors; chopper lump barrels; choice of rib type, engraving pat-

tern; some have H&H-type self-opening mechanism. Made to order in Belgium. Introduced, 1987; still imported by Wm. Larkin Moore. You may go through your whole life and never see one! Used value, $14,500 to $15,800, depending on options.

LEBEAU-COURALLY Model 1225: side-by-side; 12-, 20-, 28-ga.; 2¾", 3" chambers; 26" to 28" custom-choked barrels; weighs 6.4 lb.; custom Grand Luxe walnut stock; Holland & Holland side-lock action; double triggers; auto ejectors; color case-hardened frame;

English engraving. Made to order in Belgium. Introduced, 1987; dropped, 1988. Used value, $7350 to $7600, depending on options.

Marocchi America Model

MAROCCHI America: over/under; 12-, 20-ga.; 2¾" chambers; 26"-29" skeet barrels, 27"-32" trap, 30", 32" single barrel; select

European walnut stock; left- or right-hand palm swell; hand checkering; Schnabel or beavertail forend; medium engraving coverage on frame; custom engraving, inlays offered. Marketed in fitted hard case. Made in Italy. Introduced, 1983; dropped, 1986. Used value, $1700 to $1800.

Marocchi Contrast Model

MAROCCHI SM-28 SXS: side-by-side; 12- or 20-ga.; 2¾" chamber; totally handmade to customer's specs and dimensions. Supplied with fitted leather luggage case. Introduced, 1983; dropped, 1986. Used value, $8000 to $8250.

MAROCCHI Contrast: over/under; 12-, 20-ga.; 2¾" chambers; 26"-29" skeet barrels, 27"-32" trap; select European walnut stock; hand-rubbed wax finish; hand-checkered pistol grip, forend; left- or right-hand palm swell; Schnabel or beavertail forend; light engraving on standard grade; custom engraving, inlays at added cost. Marketed in fitted hard case. Made in Italy. Introduced, 1983; dropped, 1986. Used value, $1500 to $1600.

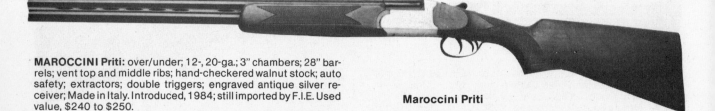

MAROCCINI Priti: over/under; 12-, 20-ga.; 3" chambers; 28" barrels; vent top and middle ribs; hand-checkered walnut stock; auto safety; extractors; double triggers; engraved antique silver receiver; Made in Italy. Introduced, 1984; still imported by F.I.E. Used value, $240 to $250.

Maroccini Priti

MAUSER Model Contest: over/under; 12-ga. only; 27½" barrels; select European walnut stock; chrome-lined barrels; receiver engraved with hunting scenes; dummy side plates; auto ejectors; single selective trigger. Manufactured in Germany. Introduced by Waidmanns Guns International, 1981; no longer imported. Used values: trap version, $900 to $950; skeet, $1400 to $1450.

MERCURY Magnum: side-by-side; 10-, 12-, 20-ga. magnums; 28", 32" barrels; triple-lock Anson & Deeley-type action; checkered pistol-grip stock of European walnut; double triggers; auto safety; extractors; safety gas ports; engraved frame. Made in Spain. Introduced, 1970; still imported by Tradewinds, Inc. Used values: 10-ga. magnum, $275 to $300; other gauges, $200 to $225.

MONTE CARLO Single: single-barrel; 12-ga. only; 32" trap barrel; hand-checkered pistol-grip stock of European walnut; beavertail forend; recoil pad; auto ejector; slide safety; gold-plated trigger.

OMEGA Folding Model Single-Shot: 12-, 16-, 28-ga., .410; 2¾", 3" chambers; 26", 28", 30" barrel lengths; full chokes; checkered beech stock; metal bead front sight; matte chromed receiver; top opening lever; folds for storage, transport. Made in Italy. Introduced,

Made in Italy. Introduced, 1968; no longer imported. Used value, $230 to $240.

1984; dropped, 1988. Used Value, $115 to $125.
   Deluxe Folding Model has same specs as standard version, except has checkered walnut stock, blued receiver, vent rib. Introduced, 1984; dropped, 1988. Used value, $150 to $160.

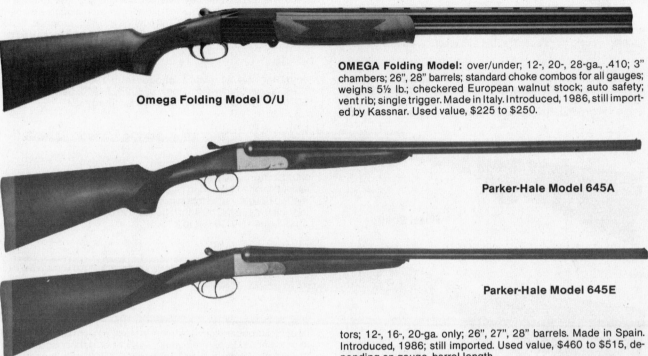

Omega Folding Model O/U

OMEGA Folding Model: over/under; 12-, 20-, 28-ga., .410; 3" chambers; 26", 28" barrels; standard choke combos for all gauges; weighs 5½ lb.; checkered European walnut stock; auto safety; vent rib; single trigger. Made in Italy. Introduced, 1986, still imported by Kassnar. Used value, $225 to $250.

Parker-Hale Model 645A

Parker-Hale Model 645E

PARKER-HALE Model 640E: side-by-side; 12-, 16-, 20-, 28-ga., .410; 2¾", 3" chambers; 25", 26", 27", 28" barrel lengths; hand-checkered, oil-finished straight-grip English-style walnut stock; splinter forend; checkered butt; silvered, engraved box-lock action; auto safety; extractors; double triggers; concave rib. Made in Spain. Introduced, 1986; still imported by Precision Sports. Used value, $375 to $400.
   Model 640A has same specs as 640 E, except for American-influenced pistol-grip stock, beavertail forend, butt plate. Made in Spain. Introduced, 1986; still imported. Used value, $425 to $450.
   Model 645E has same specs as Model 640E, except has ejec-

tors; 12-, 16-, 20-ga. only; 26", 27", 28" barrels. Made in Spain. Introduced, 1986; still imported. Used value, $460 to $515, depending on gauge, barrel length.
   Model 645A has same specs as Model 640A, except has ejectors; 12-, 16-, 20-ga.; 26", 28" barrels. Made in Spain. Introduced, 1986; still imported. Used value, $525 to $565.
   Model 645E-XXV has same specs as 645E, except has 25", 27" barrel lengths. Made in Spain. Introduced, 1986; still imported. Used value, $475 to $550, depending on gauge, barrel length.
   Model 670E-XXV has same specs as standard model, except has 27", 28" barrels, ejectors, side-locks. Made in Spain. Introduced, 1986; still imported. USed value, $1850 to $1975.
   Model 680E-XXV has same specs as 670E-XXV, except has 25" barrels; case-hardened action. Made in Spain. Introduced, 1986, still imported. Used value, $1800 to $1900.

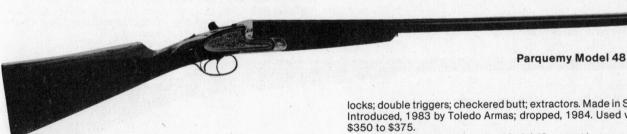

Parquemy Model 48

PARQUEMY Model 48: side-by-side; .410; 3" chambers; modified/full barrels; straight-grip European walnut stock; hand checkering; automatic ejectors; medium bead front sight; hand-engraved

locks; double triggers; checkered butt; extractors. Made in Spain. Introduced, 1983 by Toledo Armas; dropped, 1984. Used value, $350 to $375.
   Model 48E has same specs as Model 48, except has no extractors; chambered for 12-, 20-, 28-ga.; 2¾" chambers. Introduced, 1982, by Toledo Armas; dropped, 1984. Used value, $400 to $425.

PERUGINI-VISINI Classic Double: side-by-side; 12-, 20-ga.; 2¾", 3" chambers; optional barrel lengths, chokes; high-grade oil-finished straight English briar walnut stock; H&H-type hand-detachable side-locks; internal parts gold-plated; single or double triggers; auto ejectors; numerous options. Made in Italy. Introduced, 1986; was imported by Armes de Chasse, now by Wm. Larkin Moore. Used value, $8200-plus.

PERUGINI-VISINI Liberty Double: side-by-side; 12-, 20-, 28-ga.; .410; 2¾", 3" chambers; box-lock action; has same features as the classic model; made to order; many options; can be ordered in matched pairs, if you want to upset the balance of trade. Used value, $3900-plus, depending on options.

Rigby Regal Model Double

RIGBY Sidelock Double: side-by-side; in all gauges; barrel lengths, chokes to customer's specs; automatic ejectors; double triggers; hand-checkered European walnut straight-grip stock, forearm; English engraving; two grades, differing in overall quality, amount of engraving. English made. Introduced in 1885; dropped, 1955. Used values: Sandringham Grade, $7500 to $8000; Regal Grade, $12,500 to $15,000; add $750 to $1000 for fitted case.

RIGBY Box-lock Double: side-by-side; in all gauges; barrel lengths, chokes to customer's specs; automatic ejectors; double triggers; hand-checkered European walnut straight-grip stock, forearm; English engraving; in two grades, differing in amount and nature of engraving, overall quality. Introduced in 1900; dropped, 1955. Used values: Chatsworth Grade, $3500 to $4500; Sackville Grade, $3750 to $4750; add $600 to $750 for fitted case.

Rossi Squire

ROSSI Squire: side-by-side; 12-, 20-ga., .410; 26", 28" barrels; walnut-finished hardwood pistol-grip stock; double triggers; raised matted rib; beavertail forearm; twin underlugs; synchronized sliding bolts. Made in Brazil. Introduced, 1978; still imported by Interarms. Used value, $135 to $150.

Rossi Overland

ROSSI Overland: side-by-side; 12-, 20-ga., .410; 20", 26", 28" barrels; European walnut pistol-grip stock, beavertail forend; sidelock action; external hammers; Greener crossbolt; solid raised matted rib. Made in Brazil. Introduced, 1978; still imported by Interarms. Used value, $135 to $150.

Royal Arms Model 87SC

ROYAL ARMS Model 87SC: over/under; 12-ga.; 2¾" chambers; 27⅝" barrels; choke tubes; weighs 7⅜ lb.; select walnut stock; box-lock action; auto ejectors; auto safety; single selective trigger; coin-finish receiver; arabesque scroll engraving; tapered raised rib. Made in Italy. Introduced, 1987; still imported by Royal Arms International. Used value, $500 to $550.

    Model 87T Trap has same general specs as basic model, except has trap stock, other trap configurations. Introduced, 1987; still imported. Used value, $525 to $550.

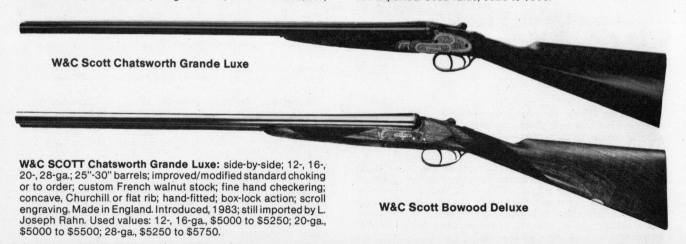

W&C Scott Chatsworth Grande Luxe

W&C SCOTT Chatsworth Grande Luxe: side-by-side; 12-, 16-, 20-, 28-ga.; 25"-30" barrels; improved/modified standard choking or to order; custom French walnut stock; fine hand checkering; concave, Churchill or flat rib; hand-fitted; box-lock action; scroll engraving. Made in England. Introduced, 1983; still imported by L. Joseph Rahn. Used values: 12-, 16-ga., $5000 to $5250; 20-ga., $5000 to $5500; 28-ga., $5250 to $5750.

W&C Scott Bowood Deluxe

W&C SCOTT Bowood Deluxe: side-by-side; has same specs as Grand Luxe, except metal, wood are lower in quality; hand-checkered pistol grip, forend. Made in England. Introduced, 1983; still imported by L. Joseph Rahn. Used values: 12-, 16-ga., $3500 to $3700; 20-ga., $4000 to $4200; 28-ga., $4200 to $4400.

W&C SCOTT Kinmount: side-by-side; similar to Bowood Deluxe, but quality of wood, metalwork is less; other features the same. Made in England. Introduced, 1983; still imported by L. Joseph Rahn. Used values: 12-, 16-ga., $2900 to $3000; 20-ga., $3250 to $3500; 28-ga., $3750 to $4000.

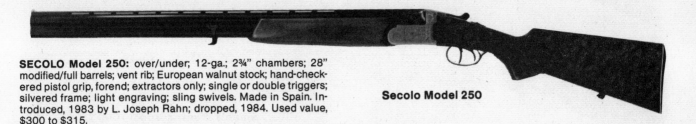

Secolo Model 250

SECOLO Model 250: over/under; 12-ga.; 2¾" chambers; 28" modified/full barrels; vent rib; European walnut stock; hand-checkered pistol grip, forend; extractors only; single or double triggers; silvered frame; light engraving; sling swivels. Made in Spain. Introduced, 1983 by L. Joseph Rahn; dropped, 1984. Used value, $300 to $315.

SECOLO Model 550 Trap: over/under; 12-ga.; 2¾" chambers, 30", 32" barrels; marketed with 5 interchangeable choke tubes; Monte Carlo-style European walnut stock; vent rib; silvered or case-hardened receiver. Made in Spain. Introduced, 1983 by L. Joseph Rahn; dropped, 1984. Used value, $550 to $600.

  Model 540 Mono Trap is same as standard Model 550, except has single upper trap barrel. Introduced, 1983 by L. Joseph Rahn; dropped, 1984. Used value, $525 to $625.

  Model 530 has same specs as Model 540, except lower barrel is installed. Introduced, 1983; dropped, 1984. Used value, $600 To $625.

  Model 560 Skeet has same specs as standard Model 550, except has skeet stock, barrels. Introduced, 1983; dropped, 1984. Used value, $600 to $625.

Senator Folding Model

SENATOR Folding Model: over/under; 12-, 20-ga.; .410; 3" chambers; 26", 28" barrels; weighs 7 lb.; European walnut stock; engraved box-lock action; vent top, middle ribs; under-lever cocking/opening system. Made in Italy. Introduced, 1986; dropped, 1988. Used value, $190 to $210.

Sile Sky Stalker

SILE Sky Stalker: folding over/under; .410; 3" chambers; 26" barrels; checkered walnut stock; Schnabel forend; folds for storage, carrying; chrome-lined bores; matted hard chrome finish on receiver. Made in Italy. Introduced, 1984; still imported by Sile. Used value, $140 to $150.

S&M 10 Gauge: over/under; 10-ga.; 3½" chambers; 28", 32½" barrels; full/full; weighs 9 lb.; checkered walnut stock; box-lock action; double triggers; extractors; matte-finished metal. Made in Europe. Introduced, 1986; still imported by Ballistic Products. Used value, $400 to $425.

Smith & Wesson Model 1000

SMITH & WESSON Model 1000: gas-operated autoloader; 12-ga. only; 2¾" chamber; 4-rd.; barrel lengths, 26" skeet, improved cylinder; 28" improved, modified, full; walnut stock, checkered pistol grip, forearm; crossbolt safety; vent rib; front, middle beads; engraved alloy receiver; pressure compensator. Introduced in 1973; dropped, 1984. Manufactured in Japan. Used value, $300 to $350.

  Model 1000 Magnum has same specs as standard Model 1000, except chambered for 12-ga., 3" shell only; 30" modified or full choke barrel; recoil pad. Imported 1977 to 1984. Used value, $325 to $350.

  Model 1000 20-Gauge is made in standard 20 and 3" 20-ga. magnum; similar to 12-ga. model except slimmed down; has self-cleaning gas system; 26", 28" barrels. Introduced, 1978; dropped,

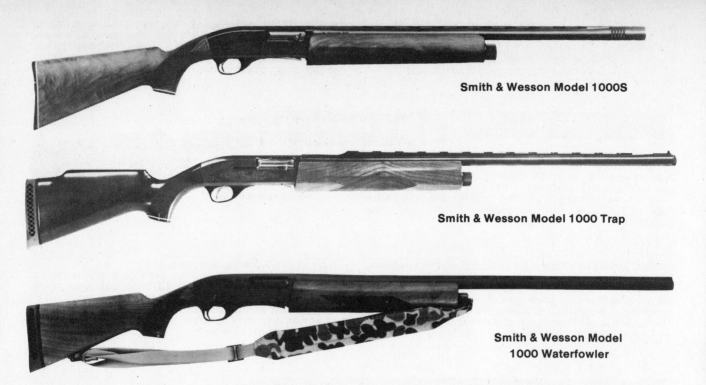

Smith & Wesson Model 1000S

Smith & Wesson Model 1000 Trap

Smith & Wesson Model 1000 Waterfowler

1984. Used values: standard, $300 to $325; magnum, $325 to $350.

Model 1000S has same basic specs as standard model, except has recessed-type skeet choke with compensator to soften recoil, reduce muzzle jump; stock has palm swell; vent rib, fluorescent red front bead; oil-finished select walnut stock. Introduced, 1979; dropped, 1984. Used value, $550 to $575.

Model 1000 Trap has same specs as standard model, except has Monte Carlo trap stock; stepped rib; white middle bead, Bradley front; shell catcher; 30" Multi-Choke barrel; steel receiver. Introduced, 1983; dropped, 1984. Used value, $400 to $425.

Model 1000 Waterfowler has same specs as standard model, except has Parkerized finished, black-oxidized bolt; dull oil stock finish; marketed with quick-detachable swivels, padded camouflage sling; 30" full-choke barrel; 3" chamber. Introduced, 1982; dropped, 1984. Used value, $375 to $395.

Smith & Wesson Model 3000

Smith & Wesson Model 3000 Waterfowler

SMITH & WESSON Model 3000: slide-action; 12-, 20-ga.; 3" chamber; 22" slug barrel with rifle sights, 26" improved, 28" modified, 30" full; plain or vent-rib barrel; Multi-Choke available; American walnut stock; crossbolt reversible safety for left-handers; dual action bars; chrome-plated bolt; steel receiver; rubber recoil

pad. Introduced 1980; dropped, 1984. Used value, $250 to $285, depending upon refinements.

Model 3000 Waterfowler is same as standard 3000, except exterior metal is Parkerized; black oxidized bolt; dull oil-finished stock; 30" full-choke barrel; 3" chamber; marketed with quick-detachable sling swivels, padded camo sling. Introduced, 1982; dropped, 1984. Used value, $275 to $300.

TECHNI-MEC Model SPL 640: folding over/under; 12-, 16-, 20-, 28-ga.; .410; 3" chambers in .410, 2¾" in all others; 26" barrels; European walnut stock, forend; gun folds for storage, transport; vent rib; chrome-lined barrels; photo-engraved, silvered receiver. Made in Italy. Introduced, 1984; still imported by L. Joseph Rahn. Used values: double-trigger model, $180 to $190; single trigger, $190 to $200.

TECHNI-MEC Model SR 692 EM: over/under; 12-, 16-, 20-ga.; 2¾", 3" chambers; 26", 28", 30" barrel lengths; checkered European walnut stock, forend; box-lock action, dummy side plates; game scene engraving; auto ejectors available; single selective trigger. Made in Italy. Introduced, 1984; dropped, 1985. Used value, $400 to $425.

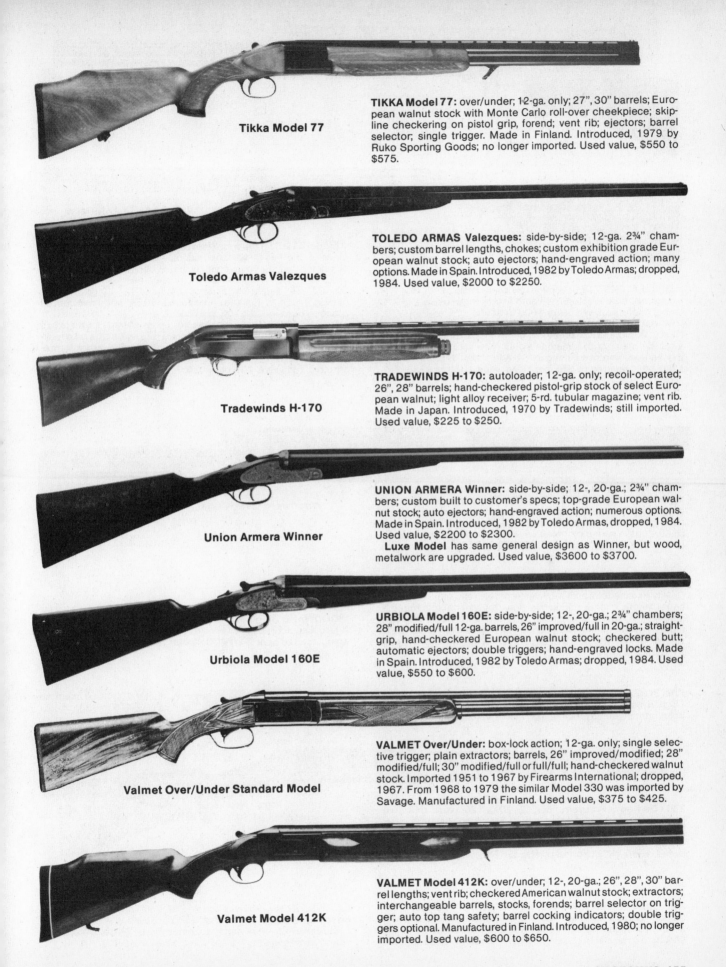

Tikka Model 77

TIKKA Model 77: over/under; 12-ga. only; 27", 30" barrels; European walnut stock with Monte Carlo roll-over cheekpiece; skipline checkering on pistol grip, forend; vent rib; ejectors; barrel selector; single trigger. Made in Finland. Introduced, 1979 by Ruko Sporting Goods; no longer imported. Used value, $550 to $575.

Toledo Armas Valezques

TOLEDO ARMAS Valezques: side-by-side; 12-ga. 2¾" chambers; custom barrel lengths, chokes; custom exhibition grade European walnut stock; auto ejectors; hand-engraved action; many options. Made in Spain. Introduced, 1982 by Toledo Armas; dropped, 1984. Used value, $2000 to $2250.

Tradewinds H-170

TRADEWINDS H-170: autoloader; 12-ga. only; recoil-operated; 26", 28" barrels; hand-checkered pistol-grip stock of select European walnut; light alloy receiver; 5-rd. tubular magazine; vent rib. Made in Japan. Introduced, 1970 by Tradewinds; still imported. Used value, $225 to $250.

Union Armera Winner

UNION ARMERA Winner: side-by-side; 12-, 20-ga.; 2¾" chambers; custom built to customer's specs; top-grade European walnut stock; auto ejectors; hand-engraved action; numerous options. Made in Spain. Introduced, 1982 by Toledo Armas, dropped, 1984. Used value, $2200 to $2300.

    Luxe Model has same general design as Winner, but wood, metalwork are upgraded. Used value, $3600 to $3700.

Urbiola Model 160E

URBIOLA Model 160E: side-by-side; 12-, 20-ga.; 2¾" chambers; 28" modified/full 12-ga. barrels; 26" improved/full in 20-ga.; straight-grip, hand-checkered European walnut stock; checkered butt; automatic ejectors; double triggers; hand-engraved locks. Made in Spain. Introduced, 1982 by Toledo Armas; dropped, 1984. Used value, $550 to $600.

Valmet Over/Under Standard Model

VALMET Over/Under: box-lock action; 12-ga. only; single selective trigger; plain extractors; barrels, 26" improved/modified; 28" modified/full; 30" modified/full or full/full; hand-checkered walnut stock. Imported 1951 to 1967 by Firearms International; dropped, 1967. From 1968 to 1979 the similar Model 330 was imported by Savage. Manufactured in Finland. Used value, $375 to $425.

Valmet Model 412K

VALMET Model 412K: over/under; 12-, 20-ga.; 26", 28", 30" barrel lengths; vent rib; checkered American walnut stock; extractors; interchangeable barrels, stocks, forends; barrel selector on trigger; auto top tang safety; barrel cocking indicators; double triggers optional. Manufactured in Finland. Introduced, 1980; no longer imported. Used value, $600 to $650.

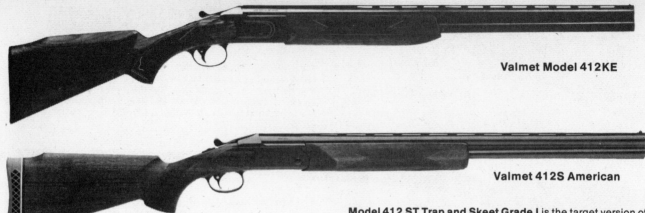

Valmet Model 412KE

Valmet 412S American

Model 412KE Target version has same basic specs as 412K, except has auto ejectors, non-auto safety. Introduced, 1980; no longer imported. Used value, $600 to $650.

Model 412S American is made in trap, skeet, field versions; similar to the 412K, except has better wood, checkering; palm swell on pistol grip; luminous sights; new forend latch spring mechanism; improved firing pin. Made in Finland. Introduced, 1980; still imported by Stoeger. Used value, $650 to $750.

Model 412 ST Trap and Skeet Grade I is the target version of Model 412S; has hand-honed action, mechanical single trigger, elongated forcing cone, stainless steel choke tubes; automatic ejectors; cocking indicators. Trap version has high-stepped rib; 30", 32", 34" single barrel; skeet model is 12-, 20-ga., with 28" barrels. Made in Finland. Introduced, 1987; still imported by Stoeger. Used value, $700 to $750.

Model 412 ST Grade II has same specs as Grade I, except has semi-fancy wood, matte nickel-finished receiver, matte blue locking bolt and lever, gold trigger, more checkering; stock is pre-drilled for recoil reducer installation. Introduced, 1987; still imported. Used value, $875 to $925.

Woodward Over/Under

WOODWARD Over/Under: marketed as Woodward Best Quality; built to customer order in any standard gauge, barrel length, choke; side-lock action; double or single triggers; auto ejectors; plain barrel or vent rib. Manufactured 1909 to WWII. Collector value. English manufacture. Used values: single trigger, $19,000 to $20,000; double triggers, $18,000 to $18,500.

WOODWARD Double: side-by-side; marketed as Woodward Best Quality Hammerless; built to customer order in any standard gauge, barrel length, choke; side-lock action; double or single triggers; automatic ejectors; produced in field, wildfowl, skeet or trap configurations. Manufactured prior to WWII. Collector value. Used values: single trigger, $12,000 to $12,250; double triggers, $11,000 to $11,250.

PIETRO ZANOLETTI Model 2000 Field: over/under; 12-ga.; 28" barrels; European walnut stock; checkered grip, forend; gold bead front sight; box-lock action; auto ejectors; double triggers;

WOODWARD Single Barrel Trap: special order; has same general mechanical specs as over/under model; vent rib; 12-ga. only. Manufactured prior to WWII. Collector value. Used value, $17,500 to $18,000.

engraved receiver. Made in Italy. Introduced, 1984; still imported by Mandall Shooting Supplies. Used value, $475 to $525.

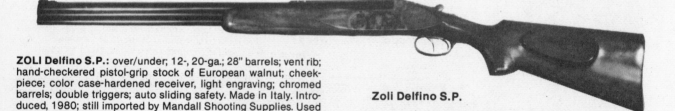

Zoli Delfino S.P.

ZOLI Delfino S.P.: over/under; 12-, 20-ga.; 28" barrels; vent rib; hand-checkered pistol-grip stock of European walnut; cheekpiece; color case-hardened receiver, light engraving; chromed barrels; double triggers; auto sliding safety. Made in Italy. Introduced, 1980; still imported by Mandall Shooting Supplies. Used value, $475 to $500.

ZOLI Silver Snipe: over/under; 12-, 20-ga.; 3" chambers; 26", 28", 30" barrels; standard choke combinations; double box-lock action; European walnut stock; hand-checkered pistol grip, forend; auto safety; vent rib; single trigger; chromed bores. Made in

Italy. Introduced, 1980; dropped, 1987. Was imported by Mandall Shooting Supplies. Used value, $575 to $600.

Golden Snipe has same specs as Silver Snipe, except has selective auto ejectors. Used value, $625 to $650.

COMMEMORATIVES

There's Need For Less Greed; Or John Wayne Was Never A Gun Salesman!

WHEN WE talk about commemorative firearms, a number of factors become increasingly evident, if one looks at the facts and the figures involved.

Before we go any further, let it be pointed out that the values included in the following pages are not for "used guns." Second-hand guns, yes, but not those that have been fired. The prices on all of these commemoratives are based on the idea that each of these firearms — be it revolver, automatic, rifle, carbine or shotgun — is in pristine, mint condition.

If you look around, you find that Americans seem to be a nation of collectors, an avocation which is expanding to other countries. Only a few days before this writing, there was a news item concerning one of the pianos played by the late Dooley Wilson as he sang, "As Time Goes By" in the movie, *Casablanca*. There are two of these pianos, since in the movie business, there is a double for almost every type of prop in case one of them doesn't work. One of these pianos sold for something like a quarter of a million bucks to a Japanese gentleman.

The ruby slippers Judy Garland wore in *The Wizard Of Oz* went for enough to buy a house, even in Southern California, when Metro-Goldwyn-Mayer cleaned out their property room and costume department a few years back. Again, there were two pairs of these shoes originally, but it seems one pair had disappeared.

But taking a look at firearms, when Colt auctioned off what they called their 150th Anniversary Exhibit Gun a couple of years back, the minimum bid accepted was $150,000. Actually, the gun sold for something like $244,000, if I recall correctly. It was for a good cause, though, since the funds helped finance the training of the 1988 U.S. Olympic shooting team. Still, consider that the buyer paid all that money for a single gun.

Colt also issued several lesser models to commemorate their century and a half of service to shooters, but none of them went for nearly that much. I haven't been able to pin down any facts, but some of these still may be available, if you talk to the right Colt salesman.

"So what does all this show biz talk have to do with the price of my John Wayne Commemorative Model 94 carbine?" some of you are asking.

Not much, when it comes right down to it. In the case of Dooley Wilson's piano, there were *two* of them. Judy Garland or someone had lost one pair of the ruby slippers; that left a *single* pair. As for the Colt 150th Anniversary Exhibition single-action, there was — and is — *one*.

In 1981, when the John Wayne commemorative carbine was introduced, the plant in New Haven was grinding them out like steel sausages. They made 50,000 of them!

The John Wayne Commemorative Model 94, as well as the Duke-inspired single-actions turned out by Colt the following year, in 1982, have increased a few dollars in value in some geographic areas. Of the Colt John Wayne Presentation Model, for example, only one hundred were made and each was priced at $20,000. If you're in the market for memorabilia, you might consider — if you have it — paying a quarter of a million for Dooley Wilson's piano, knowing there was only one other like it. But would you pay $20,000 for one of a hundred modern-made Colts, even it if did have John Wayne's likeness engraved in gold? Some of us would not.

Age also has a great deal to do with these items. Judy Garland wore these slippers in 1939, half a century ago; Dooley Wilson's piano is nearly that old. The John Wayne guns — all 50,000 of the carbines — are less than ten years old. They're not even old enough to have character!

Firearms makers have been in the "special model" or "special issue" business almost as long as there has been a gun business in this country. Sam Colt had been around only a few years, when he had two of his famed Walker Colts stamped with consecutive serial numbers and sent them off to Captain S.H. Walker, who had designed the model. The guns arrived after the captain had been slain in combat, but those may well have been the first "presentation Colts." The last I knew, one of these guns was known to exist and was valued at well over $25,000! But there were only *two* Walker Colts that were made specifically for the designer.

Such presentation pieces usually were a basic model that had been gussied up with a lot of gold inlay work, ivory grips and deep engraving, then sometimes personalized with the presentee's name,

In 1984, U.S. Repeating Arms and Colt teamed up to offer a 94 Winchester/Colt SAA commemorative set, with special matching serial numbers. Only 4400 sets were made, but there was no buying rush and today's value is less than half the original asking price of $3995 for the pair. Other commemoratives suffer similar buyer resistance.

rank and serial number. But these were unique and, in most instances, one-of-a-kind productions. They were valuable — and still are, only more so — because they were unique.

There had been a few scattered commemorative issues made in limited numbers, but the current fad, if we can still call it that, got off to a rousing start in 1961, when Bill Cherry asked Colt to produce a special replica run of the long obsolete No. 4 Derringer. Cherry operated a sporting goods store in Geneseo, Illinois, at the time and had the guns made to commemorate the 125th anniversary of the founding of his town.

In 1961, when Bill Cherry offered the little derringers at $27.50, they sold quickly, since he had ordered only 104 of them. Today, those same derringers are worth upward of $600 each; more than twenty times their original value.

Most of the early Colt and Winchester replicas have increased greatly in value. That's because they were made in low numbers. But as time went on, each manufacturer introduced more models for a specific year — and made more of each model. For a time, sales held up.

Colt and Winchester were not the only ones mining this seeming bonanza, incidentally. Some sort of ironic sign of the times was reached when the then semi-infant Charter Arms announced a special commemorative to celebrate their *fifth* year in the arms business. I don't know how many of them they sold and I can't find anyone who does.

At the other extreme, considering the number of arms companies that have folded, merged or been bought out by foreign interests in the past several decades, perhaps the fact that Charter Arms had stayed in business for half a decade was just reason to celebrate with a commemorative! Let's hope they make it to fifty years and a batch more!

This brings us full circle to the age-old law of supply and demand. Among most of the commemoratives sold in limited numbers at logical prices, values have continued to grow. But with thousands upon thousands of a specific model being turned out and original retail prices ever increasing, collectors and speculators finally didn't want to play any more.

The Winchester models dedicated to the centennial of the National Rifle Association are a case in point. Winchester never has publicized exactly how many of these rifles and muskets were manufactured, but the obvious thinking was that, with more than a million NRA members, there should be a market for a million commemorative firearms!

Wrong! Even several years later, this particular commemorative was being offered in discount houses — and they couldn't move them, either!

The fact that most of the recent commemoratives — those made in the past decade — are reselling at their original prices or for less seems to reflect general disillusionment of the collecting fraternity. Some feel they have been victimized by manufacturer greed. Actually, they've been victimized by some makers' lousy business judgment. In many instances, manufacturers have suffered more than buyers.

There has to be a happy medium for all this and a few manufacturers seem to feel they've found it. Some again are starting to pick historically important dates to commemorate and they are doing it with limited numbers.

The American public willingly paid five bucks or so to see John Wayne save the American way of life on the screen; a great way to pass a couple of hours. But there were not 50,000 of them interested in paying $600 a copy for a Model 94 carbine with a bit of engraving and a few embellishments.

It's been a hard-learned lesson.

1960

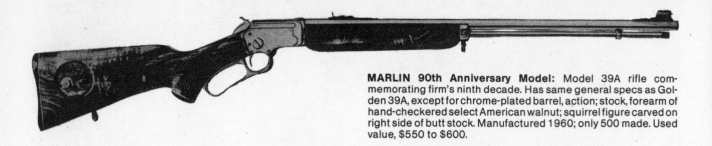

MARLIN 90th Anniversary Model: Model 39A rifle commemorating firm's ninth decade. Has same general specs as Golden 39A, except for chrome-plated barrel, action; stock, forearm of hand-checkered select American walnut; squirrel figure carved on right side of butt stock. Manufactured 1960; only 500 made. Used value, $550 to $600.

1961

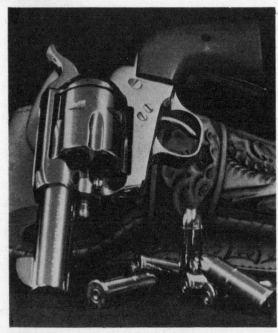

COLT Sheriff's Model: single-action Army revolver; made exclusively for Centennial Arms Corp.; "Colt Sheriff's Model .45" on left side of 3" barrel; .45 Colt only; walnut grips without medallions; 25 made with nickel finish; 478 blued; made only in 1961. Original prices: nickel, $139.50; blued, $150. Current values: nickel, $4000 to $4500; blued, $1450 to $1650.

COLT 125th Anniversary Model: single-action Army revolver; "125th Anniversary — SAA Model .45 Cal." on left side of 7½" barrel; .45 Colt only; varnished walnut grips; gold-plated Colt medallions; gold-plated hammer, trigger, trigger guard; balance blued. Originally cased in red velvet-lined box; 7390 made in 1961 only. Original retail, $150. Current value, $600 to $650.

COLT Kansas Statehood Centennial: Frontier Scout revolver; "1861 — Kansas Centennial — 1961" on left side of 4¾" barrel; .22 LR only; walnut grips; no medallions; gold plated in entirety; originally cased in velvet-lined box with Kansas state seal inlaid in lid; 6201 made in 1961 only. Original retail, $75. Current value, $275 to $325.

COLT Geneseo Anniversary: No. 4 Derringer replica; "1836 — Geneseo Anniversary Model — 1961" on left side of 2½" barrel; .22 short only; walnut grips; gold plated in entirety; originally cased in velvet/satin-lined box; made especially for Cherry's Sporting Goods, Geneseo, Illinois; 104 made in 1961 only. Original retail, $27.50. Current value, $500 to $550.

COLT Pony Express Centennial: Frontier Scout revolver; "1860-61 — Russell, Majors and Waddell/Pony Express Centennial Model — 1960-61" on left side of 4¾" barrel; .22 LR only; varnished walnut grips; gold-plated Colt medallions; gold plated in entirety; originally cased in rosewood box with gold-plated centennial medallion in lid; 1007 made in 1961 only. Original retail, $80. Current value, $425 to $475.

COLT Civil War Centennial: single-shot replica of Colt Model 1860 Army revolver; "Civil War Centennial Model — .22 Caliber Short" on left side of 6" barrel; .22 short only; varnished walnut grips; gold-plated Colt medallions; gold-plated frame, backstrap, trigger guard assembly, balance blued; originally in leatherette case; 24,114 made in 1961 only. Original retail, $32.50. Current value, $125 to $150.

1962

COLT Rock Island Arsenal Centennial: single-shot version of Colt Model 1860 Army revolver; "1862 — Rock Island Arsenal Centennial Model — 1962" on left side of 6" barrel; .22 short only; varnished walnut grips; blued finish; originally in blue and gray leatherette case; 550 made in 1962 only. Original retail, $38.50. Current value, $200 to $250.

COLT Columbus, Ohio, Sesquicentennial: Frontier Scout revolver; "1812 — Columbus Sesquicentennial — 1962" on left side of 4¾" barrel; .22 LR only; varnished walnut grips with gold-plated medallions; gold-plated in entirety; originally cased in velvet/satin-lined walnut case; 200 made in 1962 only. Original retail, $100. Current value, $550 to $600.

COLT Fort Findlay, Ohio, Sesquicentennial: Frontier Scout revolver; "1812 — Fort Findlay Sesquicentennial — 1962" on left side of 4¾" barrel; .22 LR, .22 WRFM; varnished walnut grips; gold-plated in entirety; originally cased in red velvet/satin-lined walnut box; 110 made in 1962 only. Original retail, $89.50. Current values: $600 to $625; cased pair, .22 LR, .22 WRFM, 20 made in 1962. $2500 to $2750.

COLT New Mexico Golden Anniversary: Frontier Scout revolver; "1912 — New Mexico Golden Anniversary — 1962" wiped in gold on left side of 4¾" barrel; .22 LR only; varnished walnut grips; gold-plated medallions; barrel, frame, base pin screw, ejector rod, rod tube, tube plug and screw, bolt and trigger, hammer screws blued; balance gold plated; originally cased in redwood box with yellow satin/velvet lining; 1000 made in 1962 only. Original retail, $79.95. Current value, $350 to $375.

COLT West Virginia Statehood Centennial: Frontier Scout revolver; "1863 — West Virginia Centennial — 1963" wiped in gold on left side of 4¾" barrel; .22 LR only; pearlite grips, gold-plated medallions; blued, with gold-plated backstrap, trigger guard assembly and screws, stock screw; originally cased in blonde wood box with gold velvet/satin lining; 3452 made in 1962 only. Original retail, $75. Current value, $325 to $350.

West Virginia Statehood Centennial single-action Army revolver has same legend on barrel as .22 version; 5½" barrel; .45 Colt only; same blue/gold finish as Scout version; same type of casing; 600 made in 1963 only. Original retail, $150. Current value, $800 to $850.

1963

COLT Fort McPherson, Nebraska, Centennial: No. 4 Derringer replica; "Fort McPherson/1863 — Centennial — 1963" wiped in gold on left side of 2½" barrel; .22 short only; ivorylite grips, no medallions; gold plated with blued barrel, bolt, trigger screw, hammer and screw, trigger and stock screw; originally cased in walnut-finished box, with gold velvet/satin lining; 300 made in 1963 only. Original retail, $28.95. Current value, $350 to $400.

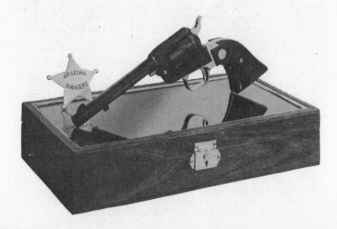

COLT Arizona Territorial Centennial: Frontier Scout revolver; "1863 — Arizona Territorial Centennial — 1963" wiped in gold on left side of 4¾" barrel; .22 LR only; pearlite grips, gold-plated medallions; gold plated, with blue barrel, frame, base pin screw, ejector rod, rod tube, tube plug and screw, bolt and trigger screws, hammer and hammer screw; originally cased in blonde-finished box, with yellow velvet/satin lining; 5355 made in 1963 only. Original retail, $75. Current value, $275 to $300.

Arizona Territorial Centennial single-action Army revolver has same legend on barrel as Scout version; 5½" barrel; .45 Colt only; same blue/gold-plated finish as Scout; same type case; 1280 made in 1963 only. Original retail, $150. Current value, $800 to $850.

COLT Carolina Charter Tercentenary: Frontier Scout revolver; "1663 — Carolina Charter Tercentenary — 1963" wiped in gold on left side of 4¾" barrel; .22 LR only; walnut grips; gold-plated medallions; gold plated, with barrel, frame, cylinder, base pin screw, ejector rod, rod tube, tube plug, tube screw, bolt, trigger and hammer screws blued; originally cased in blonde-finished box with yellow velvet/satin lining; 300 made in 1963 only. Original retail, $75. Current value, $400 to $450.

Carolina Charter Tercentenary .22/.45 Combo Set includes Frontier Scout described above, single-action Army revolver, with same legend on 5½" barrel, .45 Colt only; same finish on grips as Frontier version; larger case to fit both guns; 251 sets made in 1963 only. Original retail for set, $240. Current value, $950 to $1050.

COLT H. Cook 1 of 100: Frontier Scout/single-action Army revolvers; sold as set; "H. Cook 1 of 100" on left side of barrels; Scout has 4¾" barrel, .22 LR only; SA Army has 7½" barrel, .45 Colt only; pearlite grips; nickel-plated medallions; both nickel plated with blued frame, base pin, trigger and hammer screws; originally cased in silver-colored box with blue satin/velvet lining; 100 sets made in 1963 only for H. Cook Sporting Goods, Albuquerque, N.M. Original retail for set, $275. Current value, $1100 to $1250.

COLT Fort Stephenson, Ohio, Sesquicentennial: Frontier Scout revolver; "1813 — Fort Stephenson Sesquicentennial — 1963" wiped in silver on left side of 4¾" barrel; .22 LR only; laminated rosewood grips; nickel-plated medallions; nickel-plated finish, with blued barrel, frame, base pin screw, ejector rod, rod tube, tube plug and screw, bolt and trigger and hammer screws; originally cased in blonde-finished wood, with yellow velvet/satin lining; 200 made only in 1963. Original retail, $75. Current value, $500 to $550.

COLT Battle of Gettysburg Centennial: Frontier Scout revolver; "1863 — Battle of Gettysburg Centennial — 1963" wiped in gold on left side of 4¾" barrel; .22 LR only; walnut grips; gold-plated medallions; gold plated with blued barrel, frame, base pin screw, ejector rod tube, tube plug and screw, and bolt, trigger and hammer screws; originally cased in blonde-finished wood with yellow velvet in bottom, blue satin in lid; 1019 made in 1963 only. Original retail, $89.95. Current value, $325 to $375.

COLT Idaho Territorial Centennial: Frontier Scout revolver; "1863 — Idaho Territorial Centennial — 1963" wiped in silver on left side of 4¾" barrel; .22 LR only; pearlite grips; nickel-plated medallions; nickel plated with blue frame, barrel, base pin screw, ejector rod tube, tube plug and screw, and bolt, trigger and hammer screws; originally cased in blonde-finished wood, with gold velvet/satin lining; 902 made in 1963 only. Original retail, $75. Current value, $350 to $400.

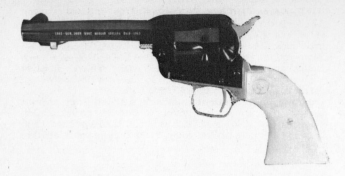

COLT General John Hunt Morgan Indian Raid: Frontier Scout revolver; "1863 — Gen. John Hunt Morgan Indian Raid — 1963" wiped in gold on left side of 4¾" barrel; .22 LR; pearlite grips, gold-plated medallions; gold plated with blued frame, barrel, cylinder, base pin screw, ejector rod, rod tube, tube plug and tube screw and bolt and trigger screw; originally cased in blonde-finished wood, with gold velvet/satin lining; 100 made in 1963 only. Original retail, $74.50. Current value, $650 to $700.

1964

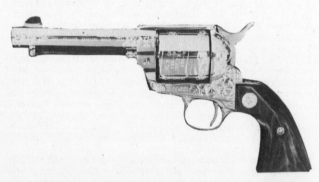

COLT Cherry's Sporting Goods 35th Anniversary: Frontier Scout/single-action Army revolvers, sold as set; "1929 — Cherry's Sporting Goods — 1964" on left side of barrel; Scout has 4¾" barrel, .22 LR only; SA Army has 4¾" barrel, .45 Colt only; both have laminated rosewood grips; gold-plated medallions; gold plated in entirety; originally cased in embossed black leatherette, with black velvet/satin lining; 100 sets made in 1964 only. Original retail, $275. Current value, $1450 to $1650.

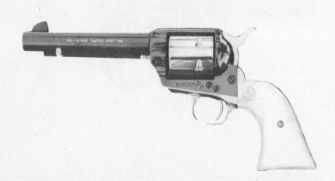

COLT Nevada Statehood Centennial: Frontier Scout revolver; "1864 — Nevada Centennial — 1964" wiped in silver on left side of 4¾" barrel; .22 LR only; pearlite grips; nickel-plated medallions; nickel-plated finish, with blued barrel, frame, base pin screw, cylin-

der, ejector rod, rod tube, tube plug and tube screw, hammer, bolt, trigger screws; originally cased in gray-finished wood with blue velvet-lined bottom, silver satin-lined lid; 3984 made in 1964 only. Original retail, $75. Used value, $300 to $325.

Nevada Statehood Centennial single-action Army revolver has same legend on barrel as Frontier Scout; 5½" barrel; .45 Colt only; grips, medallions, finish identical to Scout; same casing motif; 1688 made in 1964 only. Original retail, $150. Current value, $750 to $800.

Nevada State Centennial Frontier Scout/single-action Army set includes the two handguns described above in oversized case; 189 standard sets were made, plus 577 sets featuring extra engraved cylinders; made in 1964 only. Original retail: standard set, $240; with extra engraved cylinders, $350. Current values: standard set, $1150 to $1200; with extra engraved cylinders, $1300 to $1350.

COLT Nevada Battle Born Commemorative: Frontier Scout revolver; "1864 — Nevada 'Battle Born' — 1964" wiped in silver on left side of 4¾" barrel; .22 LR only; pearlite grips; nickel-plated medallions; nickel plated, with blued frame, barrel, base pin screw, ejector rod, tube, tube plug and screw, bolt, trigger and hammer screws; cased in blue-finished wood box, with blue velvet/satin lining; 981 made in 1964 only. Original retail, $85. Current value, $200 to $325.

Nevada Battle Born Commemorative single-action Army revolver has same legend on barrel as Frontier Scout version; 5½" barrel; .45 Colt only; same grips, finish, casing as Frontier Scout; 80 made in 1964 only. Original retail, $175. Current value, $750 to $800.

Nevada Battle Born Commemorative Frontier Scout/single-action Army set includes the two handguns previously described in oversize case; 20 sets were made in 1964 only. Original retail, $265. Current value, $1200 to $1300.

COLT Montana Territory Centennial: Frontier Scout revolver; "1864 — Montana Territory Centennial — 1964" on left side of barrel; "1889 — Diamond Jubilee Statehood — 1964" on right side; both markings wiped in gold; 4¾" barrel; .22 LR only; rosewood or pearlite grips; gold-plated medallions; gold-plated finish, except for blued barrel, frame, base pin screw, cylinder, ejector rod, rod tube, tube plug and tube screw, bolt, and trigger and hammer screws; originally cased in walnut-finished box with red velvet/satin lining; 2300 made in 1964 only. Original retail, $75. Current value, $300 to $325.

Montana Territory Centennial single-action Army revolver has same barrel markings as Frontier Scout version; 7½" barrel, .45 Colt only; same grips, finish, except frame is color case-hardened; same casing as Frontier Scout; 851 made in 1964 only. Original retail, $150. Current value, $800 to $850.

COLT Wyoming Diamond Jubilee: Frontier Scout revolver; "1890 — Wyoming Diamond Jubilee — 1965" on left side of barrel; 4¾" barrel; .22 LR only; rosewood grips, nickel-plated medallions; nickel-plated finish, except for blued barrel, frame, ejector rod, rod tube, tube plug and plug screw; cased in blonde-finished box, with blue velvet bottom lining, silver satin-lined lid; 2357 made in 1964 only. Original retail, $75. Current value, $300 to $325

COLT General Hood Centennial: Frontier Scout revolver; "1864 — General Hood's Tennessee Campaign — 1964" on left side of 4¾" barrel; .22 LR only; laminated rosewood grips, gold-plated medallions; gold-plated finish, except for blued trigger, hammer, base pin, ejector rod, rod head and screw and screws for base pin, hammer, trigger, backstrap and trigger guard; originally cased in blonde-finished wood box with green velvet/satin lining; 1503 made in 1964 only. Original retail, $75. Current value, $300 to $325.

COLT New Jersey Tercentenary: Frontier Scout revolver; "1664 — New Jersey Tercentenary — 1964" on left side of barrel; 4¾" barrel; .22 LR only; laminated rosewood grips; nickel-plated medallions; blued finish, with nickel-plated barrel, frame, ejector rod tube, tube plug and screw; originally cased in blonde-finished box with blue velvet lining in bottom, silver satin in lid; 1001 made in 1964 only. Original retail, $75. Current value, $275 to $300.

    New Jersey Tercentenary single-action Army revolver has same legend on barrel; 5½" barrel; .45 Colt only; grips, medallions, finish the same as on Frontier Scout version; same casing; 250 made in 1964 only. Original retail, $150. Current value, $850 to $900.

COLT St. Louis Bicentennial: Frontier Scout revolver; "1764 — St. Louis Bicentennial — 1964" wiped in gold on left side of 4¾" barrel; .22 LR only; laminated rosewood grips; gold-plated medallions; gold plated, except for blued frame, barrel, cylinder, ejector rod, rod tube, tube plug and screw; non-fluted cylinder; originally cased in blonde-finished wood box; yellow velvet/satin lining; 802 made in 1964 only. Original retail, $75. Current value, $300 to $325.

    St. Louis Bicentennial single-action Army revolver has same legend on barrel as Frontier Scout version; 5½" barrel; .45 Colt only; same grips, medallions, finish, casing as Scout version; 200 made in 1964 only. Original retail, $150. Current value, $800 to $850.

    St. Louis Bicentennial Frontier Scout/single-action Army set includes the two handguns described above in oversize case; 200 sets made in 1964 only. Original retail, $240. Current value, $800 to $850.

COLT California Gold Rush Commemorative: Frontier Scout revolver; "California Gold Rush Model" on left side of 4¾" barrel; .22 LR only; ivorylite grips; gold-plated medallions; gold plated in entirety; originally cased in blonde wood box; blue velvet lining in bottom, gold in lid; 500 made in 1964 only. Original retail, $79.50. Current value, $350 to $400.

    California Gold Rush single-action Army revolver has same barrel legend as Frontier Scout version; 5½" barrel; .45 Colt only; same finish, grips, casing; 130 made in 1966 only. Original retail, $175. Current value, $1250 to $1500.

COLT Pony Express Presentation: single-action Army revolver; "Russell, Majors and Waddell — Pony Express Presentation Model" on left side of barrel. Various Pony Express stop markings on backstrap; 7½" barrel; .45 Colt; walnut grips; nickel-plated medallions; nickel plated in entirety; originally cased in walnut-finished wood with transparent Lucite lid; lined with burgundy velvet; 1004 made in 1964 only. Original retail, $250. Current value, $1000 to $1100.

COLT Chamizal Treaty Commemorative: Frontier Scout revolver; "1867 Chamizal Treaty — 1964" wiped in gold on left side of 4¾" barrel; .22 LR only; pearlite grips; gold-plated medallions; gold-plated finish; blued frame, barrel, ejector rod, ejector tube, rod plug and screw, base pin and base pin screw and hammer, trigger and bolt screws; originally cased in blonde-finished wood; yellow velvet/satin lining; 450 made in 1964. Original retail, $85. Current value, $300 to $325.

    Chamizal Treaty single-action Army revolver has same legend on 5½" barrel; .45 Colt only; same grips, finish as Frontier Scout version; same type of case; 50 made in 1964. Original retail, $170. Current value, $1250 to $1350.

    Chamizal Treaty Frontier Scout/single action Army combo includes the two guns described above in one oversize case; 50 pairs made in 1965. Original retail, $280. Current value, $1850 to $2000.

COLT Col. Sam Colt Sesquicentennial Presentation: single-action Army revolver; "1815 — Col. Saml Colt Sesquicentennial Model — 1964" on left side of 7½" barrel; .45 Colt only; rosewood grips; roll-engraved scene on cylinder; nickel-plated medallions; silver-plated finish, with blued frame, barrel, ejector rod tube and screw, hammer and trigger; originally cased in varnished walnut box, with 12 dummy nickel-plated cartridges in cartridge block; burgundy velvet lining; 4750 made in 1964 only. Original retail, $225. Current value, $850 to $900.

    Sam Colt Sesquicentennial Deluxe has same specs as standard presentation model, except grips are hand-fitted rosewood with escutcheons rather than medallions; hand-engraved cylinder; case has plate marked "1 of 200"; 200 made in 1964 only. Original retail, $500. Current value, $2000 to $2100.

    Custom Deluxe model has same specs as Deluxe, except for facsimile of Samuel Colt's signature engraved on backstrap, lid of case engraved with "1 of 50"; name of purchaser engraved when requested; 50 made in 1965. Original retail, $1000. Used value, $2975 to $3050.

COLT Wyatt Earp Buntline: single-action Army revolver; "Wyatt Earp Buntline Special" on left side of 12" barrel; .45 Colt only; laminated black rosewood grips; gold-plated medallions; gold plated in entirety; originally cased in black-finished wood, lined with green velvet/satin; 150 made only in 1964. Original retail, $250. Used value, $1750 to $1850.

COLT Wichita Commemorative: Frontier Scout revolver; "1864 — Kansas Series — Wichita — 1964" wiped in silver on left side of 4¾" barrel; .22 LR only; pearlite grips; gold-plated medallions; gold plated in entirety; originally cased in blonde-finished wood; lined with red velvet/satin; 500 made in 1964 only. Original retail, $85. Current value, $300 to $325.

ITHACA Model 49 St. Louis Bicentennial: lever-action single-shot; hand-operated rebounding hammer; .22 LR, long, short; 18" barrel; Western carbine-style straight stock; open rear sight, ramp front. Only 200 manufactured in 1964. Original retail, $34.95. Current value, $250 to $275.

REMINGTON Montana Centennial: Model 600 carbine; bolt-action; 6mm Rem. only; deviates from standard Model 600 specs only in better walnut, commemorative medallion inlaid into the stock; barrel inscription reads, "1889-1964/75th Anniversary"; 1000 made in 1964 only. Original retail, $124.95. Current value, $550 to $600.

WINCHESTER Wyoming Diamond Jubilee Commemorative: Model 94 carbine; .30-30 only; 1500 made, distributed exclusively by Billings Hardware Co.; same as standard M94, except for color case-hardened, engraved receiver, commemorative inscription on barrel; brass saddle ring, loading gate; state medallion imbedded in stock; made only in 1964, with retail of $100. Current value, $1450 to $1550.

1965

COLT Dodge City Commemorative: Frontier Scout revolver; "1864 — Kansas Series — Dodge City — 1964" wiped in silver on left side of 4¾" barrel; .22 LR only; ivorylite grips; gold-plated medallions; gold-plated finish, with blued base pin and screw, ejector rod, ejector rod head, bolt and trigger screw, hammer and hammer screw, trigger; originally cased in blonde-finished wood; lined with kelly green velvet/satin; 500 made in 1965 only. Original retail, $85. Current value, $325 to $350.

COLT Colorado Gold Rush Commemorative: Frontier Scout revolver; "1858 — Colorado Gold Rush — 1878" wiped in silver on left side of 4¾" barrel; .22 LR only; laminated rosewood grips; nickel-plated medallions; gold-plated finish, with nickel-plated hammer, base pin and screw, ejector rod head, hammer and trigger screws, trigger, grip screw; originally cased in blonde-finished wood; black velvet/satin lining; 1350 made in 1965 only. Original retail, $85. Current value, $300 to $325.

COLT Oregon Trail Commemorative: Frontier Scout revolver; "Oregon Trail Model," wiped in gold, on left side of 4¾" barrel; .22 LR only; pearlite grips; gold-plated medallions; blued finish with gold-plated backstrap and trigger guard assembly and screws, hammer, trigger and screws, base pin, base pin screw and ejector rod head; originally cased in blonde-finished wood; lined with blue velvet in bottom, gold satin in lid; 1995 made only in 1965. Original retail, $75. Current value, $275 to $300.

COLT Joaquin Murrietta 1 of 1000: Frontier Scout/single-action Army combo; both have "Joaquin Murrietta 1 of 100" on left side of barrels; Scout has 4¾" barrel, .22 LR only; SAA has 5½" barrel, .45 Colt only; grips on both are pearlite, with gold-plated medallions; finish for both is gold-plated with blued barrels, frames, ejector rod tubes; originally in one oversize case of walnut-finished wood; blue velvet/satin lining; 100 sets made in 1965 only. Original retail, $350. Current value, $1450 to $1550.

COLT Forty-Niner Miner: Frontier Scout revolver; "The '49er Miner" wiped in gold on left side of 4¾" barrel; .22 LR only; laminated rosewood grips; gold-plated medallions; gold-plated finish with blued barrel, frame, backstrap and trigger guard assembly, ejector rod, tube and tube plug, ejector tube screw; originally cased in walnut-finished wood; lined with velvet in bottom, blue satin in lid; 500 made only in 1965. Original retail, $85. Current value, $300 to $325.

COLT Old Fort Des Moines Reconstruction Commemorative: Frontier Scout revolver; "Reconstruction of Old Fort Des Moines" wiped in silver on left side of 4¾" barrel; .22 LR only; pearlite grips; gold-plated medallions; gold-plated in entirety; originally cased in white-finished wood; royal purple velvet lining in bottom; white satin in lid; 700 made in 1965 only. Original retail, $89.95. Current value, $325 to $350.

   Old Fort Des Moines Reconstruction single-action Army revolver; has same legend on 5½" barrel; .45 Colt only; grips, finish the same as on Frontier Scout version; same casing; 100 made in 1965 only. Original retail, $169.95. Current value, $850 to $900.

   Old Fort Des Moines Frontier Scout/single-action Army combo has the same specs as those for two guns described above, in one oversize case; 100 sets made in 1965 only. Original retail, $289.95. Current value, $1250 to $1300.

COLT Appomattox Centennial: Frontier Scout revolver; "1865 — Appomattox Commemorative Model — 1965" wiped in silver on left side of 4¾" barrel; .22 LR only; laminated rosewood grips; nickel-plated medallions; nickel-plated finish, with blued barrel, frame, backstrap and trigger guard screws, ejector rod tube, tube plug and tube screw; originally cased in blonde-finished wood lined with blue velvet on bottom, gray satin in lid; 1001 made in 1965 only. Original retail, $75. Current value, $275 to $325.

   Appomattox Centennial Frontier single-action Army has same legend on 5½" barrel; .45 Colt only; grips, finish, casing the same as for Frontier Scout version; 250 made in 1965. Original retail, $150. Current value, $800 to $850.

   Appomattox Centennial Frontier Scout/single-action Army Combo consists of two guns described above in one oversize case; 250 sets made in 1965 only. Original retail, $240. Current value, $1100 to $1200.

COLT General Meade Campaign Commemorative: Frontier Scout revolver; "Gen. Meade Pennsylvania Campaign Model" wiped in gold on left side of 4¾" barrel; .22 LR only; ivorylite grips, gold-plated medallions; gold-plated finish; blued frame, barrel, cylinder, ejector rod tube, tube plug and screw, hammer and trigger screws; originally cased in walnut-finished wood; blue velvet lining in bottom, gold satin in lid; 1197 made in 1965 only. Original retail, $75. Current value, $300 to $325.

   General Meade Campaign single-action Army revolver has same legend on the 5½" barrel, .45 Colt only; same finish, casing as Frontier Scout version; 200 made in 1965 only. Original retail, $165. Current value, $800 to $850.

COLT St. Augustine Quadricentennial: Frontier Scout revolver; "1565 — St. Augustine Quadricentennial — 1965" wiped in gold on left side of 4¾" barrel; .22 LR only; pearlite grips; gold-plated medallions; gold-plated finish, with blued barrel, base pin, ejector rod, tube, tube plug and screw, frame, hammer and trigger screws, backstrap and trigger guard assembly and screws; cased in blonde-finished wood; gold velvet/satin lining; 500 made in 1965 only. Original retail, $85. Current value, $325 to $350.

1966

COLT Oklahoma Territory Commemorative: Frontier Scout revolver; "1890 — Oklahoma Diamond Jubilee — 1965" wiped in gold on left side of 4¾" barrel; .22 LR only laminated rosewood grips; gold-plated medallions blued finish with gold-plated backstrap and trigger guard assembly and screws, cylinder, ejector rod head, base pin and screw, bolt and trigger; cased in blonde-finished wood; red velvet/satin lining; 1343 made only in 1966. Original retail, $85. Current value, $300 to $325.

COLT Dakota Territory Commemorative: Frontier Scout revolver; "1861 — Dakota Territory — 1889" wiped in gold on left side of 4¾" barrel; .22 LR only; laminated rosewood grips; gold-plated medallions; blued finish with gold-plated backstrap and trigger guard assembly and screws, ejector rod and head, base pin, trigger, hammer, stock screw; originally cased in blonde-finished wood; red velvet/satin lining; 1000 made in 1966 only. Original retail, $85. Current value, $300 to $325.

COLT Abercrombie & Fitch Trailblazer: New Frontier single-action Army revolver; "Abercrombie & Fitch Co." wiped in gold on left side of 7½" barrel; .45 Colt only; rosewood grips; gold-plated medallions; gold-plated finish, blued barrel, cylinder, hammer, sights, ejector rod tube, ejector rod screw, case-hardened frame; roll-engraved, nonfluted cylinder; originally cased in varnished American walnut with brass-framed glass cover; bottom lined with crushed blue velvet; 200 made in 1966 with "New York" marked on butt, 100 with "Chicago" butt marking; 200 with "San Francisco" butt marking. Original retail, $275. Current value, $1950 to $2000.

COLT Indiana Sesquicentennial: Frontier Scout revolver; "1816 — Indiana Sesquicentennial — 1966" wiped in gold on left side of 4¾" barrel; .22 LR only; pearlite grips; gold-plated medallions; blued finish, with gold-plated backstrap and trigger guard assembly, base pin and screw, ejector rod head, cylinder, bolt and trigger screw, hammer and hammer screw, trigger, stock screw; originally cased in blonde-finished wood; bottom lined with gold velvet, lid with blue satin; 1500 made in 1966 only. Original retail, $85. Current value, $300 to $325.

COLT Abilene Commemorative: Frontier Scout revolver; "1866 — Kansas Series — Abilene — 1966" wiped in silver on left side of 4¾" barrel; .22 LR only; laminated rosewood grips; gold-plated

medallions; gold plated in entirety; originally cased in blonde-finished wood; blue velvet/satin lining; 500 made in 1966 only. Original retail, $95. Current value, $300 to $325.

REMINGTON 150th Anniversary Model 1100 SA: autoloading skeet shotgun; 12-ga. only; 26" barrel; vent rib; specs the same as standard Model 1100, except for stamp-engraved legend on left side of receiver: "Remington Arms Company, Inc., 1816-1966, 150th Anniversary" with corporate logo; 1000 made in 1966 only. Original retail, $185. Current value, $600 to $650.

Model 1100 TB 150th Anniversary commemorative has same specs as skeet version, except for recoil pad, 30" barrel, trap stock; same stamp-engraved legend on receiver; 1000 made in 1966 only. Original retail, $220. Current value, $650 to $675.

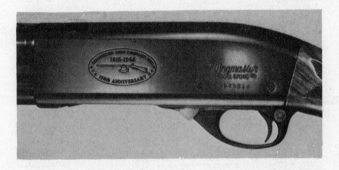

REMINGTON 150th Anniversary Model 870 SA: slide-action skeet gun; 12-ga. only; 26" barrel; vent rib; specs the same as standard Model 870, except for stamp-engraved legend on left side of receiver: "Remington Arms Company, Inc., 1816-1966, 150th Anniversary" with corporate logo; 1000 made in 1966 only. Original retail, $130. Current value, $600 to $650.

Model 870 TB 150th Anniversary commemorative has same specs as skeet version, except for recoil pad, 30" barrel, trap stock; same stamp-engraved legend on receiver; 1000 made in 1966 only. Original retail, $165. Current value, $600 to $650.

REMINGTON 150th Anniversary Model 742 ADL: autoloading rifle; .30/06 only; impressed basketweave checkering; has same specs as standard 742 ADL, except for stamp-engraved legend on left side of receiver; "Remington Arms Company Inc., 1816-1886, 150th Anniversary" with corporate logo; 1000 made in 1966 only. Original retail, $150. Current value, $350 to $400.

REMINGTON 150th Anniversary Model 760 ADL: pump-action rifle; .30/06 only; has same specs as standard 760 BDL Deluxe model, except for stamp-engraved legend on left side of receiver: "Remington Arms Company Inc., 1816-1966, 150th Anniversary," with corporate logo; 1000 made in 1966 only. Original retail, $135. Current value, $300 to $350.

REMINGTON 150th Anniversary Model 552A: autoloading rifle; .22 LR long, short; has same specs as standard Model 552, except for stamp-engraved legend on left side of receiver: "Remington Arms Company Inc., 1816-1966, 150th Anniversary," with corporate logo; 1000 made in 1966 only. Original retail, $58. Current value, $275 to $300.

REMINGTON 150th Anniversary Model 572A: slide-action rifle; .22 short, long, LR; has same specs as standard model 572, except for stamp-engraved legend on left side of receiver; "Remington Arms Company, Inc., 1816-1966, 150th Anniversary," with corporate logo; 1000 made in 1966 only. Original retail, $60. Current value, $275 to $300.

REMINGTON 150th Anniversary Nylon 66: autoloading rifle; .22 LR; has same specs as standard Nylon 66 Apache Black model, except for stamp-engraved legend on left side of receiver: "Remington Arms Company Inc., 1816-1966, 150th Anniversary," with corporate logo; 1000 made in 1966 only. Original retail, $50. Current value, $175 to $200.

WINCHESTER Nebraska Centennial Commemorative: Model 94 carbine; .30-30 only; same as standard M94 except for gold-plated loading gate, butt plate, rear barrel band, hammer; commemorative inscription on barrel, medallion in stock; only 2500 made and distributed only in Nebraska; made only in 1966. Original retail, $100. Current value, $1250 to $1300.

WINCHESTER Centennial '66 Commemorative: Model 94; rifle and carbine versions commemorate Winchester's 100th anniversary; produced in 1966 only; 100,478 were made; .30-30 only; rifle version has 26" ½-octagon barrel; full-length 8-rd. magazine; gold-plated forearm cap, receiver; post front sight, open rear; walnut stock, forearm with epoxy finish; saddle ring; brass butt plate; commemorative inscription on barrel and top tang. Retail price, $125. Used value, $400 to $425. Carbine differs only in shorter forearm, 20" barrel, 6-rd. magazine. Used value, $400 to $425. Matched set, with consecutive serial numbers, current value, $950 to $1000.

1967

COLT Bat Masterson: Frontier Scout revolver; "Lawman Series — Bat Masterson" on left side of 4¾" barrel; .22 LR only; checkered rubber eagle grips; nickel-plated finish; cased originally in black leatherette; red velvet/satin lining; 3000 made in 1967 only. Original retail, $90. Current value, $350 to $375.

Bat Masterson single-action Army has same legend on 4¾" barrel, .45 Colt only; grips, finish, casing are the same as for Frontier Scout version; 500 made in 1967 only. Original retail, $180. Current value, $850 to $900.

COLT Alamo Commemorative: Frontier Scout revolver; "Alamo Model," flanked by stars, wiped in gold on left side of 4¾" barrel; .22 LR only; ivorylite grips, with inlaid gold-plated Texas star below screw on left grip. Gold-plated finish; blued barrel, frame, ejector rod tube, tube plug and screw; originally cased in blonde-finished wood box; blue velvet/satin lining; 4250 made in 1967 only. Original retail, $85. Current value, $325 to $350.

Alamo Commemorative single-action Army has same legend on barrel; same grips, finish, but with blued barrel, frame and ejector rod tube and tube screw; same casing; 750 made in 1967 only. Original retail, $165. Current value, $800 to $850.

Alamo Commemorative Frontier Scout/single-action Army combo includes two guns described above in one oversize case; 250 sets made in 1967 only. Original retail, $265. Current value, $1100 to $1200.

COLT Coffeyville Commemorative: Frontier Scout revolver; "1866 — Kansas Series — Coffeyville — 1966" wiped in silver on left side of 4¾" barrel; .22 LR only; walnut grips; gold-plated medallions; gold-plated finish; blued backstrap and trigger guard assembly screws, base pin and screw, ejector rod, ejector rod head, hammer and hammer screw, trigger; originally cased in blonde-finished wood; black velvet/satin lining; 500 made in 1967 only. Original retail, $95. Current value, $300 to $325.

COLT Chisholm Trail Commemorative: Frontier Scout revolver; "1867 — Kansas Series — Chisholm Trail — 1967" wiped with silver on left side of 4¾" barrel; .22 LR; pearlite grips; nickel-plated medallions; blued finish, with nickel-plated backstrap and trigger guard assembly and screws, trigger, hammer, base pin, ejector rod head, stock screw; originally cased in blonde-finished wood, gold velvet/satin lining; 500 made in 1967 only. Original retail, $100. Current value, $275 to $300.

COLT Chateau Thierry Commemorative: automatic, Model 1911A1; "1917 World War I Commemorative 1967" on right side of slide; roll-engraved scene on left depicting WWI battle; 5" barrel; .45 auto; checkered walnut grips; inlaid commemorative medallions left grip inlaid with Chateau Thierry battle bar; blued finish with slide scene, serial number, banner, Colt markings wiped in gold; several features including no trigger finger relief cuts, non-grooved trigger, safety lever, adapted from original M1911 design; Standard model cased in olive drab box; Deluxe and Custom models have oiled, waxed teak cases; Deluxe model case inscribed "One of Seventy-Five/Deluxe Engraved/Chateau Thierry Commemoratives"; Custom model case inscribed "One of Twenty-Five/Custom Engraved/Chateau Thierry Commemoratives"; gun bears gold-filled signature of A.A. White, engraver; 7400 Standard versions made in 1967-68, 75 Deluxe, 25 Custom. Original retail prices: Standard, $200; Deluxe, $500; Custom, $1000. Current values: Standard, $525 to $550; Deluxe $1400 to $1500; Custom, $2250 to $2350.

REMINGTON Canadian Centennial: Model 742 rifle; autoloader; .30/06 only; same as standard model, except for impressed checkering on pistol grip; left side of receiver is engraved with maple leaves, special insignia, "1867-1967 — Canadian Centennial Gun," wiped in white; serial number is preceded by letter C; 1000 made in 1967 only. Original retail, $119.95. Current value, $500 to $525.

RUGER Canadian Centennial 10/22: Standard model of .22 rimfire rifle, with silver commemorative medal set in the stock; top of

the receiver is engraved with a design composed of the Canadian Exposition symbol, branches of the Canadian maple leaf and the words, "Canadian Centennial Guns." Issued in 1967; 4430 made. Original price, $99.50. Used value, $450 to $500.

WINCHESTER Alaskan Purchase Centennial: Model 94 rifle; sold only in Alaska; receiver is engraved in 19th Century filigree for "antique" appeal; centered in stock is the official Alaskan Purchase centennial medallion with totem pole symbol of the state; barrel is

26", with magazine capacity of 8 rds.; other facets are standard of Model 94. Introduced, 1967. Original price, $125. Current value, $1400 to $1500.

WINCHESTER Canadian Centennial: Model 64; action obviously is the Model 94; not to be confused with Winchester's Model 64 boy's rifle, discontinued in 1963. Canadian commemorative is in .30-30 caliber, with octagonal 26" rifle or 20" carbine barrel;

black-chromed receiver is engraved with maple leaf motif; forearm tip is black chromed; straight stock is finished with "antique gloss." Both versions have a dovetail bead post front sight, buckhorn rear. Carbine is equipped with saddle ring, has 6-shot magazine, the

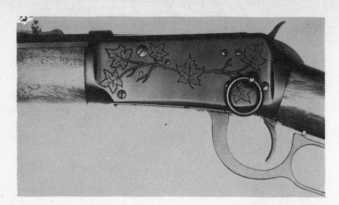

rifle, 8. Gold-filled inscription on barrel reads, "Canadian Centennial 1867-1967." Introduced in 1967. Original price for rifle or carbine, $125; matching set, with consecutive serial numbers, $275. Current values: rifle, $350 to $400; carbine, $375 to $425; matched set, $1100 to $1200.

1968

COLT Nebraska Centennial: Frontier Scout revolver; "1867 — Nebraska Centennial — 1967" on left side of 4¾" barrel; .22 LR; pearlite grips; gold-plated barrel, frame, hammer, trigger, ejector rod head, stock screw; originally cased in blonde-finished wood; lined with blue velvet in bottom, gold satin in lid; 7001 made in 1968 only. Original retail, $100. Current value, $275 to $300.

COLT Gen. Nathan Bedford Forrest: Frontier Scout revolver; "General Nathan Bedford Forrest" on left side of 4¾" barrel; .22 LR only; laminated rosewood grips; gold-plated medallions; gold-plated finish; blued cylinder, backstrap and trigger guard assembly; originally cased in dark brown leatherette; red velvet/satin lining; 3000 made in 1968-69. Original retail, $110. Current value, $275 to $300.

COLT Belleau Wood Commemorative: automatic; Model 1911A1; "1917 World War I Commemorative 1967" on right side of slide; roll engraved scene on left side of machine gun battle; 5" barrel; .45 auto only; rosewood grips inlaid with commemorative medallions; left grip inlaid with Belleau Wood battle bar; blued finish; slide scene, serial number, banner, Colt markings wiped in gold on Standard model; Deluxe version has slide, frame hand engraved, serial numbers gold-inlaid; Custom has more elaborate engraving; the same features of 1911 model adapted to Chateau Thierry model are incorporated; cases are same as Chateau Thierry model, with brass plate for Deluxe engraved "One of Seventy-Five/Deluxe Engraved/Belleau Wood Commemorative"; plate on Custom model reads "One of Twenty-Five/Custom Engraved/Belleau Wood Commemoratives"; production began in 1968, with 7400 Standard types, 75 Deluxe, 25 Custom. Original retail: Standard, $200; Deluxe, $500; Custom, $1000. Current values: Standard, $525 to $550; Deluxe, $1500 to $1600; Custom, $2250 to $2300.

COLT Pawnee Trail Commemorative: Frontier Scout revolver; "1868 — Kansas Series — Pawnee Trail — 1968" wiped in silver on left side of 4¾" barrel; .22 LR; laminated rosewood grips; nickel-plated medallions; blued finish; nickel-plated backstrap and trigger guard assembly and screws, cylinder, base pin, ejector rod head, trigger, hammer, stock screw; originally cased in blonde-finished wood; lined with blue velvet in bottom, silver satin in lid; 501 made in 1968. Original retail, $110. Current value, $275 to $300.

COLT Pat Garrett Commemorative: Frontier Scout revolver; "Lawman Series — Pat Garrett" on right side of 4¾" barrel; .22 LR only; pearlite grips; gold-plated medallions; gold-plated finish; nickel-plated barrel, frame, backstrap and trigger guard assembly, ejector rod; loading gate is gold plated; originally cased in black leatherette with gold velvet/satin lining; 3000 made in 1968 only. Original retail, $110. Current value, $325 to $350.

   Pat Garrett single-action Army revolver has same barrel legend; 5½" barrel; .45 Colt only; same grips, finish, casing as Frontier Scout version; 500 made in 1968. Original retail, $200. Current value, $850 to $900.

COLT Santa Fe Trail Commemorative: Frontier Scout revolver; "Kansas Series — Santa Fe Trail — 1968" wiped in silver on left side of 4¾" barrel; .22 LR; ivorylite grips; nickel-plated medallions; blued finish with nickel-plated backstrap and trigger guard assembly and screws, hammer, trigger, stock screw, base pin, ejector rod head; originally cased in blonde-finished wood; green velvet/satin lining; 501 made in 1968-69. Original retail, $120. Current value, $275 to $300.

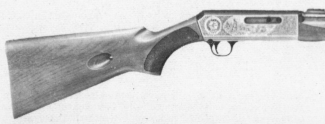

FRANCHI Centennial: semiautomatic take-down rifle, .22 LR only; commemorates 1868-1968 centennial of S.A. Luigi Franchi; centennial seal engraved on receiver; 21" barrel, 11-rd. butt-stock magazine; hand-checkered European walnut stock, forearm; open rear sight, gold bead front on ramp. Deluxe model has better grade wood, fully engraved receiver. Made only in 1968. Original retail: deluxe, $124.95; standard, $86.95. Current values: deluxe model, $450 to $475; standard model, $300 to $325.

WINCHESTER Buffalo Bill Commemorative: Model 94; available with either 20" or 26" barrel, both with bead post front sights, semi-buckhorn rear sights. Hammer, trigger, loading gate, forearm tip, saddle ring, crescent butt plate are nickel plated. Barrel, tang are inscribed respectively, "Buffalo Bill Commemorative" and "W.F. Cody — Chief of Scouts." Receiver is embellished with scrollwork. American walnut stock has Buffalo Bill Memorial Assn. medallion imbedded; rifle has 8-rd. tubular magazine, carbine, 6 rds. Introduced, 1968. Original price, $129.95. Current values: rifle, $300 to $325; carbine, $300 to $325.

WINCHESTER Illinois Sesquicentennial: Model 94; standard design, except for words, "Land of Lincoln," and a profile of Lincoln engraved on the receiver, with gold-filled inscription on barrel, "Illinois Sesquicentennial, 1818-1968"; gold-plated metal butt plate, trigger, loading gate and saddle ring. Official souvenir medallion is imbedded in the walnut stock. This was the first state commemorative to be sold outside the celebrating state by Winchester. Introduced in 1968. Original price, $110. Current value, $300 to $325.

1969

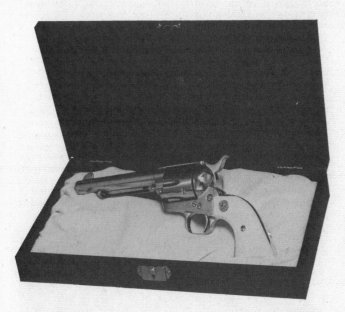

COLT Alabama Sesquicentennial: Frontier Scout revolver; "1819 — Alabama Sesquicentennial — 1969" on left side of 4¾" barrel; .22 LR only; ivorylite grips; gold-plated medallions; gold-plated finish; nickel-plated loading gate, cylinder, ejector rod, rod head, and tube, base pin and screw, bolt and trigger guard assembly screws, hammer and screw, trigger; originally cased in red leatherette-covered wood box; white velvet lining in bottom, red satin in lid; 3001 made in 1969. Original retail, $110. Current value, $300 to $325.

COLT Golden Spike: Frontier Scout revolver; "1869 — Golden Spike — 1969" on right side of 6" barrel; standard barrel markings on left; both wiped in gold; .22 LR only; sand-blasted walnut-stained fir grips; gold-plated medallions; gold-plated finish; blued barrel, frame, backstrap and trigger guard assembly and ejector tube plug and screw; originally cased in hand-stained, embossed simulated mahogany; 11,000 made in 1969. Original retail, $135. Current value, $300 to $325.

COLT Wild Bill Hickok Commemorative: Frontier Scout revolver; "Lawman Series — Wild Bill Hickok" wiped in silver on right side of 6" barrel; .22 LR only; nonfluted cylinder; pearlite grips; nickel-plated medallions; nickel-plated finish; blued barrel, frame, ejector tube screw; originally cased in black leatherette-covered box; bottom lined in blue velvet, lid in silver satin; 3000 made, production began in 1969. Original retail, $116.60. Current value, $325 to $350.

Wild Bill Hickok Commemorative single-action Army has same legend on 7½" barrel; .45 Colt only; same finish as Frontier Scout version, except for nickel-plated loading gate; same casing; 500 made, production beginning in 1969. Original retail, $220. Current value, $850 to $900.

COLT Second Battle of the Marne Commemorative: automatic, Model 1911A1; "1917 World War I Commemorative 1967"

on right side of slide; roll-engraved combat scene on left side of slide; 5" barrel; .45 auto; white French holly grips; inlaid commemorative medallions; left grip inlaid with 2nd Battle of the Marne battle bar; blue finish, with slide engraving, serial number on Standard, banner, other markings wiped in gold; Deluxe and Custom models are hand engraved, with serial numbers gold inlaid; work on Custom model is in greater detail; cases are same as others in series, except Deluxe case has brass plate inscribed "One of Seventy-Five/Deluxe Engraved/2nd Battle of the Marne Commemorative"; Custom case has same type of plate inscribed "One of Twenty-Five/Custom Engraved/2nd Battle of the Marne Commemorative"; 7400 Standard guns made in 1969; 75 Deluxe; 25 Custom. Original retail: Standard, $220; Deluxe, $500; Custom, $1000. Current values: Standard, $525 to $550; Deluxe, $1500 to $1600; Custom, $2250 to $2300.

COLT Shawnee Trail Commemorative: Frontier Scout revolver; "1869 — Kansas Series — Shawnee Trail — 1969" wiped in silver on left side of 4¾" barrel; .22 LR only; laminated rosewood grips; nickel-plated medallions; blued finish; nickel-plated backstrap and trigger guard assembly and screws, cylinder, base pin, ejector rod head, hammer, trigger and stock screw; originally cased in blonde-finished wood; red velvet/satin lining; 501 made in 1969 only. Original retail, $120. Current value, $275 to $300.

COLT Texas Ranger Commemorative: single-action Army revolver; "Texas Ranger Commemoratives/One Riot-One Ranger" wiped in silver on left side of barrel; "Texas Rangers" roll engraved on backstrap; sterling silver star, wreath on top of backstrap behind hammer; YO Ranch brand stamped on bottom of backstrap; 7½" barrel; .45 Colt only; Standard model has rosewood grips, silver miniature Ranger badge inlaid in left grip; blued finish; case-hardened frame; nickel-plated trigger guard, base pin and screw, ejector rod and head, ejector tube screw; gold-plated stock screw, stock escutcheons, medallions. First 200 are custom models, with finish, decoration to customer's desires at increasing prices; custom-finished guns had deluxe engraved serial numbers, ivory grips with star inlay; originally cased in special hand-rubbed box with drawers, glass top; red velvet lining; 200 Custom, 800 Standard guns made; production began in 1969. Original values: Custom, varying with customer's desires; Standard, $650. Current values: Standard, $850 to $900; Custom, $1450 to $1500.

COLT Arkansas Territorial Sesquicentennial: Frontier Scout revolver; "1819 — Arkansas Territory Sesquicentennial — 1969" on left side of 4¾" barrel; .22 LR only; laminated rosewood grips; gold-plated medallions; blued frame, backstrap and trigger guard assembly, ejector rod head; gold-plated stock screw nut; originally cased in blonde-finished basswood; red velvet/satin lining; 3500 made; production began in 1969. Original retail, $110. Current value, $225 to $250.

COLT Meuse Argonne Commemorative: automatic; Model 1911A1; "1917 World War I Commemorative 1967" on right side of slide; left has roll-engraved charge on pillbox on Standard; slides, frames on Deluxe, Custom models are hand engraved, serial numbers inlaid in gold; Custom model is more elaborately engraved, inlaid; 5" barrel, .45 auto only; varnished crotch walnut grips; inlaid commemorative medallions left grip inlaid with Meuse Argonne battle bar; blued finish; engraving, numbers et al., gold

wiped on Standard model; same case as earlier WWI Commemoratives; brass plate for Deluxe reads "One of Seventy-Five/Deluxe Engraved/Meuse Argonne Commemoratives"; plate on Custom case is inscribed "One of Seventy-Five/Custom Engraved/Meuse Argonne Commemoratives"; production began in 1969; 7400 Standard, 75 Deluxe, 25 Custom. Original retail: Standard, $220; Deluxe, $500; Custom, $1000. Current values: Standard, $525 to $550; Deluxe, $1500 to $1600; Custom, $2250 to $2300.

COLT California Bicentennial: Frontier Scout revolver; "1769 — California Bicentennial — 1969" on left side of 6" barrel; .22 LR only; laminated rosewood grips; gold-plated medallions; gold-plated finish; all screws nickel-plated, except base pin, grip screws; hammer, trigger also nickel plated; originally cased in California redwood; black velvet/satin lining; 5000 made in 1969-70. Original retail, $135. Current value, $275 to $300.

COLT Fort Larned Commemorative: Frontier Scout revolver; "1869 — Kansas Series — Fort Larned — 1969" on left side of 4¾" barrel; .22 LR; pearlite grips; nickel-plated medallions; nickel-plated finish; blued backstrap and trigger guard assembly, base pin and screw, cylinder, ejector rod head and tube screw, hammer and stock screw, bolt and trigger screw; originally cased in blonde-finished wood; blue velvet lining in bottom; silver satin in lid; 500 made in 1969-70. Original retail, $120. Current value, $275 to $300.

WINCHESTER Golden Spike: Model 94; features 20" barrel with twin barrel bands plated in yellow gold; yellow gold receiver, engraved with decorative scrolled border on right side, inscribed on other side with railroad spike flanked by dates, 1869 and 1969. Barrel carries "Golden Spike Commemorative" inscription; upper tang bears words "Oceans United By Rail." Butt stock, forearm are straight-line design of satin-finished American walnut, with fluted comb. Inset in stock is centennial medallion of engines of Central Pacific, Union Pacific meeting on May 10, 1869. It has straight brass butt plate, blued saddle ring; chambered for .30-30; weight is 7 lb. Introduced in 1969. Original retail price, $119.95. Current value, $300 to $325.

WINCHESTER Theodore Roosevelt Commemorative: Model 94 rifle and carbine; made in 1969 only; 49,505 manufactured; .30-30 only; rifle has 26" octagonal barrel; 6-rd. half-magazine; forearm cap, upper tang, receiver plated with white gold; receiver engraved with American eagle, "26th President 1901-1909," Roosevelt's facsimile signature; contoured lever, half pistol grip; medallion in stock. Retail price, $125. Used value, $400 to $425. Carbine differs from rifle in shorter forearm, full-length 6-rd tubular magazine; 20" barrel. Current value, $350 to $400. Matched set with consecutive serial numbers, $1000 to $1100.

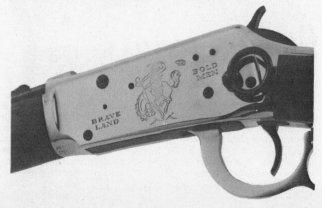

WINCHESTER Cowboy Commemorative: Model 94; receiver, upper and lower tang, lever, barrel bands are nickel plated; butt plate is stainless steel, with tang that extends over top of stock for square comb look; stock is straight grip with extended forearm of American walnut; imbedded in right side of stock is medallion of cowboy roping a steer; etched on left side of receiver, "Brave Land — Bold Men." Opposite side is engraved with coiled lariat, spurs; barrel is 20", carrying "Cowboy Commemorative"; upper tang has inscription, "Winchester Model 1894." Has adjustable semi-buckhorn rear sight, blued saddle ring; in .30-30 only. Introduced in 1969; original retail price, $125. Current value, $375 to $425.

1970

MARLIN Model 39 Century Ltd: marking Marlin Centennial, 1870 to 1970, specs are same as standard Model 39A, except for square lever, fancy walnut straight-grip uncheckered stock, forearm; 20" octagonal barrel, brass forearm cap; nameplate inset in stock, butt plate. Produced only in 1970. Original retail, $125. Current value, $275 to $300.

MARLIN Centennial Matched Pair: combines presentation-grade Model 336 centerfire, rimfire Model 39, in luggage-type case; matching serial numbers, for additional collector value. Both rifles have fancy walnut straight-grip stocks, forearms; brass forearm caps, brass butt plates, engraved receivers with inlaid medallions. Model 336 is chambered for .30-30 only, Model 39 for .22 LR, .22 long, .22 short cartridges. Only 1000 sets were manufactured in 1970. Original retail, $750. Current value, $1100 to $1250.

SAVAGE Anniversary Model 1895: replica of Savage Model 1895; hammerless lever-action; marks 75th anniversary of Savage Arms Corp. (1895-1970); .308 Win. only; 24" octagon barrel; 5-rd. rotary magazine; engraved receiver, brass-plated lever; brass butt plate; brass medallion inlaid in stock; uncheckered walnut straight-grip stock, Schnabel-type forearm. Made only in 1970; 9999 produced. Original retail, $195. Current value, $450 to $500.

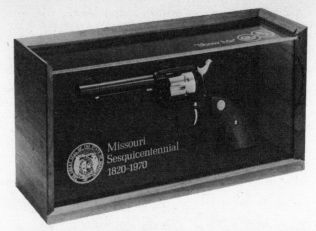

COLT World War II/European Theater: automatic; Model 1911A1; slide is marked "World War II Commemorative/European Theater of Operations" on left side; right side is roll-engraved with major sites of activity; 5" barrel; .45 auto only; bird's-eye maple grips; gold-plated medallions; nickel-plated finish in entirety; originally cased in oak box with oak cartridge block; lid removable; 7 dummy cartridges included; infantry blue velvet lining; 11,500 made; production began in 1970. Original retail, $250. Current value, $600 to $650.

COLT World War II/Pacific Theater: automatic, Model 1911A1; slide is marked "World War II Commemorative/Pacific Theater of Operations" on right side; left side roll-engraved with names of 10 major battle areas; both sides of slide bordered in roll-marked palm leaf design; 5" barrel; .45 auto only; Brazilian rosewood grips; gold-plated medallions; nickel plated in entirety; originally cased in Obichee wood; light green velvet lining; 7 nickel-plated dummy cartridges in cartridge block; 11,500 made; production began in 1970. Original retail, $250. Current value, $600 to $650.

COLT Maine Sesquicentennial: Frontier Scout revolver; "1820 — Maine Sesquicentennial — 1970" on left side of 4¾" barrel; .22 LR only; nonfluted cylinder; pearlite grips; gold-plated medallions; gold-plated finish; nickel-plated backstrap and trigger guard assembly, cylinder, base pin screw, hammer and hammer screw, ejector rod, ejector rod head, ejector tube screw, bolt and trigger screw; originally cased in natural knotty white pine; lined with royal blue velvet in bottom; light blue satin in lid; 3000 made in 1970. Original retail, $120. Current value, $275 to $300.

COLT Missouri Territorial Sesquicentennial: Frontier Scout revolver; "1820 — Missouri Sesquicentennial — 1970" wiped in gold on left side of 4¾" barrel; .22 LR only; walnut grips; gold-plated medallions; blued finish; gold-plated cylinder, loading gate, base pin, ejector rod head, ejector tube, tube screw, bolt and trigger screw, hammer, trigger, stock screw, top backstrap screws; originally cased in natural finish willow, lined in red velvet; 3000 made in 1970. Original retail, $125. Current value, $275 to $300.

Missouri Territorial Sesquicentennial single-action Army has same legend on the 5½" barrel, .45 Colt only; grips, medal-

lions, finish and plating are same as Frontier Scout version, except for case-hardened frame, loading gate; same casing; 900 made; production started in 1970. Original retail, $220. Current value, $700 to $750.

COLT Wyatt Earp Commemorative: Frontier Scout revolver; "Lawman Series — Wyatt Earp" on right side of barrel; standard model markings on left side; 12" Buntline barrel; .22 LR only; walnut grips; nickel-plated medallions blued finish; nickel-plated barrel, cylinder, ejector tube plug, ejector tube screw, rod head, base pin and base pin screw, hammer, trigger and backstrap and trigger guard assembly; originally cased in black leatherette-covered box; bottom lined with burgundy velvet; lid with red satin; 3000 made; production started in 1970. Original retail, $125. Current value, $385 to $400.

Wyatt Earp single-action Army has same legend on barrel, but wiped in silver; 16⅛" barrel; .45 Colt only; same grips, medallions as Frontier Scout version; blued finish; case-hardened frame; nickel-plated hammer, trigger, base pin, base pin crosslatch assembly; same casing as Frontier Scout; 500 made; production began in 1970. Original retail, $395. Current value, $1350 to $1400.

COLT Fort Riley Commemorative: Frontier Scout revolver, "1870 — Kansas Series — Fort Riley — 1970" wiped in black on left side of 4¾" barrel; .22 LR only; ivorylite grips; nickel-plated medallions; nickel-plated finish; blued backstrap and trigger guard assembly, cylinder, base pin and screw, ejector rod head and tube screw, bolt and trigger screw, hammer and screw, trigger, stock screw; originally cased in blonde-finished wood; black velvet/satin lining; 500 made in 1970. Original retail, $130. Current value, $275 to $300.

COLT Fort Hays Commemorative: Frontier Scout revolver; "1870 — Fort Hays — 1970" wiped in silver on left side of 4¾" barrel; .22 LR only; hard rubber grips; nickel-plated finish; blued barrel, backstrap and trigger guard assembly screws, cylinder, base pin screw, ejector tube screw, bolt and trigger screw, hammer screw, trigger; originally cased in blonde-finished wood; bottom lined with blue velvet, gold satin in lid; 500 made in 1970. Original retail, $130. Current value, $300 to $325.

WINCHESTER Lone Star Commemorative: Model 94; produced in rifle version with 26" barrel and carbine with 20" length. Receiver, upper and lower tang, lever, forearm cap, magazine tube cap all are gold plated; butt plate is crescent shaped, solid brass. Stocks are American walnut with half pistol grip, fluted comb; commemorative medal with faces of Sam Houston, Stephen F. Austin, William Travis, Jim Bowie and Davy Crockett is inset in right side of stock. Left side of receiver is engraved with star and dates, 1845, 1970; both sides are bordered with series of stars; barrel carries inscription, "Lone Star Commemorative." Upper tang has "Under Six Flags," referring to banners of Spain, France, Mexico, Texas Republic, Confederacy and United States, which have flown over territory. It has bead post front sight, semi-buckhorn rear, plus saddle ring. Introduced in 1970; original price, $140 for either rifle or carbine; $305 for matched set with consecutive serial numbers. Current values: carbine, $400 to $425; rifle, $400 to $425; matched set, $1000 to $1100.

1971

HARRINGTON & RICHARDSON Anniversary Model 1873: replica of Officer's Model 1873 Trapdoor Springfield commemorating 100th anniversary of H&R (1871-1971). Single-shot action; .45-70 only; 26" barrel; engraved receiver, breech block, hammer, lock, plate, butt plate; hand-checkered walnut stock with inlaid brass commemorative plate; peep rear sight, blade front; ramrod. Made only in 1971. Production limited to 10,000. Current value, $500 to $525.

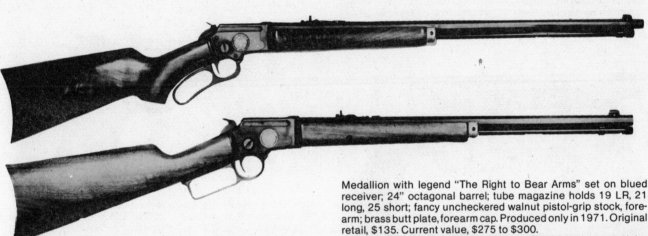

Medallion with legend "The Right to Bear Arms" set on blued receiver; 24" octagonal barrel; tube magazine holds 19 LR, 21 long, 25 short; fancy uncheckered walnut pistol-grip stock, forearm; brass butt plate, forearm cap. Produced only in 1971. Original retail, $135. Current value, $275 to $300.

    Article II carbine is same as Article II rifle, except it has straight-grip stock, square lever, shorter magazine, reduced capacity; 20" octagonal barrel. Produced only in 1971. Original retail, $135. Current value, $300 to $325.

MARLIN 39A Article II: same general specs as Model 39A; commemorates National Rifle Association Centennial, 1871-1971.

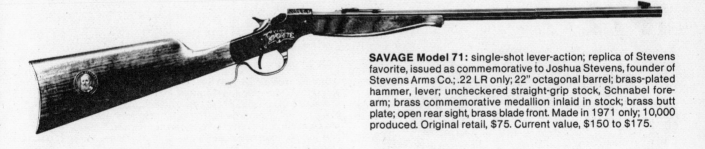

SAVAGE Model 71: single-shot lever-action; replica of Stevens favorite, issued as commemorative to Joshua Stevens, founder of Stevens Arms Co.; .22 LR only; 22" octagonal barrel; brass-plated hammer, lever; uncheckered straight-grip stock, Schnabel forearm; brass commemorative medallion inlaid in stock; brass butt plate; open rear sight, brass blade front. Made in 1971 only; 10,000 produced. Original retail, $75. Current value, $150 to $175.

WINCHESTER National Rifle Association Centennial Model: introduced in two versions: musket and rifle, both on Model 94 actions; musket resembles Model 1895 NRA musket with military lever to meet requirements for NRA match competition at turn of century; has 26" tapered, round barrel; full-length American walnut forearm; black-chromed steel butt plate; rear sight has calibrated folding rear leaf sight, blade front sight; magazine holds 7 rds.

    Rifle model resembles Model 64, also made on 94 action. Has

half magazine holding 5 rds., 24" tapered, round barrel, hooded ramp and bead post front sight, adjustable semi-buckhorn rear sight, contoured lever, blued steel forearm cap.

Both models are .30-30, have quick-detachable sling swivels; receivers are black-chromed steel; NRA seal in silver-colored metal is set in right side of stocks; left side of receivers inscribed appropriately with "NRA Centennial Musket" or "NRA Centennial Rifle." Both were introduced in 1971; retail price on each was $149.95; matched set with consecutive serial numbers, $325. Current values: musket, $325 to $350; rifle, $325 to $350; cased set, $1000 to $1100.

COLT Fort Scott Commemorative: Frontier Scout revolver; "1871 — Kansas Series — Fort Scott — 1971" on left side of 4¾" barrel; .22 LR only; checkered rubber, eagle-style grips; nickel-plated finish; blued barrel, cylinder, base pin screw, ejector tube screw, bolt and trigger screw, hammer, hammer screw, trigger; originally cased in blonde-finished wood; gold velvet/satin lining; 500 made in 1971. Original retail, $130. Current value, $275 to $300.

walnut, with inlaid NRA plate; gold velvet/satin lining; 2412 .357 magnums, 4131 .45 Colts made; production began in 1971. Original retail, $250. Current value, $700 to $750.

COLT NRA Centennial Commemorative: single-action Army; "1871 NRA Centennial 1971" wiped in gold on left side of 4¾", 5½", or 7½" barrels; .357 magnum, .45 Colt; goncalo alves grips; gold-plated NRA medallion inlays; blued finish; case-hardened frame; nickel-silver grip screw escutcheons; originally cased in

COLT NRA Centennial Commemorative: automatic; Gold Cup National Match model; "1871 NRA Centennial 1971/The First 100 Years of Service/.45 Automatic Caliber" wiped in gold on left side of slide; MK IV barrel; Eliason rear sight; 5" barrel; .45 auto only; checkered walnut grips; gold-plated NRA medallion inlays; blued, has same type of case as NRA commemorative SAA; 2500 made; production began in 1971. Original retail, $250. Current value, $600 to $650.

1972

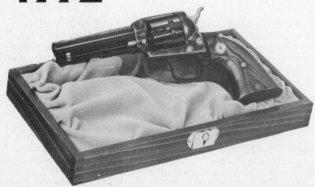

COLT Florida Territorial Sesquicentennial: Frontier Scout revolver; "1822 — Florida Territory — 1972" on left side of 4¾" barrel; .22 LR only; cypress wood grips; gold-plated medallions, blued finish; case-hardened frame; loading gate; gold-plated base pin, base pin screw, ejector rod head and screws, hammer, trigger and trigger screws; originally cased in cypress wood box; gold velvet/satin lining; 2001 made; production began in 1972. Original retail, $125. Current value, $275 to $300.

MARLIN Model 336 Zane Grey: same specs as Model 336A, except in .30-30 only; 22" octagonal barrel. Commemorates centennial of Zane Grey's birth, 1872 to 1972; commemorative medallion attached to receiver; selected uncheckered walnut pistol-grip stock, forearm; brass forearm cap, butt plate; 10,000 produced with special serial numbers, ZG1 through ZG10,000. Produced only in 1972. Original retail, $150. Current value, $375 to $400.

1973

SAKO Golden Anniversary Model: has same specs as Sako long-action Deluxe sporter; 7mm Rem magnum only; floor plate, trigger guard, receiver feature gold oak leaf, acorn decoration; hand-checkered select European walnut stock, hand-carved oak leaf pattern. Commemorates firm's 50th anniversary; only 1000 made in 1973. Current value, $1300 to $1350.

WINCHESTER Texas Ranger Commemorative: Model 94; features stock, forearm of semi-fancy walnut, with the butt stock having square comb, metal butt plate. Chambered in .30-30, tube magazine holds 6 rds.; a facsimile of Texas Ranger star badge is imbedded in the stock; saddle ring is included. Of standard grade, only 4850 were released in April 1973, all of them in the state of Texas. Another 150 Special Edition guns, at $1000 each, were released, in presentation cases, only to the Texas Ranger Association. These were hand-checkered, with full fancy walnut stocks, barrel and receiver highly polished. Magazine holds only 4 rds; gun has 16" barrel, weighs 6 lbs.; standard model weighs 7 lbs.; has 20" barrel. With Special Edition guns, commemorative star is mounted inside the presentation case instead of in the stock. Also introduced April 1973. Original prices: standard model, $134.95; Special Edition, $1000. Current values: standard model, $550 to $600; Special Edition, $3000 to $3500.

CHURCHILL One of One Thousand: bolt-action; .270 Win., 7mm Rem. magnum, .308, .30/06, .300 Win. magnum, .375 H&H magnum, .458 Win. magnum; 5-rd. magazine in standard calibers, 3 rds. in magnum; made on Mauser-type action; classic French walnut stock; hand-checkered pistol-grip, forearm; recoil pad, cartridge trap in butt; sling swivels. Manufactured in England in 1973 to commemorate Interarms' 20th anniversary. Only 1000 made. Current value, $2500 to $2750.

COLT Arizona Ranger Commemorative: Frontier Scout revolver; "Arizona Ranger Commemorative" on left side of 4¾" barrel; .22 LR only; laminated rosewood grips; nickel-plated medallions; blued finish; case-hardened frame; nickel-plated backstrap and trigger guard assembly, hammer, trigger, base pin, base pin assembly, screw for backstrap/trigger guard assembly, grips; originally cased in walnut with glass window lid; replica Arizona Ranger badge included in case; lined with maroon velvet; 3001 made; production began in 1973. Original retail, $135. Current value, $275 to $300.

COLT Peacemaker Centennial: single-action Army revolver, Frontier Six Shooter configuration; "The Frontier Six-Shooter"

etched on left side of barrel, "1873 Peacemaker Centennial 1973" roll marked on right side; 7½" barrel; .44-40 only; checkered rubber eagle-style grips; nickel-plated in entirety; originally cased in leather-covered wood box; brown velvet lining; 1500 made; production began in 1973. Original retail, $300. Current value, $800 to $850.

Peacemaker Centennial in .45 Colt Peacemaker configuration has "1873 Peacemaker Centennial 1973" roll marked on left side of 7½" barrel; .45 Colt only; one-piece varnished walnut grip; blued finish; case-hardened frame, hammer; originally cased in oiled walnut with brass-framed glass cover; maroon velvet lining; 1500 made; production began in 1973. Original retail, $300. Current value, $750 to $800.

Peacemaker Centennial .45 Colt/.44-40 combo includes both guns described above in oversize case of walnut-stained willow; lined with dark maroon velvet; matching serial numbers on guns; 500 sets made in 1973. Original retail, $625. Current value, $1850 to $1900.

REMINGTON 1973 Ducks Unlimited Commemoratives: Model 1100 autoloading shotgun; 12-ga. only; 30" barrel; full choke; vent rib. Other specs the same as standard Model 1100, except that serial number is preceded by DU; Ducks Unlimited medallion, surrounded by gilded scrollwork, is attached to left side of receiver; 500 made in 1973 only. Original retail, $230. Current value, $650 to $750.

SMITH & WESSON Texas Ranger Commemorative: Model 19 .357 Combat Magnum; 4" barrel; side plate stamped with Texas Ranger commemorative seal; unchecked goncalo alves stocks; marketed with specially designed Bowie-type knife in presentation case. Commemorated the 150th anniversary of the Texas Rangers. Reported 8000 sets made in 1973. Current value, $650 to $700.

1974

CHARLES DALY Wildlife Commemorative: over/under; 12-ga.; trap and skeet models only; has same general specs as Diamond Grade over/under; fine scrollwork on left side of receiver, duck scene engraved on right side. Manufactured in Japan 1974. Reported 500 guns made. Current value, $850 to $900.

REMINGTON 1974 Ducks Unlimited Commemorative: Model 870 pump-action, with gilded scroll receiver, special serial numbers, DU color medallion set in receiver. Made only in 1974 for auction by DU. Current value, $550 to $600.

1975

MOSSBERG Duck Stamp Commemorative: same as the Model 500DSPR Pigeon Grade 12-ga. magnum heavy duck gun; features a heavy 30" vent-rib barrel; full choke only; receiver carries an etching of a wood duck. Gun was marketed with a special wall plaque commemorating, with the shotgun, the Migratory Bird Hunting Stamp Program. Only 1000 made in 1975. Current value, $500 to $550.

1976

BROWNING Bicentennial 78: single-shot Model 78; .45-70; same specs as standard model, except for bison and eagle engraved on receiver, scroll engraving on lever, both ends of barrel, butt plate, top of receiver; high-grade walnut stock, forearm. Manufactured in Japan. Marketed with engraved hunting knife, commemorative medallion, alder presentation case. Gun and knife serial numbers match, beginning with 1776. Only 1000 sets made. Manufactured only in 1976. Current value for set, $2250 to $2500.

BROWNING Bicentennial Superposed: over/under; 12-ga.; same basic specs as standard Superposed shotgun, but side plates have engraved, gold-inlaid turkey-hunting scene on right side, U.S. flag, bald eagle on left. State markings are in gold on blue background; hand-checkered American walnut straight-grip stock, Schnabel forearm; marketed in velvet-lined walnut presentation case. Only 51 made; one for each state and District of Columbia. Manufactured in Belgium, 1976. Current value, $14,000-plus.

COLT Bicentennial Set: includes Colt SAA revolver, Python revolver and 3rd Model Dragoon revolver, with accessories; all have rosewood stocks, matching roll-engraved unfluted cylinders, blued finish, silver medallion bearing the Seal of the United States; Dragoon has silver grip frame; all revolvers in set have matching serial numbers, 0001 through 1776. Marketed with deluxe three-drawer walnut presentation case, reproduction volume of *Armsmear*. Made only in 1976. Current value for set, $1850 to $1900.

ITHACA Bicentennial Model 37: slide-action; 12-ga.; has basic specs of Model 37 Supreme, except for Bicentennial design etched into receiver, serialized USA 0001 to USA 1976; full fancy walnut stock, slide handle. Only 1976 made in 1976. Marketed in presentation case. Current value, $450 to $500.

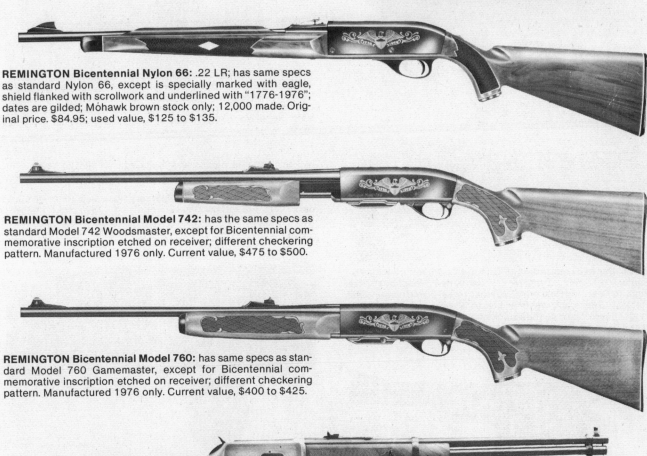

REMINGTON Bicentennial Nylon 66: .22 LR; has same specs as standard Nylon 66, except is specially marked with eagle, shield flanked with scrollwork and underlined with "1776-1976"; dates are gilded; Mohawk brown stock only; 12,000 made. Original price. $84.95; used value, $125 to $135.

REMINGTON Bicentennial Model 742: has the same specs as standard Model 742 Woodsmaster, except for Bicentennial commemorative inscription etched on receiver; different checkering pattern. Manufactured 1976 only. Current value, $475 to $500.

REMINGTON Bicentennial Model 760: has same specs as standard Model 760 Gamemaster, except for Bicentennial commemorative inscription etched on receiver; different checkering pattern. Manufactured 1976 only. Current value, $400 to $425.

WINCHESTER Bicentennial '76 Carbine: Model 94; has same general specs as standard model, except chambered for .30-30 only; engraved antique silver finish; American eagle on left side of receiver, "76" encircled with 13 stars on right side; engraved on right side of barrel is legend "Bicentennial 1776-1976." Originally marketed with wooden gun rack with simulated deer antlers, gold-colored identification plate. Reported 20,000 made in 1976. Original price, $325. Current value, $650 to $700.

RUGER Colorado Centennial Commemorative: Super Single-Six .22 convertible model; stainless steel grip frame, hammer and trigger; rosewood grip panels; marketed with two unfluted cylinders for .22 LR, .22 WRFM cartridges; inscription reads "1876 — Colorado — 1976." Marketed in lined walnut case carrying gold Ruger eagle, legend, "Ruger Colorado Centennial 1876-1976." Approximately 15,000 made in 1976. Original price, $250. Used value, $275 to $300.

WICKLIFFE '76 Commemorative: single-shot; has same specs as '76 Deluxe model, except for filled etching on sidewalls of receiver; 26" barrel only; U.S. silver dollar inlaid in stock; marketed in presentation case. Manufactured 1976 only. Only 100 made. Current value, $500 to $525.

1977

WINCHESTER Wells Fargo Model 94: has same specs as standard Model 94, except .30-30 only; antique silver-finish engraved receiver; nickel-silver stagecoach medallion inset in butt stock; checkered fancy American walnut stock, forearm; curved butt plate. Reported 20,000 made in 1977. Current value, $450 to $500.

nickel-silver anniversary seal. Included is book, *125 Years With Smith & Wesson*. Reported 9950 issued in 1977. Current value, $550 to $600.

Deluxe Edition 125th Anniversary has same specs as standard issue, except has Class A engraving, ivory stocks; anniversary medallion on box is sterling silver, book is leather-bound. Reported 50 issued in 1977. Current value, $2500 to $2750.

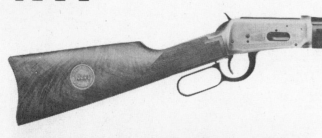

COLT Second Amendment Commemorative: Peacemaker Buntline revolver; .22 rimfire; 7½" barrel bears inscription "The Right To Keep And Bear Arms"; polished nickel-plated barrel, frame, ejector rod assembly, hammer, trigger; blued cylinder, backstrap, trigger guard; black pearlite stocks; fluted cylinder; specially serial numbered; marketed in special presentation case, carrying reproduction copy of Second Amendment to the Constitution. Reported 3000 made in 1977. Original price, $194.95. Current value, $325 to $350.

SMITH & WESSON 125th Anniversary: Model 25 revolver; .45 Colt chambering; 6½" barrel; blued finish; goncalo alves stocks; "Smith & Wesson 125th Anniversary" gold-filled on barrel; side plate has gold-filled anniversary seal; marketed in case bearing

ITHACA Ducks Unlimited Commemorative: Limited edition of Model 37 Featherlight pump action; commemorates DU 40th anniversary; 12-ga.; 30" full choke barrel; vent rib; recoil pad; Raybar front sight; commemorative grip cap; receiver engraved with DU anniversary logo, banner commemorating occasion. Also made in high-grade custom version with more elaborate etching, hand-checkered full fancy American walnut stock, custom-fitted carrying case. Reported 5000 made in 1977. Original value of standard commemorative, $255; custom version, $600. Used values: standard, $400 to $425; custom, $700 to $750.

1978

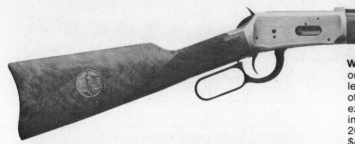

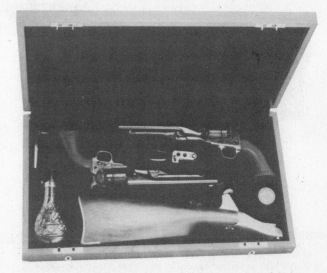

WINCHESTER Legendary Lawman: Model 94 Carbine; .30-30 only; has same specs as standard model, except for 16" barrel; full-length tube magazine; antique silver-finish barrel bands; right side of barrel bears silver-colored inscription, "Legendary Lawman"; extended forearm, straight-grip stock; nickel-silver medallion set in butt stock features sheriff standing on Western street. Reported 20,000 manufactured in 1978. Original price, $375. Current value, $425 to $450.

BROWNING Centennial Hi-Power: commemorates Browning's centennial anniversary; same as standard 9mm Hi-Power, except has oil-finished hand-checkered walnut stocks; Browning medallion inset on both sides; chrome finish; has centennial inscription with date hand-engraved on side; gold-plated trigger; fixed sights. Issued in fitted walnut case with red velvet lining. Only 3500 produced in 1978, with serial #1878D-0001 through 1878D-3500. Original price, $495. Current value, $650 to $700.

COLT U.S. Cavalry Commemorative: based on 1860 Army design; commemorates 200th anniversary of U.S. Cavalry, 1777 to 1977; blued barrel, rammer assembly, cylinder, backstrap, trigger; frame, hammer color case-hardened; brass trigger guard; one-piece walnut stocks; naval engagement scene roll marked on non-fluted cylinder; marketed with detachable walnut shoulder stock, accessories, in oiled American walnut presentation case. Reported 3000 units manufactured 1978. Original price, $995. Current value, $1000 to $1100.

WINCHESTER Antlered Game Commemorative: Built on Winchester 94 action, but with polished 20" barrel; gold-colored inscription reading "Antlered Game." Has gold-plated lever; tang and barrel bands match blue of receiver; .30-30 only. Total of 19,999 made in 1978. Original price, $374.95. Current value, $400 to $425.

1979

WINCHESTER Legendary Frontiersman: Model 94 Carbine; receiver decorated with scenes of the old frontier; silver-plated finish on receiver; polished, blued barrel, finger lever, hammer and trigger; forearm and straight-grip stock of semi-fancy American walnut; cut checkering; "Legendary Frontiersman" in silver on right side of barrel. Reported 19,999 made in 1979. Original price, $549.95 each. Used value, $475 to $500.

WINCHESTER Set of 1000 Collector Issue: Combines Model 94 in .30-30 and Model 9422 in .22 WRFM. Both have game scene engraved in receiver; levers, receivers, barrel bands are gold-plated. Marketed in red velvet-lined wooden case, with brass hardware, lock, key. Only 1000 sets made in 1979. Original price, $3000 per set. Current value, $3000 to $3200.

WINCHESTER Limited Edition II: built on standard Model 94 carbine action, but had gold plated receiver with etched game scenes on each side, gold-plated hammer, lever; rest of metal bright blued; top quality fancy walnut stock, forend. Only 1500 made in 1979. Original price, $1750. Current value, $1950 to $2000.

COLT Ned Buntline Commemorative: single-action revolver; .45 Colt; 12" barrel; built on New Frontier SAA frame; adjustable rear sight; nickel plated; black composite rubber grips; marketed in custom presentation case with six nickel-plated .45 cartridges. Reported 3000 manufactured in 1979. Original price, $900. Used value, $800 to $850.

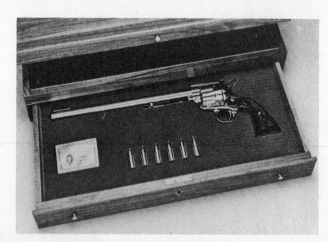

1980

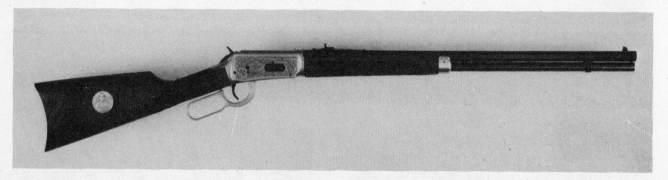

WINCHESTER Oliver Winchester Commemorative: Model 94-rifle, .38-55 Win. only; gold commemorative plaque featuring Oliver Winchester medallion inlaid in American walnut stock; gold-plated, engraved receiver, forend cap. Reported 19,999 made in 1980. Original price, $595. Used value, $525 to $550.

WICKLIFFE Big Game Commemorative: single-shot; has same specs as Wickliffe Model '76, except has glossy stock finish; gold-filled receiver etchings, chambered for .338 Win. magnum only. Only 200 made. Manufactured 1980 only. Used value, $550 to $600.

1981

WINCHESTER John Wayne Commemorative: Model 94 carbine; .32-40 Win. only; pewter-plated receiver; nickel-silver likeness of Wayne inlaid in American walnut stock; cut checkering; receiver engraved with cattle-drive scene on one side, stagecoach under attack by Indians on other; scenes are edged with titles of Wayne's films. Reported 50,000 made in 1981, some marketed by U.S. Repeating Arms. Original price, $600. Used value, $700 to $750.

BROWNING Waterfowl/Mallard Limited Edition: over/under; 12-ga.; 28" modified/full barrels; other specs are the same as Lightning Superposed model, except each gun is inscribed in gold with the Latin scientific name for the mallard, has gold mallard inlaid in receiver, with two ducks on bottom, one on trigger guard; grayed, engraved receiver; French walnut stock, forend; 24-line-per-inch checkering; oil-finished hand-rubbed wood; marketed in velvet-lined black walnut case. Only 500 made in 1981. Original price, $8800. Current value, $8700 to $8800.

COLT John M. Browning Commemorative: Model 1911; .45 auto; standard model to commemorate the 70th anniversary of the model's existence. Gold inlay on right side of slide announces the reason for manufacture, with eagle, scrollwork and Colt stallion; right side of slide also features extensive scrollwork; blued hammer and trigger, hand-checkered walnut grips. Reported 3000 made in 1981. Original sale price, $1100. Used value, $950 to $1000.

REMINGTON Chesapeake: Ducks Unlimited commemorative for 1981; Model 1100; 12-ga. magnum; 30" barrel; full choke, select American walnut stock; cut checkering recoil pad; gold-colored trigger; ivory bead front sight; left side of receiver decorated with plaque of flying duck, scrollwork, engraved gold-filled legend; furnished with foam-lined hard carrying case. Only 2400 made for DU auctions with opening bid of $950. Used value, $950 to $1000.

REMINGTON 1981 Ducks Unlimited Special: Model 1100 LT-20, 26" improved cylinder, vent-rib barrel; 2¾" chamber; left side of receiver panel carries words, "Ducks Unlimited Special," in script lettering. Right receiver panel has DU mallard head logo with scrollwork. Right side of butt stock has laser-etched reproduction of DU crest. Only 2400 made in 1981, with serial numbers 0001-DU81 to 2400-DU81, for auction by DU. Current value, $550 to $600.

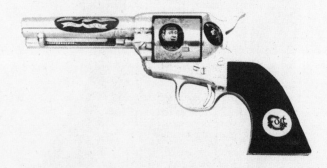

REMINGTON Atlantic DU Commemorative: Model 1100 12-ga. magnum; 32" full-choke, vent-rib barrel; right side of receiver is embossed with "Ducks Unlimited" and DU mallard head symbol; left side carries the words, "The Atlantic," surrounded by scroll markings. Made only in 1981; carries special DU serial numbers. Original price, $552. Current value, $550 to $600.

1982

BROWNING Waterfowl/Pintail Limited Edition: over/under; 12-ga.; 28" modified/full barrels; has same general specs as 1981 Mallard Limited Edition, except has hand-sculptured inlays of pin- tails in flight against background of cattails; gold-inlaid head of pintail on trigger; inscribed in gold are "American Pintail" and the scientific name, "Anas Acuta." Stock is of French walnut, with checkered butt. Marketed in velvet-lined black walnut case. Only 500 made in Belgium in 1982. Original price, $8800. Current value, $8700 to $8800.

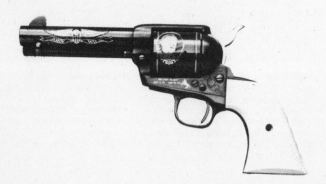

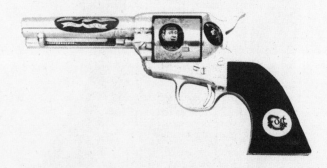

COLT John Wayne Commemorative: single-action; .45 Colt; ivory grips; etched, gold-plated portrait of Wayne on cylinder, eagle and shield on barrel with name; gold-filled Wayne signature on backstrap; marketed in presentation case. Reported 3100 made. Original price, $2995. Used value, $2000.

COLT John Wayne Deluxe: same general specs as standard commemorative, except has silver-plated, hand-engraved finish with 18-karat gold inlaid motif; two-piece ebony grips with ivory insert, gold-plated image of Wayne on horseback etched on right side of cylinder. Only 500 made. Original price, $10,000. Used value, $7500.

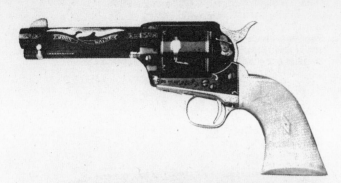

COLT John Wayne Presentation: has same general specs as standard commemorative, except blued finish, gold plating, 24-karat gold inlays, two-piece checkered ivory grips with gold inlay. Only 100 made. Original price, $20,000. Used value, $15,000.

WINCHESTER Annie Oakley 22: .22 LR, .22 WRFM; 20½" barrel; based on Model 9422; barrel inscription gold inlaid; receiver roll-engraved on right side with portrait of Annie Oakley, on left side with Oakley standing in saddle, shooting from moving horse; available with sling swivels, saddle ring on special order. Reported 6000 manufactured. Original price, $699. Used value, $700.

REMINGTON 1982 DU Special: Model 870 20-ga. lightweight; 2¾" chamber, 26" improved cylinder barrel; decorated with gold-filled scrollwork, inscribed with mallard logo, words, "Ducks Unlimited Special"; has gold-colored trigger, ivory bead front sight. Only 3000 made; serial numbers are 0001-DU82 to 3000-DU82. Original price, $550. Current value, $550 to $600.

REMINGTON River DU Commemorative: Model 870 12-ga. magnum; 30" full-choke, vent-rib barrel; dedicated to the Mississippi Flyway; left receiver panel has engraved bronze medallion of mallard duck, flanked by script lettering of gun's model and commemorative title, "The River," set off by scroll markings filled in gold color. Special serial numbers are DU82-0001 to DU82-3000. Only 3000 made. Original price, $425. Current value, $550 to $600.

RUGER Model I Limited Edition: Mark I Target Model automatic pistol of stainless steel was introduced January 1, 1982, to mark the end of production of the standard model. Pistol was marketed in the same type of wooden case and printed inner box in which the original Ruger auto was shipped at the beginning of production in 1949. Each pistol was accompanied by an exact reproduction of the original automatic pistol brochure. Barrel of each pistol was marked "1 of 5000" and the receiver roll-marked with a replica of the signature of the inventor, William B. Ruger. Only 5000 made in 1982. Original price, $435. Used value, $550 to $600.

1983

WINCHESTER Chief Crazy Horse Commemorative: built on Model 94 action; .38-55 Win.; 24" barrel; stock decorated with brass tacks; medallion in stock symbolizes united Sioux tribes;

Chief Crazy Horse inscription engraved in barrel; receiver engraved, gold filled on both sides with Indian scenes, names of Sioux tribes in English, Lakota Sioux; saddle ring. Reported 19,999 made. Original price, $600. Used value, $550.

BROWNING Waterfowl/Black Duck Limited Edition: over/under; 12-ga.; 28" modified/full barrels; has same general specs as 1981 Mallard Limited Edition, except has 24-karat black ducks inlaid in receiver; words, "Black Duck" and Latin designation "Anas Rubripes," engraved in gold within gold banners. Marketed in velvet-lined black walnut case. Only 500 made in Belgium in 1983. Original price, $8800. Current value, $8700 to $8800.

COLT Buffalo Bill Wild West Show Commemorative: SAA .45; 4¾" barrel etched with gold-plated figure of Colonel Cody on unfluted cylinder, cowboys, Indians and buffalo on barrel with commemorative inscription; two-piece walnut grips; blued finish, color case-hardened frame; marketed in cherry-stained hardwood case. Only 500 made. Original price, $1349.95. Used value, $1400.

REMINGTON Mississippi DU Commemorative: Model 870 12-ga. magnum; 32" full-choke, vent-rib barrel; right side of receiver embossed with words, "Ducks Unlimited," DU mallard head symbol; left side of receiver carries title of gun, "The Mississippi," with scrollwork. Original price, $454. Current value, $500 to $550.

1984

WINCHESTER 9422 Eagle Scout Commemorative: Similar to standard 9422 XTR, except receiver is deep etched, plated in gold; left side has Boy Scout law, right side has Boy Scout oath; frame has "1910-1985" inscription; checkered stock, forend, high-luster finish; Eagle Scout medallion embedded in right side of stock; crescent steel butt plate; gold-plated forend cap; jeweled bolt. Marketed in oak presentation case; 1000 made. Original price, $2052; used value, $2052.

WINCHESTER 9422 Boy Scout Commemorative: Similar to standard 9422, except receiver is roll-engraved, plated in antique pewter; frame carries "1910-1985" anniversary inscription, Boy Scout oath, law; lever has engraved frieze of scouting knots; "Boy Scouts of America" inscribed on barrel; medallion embedded in stock; 15,000 made. Original price, $589; used value, $589.

COLT Kit Carson Commemorative: single-action; .22 RF; based on Colt New Frontier model; 6" barrel; blued, color case-hardened frame; ivory-colored stocks; gold artwork in Western motif on barrel; marketed in custom cherry case with hardbound copy of *Kit Carson's Own Story*; 1000 made. Original price, $549; used value, $500 to $550.

WINCHESTER Grouse Model: limited edition over/under based on Model 101 configuration; custom built for the Ruffed Grouse Society; 20-ga. only; engraved scene of grouse on action; fancy walnut woodwork. Only 225 made in 1984. Current value, $1450 to $1550.

WINCHESTER/COLT 94 Set: both guns are .44-40 Win.; carbine has 20" barrel; tube magazine; 38⅛" overall length; follows basic Model 94 specs, except has horse-and-rider trademark, WC monogram etched in gold on left side; gold-etched portrait of Oliver Winchester on right; right side of barrel has rendering of original Winchester factory; additional gold scrollwork; crescent butt plate; deep-cut spade checkering; semi-gloss finish on American walnut woodwork. Colt is Peacemaker SAA model with backstrap bearing Sam Colt signature in gold; WC monogram is gold-etched on left side of cylinder; barrel bears serpentine Colt logo in gold; right side of barrel has gold etching of original Colt factory; gold-plated scrollwork; oil-finished American walnut grips; 7½" barrel; 4440 sets made. Original price, $3995; used value, $1750 to $1850.

COLT USA Edition: single-action revolver; .44-40; 7½" barrel; fluted cylinder; checkered ivory stocks with fleur-de-lis pattern; gold inlaid frame borders, outline of state or capital city on recoil shield; gold-inlaid rampant colt on loading gate; gold-inlaid "USA" on left side of barrel; two gold-inlaid barrel bands; gold-inlaid ejector tube band; silver- and gold-inlaid stars; only 100 made. Original price, $4995; used value, $3300 to $3400.

TEXAS LONGHORN South Texas Army Limited Edition: revolver; single-action; all centerfire pistol calibers; 6-rd. cylinder; 4¾" barrel; grooved top-strap rear sight, blade front; one-piece fancy walnut stocks; loading gate, ejector housing are on left side of the gun; cylinder rotates to left; color case-hardened frame; high polish blue finish; music wire coil springs; hand made; "One of One Thousand" engraved on barrel; marketed in glass-covered display case. Only 1000 made. Used value, $1500 to $1600.

COLT Theodore Roosevelt Commemorative: single-action; based on Colt SAA; 7½" barrel; .44-40; hand-fitted ivory stocks; backstrap bears gold TR monogram; barrel, cylinder hand engraved; marketed in oak presentation case; 500 made. Original price, $1695; used value, $1500 to $1600.

1985

COLT Texas Sesquicentennial: single-action; .45 Colt; built on SAA Sheriff's Model; 4" barrel; Texas legend, dates inlaid on barrel in gold; gold star in shield on cylinder; marketed in French-fitted oak presentation case; 1000 made. Original price, $1836; used value, $1800 to $1850.

    Sesquicentennial Premier also is built on SAA design; .45 Colt; 4¾" barrel; 24-karat gold-plated trigger guard, backstrap; engraved, gold-inlaid scenes of Texas history, including the Alamo; scrimshawed ivory grips; marketed in four-sided glass presentation case; 15 made. Original price, $7995; used value, $7950 to $8000.

WINCHESTER ATA Hall Of Fame Commemorative: combo trap set; 12-ga.; 34" single-barrel; 30" vent-rib over/under Winchoke barrels; engraved with Amateur Trapshooting Assn. Hall of Fame logo; serial numbered HF1 through HF250; first 60 were auction items at 1985 Grand American; marketed in fitted luggage-style case; only 250 made in 1985 in Japan by Winchester-Olin. Original price, $2795. Used value, $2750 to $2800.

1986

COLT 150th Anniversary Commemorative: Single Action Army revolver with 10" barrel, royal blue finish, authentic old-style frame with "B" engraving coverage, goncalo alves grips; anniversary logo is etched in 24K gold on backstrap, plus gold-etched signature panel. Marketed in an oak case with silver blue velvet lining; top of the lid is branded "1836 — Colt — 1986"; inside of the lid has inset 150th anniversary medallion; 1000 made with serial numbers AM-0001 through AM-1000. Made in 1986 only. Original price, $1595. Current value, $1600 to $1650.

COLT 150th Anniversary Double Diamond: Two-gun set of stainless steel, including the Python Ultimate with 6" barrel and a polished Officers Model .45 ACP automatic. Both guns carry matching serial numbers and rosewood grips as well as the Double Diamond logo. Marketed in a cherrywood presentation case with a framed glass lid; lining is black velvet. Serial numbers extend from 0001-DD through 1000-DD. Only 1000 sets made in 1986. Original retail, $1574.95. Current value, $1575 to $1600.

TEXAS LONGHORN Sesquicentennial Model: revolver; single-action; has same specs as South Texas Army Limited Edition, except with ¾-coverage engraving, antique gold, nickel finish; one-piece ivory stocks. Marketed in hand-made walnut presentation case. Only 150 made in 1986. Used value, $2500 to $2650.

COLT 150th Anniversary Engraving Sampler: Single Action Army; 4¾" barrel; blued or nickel finish; carries four styles of hand engraving; Henshaw, Nimschke, Helfricht and Colt Contemporary, with each style contained on one part of the gun; ivory grips are scrimshawed with the names of the four patterns. Made only in 1986. Original retail: blued, $1612.95; nickel, $1731.50. Current value, $1625 to $1750.

WINCHESTER 120th Anniversary Limited Edition: Model 94 carbine; .44-40 only; anniversary medallion in left side of receiver, with horse-and-rider trademark; right side of receiver carries gold-etched portrait of Oliver Winchester; signature is on the tang; right side of barrel has rendering of original Winchester factory; gold-plated scrollwork on barrel and receiver; magazine cap, front sight blade are gold-plated; has hoop-type lever, crescent butt plate. Only 1000 made in 1986. Serial numbers are WRA0001 to WRA-1000. Original price, $950. Current value, $925 to $950.

WINCHESTER Silver Anniversary Model 101: Special issue in 12-ga. only has 28" barrels, vent rib. Each gun marketed in a custom leather carrying case, complete with snap caps and silver initial plate. Only 101 made in 1986. Original price, $5200. Current value, $5750 to $6000.

1987

WINCHESTER Model 70 XTR Golden Anniversary: similar to sporter magnum, except has select walnut classic-style stock, old-style swivel bases, steel floor plate, grip cap, trigger guard; hand-engraving on barrel, receiver, magazine cover, trigger guard; inscription on barrel, "The Rifleman's Rifle 1937-1987"; hand-engraved receiver, floor plate, trigger guard, grip cap, crossbolt; chambered for .300 Win. magnum only; 500 made. Original price, $939. Current value, $925 to $950.

AMERICAN DERRINGER Texas Commemorative: has the same general specs as Model 1 Derringer, but has solid brass frame, stainless steel barrel, stag grips. Made in .38 Special, .44-40, .44 American or .45 Colt. Produced in 1987. Used value, $200 to $225.

INDEX

HANDGUNS

Walther 205 - 46
Model 33MP - 46
Model 100 Free Pistol - 46
Model 103 Free Pistol - 46
Model 110 Free Pistol - 46
Model 120 - 47
Model 150 - 47
Model 230 - 47
Model 212 Hunter - 48
Model 232 - 48

HARRINGTON & RICHARDSON
American - 48
Automatic Ejecting Model - 48
Bobby Model - 51
Expert - 50
Guardsman - 51
Hunter Model - 50
New Defender - 51
No. 199 - 51
No. 999 - 51
Premier Model - 49
Self-Loading 25 - 50
Self-Loading 32 - 51
Trapper Model - 49
USRA Model - 50
Vest Pocket Model - 48
Young American - 48
.22 Special - 50
Model 4 - 49
Model 5 - 49
Model 6 - 49
Model 40 Hammerless - 49
Model 50 Hammerless - 49
Model 504 - 54
Model 532 - 54
Model 586 - 54
Model 602 - 53
Model 604 - 53
Model 622 - 51
Model 623 - 51
Model 649 - 52
Model 650 - 52
Model 666 - 52
Model 676 - 53
Model 686 - 53
Model 732 - 51
Model 733 - 51
Model 766 - 50
Model 826 - 54
Model 829 - 54
Model 830 - 54
Model 832 - 54
Model 833 - 54
Model 900 - 52
Model 901 - 52
Model 903 - 53
Model 904 - 53
Model 905 - 53
Model 922 - 50
Model 925 - 52
Model 926 - 52
Model 929 - 51
Model 939 - 51
Model 940 - 53
Model 949 - 52
Model 950 - 52
Model 976 - 52
Model 999 - 53

HARTFORD
Repeating Pistol - 116
Target Automatic - 116
Target Single-Shot - 116

HAWES
Chief Marshal - 55
Deputy Denver Marshal - 55
Deputy Marshal - 55
Deputy Silver City Marshal - 55
Deputy Texas Marshal - 55
Favorite - 55
Federal Marshal - 55
Montana Marshal - 54
Sauer Double Action - 55
Silver City Marshal - 55
Texas Marshal - 55
Western Marshal - 54

HECKLER & KOCH
HK-4 - 56
P7 (PSP) - 57
P7-M13 - 57
P9S - 56
VP70Z - 57

HELWAN - 131

HIGH STANDARD
Camp Model - 62
Custom 10-X - 62
Derringer - 61
Double-Nine - 61
Dura-Matic - 59
Durango - 61
Field-King - 59
Flight-King - 59
High Sierra - 62
Kit Gun - 61
Longhorn - 61
Natchez - 61
Olympic - 58

Olympic ISU - 59
Plinker - 60
Posse - 61
Sentinel - 60
Sentinel Mark I - 62
Sentinel Mark II - 62
Sentinel Mark III - 62
Sentinel Mark IV - 62
Sharpshooter - 60
Sport-King - 59
Supermatic - 58
Victor - 60
Model A - 57
Model B - 57
Model C - 57
Model D - 57
Model E - 58
Model G-380 - 58
Model G-B- 58
Model G-D - 58
Model G-E - 58
Model H-A - 57
Model H-B - 57
Model H-D - 57
Model H-DM - 57
Model H-E - 58
Model S-B - 57

INDIAN ARMS
Stainless Model - 117

INTERARMS
Virginian Dragoon - 117
Dragoon Deputy - 117
Dragoon Silhouette - 117
Virginian Convertible - 131

INTERDYNAMICS
KG-99 - 117

IVER JOHNSON
American Bulldog - 66
Armsworth Model 855 - 64
Cattleman - 65
Champion - 63
Deluxe Target Model - 66
Rookie - 66
Safety Hammer Model - 62
Safety Hammerless Model - 62
Sealed Eight Supershot - 63
Sealed Eight Target - 63
Sportsman - 66
Supershot Model 844 - 63
Swing-Out Model - 66
Target 9-Shot - 63
TP22B - 66
TP25B - 66
Trailsman - 66
Trigger-Cocking Model - 63
X300 Pony - 66
22 Supershot - 63
Model 50A Sidewinder - 64
Model 55 - 64
Model 55S Cadet - 65
Model 57 - 64
Model 66 Trailsman - 64
Model 67 Viking - 65
Model 1900 - 63
Model 3000 Enforcer - 66

JANA
Bison - 117

JENNINGS
J-22 - 117

KASSNAR
M-100D - 131
Model 100TC - 131

KIMBER
Predator Hunter - 117
Predator Supergrade - 117

KLEINGUENTHER
Model R-15 - 131

KORRIPHILA
HSP 701 - 131

KORTH
9mm Auto - 132
Revolver - 132

LAHTI
Model 40 - 132
Model L-35 - 132

LAR
Grizzly - 118

LE FRANCAIS
Army Model - 132
Policeman Model - 132
Staff Officer Model - 132

LES
Model P-18 - 118

LIBERTY
Mustang - 118

LIGNOSE
Model 2 - 133
Model 2A Einhand - 133
Model 3 Einhand - 133

LJUTIC
LJ II - 118
Space Pistol - 118

LLAMA
Comanche - 68
Martial - 68
Model IIIA - 67

Model IXA - 67
Model VIII - 67
Model XA - 67
Model XI - 67
Model XV - 67
Medium Frame Model - 68
Omni - 68

LUNA
Model 300 - 133

MAB
Model A - 69
Model B - 69
Model C - 69
Model D - 69
Model E - 69
Model F - 69
Model P-15 - 69
Model R - 69

MANURHIN
PP - 133
PPK/S - 133
MR 32 Match - 133
MR 38 - 133
MR 73 - 134

MAUSER
Bolo Model 96 - 70
Parabellum - 70
Parabellum P-08 - 70
Pre-WW II Mauser-Lugers - 70
Model HSC - 70
Model HSC Super - 70
Model WTP - 70
Model 1910 Pocket Pistol - 70
Model 1914 Pocket Pistol - 70
Model 1930 - 70
Model 1934 Pocket Pistol - 70

MAXIMUM
Single-Shot - 118

MERRILL
Sportsman - 118

MITCHELL
Derringer - 118
Single Action - 118

MKE
Model TPK - 134

MORINI
Model CM-80 - 134

MOSSBERG
Abilene - 118
Brownie - 118

M-S SAFARI ARMS
Enforcer - 71
Matchmaster - 71
Unlimited - 71
Unlimited Silhouette - 71
Model 81 - 71
Model 81NM - 71
Model 81BP - 71
Model 81BP Super - 71

NAM
Mini Model - 119

NAVY ARMS
Frontier Model - 72
Frontier Target - 72
Frontier Buntline - 72
Luger Model - 72
Grand Prix - 72
Rolling Block - 72
Model 1875 - 72

NORTH AMERICAN ARMS
Model 22S - 119
Model 22LR - 119
Model 454C - 119

ODI
Viking - 119
Viking Combat Model - 119
Viking II - 119

OLYMPIC
Rapid Fire - 134

ORTGIES
Pocket Pistol - 134
.380 Auto - 134
.25 Auto - 134

PHELPS
Heritage I - 119
Eagle I - 119

PLAINFIELD
Model 71 - 120
Model 72 - 120

POCKET PARTNER
Automatic .22 - 120

RADOM
P-35 - 134

RANDALL
Service Model - 120
Compact Service Model - 120
Raider Model - 120
Curtis E. LeMay Model - 120

RAVEN - 121

RECORD-MATCH
Model 200 - 135
Model 210 - 135
Model 210A - 135

REISING
Target Model - 121

REMINGTON

Model XP-100 - 73
Model 51 - 73
Model 95 - 72
Model 1901 - 73

ROSSI
Double-Action Model - 73
Model 31 - 73
Model 51 - 73
Model 68 - 73
Model 69 - 73
Model 70 - 73
Model 84 - 74
Model 85 - 74
Model 88 - 74
Model 89 - 74
Model 511 - 74
Model 841 -74
Model 851 -74
Model 941 -74
Model 951 -74

RPM
XL Model - 121

RUGER
Bearcat - 76
GP-100 - 78
GP-141 - 78
GP-160 - 78
Hawkeye - 76
KGP-141 - 78
KGP-160 - 78
KGP-161 - 78
Mark I - 75
Mark II - 75
New Model Bisley Single Six - 78
New Model Bisley Blackhawk - 78
New Model Blackhawk - 76
New Model Blackhawk 357 Maximum - 77
New Model Super Blackhawk - 76
New Model Super Blackhawk Stainless - 77
P-85 - 78
Police Service-Six Model 107 - 76
Police Service-Six Model 108 - 76
Police Service-Six 109 - 77
Police Service-Six 707 - 77
Police Service-Six 708 - 77
Redhawk - 77
Security-Six Model 117 - 77
Security-Six Model 717 - 77
Single Six - 75
Speed-Six Model 207 - 77
Speed-Six Model 208 - 77
Speed-Six Model 909 - 77
Speed Six Model 737 - 77
Speed-Six Model 738 - 77
Speed-Six Model 739 - 77
Standard Model - 74
Super Blackhawk - 76
Super Redhawk - 77
.30 Carbine Blackhawk - 76
.357 Magnum Blackhawk - 75
.41 Magnum Blackhawk - 76
.44 Magnum Blackhawk - 76
.45 Colt - 76

RG
Super 66 - 79
Model 39 - 80
Model 74 - 80
Model 88 - 79
RG 14 - 79
RG 23 - 79
RG 26 - 79
RG 30 - 78
RG 31 - 80
RG 38S - 78
RG 57 - 78
RG 63 - 79

S.A.B. GAMBA
Model SAB G 90 - 135
Model SAB G 91 - 135

SAUER
Pocket 25 - 80
WTM - 81
Model 28 - 81
Model 38(H) - 81
Model 1913 - 80
Model 1930 - 81

SAVAGE
Model 101 - 121
Model 1910 - 121
Model 1917 - 121

SECURITY INDUSTRIES
Model PM357 - 122
Model PPM357 - 121
Model PSS38 - 121

SEDGLEY
Baby Hammerless Model - 122

SEVILLE
Sheriff's Model - 122
Silhouette - 122
Single Action - 122
Stainless Super Mag - 122

SHERIDAN
Knockabout - 122

SIG
Hammerli Model P240 - 82
Sauer Model P225 - 82

489

Sauer Model P220 - 81
Sauer Model P230 - 81
Model P210-1 - 81
Model P210-2 - 81
Model P210-5 - 81
Model P210-6 - 81

SILE
Benelli 876 - 135
Seecamp II - 122

SMITH & WESSON
Airweight Kit Gun Model 43 - 89
Military & Police Target Model - 84
Military Model of 1917 - 84
New Model No. 3 - 82
Olympic Model - 83
Perfected Model 38 - 84
Regulation Police Target Model - 85
Safety Hammerless - 83
Straightline Single-Shot Target - 85
Victory Model - 87
.22 Auto Target Model 41 - 91
.22/32 Target Model - 84
.22/32 Kit Gun - 86
.32 Auto - 91
32 - 82
35 - 84
38 - 82
.38/44 Outdoorsman Model 23 - 86
44 - 83
1950/1955 Model 25 .45 Target - 88
Model I - 83
Model 10 Military & Police - 83
Model 12 Military & Police Airweight - 88
Model 14 K-38 Masterpiece - 87
Model 15 .38 Combat Masterpiece - 88
Model 16 K-32 Masterpiece - 87
Model 17 K-22 Masterpiece - 86
Model 18 .22 Combat Masterpiece - 88
Model 19 Combat Magnum - 90
Model 20 .30/44 Heavy Duty - 85
Model 21 1950 .44 Military - 87
Model 22 1950 Army - 87
Model 24 1950 .44 Target - 88
Model 25 1950/1955 .45 Target - 87
Model 27 .357 Magnum - 86
Model 28 Highway Patrolman - 89
Model 29 .44 Magnum - 90
Model 30 Hand Ejector - 84
Model 31 Regulation Police - 84
Model 32 Terrier - 86
Model 33 Regulation Police - 85
Model 34 1953 .22/32 Kit Gun - 88
Model 35 1953 .22/32 - 89
Model 36 Chiefs Special - 88
Model 37 Chiefs Special Airweight - 89
Model 38 Bodyguard Airweight - 90
Model 39 9mm Auto - 92
Model 40 Centennial - 89
Model 48 K-23 Masterpiece WMRF - 87
Model 49 Bodyguard - 90
Model 51 1960 .22/32 Kit Gun WMRF - 91
Model 52 .38 Target Auto - 92
Model 53 .22 Magnum - 90
Model 57 .41 Magnum - 91
Model 58 .41 Magnum - 90
Model 59 9mm Auto - 92
Model 60 Stainless Chiefs Special 89
Model 61 Escort - 91
Model 63 - 89
Model 64 - 93
Model 66 Combat Magnum - 92
Model 67 K-38 - 92
Model 422 - 95
Model 439 - 93
Model 459 - 93
Model 469 - 94
Model 547 - 93
Model 581 - 94
Model 586 - 94
Model 624 - 94
Model 639 - 93
Model 645 - 94
Model 650 - 94
Model 651 - 94
Model 659 - 93
Model 681 - 94
Model 686 - 94
Model 745 - 95
Model 1891 - 83
Model 1926 .44 Military - 85
Model 1926 Target - 85

SOKOLOVSKY
.45 Automaster - 122

SPRINGFIELD ARMORY
1911-A1 - 123

S.P.A. GAMBA
Mauser 80G 15 - 135
Trident Super 4 - 135

STAR
Olympia Model - 96
Super SM - 97
Super Star Model - 96
Super Star Target Model - 96
Model A - 95
Model B - 95
Model BKM - 97

Model BKS - 97
Model CO - 95
Model DK - 97
Model F - 96
Model F Sport - 96
Model F Target - 96
Model FRS - 96
Model FM - 96
Model H - 95
Model HN - 95
Model HK - 97
Model I - 95
Model IN - 96
Model M - 96
Model PD - 97
Model S - 96
Model SI - 96
Model SI Super - 96
Model 28 - 97
Model 30M - 98
Model 30 PK - 98

STEEL CITY
Double Deuce - 123
War Eagle - 123

STERLING
Model 283 - 98
Model 284 - 98
Model 285 - 98
Model 286 - 98
Model 295 - 98
Model 300 - 98
Model 300S - 99
Model 302 - 99
Model 302S - 99
Model 400 - 99
Model 400S - 99
Model 402 - 99
Model 450 - 100
X-Caliber - 99

STEVENS
No. 10 - 123
No. 35 - 123

STEYR
Model SP - 135
Model GB - 135

STOEGER
Luger - 124

SUPER SIX
Golden Bison - 124

TANARMI
Derringer - 124
Model TA22S - 135
Model TA76 - 135

TARGA
Model GT27 - 136
Model GT32 - 136
Model GT32XE - 136
Model GT380 - 136
Model GT380XE - 136

TAURUS
Model 65 - 100
Model 66 - 101
Model 73 - 102
Model 74 - 100
Model 80 - 100
Model 82 - 100
Model 83 - 101
Model 84 - 100
Model 85 - 101
Model 86 - 100
Model 94 - 100
Model 96 Scoutmaster - 100
PT-22 - 102
PT-92 - 102
PT-99 - 102

TDE
Backup - 124

TEXAS LONGHORN
Border Special - 124
Jezebel - 124
West Texas Flat Top - 124

THOMAS
.45 - 124

THOMPSON/CENTER
Contender - 125

UBERTI
1873 Cattleman - 102
1873 Buckhorn - 102
1873 Buntline - 102
1873 Stallion - 102
1875 Army Outlaw - 103
1890 Army Outlaw - 103
Inspector - 103
Phantom SA Silhouette - 103
Rolling Block - 103

ULTRA LIGHT ARMS
Model 20 Reb Hunter - 125

UNIQUE
Kriegsmodell - 103
Model B/Cf - 104
Model DES/VO - 105
Model DES/69 - 103
Model D2 - 103
Model D6 - 103
Model L - 103
Model Mikros - 103

Model Rr - 103
Model 2000-U Match - 105

U.S. ARMS
Abilene Model - 125

VEGA
Stainless 45 - 125

WALTHER
GSP Match Model - 108
Olympia Sport Model - 107
P-5 - 108
P-38IV - 108
P-38 Military - 107
P-38K - 108
Self-Loading Model - 107
Target Model - 106
Model HP - 107
Model PP - 106
Model PPK - 106
Model 1 - 105
Model 2 - 105
Model 3 - 105
Model 4 - 105
Model 5 - 106
Model 6 - 107
Model 7 - 107
Model 8 - 108
Model 9 - 108

WARNER
Infallible Model - 125

WEATHERBY
Mark V Silhouette - 125

WEBLEY
Fosbery Automatic Revolver - 109
Mark III Police Model - 109
Mark IV Police Model - 110
Mark IV Target Model - 110
Mark IV .32 Police - 110
Police & Civilian Pocket Model - 109
Model 1906 - 109
Model 1906 .25 - 109
Model 1909 - 109
Model 1909 Single-Shot - 110
Model 1911 - 110
Model 1913 - 110

DAN WESSON
Model 8-2 - 111
Model 9-2 - 112
Model 9-2H - 111
Model 11 - 110
Model 12 - 110
Model 14 - 110
Model 14-2 - 111
Model 15 - 111
Model 15-1 - 111
Model 15-2H - 111
Model 15-2HV - 111
Model 22 - 111
Model 32M - 111
Model 40 Silhouette - 112
Model 41V - 111
Model 44V - 112

WICHITA
Classic - 126
Hunter - 126
International - 126
Silhouette - 126

WILKINSON
Diana - 126
Linda - 126
Sherry - 125

WHITNEY
Wolverine - 126

RIFLES

ACKLEY
Standard Model - 277

ALPHA
Model 1 - 278
Custom Model - 278

ALPINE
Sporter - 287

AMERICAN FIREARMS
Stainless Model - 278

AMT
Lightning 25/22 - 278

ANSCHUTZ
Achiever - 145
Kadett - 145
Mark 2000 - 142
Model 54.18 - 143
Model 64 - 140
Model 520 - 144
Model 1403D - 143
Model 1407 - 140
Model 1408 - 141
Model 1411 - 141
Model 1413 - 141
Model 1416 Deluxe - 144
Model 1418D Deluxe - 144
Model 1422D Classic - 144
Model 1432 - 141
Model 1432D - 142
Model 1433 - 141

Model 1516 Deluxe - 144
Model 1518 - 142
Model 1518D Deluxe - 144
Model 1522 Classic - 144
Model 1532D - 142
Model 1533 - 142
Model 1803D - 143
Model 1807 Match - 143
Model 1808ED - 143
Model 1810 Super Match II - 145
Model 1811 Match - 142
Model 1813 Super Match - 142
Model 1827B Biathlon - 143

ARMALITE
AR-7 Explorer - 279
Custom AR-7 - 279

ARMSCOR
Model 14P - 145
Model 20P - 145
Model 1500 - 145
Model 1600 - 145
Model 2000 - 145

ARMSPORT
Emperor 4000 - 288
2801 - 288

BERETTA
Express S689 - 288
Model 500 - 288
Sporting Carbine - 288

BIG HORN
Custom - 279

BORTMESS
Big Horn - 279
Classic - 279
Omega - 279

BRNO
Hornet - 146
Model I - 146
Model II - 146
Model 21H - 146
Model 22F - 146
Super Express - 147
ZH Series 300 - 146
ZKK 600 - 147

BROWNING
A-Bolt - 151
BAR - 148
BAR-22 - 149
BLR - 149
BL-22 - 148
BBR - 150
BPR-22 - 148
B-78 - 148
B-92 - 148
Continental - 150
Express - 150
Grade I Autoloader .22 - 147
Grade II Autoloader .22 - 147
Grade III Autoloader .22 - 147
High-Power Safari Grade - 147
Model T-1 T-Bolt - 148
Model T-2 - 148
Model 71 - 151
Model 78 - 148
Model 1885 - 150
Model 1895 - 150

BSA
Centurion - 152
CF-2 - 154
CF-2 Stutzen - 154
Imperial - 153
Majestic Deluxe - 153
Martini-International Heavy Pattern - 152
Martini-International Light Pattern - 152
Martini ISU Match - 153
Martini-International Mark II - 153
Martini-International Mark III - 153
Model 12/15 - 152
Monarch Deluxe - 153
Parker Model 12/15 - 152
Model 15 - 152
No. 12 - 151
No. 13 - 152

CABANAS
Laser Model - 155
Leyre Model - 154
Master Model - 154
Varmint Model - 154
Model 82 - 154
Model R83 - 154

CENTURY
Centurion 14 - 155
Enfield Sporter #4 - 155
Swedish Sporter #38 - 155
Weekender - 155

CHAPUIS
Express Model - 288

CHIPMUNK
Single-Shot - 279

CHURCHILL
Highlander - 288
Regent Combo - 288

CLAYCO
Model 4 - 289

CLERKE
Hi-wall - 279

WINCHESTER
Double Express - 277
High-Wall Sporter - 261
Lee Musket - 263
Low-Wall Sporter - 261
Ranger - 277
Super Grade Combo - 277
Model 02 - 263
Model 03 - 264
Model 04 - 263
Model 05 - 264
Model 07 - 264
Model 10 - 264
Model 17 - 264
Model 43 - 272
Model 47 - 273
Model 52 - 264
Model 54 - 264
Model 55 - 273
Model 55 Center-fire - 266
Model 56 - 266
Model 57 - 267
Model 58 - 267
Model 59 - 267
Model 60 - 267
Model 60A - 267
Model 61 - 267
Model 62 - 267
Model 63 - 268
Model 64 - 268
Model 65 - 268
Model 67 - 268
Model 68 - 269
Model 69 - 269
Model 70 - 270
Model 70A - 275
Model 70 XTR - 271
Model 71 - 271
Model 72 - 272
Model 73 - 260
Model 74 - 272
Model 75 Sporter - 272
Model 77 - 272
Model 88 - 273
Model 90 - 261
Model 92 - 261
Model 94 - 261
Model 95 - 263
Model 99 - 263
Model 100 - 273
Model 121 - 274
Model 131 - 274
Model 141 - 275
Model 150 - 275
Model 190 - 276
Model 250 - 273
Model 255 - 273
Model 270 - 274
Model 275 - 274
Model 290 - 274
Model 310 - 275
Model 320 - 275
Model 670 - 276
Model 677 - 268
Model 697 - 269
Model 770 - 276
Model 1886 - 261
Model 1900 - 263
Model 1906 - 264
Model 9422 - 276
WINSLOW
Bolt Action - 287
A. ZOLI
O/U Combo - 301

SHOTGUNS

ARIZAGA
Model 31 - 442
ARMALITE
AR-17 Golden Gun - 431
ARMSCOR
Model 30
ARMSPORT
Goosegun - 306
Western - 306
Model 1050 - 306
Model 2500 - 306
Model 2700 - 306
Model 2751 - 306
Model 2755 - 306
Model 2900 Tri-Barrel - 306
ASTRA
Model 650 - 443
Model 750 - 443
AYA
Bolero - 307
Matador - 307
Matador II - 307
No. 1 - 307
No. 2 - 308
No. 4 Deluxe - 308
XXV/SL - 307
XXV/BL - 307

Model 2 - 308
Model 37 Super - 307
Model 53E - 307
Model 56 - 307
Model 76 - 308
Model 76 410 - 308
Model 117 - 308
BABY BRETTON
Deluxe - 443
BAIKAL
IJ-27EIC - 309
IJ-58MAE - 309
MC-5-105 - 308
MC-7 - 308
MC-8-0 - 308
MC-109 - 309
MC-110 - 309
MC-111 - 309
BAKER
Batavia Leader - 309
Batavia Special - 309
Batavia Ejector - 309
Black Beauty Special - 310
Grade R - 310
Grade S - 310
BEEMAN
Fabarm - 443
BENELLI
Autoloader - 443
123-SL-80 - 443
Super 90 - 444
BJG
10 Gauge Magnum - 444
BERETTA
FS-1 - 311
Gold Lark - 311
Gold Pigeon - 311
Golden Snipe - 311
Golden Snipe Deluxe - 311
Grade 100 - 311
Grade 200 - 311
Mark II - 314
Ruby Lark - 311
Ruby Pigeon - 311
Silver Hawk Featherweight - 310
Silver Hawk Magnum - 311
Silver Lark - 311
Silver Snipe - 311
Silver Pigeon - 311
SO2 Presentation - 312
SO3 Presentation - 312
SO4 Presentation - 312
SO5 Presentation - 312
SO6 Presentation - 312
SO7 Presentation - 312
Model Asel - 310
Model A-301 - 314
Model A-302 - 314
Model A-303 - 314
Model AL-2 - 314
Model AL-3 - 314
Model BL-1 - 313
Model BL-2 - 313
Model BL-3 - 313
Model BL-4 - 313
Model BL-5 - 313
Model BL-6 - 313
Model GR-2 - 312
Model GR-3 - 314
Model GR-4 - 313
Model S55B - 314
Model S56E - 314
Model S58 Skeet - 315
Model S58 Trap - 315
Model SL-2 - 313
Model TR-1 - 313
Model TR-2 - 313
Model 57E - 311
Model 409PB - 310
Model 410 - 310
Model 410E - 310
Model 411E - 310
Model 424 - 314
Model 426E - 314
Model 626 - 315*
Model 627EL - 315
Model 680 - 315
Model 685 - 315
Model 686 - 315
Model 687 - 315
BERNARDELLI
Brescia - 316
Deluxe Holland - 316
Elio - 316
Game Cock - 317
Holland - 316
Italia - 316
Las Palomas - 317
Roma - 315
System Holland H - 317
St. Uberto 1 - 316
St. Uberto 2 - 316
St. Uberto 3 - 316
XXVSL - 317
BOSS
Double Barrel - 444

Over/Under - 444
BREDA
Autoloader - 444
BRNO
Super - 317
ZH 301 - 318
ZP 149 - 317
ZP 349 - 317
500 - 317
BROWNING
A-500 - 324
American Grade I - 321
American Special - 321
Auto-5 - 318
Auto-5 Light - 318
B-80 - 323
BPS - 323
BSS - 321
BT 99 - 321
Citori - 322
Double Auto - 321
Liege - 322
ST-100 - 323
Superposed - 319
Superposed Super-Light - 321
Twelvette - 321
Twentyweight - 321
B-2000 - 322
CAPRINUS
Sweden - 444
CHAPUIS
Progress - 445
CHURCHILL
Field Model - 324
Premier Over/Under - 324
Premier Quality - 324
Utility Model - 324
XXV Premier - 324
XXV Imperial - 324
XXV Hercules - 324
XXV Regal - 324
CHURCHILL/KASSNAR
Deerfield - 326
Monarch - 326
Regent Auto - 326
Regent Flyweight - 326
Regent O/U - 325
Regent S/S - 325
Regent Trap/Skeet - 325
Windsor Auto - 325
Windsor Flyweight - 326
Windsor O/U - 325
Windsor S/S - 325
CLAYCO
Model 6 - 445
COGSWELL & HARRISON
Ambassador - 327
Avant Tout - 326
Avant Tout Rex - 327
Avant Tout Sandhurst - 326
Huntic Model - 327
Markor Model - 327
Primac Model - 326
Victor Model - 327
COLT
Coltsman Pump Model - 327
Custom Double Barrel - 327
Magnum Auto - 327
Sauer Drilling - 327
Ultra Light Auto - 327
CONTENTO
Grade I - 445
Lusso Grade - 445
Extra Lusso - 445
CRUCELEGUI HERMANOS
Model 150 - 445
CHARLES DALY
Auto - 330
Diamond Grade - 331
Diamond Grade O/U - 331
Diamond-Regent Grade - 329
Empire Double - 330
Empire Quality Over/Under - 328
Empire Quality Trap - 329
Field Auto - 331
Field Grade - 329
Field III - 331
Hammerless Double Barrel - 328
Hammerless Drilling - 329
Model 100 Commander - 329
Model 200 Commander - 329
Multi-XII - 331
Novamatic Lightweight - 330
Presentation Grade - 331
Sextuple Trap - 329
Superior Grade - 329
Superior Trap - 330
Superior II - 331
Venture Grade - 330
DARNE
Bird-Hunter - 445
Pheasant Hunter - 445
Quail-Hunter Supreme - 445
DAVIDSON
Model 63B - 331
Model 63B Magnum - 331

Model 69SL - 331
Model 73 - 331
DIARM
Bristol - 332
Competition - 332
Derby Model - 333
Model Excelsior - 332
Model Royal - 333
Silver I - 332
Silver II - 332
Turkey Special - 333
Waterfowl Special - 332
Waterfowl Special 10 - 333
York - 333
ERA
Bird Hunter - 445
Full Limit - 446
Winner - 446
ERBI
Model 76ST - 446
Model 76AJ - 446
Model 80 - 446
EXEL
Model 51 - 334
Model 201 - 333
Model 202 - 333
Model 203 - 333
Model 204 - 334
Model 205 - 334
Model 206 - 334
Model 207 - 334
Model 208 - 334
Model 209 - 334
Model 210 - 334
Model 300 - 334
FERLACH
Constant Companion - 446
FERLIB
Model FVII - 446
F.I.E.
Brute - 334
CBC - 334
Hamilton & Hunter - 335
SOB - 334
SSS Model - 335
FOX
A.H. Fox Model - 335
FA-1 - 336
FP-1 - 336
Model B - 336
Single-Barrel Trap Model - 336
Sterlingworth - 335
Super Fox - 336
FRANCHI
Airon Model - 338
Alcione Super Deluxe - 341
Aristocrat Trap Model - 339
Astore Model - 338
Custom Sidelock Model - 338
Diamond Grade - 341
Dynamic 12 - 339
Eldorado - 338
Falconet - 339
Hunter Model Autoloader - 337
Imperiale Monte Carlo Extra - 340
PG-80 Prestige - 341
Peregrin Model 451 - 340
Silver King Aristocrat - 339
Slug Gun - 338
Standard Autoloader - 337
Model 48/AL - 340
Model 400 - 340
Model 500 - 340
Model 520 Deluxe - 340
Model 520 Eldorado Gold - 340
Model 530 - 340
Model 2003 Trap - 340
Model 2004 Trap - 340
Model 2005 Trap Set - 340
Model 3000/2 - 340
FRANCOTTE
A&F Series - 341
Model SOB.E/11082 - 343
Model 9/40E/38321 - 342
Model 9/40.SE - 342
Model 10/18E/628 - 342
Model 11/18E - 342
Model 120.HE/328 - 342
Model 4996 - 342
Model 6886 - 341
Model 6930 - 342
Model 6982 - 342
Model 8446 - 341
Model 8455 - 342
Model 8457 - 342
Model 9261 - 342
Model 10594 - 342
GALEF
Companion - 343
Monte Carlo Trap - 343
Zabala - 343
Zoli Golden Snipe - 343
Zoli Silver Hawk - 343
Zoli Silver Snipe - 343
GAMBA
Ambassador - 344

Edinburgh - 344
Europe 2000 - 344
Grifone - 344
Hunter Super - 344
London Model - 344
LS 2000 - 344
Milano 3 - 344
Model Grinta - 344
Oxford 90 - 344
Principessa - 344
Victory Skeet - 344
Victory Trap - 344

GARBI
Special Model - 345
Model 51A - 345
Model 60A - 345
Model 62A - 345
Model 71 - 345
Model 101 - 345
Model 102 - 345
Model 103A - 345
Model 110 - 345
Model 200 - 345

GARCIA
Bronco - 446
Bronco 22/410 - 446

GIB
Magnum - 446

GOLDEN EAGLE
Model 5000 - 447

GOROSABEL
Model Blackpoint - 447
Model Silverpoint - 447
Model 501 - 448
Model 502 - 448
Model 503 - 447

GREENER
Crown Model - 346
Empire Model - 346
Far-Killer Model - 346
General Purpose - 346
Jubilee Model - 346
Sovereign Model - 346

GREIFELT
Grade No. 1 - 347
Grade No. 3 - 347
Model 22 - 347
Model 103 - 347
Model 143E - 347
Over/Under Combo Model - 347

HARRINGTON & RICHARDSON
Bay State No. 7 - 348
Folding Model - 348
Harrich No. 1 - 350
No 3 - 347
No. 5 - 347
No. 6 - 347
No. 8 - 348
No. 48 Topper - 348
No. 488 Topper Deluxe - 348
Topper Model 058 - 349
Topper Model 088 - 349
Topper Model 098 - 349
Model 099 Deluxe - 351
Model 148 Topper - 348
Model 158 Topper - 348
Model 159 - 349
Model 162 - 350
Model 176 - 351
Model 176 10-Ga. Slug - 351
Model 176 Magnum - 351
Model 188 Topper Deluxe - 348
Model 198 Topper Deluxe - 349
Model 348 - 349
Model 349 - 349
Model 351 - 349
Model 400 - 349
Model 401 - 349
Model 402 - 349
Model 403 - 350
Model 404 - 350
Model 440 - 350
Model 442 - 350
Model 459 - 349
Model 480 Jr. Topper - 348
Model 488 Topper Deluxe - 348
Model 490 - 349
Model 490 Greenwing - 351
Model 490 Topper - 351
Model 580 Jr. Topper - 348
Model 590 Topper - 349
Model 1212 - 350

HEYM
Model 55/77 - 448
Model 55/77FSS - 448

HIGH-STANDARD
Flite-King Brush Gun - 354
Flite-King Brush Deluxe (1966) - 355
Flite-King Deluxe (1966) - 354
Flite-King Deluxe Rib - 353
Flite-King Deluxe Rib (1966) - 355
Flite-King Deluxe Skeet (1966) - 355
Flite-King Field Model - 353
Flite-King Skeet - 354
Flite-King Special - 353
Flite-King Trap - 355

Flite-King Trophy - 354
Flite-King 16 Series - 354
Flite-King 410 Series - 354
Shadow Auto - 355
Shadow Indy - 355
Shadow Seven - 355
Supermatic Deer Model - 352
Supermatic Deluxe - 352
Supermatic Duck Model - 352
Supermatic Field Model - 351
Supermatic Skeet - 352
Supermatic Special - 352
Supermatic Trap - 352
Supermatic Trophy Model - 352

HOLLAND & HOLLAND
Badminton Model - 356
Dominion Model - 356
Model Deluxe - 356
New Royal Model - 356
Northwood Game Model - 356
Riviera Model - 356
Royal Model - 356
Royal Over/Under - 356
Super Trap - 356

HUNTER
Fulton - 442
Special - 442

IGA
Standard Model - 448
Coach Model - 448

INDUSTRIAS DANOK
Red Prince Model - 448

ITHACA
5E - 364
Competition I - 361
Hammerless Double Field Grade - 357
Hammerless Double No. 2 - 357
Hammerless Double No. 4 - 357
Hammerless Double No. 5 - 358
Hammerless Double No. 7 - 358
Hammerless Double $2000 Grade - 358
Light Game Model - 363
LSA-55 Turkey Gun - 363
Mag 10 - 363
Mirage - 361
MX-8 - 361
One Barrel Trap Gun - 358
Single-Barrel Victory Model - 358
SKB Century - 363
SKB Model 100 - 360
SKB Model 150 - 360
SKB Model 200E - 360
SKB Model 280 - 360
SKB Model 500 - 360
SKB Model 600 - 361
SKB Model 680 English - 360
SKB Model 700 - 361
SKB Model 880 Crown Grade - 364
Model XL 300 - 363
Model XL 900 - 363
Model 37 - 358
Model 51 - 362
Model 66 - 360
Model 300 - 361
Model 900 Deluxe - 361
SE Grade - 363

IVER JOHNSON
Champion Grade - 364
Hercules Grade - 365
Matted Rib Grade - 364
Silver Shadow - 365
Skeeter Model - 365
Special Trap Model - 365
Super Trap Model - 365

KASSNAR
FIAS SK-1 - 366
FIAS SK-3 - 366
FIAS SK-4D - 366
Fox - 366
Omega - 366
Omega O/U - 366
Omega SS - 366
Squires-Bingham 30D - 366
Zabala Double - 366

KAWAGUCHIYA
KFC FG - 448
KFC M-250 - 448
KFC OT-Trap-E1 - 448

KESSLER
Lever-Matic - 442
Three-Shot Repeater - 442

KLEINGUENTHER
Brescia - 449
Condor - 449
Condor Trap - 449

KRIEGHOFF
Model 32 - 367
Model 32 Single-Barrel Trap - 367
Model 32 Skeet Set - 367
Neptun - 367
Neptun-Primus - 367
Single-Barrel Trap - 368
Teck - 368
Teck Combo - 368
Trumpf - 367
Ulm - 367

Ulm Combo - 367
Ulm-Primus - 367
Ulm-Primus Combo - 368
Vandalia Trap - 368

LANBER
Model 208 - 449
Model 844 - 449
Model 2004 - 449
Model 2008 - 449

LAURONA
Super Model - 449

LEFEVRE
Double Hammerless - 369
Grade A - 370
Grade A Skeet - 370
Hammerless Double Sidelock - 368
Long Range - 369
Nitro Special - 369
Single Barrel Trap - 369

MIGUEL LARRANAGA
Traditional - 450

LEBEAU-COURALLY
Boxlock Model - 450
Sidelock Model - 450
Model 1225 - 450

LJUTIC
Bi-Gun - 370
Bi-Gun Combo - 370
Bi-Matic - 371
Dyna Trap II - 371
Four Barrel Skeet - 370
LXT Mono Gun - 370
Mono Gun - 370
Space Gun - 371

MANUFRANCE
Auto - 371
222 Robust Field - 371
254 Robust Deluxe - 371
979 Falcor - 371
1977 Falcor - 372
1985 Falcor Trap - 372
1987 Falcor Skeet - 372

MARLIN
Glenfield Model 60G - 375
Glenfield 788 - 376
Premier Mark I - 375
Model 16 - 372
Model 17 - 372
Model 19 - 372
Model 21 Trap - 372
Model 24 - 374
Model 26 - 373
Model 26 Brush - 373
Model 28 - 373
Model 30 - 374
Model 31A - 373
Model 42A - 373
Model 43A - 373
Model 44A - 374
Model 49 - 374
Model 50 - 376
Model 53 - 374
Model 55 - 374
Model 59 Olympic - 375
Model 60 - 374
Model 63A - 374
Model 90 - 374
Model 120 Magnum - 375
Model 410 - 374
Model 1898 - 372
Model 5510 - 375

MAROCCHI
American - 450
Contrast - 450
SM28 SXS - 450

MAROCCINI
Priti - 450

MAUSER
Model Contest - 450

MAUSER-BAUER
Model 71E - 377
Model 72E - 377
Model 496 - 377
Model 580 - 377
Model 610 Phantom - 377
Model 620 - 377

MERCURY
Magnum - 450
Model Contest - 450

MERKEL
Model 47S - 380
Model 100 - 378
Model 101 - 378
Model 127 - 380
Model 130 - 380
Model 147E - 380
Model 200 - 378
Model 201 - 378
Model 202 - 379
Model 203 - 379
Model 204E - 379
Model 300 - 379
Model 301 - 379
Model 302 - 379
Model 303E - 379
Model 304E - 379

Model 400 - 378

MIIDA
Grandee GRS Skeet - 381
Grandee GRT Trap - 381
Model 612 - 380
Model 2100 Skeet - 380
Model 2200 Trap - 380
Model 2300 Trap - 380
Model 2200 Skeet - 380

MONTE CARLO
Single - 451

MORONNE
Model 46 - 442

MOSSBERG
Model 83D - 381
Model 85D - 381
Model 183D - 381
Model 185D - 381
Model 190D - 381
Model 195D - 382
Model 195K - 382
Model 200D - 382
Model 200K - 382
Model 385K - 384
Model 390K - 384
Model 395K - 384
Model 500ALD - 383
Model 500ATP6 - 383
Model 500 Field - 383
Model 1000 - 384
Model 5500 - 384

NAVY ARMS
Model 83 - 384
Model 84 - 384
Model 95 - 385
Model 96 - 385
Model 100 - 385
Model 105 - 385
Model 150 - 385
Model 410 - 385
Model 600 - 385

NEW HAVEN
Model 273 - 385
Model 283 - 385
Model 285 - 385
Model 290 - 385
Model 295 - 385
Model 495 - 386
Model 600 - 385
Model 600AST Slugster - 386

NOBLE
Model 40 - 386
Model 50 - 386
Model 60 - 386
Model 65 - 386
Model 66RCLP - 386
Model 70 - 387
Model 80 - 387
Model 160 Deergun - 387
Model 166 Deergun - 387
Model 200 - 388
Model 300 - 388
Model 390 Deergun - 389
Model 400 - 388
Model 420 - 387
Model 450E - 388
Model 520 - 389
Model 550 - 389
Model 602 - 386
Model 662 - 388
Model 757 - 389

OMEGA
Deluxe Folding Model - 451
Folding O/U - 451
Folding Single-Shot - 451

PARKER
DHE - 390
Model 920 Hammerless - 390
Single-Barrel Trap - 390
Trojan - 390

PARKER-HALE
Model 640 - 451
Model 645 - 451
Model 645E-XXV - 451
Model 670E-XXV - 451
Model 680E-XXV - 451

PARQUEMY
Model 48 - 451

PEDERSEN
Model 4000 - 392
Model 4500 - 392
Series 1000 - 391
Series 2000 - 391
1500 - 391
2500 - 391

PERAZZI
Competition I Trap - 392
Competition IV - 393
Light Game Model - 393
Mirage Trap - 393
Mirage Live Bird Model - 393
Mirage Skeet - 392
MT-6 Trap - 392
MT-8 Trap - 392
MX-8 Trap - 392

COMMEMORATIVES